The Complete

BIBLICAL LIBRARY

The Complete
BIBLICAL
LIBRARY

THE NEW TESTAMENT STUDY BIBLE

HEBREWS through JUDE

The Complete BIBLICAL LIBRARY

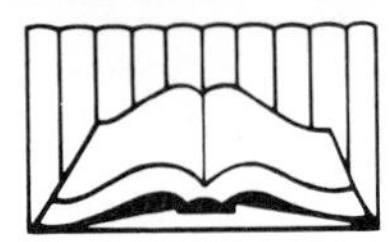

The Complete Biblical Library, part 1, a 16-volume study series on the New Testament. Volume 9: STUDY BIBLE, HEBREWS—JUDE. Printed in the United States of America 1989 by R.R. Donnelley and Sons Company, Chicago, Illinois 60606. Library of Congress Catalog Card Number 89-62160 International Standard Book Number 0-88243-369-5.

THE NEW TESTAMENT
Study Bible, Greek-English Dictionary, Harmony of the Gospels

THE OLD TESTAMENT
Study Bible, Hebrew-English Dictionary

THE BIBLE ENCYCLOPEDIA

INTERNATIONAL EDITOR
THORALF GILBRANT

Executive Editor: Ralph W. Harris, M.A.
Computer Systems: Tor Inge Gilbrant

NATIONAL EDITORS

U.S.A.
Stanley M. Horton, Th.D.

NORWAY
Erling Utnem, Bishop
Arthur Berg, B.D.

DENMARK
Jorgen Glenthoj, Th.M.

SWEDEN
Hugo Odeberg, Ph.D., D.D.
Bertil E. Gartner, D.D.
Thorsten Kjall, M.A.
Stig Wikstrom, D.Th.M.

FINLAND
Aapelii Saarisalo, Ph.D.
Valter Luoto, Pastor
Matti Liljequist, B.D.

HOLLAND
Herman ter Welle, Pastor
Henk Courtz, Drs.

Project Coordinator: William G. Eastlake

INTERNATIONAL AND INTERDENOMINATIONAL BIBLE STUDY SYSTEM

THE NEW TESTAMENT STUDY BIBLE HEBREWS–JUDE

Executive Editor: Ralph W. Harris, M.A.

Editor: Stanley M. Horton, Th.D.

Managing Editor: Gayle Garrity Seaver, J.D.

THE COMPLETE BIBLICAL LIBRARY
Springfield, Missouri, U.S.A.

Table of Contents

VERSE-BY-VERSE COMMENTARY

PAUL O. WRIGHT, Th.D. **Hebrews**
HARDY W. STEINBERG, B.A. **James**
ROBERT C. CUNNINGHAM, M.A. **1, 2 Peter**
JOHN D. BECHTLE, D.Min. **1, 2, 3 John, Jude**

VARIOUS VERSIONS

GERARD J. FLOKSTRA, JR., D.Min.

BOARD OF REVIEW

Zenas Bicket, Ph.D.
Charles Harris, Ed.D.
Jesse Moon, D.Min.
Opal Reddin, D.Min.

STAFF

Editor of Greek-English Dictionary: Denis Vinyard, M.Div.

Editor of the Old Testament: Don Williams, M.Div.

Production Coordinator: Cynthia Riemenschneider

Senior Editors: Gary Leggett, M.A.; Dorothy B. Morris

Editorial Team: Paul Ash, B.A.; Lloyd Anderson; Betty Bates; Faye Faucett; Norma Gott; Charlotte Gribben; Faith Horton, B.A.; Mary Jane Jaynes; Connie Leggett; Brenda Lochner; Marietta Vinyard

Art Director: Terry Van Someren, B.F.A.

Layout Artist: Jim Misloski, B.A.

Word Processing and Secretarial: Sonja Jensen; Patti Christensen; Rochelle Holman; Rachel Wisehart, B.A.

Introduction

This volume of the *Study Bible* is part of a 16-volume set titled *The Complete Biblical Library.* It is an ambitious plan to provide all the information one needs for a basic understanding of the New Testament—useful for scholars but also for students and lay people.

In addition to the Harmony, *The Complete Biblical Library* provides a 9-volume *Study Bible* and a 6-volume *Greek-English Dictionary.* They are closely linked. You will find information about the *Study Bible*'s features later in the Introduction. The *Greek-English Dictionary* lists all the Greek words of the New Testament in their alphabetic order, provides a concordance showing each place the words appear in the New Testament, and includes an article explaining the background, significance, and meaning of the words.

FEATURES OF THE STUDY BIBLE

The *Study Bible* is a unique combination of study materials which will help both the scholar and the layman achieve a better understanding of the New Testament and the language in which it was written. All of these helps are available in various forms but bringing them together in combination will save many hours of research. Most scholars do not have in their personal libraries all the volumes necessary to provide the information so readily available here.

The editors of *The Complete Biblical Library* are attempting an unusual task: to help scholars in their research but also to make available to laymen the tools by which to acquire knowledge which up to this time has been available only to scholars.

Following are the major divisions of the *Study Bible*:

Overview

Each volume contains an encyclopedic survey of the New Testament book. It provides a general outline, discusses matters about which there may be a difference of opinion, and provides background information regarding the history, culture, literature, and philosophy of the era covered by the book.

Interlinear

Following the overall principle of providing help for both the scholar and the layman, we supply a unique *Interlinear.* Most interlinears, if not all, give merely the Greek text and the meanings of the words. Our *Interlinear* contains *five* parts:

1. *Greek Text.* Our Greek text is a comparative text which includes both the traditional text type and the text which is common in modern textual editions.

2. *Grammatical Forms.* These are shown above each Greek word, alongside its assigned number. This information is repeated, along with the Greek word, in the *Greek-English Dictionary* where more details may be found.

3. *Transliteration.* No other interlinears provide this. Its purpose is to familiarize laymen with the proper pronunciation of Greek words so they will feel comfortable when using them in teaching situations. Complete information on pronunciation is found on the page showing the Greek and Hebrew alphabets.

4. *Translation.* The basic meaning of each Greek word is found beneath it. Rather than merely accepting the work of past interlinears, we have assigned scholars to upgrade words to a more modern description. See a later section for the principles we have followed in translation of the Greek words in our *Interlinear.*

5. *Assigned Numbers.* The unique numbering system of *The Complete Biblical Library* makes cross-reference study between the *Study Bible* and the *Greek-English Dictionary* the ultimate in simplicity. Each Greek word has been assigned a number. *Alpha* is the first word in alphabetic order as well as the first letter of the Greek alphabet, so the number *1* has been assigned to it. The rest of the almost 5,000 words follow in numerical and alphabetic sequence.

The *Greek-English Dictionary* follows the same plan with each word listed in alphabetic sequence. If a student desires further study on a certain word, he can find its number above it and locate it in the dictionary. In moments he has access to all the valuable information he needs for a basic understanding of that word.

Textual Apparatus

As said above, our Greek text is a comparative text. A text based only upon the *Textus Receptus* is not adequate for today's needs. Also, an eclectic text—using the "best" from various text types—will not be satisfactory, because such an approach may be quite subjective, with decisions influenced by the personal viewpoint of the scholar. Our text is a combination of both the main types of the Greek New Testament text. We have the *Textus Receptus*, a Stephanus text, based on the Byzantine text type. When there are important variants which differ from the *Textus Receptus*, they are included within brackets in the text. In the narrow column to the left of the *Interlinear*, the sources of the variants are listed. This will provide a fascinating study for a scholar and student, and will save him innumerable hours of research.

Verse-by-Verse Commentary

Many Bible-loving scholars have combined their knowledge, study, and skills to provide this. It is not an exhaustive treatment (many other commentaries are available for that), but again it provides a basic understanding of every verse in the New Testament. It does not usually deal with textual criticism (that can be dealt with in another arena), but it opens up the nuances of the Greek New Testament as written by the inspired writers.

Various Versions

This offers a greatly amplified New Testament. Each verse is broken down into its phrases; the King James Version is shown in boldface type; then from more than 60 other versions we show various ways the Greek of that phrase may be translated. The Greek of the First Century was such a rich language that to obtain the full meaning of words, several synonyms may be needed.

TRANSLATION OF GREEK WORDS

No word-for-word translation can be fully "literal" in the sense of expressing all the nuances of the original language. Rather, our purpose is to help the student find the English word which most correctly expresses the original Greek word in that particular context. The Greek language is so rich in meaning that the same word may have a slightly different meaning in another context.

In any language idioms offer a special translation problem. According to the dictionary, this is an expression which has "a meaning which cannot be derived from the conjoined meanings of its elements." The Greek language abounds in such phrases which cannot be translated literally.

We have come to what we consider a splendid solution to the problem, whether the translation should be strictly literal or abound in a plethora of idiomatic expressions. From more than 60 translations, the *Various Versions* column presents the various ways phrases have been translated. Here the student will find the translations of the idioms. This enables us to make our English line in the *Interlinear* strictly literal. The student will have available both types of translation—and will have a fresh appreciation for the struggles through which translators go.

HOW THE NEW TESTAMENT CAME TO US

Volume 1 of *The Complete Biblical Library*, the *Harmony of the Gospels*, contains information on how the four Gospels came into being. The preponderance of proof points to the fact that the rest of the New Testament was written before A.D. 100. Like the Gospels, it was written in Greek, the universal language of that era. It was qualified in a special way for this purpose. Probably no other language is so expressive and able to provide such fine nuances of meaning.

Yet the New Testament Greek is not the perfectly structured form of the language from the old classical period. It is the more simple Koine Greek from the later Hellenistic age. This had become the lingua franca of the Hellenistic and Roman world. The Egyptian papyri have shown that the language which the New Testament writers used was the common language of the people. It seems as though God accomodated himself to a form of communication which would make His Word most readily accepted and easily understood.

At the same time we should recognize that the language of the Greek New Testament also is a *religious language*, with a tradition going back a couple of centuries to the Septuagint, the Greek translation of the Old Testament.

The Manuscripts

None of the original manuscripts (handwritten documents) still exist. Even in the First Century they must have often been copied so as to share their treasured truths with numerous congregations of believers. The original documents then soon became worn out through use. Evidently, only copies of the New Testament still exist.

Over 5,000 manuscripts of the New Testament have been discovered up to the present time. Most of them are small fragments of verses or chapters, a few books of the New Testament, some copies of the Gospels. Very few contain all or nearly all of the New Testament.

The manuscripts have come to us in various forms: (1) Egyptian papyri, (2) majuscules, (3) minuscules, (4) writings of the Early Church fathers, (5) lectionaries, and (6) early versions.

The Egyptian Papyri

These are the oldest copies of parts of the Greek New Testament. The earliest are dated about A.D. 200, a few even earlier, and the youngest are from the Seventh Century. Most of them date back to the Third, Fourth and Fifth Centuries of the Christian Era.

They were found in the late 1800s in Egypt. The dry climatic conditions of that country enabled them to be preserved. The largest fragments contain only a few dozen pages, while the smallest are the size of a postage stamp.

The papyri are listed in the back of this volume under the heading "Manuscripts."

The Majuscules

These are the second oldest kind of copies of New Testament manuscripts. They received this description because they were written in majuscules; that is, large letters (the uncials are a form of majuscules). Three major majuscules are the following:

1. Codex Aleph, also called Codex Sinaiticus, because it was discovered in the mid-1840s by the great scholar Tischendorf at St. Catharine's Monastery, located at the foot of Mount Sinai. Numbered 01, it contains all the New Testament and is dated in the Fourth Century.

2. Codex A, numbered 02, is named Alexandrinus, because it came from Alexandria in Egypt. In the Gospels, this manuscript is the foremost witness to the Byzantine text type.

3. Codex B, 03, is called Codex Vaticanus, because it is in the Vatican library. Along with the Sinaiticus, it is the main witness for the Egyptian text type. However, it is important to realize there are more than 3,000 differences between these 2 manuscripts in the Gospels alone (Hoskier).

See the list of majuscules in the back of this volume, under "Manuscripts."

The Minuscules

This is a kind of manuscript written in small letters. They are only a few hundred years old, beginning with the Ninth Century. Most come from the 12th to the 14th Century A.D. They form, by far, the greatest group of the New Testament manuscripts, numbering almost 2,800.

The minuscules represent the unbroken text tradition in the Greek Orthodox Church, and about 90 percent of them belong to the Byzantine text group. They are numbered 1, 2, 3, etc.

Lectionaries and Church Fathers

Lectionaries include manuscripts which were not Scripture themselves but contain Scripture quotations, used for the scheduled worship services of the annual church calendar. These are numbered consecutively and are identified by *lect*.

Practically all the New Testament could be retrieved from the writings of early Christian leaders, called church fathers. These lists are located in the back of this volume.

Early Versions

Translations of the New Testament from Greek are also of value. They are listed under "Manuscripts" in the back of this volume. The best known is the Latin Vulgate by Jerome.

Major Greek Texts

From the manuscripts which have just been described, various types of Greek texts have been formed:

The Western text can possibly be traced back to the Second Century. It was used mostly in Western Europe and North Africa. It tends to add to the text and makes long paraphrases of it. Today some scholars do not recognize it as a special text type.

The Caesarean text may have originated in Egypt and was brought, it is believed, to the city of Caesarea in Palestine. Later, it was carried to Jerusalem, then by Armenian missionaries into a province in the kingdom of Georgia, now a republic of the U.S.S.R. Some scholars consider it a mixture of other text types.

The two most prominent text types, however, are the Egyptian (also called the Alexandrian) and the Byzantine. These are the major ones considered in our *Interlinear* and *Textual Apparatus*. Except for the papyrus texts which are highly varied, these are the only text families which have any degree of support. References to numerous text groups which were so common a few decades ago must now probably be considered out of date. At any rate, out of practical considerations, we have kept the Byzantine and Egyptian (Alexandrian) as fixed text groups in our *Textual Apparatus*. Following is historical information about them.

The Byzantine Text

Many titles have been applied to this text type. It has been called the *K* (Koine), Syrian, Antiochian, and Traditional. It is generally believed to have been produced at Antioch in Syria, then taken to Byzantium, later known as Constantinople. For about 1,000 years, while the Byzantine Empire ruled the Middle East, this was the text used by the Greek Orthodox Church. It also influenced Europe.

Because of this background it became the basis for the first printed text editions, among others the famous *Textus Receptus*, called "the acknowledged text."

The Byzantine text form is also called the Majority text, since 80 to 90 percent of all existing manuscripts are represented in this text, though most of them are quite recent and evidently copies of earlier manuscripts. Like the Egyptian text, the Byzantine text can be traced back to the Fourth Century. It also contains some readings which seem to be the same as some papyri which can be traced back to a much earlier time. Among the oldest majuscules the Byzantine is, among others, represented by Codex Alexandrinus (02, A), 07, 08, 09, 010, 011, 012, 013, 015, and others.

The Egyptian Text

This text type originated in Egypt and is the one which gained the highest recognition and acceptance there in the Fourth Century. It was produced mainly by copyists in Alexandria, from which it received the name *Alexandrian*. This text form is represented mostly by two codices: Sinaiticus (01, Aleph) and Vaticanus (03, B) from the Fourth Century, also from Codex Ephraemi (04, C) from the Fifth Century. The use of this text type ceased about the year 450 but lived on in the Latin translation, the Vulgate version.

Printed Greek Texts

The invention of printing about 1450 opened the door for wider distribution of the Scriptures. In 1516 Erasmus, a Dutch scholar, produced the first *printed* Greek New Testament. It was based on the Byzantine text type, with most of the New Testament coming from manuscripts dated at about the 12th Century. He did his work very hurriedly, finishing his task in just a few months. His second edition, produced in 1519 with some of the mistakes corrected, became the basis for translations into German by Luther and into English by Tyndale.

A printed Greek New Testament was produced by a French printer, Stephanus, in 1550. His edition and those produced by Theodore Beza, of Geneva, between 1565 and 1604, based on the Byzantine text, have been entitled the *Textus Receptus.* That description, however, originated with the text produced by Elzevir. He described his second edition of 1633 by the Latin phrase *Textus Receptus,* or the "Received Text"; that is, the one accepted generally as the correct one.

A list of the printed editions of the Greek text is found in the section describing the relationship of the *Interlinear* and the *Textual Apparatus.*

Contribution of Westcott and Hort

Two British scholars, Westcott and Hort, have played a prominent role in deciding which text type should be used. They (especially Hort) called the Byzantine text "corrupt," because of the young age of its supporting manuscripts and proceeded to develop their own text (1881-86). It was really a restoration of the Egyptian text from the Fourth Century. It depended mainly on two codices, Sinaiticus and Vaticanus, but was also supported by numerous majuscules such as 02, 04, 019, 020, 025, 032, 033, 037, and 044.

Westcott and Hort opposed the *Textus Receptus* because it was based on the Byzantine text form. Most scholars agreed with their contention, and the *Textus Receptus* fell into disrepute. However, Westcott and Hort made their assumptions before the Greek papyri were discovered, and in recent years some scholars have come to the defense of the Byzantine text and the *Textus Receptus.* They have learned that some of the readings in the Byzantine text are the same as those found in the earliest papyri, dated about A.D. 200 and even earlier (p45, p46, p64 and p66, for example). This seems to take the Byzantine text back at least as far as the Egyptian.

Two important statements must be made: (1) We should always remember there are good men and scholars on both sides of the controversy, and their major concern is to obtain as pure a text as possible, to reassure Bible students that the New Testament we now possess conforms to that written in the First Century. (2) Since it was the original writings which were inspired by the Holy Spirit, it is important for us to ascertain as closely as possible how well our present-day text agrees with the original writings. It should alleviate the fears some may have as to whether we have the true gospel enunciated in the First Century to know that most of the differences in the Greek text (about 1 percent of the total) are minor in nature and do not affect the great Christian doctrines we hold dear. Significant differences may be found in only a very few cases.

We have consciously avoided polemics in the area of textual criticism. There is legitimacy for such discussion, but *The Complete Biblical Library* is not the arena for such a conflict. (1) Often the opposing views are conjectural. (2) There is insufficient space to treat subjects adequately and to raise questions without answering them fully leads to confusion.

LITERARY AND BIBLICAL STANDARDS

Several hundred people, highly qualified scholars and specialists in particular fields have participated in producing *The Complete Biblical Library.* Great care has been taken to maintain high standards of scholarship and ethics. By involving scholars in Boards of Review for the *Study Bible* and the *Greek-English Dictionary,* we added an extra step to the editorial process. We have been particularly concerned about giving proper credit for citations from other works and have instructed our writers to show care in this regard. Any deviation from this principle has been inadvertent and not intentional.

Obviously, with writers coming from widely differing backgrounds, there are differences of opinion as to how to interpret certain passages.

We have tried to be just. When there are strong differences on the meaning of a particular passage, we have felt it best to present the contrasting viewpoints.

STUDY HELPS

As you come to the Scripture section of this volume, you will find correlated pages for your study. The facing pages are designed to complement each other, so you will have a better understanding of the Word of God than ever before. Each two-page spread will deal with a group of verses.

On the left-hand page is the *Interlinear* with its fivefold helps: (1) the Greek text in which the New Testament was written; (2) the transliteration, showing how to pronounce each word; (3) the basic meaning of each word; (4) next to Greek words an assigned number (you will need this number to learn more about the word in the *Greek-English Dictionary*, companion to the *Study Bible*); and (5) the grammatical forms of each Greek word. The left-hand page also contains a column called the *Textual Apparatus*. This column is explained later.

The right-hand page contains two features. The *Verse-by-Verse Commentary* refers to each verse, except when occasionally it deals with some closely related verses. The *Various Versions* column provides an expanded understanding of the various ways Greek words or phrases can be translated. The phrase from the King James Version appears first in boldface print, then other meaningful ways the Greek language has been translated. This feature will bring to you the riches of the language in which the New Testament first appeared.

General Abbreviations

In a work of this nature it is necessary to use some abbreviations in order to conserve space. In deference to the Scriptures it is our custom not to abbreviate the titles of the books of the Bible, but abbreviations are used elsewhere. Becoming familiar with them will enable you to pursue in-depth study more effectively.

The following are general abbreviations which you will find used throughout the book:

cf.	compared to or see
ibid.	in the same place
id.	the same
idem	the same
i.e.	that is
e.g.	for example
f. ff.	and following page or pages
sic	intended as written
MS(S)	manuscript(s)
ET	editor's translation

Greek and Hebrew Alphabets with Pronunciation Guide

Some readers may want to become better acquainted with the Greek and Hebrew alphabets (the latter the language of the Old Testament). If so, the following lists will be of service to you.

Greek

Α	α	alpha	a	(father)
Β	β	beta	b	
Γ	γ	gamma	g	(got)
Δ	δ	delta	d	
Ε	ε	epsilon	e	(get)
Ζ	ζ	zeta	z	dz (leads)
Η	η	eta	e	(ate)
Θ	θ	theta	th	(thin)
Ι	ι	iota	i	(sin or machine)
Κ	κ	kappa	k	
Λ	λ	lambda	l	
Μ	μ	mu	m	
Ν	ν	nu	n	
Ξ	ξ	xi	x	
Ο	ο	omicron	o	(lot)
Π	π	pi	p	
Ρ	ρ	rho	r	
Σ	σ,s[1]	sigma	s	
Τ	τ	tau	t	
Υ	υ	upsilon	u	German ü
Φ	φ	phi	ph	(philosophy)
Χ	χ	chi	ch	(chaos)
Ψ	ψ	psi	ps	(lips)
Ω	ω	omega	o	(ocean)

Hebrew

א	aleph	’[2]	
ב	beth	b, bh	(v)[3]
ג	gimel	g, gh	
ד	daleth	d, dh	(they)[3]
ה	he	h	
ו	waw	w	
ז	zayin	z	
ח	heth	h	(kh)
ט	teth	t	
י	yod	y	
כ ך	kaph	k, kh	
ל	lamed	l	
מ ם	mem	m	
נ ן	nun	n	
ס	samekh	s	
ע	ayin	‘	
פ ף	pe	p, ph	
צ ץ	sadhe	s	(ts)
ק	qoph	q	
ר	resh	r	
שׂ	sin	s	
שׁ	shin	sh	
ת	taw	t, th	(thing)[3]

Greek Pronunciation Rules

Before another *g*, or before a *k* or a *ch*, *g* is pronounced and spelled with an *n*, in the transliteration of the Greek word.

In the Greek, *s* is written at the end of a word, elsewhere it appears as σ. The rough breathing mark (‘) indicates that an *h*-sound is to be pronounced before the initial vowel or diphthong. The smooth breathing mark (’) indicates that no such *h*-sound is to be pronounced.

There are three accents, the acute (—́), the circumflex (—̂) and the grave (—̀). These stand over a vowel and indicate that stress in pronunciation is to be placed on the syllable having any one of the accents.

Pronouncing Diphthongs

ai is pronounced like *ai* in aisle
ei is pronounced like *ei* in eight
oi is pronounced like *oi* in oil
au is pronounced like *ow* in cow
eu is pronounced like *eu* in feud
ou is pronounced like *oo* in food
ui is pronounced like *ui* in suite (sweet)

1. Where two forms of a letter are given, the one at the right is used at the end of a word.
2. Not represented in transliteration when the initial letter.
3. Letters underscored represent pronunciation of the second form only.

Old and New Testament Books and Apocrypha

As a service to you, we have listed the books of the Bible in their order. The Apocrypha is a series of books which were included in the Vulgate version (the Latin translation of the Bible endorsed by the Roman Catholic Church). Though not considered part of the canon by either the Jews or Protestants, they give interesting insights, on occasion, concerning the times with which they deal. They are not on the same level as the 66 books of our canon. These lists are located in the back of the book.

Bibliographic Citations

The Complete Biblical Library has adopted a system of coordinated citations in the text and bibliography material which accommodates every type of reader. For the sake of simplicity and space, information given in the text to document a source is minimal, often including only the last name of the writer, or a shortened title and a page number.

Those who would like to research the subject more deeply can easily do so by looking in the Bibliography in the back of the book under the last name or shortened title. The Bibliography lists complete information necessary to locate the source in a library, supplemented by the page number given in the citation in the text.

RELATIONSHIP OF THE INTERLINEAR AND THE TEXTUAL APPARATUS

The Greek text of the *Study Bible* provides a means of collating the traditional texts with modern text editions; that is, comparing them critically to discover their degree of similarity or divergence. The *Textual Apparatus* column provides information as to which manuscripts or groups of manuscripts support certain readings. Some scholarly works use an eclectic text, selecting from various sources the text they consider to be the best. In our view, our comparative text provides a better system for considering the relative merits of the major texts.

The *Textual Apparatus* refers to many different manuscripts but to just two text groups, the Byzantine and the Egyptian, also known as Alexandrian. Except for the papyri texts, which are highly varied, these two text families are the only ones which have a significant degree of support. Reference to many different text groups is now becoming passé. Using only the byz (Byzantine) and eg (Egyptian) text groups makes the work of the researcher less complicated and provides an adequate system of reference.

The *Interlinear* uses the Stephanus text as its basis but is not confined to it. Actually, most of the Greek text is the same in all the text types. For easy comparison variants are inserted in the text and are then considered in the *Textual Apparatus* column, which provides their background in the major and minor manuscripts.

Abbreviations and Signs Used in the Textual Apparatus

Using the information which follows you will be able to identify the variants and their sources and to compare them with the basic text and other variants.

Txt	The Greek text used, the TR
byz	Byzantine text form
eg	Egyptian text form
p 1, etc.	Papyrus manuscripts
01, etc.	Majuscule manuscripts
1, etc.	Minuscule manuscripts
lect	Lectionaries
org	Reading of original copier
corr 1, etc.	Change by another person
( )	Supports in principle
sa	Sahidic
bo	Bohairic

Printed Editions of the Greek Text (with abbreviations)

Steph	Stephanus, 1550
Beza	Beza, 1564-1604
Elzev	Elzevir, 1624
Gries	Griesbach, 1805
Lach	Lachmann, 1842-50
Treg	Tregelles, 1857-72
Alf	Alford, 1862-71
Tisc	Tischendorf, 1865-95
Word	Wordsworth, 1870
We/Ho	Westcott and Hort, 1881-86
Wey	Weymouth, 1885
Weis	Weiss, 1894-1900
Sod	von Soden, 1902-10
H/Far	Hodges and Farstad (Majority text)
☆	various modern text editions
UBS	United Bible Society

Understanding the Codes in the Greek Text and the Textual Apparatus

Definitions:

TR. The *Textus Receptus*, the basic text of this *Interlinear*.

Reading. A word or phrase from a Greek text.

Variant. A reading which differs from the TR.

The *Textual Apparatus* contains two divisions for analyzing the text when variants occur: *Txt*, meaning the TR (*Textus Receptus*); and *Var*, meaning variants, readings which differ from the TR. Under these two headings are listed the manuscripts which support either the TR or the variant.

Illustrations:

The following examples from Luke 10:19-21 show how to understand the relationship between the Greek text and the *Textual Apparatus*.

The half-parenthesis indicates that the next word begins a TR reading for which a variant is shown. See example A.

The variant itself is enclosed in brackets (note the example of this at the beginning of verse 19). The text (TR) reads, "I give . . . , " but the variant reads, "I have given . . . ." See example B.

The small *a* at the beginning of the bracket refers back to the *Textual Apparatus* column, showing it is the first variant in that particular verse. See example C. Only those variants identified by *a, b, c,* etc., are considered in the *Textual Apparatus*.

The star following the *a* means that the variant is used in some modern text editions, such as the UBS text. See example D.

Note that in variant *b* of verse 19 the star appears before the TR word. This means that in this case UBS and/or others do not follow the variant but read the same as the TR. See example E.

In verse 20, variant *a* appears between two half-parentheses, showing *mallon* ("rather") is not included in some texts. The TR reads, "Rejoice but rather that . . . ," while the variant (without *mallon*) reads, "Rejoice but that . . . ." See example F.

It is important to recognize that the star in the *Textual Apparatus* for verse 20 means that UBS and other modern texts support the variant reading. If the UBS supported the TR, the star would have appeared under the *Txt* heading. See example G.

Sometimes there is more than one variant reading, as in variant *b* of verse 20. In such cases they are numbered in order (see the *2* before the star in the second reading). This shows the difference and also provides an easy reference in the *Textual Apparatus*. See example H.

In verse 21, variant *a* presents a case where the word *en* ("in") is not a part of the TR but appears in other texts. The + sign indicates this. See example I.

Understanding the Codes in the Greek Text and the Textual Apparatus

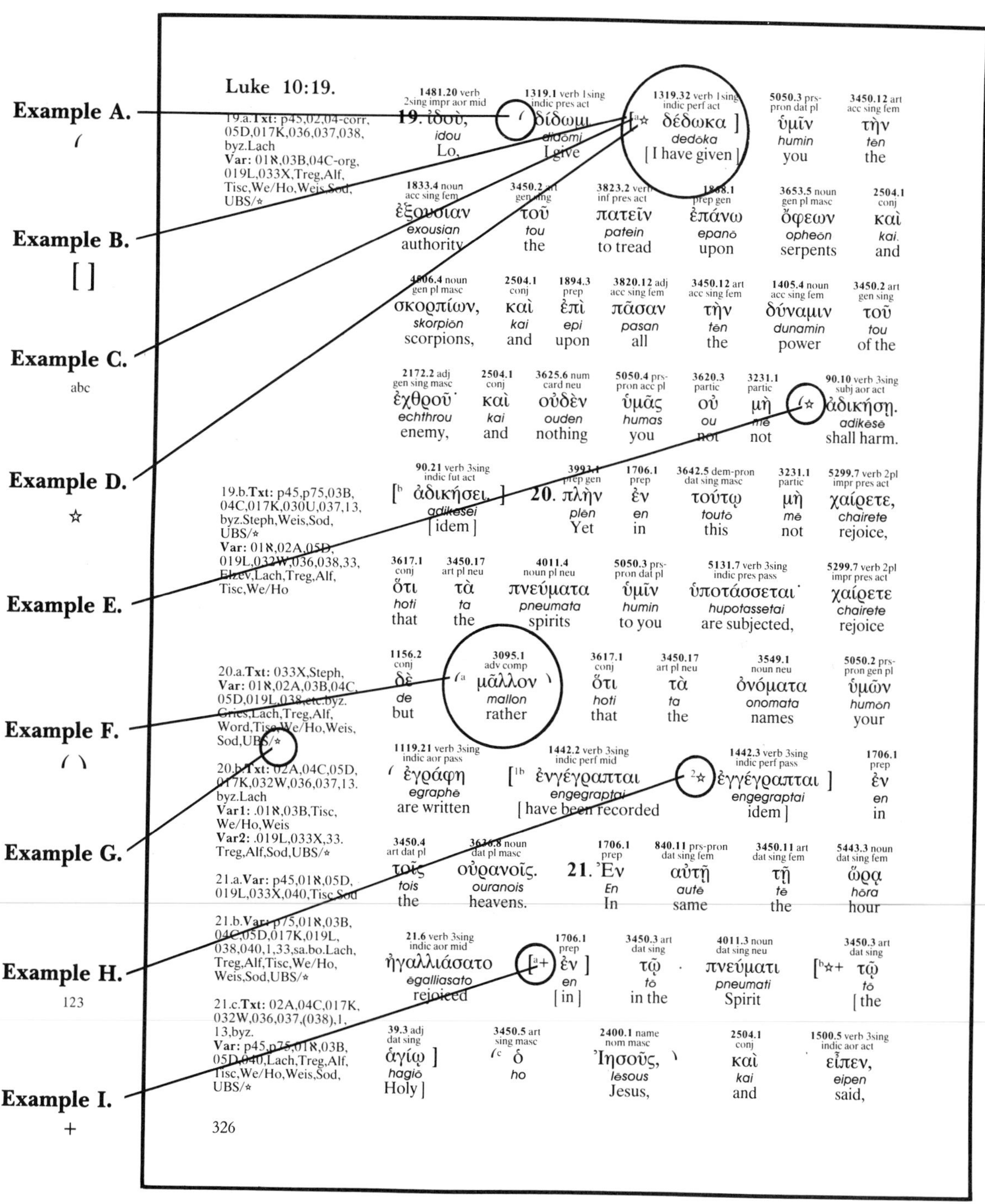

THE EPISTLE TO THE
HEBREWS

Expanded Interlinear
Textual Critical Apparatus
Verse-by-Verse Commentary
Various Versions

3450.9 art nom sing fem	4242.1 prep	1439.4 name acc pl masc	1976.1 noun nom sing fem
Ἡ	Πρὸς	Ἑβραίους	Ἐπιστολή
Hē	*Pros*	*Hebraious*	*Epistolē*
The	To	Hebrews	Epistle

Textual Apparatus

	4041.1 adv	2504.1 conj	4047.1 adv	3682.1 adv	3450.5 art nom sing masc
1:1.	Πολυμερῶς	καὶ	πολυτρόπως	πάλαι	ὁ
	Polumerōs	*kai*	*polutropōs*	*palai*	*ho*
	In many parts	and	in many ways	of old	

2296.1 noun nom sing masc	2953.34 verb nom sing masc part aor act	3450.4 art dat pl	3824.8 noun dat pl masc	1706.1 prep	3450.4 art dat pl
θεὸς	λαλήσας	τοῖς	πατράσιν	ἐν	τοῖς
theos	*lalēsas*	*tois*	*patrasin*	*en*	*tois*
God	having spoken	to the	fathers	by	the

1.a.**Txt:** Steph
Var: 01א,02A,03B
018K,020L,025P,33,byz.
Gries,Lach,Treg,Alf
Word,Tisc,We/Ho,Weis
Sod,UBS/☆

4254.6 noun dat pl masc	1894.2 prep	2057.1 adj gen pl	2057.2 adj gen sing	3450.1 art gen pl
προφήταις,	ἐπ'	ʻ ἐσχάτων	[a☆ ἐσχάτου]	τῶν
prophētais	*ep'*	*eschatōn*	*eschatou*	*tōn*
prophets,	in	last	[idem]	the

2232.6 noun gen pl fem	3642.2 dem-pron gen pl	2953.27 verb 3sing indic aor act	2231.3 prs-pron dat 1pl	1706.1 prep	5048.3 noun dat sing masc
ἡμερῶν	τούτων,	ἐλάλησεν	ἡμῖν	ἐν	υἱῷ,
hēmerōn	*toutōn*	*elalēsen*	*hēmin*	*en*	*huiō*
days	these,	spoke	to us	by	a Son,

3614.6 rel-pron acc sing masc	4935.10 verb 3sing indic aor act	2791.2 noun acc sing masc	3820.4 adj gen pl	1217.1 prep
2. ὃν	ἔθηκεν	κληρονόμον	πάντων,	δι'
hon	*ethēken*	*klēronomon*	*pantōn*	*di'*
whom	he appointed	heir	of all,	through

3614.2 rel-pron gen sing	2504.1 conj	3450.8 art acc pl masc	163.6 noun acc pl masc	4020.24 verb 3sing indic aor act	4020.24 verb 3sing indic aor act
οὗ	καὶ	ʻ τοὺς	αἰῶνας	ἐποίησεν,	[☆ ἐποίησεν
hou	*kai*	*tous*	*aiōnas*	*epoiēsen*	*epoiēsen*
whom	also	the	ages	he made:	[he made

3450.8 art acc pl masc	163.6 noun acc pl masc	3614.5 rel-pron nom sing masc	1498.21 verb nom sing masc part pres act	537.1 noun sing neu
τοὺς	αἰῶνας·]	3. ὃς	ὢν	ἀπαύγασμα
tous	*aiōnas*	*hos*	*ōn*	*apaugasma*
the	ages:]	who	being	effulgence

3450.10 art gen sing fem	1385.2 noun gen sing fem	2504.1 conj	5317.1 noun nom sing masc	3450.10 art gen sing fem	5125.2 noun gen sing fem
τῆς	δόξης	καὶ	χαρακτὴρ	τῆς	ὑποστάσεως
tēs	*doxēs*	*kai*	*charaktēr*	*tēs*	*hupostaseōs*
of the	glory	and	exact expression	of the	substance

840.3 prs-pron gen sing	5179.7 verb nom sing masc part pres act	4885.1 conj	3450.17 art pl neu	3820.1 adj	3450.3 art dat sing
αὐτοῦ,	φέρων	τε	τὰ	πάντα	τῷ
autou	*pherōn*	*te*	*ta*	*panta*	*tō*
his,	upholding	and	the	all things	by the

THE EPISTLE TO THE
HEBREWS

1:1. The majestic opening words of this epistle set the tone for the entire book. They subtly contrast the former ancient revelation, the Mosaic covenant, with the final, present revelation in Jesus Christ, the new covenant. Under the old covenant God spoke to the Hebrew fathers by the prophets. This self-disclosure was periodic and partial in nature. It was spread out over at least 10 centuries and given by various means. Sometimes God directly intervened in history; sometimes the Holy Spirit worked internally in the minds of the prophetic writers; sometimes God revealed himself through visions or dreams; often God's message was delivered by angels. Such revelations were preparatory and piecemeal. And they were given in the past.

1:2,3. But the divine disclosure which has been made in Jesus Christ is substantially different. First of all, it is current. It has taken place "in these last days," and it has been given to believers. Secondly, it is cumulative. It completes what was begun in the Old Testament. The phrase "in these last days" is messianic and points out that in the Son there is the fulfillment of what was only promised by the old covenant. It is the equivalent of saying that in the Son God has spoken His final message of salvation. All that is needed for salvation has been revealed in the Son. Finally, the inspired writer emphasized the Christological nature of this revelation. By omitting the article on the word "Son" (*huiō*) he pointed to the essential characteristic of the messenger. It is in such a person as His Son that God has spoken His ultimate word of salvation. Only such a One could bring redemption to a lost race.

The text enumerates nine factors which demonstrate the superiority of the Son as the divine messenger. (1) He is "heir of all things." These words echo the commission given to Adam (Genesis 1:28), ring with the promise of Psalm 2:7,8, and sparkle with the dignity of man described in Psalm 8:5,6. Certainly they resound with overtones of the Cross. Jesus told of the vineyard owner (Matthew 21:37,38) who finally sent his son, saying, "They will reverence my son," only to hear the evil tenants reply, "This is the heir; come, let us kill him, and let us seize on his inheritance." This reflects the attitude Jesus faced while here on earth. (2) The Son is the agent by whom God created the universe and the ages of time through which it passes.

(3) Christ is the flashing forth of the Father's glory; like a brilliant ray from the sun, He reveals God's perfections. (4) Like the impres-

Various Versions

1. God, who at sundry times and in divers manners spake in time past, unto the fathers by the prophets: Long ago God spoke, *Beck* . . . It was bit by bit...in olden times, *Williams* . . . It was in a number of stages and in a variety of ways, *Adams* . . . in ancient days spoke to our ancestors...at many different times, *Montgomery* . . . and many modes, *Concordant* . . . by various methods, *Wilson* . . . to our early fathers, *NLT.*

2. Hath in these last days spoken unto us: . . . in these latter days, *Williams.*

by [his] Son: . . . in One who by nature is, *Wuest* . . . through a Son, *Williams.*

whom he hath appointed heir of all things: And He has been given everything for a heritage, *Norlie* . . . appointed lawful owner of everything, *Williams.*

by whom also he made the worlds: . . . of whom also he constituted the ages, *Wilson* . . . It was through him that God made the universe, *TNT.*

3. Who being the brightness of [his] glory: He radiates, *TNT* . . . who shines with God's glory, *Beck* . . . as he is the reflection of his glory, *Klingensmith* . . . being an emanation of God's glory, *Montgomery* . . . being an Effulgence, *Wilson.*

and the express image of his person: . . . the perfect representation of, *Adams, Williams* . . . and the exact image of God's nature, *Norlie* . . . and an exact Impress of his substance, *Wilson* . . . the exact picture of God's real being, *SEB* . . . the exact reproduction of His essence, *Wuest* . . . The Son is as God is in every way, *NLT* . . . and stamp of his substance, *Montgomery* . . . and the embodiment of the divine nature, *TCNT.*

Hebrews 1:4

3.a.**Txt:** 06D-corr 015H-corr,018K,020L byz.sa.bo.Sod **Var:** 01א,02A,03B 015H-org,025P,33,it. Lach,Treg,Alf,Tisc We/Ho,Weis,UBS/☆

3.b.**Txt:** 06D-corr,018K 020L,byz. **Var:** 01א-org,02A,03B 06D-org,025P,bo.Lach Treg,Alf,Word,Tisc We/Ho,Weis,UBS/☆

4.a.**Var:** p46,03B

4343.3 noun dat sing neu	**3450.10** art gen sing fem	**1405.2** noun gen sing fem	**840.3** prs-pron gen sing	**1217.1** prep	**1431.4** prs-pron gen sing
ῥήματι	τῆς	δυνάμεως	αὐτοῦ,	(a δι'	ἑαυτοῦ \
rhēmati	*tēs*	*dunameōs*	*autou*	*di'*	*heautou*
word	of the	power	his,	by	himself

2484.2 noun acc sing masc	**4020.69** verb nom sing masc part aor mid	**3450.1** art gen pl	**264.6** noun gen pl fem	**3450.1** art gen pl
καθαρισμὸν	(ποιησάμενος	τῶν	ἁμαρτιῶν	[☆ τῶν
katharismon	*poiēsamenos*	*tōn*	*hamartiōn*	*tōn*
purification	having made	of the	sins	[of the

264.6 noun gen pl fem	**4020.69** verb nom sing masc part aor mid	**2231.2** prs-pron gen 1pl	**2495.3** verb 3sing indic aor act	**1706.1** prep
ἁμαρτιῶν	ποιησάμενος]	(b ἡμῶν, \	ἐκάθισεν	ἐν
hamartiōn	*poiēsamenos*	*hēmōn*	*ekathisen*	*en*
sins	having made]	our,	sat down	on

1182.5 adj dat sing fem	**3450.10** art gen sing fem	**3142.2** noun gen sing fem	**1706.1** prep	**5146.2** adj dat pl masc	**4965.8** dem-pron dat sing neu
δεξιᾷ	τῆς	μεγαλωσύνης	ἐν	ὑψηλοῖς,	4. τοσούτῳ
dexia	*tēs*	*megalōsunēs*	*en*	*hupsēlois*	*tosoutō*
right hand	of the	greatness	on	high,	by so much

2882.2 adj comp nom sing masc	**1090.53** verb nom sing masc part aor mid	**3450.1** art gen pl	**32.6** noun gen pl masc	**3607.7** rel-pron dat sing neu
κρείττων	γενόμενος	(a τῶν \	ἀγγέλων	ὅσῳ
kreittōn	*genomenos*	*tōn*	*angelōn*	*hosō*
better	having become	than the	angels,	as much as

1307.4 adj comp sing neu	**3706.1** prep	**840.8** prs-pron acc pl masc	**2789.9** verb 3sing indic perf act	**3549.2** noun sing neu
διαφορώτερον	παρ'	αὐτοὺς	κεκληρονόμηκεν	ὄνομα.
diaphorōteron	*par'*	*autous*	*keklēronomēken*	*onoma*
more excellent	beyond	them	he has inherited	a name.

4949.2 intr-pron dat sing	**1056.1** conj	**1500.5** verb 3sing indic aor act	**4077.1** adv	**3450.1** art gen pl	**32.6** noun gen pl masc
5. Τίνι	γὰρ	εἶπέν	ποτε	τῶν	ἀγγέλων,
Tini	*gar*	*eipen*	*pote*	*tōn*	*angelōn*
To which	for	said he	ever	of the	angels,

5048.1 noun nom sing masc	**1466.2** prs-pron gen 1sing	**1498.3** verb 2sing indic pres act	**4622.1** prs-pron nom 2sing	**1466.1** prs-pron nom 1sing
Υἱός	μου	εἶ	σύ,	ἐγὼ
Huios	*mou*	*ei*	*su*	*egō*
Son	my	are	you:	I

4449.1 adv	**1074.8** verb 1sing indic perf act	**4622.4** prs-pron acc 2sing	**2504.1** conj	**3687.1** adv	**1466.1** prs-pron nom 1sing
σήμερον	γεγέννηκά	σε;	καὶ	πάλιν,	Ἐγὼ
sēmeron	*gegennēka*	*se*	*kai*	*palin*	*Egō*
today	have begotten	you?	and	again,	I

1498.38 verb 1sing indic fut mid	**840.4** prs-pron dat sing	**1519.1** prep	**3824.4** noun acc sing masc	**2504.1** conj	**840.5** prs-pron nom sing masc
ἔσομαι	αὐτῷ	εἰς	πατέρα,	καὶ	αὐτὸς
esomai	*autō*	*eis*	*patera*	*kai*	*autos*
will be	to him	for	Father,	and	he

1498.40 verb 3sing indic fut mid	**1466.4** prs-pron dat 1sing	**1519.1** prep	**5048.4** noun acc sing masc	**3615.1** conj	**1156.2** conj
ἔσται	μοι	εἰς	υἱόν;	6. ὅταν	δὲ
estai	*moi*	*eis*	*huion*	*hotan*	*de*
shall be	to me	for	Son?	When	and

sion made in wax by a signet ring, He is the exact expression of God's character in human form. There is not one feature of God's character that is not displayed in His Son. (5) By His powerful utterance, He upholds the universe, that is, He carries it along to its final destiny. He is the Lord of history. But He is more than a revealer of knowledge. (6) He has already by himself effected the cleansing and removal of the believer's sins. He is the Redeemer. (7) He sits and rules as absolute Sovereign and (8) as Intercessor at God's right hand.

and upholding all things by the word of his power: He sustains everything by His powerful word, *Adams* . . . continues to uphold, *Williams* . . . upholds the universe, *TNT* . . . besides carrying on all by his powerful declaration, *Concordant* . . . and sustaining, guiding, and propelling all things by, *Wuest* . . . sustaining the Universe by the expression of His mighty Will, *Wade* . . . through the powerful mandate of God, *Noli.*

when he had by himself purged our sins: He made an expiation for the sins of men, *Montgomery* . . . After he had provided a cleansing from sin, *SEB* . . . procured man's purification from sins, *Williams.*

sat down on the right hand of the Majesty on high: . . . has taken his seat, *Montgomery* . . . he sat at the right of the Greatness in the Highest, *Klingensmith* . . . of Almighty God in heaven, *TNT.*

1:4. The ninth characteristic of the Son used to emphasize His superiority is His name, "Son." The name *Son* is inherently superior to the name *angel.* It was as the Son of Man that Jesus entered into the messianic office through His incarnation, suffering, and resurrection. The eternal deity of Jesus as the Son of God and His human sonship is not the consideration at this point, but rather His messianic sonship which is dependent on His divine-human personhood. To be Messiah He had to be the God-man.

The rest of chapter 1 elaborates on the superiority of the Son to the angels. Some recent interpreters think this argument is directed at the influence of the Essenes of the Qumran community on the Jewish Christian readers of this letter. This is possible, but the argument in the context emphasizes the superiority of the gospel to the Law. In the light of Psalm 68:17, Galatians 3:19, Acts 7:38, and the Septuagint rendering of Deuteronomy 33:2, it is clear that the Jews heavily emphasized the mediation of the angels in the giving of the Law. To professing Jewish Christians who might be tempted to revert to Judaism, the Son's superiority to the angels was an important matter.

Angels were so prominent in ancient Israel's history, its people were tempted to worship them, but to do so would be to worship the creature rather than the Creator (Romans 1:25). Paul warned the Colossians not to show devotion to angels (Colossians 2:18). John said of the heavenly messenger who showed him many things, "And when I had heard and seen, I fell down to worship before the feet of the angel which showed me these things. Then saith he unto me, See thou do it not: for I am thy fellow servant" (Revelation 22:8,9).

4. Being made so much better than the angels: . . . being thereby shewn to be, *Wade* . . . proving Himself to be as much, *Williams* . . . He became as much superior, *Adams* . . . became as much greater than, *Beck.*

as he hath by inheritance: . . . that he has inherited, *Montgomery.*

obtained a more excellent name than they: . . . a greater name than theirs, *NLT* . . . has received a title, *SEB* . . . having shown himself as much greater than the angels as the Name that he has inherited surpasses theirs, *TCNT* . . . a name far beyond them, *Klingensmith* . . . far greater than the angels with their inferior name, *TNT* . . . is more exalted than theirs, *Wade* . . . is more distinguished than theirs, *Noli.*

1:5. Psalm 2:7 is quoted to point out the contrast between the Son and the angels. Although the angels as a group are called the "sons of God" in the Old Testament (Genesis 6:2; Job 1:6; 2:1; 38:7), no angel ever is called "Son." The Father, however, calls Jesus "Son" at His baptism and at the Transfiguration. God promised David a son who would establish David's house, throne, and kingdom forever (2 Samuel 7:13,14). And David knew about and looked for a greater Son than Solomon (Psalm 89).

5. For unto which of the angels said he at any time: God never said to any, *TNT* . . . did he ever say, *Wilson.*

Thou art my Son, this day have I begotten thee?: I have fathered you, *SEB* . . . I am Your Father, *Beck* . . . today I have become your Father? *Williams.*

And again, I will be to him a Father, and he shall be to me a Son?: I will become His Father, and He shall become my Son, *Williams.*

Hebrews 1:7

3687.1 adv	1507.3 verb 3sing subj aor act	3450.6 art acc sing masc	4274.2 adj acc sing masc	1519.1 prep	3450.12 art acc sing fem
πάλιν	εἰσαγάγῃ	τὸν	πρωτότοκον	εἰς	τὴν
palin	*eisagagē*	*ton*	*prōtotokon*	*eis*	*tēn*
again	he brings in	the	firstborn	into	the

3487.4 noun acc sing fem	2978.5 verb 3sing indic pres act	2504.1 conj	4210.16 verb 3pl impr aor act	840.4 prs-pron dat sing
οἰκουμένην,	λέγει,	Καὶ	προσκυνησάτωσαν	αὐτῷ
oikoumenēn	*legei*	*Kai*	*proskunēsatōsan*	*autō*
habitable world,	he says,	And	let worship	him

3820.7 adj nom pl masc	32.5 noun nom pl masc	2296.2 noun gen sing masc	2504.1 conj	4242.1 prep	3173.1 conj	3450.8 art acc pl masc
πάντες	ἄγγελοι	θεοῦ.	7. Καὶ	πρὸς	μὲν	τοὺς
pantes	*angeloi*	*theou*	*Kai*	*pros*	*men*	*tous*
all	angels	of God.	And	as to		the

32.8 noun acc pl masc	2978.5 verb 3sing indic pres act	3450.5 art nom sing masc	4020.15 verb nom sing masc part pres act	3450.8 art acc pl masc
ἀγγέλους	λέγει,	Ὁ	ποιῶν	τοὺς
angelous	*legei*	*Ho*	*poiōn*	*tous*
angels	he says,	The	making	the

32.8 noun acc pl masc	840.3 prs-pron gen sing	4011.4 noun pl neu	2504.1 conj	3450.8 art acc pl masc	2985.4 noun acc pl masc
ἀγγέλους	αὐτοῦ	πνεύματα,	καὶ	τοὺς	λειτουργοὺς
angelous	*autou*	*pneumata*	*kai*	*tous*	*leitourgous*
angels	his	spirits,	and	the	ministers

840.3 prs-pron gen sing	4300.2 noun gen sing neu	5232.4 noun acc sing fem	4242.1 prep	1156.2 conj	3450.6 art acc sing masc	5048.4 noun acc sing masc
αὐτοῦ	πυρὸς	φλόγα·	8. πρὸς	δὲ	τὸν	υἱόν,
autou	*puros*	*phloga*	*pros*	*de*	*ton*	*huion*
his	of fire	a flame;	as to	but	the	Son,

3450.5 art nom sing masc	2339.1 noun nom sing masc	4622.2 prs-pron gen 2sing	3450.5 art nom sing masc	2296.1 noun nom sing masc	1519.1 prep
Ὁ	θρόνος	σου,	ὁ	θεός,	εἰς
Ho	*thronos*	*sou*	*ho*	*theos*	*eis*
The	throne	your,		God,	to

8.a.**Var:** 01א,02A,03B 33,Treg,Alf,Tisc,We/Ho Weis,Sod,UBS/☆

8.b.**Var:** 01א-corr,02A 03B,33,Lach,Treg,Tisc We/Ho,Weis,Sod UBS/☆

8.c.**Txt:** 06D,018K,020L 025P,byz.
Var: 01א,02A,03B,33 Lach,Treg,Tisc,We/Ho Weis,Sod,UBS/☆

8.d.**Txt:** 02A,06D,018K 020L,025P,etc.byz.it.sa. bo.Tisc,Sod
Var: p46,01א,03B We/Ho,Weis,UBS/☆

3450.6 art acc sing masc	163.3 noun acc sing masc	3450.2 art gen sing	163.1 noun gen sing masc	2504.1 conj	3450.9 art nom sing fem
τὸν	αἰῶνα	τοῦ	αἰῶνος·	[a☆+ καὶ	ἡ]
ton	*aiōna*	*tou*	*aiōnos*	*kai*	*hē*
the	age	of the	age.	[and	the]

4321.1 noun nom sing fem	3450.10 art gen sing fem	2099.1 noun gen sing fem	3450.9 art nom sing fem	4321.1 noun nom sing fem
ῥάβδος	[b☆+ τῆς]	εὐθύτητος	⸂c ἡ ⸃	ῥάβδος
rhabdos	*tēs*	*euthutētos*	*hē*	*rhabdos*
A sceptre	[of the]	of uprightness	the	sceptre

3450.10 art gen sing fem	926.1 noun fem	4622.2 prs-pron gen 2sing	840.3 prs-pron gen sing	25.13 verb 2sing indic aor act
τῆς	βασιλείας	⸂ σου.	[d αὐτοῦ]	9. ἠγάπησας
tēs	*basileias*	*sou*	*autou*	*ēgapēsas*
of the	kingdom	your.	[his.]	You did love

1336.4 noun acc sing fem	2504.1 conj	3268.12 verb 2sing indic aor act	455.4 noun acc sing fem	1217.2 prep
δικαιοσύνην	καὶ	ἐμίσησας	ἀνομίαν.	διὰ
dikaiosunēn	*kai*	*emisēsas*	*anomian*	*dia*
righteousness	and	did hate	lawlessness;	because of

1:6. Here the third Old Testament quotation is taken from the Septuagint. This form of the Deuteronomy 32:43 quotation has also been discovered in a Hebrew fragment of the passage found among the Dead Sea Scrolls (Cross, pp.182-184). The context of Deuteronomy is one of judgment, vengeance, and reward, and the angels are worshiping Jehovah. Since Jesus Christ the Son will execute the Father's final judgment, the reference in Deuteronomy implies the deity of the Son and shows His superiority to the angels, because they are commanded to fall down and worship Him.

In this verse the Son is called "first-begotten" (*prōtotokon*). Paul said Christ was the first begotten or "firstborn from the dead" (Colossians 1:18). John wrote the same (Revelation 1:5). Here "first-born" is an expression meaning Christ's resurrection from the dead. In 12:23 the word "firstborn" is used for the perfected Christian church in heaven. There it appears in the plural and includes all the believers who are a firstfruit for God.

Prōtotokon refers to either superiority in rank or first in time. Hebrews 1:5 spoke of Christ as the "begotten" in a quote from Psalm 2:7. The Father said to the Son, "This day have I begotten thee," but the statement refers not to a literal birth. Rather, it points to a position of rank. God later declared of the Messiah, "Also I will make him my firstborn, higher than the kings of the earth" (Psalm 89:27). Here "firstborn" suggests being "supreme in rank" rather than "first in time." In other words, God would make His Son as the Messiah higher than all other kings of the earth. Hebrews had a similar message as to His being superior to angels.

1:7. The fourth quote comes from Psalm 104:4 and is contrasted with the fifth quotation given in verse 8. These words depict the angels as the messengers and ministers of God. They are beings created to perform His service. By portraying them in this capacity, the Psalmist likens them to wind and flames. This imagery stresses the fleeting, temporary, and changeable character of the angels' service to God.

1:8,9. To spotlight the Son's position over against the subservience of the angels, the inspired writer next cited Psalm 45:6,7. This prophetic and messianic psalm speaks about the God-man, the Son. He was to come from the house of David, a dynasty with which God had made an extraordinary covenant (2 Samuel 7:13,14), a covenant which would only be fulfilled in Jesus the Messiah. In Psalm 45, the Messiah is designated "God." He is promised an eternal throne. His rule is described as just. He is portrayed as One who is personally committed to righteousness. He has been anointed royally and crowned with joy.

Later, 12:2 describes the way this joy came—through suffering. The joy of believers can come this way also, as 12:3-11 points out.

6. And again, when he bringeth in the first begotten into the world: And further...into the habitable world, *Montgomery* . . . when he introduces this...into the universe, *Noli* . . . when God is about to send, *TNT* . . . when He brings the First-born into the world of men, *Wade*. . . His First-born, *Adams* . . . into the inhabited earth, *Concordant.*

he saith, And let all the angels of God worship him: He declares...all God's angels must worship Him, *Wade* . . . will bow before him, *Noli.*

7. And of the angels he saith: Now referring to the angels He says, *Adams* . . . when speaking of angels, *TNT* . . . speaking of their mutability, *Wade.*

Who maketh his angels spirits: He makes the winds his angels, *TCNT* . . . He turns His angels, *Williams* . . . into winds, *Montgomery.*

and his ministers a flame of fire: And His attendants, *Williams* . . . and his servants, *TNT* . . . And his public officers flaming fire, *Klingensmith* . . . His Ministrants into lightning-flame, *Wade* . . . and the lightnings are his servants, *Noli.*

8. But unto the Son [he saith]: But referring to, *Adams* . . . regarding, *Williams* . . . when speaking of the Son, *TNT* . . . Who is unchanging, *Wade.*

Thy throne, O God, [is] for ever and ever: Thy throne is God's throne, lasting for ever, *Wade* . . . will last, *TNT* . . . will stand forever, *Williams* . . . is from everlasting to everlasting, *Norlie.*

a sceptre of righteousness [is] the sceptre of thy kingdom: . . . and the rod of Your empire, *Adams* . . . the scepter of equity, *Wuest* . . . an equitable rule is Thy rule of Thy Dominion, *Wade* . . . Your royal sceptre stands for, *TNT* . . . the scepter of justice, *Montgomery* . . . You rule your kingdom fairly, *SEB.*

9. Thou hast loved righteousness, and hated iniquity: . . . loved justice, *Wade* . . . loved right and hated wrong, *Beck* . . . hated lawlessness, *Montgomery, Klingensmith* . . . and hated wickedness, *TCNT* . . . and hated what is wrong, *SEB.*

Hebrews 1:10

3642.17 dem-pron sing neu	5383.2 verb 3sing indic aor act	4622.4 prs-pron acc 2sing	3450.5 art nom sing masc	2296.1 noun nom sing masc	3450.5 art nom sing masc
τοῦτο	ἔχρισέν	σε	ὁ	θεός,	ὁ
touto	*echrisen*	*se*	*ho*	*theos*	*ho*
this	anointed	you		God	

2296.1 noun nom sing masc	4622.2 prs-pron gen 2sing	1624.3 noun sing neu	20.2 noun gen sing fem	3706.2 prep	3450.8 art acc pl masc
θεός	σου	ἔλαιον	ἀγαλλιάσεως	παρὰ	τοὺς
theos	*sou*	*elaion*	*agalliaseōs*	*para*	*tous*
God	your	with oil	of exultation	above	the

3223.3 adj acc pl masc	4622.2 prs-pron gen 2sing	2504.1 conj	4622.1 prs-pron nom 2sing	2567.1 prep	741.7 noun acc pl fem
μετόχους	σου.	**10.** Καί,	Σὺ	κατ'	ἀρχάς,
metochous	*sou*	*Kai*	*Su*	*kat'*	*archas*
companions	your.	And,	You	in	the beginning,

2935.5 noun voc sing masc	3450.12 art acc sing fem	1087.4 noun acc sing fem	2288.1 verb 2sing indic aor act	2504.1 conj	2024.4 noun pl neu
κύριε,	τὴν	γῆν	ἐθεμελίωσας,	καὶ	ἔργα
kurie	*tēn*	*gēn*	*ethemeliōsas*	*kai*	*erga*
Lord,	the	earth	did found,	and	works

3450.1 art gen pl	5331.6 noun gen pl fem	4622.2 prs-pron gen 2sing	1498.7 verb 3pl indic pres act	3450.7 art nom pl masc	3636.6 noun nom pl masc
τῶν	χειρῶν	σού	εἰσιν	οἱ	οὐρανοί·
tōn	*cheirōn*	*sou*	*eisin*	*hoi*	*ouranoi*
of the	hands	your	are	the	heavens.

840.7 prs-pron nom pl masc	616.29 verb 3pl indic fut mid	4622.1 prs-pron nom 2sing	1156.2 conj	1259.1 verb 2sing indic pres act
11. αὐτοὶ	ἀπολοῦνται,	σὺ	δὲ	διαμένεις·
autoi	*apolountai*	*su*	*de*	*diameneis*
They	shall perish,	you	but	continue;

2504.1 conj	3820.7 adj nom pl masc	5453.1 conj	2416.1 noun sing neu	3869.4 verb 3pl indic fut pass
καὶ	πάντες	ὡς	ἱμάτιον	παλαιωθήσονται,
kai	*pantes*	*hōs*	*himation*	*palaiōthēsontai*
and	all	as	a garment	shall grow old,

2504.1 conj	5448.1 adv	3881.2 noun sing neu	1654.1 verb 2sing indic fut act	840.8 prs-pron acc pl masc
12. καὶ	ὡσεὶ	περιβόλαιον	ἑλίξεις	αὐτούς,
kai	*hōsei*	*peribolaion*	*helixeis*	*autous*
and	as	a covering	you shall roll up	them,

12.a.Var: p46,01ℵ,02A 03B,06D-org,Lach,Treg We/Ho,Weis,Sod UBS/★

5453.1 conj	2416.1 noun sing neu	2504.1 conj	234.5 verb 3pl indic fut pass	4622.1 prs-pron nom 2sing
[a☆+ ὡς	ἱμάτιον]	καὶ	ἀλλαγήσονται·	σὺ
hōs	*himation*	*kai*	*allagēsontai*	*su*
[as	a garment]	and	they shall be changed;	you

1156.2 conj	3450.5 art nom sing masc	840.5 prs-pron nom sing masc	1498.3 verb 2sing indic pres act	2504.1 conj	3450.17 art pl neu
δὲ	ὁ	αὐτὸς	εἶ,	καὶ	τὰ
de	*ho*	*autos*	*ei*	*kai*	*ta*
but	the	same	are,	and	the

2073.3 noun pl neu	4622.2 prs-pron gen 2sing	3620.2 partic	1574.3 verb 3pl indic fut act	4242.1 prep	4949.1 intr-pron
ἔτη	σου	οὐκ	ἐκλείψουσιν.	**13.** Πρὸς	τίνα
etē	*sou*	*ouk*	*ekleipsousin*	*Pros*	*tina*
years	your	not	shall fail.	To	which

The word *metochous*, translated "fellows" in 1:9, is translated "partakers" in 12:8. By sharing in Christ's sufferings we share also in His joy. Because of salvation believers have been endowed with an inexpressibly glorious joy (1 Peter 1:8), but the joy brought by sharing in the sufferings of Christ is even greater. The same truth is expressed in 1 Peter 4:13, though the word "partakers" comes from a different Greek word: "Rejoice, inasmuch as ye are partakers of Christ's sufferings; that, when his glory shall be revealed, ye may be glad also with exceeding joy."

1:10,11. Next the inspired writer of Hebrews hurled a long quote from Psalm 102:25-27 at his readers with scarcely any introduction. He used only the word "and." Since the Son is the Father's agent in creating the universe and the ages through which it progresses (see 1:2), these words about Jehovah the Creator are fittingly used of Jesus Christ the Son.

Once again the Septuagint version is employed. There are some minor differences between Hebrews 1:10-12 and Psalm 102:25-27. The meaning and substance, however, are the same. In Psalm 102:24 it is "God" who is addressed, but in 102:22 He is identified as "Lord," which is the translation of the Hebrew word for *Jehovah*. In the Septuagint He is addressed as "Lord," that is, *kurion*. Consistent with his understanding of the Old Testament the writer to the Hebrews recognized Jesus is God and freely used passages of Scripture which speak about Jehovah in talking about Him. In the reference in Psalms these words were addressed by the Lord to the one who offered the prayer at the beginning of the psalm. Yet the Lord addressed part of His answer to the Lord. To whom else could such words be directed? Who else but the Son is both Creator and Lord? In contrast with the creation and the angels, He is the eternal, unchanging Son.

He existed before the universe because He created it. It is not everlasting; He is. It is affected by the process of aging. Like a fragile garment susceptible to humidity, sunlight, and the jaws of the moths, the physical creation will shrivel, decay, dry out, and crumble. But Jesus Christ our Lord, the eternal Son of God, creator of all, shall remain forever and ever. Since He is Jehovah God, there is no reason to puzzle or wonder why created beings like the angels will bow down and worship Him, confessing Him Lord of lords.

1:12. The imagery continues here in the quotation. The sky and the earth will be collapsed like clothing in the hands of the Lord. He is unchangeable. He does not lose His strength in an aging process.

1:13. Finally, the inspired writer employed his favorite passage from the Old Testament, Psalm 110:1. The question is asked: To

therefore God, [even] thy God, hath anointed thee: This is why God, your God, called you, *TNT* . . . hath welcomed Thee, *Wade.*

with the oil of gladness above thy fellows: . . . with the sacred oil above your companions, *Noli* . . . with the festal oil more abundantly than, *TCNT* . . . with the oil of Exultation beyond thy associates, *Wilson* . . . the oil of rejoicing above your friends, *Klingensmith* . . . With tokens of joy beyond the Angels Thy associates, *Wade* . . . gave you the joy of being anointed king...and not your companions, *TNT* . . . has made you king over your friends, *SEB* . . . beyond Your companions, *Adams* . . . beyond thy comrades, *Montgomery* . . . Thy partners, *Concordant.*

10. And, Thou, Lord, in the beginning hast laid the foundation of the earth: . . . founded the earth, *Williams.*

and the heavens are the works of thine hands: With your own hands you made, *TNT* . . . the sky, *Wade.*

11. They shall perish; but thou remainest: They will be destroyed, *Adams* . . . you remain permanently, *Wuest* . . . You will always be here, *NLT* . . . yet Thou art continuing, *Concordant* . . . but you will continue, *SEB.*

and they all shall wax old as doth a garment: . . . all will grow time-worn, *Wade* . . . will grow old, *Williams* . . . and worn out as a garment, *Wuest* . . . as clothes become old, *TNT.*

12. And as a vesture shalt thou fold them up: You will roll them up like a robe, *Adams* . . . like a blanket, *Beck* . . . like a cloak, *TNT* . . . like a mantle, *Wade.*

and they shall be changed: . . . like the changing of one's coat, *Williams* . . . you will change them, *Noli.*

but thou art the same: . . . you remain, *TNT* . . . Thou continuest the same, *Wade.*

and thy years shall not fail: . . . will not come to an end, *Adams* . . . your years have no end, *Noli* . . . your years will never cease, *Williams* . . . You will never get old, *SEB* . . . will never end, *Beck* . . . you will never die, *TNT.*

1156.2 conj	**3450.1** art gen pl	**32.6** noun gen pl masc	**2029.3** verb 3sing indic perf act	**4077.1** adv	**2493.4** verb 2sing impr pres mid
δὲ	τῶν	ἀγγέλων	εἴρηκέν	ποτε,	Κάθου
de	*tōn*	*angelōn*	*eirēken*	*pote*	*Kathou*
but	of the	angels	has he said	ever,	Sit

1523.2 prep gen	**1182.7** adj gen pl neu	**1466.2** prs-pron gen 1sing	**2175.1** conj	**300.1** partic	**4935.12** verb 1sing subj aor act	**3450.8** art acc pl masc
ἐκ	δεξιῶν	μου,	ἕως	ἂν	θῶ	τοὺς
ek	*dexiōn*	*mou*	*heōs*	*an*	*thō*	*tous*
at	right hand	my	until	I	place	the

2172.7 adj acc pl masc	**4622.2** prs-pron gen 2sing	**5124.1** noun sing neu	**3450.1** art gen pl	**4087.5** noun gen pl masc	**4622.2** prs-pron gen 2sing
ἐχθρούς	σου	ὑποπόδιον	τῶν	ποδῶν	σου;
echthrous	*sou*	*hupopodion*	*tōn*	*podōn*	*sou*
enemies	your	a footstool	for the	feet	your?

3644.1 adv	**3820.7** adj nom pl masc	**1498.7** verb 3pl indic pres act	**2984.1** adj pl neu	**4011.4** noun pl neu
14. οὐχὶ	πάντες	εἰσὶν	λειτουργικὰ	πνεύματα,
ouchi	*pantes*	*eisin*	*leitourgika*	*pneumata*
Not	all	are they	ministering	spirits,

1519.1 prep	**1242.4** noun acc sing fem	**643.23** verb pl neu part pres mid	**1217.2** prep	**3450.8** art acc pl masc
εἰς	διακονίαν	ἀποστελλόμενα	διὰ	τοὺς
eis	*diakonian*	*apostellomena*	*dia*	*tous*
for	service	being sent forth	on account of	those

3165.14 verb acc pl masc part pres act	**2789.3** verb inf pres act	**4843.3** noun acc sing fem	**1217.2** prep
μέλλοντας	κληρονομεῖν	σωτηρίαν;	**2:1.** Διὰ
mellontas	*klēronomein*	*sōtērian*	*Dia*
being about	to inherit	salvation?	On account of

3642.17 dem-pron sing neu	**1158.1** verb 3sing indic pres act	**3917.2** adv comp	**2231.4** prs-pron acc 1pl	**4196.5** verb inf pres act
τοῦτο	δεῖ	περισσοτέρως	ʻ ἡμᾶς	προσέχειν
touto	*dei*	*perissoterōs*	*hēmas*	*prosechein*
this	it is necessary for	more abundantly	us	to give heed

4196.5 verb inf pres act	**2231.4** prs-pron acc 1pl	**3450.4** art dat pl	**189.50** verb dat pl neu part aor pass
[☆ προσέχειν	ἡμᾶς]	τοῖς	ἀκουσθεῖσιν,
prosechein	*hēmas*	*tois*	*akoustheisin*
[to give heed	us]	to the things	having been heard,

3246.1 partic	**3762.1** verb 1pl subj aor act	**3762.2** verb 1pl subj aor act	**1479.1** conj
μήποτε	ʻ παραῤῥυῶμεν.	[☆ παραρυῶμεν.]	**2.** εἰ
mēpote	*pararrhuōmen*	*pararuōmen*	*ei*
lest at any time	we should slip away.	[idem]	If

1056.1 conj	**3450.5** art nom sing masc	**1217.1** prep	**32.6** noun gen pl masc	**2953.53** verb nom sing masc part aor pass	**3030.1** noun nom sing masc
γὰρ	ὁ	δι'	ἀγγέλων	λαληθεὶς	λόγος
gar	*ho*	*di'*	*angelōn*	*lalētheis*	*logos*
for	the	by	angels	having been spoken	word

1090.33 verb 3sing indic aor mid	**942.1** adj nom sing masc	**2504.1** conj	**3820.9** adj nom sing fem	**3709.1** noun nom sing fem	**2504.1** conj
ἐγένετο	βέβαιος,	καὶ	πᾶσα	παράβασις	καὶ
egeneto	*bebaios*	*kai*	*pasa*	*parabasis*	*kai*
was	confirmed,	and	every	transgression	and

what angel did Jehovah ever offer the place of favor and blessing in absolute sovereignty over His conquered enemies? To what angel was the office of king in the messianic kingdom ever given? Undoubtedly this passage was in mind back in verse 3 when the Son was described as having "sat down on the right hand of the Majesty on high."

The warrant for understanding this text as a reference to the Son comes from Jesus Christ himself. In His confrontation with His enemies during Passion Week after He had turned all their trick questions back on them, He inquired of them, "What think ye of Christ? whose son is he?" (Matthew 22:42). After they replied that the Messiah was a descendant of David, Jesus asked how it could be that David called the Messiah "Lord" in Psalm 110:1. They of course did not reply. Logically, since the Messiah could be both "Lord" and a human descendant of David, He would have to be both God and man at the same time. This psalm's implications for the Son are used here to underscore His exaltation, power, royal station, and sovereignty as supports for the superiority and finality of the divine revelation which centers in Him. At the same time, the idea that the Son is now sitting in heaven waiting for His ultimate victory is introduced.

1:14. Here the final touch to the argument was added. The angels are not only inferior to the Son; they might also be considered inferior to believers, at least in the sense that they are sent out continually to serve human beings who are destined to inherit salvation. The arguments in verses 4-14 show that Jesus the Son is better than the angels because: (1) God has designated Him individually as His messianic Son and declared Him to be His Son in power by resurrection from the dead; (2) angels are commanded to worship the Son; (3) He is God; (4) He is eternal and unchanging; (5) He is personally righteous and rules in absolute equity; (6) He is the Creator; (7) He is seated securely at the right hand of God, awaiting the day when He will rule the universe in absolute sovereignty.

2:1. On the basis of the Son's superiority to the angels, the first of several stern warnings is issued. Because God has spoken in such an exalted way of His Son, Christians must be careful lest they drift away from the sure anchorage of revelation in the Son. The picture is one of a ship slipping by its anchorage in a protected harbor.

2:2. As was shown in the commentary on 1:4, angels were present on Mount Sinai and mediated in the giving of the Law. That Law fixed a firm penalty for transgression and disobedience. That is the "word spoken by angels." Under it sin incurred the penalty of physical death.

13. But to which of the angels said he at any time: God never said to any angel, *NLT.*

Sit on my right hand: Just keep your seat, *Williams.*

until I make thine enemies thy footstool?: . . . make your foes a footstool for your feet? *Williams.*

14. Are they not all ministering spirits: . . . are simply spirits in the service of God, *TNT* . . . all attending spirits, *Williams.*

sent forth to minister: . . . sent to help, *TNT* . . . commissioned for service, *Concordant* . . . sent on a commission, *Wuest* . . . sent off to serve for the benefit, *Adams* . . . to minister to their needs? *TCNT.*

for them who shall be heirs of salvation?: . . . those who are going to be saved? *Beck* . . . those who are to enter into salvation, *TNT* . . . for the sake of those who are going to be unceasing possessors of salvation? *Williams.*

1. Therefore we ought to give the more earnest heed: On this account it behoves us to attend more earnestly, *Wilson* . . . That is why we should listen all the more carefully, *Beck* . . . we ought to give, *TCNT* . . . we have to pay much closer attention, *Klingensmith* . . . we must pay all the more attention, *Adams* . . . even closer attention, *TNT* . . . listen all the more to, *NLT.*

to the things which we have heard: . . . to the message once heard, *Williams.*

lest at any time we should let [them] slip: . . . to keep from drifting to one side, *Williams* . . . we won't drift away from it, *Adams* . . . for fear we should drift away, *Montgomery* . . . so that we do not drift from our course, *TNT.*

2. For if the word spoken by angels was stedfast: . . . if the message spoken through, *Williams* . . . the word of the Law...was so binding, *TNT* . . . had its authority confirmed, *TCNT* . . . was certain, *Adams* . . . proved to be valid, *Norlie.*

and every transgression and disobedience: . . . and every violation and infraction of it, *Williams* . . . that anyone who broke it or disobeyed it, *TNT.*

3737.1 noun nom sing fem	2956.14 verb 3sing indic aor act	1722.1 adj sing	3269.1 noun acc sing fem	4316.1 adv
παρακοὴ	ἔλαβεν	ἔνδικον	μισθαποδοσίαν,	3. πῶς
parakoē	*elaben*	*endikon*	*misthapodosian*	*pōs*
disobedience	received	just	recompense,	how

2231.1 prs-pron nom 1pl	1614.6 verb 1pl indic fut mid	4930.3 dem-pron gen sing fem	270.2 verb nom pl masc part aor act	4843.2 noun gen sing fem
ἡμεῖς	ἐκφευξόμεθα	τηλικαύτης	ἀμελήσαντες	σωτηρίας;
hēmeis	*ekpheuxometha*	*tēlikautēs*	*amelēsantes*	*sōtērias*
we	shall escape	so great	having neglected	a salvation?

3610.3 rel-pron nom sing fem	741.4 noun acc sing fem	2956.29 verb nom sing fem part aor act	2953.51 verb inf pres mid	1217.2 prep
ἥτις,	ἀρχὴν	λαβοῦσα	λαλεῖσθαι	διὰ
hētis	*archēn*	*labousa*	*laleisthai*	*dia*
which	a commencement	having received	to be spoken	by

3450.2 art gen sing	2935.2 noun gen sing masc	5097.3 prep	3450.1 art gen pl	189.33 verb gen pl masc part aor act	1519.1 prep	2231.4 prs-pron acc 1pl
τοῦ	κυρίου,	ὑπὸ	τῶν	ἀκουσάντων	εἰς	ἡμᾶς
tou	*kuriou*	*hupo*	*tōn*	*akousantōn*	*eis*	*hēmas*
the	Lord,	by	the	having heard	to	us

943.7 verb 3sing indic aor pass	4751.1 verb gen sing masc part pres act	3450.2 art gen sing	2296.2 noun gen sing masc
ἐβεβαιώθη,	4. συνεπιμαρτυροῦντος	τοῦ	θεοῦ
ebebaiōthē	*sunepimarturountos*	*tou*	*theou*
was confirmed;	bearing witness with		God

4447.4 noun dat pl neu	4885.1 conj	2504.1 conj	4907.3 noun dat pl neu	2504.1 conj	4024.3 adj dat pl fem	1405.7 noun dat pl fem
σημείοις	τε	καὶ	τέρασιν,	καὶ	ποικίλαις	δυνάμεσιν,
sēmeiois	*te*	*kai*	*terasin*	*kai*	*poikilais*	*dunamesin*
by signs	both	and	wonders,	and	various	acts of power,

2504.1 conj	4011.2 noun gen sing neu	39.2 adj gen sing	3180.2 noun dat pl masc	2567.3 prep	3450.12 art acc sing fem
καὶ	πνεύματος	ἁγίου	μερισμοῖς	κατὰ	τὴν
kai	*pneumatos*	*hagiou*	*merismois*	*kata*	*tēn*
and	of Spirit	Holy	distributions,	according to	the

840.3 prs-pron gen sing	2285.1 noun acc sing fem	3620.3 partic	1056.1 conj	32.7 noun dat pl masc	5131.2 verb 3sing indic aor act
αὐτοῦ	θέλησιν.	5. Οὐ	γὰρ	ἀγγέλοις	ὑπέταξεν
autou	*thelēsin*	*Ou*	*gar*	*angelois*	*hupetaxen*
his	will.	Not	for	to angels	did he subject

3450.12 art acc sing fem	3487.4 noun acc sing fem	3450.12 art acc sing fem	3165.16 verb acc sing fem part pres act	3875.1 prep
τὴν	οἰκουμένην	τὴν	μέλλουσαν,	περὶ
tēn	*oikoumenēn*	*tēn*	*mellousan*	*peri*
the	habitable world	the	being about to come,	of

3614.10 rel-pron gen sing fem	2953.4 verb 1pl indic pres act	1257.6 verb 3sing indic aor mid	1156.2 conj	4084.1 adv
ἧς	λαλοῦμεν·	6. διεμαρτύρατο	δέ	πού
hēs	*laloumen*	*diemarturato*	*de*	*pou*
which	we speak;	fully testified	but	somewhere

4948.3 indef-pron nom sing	2978.15 verb nom sing masc part pres act	4949.9 intr-pron sing neu	1498.4 verb 3sing indic pres act	442.1 noun nom sing masc
τις	λέγων,	Τί	ἐστιν	ἄνθρωπος,
tis	*legōn*	*Ti*	*estin*	*anthrōpos*
one	saying,	What	is	man,

2:3. If the Mosaic covenant firmly fixed the death penalty and it was mediated only by angels, what about the penalty for neglect of the new covenant which has been established by the Son who is himself God, eternal, unchanging, righteous, the Creator, and the sovereign Judge? If the greater message is neglected will there not be a greater penalty? The words are emphatic—those who live in this final age of human history when God himself was revealed in the Son—how shall they escape? Those who neglect the message of the Son face a fate worse than physical death; they will endure the spiritual death of eternal torment and separation from God. The description of Revelation 14:11 is graphic: "And the smoke of their torment ascendeth up for ever and ever: and they have no rest day nor night." Jesus spoke more about hell than all of the apostles and prophets combined. He, the Lord, brought this gospel message, and His words were attested by eyewitnesses.

2:4. Furthermore, these eyewitnesses have been attested by God the Father who put His stamp of approval on their testimony by pouring out the miraculous events which accompanied the apostolic preaching in the founding and establishment of the Church on the Day of Pentecost: in Samaria, in the home of Cornelius, in Ephesus upon the conversion of John the Baptist's disciples, and on many other occasions recorded in Acts. The Messianic Age is the age of the fullness of the Holy Spirit. Those who put their trust in Jesus Christ drink of the fullness of the Spirit. The apostolic message came from the Son who has sent the Spirit to fill and empower believers and to distribute spiritual gifts in the body of Christ sovereignly as He wills.

2:5. Having sternly warned his audience of the dire consequences facing those who disregard the gospel of God's beloved Son, the writer returned to the theme of the Son's present seating at the Father's right hand. He did this in order to further advance his comparison of the Son and the angels, but also to show that the full exaltation of the Son had not yet been completed. It will be shown that the world to come will not be put in subjection to angels but to the exalted Son of Man.

2:6. Only in Christ, as sitting with Him on His throne, can man rise to a position higher than the angels. At present he has a lower status than the angels, and since any superiority of mankind to angels is not readily apparent, and since the Son became a man, there would be some questions arising in the minds of those who received this epistle: In the light of His becoming flesh and experiencing hunger, exhaustion, pain, suffering, and crucifixion, how can the Son be superior? Are not the angels superior to men and so to Him?

received a just recompense of reward: . . . received its full punishment, *Adams* . . . met with its just retribution, *Montgomery* . . . received fair punishment, *SEB.*

3. How shall we escape: . . . how is it possible for us to escape, *Wuest.*

if we neglect so great salvation: . . . if we disregard, *TCNT.*

which at the first began to be spoken by the Lord: It was at the outset declared, *Adams.*

and was confirmed unto us by them that heard [him]: . . . the people who heard him showed us that it was true, *SEB* . . . guaranteed its truth to us, *Beck.*

4. God also bearing [them] witness: . . . testified to it by signs, *Adams* . . . God also bearing joint-testimony, *Wuest* . . . God proved what they said was true, *NLT* . . . co-attesting both by, *Wilson* . . . corroborating their testimony, *Montgomery* . . . has also confirmed their testimony, *Norlie.*

both with signs and wonders: . . . by showing us special things, *NLT* . . . amazing things, *SEB.*

and with divers miracles: . . . by various powerful deeds, *Concordant* . . . and different kinds of powers, *SEB* . . . and many great powers, *Klingensmith.*

and gifts of the Holy Ghost: . . . as well as by imparting the holy Spirit, *TCNT.*

according to his own will?: . . . measured out according to, *Klingensmith* . . . imparted in accordance with, *Montgomery* . . . distributed as He wished, *Adams* . . . as he saw best, *TCNT* . . . as He saw fit, *Norlie.*

5. For unto the angels hath he not put in subjection the world to come: . . . did not put the future world, *SEB* . . . the control of that Future World, *TCNT.*

whereof we speak:

6. But one in a certain place testified, saying: Instead, the Holy Writings say, *NLT* . . . There is a Scripture passage that says, *Norlie* . . . But somewhere someone had declared, *Beck.*

Hebrews 2:7

3617.1 conj	3267.1 verb 2sing indic pres mid	840.3 prs-pron gen sing	2211.1 conj	5048.1 noun nom sing masc	442.2 noun gen sing masc
ὅτι	μιμνῄσκῃ	αὐτοῦ˙	ἢ	υἱὸς	ἀνθρώπου,
hoti	*mimnēskē*	*autou*	*ē*	*huios*	*anthrōpou*
that	you are mindful	of him,	or	son	of man,

3617.1 conj	1964.1 verb 2sing indic pres mid	840.6 prs-pron acc sing masc	1628.1 verb 2sing indic aor act	840.6 prs-pron acc sing masc
ὅτι	ἐπισκέπτῃ	αὐτόν˙	7. ἠλάττωσας	αὐτὸν
hoti	*episkeptē*	*auton*	*ēlattōsas*	*auton*
that	you visit	him?	You did make lower	him

1017.2 adj sing neu	4948.10 indef-pron sing neu	3706.1 prep	32.8 noun acc pl masc	1385.3 noun dat sing fem	2504.1 conj	4940.3 noun dat sing fem
βραχύ	τι	παρ'	ἀγγέλους˙	δόξῃ	καὶ	τιμῇ
brachu	*ti*	*par'*	*angelous*	*doxē*	*kai*	*timē*
little	some	than	angels;	with glory	and	honor

7.a.**Txt:** 01ℵ,02A,04C 06D-org,025P,it.sa.bo. We/Ho
Var: p46,03B,06D-corr 018K,020L,Gries,Alf Tisc,Weis,Sod,UBS/☆

4588.1 verb 2sing indic aor act	840.6 prs-pron acc sing masc	2504.1 conj	2497.3 verb 2sing indic aor act	840.6 prs-pron acc sing masc
ἐστεφάνωσας	αὐτόν,	(a καὶ	κατέστησας	αὐτὸν
estephanōsas	*auton*	*kai*	*katestēsas*	*auton*
you did crown	him,	and	did set	him

1894.3 prep	3450.17 art pl neu	2024.4 noun pl neu	3450.1 art gen pl	5331.6 noun gen pl fem	4622.2 prs-pron gen 2sing	3820.1 adj
ἐπὶ	τὰ	ἔργα	τῶν	χειρῶν	σου˙)	8. πάντα
epi	*ta*	*erga*	*tōn*	*cheirōn*	*sou*	*panta*
over	the	works	of the	hands	your;	all things

5131.1 verb 2sing indic aor act	5108.1 prep	3450.1 art gen pl	4087.5 noun gen pl masc	840.3 prs-pron gen sing	1706.1 prep
ὑπέταξας	ὑποκάτω	τῶν	ποδῶν	αὐτοῦ.	Ἐν
hupetaxas	*hupokatō*	*tōn*	*podōn*	*autou*	*En*
you did subject	under	the	feet	his.	In

8.a.**Txt:** p46,02A,04C byz.Sod
Var: 01ℵ,03B,06D,044 1739

1056.1 conj	3450.3 art dat sing	3450.3 art dat sing	1056.1 conj	5131.6 verb inf aor act	840.4 prs-pron dat sing	3450.17 art pl neu
(γὰρ	τῷ	[a☆ τῷ	γὰρ]	ὑποτάξαι	αὐτῷ	τὰ
gar	*tō*	*tō*	*gar*	*hupotaxai*	*autō*	*ta*
for	the	[the	for]	to subject	to him	the

3820.1 adj	3625.6 num card neu	856.10 verb 3sing indic aor act	840.4 prs-pron dat sing	503.3 adj sing neu
πάντα,	οὐδὲν	ἀφῆκεν	αὐτῷ	ἀνυπότακτον˙
panta	*ouden*	*aphēken*	*autō*	*anupotakton*
all things,	nothing	he left	to him	unsubject.

8.b.**Var:** p46,03B,We/Ho

3431.1 adv	1156.2 conj	3632.1 adv	3571.4 verb 1pl indic pres act	840.4 prs-pron dat sing	3450.17 art pl neu	3820.1 adj
νῦν	δὲ	οὔπω	ὁρῶμεν	(b αὐτῷ)	τὰ	πάντα
nun	*de*	*oupō*	*horōmen*	*autō*	*ta*	*panta*
Now	but	not yet	do we see	to him	the	all things

5131.22 verb pl neu part perf mid	3450.6 art acc sing masc	1156.2 conj	1017.2 adj sing neu	4948.10 indef-pron sing neu	3706.1 prep
ὑποτεταγμένα˙	9. τὸν	δὲ	βραχύ	τι	παρ'
hupotetagmena	*ton*	*de*	*brachu*	*ti*	*par'*
subjected;	the	but	little	some	than

32.8 noun acc pl masc	1628.3 verb acc sing masc part perf mid	984.5 verb 1pl indic pres act	2400.3 name acc masc
ἀγγέλους	ἠλαττωμένον	βλέπομεν	Ἰησοῦν
angelous	*ēlattōmenon*	*blepomen*	*Iēsoun*
angels	having been made lower	we see	Jesus

With these objections in mind, Psalm 8:4-6 was cited. Here David proclaimed the dignity, nobility, and greatness of man. He was awestruck by the splendor of the heavens and felt dwarfed by their majesty (Psalm 8:3). He marveled that the Lord should have any concern for mankind and was amazed that He should visit the feeble human race for the purpose of healing their weaknesses. As Asaph put it in Psalm 80:17, men pray, "Let thy hand be upon the man of thy right hand, upon the son of man whom thou madest strong for thyself." The term "son of man" is freighted with significance. It speaks of the ideal man. It was Jesus' favorite self-designation and visualizes Him as the ideal man, the last Adam who has come to undo the consequences of Adam's fall.

2:7. God created the human race in His own image. He created mankind a little lower than the angels and ordained them to rule over the earth (Genesis 1:26-31). Instead, they sinned and now find themselves degraded. The emphasis is upon the humiliation of man. As a result of Adam's disobedience, men have been cursed. Even though God gave this dominion to man and not to the angelic hosts, the Lord expelled him from Eden's paradise and subjected him to sorrow and suffering (Genesis 3:14-24).

2:8. Man's situation is tragic. He does not have dominion over the earth. His efforts to master the earth are cursed by sweat and drudgery. He is subject to the destructive powers of natural disasters: hurricanes, tornadoes, tidal waves, floods, volcanic eruptions, and earthquakes. He is ravaged by disease and grows old. In the end he is conquered by death. What a tragedy!

By application and practice of his God-given abilities, by conscious deliberation, by systematic calculation based on his powers of observation, by employing his creative powers, man is supposed to exercise dominion in the service of God for His glory. Yet he does not. He is staring down the barrel of nuclear destruction and radiation sickness. Millions starve to death. Everywhere man is confronted by wretchedness, depravity, misery, despair, and sinfulness. At the present time, he does not see the nobility and dignity of the human race evident in the subjugation of all his enemies. There are many foes left to conquer.

It is a sad scene: man, created with such dignity and such a noble destiny, ruined by the Fall and degraded by the ravages of sin. But, thankfully, the last chapter has not been written.

2:9. The original readers of this epistle did not see a triumphant human race ruling in dignity over the earth. Nor did they see a victorious Messiah when they looked about. Indeed, they saw the Son, Jesus, who had recently been crucified in a criminal execution. It is not only the race which has been humbled by God; the Son has also been humiliated. In His death He was "made a little lower than the angels."

What is man, that thou art mindful of him?: . . . that You remember him, *Adams, Klingensmith* . . . that thou should'st remember him? *TCNT* . . . that you should think of him, *Williams.*

or the son of man, that thou visitest him?: Or any man, that thou carest for him? *Montgomery* . . . in order to come to his aid? *Wuest* . . . that You look out for him? *Norlie* . . . That thou dost regard him? *Wilson* . . . that you should care for Him? *Williams* . . . that you should show concern for him? *TNT.*

7. Thou madest him a little lower than the angels: . . . inferior to angels, *Williams.*

thou crownedst him with glory and honour:

and didst set him over the works of thy hands: And hast set him to govern, *Montgomery* . . . Thou hast appointed him over, *Wade.*

8. Thou hast put all things in subjection under his feet: You put everything under his control, *SEB* . . . Thou hast reduced all things, *Wade* . . . and subjected everything beneath his feet, *Adams.*

For in that he put all in subjection under him: Subjected...means that, *TNT* . . . by reducing, *Wade* . . . when He gave Him authority over everything, *Williams.*

he left nothing [that is] not put under him: He left nothing outside His control, *Beck* . . . did not leave a single thing that was not put under His authority, *Williams* . . . not even the angels—exempt from subjection to his control, *Wade.*

But now we see not yet all things put under him: But as conditions are...we do not yet see all things reduced to subjection under him, *Wade* . . . we do not see everything actually under His authority, *Williams.*

9. But we see Jesus, who was made a little lower than the angels: . . . though we do behold Him, *Wade* . . . What we do see is Jesus...made for a little while, *TNT* . . . Who for a short time was, *Adams* . . . who was made inferior, *Williams* . . . a little lower than heavenly messengers, *Klingensmith.*

1217.2 prep	3450.16 art sing neu	3667.1 noun sing neu	3450.2 art gen sing	2265.2 noun gen sing masc
διὰ	τὸ	πάθημα	τοῦ	θανάτου
dia	to	pathēma	tou	thanatou
on account of	the	suffering	of the	death

1385.3 noun dat sing fem	2504.1 conj	4940.3 noun dat sing fem	4588.3 verb acc sing masc part perf mid	3567.1 conj
δόξῃ	καὶ	τιμῇ	ἐστεφανωμένον,	ὅπως
doxē	kai	timē	estephanōmenon	hopōs
with glory	and	with honor	having been crowned;	so that by

5322.3 noun dat sing fem	2296.2 noun gen sing masc	5065.1 prep	3820.2 adj gen sing	1083.4 verb 3sing subj aor mid	2265.2 noun gen sing masc
χάριτι	θεοῦ	ὑπὲρ	παντὸς	γεύσηται	θανάτου.
chariti	theou	huper	pantos	geusētai	thanatou
grace	of God	for	everyone	he might taste	death.

4100.3 verb 3sing indic imperf act	1056.1 conj	840.4 prs-pron dat sing	1217.1 prep	3614.6 rel-pron acc sing masc	3450.17 art pl neu
10. Ἔπρεπεν	γὰρ	αὐτῷ,	δι'	ὃν	τὰ
Eprepen	gar	autō	di'	hon	ta
It was becoming	for	to him,	for	whom	the

3820.1 adj	2504.1 conj	1217.1 prep	3614.2 rel-pron gen sing	3450.17 art pl neu	3820.1 adj	4044.8 adj acc pl masc
πάντα	καὶ	δι'	οὗ	τὰ	πάντα,	πολλοὺς
panta	kai	di'	hou	ta	panta	pollous
all things	and	by	whom	the	all things,	many

5048.9 noun acc pl masc	1519.1 prep	1385.4 noun acc sing fem	70.13 verb acc sing masc part aor act	3450.6 art acc sing masc	742.1 noun acc sing masc
υἱοὺς	εἰς	δόξαν	ἀγαγόντα,	τὸν	ἀρχηγὸν
huious	eis	doxan	agagonta	ton	archēgon
sons	to	glory	having brought,	the	leader

3450.10 art gen sing fem	4843.2 noun gen sing fem	840.1 prs-pron gen pl	1217.2 prep	3667.3 noun gen pl neu	4896.5 verb inf aor act
τῆς	σωτηρίας	αὐτῶν	διὰ	παθημάτων	τελειῶσαι.
tēs	sōtērias	autōn	dia	pathēmatōn	teleiōsai
of the	salvation	their	through	sufferings	to make perfect.

3450.5 art nom sing masc	4885.1 conj	1056.1 conj	37.3 verb nom sing masc part pres act	2504.1 conj	3450.7 art nom pl masc	37.11 verb nom pl masc part pres mid
11. ὁ	τε	γὰρ	ἁγιάζων	καὶ	οἱ	ἁγιαζόμενοι,
ho	te	gar	hagiazōn	kai	hoi	hagiazomenoi
The	both	for	sanctifying	and	the	being sanctified

1523.1 prep gen	1518.1 num card gen	3820.7 adj nom pl masc	1217.1 prep	3614.12 rel-pron acc sing fem	155.3 noun acc sing fem	3620.2 partic
ἐξ	ἑνὸς	πάντες·	δι'	ἣν	αἰτίαν	οὐκ
ex	henos	pantes	di'	hēn	aitian	ouk
of	one	all;	for	which	cause	not

1855.2 verb 3sing indic pres mid	79.9 noun acc pl masc	840.8 prs-pron acc pl masc	2535.7 verb inf pres act	2978.15 verb nom sing masc part pres act
ἐπαισχύνεται	ἀδελφοὺς	αὐτοὺς	καλεῖν,	12. λέγων,
epaischunetai	adelphous	autous	kalein	legōn
he is ashamed	brothers	them	to call,	saying,

514.11 verb 1sing indic fut act	3450.16 art sing neu	3549.2 noun sing neu	4622.2 prs-pron gen 2sing	3450.4 art dat pl	79.8 noun dat pl masc
Ἀπαγγελῶ	τὸ	ὄνομά	σου	τοῖς	ἀδελφοῖς
Apangelō	to	onoma	sou	tois	adelphois
I will declare	the	name	your	to the	brothers

But the epistle looks beyond the Son's temporary humiliation to the objective which God the Father pursued in the Son's death. The results of Jesus' death are "glory and honor," the same crown which the Lord intended for mankind (Psalm 8:5). By suffering the particular death which He experienced at Calvary, the Son became a channel for the grace of God. His death is described as a "taste" because it was a real but temporary experience. Jesus did not remain dead. His death, moreover, had purpose and significance for the whole human race. It was a death which He died for others. It was substitutionary. The text says Jesus died "for every man." The phrase *huper pantos* means "in the place of every man."

2:10. Here we are introduced to the great heart of God. It is entirely appropriate for the Creator and Sustainer of all things in the universe to direct His Son along a path of suffering in pursuit of His objective for mankind. The "many sons" whom He is glorifying are the human beings who will be restored from the effects of the Fall and will exercise dominion over the earth. This restoration will be achieved by the "captain," that is, the *archēgon*, the pioneer of their deliverance—Jesus the Son. Because of God's love, He became a trailblazer in respect to man's salvation. He opened up the way to God in heaven. The perfection spoken of here is not a moral perfection. There is no suggestion that Jesus had moral defects which were remedied by His suffering. As will be seen in the following verses and in 5:8,9, it is His qualification for entrance into the high priesthood as a man which is in view.

2:11. Both the priest who sets apart the people and the people who are set apart must be "all of one," that is, out of the same group. To represent the human race, the Son had to become flesh. Since He came to sanctify believers as their priest, the humiliation involved in His becoming one of them and dying for them did not stop Him. Identifying with sinners as brothers caused Him no shame. His suffering as one with them and for them was prophesied.

What a beautiful statement: "He is not ashamed to call them brethren." Christ had many reasons to be ashamed of the race to which He belonged. In His own line were murderers, adulterers, liars. Again we see the grace of God demonstrated.

2:12. Here Psalm 22:22 is cited. As the source of Jesus' agonized cry, "My God, my God, why hast thou forsaken me?" (Psalm 22:1), the first part of this psalm is a lament and a cry for deliverance. In the second part, beginning with 22:22, the lament is followed by words of thanksgiving. The same Jesus, who lamented His aban-

for the suffering of death: . . . because of the death he suffered, *TNT.*

crowned with glory and honour: . . . wreathed with, *Concordant.*

that he by the grace of God: By God's gracious love he did this, *SEB* . . . that by God's favor, *Williams.*

should taste death for every man: He might experience death, *Williams* . . . tasted the bitterness of death, *Norlie* . . . might die for everyone, *TNT* . . . for all sorts of people, *Adams* . . . for the sake of everyone, *Concordant* . . . for every person, *Klingensmith.*

10. For it became him: For it befitted him, *Montgomery* . . . It fitted Him well, *Beck* . . . It was appropriate for Him, *Williams.*

for whom [are] all things, and by whom [are] all things: . . . by Whom everything exists, *Adams* . . . created all things for his own purposes, *TNT* . . . who is the Final Goal and the First Cause of the universe, *Williams.*

in bringing many sons unto glory: . . . in conducting Many Sons, *Wilson* . . . many children to glory, *Williams.*

to make the captain of their salvation: . . . to make Jesus a perfect Leader, *NLT* . . . to perfect the Inaugurator, *Concordant* . . . him who leads them to salvation, *TNT* . . . the Pioneer of their salvation, *Montgomery.*

perfect through sufferings: . . . achieve perfection through suffering, *Norlie* . . . through the process of suffering, *Williams.*

11. For both he that sanctifieth and they who are sanctified: . . . he who purifies, *TCNT* . . . the one who cleanses them from sin, *TNT* . . . and those who are being hallowed, *Concordant.*

[are] all of one: . . . all spring from, *Williams* . . . all one common origin, *Norlie* . . . all have one Father, *Beck.*

for which cause he is not ashamed to call them brethren: That is why, *TNT.*

12. Saying, I will declare thy name unto my brethren: . . . when He says, *Williams* . . . I will announce, *Adams* . . . I will proclaim, *TNT.*

1466.2 prs-pron gen 1sing	**1706.1** prep	**3189.1** adj dat sing	**1564.1** noun fem	**5053.2** verb 1sing indic fut act	**4622.4** prs-pron acc 2sing
μου,	ἐν	μέσῳ	ἐκκλησίας	ὑμνήσω	σε.
mou	*en*	*mesō*	*ekklēsias*	*humnēsō*	*se*
my;	in	midst	of assembly	I will sing praise	to you.

2504.1 conj	**3687.1** adv	**1466.1** prs-pron nom 1sing	**1498.38** verb 1sing indic fut mid	**3844.13** verb nom sing masc part perf act	**1894.2** prep
13. καὶ	πάλιν,	Ἐγὼ	ἔσομαι	πεποιθὼς	ἐπ'
kai	*palin*	*Egō*	*esomai*	*pepoithōs*	*ep'*
And	again,	I	will be	having trusted	in

840.4 prs-pron dat sing	**2504.1** conj	**3687.1** adv	**1481.20** verb 2sing impr aor mid	**1466.1** prs-pron nom 1sing	**2504.1** conj	**3450.17** art pl neu
αὐτῷ.	καὶ	πάλιν,	Ἰδοὺ	ἐγὼ	καὶ	τὰ
autō	*kai*	*palin*	*Idou*	*egō*	*kai*	*ta*
him.	And	again,	Behold	I	and	the

3676.3 noun nom pl neu	**3614.17** rel-pron pl neu	**1466.4** prs-pron dat 1sing	**1319.14** verb 3sing indic aor act	**3450.5** art nom sing masc	**2296.1** noun nom sing masc
παιδία	ἅ	μοι	ἔδωκεν	ὁ	θεός.
paidia	*ha*	*moi*	*edōken*	*ho*	*theos*
children	which	me	gave		God.

1878.1 conj	**3631.1** partic	**3450.17** art pl neu	**3676.3** noun nom pl neu	**2814.8** verb 3sing indic perf act
14. Ἐπεὶ	οὖν	τὰ	παιδία	κεκοινώνηκεν
Epei	*oun*	*ta*	*paidia*	*kekoinōnēken*
Since	therefore	the	children	have shared

4418.2 noun gen sing fem	**2504.1** conj	**129.2** noun gen sing neu	**129.2** noun gen sing neu	**2504.1** conj	**4418.2** noun gen sing fem
‛ σαρκός	καὶ	αἵματος,	[☆ αἵματος	καὶ	σαρκός,]
sarkos	*kai*	*haimatos*	*haimatos*	*kai*	*sarkos*
of flesh	and	blood,	[blood	and	flesh,]

2504.1 conj	**840.5** prs-pron nom sing masc	**3759.1** adv	**3218.6** verb 3sing indic aor act	**3450.1** art gen pl	**840.1** prs-pron gen pl
καὶ	αὐτὸς	παραπλησίως	μετέσχεν	τῶν	αὐτῶν,
kai	*autos*	*paraplēsiōs*	*meteschen*	*tōn*	*autōn*
also	he	in like manner	took part in	the	same,

2419.1 conj	**1217.2** prep	**3450.2** art gen sing	**2265.2** noun gen sing masc	**2643.3** verb 3sing subj aor act	**3450.6** art acc sing masc
ἵνα	διὰ	τοῦ	θανάτου	καταργήσῃ	τὸν
hina	*dia*	*tou*	*thanatou*	*katargēsē*	*ton*
that	through	the	death	he might annul	the

3450.16 art sing neu	**2877.1** noun sing neu	**2174.15** verb part pres act	**3450.2** art gen sing	**2265.2** noun gen sing masc	**4969.1** verb 3sing indic pres act
τὸ	κράτος	ἔχοντα	τοῦ	θανάτου,	‛ τουτέστιν
to	*kratos*	*echonta*	*tou*	*thanatou*	*toutestin*
the	might	having	of the	death,	that is,

3642.16 dem-pron sing neu	**1498.4** verb 3sing indic pres act	**3450.6** art acc sing masc	**1222.4** adj acc sing masc	**2504.1** conj
[☆ τοῦτ'	ἔστιν]	τὸν	διάβολον,	15. καὶ
tout'	*estin*	*ton*	*diabolon*	*kai*
[this	is]	the	devil;	and

521.1 verb 3sing subj aor act	**3642.8** dem-pron acc pl masc	**3607.2** rel-pron nom pl masc	**5238.3** noun dat sing masc	**2265.2** noun gen sing masc	**1217.2** prep
ἀπαλλάξῃ	τούτους	ὅσοι	φόβῳ	θανάτου	διὰ
apallaxē	*toutous*	*hosoi*	*phobō*	*thanatou*	*dia*
might set free	those	whosoever	by fear	of death	through

donment by the Father while on the cross bearing our sins, is seen in this messianic psalm praising God for deliverance in the midst of His brethren, the assembled saints.

in the midst of the church will I sing praise unto thee: I will join the congregation in singing your praise, *TNT* . . . in the midst of the congregation, *Norlie, Williams*. . . I will sing a hymn to You, *Adams* . . . shall I be singing hymns, *Concordant*. . . I will sing to You in the middle of the congregation, *SEB.*

2:13. Next the inspired writer cites words from Isaiah 8:18. In the context of Isaiah 8, the prophet spoke these words to the nation of Israel which had rejected the message he brought from Jehovah. In the face of his rejection, Isaiah declared that he had put his trust in the Lord. This same attitude and these same circumstances were true in the life of Jesus. He came to His own people, Israel, and they crucified Him. In the hour of His trial, Jesus identified himself with other men by putting His trust in the Lord. Psalm 22:24 indicates that the Lord did not turn from the afflicted, "But when he cried unto him, he heard." As a man, in His loneliest hour, Jesus the Son put His trust in the Father.

This verse continues to quote from Isaiah 8:18: "Behold, I and the children whom the Lord hath given me are for signs and for wonders in Israel from the Lord of hosts, which dwelleth in mount Zion." Even though the people rejected Isaiah, his preaching and his children and their symbolic names stood as a continuing witness to the unbelieving Jews: *Isaiah* means "Jehovah is salvation"; *Shear-jashub* means "a remnant will return"; *Mahershalalhashbaz* means "hasten booty, speed plunder." Likewise, the professing Jewish Christians who were in danger of rejecting the Son were to look to the meaning of His name. *Jesus* means "Saviour." The Son and His children are those who put their trust in the Lord.

13. And again, I will put my trust in him: I myself, like others, *Wade* . . . I will confide in him, *Wilson.*

And again, Behold I and the children which God hath given me: Here I am and the children, *Williams.*

2:14. Having argued that the Son needed to become a man in order to qualify for the priesthood by identifying with the race He came to represent, the inspired writer stated the fact simply: the Son has actually become a man.

The incarnation! What an event! What a concept! Only an all-wise God could have conceived such a plan, to stoop down as it were, in order to raise man from his hopelessness.

In the second half of the verse there begins the examination of the consequences of Christ's qualifying for the priesthood. Three powerful results of Christ's high-priestly work are presented. One is given in verse 14, another in verse 15, and the third in verses 17 and 18. First of all, Jesus Christ shattered the power of the devil (1 John 3:8; Colossians 2:15). Jesus marched into Satan's fortress of death, disarmed him, chained him, and robbed him of his captives.

14. Forasmuch then as the children: Since then, *Williams.*

are partakers of flesh and blood: . . . since human nature is the common heritage, *TCNT* . . . share our mortal nature, *Williams.*

he also himself likewise took part of the same: . . . in like manner, participated in the same, *Wade* . . . also shared in their humanity, *SEB* . . . took on Himself a full share of the same, *Williams* . . . shared their human nature in the same way, *TNT.*

that through death: . . . in order that He by His death, *Williams* . . . His purpose was, *TNT* . . . which His possession of the same physical nature rendered possible, *Wade.*

he might destroy him that had the power of death: . . . he might vanquish, *Wilson* . . . might put a stop to the power of, *Williams* . . . he might render powerless, *Montgomery, TCNT* . . . to depose, *TNT* . . . by death cancel out him who has the strength of death, *Klingensmith* . . . He might render inoperative the one having the dominion of, *Wuest* . . . who has the might of death, *Concordant* . . . who has in Death the instrument of his sway, *Wade.*

that is, the devil:

2:15. Secondly, the sufferings and death of Jesus save the prisoners of fear. The fear of death enslaves. Men who fear death will

15. And deliver them who through fear of death: . . . and set at liberty...because of their dread of death, *Williams* . . . that He might set free those, *Norlie* . . . and release those, *TNT* . . . terrified by death, *Beck* . . . were subject to the fear of, *Wade.*

3820.2 adj gen sing	3450.2 art gen sing	2180.19 verb inf pres act	1761.3 adj nom pl masc	1498.37 verb 3pl indic imperf act	1391.1 noun gen sing fem
παντὸς	τοῦ	ζῆν	ἔνοχοι	ἦσαν	δουλείας.
pantos	*tou*	*zēn*	*enochoi*	*ēsan*	*douleias*
all	the	lifetime	subject	were	to bondage.

3620.3 partic	1056.1 conj	1216.1 partic	32.6 noun gen pl masc	1934.1 verb 3sing indic pres mid
16. οὐ	γὰρ	δήπου	ἀγγέλων	ἐπιλαμβάνεται,
ou	*gar*	*dēpou*	*angelōn*	*epilambanetai*
Not	for	indeed	of angels	he takes upon himself,

233.2 conj	4543.2 noun gen sing neu	11.1 name masc	1934.1 verb 3sing indic pres mid
ἀλλὰ	σπέρματος	Ἀβραὰμ	ἐπιλαμβάνεται.
alla	*spermatos*	*Abraam*	*epilambanetai*
but	of seed	of Abraham	he takes upon himself.

3468.1 adv	3648.9 verb 3sing indic imperf act	2567.3 prep	3820.1 adj	3450.4 art dat pl	79.8 noun dat pl masc
17. ὅθεν	ὤφειλεν	κατὰ	πάντα	τοῖς	ἀδελφοῖς
hothen	*ōpheilen*	*kata*	*panta*	*tois*	*adelphois*
Wherefore	he had to	in	all things	to the	brothers

3529.7 verb inf aor pass	2419.1 conj	1642.1 adj nom sing masc	1090.40 verb 3sing subj aor mid	2504.1 conj	3964.2 adj nom sing masc
ὁμοιωθῆναι,	ἵνα	ἐλεήμων	γένηται	καὶ	πιστὸς
homoiōthēnai	*hina*	*eleēmōn*	*genētai*	*kai*	*pistos*
to be made like,	that	a merciful	he might be	and	faithful

744.1 noun nom sing masc	3450.17 art pl neu	4242.1 prep	3450.6 art acc sing masc	2296.4 noun acc sing masc	1519.1 prep
ἀρχιερεὺς	τὰ	πρὸς	τὸν	θεόν,	εἰς
archiereus	*ta*	*pros*	*ton*	*theon*	*eis*
high priest	the things	relating to		God,	for

3450.16 art sing neu	2409.1 verb inf pres mid	3450.15 art acc pl fem	264.1 noun fem	3450.2 art gen sing
τὸ	ἱλάσκεσθαι	τὰς	ἁμαρτίας	τοῦ
to	*hilaskesthai*	*tas*	*hamartias*	*tou*
the	to make propitiation for	the	sins	of the

2967.2 noun gen sing masc	1706.1 prep	3614.3 rel-pron dat sing	1056.1 conj	3819.19 verb 3sing indic perf act	840.5 prs-pron nom sing masc
λαοῦ.	**18.** ἐν	ᾧ	γὰρ	πέπονθεν	αὐτὸς
laou	*en*	*hō*	*gar*	*peponthen*	*autos*
people;	in	which	for	he has suffered	himself

3847.18 verb nom sing masc part aor pass	1404.4 verb 3sing indic pres mid	3450.4 art dat pl	3847.13 verb dat pl masc part pres mid
πειρασθείς,	δύναται	τοῖς	πειραζομένοις
peirastheis	*dunatai*	*tois*	*peirazomenois*
having been tempted,	he is able	the	being tempted

990.6 verb inf aor act	3468.1 adv	79.6 noun nom pl masc	39.7 adj nom pl masc	2794.2 noun gen sing fem
βοηθῆσαι.	**3:1.** Ὅθεν,	ἀδελφοὶ	ἅγιοι,	κλήσεως
boēthēsai	*Hothen*	*adelphoi*	*hagioi*	*klēseōs*
to help.	Wherefore,	brothers	holy,	of calling

2016.1 adj gen sing	3223.1 adj nom pl masc	2627.5 verb 2pl impr aor act	3450.6 art acc sing masc	646.3 noun acc sing masc
ἐπουρανίου	μέτοχοι,	κατανοήσατε	τὸν	ἀπόστολον
epouraniou	*metochoi*	*katanoēsate*	*ton*	*apostolon*
heavenly	partakers,	consider	the	apostle

force themselves to do things that nothing else could force them to do. For sinful men the fearful judgment of the living God stands beyond the grave. But Christ delivers believers.

2:16. The work of Christ influences the whole universe (Ephesians 1:10), but His redemptive work was not done for angels but for mankind. The author pointed out that the Son identified himself not with angels but with the nation of Israel, the descendants of Abraham and for those who have his faith.

2:17. Finally, by His death and resurrection, Jesus Christ has *secured the priesthood for sinners.* The text presents two aspects of that priesthood. Jesus Christ the "merciful and faithful high priest" has by His death provided a *covering for sins.* Believers have been covered by His blood and His righteous life. He has paid the penalty for their sins. The word *hilaskesthai* looks at the propitiatory aspect of Christ's work. It refers to the satisfaction of God's wrath by Christ's sacrifice. The wrath of God due to the sinner has been diverted from the sinner and fallen on Jesus. The word is loaded with the imagery of the sacrifice and blood sprinkled on the lid of the ark of the covenant on the Day of Atonement. As that blood ceremonially covered the sins of Israel on a yearly basis, so the blood of Jesus actually and effectively covers "the sins of the whole world" (1 John 2:2). God the Son was sent by the Father to take the wrath of the Father upon himself in order that sinners who put their trust in Him might be declared righteous and reconciled to their God.

2:18. The propitiation secured by Jesus' sacrifice does not, however, exhaust the effects of His priesthood. Christians have only begun to experience its benefits when they enjoy forgiveness.

The Son provides *comfort in suffering.* In becoming a priest, Jesus blazed a trail by obeying the Father's will in His sufferings. Believers cannot experience anything that He has not already experienced. He endured all the hardships that mankind can suffer. Having been tempted, He knows the force of the temptations which assail them. He suffered and triumphed over His sufferings. He comforts His own and gives them grace sufficient to overcome their strongest temptations.

3:1. After concluding his discussion of the relationship between Jesus' sufferings and His superiority to the angels, the inspired writer began a brief presentation of the Son's superiority to Moses. The assertion that the message of the Son is superior to the message of the angels delivered on Mount Sinai (2:1-3) raises questions about the place of Moses who was also associated with the Law given at Sinai. Therefore, the readers of the epistle are asked to consider

were all their lifetime subject to bondage: . . . held in Slavery, *Wilson* . . . were subjected to slavery throughout their entire lifetime, *Adams* . . . lived their whole lifetime in bondage, *Norlie* . . . We no longer need to be chained to this fear, *NLT.*

16. For verily he took not on [him the nature of] angels: For of course it is not angels, *Williams* . . . It is clear He didn't come to help angels, *Beck.*

but he took on [him] the seed of Abraham: . . . but descendants of Abraham, *Williams.*

17. Wherefore in all things it behoved him: And consequently it was necessary, *TCNT* . . . This is why he had to, *TNT.*

to be made like unto [his] brethren: He had to be made like His brothers, *Williams* . . . had to be made in all respects, *TNT.*

that he might be a merciful and faithful high priest in things [pertaining] to God: . . . that he might serve God...with compassion and faithfulness, *TNT* . . . become a compassionate, *Montgomery* . . . a sympathetic High Priest, *Williams* . . . in what is related to God, *Adams.*

to make reconciliation for the sins of the people: . . . in order to, *Wilson* . . . make propitiation, *Adams* . . . and pay for the sins, *Beck* . . . for the purpose of expiating the sins of his People, *TCNT* . . . to atone for the people's sins, *TNT.*

18. For in that he himself hath suffered being tempted: It is because he himself has been tested by suffering, *TNT.*

he is able to succour them that are tempted: . . . is also able instantly, *Montgomery* . . . He is able to help those, *Adams* . . . to give immediate help to any, *Williams* . . . those who are now being tested in the same way, *TNT.*

1. Wherefore, holy brethren: My fellow-Christians, *Norlie* . . . For these reasons, *Klingensmith* . . . my Christian brothers, *Williams.*

partakers of the heavenly calling: . . . you who share in God's calling, *SEB* . . . partners of a celestial calling, *Concordant.*

Hebrews 3:2

1.a.**Txt:** 04C-corr 06D-corr,018K,020L byz.
Var: 01א,02A,03B 04C-org,06D-org,025P 33,Gries,Lach,Treg,Alf Word,Tisc,We/Ho,Weis Sod,UBS/*

2504.1 conj	**744.4** noun acc sing masc	**3450.10** art gen sing fem	**3534.1** noun gen sing fem	**2231.2** prs-pron gen 1pl	**5382.4** name acc masc
καὶ	ἀρχιερέα	τῆς	ὁμολογίας	ἡμῶν	⸀a Χριστὸν ⸌
kai	*archierea*	*tēs*	*homologias*	*hēmōn*	*Christon*
and	high priest	of the	confession	our,	Christ

2400.3 name acc masc	**3964.1** adj sing	**1498.18** verb part pres act	**3450.3** art dat sing	**4020.38** verb dat sing masc part aor act	**840.6** prs-pron acc sing masc
Ἰησοῦν·	2. πιστὸν	ὄντα	τῷ	ποιήσαντι	αὐτὸν,
Iēsoun	*piston*	*onta*	*tō*	*poiēsanti*	*auton*
Jesus,	faithful	being	to the	having appointed	him,

2.a.**Txt:** 01א,02A,04C 06D,044,byz.
Var: p13,p46-vid,03B We/Ho

5453.1 conj	**2504.1** conj	**3337.1** name nom masc	**3338.1** name nom masc	**1706.1** prep	**3513.3** adj dat sing	**3450.3** art dat sing
ὡς	καὶ	⸀ Μωσῆς	[* Μωϋσῆς]	ἐν	⸀a ὅλῳ ⸌	τῷ
hōs	*kai*	*Mōsēs*	*Mōusēs*	*en*	*holō*	*tō*
as	also	Moses	[idem]	in	all	the

3486.3 noun dat sing masc	**840.3** prs-pron gen sing	**3979.7** adj comp gen sing fem	**1056.1** conj	**1385.2** noun gen sing fem	**3642.4** dem-pron nom sing masc
οἴκῳ	αὐτοῦ.	3. πλείονος	γὰρ	⸀ δόξης	οὗτος
oikō	*autou*	*pleionos*	*gar*	*doxēs*	*houtos*
house	his.	Of more	for	glory	this

3642.4 dem-pron nom sing masc	**1385.2** noun gen sing fem	**3706.2** prep	**3337.6** name acc masc	**3338.1** name nom masc
[* οὗτος	δόξης]	παρὰ	⸀ Μωσῆν	[* Μωϋσῆς]
houtos	*doxēs*	*para*	*Mōsēn*	*Mōusēs*
[this	glory]	than	Moses	[idem]

511.6 verb 3sing indic perf mid	**2567.2** prep	**3607.1** rel-pron sing	**3979.1** adj comp	**4940.4** noun acc sing fem
ἠξίωται,	καθ'	ὅσον	πλείονα	τιμὴν
ēxiōtai	*kath'*	*hoson*	*pleiona*	*timēn*
has been counted worthy,	by	how much	more	honor

2174.4 verb 3sing indic pres act	**3450.2** art gen sing	**3486.2** noun gen sing masc	**3450.5** art nom sing masc	**2650.2** verb nom sing masc part aor act
ἔχει	τοῦ	οἴκου	ὁ	κατασκευάσας
echei	*tou*	*oikou*	*ho*	*kataskeuasas*
has	than the	house	the	having built

840.6 prs-pron acc sing masc	**3820.6** adj nom sing masc	**1056.1** conj	**3486.1** noun nom sing masc	**2650.4** verb 3sing indic pres mid
αὐτόν·	4. πᾶς	γὰρ	οἶκος	κατασκευάζεται
auton	*pas*	*gar*	*oikos*	*kataskeuazetai*
it.	Every	for	house	is being built

4.a.**Txt:** 04C-corr 06D-corr,020L,025P,byz.
Var: 01א,02A,03B 04C-org,06D-org,018K 33,Lach,Treg,Alf,Word Tisc,We/Ho,Weis,Sod UBS/*

5097.3 prep	**4948.1** indef-pron gen sing	**3450.5** art nom sing masc	**1156.2** conj	**3450.17** art pl neu	**3820.1** adj
ὑπό	τινος·	ὁ	δὲ	⸀a τὰ ⸌	πάντα
hupo	*tinos*	*ho*	*de*	*ta*	*panta*
by	someone;	the	but	the	all things

2650.2 verb nom sing masc part aor act	**2296.1** noun nom sing masc	**2504.1** conj	**3337.1** name nom masc	**3338.1** name nom masc
κατασκευάσας	θεός.	5. καὶ	⸀ Μωσῆς	[* Μωϋσῆς]
kataskeuasas	*theos*	*kai*	*Mōsēs*	*Mōusēs*
being built	God.	And	Moses	[idem]

3173.1 conj	**3964.2** adj nom sing masc	**1706.1** prep	**3513.3** adj dat sing	**3450.3** art dat sing	**3486.3** noun dat sing masc	**840.3** prs-pron gen sing
μὲν	πιστὸς	ἐν	ὅλῳ	τῷ	οἴκῳ	αὐτοῦ
men	*pistos*	*en*	*holō*	*tō*	*oikō*	*autou*
indeed	faithful	in	all	the	house	his

Jesus the Messiah who is designated "the Apostle and High Priest of our profession." As Apostle He was sent by the Father to reveal the Father to men; as High Priest He represents men to the Father.

Jesus the Christ, the Messiah, is a two-way mediator. In this twofold mediation, He parallels Moses who was sent by Jehovah to deliver the Law to Israel and who also on several occasions interceded with Jehovah on Israel's behalf as their representative. Just as Israel acknowledged Moses as a mediator between themselves and the Lord, so believers confess Jesus Christ as the Mediator between themselves and the Father.

3:2. A further point of likeness between Jesus and Moses is singled out here: both were "faithful" to God in the responsibilities which He gave to them. The sphere of their work is identified by the term "house" which is picked up in the next verse when the inspired writer moved away from points of similarity.

3:3. "For" introduces the reason the readers of the epistle should set their minds upon Jesus. Jesus surpasses Moses. "Counted worthy" conjures up pictures of a balance scale. The parallels between Moses and Jesus now move from comparison to contrast. The weight of Jesus' glory is greater than Moses' to the same degree that the contractor who constructs a house has greater honor than the house.

3:4. "For" in this verse ushers in the explanation of the "house" illustration. Houses do not materialize from nothing; each has been built by someone. The house in view here is *panta*, the totality of all existing things, the entire universe. God is its builder. He is clearly greater than Moses. The context provides clear interpretation of these words. The Son is the Father's agent in creation (1:2). He is addressed as God (1:8). He is portrayed as Creator (1:10-12). Jesus' glory far surpasses the glory of Moses, because He is the builder of the house, the Creator of the universe.

3:5. Moses' status and significance were not examined. His faithfulness (introduced in verse 2) was addressed. This is not the writer's personal opinion; it is the judgment of the Lord. Numbers 12 gives the account of Miriam and Aaron complaining against Moses. In response to them, Jehovah spoke in Moses' defense. He declared that Moses was superior to the prophets because he received God's words directly, not in visions and dreams. In proclaiming Moses' superiority, He says, "My servant Moses is not so, who is faithful in all mine house" (Numbers 12:7). The passage is almost cited verbatim here. "Mine house" is changed to "his house" because the writer was reporting God's evaluation indirectly.

consider the Apostle and High Priest of our profession, Christ Jesus: . . . contemplate, *Noli* . . . think carefully on, *Klingensmith* . . . attentively regard Jesus, *Wilson* . . . fix your eyes on...the Apostle and High Priest of our Religion, *TCNT* . . . fix your thoughts then upon Jesus, *Montgomery* . . . the Messenger and High Priest whom we profess to follow, *Williams* . . . in our confession of Faith, *Wade.*

2. Who was faithful to him that appointed him: . . . to see how faithful He was to God, *Williams.*

as also Moses [was faithful] in all his house: . . . in all the house of God, *Williams* . . . all God's household, *TNT.*

3. For this [man] was counted worthy of more glory than Moses: . . . is held in greater regard, *TCNT* . . . is judged to be worthy of, *Williams* . . . has been considered worthy of greater honor, *Adams* . . . of greater glory, *Montgomery.*

inasmuch as he who hath builded the house: . . . just as the founder of a household, *TNT* . . . as He Who constructs it, *Concordant* . . . A builder, *SEB* . . . he who has organized a household, *Wade.*

hath more honour than the house: . . . has greater glory than, *Williams* . . . deserves more praise, *SEB* . . . is more than the household itself, *TNT* . . . enjoys more honour than the household, *Wade.*

4. For every house is builded by some [man]: . . . is organized by, *Wade* . . . is built by somebody, *Williams* . . . is founded by someone, *TNT.*

but he that built all things [is] God: . . . he who built the universe, *Montgomery* . . . but the builder and furnisher of the universe, *Williams* . . . but God is the founder of everything, *TNT* . . . organized the Universe, *Wade.*

5. And Moses verily [was] faithful in all his house, as a servant: The loyalty of Moses was, *Noli* . . . as an attendant, *Concordant* . . . it was as a servant that Moses was faithful, *TNT* . . . in the administration of the whole of God's Household, *Wade.*

Hebrews 3:6

5453.1 conj	2301.1 noun nom sing masc	1519.1 prep	3115.1 noun sing neu	3450.1 art gen pl
ὡς	θεράπων,	εἰς	μαρτύριον	τῶν
hōs	*therapōn*	*eis*	*marturion*	*tōn*
as	a ministering servant,	for	a testimony	of the things

2953.61 verb gen pl neu part fut pass	5382.1 name nom masc	1156.2 conj	5453.1 conj	5048.1 noun nom sing masc	1894.3 prep
λαληθησομένων·	6. Χριστὸς	δὲ	ὡς	υἱὸς	ἐπὶ
lalēthēsomenōn	*Christos*	*de*	*hōs*	*huios*	*epi*
going to be spoken;	Christ	but	as	Son	over

6.a.**Txt:** p13,01ℵ,02A 03B,04C,06D-corr2 016I,044,byz.We/Ho
Var: p46,06D-org,6 0121b,1739

3450.6 art acc sing masc	3486.4 noun acc sing masc	840.3 prs-pron gen sing	3614.2 rel-pron gen sing	3614.5 rel-pron nom sing masc	3486.1 noun nom sing masc
τὸν	οἶκον	αὐτοῦ,	⸂☆ οὗ	[a ὅς]	οἶκός
ton	*oikon*	*autou*	*hou*	*hos*	*oikos*
the	house	his,	whose	[which]	house

6.b.**Txt:** 01ℵ-corr,02A 04C,06D-corr,018K 020L,byz.Sod
Var: 01ℵ-org,03B 06D-org,025P,33,Treg Alf,Tisc,We/Ho,Weis UBS/☆

1498.5 verb 1pl indic pres act	2231.1 prs-pron nom 1pl	1430.1 conj	1430.1 partic	3450.12 art acc sing fem
ἐσμεν	ἡμεῖς,	⸂ ἐάνπερ	[b☆ ἐὰν]	τὴν
esmen	*hēmeis*	*eanper*	*ean*	*tēn*
are	we,	if indeed	[if]	the

3816.4 noun acc sing fem	2504.1 conj	3450.16 art sing neu	2715.1 noun sing neu	3450.10 art gen sing fem	1667.2 noun gen sing fem
παῤῥησίαν	καὶ	τὸ	καύχημα	τῆς	ἐλπίδος
parrhēsian	*kai*	*to*	*kauchēma*	*tēs*	*elpidos*
confidence	and	the	boasting	of the	hope

6.c.**Txt:** 01ℵ,02A,04C 06D,044,0121b,bo.byz. We/Ho,Sod
Var: p13,p46,03B,sa. UBS/☆

3230.1 prep	4904.2 noun gen sing neu	942.3 adj acc sing fem	2692.9 verb 1pl subj aor act	1346.1 conj
⸂c μέχρι	τέλους	βεβαίαν⸃	κατάσχωμεν.	7. Διό,
mechri	*telous*	*bebaian*	*kataschōmen*	*Dio*
unto	end	firm	we should hold.	Wherefore,

2503.1 conj	2978.5 verb 3sing indic pres act	3450.16 art sing neu	4011.1 noun sing neu	3450.16 art sing neu	39.1 adj sing
καθὼς	λέγει	τὸ	πνεῦμα	τὸ	ἅγιον,
kathōs	*legei*	*to*	*pneuma*	*to*	*hagion*
even as	says	the	Spirit	the	Holy,

4449.1 adv	1430.1 partic	3450.10 art gen sing fem	5292.2 noun gen sing fem	840.3 prs-pron gen sing	189.26 verb 2pl subj aor act
Σήμερον	ἐὰν	τῆς	φωνῆς	αὐτοῦ	ἀκούσητε,
Sēmeron	*ean*	*tēs*	*phōnēs*	*autou*	*akousēte*
Today	if	the	voice	his	you will hear,

3231.1 partic	4500.2 verb 2pl subj aor act	3450.15 art acc pl fem	2559.1 noun fem	5050.2 prs-pron gen 2pl	5453.1 conj	1706.1 prep
8. μὴ	σκληρύνητε	τὰς	καρδίας	ὑμῶν,	ὡς	ἐν
mē	*sklērunēte*	*tas*	*kardias*	*humōn*	*hōs*	*en*
not	harden	the	hearts	your,	as	in

3450.3 art dat sing	3755.1 noun dat sing masc	2567.3 prep	3450.12 art acc sing fem	2232.4 noun acc sing fem	3450.2 art gen sing
τῷ	παραπικρασμῷ,	κατὰ	τὴν	ἡμέραν	τοῦ
tō	*parapikrasmō*	*kata*	*tēn*	*hēmeran*	*tou*
the	rebellion,	in	the	day	of the

3848.2 noun gen sing masc	1706.1 prep	3450.11 art dat sing fem	2031.2 noun dat sing fem	3619.1 adv	3847.7 verb 3pl indic aor act
πειρασμοῦ	ἐν	τῇ	ἐρήμῳ,	9. οὗ	ἐπείρασαν
peirasmou	*en*	*tē*	*erēmō*	*hou*	*epeirasan*
temptation,	in	the	wilderness,	where	tempted

In the last part of the verse, two contrasts are drawn. Moses is classified by the Lord as "a servant." The term *therapōn* does not carry the connotations of slavery or menial service; rather, it is associated with dignity and personal service. Yet it does indicate that Moses was responsible and accountable to the Lord as a subordinate not born in the family. Finally, Moses testified of "things which were to be spoken after." The revelation which he received from Jehovah was inferior to the revelation spoken in the Son because that word was God's final message of salvation (1:1,2).

for a testimony of those things which were to be spoken after: . . . being included among its members for the purpose of bearing testimony to the Truths that were afterwards to be communicated, *Wade* . . . bore witness to what God would say, *TNT* . . . that would be disclosed in the future, *Adams* . . . to a Message still to come, *TCNT.*

3:6. Christ's superiority to Moses is stated simply. He is not a servant; He is "a son." He is not "in" the house; He is "over" it. It is not someone else's house; it is "his own house," the one He himself created. Those who profess faith in Jesus Christ are His creation, if their confidence is strong enough to boldly maintain their hope in Jesus' future restoration of mankind's lost "glory" and "honor."

6. But Christ as a son over his own house: . . . but Christ was faithful as a son, *TNT.*

whose house are we: We are His family, *Beck* . . . we are that house, *Williams* . . . ruling over God's household, *TNT.*

if we hold fast: . . . if we hold firmly, *Adams* . . . if we should be retaining the boldness, *Concordant* . . . if only we keep, *TNT* . . . keep up our courage, *Norlie.*

the confidence and the rejoicing of the hope: . . . our confidence and pride in the hope that is ours, *TNT* . . . and the joy that hope inspires, *Williams.*

firm unto the end: . . . unshaken to, *TCNT* . . . unto the consummation, *Concordant* . . . the very end, *Williams.*

3:7. Verse 6 introduced a long section of application which consists of encouragement, exhortation, and warning. It extends to 4:13. Those who received this epistle were professing Jewish believers who were under great pressure to abandon their profession of faith in Jesus as the Messiah. Their exact situation is not known, but it is fairly easy to imagine some of the trials that pressured them: family and religious ties to Judaism, ostracism by their peers, economic sanctions, famine, poverty, loneliness, religious persecution, and perhaps the threat of martyrdom.

To underscore the danger of their turning back, the inspired writer pointed out the parallel between their situation and that of those who were with Moses in the wilderness. Moses was a great servant of the Lord, but almost all who followed him died in the wilderness and never entered the Promised Land. Jesus is the Son and the revealer of a superior message. Those who fail to follow Him by faith wherever He leads them will also fail to enter into the realization of that which He has promised to them.

As a foundation for this extended warning, the writer fully quoted Psalm 95:7-11. First of all, he introduced the quote in a notable manner. "Wherefore" indicates that the passage is cited in support of the conditionality of hope. Secondly, the introductory phrase "as the Holy Ghost saith" reveals his high view of the Old Testament. The words of Psalm 95 are presented as the work of God the Holy Spirit, and they spoke with divine authority to the professing Hebrew Christians of the First Century, even though they were written to their ancestors several centuries beforehand.

7. Wherefore (as the Holy Ghost saith:

To day if ye will hear his voice: Listen to his voice today, *TNT* . . . if you hear Him speak, *Beck.*

8. Harden not your hearts, as in the provocation: . . . don't close your minds as it happened when the people provoked me, *Beck* . . . don't let your hearts become stubborn, as you did during the rebellion, *SEB* . . . Do not be stubborn as you once were when you rebelled against him, *TNT* . . . as they did in provoking me, *Williams* . . . as in the revolt, *Adams* . . . when they turned against Me, *NLT.*

in the day of temptation in the wilderness: . . . during the day of testing in the desert, *Adams* . . . that day when you put him to the test in the desert, *TNT.*

3:8,9. Since the interpretation and application of these words is drawn out in 3:12 to 4:13, only a few historical notations are given here. Psalm 95 begins with a call to worship Jehovah followed by the quotation in this verse, a warning against disobedience to the

9. When your fathers tempted me, proved me: Where your forefathers found I stood their test, *Williams* . . . tried my forbearance, *Montgomery* . . . when they tried my patience, *TCNT* . . . and tested Me, *Norlie.*

9.a.**Txt:** 01ℵ-corr 06D-corr,018K,020L 025P,byz.bo.Sod
Var: 01ℵ-org,02A,03B 04C,06D-org,33,Lach Treg,Alf,Word,Tisc We/Ho,Weis,UBS/☆

9.b.**Txt:** 01ℵ-corr 06D-corr,018K,020L byz.
Var: 01ℵ-org,02A,03B 04C,06D-org,025P,33 Lach,Treg,Alf,Word Tisc,We/Ho,Weis,Sod UBS/☆

10.a.**Txt:** 04C,06D-corr 018K,020L,025P,byz.bo.
Var: 01ℵ,02A,03B 06D-org,33,Lach,Treg Alf,Word,Tisc,We/Ho Weis,Sod,UBS/☆

1466.6 prs-pron acc 1sing	**3450.7** art nom pl masc	**3824.6** noun nom pl masc	**5050.2** prs-pron gen 2pl	**1375.10** verb 3pl indic aor act	**1466.6** prs-pron acc 1sing
⸂[a] με ⸃	οἱ	πατέρες	ὑμῶν,	⸀ ἐδοκίμασάν	με,
me	*hoi*	*pateres*	*humōn*	*edokimasan*	*me*
me	the	fathers	your,	proved	me,

1706.1 prep	**1375.1** noun dat sing fem	**2504.1** conj	**1481.1** verb indic aor act	**3450.17** art pl neu	**2024.4** noun pl neu
[[b]☆ ἐν	δοκιμασίᾳ]	καὶ	εἶδον	τὰ	ἔργα
en	*dokimasia*	*kai*	*eidon*	*ta*	*erga*
[in	proving]	and	saw	the	works

1466.2 prs-pron gen 1sing	**4910.2** num card	**4910.2** num card	**2073.3** noun pl neu
μου	⸀ τεσσαράκοντα	[☆ τεσσαράκοντα]	ἔτη·
mou	*tessarakonta*	*tessarakonta*	*etē*
my	forty	[idem]	years.

1346.1 conj	**4218.1** verb 1sing indic aor act	**3450.11** art dat sing fem	**1067.3** noun dat sing fem	**1552.11** dem-pron dat sing fem
10. διὸ	προσώχθισα	τῇ	γενεᾷ	⸀ ἐκείνῃ
dio	*prosōchthisa*	*tē*	*genea*	*ekeinē*
Wherefore	I was indignant	with the	generation	that,

3642.11 dem-pron dat sing fem	**2504.1** conj	**1500.3** verb indic aor act	**103.1** adv	**3966.12** verb 3pl indic pres mid	**3450.11** art dat sing fem
[[a]☆ ταύτῃ]	καὶ	εἶπον,	Ἀεὶ	πλανῶνται	τῇ
tautē	*kai*	*eipon*	*Aei*	*planōntai*	*tē*
[this]	and	said,	Always	they err	in the

2559.3 noun dat sing fem	**840.7** prs-pron nom pl masc	**1156.2** conj	**3620.2** partic	**1091.18** verb 3pl indic aor act	**3450.15** art acc pl fem	**3461.8** noun acc pl fem
καρδίᾳ·	αὐτοὶ	δὲ	οὐκ	ἔγνωσαν	τὰς	ὁδούς
kardia	*autoi*	*de*	*ouk*	*egnōsan*	*tas*	*hodous*
heart;	they	and	not	did know	the	ways

1466.2 prs-pron gen 1sing	**5453.1** conj	**3523.5** verb 1sing indic aor act	**1706.1** prep	**3450.11** art dat sing fem	**3572.3** noun dat sing fem
μου·	**11.** ὡς	ὤμοσα	ἐν	τῇ	ὀργῇ
mou	*hōs*	*ōmosa*	*en*	*tē*	*orgē*
my;	so	I swore	in	the	wrath

1466.2 prs-pron gen 1sing	**1479.1** conj	**1511.39** verb 3pl indic fut mid	**1519.1** prep	**3450.12** art acc sing fem	**2633.2** noun acc sing fem
μου,	Εἰ	εἰσελεύσονται	εἰς	τὴν	κατάπαυσίν
mou	*Ei*	*eiseleusontai*	*eis*	*tēn*	*katapausin*
my,	If	they shall enter	into	the	rest

1466.2 prs-pron gen 1sing	**984.1** verb 2pl pres act	**79.6** noun nom pl masc	**3246.1** partic	**1498.40** verb 3sing indic fut mid
μου.	**12.** Βλέπετε,	ἀδελφοί,	μήποτε	ἔσται
mou	*Blepete*	*adelphoi*	*mēpote*	*estai*
my.	Take heed,	brothers,	lest perhaps	shall be

1706.1 prep	**4948.2** indef-pron dat sing	**5050.2** prs-pron gen 2pl	**2559.2** noun nom sing fem	**4050.10** adj	**565.2** noun gen sing fem	**1706.1** prep
ἔν	τινι	ὑμῶν	καρδία	πονηρὰ	ἀπιστίας	ἐν
en	*tini*	*humōn*	*kardia*	*ponēra*	*apistias*	*en*
in	anyone	of you	a heart	wicked	of unbelief	in

3450.3 art dat sing	**861.9** verb inf aor act	**570.3** prep	**2296.2** noun gen sing masc	**2180.11** verb gen sing part pres act	**233.2** conj
τῷ	ἀποστῆναι	ἀπὸ	θεοῦ	ζῶντος·	**13.** ἀλλὰ
tō	*apostēnai*	*apo*	*theou*	*zōntos*	*alla*
the	departing	from	God	living.	But

Lord. The words just prior to the quote include the statement, "We are the people of his pasture" (Psalm 95:7), an idea in line with the inspired writer's application: this is the way believers must behave, if they are to be God's house. The "if" clause of verse 7 recalls Exodus 19:5 and Deuteronomy 5:25. "Harden not" evokes images of Pharaoh's and Israel's rebellions. "The provocation" hints at the incident in Exodus 17 which occurred at a place Moses called Massah and Meribah, meaning "temptation" and "strife," "because they tempted the Lord . . . " (Exodus 17:7). In spite of God's goodness in always providing their needs, such events were repeated for 40 years (e.g., Numbers 20:1-13).

3:10. Murmurings against Jehovah characterized the entire wilderness generation. The Lord continually punished the guilty, and eventually His patient long-suffering ended. Israel did not focus her heart on Him; as a result they did not obey Him.

3:11. Israel had grieved God by their murmurings and disobedience. Finally, His grief changed to anger, when they turned back from entering Canaan at Kadesh-barnea. The Lord swore an oath prohibiting them from ever setting foot in the "Promised Land" of rest (Numbers 14:23). They wandered for a total of 40 years until all that generation had perished in the wilderness.

3:12. Addressing the professing Jewish Christian readers as "brethren," the writer began to apply Psalm 95 by telling them to watch out in case any of them had an "evil heart" which he identified as a heart characterized by unbelief. In using the word "heart," he was not talking merely of their emotional nature. "Heart" referred to the core of their being. The action of such an evil heart is described by the phrase *en tō apostēnai* which speaks of their turning aside from God. Unbelief abandons God and rebels against Him. The God they were in danger of leaving was not some idol; He is the "living" God. The whole tenor of the argument to this point argues that if they abandoned their belief in the Son, they would be rebelling against God as the wilderness generation did in Moses' day.

3:13. The danger of rebellion was so great that the writer asked the believers to admonish and encourage each other on a daily basis. The verb *parakaleite* echoes both the negative and positive elements associated with exhortation. Its meaning can be illustrated

and saw my works forty years: . . . they watched me at work, *TNT* . . . were acquainted with My acts, *Concordant* . . . my marvellous deeds during so many years, *Wade.*

10. Wherefore I was grieved with that generation: That is why I became angry with the people of that time, *TNT* . . . I am disgusted with, *Concordant* . . . I was sore displeased, *Montgomery* . . . I was indignant with, *Williams.*

and said, They do alway err in [their] heart: Their hearts are always going astray, *Adams, Williams* . . . They always think wrong thoughts, *NLT* . . . Their hearts always wander away, *SEB* . . . They are always wandering, *Montgomery* . . . Their hearts are always straying, *TCNT.*

and they have not known my ways: . . . but they did not acknowledge my ways, *Wilson* . . . they have never come to know, *Williams* . . . they do not understand, *TNT* . . . and never have learned My paths, *Beck.*

11. So I sware in my wrath: As I shewed when I swore, *Wade* . . . in my indignation, *Wilson* . . . So in My anger I took oath, *Norlie, Williams* . . . while I was angry, I made a vow, *SEB* . . . I swore, *TNT.*

They shall not enter into my rest.): . . . that they would never come in and rest with me, *TNT* . . . not be admitted to, *Williams.*

12. Take heed, brethren, lest there be: Consequently, I repeat, *Wade* . . . Watch out, brothers, *Adams* . . . Brothers, be careful, *SEB* . . . See to it, *Williams.*

in any of you an evil heart of unbelief: . . . a wicked and faithless heart, *TCNT* . . . no wicked, unbelieving heart is found, *Williams.*

in departing from the living God: . . . as shown by your turning away from, *Williams* . . . by apostatizing, *Wilson* . . . should fall away from, *TNT* . . . that pulls away from, *SEB* . . . manifesting itself in apostasy from, *Montgomery* . . . that would turn you away from, *Adams.*

13. But exhort one another daily: On the contrary, *Wade* . . . What you should do...is to en-

3731.6 verb 2pl impr pres act	1431.8 prs-pron acc pl masc	2567.2 prep	1524.7 adj acc sing fem	2232.4 noun acc sing fem	884.1 conj
παρακαλεῖτε	ἑαυτοὺς	καθ'	ἑκάστην	ἡμέραν,	ἄχρις
parakaleite	*heautous*	*kath'*	*hekastēn*	*hēmeran*	*achris*
encourage	yourselves	by	every	day	until

3614.2 rel-pron gen sing	3450.16 art sing neu	4449.1 adv	2535.26 verb 3sing indic pres mid	2419.1 conj	3231.1 partic
οὗ	τὸ	Σήμερον	καλεῖται,	ἵνα	μὴ
hou	*to*	*Sēmeron*	*kaleitai*	*hina*	*mē*
which	the	today	it is being called,	that	not

13.a.**Txt:** p13,01ℵ,02A 04C,015H,025P,044 0121b,33,81,104,629 1241,1739,1881,2646 **Var:** 03B,06D,byz.

4500.3 verb 3sing subj aor pass	4948.3 indef-pron nom sing	1523.1 prep gen	5050.2 prs-pron gen 2pl	5050.2 prs-pron gen 2pl	1523.1 prep gen
σκληρυνθῇ	ʿ☆ τις	ἐξ	ὑμῶν	[a ὑμῶν	ἐξ
sklērunthē	*tis*	*ex*	*humōn*	*humōn*	*ex*
may be hardened	any	of	you	[you	of

4948.3 indef-pron nom sing	535.3 noun dat sing fem	3450.10 art gen sing fem	264.1 noun fem	3223.1 adj nom pl masc
τις]	ἀπάτῃ	τῆς	ἁμαρτίας·	14. μέτοχοι
tis	*apatē*	*tēs*	*hamartias*	*metochoi*
any]	by deceitfulness	of the	sin.	Companions

1056.1 conj	1090.4 verb 1pl indic perf act	3450.2 art gen sing	5382.2 name gen masc	3450.2 art gen sing	5382.2 name gen masc
γὰρ	ʿ γεγόναμεν	τοῦ	Χριστοῦ,	[☆ τοῦ	Χριστοῦ
gar	*gegonamen*	*tou*	*Christou*	*tou*	*Christou*
for	we have become	of the	Christ,	[of the	Christ

1090.4 verb 1pl indic perf act	1430.1 conj	3450.12 art acc sing fem	741.4 noun acc sing fem	3450.10 art gen sing fem
γεγόναμεν,]	ἐάνπερ	τὴν	ἀρχὴν	τῆς
gegonamen	*eanper*	*tēn*	*archēn*	*tēs*
we have become,]	if indeed	the	beginning	of the

5125.2 noun gen sing fem	3230.1 prep	4904.2 noun gen sing neu	942.3 adj acc sing fem	2692.9 verb 1pl subj aor act
ὑποστάσεως	μέχρι	τέλους	βεβαίαν	κατάσχωμεν·
hupostaseōs	*mechri*	*telous*	*bebaian*	*kataschōmen*
assurance	unto	end	firm	we should hold;

1706.1 prep	3450.3 art dat sing	2978.38 verb inf pres mid	4449.1 adv	1430.1 partic	3450.10 art gen sing fem
15. ἐν	τῷ	λέγεσθαι,	Σήμερον	ἐὰν	τῆς
en	*tō*	*legesthai*	*Sēmeron*	*ean*	*tēs*
in	the	to be said,	Today	if	the

5292.2 noun gen sing fem	840.3 prs-pron gen sing	189.26 verb 2pl subj aor act	3231.1 partic	4500.2 verb 2pl subj aor act	3450.15 art acc pl fem
φωνῆς	αὐτοῦ	ἀκούσητε,	Μὴ	σκληρύνητε	τὰς
phōnēs	*autou*	*akousēte*	*Mē*	*sklērunēte*	*tas*
voice	his	you should hear,	not	harden	the

2559.1 noun fem	5050.2 prs-pron gen 2pl	5453.1 conj	1706.1 prep	3450.3 art dat sing	3755.1 noun dat sing masc
καρδίας	ὑμῶν,	ὡς	ἐν	τῷ	παραπικρασμῷ.
kardias	*humōn*	*hōs*	*en*	*tō*	*parapikrasmō*
hearts	your,	as	in	the	rebellion.

4949.6 intr-pron nom pl masc	1056.1 conj	189.32 verb nom pl masc part aor act	3754.1 verb 3pl indic aor act	233.1 conj	3620.3 partic
16. τίνες	γὰρ	ἀκούσαντες	παρεπίκραναν;	ἀλλ'	οὐ
tines	*gar*	*akousantes*	*parepikranan*	*all'*	*ou*
Some	for	having heard	rebelled,	but	not

by picturing someone running alongside a long-distance runner and exhorting him to finish the course in the face of his fatigue and exhaustion. There is a warning about the effects of quitting, but there is a sense of unity and a spirit of hope which comes to the fore. In his comments on Psalm 95, the writer emphasizes the sense of urgency and immediacy attached to the word "Today." The danger of turning from the Son must be attended to on a daily basis, because the sin of unbelief sneaks up on a believer. Little by little an individual can be hardened and become unaware.

3:14. The prize in a race does not go to those who start out quickly. Those who finish are the ones who are honored. Over the centuries some controversy has arisen over the meaning of the phrase *metochoi gar . . . tou Christou* ("partakers of Christ"). Most interpreters have taken it to mean "companions with Christ," seeing it as a reference to the believer's participation with Christ in the Kingdom. Some, however, have interpreted it as a reference to the Christian's union with Christ. The context seems to argue in favor of the first meaning. The participation under consideration is something in the future. When a believer maintains the faith that brought salvation until the end of this life, either until death or the Second Coming, he will most certainly participate with the Son in His kingdom. Participation in the promised kingdom of God is not dependent upon a profession of faith alone; it is conditioned upon displaying the reality of that profession by living a life which continues following after God.

History has often recorded the failure of those who seemingly started out well but dropped out along the way. The history of the kingdom of Judah illustrates this. Time after time a king would begin his reign seeking to please God, but because of evil influences would turn away from Jehovah. Only those who persist in finding and obeying the will of God can expect to achieve the prize which God has designed for them. "Steadfast" must be the watchword for the follower of Christ.

3:15. Returning to Psalm 95:7,8, the inspired writer continued his theme of the urgency and immediacy of the danger of unbelief. The implication both here and in verse 13 is that the time will come when the opportunity for genuine belief will be past. Belief must be exercised while the gospel invitation stands open.

3:16. Some who heard God's promise and warnings bitterly rebelled against Him anyway. Not all who experienced God's gracious deliverance from Egypt rebelled against Him in the wilderness. Failure was not inevitable; it was the result of personal choice.

courage one another every day, *TNT* . . . continue to encourage, *Williams.*

while it is called To day: . . . as long as there lasts the interval which is called, *Wade* . . . as long as "Today" shall last, *Williams.*

lest any of you be hardened: . . . made stubborn against God, *TNT.*

through the deceitfulness of sin: . . . by the seduction of sin, *Concordant* . . . by a Delusion of sin, *Wilson* . . . by the trickery of sin, *Klingensmith* . . . by sin's deceiving ways, *Williams.*

14. For we are made partakers of Christ: We have become Companions of, *TCNT* . . . We share in Christ, *Beck* . . . we shall have become Christ's partners, *TNT* . . . become real sharers, *Williams.*

if we hold the beginning of our confidence stedfast unto the end: . . . we only remain so, provided we retain unshaken to the end the confidence which we had at first, *Wade* . . . if we hold our first title deed firm, *Montgomery* . . . the assumption confirmed unto the consummation, *Concordant* . . . if we keep firm to the end the faith we had at first, *Williams.*

15. While it is said: With regard to the declaration, *Wilson* . . . Scripture says to us also, *TNT* . . . This warning is still being uttered, *Wade* . . . and yet the warning continues to be spoken, *Williams.*

To day if ye will hear his voice: Listen to his voice today, *TNT.*

harden not your hearts, as in the provocation: Do not continue to harden your hearts, *Montgomery* . . . Do not be stubborn as you once were when you rebelled against him, *TNT* . . . as in the revolt, *Adams* . . . as in the embitterment, *Concordant* . . . as in the rebellion, *Norlie* . . . as they did in provoking me, *Williams* . . . as when ye exasperated me, *Wade.*

16. For some, when they had heard, did provoke: . . . who was it that heard and yet provoked Him? *Williams* . . . Who listened to his voice and rebelled? *TNT* . . . For who were they who, after hearing God speak, exasperated Him? *Wade.*

3820.7 adj nom pl masc	**3450.7** art nom pl masc	**1814.15** verb nom pl masc part aor act	**1523.1** prep gen	**125.2** name gen fem	**1217.2** prep
πάντες	οἱ	ἐξελθόντες	ἐξ	Αἰγύπτου	διὰ
pantes	*hoi*	*exelthontes*	*ex*	*Aiguptou*	*dia*
all	the	having come out	from	Egypt	by

3337.2 name gen masc	**3338.2** name gen masc	**4949.7** intr-pron dat pl masc	**1156.2** conj	**4218.2** verb 3sing indic aor act
ᶠ Μωσέως.	[☆ Μωϋσέως;]	**17.** τίσιν	δὲ	προσώχθισεν
Mōseōs	*Mōuseōs*	*tisin*	*de*	*prosōchthisen*
Moses.	[idem]	With whom	and	was he indignant

4910.2 num card	**4910.1** num card	**2073.3** noun pl neu	**3644.1** adv	**3450.4** art dat pl
ᶠ τεσσαράκοντα	[τεσσεράκοντα]	ἔτη;	οὐχὶ	τοῖς
tessarakonta	*tesserakonta*	*etē*	*ouchi*	*tois*
forty	[idem]	years?	Not	with the

262.19 verb dat pl masc part aor act	**3614.1** rel-pron gen pl	**3450.17** art pl neu	**2939.1** noun pl neu	**3959.5** verb 3sing indic aor act	**1706.1** prep
ἁμαρτήσασιν,	ὧν	τὰ	κῶλα	ἔπεσεν	ἐν
hamartēsasin	*hōn*	*ta*	*kōla*	*epesen*	*en*
having sinned,	of whom	the	corpses	fell	in

3450.11 art dat sing fem	**2031.2** noun dat sing fem	**4949.7** intr-pron dat pl masc	**1156.2** conj	**3523.6** verb 3sing indic aor act	**3231.1** partic
τῇ	ἐρήμῳ;	**18.** τίσιν	δὲ	ὤμοσεν	μὴ
tē	*erēmō*	*tisin*	*de*	*ōmosen*	*mē*
the	wilderness?	To whom	and	swore he	not

1511.40 verb inf fut mid	**1519.1** prep	**3450.12** art acc sing fem	**2633.2** noun acc sing fem	**840.3** prs-pron gen sing	**1479.1** conj
εἰσελεύσεσθαι	εἰς	τὴν	κατάπαυσιν	αὐτοῦ,	εἰ
eiseleusesthai	*eis*	*tēn*	*katapausin*	*autou*	*ei*
to enter	into	the	rest	his,	if

3231.1 partic	**3450.4** art dat pl	**540.9** verb dat pl masc part aor act	**2504.1** conj	**984.5** verb 1pl indic pres act	**3617.1** conj
μὴ	τοῖς	ἀπειθήσασιν;	**19.** καὶ	βλέπομεν	ὅτι
mē	*tois*	*apeithēsasin*	*kai*	*blepomen*	*hoti*
not	to the	having disobeyed?	And	we see	that

3620.2 partic	**1404.27** verb 3pl indic aor pass	**1511.21** verb inf aor act	**1217.1** prep	**565.4** noun acc sing fem
οὐκ	ἠδυνήθησαν	εἰσελθεῖν	δι'	ἀπιστίαν.
ouk	*ēdunēthēsan*	*eiselthein*	*di'*	*apistian*
not	they were able	to enter in	on account of	unbelief.

5236.16 verb 1pl subj aor pass	**3631.1** partic	**3246.1** partic	**2611.9** verb gen sing fem part pres mid
4:1. Φοβηθῶμεν	οὖν	μήποτε	καταλειπομένης
Phobēthōmen	*oun*	*mēpote*	*kataleipomenēs*
We should fear	therefore	lest perhaps	being left

1845.1 noun fem	**1511.21** verb inf aor act	**1519.1** prep	**3450.12** art acc sing fem	**2633.2** noun acc sing fem	**840.3** prs-pron gen sing
ἐπαγγελίας	εἰσελθεῖν	εἰς	τὴν	κατάπαυσιν	αὐτοῦ
epangelias	*eiselthein*	*eis*	*tēn*	*katapausin*	*autou*
a promise	to enter	into	the	rest	his

1374.7 verb 3sing subj pres act	**4948.3** indef-pron nom sing	**1523.1** prep gen	**5050.2** prs-pron gen 2pl	**5139.8** verb inf perf act	**2504.1** conj
δοκῇ	τις	ἐξ	ὑμῶν	ὑστερηκέναι.	**2.** καὶ
dokē	*tis*	*ex*	*humōn*	*husterēkenai*	*kai*
might seem	any	of	you	to have come short.	Indeed

3:17. A series of rhetorical questions begins to drive home the lesson of Israel in the wilderness. Which Israelites disgusted and angered Jehovah during those 40 years of trial in the desert? The account written by the eyewitness Moses is clear. The corpses strewn across the pages of the Pentateuch and the Sinai peninsula are the corpses of the Children of Israel who tested God's patience by repeated acts of sin. Their bleaching bones testified to their disobedience.

3:18. The verse begins with another question with an obvious answer. This time the focus is on the penalty and the nature of the sin which led to the death of so many in the wilderness. Those who died are characterized as those who were prohibited from entrance into Canaan by the oath of the living God. The essence of the sin which brought down the wrath of God upon them was unbelief. Instead of zeroing in on the rebellion, backbiting, complaining, grumbling, murmuring, and defiance which fill the pages of the Old Testament record of Israel's wilderness experience, the writer looked at the source of these acts of sin: deep inside, underneath it all, was their refusal to believe God.

3:19. In case some did not get the point, it was repeated forcefully. God drew a line, and the disobedient Children of Israel were not able to cross it. They could not leave the wilderness and enter Canaan because they did not take God at His word. It was their unbelief which kept them from entering into the rest which the Lord had promised.

4:1. Since God keeps His word and punishes unbelief by denying "rest" to those who do not trust Him, those who profess faith in the Son ought to fear God. This is what the Son himself taught His disciples (Matthew 10:28) when He said: "And fear not them which kill the body, but are not able to kill the soul: but rather fear him which is able to destroy both soul and body in hell." After all, it was the Son who promised rest to those who would come unto Him: "Come unto me, all ye that labor and are heavy laden, and I will give you rest. Take my yoke upon you, and learn of me; for I am meek and lowly in heart: and ye shall find rest unto your souls" (Matthew 11:28,29).

At this juncture, the inspired writer began to ring the changes on the word "rest" which appeared in the last verse of his citation from Psalm 95 (Hebrews 3:11). He used the word *katapausin* which is found in the Septuagint translation of the psalm and is related to the word *anapausin* employed in Matthew 11:29. In this verse he was concentrating on the danger which threatened some of those to whom he was writing the epistle. Like the Children of Israel in Moses' day, they might never experience God's promised rest.

howbeit not all that came out of Egypt by Moses: Was it not all, *Williams* . . . under the leadership of Moses? *Wade.*

17. But with whom was he grieved forty years?: . . . with whom was God incensed, *Norlie* . . . was God angry, *TNT* . . . was He deeply displeased during so many years? *Wade.*

[was it] not with them that had sinned:

whose carcases fell in the wilderness?: . . . whose dead bodies, *Montgomery* . . . whose corpses fell, *Adams* . . . whose bodies dropped dead in the desert? *Beck.*

18. And to whom sware he: To whom did He take oath, *Williams.*

that they should not enter into his rest: . . . that they should not be admitted to, *Williams* . . . that they would never come in and rest with him? *TNT.*

but to them that believed not?: . . . except to the stubborn? *Concordant* . . . Those who did not obey God! *SEB* . . . to those who disobeyed? *Beck, TNT.*

19. So we see that they could not enter in: . . . could not be admitted to it, *Williams* . . . they were precluded from entering, *Wade.*

because of unbelief: . . . because they did not believe, *TNT* . . . it was through mistrust, *Wade.*

1. Let us therefore fear, lest: . . . the one thing we should fear, *TNT* . . . be on our guard, *Montgomery* . . . we must be apprehensive, *Wade.*

a promise being left [us] of entering into his rest: . . . as long as God's promise that we should go in and rest with him still stands, *TNT* . . . though there is a promise still standing, *TCNT* . . . The same promise of going into God's rest is still for us, *NLT* . . . the promise for us to be admitted, *Williams* . . . still remains open, *Norlie.*

any of you should seem to come short of it: . . . may be found, *Williams* . . . seeming to be deficient, *Concordant* . . . some of you might not make it, *SEB* . . . failed to satisfy the conditions governing entrance, *Wade* . . . may be judged to have missed, *Beck* . . . one of you should think he has missed his chance, *TNT.*

Hebrews 4:3

1056.1 conj	1498.5 verb 1pl indic pres act	2076.26 verb nom pl masc part perf mid	2481.1 conj
γάρ	ἐσμεν	εὐηγγελισμένοι,	καθάπερ
gar	*esmen*	*euēngelismenoi*	*kathaper*
for	we are	having had good news announced	even as

2519.4 dem-pron nom pl masc	233.1 conj	3620.2 partic	5456.3 verb 3sing indic aor act	3450.5 art nom sing masc	3030.1 noun nom sing masc
κἀκεῖνοι·	ἀλλ'	οὐκ	ὠφέλησεν	ὁ	λόγος
kakeinoi	*all'*	*ouk*	*ōphelēsen*	*ho*	*logos*
also they;	but	not	did profit	the	word

3450.10 art gen sing fem	187.2 noun gen sing fem	1552.8 dem-pron acc pl masc	3231.1 partic	4637.2 verb nom sing masc part perf mid
τῆς	ἀκοῆς	ἐκείνους,	μὴ	⸀ συγκεκραμένος
tēs	*akoēs*	*ekeinous*	*mē*	*sunkekramenos*
of the	report	those,	not	having been mixed with

2.a.**Txt:** Steph
Var: 01ℵ,UBS/⋆

4637.5 verb acc pl masc part perf mid	3450.11 art dat sing fem	3963.3 noun dat sing fem	3450.4 art dat pl	189.34 verb dat pl masc part aor act
[ᵃ⋆ συγκεκερασμένους]	τῇ	πίστει	τοῖς	ἀκούσασιν.
sunkekerasmenous	*tē*	*pistei*	*tois*	*akousasin*
[idem]	the	faith	in the	having heard.

3.a.**Txt:** p13,p46,03B 06D,08E,018K,020L 025P,044,We/Ho,byz.
Var: 01ℵ,02A,04C 0121b,81,104,365,1739 1881,2464

3.b.**Txt:** 01ℵ,02A,04C 06D-corr2,044,0121b byz.We/Ho,UBS/⋆
Var: p13-vid,p46,03B 06D-org

1511.27 verb 1pl indic pres mid	1056.1 conj	3631.1 partic	1519.1 prep	3450.12 art acc sing fem
3. εἰσερχόμεθα	⸂⋆ γὰρ	[ᵃ οὖν]	εἰς	⸂ᵇ τὴν ⸃
eiserchometha	*gar*	*oun*	*eis*	*tēn*
We enter	for	[therefore]	into	the

2633.2 noun acc sing fem	3450.7 art nom pl masc	3961.31 verb nom pl masc part aor act	2503.1 conj	2029.3 verb 3sing indic perf act
κατάπαυσιν	οἱ	πιστεύσαντες,	καθὼς	εἴρηκεν,
katapausin	*hoi*	*pisteusantes*	*kathōs*	*eirēken*
rest,	the	having believed;	as	he has said,

5453.1 conj	3523.5 verb 1sing indic aor act	1706.1 prep	3450.11 art dat sing fem	3572.3 noun dat sing fem	1466.2 prs-pron gen 1sing	1479.1 conj
Ὡς	ὤμοσα	ἐν	τῇ	ὀργῇ	μου,	Εἰ
Hōs	*ōmosa*	*en*	*tē*	*orgē*	*mou*	*Ei*
So	I swore	in	the	wrath	my,	If

1511.39 verb 3pl indic fut mid	1519.1 prep	3450.12 art acc sing fem	2633.2 noun acc sing fem	1466.2 prs-pron gen 1sing
εἰσελεύσονται	εἰς	τὴν	κατάπαυσίν	μου·
eiseleusontai	*eis*	*tēn*	*katapausin*	*mou*
they shall enter	into	the	rest	my;

2514.1 adv	3450.1 art gen pl	2024.5 noun gen pl neu	570.3 prep	2573.1 noun gen sing fem	2862.2 noun gen sing masc
καίτοι	τῶν	ἔργων	ἀπὸ	καταβολῆς	κόσμου
kaitoi	*tōn*	*ergōn*	*apo*	*katabolēs*	*kosmou*
and yet	the	works	from	foundation	of world

1090.60 verb gen pl neu part aor pass	2029.3 verb 3sing indic perf act	1056.1 conj	4084.1 adv	3875.1 prep
γενηθέντων.	4. Εἴρηκεν	γάρ	που	περὶ
genēthentōn	*Eirēken*	*gar*	*pou*	*peri*
having been done.	He has said	for	somewhere	concerning

3450.10 art gen sing fem	1436.3 num ord gen sing fem	3643.1 adv	2504.1 conj	2634.1 verb 3sing indic aor act	3450.5 art nom sing masc
τῆς	ἑβδόμης	οὕτως,	Καὶ	κατέπαυσεν	ὁ
tēs	*hebdomēs*	*houtōs*	*Kai*	*katepausen*	*ho*
the	seventh	thus,	And	rested	

4:2. Once again a section of explanation begins with the word "For." The writer specifically drew a parallel between his readers and the Hebrews in the wilderness. Both groups had good news preached to them. Obviously, Israel had been delivered from slavery in Egypt and was to gain entrance to the land of Abraham, Isaac, and Jacob. The good news preached to the readers of this epistle was spoken by God in His Son (1:2; 2:3). The fact that the Israelites heard the message with their own ears, however, did not do them the slightest bit of good. Physical hearing was not enough to bring the experience of the reality of Canaan to fruition. The seed of that promise had to fall into good ground where it was received in faith before it could bear fruit in their lives. But, sad to say, even though they heard the words, and the meaning of the words may have entered into their understanding, there was no enjoyment of the promise in actual experience, because the message was not united with faith in the Children of Israel who heard it. They needed faith as well as hearing.

4:3. For those who believe today, the opposite is true. Believers are in the process of entering into rest. The linear action of the verb *eiserchometha* emphasizes the process in those who "have believed." The tense of *pisteusantes* ("having believed") refers to the moment of genuine conversion. Here the writer repeats the part of Psalm 95 already cited in Hebrews 3:11. Although the English text of 3:11 and the part of 4:3 containing the quote are different, the Greek text is exactly the same. The "if" appears in 4:3 because here the Greek has been translated more literally and shows the idiomatic form of an oath made in the Hebrew language. The rather cryptic ending of verse 3 seems to heighten the sense of tragedy. Israel was, by their own sin and God's punishing oath, kept from entering into the divine rest which had been available ever since God himself had rested from His work in creation. They brought judgment upon themselves.

4:4. Here (as in 2:6) is demonstrated complete trust in the divine authority and authorship of the Old Testament. The human author of this passage is not specifically identified. This approach shows respect for the readers' familiarity with the contents of the Pentateuch and other Old Testament Scriptures. They were well aware of the source of this quotation from Genesis 2:2. "For," which introduces this verse, indicates that the inspired writer is clarifying the previous sentence.

Anyone who knew the Genesis account of creation knew that after 6 days of creative activity God had completed His work and rested on the seventh day. Most people had not recognized the implications of God's rest other than in regard to its relationship to Israel's resting on the Sabbath. Apparently the inspired writer

2. For unto us was the gospel preached: For we have had the good news, *Williams* . . . communicated to us, *Wade.*

as well as unto them: . . . just as it was to those men of old, *TNT* . . . they received the Gospel, *Noli* . . . even as they had, *Wade.*

but the word preached did not profit them: . . . the proclamation of the Gospel, *Noli* . . . the preaching that they heard, *TNT* . . . but the message heard did them no good, *Williams* . . . was of no service to them, *Wade.*

not being mixed with faith in them that heard [it]: . . . because when they heard it, *Noli* . . . it was not inwardly assimilated through faith by the hearers, *Wade* . . . not having been blended, *Concordant* . . . of those who were attentive to it, *TCNT* . . . they did not believe it, *Norlie* . . . they were not by faith made one with those who heeded it, *Williams* . . . in their hearts, *TNT.*

3. For we which have believed do enter into rest: . . . are being admitted to, *Williams* . . . into that promised Rest we who have reposed faith in God are in the course of entering, *Wade* . . . are going into rest with him because we are believers, *TNT* . . . We enter his rest only if we believe, *Noli.*

as he said: Scripture says, *TNT* . . . just as He has implied in the words, *Wade.*

As I have sworn in my wrath, if they shall enter into my rest: As in my anger I took oath, *Williams* . . . In my anger I swore that they would never come in and rest with me, *TNT.*

although the works were finished from the foundation of the world: . . . even though His works had been completed, *Adams* . . . All His works had been planned before, *Norlie* . . . at the creation, *Williams* . . . though ever since the creation of the world God's work had been finished, *TNT* . . . after the foundation, *Wade.*

4. For he spake in a certain place of the seventh [day] on this wise: For this is what Scripture says somewhere, *TNT* . . . somewhere He speaks of, *Williams* . . . as you know, concerning the Seventh Day the Divine Spirit has spoken thus, *Wade.*

Hebrews 4:5

2296.1 noun nom sing masc	1706.1 prep	3450.11 art dat sing fem	2232.3 noun dat sing fem	3450.11 art dat sing fem	1436.4 num ord dat sing fem
θεὸς	ἐν	τῇ	ἡμέρᾳ	τῇ	ἑβδόμῃ
theos	*en*	*tē*	*hēmera*	*tē*	*hebdomē*
God	on	the	day	the	seventh

570.3 prep	3820.4 adj gen pl	3450.1 art gen pl	2024.5 noun gen pl neu	840.3 prs-pron gen sing	2504.1 conj	1706.1 prep
ἀπὸ	πάντων	τῶν	ἔργων	αὐτοῦ·	5. καὶ	ἐν
apo	*pantōn*	*tōn*	*ergōn*	*autou*	*kai*	*en*
from	all	the	works	his:	and	in

5.a.**Txt:** p46,01ℵ,02A 03B,04C,06D-corr2,044 byz.
Var: p13,06D-org,81 629,1739,bo.

3642.5 dem-pron dat sing masc	3687.1 adv	1479.1 conj	1511.39 verb 3pl indic fut mid	1519.1 prep	3450.12 art acc sing fem
τούτῳ	πάλιν,	⸂[a] Εἰ ⸃	εἰσελεύσονται	εἰς	τὴν
toutō	*palin*	*Ei*	*eiseleusontai*	*eis*	*tēn*
this	again,	If	they shall enter	into	the

2633.2 noun acc sing fem	1466.2 prs-pron gen 1sing	1878.1 conj	3631.1 partic	614.3 verb 3sing indic pres mid
κατάπαυσίν	μου.	6. Ἐπεὶ	οὖν	ἀπολείπεται
katapausin	*mou*	*Epei*	*oun*	*apoleipetai*
rest	my.	Since	therefore	it remains

4948.9 indef-pron acc pl masc	1511.21 verb inf aor act	1519.1 prep	840.12 prs-pron acc sing fem	2504.1 conj	3450.7 art nom pl masc
τινὰς	εἰσελθεῖν	εἰς	αὐτήν,	καὶ	οἱ
tinas	*eiselthein*	*eis*	*autēn*	*kai*	*hoi*
some	to enter	into	it,	and	the

4245.2 adj comp sing neu	2076.21 verb nom pl masc part aor pass	3620.2 partic	1511.1 verb indic aor act	1217.1 prep
πρότερον	εὐαγγελισθέντες	οὐκ	εἰσῆλθον	δι'
proteron	*euangelisthentes*	*ouk*	*eisēlthon*	*di'*
formerly	having heard good news	not	did enter in	on account of

539.3 noun acc sing fem	3687.1 adv	4948.5 indef-pron	3587.1 verb 3sing indic pres act	2232.4 noun acc sing fem
ἀπείθειαν,	7. πάλιν	τινὰ	ὁρίζει	ἡμέραν,
apeitheian	*palin*	*tina*	*horizei*	*hēmeran*
disobedience,	again	a certain	he determines	day,

4449.1 adv	1706.1 prep	1132.1 name masc	2978.15 verb nom sing masc part pres act	3196.3 prep	4965.1 dem-pron acc sing
Σήμερον,	ἐν	Δαβὶδ	λέγων,	μετὰ	τοσοῦτον
Sēmeron	*en*	*Dabid*	*legōn*	*meta*	*tosouton*
Today,	in	David	saying,	after	so long

7.a.**Txt:** 06D-corr,018K 020L,byz.
Var: 01ℵ,02A,04C 06D-org,025P,33,Lach Treg,Alf,Word,Tisc We/Ho,Weis,Sod UBS/☆

5385.4 noun acc sing masc	2503.1 conj	2029.15 verb 3sing indic perf mid	4136.6 verb 3sing indic perf mid
χρόνον,	καθὼς	⸂ εἴρηται,	[[a]☆ προείρηται,]
chronon	*kathōs*	*eirētai*	*proeirētai*
a time,	according as	it has been said,	[he has previously said,]

4449.1 adv	1430.1 partic	3450.10 art gen sing fem	5292.2 noun gen sing fem	840.3 prs-pron gen sing	189.26 verb 2pl subj aor act
Σήμερον	ἐὰν	τῆς	φωνῆς	αὐτοῦ	ἀκούσητε,
Sēmeron	*ean*	*tēs*	*phōnēs*	*autou*	*akousēte*
Today,	if	the	voice	his	you should hear,

3231.1 partic	4500.2 verb 2pl subj aor act	3450.15 art acc pl fem	2559.1 noun fem	5050.2 prs-pron gen 2pl	1479.1 conj	1056.1 conj
μὴ	σκληρύνητε	τὰς	καρδίας	ὑμῶν.	8. Εἰ	γὰρ
mē	*sklērunēte*	*tas*	*kardias*	*humōn*	*Ei*	*gar*
not	harden	the	hearts	your.	If	for

of Hebrews had given it a great deal of thought, and he was about to tie in the idea of God's resting with Psalm 95 and Canaan's conquest.

4:5. For a fourth time the writer refers to God's oath prohibiting the wilderness generation's entrance into Canaan (3:11,18; 4:3). Undoubtedly, this emphasized that it was God's judgment which kept them from entering the Promised Land, but there is something further: "my rest" focuses on it as a rest which comes from and belongs peculiarly to God. It is, moreover, a rest which He makes available to those who determine to follow after Him.

4:6. Since it is God's rest and not man's rest, it still exists and is available for others (*tinas,* "some," an indefinite pronoun) to experience. Those to whom the invitation was originally extended did not experience God's rest because they did not believe the promises which God made to them. They wanted to go back to Egypt. They couldn't trust God to conquer the giants in Canaan. The word translated "preached" (*euangelisthentes*) means to announce good news or news of a victory. It points out the parallelism between the Christian gospel (*euangelion*) preached to the Hebrew readers of this epistle and the promise of conquest over the Canaanites given to their forefathers in the wilderness.

4:7. This verse refers again to the quotation from Psalm 95 and points out that God *is* (present tense) setting a limit (*horizei*) on His offer of rest. It will not always be available. Yet it was not a onetime offer of rest made only to the Jews in the wilderness. To prove this point, the writer reminded his readers that the words he has quoted were written by David, not by Moses; that is, they were written over 400 years after the time of the Exodus and wilderness wanderings. Although David wrote the psalm, it was God who was speaking "in David."

Most important of all, God is still speaking (the participle *legōn* is in the present tense), and the time limit which He sets is expressed in the word "Today" (*Sēmeron*). The implication is clear. God is still speaking and offering His rest through the words of David in Psalm 95, even "after so long a time." More than 400 years after Moses and the Children of Israel perished in the wilderness, God in David offers His rest, saying, "To-day."

4:8. It would be hard for first-century believers to accept this truth. After all, they were not wandering around in the wilderness murmuring against God's miraculous provision of water, manna, and quail. What did God's oath, swearing to keep the wilderness generation from the Promised Land, have to do with first-century Hebrew Christians?

And God did rest the seventh day from all his works: . . . from all He had done, *Beck.*

5. And in this [place] again: . . . while in this passage again He says, *Williams* . . . But Scripture also says, *TNT* . . . in the passage just quoted, *Wade.*

If they shall enter into my rest: They shall never come in and rest with me, *TNT.*

6. Seeing therefore it remaineth that some must enter therein: It still remains true that some will enter it, *Norlie* . . . Clearly then it is still open for some to go in and rest with him, *TNT* . . . there is still in reserve an opportunity for some to enter, *Wade* . . . some are being admitted to it, *Williams.*

and they to whom it was first preached: . . . and those who previously had the good news announced, *Adams* . . . who first had the good news told, *Williams* . . . to whom the Good News was formerly communicated, *Wade.*

entered not in because of unbelief: . . . were precluded from entering on account of their disobedience, *Wade* . . . disbelieved and did not go in, *TNT* . . . were not admitted because of disobedience, *Williams.*

7. Again, he limiteth a certain day: He is again specifying, *Concordant* . . . He again...makes definite reference, *Wade* . . . once again God appoints a day, *TNT* . . . marks out a certain day, *Adams* . . . so He sets another day, *Beck* . . . He again fixes a definite day, *Williams.*

saying in David, To day, after so long a time: . . . speaking after a long interval, *TCNT* . . . saying long afterward through, *Williams* . . . after ever so long an interval, *Wade* . . . many years later, *TNT.*

as it is said: . . . using the words quoted above, *TNT* . . . in words that have been quoted before, *Wade.*

To day if ye will hear his voice, harden not your hearts: . . . you must listen to his voice, *TNT* . . . You must not harden, *Williams* . . . don't let your hearts become stubborn, *SEB.*

8. For if Jesus had given them rest: . . . if Joshua had really given them, *Williams.*

840.8 prs-pron acc pl masc	2400.1 name nom masc	2634.1 verb 3sing indic aor act	3620.2 partic	300.1 partic	3875.1 prep
αὐτοὺς	Ἰησοῦς	κατέπαυσεν,	οὐκ	ἂν	περὶ
autous	*Iēsous*	*katepausen*	*ouk*	*an*	*peri*
them	Jesus	gave rest,	not		concerning

241.10 adj gen sing fem	2953.45 verb 3sing indic imperf act	3196.3 prep	3642.18 dem-pron pl neu	2232.1 noun fem
ἄλλης	ἐλάλει	μετὰ	ταῦτα	ἡμέρας·
allēs	*elalei*	*meta*	*tauta*	*hēmeras*
another	would he have spoken	afterwards	these	days.

679.1 partic	614.3 verb 3sing indic pres mid	4377.1 noun nom sing masc	3450.3 art dat sing
9. ἄρα	ἀπολείπεται	σαββατισμὸς	τῷ
ara	*apoleipetai*	*sabbatismos*	*tō*
Then	remains	an observance of the Sabbath	to the

2967.3 noun dat sing masc	3450.2 art gen sing	2296.2 noun gen sing masc	3450.5 art nom sing masc	1056.1 conj	1511.13 verb nom sing masc part aor act
λαῷ	τοῦ	θεοῦ.	10. ὁ	γὰρ	εἰσελθὼν
laō	*tou*	*theou*	*ho*	*gar*	*eiselthōn*
people		of God.	The	for	having entered

1519.1 prep	3450.12 art acc sing fem	2633.2 noun acc sing fem	840.3 prs-pron gen sing	2504.1 conj	840.5 prs-pron nom sing masc
εἰς	τὴν	κατάπαυσιν	αὐτοῦ,	καὶ	αὐτὸς
eis	*tēn*	*katapausin*	*autou*	*kai*	*autos*
into	the	rest	his,	also	he

2634.1 verb 3sing indic aor act	570.3 prep	3450.1 art gen pl	2024.5 noun gen pl neu	840.3 prs-pron gen sing	5450.1 conj	570.3 prep
κατέπαυσεν	ἀπὸ	τῶν	ἔργων	αὐτοῦ,	ὥσπερ	ἀπὸ
katepausen	*apo*	*tōn*	*ergōn*	*autou*	*hōsper*	*apo*
rested	from	the	works	his,	as	from

3450.1 art gen pl	2375.1 adj gen pl	3450.5 art nom sing masc	2296.1 noun nom sing masc	4557.4 verb 1pl subj aor act
τῶν	ἰδίων	ὁ	θεός.	11. Σπουδάσωμεν
tōn	*idiōn*	*ho*	*theos*	*Spoudasōmen*
the	his own		God.	We should be diligent

3631.1 partic	1511.21 verb inf aor act	1519.1 prep	1552.12 dem-pron acc sing fem	3450.12 art acc sing fem	2633.2 noun acc sing fem
οὖν	εἰσελθεῖν	εἰς	ἐκείνην	τὴν	κατάπαυσιν,
oun	*eiselthein*	*eis*	*ekeinēn*	*tēn*	*katapausin*
therefore	to enter	into	that	the	rest,

2419.1 conj	3231.1 partic	1706.1 prep	3450.3 art dat sing	840.4 prs-pron dat sing	4948.3 indef-pron nom sing	5100.1 noun dat sing neu
ἵνα	μή	ἐν	τῷ	αὐτῷ	τις	ὑποδείγματι
hina	*mē*	*en*	*tō*	*autō*	*tis*	*hupodeigmati*
so that	not	in	the	same	anyone	example

3959.7 verb 3sing subj aor act	3450.10 art gen sing fem	539.1 noun gen sing fem	2180.10 verb sing part pres act	1056.1 conj
πέσῃ	τῆς	ἀπειθείας.	12. Ζῶν	γὰρ
pesē	*tēs*	*apeitheias*	*Zōn*	*gar*
may fall	of the	disobedience.	Living	for

3450.5 art nom sing masc	3030.1 noun nom sing masc	3450.2 art gen sing	2296.2 noun gen sing masc	2504.1 conj	1740.1 adj nom sing	2504.1 conj
ὁ	λόγος	τοῦ	θεοῦ	καὶ	ἐνεργής,	καὶ
ho	*logos*	*tou*	*theou*	*kai*	*energēs*	*kai*
the	word		of God	and	effective,	and

To meet this response, a further explanation was given of the analysis of Psalm 95. Since God through David says "Today," it is necessary to conclude that the Israelites who entered Canaan under Joshua did not experience God's rest either. Otherwise, God would not still be offering His rest through David by saying "Today." (*Joshua* and *Jesus* are the same name, and the reference here is to the Old Testament Joshua, not to Jesus Christ. See the NIV translation of 4:8.)

4:9. With great confidence, the inspired writer drew the conclusion and marked it off by the word "therefore," a logical connective that hints at the inescapability of the logic used. Beyond the time of Israel's conquest of Canaan under Joshua, a Sabbath Day's rest remains for "the people of God." This term links God's offer of rest with His rest on the Sabbath or seventh day referred to in verse 4 (cf. Genesis 2:2). This rest is available not just to Israelites, but to all who may be designated "people of God," Jew and Gentile alike.

4:10. This verse offers some explanation of the use of the term "his rest" (*katapausin autou*). The person who experiences God's rest is the one who has "ceased from his own works, as God did from his." God's rest was not a cessation of all His activity. He ceased His creation, but He continued to sustain it and take an active part and interest in it, as is seen in His relationship with Adam and Eve (Genesis 3:8ff.). God created the human race and placed it upon earth so He could maintain a unique relationship with those whom He had created in His own image. God's rest certainly included the maintenance of His fellowship with mankind.

4:11. A restoration to fellowship between human beings and their Creator is the result of the Son's work, but, as is seen in 2:8,9, this yet remains to be fully accomplished. Entrance into God's rest is still in the future. It is the consummation of Jesus' work. It is neither the new birth nor entrance into heaven at death. It is entrance into and full participation in the eternal kingdom of God established at the second coming of Jesus Christ. (For a full discussion of this interpretation consult Kaiser, pp.153-175.) The verb "labor" (*spoudasōmen*) issues a strong exhortation for the readers to diligently apply themselves by doing everything they possibly can to secure their entrance into God's eternal rest, lest they die in unbelief as the Israelites did in the desert.

4:12. God's warning from Psalm 95 is still in force. The Word is "quick," meaning "alive" (*zōn* emphatically stands first in the verse). It is "powerful," meaning "active." It is "sharper than any two-edged sword" because it penetrates more than the physical body. It is comprehensive in its effects. It reaches into all the various

then would he not afterward have spoken of another day: God would not have continued to speak of another day, *TNT* ... of another and later Day, *Wade.*

9. There remaineth therefore: At any rate, *Norlie* ... There is still in reserve, then, *Wade* ... is still open for, *TNT.*

a rest to the people of God: ... there is a keeping of sabbath still open for God's people, *SEB* ... a sabbath of rest is still awaiting God's people, *Williams.*

10. For he that is entered into his rest: ... if anyone goes in and rests with God, *TNT.*

he also hath ceased from his own works, as God [did] from his: ... has rested from his works, *Williams* ... himself rests altogether from his works, *Wade* ... just as God stopped working, *Adams.*

11. Let us labour therefore to enter into that rest: So let us be alert, *Klingensmith* ... let us make every effort, *Adams* ... be earnest to enter, *Montgomery* ... then strive diligently, *Norlie* ... We should be eager, therefore, to enter that perfect Rest, *Wade* ... Let us do our utmost then to enter that rest, *TNT* ... let us do our best to be admitted to, *Williams.*

lest any man fall: ... so that not one of us may fail, *Williams.*

after the same example of unbelief: ... through being disobedient as they were, *TNT* ... through such disobedience as is illustrated by the example just given, *Wade* ... through the same sort of, *Williams* ... by the same pattern of disobedience, *Adams.*

12. For the word of God [is] quick, and powerful: God's Message is a living and active power, *TCNT* ... the Divine Reason, *Wade* ... is alive and full of power in action, *Williams* ... lives and is active, *Beck* ... and workable, *Klingensmith* ... and energetic, *Wilson.*

and sharper than any twoedged sword: ... and keener than any two-edged blade, *Wade* ... and more cutting than Any two-edged Sword, *Wilson* ... any double-edged sword, *Williams* ... a sword that cuts both ways, *NLT.*

Hebrews 4:13

4961.1 adj comp nom sing masc	5065.1 prep	3820.12 adj acc sing fem	3134.4 noun acc sing fem	1359.2 adj acc sing fem	2504.1 conj
τομώτερος	ὑπὲρ	πᾶσαν	μάχαιραν	δίστομον,	καὶ
tomōteros	*huper*	*pasan*	*machairan*	*distomon*	*kai*
sharper	beyond	every	sword	two edged,	even

12.a.**Txt:** 06D,018K,byz.
Var: 01ℵ,02A,03B,04C
015H,020L,025P,33
Lach,Treg,Alf,Word
Tisc,We/Ho,Weis,Sod
UBS/⋆

1332.1 verb nom sing masc part pres mid	884.2 conj	3180.1 noun gen sing masc	5425.2 noun gen sing fem	4885.1 conj	2504.1 conj
διϊκνούμενος	ἄχρι	μερισμοῦ	ψυχῆς	⸂[a] τε ⸃	καὶ
diiknoumenos	*achri*	*merismou*	*psuchēs*	*te*	*kai*
penetrating	to	division	soul	both	and

4011.2 noun gen sing neu	713.1 noun gen pl masc	4885.1 conj	2504.1 conj	3314.1 noun gen pl masc	2504.1 conj	2897.1 adj nom sing masc
πνεύματος,	ἁρμῶν	τε	καὶ	μυελῶν,	καὶ	κριτικὸς
pneumatos	*harmōn*	*te*	*kai*	*muelōn*	*kai*	*kritikos*
of spirit,	of joints	both	and	marrows,	and	a discerner

1745.2 noun gen pl fem	2504.1 conj	1755.2 noun gen pl fem	2559.1 noun fem	2504.1 conj	3620.2 partic
ἐνθυμήσεων	καὶ	ἐννοιῶν	καρδίας·	**13.** καὶ	οὐκ
enthumēseōn	*kai*	*ennoiōn*	*kardias*	*kai*	*ouk*
of thoughts	and	intents	of heart.	And	not

1498.4 verb 3sing indic pres act	2909.1 noun nom sing fem	845.1 adj nom sing fem	1783.1 prep	840.3 prs-pron gen sing
ἔστιν	κτίσις	ἀφανὴς	ἐνώπιον	αὐτοῦ·
estin	*ktisis*	*aphanēs*	*enōpion*	*autou*
there is	a created thing	unapparent	before	him;

3820.1 adj	1156.2 conj	1125.7 adj pl neu	2504.1 conj	4975.1 verb pl neu part perf mid	3450.4 art dat pl
πάντα	δὲ	γυμνὰ	καὶ	τετραχηλισμένα	τοῖς
panta	*de*	*gumna*	*kai*	*tetrachēlismena*	*tois*
all things	but	naked	and	having been laid bare	to the

3652.7 noun dat pl masc	840.3 prs-pron gen sing	4242.1 prep	3614.6 rel-pron acc sing masc	2231.3 prs-pron dat 1pl	3450.5 art nom sing masc
ὀφθαλμοῖς	αὐτοῦ,	πρὸς	ὃν	ἡμῖν	ὁ
ophthalmois	*autou*	*pros*	*hon*	*hēmin*	*ho*
eyes	his,	with	whom	our	the

3030.1 noun nom sing masc	2174.19 verb nom pl masc part pres act	3631.1 partic	744.4 noun acc sing masc	3144.4 adj acc sing masc
λόγος.	**14.** Ἔχοντες	οὖν	ἀρχιερέα	μέγαν
logos	*Echontes*	*oun*	*archierea*	*megan*
account.	Having	therefore	high priest	great

1324.9 verb acc sing masc part perf act	3450.8 art acc pl masc	3636.9 noun acc pl masc	2400.3 name acc masc	3450.6 art acc sing masc
διεληλυθότα	τοὺς	οὐρανούς,	Ἰησοῦν	τὸν
dielēluthota	*tous*	*ouranous*	*Iēsoun*	*ton*
having passed through	the	heavens,	Jesus	the

5048.4 noun acc sing masc	3450.2 art gen sing	2296.2 noun gen sing masc	2875.4 verb 1pl subj pres act	3450.10 art gen sing fem
υἱὸν	τοῦ	θεοῦ,	κρατῶμεν	τῆς
huion	*tou*	*theou*	*kratōmen*	*tēs*
Son		of God,	we should hold fast	the

3534.1 noun gen sing fem	3620.3 partic	1056.1 conj	2174.5 verb 1pl indic pres act	744.4 noun acc sing masc	3231.1 partic
ὁμολογίας.	**15.** οὐ	γὰρ	ἔχομεν	ἀρχιερέα	μὴ
homologias	*ou*	*gar*	*echomen*	*archierea*	*mē*
confession.	Not	for	have we	a high priest	not

parts and functions of the individual and makes judgments. The emphasis is not upon the separation of one part from another, but upon the penetration of all the individual parts, even down to the innermost secrets and purposes which are hidden in the core of an individual's consciousness, away from the eyes of other people.

4:13. As has been evident throughout this epistle, virtually no distinction has been made between God and the Scriptures. When the Scriptures speak, God is speaking. In this verse the dynamic, living quality of God's Word in Psalm 95 is attributed to God himself. The challenge to believe and not harden one's heart "Today" while there is still time relates to the powerful all-encompassing authority of that Word to sit in judgment on every creature.

The term "opened" (*tetrachēlismena*) is full of illustrative potential. Literally, it refers to bending the neck backward so the face is looking upwards. It is used sometimes to describe the act of falling prostrate naked before someone. In its figurative use it means to lay bare. Any of these usages fit the context of this verse. God has the power and authority to sit in judgment over all human behavior: each person must grovel helplessly before Him in judgment. His judgment is efficient and inescapable.

4:14. Having come to the end of his warning which began in 3:7, the inspired writer applied its challenge to the theme of the superiority of Jesus the Son as it is displayed in His high-priestly ministry. He is not an ordinary, run-of-the-mill high priest. He is "great" because He is the Son, exalted and sitting at the Father's right hand until He returns victorious over all of His enemies to establish His eternal rest.

Here there is a foreshadowing of an argument that will be stated explicitly later on (9:11,24; 10:20): Jesus did not pass through the cloth veil of the temple into a sanctuary built by men; indeed, He has entered into God's heavenly sanctuary and is seated there until His return. In light of these facts, Christians must hold on to their profession of faith in Him unto the very end in spite of all the trials that surround them. He is Jesus—our Deliverer.

4:15. The reason Christians must cling to their profession of Jesus as their Messiah and God is given here. He is one with us. He became a man and is, therefore, able to understand human frailties and weaknesses. The word "infirmities" (*astheneiais*) includes both moral and physical weaknesses. The verb used (*sumpathēsai*) indicates that Jesus is able to empathize with believers because He has experienced the limitations and feelings that are common to all humans.

piercing even to the dividing asunder of soul and spirit: It can slice between, *SEB* . . . It is a judge of, *Klingensmith* . . . penetrating deeply enough to split soul and spirit, *Adams* . . . cutting through even to a Separation of Life and Breath, *Wilson* . . . even to the severance of soul from spirit, *Montgomery.*

and of the joints and marrow: and [is] a discerner of the thoughts and intents of the heart: It is keen in judging the thoughts, *Norlie* . . . It can tell the difference between the desires and the intentions of the human mind, *SEB* . . . and detecting the inmost thoughts, *TCNT* . . . and is a sifter and analyzer of the reflections and conceptions of the heart, *Wuest* . . . is a judge of the sentiments and thoughts of the heart, *Concordant* . . . the very thoughts, *Montgomery.*

13. Neither is there any creature that is not manifest in his sight: No created being can escape God's notice, *Norlie* . . . before Him no creature can hide, *Adams* . . . can hide from Him, *Beck.*

but all things [are] naked and opened unto the eyes of him: Everything is exposed and laid bare, *TCNT* . . . and vulnerable to, *Adams* . . . and helpless before the eyes, *Beck* . . . and laid prostrate before, *Montgomery.*

with whom we have to do: We must give an answer to God, *SEB* . . . to Whom we are accountable, *Concordant.*

14. Seeing then that we have a great high priest: We have a great Religious leader, *NLT.*

that is passed into the heavens, Jesus the Son of God: . . . who has gone through the heavens, *Beck.*

let us hold fast [our] profession: . . . we should firmly retain the confession, *Wilson* . . . Let us keep our trust in Jesus Christ, *NLT* . . . hold fast to our faith in Him, *Norlie* . . . cling to, *Beck.*

15. For we have not an high priest which cannot: . . . who isn't able, *Adams.*

be touched with the feeling of our infirmities: . . . suffer with, *Klingensmith* . . . sympathize with our weaknesses, *Adams.*

Hebrews 4:16

1404.15 verb acc sing masc part pres mid	4685.2 verb inf aor act	3450.14 art dat pl fem	763.6 noun dat pl fem	2231.2 prs-pron gen 1pl
δυνάμενον	συμπαθῆσαι	ταῖς	ἀσθενείαις	ἡμῶν,
dunamenon	*sumpathēsai*	*tais*	*astheneiais*	*hēmōn*
being able	to sympathize	with the	weaknesses	our,

15.a.**Txt:** 04C,018K 020L,025P,byz.Sod,01ℵ 02A,03B,06D,Elzev Gries,Lach,Treg,Alf Word,Tisc,We/Ho,Weis UBS/☆

3847.20 verb acc sing masc part perf mid	3847.23 verb acc sing masc part perf mid	1156.2 conj	2567.3 prep	3820.1 adj
⸀ πεπειραμένον	[a☆ πεπειρασμένον]	δὲ	κατὰ	πάντα
pepeiramenon	*pepeirasmenon*	*de*	*kata*	*panta*
having been tempted	[idem]	but	in	all things

2567.2 prep	3528.1 noun acc sing fem	5400.1 prep	264.1 noun fem	4193.12 verb 1pl subj pres mid
καθ’	ὁμοιότητα	χωρὶς	ἁμαρτίας.	16. προσερχώμεθα
kath'	*homoiotēta*	*chōris*	*hamartias*	*proserchōmetha*
according to	likeness,	without	sin.	We should come

3631.1 partic	3196.3 prep	3816.2 noun gen sing fem	3450.3 art dat sing	2339.3 noun dat sing masc	3450.10 art gen sing fem	5322.2 noun gen sing fem
οὖν	μετὰ	παῤῥησίας	τῷ	θρόνῳ	τῆς	χάριτος,
oun	*meta*	*parrhēsias*	*tō*	*thronō*	*tēs*	*charitos*
therefore	with	confidence	to the	throne	to the	grace,

16.a.**Txt:** 04C-corr 06D-corr,020L,byz.
Var: 01ℵ,02A,03B 04C-org,06D-org,018K 025P,33,Lach,Treg,Alf Word,Tisc,We/Ho,Weis Sod,UBS/☆

2419.1 conj	2956.19 verb 1pl subj aor act	1643.1 noun acc sing masc	1643.2 noun sing neu	2504.1 conj	5322.4 noun acc sing fem
ἵνα	λάβωμεν	⸀ ἔλεον,	[a☆ ἔλεος]	καὶ	χάριν
hina	*labōmen*	*eleon*	*eleos*	*kai*	*charin*
that	we may receive	mercy,	[idem]	and	grace

2128.13 verb 1pl subj aor act	1519.1 prep	2102.2 adj acc sing fem	989.1 noun acc sing fem	3820.6 adj nom sing masc	1056.1 conj
εὕρωμεν	εἰς	εὔκαιρον	βοήθειαν.	5:1. Πᾶς	γὰρ
heurōmen	*eis*	*eukairon*	*boētheian*	*Pas*	*gar*
may find	for	opportune	help.	Every	for

744.1 noun nom sing masc	1523.1 prep gen	442.7 noun gen pl masc	2956.37 verb nom sing masc part pres mid	5065.1 prep
ἀρχιερεὺς	ἐξ	ἀνθρώπων	λαμβανόμενος,	ὑπὲρ
archiereus	*ex*	*anthrōpōn*	*lambanomenos*	*huper*
high priest	from among	men	being taken	for

442.7 noun gen pl masc	2497.9 verb 3sing indic pres mid	3450.17 art pl neu	4242.1 prep	3450.6 art acc sing masc
ἀνθρώπων	καθίσταται	τὰ	πρὸς	τὸν
anthrōpōn	*kathistatai*	*ta*	*pros*	*ton*
men	is being appointed	the things	relating to	

1.a.**Var:** 03B,06D-corr1 044,We/Ho

2296.4 noun acc sing masc	2419.1 conj	4232.4 verb 3sing subj pres act	1428.3 noun pl neu	4885.1 conj	2504.1 conj	2355.1 noun fem
θεόν,	ἵνα	προσφέρῃ	δῶρά	⸂a τε ⸃	καὶ	θυσίας
theon	*hina*	*prospherē*	*dōra*	*te*	*kai*	*thusias*
God,	that	he may offer	gifts	both,	and	sacrifices

5065.1 prep	264.6 noun gen pl fem	3226.1 verb inf pres act	1404.13 verb nom sing masc part pres mid	3450.4 art dat pl
ὑπὲρ	ἁμαρτιῶν,	2. μετριοπαθεῖν	δυνάμενος	τοῖς
huper	*hamartiōn*	*metriopathein*	*dunamenos*	*tois*
for	sins;	to deal gently with	being able	with the

49.4 verb dat pl part pres act	2504.1 conj	3966.14 verb dat pl masc part pres mid	1878.1 conj	2504.1 conj	840.5 prs-pron nom sing masc
ἀγνοοῦσιν	καὶ	πλανωμένοις,	ἐπεὶ	καὶ	αὐτὸς
agnoousin	*kai*	*planōmenois*	*epei*	*kai*	*autos*
being ignorant	and	erring,	since	also	himself

Furthermore, although He never succumbed to any temptation and never sinned, He was subjected to the full gamut of temptations to evil. This means that He was tested and tried but that He never committed a sin or was enticed by evil in His mind to the extent that He approved of it. He understands the power of temptation, and He also knows the stratagems by which it is successfully resisted.

but was in all points tempted like as [we are: . . . but One Who has been tried in all respects, *Concordant* . . . tested in every spot that we are, *Klingensmith* . . . and in every respect, *Norlie* . . . in every way just as we are, *Beck.*

yet] without sin: . . . yet He never sinned, *Norlie* . . . yet without committing any sin, *Williams* . . . but he did not sin, *TNT.*

4:16. Because the Son knows the power of sin and the means of success over temptation, believers can come to Him in prayer with confidence in His wisdom and ability to help when they are confronted with temptation. The readers of this epistle were facing the temptation to abandon their profession of faith in the face of ridicule and persecution. Most assuredly, the Son, who was abandoned by His disciples and forsaken by the Father while on the cross, understands the needs of those who are tempted to forsake Him in the hour of trial.

The word "boldly" (*parrhēsias*) conveys a sense of openness, freedom, and confidence. When Christians come to God in prayer through the Son, they receive not justice, but God's grace and mercy. This is available because of Jesus Christ's sacrifice on the cross. The help that is available through such prayers is timely (*eukairon*), that is, it exactly fits the need at the right moment.

16. Let us therefore come boldly unto the throne of grace: . . . let us approach, *TNT* . . . let us continue coming with courage to the throne of God's unmerited favor, *Williams.*

that we may obtain mercy: . . . we may receive, *TNT.*

and find grace to help in time of need: . . . just when we need it, *Adams* . . . for seasonable help, *Wuest* . . . and to find His spiritual strength, *Williams* . . . and get help for the days ahead, *Norlie* . . . and we may find favor for needed help, *Klingensmith* . . . and find help through his grace, *TNT.*

5:1. Having hinted at Christ's priesthood in the prologue (1:3) and having mentioned it explicitly in 2:17, the inspired writer began to argue in earnest for the superiority of Jesus' priesthood over the Aaronic priesthood. He began by presenting the qualifications for the priesthood in 5:1-4 and then proceeded to point out how Jesus Christ has met these qualifications. In verse 1 he noted that, first of all, a high priest must be human (he had already underscored Christ's humanity in 2:10-18). Secondly, a high priest was ordained to represent men in their relationship to God, more specifically in regard to the offering of sacrifice in connection with sins (another truth already introduced but not yet elaborated; see 1:3 and 2:17).

1. For every high priest taken from among men: . . . who is chosen from, *Norlie* . . . selected from men, *Beck.*

is ordained for men in things [pertaining] to God: . . . is appointed to officiate on behalf of men, *Williams* . . . is appointed to represent men in matters related to God, *Adams* . . . to serve before God, *TNT.*

that he may offer both gifts and sacrifices for sins: . . . and sin-offerings, *Williams.*

5:2. The third essential for qualification to the high priesthood related to the character of the high priest. He was a special kind of human being. The verb translated "have compassion" (*metriopathein*) means to deal gently with someone. The Aaronic high priests were able to offer sacrifice for those who committed sins in ignorance or who sinned without premeditation or presumption, but no provision was made for those who sinned deliberately (Numbers 15:28-30). This provision for the ignorant and wandering involved the Aaronic high priest in magnanimous treatment of these two groups because the high priests themselves were also encircled (*perikeitai*) by the same chains of weakness.

2. Who can have compassion on: Such a one is capable of dealing tenderly with, *Williams* . . . He can bear gently, *TNT* . . . he can gently handle people, *SEB* . . . He must also have patience, *Klingensmith* . . . is able to deal gently with, *Montgomery.*

the ignorant, and on them that are out of the way: . . . the ignorant and erring ones, *Williams.*

for that he himself also is compassed with infirmity: . . . is troubled with weakness, *Beck* . . . is inextricably involved in weakness, *Adams* . . . encompassed with moral weakness, *Montgomery* . . . is subject to weakness, *Williams.*

Hebrews 5:3

3.a.**Txt:** 04C-corr 06D-corr,018K,020L byz.
Var: 01ℵ,02A,03B 04C-org,06D-org,025P 33,Lach,Treg,Alf,Word Tisc,We/Ho,Weis,Sod UBS/☆

3.b.**Txt:** 01ℵ,02A,04C 06D-corr2,byz.Tisc We/Ho,Sod
Var: p46,03B,06D-org

3.c.**Txt:** 04C-corr 06D-corr,018K,020L byz.
Var: 01ℵ,02A,03B 04C-org,06D-org,025P 33,Lach,Treg,Alf,Word Tisc,We/Ho,Weis,Sod UBS/☆

4.a.**Txt:** 04C-corr,020L 025P,Steph
Var: 01ℵ,02A,03B 04C-org,06D,018K,byz. Gries,Lach,Treg,Alf Word,Tisc,We/Ho,Weis Sod,UBS/☆

4.b.**Txt:** 01ℵ-corr 04C-corr,06D-corr,018K 020L,025P,byz.
Var: 01ℵ-org,02A,03B 06D-org,33,Alf,Tisc We/Ho,Weis,Sod UBS/☆

4.c.**Txt:** Steph
Var: 01ℵ,02A,03B,04C 06D,018K,020L,025P byz.Gries,Lach,Treg,Alf Word,Tisc,We/Ho,Weis Sod,UBS/☆

3892.2 verb 3sing indic pres mid	**763.4** noun acc sing fem	**2504.1** conj	**1217.2** prep	**3642.12** dem-pron acc sing fem
περίκειται	ἀσθένειαν·	**3.** καὶ	⸂ διὰ	ταύτην
perikeitai	*astheneian*	*kai*	*dia*	*tautēn*
is encompassed with	weakness;	and	on account of	this

1217.1 prep	**840.12** prs-pron acc sing fem	**3648.3** verb 3sing indic pres act	**2503.1** conj	**3875.1** prep	**3450.2** art gen sing
[a☆ δι’	αὐτὴν]	ὀφείλει,	καθὼς	περὶ	τοῦ
di’	*autēn*	*opheilei*	*kathōs*	*peri*	*tou*
[because of	it]	he ought,	even as	for	the

2967.2 noun gen sing masc	**3643.1** adv	**2504.1** conj	**3875.1** prep	**1431.4** prs-pron gen sing	**840.3** prs-pron gen sing
λαοῦ,	οὕτως	καὶ	περὶ	⸂ ἑαυτοῦ	[b☆ αὐτοῦ]
laou	*houtōs*	*kai*	*peri*	*heautou*	*autou*
people,	so	also	for	himself	[him]

4232.10 verb inf pres act	**5065.1** prep	**3875.1** prep	**264.6** noun gen pl fem	**2504.1** conj
προσφέρειν	⸂ ὑπὲρ	[c☆ περὶ]	ἁμαρτιῶν.	**4.** Καὶ
prospherein	*huper*	*peri*	*hamartiōn*	*Kai*
to offer	for	[concerning]	sins.	And

3620.1 partic	**1431.5** prs-pron dat sing masc	**4948.3** indef-pron nom sing	**2956.4** verb 3sing indic pres act	**3450.12** art acc sing fem	**4940.4** noun acc sing fem	**233.2** conj
οὐχ	ἑαυτῷ	τις	λαμβάνει	τὴν	τιμήν,	ἀλλὰ
ouch	*heautō*	*tis*	*lambanei*	*tēn*	*timēn*	*alla*
not	to himself	anyone	takes	the	honor,	but

3450.5 art nom sing masc	**2535.30** verb nom sing masc part pres mid	**5097.3** prep	**3450.2** art gen sing	**2296.2** noun gen sing masc	**2481.1** conj
⸂a ὁ ⸃	καλούμενος	ὑπὸ	τοῦ	θεοῦ,	⸂ καθάπερ
ho	*kaloumenos*	*hupo*	*tou*	*theou*	*kathaper*
the	being called	by		God,	even as

2502.1 conj	**2504.1** conj	**3450.5** art nom sing masc	**2.1** name masc	**3643.1** adv	**2504.1** conj
[b☆ καθώσπερ]	καὶ	⸂c ὁ ⸃	Ἀαρών.	**5.** Οὕτως	καὶ
kathōsper	*kai*	*ho*	*Aarōn*	*Houtōs*	*kai*
[idem]	also		Aaron.	Thus	also

3450.5 art nom sing masc	**5382.1** name nom masc	**3620.1** partic	**1431.6** prs-pron acc sing masc	**1386.9** verb 3sing indic aor act	**1090.62** verb inf aor pass
ὁ	Χριστὸς	οὐχ	ἑαυτὸν	ἐδόξασεν	γενηθῆναι
ho	*Christos*	*ouch*	*heauton*	*edoxasen*	*genēthēnai*
the	Christ	not	himself	did glorify	to become

744.4 noun acc sing masc	**233.1** conj	**3450.5** art nom sing masc	**2953.34** verb nom sing masc part aor act	**4242.1** prep	**840.6** prs-pron acc sing masc
ἀρχιερέα,	ἀλλ’	ὁ	λαλήσας	πρὸς	αὐτόν,
archierea	*all’*	*ho*	*lalēsas*	*pros*	*auton*
a high priest;	but	the	having said	to	him,

5048.1 noun nom sing masc	**1466.2** prs-pron gen 1sing	**1498.3** verb 2sing indic pres act	**4622.1** prs-pron nom 2sing	**1466.1** prs-pron nom 1sing	**4449.1** adv
Υἱός	μου	εἶ	σύ,	ἐγὼ	σήμερον
Huios	*mou*	*ei*	*su*	*egō*	*sēmeron*
Son	my	are	you,	I	today

1074.8 verb 1sing indic perf act	**4622.4** prs-pron acc 2sing	**2503.1** conj	**2504.1** conj	**1706.1** prep	**2066.2** adj dat sing
γεγέννηκά	σε.	**6.** καθὼς	καὶ	ἐν	ἑτέρῳ
gegennēka	*se*	*kathōs*	*kai*	*en*	*heterō*
have begotten	you.	Even as	also	in	another

5:3. Because the high priests of the Aaronic priesthood were guilty of wandering and committed sins of ignorance, they found it necessary to offer sacrifices not only for the sins of the Children of Israel but also for their own personal acts of sin. These personal sacrifices offered up by the high priests were not something done voluntarily. They were absolutely necessary; the word "ought" (*opheilei*) indicates their obligation. In the use of the present infinitive "to offer" (*prospherein*), there may be a foreshadowing of the later emphasis on the daily necessity of such sacrifices (7:27). Daily sinning required that they seek forgiveness each day.

5:4. The fourth essential qualification for the high priesthood was that the appointment was divine. Aaron did not elect himself to be the high priest. Self-initiative did not qualify one for the priesthood. It was an office and honor that only God could bestow. The background of Aaron's appointment as the high priest for Israel was God's choice of the tribe of Levi to be the priestly tribe. All the Levites stood in a special relationship to God, with special responsibilities. They had certain assigned duties in relation to the tabernacle. Aaron was the logical choice then for the office of high priest.

5:5. So Christ's appointment was not from any ambition or self-initiative on His part. He did not thrust himself forward or lobby for the position. His elevation to the office of High Priest came from the Father, the One who said, "Thou art my Son, today have I begotten thee." These words hark back to the first argument for the Son's superiority to the angels. In Hebrews 1:5 these same words from Psalm 2:7 are quoted. At Jesus' baptism the Father identified Him as "my beloved Son, in whom I am well pleased" (Mark 1:11). The same words were spoken by the Father at the Transfiguration (Matthew 17:5). The reference seems to be to the Father's launching Jesus in His messianic sonship, not to His eternal generation or human birth. Eternally, He is the Son of God, the Second Person of the Trinity. From a human standpoint He was the son of Mary, born in Bethlehem. Messianically, He became the Messiah once He had met the qualifications for the priesthood.

5:6. Here the inspired writer introduced his favorite Old Testament quotation from Psalm 110:4—the psalm he cited the most. He referred to it again and again. The purpose was to introduce the Melchizedekian priesthood as the messianic priesthood which stands in contrast to the Aaronic priesthood. The eternality of this priesthood as indicated by the words "for ever" will be drawn out later on in the epistle (7:24-28).

3. And by reason hereof he ought: . . . and because of that weakness, *TNT* . . . being feeble, he has to make sin-offerings, *BB* . . . he is obligated, *Adams* . . . he obliged himself, *Noli.*

as for the people, so also for himself, to offer for sins: . . . to offer sin-offerings, not only for the people but for himself as well, *Williams* . . . for himself also, just as he does for the people, *TNT* . . . on behalf of himself, just as he does on behalf of the People, *Wade.*

4. And no man taketh this honour unto himself: No one of his own accord assumes this honor, *Norlie* . . . And no one presumes to take for himself this honourable office, *Wade* . . . no one takes this office upon himself, *TNT.*

but he that is called of God, as [was] Aaron: . . . unless he is called...as Aaron was, *Noli* . . . but, on the contrary, *Adams* . . . is called to it by God, *Williams* . . . given authority by God, *BB.*

5. So also Christ: In the same way, *SEB, BB* . . . Even Christ, *Noli* . . . Thus also the Messiah, *Fenton.*

glorified not himself to be made an high priest: . . . didn't exalt Himself, *Adams* . . . did not Himself decree, *Fenton* . . . did not of himself assume the dignity of, *TCNT* . . . did not take upon Himself, *Williams* . . . did not invest himself with the glory of the high priest, *Noli* . . . did not claim for Himself the dignity of being made, *Wade* . . . the honour of becoming, *TNT.*

but he that said unto him: On the contrary, he was invested by God, who said, *Noli* . . . but He was raised to that dignity by Him Who said, *Wade* . . . but on the contrary, *Montgomery* . . . he was made high priest by God who said to him, *TNT* . . . but it was God who said, *Williams.*

Thou art my Son, to day have I begotten thee: I have today become your Father, *Williams.*

6. As he saith also in another [place]: . . . just as He says likewise in a second passage, *Wade* . . . as in a different place, *Concordant* . . . in another passage, *Williams.*

2978.5 verb 3sing indic pres act	**4622.1** prs-pron nom 2sing	**2385.1** noun nom sing masc	**1519.1** prep	**3450.6** art acc sing masc	**163.3** noun acc sing masc
λέγει,	Σὺ	ἱερεὺς	εἰς	τὸν	αἰῶνα
legei	*Su*	*hiereus*	*eis*	*ton*	*aiōna*
he says,	You	a priest	unto	the	age

2567.3 prep	**3450.12** art acc sing fem	**4861.2** noun acc sing fem	**3168.1** name masc	**3614.5** rel-pron nom sing masc	**1706.1** prep
κατὰ	τὴν	τάξιν	Μελχισέδεκ.	7. Ὃς	ἐν
kata	*tēn*	*taxin*	*Melchisedek*	*Hos*	*en*
according to	the	order	of Melchizedek.	Who	in

3450.14 art dat pl fem	**2232.7** noun dat pl fem	**3450.10** art gen sing fem	**4418.2** noun gen sing fem	**840.3** prs-pron gen sing	**1157.6** noun acc pl fem
ταῖς	ἡμέραις	τῆς	σαρκὸς	αὐτοῦ	δεήσεις
tais	*hēmerais*	*tēs*	*sarkos*	*autou*	*deēseis*
the	days	the	flesh	his	supplications

4885.1 conj	**2504.1** conj	**2404.1** noun acc pl fem	**4242.1** prep	**3450.6** art acc sing masc	**1404.15** verb acc sing masc part pres mid	**4834.3** verb inf pres act
τε	καὶ	ἱκετηρίας	πρὸς	τὸν	δυνάμενον	σῴζειν
te	*kai*	*hiketērias*	*pros*	*ton*	*dunamenon*	*sōzein*
both	and	entreaties	to	the	being able	to save

840.6 prs-pron acc sing masc	**1523.2** prep gen	**2265.2** noun gen sing masc	**3196.3** prep	**2879.2** noun gen sing fem	**2451.7** adj gen sing fem
αὐτὸν	ἐκ	θανάτου,	μετὰ	κραυγῆς	ἰσχυρᾶς
auton	*ek*	*thanatou*	*meta*	*kraugēs*	*ischuras*
him	from	death,	with	crying	strong

2504.1 conj	**1139.2** noun gen pl neu	**4232.17** verb nom sing masc part aor act	**2504.1** conj	**1508.2** verb nom sing masc part aor pass
καὶ	δακρύων	προσενέγκας,	καὶ	εἰσακουσθεὶς
kai	*dakruōn*	*prosenenkas*	*kai*	*eisakoustheis*
and	tears	having offered,	and	having been heard

570.3 prep	**3450.10** art gen sing fem	**2105.1** noun gen sing fem	**2510.1** conj	**1498.21** verb nom sing masc part pres act
ἀπὸ	τῆς	εὐλαβείας,	8. καίπερ	ὢν
apo	*tēs*	*eulabeias*	*kaiper*	*ōn*
because	of the	reverence;	though	being

5048.1 noun nom sing masc	**3101.8** verb 3sing indic aor act	**570.1** prep	**3614.1** rel-pron gen pl	**3819.11** verb 3sing indic aor act
υἱός,	ἔμαθεν	ἀφ'	ὧν	ἔπαθεν
huios	*emathen*	*aph'*	*hōn*	*epathen*
a son,	he learned,	from	things which	he suffered,

3450.12 art acc sing fem	**5056.4** noun acc sing fem	**2504.1** conj	**4896.12** verb nom sing masc part aor pass	**1090.33** verb 3sing indic aor mid
τὴν	ὑπακοήν,	9. καὶ	τελειωθεὶς	ἐγένετο
tēn	*hupakoēn*	*kai*	*teleiōtheis*	*egeneto*
the	obedience;	and	having been perfected	became

3450.4 art dat pl	**5057.2** verb dat pl masc part pres act	**840.4** prs-pron dat sing	**3820.5** adj dat pl	**3820.5** adj dat pl	**3450.4** art dat pl
‘ τοῖς	ὑπακούουσιν	αὐτῷ	πᾶσιν	[☆ πᾶσιν	τοῖς
tois	*hupakouousin*	*autō*	*pasin*	*pasin*	*tois*
to the	obeying	him	all,	[all	to the

5057.2 verb dat pl masc part pres act	**840.4** prs-pron dat sing	**157.1** adj nom sing masc	**4843.2** noun gen sing fem	**164.2** adj gen sing
ὑπακούουσιν	αὐτῷ]	αἴτιος	σωτηρίας	αἰωνίου·
hupakouousin	*autō*	*aitios*	*sōtērias*	*aiōniou*
obeying	him]	source	of salvation	eternal;

5:7. At this point the epistle abruptly alludes to a historical incident in the life of Jesus with the phrase "in the days of his flesh." The allusion relates to the discussion of the essential qualifications for the high priesthood. It offers an example of the humanity and weakness of the Son which qualifies Him as a compassionate Person who is able to offer up effective prayers to God in heaven.

The situation alluded to is graphically described. It was a situation in which Jesus did face suffering unto death. His prayers were not normal petitions but "entreaties" (*hiketērias*) for the deliverance of His life, and they were uttered with strong emotion, loud cries, and tears. The incident which seems to fit this description is the prayer offered in Gethsemane when Jesus sweat "as it were great drops of blood" (Luke 22:44). The emphasis here is on Jesus' humanity and oneness with men in His agony.

The final words "was heard in that he *feared*" refer to Jesus' reverential piety and trust of God, because the word for *fear* is *eulabeias,* not *phobos.* Jesus was heard in His being strengthened to do His Father's will.

5:8. This verse presents an extremely difficult statement. In spite of Jesus Christ's divine messianic sonship, in spite of His being God and the promised blessed Deliverer-King, He was subjected to the humiliation, shame, fear, pain, instruction, and discipline of suffering as a human being. But what does it mean that He "learned . . . obedience by the things which he suffered"?

As God, the Son was omniscient. When He became flesh, He set aside the independent use of His divine attributes and the independent exercise of His will. Thus Luke could describe Him as growing "in wisdom and stature" (Luke 2:52). He did not increase in knowledge as God, but, as the God-man, He grew physically and mentally. So as the God-man, Jesus learned experientially what it means to obey the Father's will, when He suffered as a human in Gethsemane and at Calvary.

5:9. The obedience experienced in Jesus' suffering is here described by the past participle "being made perfect" (*teleiōtheis*). This verb is used in the Septuagint to describe the consecration of the hands of the high priest (Exodus 29:9,29,33,35; Leviticus 4:5; 8:33; 16:32) and once of the consecration of the high priest to service (Leviticus 21:10). After being consecrated to the high priesthood by experiencing the sufferings common to humanity, Jesus then became the cause (*aitios*) of everlasting deliverance to all of those who, unlike the Children of Israel in the wilderness, obey Him. In the New Testament obedience is often used as a synonym for belief (as in "obeying the truth" [1 Peter 1:22] and "they have not all obeyed the gospel" [Romans 10:16]).

5:10. Now comes the reminder, on the basis of the quotation from Psalm 110:4 introduced in Hebrews 5:6, that the Son's eternal

Thou [art] a priest for ever after the order of Melchisedec: . . . a priest for all time, *TCNT* . . . according to the ordination of, *Klingensmith* . . . to the order of, *Wilson* . . . in the category of Melchizedek, *SEB* . . . Belonging to the rank of, *Williams.*

7. Who in the days of his flesh: . . . in the days of his earthly life, *TCNT* . . . In His humble life on earth, *Beck* . . . For during His human life, *Williams.*

when he had offered up prayers and supplications: He offered specific requests, *Adams* . . . offered up special, definite petitions, *Wuest* . . . offering both petitions and, *Concordant* . . . and entreaties, *Norlie, Williams.*

with strong crying and tears: . . . crying aloud with tears, *Williams.*

unto him that was able to save him from death: . . . who had power to save him, *Klingensmith* . . . out of death, *Williams.*

and was heard in that he feared: . . . because of His reverence, *Adams* . . . because of His beautiful spirit of worship, *Williams* . . . Because of His reverent submission to God, *Norlie.*

8. Though he were a Son: . . . although he was the Son of God, *Noli* . . . Son though he was, *Wade.*

yet learned he obedience by the things which he suffered: He found out from what He suffered what it means to obey, *Beck* . . . He learned from what He suffered how to, *Williams.*

9. And being made perfect, he became: And when He was finished, *Beck* . . . and because He was perfectly qualified for it, *Williams.*

the author of eternal salvation unto all them that obey him: . . . responsible for, *Klingensmith* . . . the source of, *Norlie* . . . the Origin of, *Adams* . . . of endless salvation, *Williams.*

10. Called of God an high priest: . . . and He was introduced by, *Adams* . . . God has pronounced him, *Norlie* . . . having been declared by God, *Wilson* . . . being proclaimed by God, *Beck* . . . since He had received from God the title of, *Williams.*

4174.1 verb nom sing masc part aor pass	5097.3 prep	3450.2 art gen sing	2296.2 noun gen sing masc	744.1 noun nom sing masc
10. προσαγορευθεὶς	ὑπὸ	τοῦ	θεοῦ	ἀρχιερεὺς
prosagoreutheis	*hupo*	*tou*	*theou*	*archiereus*
having been proclaimed	by		God	high priest

2567.3 prep	3450.12 art acc sing fem	4861.2 noun acc sing fem	3168.1 name masc	3875.1 prep
κατὰ	τὴν	τάξιν	Μελχισέδεκ.	11. Περὶ
kata	*tēn*	*taxin*	*Melchisedek*	*Peri*
according to	the	order	of Melchizedek.	Concerning

3614.2 rel-pron gen sing	4044.5 adj nom sing masc	2231.3 prs-pron dat 1pl	3450.5 art nom sing masc	3030.1 noun nom sing masc	2504.1 conj
οὗ	πολὺς	ἡμῖν	ὁ	λόγος	καὶ
hou	*polus*	*hēmin*	*ho*	*logos*	*kai*
whom	much	our	the	discourse	and

1414.1 adj nom sing masc	2978.24 verb inf pres act	1878.1 conj	3438.1 adj nom pl masc	1090.5 verb 2pl indic perf act
δυσερμήνευτος	λέγειν,	ἐπεὶ	νωθροὶ	γεγόνατε
dusermēneutos	*legein*	*epei*	*nōthroi*	*gegonate*
difficult in interpretation	to speak,	since	sluggish	you have become

3450.14 art dat pl fem	187.6 noun dat pl fem	2504.1 conj	1056.1 conj	3648.7 verb nom pl masc part pres act	1498.32 verb inf pres act
ταῖς	ἀκοαῖς.	12. καὶ	γὰρ	ὀφείλοντες	εἶναι
tais	*akoais*	*kai*	*gar*	*opheilontes*	*einai*
in the	hearing.	Indeed	for	owing	to be

1314.4 noun nom pl masc	1217.2 prep	3450.6 art acc sing masc	5385.4 noun acc sing masc	3687.1 adv	5367.3 noun acc sing fem
διδάσκαλοι	διὰ	τὸν	χρόνον,	πάλιν	χρείαν
didaskaloi	*dia*	*ton*	*chronon*	*palin*	*chreian*
teachers	because of	the	time,	again	need

2174.2 verb 2pl pres act	3450.2 art gen sing	1315.10 verb inf pres act	5050.4 prs-pron acc 2pl	4948.5 indef-pron	3450.17 art pl neu	4598.1 noun pl neu
ἔχετε	τοῦ	διδάσκειν	ὑμᾶς	τινὰ	τὰ	στοιχεῖα
echete	*tou*	*didaskein*	*humas*	*tina*	*ta*	*stoicheia*
you have	of the	to teach	you	what	the	elements

3450.10 art gen sing fem	741.2 noun gen sing fem	3450.1 art gen pl	3025.1 noun gen pl neu	3450.2 art gen sing	2296.2 noun gen sing masc	2504.1 conj
τῆς	ἀρχῆς	τῶν	λογίων	τοῦ	θεοῦ·	καὶ
tēs	*archēs*	*tōn*	*logiōn*	*tou*	*theou*	*kai*
of the	beginning	of the	oracles		of God,	and

12.a.**Txt:** 01ℵ-corr,02A 03B-org,06D,018K 020L,025P,byz.Weis **Var:** 01ℵ-org,03B-corr 04C,33,bo.Tisc,We/Ho Sod,UBS/⋆

1090.5 verb 2pl indic perf act	5367.3 noun acc sing fem	2174.19 verb nom pl masc part pres act	1044.1 noun gen sing neu	2504.1 conj	3620.3 partic
γεγόνατε	χρείαν	ἔχοντες	γάλακτος,	(a καὶ)	οὐ
gegonate	*chreian*	*echontes*	*galaktos*	*kai*	*ou*
have become	need	having	of milk,	and	not

4582.4 adj gen sing fem	5001.2 noun gen sing fem	3820.6 adj nom sing masc	1056.1 conj	3450.5 art nom sing masc	3218.4 verb nom sing masc part pres act
στερεᾶς	τροφῆς.	13. πᾶς	γὰρ	ὁ	μετέχων
stereas	*trophēs*	*pas*	*gar*	*ho*	*metechōn*
of solid	food;	everyone	for	the	partaking

1044.1 noun gen sing neu	548.1 adj nom sing masc	3030.2 noun gen sing masc	1336.2 noun gen sing fem	3378.1 adj nom sing masc
γάλακτος	ἄπειρος	λόγου	δικαιοσύνης·	νήπιος
galaktos	*apeiros*	*logou*	*dikaiosunēs*	*nēpios*
of milk	without experience	in word	of righteousness,	an infant

high priesthood is not Aaronic but patterned after that of Melchizedek. The emphasis in verses 6, 9, and 10 falls on the eternality of His high-priestly work.

5:11,12. In these verses the inspired writer indicated that he desired to expand on Christ's Melchizedekian priesthood, but that the spiritual condition of his readers prevented him from doing so. The information he wished to convey was difficult to interpret and explain (*dusermēneutos*), and they were sluggish and slothful (*nōthroi*) in their listening.

The implication is that a grasp of deep spiritual truth is dependent in part on the diligence of the believer in listening. The readers of the epistle had been believers long enough to have advanced to the function of teaching, but they had not. Instead, they found themselves in need of being once again taught the *stoicheia*, the ABCs of God's self-disclosure. They had not advanced normally in their spiritual growth. They should have been chewing on tough meat like mature adults, but instead they were retarded. They had to be taught the baby lessons designed for new Christians.

Paul instructed the Corinthians as Hebrews does here: "I have fed you with milk, and not with meat: for hitherto ye were not able to bear it, neither yet now are ye able" (1 Corinthians 3:2). The sad thing is those of both groups were not the only ones who suffered from their lack of spiritual maturity. Recognizing this, Pfeiffer wrote, "Immature Christians not only hurt themselves, by robbing themselves of the spiritual benefits which accompany maturity, but they rob others also. Christians should be 'teachers' (5:12), sharing their spiritual blessings with others, both within and without the Church. It is the entire Church that has been called to a teaching ministry, although some individuals have special gifts (Ephesians 4:11-12). The Great Commission includes the command, 'teach all nations' (Matthew 28:19)" (pp.46,47).

5:13. The vivid imagery of verse 12 is expanded here. They needed milk; that is, to have the basic principles of the gospel message explained to them. Because they had not fully grasped these first principles, they were unable to comprehend the deeper truths of the Word of God. The term "unskilful" translates *apeiros* which means "not tested," the idea being that the Hebrews were not able because they did not have enough experience.

5:14. The other side of the coin is examined in this verse. Tough meat is for the *teleiōn*, those who have matured, who in turn are described as "those who by reason of use have their senses exercised to discern both good and evil." The imagery here switches to the

after the order of Melchisedec: ... with the rank of, *Williams.*

11. Of whom we have many things to say: I have much to say to you about Him, *Williams* ... our discourse will be long, *Wade.*

and hard to be uttered: ... of difficult interpretation, *Wilson* ... but it is difficult to make it clear to you, *Williams* ... hard to make intelligible to you, *Wade.*

seeing ye are dull of hearing: ... so slow to learn, *TCNT* ... seeing that you seem sluggish in spiritual understanding, *Norlie* ... since you have become so dull in your spiritual senses, *Williams* ... slow of apprehension, *Wade.*

12. For when for the time ye ought to be teachers: ... in view of the time that has elapsed, *Wade* ... You should have become teachers a long time ago, *SEB* ... although you ought to be teachers of others because you have been Christians so long, *Williams.*

ye have need that one teach you again: ... you actually need someone to teach you over and over again, *Williams.*

which [be] the first principles of the oracles of God: ... what are the rudimentary elements, *Concordant* ... to teach you the ABC of God's Word again, *Beck* ... the very alphabet of the Divine Revelation, *TCNT* ... the elementary principles of God's revelation, *Adams* ... the very elements of the truths that God has given us, *Williams.*

and are become such as have need of milk, and not of strong meat: ... you have come to need milk, *TNT* ... you are in constant need of milk instead of, *Williams* ... not solid food, *Adams* ... solid nourishment, *Concordant.*

13. For every one that useth milk: ... anyone who lives on milk, *TNT.*

[is] unskilful in the word of righteousness: ... is inexperienced in the message of rightdoing, *Williams* ... has no experience of the message of righteousness, *TNT.*

for he is a babe: ... he is only an infant, *Williams.*

Hebrews 5:14

1056.1 conj	1498.4 verb 3sing indic pres act	4894.4 adj gen pl masc	1156.2 conj	1498.4 verb 3sing indic pres act	3450.9 art nom sing fem
γάρ	ἐστιν˙	14. τελείων	δέ	ἐστιν	ἡ
gar	*estin*	*teleiōn*	*de*	*estin*	*hē*
for	he is;	full grown	but	is	the

4582.3 adj nom sing fem	5001.1 noun nom sing fem	3450.1 art gen pl	1217.2 prep	3450.12 art acc sing fem	1824.1 noun acc sing fem
στερεὰ	τροφή,	τῶν	διὰ	τὴν	ἕξιν
sterea	*trophē*	*tōn*	*dia*	*tēn*	*hexin*
solid	food,	the	on account of	the	practice

3450.17 art pl neu	145.1 noun pl neu	1122.4 verb pl neu part perf mid	2174.20 verb gen pl masc part pres act	4242.1 prep
τὰ	αἰσθητήρια	γεγυμνασμένα	ἐχόντων	πρὸς
ta	*aisthētēria*	*gegumnasmena*	*echontōn*	*pros*
the	senses	having been trained	having	for

1247.1 noun acc sing fem	2541.9 adj gen sing neu	4885.1 conj	2504.1 conj	2527.8 adj gen sing neu	1346.1 conj
διάκρισιν	καλοῦ	τε	καὶ	κακοῦ.	6:1. Διὸ
diakrisin	*kalou*	*te*	*kai*	*kakou*	*Dio*
distinguishing	good	both	and	evil.	Wherefore,

856.19 verb nom pl masc part aor act	3450.6 art acc sing masc	3450.10 art gen sing fem	741.2 noun gen sing fem	3450.2 art gen sing	5382.2 name gen masc
ἀφέντες	τὸν	τῆς	ἀρχῆς	τοῦ	Χριστοῦ
aphentes	*ton*	*tēs*	*archēs*	*tou*	*Christou*
having left	the	of the	beginning	of the	Christ

3030.4 noun acc sing masc	1894.3 prep	3450.12 art acc sing fem	4895.2 noun acc sing fem	5179.23 verb 1pl subj pres mid
λόγον,	ἐπὶ	τὴν	τελειότητα	φερώμεθα˙
logon	*epi*	*tēn*	*teleiotēta*	*pherōmetha*
discourse,	to	the	full growth	we should go on;

3231.1 partic	3687.1 adv	2287.4 noun acc sing masc	2569.1 verb nom pl masc part pres mid	3211.1 noun gen sing fem
μὴ	πάλιν	θεμέλιον	καταβαλλόμενοι	μετανοίας
mē	*palin*	*themelion*	*kataballomenoi*	*metanoias*
not	again	a foundation	laying	of repentance

570.3 prep	3361.2 adj gen pl	2024.5 noun gen pl neu	2504.1 conj	3963.2 noun gen sing fem	1894.3 prep	2296.4 noun acc sing masc
ἀπὸ	νεκρῶν	ἔργων,	καὶ	πίστεως	ἐπὶ	θεόν,
apo	*nekrōn*	*ergōn*	*kai*	*pisteōs*	*epi*	*theon*
from	dead	works,	and	faith	in	God,

903.1 noun gen pl masc	1316.2 noun gen sing fem	1921.1 noun gen sing fem	4885.1 conj	5331.6 noun gen pl fem
2. βαπτισμῶν	διδαχῆς,	ἐπιθέσεώς	τε	χειρῶν,
baptismōn	*didachēs*	*epitheseōs*	*te*	*cheirōn*
of baptisms	of doctrine,	of laying on	and	of hands,

2.a.**Txt:** 01ℵ,02A,04C 06D-corr,018K,020L,etc. byz.Tisc,Sod
Var: 03B,06D-org,025P We/Ho,Weis,UBS/☆

384.2 noun gen sing fem	4885.1 conj	3361.2 adj gen pl	2504.1 conj	2890.2 noun gen sing neu	164.2 adj gen sing
ἀναστάσεώς	(a τε)	νεκρῶν,	καὶ	κρίματος	αἰωνίου.
anastaseōs	*te*	*nekrōn*	*kai*	*krimatos*	*aiōniou*
of resurrection	and	of dead,	and	of judgment	eternal;

3.a.**Txt:** p46,01ℵ,03B 016I,018K,020L,0122,6 33,629,630,1241,1739 1881,2464,bo.Sod
Var: 02A,04C,06D,025P 044,81,104,365,2495

2504.1 conj	3642.17 dem-pron sing neu	4020.53 verb 1pl indic fut act	4020.30 verb 1pl subj aor act	1430.1 conj
3. καὶ	τοῦτο	(☆ ποιήσομεν,	[a ποιήσωμεν,]	ἐάνπερ
kai	*touto*	*poiēsomen*	*poiēsōmen*	*eanper*
and	this	will we do,	[we may do,]	if indeed

gymnasium. The development of Christian discernment is likened to the training of an athlete's skills by the discipline of practice. The Hebrew believers had not received spiritual insight because they had not been wrestling with spiritual truths. Hence they were not able to separate good from evil.

14. But strong meat belongeth to them that are of full age: Solid food is for mature people, *Adams* . . . belongs to full-grown men, *Williams* . . . is for advanced Christians, *TCNT* . . . for grown-up people, *Beck.*

[even] those who by reason of use have their senses exercised: Their minds are exercised by habit, *Klingensmith* . . . whose senses are habitually in training to distinguish between, *Norlie* . . . for those who by constant practise have their faculties trained, *Montgomery* . . . who on account of constant use have their faculties trained, *Williams.*

to discern both good and evil: . . . to tell the difference between right and wrong, *SEB* . . . for discriminating between the ideal, *Concordant.*

6:1. In the light of their situation, the Hebrew believers were challenged to do what they had been avoiding: to leave *ton tēs archēs tou Christou logon,* the word of the beginning of the Messiah. This phrase is the equivalent of the *stoicheia,* the first principles of God's self-revelation mentioned in 5:12. They needed to go beyond an elementary understanding of the difference between Judaism and Christian messianic teaching. The challenge was to go on to a deep, mature understanding of the implications of their confession of faith in Jesus as the Messiah.

There are great depths of truth to be discovered. They were not to lay "again the foundation." These basic gospel truths are the foundation for Christian living and should not be forgotten. However, our Christian knowledge should not be limited to a few truths found in the Word of God. In 1 Corinthians 3:10 Paul states that we should build upon this foundation—the same thought expressed in these verses.

In 6:1,2 the inspired writer identified the six ABCs of messianic teachings upon which the superstructure was to be built. The first foundational truth mentioned is "repentance from dead works." The phrase "dead works" appears again in 9:14. In both places it seems best to take it as a reference to reliance upon good works as the means or cause of one's salvation. Repentance would then be the recognition that one's good works have no power to save because they are dead. They cannot produce eternal life. Those who have truly repented have stopped relying on their own good works for salvation. On the contrary, they have discovered the second of the messianic ABCs. They have turned away from their own works and trusted God to give them eternal life. Their faith is not in themselves but in the power of the living God.

1. Therefore leaving the principles of the doctrine of Christ: Let us now dismiss the question of elementary Christian instruction, *Norlie* . . . let us once for all quit the elementary teaching, *Williams* . . . leaving the elementary teachings, *Adams.*

let us go on unto perfection: . . . and continue progressing toward, *Williams* . . . we should progress towards maturity, *Wilson* . . . go on to completion, *Klingensmith* . . . go on to more mature things, *SEB* . . . toward maturity, *Adams.*

not laying again the foundation: . . . let us stop relaying a foundation, *Williams* . . . We do not need to teach these first truths again, *NLT.*

of repentance from dead works, and of faith toward God: . . . turning away from depending on dead human efforts, *SEB* . . . from works that mean only death, *Williams.*

6:2. This verse lists four more of the initial doctrines of messianic faith: baptism, laying on of hands, resurrection, and judgment. All six of the doctrines listed in verses 1 and 2 are not distinctives of Christianity as opposed to a true messianic Judaism. A Jew who carefully read his Old Testament would have understood all six of these teachings.

2. Of the doctrine of baptisms, and of laying on of hands: . . . the Doctrine of Immersions, *Wilson* . . . of teaching about baptisms, *Adams* . . . about ceremonial washings, *Williams* . . . besides the imposition of hands, *Concordant.*

and of resurrection of the dead, and of eternal judgment: . . . and a final judgement, *TCNT.*

6:3. At this point, the inspired writer professed the expectation that both he and his readers would advance beyond the ABCs if

3. And this will we do, if God permit: And we will progress, *Williams.*

1994.2 verb 3sing subj pres act	3450.5 art nom sing masc	2296.1 noun nom sing masc	101.3 adj sing neu	1056.1 conj	3450.8 art acc pl masc
ἐπιτρέπῃ	ὁ	θεός.	4. Ἀδύνατον	γὰρ	τοὺς
epitrepē	*ho*	*theos*	*Adunaton*	*gar*	*tous*
permit		God.	Impossible	for,	the

526.1 adv	5297.9 verb acc pl masc part aor pass	1083.7 verb acc pl masc part aor mid	4885.1 conj	3450.10 art gen sing fem
ἅπαξ	φωτισθέντας,	γευσαμένους	τε	τῆς
hapax	*phōtisthentas*	*geusamenous*	*te*	*tēs*
once	having been enlightened,	having tasted	and	of the

1424.2 noun gen sing fem	3450.10 art gen sing fem	2016.1 adj gen sing	2504.1 conj	3223.3 adj acc pl masc	1090.56 verb acc pl masc part aor pass
δωρεᾶς	τῆς	ἐπουρανίου,	καὶ	μετόχους	γενηθέντας
dōreas	*tēs*	*epouraniou*	*kai*	*metochous*	*genēthentas*
gift	the	heavenly,	and	partakers	having become

4011.2 noun gen sing neu	39.2 adj gen sing	2504.1 conj	2541.1 adj sing	1083.7 verb acc pl masc part aor mid
πνεύματος	ἁγίου,	5. καὶ	καλὸν	γευσαμένους
pneumatos	*hagiou*	*kai*	*kalon*	*geusamenous*
of Spirit	Holy,	and	good	having tasted

2296.2 noun gen sing masc	4343.1 noun sing neu	1405.5 noun pl fem	4885.1 conj	3165.9 verb gen sing part pres act
θεοῦ	ῥῆμα	δυνάμεις	τε	μέλλοντος
theou	*rhēma*	*dunameis*	*te*	*mellontos*
of God	word	works of power	and	being about to come

163.1 noun gen sing masc	2504.1 conj	3756.1 verb acc pl masc part aor act	3687.1 adv	338.1 verb inf pres act
αἰῶνος,	6. καὶ	παραπεσόντας,	πάλιν	ἀνακαινίζειν
aiōnos	*kai*	*parapesontas*	*palin*	*anakainizein*
age,	and	having fallen away,	again	to renew

1519.1 prep	3211.2 noun acc sing fem	386.1 verb acc pl masc part pres act	1431.7 prs-pron dat pl masc	3450.6 art acc sing masc
εἰς	μετάνοιαν,	ἀνασταυροῦντας	ἑαυτοῖς	τὸν
eis	*metanoian*	*anastaurountas*	*heautois*	*ton*
to	repentance,	crucifying	for themselves	the

5048.4 noun acc sing masc	3450.2 art gen sing	2296.2 noun gen sing masc	2504.1 conj	3718.1 verb acc pl masc part pres act
υἱὸν	τοῦ	θεοῦ	καὶ	παραδειγματίζοντας.
huion	*tou*	*theou*	*kai*	*paradeigmatizontas*
Son		of God,	and	exposing publicly.

1087.1 noun nom sing fem	1056.1 conj	3450.9 art nom sing fem	3956.22 verb nom sing fem part aor act	3450.6 art acc sing masc	1894.2 prep
7. γῆ	γὰρ	ἡ	πιοῦσα	τὸν	ἐπ'
gē	*gar*	*hē*	*piousa*	*ton*	*ep'*
Ground	for	the	having drunk	the	upon

840.10 prs-pron gen sing fem	4038.1 adv	2048.42 verb sing part pres mid	2048.42 verb sing part pres mid	4038.1 adv
αὐτῆς	ʻ πολλάκις	ἐρχόμενον	[☆ ἐρχόμενον	πολλάκις]
autēs	*pollakis*	*erchomenon*	*erchomenon*	*pollakis*
it	often	coming	[coming	often]

5046.2 noun acc sing masc	2504.1 conj	4936.3 verb nom sing fem part pres act	1001.1 noun acc sing fem	2090.2 adj sing	1552.7 dem-pron dat pl masc
ὑετόν,	καὶ	τίκτουσα	βοτάνην	εὔθετον	ἐκείνοις
hueton	*kai*	*tiktousa*	*botanēn*	*eutheton*	*ekeinois*
rain,	and	producing	plant	fit	for those

God allowed them to live long enough, provided their hope and professions were genuine.

6:4-6. These three verses must be among the most difficult to understand in the entire Bible. For those who teach "eternal security," it must be strange to find such a strong warning against apostasy. For those who believe a Christian can lose his salvation, it must be just as problematic to read that such a falling away is irretrievable.

Christians of the Arminian persuasion who believe in "freewill choice" will assert the writer is here speaking of genuine believers who fall away and lose their salvation. Objection: How does this agree with what Jesus said, that He gave them His own eternal life, they shall never perish, and no one can pluck them out of His or His Father's hand (John 10:28,29)?

Christians who follow the Calvinistic viewpoint will have different explanations, of which two are the most common: (1) Those referred to here are not true believers who fall away, but religious people who have not been born again, yet have a knowledge of the gospel. Objection: How then explain (a) that the context contains five distinct expressions which elsewhere in the Bible are used of true believers? (b) Why should backsliding from a fake and dead religious knowledge be an unforgivable and irretrievable sin? (c) And why should the Christian readers of this epistle be warned against something of which only unbelievers could be guilty?

(2) Others with a Calvinistic background will admit that the text must refer to born-again Christians who fall away, but the backsliding in view is not the kind which would deprive them of salvation, but only from fruitful Christian service. Objection: How is it possible that a man who is continually crucifying the Son of God and is exposing Him to public ridicule (*paradeigmatizontas*), can at the same time be a true Christian, possessing eternal life?

It is plain to see that the great problems arise in connection with the various interpretations, and it is the responsibility of each one to decide how much doctrinal considerations should be allowed to influence a proper exegesis of the text.

In regard to the statement that such people cannot be renewed again to repentance, notice that God himself cannot be blamed for this impossibility of repentance. Rather, the impossibility should be related to the fact that these apostates are continually recrucifying Jesus themselves and continuing to expose Him to public ridicule. How could people like this, who continue to reject the only means of salvation, possibly be saved?

6:7,8. Most likely the Lord's Parable of the Sower and the kinds of ground (Matthew 13:18-23; Luke 8:4-15) is the background of the illustration. Those whose profession endures and produces

4. For [it is] impossible for those who were once enlightened: Some people once had the light, *SEB.*

and have tasted of the heavenly gift: . . . tasting the celestial gratuity, *Concordant* . . . have experienced the gift from heaven, *Williams.*

and were made partakers of the Holy Ghost: . . . and have become sharers of, *Adams, Norlie* . . . and have become companions of, *Wuest* . . . and came to share in, *TCNT* . . . who had the Holy Spirit just as others did, *Beck.*

5. And have tasted the good word of God: . . . and have experienced how good God's message is, *Williams.*

and the powers of the world to come: . . . and the miracles of the coming age, *Adams* . . . and the mighty powers of the age to come, *Williams* . . . of the Future Age, *Montgomery* . . . the future world, *SEB.*

6. If they shall fall away: . . . have fallen by the wayside, *Williams.*

to renew them again unto repentance: . . . to keep on restoring them to their first repentance, *Williams.*

seeing they crucify to themselves the Son of God afresh: . . . since they continue...to their detriment, *Williams* . . . they repeatedly crucify, *Montgomery* . . . they nail the Son of God to the cross again, *SEB.*

and put [him] to an open shame: . . . and have exposed Him publicly to shame, *Norlie* . . . and expose him to, *Montgomery* . . . all over again and publicly disgrace Him, *Adams* . . . exposing him to open contempt, *TCNT* . . . and hold Him up for mockery, *Beck.*

7. For the earth which drinketh in the rain that cometh oft upon it: . . . a piece of ground, *Williams.*

and bringeth forth herbs: . . . and produces plants, *Beck* . . . bears vegetation, *Adams.*

meet for them by whom it is dressed: . . . that is useful to, *Adams* . . . for those who have tilled it, *Norlie* . . . for the people who farm it, *SEB* . . . for whom also it is cultivated, *Wilson.*

1217.1 prep	3614.8 rel-pron acc pl masc	2504.1 conj	1084.1 verb 3sing indic pres mid	3205.1 verb 3sing indic pres act
δι’	οὓς	καὶ	γεωργεῖται,	μεταλαμβάνει
di'	*hous*	*kai*	*geōrgeitai*	*metalambanei*
for sake of	whom	also	it is being filled,	partakers

2110.2 noun gen sing fem	570.3 prep	3450.2 art gen sing	2296.2 noun gen sing masc	1613.1 verb nom sing fem part pres act	1156.2 conj
εὐλογίας	ἀπὸ	τοῦ	θεοῦ˙	**8.** ἐκφέρουσα	δὲ
eulogias	*apo*	*tou*	*theou*	*ekpherousa*	*de*
of blessing	from		God;	bringing forth	but

171.3 noun acc pl fem	2504.1 conj	4987.2 noun acc pl masc	95.1 adj nom sing	2504.1 conj	2641.2 noun gen sing fem
ἀκάνθας	καὶ	τριβόλους,	ἀδόκιμος	καὶ	κατάρας
akanthas	*kai*	*tribolous*	*adokimos*	*kai*	*kataras*
thorns	and	thistles	rejected	and	a curse

1445.1 adv	3614.10 rel-pron gen sing fem	3450.16 art sing neu	4904.1 noun sing neu	1519.1 prep	2711.1 noun acc sing fem
ἐγγύς,	ἧς	τὸ	τέλος	εἰς	καῦσιν.
engus	*hēs*	*to*	*telos*	*eis*	*kausin*
near to,	of which	the	end	for	burning.

3844.29 verb 1pl indic perf mid	1156.2 conj	3875.1 prep	5050.2 prs-pron gen 2pl	27.6 adj pl masc	3450.17 art pl neu
9. Πεπείσμεθα	δὲ	περὶ	ὑμῶν,	ἀγαπητοί,	τὰ
Pepeismetha	*de*	*peri*	*humōn*	*agapētoi*	*ta*
We are persuaded	but	concerning	you,	beloved,	the

2882.3 adj comp	2882.7 adj comp pl neu	2504.1 conj	2174.50 verb pl neu part pres mid	4843.2 noun gen sing fem
⸀ κρείττονα	[☆ κρείσσονα]	καὶ	ἐχόμενα	σωτηρίας,
kreittona	*kreissona*	*kai*	*echomena*	*sōtērias*
better things,	[idem]	and	having	salvation,

1479.1 conj	2504.1 conj	3643.1 adv	2953.4 verb 1pl indic pres act	3620.3 partic	1056.1 conj	93.1 adj nom sing masc
εἰ	καὶ	οὕτως	λαλοῦμεν˙	**10.** οὐ	γὰρ	ἄδικος
ei	*kai*	*houtōs*	*laloumen*	*ou*	*gar*	*adikos*
if	even	thus	we speak.	Not	for	unrighteous

3450.5 art nom sing masc	2296.1 noun nom sing masc	1935.5 verb inf aor mid	3450.2 art gen sing	2024.2 noun gen sing neu	5050.2 prs-pron gen 2pl
ὁ	θεὸς	ἐπιλαθέσθαι	τοῦ	ἔργου	ὑμῶν
ho	*theos*	*epilathesthai*	*tou*	*ergou*	*humōn*
	God	to forget	the	work	your

2504.1 conj	3450.2 art gen sing	2845.2 noun gen sing masc	3450.10 art gen sing fem	26.2 noun gen sing fem	3614.10 rel-pron gen sing fem
καὶ	⸀a τοῦ	κόπου ⸌	τῆς	ἀγάπης	⸀☆ ἧς
kai	*tou*	*kopou*	*tēs*	*agapēs*	*hēs*
and	the	labor	of the	love	which

3614.12 rel-pron acc sing fem	1715.5 verb 2pl indic aor mid	1519.1 prep	3450.16 art sing neu	3549.2 noun sing neu	840.3 prs-pron gen sing
[b ἣν]	ἐνεδείξασθε	εἰς	τὸ	ὄνομα	αὐτοῦ,
hēn	*enedeixasthe*	*eis*	*to*	*onoma*	*autou*
[idem]	you did show	to	the	name	his,

1241.12 verb nom pl masc part aor act	3450.4 art dat pl	39.8 adj dat pl masc	2504.1 conj	1241.5 verb nom pl masc part pres act
διακονήσαντες	τοῖς	ἁγίοις	καὶ	διακονοῦντες.
diakonēsantes	*tois*	*hagiois*	*kai*	*diakonountes*
having served	to the	saints	and	serving.

10.a.**Txt:** 06D-corr,018K 020L,byz.bo.
Var: 01ℵ,02A,03B,04C 06D-org,025P,33,Gries Lach,Treg,Alf,Word Tisc,We/Ho,Weis,Sod UBS/☆

10.b.**Txt:** 01ℵ,02A 03B-org,06D,byz.
Var: p46,03B-corr2 1739,1881,2495

fruit are the good ground. Fruit is blessed and weeds are cursed by God. The application seems clear enough. Not all who initially hear the message of God spoken in His Son actually have the roots of faith.

6:9. Having confronted believers with the terrible end awaiting those who turn back (apostatize) from their profession of faith in the Son, the inspired writer declared that he did not think the readers of this epistle were the kind of ground that only produces thistles and weeds. Even though he had issued a stern warning about God's judgment upon those who turn back from Jesus Christ, he indicated confidence that their lives showed evidence of real faith which produces the genuine fruits of salvation and maturity in Christ. Although he is concerned about the possibility of some in their midst apostatizing, his basic anxiety relates to their failure to reach maturity.

6:10. Once again, the word "For" which begins the verse indicates that the inspired writer was offering an explanation of the statement which he had just made. He had stated the basis for confidence in the reality of their salvation. It was grounded in two realities: the nature of God and the characteristics of faith displayed in their lives.

First, God is righteous and just. He keeps His promises. He declares those who trust in Jesus Christ to be righteous. He covers their sins and delivers them from the consequences of their transgressions. He promises life eternal to all who believe in Jesus Christ His Son, and He will make good His promise. Second, in spite of the spiritual immaturity of the believers who received this epistle (5:11-14), they displayed the fruits of genuine faith by their actions. They displayed love by exhausting themselves in deeds of love (*tou kopou tēs agapēs*) directed toward their fellow believers. What they have done for God's children has, of course, been done for Him and for the Son (Matthew 25:40). Their works sprang not from a desire to gain merit in God's sight, but out of love for Him and His people, from a genuine desire to please Him.

This life-style of giving was not a onetime thing. It continued to characterize their behavior, for they "have ministered to the saints" in the past, and even now they "do minister." The continuation of their labor of love was an evidence of their enduring faith.

6:11. Having taken note of their love, the inspired writer pointed out other areas of their lives where they needed to work hard on the cultivation of other Christian virtues which are indicative of maturity. It is imperative that believers display the same careful concern and painstaking effort in the development of full assurance in regard to the Christian's hope—the victorious reign of Jesus Christ at the end of this age. There is high emotional intensity in the words "desire" (*epithumoumen*) and "diligence" (*spoudēn*). The

receiveth blessing from God: . . . shares a blessing, *Wade.*

8. But that which beareth thorns and briers: . . . if it continues to yield, *Williams* . . . if that soil produces, *TNT* . . . But land which produces thorny weeds and thorn bushes, *SEB* . . . But if it gives nothing but weeds, it is worth nothing, *NLT* . . . and thistles, *Adams.*

[is] rejected, and [is] nigh unto cursing: . . . it is regarded as, *TCNT* . . . considered worthless, *Montgomery, Williams* . . . disqualified, *Concordant* . . . has no value, *Norlie* . . . verging on the state of a land accursed, *Wade* . . . under God's curse, *TNT.*

whose end [is] to be burned: . . . its end is, *Wade* . . . its final fate is burning, *Williams* . . . and will finish in flames, *TNT.*

9. But, beloved, we are persuaded better things of you: But in your case, my dearly loved friends...we are sure of, *Williams* . . . we have no doubt about you, *TNT* . . . are convinced, *Wade.*

and things that accompany salvation: You know what is good and leads to your salvation, *TNT* . . . conditions conducing to, *Wade* . . . that point to, *Williams.*

though we thus speak: . . . even though we speak in such a tone, *Williams* . . . though we speak thus gravely, *Wade.*

10. For God [is] not unrighteous to forget your work: . . . is not so unjust as to forget the work you have done, *Williams.*

and labour of love, which ye have showed toward his name: . . . the love you have shown His name, *Williams* . . . the love which you have evinced, *Wade* . . . for him, *TNT.*

in that ye have ministered to the saints, and do minister: . . . in the service you have rendered for your fellow-Christians, and still are doing, *Williams* . . . when you serve the saints, *Concordant* . . . by serving His saints in the past and at present, *Adams* . . . in your past and present service to his people, *TNT.*

11. And we desire that every one of you: Now we are yearning, *Concordant* . . . We are very eager that each one of you, *TNT.*

1922.2 verb 1pl indic pres act	1156.2 conj	1524.1 adj sing	5050.2 prs-pron gen 2pl	3450.12 art acc sing fem
11. ἐπιθυμοῦμεν	δὲ	ἕκαστον	ὑμῶν	τὴν
epithumoumen	*de*	*hekaston*	*humōn*	*tēn*
We desire	but	each	of you	the

840.12 prs-pron acc sing fem	1715.3 verb inf pres mid	4561.3 noun acc sing fem	4242.1 prep	3450.12 art acc sing fem
αὐτὴν	ἐνδείκνυσθαι	σπουδὴν	πρὸς	τὴν
autēn	*endeiknusthai*	*spoudēn*	*pros*	*tēn*
same	to show	diligence	to	the

3996.3 noun acc sing fem	3450.10 art gen sing fem	1667.2 noun gen sing fem	884.2 conj	4904.2 noun gen sing neu	2419.1 conj
πληροφορίαν	τῆς	ἐλπίδος	ἄχρι	τέλους·	12. ἵνα
plērophorian	*tēs*	*elpidos*	*achri*	*telous*	*hina*
full assurance	of the	hope	unto	end;	that

3231.1 partic	3438.1 adj nom pl masc	1090.42 verb 2pl subj aor mid	3266.1 noun nom pl masc	1156.2 conj	3450.1 art gen pl	1217.2 prep
μὴ	νωθροὶ	γένησθε,	μιμηταὶ	δὲ	τῶν	διὰ
mē	*nōthroi*	*genēsthe*	*mimētai*	*de*	*tōn*	*dia*
not	sluggish	you be,	imitators	but	of the	through

3963.2 noun gen sing fem	2504.1 conj	3087.2 noun gen sing fem	2789.2 verb gen pl masc part pres act	3450.15 art acc pl fem
πίστεως	καὶ	μακροθυμίας	κληρονομούντων	τὰς
pisteōs	*kai*	*makrothumias*	*klēronomountōn*	*tas*
faith	and	long patience	inherited	the

1845.1 noun fem	3450.3 art dat sing	1056.1 conj	11.1 name masc	1846.5 verb nom sing masc part aor mid
ἐπαγγελίας.	13. Τῷ	γὰρ	Ἀβραὰμ	ἐπαγγειλάμενος
epangelias	*Tō*	*gar*	*Abraam*	*epangeilamenos*
promises.		For	to Abraham	having promised

3450.5 art nom sing masc	2296.1 noun nom sing masc	1878.1 conj	2567.1 prep	3625.1 num card gen	2174.44 verb 3sing indic imperf act
ὁ	θεός,	ἐπεὶ	κατ'	οὐδενὸς	εἶχεν
ho	*theos*	*epei*	*kat'*	*oudenos*	*eichen*
	God,	since	by	no one	he was having

3157.3 adj comp gen sing	3523.10 verb inf aor act	3523.6 verb 3sing indic aor act	2567.2 prep	1431.4 prs-pron gen sing	2978.15 verb nom sing masc part pres act
μείζονος	ὀμόσαι,	ὤμοσεν	καθ'	ἑαυτοῦ,	14. λέγων,
meizonos	*omosai*	*ōmosen*	*kath'*	*heautou*	*legōn*
greater	to swear,	swore	by	himself,	saying,

14.a.**Txt:** 018K,020L-org byz.
Var: 01ℵ,02A,03B 06D-org,025P,33,Lach Treg,Alf,Tisc,We/Ho Weis,Sod,UBS/⋆

2212.1 partic	1479.1 conj	3244.1 partic	2108.3 verb nom sing masc part pres act	2108.11 verb 1sing indic fut act	4622.4 prs-pron acc 2sing
ʼ Ἦ	[a⋆ Εἰ]	μὴν	εὐλογῶν	εὐλογήσω	σε,
Ē	*Ei*	*mēn*	*eulogōn*	*eulogēsō*	*se*
	[If]	Surely	blessing	I will bless	you,

2504.1 conj	3989.1 verb nom sing masc part pres act	3989.4 verb 1sing indic fut act	4622.4 prs-pron acc 2sing	2504.1 conj	3643.1 adv
καὶ	πληθύνων	πληθυνῶ	σε·	15. καὶ	οὕτως
kai	*plēthunōn*	*plēthunō*	*se*	*kai*	*houtōs*
and	multiplying	I will multiply	you;	and	thus

3086.6 verb nom sing masc part aor act	1997.1 verb 3sing indic aor act	3450.10 art gen sing fem	1845.1 noun fem
μακροθυμήσας	ἐπέτυχεν	τῆς	ἐπαγγελίας.
makrothumēsas	*epetuchen*	*tēs*	*epangelias*
having had long patience	he obtained	the	promise.

latter term indicates that believers are to make every effort to display their confidence in the promised but as yet unrealized subjugation of the universe to the Son (2:8,9). Apparently some of the Christians at that time had begun to waver in their "full assurance of hope" concerning the glorious second coming of Christ to rule over His kingdom. The display of confidence in the Lord's second coming is a hallmark of Christian maturity.

6:12. The inspired writer charged these believers with a sluggish laziness, calling them *nōthroi* (see also 5:11). He urged them to put an end to such sloth by observing and imitating the patriarchs of Genesis, who "through faith and patience inherit the promises" of God after an earthly pilgrimage characterized by faith in the midst of lives marked by long-suffering (*makrothumias*) without reward.

6:13. The ground of Christian confidence in the face of as yet unrealized promises from God is found in the patriarchs' experience of God's character. First, God based His promise to Abraham on an oath. Oaths are not lightly undertaken. They are solemn matters of business and courtroom procedure, designed to emphasize the seriousness of the matter and to secure honesty between parties to an agreement or testimony. Since God can swear by no one greater, He swore by His own character and greatness when He made His promise to Abraham (Genesis 22:16) concerning the blessing and numbering of his descendants. God takes His promises seriously.

6:14. This particular promise of God to Abraham was cited as the writer quoted Genesis 22:17. The reference is to God's promise to richly bless the descendants of Abraham and Isaac while at the same time increasing their number incalculably.

6:15. God kept this mind-staggering promise. Because of their advanced ages and Sara's history of barrenness, both parents laughed at God's promise. But, according to that promise, Sarah conceived and bore Isaac, and through Isaac's son Jacob the Lord increased and enriched Abraham's descendants, the nation of Israel—after Abraham had suffered long (*makrothumēsas*).

6:16. Continuing the explanation of the grounds of a believer's confidence in God's promises, the writer analyzed the purpose of

do show the same diligence: . . . to continue to show the same earnestness, *Williams* . . . you should go on showing the same zeal, *TNT.*

to the full assurance of hope unto the end: . . . until the consummation, *Concordant* . . . to the very end, *Williams* . . . until your hope is fully and finally realized, *TNT.*

12. That ye be not slothful: Then do not become slack, *Montgomery* . . . Do not be lazy, *Klingensmith* . . . so that you may not grow careless, *Williams.*

but followers of them who through faith and patience: We want you to be like those who, *TNT* . . . follow the example of those who through their faith and patient endurance, *Williams.*

inherit the promises: . . . are now possessors of the blessings promised, *Williams* . . . are now taking possession of God's promises, *TNT.*

13. For when God made promise to Abraham:

because he could swear by no greater, he sware by himself: He took the oath by Himself, *Norlie.*

14. Saying, Surely blessing I will bless thee: . . . declaring, Assuredly, *Wade* . . . I will certainly bless you, *TNT.*

and multiplying I will multiply thee: For sure, I will give you many children, *NLT* . . . I will increase you, and increase you, *Montgomery* . . . I will certainly bless you over and over again, *Williams* . . . and increase thy numbers, *TCNT* . . . I will surely give you many descendants, *SEB.*

15. And so, after he had patiently endured: . . . in reliance upon this pledge...through his patience, *Wade* . . . after patiently waiting, *TCNT.*

he obtained the promise: . . . he got what was promised, *Adams* . . . Abraham got what God promised, *Beck.*

16. For men verily swear by the greater: For it is a custom among men to take oath by something greater than themselves, *Williams* . . . Men swear by one who is greater than themselves, *TNT.*

Hebrews 6:16

16.a.**Txt:** 04C,06D-corr 018K,020L,byz.bo. **Var:** 01ℵ,02A,03B 06D-org,025P,Lach Treg,Tisc,We/Ho,Weis Sod,UBS/⋆

442.6 noun nom pl masc	**3173.1** conj	**1056.1** conj	**2567.3** prep	**3450.2** art gen sing	**3157.3** adj comp gen sing
16. ἄνθρωποι	(a μὲν)	γὰρ	κατὰ	τοῦ	μείζονος
anthrōpoi	*men*	*gar*	*kata*	*tou*	*meizonos*
Men	indeed	for	by	the	greater

3523.2 verb 3pl indic pres act	**2504.1** conj	**3820.10** adj gen sing fem	**840.2** prs-pron dat pl	**482.1** noun gen sing fem	**3872.1** noun sing neu
ὀμνύουσιν,	καὶ	πάσης	αὐτοῖς	ἀντιλογίας	πέρας
omnuousin	*kai*	*pasēs*	*autois*	*antilogias*	*peras*
swear,	and	of all	to them	controversy	an end

1519.1 prep	**944.2** noun acc sing fem	**3450.5** art nom sing masc	**3590.1** noun nom sing masc	**1706.1** prep	**3614.3** rel-pron dat sing
εἰς	βεβαίωσιν	ὁ	ὅρκος·	**17.** ἐν	ᾧ
eis	*bebaiōsin*	*ho*	*horkos*	*en*	*hō*
for	confirmation	the	oath.	In	which

3917.3 adv comp	**1007.8** verb nom sing masc part pres mid	**3450.5** art nom sing masc	**2296.1** noun nom sing masc	**1910.4** verb inf aor act
περισσότερον	βουλόμενος	ὁ	θεὸς	ἐπιδεῖξαι
perissoteron	*boulomenos*	*ho*	*theos*	*epideixai*
more abundantly	desiring		God	to show

3450.4 art dat pl	**2791.4** noun dat pl masc	**3450.10** art gen sing fem	**1845.1** noun fem	**3450.16** art sing neu
τοῖς	κληρονόμοις	τῆς	ἐπαγγελίας	τὸ
tois	*klēronomois*	*tēs*	*epangelias*	*to*
to the	heirs	of the	promise	the

274.1 adj sing neu	**3450.10** art gen sing fem	**1005.2** noun gen sing fem	**840.3** prs-pron gen sing	**3185.1** verb 3sing indic aor act
ἀμετάθετον	τῆς	βουλῆς	αὐτοῦ,	ἐμεσίτευσεν
ametatheton	*tēs*	*boulēs*	*autou*	*emesiteusen*
unchangeableness	of the	counsel	his,	interposed

3590.3 noun dat sing masc	**2419.1** conj	**1217.2** prep	**1411.3** num card	**4088.4** noun gen pl neu	**274.2** adj gen pl neu
ὅρκῳ,	**18.** ἵνα	διὰ	δύο	πραγμάτων	ἀμεταθέτων,
horkō	*hina*	*dia*	*duo*	*pragmatōn*	*ametathetōn*
by an oath,	that	by	two	things	unchangeable,

18.a.**Txt:** 03B,06D,044 byz. **Var:** p46,01ℵ,02A,04C 025P,33,1739,1881 2495,Sod

1706.1 prep	**3614.4** rel-pron dat pl	**101.3** adj sing neu	**5409.7** verb inf aor mid	**3450.6** art acc sing masc	**2296.4** noun acc sing masc
ἐν	οἷς	ἀδύνατον	ψεύσασθαι	[a+ τὸν]	θεόν,
en	*hois*	*adunaton*	*pseusasthai*	*ton*	*theon*
in	which	impossible	to lie		God,

2451.8 adj acc sing fem	**3735.4** noun acc sing fem	**2174.8** verb 1pl subj pres act	**3450.7** art nom pl masc	**2672.2** verb nom pl masc part aor act
ἰσχυρὰν	παράκλησιν	ἔχωμεν	οἱ	καταφυγόντες
ischuran	*paraklēsin*	*echōmen*	*hoi*	*kataphugontes*
strong	encouragement	we might have	the	having fled for refuge

2875.20 verb inf aor act	**3450.10** art gen sing fem	**4154.4** verb gen sing fem part pres mid	**1667.2** noun gen sing fem	**3614.12** rel-pron acc sing fem
κρατῆσαι	τῆς	προκειμένης	ἐλπίδος·	**19.** ἣν
kratēsai	*tēs*	*prokeimenēs*	*elpidos*	*hēn*
to lay hold on	the	setting before	hope,	which

5453.1 conj	**44.1** noun acc sing fem	**2174.5** verb 1pl indic pres act	**3450.10** art gen sing fem	**5425.2** noun gen sing fem	**798.1** adj acc sing fem
ὡς	ἄγκυραν	ἔχομεν	τῆς	ψυχῆς	ἀσφαλῆ
hōs	*ankuran*	*echomen*	*tēs*	*psuchēs*	*asphalē*
as	an anchor	we have	of the	soul	certain

an oath in human affairs. In matters over which there is some strife, i.e., in disputes (*antilogias*), oaths are introduced to end or mark the boundary (*peras*) for the purpose of establishing and confirming agreement. In taking oaths, men swear by God who is greater than they are. They do so in order to convince other men that they are truthful and intend to abide by their promises.

6:17. The implication here is that God, even though He is not like men, confirmed His promise to Abraham and his descendants by an oath. That oath underscored God's unchangeableness, "the immutability of his counsel." To do this He accommodated himself to the human custom of emphasizing one's word by means of an oath, thus communicating the solemnity and import of His promise. His oath was to grant assurance to Abraham's heirs.

6:18. This assurance flows from two unchanging realities. The first is clearly stated: God cannot lie. The certainty of a promise is rooted in the nature of the one who makes it. In this case it is the Lord, the all-powerful Creator, the righteous Judge of all men, who made the promise. His word is His bond. If He says it, without doubt, it will be accomplished.

The second unchanging reality is implied in the oath. Even though God cannot lie, He has taken the additional step of interjecting an oath based on His own unchanging nature. The purpose of the oath was to strengthen the assurance of those who are to inherit the promises. God's promise and His oath are true because He cannot deny His own righteous character. It does not change.

The result of God's promise and oath is our "strong consolation." The unchanging character of God assures the believer of the fulfillment of everything which He has promised. Christians who have fled from the wrath due them because of their sins have seized upon the hope which God the Father has offered in His Son, Jesus Christ. Since it is not yet fully realized, it is hope. It is "set before us" as the promise was to the patriarchs. It is grounded in God's immutability, even though it is unfulfilled as yet. The promise of the subjection of the universe to Jesus at the end of this current age provides believers with admonition and encouragement to endure in the midst of current trials and sufferings.

6:19. The hope that all things will be subordinated to the Son serves as an anchor for the believers' lives. It is a source of stability in the seas of life. Circumstances change, but Christians have a firm, unchanging hope. It is both certain and steady because it partakes of the eternal; it "entereth into that within the veil," a reference to the Son's priesthood.

and an oath for confirmation [is] to them an end of all strife: . . . to silence anyone who opposes them, *Beck* . . . the oath is final for confirmation, *Montgomery* . . . This confirms agreements, *SEB* . . . ends all arguments, *Adams* . . . puts an end to further questioning, *Norlie* . . . settles any dispute, *Williams* . . . terminates Every Dispute among them, *Wilson.*

17. Wherein God, willing more abundantly to show: . . . because God wanted to make the strongest demonstration of, *Williams.*

unto the heirs of promise:

the immutability of his counsel: . . . the unchangeable nature of, *Adams* . . . the unchangeableness of, *TCNT* . . . the unchangeable character of His purpose, *Williams.*

confirmed [it] by an oath: He interposed with an oath, *Williams.*

18. That by two immutable things: . . . so that by Two unalterable Things, *Wilson* . . . that through the instrumentality of two immutable facts, *Wuest* . . . two unchangeable things, *Beck, Williams.*

in which [it was] impossible for God to lie: . . . for God cannot possibly tell a lie, *Norlie* . . . to break faith, *Montgomery* . . . to prove false, *Williams.*

we might have a strong consolation: . . . may have strong encouragement, *Klingensmith.*

who have fled for refuge: . . . fled for shelter, *Klingensmith* . . . who have taken refuge with Him, *Williams.*

to lay hold upon the hope set before us: . . . to make us seize upon the hope that lies ahead of us, *Williams.*

19. Which [hope] we have as an anchor of the soul: . . . like an anchor for our lives, *Beck.*

both sure and stedfast: . . . both secure and confirmed, *Concordant* . . . secure and strong, *Montgomery* . . . and safe, *Williams* . . . It will never move, *NLT.*

and which entereth into that within the veil: . . . which reaches up behind the heavenly veil, *Williams* . . . on the inner side of the curtain, *Adams.*

4885.1 conj	2504.1 conj	942.3 adj acc sing fem	2504.1 conj	1511.35 verb acc sing fem part pres mid	1519.1 prep	3450.16 art sing neu
τε	καὶ	βεβαίαν,	καὶ	εἰσερχομένην	εἰς	τὸ
te	*kai*	*bebaian*	*kai*	*eiserchomenēn*	*eis*	*to*
both	and	firm,	and	entering	into	the

2061.2 adj comp sing neu	3450.2 art gen sing	2635.2 noun gen sing neu	3562.1 adv	4133.1 adj nom sing masc
ἐσώτερον	τοῦ	καταπετάσματος,	20. ὅπου	πρόδρομος
esōteron	*tou*	*katapetasmatos*	*hopou*	*prodromos*
within	the	veil;	where	forerunner

5065.1 prep	2231.2 prs-pron gen 1pl	1511.3 verb 3sing indic aor act	2400.1 name nom masc	2567.3 prep	3450.12 art acc sing fem
ὑπὲρ	ἡμῶν	εἰσῆλθεν	Ἰησοῦς,	κατὰ	τὴν
huper	*hēmōn*	*eisēlthen*	*Iēsous*	*kata*	*tēn*
for	us	entered	Jesus,	according to	the

4861.2 noun acc sing fem	3168.1 name masc	744.1 noun nom sing masc	1090.53 verb nom sing masc part aor mid	1519.1 prep
τάξιν	Μελχισέδεκ	ἀρχιερεὺς	γενόμενος	εἰς
taxin	*Melchisedek*	*archiereus*	*genomenos*	*eis*
order	of Melchizedek	a high priest	having become	for

3450.6 art acc sing masc	163.3 noun acc sing masc	3642.4 dem-pron nom sing masc	1056.1 conj	3450.5 art nom sing masc	3168.1 name masc
τὸν	αἰῶνα.	7:1. Οὗτος	γὰρ	ὁ	Μελχισέδεκ,
ton	*aiōna*	*Houtos*	*gar*	*ho*	*Melchisedek*
the	age.	This	for		Melchizedek,

928.1 noun nom sing masc	4389.1 name fem	2385.1 noun nom sing masc	3450.2 art gen sing	2296.2 noun gen sing masc	3450.2 art gen sing
βασιλεὺς	Σαλήμ,	ἱερεὺς	τοῦ	θεοῦ	τοῦ
basileus	*Salēm*	*hiereus*	*tou*	*theou*	*tou*
king	of Salem,	priest		of God	the

1.a.**Txt:** p46,04C-org 020L,025P,044,byz. **Var:** 01ℵ,02A,03B 04C-corr2,06D,08E 018K,33

5148.2 adj sup gen sing masc	3450.5 art nom sing masc	3614.5 rel-pron nom sing masc	4727.2 verb nom sing masc part aor act	11.1 name masc
ὑψίστου,	☆ ὁ	[a ὅς]	συναντήσας	Ἀβραὰμ
hupsistou	*ho*	*hos*	*sunantēsas*	*Abraam*
most high,	the	[who]	having met	Abraham

5128.3 verb dat sing masc part pres act	570.3 prep	3450.10 art gen sing fem	2843.1 noun gen sing fem	3450.1 art gen pl	928.7 noun gen pl masc
ὑποστρέφοντι	ἀπὸ	τῆς	κοπῆς	τῶν	βασιλέων,
hupostrephonti	*apo*	*tēs*	*kopēs*	*tōn*	*basileōn*
returning	from	the	slaughter	of the	kings,

2504.1 conj	2108.9 verb nom sing masc part aor act	840.6 prs-pron acc sing masc	3614.3 rel-pron dat sing	2504.1 conj	1176.4 num ord acc sing fem
καὶ	εὐλογήσας	αὐτόν·	2. ᾧ	καὶ	δεκάτην
kai	*eulogēsas*	*auton*	*hō*	*kai*	*dekatēn*
and	having blessed	him;	to whom	also	a tenth

570.3 prep	3820.4 adj gen pl	3177.1 verb 3sing indic aor act	11.1 name masc	4270.1 adv	3173.1 conj
ἀπὸ	πάντων	ἐμέρισεν	Ἀβραάμ·	πρῶτον	μὲν
apo	*pantōn*	*emerisen*	*Abraam*	*prōton*	*men*
of	all	divided	Abraham;	first	

2043.2 verb nom sing masc part pres mid	928.1 noun nom sing masc	1336.2 noun gen sing fem	1884.1 adv	1156.2 conj
ἑρμηνευόμενος	βασιλεὺς	δικαιοσύνης	ἔπειτα	δὲ
hermēneuomenos	*basileus*	*dikaiosunēs*	*epeita*	*de*
being interpreted	king	of righteousness,	then	and

6:20. The allusion to the sanctuary, the Holy of Holies which existed beyond the veil of both the tabernacle and the Jerusalem temple, directs attention to the high priestly work of Jesus Christ. Once a year on the Day of Atonement, the high priest sprinkled the blood of sacrifice upon the lid of the ark of the covenant. This reference provides a transition from the warning and explanation (5:11 to 6:19) back to the subject of Jesus' superiority to the Aaronic high priesthood, begun in 5:1.

As High Priest, Jesus has entered into the Holy of Holies in heaven as our forerunner (*prodromos*). Like a scout or pioneer He has gone on before, and believers are to follow His path. On the basis of His entrance, believers can follow Him into the very presence of God. According to Romans 8:34, He is there making intercession for us. He has met all the requirements for a high priest (5:1-10). His work, however, is not effective only from one annual Day of Atonement to another; instead, it is "for ever." It is not patterned after the work of Aaron and his descendants, but (as has already been pointed out by the citation from Psalm 110) it is modeled after the priesthood observed in the instance of Melchizedek found in Genesis 14:18-20.

7:1. The sentence begun in this verse is completed in verse 3. Essentially it declares that Melchizedek remains a priest in perpetuity. Verses 1 and 2 add several other observations about Melchizedek. Before commenting on this, a few words are to be said about the relationship between this epistle and intertestamental Jewish literature. In the *Testaments of the Twelve Patriarchs* (ca. 135–105 B.C.) there is an expectation of two messianic figures: one royal from Judah and one priestly from Levi. Fragments from cave 1 at Qumran (ca. A.D. 50) represent Melchizedek as the champion and deliverer of the Jewish remnant and attribute to him functions that are elsewhere in Qumranic literature ascribed to the archangel Michael. It is possible that a combination of teachings like these are being combated by the teaching in this part of Hebrews. The inspired writer began by identifying Melchizedek as the priestly king of Salem who met Abraham after his defeat of Chedorla-omer and his federation of kings (see Genesis 14).

7:2. Verse 2 indicates three things about Melchizedek. First, Abraham paid a tithe of all the spoils of his victory to Melchizedek. Second, the etymology of the name Melchizedek is *melek*, Hebrew for "king," and *tsadîq*, Hebrew for "righteousness." Literally, the name is "king of righteousness" or *righteousness* is king. Third, he was the "King of Salem." "Salem" is Hebrew for "peace." So Melchizedek was also the "King of peace." These facts are significant because Jesus' high priesthood is patterned after the priesthood of Melchizedek who was a type of Christ.

20. Whither the forerunner is for us entered, [even] Jesus: Jesus has gone there as, *Noli* . . . where Jesus has blazed the way for us, *Williams* . . . where Jesus went in before us on our behalf, *TNT* . . . has entered for us, *Fenton.*

made an high priest for ever after the order of Melchisedec: . . . for he has become, *TNT* . . . having become, as we have seen, *Phillips* . . . becoming Chief Priest, *Concordant* . . . with the rank of, *Williams* . . . according to the order of, *Noli, Fenton.*

1. For this Melchisedec, king of Salem:

priest of the most high God: . . . of the Highest God, *Fenton.*

who met Abraham returning from the slaughter of the kings: . . . when he returned from the defeat, *Adams* . . . on his way back after, *TNT* . . . returning from the combat with, *Concordant* . . . when the latter was returning from smiting the kings, *Wade* . . . coming back from beating the kings, *Klingensmith* . . . from defeating the kings, *Beck* . . . after putting the kings to death, *BB.*

and blessed him: . . . bestowed his blessing, *Wade* . . . put his blessing on him, *Williams.*

2. To whom also Abraham gave a tenth part of all: So Abraham gave him, *TNT* . . . set apart a tenth, *Fenton* . . . apportioned a tithe of all the spoil, *Montgomery* . . . contributed a tenth of all his spoils, *Williams* . . . gave him a tribute, *Phillips* . . . As a tribute, *Noli* . . . of everything which he had, *BB.*

first being by interpretation King of righteousness: . . . this is the translation of his name, *Wade* . . . being first named, *BB* . . . whose name is interpreted as, *Fenton* . . . who first of all, in accordance with the meaning of his name, *Williams* . . . His name means "first king of righteousness," *Noli* . . . king of what is right, *SEB* . . . of Justice, *Klingensmith.*

and after that also King of Salem, which is, King of peace: And secondly, *Wade* . . . and his other title, *Phillips* . . . and then in addition...that is to say, *BB* . . . By translation of this name, *Norlie* . . . he is also, *TNT* . . . which means, *Williams.*

2504.1 conj	928.1 noun nom sing masc	4389.1 name fem	3614.16 rel-pron sing neu	1498.4 verb 3sing indic pres act	928.1 noun nom sing masc
καὶ	βασιλεὺς	Σαλήμ,	ὅ	ἐστιν	βασιλεὺς
kai	*basileus*	*Salēm*	*ho*	*estin*	*basileus*
also	king	of Salem,	which	is	king

1503.2 noun gen sing fem	536.1 adj nom sing masc	280.1 adj nom sing masc	35.1 adj nom sing masc	3250.1 conj
εἰρήνης·	3. ἀπάτωρ,	ἀμήτωρ,	ἀγενεαλόγητος·	μήτε
eirēnēs	*apatōr*	*amētōr*	*agenealogētos*	*mēte*
of peace;	without father,	without mother,	without genealogy;	neither

741.4 noun acc sing fem	2232.6 noun gen pl fem	3250.1 conj	2205.2 noun gen sing fem	4904.1 noun sing neu	2174.17 verb nom sing masc part pres act
ἀρχὴν	ἡμερῶν,	μήτε	ζωῆς	τέλος	ἔχων·
archēn	*hēmerōn*	*mēte*	*zōēs*	*telos*	*echōn*
beginning	of days	nor	of life	end	having,

864.1 verb nom sing masc part perf mid	1156.2 conj	3450.3 art dat sing	5048.3 noun dat sing masc	3450.2 art gen sing	2296.2 noun gen sing masc
ἀφωμοιωμένος	δὲ	τῷ	υἱῷ	τοῦ	θεοῦ,
aphōmoiōmenos	*de*	*tō*	*huiō*	*tou*	*theou*
having been made like	but	to the	Son		of God,

3176.1 verb 3sing indic pres act	2385.1 noun nom sing masc	1519.1 prep	3450.16 art sing neu	1330.1 adj sing neu	2311.1 verb 2pl pres act
μένει	ἱερεὺς	εἰς	τὸ	διηνεκές.	4. Θεωρεῖτε
menei	*hiereus*	*eis*	*to*	*diēnekes*	*Theōreite*
abides	a priest	in	the	perpetuity.	Consider

4.a.**Txt:** 01א,02A,04C 06D-corr,018K,020L 025P,byz.Tisc,Sod
Var: 03B,06D-org,bo. Lach,Treg,We/Ho,Weis UBS/☆

1156.2 conj	3941.1 intr-pron nom sing masc	3642.4 dem-pron nom sing masc	3614.3 rel-pron dat sing	2504.1 conj	1176.4 num ord acc sing fem
δὲ	πηλίκος	οὗτος	ᾧ	(a καὶ)	δεκάτην
de	*pēlikos*	*houtos*	*hō*	*kai*	*dekatēn*
now	how great	this,	to whom	even	a tenth

11.1 name masc	1319.14 verb 3sing indic aor act	1523.2 prep gen	3450.1 art gen pl	203.1 noun gen pl neu	3450.5 art nom sing masc
Ἀβραὰμ	ἔδωκεν	ἐκ	τῶν	ἀκροθινίων	ὁ
Abraam	*edōken*	*ek*	*tōn*	*akrothiniōn*	*ho*
Abraham	gave	out of	the	spoils	the

3828.1 noun nom sing masc	2504.1 conj	3450.7 art nom pl masc	3173.1 conj	1523.2 prep gen	3450.1 art gen pl
πατριάρχης.	5. καὶ	οἱ	μὲν	ἐκ	τῶν
patriarchēs	*kai*	*hoi*	*men*	*ek*	*tōn*
patriarch.	And	the	indeed	from among	the

5048.7 noun gen pl masc	2991.1 name masc	3450.12 art acc sing fem	2381.2 noun acc sing fem	2956.9 verb nom pl masc part pres act
υἱῶν	Λευὶ	τὴν	ἱερατείαν	λαμβάνοντες,
huiōn	*Leui*	*tēn*	*hierateian*	*lambanontes*
sons	of Levi,	the	priesthood	receiving,

1769.3 noun acc sing fem	2174.6 verb 3pl indic pres act	581.3 verb inf pres act	3450.6 art acc sing masc	2967.4 noun acc sing masc
ἐντολὴν	ἔχουσιν	ἀποδεκατοῦν	τὸν	λαὸν
entolēn	*echousin*	*apodekatoun*	*ton*	*laon*
commandment	have	to take tithes from	the	people

2567.3 prep	3450.6 art acc sing masc	3414.4 noun acc sing masc	4969.1 verb	3642.16 dem-pron sing neu
κατὰ	τὸν	νόμον,	(τουτέστιν,	[☆ τοῦτ'
kata	*ton*	*nomon*	*toutestin*	*tout'*
according to	the	law,	that is	[this

7:3. Melchizedek is mentioned in only two places in the Old Testament (Genesis 14; Psalm 110). No mention is made of his origin, his parents, or his descendants. There is no record of his birth or his death. He simply appears in the Biblical text as a priest from Salem who appeared before Abraham, praising God. He is likened to the Son of God whose perpetual priesthood is eternal by divine decree. Some interpreters have seen Melchizedek as a preincarnate appearance of the Second Person of the Trinity, but it seems best to let the text stand in its most natural sense. "Made like unto the Son of God" means that a parallel exists between Melchizedek and Jesus.

7:4. The writer calls attention to the greatness of Melchizedek: namely, that Abraham—the father of the Jewish nation, and the spiritual father of all who believe, the one whose seed was to be multiplied and blessed materially—paid tithes to someone else, to Melchizedek, who must have been a great man indeed.

7:5,6. According to the Mosaic law which governed Jewish life, it was the descendants of Levi whom Jehovah designated to receive the tithe offerings of the nation of Israel (Numbers 18:21,26). These Levitical priests were descendants of Abraham through Isaac and Jacob and, as is pointed out in 7:11, they were the priesthood associated with Moses' brother Aaron.

All of this shows the superiority of the priesthood of Melchizedek to that of Aaron, in part, because of priority in time. Besides this, though, the account demonstrates tithing existed before the Law. Abraham paid a tithe of the spoils of victory in battle to show his gratitude, and not because some law required it of him. Jacob vowed to tithe financial blessings from God long before the law of Moses demanded it. In response to a promise of the Lord's goodness that would come to him, he said, "Of all that thou shalt give me I will surely give the tenth unto thee" (Genesis 28:22).

Akrothiniōn for "spoils" in verse 4 here suggests a high view of tithing. It refers literally to "first-fruits." Thus Abraham gave "the first of spoils" to Melchizedek. So tithing is in keeping with the ancient exhortation, "Honor the Lord with thy substance, and with the firstfruits of all thine increase" (Proverbs 3:9).

Melchizedek, however, was not a member of the Aaronic, Levitical priesthood. That priesthood was given to men who were descendants of Abraham. Melchizedek, being a contemporary of Abraham, therefore, possessed some other kind of priesthood. Moreover, that priesthood obviously preceded the formation of the Aaronic priesthood which was not established until the time of Moses, hundreds of years after Abraham. By some other authority than that of the Mosaic law, Abraham, the father of the Children of Israel, had tithes levied on him by this stranger, the mysterious

3. Without father, without mother, without descent: There is no record...There is no genealogy, *Norlie* . . . or ancestral lineage, *Adams* . . . no ancestry, *Williams* . . . without a genealogy, *Concordant* . . . without a family tree, *Klingensmith* . . . or line of ancestors, *Beck* . . . designated by name, no recorded genealogy, *Wade.*

having neither beginning of days, nor end of life: . . . we don't know when he was born or how long he lived, *SEB* . . . no reference to, *TNT* . . . no specified beginning of existence, *Wade* . . . no date of birth or death, *Norlie* . . . nor termination of life, *Wuest* . . . no end to his life, *Williams.*

but made like unto the Son of God: In this he resembles, *TCNT* . . . but resembling the Son of God, *Montgomery.*

abideth a priest continually: . . . remains a priest perpetually, *Adams, Wilson* . . . remains a priest continually, *Wuest* . . . is remaining a priest to a finality, *Concordant* . . . he remains a priest for all time, *TNT* . . . he stays a priest without ending, *Klingensmith* . . . as priest continues on and on with no successor, *Williams.*

4. Now consider how great this man [was]: . . . observe how great was the dignity of this man, *Wade.*

unto whom even the patriarch Abraham gave the tenth of the spoils: . . . the Old Father Abraham gave a tenth of what he captured, *Klingensmith* . . . of all he had taken in the war, *NLT* . . . the best of the booty, *Concordant.*

5. And verily they that are of the sons of Levi: . . . those of the descendants of Levi, *Williams.*

who receive the office of the priesthood: . . . who accept, *Williams.*

have a commandment to take tithes of the people according to the law: . . . are authorized by the Law, *Montgomery* . . . are commanded to exact tenths, *Wade* . . . to collect a tenth from the people, *Williams.*

that is, of their brethren: . . . from other Israelites, *Beck* . . . from their fellow-Israelites, *TNT* . . . from their own brothers, *Williams.*

1498.4 verb 3sing indic pres act	3450.8 art acc pl masc	79.9 noun acc pl masc	840.1 prs-pron gen pl	2510.1 conj	1814.26 verb acc pl masc part perf act
ἔστιν]	τοὺς	ἀδελφοὺς	αὐτῶν,	καίπερ	ἐξεληλυθότας
estin	*tous*	*adelphous*	*autōn*	*kaiper*	*exelēluthotas*
is]	the	brothers	their,	though	having come

1523.2 prep gen	3450.10 art gen sing fem	3613.1 noun gen sing fem	11.1 name masc	3450.5 art nom sing masc	1156.2 conj	3231.1 partic
ἐκ	τῆς	ὀσφύος	Ἀβραάμ·	**6.** ὁ	δὲ	μὴ
ek	*tēs*	*osphuos*	*Abraam*	*ho*	*de*	*mē*
out of	the	loins	of Abraham;	the	but	no

6.a.**Txt:** 02A,06D-corr 018K,020L,025P,byz. Sod
Var: 01ℵ,03B,04C 06D-org,33,Lach,Treg Alf,Tisc,We/Ho,Weis UBS/☆

1068.1 verb nom sing masc part pres mid	1523.1 prep gen	840.1 prs-pron gen pl	1177.1 verb 3sing indic perf act	3450.6 art acc sing masc
γενεαλογούμενος	ἐξ	αὐτῶν	δεδεκάτωκεν	⌜a τὸν ⌝
genealogoumenos	*ex*	*autōn*	*dedekatōken*	*ton*
reckoning genealogy	from	them	has tithed	

11.1 name masc	2504.1 conj	3450.6 art acc sing masc	2174.15 verb part pres act	3450.15 art acc pl fem	1845.1 noun fem
Ἀβραάμ,	καὶ	τὸν	ἔχοντα	τὰς	ἐπαγγελίας
Abraam	*kai*	*ton*	*echonta*	*tas*	*epangelias*
Abraham,	and	the	having	the	promises,

6.b.**Txt:** 01ℵ,03B,06D byz.
Var: 02A,04C,025P,044 81,104,365,1739,1881 2495

2108.10 verb 3sing indic perf act	2108.7 verb 3sing indic aor act	5400.1 prep	1156.2 conj	3820.10 adj gen sing fem
⌜☆ εὐλόγηκεν·	[b εὐλόγησεν·]	**7.** χωρὶς	δὲ	πάσης
eulogēken	*eulogēsen*	*chōris*	*de*	*pasēs*
has blessed.	[blessed.]	Without from	but	any

482.1 noun gen sing fem	3450.16 art sing neu	1629.3 adj comp sing neu	5097.3 prep	3450.2 art gen sing	2882.1 adj comp gen sing
ἀντιλογίας	τὸ	ἔλαττον	ὑπὸ	τοῦ	κρείττονος
antilogias	*to*	*elatton*	*hupo*	*tou*	*kreittonos*
contradiction	the	inferior	by	the	superior

2108.13 verb 3sing indic pres mid	2504.1 conj	5436.1 adv	3173.1 conj	1176.5 num ord acc pl fem	594.7 verb nom pl masc part pres act
εὐλογεῖται.	**8.** καὶ	ὧδε	μὲν	δεκάτας	ἀποθνήσκοντες
eulogeitai	*kai*	*hōde*	*men*	*dekatas*	*apothnēskontes*
is being blessed.	And	here		tithes	dying

442.6 noun nom pl masc	2956.6 verb 3pl indic pres act	1550.1 adv	1156.2 conj	3113.32 verb nom sing masc part pres mid	3617.1 conj
ἄνθρωποι	λαμβάνουσιν·	ἐκεῖ	δέ,	μαρτυρούμενος	ὅτι
anthrōpoi	*lambanousin*	*ekei*	*de*	*marturoumenos*	*hoti*
men	receive;	there	but	being witnessed of	that

2180.1 verb sing indic pres act	2504.1 conj	5453.1 conj	2015.1 noun sing neu	1500.21 verb inf aor act	1217.2 prep	1217.1 prep
ζῇ.	**9.** καὶ	ὡς	ἔπος	εἰπεῖν,	⌜ διὰ	[☆ δι']
zē	*kai*	*hōs*	*epos*	*eipein*	*dia*	*di'*
he lives;	and,	so	a word	to speak,	through	[idem]

9.a.**Txt:** 06D-corr,018K 020L,025P,33,byz.bo. Sod
Var: 02A,UBS/☆

11.1 name masc	2504.1 conj	2991.1 name masc	2992.1 name nom masc	3450.5 art nom sing masc	1176.5 num ord acc pl fem
Ἀβραὰμ	καὶ	⌜ Λευῒ	[a Λευὶς]	ὁ	δεκάτας
Abraam	*kai*	*Leui*	*Leuis*	*ho*	*dekatas*
Abraham,	also	Levi,	[idem]	the	tithes

2956.8 verb nom sing masc part pres act	1177.2 verb 3sing indic perf mid	2068.1 adv	1056.1 conj	1706.1 prep	3450.11 art dat sing fem
λαμβάνων	δεδεκάτωται·	**10.** ἔτι	γὰρ	ἐν	τῇ
lambanōn	*dedekatōtai*	*eti*	*gar*	*en*	*tē*
receiving,	has been tithed.	Yet	for	in	the

Melchizedek, a priest of unknown origin and of an unknown priesthood.

Furthermore, this inscrutable personage possessed the power to issue blessings to Abraham. Genesis 14:19 says, "And he blessed him, and said, Blessed be Abram of the most high God, possessor of heaven and earth." God had made Abraham exceedingly rich. He had just been blessed by God in his attempt to liberate Lot and the possessions of the kings of Sodom and Gomorrah from Chedorla-omer and the kings who were with him. This Abraham was blessed by Melchizedek. Melchizedek must have been very great indeed.

7:7. There is no dispute. The man who receives a blessing is the lesser of the two. The man who does the blessing is greater than the one who is blessed. On the basis of this argument, although Abraham was very great, since Melchizedek blessed Abraham, it logically follows that Melchizedek was the greater of the two.

7:8. This verse contrasts the Old Testament record concerning Melchizedek and the Levitical priests. "Here" refers to the record of the Levitical priests. They were dying men. The Old Testament contains the genealogical records of the Levitical priesthood. One high priest succeeded another, replacing the one who had just died. "There" refers to the record of Melchizedek given in Genesis 14. That record mentions only that he is living; it does not record his death. There is no definite record of his predecessor or of his successor. The Scripture still testifies of this to those who read it (*marturoumenos*).

7:9. Indeed, since Levi was a descendant of Abraham, he in some way could be considered to have paid tithes to Melchizedek. The phrase "as I may so say" does not indicate that the writer of Hebrews was indicating that Levi actually paid tithes to Melchizedek. Only in a nonliteral way of looking at the situation, it could be said that he did so. Abraham was the spiritual and physical progenitor of Levi; in this respect he was greater than Levi. Since Abraham paid a tithe to Melchizedek who was greater than himself, then in a manner of speaking, Melchizedek was greater than Levi.

7:10. The unique line of argument begun in the previous verse is concluded here. Since Levi was seminally descended from Abra-

though they come out of the loins of Abraham: . . . they are Abraham's descendants, *Adams* . . . they have sprung from, *Williams.*

6. But he whose descent is not counted from them: . . . but He whose pedegree is not derived, *Wilson* . . . this man who had no Levitical genealogy, *Montgomery* . . . the man whose ancestry is not traced from them, *Williams* . . . was not a descendant of Levi, *SEB* . . . was outside their line of descent, *Beck.*

received tithes of Abraham: . . . collected a tenth, *Williams* . . . a tenth part from, *TNT.*

and blessed him that had the promises: . . . and put his blessing on the man who had, *Williams.*

7. And without all contradiction: Everyone would agree, *SEB* . . . it is beyond all dispute, *Adams* . . . all controversy, *Montgomery* . . . Unquestionably, *TNT.*

the less is blessed of the better: . . . that a more important person, *SEB* . . . the inferior, *TNT* . . . blessings come down from the superior ones to the inferior, *Norlie* . . . it is the superior who blesses the inferior, *TCNT* . . . by the greater, *Adams.*

8. And here men that die receive tithes: . . . mortal men collect the tenth, *Williams* . . . are receiving the tenth part, *TNT.*

but there he [receiveth them], of whom it is witnessed: . . . it is attested, *Montgomery.*

that he liveth: . . . a man affirmed by Scripture to be still living, *TNT* . . . lives on, *Williams.*

9. And as I may so say: I might almost say, *Williams* . . . Indeed it might be said, *TNT.*

Levi also, who receiveth tithes, payed tithes in Abraham: . . . who now collects the tenth, through Abraham paid the tenth, *Williams* . . . the man who received a tenth part, has paid it, *TNT.*

10. For he was yet in the loins of his father: . . . he was in the body of his ancestor, *Beck* . . . he was a vital part of his forefather though yet unborn, *Williams.*

when Melchisedec met him:

Hebrews 7:11

3613.2 noun dat sing fem	3450.2 art gen sing	3824.2 noun gen sing masc	1498.34 verb sing indic imperf act	3616.1 conj	4727.1 verb 3sing indic aor act
ὀσφύϊ	τοῦ	πατρὸς	ἦν,	ὅτε	συνήντησεν
osphui	*tou*	*patros*	*ēn*	*hote*	*sunēntēsen*
loins	of the	father	he was	when	met

10.a.**Txt:** 02A,04C-corr 06D-corr,018K,020L 025P,byz.Tisc,Sod **Var:** 01ℵ,03B,04C-org 06D-org,Lach,Treg,Alf We/Ho,Weis,UBS/⋆

840.4 prs-pron dat sing	3450.5 art nom sing masc	3168.1 name masc	1479.1 conj	3173.1 conj	3631.1 partic
αὐτῷ	⌜a ὁ ⌝	Μελχισέδεκ.	**11.** Εἰ	μὲν	οὖν
autō	*ho*	*Melchisedek*	*Ei*	*men*	*oun*
him		Melchizedek.	If	indeed	then

4897.1 noun nom sing fem	1217.2 prep	3450.10 art gen sing fem	2994.1 name-adj gen fem	2396.1 noun gen sing fem	1498.34 verb sing indic imperf act
τελείωσις	διὰ	τῆς	Λευϊτικῆς	ἱερωσύνης	ἦν,
teleiōsis	*dia*	*tēs*	*Leuitikēs*	*hierōsunēs*	*ēn*
perfection	by	the	Levitical	priesthood	were,

11.a.**Txt:** 06D-corr,018K byz. **Var:** 01ℵ,02A,03B,04C 06D-org,020L,025P,33 Lach,Treg,Alf,Word Tisc,We/Ho,Weis,Sod UBS/⋆

3450.5 art nom sing masc	2967.1 noun nom sing masc	1056.1 conj	1894.2 prep	840.11 prs-pron dat sing fem	840.10 prs-pron gen sing fem
ὁ	λαὸς	γὰρ	ἐπ'	⌜ αὐτῇ	[a⋆ αὐτῆς]
ho	*laos*	*gar*	*ep'*	*autē*	*autēs*
the	people	for	upon	it	[idem]

11.b.**Txt:** 06D-corr,018K 020L,byz.Sod **Var:** 01ℵ,02A,03B,04C 06D-org,025P,33,Lach Treg,Alf,Word,Tisc We/Ho,Weis,UBS/⋆

3412.2 verb 3sing indic plperf pass	3412.1 verb 3sing indic perf mid	4949.3 intr-pron nom sing	2068.1 adv
⌜ νενομοθέτητο,	[b⋆ νενομοθέτηται,]	τίς	ἔτι
nenomothetēto	*nenomothetētai*	*tis*	*eti*
had received law,	[idem]	what	still

5367.2 noun nom sing fem	2567.3 prep	3450.12 art acc sing fem	4861.2 noun acc sing fem	3168.1 name masc	2066.1 adj sing
χρεία	κατὰ	τὴν	τάξιν	Μελχισέδεκ	ἕτερον
chreia	*kata*	*tēn*	*taxin*	*Melchisedek*	*heteron*
need	according to	the	order	of Melchizedek	another

448.19 verb inf pres mid	2385.3 noun acc sing masc	2504.1 conj	3620.3 partic	2567.3 prep	3450.12 art acc sing fem
ἀνίστασθαι	ἱερέα,	καὶ	οὐ	κατὰ	τὴν
anistasthai	*hierea*	*kai*	*ou*	*kata*	*tēn*
to arise	priest;	and	not	according to	the

4861.2 noun acc sing fem	2.1 name masc	2978.38 verb inf pres mid	3216.4 verb gen sing fem part pres mid	1056.1 conj
τάξιν	Ἀαρὼν	λέγεσθαι;	**12.** μετατιθεμένης	γὰρ
taxin	*Aarōn*	*legesthai*	*metatithemenēs*	*gar*
order	of Aaron	to be named?	Being changed	for

3450.10 art gen sing fem	2396.1 noun gen sing fem	1523.1 prep gen	316.2 noun gen sing fem	2504.1 conj	3414.2 noun gen sing masc
τῆς	ἱερωσύνης,	ἐξ	ἀνάγκης	καὶ	νόμου
tēs	*hierōsunēs*	*ex*	*anankēs*	*kai*	*nomou*
the	priesthood,	from	necessity	also	of law

3201.1 noun nom sing fem	1090.14 verb 3sing indic pres mid	1894.1 prep	3614.6 rel-pron acc sing masc	1056.1 conj
μετάθεσις	γίνεται.	**13.** ἐφ'	ὃν	γὰρ
metathesis	*ginetai*	*eph'*	*hon*	*gar*
a change	takes place.	With respect to	whom	for

2978.28 verb 3sing indic pres mid	3642.18 dem-pron pl neu	5279.1 noun gen sing fem	2066.10 adj gen sing fem	3218.7 verb 3sing indic perf act	570.1 prep
λέγεται	ταῦτα,	φυλῆς	ἑτέρας	μετέσχηκεν,	ἀφ'
legetai	*tauta*	*phulēs*	*heteras*	*meteschēken*	*aph'*
are being said	these things,	a tribe	different	has part in,	of

ham through his son Isaac and his grandson Jacob, Levi was in this manner present and paying tithes with Abraham his great-grandfather.

7:11. At this point the writer began to move from the contrast between Melchizedek and the Levitical priests to the goal of his whole argument: the contrast between the Levitical priesthood and the high priestly accomplishments of Jesus the Son of God. If the Levitical priesthood had been able to effect perfection, there would have been no need "that another priest (Jesus) should rise after the order of Melchizedek." This reasoning assumes that the priesthood needed to be perfect if it was to be efficacious. It also assumes that the Levitical priesthood was imperfect.

Perhaps most important of all to the line of argument, there is the assumption that the Mosaic law and the Levitical priesthood were inextricably linked. If the Aaronic high priests and their ministrations could not bring in the age of perfection and the messianic restoration of Eden's paradise, neither could the statutes, rites, ceremonies, and penalties of the Mosaic code establish a basis for the promised age.

The word *teleiōsis* ("perfection") means the completing or finishing of anything, so nothing imperfect is left and nothing has been omitted. In reference to the Levitical priesthood, it means fulfilling the purpose for which the priesthood was established; that is, providing a system whereby the people could come to God in an acceptable way and find full pardon. This "perfection" the Levitical law could never accomplish.

7:12. Since the Mosaic covenant and its legislation are so closely intertwined with the Levitical priesthood, a change of priesthood (from Levitical to Melchizedekian) also necessitated a change of legal systems. At this point the new legal system or new covenant was not identified. That was held in abeyance until the development of the contrast between the Aaronic priesthood and the priesthood of Melchizedek, exemplified in Jesus Christ. The new covenant was explicitly introduced in 8:6.

7:13. Under the Mosaic covenant the priests were to come from the tribe of Levi and the line of Aaron, but the new High Priest of whom this epistle speaks, Jesus Christ, did not come from the tribe of Levi. Jesus Christ, therefore, is by necessity a Priest under a different system from the one instituted by Moses. Under Moses no one from Judah, Jesus' tribe, was eligible to perform priestly duties at the altars of the temple or tabernacle. Jesus, a new kind of Priest, works under a new system.

11. If therefore perfection were by the Levitical priesthood: . . . the spiritual perfecting of men had been possible through the functions of, *Wade* . . . had been attainable through, *TCNT* . . . had fulfilled its purpose, *TNT* . . . had been reached through, *Williams.*

(for under it the people received the law,): . . . for on it as a basis even the law was enacted for the people, *Williams* . . . was the basis on which a Legal system for the Jewish People was constituted, *Wade* . . . with which the giving of the Law to the people was closely linked, *TNT.*

what further need [was there] that another priest should rise: . . . what...need would there have been for another kind of, *TNT* . . . why did another priest still need to come, *Beck* . . . of appointing a different priest, *Williams.*

after the order of Melchisedec: . . . with the rank of, *Williams.*

and not be called after the order of Aaron?: . . . and for him not to be described as, *TNT* . . . instead of designating one with the rank of, *Williams* . . . rather than to be named after, *Adams* . . . described as having a different rank from, *Wade* . . . after the ordination of, *Klingensmith* . . . instead of through Aaron's priesthood? *SEB.*

12. For the priesthood being changed: When a different person is made priest, *Beck* . . . when a change in the priesthood takes place, *Williams* . . . being transferred, *Concordant.*

there is made of necessity a change also of the law: . . . a change in its law necessarily takes place, *Williams* . . . there should also be a change of the Law, *TNT.*

13. For he of whom these things are spoken: . . . of whom this is said, *Williams.*

pertaineth to another tribe: . . . became a member of, *Williams* . . . are said belonged to a different tribe, *Adams.*

of which no man gave attendance at the altar: . . . from which no one has come to serve at the altar, *TNT* . . . no member of which ever officiated, *Williams* . . . has ever attended as priest, *Wade* . . . could serve, *SEB.*

Hebrews 7:14

13.a.**Txt:** 01ℵ,03B,06D 044,byz.
Var: p46,02A,04C,33,81 1739

3614.10 rel-pron gen sing fem	**3625.2** num card nom masc	**4196.6** verb 3sing indic perf act	**4196.8** verb 3sing indic aor act
ἧς	οὐδεὶς	ʻ☆ προσέσχηκεν	[a προσέσχεν]
hēs	*oudeis*	*proseschēken*	*proseschen*
which	no one	has given attendance	[gave attendance]

3450.3 art dat sing	**2356.3** noun dat sing neu	**4130.2** adj sing neu	**1056.1** conj	**3617.1** conj	**1523.1** prep gen
τῷ	θυσιαστηρίῳ·	**14.** πρόδηλον	γὰρ	ὅτι	ἐξ
tō	*thusiastēriō*	*prodēlon*	*gar*	*hoti*	*ex*
at the	altar.	Clear	for	that	out of

2430.2 name masc	**391.6** verb 3sing indic perf act	**3450.5** art nom sing masc	**2935.1** noun nom sing masc	**2231.2** prs-pron gen 1pl	**1519.1** prep
Ἰούδα	ἀνατέταλκεν	ὁ	κύριος	ἡμῶν,	εἰς
Iouda	*anatetalken*	*ho*	*kurios*	*hēmōn*	*eis*
Judah	has sprung	the	Lord	our,	as to

3614.12 rel-pron acc sing fem	**5279.2** noun acc sing fem	**3625.6** num card neu	**3875.1** prep	**2396.1** noun gen sing fem
ἣν	φυλὴν	ʻ οὐδὲν	περὶ	ἱερωσύνης
hēn	*phulēn*	*ouden*	*peri*	*hierōsunēs*
which	tribe	nothing	concerning	priesthood

14.a.**Txt:** 06D-corr,018K 020L,byz.
Var: 01ℵ-org,02A,03B 04C-org,06D-org,025P 33,Lach,Treg,Alf,Word Tisc,We/Ho,Weis,Sod UBS/☆

3875.1 prep	**2385.5** noun gen pl masc	**3625.6** num card neu	**3337.1** name nom masc	**3338.1** name nom masc
[a☆ περὶ	ἱερέων	οὐδὲν]	ʻ Μωσῆς	[☆ Μωϋσῆς]
peri	*hiereōn*	*ouden*	*Mōsēs*	*Mōusēs*
[concerning	priesthood	nothing]	Moses	[idem]

2953.27 verb 3sing indic aor act	**2504.1** conj	**3917.3** adv comp	**2068.1** adv	**2583.1** adj sing neu
ἐλάλησεν.	**15.** Καὶ	περισσότερον	ἔτι	κατάδηλόν
elalēsen	*Kai*	*perissoteron*	*eti*	*katadēlon*
spoke.	And	more abundantly	yet	quite obvious

1498.4 verb 3sing indic pres act	**1479.1** conj	**2567.3** prep	**3450.12** art acc sing fem	**3528.1** noun acc sing fem
ἐστιν,	εἰ	κατὰ	τὴν	ὁμοιότητα
estin	*ei*	*kata*	*tēn*	*homoiotēta*
it is,	since	according to	the	similarity

3168.1 name masc	**448.17** verb 3sing indic pres mid	**2385.1** noun nom sing masc	**2066.5** adj nom sing masc	**3614.5** rel-pron nom sing masc
Μελχισέδεκ	ἀνίσταται	ἱερεὺς	ἕτερος,	**16.** ὃς
Melchisedek	*anistatai*	*hiereus*	*heteros*	*hos*
of Melchizedek	arises	a priest	different,	who

16.a.**Txt:** 04C-corr 06D-corr,018K,byz.
Var: 01ℵ,02A,03B 04C-org,06D-org,020L 025P,33,Lach,Treg,Alf Word,Tisc,We/Ho,Weis Sod,UBS/☆

3620.3 partic	**2567.3** prep	**3414.4** noun acc sing masc	**1769.2** noun gen sing fem	**4416.4** adj gen sing fem
οὐ	κατὰ	νόμον	ἐντολῆς	ʻ σαρκικῆς
ou	*kata*	*nomon*	*entolēs*	*sarkikēs*
not	according to	law	of commandment	fleshly

4417.4 adj gen sing fem	**1090.3** verb 3sing indic perf act	**233.2** conj	**2567.3** prep	**1405.4** noun acc sing fem
[a☆ σαρκίνης]	γέγονεν,	ἀλλὰ	κατὰ	δύναμιν
sarkinēs	*gegonen*	*alla*	*kata*	*dunamin*
[idem]	has become,	but	according to	power

17.a.**Txt:** 04C,06D-corr 018K,020L,byz.
Var: 01ℵ,02A,03B 06D-org,025P,33,sa.bo. Lach,Treg,Alf,Word Tisc,We/Ho,Weis,Sod UBS/☆

2205.2 noun gen sing fem	**177.1** adj gen sing fem	**3113.3** verb 3sing indic pres act	**3113.41** verb 3sing indic pres mid
ζωῆς	ἀκαταλύτου·	**17.** ʻ μαρτυρεῖ	[a☆ μαρτυρεῖται]
zōēs	*akatalutou*	*marturei*	*martureitai*
of life	indestructible	He testifies	[It is being testified]

7:14. The evidence provided by the genealogy of Jesus in both Matthew and Luke traces His human ancestry back to the house of Judah on both the side of Joseph and His mother, Mary. It demonstrates that He is a legitimate claimant to the throne of David and that He is qualified by birth to be the Messiah. At the same time, however, that human genealogy disqualified Him from any possibility of serving as a priest in the Jewish temple. That was the right of Levites.

7:15. Beyond the silence of the Mosaic legislation in regard to a priestly Messiah or a royal priesthood out of the descendants of Judah, there is something even more evident. It was so plain that it had been noticed and had led to some of the speculation noted earlier (7:1). There were some Jews among the Essenes of Qumran and elsewhere who understood some of the messianic implications of Psalm 110. For they did expect some kind of an angelic Melchizedek to appear and deliver the holy Jewish remnant at the end of the age. Of him it is written, "And Melkizedek will avenge the vengeance of the judgments of God" (G. Vermes, p.267). In the *Testaments of the Twelve Patriarchs* 18:2, Levi predicts "then the Lord will raise up a new priest." Psalm 110:4 speaks of the Messiah as a priest like Melchizedek, but on the basis of the Mosaic law the Jews had not been able to understand how Messiah could be both King and Priest. Hebrews 7 shows how Jesus can be both.

7:16. In this verse the inspired writer described the other (*heteros*) priest, i.e., another of a different type. This new priest's elevation to the priesthood was according to the statutes of another kind of law. Strong emphasis is placed on the permanency and current efficacy of this new priest. First of all, the verb "who is made" translates the Greek word *gegonen* which by its tense refers to a past action that has results enduring to the time of the writing. Through His incarnation and suffering Christ became a Priest and He remains a Priest. The Levitical priests under the Mosaic law were determined according to *sarkikēs*, a term which relates to the flesh. Here it is used not in reference to the sin nature but in regard to the fact that Aaronic priests were determined by their descent. There is the implication that the priesthood passed from one generation to another. Levitical priests died and were succeeded by their descendants. The "new priest," however, exists not by commandment but by power. And what a power it is: the power not of death and succession, but "the power of an endless life." Not just any life, but life which is *akatalutou*, life which cannot be dissolved. He lives forever!

7:17. The proof adduced for the eternal life of this "new priest" was taken from Psalm 110:4. The Lord himself had said that the

14. For [it is] evident that our Lord sprang out of Judah: For it is taken for granted that, *Concordant* . . . for it is very plain, *Wilson* . . . it is quite clear that our Lord descended from, *TNT.*

of which tribe Moses spake nothing concerning priesthood: Moses said nothing about priests in connection with this tribe, *TNT.*

15. And it is yet far more evident: The matter is, *TNT* . . . still more superabundantly sure, *Concordant* . . . yet more abundantly clear, *Montgomery* . . . it becomes even plainer, *SEB* . . . That point is much clearer still, *Beck* . . . it is still more overwhelmingly clear, *Williams* . . . appears still more manifest, *Wade.*

for that after the similitude of Melchisedec: . . . one analogous to, *Wade* . . . in the likeness of, *Williams.*

there ariseth another priest: . . . different type, *Wade* . . . another kind of priest...arises, *TNT.*

16. Who is made: . . . is appointed, *Williams.*

not after the law of a carnal commandment: . . . not appointed according to a Law, *Beck* . . . of a transitory enactment, *Montgomery* . . . does not depend on a system of earthly commandments, *TNT* . . . not on the basis of a physical qualification, *Williams* . . . not because of human rules and laws, *SEB* . . . that required fleshly qualifications, *Adams* . . . of a fleshy precept, *Concordant.*

but after the power of an endless life: . . . but rather according to the power of an indestructible life, *Adams* . . . according to the energy of an indissoluble life, *Montgomery* . . . flowing from a life that cannot end, *Williams* . . . but by the power of a life that cannot be destroyed, *SEB* . . . a life that nothing can destroy, *TNT* . . . of immortal life, *Norlie* . . . of an imperishable Life, *Wilson.*

17. For he testifieth: For the Psalmist testifies, *Norlie* . . . For the Scripture bears witness, *Williams* . . . for Scripture affirms, *TNT* . . . for his possession of this is evidenced by the statement, *Wade.*

1056.1 conj	**3617.1** conj	**4622.1** prs-pron nom 2sing	**2385.1** noun nom sing masc	**1519.1** prep	**3450.6** art acc sing masc	**163.3** noun acc sing masc
γὰρ,	Ὅτι	Σὺ	ἱερεὺς	εἰς	τὸν	αἰῶνα
gar	*Hoti*	*Su*	*hiereus*	*eis*	*ton*	*aiōna*
for,		You	a priest	for	the	age

2567.3 prep	**3450.12** art acc sing fem	**4861.2** noun acc sing fem	**3168.1** name masc	**115.1** noun nom sing fem
κατὰ	τὴν	τάξιν	Μελχισέδεκ.	**18.** Ἀθέτησις
kata	*tēn*	*taxin*	*Melchisedek*	*Athetēsis*
after	the	order	of Melchizedek.	A putting away

3173.1 conj	**1056.1** conj	**1090.14** verb 3sing indic pres mid	**4113.5** verb gen sing fem part pres act	**1769.2** noun gen sing fem
μὲν	γὰρ	γίνεται	προαγούσης	ἐντολῆς,
men	*gar*	*ginetai*	*proagousēs*	*entolēs*
	for	there is	of the going before	commandment,

1217.2 prep	**3450.16** art sing neu	**840.10** prs-pron gen sing fem	**766.7** adj sing neu	**2504.1** conj
διὰ	τὸ	αὐτῆς	ἀσθενὲς	καὶ
dia	*to*	*autēs*	*asthenes*	*kai*
because of	the	its	weakness	and

508.2 adj sing neu	**3625.6** num card neu	**1056.1** conj	**4896.2** verb 3sing indic aor act	**3450.5** art nom sing masc
ἀνωφελές,	**19.** οὐδὲν	γὰρ	ἐτελείωσεν	ὁ
anōpheles	*ouden*	*gar*	*eteleiōsen*	*ho*
unprofitableness,	nothing	for	perfected	the

3414.1 noun nom sing masc	**1883.1** noun nom sing fem	**1156.2** conj	**2882.1** adj comp gen sing	**1667.2** noun gen sing fem	**1217.1** prep
νόμος,	ἐπεισαγωγὴ	δὲ	κρείττονος	ἐλπίδος,	δι'
nomos	*epeisagōgē*	*de*	*kreittonos*	*elpidos*	*di'*
law,	introduction	and	of a better	hope	by

3614.10 rel-pron gen sing fem	**1443.1** verb 1pl indic pres act	**3450.3** art dat sing	**2296.3** noun dat sing masc	**2504.1** conj	**2567.2** prep
ἧς	ἐγγίζομεν	τῷ	θεῷ.	**20.** Καὶ	καθ'
hēs	*engizomen*	*tō*	*theō*	*Kai*	*kath'*
which	we draw near		to God.	And	by

3607.1 rel-pron sing	**3620.3** partic	**5400.1** prep	**3591.1** noun gen sing fem	**3450.7** art nom pl masc
ὅσον	οὐ	χωρὶς	ὁρκωμοσίας·	οἱ
hoson	*ou*	*chōris*	*horkōmosias*	*hoi*
how much	not	apart from	swearing of an oath,	the

3173.1 conj	**1056.1** conj	**5400.1** prep	**3591.1** noun gen sing fem	**1498.7** verb 3pl indic pres act	**2385.4** noun pl masc
μὲν	γὰρ,	χωρὶς	ὁρκωμοσίας	εἰσὶν	ἱερεῖς
men	*gar*	*chōris*	*horkōmosias*	*eisin*	*hiereis*
	for	without	swearing of an oath	are	priests

1090.8 verb nom pl masc part perf act	**3450.5** art nom sing masc	**1156.2** conj	**3196.3** prep	**3591.1** noun gen sing fem
γεγονότες,	**21.** ὁ	δὲ	μετὰ	ὁρκωμοσίας,
gegonotes	*ho*	*de*	*meta*	*horkōmosias*
having become,	the	but	with	swearing of an oath,

1217.2 prep	**3450.2** art gen sing	**2978.14** verb gen sing part pres act	**4242.1** prep	**840.6** prs-pron acc sing masc	**3523.6** verb 3sing indic aor act
διὰ	τοῦ	λέγοντος	πρὸς	αὐτόν,	Ὤμοσεν
dia	*tou*	*legontos*	*pros*	*auton*	*Ōmosen*
by	the	saying,	as to	him,	swore

Messiah is eternally a priest of the Melchizedekian order. For all who trust the Lord, His Word settles the issue. No further proof is needed.

Thou [art] a priest for ever after the order of Melchisedec: . . . with the rank of, *Williams.*

7:18. This verse begins a contrast which is completed in verse 19. A contrast is made between the ineffectiveness of the Law and the hope offered by the new covenant (7:22). On the one hand, the previous commandment, i.e., the one "going before," is canceled. The term *athetēsis* is found frequently in the legal papyri of the New Testament period. It refers to cancellation or annulment of contracts for various causes. Often it is associated with inefficiency, inability, and unfitness. In this verse it refers to the just mentioned weakness of the dying Levitical priests. Their humanity made them inadequate.

18. For there is verily a disannulling of the commandment going before: The old rule was done away with, *SEB* . . . The earlier rule is canceled, *Beck* . . . For indeed an Abrogation of the Preceding Commandment, *Wilson* . . . of a prior Code of commands, *Wade* . . . the rescinding of a previous regulation, *Williams* . . . The previous commandment has been set aside, *TNT* . . . a former commandment is set aside, *Adams* . . . there is coming to be a repudiation of the preceding precept, *Concordant* . . . there is a setting aside, *Montgomery.*

for the weakness and unprofitableness thereof: . . . because it was weak and ineffective, *Norlie, Williams* . . . because of its ...futility, *Wade.*

7:19. "The law made nothing perfect" is a startling statement. It could not remedy the consequences of Adam's fall. It could not eradicate sin, conquer death, or cleanse consciences from moral guilt before the Lord. It could provoke sin, reveal it, and condemn it. It could deal with sin only in an external ceremonial way, but it was powerless to overcome sin and its results. Its priests entered into an earthly sanctuary once a year, but they died eventually because of sin's unbroken sway. Jesus, the new, undying Priest of the Melchizedekian order, however, brought in a much better hope—a hope by which believers are now actually drawing near to God himself. Through the Son Christians are able daily and continuously to enter into the very presence of God.

19. For the law made nothing perfect: . . . the Law completely failed to fulfill its purpose, *TNT* . . . brought nothing to spiritual perfection, *Wade.*

but the bringing in of a better hope [did]: . . . is brought to us, *Williams* . . . the introduction of, *Wade.*

by the which we draw nigh unto God: . . . in the strength of which, *Wade* . . . through which we have approach to God, *Williams* . . . it brings us close to God, *Beck.*

7:20. As with God's promise to Abraham (6:13), this new priesthood is doubly certified because it was established by an oath. The value of an oath depends on the character of the one making it. Since the maker of this covenant was God, who is completely holy and righteous, the oath is sure.

20. And inasmuch as not without an oath [he was made priest]: . . . by so much as He was not appointed without God's taking an oath, *Williams.*

21. (For those priests were made without an oath: . . . were appointed, *Williams.*

but this with an oath by him that said unto him: He became a priest with an oath, through the One who says to him, *TNT.*

The Lord sware and will not repent: . . . took oath, *Williams* . . . He will never change it, *SEB* . . . and will not change His mind, *Adams, Wuest* . . . will not change His decision, *Wade* . . . will not be regretting it, *Concordant* . . . and will never be sorry for it, *Klingensmith* . . . and he will not go back on his word, *TNT.*

7:21. For the first time the writer cited all of Psalm 110:4, revealing that the Melchizedekian priesthood of the Messiah was established by a divine oath. The implication seems to be the same as the argument articulated previously in his presentation of the Abrahamic covenant (6:13-20). God himself has singled out the importance of the Melchizedekian order by underscoring its establishment with an oath. He did not do this when He established the Levitical priesthood.

Hebrews 7:22

21.a.**Txt:** 01ℵ-corr,02A 06D,018K,020L,025P byz.bo.
Var: 01ℵ-org,02A,04C 33,sa.Treg,Alf,Tisc We/Ho,Weis,Sod UBS/☆

22.a.**Txt:** 01ℵ-corr 06D-corr,018K,020L byz.
Var: 01ℵ-org,02A,03B 04C,06D-org,025P,33 Lach,Treg,Alf,Word Tisc,We/Ho,Weis,Sod UBS/☆

22.b.**Var:** 01ℵ-org,03B 04C-org,Alf,Tisc,We/Ho Weis,UBS/☆

2935.1 noun nom sing masc	**2504.1** conj	**3620.3** partic	**3208.4** verb 3sing indic fut pass	**4622.1** prs-pron nom 2sing	**2385.1** noun nom sing masc
κύριος	καὶ	οὐ	μεταμεληθήσεται,	Σὺ	ἱερεὺς
kurios	*kai*	*ou*	*metamelēthēsetai*	*Su*	*hiereus*
Lord,	and	not	will change mind,	You	a priest

1519.1 prep	**3450.6** art acc sing masc	**163.3** noun acc sing masc	**2567.3** prep	**3450.12** art acc sing fem	**4861.2** noun acc sing fem
εἰς	τὸν	αἰῶνα	⸀a κατὰ	τὴν	τάξιν
eis	*ton*	*aiōna*	*kata*	*tēn*	*taxin*
for	the	age	according to	the	order

3168.1 name masc	**2567.3** prep	**4965.1** dem-pron acc sing	**4965.10** dem-pron sing neu
Μελχισεδέκ·⸁	22. κατὰ	⸀ τοσοῦτον	[a☆ τοσοῦτο]
Melchisedek	*kata*	*tosouton*	*tosouto*
of Melchizedek,	by	so much	[idem]

2504.1 conj	**2882.1** adj comp gen sing	**1236.2** noun gen sing fem	**1090.3** verb 3sing indic perf act	**1444.1** adj nom sing masc
[b☆+ καὶ]	κρείττονος	διαθήκης	γέγονεν	ἔγγυος
kai	*kreittonos*	*diathēkēs*	*gegonen*	*enguos*
[even]	of a better	covenant	has become	surety

2400.1 name nom masc	**2504.1** conj	**3450.7** art nom pl masc	**3173.1** conj	**3979.5** adj comp nom pl masc	**1498.7** verb 3pl indic pres act
Ἰησοῦς.	23. Καὶ	οἱ	μὲν	πλείονές	εἰσιν
Iēsous	*Kai*	*hoi*	*men*	*pleiones*	*eisin*
Jesus.	And	the		many	are

1090.8 verb nom pl masc part perf act	**2385.4** noun pl masc	**1217.2** prep	**3450.16** art sing neu	**2265.3** noun dat sing masc
γεγονότες	ἱερεῖς	διὰ	τὸ	θανάτῳ
gegonotes	*hiereis*	*dia*	*to*	*thanatō*
having become	priests	on account of	the	by death

2940.11 verb inf pres mid	**3748.1** verb inf pres act	**3450.5** art nom sing masc	**1156.2** conj	**1217.2** prep
κωλύεσθαι	παραμένειν·	24. ὁ	δὲ,	διὰ
kōluesthai	*paramenein*	*ho*	*de*	*dia*
to be hindered from	to continue;	the	but,	because of

3450.16 art sing neu	**3176.15** verb inf pres act	**840.6** prs-pron acc sing masc	**1519.1** prep	**3450.6** art acc sing masc	**163.3** noun acc sing masc
τὸ	μένειν	αὐτὸν	εἰς	τὸν	αἰῶνα,
to	*menein*	*auton*	*eis*	*ton*	*aiōna*
the	to abide	his	for	the	age,

527.1 adj acc sing fem	**2174.4** verb 3sing indic pres act	**3450.12** art acc sing fem	**2396.2** noun acc sing fem	**3468.1** adv
ἀπαράβατον	ἔχει	τὴν	ἱερωσύνην·	25. ὅθεν
aparabaton	*echei*	*tēn*	*hierōsunēn*	*hothen*
without end	has	the	priesthood.	Hence

2504.1 conj	**4834.3** verb inf pres act	**1519.1** prep	**3450.16** art sing neu	**3700.1** adj sing neu	**1404.4** verb 3sing indic pres mid
καὶ	σῴζειν	εἰς	τὸ	παντελὲς	δύναται
kai	*sōzein*	*eis*	*to*	*panteles*	*dunatai*
also	to save	to	the	entire	he is able

3450.8 art acc pl masc	**4193.16** verb acc pl masc part pres mid	**1217.1** prep	**840.3** prs-pron gen sing	**3450.3** art dat sing
τοὺς	προσερχομένους	δι'	αὐτοῦ	τῷ
tous	*proserchomenous*	*di'*	*autou*	*tō*
the	approaching	by	him	

7:22. This verse gives the name of this undying, oath-established Priest—Jesus (last named in 6:20). The emphasis upon this identification is inescapable. Literally, the word order of the verse is: "In proportion to the degree that this is a better covenant, He is become a guarantee, Jesus" (author's translation). The term "surety" (*enguos*) speaks of a bond for bail or a marriage dowry. The certainty of the efficacy of the new and better covenant is linked to the superiority of the new covenant, which in turn is inherent in the nature of the Son, Jesus. Everything He touches is better: His name and inheritance (1:4); the hope which He offers (7:7); the covenant which He established (7:22); the sacrifices which He offers (9:23); and the benefits which He brings (10:34; 11:16,35,40; 12:24).

7:23. This verse begins to spell out the things implied by *sarkikēs* in verse 16. The one undying Priest, Jesus, is superior to the many dying priests of the Levitical order. Because they were mortal, there were continual changes in the priesthood. Because Jesus is alive forevermore, His priesthood is an unchanging one.

7:24. Although Jesus died, He did not remain dead. He lives. His priesthood is a permanent priesthood. Because of His indissoluble life (7:16), His ministry remains *aparabaton*. This term may have both meanings in view: Jesus' priesthood is both unchangeable and nontransferable because He himself is eternal.

7:25. At this point the writer emphasized the staggering relevance of Jesus' eternal priesthood. Since Jesus is alive forever, He is able to function as the believers' Priest eternally. His chief purpose as Priest is summed up by the word *entunchanein*. This term means that Jesus meets with God the Father in order to represent believers and to ask Him to act graciously on their behalf. As a living, eternal Priest He intercedes for believers. The power of His indissoluble life enables Him to keep on delivering those who are His because, unlike the priests who stopped functioning at death, His ministry continues on.

The phrase "to the uttermost" translates *eis to panteles*. This phrase could be rendered by the English word *finally*. It includes the idea of completeness and totality, but it also has connotations of time. The deliverance effected by Jesus' intercession is both thorough and final. At the end of time the believer's salvation will be total. None of a Christian's needs are beyond the scope of His deliverance. But the inspired writer was careful to maintain a proper perspective on the necessity of faith. Deliverance is for those who keep on coming to God through Jesus alone.

Thou [art] a priest for ever after the order of Melchisedec:):

22. By so much: . . . this implies that, *Wade.*

was Jesus made a surety of a better testament: This makes Jesus a guarantee of, *Norlie* . . . the Covenant for which Jesus has become Surety, *Wade* . . . become the guarantee of a better covenant, *Adams, Williams* . . . has Jesus become a Pledge, *Wilson* . . . become the sponsor of a better covenant, *Concordant.*

23. And they truly were many priests: There is another point, *TNT* . . . there was a succession of priests, *Norlie* . . . Many priests were needed to continue the line, *SEB* . . . have become numerous, *Williams.*

because they were not suffered to continue by reason of death: . . . they have been prevented by death from continuing, *Montgomery, Williams* . . . for death stopped them from staying on, *Norlie* . . . on account of being hindered by Death, *Wilson* . . . from remaining in office, *TNT.*

24. But this [man], because he continueth ever: . . . in consequence of His continuing to exist for ever, *Wade.*

hath an unchangeable priesthood: . . . holds his priesthood inviolable, *Montgomery* . . . has an inviolate priesthood, *Concordant* . . . he has a priesthood which cannot pass to another, *TNT* . . . because He Himself lives on forever, *Williams* . . . He never passes on his priestly work to others, *SEB* . . . which is untransferable, *Wuest.*

25. Wherefore he is able also to save them to the uttermost: . . . and hence, *Wade* . . . he is also able for all time, *TNT* . . . makes Him able to save completely, *Adams* . . . any and all, *Williams.*

that come unto God by him: . . . who approach God, *Norlie.*

seeing he ever liveth to make intercession for them: . . . because he is alive always to turn to God on their behalf, *TNT* . . . He lives forever to pray for them, *NLT* . . . to intercede for them, *Montgomery* . . . to interpose on their behalf, *Wilson.*

Hebrews 7:26

2296.3 noun	3704.1	2180.10 verb	1519.1	3450.16 art	1777.2 verb
dat sing masc	adv	sing part pres act	prep	sing neu	inf pres act
θεῷ,	πάντοτε	ζῶν	εἰς	τὸ	ἐντυγχάνειν
theō	*pantote*	*zōn*	*eis*	*to*	*entunchanein*
to God,	always	living	for	the	to intercede

26.a.**Var:** 02A,03B,06D Lach,Treg,Alf,Word Tisc,We/Ho,Weis,Sod UBS/☆

5065.1	840.1 prs-	4955.4 dem-pron	1056.1	2231.3 prs-	2504.1
prep	pron gen pl	nom sing masc	conj	pron dat 1pl	conj
ὑπὲρ	αὐτῶν.	**26.** Τοιοῦτος	γὰρ	ἡμῖν	[a☆+ καὶ]
huper	*autōn*	*Toioutos*	*gar*	*hēmin*	*kai*
for	them.	Such	for	us	[also]

4100.3 verb 3sing	744.1 noun	3603.1 adj	170.1 adj	281.1 adj
indic imperf act	nom sing masc	nom sing masc	nom sing masc	nom sing
ἔπρεπεν	ἀρχιερεύς,	ὅσιος,	ἄκακος,	ἀμίαντος,
eprepen	*archiereus*	*hosios*	*akakos*	*amiantos*
became	a high priest,	holy,	without evil,	undefiled,

5398.11 verb nom sing	570.3	3450.1	266.5 adj	2504.1
masc part perf mid	prep	art gen pl	gen pl masc	conj
κεχωρισμένος	ἀπὸ	τῶν	ἁμαρτωλῶν,	καὶ
kechōrismenos	*apo*	*tōn*	*hamartōlōn*	*kai*
having been separated	from	the	sinners,	and

5146.5 adj comp	3450.1	3636.7 noun	1090.53 verb nom	3614.5 rel-pron
nom sing masc	art gen pl	gen pl masc	sing masc part aor mid	nom sing masc
ὑψηλότερος	τῶν	οὐρανῶν	γενόμενος·	**27.** ὃς
hupsēloteros	*tōn*	*ouranōn*	*genomenos*	*hos*
higher	than the	heavens	having become:	who

3620.2	2174.4 verb 3sing	2567.2	2232.4 noun	316.4 noun	5450.1	3450.7 art
partic	indic pres act	prep	acc sing fem	acc sing fem	conj	nom pl masc
οὐκ	ἔχει	καθ'	ἡμέραν	ἀνάγκην,	ὥσπερ	οἱ
ouk	*echei*	*kath'*	*hēmeran*	*anankēn*	*hōsper*	*hoi*
not	has	by	day	necessity,	as	the

744.5 noun	4245.2 adj	5065.1	3450.1	2375.1	264.6 noun
pl masc	comp sing neu	prep	art gen pl	adj gen pl	gen pl fem
ἀρχιερεῖς,	πρότερον	ὑπὲρ	τῶν	ἰδίων	ἁμαρτιῶν
archiereis	*proteron*	*huper*	*tōn*	*idiōn*	*hamartiōn*
high priests,	first	for	the	his own	sins

2355.1	397.3 verb	1884.1	3450.1	3450.2 art	2967.2 noun	3642.17 dem-
noun fem	inf pres act	adv	art gen pl	gen sing	gen sing masc	pron sing neu
θυσίας	ἀναφέρειν,	ἔπειτα	τῶν	τοῦ	λαοῦ·	τοῦτο
thusias	*anapherein*	*epeita*	*tōn*	*tou*	*laou*	*touto*
sacrifices	to offer up,	then	for the	of the	people;	this

1056.1	4020.24 verb 3sing	2160.1	1431.6 prs-pron	397.5 verb nom sing
conj	indic aor act	adv	acc sing masc	masc part aor act
γὰρ	ἐποίησεν	ἐφάπαξ	ἑαυτὸν	⸀☆ ἀνενέγκας.
gar	*epoiēsen*	*ephapax*	*heauton*	*anenenkas*
for	he did	once for all,	himself	having offered up.

27.a.**Txt:** p46,03B,04C 06D,08E,018K,020L 025P,044,byz. **Var:** 01ℵ,02A,016I,33 365,Tisc

4232.17 verb nom	3450.5 art	3414.1 noun	1056.1	442.9 noun
sing masc part aor act	nom sing masc	nom sing masc	conj	acc pl masc
[a προσενέγκας]	**28.** ὁ	νόμος	γὰρ	ἀνθρώπους
prosenenkas	*ho*	*nomos*	*gar*	*anthrōpous*
[idem]	The	law	for	men

2497.1 verb 3sing	744.5 noun	2174.21 verb acc pl	763.4 noun	3450.5 art
indic pres act	pl masc	masc part pres act	acc sing fem	nom sing masc
καθίστησιν	ἀρχιερεῖς	ἔχοντας	ἀσθένειαν·	ὁ
kathistēsin	*archiereis*	*echontas*	*astheneian*	*ho*
constitutes	high priests,	have	weakness;	the

7:26. Verse 26 continues to summarize the superiority of Jesus as a Melchizedekian High Priest. It is fitting for Christians to have a High Priest with such qualifications. Unlike the Levitical priests, He is holy, sinless, and innocent in His own person. In His relationships with others, He is perfect. In His humanity He was unlike other men because He is sinless. He has moral perfection. Exalted, He ministers in heaven.

7:27. Unlike the Levitical priests, Jesus does not have to offer sacrifices for His own sins. His sinless perfection eliminates any need for atonement for himself. But there is something more important. The power of His indissoluble life renders His sacrificial death for others far more efficacious than any of the animal sacrifices offered by Aaronic priests. They offered sacrifices for themselves and their people day after day. Jesus had to offer himself only once.

7:28. The Mosaic law established priests with sinful weaknesses, but the divine oath of Psalm 110:4, which came after the Mosaic covenant, established the Son as an eternal Priest. Seated at the right hand of God and addressed as Son, His priesthood is perfect—without limits. This is the One to whom we can come with our needs, knowing He is completely able to provide help.

Jesus' intercession for believers can be aptly illustrated by an incident from antiquity. In classical Greece in a certain city state there were two brothers. They were as different as night is from day. Amyntas was the hero of the city. He had led them to victory in battle. He had defended them at the jeopardy of his own life. His brother Aeschylus was a ne'er-do-well and a blackguard. Aeschylus' double-dealing and treacherous ways caught up with him. He was brought to trial before the assembly of citizens. The evidence against him was both overwhelming and undisputed. There was no doubt: Aeschylus was guilty of treason. He would be banished from the presence of the citizenry and his family forever.

The laws, however, entitled him to a defense, and he had chosen his brother Amyntas for his advocate. The prosecution rested its case, and it was time for Amyntas to defend Aeschylus. Every eye was upon him as he took his place on the stage in the center of the town's amphitheater. What would he say? What could he say in defense of his guilty brother? He said nothing. As all the citizens anxiously waited, Amyntas withdrew his right arm from his cloak and slowly raised its scarred stump for all to see, reminding them of the price he had paid in defense of their freedom. When he returned to his seat, the citizenry, stunned and stirred, acquitted Aeschylus. So it is when Jesus pleads the believer's cause. His very life intercedes. It is Christ, crucified and risen, who makes intercession.

26. For such an high priest became us: This was the High Priest we needed, *TCNT* . . . Such was the divine High priest we needed, *Noli* . . . We needed just such a High Priest, *Norlie* . . . A high priest of such a kind does indeed meet our need, *TNT* . . . was appropriate to our needs and conditions, *Wade.*

[who is] holy, harmless, undefiled: . . . innocent, unstained, *Adams, Williams* . . . saintly, *Wade* . . . immaculate, *Noli.*

separate from sinners: . . . sinless, *Noli* . . . sundered from the sinful, *Wade* . . . is different from sinful men, *NLT* . . . far removed from sinful men, *Williams.*

and made higher than the heavens: . . . raised higher than, *Norlie* . . . and exalted above the heavens, *Montgomery* . . . and elevated far above the very heavens, *Williams.*

27. Who needeth not daily, as those high priests: . . . has no need, like those human high priests, *Noli* . . . is not daily under the necessity, *Wade* . . . as did the Levitical priests, *Williams.*

to offer up sacrifice, first for his own sins: . . . offer sacrifices daily, *TNT.*

and then for the people's: . . . and next for those of, *Wade.*

for this he did once, when he offered up himself: For this sacrifice was made once for all, *Montgomery* . . . this latter is just what He did once for all, *Williams* . . . He made one sacrifice for all mankind, *Noli* . . . for all time, *SEB.*

28. For the law maketh men high priests which have infirmity: . . . appoints to the high priesthood men full of imperfections, *Noli* . . . men high priests who have weakness, *Adams* . . . human beings subject to weakness, *TNT* . . . men who are subject to moral and physical infirmity, *Wade* . . . these men are not perfect, *SEB.*

but the word of the oath, which was since the law: . . . but the assertion about the taking of an oath, which was spoken after the time of the law, *Williams* . . . the declaration in God's oathtaking, which occurred later than the Law, *Wade* . . . which came later than the Law, *TNT.*

Hebrews 8:1

3030.1 noun nom sing masc	**1156.2** conj	**3450.10** art gen sing fem	**3591.1** noun gen sing fem	**3450.10** art gen sing fem	**3196.3** prep
λόγος	δὲ	τῆς	ὁρκωμοσίας	τῆς	μετὰ
logos	*de*	*tēs*	*horkōmosias*	*tēs*	*meta*
word	but	of the	swearing of the oath,	the	after

3450.6 art acc sing masc	**3414.4** noun acc sing masc	**5048.4** noun acc sing masc	**1519.1** prep	**3450.6** art acc sing masc	**163.3** noun acc sing masc
τὸν	νόμον,	υἱὸν	εἰς	τὸν	αἰῶνα
ton	*nomon*	*huion*	*eis*	*ton*	*aiōna*
the	law,	a Son	for	the	age

4896.15 verb acc sing masc part perf mid	**2745.1** noun sing neu	**1156.2** conj	**1894.3** prep	**3450.4** art dat pl
τετελειωμένον.	**8:1.** Κεφάλαιον	δὲ	ἐπὶ	τοῖς
teteleiōmenon	*Kephalaion*	*de*	*epi*	*tois*
having been perfected.	A summary	now	of	the things

2978.36 verb dat pl neu part pres mid	**4955.2** dem-pron sing	**2174.5** verb 1pl indic pres act	**744.4** noun acc sing masc	**3614.5** rel-pron nom sing masc
λεγομένοις,	τοιοῦτον	ἔχομεν	ἀρχιερέα,	ὃς
legomenois	*toiouton*	*echomen*	*archierea*	*hos*
being spoken of,	such	we have	a high priest,	who

2495.3 verb 3sing indic aor act	**1706.1** prep	**1182.5** adj dat sing fem	**3450.2** art gen sing	**2339.2** noun gen sing masc	**3450.10** art gen sing fem
ἐκάθισεν	ἐν	δεξιᾷ	τοῦ	θρόνου	τῆς
ekathisen	*en*	*dexia*	*tou*	*thronou*	*tēs*
sat down	on	right hand	of the	throne	of the

3142.2 noun gen sing fem	**1706.1** prep	**3450.4** art dat pl	**3636.8** noun dat pl masc	**3450.1** art gen pl	**39.4** adj gen pl
μεγαλωσύνης	ἐν	τοῖς	οὐρανοῖς,	**2.** τῶν	ἁγίων
megalōsunēs	*en*	*tois*	*ouranois*	*tōn*	*hagiōn*
greatness	in	the	heavens;	of the	holies

2985.1 noun nom sing masc	**2504.1** conj	**3450.10** art gen sing fem	**4488.2** noun gen sing fem	**3450.10** art gen sing fem	**226.6** adj gen sing fem
λειτουργὸς,	καὶ	τῆς	σκηνῆς	τῆς	ἀληθινῆς,
leitourgos	*kai*	*tēs*	*skēnēs*	*tēs*	*alēthinēs*
minister,	and	of the	tabernacle	the	true

2.a.**Txt:** 02A,06D-corr 018K,020L,025P,byz. Sod
Var: 01ℵ,03B,06D-org 33,Lach,Treg,Alf,Word Tisc,We/Ho,Weis UBS/*

3614.12 rel-pron acc sing fem	**3939.1** verb 3sing indic aor act	**3450.5** art nom sing masc	**2935.1** noun nom sing masc	**2504.1** conj	**3620.2** partic
ἣν	ἔπηξεν	ὁ	κύριος,	(a καὶ)	οὐκ
hēn	*epēxen*	*ho*	*kurios*	*kai*	*ouk*
which	pitched	the	Lord	and	not

442.1 noun nom sing masc	**3820.6** adj nom sing masc	**1056.1** conj	**744.1** noun nom sing masc	**1519.1** prep	**3450.16** art sing neu
ἄνθρωπος.	**3.** Πᾶς	γὰρ	ἀρχιερεὺς	εἰς	τὸ
anthrōpos	*Pas*	*gar*	*archiereus*	*eis*	*to*
man.	Every	for	high priest	for	the

4232.10 verb inf pres act	**1428.3** noun pl neu	**4885.1** conj	**2504.1** conj	**2355.1** noun fem
προσφέρειν	δῶρά	τε	καὶ	θυσίας
prospherein	*dōra*	*te*	*kai*	*thusias*
to offer	gifts	both	and	sacrifices

2497.9 verb 3sing indic pres mid	**3468.1** adv	**314.3** adj sing neu	**2174.29** verb inf pres act	**4948.10** indef-pron sing neu
καθίσταται·	ὅθεν	ἀναγκαῖον	ἔχειν	τι
kathistatai	*hothen*	*anankaion*	*echein*	*ti*
is being appointed;	hence	necessary	to have	something

8:1. Chapter 8 begins with a clarification of the argument the inspired writer has been presenting by singling out the main thrust of that argument up to this point. The divine oath of Psalm 110:4 which prophesied of the establishment of an eternal Melchizedekian priesthood had now, in the lifetime of those to whom the Epistle to the Hebrews was written, been fulfilled. Such a Priest is not a figment of wishful thinking or speculation. He is now a reality. He is the believer's possession. The waiting is over. Jesus has risen and sits exalted on the right hand of God. He has completed everything necessary for the atonement of the sins of the whole human race and has sat down in God's heavenly sanctuary in the place of preference and blessing. All of God's favor and authority are His to command. He does not stand or bow in the presence of God as a sinful priest must. He is seated, because He is the Son, and His sacrifice is completed. Although He represents men who are upon the earth, He is not ministering in an earthly temple or tabernacle; He deals with spiritual realities in God's heavenly abode.

8:2. Christ's priestly service (*leitourgos*) occurs in the Holy of Holies and the true (that is, genuine) tabernacle. This is not the tent which Israel pitched in the wilderness of Sinai; it is a tabernacle which has been set up by the Lord himself. The contrast is between the earthly and the heavenly, the temporal and the eternal, the human and the divine, the external physical and the spiritually real.

8:3. All high priests appointed by God had certain common responsibilities and tasks to perform. They were all appointed to offer gifts and sacrifices to God on behalf of the people whom they represented. This aspect of priestly service has been alluded to and hinted at previously (2:17) and expressly mentioned but not commented upon (5:1).

It is important to understand the necessity of sacrificial offerings and gifts as the principal function of any priesthood. To this point, however, the writer has compared and contrasted the personal qualifications of the Son with the personal qualifications of the descendants of Aaron who formed the Levitical priesthood under the aegis of the Mosaic covenant. He has demonstrated the personal superiority of the Son to these priests and their priesthood. Now it is imperative that he demonstrate the superiority of Jesus' priestly ministry over the ministry performed by the Levitical priesthood. It was broached at the end of the previous section (7:27), but in this chapter he begins a presentation in minute and painstaking detail.

8:4. It has been demonstrated that Jesus was not qualified as a priest under the Mosaic code. The earthly priesthood was assigned

[maketh] the Son, who is consecrated for evermore: . . . appoint for ever the perfected Son, *TNT* . . . appoints as High Priest a Son who has been rendered perfect for ever, *Wade* . . . appoints a Son who is perfectly qualified to be High Priest forever, *Williams.*

1. Now of the things which we have spoken [this is] the sum: Now the important thing is this, *NLT* . . . to crown what we have been saying, *Wade* . . . The chief thing, however, *Wilson* . . . The pith of all, *Montgomery* . . . This is the point of what is being said, *SEB* . . . the main point in what I am saying is this, *Williams.*

We have such an high priest: . . . a Religious Leader Who had made the way for man to go to God, *NLT* . . . such as I have described, *TCNT.*

who is set on the right hand: . . . one who has taken His seat, *Williams* . . . has sat down, *Wade.*

of the throne of the Majesty in the heavens: . . . of God's majestic throne in heaven, *Williams.*

2. A minister of the sanctuary: . . . where he serves in the sanctuary, *TNT* . . . and acts as Officiating Minister in the Heavenly sanctuary, *Wade* . . . as officiating Priest, *Williams* . . . who ministers now in the sanctuary, *Norlie* . . . to serve as priest in the holy place, *Beck.*

and of the true tabernacle, which the Lord pitched, and not man: . . . the genuine one, *Wuest* . . . this being the Real Tabernacle, *Wade* . . . which is also the true tent of worship, *Williams* . . . which the Lord, not man, set up, *TNT.*

3. For every high priest is ordained to offer gifts and sacrifices: . . . is appointed, *Williams* . . . to present both bloodless Offerings, *Wade.*

wherefore [it is] of necessity that this man: . . . and accordingly it is essential that Jesus, too, *Wade* . . . our high priest too must, *TNT.*

have somewhat also to offer: . . . should have an Offering to present, *Wade.*

4. For if he were on earth: However, if He were still on earth, *Williams.*

Hebrews 8:4

2504.1 conj	3642.6 dem-pron acc sing masc	3614.16 rel-pron sing neu	4232.15 verb 3sing subj aor act	1479.1 conj	3173.1 conj
καὶ	τοῦτον	ὃ	προσενέγκῃ.	4. εἰ	μὲν
kai	*touton*	*ho*	*prosenenkē*	*ei*	*men*
also	this	which	he may offer.	If	indeed

4.a.**Txt:** 06D-corr,018K 020L,byz.Sod
Var: 01ℵ,02A,03B 06D-org,025P,33,bo. Lach,Treg,Alf,Word Tisc,We/Ho,Weis UBS/☆

1056.1 conj	3631.1 partic	1498.34 verb sing indic imperf act	1894.3 prep	1087.2 noun gen sing fem	3624.2 adv
ʼ γὰρ	[a☆ οὖν]	ἦν	ἐπὶ	γῆς,	οὐδ’
gar	*oun*	*ēn*	*epi*	*gēs*	*oud’*
for	[therefore]	he were	on	earth,	not even

4.b.**Txt:** 06D-corr,018K 020L,byz.
Var: 01ℵ,02A,03B 06D-org,025P,33,bo. Lach,Treg,Alf,Word Tisc,We/Ho,Weis,Sod UBS/☆

300.1 partic	1498.34 verb sing indic imperf act	2385.1 noun nom sing masc	1498.20 verb gen pl part pres act	3450.1 art gen pl
ἂν	ἦν	ἱερεύς,	ὄντων	ʼb τῶν
an	*ēn*	*hiereus*	*ontōn*	*tōn*
would	he be	a priest,	being	the

4.c.**Txt:** 01ℵ-corr,06D 018K,020L,025P,byz. Sod
Var: 01ℵ-org,02A,03B 33,Lach,Treg,Alf,Tisc We/Ho,Weis,UBS/☆

2385.5 noun gen pl masc	3450.1 art gen pl	4232.9 verb gen pl masc part pres act	2567.3 prep	3450.6 art acc sing masc
ἱερέων ˎ	τῶν	προσφερόντων	κατὰ	ʼc τὸν ˎ
hiereōn	*tōn*	*prospherontōn*	*kata*	*ton*
priests	the	offering	according to	the

3414.4 noun acc sing masc	3450.17 art pl neu	1428.3 noun pl neu	3610.2 rel-pron nom pl masc	5100.1 noun dat sing neu	2504.1 conj
νόμον	τὰ	δῶρα,	5. οἵτινες	ὑποδείγματι	καὶ
nomon	*ta*	*dōra*	*hoitines*	*hupodeigmati*	*kai*
law	the	gifts,	who	representation	and

4494.2 noun dat sing fem	2973.2 verb 3pl indic pres act	3450.1 art gen pl	2016.2 adj gen pl	2503.1 conj
σκιᾷ	λατρεύουσιν	τῶν	ἐπουρανίων,	καθὼς
skia	*latreuousin*	*tōn*	*epouraniōn*	*kathōs*
shadow	serve	of the	heavenlies,	according as

5372.7 verb 3sing indic perf mid	3337.1 name nom masc	3338.1 name nom masc	3165.12 verb nom sing masc part pres act
κεχρημάτισται	ʼ Μωσῆς	[☆ Μωϋσῆς]	μέλλων
kechrēmatistai	*Mōsēs*	*Mōusēs*	*mellōn*
was divinely instructed	Moses	[idem]	being about

1989.3 verb inf pres act	3450.12 art acc sing fem	4488.4 noun acc sing fem	3571.5 verb 2sing impr pres act	1056.1 conj	5183.2 verb 3sing indic pres act
ἐπιτελεῖν	τὴν	σκηνήν,	Ὅρα	γάρ	φησίν,
epitelein	*tēn*	*skēnēn*	*Hora*	*gar*	*phēsin*
to construct	the	tabernacle;	see,	for,	says he,

5.a.**Txt:** Steph
Var: 01ℵ,02A,03B,06D 018K,020L,025P,byz. Lach,Treg,Alf,Word Tisc,We/Ho,Weis,Sod UBS/☆

4020.28 verb 2sing subj aor act	4020.51 verb 2sing indic fut act	3820.1 adj	2567.3 prep	3450.6 art acc sing masc
ʼ ποιήσῃς	[a☆ ποιήσεις]	πάντα	κατὰ	τὸν
poiēsēs	*poiēseis*	*panta*	*kata*	*ton*
you make	[you will make]	all things	according to	the

5020.2 noun acc sing masc	3450.6 art acc sing masc	1161.13 verb acc sing masc part aor pass	4622.3 prs-pron dat 2sing	1706.1 prep	3450.3 art dat sing
τύπον	τὸν	δειχθέντα	σοι	ἐν	τῷ
tupon	*ton*	*deichthenta*	*soi*	*en*	*tō*
pattern	the	having been shown	you	in	the

3598.3 noun dat sing neu	3432.1 adv	3431.1 adv	1156.2 conj	1307.3 adj comp gen sing fem
ὄρει.	6. ʼ νυνὶ	[νῦν]	δὲ	διαφορωτέρας
orei	*nuni*	*nun*	*de*	*diaphorōteras*
mountain.	Now	[idem]	but	a more excellent

to the descendants of Aaron (7:5,6). Other than His sacrifice on the cross, Jesus' incarnation and suffering have already been presented as preparation for priestly service (2:9-18; 5:7-9). His priestly service is performed not on earth but in heaven.

This verse has some bearing on attempts to date the writing of the epistle. Since there is reference to the ministry of the Levitical priests, they would still have been serving. This ministry ceased after the Romans destroyed the Jerusalem temple in A.D. 70, so it would seem logical to believe this letter was written before A.D. 70.

8:5. This verse presents and examines the nature of the ministry of the Levitical priests. Their priestly service was secondary to the heavenly. It was only a copy (*hupodeigma*) and shadow of the heavenly realities. The evaluation of their service was based upon the Old Testament record. When Jehovah instructed Moses to begin the construction of the tabernacle, He said, "And look that thou make them after their pattern, which was showed thee in the mount" (Exodus 25:40). The tabernacle was patterned after heavenly realities revealed to Moses. The Levitical tabernacle, therefore, was not the real thing but only a copy of the heavenly reality.

The basic appeal of ritualistic religion is to the flesh rather than to the spirit of man. Its pageantry stirs his human emotions. That which he sees holds aesthetic meaning for him. He likes the beauty and grace of the routine its ministers go through. It is all a work of art to him. Soon after God instituted it, Israel had reduced the forms of worship in Judaism to mere ritual.

To warn the Hebrews against turning back to the pageantry of Judaism, the writer played down the splendor of its temple and referred to the tabernacle, *skēnēn*, literally "tent," instead. He said worship there was but a shadow of the real. To focus on it was like following the shade of a man walking in the sun rather than the person himself. In Hebrews that Person was Jesus. Why return to the shadow of a man when you have the Man? This was his question.

8:6. To the degree that Jesus has been established as "the mediator" of a better covenant set up on the basis of better promises—to that same degree He has obtained a "more excellent" priestly ministry. The inspired writer has shown Jesus to be a messenger who is superior to the angelic messengers of the old covenant, and he has shown Him to be a superior priest because of His indissoluble life. The implication has been all along that a superior messenger and a superior priesthood mean a superior covenant.

In order to demonstrate the superiority of the new covenant the inspired writer next identified and analyzed the new covenant. He laid bare the promises of that covenant in order to compare them with the promises of the Mosaic covenant. In this way he showed

he should not be a priest: He wouldn't be, *Adams* . . . He would not even be, *Concordant.*

seeing that there are priests that offer gifts according to the law: . . . since there exist Priests who present the gifts prescribed by Law, *Wade* . . . there are those who officiate in accordance with the law in offering the gifts, *Williams* . . . demanded by the Law, *Beck.*

5. Who serve unto the example and shadow of heavenly things: They are performing a service, *TNT* . . . yet they officiate in a sanctuary that is a mere copy, *Williams* . . . a mere sketch and outline, *Wade* . . . of the heavenly reality, *Montgomery.*

as Moses was admonished of God: This is evident from the warning, *Adams* . . . Moses has been apprized, *Concordant*. . . as Moses...was warned, *Williams.*

when he was about to make the tabernacle: . . . when about to be completing the tabernacle, *Concordant* . . . when he was about to make the tent of worship, *Williams* . . . when he was about to erect the tent was instructed to do, *TNT.*

for, See, saith he, [that] thou make all things: Be careful to make all of it, *Beck* . . . See to it that you make it all, *Williams* . . . that you do everything, *TNT.*

according to the pattern showed to thee in the mount: . . . after the model shewn to thee, *Wade* . . . just like the pattern shown you on the mountain, *Williams.*

6. But now hath he obtained a more excellent ministry: But as it is, Jesus has obtained a far superior ministry, *TNT* . . . But Christ has a more perfect work, *NLT*. . . Jesus has received a ministry that is better than theirs, *SEB* . . . He has entered upon a priestly service as much superior to theirs, *Williams* . . . a Superior Service, *Wilson.*

by how much also he is the mediator of a better covenant: . . . as the covenant of which He is the Mediator is superior to theirs, *Williams* . . . in proportion as the "covenant" of which He is the Intermediary is superior to the earlier, *Wade.*

6.a.**Txt:** 01ℵ-corr,03B 06D-corr,byz.Weis
Var: 01ℵ-org,02A 06D-org,018K,020L Lach,Alf,Word,Tisc We/Ho,UBS/⋆

5018.10 verb 3sing indic perf act	**5018.11** verb 3sing indic perf act	**2983.1** noun gen sing fem	**3607.7** rel-pron dat sing neu
ʻ τέτευχεν	[a⋆ τέτυχεν]	λειτουργίας,	ὅσῳ
teteuchen	*tetuchen*	*leitourgias*	*hosō*
he has obtained	[idem]	ministry	by so much as

2504.1 conj	**2882.1** adj comp gen sing	**1498.4** verb 3sing indic pres act	**1236.2** noun gen sing fem	**3186.1** noun nom sing masc
καὶ	κρείττονός	ἐστιν	διαθήκης	μεσίτης,
kai	*kreittonos*	*estin*	*diathēkēs*	*mesitēs*
also	of a better	he is	covenant	mediator,

3610.3 rel-pron nom sing fem	**1894.3** prep	**2882.4** adj comp dat pl fem	**1845.7** noun dat pl fem	**3412.1** verb 3sing indic perf mid
ἥτις	ἐπὶ	κρείττοσιν	ἐπαγγελίαις	νενομοθέτηται.
hētis	*epi*	*kreittosin*	*epangeliais*	*nenomothetētai*
which	upon	better	promises	has been established.

1479.1 conj	**1056.1** conj	**3450.9** art nom sing fem	**4272.9** num ord nom sing fem	**1552.9** dem-pron nom sing fem	**1498.34** verb sing indic imperf act
7. Εἰ	γὰρ	ἡ	πρώτη	ἐκείνη	ἦν
Ei	*gar*	*hē*	*prōtē*	*ekeinē*	*ēn*
If	for	the	first	that	were

271.1 adj nom sing	**3620.2** partic	**300.1** partic	**1202.5** num ord gen sing fem	**2195.29** verb 3sing indic imperf pass	**4964.1** noun nom sing masc
ἄμεμπτος,	οὐκ	ἂν	δευτέρας	ἐζητεῖτο	τόπος.
amemptos	*ouk*	*an*	*deuteras*	*ezēteito*	*topos*
faultless,	not		for a second	was being sought	place.

8.a.**Txt:** p46,01ℵ-corr 03B,06D-corr,020L,byz. Weis
Var: 01ℵ-org,02A 06D-org,016I,018K 025P,33,it.sa.bo.Lach Tisc,We/Ho,Sod,UBS/⋆

3171.2 verb nom sing masc part pres mid	**1056.1** conj	**840.2** prs-pron dat pl	**840.8** prs-pron acc pl masc	**2978.5** verb 3sing indic pres act
8. μεμφόμενος	γὰρ	ʻ αὐτοῖς	[a⋆ αὐτοὺς]	λέγει,
memphomenos	*gar*	*autois*	*autous*	*legei*
Finding fault	for,	to them	[idem]	he says,

1481.20 verb 2sing impr aor mid	**2232.5** noun nom pl fem	**2048.36** verb 3pl indic pres mid	**2978.5** verb 3sing indic pres act	**2935.1** noun nom sing masc	**2504.1** conj
Ἰδοὺ,	ἡμέραι	ἔρχονται,	λέγει	κύριος,	καὶ
Idou	*hēmerai*	*erchontai*	*legei*	*kurios*	*kai*
Lo,	days	are coming,	says	Lord,	and

4783.4 verb 1sing indic fut act	**1894.3** prep	**3450.6** art acc sing masc	**3486.4** noun acc sing masc	**2447.1** name masc	**2504.1** conj
συντελέσω	ἐπὶ	τὸν	οἶκον	Ἰσραὴλ	καὶ
suntelesō	*epi*	*ton*	*oikon*	*Israēl*	*kai*
I will ratify	as regards	the	house	of Israel	and

1894.3 prep	**3450.6** art acc sing masc	**3486.4** noun acc sing masc	**2430.2** name masc	**1236.4** noun acc sing fem	**2508.5** adj acc sing fem
ἐπὶ	τὸν	οἶκον	Ἰούδα	διαθήκην	καινήν·
epi	*ton*	*oikon*	*Iouda*	*diathēkēn*	*kainēn*
as regards	the	house	of Judah	a covenant	new;

3620.3 partic	**2567.3** prep	**3450.12** art acc sing fem	**1236.4** noun acc sing fem	**3614.12** rel-pron acc sing fem	**4020.22** verb 1sing indic aor act
9. οὐ	κατὰ	τὴν	διαθήκην	ἣν	ἐποίησα
ou	*kata*	*tēn*	*diathēkēn*	*hēn*	*epoiēsa*
not	according to	the	covenant	which	I made

3450.4 art dat pl	**3824.8** noun dat pl masc	**840.1** prs-pron gen pl	**1706.1** prep	**2232.3** noun dat sing fem	**1934.6** verb gen sing masc part aor mid
τοῖς	πατράσιν	αὐτῶν,	ἐν	ἡμέρᾳ	ἐπιλαβομένου
tois	*patrasin*	*autōn*	*en*	*hēmera*	*epilabomenou*
with the	fathers	their,	in	day	of taking hold of

the promises of the new covenant were superior—not because they were more reliable (both came from God who cannot lie) but because the goals which they were designed to accomplish were superior to the objectives set up for the Mosaic law.

8:7. The very fact that God set up a second covenant indicates that the first covenant was indeed lacking something. The second covenant provides clues to this weakness.

8:8. The purpose of quoting the new covenant from Jeremiah 31:31-34 is manifold. For one thing, it was necessary to show that the temporary nature of the Mosaic covenant was known to the prophets. It was also the divine intention to supersede the law of Moses. An analysis of the provisions of the new covenant was necessary in order to prove its superiority to the Sinaitic code.

In introducing the Old Testament quotation the inspired writer set the stage with an introductory formula which identified the context in which the new covenant was given by the Lord. It also highlights the contention that the old covenant was seriously deficient. The announcement of the new covenant arose in a situation where Jehovah was excoriating Israel for its sinfulness and pronouncing judgment upon the nation because of its failure to keep the Law. Immediately after giving a death sentence for sin, Jehovah announced that at some time in the future He would establish a new covenant with both Israel and the house of Judah, thus reuniting the divided kingdom.

Though Jehovah made the new covenant with Israel, its provisions belong to any who meet its conditions. National Israel refused to accept it in the First Century by rejecting Jesus as the Messiah. Regardless, His death put His covenant or will into effect. Individual Jews believed and received, including the recipients of this letter (Romans 11:5). However, they constituted only a "remnant." In the future so many Jewish people will believe on Jesus that one might even say "all" Israel will be saved (Romans 11:26). In the meantime, any who receive Jesus partake of the benefits of the covenant.

8:9. In this verse the quotation contrasts the nature of the new covenant with the old and brings forward at least one reason why the Lord determined to create a new covenant with His people Israel. Jehovah said the new covenant would be different. It would not operate according to the same standard as the covenant which He established with the Children of Israel when He led them out of Egypt through the Red Sea on dry land. This new covenant would be set up because of Israel's failure to keep the Sinaitic

which was established upon better promises: . . . which has been enacted upon, *Montgomery* . . . it has been established on the basis of, *TNT* . . . being constituted on the basis of better Promises, *Wade* . . . which rests upon better promises, *Norlie* . . . God has based it on better promises, *Beck* . . . it has been enacted upon superior promises, *Williams* . . . based on nobler promises from heaven, *Noli.*

7. For if that first [covenant] had been faultless: . . . if the former covenant, *TNT* . . . if the carrying-out of that first Covenant...had afforded no ground for censure, *Wade* . . . had been perfect, *Norlie* . . . had been unimpeachable, *Noli.*

then should no place have been sought for the second: God would not have been seeking a place for a second, *TNT* . . . there would have been no need for, *Montgomery, Noli* . . . there would have been no occasion, *Norlie* . . . could have been no room for a second one, *Williams.*

8. For finding fault with them, he saith: For, blaming them, *Concordant* . . . because He was dissatisfied with His people, *Williams* . . . He finds fault with his people, saying, *TNT* . . . God himself impeached it and denounced our forefathers for its invalidation, saying, *Noli.*

Behold, the days come, saith the Lord: Lo, *Wade* . . . the time is coming, *Williams.*

when I will make a new covenant: . . . when I will complete, *Adams* . . . when I will conclude, *TNT, Wade* . . . a new agreement, *SEB.*

with the house of Israel and with the house of Judah:

9. Not according to the covenant that I made with their fathers: It won't be like the covenant that, *Adams* . . . Not on the lines of the covenant which, *Wade* . . . will be different from the covenant, *Noli* . . . unlike the one that I made with their forefathers, *Williams.*

in the day when I took them by the hand:

to lead them out of the land of Egypt: . . . to bring them, *TNT* . . . lead them forth, *Wade.*

Hebrews 8:10

1466.2 prs-pron gen 1sing	**3450.10** art gen sing fem	**5331.2** noun gen sing fem	**840.1** prs-pron gen pl	**1790.7** verb inf aor act	**840.8** prs-pron acc pl masc	**1523.2** prep gen
μου	τῆς	χειρὸς	αὐτῶν	ἐξαγαγεῖν	αὐτοὺς	ἐκ
mou	*tēs*	*cheiros*	*autōn*	*exagagein*	*autous*	*ek*
my	the	hand	their	to lead	them	out of

1087.2 noun gen sing fem	**125.2** name gen fem	**3617.1** conj	**840.7** prs-pron nom pl masc	**3620.2** partic	**1682.3** verb 3pl indic aor act
γῆς	Αἰγύπτου·	ὅτι	αὐτοὶ	οὐκ	ἐνέμειναν
gēs	*Aiguptou*	*hoti*	*autoi*	*ouk*	*enemeinan*
land	of Egypt;	because	they	not	did continue

1706.1 prep	**3450.11** art dat sing fem	**1236.3** noun dat sing fem	**1466.2** prs-pron gen 1sing	**2476.3** prs-pron nom	**270.3** verb 1sing indic aor act
ἐν	τῇ	διαθήκῃ	μου,	κἀγὼ	ἠμέλησα
en	*tē*	*diathēkē*	*mou*	*kagō*	*ēmelēsa*
in	the	covenant	my,	and I	disregarded

840.1 prs-pron gen pl	**2978.5** verb 3sing indic pres act	**2935.1** noun nom sing masc	**3617.1** conj	**3642.9** dem-pron nom sing fem	**3450.9** art nom sing fem
αὐτῶν,	λέγει	κύριος.	**10.** ὅτι	αὕτη	ἡ
autōn	*legei*	*kurios*	*hoti*	*hautē*	*hē*
them,	says	Lord.	Because	this	the

10.a.**Var:** 02A,06D,044

1236.1 noun nom sing fem	**1466.2** prs-pron gen 1sing	**3614.12** rel-pron acc sing fem	**1297.5** verb 1sing indic fut mid	**3450.3** art dat sing
διαθήκη	[a+ μου]	ἣν	διαθήσομαι	τῷ
diathēkē	*mou*	*hēn*	*diathēsomai*	*tō*
covenant	[my]	which	I will covenant	with the

3486.3 noun dat sing masc	**2447.1** name masc	**3196.3** prep	**3450.15** art acc pl fem	**2232.1** noun fem	**1552.15** dem-pron acc pl fem
οἴκῳ	Ἰσραὴλ	μετὰ	τὰς	ἡμέρας	ἐκείνας,
oikō	*Israēl*	*meta*	*tas*	*hēmeras*	*ekeinas*
house	of Israel	after	the	days	those,

2978.5 verb 3sing indic pres act	**2935.1** noun nom sing masc	**1319.5** verb nom sing masc part pres act	**3414.5** noun acc pl masc	**1466.2** prs-pron gen 1sing	**1519.1** prep
λέγει	κύριος,	διδοὺς	νόμους	μου	εἰς
legei	*kurios*	*didous*	*nomous*	*mou*	*eis*
says	Lord,	giving	laws	my	into

3450.12 art acc sing fem	**1265.3** noun acc sing fem	**840.1** prs-pron gen pl	**2504.1** conj	**1894.3** prep	**2559.1** noun fem	**840.1** prs-pron gen pl
τὴν	διάνοιαν	αὐτῶν	καὶ	ἐπὶ	καρδίας	αὐτῶν
tēn	*dianoian*	*autōn*	*kai*	*epi*	*kardias*	*autōn*
the	mind	their,	also	upon	hearts	their

10.b.**Var:** p46,03B,044

1909.1 verb 1sing indic fut act	**1119.6** verb 1sing act	**840.8** prs-pron acc pl masc	**2504.1** conj	**1498.38** verb 1sing indic fut mid
(☆ ἐπιγράψω	[b γράψω]	αὐτούς·	καὶ	ἔσομαι
epigrapsō	*grapsō*	*autous*	*kai*	*esomai*
I will inscribe	[I will write]	them;	and	I will be

840.2 prs-pron dat pl	**1519.1** prep	**2296.4** noun acc sing masc	**2504.1** conj	**840.7** prs-pron nom pl masc	**1498.43** verb 3pl indic fut mid	**1466.4** prs-pron dat 1sing
αὐτοῖς	εἰς	θεόν,	καὶ	αὐτοὶ	ἔσονταί	μοι
autois	*eis*	*theon*	*kai*	*autoi*	*esontai*	*moi*
to them	for	God,	and	they	shall be	to me

1519.1 prep	**2967.4** noun acc sing masc	**2504.1** conj	**3620.3** partic	**3231.1** partic	**1315.16** verb 3pl subj aor act	**1524.3** adj nom sing masc
εἰς	λαόν.	**11.** καὶ	οὐ	μὴ	διδάξωσιν	ἕκαστος
eis	*laon*	*kai*	*ou*	*mē*	*didaxōsin*	*hekastos*
for	people.	And	not	not	shall they teach	each

covenant. They did not abide in the covenant of the Lord. Since they did not dwell in His covenant, He left them to their own devices and allowed them to suffer the consequences of their rebellion.

8:10. At this juncture Jehovah began to outline the provisions of the new covenant. The nation of Israel was identified as the second party to the covenant. The new covenant would be established "after those days" which (in the context of Jeremiah 31:29) refers to the time when Jehovah would pour out His judgment on Israel because of their sins. This identifies it as sometime after the Babylonian captivity and return to Palestine.

Having indicated when and with whom He would make His new covenant, the Lord enunciated its terms. The first of these was very different from any provision found in the Mosaic law. He said, "I will put my laws into their mind, and write them in their hearts." These laws were not to be external as were those given to Moses on tablets of stone. They would be internalized in the mind, consciousness, and emotional center of the entire nation. The end result would be that Israel would actually become what God had always desired them to be: His people (Exodus 6:7).

Ezekiel joined Jeremiah in promising a day when God would internalize Israel's religion (Ezekiel 36:25-27). He promised cleansing from moral filthiness. The Lord would give a new heart, a tender one of flesh, to replace a hard one of stone. Thus both prophets promised an experience of heartfelt religion. Ezekiel further declared God would put a new spirit within. This makes possible a walk according to God's laws. With the Psalmist one can say, "I delight to do thy will, O my God: yea, thy law is within my heart" (Psalm 40:8). We can live by internal constraint, not external restraint.

Ezekiel and Jeremiah use "spirit," "heart," and "mind" as synonyms. Rather than finding a distinction between "putting laws in the mind" and "writing them on the heart," it is more correct to see the expressions as forming a Hebrew parallelism. Taylor wrote, "In 10:16 the two terms are inverted; this suggests that the writer thinks of the two clauses as a simple parallelism, and *mind* and *heart* as synonyms. In 8:10 the laws are inscribed in the heart, while they are put into the mind; but in 10:16 they are inscribed on the mind and put into the heart" (*Beacon Bible Commentary*, p.98).

8:11. The personal relationship which God desires with His people, "to them a God" and "to me a people" (verse 10), was further heightened by the description of the covenantal terms revealed in this verse. The need for mediation between God and men found in the priests and teachers of the old covenant would be eliminated under the new agreement. No longer would people need to admonish one another to come to know the Lord, because all of them

because they continued not in my covenant: . . . they did not follow the Old Way of Worship, *NLT* . . . did not abide by, *Barclay* . . . on their part, did not adhere to my covenant, *Wade* . . . But they did not stick to their agreement, *Norlie* . . . they did not keep the agreement with me, *BB* . . . they themselves repudiated my old covenant, *Noli* . . . they have not been loyal to My covenant, *Beck* . . . they did not abide by their covenant with me, *Williams* . . . they remained not in My plan, *Fenton.*

and I regarded them not, saith the Lord: And I would not listen to them, *Klingensmith* . . . and I left them alone, *Adams* . . . So I, on my side, paid no regard to them, *Wade* . . . I also did not take care of them, *Swann* . . . I let them go their own way, *Barclay* . . . I was sorry for them, *Fenton* . . . paid no attention to them, *SEB* . . . So I did not care for them, *Williams* . . . I ceased to care, *TNT* . . . So I had to repudiate them also, *Noli* . . . I gave them up, *BB.*

10. For this [is] the covenant that I will make with the house of Israel: . . . this is the agreement, *BB* . . . This, then, is the settlement I will make, *Fenton* . . . that I will contract, *Adams* . . . to which I will commit myself for, *Wade.*

after those days, saith the Lord: . . . in the future, *SEB, Noli* . . . In those days, *Williams.*

I will put my laws into their mind: I will impress, *Wade, Noli* . . . to their comprehension, *Concordant* . . . into their understanding, *Fenton.*

and write them in their hearts: I will inscribe them, *Wade.*

and I will be to them a God: Then I will be their God, *Noli.*

and they shall be to me a people: . . . they will be my people, *Noli.*

11. And they shall not teach every man his neighbour: No man shall teach, *TNT* . . . there will be no need, *BB* . . . there will be no necessity, *Barclay* . . . nevermore will each one need to teach, *Williams* . . . Then they will not have to teach their neighbors, *Noli* . . . to instruct, *TCNT* . . . his fellow citizen, *Montgomery* . . . his friend, *Fenton.*

11.a.**Txt:** 025P,it.Steph
Var: p46,01ℵ,02A,03B
06D,018K,020L,33,byz.
sa.bo.Gries,Lach,Treg
Alf,Word,Tisc,We/Ho
Weis,Sod,UBS/☆

3450.6 art acc sing masc	**3999.1** adv	**4037.4** noun acc sing masc	**840.3** prs-pron gen sing	**2504.1** conj	**1524.3** adj nom sing masc
τὸν	⸂ πλησίον	[a☆ πολίτην]	αὐτοῦ,	καὶ	ἕκαστος
ton	*plēsion*	*politēn*	*autou*	*kai*	*hekastos*
the	neighbor	[citizen]	his,	and	each

3450.6 art acc sing masc	**79.4** noun acc sing masc	**840.3** prs-pron gen sing	**2978.15** verb nom sing masc part pres act	**1091.24** verb 2sing impr aor act
τὸν	ἀδελφὸν	αὐτοῦ,	λέγων,	Γνῶθι
ton	*adelphon*	*autou*	*legōn*	*Gnōthi*
the	brother	his,	saying,	Know

3450.6 art acc sing masc	**2935.4** noun acc sing masc	**3617.1** conj	**3820.7** adj nom pl masc	**3471.26** verb 3pl indic fut act	**1466.6** prs-pron acc 1sing
τὸν	κύριον·	ὅτι	πάντες	εἰδήσουσίν	με,
ton	*kurion*	*hoti*	*pantes*	*eidēsousin*	*me*
the	Lord;	because	all	shall know	me,

11.b.**Txt:** 06D-corr,020L
byz.bo.
Var: 01ℵ,02A,03B
06D-org,018K,025P,33
Lach,Treg,Alf,Tisc
We/Ho,Weis,Sod
UBS/☆

570.3 prep	**3262.4** adj gen sing masc	**840.1** prs-pron gen pl	**2175.1** conj	**3144.3** adj gen sing masc	**840.1** prs-pron gen pl
ἀπὸ	μικροῦ	⸂b αὐτῶν ⸃	ἕως	μεγάλου	αὐτῶν·
apo	*mikrou*	*autōn*	*heōs*	*megalou*	*autōn*
from	little	of them	to	great	of them.

3617.1 conj	**2412.1** adj nom sing masc	**1498.38** verb 1sing indic fut mid	**3450.14** art dat pl fem	**92.5** noun dat pl fem
12. ὅτι	ἵλεως	ἔσομαι	ταῖς	ἀδικίαις
hoti	*hileōs*	*esomai*	*tais*	*adikiais*
Because	merciful	I will be	to the	unrighteousnesses

12.a.**Txt:** 01ℵ-corr,02A
06D,018K,020L,025P
byz.
Var: 01ℵ-org,03B,33,bo.
Treg,Alf,Tisc,We/Ho
Weis,Sod,UBS/☆

840.1 prs-pron gen pl	**2504.1** conj	**3450.1** art gen pl	**264.6** noun gen pl fem	**840.1** prs-pron gen pl	**2504.1** conj	**3450.1** art gen pl
αὐτῶν,	καὶ	τῶν	ἁμαρτιῶν	αὐτῶν	⸂a καὶ	τῶν
autōn	*kai*	*tōn*	*hamartiōn*	*autōn*	*kai*	*tōn*
their,	and	the	sins	their	and	the

455.6 noun gen pl fem	**840.1** prs-pron gen pl	**3620.3** partic	**3231.1** partic	**3279.5** verb 1sing subj aor pass	**2068.1** adv
ἀνομιῶν	αὐτῶν ⸃	οὐ	μὴ	μνησθῶ	ἔτι.
anomiōn	*autōn*	*ou*	*mē*	*mnēsthō*	*eti*
lawlessnesses	their	not	not	I may remember	more.

1706.1 prep	**3450.3** art dat sing	**2978.24** verb inf pres act	**2508.5** adj acc sing fem	**3869.1** verb 3sing indic perf act	**3450.12** art acc sing fem
13. ἐν	τῷ	λέγειν	Καινὴν,	πεπαλαίωκεν	τὴν
en	*tō*	*legein*	*Kainēn*	*pepalaiōken*	*tēn*
In	the	to say	New,	he has made old	the

4272.12 num ord acc sing fem	**3450.16** art sing neu	**1156.2** conj	**3869.2** verb sing neu part pres mid	**2504.1** conj	**1088.1** verb sing neu part pres act
πρώτην·	τὸ	δὲ	παλαιούμενον	καὶ	γηράσκον
prōtēn	*to*	*de*	*palaioumenon*	*kai*	*gēraskon*
first;	the	but	being made old	and	growing aged

1.a.**Txt:** 06D,025P,Steph
Var: 01ℵ,03B,020L,Tisc
We/Ho,Weis,Sod
UBS/☆

1445.1 adv	**847.1** noun gen sing masc	**2174.44** verb 3sing indic imperf act	**2174.45** verb 3sing indic imperf act	**3173.1** conj
ἐγγὺς	ἀφανισμοῦ.	**9:1.** ⸂ Εἶχεν	[a☆ Εἶχε]	μὲν
engus	*aphanismou*	*Eichen*	*Eiche*	*men*
near	disappearing.	Was having	[idem]	indeed

1.b.**Txt:** byz.
Var: 01ℵ,02A,03B,06D
018K,020L,025P,Gries
Lach,Treg,Alf,Word
Tisc,We/Ho,Weis,Sod
UBS/☆

3631.1 partic	**2504.1** conj	**3450.9** art nom sing fem	**4272.9** num ord nom sing fem	**4488.1** noun nom sing fem	**1339.3** noun pl neu
οὖν	καὶ	ἡ	πρώτη	⸂b σκηνὴ ⸃	δικαιώματα
oun	*kai*	*hē*	*prōtē*	*skēnē*	*dikaiōmata*
therefore	also	the	first	tabernacle	ordinances

would have firsthand experience knowing the Lord. In having access to the Lord, all, from the most powerful and influential to the least important, would be on an equal basis.

8:12. Jehovah next declared the greatest provision of the new covenant, something not found in the Mosaic law—provision for the forgiveness of sins. Under the new covenant He promised to show mercy to their unrighteousness. He also declared that He would not hold their lawlessness against them.

The intention was not to deny there could be an experience of forgiveness in the time of the old covenant. Obviously David knew the blessing of forgiveness, and the knowledge of justification by faith was available since the time of Abraham. Yet these things were not based on any provisions which God had built into the Mosaic covenant. They grew out of the covenant which the Lord had made with Abraham. The sacrificial system administered by the Levitical priesthood did not cleanse consciences of moral guilt or deal with the penalty of sin. They only provided ceremonial cleansing on an annual basis. God does not change. His merciful and gracious character are seen in the Old Testament Scriptures (Micah 7:18) and revealed in the Mosaic law, but in the new covenant there is a complete forgiveness, only foreshadowed in the old. Along with this comes a freedom from fear and from the power of man's fallen nature not known under the old covenant.

8:13. Verse 13 gives the writer's concluding remarks on his citation of the new covenant text from Jeremiah 31:31-34. But this only serves as a launching pad for the main discussion of its superiority which is developed in chapters 9 and 10. The main contention at this point was that the announcement of a new covenant and the introduction of the Son necessitated the cancellation of the Mosaic covenant (7:11,18; 8:7). The new and the old are incompatible. They cannot coexist. The new antiquates the old. Being obsolete, the old was near its vanishing point. It was gone—in A.D. 70.

9:1. This verse begins with the Greek word *eichen* which means "had." It is significant that the Mosaic covenant is referred to in the past tense, for it has just been depicted as being on the verge of disappearing. Exodus 25:40 was cited in Hebrews 8:5, and chapter 9 proceeds to describe the copies which Moses was commanded to make for the wilderness tabernacle. This was in order to describe the Levitical priesthood's divine service in the offering of sacrifice on the Day of Atonement. Verse 1 refers to the old covenant as "the first." It had regulations (*dikaiōmata*) which governed the service performed by its priests. It possessed not the genuine heavenly sanctuary but the holy place which was worldly (*to te hagion kosmikon*); its sanctuary was an earthbound, man-made copy of the heavenly original shown to Moses (9:24).

and every man his brother, saying, Know the Lord: . . . each one teach his brother, *Williams* . . . Acquaint thee with the Lord, *Wade.*

for all shall know me, from the least to the greatest: . . . because from small to great, *TNT* . . . all shall be acquainted with Me, *Concordant* . . . From the lowest to the highest, *Williams.*

12. For I will be merciful to their unrighteousness: . . . will pardon their misdeeds, *Norlie* . . . upon their wrong-doings, *Montgomery* . . . to their deeds of wrong, *Williams* . . . to their iniquities, *Wade.*

and their sins and their iniquities will I remember no more: . . . never, never any more will I recall their sins, *Williams.*

13. In that he saith, A new [covenant]: In speaking of a new covenant, *Williams* . . . By saying 'new,' *TNT* . . . a covenant of a new type, *Wade.*

he hath made the first old: He has pronounced, *Wade* . . . made the first obsolete, *Adams.*

Now that which decayeth and waxeth old: . . . and whatever is obsolete and antiquated, *Williams* . . . growing old and decrepit, *Concordant* . . . that which grows old and creaky, *Klingensmith* . . . and feeble, *Norlie.*

[is] ready to vanish away: . . . is about ready to disappear, *Norlie* . . . is fast disappearing, *Klingensmith* . . . It will never be used again, *NLT* . . . is not far from disappearing, *TNT* . . . is on the point of disappearing, *TCNT* . . . is on the verge of vanishing, *Williams* . . . disappearing altogether, *Wade.*

1. Then verily the first [covenant] had also: So indeed, *Williams.*

ordinances of divine service: There were special ways of worship and a special holy place, *NLT* . . . regulations of worship, *Adams* . . . for divine worship, *TCNT* . . . of public worship, *Montgomery.*

and a worldly sanctuary: . . . and it had its sanctuary, an earthly one, *TNT* . . . and the earthly holy place, *Beck* . . . one that shared the nature of the material world, *Wade.*

Hebrews 9:2

2972.1 noun fem	3450.16 art sing neu	4885.1 conj	39.1 adj sing	2859.2 adj sing neu	4488.1 noun nom sing fem
λατρείας,	τό	τε	ἅγιον	κοσμικόν.	2. σκηνὴ
latreias	*to*	*te*	*hagion*	*kosmikon*	*skēnē*
of service,	the	and	sanctuary,	a worldly.	A tabernacle

1056.1 conj	2650.6 verb 3sing indic aor pass	3450.9 art nom sing fem	4272.9 num ord nom sing fem	1706.1 prep	3614.11 rel-pron dat sing fem
γὰρ	κατεσκευάσθη	ἡ	πρώτη,	ἐν	ᾗ
gar	*kateskeuasthē*	*hē*	*prōtē*	*en*	*hē*
for	was prepared,	the	first,	in	which

3614.9 rel-pron nom sing fem	4885.1 conj	3059.2 noun nom sing fem	2504.1 conj	3450.9 art nom sing fem	4971.1 noun nom sing fem
ἥ	τε	λυχνία	καὶ	ἡ	τράπεζα
hē	*te*	*luchnia*	*kai*	*hē*	*trapeza*
the	both	lampstand	and	the	table

2504.1 conj	3450.9 art nom sing fem	4145.1 noun nom sing fem	3450.1 art gen pl	735.6 noun gen pl masc	3610.3 rel-pron nom sing fem
καὶ	ἡ	πρόθεσις	τῶν	ἄρτων,	ἥτις
kai	*hē*	*prothesis*	*tōn*	*artōn*	*hētis*
and	the	presentation	of the	loaves,	which

2978.28 verb 3sing indic pres mid	39.10 adj nom sing fem	3196.3 prep	1156.2 conj	3450.16 art sing neu	1202.8 num ord sing neu
λέγεται	ἅγια·	3. μετὰ	δὲ	τὸ	δεύτερον
legetai	*hagia*	*meta*	*de*	*to*	*deuteron*
is being called	holy;	after	but	the	second

2635.1 noun sing neu	4488.1 noun nom sing fem	3450.9 art nom sing fem	2978.33 verb nom sing fem part pres mid	39.10 adj nom sing fem
καταπέτασμα	σκηνὴ	ἡ	λεγομένη	[a☆ ἅγια
katapetasma	*skēnē*	*hē*	*legomenē*	*hagia*
veil	a tabernacle	the	called	holy

3.a.**Txt:** 01ℵ-org,02A 06D-org,byz.
Var: 01ℵ-corr2,03B 06D-corr1,018K,020L 1241

39.4 adj gen pl	3450.17 art pl neu	39.10 adj nom sing fem	3450.1 art gen pl	39.4 adj gen pl	5387.1 adj sing
ἁγίων,	[a τὰ	ἅγια	τῶν	ἁγίων,]	4. χρυσοῦν
hagiōn	*ta*	*hagia*	*tōn*	*hagiōn*	*chrusoun*
of holies,	[the	holy	of the	holies,]	a golden

2174.22 verb nom sing fem part pres act	2346.1 noun sing neu	2504.1 conj	3450.12 art acc sing fem	2759.3 noun acc sing fem	3450.10 art gen sing fem
ἔχουσα	θυμιατήριον,	καὶ	τὴν	κιβωτὸν	τῆς
echousa	*thumiatērion*	*kai*	*tēn*	*kibōton*	*tēs*
having	censer,	and	the	ark	of the

1236.2 noun gen sing fem	3891.3 verb acc sing fem part perf mid	3702.1 adv	5388.3 noun dat sing neu
διαθήκης	περικεκαλυμμένην	πάντοθεν	χρυσίῳ,
diathēkēs	*perikekalummenēn*	*pantothen*	*chrusiō*
covenant,	having been covered round	in every part	with gold,

1706.1 prep	3614.11 rel-pron dat sing fem	4564.1 noun nom sing fem	5387.3 adj nom sing fem	2174.22 verb nom sing fem part pres act	3450.16 art sing neu
ἐν	ᾗ	στάμνος	χρυσῆ	ἔχουσα	τὸ
en	*hē*	*stamnos*	*chrusē*	*echousa*	*to*
in	which	pot	golden	having	the

3103.1 noun neu	2504.1 conj	3450.9 art nom sing fem	4321.1 noun nom sing fem	2.1 name masc	3450.9 art nom sing fem
μάννα,	καὶ	ἡ	ῥάβδος	Ἀαρὼν	ἡ
manna	*kai*	*hē*	*rhabdos*	*Aarōn*	*hē*
manna,	and	the	rod	of Aaron	the

9:2. Here the inspired writer recounts for Jewish believers the details of worship at the tabernacle. The intent is to show God provided a better approach through Jesus. Previously he had shown Christ as a better messenger than the prophets or angels; a better apostle than Moses or Joshua; as our High Priest, better than Aaron; and offering a better covenant to Israel. Now he emphasizes Jesus brought better provisions for worship.

He had respect for worship in Judaism, but by the Spirit he said some shocking things to prevent believers in Israel from turning back to the old means of access to God. As Carter observed, "The tabernacle was intended of God as a *means* of worship, *not* as an *object* of worship. It was intended as a symbol to direct their thoughts and devotion to the realities of the coming Messiah which it symbolized" (*The Wesleyan Bible Commentary*, p.109).

Verse 2 describes the furniture found in the outer sanctuary or Holy Place which was designated as "the first." With the Old Testament Scriptures as his authority and its record of the institution of tabernacle worship in the Mosaic law, the writer portrayed not the temple but the *skēnē*, i.e., the tabernacle or tent which was moved around with Israel in their wanderings. Since the Hebrews were familiar with this setup, the contents of the outer sanctuary or Holy Place were merely itemized without further commentary. The first sanctuary of the tabernacle housed a lampstand, a table, and the bread known as shewbread or the "bread of the Presence." Details concerning their specifications, construction, and placement are found in Exodus 25, 37, and 40.

9:3,4. These verses describe the inner sanctuary's contents. The words used are *Hagia Hagiōn*, the Holy of Holies. The entrances to both the inner and outer holy places were covered by veils. The gold censer or altar of incense (*thumiatērion*) was not in the Holy of Holies. It stood before the entrance to the inner sanctuary and thus was in the Holy Place. But the smoke of the incense burned upon it was designed to penetrate the veil and permeate the Holy of Holies as it ascended before the ark of the covenant.

Since this intimate association existed between the altar of incense and the ark of the covenant, they are tied together by the use of the same participle (*echousa* translated "which had") in reference to both. The ark was "overlaid round about with gold" (*perikekalummenēn pantothen*), meaning it was overlaid with gold both on the outside and the inside.

Three items were kept inside the ark of the covenant: a golden urn filled with manna as a reminder of God's provision in the wilderness, Aaron's rod which had budded, and the tablets of the Decalogue. By the time of the dedication of Solomon's Temple, two of these items had disappeared (see 1 Kings 8:9). We are not told when this occurred, but it may have happened during the period of 7 months when the ark was in exile in the land of the Philistines (see 1 Samuel 5 and 6).

2. For there was a tabernacle made; the first: The sanctuary was built, *SEB* . . . there was constructed a Tabernacle—consisting, first, of a Front Tent, *Wade* . . . outer part of the tent, *Williams* . . . a tent was constructed, *TNT.*

wherein [was] the candlestick, and the table, and the show-bread: . . . containing, *Wade* . . . where the lampstand and the table with the Bread of the Presence were, *TNT* . . . was equipped with the lamp and table, *Williams* . . . and the presentation bread, *Adams* . . . and the holy bread was on it, *NLT* . . . the oblation bread, *Noli.*

which is called the sanctuary: . . . which is termed the holy place, *Concordant* . . . The Holy of Holies, *Wade.*

3. And after the second veil: Behind the second curtain, *Beck, Wade* . . . beyond which was, *TNT.*

the tabernacle which is called the Holiest of all: . . . there came a Rear Tent, *Wade* . . . is the tent that is called the holy of holies, *Williams* . . . known as the Inner Sanctuary, *TCNT.*

4. Which had the golden censer: This room contained the golden altar, *SEB* . . . In it were a golden altar for burning incense, *TNT* . . . golden incense-altar, *Williams* . . . where special perfume was burned, *NLT.*

and the ark of the covenant overlaid round about with gold: . . . the chest for the covenant, *Williams* . . . covered all over, *Montgomery* . . . completely covered, *Beck* . . . covered on all sides with gold, *Noli* . . . with gold plating, *Wade.*

wherein [was] the golden pot that had manna: . . . a golden jar, *Williams, TNT* . . . the Golden Casket containing, *Wade* . . . it contained the golden urn with the manna, *Noli.*

and Aaron's rod that budded: . . . staff which germinates, *Concordant* . . . which blossomed, *Wilson* . . . which sprouted, *TNT.*

and the tables of the covenant: . . . the tablets on which the covenant was written, *Williams* . . . the stone tablets of the covenant, *TNT* . . . inscribed with the Covenant, *Wade.*

978.3 verb nom sing fem part aor act	**2504.1** conj	**3450.13** art nom pl fem	**3970.1** noun nom pl fem	**3450.10** art gen sing fem	**1236.2** noun gen sing fem
βλαστήσασα,	καὶ	αἱ	πλάκες	τῆς	διαθήκης˙
blastēsasa	*kai*	*hai*	*plakes*	*tēs*	*diathēkēs*
having sprouted,	and	the	tablets	of the	covenant;

5.a.**Txt:** 018K,020L,byz. Sod
Var: 01ℵ,06D-org,Alf UBS/☆

5068.1 prep	**1156.2** conj	**840.10** prs-pron gen sing fem	**5338.1** noun nom pl masc	**5338.3** noun nom pl masc
5. ὑπεράνω	δὲ	αὐτῆς	ʻ χερουβὶμ	[a☆ χερουβεὶν]
huperanō	*de*	*autēs*	*cheroubim*	*cheroubein*
above	and	it	cherubim	[idem]

1385.2 noun gen sing fem	**2653.1** verb pl neu part pres act	**3450.16** art sing neu	**2411.1** adj sing neu	**3875.1** prep
δόξης	κατασκιάζοντα	τὸ	ἱλαστήριον˙	περὶ
doxēs	*kataskiazonta*	*to*	*hilastērion*	*peri*
of glory	overshadowing	the	mercy seat;	concerning

3614.1 rel-pron gen pl	**3620.2** partic	**1498.4** verb 3sing indic pres act	**3431.1** adv	**2978.24** verb inf pres act	**2567.3** prep	**3183.1** noun sing neu
ὧν	οὐκ	ἔστιν	νῦν	λέγειν	κατὰ	μέρος.
hōn	*ouk*	*estin*	*nun*	*legein*	*kata*	*meros*
which	not	it is	now	to speak	in	detail.

3642.2 dem-pron gen pl	**1156.2** conj	**3643.1** adv	**2650.8** verb gen pl neu part perf mid	**1519.1** prep	**3173.1** conj
6. Τούτων	δὲ	οὕτως	κατεσκευασμένων,	εἰς	μὲν
Toutōn	*de*	*houtōs*	*kateskeuasmenōn*	*eis*	*men*
These things	now	thus	having been prepared,	into	

3450.12 art acc sing fem	**4272.12** num ord acc sing fem	**4488.4** noun acc sing fem	**1269.1** adv	**1217.2** prep
τὴν	πρώτην	σκηνὴν	ʻ διαπαντὸς	[☆ διὰ
tēn	*prōtēn*	*skēnēn*	*diapantos*	*dia*
the	first	tabernacle	at all times	[through

3820.2 adj gen sing	**1510.1** verb 3pl indic pres act	**3450.7** art nom pl masc	**2385.4** noun pl masc	**3450.15** art acc pl fem	**2972.1** noun fem
παντὸς]	εἰσίασιν	οἱ	ἱερεῖς	τὰς	λατρείας
pantos	*eisiasin*	*hoi*	*hiereis*	*tas*	*latreias*
all]	enter	the	priests,	the	services

1989.2 verb nom pl masc part pres act	**1519.1** prep	**1156.2** conj	**3450.12** art acc sing fem	**1202.7** num ord acc sing fem	**526.1** adv
ἐπιτελοῦντες˙	**7.** εἰς	δὲ	τὴν	δευτέραν	ἅπαξ
epiteleountes	*eis*	*de*	*tēn*	*deuteran*	*hapax*
accomplishing;	into	but	the	second	once

3450.2 art gen sing	**1747.1** noun gen sing masc	**3304.2** adj nom sing masc	**3450.5** art nom sing masc	**744.1** noun nom sing masc	**3620.3** partic
τοῦ	ἐνιαυτοῦ	μόνος	ὁ	ἀρχιερεύς,	οὐ
tou	*eniautou*	*monos*	*ho*	*archiereus*	*ou*
the	year	alone	the	high priest,	not

5400.1 prep	**129.2** noun gen sing neu	**3614.16** rel-pron sing neu	**4232.2** verb 3sing indic pres act	**5065.1** prep	**1431.4** prs-pron gen sing
χωρὶς	αἵματος,	ὃ	προσφέρει	ὑπὲρ	ἑαυτοῦ
chōris	*haimatos*	*ho*	*prospherei*	*huper*	*heautou*
apart from	blood,	which	he offers	for	himself

2504.1 conj	**3450.1** art gen pl	**3450.2** art gen sing	**2967.2** noun gen sing masc	**50.1** noun gen pl neu	**3642.17** dem-pron sing neu
καὶ	τῶν	τοῦ	λαοῦ	ἀγνοημάτων˙	**8.** τοῦτο
kai	*tōn*	*tou*	*laou*	*agnoēmatōn*	*touto*
and	the	of the	people	sins of ignorance:	this

9:5. Fashioned on the lid of the ark of the covenant were the "cherubim of glory," angelic guardians. Their function was to guard the presence of Jehovah. For the Lord was indeed *the* "Glory." The lid which these figures overshadowed was called the mercy seat.

The Septuagint term *hilastērion*, used here for "mercy seat," reminded believers of the sacrifices and rituals performed once a year on the Day of Atonement. On that day when the high priest entered into the Holiest of Holies and sprinkled sacrificial blood on the lid of the ark, it ceremonially covered the sins of the nation of Israel until the next Day of Atonement.

Later on in the epistle this imagery brings into sharper focus the contrast between it and the sacrificial death of Jesus at Calvary. This seed so deftly planted by the Holy Spirit will be harvested later.

9:6. The opening words of this verse clearly indicate that only a cursory treatment will be given to the physical aspects of the tabernacle's furniture and sanctuaries in the light the previous citation of Exodus 25:40 (Hebrews 8:5). They were inferior copies of the heavenly realities.

The first four words of this verse (*Toutōn de houtōs kateskeuasmenōn*) could be translated "Now when these things were constructed thus," that is, when Moses had carried out the Lord's command and built the tabernacle and its furnishings according to the pattern which had been shown to him on Mount Sinai. So, after the copies were made, the priests began to perform their priestly duties. The service which they provided continually on a daily basis (as signified by *diapantos*) was, however, only performed in the first or outer sanctuary.

9:7. Entrance into the inner sanctum, the Holy of Holies, the place where the cherubim overshadowed the lid of the ark as guardians of the Shekinah glory that symbolized Jehovah's presence, was limited to only the high priest. Ordinary priests were not allowed to enter. Moreover, even the high priest was rigidly restricted in his access to the innermost sanctuary of the tabernacle. He could not march into the presence of the Lord anytime he felt like it. Only once a year, on the 10th of Tishri—the Day of Atonement—was the high priest allowed to enter "the holiest of all" (verse 3). (See Exodus 30:10 and Leviticus 16:34.) Before he could do so, he had to observe the sacrificial rites and ceremonies outlined in Leviticus 16. Blood had to be shed for him and the people.

9:8. The word "this" refers back to the description in the previous verses of the once a year ministry of the high priest on the Day of

5. And over it the cherubims of glory: And above it, *Adams* . . . above the chest were the winged creatures, the symbols of God's glorious presence, *Williams* . . . were the angels of glory, *Beck* . . . who revealed God's glory, *TNT.*

shadowing the mercyseat: . . . overshadowing the propitiatory shelter, *Concordant* . . . the place of reconciliation, *TNT.*

of which we cannot now speak particularly: But now is not the time to talk about every detail of these things, *SEB* . . . it isn't possible to speak in detail about these things, *Adams* . . . of which I cannot now speak in detail, *Williams.*

6. Now when these things were thus ordained: Under these arrangements, *TNT* . . . Such then were the arrangements, *Montgomery* . . . But that is how it was arranged, *Beck* . . . With these arrangements completed in this way, *Williams.*

the priests went always into the first tabernacle: . . . continually enter the outer tent, *TNT* . . . regularly go into the outer part of the tent of worship, *Williams.*

accomplishing the service [of God]: . . . in conducting their official services, *Williams* . . . when they carry out the duties of their service, *TNT* . . . performing the divine service, *Concordant* . . . in the discharge of their sacred duties, *TCNT.*

7. But into the second: . . . but into the inner tent, *Montgomery* . . . into the inner room, *Norlie.*

[went] the high priest alone once every year: . . . nobody but the high priest may go, *Williams* . . . once annually, *Wilson.*

not without blood, which he offered for himself: . . . and never without blood which he offers for himself, *Williams* . . . He always takes blood with him, *TNT.*

and [for] the errors of the people: . . . and the people's sins of ignorance, *Adams* . . . and for the sins committed in ignorance by the people, *Williams.*

8. The Holy Ghost this signifying: . . . making it evident, *Concordant* . . . teaching by this, *Montgomery* . . . was showing, *Williams.*

1207.2 verb gen sing neu part pres act	3450.2 art gen sing	4011.2 noun gen sing neu	3450.2 art gen sing	39.2 adj gen sing	3247.1 adv
δηλοῦντος	τοῦ	πνεύματος	τοῦ	ἁγίου,	μήπω
dēlountos	*tou*	*pneumatos*	*tou*	*hagiou*	*mēpō*
signifying	the	Spirit	the	Holy,	not yet

5157.20 verb inf perf mid	3450.12 art acc sing fem	3450.1 art gen pl	39.4 adj gen pl	3461.4 noun acc sing fem	2068.1 adv
πεφανερῶσθαι	τὴν	τῶν	ἁγίων	ὁδὸν	ἔτι
pephanerōsthai	*tēn*	*tōn*	*hagiōn*	*hodon*	*eti*
to be made manifest	the	of the	holies	way,	still

3450.10 art gen sing fem	4272.10 num ord gen sing fem	4488.2 noun gen sing fem	2174.23 verb gen sing fem part pres act	4565.4 noun acc sing fem
τῆς	πρώτης	σκηνῆς	ἐχούσης	στάσιν·
tēs	*prōtēs*	*skēnēs*	*echousēs*	*stasin*
the	first	tabernacle	having	a standing;

3610.3 rel-pron nom sing fem	3712.1 noun nom sing fem	1519.1 prep	3450.6 art acc sing masc	2511.4 noun acc sing masc	3450.6 art acc sing masc
9. ἥτις	παραβολὴ	εἰς	τὸν	καιρὸν	τὸν
hētis	*parabolē*	*eis*	*ton*	*kairon*	*ton*
which	a symbol	for	the	time	the

9.a.**Txt:** 06D-corr,018K 020L,025P,byz. **Var:** 01ℵ,02A,03B 06D-org,33,Lach,Treg Alf,Word,Tisc,We/Ho Weis,Sod,UBS/☆

1748.3 verb acc sing masc part perf act	2567.2 prep	3614.6 rel-pron acc sing masc	3614.12 rel-pron acc sing fem	1428.3 noun pl neu	4885.1 conj
ἐνεστηκότα,	καθ'	ʼ ὃν	[a☆ ἣν]	δῶρά	τε
enestēkota	*kath'*	*hon*	*hēn*	*dōra*	*te*
having been present,	in	which	[idem]	gifts	both

2504.1 conj	2355.5 noun nom pl fem	4232.22 verb 3pl indic pres mid	3231.1 partic	1404.20 verb nom pl fem part pres mid	2567.3 prep
καὶ	θυσίαι	προσφέρονται,	μὴ	δυνάμεναι	κατὰ
kai	*thusiai*	*prospherontai*	*mē*	*dunamenai*	*kata*
and	sacrifices	are being offered,	not	being able	as to

4743.4 noun acc sing fem	4896.5 verb inf aor act	3450.6 art acc sing masc	2973.4 verb acc sing masc part pres act	3303.1 adv
συνείδησιν	τελειῶσαι	τὸν	λατρεύοντα,	10. μόνον
suneidēsin	*teleiōsai*	*ton*	*latreuonta*	*monon*
conscience	to perfect	the	serving,	only

10.a.**Txt:** 01ℵ-corr,03B 06D-corr,018K,020L byz.it.Weis **Var:** p46,01ℵ-org,02A 06D-org,025P,33,sa.bo. Gries,Lach,Alf,Word Tisc,We/Ho,Sod,UBS/☆

1894.3 prep	1026.6 noun dat pl neu	2504.1 conj	4048.2 noun dat pl neu	2504.1 conj	1307.1 adj dat pl masc
ἐπὶ	βρώμασιν	καὶ	πόμασιν	καὶ	διαφόροις
epi	*brōmasin*	*kai*	*pomasin*	*kai*	*diaphorois*
in	foods	and	drinks	and	varieties

10.b.**Txt:** 06D-corr,018K 020L,byz.it. **Var:** p46,01ℵ,02A,03B 025P,33,sa.bo.Lach Treg,Alf,Word,Tisc We/Ho,Weis,Sod UBS/☆

903.2 noun dat pl masc	2504.1 conj	1339.4 noun dat pl neu	1339.3 noun pl neu
βαπτισμοῖς,	ʼa καὶ ˋ	ʼ δικαιώμασιν	[b☆ δικαιώματα]
baptismois	*kai*	*dikaiōmasin*	*dikaiōmata*
washings,	and	ordinances	[idem]

4418.2 noun gen sing fem	3230.1 prep	2511.2 noun gen sing masc	1351.1 noun gen sing fem	1930.4 verb pl neu part pres mid
σαρκός,	μέχρι	καιροῦ	διορθώσεως	ἐπικείμενα.
sarkos	*mechri*	*kairou*	*diorthōseōs*	*epikeimena*
of flesh,	until	time	of setting things right	being imposed.

5382.1 name nom masc	1156.2 conj	3716.7 verb nom sing masc part aor mid	744.1 noun nom sing masc	3450.1 art gen pl
11. Χριστὸς	δὲ	παραγενόμενος	ἀρχιερεὺς	τῶν
Christos	*de*	*paragenomenos*	*archiereus*	*tōn*
Christ	but	having come	high priest	of the

Atonement. The ceremonies performed on that day were intended by the Holy Spirit to indicate that entrance into the very presence of God in heaven was severely limited. As long as the Levitical rites and ceremonies were practiced, access into the presence of God "was not yet made manifest." Men were not free to come to God at any time; they were restricted to the once a year, symbolic rites.

9:9. Controversy has arisen over the meaning of the first statement in this verse. The King James translators saw the Levitical rites as a "figure" (*parabolē*) for the Children of Israel. They indicated this by translating the participle *enestēkota* as "the time then present." It is possible that this refers to the time period after the establishment of the new covenant, *the time now present.* If it has the first meaning, the text would be saying that the ceremonies had a parabolic significance to those who practiced them. If it is the latter, then it means that they have parabolic significance to those under the new covenant. This latter sense seems to fit the argument better. The thrust of the rest of the verse is clear: the rites performed by the high priest under the Levitical system had no power to consecrate or cleanse the consciences of the high priest or those he represented.

God meant conscience to serve man well. It is not self-imposed or man would rid himself of it. To the Romans Paul wrote, "I lie not, my conscience also bearing me witness in the Holy Ghost" (Romans 9:1). Still, it can become defiled (1 Corinthians 8:7) as well as seared and leave one insensible (1 Timothy 4:2). Since to a degree it is fallible, "Let your conscience be your guide" is not a safe maxim. It needs cleansing; God has provided for that through Jesus.

9:10. Indeed, the Levitical offerings were limited to physical, external practices. They were only intended to be temporary. The extent of their power dealt "only" with food (*brōmasin*) and drink, and various ritual ablutions, and other regulations (*dikaiōmasin*) for the physical body (*sarkos*). These are mentioned in contrast to the conscience (9:9). The final phrase appears nowhere else in the Septuagint or New Testament. In its context, however, *mechri kairou diorthōseōs* can only refer to the fact that these regulations were set up temporarily until the divinely appointed time of the reconstruction of things under the new covenant.

9:11. This verse begins a sentence which is not completed until verse 12. It expressly declares the result of the Son's high priestly ministry is the completion of eternal redemption. Since Christ has been placed in the office of High Priest, not on earth as Aaron but as a Melchizedekian priest in the genuine sanctuary of heaven (9:24), He has inaugurated the "good things" promised by the new covenant. They are no longer future ("things to come"). The sanc-

that the way into the holiest of all was not yet made manifest: . . . there was as yet no access to the real sanctuary, *Williams* . . . the way into the sanctuary was not revealed, *TNT* . . . was not made plain, *Klingensmith* . . . had not yet been opened, *SEB* . . . has not yet been disclosed, *Montgomery.*

while as the first tabernacle was yet standing: . . . as long as the outside tent and its Old Way of Worship were being used, *NLT* . . . while the old covenant was still in force, *Norlie* . . . while the outer tent was still in existence, *Williams, TNT.*

9. Which [was] a figure for the time then present: This is symbolic for today, *SEB* . . . for it is merely a symbol of the present time, *Williams* . . . pointing to the present, *TNT.*

in which were offered both gifts and sacrifices: . . . it means, *TNT* . . . in connection with which gifts and sacrifices are repeatedly offered, *Williams.*

that could not make him that did the service perfect: . . . they cannot make...the worshiper perfect, *Williams.*

as pertaining to the conscience: . . . inwardly, *TNT.*

10. [Which stood] only in meats and drinks, and divers washings: . . . since they were concerned only with food and drink and ritual washings of different kinds, *TNT* . . . since they deal only with food and drink and various washings, *Williams.*

and carnal ordinances: . . . that is, with mere material regulations, *Williams* . . . and other things to do with the body, *NLT* . . . external ceremonies, *TCNT.*

imposed [on them] until the time of reformation: . . . which are in force only until the time of setting things straight, *Williams* . . . until the time of correction, *Adams* . . . the time set up for making all things right, *Klingensmith* . . . when things would be set right, *Beck.*

11. But Christ being come an high priest of good things to come: . . . when Christ came as the High Priest of good things that have already taken place, *Williams.*

11.a.**Txt:** 01ℵ,02A 06D-corr,018K,020L 025P,byz.Tisc,Sod
Var: 03B,06D-org,1739 Lach,We/Ho,Weis UBS/☆

3165.11 verb gen pl part pres act	**1090.49** verb gen pl part aor mid	**18.1** adj gen pl	**1217.2** prep	**3450.10** art gen sing fem
ʻ μελλόντων	[a☆ γενομένων]	ἀγαθῶν,	διὰ	τῆς
mellontōn	*genomenōn*	*agathōn*	*dia*	*tēs*
coming	[having come]	good things,	by	the

3157.3 adj comp gen sing	**2504.1** conj	**4894.7** adj comp gen sing fem	**4488.2** noun gen sing fem	**3620.3** partic	**5335.3** adj gen sing fem
μείζονος	καὶ	τελειοτέρας	σκηνῆς,	οὐ	χειροποιήτου,
meizonos	*kai*	*teleioteras*	*skēnēs*	*ou*	*cheiropoiētou*
greater	and	more perfect	tabernacle,	not	made by hand,

4969.1 verb	**3642.16** dem-pron sing neu	**1498.4** verb 3sing indic pres act	**3620.3** partic	**3642.10** dem-pron gen sing fem	**3450.10** art gen sing fem
ʻ τουτέστιν	[☆ τοῦτ’	ἔστιν]	οὐ	ταύτης	τῆς
toutestin	*tout’*	*estin*	*ou*	*tautēs*	*tēs*
that is,	[this	is]	not	of this	the

2909.2 noun gen sing fem	**3624.1** conj	**1217.1** prep	**129.2** noun gen sing neu	**4970.1** noun gen pl masc	**2504.1** conj	**3311.3** noun gen pl masc
κτίσεως,	**12.** οὐδὲ	δι’	αἵματος	τράγων	καὶ	μόσχων,
ktiseōs	*oude*	*di’*	*haimatos*	*tragōn*	*kai*	*moschōn*
creation,	nor	by	blood	of goats	and	calves,

1217.2 prep	**1156.2** conj	**3450.2** art gen sing	**2375.2** adj gen sing	**129.2** noun gen sing neu	**1511.3** verb 3sing indic aor act	**2160.1** adv
διὰ	δὲ	τοῦ	ἰδίου	αἵματος	εἰσῆλθεν	ἐφάπαξ
dia	*de*	*tou*	*idiou*	*haimatos*	*eisēlthen*	*ephapax*
by	but	the	his own	blood,	entered	once for all

1519.1 prep	**3450.17** art pl neu	**39.16** adj pl neu	**164.6** adj acc sing fem	**3057.1** noun acc sing fem	**2128.40** verb nom sing masc part aor mid
εἰς	τὰ	ἅγια,	αἰωνίαν	λύτρωσιν	εὑράμενος.
eis	*ta*	*hagia*	*aiōnian*	*lutrōsin*	*heuramenos*
into	the	holies,	eternal	redemption	having found.

1479.1 conj	**1056.1** conj	**3450.16** art sing neu	**129.1** noun sing neu	**4873.2** noun gen pl masc	**2504.1** conj	**4970.1** noun gen pl masc
13. εἰ	γὰρ	τὸ	αἷμα	ʻ ταύρων	καὶ	τράγων,
ei	*gar*	*to*	*haima*	*taurōn*	*kai*	*tragōn*
If	for	the	blood	of bulls	and	of goats

4970.1 noun gen pl masc	**2504.1** conj	**4873.2** noun gen pl masc	**2504.1** conj	**4553.1** noun nom sing fem	**1146.1** noun gen sing fem
[☆ τράγων	καὶ	ταύρων]	καὶ	σποδὸς	δαμάλεως
tragōn	*kai*	*taurōn*	*kai*	*spodos*	*damaleōs*
[of goats	and	of bulls]	and	ashes	of a heifer

4329.1 verb nom sing fem part pres act	**3450.8** art acc pl masc	**2813.7** verb acc pl masc part perf mid	**37.2** verb 3sing indic pres act	**4242.1** prep
ῥαντίζουσα	τοὺς	κεκοινωμένους,	ἁγιάζει	πρὸς
rhantizousa	*tous*	*kekoinōmenous*	*hagiazei*	*pros*
sprinkling	the	having been defiled,	sanctifies	for

3450.12 art acc sing fem	**3450.10** art gen sing fem	**4418.2** noun gen sing fem	**2486.1** noun acc sing fem	**4073.9** intr-pron dat sing neu
τὴν	τῆς	σαρκὸς	καθαρότητα,	**14.** πόσῳ
tēn	*tēs*	*sarkos*	*katharotēta*	*posō*
the	of the	flesh	purity,	how much

3095.1 adv comp	**3450.16** art sing neu	**129.1** noun sing neu	**3450.2** art gen sing	**5382.2** name gen masc	**3614.5** rel-pron nom sing masc
μᾶλλον	τὸ	αἷμα	τοῦ	Χριστοῦ,	ὃς
mallon	*to*	*haima*	*tou*	*Christou*	*hos*
rather	the	blood	of the	Christ	who

tuary in which He performs His priestly ministry is not part of the physical creation ("this building") nor is it something which like the Levitical tabernacle was constructed by human effort, "made with hands" (cf. Acts 7:44-49).

9:12. The comparison pointing out the superiority of Christ the Son's priestly offering is continued in this verse. He did not offer the blood of animals in His sacrifice. Rather, by His very own blood, the blood of the Son, described in verses 11-14, He entered into the holy sanctuary—heaven itself. And He did not do this year after year; He did it only "once." So powerful was His blood that it effected an everlasting redemption from the curse of sin.

9:13. The sacrifices of animals under the old covenant were not useless. After all, they were appointed by God. The sacrifices commanded to be performed annually on the Day of Atonement (Leviticus 16:14-16) and the ceremonies in which the ashes of a sacrificed heifer were mixed with water and sprinkled by the priest upon those ceremonially unclean (Numbers 19:2,17-19) provided sanctification, that is, ritual cleansing for the external, physical body ("flesh").

The point is not that these sacrifices had no power whatsoever, but that their power was restricted and small in contrast to the power displayed in the single sacrifice of the Lord Jesus Christ. The argument then is from the smaller to the greater, from the weaker to the more powerful. If these earthly sacrifices had earthly consequences, then the sacrifice of the Son offered in heaven has heavenly, eternal consequences.

9:14. By a rhetorical question then, the inference is drawn concerning the superiority of the Son's sacrifice. To the degree that His blood is superior, to that same degree His sacrifice is more powerful in its effects. Christ, the Messiah, offered himself to God the Father as a perfect, unblemished sacrifice, for He was sinless (4:15). His sacrifice was not passive. The animals in the Old Testament were in every sense victims, but Jesus voluntarily laid down His life for the sheep (John 10:17,18), indicating the greatness of His love. He was a victor!

This tremendous sacrifice was accomplished through the agency of the "eternal Spirit." Interpreters have disputed the exact meaning of this phrase. Many take it as a reference to some ministry of the Holy Spirit to Jesus during His crucifixion. Others see it as a reference to Jesus' eternal nature in His sonship as Second Person of the Trinity. The Greek phrase *dia pneumatos aiōniou* has no article with it and literally means "through eternal spirit." Since the argument is for the superior effects of Christ's sacrifice on the basis

by a greater and more perfect tabernacle: He went by way of that greater and more perfect tent of worship, *Williams* . . . through the Superior and more Perfect Tabernacle, *Wade.*

not made with hands: . . . reared by, *Wade* . . . not made by human hands, *Williams.*

that is to say, not of this building: I mean, no part of, *Wade* . . . not of this material creation, *Montgomery* . . . not belonging to this physical creation, *Norlie* . . . not a part of this world, *SEB* . . . not a part of our created world, *Beck.*

12. Neither by the blood of goats and calves:

but by his own blood he entered in: . . . with the accompaniment...of His own Blood, *Wade* . . . with His own blood He...went into, *Williams.*

once into the holy place: . . . once for all...the real sanctuary, *Williams.*

having obtained eternal redemption [for us]: . . . and pay a price that frees us forever, *Beck* . . . and secured our eternal redemption, *Williams* . . . eternal deliverance, *TNT* . . . everlasting forgiveness, *SEB.*

13. For if the blood of bulls and of goats:

and the ashes of an heifer sprinkling the unclean: . . . sprinkling those who are ceremonially unclean, *Williams* . . . the latter being sprinkled on those who have incurred physical defilement, *Wade* . . . of polluted persons, *Adams* . . . the contaminated, *Concordant.*

sanctifieth to the purifying of the flesh: . . . is hallowing to the cleanness of, *Concordant* . . . were sufficient to make the body pure again, *Norlie* . . . become sanctifying agencies for effecting ceremonial purification, *Wade* . . . purifies them with physical cleansing, *Williams* . . . and free them from ritual uncleanness, *TNT.*

14. How much more shall the blood of Christ: . . . more effectively, *Wade* . . . of the Anointed one, *Wilson.*

who through the eternal Spirit: Who by means of, *Adams* . . . eternal in its potency, *Wade.*

Hebrews 9:15

14.a.**Txt:** p46,01ℵ-org 03B,06D-corr2,byz. **Var:** 01ℵ-corr2,06D-org 025P,81,104,326,365 629,630,2464,bo.

1217.2 prep	**4011.2** noun gen sing neu	**164.2** adj gen sing	**39.2** adj gen sing	**1431.6** prs-pron acc sing masc
διὰ	πνεύματος	ʻ☆ αἰωνίου	[a ἁγίου]	ἑαυτὸν
dia	*pneumatos*	*aiōniou*	*hagiou*	*heauton*
through	Spirit	eternal	[Holy]	himself

4232.12 verb 3sing indic aor act	**297.2** adj acc sing masc	**3450.3** art dat sing	**2296.3** noun dat sing masc	**2483.11** verb 3sing indic fut act
προσήνεγκεν	ἄμωμον	τῷ	θεῷ,	καθαριεῖ
prosēnenken	*amōmon*	*tō*	*theō*	*kathariei*
offered	spotless		to God,	shall purify

14.b.**Txt:** 01ℵ,06D-corr 020L,33,byz.sa.Tisc,Sod **Var:** 02A,06D-org,018K 025P,Lach,Alf,Word We/Ho,Weis,UBS/☆

3450.12 art acc sing fem	**4743.4** noun acc sing fem	**5050.2** prs-pron gen 2pl	**2231.2** prs-pron gen 1pl	**570.3** prep	**3361.2** adj gen pl
τὴν	συνείδησιν	ʻ ὑμῶν	[b☆ ἡμῶν]	ἀπὸ	νεκρῶν
tēn	*suneidēsin*	*humōn*	*hēmōn*	*apo*	*nekrōn*
the	conscience	your	[our]	from	dead

2024.5 noun gen pl neu	**1519.1** prep	**3450.16** art sing neu	**2973.9** verb inf pres act	**2296.3** noun dat sing masc	**2180.12** verb dat sing masc part pres act
ἔργων,	εἰς	τὸ	λατρεύειν	θεῷ	ζῶντι;
ergōn	*eis*	*to*	*latreuein*	*theō*	*zōnti*
works	for	the	to serve	God	living!

2504.1 conj	**1217.2** prep	**3642.17** dem-pron sing neu	**1236.2** noun gen sing fem	**2508.4** adj gen sing fem	**3186.1** noun nom sing masc
15. Καὶ	διὰ	τοῦτο	διαθήκης	καινῆς	μεσίτης
Kai	*dia*	*touto*	*diathēkēs*	*kainēs*	*mesitēs*
And	because of	this	of a covenant	new	mediator

1498.4 verb 3sing indic pres act	**3567.1** conj	**2265.2** noun gen sing masc	**1090.50** verb gen sing part aor mid	**1519.1** prep
ἐστίν,	ὅπως	θανάτου	γενομένου,	εἰς
estin	*hopōs*	*thanatou*	*genomenou*	*eis*
he is,	so that,	death	having taken place	for

623.3 noun acc sing fem	**3450.1** art gen pl	**1894.3** prep	**3450.11** art dat sing fem	**4272.11** num ord dat sing fem	**1236.3** noun dat sing fem
ἀπολύτρωσιν	τῶν	ἐπὶ	τῇ	πρώτῃ	διαθήκῃ
apolutrōsin	*tōn*	*epi*	*tē*	*prōtē*	*diathēkē*
redemption	of the	under	the	first	covenant

3709.4 noun gen pl fem	**3450.12** art acc sing fem	**1845.4** noun acc sing fem	**2956.21** verb 3pl subj aor act	**3450.7** art nom pl masc
παραβάσεων,	τὴν	ἐπαγγελίαν	λάβωσιν	οἱ
parabaseōn	*tēn*	*epangelian*	*labōsin*	*hoi*
transgressions,	the	promise	might receive	the

2535.47 verb nom pl masc part perf mid	**3450.10** art gen sing fem	**164.2** adj gen sing	**2790.2** noun gen sing fem	**3562.1** adv
κεκλημένοι	τῆς	αἰωνίου	κληρονομίας.	**16.** ὅπου
keklēmenoi	*tēs*	*aiōniou*	*klēronomias*	*hopou*
having been called	of the	eternal	inheritance.	Where

1056.1 conj	**1236.1** noun nom sing fem	**2265.4** noun acc sing masc	**316.1** noun nom sing fem	**5179.27** verb inf pres mid	**3450.2** art gen sing
γὰρ	διαθήκη,	θάνατον	ἀνάγκη	φέρεσθαι	τοῦ
gar	*diathēkē*	*thanaton*	*anankē*	*pheresthai*	*tou*
for	a covenant,	death	necessary	to come in	of the

1297.4 verb gen sing masc part aor mid	**1236.1** noun nom sing fem	**1056.1** conj	**1894.3** prep	**3361.6** adj dat pl masc
διαθεμένου·	**17.** διαθήκη	γὰρ	ἐπὶ	νεκροῖς
diathemenou	*diathēkē*	*gar*	*epi*	*nekrois*
having made covenant.	A will	for	in the	case of dead

of His personal superiorities, it seems best to understand this as a reference to the indissoluble life inherent in the eternal Son (7:16).

By means of offering His eternal life, i.e., "Spirit," He was able to cleanse (*katharie*i) the believer's conscience from "dead works," that is, reliance on one's own efforts to obtain merit before God (6:1). They are freed from bondage to this guilt.

offered himself without spot to God: He gave Himself as a perfect gift to God, *NLT* . . . offers Himself flawless to God, *Concordant* . . . a spotless offering to God, *Williams.*

purge your conscience from dead works: . . . purify your consciences, *Williams* . . . cleanse your conscience, *Montgomery* . . . from dead human efforts, *SEB.*

to serve the living God?: . . . the ever-living, *Williams.*

9:15. Because Jesus Christ is the Son of God, His blood is superior to the blood of animals and makes the new covenant superior to the old. A superior sacrifice was needed to establish a superior covenant. His death made Him the Mediator (*mesitēs*) of the new covenant. Generally, the term *mesitēs* is taken in the sense of go-between, but in this context as well as those of 8:6 and 12:24 it may be interpreted as referring to Jesus as a surety or guarantee of the new covenant. Because His blood is superior to that of animals, He was able to become the surety for God's new and superior covenant.

Interpreters dispute the use of the term *diathēkēs* ("testament") in 9:15-18. Some say it means "will" in all these uses. Others say it means "covenant." Most recent interpreters think there is a play upon both meanings of the word. In the Septuagint and in one instance in Aristophanes' comedy *Birds* (414 B.C.), it is used of a compact between two parties, one of whom clearly dominates and fixes the terms of agreement. In the Septuagint it refers to God's "treaties" or covenants with men. By the time the New Testament was written, however, the term *sunthēkē* was generally used by the Greeks to describe contracts, and *diathēkē* was universally used to speak of a man's last will and testament.

The blood of animals could not bring salvation; the shedding of the Son's blood did. It made possible "the redemption of the transgressions" of those who sinned under the Mosaic law. Because of Christ's sacrifice it was possible for them to receive the eternal inheritance which they had been promised in the covenant God made with their forefather Abraham. By linking the discussion to the promise made to Abraham, the idea of an inheritance was introduced and paved the way for the play on the use of the term *diathēkē* as a last will and testament.

15. And for this cause he is the mediator of the new testament: So, because of this, *Adams* . . . this is why, *Williams* . . . he is a go-between, *Klingensmith.*

that by means of death, for the redemption: . . . in order that, after He had suffered death for securing redemption, *Williams* . . . was the price to set them free from sin, *SEB* . . . He paid the ransom to free people, *Beck.*

of the transgressions [that were] under the first testament: . . . from the offenses committed under the first covenant, *Williams.*

they which are called might receive: . . . those who had been invited to share it might obtain, *Williams.*

the promise of eternal inheritance:

9:16. An inheritance is what is passed on to the heirs after the one who promises it to them in his will dies. The heirs do not receive what is promised until the one who makes the will passes away.

16. For where a testament [is]: Where there is a will, *Adams* . . . For when a will is made, *Williams.*

there must also of necessity be the death of the testator: That will is worthless, unless someone can prove that a person died, *SEB* . . . it is necessary that the death of him who makes it be proved, *Williams.*

9:17. The effectiveness (*bebaia*) of a will is dependent upon the death of the one who made it. The promise is not carried out while he is alive. Although it is not expressly stated here, the imagery points to Jesus as the testator who made the promise to Abraham and who activated it by His own death.

17. For a testament [is] of force after men are dead: That piece of paper, *NLT* . . . For a will goes into force only, *Norlie* . . . For a will is valid only after a man is dead, *Williams.*

otherwise it is of no strength at all while the testator liveth: . . . it is never valid when that which ratifies it is alive, *Wilson* . . . means nothing as long as he is alive, *NLT* . . . as long as the one who made it is still living, *Beck* . . . is still alive, *Adams.*

942.2 adj nom sing fem	**1878.1** conj	**3246.1** partic	**2453.2** verb 3sing indic pres act	**3616.1** conj	**2180.1** verb sing indic pres act
βεβαία,	ἐπεὶ	μήποτε	ἰσχύει	ὅτε	ζῇ
bebaia	*epei*	*mēpote*	*ischuei*	*hote*	*zē*
affirmed,	since	in no way	it is of force	when	is living

3450.5 art nom sing masc	**1297.3** verb nom sing masc part aor mid	**3468.1** adv	**3624.2** adv	**3624.1** conj
ὁ	διαθέμενος.	**18.** ὅθεν	⸀ οὐδ'	[☆ οὐδὲ]
ho	*diathemenos*	*hothen*	*oud'*	*oude*
the	having made covenant.	Hence	neither	[idem]

3450.9 art nom sing fem	**4272.9** num ord nom sing fem	**5400.1** prep	**129.2** noun gen sing neu	**1450.2** verb 3sing indic perf mid
ἡ	πρώτη	χωρὶς	αἵματος	ἐγκεκαίνισται.
hē	*prōtē*	*chōris*	*haimatos*	*enkekainistai*
the	first	apart from	blood	has been inaugurated.

2953.54 verb gen sing fem part aor pass	**1056.1** conj	**3820.10** adj gen sing fem	**1769.2** noun gen sing fem	**2567.3** prep
19. λαληθείσης	γὰρ	πάσης	ἐντολῆς	κατὰ
lalētheisēs	*gar*	*pasēs*	*entolēs*	*kata*
Having been spoken	for	every	commandment	according to

19.a.**Var:** 01ℵ-corr,02A 04C,06D-org,020L,33 Lach,Treg,Alf,Word We/Ho,Weis,Sod UBS/☆

3450.6 art acc sing masc	**3414.4** noun acc sing masc	**5097.3** prep	**3338.2** name gen masc	**3820.3** adj dat sing	**3450.3** art dat sing
[a☆+ τὸν]	νόμον	ὑπὸ	Μωϋσέως	παντὶ	τῷ
ton	*nomon*	*hupo*	*Mōuseōs*	*panti*	*tō*
[the]	law	by	Moses	to all	the

2967.3 noun dat sing masc	**2956.25** verb nom sing masc part aor act	**3450.16** art sing neu	**129.1** noun sing neu	**3450.1** art gen pl	**3311.3** noun gen pl masc
λαῷ,	λαβὼν	τὸ	αἷμα	τῶν	μόσχων
laō	*labōn*	*to*	*haima*	*tōn*	*moschōn*
people,	having taken	the	blood	of the	calves

19.b.**Var:** 01ℵ-org,02A 04C,06D,sa.Lach,Treg Alf,Word,Tisc,We/Ho Weis,Sod,UBS/☆

2504.1 conj	**3450.1** art gen pl	**4970.1** noun gen pl masc	**3196.3** prep	**5045.2** noun gen sing neu	**2504.1** conj	**2037.2** noun gen sing neu
καὶ	[b☆+ τῶν]	τράγων,	μετὰ	ὕδατος	καὶ	ἐρίου
kai	*tōn*	*tragōn*	*meta*	*hudatos*	*kai*	*eriou*
and	[of the]	of goats,	with	water	and	wool

2820.2 adj gen sing neu	**2504.1** conj	**5138.1** noun gen sing masc	**840.15** prs-pron sing neu	**4885.1** conj	**3450.16** art sing neu
κοκκίνου	καὶ	ὑσσώπου	αὐτό	τε	τὸ
kokkinou	*kai*	*hussōpou*	*auto*	*te*	*to*
scarlet	and	hyssop,	itself	both	the

968.1 noun sing neu	**2504.1** conj	**3820.1** adj	**3450.6** art acc sing masc	**2967.4** noun acc sing masc	**4329.2** verb 3sing indic aor act
βιβλίον	καὶ	πάντα	τὸν	λαὸν	ἐρράντισεν,
biblion	*kai*	*panta*	*ton*	*laon*	*errhantisen*
book	and	all	the	people	he sprinkled,

2978.15 verb nom sing masc part pres act	**3642.17** dem-pron sing neu	**3450.16** art sing neu	**129.1** noun sing neu	**3450.10** art gen sing fem	**1236.2** noun gen sing fem
20. λέγων,	Τοῦτο	τὸ	αἷμα	τῆς	διαθήκης
legōn	*Touto*	*to*	*haima*	*tēs*	*diathēkēs*
saying,	This	the	blood	of the	covenant

3614.10 rel-pron gen sing fem	**1765.3** verb 3sing indic aor mid	**4242.1** prep	**5050.4** prs-pron acc 2pl	**3450.5** art nom sing masc	**2296.1** noun nom sing masc
ἧς	ἐνετείλατο	πρὸς	ὑμᾶς	ὁ	θεός·
hēs	*eneteilato*	*pros*	*humas*	*ho*	*theos*
which	enjoined	to	you		God.

9:18,19. The necessity of a death in the carrying out of any settlement based upon a divine *diathēkē* is illustrated by the procedures used when God established the first covenant, that is, the Mosaic covenant, with the Children of Israel at Sinai. The record found in Exodus 24:5-8 is clear. When the Lord inaugurated (*enkekainistai*) the Mosaic covenant, animals were sacrificed, and their blood was used in the ceremonies and rites accompanying the ratification of the compact.

To speak vividly, in type, of the death of Christ which was to come, Jehovah instructed Moses that animals must lose their lives at the institution of His first covenant with Israel. To stand in solemn assembly and watch them die for their sins, knowing they had done no wrong, must have had a sobering effect on the worshipers. They may have wept as eyes focused on the cutting of each creature's throat while a priest caught his blood in an appropriate container. Exodus says, "Moses took half of the blood, and put it in basins; and half of the blood he sprinkled on the altar" (Exodus 24:6). It was a dramatic picture of redemption.

Silence settled over the congregation of Israel as Moses read from the book of the old covenant. Then the great leader of God's people placed the scroll in a conspicuous place and sprinkled some of the blood from the bowl on it. The rest of the second half of the blood Moses used in a ceremony one would have to experience to sense its full impact. Scripture says, "And Moses took the blood, and sprinkled it on the people, and said, Behold the blood of the covenant, which the Lord hath made with you concerning all these words" (Exodus 24:8). Understandably, those present responded, "All that the Lord hath said will we do, and be obedient" (Exodus 24:7).

9:20. The description of the inauguration of the Mosaic covenant given by the writer was not a word-for-word or step-by- step quotation from the Old Testament account. The basic purpose in alluding to the inauguration of the Mosaic covenant seems to be found in the words "the blood of the testament." They come directly from Exodus 24:8 which uses the word "covenant." They form the proof of the argument. When God establishes a covenant (*diathēkē*), blood must be shed. The inspired writer links the establishing of the first covenant with the new covenant by combining the words of Exodus 24:8 with words spoken by our Lord Jesus Christ when He was about to inaugurate the new covenant: "This" and "which God hath enjoined unto you." Compare Hebrews 9:20 with Mark 14:24; Matthew 26:28; Luke 22:20; 1 Corinthians 11:25. The word "this" (*touto*) appears in all the records of Jesus' establishment of the Lord's Supper. The other words are a paraphrase of Exodus 24:8.

9:21. This verse moves beyond the inauguration of the Mosaic covenant to describe events that occurred later: the consecration

18. Whereupon neither the first [testament] was dedicated without blood: That is why, *TNT* . . . As a matter of fact, *Noli* . . . Consequently, *Wade* . . . It was for this very reason, *Barclay* . . . the first Agreement of God's will was not put into force, *Phillips* . . . neither the former was renewed without blood, *Fenton* . . . neither was the first testament inaugurated without blood, *Wuest* . . . not even the first covenant was ratified without the use of blood, *Williams* . . . was not in effect until blood sealed it, *SEB.*

19. For when Moses had spoken: . . . having been repeated by, *Fenton* . . . had announced, *Barclay* . . . had been communicated...by Moses, *Wade* . . . had been proclaimed by Moses, *TNT* . . . had promulgated, *Noli.*

every precept to all the people according to the law: . . . had given all the rules of the law, *BB* . . . every regulation in the law...to all the people, *Williams* . . . told the people of every command, *Phillips* . . . every commandment comprised in the Law, *Wade.*

he took the blood of calves and of goats: . . . of the sacrificed calves, *Noli* . . . young oxen, *BB.*

with water, and scarlet wool, and hyssop: . . . together with the water, *Wade* . . . crimson wool, and a bunch of, *Williams* . . . red wool, *BB.*

and sprinkled both the book and all the people: . . . put it on the book itself, *BB* . . . the Lawbook, *Wade* . . . both the scroll itself and the entire people, *Concordant* . . . the book containing the law and all the people, *Williams.*

20. Saying, This [is] the blood of the testament: . . . declaring This is the Blood making binding the Covenant, *Wade* . . . This blood seals the agreement, *SEB* . . . is the sign of the agreement, *BB* . . . that ratifies the covenant, *Williams.*

which God hath enjoined unto you: . . . that God commanded you to obey, *SEB* . . . commanded me to make with you, *Williams* . . . has prescribed for you, *Norlie* . . . ordered you to keep, *Adams* . . . which God has concluded with you, *Fenton* . . . which God makes for you, *Phillips.*

2504.1 conj	3450.12 art acc sing fem	4488.4 noun acc sing fem	1156.2 conj	2504.1 conj	3820.1 adj	3450.17 art pl neu
21. καὶ	τὴν	σκηνὴν	δὲ	καὶ	πάντα	τὰ
kai	tēn	skēnēn	de	kai	panta	ta
And	the	tabernacle	too	and	all	the

4487.3 noun pl neu	3450.10 art gen sing fem	2983.1 noun gen sing fem	3450.3 art dat sing	129.3 noun dat sing neu	3532.1 adv
σκεύη	τῆς	λειτουργίας	τῷ	αἵματι	ὁμοίως
skeuē	tēs	leitourgias	tō	haimati	homoiōs
vessels	of the	ministration	with	blood	in like manner

4329.2 verb 3sing indic aor act	2504.1 conj	4827.1 adv	1706.1 prep	129.3 noun dat sing neu	3820.1 adj
ἐῤῥάντισεν.	22. καὶ	σχεδὸν	ἐν	αἵματι	πάντα
errhantisen	kai	schedon	en	haimati	panta
he sprinkled;	and	almost	with	blood	all things

2483.12 verb 3sing indic pres mid	2567.3 prep	3450.6 art acc sing masc	3414.4 noun acc sing masc	2504.1 conj	5400.1 prep
καθαρίζεται	κατὰ	τὸν	νόμον,	καὶ	χωρὶς
katharizetai	kata	ton	nomon	kai	chōris
are being purified	according to	the	law,	and	apart from

130.1 noun gen sing fem	3620.3 partic	1090.14 verb 3sing indic pres mid	852.1 noun nom sing fem	316.1 noun nom sing fem
αἱματεκχυσίας	οὐ	γίνεται	ἄφεσις.	23. Ἀνάγκη
haimatekchusias	ou	ginetai	aphesis	Anankē
blood shedding	no	there is	remission.	Necessary

3631.1 partic	3450.17 art pl neu	3173.1 conj	5100.3 noun pl neu	3450.1 art gen pl	1706.1 prep	3450.4 art dat pl
οὖν	τὰ	μὲν	ὑποδείγματα	τῶν	ἐν	τοῖς
oun	ta	men	hupodeigmata	tōn	en	tois
then	the		representations	of the things	in	the

3636.8 noun dat pl masc	3642.3 dem-pron dat pl	2483.14 verb inf pres mid	840.16 prs-pron pl neu	1156.2 conj
οὐρανοῖς	τούτοις	καθαρίζεσθαι,	αὐτὰ	δὲ
ouranois	toutois	katharizesthai	auta	de
heavens	with these	to be purified,	themselves	but

3450.17 art pl neu	2016.7 adj pl neu	2882.4 adj comp dat pl fem	2355.7 noun dat pl fem	3706.2 prep	3642.15 dem-pron acc pl fem
τὰ	ἐπουράνια	κρείττοσιν	θυσίαις	παρὰ	ταύτας.
ta	epourania	kreittosin	thusiais	para	tautas
the	heavenlies	with better	sacrifices	than	these.

3620.3 partic	1056.1 conj	1519.1 prep	5335.4 adj pl neu	39.16 adj pl neu	1511.3 verb 3sing indic aor act
24. οὐ	γὰρ	εἰς	χειροποίητα	⸉ ἅγια	εἰσῆλθεν
ou	gar	eis	cheiropoiēta	hagia	eisēlthen
Not	for	into	made by hands	holies	entered

24.a.**Txt:** 04C-corr 06D-corr,018K,020L 025P,byz.
Var: 01ℵ,02A,04C-org 06D-org,33,Lach,Treg Alf,Word,Tisc,We/Ho Weis,Sod,UBS/⋆

1511.3 verb 3sing indic aor act	39.16 adj pl neu	3450.5 art nom sing masc	5382.1 name nom masc	496.2 adj pl neu	3450.1 art gen pl
[⋆ εἰσῆλθεν	ἅγια]	⸂a ὁ ⸃	Χριστός,	ἀντίτυπα	τῶν
eisēlthen	hagia	ho	Christos	antitupa	tōn
[entered	holies]	the	Christ,	figures	of the

226.8 adj gen pl neu	233.1 conj	1519.1 prep	840.6 prs-pron acc sing masc	3450.6 art acc sing masc	3636.4 noun acc sing masc	3431.1 adv
ἀληθινῶν,	ἀλλ'	εἰς	αὐτὸν	τὸν	οὐρανόν,	νῦν
alēthinōn	all'	eis	auton	ton	ouranon	nun
true,	but	into	itself	the	heaven,	now

of the tabernacle and its sacred vessels. No specific references are cited. The emphasis is on the place of sacrificial blood in the rites associated with the Mosaic law. By divine commandment blood was pervasive in the observance of the old covenant.

9:22. Two more pieces of evidence are here presented for the contention concerning the preeminence of blood sacrifice under the old covenant. The use of blood sacrifice in ceremonial rites of cleansing and in sacrifices for the ceremonial remission of sin is cited. In almost all cases of ritual cleansing of ceremonially defiled persons and objects a blood sacrifice was commanded.

Scholars point out three exceptions to this law: (1) Poor people were allowed to bring a meal offering for their sin offering (Leviticus 5:11); (2) Metal weapons taken as the spoils of war were to be cleansed by fire (Numbers 31:50); (3) When the nation of Israel was cleansed after the rebellion of Korah, incense is mentioned but not blood sacrifice (Numbers 16:46). Otherwise, all instances of cleansing involved animal sacrifice of some kind.

The second evidence, found in Leviticus 17:11, says the Lord has given sacrificial blood to make atonement for human lives. There may be ritual cleansing that is bloodless, but there can be no forgiveness of sin without sacrificial bloodshed. These sacrifices typified the death of Jesus, the Lamb of God, who gave His life for the whole world.

9:23. Moses only copied the tabernacle and its furnishings after the heavenly articles revealed to him on Mount Sinai; therefore, it was appropriate for the sacrifices offered on these earthly altars to be sheep and bulls and goats. The ceremonial cleansing of the Law only cleansed earthly and physical things. Heaven needed a sacrifice that was better.

9:24. That the heavenly realities shown to Moses on Mount Sinai needed to be cleansed with better sacrifices than the blood of bulls and goats was demonstrated by the ascension of Jesus Christ into heaven itself. He is seated in the heavens at the right hand of God the Father. It is there that He makes priestly intercession for His people. He did not enter into the Holy of Holies here on earth. He did not deal with the earthly figures and copies. He had to do with the genuine articles. His high priestly ministry takes place in "heaven itself." Moreover, what He does in heaven is "to appear in the presence of God for us." And He is doing it "now." So the contrast with the ministry and sacrifices of the Aaronic high priesthood advances. Not animals, but the Son; not on earth in a tent, but in heaven in the very presence of God.

21. Moreover he sprinkled with blood: In the same way, *NLT.*

both the tabernacle, and all the vessels of the ministry: . . . the tent and all the utensils of the priestly service, *Williams* . . . and all the vessels of worship, *Adams* . . . all the vessels of service, *Montgomery* . . . and all the tools for service, *Klingensmith* . . . All the utensils of the public service, *Wilson* . . . utensils used in divine worship, *Norlie.*

22. And almost all things are by the law purged with blood: . . . under the law, *Williams* . . . purified by Blood, *Wilson.*

and without shedding of blood is no remission: . . . and without an Effusion of Blood no Forgiveness takes place, *Wilson* . . . there is not forgiveness of sins, *Adams* . . . Sins are not forgiven unless blood is given, *NLT* . . . no sins are forgiven, *Beck* . . . no forgiveness is granted, *Williams* . . . is coming no pardon, *Concordant* . . . no forgiveness was to be obtained, *TCNT.*

23. [It was] therefore necessary: . . . on the one hand, *Williams.*

that the patterns of things in the heavens: . . . that the copies of the heavenly things, *Montgomery* . . . the copies of the original things in heaven, *Williams* . . . But the highest things needed, *Klingensmith.*

should be purified with these: . . . by these rites, *Norlie* . . . with such sacrifices, *Williams.*

but the heavenly things themselves with better sacrifices than these: . . . the original things themselves in heaven, *Williams* . . . required nobler sacrifices, *Montgomery.*

24. For Christ is not entered into the holy places made with hands: . . . a sanctuary made by human hands, *Williams.*

[which are] the figures of the true: . . . and just a copy of the real thing, *Beck* . . . that is a picture of, *Adams* . . . representations of, *Concordant.*

but into heaven itself: . . . it was into heaven itself that He went, *Williams.*

now to appear in the presence of God for us: . . . on our behalf, *Adams.*

Hebrews 9:25

1702.8 verb inf aor pass	3450.3 art dat sing	4241.3 noun dat sing neu	3450.2 art gen sing	2296.2 noun gen sing masc	5065.1 prep
ἐμφανισθῆναι	τῷ	προσώπῳ	τοῦ	θεοῦ	ὑπὲρ
emphanisthēnai	*tō*	*prosōpō*	*tou*	*theou*	*huper*
to appear	in the	face		of God	for

2231.2 prs-pron gen 1pl		3624.2 adv	2419.1 conj	4038.1 adv	4232.4 verb 3sing subj pres act	1431.6 prs-pron acc sing masc
ἡμῶν·	**25.**	οὐδ'	ἵνα	πολλάκις	προσφέρῃ	ἑαυτόν,
hēmōn		*oud'*	*hina*	*pollakis*	*prospherē*	*heauton*
us:		nor	that	often	he should offer	himself,

5450.1 conj	3450.5 art nom sing masc	744.1 noun nom sing masc	1511.26 verb 3sing indic pres mid	1519.1 prep	3450.17 art pl neu
ὥσπερ	ὁ	ἀρχιερεὺς	εἰσέρχεται	εἰς	τὰ
hōsper	*ho*	*archiereus*	*eiserchetai*	*eis*	*ta*
even as	the	high priest	enters	into	the

39.16 adj pl neu	2567.1 prep	1747.2 noun acc sing masc	1706.1 prep	129.3 noun dat sing neu	243.1 adj dat sing		1878.1 conj
ἅγια	κατ'	ἐνιαυτὸν	ἐν	αἵματι	ἀλλοτρίῳ·	**26.**	ἐπεὶ
hagia	*kat'*	*eniauton*	*en*	*haimati*	*allotriō*		*epei*
holies	by	year	with	blood	another's;		since

1158.6 verb 3sing indic imperf act	840.6 prs-pron acc sing masc	4038.1 adv	3819.18 verb inf aor act	570.3 prep
ἔδει	αὐτὸν	πολλάκις	παθεῖν	ἀπὸ
edei	*auton*	*pollakis*	*pathein*	*apo*
it was necessary for	him	often	to have suffered	from

2573.1 noun gen sing fem	2862.2 noun gen sing masc	3431.1 adv	3432.1 adv	1156.2 conj	526.1 adv
καταβολῆς	κόσμου·	ʻ νῦν	[☆ νυνὶ]	δὲ	ἅπαξ
katabolēs	*kosmou*	*nun*	*nuni*	*de*	*hapax*
foundation	of world.	Now	[idem]	but	once

1894.3 prep	4782.3 noun dat sing fem	3450.1 art gen pl	163.4 noun gen pl masc	1519.1 prep	115.2 noun acc sing fem
ἐπὶ	συντελείᾳ	τῶν	αἰώνων,	εἰς	ἀθέτησιν
epi	*sunteleia*	*tōn*	*aiōnōn*	*eis*	*athetēsin*
in	consummation	of the	ages,	for	putting away

26.a.**Var:** 01ℵ,02A,025P 33,sa.bo.Lach,Treg We/Ho,Weis,Sod UBS/☆

3450.10 art gen sing fem	264.1 noun fem	1217.2 prep	3450.10 art gen sing fem	2355.1 noun fem
[ᵃ☆+ τῆς]	ἁμαρτίας,	διὰ	τῆς	θυσίας
tēs	*hamartias*	*dia*	*tēs*	*thusias*
[of the]	of sin	by	the	sacrifice

840.3 prs-pron gen sing	5157.18 verb 3sing indic perf mid		2504.1 conj	2567.2 prep	3607.1 rel-pron sing
αὐτοῦ	πεφανέρωται.	**27.**	καὶ	καθ'	ὅσον
autou	*pephanerōtai*		*kai*	*kath'*	*hoson*
his	he has been manifested.		And	for	as much as

601.1 verb 3sing indic pres mid	3450.4 art dat pl	442.8 noun dat pl masc	526.1 adv	594.20 verb inf aor act	3196.3 prep
ἀπόκειται	τοῖς	ἀνθρώποις	ἅπαξ	ἀποθανεῖν,	μετὰ
apokeitai	*tois*	*anthrōpois*	*hapax*	*apothanein*	*meta*
it is apportioned	for the	men	once	to die,	after

28.a.**Var:** 01ℵ,02A,04C 06D,018K,020L,025P byz.sa.bo.Gries,Lach Treg,Alf,Word,Tisc We/Ho,Weis,Sod UBS/☆

1156.2 conj	3642.17 dem-pron sing neu	2893.1 noun nom sing fem		3643.1 adv	2504.1 conj	3450.5 art nom sing masc
δὲ	τοῦτο	κρίσις·	**28.**	οὕτως	[ᵃ☆+ καὶ]	ὁ
de	*touto*	*krisis*		*houtōs*	*kai*	*ho*
and	this,	judgment;		thus	[also]	the

9:25. Another element of contrast is that Jesus did not have to offer himself as a sacrifice on more than one occasion. The high priests of the Levitical order were commanded by the Lord to enter into the sanctuary once every year (Leviticus 16). Furthermore, this annual sacrifice did not involve the sacrifice of themselves; they instead offered the blood shed by other victims, the animals previously mentioned. In every way this epistle proves that the work and sacrifice of God's Son, Jesus Christ the Lord, is definitely superior to those of the old covenant.

9:26. If Jesus had been on the same level as the Levitical priests, it would have been necessary for Him to have suffered many times "since the foundation of the world." This statement is a bit puzzling and, in the end, mind-boggling. Since the Son is also the Creator, He was also available at the foundation of the world. Yet this does not seem to be the intended meaning. The argument is the value of Christ's self-sacrifice contrasted to the value of the animal sacrifices required by the Mosaic law. Obviously, the self-sacrifice by its very nature could only be performed once. If it had only the same power as the annual sacrifices, it would have had to be repeated over and over from the beginning of time to equal the value of the animal sacrifices.

This, however, has not been the case. Because He is the eternal Son of God, Jesus accomplished more than all of the sacrificed animals by sacrificing himself only once. In Him the Father has spoken finally "in these last days" (1:2). His single sacrifice has ushered in "the end of the world" (literally the Greek says "the end of the ages"). He has by His atonement begun the final age of human history. By offering himself, He has accomplished what all of the animal sacrifices failed to do: the annulment (*athetēsin*) of sin. For as Horatius Bonar declares in his hymn, "Richer blood has flow'd from nobler veins to purge the soul from guilt and cleanse the reddest stains."

9:27. Since Jesus has "put away sin," there remains no more need for sacrifice. He does not need to sacrifice himself over and over again, and believers do not need to continue to offer blood sacrifices. The ritual sacrifices of the Mosaic system served God's intended purpose. The old covenant was "ready to vanish away" (8:13). Shortly after this epistle was written, the animal sacrifices of Judaism ceased with the destruction of the Jerusalem temple in A.D. 70. (The Jews did offer sacrifices on the ruins of the temple for a short while until the Romans stopped them.) Christ died once for all, and the next item on His agenda is "the judgment." But He will be the Judge.

9:28. So Jesus Christ, God's Son, was offered once in death. And what a death it was: a substitutionary death. The words used here are graphic. He was offered "to bear the sins of many." God placed

25. Nor yet that he should offer himself often: Nor has He done so for the purpose of offering himself in sacrifice frequently, *Wade* . . . offer Himself repeatedly, *Adams* . . . has not given Himself many times, *NLT* . . . He did not have to make an offering of Himself again and again, *Norlie* . . . not to sacrifice Himself over and over again, *Beck.*

as the high priest entereth into the holy place every year: . . . enters the sanctuary, *TNT.*

with blood of others: . . . with an offering of, *TNT* . . . with blood that is not his own, *Williams, Wade.*

26. For then must he often have suffered: . . . if that had been the case, He would have had to suffer over and over again, *Williams* . . . seeing that otherwise Christ would have had to suffer death repeatedly, *Wade.*

since the foundation of the world: . . . from the time of the creation, *Norlie* . . . from the beginning of the universe, *Klingensmith.*

but now once: . . . as it is, once, *Williams* . . . for all time, *NLT.*

in the end of the world hath he appeared: He has manifested Himself once for all at the Consummation of the World's successive Ages, *Wade* . . . He has appeared, *Adams* . . . at the perfect completion of the ages, *Klingensmith* . . . at the end of the ages, *Montgomery* . . . at a Completion of the Ages, *Wilson* . . . he has been revealed, *TNT.*

to put away sin by the sacrifice of himself: . . . get rid of sin, *Beck* . . . that sin may be set aside, *TNT* . . . to abolish sin through the sacrifice of Himself, *Wade.*

27. And as it is appointed unto men once to die: Indeed, just as men must die but once, *Williams* . . . Men are destined once, *Norlie* . . . inasmuch as the destiny in store for men is to die only once, *Wade.*

but after this the judgment: . . . they face judgment, *Adams* . . . be judged, *Williams.*

28. So Christ: . . . so too, *TNT.*

was once offered to bear the sins of many: . . . once for all to take away the sins, *Williams.*

Hebrews 10:1

5382.1 name nom masc	526.1 adv	4232.25 verb nom sing masc part aor pass	1519.1 prep	3450.16 art sing neu	4044.1 adj gen pl
Χριστός	ἅπαξ	προσενεχθεὶς	εἰς	τὸ	πολλῶν
Christos	*hapax*	*prosenechtheis*	*eis*	*to*	*pollōn*
Christ,	once	having been offered	for	the	of many

397.6 verb inf aor act	264.1 noun fem	1523.2 prep gen	1202.1 num ord gen sing	5400.1 prep	264.1 noun fem
ἀνενεγκεῖν	ἁμαρτίας,	ἐκ	δευτέρου	χωρὶς	ἁμαρτίας
anenenkein	*hamartias*	*ek*	*deuterou*	*chōris*	*hamartias*
to bear	sins,	of	second time	apart from	sin

3571.30 verb 3sing indic fut pass	3450.4 art dat pl	840.6 prs-pron acc sing masc	549.4 verb dat pl masc part pres mid	1519.1 prep
ὀφθήσεται	τοῖς	αὐτὸν	ἀπεκδεχομένοις	εἰς
ophthēsetai	*tois*	*auton*	*apekdechomenois*	*eis*
shall appear	to those that	him	awaiting	for

4843.3 noun acc sing fem	4494.3 noun acc sing fem	1056.1 conj	2174.17 verb nom sing masc part pres act	3450.5 art nom sing masc
σωτηρίαν.	**10:1.** Σκιὰν	γὰρ	ἔχων	ὁ
sōtērian	*Skian*	*gar*	*echōn*	*ho*
salvation.	A shadow	for	having	the

3414.1 noun nom sing masc	3450.1 art gen pl	3165.11 verb gen pl part pres act	18.1 adj gen pl	3620.2 partic	840.12 prs-pron acc sing fem
νόμος	τῶν	μελλόντων	ἀγαθῶν,	οὐκ	αὐτὴν
nomos	*tōn*	*mellontōn*	*agathōn*	*ouk*	*autēn*
law	of the	coming	good things,	not	itself

3450.12 art acc sing fem	1494.4 noun acc sing fem	3450.1 art gen pl	4088.4 noun gen pl neu	2567.1 prep	1747.2 noun acc sing masc
τὴν	εἰκόνα	τῶν	πραγμάτων,	κατ'	ἐνιαυτὸν
tēn	*eikona*	*tōn*	*pragmatōn*	*kat'*	*eniauton*
the	image	of the	things,	by	year

1.a.**Txt:** p46,02A,04C 06D,08E,015H,018K 020L,byz.
Var: 01ℵ,025P

3450.14 art dat pl fem	840.14 prs-pron dat pl fem	2355.7 noun dat pl fem	840.1 prs-pron gen pl	3614.15 rel-pron acc pl fem
ταῖς	αὐταῖς	θυσίαις	[a+ αὐτῶν]	ἃς
tais	*autais*	*thusiais*	*autōn*	*has*
with the	same	sacrifices	[their]	which

4232.1 verb 3pl indic pres act	1519.1 prep	3450.16 art sing neu	1330.1 adj sing neu	3626.1 adv
προσφέρουσιν	εἰς	τὸ	διηνεκὲς	οὐδέποτε
prospherousin	*eis*	*to*	*diēnekes*	*oudepote*
they offer	to	the	perpetuity	never

1.b.**Txt:** p46,06D-org 08E,015H,018K,020L 044,326,365,629,630 1739,1881,byz.
Var: 01ℵ,02A,04C 06D-corr1,025P,33,81 104,614,1241,2495

1404.4 verb 3sing indic pres mid	1404.7 verb 3pl indic pres mid	3450.8 art acc pl masc	4193.16 verb acc pl masc part pres mid
(b☆ δύναται	[b δύνανται]	τοὺς	προσερχομένους
dunatai	*dunantai*	*tous*	*proserchomenous*
is able	[are able]	the	approaching

4896.5 verb inf aor act	1878.1 conj	3620.2 partic	300.1 partic	3835.7 verb 3pl indic aor mid
τελειῶσαι.	**2.** ἐπεὶ	οὐκ	ἂν	ἐπαύσαντο
teleiōsai	*epei*	*ouk*	*an*	*epausanto*
to perfect.	Since	not	would	they have ceased

4232.23 verb nom pl fem part pres mid	1217.2 prep	3450.16 art sing neu	3235.5 num card acc fem	2174.29 verb inf pres act
προσφερόμεναι,	διὰ	τὸ	μηδεμίαν	ἔχειν
prospheromenai	*dia*	*to*	*mēdemian*	*echein*
being offered,	on account of	the	not any	to have

upon Him "the sins of many." He carried away, bore the burden, and removed (*anenenkein*) sins for the many. The sins of all who will believe were laid on Him. He has borne the penalty for sin (i.e., for the many of those who believe), and they do not have to look forward to judgment. Instead, believers, those who look for Him, discover that for them Jesus will "appear the second time without sin unto salvation." By His one sacrifice, He has removed believers' sins forever. When He returns He will not come as a sacrifice, nor will He come to condemn and remind believers of their sins; He will come to bring what He promised: the inheritance secured and guaranteed by His atoning death—the believers' eternal salvation.

10:1. In the first four verses of chapter 10, the argument for the superiority of Jesus' once-for-all sacrifice is emphasized by the references to the inadequacies of the Levitical sacrifices. Added to the reiteration of points made previously, fresh insights are given.

First of all, the inspired writer put the two covenants in their proper relationship. The new was portrayed as "the very image of the things" (*autēn tēn eikona tōn pragmatōn*); that is, it is the reality, the embodiment of the real thing. The old, the Mosaic law, was but the shadow cast by the new covenant. In the Law there was only the rough outline of the new covenant but not all its colors and details. The new covenant was also called "good things to come." This emphasized its quality as "good" and underscored the fact that it brought into existence things that did not exist under the old covenant.

The chief point of contrast was made in regard to the sacrificial system enacted by the Mosaic law. The phrase "those sacrifices" refers to the animal sacrifices mentioned in chapter 9, particularly those offered annually on the 10th of Tishri, the Day of Atonement. They were inadequate because they could not perfect those who offered them.

10:2. The inadequacy of the Levitical sacrifices is obvious. They did not deal with sin in any final sense. The fact that they had to be offered over and over again on an annual basis is proof of this contention. If they had been effective in a final sense, they would not have been repeated year after year. Having made this point clear, the writer then proceeded to identify further the nature of their inadequacy. If those who offered sacrifices under the Levitical system had actually been once for all (*hapax*) purified (*kekatharmenous*), literally had been cleansed and remained cleansed of their sins, they would not still have had any awareness of their sinful guilt before God. It is clear, however, that they were continually aware of their guilt before God because their consciousness of guilt forced them to keep on offering animal sacrifices, not only on Yom Kippur, the Day of Atonement, but on various occasions between the annual Day of Atonement.

and unto them that look for him: ... those who are eagerly waiting for Him, *Williams* ... to those who are awaiting him, *TNT.*

shall he appear the second time without sin: ... again He will appear, without having anything to do with sin, *Williams* ... not as a sin-bearer, *Norlie* ... not to deal with sin, *TNT* ... no longer burdened by human sin, *Wade.*

unto salvation: ... but to bring salvation to, *TNT* ... to bring them final salvation, *Williams* ... for the accomplishment of their Salvation, *Wade.*

1. For the law having a shadow of good things to come: ... since the law cast only a shadow of the blessings to come, *Williams* ... is like a picture, *NLT* ... only a shadow of the benefits in store for the godly, *Norlie* ... having only a dim outline of the good things in the future, *Beck* ... since it provides only an outline of, *Wade* ... It only foreshadows blessings that are to come, *TNT.*

[and] not the very image of the things: ... and not a perfect reproduction of the Reality of those Blessings, *Wade* ... is not identical with actual realities, *TNT* ... and not their very substance, *Montgomery* ... did not possess the reality itself of those blessings, *Williams.*

can never with those sacrifices: ... by a repetition of the same sacrifices, *Wade.*

which they offered year by year continually: ... by a constant repetition of the same sacrifices, *TNT* ... repeated endlessly year after year, *Beck* ... that are perpetually offered, *Williams.*

make the comers thereunto perfect: ... make worshippers perfect, *TNT* ... make perfect those who come to worship, *Williams* ... can never...render perfect those who approach to worship, *Wade.*

2. For then would they not have ceased to be offered?: ... otherwise, would not such sacrifices (I ask) have ceased to be presented, *Wade* ... If that were possible, the sacrifices would no longer be offered, *TNT.*

because that the worshippers once purged: ... because those who offered them, having once been purified, *Williams.*

Hebrews 10:3

2.a.**Txt:** 020L,byz.
Var: 01א,06D,018K 025P,33,Treg,Alf,Word Tisc,We/Ho,Weis,Sod UBS/☆

2068.1 adv	4743.4 noun acc sing fem	264.6 noun gen pl fem	3450.8 art acc pl masc	2973.6 verb acc pl masc part pres act
ἔτι	συνείδησιν	ἁμαρτιῶν	τοὺς	λατρεύοντας,
eti	*suneidēsin*	*hamartiōn*	*tous*	*latreuontas*
longer	conscience	of sins	the	serving

526.1 adv	2480.2 verb acc pl masc part perf mid	2483.19 verb acc pl masc part perf mid	233.1 conj
ἅπαξ	‹ κεκαθαρμένους;	[a☆ κεκαθαρισμένους;]	3. ἀλλ'
hapax	*kekatharmenous*	*kekatharismenous*	*all'*
once	having been cleansed?	[idem]	But

1706.1 prep	840.14 prs-pron dat pl fem	363.1 noun nom sing fem	264.6 noun gen pl fem	2567.1 prep	1747.2 noun acc sing masc
ἐν	αὐταῖς	ἀνάμνησις	ἁμαρτιῶν	κατ'	ἐνιαυτόν.
en	*autais*	*anamnēsis*	*hamartiōn*	*kat'*	*eniauton*
in	them	a remembrance	of sins	by	year.

101.3 adj sing neu	1056.1 conj	129.1 noun sing neu	4873.2 noun gen pl masc	2504.1 conj	4970.1 noun gen pl masc
4. ἀδύνατον	γὰρ	αἷμα	ταύρων	καὶ	τράγων
adunaton	*gar*	*haima*	*taurōn*	*kai*	*tragōn*
Impossible	for	blood	of bulls	and	of goats

844.2 verb inf pres act	264.1 noun fem	1346.1 conj	1511.31 verb nom sing masc part pres mid	1519.1 prep
ἀφαιρεῖν	ἁμαρτίας.	5. Διὸ	εἰσερχόμενος	εἰς
aphairein	*hamartias*	*Dio*	*eiserchomenos*	*eis*
to take away	sins.	Wherefore	coming	into

3450.6 art acc sing masc	2862.4 noun acc sing masc	2978.5 verb 3sing indic pres act	2355.4 noun acc sing fem	2504.1 conj	4234.4 noun acc sing fem
τὸν	κόσμον	λέγει,	Θυσίαν	καὶ	προσφορὰν
ton	*kosmon*	*legei*	*Thusian*	*kai*	*prosphoran*
the	world	he says,	Sacrifice	and	offering

3620.2 partic	2286.21 verb 2sing indic aor act	4835.1 noun sing neu	1156.2 conj	2645.5 verb 2sing indic aor mid	1466.4 prs-pron dat 1sing
οὐκ	ἠθέλησας,	σῶμα	δὲ	κατηρτίσω	μοι·
ouk	*ēthelēsas*	*sōma*	*de*	*katērtisō*	*moi*
not	you will,	a body	but	you did prepare	me.

3509.2 noun pl neu	2504.1 conj	3875.1 prep	264.1 noun fem	3620.2 partic
6. ὁλοκαυτώματα	καὶ	περὶ	ἁμαρτίας	οὐκ
holokautōmata	*kai*	*peri*	*hamartias*	*ouk*
Burnt offerings	and	for	sin	not

2085.6 verb 2sing indic aor act	4966.1 adv	1500.3 verb indic aor act	1481.20 verb 2sing impr aor mid	2223.1 verb 1sing indic pres act
εὐδόκησας.	7. τότε	εἶπον,	Ἰδοὺ	ἥκω,
eudokēsas	*tote*	*eipon*	*Idou*	*hēkō*
you delighted in.	Then	I said,	Lo,	I come,

1706.1 prep	2749.1 noun dat sing fem	968.2 noun gen sing neu	1119.22 verb 3sing indic perf mid	3875.1 prep	1466.3 prs-pron gen 1sing
ἐν	κεφαλίδι	βιβλίου	γέγραπται	περὶ	ἐμοῦ,
en	*kephalidi*	*bibliou*	*gegraptai*	*peri*	*emou*
in	roll	of book	it is written	of	me,

3450.2 art gen sing	4020.41 verb inf aor act	3450.5 art nom sing masc	2296.1 noun nom sing masc	3450.16 art sing neu	2284.1 noun sing neu
τοῦ	ποιῆσαι,	ὁ	θεός,	τὸ	θέλημά
tou	*poiēsai*	*ho*	*theos*	*to*	*thelēma*
the	to do,	God,	the	will

10:3,4. Verse 3 comments on the effect of the sacrifices offered in the annual ceremonies of Yom Kippur. Unlike the new covenant's Lord's Supper, the sacrifices of the Day of Atonement did not provide a remembrance of forgiveness. Instead they provoked remembrance of sins committed. They were not designed to instill gratitude; they served to create guilt feelings.

The reason the animal sacrifices of the Levitical system created guilt feelings was inherent in their very nature. They did not possess the power necessary to remove the moral guilt of mankind's offense against God.

10:5-7. Much controversial discussion has been generated by the quotation of Psalm 40:6-8 in Hebrews 10:5-7. It revolves around three questions: (1) how the psalm is used, (2) the meaning of the psalm; (3) the differences between the Hebrew of the Masoretic text and the Greek language of the Septuagint and that which is used in the Epistle to the Hebrews. The differences can be explained by recognizing the Greek as a paraphrase rather than a direct quotation of the Hebrew. In the English version of the Old Testament, Psalm 40:6 reads, "Mine ears hast thou opened," while Hebrews 10:5 says, "A body hast thou prepared me." Most contemporary commentators think the quotation in Hebrews substitutes "body" for "ears" as a whole for the part. However, this interpreter feels both Psalm 40 and Hebrews refer to the custom described in Exodus 21:6 and Deuteronomy 15:17.

In those verses there is a description of a slave who has been set free by his master but who wants to continue to serve him out of love. As a sign of his voluntary servitude, he has his ears digged or pierced. This fits the argument of Hebrews at this point quite well. It also explains the paraphrase and its use of "body" for "ears." In Koine Greek the word *body* is often used as a synonym for *slave* (see M-M, "soma"). The point is that God did not prefer an animal sacrifice; He preferred the voluntary, loving servitude of Israel's obedience as a living sacrifice as opposed to empty ritual sacrifices.

The paraphrased citation of Psalm 40:6-8 is offered as an illustration of the attitude exhibited by Jesus Christ. In His incarnation He displayed the attitude which the Lord sought in Israel. He wanted the sons of Abraham to demonstrate voluntary obedience. In laying down His life as an atonement for the sins of mankind, Jesus displayed the attitude of voluntary servitude exhibited in Psalm 40:6-8, Exodus 21:1-6, and Deuteronomy 15:12-17. This willingness to serve God voluntarily by sacrificing himself (along with His superiority as God's unique, one-of-a-kind Son) makes Jesus' sacrifice superior to the sacrifice of bulls and goats.

This attitude was exemplified by Jesus after His entrance into the world as a man, for the word *hēkō* means that He had already entered into the world when He echoed the words of Psalm 40:7 (*hēkō* could be translated "I have come").

The phrase "volume of the book" refers to the requirements of the law of God revealed in the Mosaic covenant. It does not refer to the external rituals and ceremonies of the Law but to its spiritual

should have had no more conscience of sins: They would not feel guilty, *SEB* . . . would have had no further consciousness, *Williams* . . . and would no longer have a sense of guilt, *TNT.*

3. But in those [sacrifices: . . . in fact the opposite happens, *TNT* . . . On the other hand, through these sacrifices, *Williams.*

there is] a remembrance again [made] of sins every year: . . . there is given a real reminder of their sins, *Williams* . . . only serve to remind people every year, *TNT.*

4. For [it is] not possible that the blood of bulls and of goats: . . . the blood...is unable to, *Williams.*

should take away sins: . . . to be eliminating sins, *Concordant* . . . can never take sins away, *TNT.*

5. Wherefore when he cometh into the world, he saith: Consequently, *Adams* . . . It is for this reason, *Montgomery* . . . This is why, when Christ was coming...he said to God, *TNT.*

Sacrifice and offering thou wouldest not: It was not a sacrifice and an offering that you wanted, *TNT.*

but a body hast thou prepared me: Yet a body dost Thou adapt to Me, *Concordant.*

6. In burnt offerings and [sacrifices] for sin thou hast had no pleasure: You weren't pleased with, *Adams* . . . No, you never cared for, *Norlie* . . . you never took delight, *Williams* . . . You found no pleasure in, *TNT.*

7. Then said I, Lo, I come: See, I have come, *Williams* . . . Here I am, O God, *TNT.*

(in the volume of the book it is written of me,): . . . the writing in the scroll, *Beck* . . . In the roll of, *Adams* . . . In the summary of the scroll, *Concordant* . . . in the first part of the scroll, *SEB* . . . just as the Scripture writes about me, *Williams.*

to do thy will, O God: . . . what you want, *Beck.*

8. Above when he said: First He says, *Beck* . . . Although at first, *Williams.*

Hebrews 10:8

8.a.**Txt:** 01ℵ-corr 06D-corr,018K,020L byz.
Var: 01ℵ-org,02A,04C 06D-org,025P,33,sa.bo. Lach,Treg,Alf,Word Tisc,We/Ho,Weis,Sod UBS/☆

8.b.**Txt:** 01ℵ-corr 06D-corr,018K,020L byz.
Var: 01ℵ-org,02A,04C 06D-org,025P,33,sa.bo. Lach,Treg,Alf,Word Tisc,We/Ho,Weis,Sod UBS/☆

4622.2 prs-pron gen 2sing	**507.1** adv comp	**2978.15** verb nom sing masc part pres act	**3617.1** conj	**2355.4** noun acc sing fem
σου.	**8.** ᾿Ανώτερον	λέγων,	῞Οτι	⌜ Θυσίαν
sou	*Anōteron*	*legōn*	*Hoti*	*Thusian*
your.	Above	saying,		Sacrifice

2355.1 noun fem	**2504.1** conj	**4234.4** noun acc sing fem	**4234.5** noun acc pl fem	**2504.1** conj
[a☆ Θυσίας]	καὶ	⌜ προσφορὰν	[b☆ προσφορὰς]	καὶ
Thusias	*kai*	*prosphoran*	*prosphoras*	*kai*
[Sacrifices]	and	offering	[offerings]	and

3509.2 noun pl neu	**2504.1** conj	**3875.1** prep	**264.1** noun fem	**3620.2** partic	**2286.21** verb 2sing indic aor act
ὁλοκαυτώματα	καὶ	περὶ	ἁμαρτίας	οὐκ	ἠθέλησας,
holokautōmata	*kai*	*peri*	*hamartias*	*ouk*	*ēthelēsas*
burnt offerings	and	for	sin	not	you will,

8.c.**Txt:** 06D,018K,020L 025P,byz.
Var: 01ℵ,02A,04C,33 Lach,Treg,Tisc,We/Ho Weis,Sod,UBS/☆

3624.1 conj	**2085.6** verb 2sing indic aor act	**3610.4** rel-pron nom pl fem	**2567.3** prep	**3450.6** art acc sing masc
οὐδὲ	εὐδόκησας,	αἵτινες	κατὰ	⌜c τὸν ⌝
oude	*eudokēsas*	*haitines*	*kata*	*ton*
nor	delighted in,	which	according to	the

3414.4 noun acc sing masc	**4232.22** verb 3pl indic pres mid	**4966.1** adv	**2029.3** verb 3sing indic perf act	**1481.20** verb 2sing impr aor mid
νόμον	προσφέρονται,	**9.** τότε	εἴρηκεν,	Ἰδοὺ
nomon	*prospherontai*	*tote*	*eirēken*	*Idou*
law	are being offered;	then	he has said,	Lo,

9.a.**Txt:** 01ℵ-corr,020L byz.
Var: 01ℵ-org,02A,04C 06D,018K,025P,33 Gries,Lach,Treg,Alf Word,Tisc,We/Ho,Weis Sod,UBS/☆

2223.1 verb 1sing indic pres act	**3450.2** art gen sing	**4020.41** verb inf aor act	**3450.5** art nom sing masc	**2296.1** noun nom sing masc	**3450.16** art sing neu
ἥκω	τοῦ	ποιῆσαι	⌜a ὁ	Θεός ⌝	τὸ
hēkō	*tou*	*poiēsai*	*ho*	*Theos*	*to*
I come,	the	to do,		God,	the

2284.1 noun sing neu	**4622.2** prs-pron gen 2sing	**335.1** verb 3sing indic pres act	**3450.16** art sing neu	**4272.2** num ord sing	**2419.1** conj
θέλημά	σου.	ἀναιρεῖ	τὸ	πρῶτον,	ἵνα
thelēma	*sou*	*anairei*	*to*	*prōton*	*hina*
will	your.	He takes away	the	first,	that

3450.16 art sing neu	**1202.8** num ord sing neu	**2449.8** verb 3sing subj aor act	**1706.1** prep	**3614.3** rel-pron dat sing
τὸ	δεύτερον	στήσῃ·	**10.** ἐν	ᾧ
to	*deuteron*	*stēsē*	*en*	*hō*
the	second	he may establish;	by	which

10.a.**Txt:** 06D-corr,018K 020L,byz.
Var: 01ℵ,02A,04C 06D-org,025P,33,Elzev Gries,Lach,Treg,Alf Word,Tisc,We/Ho,Weis Sod,UBS/☆

2284.3 noun dat sing neu	**37.17** verb nom pl masc part perf mid	**1498.5** verb 1pl indic pres act	**3450.7** art nom pl masc	**1217.2** prep
θελήματι	ἡγιασμένοι	ἐσμὲν	⌜a οἱ ⌝	διὰ
thelēmati	*hēgiasmenoi*	*esmen*	*hoi*	*dia*
will	having been sanctified	we are	the	through

10.b.**Txt:** Steph
Var: 01ℵ,02A,04C,06D 018K,020L,025P,byz. Gries,Lach,Treg,Alf Word,Tisc,We/Ho,Weis Sod,UBS/☆

3450.10 art gen sing fem	**4234.2** noun gen sing fem	**3450.2** art gen sing	**4835.2** noun gen sing neu	**3450.2** art gen sing	**2400.2** name masc
τῆς	προσφορᾶς	τοῦ	σώματος	⌜b τοῦ ⌝	Ἰησοῦ
tēs	*prosphoras*	*tou*	*sōmatos*	*tou*	*Iēsou*
the	offering	of the	body		of Jesus

5382.2 name gen masc	**2160.1** adv	**2504.1** conj	**3820.6** adj nom sing masc	**3173.1** conj	**2385.1** noun nom sing masc
Χριστοῦ	ἐφάπαξ.	**11.** Καὶ	πᾶς	μὲν	ἱερεὺς
Christou	*ephapax*	*Kai*	*pas*	*men*	*hiereus*
Christ	once for all.	And	every		priest

demands upon the Children of Israel. In Psalm 40:8 David made this clear by adding, "Thy law is within my heart," words reminiscent of the promise of the new covenant (Jeremiah 31:33). Jesus came voluntarily to meet the requirements of the Law's precepts and of its messianic prophecies. Most specifically He came to die as the Seed of the woman who crushes Satan's head (Genesis 3:15).

10:8. Parts of the quotation from Psalm 40 were repeated for the purpose of clearly contrasting the old covenant with the new covenant. As in the previous citation, the emphasis falls upon the Lord's lack of pleasure in the ceremonial sacrifice of animals as offerings for sin. God had required them, but not for the purposes Israel had supposed. As noted already (10:3), they reminded Israel of sin without removing the guilt of sin.

10:9. But when the Son entered into the human condition saying, "Lo, I come to do thy will, O God," the situation was changed dramatically. That which existed under the old Mosaic law began to pass away; in its place the Lord established the new covenant prophesied by Jeremiah and Ezekiel. Willing to carry out the will of God, the Son of God, Jesus Christ, replaced the Mosaic covenant established at Mount Sinai and set up the new covenant instituted at Mount Calvary.

10:10. This verse specifically identifies the will of God and clearly sets forth the results of the Son's obedience to that will. In no uncertain terms, the death of Jesus Christ is described as "the offering of the body of Jesus Christ once for all." These words highlight the voluntary, sacrificial nature of His death and underscore its superiority and permanence. He offered one sacrifice, and its consequences are permanent. The phrase *hēgiasmenoi esmen* is also emphatic. It means that by Christ's death believers have been and remain sanctified.

10:11. Verses 11-18 summarize the arguments concerning the superiority of the Son's high priestly sacrifice. The contrasts given in this passage have all been stated before either directly or by implication. The priests of the Levitical order stood. Jesus is seated in heaven. Their service was daily, but Jesus sacrificed only once. They repeatedly offered the same kind of animal sacrifices which did not even possess the remotest possibility of taking away sin and its consequences.

Sacrifice and offering and burnt offerings and [offering] for sin: . . . and sin-offerings, *TNT* . . . offerings for sin which are prescribed by the Law, *Noli.*

thou wouldest not, neither hadst pleasure [therein]: . . . neither desires nor takes pleasure in, *Noli* . . . you neither wish nor enjoy, *Klingensmith* . . . You did not want or find pleasure in, *TNT* . . . You were not pleased with these things, *SEB* . . . You never wished or took delight in, *Williams.*

which are offered by the law: . . . all of which are repeatedly offered in accordance with the law, *Williams* . . . which are prescribed by the Law, *Noli.*

9. Then said he, Lo, I come to do thy will, O God: He afterward said, *Williams* . . . Here I am, O God, ready to do, *TNT* . . . I have come to do what You want, *SEB.*

He taketh away the first, that he may establish the second: He is despatching the first, *Concordant* . . . He negatives the first kind of sacrifice in order to substitute the second, *Wade* . . . So Jesus Christ abolishes the first...to establish the second, *TNT* . . . He is taking away the first to let the second take its place, *Williams* . . . The former statement is set aside to be replaced by the latter, *TCNT* . . . God took away the first group of sacrifices, *SEB.*

10. By the which will we are sanctified: In accordance with this divine will, *Noli* . . . it is by the fulfilment of this Will of God that we have been Hallowed, *Wade* . . . It is by this will of God that we are consecrated, *Williams* . . . we are cleansed and set apart for his service, *TNT.*

through the offering of the body of Jesus Christ once [for all]: . . . once, and once only, *Adams* . . . Because he did what God wanted him to do and offered his body, *TNT* . . . by the sacrifice of the body, *Noli.*

11. And every priest standeth daily ministering: Every other priest stands officiating, *Williams* . . . is celebrating his service daily, *Noli* . . . Every Jewish priest stands, *TNT* . . . day after day, *Montgomery.*

2449.18 verb 3sing indic perf act	2567.2 prep	2232.4 noun acc sing fem	2982.1 verb nom sing masc part pres act	2504.1 conj	3450.15 art acc pl fem
ἕστηκεν	καθ'	ἡμέραν	λειτουργῶν,	καὶ	τὰς
hestēken	*kath'*	*hēmeran*	*leitourgōn*	*kai*	*tas*
has stood	by	day	ministering,	and	the

840.13 prs-pron acc pl fem	4038.1 adv	4232.7 verb nom sing masc part pres act	2355.1 noun fem	3610.4 rel-pron nom pl fem
αὐτὰς	πολλάκις	προσφέρων	θυσίας,	αἵτινες
autas	*pollakis*	*prospherōn*	*thusias*	*haitines*
same	often	offering	sacrifices,	which

3626.1 adv	1404.7 verb 3pl indic pres mid	3877.2 verb inf aor act	264.1 noun fem	840.5 prs-pron nom sing masc
οὐδέποτε	δύνανται	περιελεῖν	ἁμαρτίας·	**12.** ʻ αὐτὸς
oudepote	*dunantai*	*perielein*	*hamartias*	*autos*
never	are able	to take away	sins.	He

12.a.**Txt:** 06D-corr,018K 020L,byz.
Var: 01א,02A,04C 06D-org,025P,33,Lach Treg,Alf,Word,Tisc We/Ho,Weis,Sod UBS/☆

3642.4 dem-pron nom sing masc	1156.2 conj	1518.8 num card acc fem	5065.1 prep	264.6 noun gen pl fem	4232.17 verb nom sing masc part aor act
[a☆ οὗτος]	δὲ	μίαν	ὑπὲρ	ἁμαρτιῶν	προσενέγκας
houtos	*de*	*mian*	*huper*	*hamartiōn*	*prosenenkas*
[This]	but,	one	for	sins	having offered

2355.4 noun acc sing fem	1519.1 prep	3450.16 art sing neu	1330.1 adj sing neu	2495.3 verb 3sing indic aor act	1706.1 prep	1182.5 adj dat sing fem
θυσίαν,	εἰς	τὸ	διηνεκὲς	ἐκάθισεν	ἐν	δεξιᾷ
thusian	*eis*	*to*	*diēnekes*	*ekathisen*	*en*	*dexia*
sacrifice,	in	the	perpetuity	sat down	at	right hand

3450.2 art gen sing	2296.2 noun gen sing masc	3450.16 art sing neu	3036.8 adj sing neu	1538.4 verb nom sing masc part pres mid	2175.1 conj
τοῦ	θεοῦ,	**13.** τὸ	λοιπὸν	ἐκδεχόμενος	ἕως
tou	*theou*	*to*	*loipon*	*ekdechomenos*	*heōs*
	of God,	the	remaining	awaiting	until

4935.35 verb 3pl subj aor pass	3450.7 art nom pl masc	2172.5 adj nom pl masc	840.3 prs-pron gen sing	5124.1 noun sing neu	3450.1 art gen pl	4087.5 noun gen pl masc
τεθῶσιν	οἱ	ἐχθροὶ	αὐτοῦ	ὑποπόδιον	τῶν	ποδῶν
tethōsin	*hoi*	*echthroi*	*autou*	*hupopodion*	*tōn*	*podōn*
be placed	the	enemies	his	a footstool	of the	feet

840.3 prs-pron gen sing	1518.7 num card dat fem	1056.1 conj	4234.3 noun dat sing fem	4896.6 verb 3sing indic perf act	1519.1 prep
αὐτοῦ.	**14.** μιᾷ	γὰρ	προσφορᾷ	τετελείωκεν	εἰς
autou	*mia*	*gar*	*prosphora*	*teteleiōken*	*eis*
his.	By one	for	offering	he has perfected	in

3450.16 art sing neu	1330.1 adj sing neu	3450.8 art acc pl masc	37.12 verb acc pl masc part pres mid	3113.3 verb 3sing indic pres act
τὸ	διηνεκὲς	τοὺς	ἁγιαζομένους.	**15.** Μαρτυρεῖ
to	*diēnekes*	*tous*	*hagiazomenous*	*Marturei*
the	perpetuity	the	being sanctified.	Bears witness

1156.2 conj	2231.3 prs-pron dat 1pl	2504.1 conj	3450.16 art sing neu	4011.1 noun sing neu	3450.16 art sing neu	39.1 adj sing
δὲ	ἡμῖν	καὶ	τὸ	πνεῦμα	τὸ	ἅγιον·
de	*hēmin*	*kai*	*to*	*pneuma*	*to*	*hagion*
and	to us	also	the	Spirit	the	Holy;

15.a.**Txt:** 018K,020L,byz.
Var: 01א,02A,04C,06D 025P,33,bo.Lach,Treg Alf,Word,Tisc,We/Ho Weis,Sod,UBS/☆

3196.3 prep	1056.1 conj	3450.16 art sing neu	4136.4 verb inf perf act	2029.17 verb inf perf act
μετὰ	γὰρ	τὸ	ʻ προειρηκέναι,	[a☆ εἰρηκέναι,]
meta	*gar*	*to*	*proeirēkenai*	*eirēkenai*
after	for	the	to have said before,	[to have said,]

10:12. In contrast to the descendants of Levi and Aaron, "this man," the Son of God, offered one sacrifice—himself. It took care of sins forever. When His sacrifice was completed, He had no need of offering another. It could not be repeated; it did not need to be. It was not offered to the Lord in some earthly sanctuary. Rather, His sacrificed and resurrected body ascended to the heavenly sanctuary where He is sitting at the right hand of the Father in honor of His finished work.

10:13. These words allude to the often quoted beginning of Psalm 110. Jesus is seated at God's right hand because the Father has asked Him to sit there until all of His enemies have been subdued. So Jesus, who is an eternal Melchizedekian priest, sits in heaven, eagerly looking forward to the time when His enemies shall become "his footstool." Then He shall be not only the believers' High Priest but King of kings and Lord of lords.

10:14. Jesus is able to sit in the heavenly sanctuary because there is nothing more for Him to do in regard to making offering for human sin. He could truly announce, "It is finished!" By His one sacrifice He accomplished what all the offerings of lambs, bulls, and goats sacrificed under the Mosaic law could never accomplish. The Law and its sacrifices could not perfect those who worshiped under their aegis (7:19; 9:9; 10:1), but the solitary offering of the Son has perpetually perfected believers, that is, *tous hagiazomenous* (the ones who are being sanctified). The work of Christ's one sacrifice continues to sanctify believers; there is no need for a repetition of His sacrifice.

10:15. To close the doctrinal argument for the superiority of the atoning sacrifice of Jesus Christ, the inspired writer returned to Jeremiah 31 and the prophecy of the new covenant. The comments in this verse are dependent upon the sequential order of the statements made in Jeremiah 31. First, it is noted that Jeremiah's words were divinely inspired. The Holy Spirit was their ultimate Author.

Second, the words quoted in verse 16 (Jeremiah 31:33) were written before the words alluded to in verse 17 (Jeremiah 31:34). The point made in this verse is that the Spirit promised *both* the internalization of the Law *and* the forgiveness of sin.

10:16. Jeremiah 31:33 was cited to remind believers that the divinely instituted new covenant promised to internalize God's laws,

and offering oftentimes the same sacrifices: . . . offering repeatedly, *TNT* . . . over and over again, *Williams.*

which can never take away sins: . . . although they are unable to take away our sins, *Williams* . . . which can never actually take away sins, *Norlie* . . . can never remove, *TNT.*

12. But this man: . . . this One, *Williams* . . . this priest, *TNT.*

after he had offered one sacrifice for sins for ever: . . . having offered One Enduring Sacrifice, *Wilson* . . . for sins for all time, *TNT* . . . offering for all time, *Adams* . . . once for all and for all time, *Williams* . . . availing in perpetuity, *Wade.*

sat down on the right hand of God: . . . sat down in perpetuity on, *Wuest* . . . has taken His seat, *Wade* . . . took His seat at God's right hand, *Williams.*

13. From henceforth expecting: Since then He has been awaiting the day, *Norlie* . . . waiting henceforward, *Wade* . . . from that time waiting, *Williams.*

till his enemies be made his footstool: . . . may be placed underneath his feet, *Wilson* . . . made the footstool of His feet, *Williams, Wade.*

14. For by one offering he hath perfected for ever: . . . by that one sacrifice, *Williams* . . . by one single offering, *TNT* . . . He has brought to completion forever, *Wuest* . . . he has permanently perfected, *Wilson* . . . perfected in perpetuity, *Wade.*

them that are sanctified: . . . those who are consecrated to Him, *Williams* . . . those who are being set apart, *Adams* . . . those whom he cleanses and sets apart for his service, *TNT* . . . for God-like living, *NLT.*

15. [Whereof] the Holy Ghost also is a witness to us: . . . assures us of this, *Beck* . . . gives us the testimony, *Williams.*

for after that he had said before: First he says, *TNT* . . . after saying, *Williams* . . . after affirming, *Wade.*

16. This [is] the covenant that I will make with them: . . . to which I will commit myself, *Wade.*

3642.9 dem-pron nom sing fem	3450.9 art nom sing fem	1236.1 noun nom sing fem	3614.12 rel-pron acc sing fem	1297.5 verb 1sing indic fut mid
16. Αὕτη	ἡ	διαθήκη	ἣν	διαθήσομαι
Hautē	*hē*	*diathēkē*	*hēn*	*diathēsomai*
This	the	covenant	which	I will covenant

4242.1 prep	840.8 prs-pron acc pl masc	3196.3 prep	3450.15 art acc pl fem	2232.1 noun fem	1552.15 dem-pron acc pl fem
πρὸς	αὐτοὺς	μετὰ	τὰς	ἡμέρας	ἐκείνας,
pros	*autous*	*meta*	*tas*	*hēmeras*	*ekeinas*
toward	them	after	the	days	those,

2978.5 verb 3sing indic pres act	2935.1 noun nom sing masc	1319.5 verb nom sing masc part pres act	3414.5 noun acc pl masc	1466.2 prs-pron gen 1sing	1894.3 prep
λέγει	κύριος,	διδοὺς	νόμους	μου	ἐπὶ
legei	*kurios*	*didous*	*nomous*	*mou*	*epi*
says	Lord:	giving	laws	my	into

16.a.**Txt:** 06D-corr,018K 020L,byz.bo.Sod
Var: 01ℵ,02A,04C 06D-org,025P,33,Lach Treg,Alf,Word,Tisc We/Ho,Weis,UBS/☆

2559.1 noun fem	840.1 prs-pron gen pl	2504.1 conj	1894.3 prep	3450.1 art gen pl	1265.4 noun gen pl fem	3450.12 art acc sing fem
καρδίας	αὐτῶν,	καὶ	ἐπὶ	ʼ τῶν	διανοιῶν	[a☆ τὴν
kardias	*autōn*	*kai*	*epi*	*tōn*	*dianoiōn*	*tēn*
hearts	their,	also	into	the	minds	[the

1265.3 noun acc sing fem	840.1 prs-pron gen pl	1909.1 verb 1sing indic fut act	840.8 prs-pron acc pl masc	2504.1 conj	3450.1 art gen pl
διάνοιαν]	αὐτῶν	ἐπιγράψω	αὐτούς·	17. καὶ	τῶν
dianoian	*autōn*	*epigrapsō*	*autous*	*kai*	*tōn*
mind]	their	I will inscribe	them;	and	the

264.6 noun gen pl fem	840.1 prs-pron gen pl	2504.1 conj	3450.1 art gen pl	455.6 noun gen pl fem	840.1 prs-pron gen pl
ἁμαρτιῶν	αὐτῶν	καὶ	τῶν	ἀνομιῶν	αὐτῶν
hamartiōn	*autōn*	*kai*	*tōn*	*anomiōn*	*autōn*
sins	their	and	the	lawlessnesses	their

17.a.**Txt:** 01ℵ-corr 06D-corr,018K,020L 025P,byz.
Var: 01ℵ-org,02A,04C 06D-org,33,Lach,Treg Alf,Tisc,We/Ho,Weis Sod,UBS/☆

3620.3 partic	3231.1 partic	3279.5 verb 1sing subj aor pass	3279.12 verb 1sing indic fut pass	2068.1 adv
οὐ	μὴ	ʼ μνησθῶ	[a☆ μνησθήσομαι]	ἔτι.
ou	*mē*	*mnēsthō*	*mnēsthēsomai*	*eti*
not	not	may I remember	[will I remember]	any more.

3562.1 adv	1156.2 conj	852.1 noun nom sing fem	3642.2 dem-pron gen pl	3629.1 adv	4234.1 noun nom sing fem
18. ὅπου	δὲ	ἄφεσις	τούτων,	οὐκέτι	προσφορὰ
hopou	*de*	*aphesis*	*toutōn*	*ouketi*	*prosphora*
Where	but	remission	of these,	no longer	an offering

3875.1 prep	264.1 noun fem	2174.19 verb nom pl masc part pres act	3631.1 partic	79.6 noun nom pl masc
περὶ	ἁμαρτίας.	19. Ἔχοντες	οὖν,	ἀδελφοί,
peri	*hamartias*	*Echontes*	*oun*	*adelphoi*
for	sin.	Having	therefore,	brothers,

3816.4 noun acc sing fem	1519.1 prep	3450.12 art acc sing fem	1513.3 noun acc sing fem	3450.1 art gen pl	39.4 adj gen pl
παῤῥησίαν	εἰς	τὴν	εἴσοδον	τῶν	ἁγίων
parrhēsian	*eis*	*tēn*	*eisodon*	*tōn*	*hagiōn*
confidence	for	the	entrance into	the	holies

1706.1 prep	3450.3 art dat sing	129.3 noun dat sing neu	2400.2 name masc	3614.12 rel-pron acc sing fem	1450.1 verb 3sing indic aor act
ἐν	τῷ	αἵματι	Ἰησοῦ,	20. ἣν	ἐνεκαίνισεν
en	*tō*	*haimati*	*Iēsou*	*hēn*	*enekainisen*
by	the	blood	of Jesus,	which	he dedicated

and that God himself promised to write His laws in the minds and hearts of His people sometime after their Babylonian captivity.

10:17. Third, there is the reminder that in the institution of the same covenant God promised to forgive Israel's sins and never to remember them (Jeremiah 31:34).

10:18. Finally, there is the conclusion of the whole argument as far as Jewish Christians' continuance in the practices of the old covenant is concerned. If sins have been remitted, there is no further need for any sacrifices. The Old Testament sacrifices continued as a reminder of sin (10:3). Christ's one self-sacrifice has taken care of sins forever. Therefore, there is now no more need for sacrifice.

The implication is that the ritual sacrifices offered in the temple at that time were unnecessary and would soon cease. They were on the brink of extinction (8:13). Why should Jewish Christians persist in offering animal sacrifices? Christ put an end to animal sacrifices for sins. The stirring melody and opening words of Horatius Bonar's magnificent hymn comes to mind: "No blood, no altar now, the Sacrifice is o'er! No flame, no smoke ascends on high, the lamb is slain no more."

10:19. This verse begins the final section of the epistle—an extended section of application and warning which basically argues that since Christ is a superior messenger who mediates a superior message through His superior high priestly atonement, believers ought to do the following things lest they apostatize and suffer damnation. The first of a series of exhortations begins in verse 22. Verses 19-21 summarize the grounds upon which the entreaties are founded.

Christians are in a different position than Israel was under the old covenant. The access which they had to God was extremely limited. Their high priestly representative could enter into the "holiest" only once a year, and his efforts achieved only ceremonial results. Believers live under the new covenant, however, because of the blood shed by Jesus the Son, and they have access to the inner sanctum of heaven itself. They may enter into the very presence of God with "boldness" (*parrhēsian*). This word has connotations of freedom, frankness, openness, and confidence. Believers have been set free from fear. They recognize that the divine Judge is their Father, who loves and forgives and comes to their rescue because of Jesus' shed blood.

10:20. Access into the presence of God through the atoning death of Jesus is called "a new and living way." As once a year the veil

after those days, saith the Lord: In those last days, *Williams.*
I will put my laws into their hearts: I will impress my laws on their hearts, *Wade.*
and in their minds will I write them: And will inscribe them, *Montgomery* . . . upon their mind, *Wade.*

17. And their sins and iniquities: Then he adds, *Noli* . . . and lawless ways, *Norlie* . . . and their lawless acts, *TNT* . . . and deeds of wrong, *Williams* . . . and their offences, *Wade.*
will I remember no more: I will never, never any more recall, *Williams* . . . I will forget, *Noli* . . . I will keep no more memory of, *BB.*

18. Now where remission of these [is: Consequently, when sins are remitted by God, *Noli* . . . When these people are forgiven, *SEB* . . . where there is a pardon of these, *Concordant* . . . forgiveness of these, *Wade* . . . Where these have been forgiven, *TNT.*
there is] no more offering for sin: . . . no more need of an offering, *Williams* . . . there is no longer any need for, *TNT* . . . there is no longer any room for any sacrifice for sin, *Noli.*

19. Having therefore, brethren: Since then, my brothers, *Williams* . . . So now, brothers, *TNT* . . . being able, *BB.*
boldness to enter into the holiest by the blood of Jesus: . . . to go into the holy place without fear, *BB* . . . we can boldly enter the sanctuary through the blood of Jesus, *Noli* . . . we may with complete freedom pass through the curtain into the sanctuary, *TNT* . . . we have free access to the real sanctuary, *Williams* . . . we have a cheerful confidence, *Montgomery* . . . we have...confidence for approaching, through the Blood of Jesus, the entry into the Holy of Holies, *Wade.*

20. By a new and living way, which he hath consecrated for us: . . . an entry which, *Wade* . . . that He inaugurated for us, *Adams* . . . He opened for us, *Beck, Williams.*

Hebrews 10:21

2231.3 prs-pron dat 1pl	3461.4 noun acc sing fem	4230.1 adj acc sing fem	2504.1 conj	2180.17 verb acc sing fem part pres act	1217.2 prep
ἡμῖν	ὁδὸν	πρόσφατον	καὶ	ζῶσαν	διὰ
hēmin	*hodon*	*prosphaton*	*kai*	*zōsan*	*dia*
for us	a way	newly made	and	living	through

3450.2 art gen sing	2635.2 noun gen sing neu	4969.1 verb	3642.16 dem-pron sing neu	1498.4 verb 3sing indic pres act
τοῦ	καταπετάσματος,	' τουτέστιν	[☆ τοῦτ'	ἔστιν]
tou	*katapetasmatos*	*toutestin*	*tout'*	*estin*
the	veil,	that is,	[this	is]

3450.10 art gen sing fem	4418.2 noun gen sing fem	840.3 prs-pron gen sing	2504.1 conj	2385.3 noun acc sing masc	3144.4 adj acc sing masc	1894.3 prep
τῆς	σαρκὸς	αὐτοῦ,	21. καὶ	ἱερέα	μέγαν	ἐπὶ
tēs	*sarkos*	*autou*	*kai*	*hierea*	*megan*	*epi*
the	flesh	his;	and	a priest	great	over

3450.6 art acc sing masc	3486.4 noun acc sing masc	3450.2 art gen sing	2296.2 noun gen sing masc	4193.12 verb 1pl subj pres mid
τὸν	οἶκον	τοῦ	θεοῦ,	22. προσερχώμεθα
ton	*oikon*	*tou*	*theou*	*proserchōmetha*
the	house		of God,	we should approach

3196.3 prep	226.6 adj gen sing fem	2559.1 noun fem	1706.1 prep	3996.2 noun dat sing fem	3963.2 noun gen sing fem
μετὰ	ἀληθινῆς	καρδίας	ἐν	πληροφορίᾳ	πίστεως,
meta	*alēthinēs*	*kardias*	*en*	*plērophoria*	*pisteōs*
with	a true	heart,	in	full assurance	of faith,

22.a.**Txt:** 01ℵ-corr 06D-corr,018K,020L byz.
Var: 01ℵ-org,02A,04C 06D-org,025P,Lach Treg,Alf,Tisc,We/Ho Weis,Sod,UBS/☆

4329.3 verb nom pl masc part perf mid	4329.6 verb nom pl masc part perf mid	3450.15 art acc pl fem	2559.1 noun fem
' ἐρραντισμένοι	[a☆ ῥεραντισμένοι]	τὰς	καρδίας
errhantismenoi	*rherantismenoi*	*tas*	*kardias*
having been sprinkled	[idem]	the	hearts

570.3 prep	4743.2 noun gen sing fem	4050.11 adj gen sing fem	2504.1 conj	3040.6 verb nom pl masc part perf mid
ἀπὸ	συνειδήσεως	πονηρᾶς,	καὶ	' λελουμένοι
apo	*suneidēseōs*	*ponēras*	*kai*	*leloumenoi*
from	a conscience	wicked,	and	having been washed

22.b.**Txt:** 02A,04C 06D-corr,018K,020L byz.
Var: 01ℵ,06D-org,025P Tisc,We/Ho,Weis,Sod UBS/☆

3040.7 verb nom pl masc part perf mid	3450.16 art sing neu	4835.1 noun sing neu	5045.3 noun dat sing neu	2485.2 adj dat sing
[b☆ λελουσμένοι]	τὸ	σῶμα	ὕδατι	καθαρῷ·
lelousmenoi	*to*	*sōma*	*hudati*	*katharō*
[idem]	the	body	with water	clean.

2692.3 verb 1pl subj pres act	3450.12 art acc sing fem	3534.2 noun acc sing fem	3450.10 art gen sing fem	1667.2 noun gen sing fem
23. κατέχωμεν	τὴν	ὁμολογίαν	τῆς	ἐλπίδος
katechōmen	*tēn*	*homologian*	*tēs*	*elpidos*
We should hold fast	the	confession	of the	hope

184.1 adj acc sing fem	3964.2 adj nom sing masc	1056.1 conj	3450.5 art nom sing masc	1846.5 verb nom sing masc part aor mid	2504.1 conj
ἀκλινῆ,	πιστὸς	γὰρ	ὁ	ἐπαγγειλάμενος·	24. καὶ
aklinē	*pistos*	*gar*	*ho*	*epangeilamenos*	*kai*
unwavering,	faithful	for	the	having promised;	and

2627.2 verb 1pl subj pres act	238.3 prs-pron acc pl masc	1519.1 prep	3810.2 noun acc sing masc	26.2 noun gen sing fem
κατανοῶμεν	ἀλλήλους	εἰς	παροξυσμὸν	ἀγάπης
katanoōmen	*allēlous*	*eis*	*paroxusmon*	*agapēs*
we should consider	one another	for	provoking	love

opened to admit the Levitical high priest, so the veil of His flesh has opened to provide access to God at any time.

10:21. Furthermore, the One who serves as High Priest is not an underling called to *serve in* the house of God (3:1-6). Indeed, He is the Son who by right of His divine inheritance *rules over* the house of God.

10:22. There is no more need to offer animal sacrifices. The believers' sins are forgiven permanently. Jesus' blood allows them to enter into God's presence at any time. Jesus is God's sovereign soon-to-be-ruling Son. Christians should live lives that are characterized by three activities: prayer (10:22), perseverance (10:23), and encouragement(10:24,25). These three activities are enjoined on Christians by three cohortative subjunctive verb forms which appear in our English text following the words "let us." By the verb *proserchōmetha,* believers are entreated to keep on coming near to God in prayer. A believers' life should be consistently characterized by doing this. This is a high privilege. Unlike those under the Levitical system whose high priestly representatives could only have direct contact with God once a year on the annual Day of Atonement, believers through Jesus Christ have access to God at any time.

Christians should make the most of their unique opportunity, because they have a cleansing that is both ceremonial (in the ordinance of baptism) and actual (in the removal of the moral guilt of their consciences). Since they are thus cleansed by Christ's blood, they can come to God with a genuinely open heart, with no pretense, absolutely confident that He will welcome them and hear them because they have trusted His Son Jesus Christ as their atoning sacrifice.

10:23. Christians are enjoined by the verb *katechōmen* to keep on possessing the confession of their *elpidos aklinē,* that is, to persevere in maintaining their unwavering hope. Jesus who suffered and died for them is now seated at the right hand of God the Father. They do not yet see Him in all His power and kingdom glory (2:8), but they look for Him to return as King of kings and Lord of lords. They must persist in this hope because God is trustworthy. They can rely upon Him to keep His Word. He cannot lie, and He has sworn by oath that Jesus is an eternal Melchizedekian priest-king.

10:24,25. Christians are exhorted by the verb *katanoōmen* to be constantly aware of one another and the need to stimulate one

through the veil, that is to say, his flesh: . . . through the curtain, *Adams* . . . the Rent Curtain...which separated Him from the immediate Presence of God and which was rent on the Cross, *Wade* . . . He opened the curtain, which was His own body, *NLT* . . . His physical nature, *Williams* . . . by means of his own body, *TNT.*

21. And [having] an high priest over the house of God: . . . and since in Him we have a Great Priest, *Williams* . . . over God's household, *TNT.*

22. Let us draw near with a true heart in full assurance of faith: . . . let us continue to draw near...with sincere hearts and perfect faith, *Williams* . . . let us now approach Him...with unwavering faith, *Norlie* . . . approach God with our guilty consciences cleansed, *TNT* . . . sincere in our hearts and convinced in our faith, *Beck.*

having our hearts sprinkled from an evil conscience: . . . with our hearts cleansed from the sense of sin, *Williams* . . . to rid us of, *Adams* . . . should be made pure from a guilty conscience, *SEB.*

and our bodies washed with pure water: . . . bathed in clean water, *Concordant, Williams.*

23. Let us hold fast the profession of [our] faith without wavering: . . . keep on holding to the hope that we profess, *Williams* . . . the hope which we have professed and never turn away from it, *TNT* . . . without swaying, *Adams* . . . never in doubt, *Norlie* . . . without twisting, *Klingensmith.*

(for he [is] faithful that promised;): . . . and He is dependable, *SEB* . . . God has given his promise and he can be trusted, *TNT.*

24. And let us consider one another: We must try to think, *TNT.*

to provoke unto love and to good works: . . . let us take one another into our thoughts with the aim of stimulating mutual love and good deeds, *Wade* . . . how we can stimulate one another, *Beck* . . . so as to arouse one another, *Norlie* . . . .as to stimulate one another to love, *Williams* . . . and do good, *TNT.*

2504.1 conj	2541.12 adj gen pl neu	2024.5 noun gen pl neu	3231.1 partic	1452.1 verb nom pl masc part pres act	3450.12 art acc sing fem
καὶ	καλῶν	ἔργων,	25. μὴ	ἐγκαταλείποντες	τὴν
kai	*kalōn*	*ergōn*	*mē*	*enkataleipontes*	*tēn*
and	good	works;	not	forsaking	the

1981.2 noun acc sing fem	1431.2 prs-pron gen pl	2503.1 conj	1478.1 noun sing neu	4948.8 indef-pron dat pl masc
ἐπισυναγωγὴν	ἑαυτῶν,	καθὼς	ἔθος	τισίν,
episunagōgēn	*heautōn*	*kathōs*	*ethos*	*tisin*
assembling together	of ourselves,	even as	custom	with some;

233.2 conj	3731.9 verb nom pl masc part pres act	2504.1 conj	4965.8 dem-pron dat sing neu	3095.1 adv comp	3607.7 rel-pron dat sing neu
ἀλλὰ	παρακαλοῦντες·	καὶ	τοσούτῳ	μᾶλλον	ὅσῳ
alla	*parakalountes*	*kai*	*tosoutō*	*mallon*	*hosō*
but	encouraging,	and	by so much	more	as

984.1 verb 2pl pres act	1443.7 verb acc sing fem part pres act	3450.12 art acc sing fem	2232.4 noun acc sing fem	1583.1 adv
βλέπετε	ἐγγίζουσαν	τὴν	ἡμέραν.	26. Ἑκουσίως
blepete	*engizousan*	*tēn*	*hēmeran*	*Hekousiōs*
you see	drawing near	the	day.	Willingly

1056.1 conj	262.7 verb gen pl masc part pres act	2231.2 prs-pron gen 1pl	3196.3 prep	3450.16 art sing neu	2956.31 verb inf aor act
γὰρ	ἁμαρτανόντων	ἡμῶν	μετὰ	τὸ	λαβεῖν
gar	*hamartanontōn*	*hēmōn*	*meta*	*to*	*labein*
for	sinning	we	after	the	to receive

3450.12 art acc sing fem	1907.4 noun acc sing fem	3450.10 art gen sing fem	223.2 noun gen sing fem	3629.1 adv	3875.1 prep
τὴν	ἐπίγνωσιν	τῆς	ἀληθείας,	οὐκέτι	περὶ
tēn	*epignōsin*	*tēs*	*alētheias*	*ouketi*	*peri*
the	knowledge	of the	truth,	no longer	for

264.6 noun gen pl fem	614.3 verb 3sing indic pres mid	2355.2 noun nom sing fem	5235.1 adj nom sing fem	1156.2 conj	4948.3 indef-pron nom sing
ἁμαρτιῶν	ἀπολείπεται	θυσία·	27. φοβερὰ	δέ	τις
hamartiōn	*apoleipetai*	*thusia*	*phobera*	*de*	*tis*
sins	remains	a sacrifice,	a fearful	but	certain

1548.1 noun nom sing fem	2893.2 noun gen sing fem	2504.1 conj	4300.2 noun gen sing neu	2188.1 noun sing	2052.14 verb inf pres act
ἐκδοχὴ	κρίσεως,	καὶ	πυρὸς	ζῆλος	ἐσθίειν
ekdochē	*kriseōs*	*kai*	*puros*	*zēlos*	*esthiein*
expectation	of judgment,	and	of fire	fervor	to devour

3165.9 verb gen sing part pres act	3450.8 art acc pl masc	5064.1 adj acc pl masc	114.7 verb nom sing masc part aor act	4948.3 indef-pron nom sing
μέλλοντος	τοὺς	ὑπεναντίους.	28. ἀθετήσας	τις
mellontos	*tous*	*hupenantious*	*athetēsas*	*tis*
being about	the	adversaries.	Having set aside	any one

3414.4 noun acc sing masc	3337.2 name gen masc	3338.2 name gen masc	5400.1 prep	3490.2 noun gen pl masc
νόμον	ʻ Μωσέως	[☆ Μωϋσέως]	χωρὶς	οἰκτιρμῶν
nomon	*Mōseōs*	*Mōuseōs*	*chōris*	*oiktirmōn*
law	of Moses,	[idem]	without	compassions

1894.3 prep	1411.1 num card dat	2211.1 conj	4980.3 num card dat	3116.6 noun dat pl masc	594.2 verb 3sing indic pres act
ἐπὶ	δυσὶν	ἢ	τρισὶν	μάρτυσιν	ἀποθνήσκει·
epi	*dusin*	*ē*	*trisin*	*martusin*	*apothnēskei*
on	two	or	three	witnesses	dies:

another to loving behavior and good works. The word translated "provoke" is *paroxusmon.* It refers to sharp contention and argument, suggesting that believers must sharply confront one another with their responsibility. If such admonition is to take place, Christians must meet together on a regular basis. A Christian cannot profit from the gifts of others unless he fellowships with them. Apparently those receiving this epistle were withdrawing from the fellowship of the whole congregation in favor of their miniflock. In the light of the approaching day (a reference to the return of the Lord in judgment with some implications for the nearness of Jerusalem's destruction), the gathering of all was urged.

10:26. Having strongly admonished believers to prayer, perseverance, and provocation, the inspired writer now added a stern warning. If believers fail to appropriate the blessings of the new covenant, they are placing themselves in jeopardy of a worse fate than the fate of unbelieving Israelites in the wilderness. If Christians sin willfully (*hekousiōs* means "freely, without coercion") after having experienced the full knowledge of the truth concerning the superiority and finality of revelation and redemption in God's Son Jesus Christ our Lord, then there is no other sacrifice available for the forgiveness of sins.

This verse has been misused to buttress the teaching that there is no forgiveness of deliberate sins committed after one has become a Christian. The writer is dealing with apostasy, not backsliding. In the context it was addressed to Hebrew Christians who were in danger of apostatizing from their profession of Jesus as Messiah. The inspired writer assured them that if they turned aside from Calvary's atoning sacrifice and returned to Judaism, they would not be able to procure forgiveness of sins and have free access to heaven. Christ's sacrifice is the only one that removes sin and secures access to the Throne of Grace. Through Him we may come to the Father in prayer.

10:27. For those who deliberately reject Christ's atoning sacrifice only judgment remains. It is vividly described as *phobera*, terrifying, "fiery indignation," a judgment which is destructive because it literally eats up (*esthiein*) those who are against Jesus Christ.

10:28. As in the previous warnings issued (2:2,3; 3:7 to 4:11), comparisons and contrasts between the judgments under the Mosaic law and those under the new covenant are drawn. Those who ignored and broke the Law given through Moses found no mercy when their trespasses were verified by the testimony of two or three eyewitnesses (Deuteronomy 17:2-6). The crime specifically mentioned in the Deuteronomy 17 passage is that of idolatry. Turning aside from the Son of God and His atoning sacrifice is certainly a form of idolatry. It is turning from the true God to a powerless substitute.

25. Not forsaking the assembling of ourselves together: We must not abandon our practice of meeting together, *Adams* . . . Do not quit meeting together, *SEB* . . . Let us not neglect meeting together, *Klingensmith* . . . stop neglecting our meeting, *Williams.*

as the manner of some [is]: . . . according as the custom of some is, *Concordant* . . . as some have the habit, *Klingensmith* . . . as some do, *Williams.*

but exhorting [one another]: . . . but rather let us encourage one another, *Norlie.*

and so much the more, as ye see the day approaching: . . . as you behold, *Montgomery* . . . as you see the day drawing near, *Adams* . . . the day of His return coming near, *NLT.*

26. For if we sin wilfully: If we deliberately go on sinning, *Adams* . . . if we should voluntarily sin, *Wilson* . . . if we go willfully sinning, *Williams.*

after that we have received the knowledge of the truth:

there remaineth no more sacrifice for sins: . . . there is no sacrifice left to be offered for our sins, *Williams.*

27. But a certain fearful looking for of judgment: . . . but only a fearful anticipation, *Adams* . . . only a terrible waiting for judgment, *SEB* . . . only a terrifying prospect of judgment, *Williams* . . . expectation of, *Montgomery.*

and fiery indignation, which shall devour the adversaries: . . . the hot fires of hell will burn up those who work against God, *NLT* . . . and a fiery hatred which eventually will consume those who hate Christ, *Norlie* . . . which is going to devour God's enemies, *Williams.*

28. He that despised Moses' law: Anyone repudiating Moses' law, *Concordant* . . . Any one who set at naught, *Montgomery* . . . Anyone who violates, *Beck.*

died without mercy under two or three witnesses:

29. Of how much sorer punishment, suppose ye: How much worse do you think, *Adams* . . . how much Worse Punishment, *Wilson.*

4073.9 intr-pron dat sing neu	1374.1 verb 2pl pres act	5337.2 adj comp gen sing fem	511.7 verb 3sing indic fut pass
29. πόσῳ	δοκεῖτε	χείρονος	ἀξιωθήσεται
posō	dokeite	cheironos	axiōthēsetai
how much	think you	worse	shall he be counted worthy of

4946.1 noun gen sing fem	3450.5 art nom sing masc	3450.6 art acc sing masc	5048.4 noun acc sing masc	3450.2 art gen sing	2296.2 noun gen sing masc
τιμωρίας	ὁ	τὸν	υἱὸν	τοῦ	θεοῦ
timōrias	ho	ton	huion	tou	theou
punishment	the	the	Son		of God

2632.3 verb nom sing masc part aor act	2504.1 conj	3450.16 art sing neu	129.1 noun sing neu	3450.10 art gen sing fem
καταπατήσας,	καὶ	τὸ	αἷμα	τῆς
katapatēsas	kai	to	haima	tēs
having trampled upon,	and	the	blood	of the

1236.2 noun gen sing fem	2812.1 adj sing	2216.15 verb nom sing masc part aor mid	1706.1 prep	3614.3 rel-pron dat sing
διαθήκης	κοινὸν	ἡγησάμενος	ἐν	ᾧ
diathēkēs	koinon	hēgēsamenos	en	hō
covenant	common	having esteemed	in	which

37.13 verb 3sing indic aor pass	2504.1 conj	3450.16 art sing neu	4011.1 noun sing neu	3450.10 art gen sing fem	5322.2 noun gen sing fem
ἡγιάσθη,	καὶ	τὸ	πνεῦμα	τῆς	χάριτος
hēgiasthē	kai	to	pneuma	tēs	charitos
he was sanctified,	and	the	Spirit	of the	grace

1780.1 verb nom sing masc part aor act	3471.5 verb 1pl indic perf act	1056.1 conj	3450.6 art acc sing masc	1500.18 verb acc sing masc part aor act
ἐνυβρίσας;	30. οἴδαμεν	γὰρ	τὸν	εἰπόντα,
enubrisas	oidamen	gar	ton	eiponta
having insulted!	We know	for	the	having said,

30.a.**Txt:** 01ℵ-corr,02A 06D-corr,018K,020L byz.
Var: 01ℵ-org,06D-org 025P,33,bo.Treg,Tisc We/Ho,Weis,Sod UBS/⋆

1466.5 prs-pron dat 1sing	1544.1 noun nom sing fem	1466.1 prs-pron nom 1sing	464.2 verb 1sing indic fut act	2978.5 verb 3sing indic pres act
Ἐμοὶ	ἐκδίκησις,	ἐγὼ	ἀνταποδώσω,	(a λέγει
Emoi	ekdikēsis	egō	antapodōsō	legei
To me	vengeance;	I	will recompense,	says

2935.1 noun nom sing masc	2504.1 conj	3687.1 adv	2935.1 noun nom sing masc	2892.25 verb 3sing indic fut act	2892.25 verb 3sing indic fut act
κύριος·)	καὶ	πάλιν,	(Κύριος	κρινεῖ	[⋆ κρινεῖ
kurios	kai	palin	Kurios	krinei	krinei
Lord:	and	again,	Lord	will judge	[will judge

2935.1 noun nom sing masc	3450.6 art acc sing masc	2967.4 noun acc sing masc	840.3 prs-pron gen sing	5235.2 adj sing neu
κύριος]	τὸν	λαὸν	αὐτοῦ.	31. Φοβερὸν
kurios	ton	laon	autou	Phoberon
Lord]	the	people	his.	A fearful thing

3450.16 art sing neu	1690.4 verb inf aor act	1519.1 prep	5331.8 noun acc pl fem	2296.2 noun gen sing masc	2180.11 verb gen sing part pres act
τὸ	ἐμπεσεῖν	εἰς	χεῖρας	θεοῦ	ζῶντος.
to	empesein	eis	cheiras	theou	zōntos
the	to fall	into	hands	of God	living.

362.3 verb 2pl impr pres mid	1156.2 conj	3450.15 art acc pl fem	4245.2 adj comp sing neu	2232.1 noun fem
32. Ἀναμιμνῄσκεσθε	δὲ	τὰς	πρότερον	ἡμέρας,
Anamimnēskesthe	de	tas	proteron	hēmeras
Call to remembrance	but	the	former	days

10:29. In the light of the severity of punishment given to idolators under the old covenant, how much greater punishment will God mete out to those who have trampled God's Son under their feet? Moses was only a servant, but Jesus is the Son and heir over the house of God (3:1-6). To apostatize is to treat the blood of Jesus, the blood of the new covenant, as a common thing (*koinon*, defiled or profane, something which everyone has access to; for example, a threshold). Finally, it is to treat the Holy Spirit, "the Spirit of grace," in an insolent and arrogant manner (*enubrisas*). The implication of the question "shall he be thought worthy," which is embodied in the verb *axiōthēsetai*, is: what magnitude of punishment fits the crime? When Christ put forth this same idea in parable form to His enemies, He said the Father would "miserably destroy those wicked men" (Matthew 21:41).

10:30. The answer to the question of verse 29 is evident. The God of the old and new covenants has not changed. The God of the new covenant is the same God who spoke through Moses and the prophets. In warning Israel about the consequences of disobeying the Mosaic law by turning aside to worship idols, He told them that vengeance and repayment were His prerogatives (Deuteronomy 32:35). He also declared that He would judge Israel for their departure from the Sinaitic covenant (Deuteronomy 32:36).

10:31. To be caught in the web of God's active judgment is a terrifying prospect. (The word *phoberon*, "terrifying," is used also in verse 27.) But that is the only fate that awaits those who turn aside from the new covenant blessings procured by the blood of God's beloved Son, rejecting His sacrifice.

Some people find it difficult to believe a loving God would send judgment. But the One who is the very essence of love is also holy and righteous. When the limits of His mercy have been exceeded, nothing is left but to receive His just judgment. His hands of blessing are beyond description, but when His hands are used in judgment, the expression "fearful thing" is most appropriate.

10:32. In the face of the prospect of fiery judgment from the hands of the living God, Hebrew believers were asked to reflect on the time when they were initiated into the Christian community after having been enlightened concerning the claims of Jesus the Son. Their profession of faith embroiled them in a great struggle (*athlēsin*). In that struggle they were subjected to many different kinds of suffering. Intense as that experience was, they had managed to endure it to the end. In their early experience of suffering for the sake of Jesus Christ they had borne up well under pressure.

shall he be thought worthy: . . . will he be adjudged to deserve, *Wade* . . . a man will deserve, *TNT* . . . one deserves, *Williams.*

who hath trodden under foot the Son of God: . . . who have trampled, *TCNT.*

and hath counted the blood of the covenant, wherewith he was sanctified, an unholy thing: . . . treated the blood of the covenant as of no account—the very blood which had cleansed him, *TNT* . . . and has attached no sacred significance to the Blood, *Wade* . . . counts as a common thing, *Williams* . . . and has profaned that covenant blood, *Montgomery* . . . by which he is hallowed contaminating, *Concordant* . . . is worth nothing? *NLT.*

and hath done despite unto the Spirit of grace?: . . . and outrages, *Concordant* . . . and have heaped insults on the gracious Spirit, *TCNT* . . . insults the Spirit of love? *Beck* . . . the Spirit that grants God's unmerited favor? *Williams.*

30. For we know him that hath said:

Vengeance [belongeth] unto me, I will recompense, saith the Lord: To me is justice, *Klingensmith* . . . I have the right to punish, *Beck* . . . Revenge belongs to Me, *SEB* . . . Retribution is Mine, *Wilson* . . . I will repay, *Adams* . . . I will pay back! *Williams* . . . To me belongs the infliction, *Wade.*

And again, The Lord shall judge his people: . . . will be His people's judge, *Williams* . . . will pass judgment, *Wade.*

31. [It is] a fearful thing to fall into the hands of the living God: The very worst thing that can happen to a man, *NLT* . . . a fearful experience, *Adams* . . . It is a terrifying thing, *Williams.*

32. But call to remembrance the former days, in which: Remember what happened in those earlier days, *TNT* . . . you must continue to remember, *Williams.*

after ye were illuminated: . . . when first you received the light, *Williams* . . . after having been enlightened, *Montgomery* . . . after you had received the light of God, *TNT.*

Hebrews 10:33

1706.1 prep	3614.14 rel-pron dat pl fem	5297.8 verb nom pl masc part aor pass	4044.12 adj acc sing fem	119.1 noun acc sing fem
ἐν	αἷς	φωτισθέντες	πολλὴν	ἄθλησιν
en	*hais*	*phōtisthentes*	*pollēn*	*athlēsin*
in	which	having been enlightened,	much	conflict

5116.8 verb 2pl indic aor act	3667.3 noun gen pl neu	3642.17 dem-pron sing neu	3173.1 conj	3543.3 noun dat pl masc
ὑπεμείνατε	παθημάτων·	33. τοῦτο	μὲν,	ὀνειδισμοῖς
hupemeinate	*pathēmatōn*	*touto*	*men*	*oneidismois*
you endured	of sufferings;	this,		in reproaches

4885.1 conj	2504.1 conj	2324.7 noun dat pl fem	2278.1 verb nom pl masc part pres mid	3642.17 dem-pron sing neu	1156.2 conj
τε	καὶ	θλίψεσιν	θεατριζόμενοι·	τοῦτο	δὲ
te	*kai*	*thlipsesin*	*theatrizomenoi*	*touto*	*de*
both	and	tribulations	being made a spectacle;	this	and,

2817.3 noun nom pl masc	3450.1 art gen pl	3643.1 adv	388.4 verb gen pl masc part pres mid	1090.54 verb nom pl masc part aor pass
κοινωνοὶ	τῶν	οὕτως	ἀναστρεφομένων	γενηθέντες·
koinōnoi	*tōn*	*houtōs*	*anastrephomenōn*	*genēthentes*
partners	of the	thus	passing through	having become.

34.a.**Txt:** 01ℵ,06D-corr 018K,020L,025P,byz. **Var:** 02A,06D-org,015H 33,it.sa.bo.Gries,Lach Treg,Alf,Word,Tisc We/Ho,Weis,Sod UBS/☆

2504.1 conj	1056.1 conj	3450.4 art dat pl	1193.5 noun dat pl	1466.2 prs-pron gen 1sing	1192.6 noun dat pl masc
34. καὶ	γὰρ	τοῖς	ʻ δεσμοῖς	μου	[a☆ δεσμίοις]
kai	*gar*	*tois*	*desmois*	*mou*	*desmiois*
Both	for	with the	bonds	my	[bonds]

4685.1 verb 2pl indic aor act	2504.1 conj	3450.12 art acc sing fem	718.2 noun acc sing fem	3450.1 art gen pl
συνεπαθήσατε,	καὶ	τὴν	ἁρπαγὴν	τῶν
sunepathēsate	*kai*	*tēn*	*harpagēn*	*tōn*
you sympathized,	and	the	plunder	the

34.b.**Txt:** Steph **Var:** 01ℵ,02A,06D 015H,018K,020L,025P bo.Gries,Lach,Treg,Alf Word,Tisc,We/Ho,Weis Sod,UBS/☆

5062.10 verb gen pl neu part pres act	5050.2 prs-pron gen 2pl	3196.3 prep	5315.2 noun gen sing fem	4185.7 verb 2pl indic aor mid
ὑπαρχόντων	ὑμῶν	μετὰ	χαρᾶς	προσεδέξασθε,
huparchontōn	*humōn*	*meta*	*charas*	*prosedexasthe*
belonging	your	with	joy	you received,

34.c.**Txt:** 06D,018K 020L,byz. **Var:** 01ℵ,02A,Lach Treg,Tisc,We/Ho,Weis UBS/☆

1091.12 verb nom pl masc part pres act	2174.29 verb inf pres act	1706.1 prep	1431.8 prs-pron acc pl masc	2882.3 adj comp
γινώσκοντες	ἔχειν	ʻb ἐν ʼ	ʻ ἑαυτοὺς	κρείττονα
ginōskontes	*echein*	*en*	*heautous*	*kreittona*
knowing	to have	in	yourselves	a better

34.d.**Txt:** 01ℵ-corr 06D-corr,015H-corr 018K,020L,025P,byz. **Var:** 01ℵ-org,02A 06D-org,015H-org,33,bo. Lach,Treg,Alf,Word Tisc,We/Ho,Weis,Sod UBS/☆

1431.7 prs-pron dat pl masc	2882.7 adj comp pl neu	5061.1 noun acc sing fem	1706.1 prep	3636.8 noun dat pl masc
[c ἑαυτοῖς	κρείσσονα]	ὕπαρξιν	ʻd ἐν	οὐρανοῖς ʼ
heautois	*kreissona*	*huparxin*	*en*	*ouranois*
[for yourselves	a better]	possession	in	heavens

2504.1 conj	3176.13 verb acc sing fem part pres act	3231.1 partic	572.1 verb 2pl subj aor act	3631.1 partic	3450.12 art acc sing fem
καὶ	μένουσαν.	35. μὴ	ἀποβάλητε	οὖν	τὴν
kai	*menousan*	*mē*	*apobalēte*	*oun*	*tēn*
and	abiding.	Not	cast away	therefore	the

3816.4 noun acc sing fem	5050.2 prs-pron gen 2pl	3610.3 rel-pron nom sing fem	2174.4 verb 3sing indic pres act	3269.1 noun acc sing fem
παῤῥησίαν	ὑμῶν,	ἥτις	ἔχει	ʻ μισθαποδοσίαν
parrhēsian	*humōn*	*hētis*	*echei*	*misthapodosian*
confidence	your,	which	has	recompense

10:33. The description of the Hebrew Christians' first subjection to religious persecution is now made even more specific. They had become a spectacle for others to mock. The verb *theatrizomenoi* carries connotations of being abused in public. It is further qualified by the terms *thlipsesin* (which refers to being narrowly confined by pressure) and *oneidismois* ("abuse, reproach, insult, and shame"). They had experienced this suffering because they had become *koinōnoi* ("partners") with those who were already being persecuted in his way. The implication is that those who evangelized them were already being persecuted and that by responding to their message these believers were also receiving similar public castigation.

10:34. At this juncture the inspired writer revealed that he himself was in prison at the time of their conversion. The implication is that he had something to do with their conversion also. The thrust of his purpose in asking them to recall the time of their conversion and the persecution which followed it is then made clear. He wished them to remember two things: (1) the way in which they responded to that persecution; (2) the knowledge which helped them to respond in such a manner. They had sympathized with him in his imprisonment, and they had experienced joy when robbed of their possessions. They had been able to do this because they possessed in heaven something which was both better and more permanent than what they lost.

Their patience in persecution was a great thing; enduring it without murmuring, still greater; their rejoicing in it greatest of all.

10:35,36. Since the atoning sacrifice of Jesus Christ provided them with confidence (*parrhēsian*, this is the same "boldness" referred to in 10:19), they were admonished not to throw it away because it had the prospect, not of fiery judgment, but of great reward. Those who trust in the Son will enter into eternal rest as recipients of God's eternal salvation. Such an inheritance should not be abandoned. Nothing should be done to jeopardize it.

In order for believers to be certain about receiving this "great recompense of reward," one thing is needed: patience. *Hupomonēs* describes one particular aspect of patience, the quality of endurance. It speaks about enduring the afflictions and trials until those troubles are ended. Patient endurance to the end will receive the reward. Believers must respond to the current crises in their lives in the same way they reacted when they first professed faith in the Son of God (10:32-34). With the eyes of faith, they must look beyond their present circumstances to the glory of their future inheritance. Just as Jesus came to do the Father's will and knew it would involve Him in suffering and death, so believers discover that for them God's will also involves suffering. When they have

ye endured a great fight of afflictions: You suffered much, *NLT* . . . You won a great contest of suffering, *SEB* . . . endured so great a struggle with persecution, *Williams* . . . Though it was a hard and painful struggle, you remained steadfast, *TNT*.

33. Partly, whilst ye were made a gazingstock: You were not only made, *TNT* . . . by being exposed as a public spectacle, *Williams*.

both by reproaches and afflictions: . . . to insults and violent sufferings, *Williams*.

and partly, whilst ye became companions of them that were so used: . . . having become Joint-participators, *Wilson* . . . you deliberately shared the lot of others who were being treated in this way, *TNT* . . . by showing yourselves ready to share with those who were living in this condition, *Williams*.

34. For ye had compassion of me in my bonds: For you took pity on the prisoners, *Norlie* . . . you showed sympathy with those who were in prison, *Williams* . . . You suffered with those in prison, *TNT*.

and took joyfully the spoiling of your goods: . . . you took it cheerfully, *Beck* . . . and cheerfully accepted the plundering of your goods, *Norlie* . . . submitted to the violent seizure of your property, *Williams* . . . the confiscation, *Montgomery* . . . the seizure of your possessions, *Wilson*.

knowing in yourselves that ye have in heaven: . . . because you knew you owned, *SEB* . . . you possessed, *TNT*.

a better and an enduring substance: . . . have better and permanent property, *Concordant* . . . better things which last, *SEB* . . . even lasting possessions, *Montgomery* . . . one that was lasting, *Williams*.

35. Cast not away therefore your confidence: So then, don't throw away, *Adams* . . . do not fling away, *Montgomery* . . . Then don't lose your courage, *Beck* . . . you must never give up your confident courage, *Williams* . . . your trust, *NLT*.

which hath great recompense of reward: . . . for it holds a rich reward for you, *Williams*.

3144.12 adj acc sing fem	**3144.12** adj acc sing fem	**3269.1** noun acc sing fem	**5119.2** noun gen sing fem
μεγάλην.	[☆ μεγάλην	μισθαποδοσίαν,]	**36.** ὑπομονῆς
megalēn	*megalēn*	*misthapodosian*	*hupomonēs*
great.	[great	recompense,]	Of endurance

1056.1 conj	**2174.2** verb 2pl pres act	**5367.3** noun acc sing fem	**2419.1** conj	**3450.16** art sing neu	**2284.1** noun sing neu	**3450.2** art gen sing
γὰρ	ἔχετε	χρείαν,	ἵνα	τὸ	θέλημα	τοῦ
gar	*echete*	*chreian*	*hina*	*to*	*thelēma*	*tou*
for	you have	need,	that	the	will	

2296.2 noun gen sing masc	**4020.39** verb nom pl masc part aor act	**2837.7** verb 2pl subj aor mid	**3450.12** art acc sing fem	**1845.4** noun acc sing fem
θεοῦ	ποιήσαντες	κομίσησθε	τὴν	ἐπαγγελίαν.
theou	*poiēsantes*	*komisēsthe*	*tēn*	*epangelian*
of God	having done	you may receive	the	promise.

2068.1 adv	**1056.1** conj	**3261.1** adv	**3607.1** rel-pron sing	**3607.1** rel-pron sing	**3450.5** art nom sing masc	**2048.44** verb nom sing masc part pres mid
37. ἔτι	γὰρ	μικρὸν	ὅσον	ὅσον,	ὁ	ἐρχόμενος
eti	*gar*	*mikron*	*hoson*	*hoson*	*ho*	*erchomenos*
Yet	for	a little	which	which,	the	coming

37.a.**Txt:** 01א-corr,02A 06D-corr,015H,018K 020L,etc.byz.Sod **Var:** 01א-org,06D-org Treg,Tisc,We/Ho,Weis UBS/☆

2223.7 verb 3sing indic fut act	**2504.1** conj	**3620.3** partic	**5384.4** verb 3sing indic fut act	**5384.5** verb 3sing indic fut act	**3450.5** art nom sing masc
ἥξει,	καὶ	οὐ	ʻ χρονίει·	[a☆ χρονίσει·]	**38.** ὁ
hēxei	*kai*	*ou*	*chroniei*	*chronisei*	*ho*
will come,	and	not	will delay.	[idem]	The

38.a.**Var:** p46,01א,02A 015H-org,it.sa.Lach Treg,Alf,Tisc,We/Ho Weis,Sod,UBS/☆

1156.2 conj	**1337.3** adj nom sing masc	**1466.2** prs-pron gen 1sing	**1523.2** prep gen	**3963.2** noun gen sing fem	**2180.29** verb 3sing indic fut mid
δὲ	δίκαιός	[a☆+ μου]	ἐκ	πίστεως	ζήσεται·
de	*dikaios*	*mou*	*ek*	*pisteōs*	*zēsetai*
but	just	[my]	by	faith	shall live;

2504.1 conj	**1430.1** partic	**5126.3** verb 3sing subj aor mid	**3620.2** partic	**2085.2** verb 3sing indic pres act	**3450.9** art nom sing fem
καὶ	ἐὰν	ὑποστείληται,	οὐκ	εὐδοκεῖ	ἡ
kai	*ean*	*huposteilētai*	*ouk*	*eudokei*	*hē*
and	if	he draw back,	not	delights	the

5425.1 noun nom sing fem	**1466.2** prs-pron gen 1sing	**1706.1** prep	**840.4** prs-pron dat sing	**2231.1** prs-pron nom 1pl	**1156.2** conj
ψυχή	μου	ἐν	αὐτῷ.	**39.** ἡμεῖς	δὲ
psuchē	*mou*	*en*	*autō*	*hēmeis*	*de*
soul	my	in	him.	We	but

3620.2 partic	**1498.5** verb 1pl indic pres act	**5127.1** noun gen sing fem	**1519.1** prep	**677.3** noun acc sing fem	**233.2** conj
οὐκ	ἐσμὲν	ὑποστολῆς	εἰς	ἀπώλειαν,	ἀλλὰ
ouk	*esmen*	*hupostolēs*	*eis*	*apōleian*	*alla*
not	are	of drawing back	to	destruction,	but

3963.2 noun gen sing fem	**1519.1** prep	**3910.2** noun acc sing fem	**5425.2** noun gen sing fem	**1498.4** verb 3sing indic pres act
πίστεως	εἰς	περιποίησιν	ψυχῆς.	**11:1.** Ἔστιν
pisteōs	*eis*	*peripoiēsin*	*psuchēs*	*Estin*
of faith	to	saving	soul.	Is

1156.2 conj	**3963.1** noun nom sing fem	**1666.17** verb gen pl neu part pres mid	**5125.1** noun nom sing fem	**4088.4** noun gen pl neu
δὲ	πίστις	ἐλπιζομένων	ὑπόστασις,	πραγμάτων
de	*pistis*	*elpizomenōn*	*hupostasis*	*pragmatōn*
now	faith	of being hoped for	assurance,	of things

"done the will of God," however, they will actually go beyond their knowledge of God's promise and receive it for themselves in their personal experience.

10:37,38. To fix his admonition firmly in their minds, the inspired writer turned to another quotation from the Old Testament. With the words "For yet a little while," he alluded to Isaiah 26:20 which has a parallel context to that of Hebrews. In both cases believing Jews were suffering hardship and being encouraged to wait patiently for the fulfillment of God's promise.

The rest of the quotation comes from the Septuagint text of Habakkuk 2:3,4. Just as the Lord told Habakkuk not to worry about the Babylonians escaping judgment but to trust Him and wait for the coming of the messianic fulfillment, so verses 37 and 38 admonish and encourage believers.

They may think the Son's coming has been delayed, but this is not so: His return is certain and will take place according to God's schedule. If a believer turns back (*huposteilētai* is here used with the meaning "apostatize"), God is displeased. The one who apostatizes, i.e., abandons his profession of faith in the Son to return to Judaism and its animal sacrifices, will not receive the promised inheritance in glory.

10:39. After firmly issuing the fourth warning (10:26-38), the inspired writer again indicated that the majority of those to whom the epistle was written were not included in the group who actually would apostatize. By using the pronoun "we" throughout this section, he included himself with them (9:24; 10:10,22-24,26,30). They were not such as those who turned back to destruction. The word translated "perdition" is *apōleian*; it occurs 17 other places in the New Testament where it is translated as "damnation," "destruction," "perdition," "pernicious way," "waste," and "damnable." The end of those who turn back from faith in Jesus Christ the Son is eternal damnation. The inspired writer, however, indicated that he and those to whom the epistle was written were true believers."

11:1. The danger about which the inspired writer warned springs from the sin of unbelief. The antidote for this dread poison is faith. First of all a brief description of faith is given in verses 1-3. The word translated "substance" is *hupostasis*; it could also be translated "essence" or "confidence." It is modified by the phrase "of things hoped for." Its best meaning seems to be that faith is that which *underlies* the inheritance which believers expect to receive. Secondly, the writer declares that faith is the evidence which gives proof of the existence of the unseen world.

36. For ye have need of patience: You need to have endurance, *SEB.*
that, after ye have done the will of God: . . . to carry out the will of God, *Williams.*
ye might receive the promise: . . . you may obtain, *Adams* . . . the blessing, *Williams.*

37. For yet a little while: It is just a short time, *Adams.*
and he that shall come will come, and will not tarry: God will come. He will not be late, *SEB* . . . will be arriving and not delaying, *Concordant* . . . will not put it off, *Klingensmith.*

38. Now the just shall live by faith: Meantime my righteous servant will live on by faith, *Williams.*
but if [any man] draw back, my soul shall have no pleasure in him: If anyone turns back, *NLT* . . . And if he shrinks back, *Norlie* . . . I won't be pleased with him, *Adams* . . . has no delight in him, *Williams.*

39. But we are not of them who draw back unto perdition: . . . of those shrinking back, *Concordant* . . . not of a disposition to draw back so as to perish, *Williams* . . . into destruction, *Adams* . . . to their Ruin, *TCNT.*
but of them that believe to the saving of the soul: . . . has faith that leads to the preservation of the souls, *Adams* . . . unto the gaining of the soul, *Montgomery* . . . in order to a Preservation of Life, *Wilson.*

1. Now faith is the substance of things hoped for: . . . is a Basis of things hoped for, *Wilson* . . . is the real part of things, *Klingensmith* . . . is the assurance of, *Williams* . . . is a solidly grounded certainty about, *Adams* . . . is the title-deed, *Montgomery* . . . is an assumption of what is being expected, *Concordant* . . . is confidence in the realization of one's hopes, *TCNT.*
the evidence of things not seen: . . . the proof of the reality of the things, *Williams* . . . It is being sure of what we cannot see, *NLT* . . . It is the proof we do not see, *Klingensmith* . . . a conviction regarding things which are not yet visible, *TCNT.*

1637.1 noun nom sing masc	3620.3 partic	984.26 verb gen pl neu part pres mid	1706.1 prep	3642.11 dem-pron dat sing fem	1056.1 conj
ἔλεγχος	οὐ	βλεπομένων.	2. ἐν	ταύτῃ	γὰρ
elenchos	*ou*	*blepomenōn*	*en*	*tautē*	*gar*
conviction	not	being seen.	By	this	for

3113.37 verb 3pl indic aor pass	3450.7 art nom pl masc	4104.5 adj comp nom pl masc	3963.3 noun dat sing fem
ἐμαρτυρήθησαν	οἱ	πρεσβύτεροι.	3. Πίστει
emarturēthēsan	*hoi*	*presbuteroi*	*Pistei*
were borne witness to	the	elders.	By faith

3401.1 verb 1pl indic pres act	2645.9 verb inf perf mid	3450.8 art acc pl masc	163.6 noun acc pl masc	4343.3 noun dat sing neu
νοοῦμεν	κατηρτίσθαι	τοὺς	αἰῶνας	ῥήματι
nooumen	*katērtisthai*	*tous*	*aiōnas*	*rhēmati*
we apprehend	to have been framed	the	worlds	by word

2296.2 noun gen sing masc	1519.1 prep	3450.16 art sing neu	3231.1 partic	1523.2 prep gen	5154.12 verb gen pl neu part pres mid	3450.17 art pl neu
θεοῦ,	εἰς	τὸ	μὴ	ἐκ	φαινομένων	ʼ τὰ
theou	*eis*	*to*	*mē*	*ek*	*phainomenōn*	*ta*
of God,	so	the	not	from	appearing	the things

3.a.**Txt:** 06D-corr,018K 020L,byz.
Var: 01ℵ,02A,06D-org 025P,33,bo.Lach,Treg Alf,Tisc,We/Ho,Weis Sod,UBS/☆

984.25 verb pl neu part pres mid	3450.16 art sing neu	984.28 verb sing neu part pres mid	1090.13 verb inf perf act
βλεπόμενα	[a☆ τὸ	βλεπόμενον]	γεγονέναι.
blepomena	*to*	*blepomenon*	*gegonenai*
being seen	[the thing	being seen]	to have become.

3963.3 noun dat sing fem	3979.1 adj comp	2355.4 noun acc sing fem	6.2 name masc	3706.2 prep
4. Πίστει	πλείονα	θυσίαν	Ἄβελ	παρὰ
Pistei	*pleiona*	*thusian*	*Habel*	*para*
By faith	a more excellent	sacrifice	Abel	than

2506.1 name masc	4232.12 verb 3sing indic aor act	3450.3 art dat sing	2296.3 noun dat sing masc	1217.1 prep	3614.10 rel-pron gen sing fem
Κάϊν	προσήνεγκεν	τῷ	θεῷ,	δι'	ἧς
Kain	*prosēnenken*	*tō*	*theō*	*di'*	*hēs*
Cain	offered		to God,	by	which

3113.36 verb 3sing indic aor pass	1498.32 verb inf pres act	1337.3 adj nom sing masc	3113.8 verb gen sing masc part pres act
ἐμαρτυρήθη	εἶναι	δίκαιος,	μαρτυροῦντος
emarturēthē	*einai*	*dikaios*	*marturountos*
he was borne witness to	to be	righteous,	bearing witness

4.a.**Txt:** p13,p46 01ℵ-corr2,06D-corr2 08E,018K,020L,025P 044,bo.byz.
Var: 01ℵ-org,02A 06D-org,33,326

1894.3 prep	3450.4 art dat pl	1428.4 noun dat pl neu	840.3 prs-pron gen sing	3450.2 art gen sing	2296.2 noun gen sing masc	3450.3 art dat sing
ἐπὶ	τοῖς	δώροις	αὐτοῦ	ʼ☆ τοῦ	θεοῦ·	[a τῷ
epi	*tois*	*dōrois*	*autou*	*tou*	*theou*	*tō*
to	the	gifts	his		God,	

2296.3 noun dat sing masc	2504.1 conj	1217.1 prep	840.10 prs-pron gen sing fem	594.15 verb nom sing masc part aor act	2068.1 adv
θεῷ·]	καὶ	δι'	αὐτῆς	ἀποθανὼν	ἔτι
theō	*kai*	*di'*	*autēs*	*apothanōn*	*eti*
[to God,]	and	through	it,	having died,	yet

4.b.**Txt:** 06D,018K,020L byz.Sod
Var: 01ℵ,02A,025P,33 bo.Gries,Lach,Treg,Alf Word,Tisc,We/Ho,Weis UBS/☆

2953.47 verb 3sing indic pres mid	2953.2 verb 3sing indic pres act	3963.3 noun dat sing fem	1786.2 name masc	3216.5 verb 3sing indic aor pass
ʼ λαλεῖται.	[b☆ λαλεῖ.]	5. Πίστει	Ἐνὼχ	μετετέθη
laleitai	*lalei*	*Pistei*	*Enōch*	*metetethē*
speaks.	[idem]	By faith	Enoch	was translated

11:2,3. In these verses two more characteristics of faith are given: (1) It is the means by which the elders (the Old Testament heroes of faith discussed in this chapter) gained their favorable testimonies. (2) It is the means by which believers are able to understand the world which is seen and to grasp its relationship to the unseen world.

11:4. Verses 4-7 present faith as the means by which Abel, Enoch, and Noah were declared righteous. This brief section emphasizes the necessity of faith as the means of pleasing God and stresses the resultant righteousness displayed in the lives of these three men of faith.

As to Abel, many have inferred that his sacrifice was acceptable because it was a blood offering. He brought an offering from his flock while Cain presented one from his field.

However, this difference in the two sacrifices stands out as only one among others. Further, God later permitted even a sin offering that was bloodless. The poorest of the poor could sacrifice a handful of flour for his sins and find favor with the Lord. As God explained to Moses, "But if he be not able to bring two turtledoves, or two young pigeons, then he that sinned shall bring for his offering the tenth part of an ephah of fine flour for a sin offering" (Leviticus 5:11). Recognizing this, the writer of Hebrews declared, "And almost all things are by the law purged with blood" (9:22). Under the inspiration of the Spirit, though, he went on to rightly place the emphasis on blood sacrifice. He wrote, "And without shedding of blood is no remission" (ibid.).

The offerings of Cain and Abel also contained qualitative differences. *Pleiona,* translated "more excellent," simply means "more" in some qualitative sense. Genesis indicates Abel carefully selected "of the firstlings of his flock and of the fat thereof" (Genesis 4:4) while Cain simply "brought of the fruit of the ground" whatever his hand happened to find (Genesis 4:3). Still, the most important difference between Cain and Abel in their worship to God concerns the element of faith. Hebrews makes clear what Genesis only implies. The significant things is Abel offered his sacrifice "by faith." That faith demonstrated itself as he presented a first-class blood offering. The Lord counted his faith as righteousness. The inspired record of this incident still testifies to Abel's life of faith. That life serves as an example for others of all times.

11:5. These comments on Enoch follow the Septuagint, not the Hebrew Masoretic text. In Genesis 5:24 the English Old Testament translated from the Hebrew reads: "He was not; for God took him." The Septuagint says Enoch "was not found, because God had translated him" and "he pleased God." Neither text expressly mentions faith. Since faith is the only means by which sinful men can please God, Enoch must have lived a life characterized by faith, because the Scriptures declare his life was pleasing to God. Both the Hebrew text and the Septuagint indicate that God did not take

2. For by it the elders obtained a good report: It was for their faith that our ancestors won God's approval, *TNT* . . The elders had this kind of faith long ago. It pleased God, *SEB* . . . the Ancients were attested, *Wilson* . . . The men of long ago won approval for their faith, *Beck.*

3. Through faith we understand:

that the worlds were framed by the word of God: . . . that the universe, *Adams* . . . was fashioned by, *Montgomery* . . . the worlds were created, beautifully co-ordinated, and now exist, *Williams* . . . made by God's word, *TNT.*

so that things which are seen were not made of things which do appear: . . . the things that we see did not evolve out of existing matter, *Norlie* . . . so that what we see came into being from what we cannot see, *TNT* . . . did not develop out of mere matter, *Williams* . . . not made out of what is visible, *Montgomery* . . . that are apparent to us, *Adams.*

4. By faith Abel offered unto God a more excellent sacrifice than Cain: . . . brought to God a better sacrifice, *Beck* . . . a greater sacrifice, *TNT* . . . more acceptable to God than Cain did, *Williams.*

by which he obtained witness that he was righteous: . . . by it he was approved as an upright man, *Williams.*

God testifying of his gifts: . . . by accepting his gifts, *Montgomery* . . . showed approval of, *TNT* . . . since God approved him for the offering he made, *Williams.*

and by it he being dead yet speaketh: . . . by it he still continues to speak, though dead, *Williams.*

5. By faith Enoch was translated: Faith caused Enoch to be taken up, *Norlie* . . . was transferred, *Concordant* . . . was removed to another place, *Adams* . . . was transplanted from earth, *Williams* . . . was taken up from the earth, *NLT* . . . was taken away, *TNT.*

that he should not see death: . . . without dying, *NLT* . . . so that he did not experience dying, *Williams.*

3450.2 art gen sing	3231.1 partic	1481.19 verb inf aor act	2265.4 noun acc sing masc	2504.1 conj	3620.1 partic	2128.43 verb 3sing indic imperf pass
τοῦ	μὴ	ἰδεῖν	θάνατον,	καὶ	οὐχ	⸀ εὑρίσκετο,
tou	*mē*	*idein*	*thanaton*	*kai*	*ouch*	*heurisketo*
the	not	to see	death,	and	not	was being found,

5.a.**Txt:** 018K,020L 025P,byz.
Var: 01ℵ,02A,06D,Lach Treg,Alf,Word,Tisc We/Ho,Weis,Sod UBS/⋆

2128.49 verb 3sing indic imperf mid	1354.1 conj	3216.2 verb 3sing indic aor act	840.6 prs-pron acc sing masc	3450.5 art nom sing masc
[a⋆ ηὑρίσκετο]	διότι	μετέθηκεν	αὐτὸν	ὁ
hēurisketo	*dioti*	*metethēken*	*auton*	*ho*
[idem]	because	translated	him	

2296.1 noun nom sing masc	4112.1 prep	1056.1 conj	3450.10 art gen sing fem	3201.2 noun gen sing fem
θεός·	πρὸ	γὰρ	τῆς	μεταθέσεως
theos	*pro*	*gar*	*tēs*	*metatheseōs*
God;	before	for	the	translation

5.b.**Txt:** 01ℵ-corr 06D-corr,018K,020L byz.
Var: 01ℵ-org,02A 06D-org,025P,33,Lach Treg,Alf,Tisc,We/Ho Weis,Sod,UBS/⋆

840.3 prs-pron gen sing	3113.39 verb 3sing indic perf mid	2079.2 verb indic perf act
⸂b αὐτοῦ ⸃	μεμαρτύρηται	⸀ εὐηρεστηκέναι
autou	*memarturētai*	*euērestēkenai*
his	he has been borne witness to	to have well pleased

5.c.**Txt:** 01ℵ,06D,025P byz.Tisc,Sod
Var: 02A,018K,020L,33 Lach,Alf,We/Ho,Weis UBS/⋆

2079.4 verb inf perf act	3450.3 art dat sing	2296.3 noun dat sing masc	5400.1 prep	1156.2 conj
[c⋆ εὐαρεστηκέναι]	τῷ	θεῷ,	**6.** χωρὶς	δὲ
euarestēkenai	*tō*	*theō*	*chōris*	*de*
[idem]		God.	Apart from	but

3963.2 noun gen sing fem	101.3 adj sing neu	2079.1 verb inf aor act	3961.36 verb inf aor act
πίστεως	ἀδύνατον	εὐαρεστῆσαι·	πιστεῦσαι
pisteōs	*adunaton*	*euarestēsai*	*pisteusai*
faith	impossible	to well please.	To believe

6.a.**Txt:** p46,01ℵ-corr 06D-org,08E,018K 020L,025P,byz.
Var: p13,01ℵ-org 06D-corr2,016I,33,1912 Tisc,33,Lach,Alf,We/Ho Weis,UBS/⋆

1056.1 conj	1158.1 verb 3sing indic pres act	3450.6 art acc sing masc	4193.14 verb acc sing masc part pres mid	3450.3 art dat sing
γὰρ	δεῖ	τὸν	προσερχόμενον	⸂a τῷ ⸃
gar	*dei*	*ton*	*proserchomenon*	*tō*
for	it is necessary for	the	approaching	

2296.3 noun dat sing masc	3617.1 conj	1498.4 verb 3sing indic pres act	2504.1 conj	3450.4 art dat pl	1554.2 verb dat pl masc part pres act
θεῷ.	ὅτι	ἔστιν,	καὶ	τοῖς	ἐκζητοῦσιν
theō	*hoti*	*estin*	*kai*	*tois*	*ekzētousin*
to God,	that	he is,	and	for the	seeking out

840.6 prs-pron acc sing masc	3270.1 noun nom sing masc	1090.14 verb 3sing indic pres mid	3963.3 noun dat sing fem
αὐτὸν	μισθαποδότης	γίνεται.	**7.** Πίστει
auton	*misthapodotēs*	*ginetai*	*Pistei*
him	a rewarder	he becomes.	By faith

5372.5 verb nom sing masc part aor pass	3437.1 name masc	3875.1 prep	3450.1 art gen pl	3237.1 adv
χρηματισθεὶς	Νῶε	περὶ	τῶν	μηδέπω
chrēmatistheis	*Nōe*	*peri*	*tōn*	*mēdepō*
having been divinely instructed	Noah	concerning	the things	not yet

984.26 verb gen pl neu part pres mid	2106.1 verb nom sing masc part aor pass	2650.1 verb 3sing indic aor act
βλεπομένων,	εὐλαβηθεὶς	κατεσκεύασεν
blepomenōn	*eulabētheis*	*kateskeuasen*
being seen,	having been moved with reverence	prepared

Enoch in death but by a miraculous removal from this life which changed him from a mortal man to an immortal. Since the Bible says "Enoch walked with God" (Genesis 5:22,24), it is clear that he was a man of faith. God's Word testifies to Enoch's God-pleasing obedience. Habakkuk 2:4 provides the link between faith and God's being pleased with men (Hebrews 10:38).

The Bible never separates faith from obedience. Indeed, Paul wrote of the "obedience of faith" (Romans 16:26). When a sinner is genuinely converted, his changed life-style indicates the reality of his faith. Then through the years his confidence in God causes him to walk softly before the Lord in obedience to His commandments. He stands in awe at Jesus' words, "Why call ye me, Lord, Lord, and do not the things which I say?" (Luke 6:46). Keeping the commandments of God gives him "the answer of a good conscience toward God" (1 Peter 3:21).

Enoch's experience fit this pattern. Commenting on it Taylor wrote, "God's Spirit witnessed that all was well; no last-minute adjustments were needed. Here again the part faith played was indirect—faith, in itself, cannot translate anybody to heaven. But Enoch's walk with God was by faith, and the translation was God's sovereign reward for his faithfulness in so walking" (*Beacon Bible Commentary*, p.140).

11:6. This verse enunciates the principle drawn from the Septuagint version of Habakkuk 2:4 ("the just shall live by faith") and is demonstrated by the Biblical account of Enoch's life. Apart from faith no man can receive God's approval. Whoever comes to God, i.e., prays and worships, must do two things if his worship is to be accepted as were the sacrifice of Abel and the life of Enoch. They must believe *both* that God exists *and* that He rewards those who earnestly seek Him. The Hebrews to whom this epistle was written believed in God's existence, but some of them apparently were wondering whether or not Jesus was truly the Messiah and if He was going to return to set up the kingdom of God. They were assured that if they continued to walk with God, they would also obtain a testimony to their own righteousness before God. The same is true for believers today.

11:7. Noah, after receiving a divine admonition (*chrēmatistheis*, used also of Moses in 8:5), responded obediently in faith out of his reverence for God (*eulabētheis*). Noah's building the ark displayed faith as a response to God's instructions. God spoke and Noah obeyed Him. His obedience was remarkable. It clearly displayed one of the main characteristics of faith described in verses 1-3. God's admonition to Noah described things which had not yet occurred, but since Noah knew and trusted God, he built the ark in the face of mockery and opposition. The absurdity of building a huge ship far from the sea in preparation for a worldwide flood daunted Noah not in the least. His trust in God informed and undergirded him. The coming deluge was not a laughing matter;

and was not found, because God had translated him: . . . no remains of him could anywhere be found, *Wade* . . . had conveyed him, *Wuest* . . . because God had taken him to heaven, *SEB* . . . taken him away, *TNT.*

for before his translation he had this testimony: We know that this was due to his faith, *TNT* . . . before he was transplanted from earth evidence was given him, *Williams* . . . stands in the Scriptures his good record, *Wade.*

that he pleased God: . . . he was well-pleasing to God, *BB.*

6. But without faith [it is] impossible to please [him]: . . . it is not possible to be well-pleasing to him, *BB.*

for he that cometh to God must believe: . . . anyone who approaches God must believe, *Williams* . . . who comes near to God, *Noli* . . . First, to believe, *Norlie* . . . must have faith, *TNT.*

that he is: . . . that He exists, *Adams, TNT* . . . that there is a God, *Williams.*

and [that] he is a rewarder of them that diligently seek him: . . . and proves a Rewarder, *Wade* . . . that He gives rewards to all who earnestly try to find Him, *Williams* . . . of those who are seeking Him out, *Concordant* . . . to the one who keeps on looking for Him, *NLT* . . . to the people who are searching for Him, *SEB.*

7. By faith Noah: Through his faith, *Wade.*

being warned of God of things not seen as yet: . . . having been divinely admonished, *Wilson* . . . received God's warning about events which at the time belonged to the future, *TNT* . . . being divinely warned about a catastrophe which was not yet within sight, *Wade* . . . of the impending disaster, *Noli.*

moved with fear, prepared an ark to the saving of his house: . . . proceeded conscientiously to construct an Ark for the preservation of his household, *Wade* . . . He listened carefully to what God said, *TNT* . . . with reverential care prepared, *Wuest* . . . in reverence prepared an ark for saving his family, *Williams* . . . he built a large boat, *NLT* . . . constructs an ark, *Concordant.*

Hebrews 11:8

2759.3 noun acc sing fem	1519.1 prep	4843.3 noun acc sing fem	3450.2 art gen sing	3486.2 noun gen sing masc	840.3 prs-pron gen sing	1217.1 prep
κιβωτὸν	εἰς	σωτηρίαν	τοῦ	οἴκου	αὐτοῦ·	δι'
kibōton	*eis*	*sōtērian*	*tou*	*oikou*	*autou*	*di'*
an ark	for	salvation	of the	house	his;	by

3614.10 rel-pron gen sing fem	2602.4 verb 3sing indic aor act	3450.6 art acc sing masc	2862.4 noun acc sing masc	2504.1 conj	3450.10 art gen sing fem
ἧς	κατέκρινεν	τὸν	κόσμον,	καὶ	τῆς
hēs	*katekrinen*	*ton*	*kosmon*	*kai*	*tēs*
which	he condemned	the	world,	and	of the

2567.3 prep	3963.4 noun acc sing fem	1336.2 noun gen sing fem	1090.33 verb 3sing indic aor mid	2791.1 noun nom sing masc
κατὰ	πίστιν	δικαιοσύνης	ἐγένετο	κληρονόμος.
kata	*pistin*	*dikaiosunēs*	*egeneto*	*klēronomos*
according to	faith	righteousness	became	heir.

8.a.**Txt:** 01ℵ,06D-corr2 044,byz.
Var: p46,02A,06D-org 33,1739,1881,Sod

3963.3 noun dat sing fem	3450.5 art nom sing masc	2535.30 verb nom sing masc part pres mid	11.1 name masc	5057.5 verb 3sing indic aor act
8. Πίστει	[[a]+ ὁ]	καλούμενος	Ἀβραὰμ	ὑπήκουσεν
Pistei	*ho*	*kaloumenos*	*Abraam*	*hupēkousen*
By faith	[the]	being called	Abraham	obeyed

8.b.**Txt:** 01ℵ-corr 06D-corr,018K,020L,etc. byz.Sod
Var: 01ℵ-org,02A 06D-org,025P,33,Lach Treg,Alf,Tisc,We/Ho Weis,UBS/⋆

1814.20 verb inf aor act	1519.1 prep	3450.6 art acc sing masc	4964.4 noun acc sing masc	3614.6 rel-pron acc sing masc	3165.21 verb 3sing indic imperf act
ἐξελθεῖν	εἰς	([b] τὸν)	τόπον	ὃν	ἤμελλεν
exelthein	*eis*	*ton*	*topon*	*hon*	*ēmellen*
to go out	into	the	place	which	he was about

2956.10 verb inf pres act	1519.1 prep	2790.3 noun acc sing fem	2504.1 conj	1814.3 verb 3sing indic aor act	3231.1 partic
λαμβάνειν	εἰς	κληρονομίαν,	καὶ	ἐξῆλθεν,	μὴ
lambanein	*eis*	*klēronomian*	*kai*	*exēlthen*	*mē*
to receive	for	an inheritance,	and	went out,	not

1971.5 verb nom sing masc part pres mid	4085.1 adv	2048.34 verb 3sing indic pres mid	3963.3 noun dat sing fem	3801.2 verb 3sing indic aor act
ἐπιστάμενος	ποῦ	ἔρχεται.	**9.** Πίστει	παρῴκησεν
epistamenos	*pou*	*erchetai*	*Pistei*	*parōkēsen*
knowing	where	he is going.	By faith	he sojourned

9.a.**Txt:** 06D-org,Steph
Var: 01ℵ,02A,06D-corr 018K,020L,Lach,Treg Alf,Tisc,We/Ho,Weis Sod,UBS/⋆

1519.1 prep	3450.10 art gen sing fem	1087.4 noun acc sing fem	3450.10 art gen sing fem	1845.1 noun fem	5453.1 conj
εἰς	([a] τῆς)	γῆν	τῆς	ἐπαγγελίας,	ὡς
eis	*tēs*	*gēn*	*tēs*	*epangelias*	*hōs*
in	the	land	of the	promise,	as

243.6 adj acc sing fem	1706.1 prep	4488.5 noun dat pl fem	2700.12 verb nom sing masc part aor act	3196.3 prep	2439.1 name masc
ἀλλοτρίαν,	ἐν	σκηναῖς	κατοικήσας	μετὰ	Ἰσαὰκ
allotrian	*en*	*skēnais*	*katoikēsas*	*meta*	*Isaak*
a stranger,	in	tents	having dwelt	with	Isaac

2504.1 conj	2361.1 name masc	3450.1 art gen pl	4640.2 adj gen pl masc	3450.10 art gen sing fem	1845.1 noun fem
καὶ	Ἰακὼβ	τῶν	συγκληρονόμων	τῆς	ἐπαγγελίας
kai	*Iakōb*	*tōn*	*sunklēronomōn*	*tēs*	*epangelias*
and	Jacob,	the	joint heirs	of the	promise

3450.10 art gen sing fem	840.10 prs-pron gen sing fem	1538.7 verb 3sing indic imperf mid	1056.1 conj	3450.12 art acc sing fem	3450.8 art acc pl masc
τῆς	αὐτῆς·	**10.** ἐξεδέχετο	γὰρ	τὴν	τοὺς
tēs	*autēs*	*exedecheto*	*gar*	*tēn*	*tous*
the	same;	he was waiting	for	the	the

it was a certainty. So it is with the second coming of Jesus Christ. The world may mock, but the King will come and all will acknowledge that He is Lord. By his faith Noah accomplished three things: (1) He delivered his family from the flood; (2) His obedience contrasted with the unbelief of his contemporaries who died in the flood; (3) He became a recipient of the by-faith righteousness of God.

11:8. The second section of Old Testament heroes begins here; 11:8-22 presents the patriarchs from Abraham to Joseph. They are all represented as pilgrim-sojourners who "all died in faith, not having received the promises" (11:13). The emphasis is upon their endurance and hope in the face of life's trials.

Most appropriately the section begins with Abraham who is the "father of all them that believe" (Romans 4:11). As in the case of Noah, Abraham's faith was demonstrated by his response to a word from the Lord. He was living in Ur, but God "called" him to leave for an unknown destination. His by-faith response was obedience. Interestingly, there is no mention of Abraham's hesitations or miscues. The emphasis is upon Abraham's long term adherence to the principle of believing and obeying God. When all is said and done, even though he was ignorant of his final destination, Abraham believed God would finally bring to pass all the things included in His promise. On the basis of this trust in God, Abraham acted. He knew by faith that the things which he could not see were realities dependent upon God's faithfulness.

11:9. Abraham did get to see the land of Canaan which the Lord had promised to give to him and his descendants, but he never actually settled there or received title deed to it as his personal possession. He traveled within its borders as a nomad. He was a foreigner; *allotrian* refers to the fact that the land where he "sojourned" was "a strange country" to him. This fact is underlined by his life-style: he and his family lived in tents and followed their herds. His son and grandson lived in the same manner. In the light of these facts, it is apparent that all three of these patriarchs died without actually receiving the land which had been promised to Abraham as part of his inheritance from God. Therefore, all of them were only heirs in prospect, not actual inheritors while they lived upon the earth.

11:10. These patriarchs were richly blessed by God. They possessed vast wealth, and their family was large and powerful. They walked with the Lord and were obviously blessed by Him. Yet they did not receive all which He had promised. In spite of this they remained faithful to the Lord. Why? Since they were men of faith, they were able to gaze beyond the world which they experienced through their senses. They understood that the world in which they lived was not their ultimate home. Abraham eagerly antici-

by the which he condemned the world: . . . and by his faith, *Williams* . . . His faith was a judgement on the world, *TNT.*

and became heir of the righteousness which is by faith: By means of it he entered into possession of, *TNT* . . . an heir of the justification that comes by faith, *Norlie* . . . and became possessor of the uprightness that results from faith, *Williams.*

8. By faith Abraham, when he was called: It was faith that enabled, *TCNT* . . . on being called, *Williams.*

to go out into a place which he should after receive for an inheritance, obeyed: . . . obeyed God's call to go out to a country which one day God would give him to be his own, *TNT* . . . in starting off for a country which he was to receive as his own, *Williams.*

and he went out, not knowing whither he went: He left his home, *NLT* . . . and he did it in spite of the fact that he did not know where he was going, *Williams* . . . not having the faintest idea about where he was going, *Adams.*

9. By faith he sojourned in the land of promise: Faith kept him there in the promised land, *Norlie* . . . he made his temporary home in the land that God had promised, *Williams.*

as [in] a strange country: . . . lived as a stranger, *Beck* . . . lived as a foreigner, *SEB* . . . as an alien, *Montgomery* . . . he settled, like a stranger in a foreign land, *TNT* . . . as in an alien land, *Concordant* . . . although a land inhabited by others, *Williams.*

dwelling in tabernacles with Isaac and Jacob: . . . living merely in tents, *Williams* . . . as Isaac and Jacob did, *TNT.*

the heirs with him of the same promise: . . . who were to share the promise with him, *Williams* . . . to whom God had also made the same promise, *TNT.*

10. For he looked for a city which hath foundations: . . . he continually looked for, *Montgomery* . . . he was confidently looking forward to, *Williams* . . . was waiting for the city, *TNT* . . . that could not be moved, *NLT.*

Hebrews 11:11

2287.6 noun acc pl masc	2174.25 verb acc sing fem part pres act	4032.4 noun acc sing fem	3614.10 rel-pron gen sing fem	4927.1 noun nom sing masc
θεμελίους	ἔχουσαν	πόλιν,	ἧς	τεχνίτης
themelious	*echousan*	*polin*	*hēs*	*technitēs*
foundations	having	city,	of which	architect

2504.1 conj	1211.1 noun nom sing masc	3450.5 art nom sing masc	2296.1 noun nom sing masc	3963.3 noun dat sing fem	2504.1 conj
καὶ	δημιουργὸς	ὁ	θεός.	11. Πίστει	καὶ
kai	*dēmiourgos*	*ho*	*theos*	*Pistei*	*kai*
and	constructor		God.	By faith	also

11.a.**Txt:** p13-vid,01ℵ 02A,06D-corr2,byz.Tisc Sod
Var: p46,06D-org,044

840.9 prs-pron nom sing fem	4421.1 name nom fem	4574.1 adj nom sing fem	1405.4 noun acc sing fem	1519.1 prep
αὐτὴ	Σάῤῥα	[a+ στεῖρα]	δύναμιν	εἰς
autē	*Sarrha*	*steira*	*dunamin*	*eis*
herself	Sarah	[barren]	power	for

2573.2 noun acc sing fem	4543.2 noun gen sing neu	2956.14 verb 3sing indic aor act	2504.1 conj	3706.2 prep
καταβολὴν	σπέρματος	ἔλαβεν,	καὶ	παρὰ
katabolēn	*spermatos*	*elaben*	*kai*	*para*
conception	of seed	received,	and	beyond

11.b.**Txt:** 01ℵ-corr 06D-corr,018K,020L 025P,byz.
Var: 01ℵ-org,02A 06D-corr,33,sa.bo.Gries Lach,Treg,Alf,Tisc We/Ho,Weis,Sod UBS/☆

2511.4 noun acc sing masc	2227.1 noun gen sing fem	4936.4 verb 3sing indic aor act	1878.1 conj	3964.1 adj sing
καιρὸν	ἡλικίας	ʼb ἔτεκεν, ʽ	ἐπεὶ	πιστὸν
kairon	*hēlikias*	*eteken*	*epei*	*piston*
age	seasonable	gave birth;	since	faithful

2216.13 verb 3sing indic aor mid	3450.6 art acc sing masc	1846.6 verb acc sing masc part aor mid	1346.1 conj	2504.1 conj
ἡγήσατο	τὸν	ἐπαγγειλάμενον·	12. διὸ	καὶ
hēgēsato	*ton*	*epangeilamenon*	*dio*	*kai*
she esteemed	the	having promised.	Wherefore	also

12.a.**Txt:** 01ℵ,06D-corr 020L,byz.Tisc,We/Ho
Var: 02A,06D-org,018K 025P,33,Lach,Alf,Weis Sod,UBS/☆

570.1 prep	1518.1 num card gen	1074.15 verb 3pl indic aor pass	1090.37 verb 3pl indic aor pass	2504.1 conj
ἀφ'	ἑνὸς	ʼ ἐγεννήθησαν,	[a ἐγενήθησαν,]	καὶ
aph'	*henos*	*egennēthēsan*	*egenēthēsan*	*kai*
from	one	were born,	[idem]	and

3642.18 dem-pron pl neu	3362.2 verb gen sing masc part perf mid	2503.1 conj	3450.17 art pl neu	792.2 noun pl neu
ταῦτα	νενεκρωμένου,	καθὼς	τὰ	ἄστρα
tauta	*nenekrōmenou*	*kathōs*	*ta*	*astra*
that	of having become dead,	even as	the	stars

12.b.**Txt:** Steph
Var: 01ℵ,02A,06D 018K,020L,025P,33,byz. Gries,Lach,Treg,Alf Word,Tisc,We/Ho,Weis Sod,UBS/☆

3450.2 art gen sing	3636.2 noun gen sing masc	3450.3 art dat sing	3988.3 noun dat sing neu	2504.1 conj	5448.1 adv	5453.1 conj
τοῦ	οὐρανοῦ	τῷ	πλήθει,	καὶ	ʼ ὡσεὶ	[b☆ ὡς
tou	*ouranou*	*tō*	*plēthei*	*kai*	*hōsei*	*hōs*
of the	heaven	in the	multitude,	and	as	[as

3450.9 art nom sing fem	283.1 noun nom sing fem	3450.9 art nom sing fem	3706.2 prep	3450.16 art sing neu	5327.1 noun sing neu	3450.10 art gen sing fem
ἡ]	ἄμμος	ἡ	παρὰ	τὸ	χεῖλος	τῆς
hē	*ammos*	*hē*	*para*	*to*	*cheilos*	*tēs*
the]	sand	the	by	the	shore	of the

2258.2 noun gen sing fem	3450.9 art nom sing fem	380.1 adj nom sing fem	2567.3 prep	3963.4 noun acc sing fem
θαλάσσης	ἡ	ἀναρίθμητος.	13. Κατὰ	πίστιν
thalassēs	*hē*	*anarithmētos*	*Kata*	*pistin*
sea	the	countless.	In	faith

pated (*exedecheto* means "to welcome, to look forward to something") something far superior to the things which he observed in the Canaan of his day. He expected a way of life (*polin* means far more than "city") that was permanently designed and created by God, the divine craftsman (*technitēs*). He expected not *high tech* but *divine tech*!

whose builder and maker [is] God: . . . that had God for its Architect, *Adams* . . . and Constructor, *Wade* . . . is the Designer and Architect, *Wilson* . . . the city designed and made by, *TNT.*

11:11. Abraham's wife Sarah was not exposed for her frailties (laughing at God's promise of a child or giving Hagar to Abraham so that he might have a son). She is remembered because of what she accomplished through her faith in the Lord. Her initial response to the divine declaration that she would give birth to a son in her advanced age may have been laughter, but in the end she conceived and bore Abraham the son whom God had promised. Through her act of obedience she was empowered by God to become pregnant in spite of her age and her lifelong barrenness. Her behavior flowed from her faith in God. After God had reiterated His promise to Abraham and Sarah, she considered who God was and what He had already done for them. He had always kept His promises in the past, so she trusted Him to keep this promise and by her obedience conceived and bore the miracle child Isaac.

11. Through faith also Sara herself received strength to conceive seed: . . . also obtained power, *Concordant* . . . received power, *Montgomery* . . . for Conception, *Wilson* . . . to become pregnant, *Williams.*

and was delivered of a child when she was past age: . . . and actually gave birth to a child, although she was past the time of life for it, *Williams* . . . though she was unable to have children and was in any case, *TNT* . . . beyond the period of her prime, *Concordant* . . . though she was past the normal time of life for motherhood, *Wade.*

because she judged him faithful who had promised: . . . because she considered Him Who promised trustworthy, *Adams* . . . she thought that He who made her the promise was to be trusted, *Williams* . . . could be trusted to redeem His promise, *Wade.*

11:12. This verse emphatically stresses the astronomical results of Abraham and Sarah's trusting God for the promised son. The best way to emphasize their faith is to render a literal translation of the word order found in this verse: "Wherefore even from one man they were being born, even from one who had died in regard to such things, even as the stars of the heaven in their multitude and as the sand beside the shore of the sea, the sand innumerable!" (translation by the author). Faith in God's promises brings amazing results.

12. Therefore sprang there even of one: . . . and consequently from a single individual, *Wade* . . . from one man, *Williams, TNT.*

and him as good as dead: . . . him practically dead, *Montgomery* . . . and that dead as to any prospects for offspring, *Williams* . . . and that, too, one whose physical vigour had decayed, *Wade.*

[so many] as the stars of the sky in multitude: . . . there sprang descendants, *Wade* . . . came descendants as numerous as, *TNT* . . . a people as numberless as the stars in the sky, *Williams.*

and as the sand which is by the sea shore innumerable: . . . as countless as the grains of sand on the seashore, *TNT* . . . that nobody can count, *Beck.*

11:13. Without exception, all of these patriarchal figures died *kata pistin* (in accordance with the standards of a life of faith) without ever having actually received the promise which God had made to Abraham (Genesis 12:1-3). They never possessed Canaan as their own property. They were blessed by God, but they never saw the greatness of the nation of Israel or the countless numbers of their descendants. Nor did they live to see the whole world blessed in the seed of Abraham: Jesus Christ, God's Son.

Yet they did have an inkling, a clue as to what was happening and what was going to happen. Dimly through the eyes of faith, although they were far, far away (*porrhōthen* means "a long way off"), they had a faint understanding of the great things God would do. And the little understanding which they had was "embraced" (*aspasamenoi* literally means "greeted") by them.

13. These all died in faith: . . . all died victoriously as a result of their faith, *Williams* . . . died having faith, *SEB* . . . dominated by faith, *Wuest* . . . still believing, *Norlie* . . . sustained by their faith, *Wade.*

594.9 verb indic aor act ἀπέθανον *apethanon* died · 3642.7 dem-pron nom pl masc οὗτοι *houtoi* these · 3820.7 adj nom pl masc πάντες, *pantes* all, · 3231.1 partic μὴ *mē* not · 2956.27 verb nom pl masc part aor act ʼ λαβόντες *labontes* having received

2837.11 verb nom pl masc part aor mid [a☆ κομισάμενοι] *komisamenoi* [having obtained] · 3450.15 art acc pl fem τὰς *tas* the · 1845.1 noun fem ἐπαγγελίας, *epangelias* promises, · 233.2 conj ἀλλὰ *alla* but · 4066.1 adv πόῤῥωθεν *porrhōthen* from afar

840.13 prs-pron acc pl fem αὐτὰς *autas* them · 1481.17 verb nom pl masc part aor act ἰδόντες, *idontes* having seen, · 2504.1 conj ʼb καὶ *kai* and · 3844.27 verb nom pl masc part aor pass πεισθέντες, ʽ *peisthentes* having been persuaded, · 2504.1 conj καὶ *kai* and

776.11 verb nom pl masc part aor mid ἀσπασάμενοι, *aspasamenoi* having embraced, · 2504.1 conj καὶ *kai* and · 3533.11 verb nom pl masc part aor act ὁμολογήσαντες *homologēsantes* having confessed · 3617.1 conj ὅτι *hoti* that · 3443.3 adj nom pl masc ξένοι *xenoi* strangers

2504.1 conj καὶ *kai* and · 3789.1 adj nom pl masc παρεπίδημοί *parepidēmoi* sojourners · 1498.7 verb 3pl indic pres act εἰσιν *eisin* they are · 1894.3 prep ἐπὶ *epi* on · 3450.10 art gen sing fem τῆς *tēs* the · 1087.2 noun gen sing fem γῆς. *gēs* earth.

14. 3450.7 art nom pl masc οἱ *hoi* The · 1056.1 conj γὰρ *gar* for · 4955.14 dem-pron acc pl neu τοιαῦτα *toiauta* such things · 2978.16 verb nom pl masc part pres act λέγοντες, *legontes* saying, · 1702.1 verb 3pl indic pres act ἐμφανίζουσιν *emphanizousin* make manifest

3617.1 conj ὅτι *hoti* that · 3830.2 noun acc sing fem πατρίδα *patrida* own country · 1919.5 verb 3pl indic pres act ʼ☆ ἐπιζητοῦσιν. *epizētousin* they are seeking. · 3285.10 verb 3pl indic pres act [a μνημονεύουσιν *mnēmoneuousin* [they are remembering

15. 2504.1 conj καὶ *kai* And · 1479.1 conj εἰ *ei* if · 3173.1 conj μὲν *men* indeed · 1552.10 dem-pron gen sing fem ἐκείνης *ekeinēs* that · 3285.9 verb 3pl indic imperf act ἐμνημόνευον *emnēmoneuon* they were remembering · 570.1 prep ἀφ' *aph'* from

3614.10 rel-pron gen sing fem ἧς *hēs* where · 1814.1 verb indic aor act ʼ ἐξῆλθον, *exēlthon* they came out, · 1530.1 verb 3pl indic aor act [a☆ ἐξέβησαν,] *exebēsan* [idem] · 2174.42 verb indic imperf act εἶχον *eichon* they were having

300.1 partic ἂν *an* · 2511.4 noun acc sing masc καιρὸν *kairon* opportunity · 342.1 verb inf aor act ἀνακάμψαι· *anakampsai* to return; · **16.** 3432.1 adv ʼ νυνὶ *nuni* now · 3431.1 adv [☆ νῦν] *nun* [idem] · 1156.2 conj δὲ *de* but

2882.1 adj comp gen sing κρείττονος *kreittonos* a better · 3576.2 verb 3pl indic pres mid ὀρέγονται, *oregontai* they stretch forward to, · 4969.1 verb ʼ τουτέστιν, *toutestin* that is, · 3642.16 dem-pron sing neu [☆ τοῦτ' *tout'* [this

13.a.**Txt:** 01ℵ-corr,06D 018K,020L,byz.Weis **Var:** 01ℵ-org,025P,33 Treg,Tisc,We/Ho,Sod UBS/☆

13.b.**Txt:** Steph **Var:** 01ℵ,02A,06D 018K,020L,025P,byz.sa. bo.Gries,Lach,Treg,Alf Word,Tisc,We/Ho,Weis Sod,UBS/☆

14.a.**Txt:** 01ℵ-corr2,02A 06D-corr1,byz. **Var:** p46,01ℵ-org 06D-org,044,81 1739-org,1881

15.a.**Txt:** 01ℵ-corr 06D-corr,018K,020L byz. **Var:** 01ℵ-org,02A 06D-org,025P,33,Lach Treg,Alf,Word,Tisc We/Ho,Weis,Sod UBS/☆

God gave them a glimmer of light, and they received it warmly and respectfully. They understood and believed that at some time in the future God was going to fulfill His spectacular promises. They had convictions; they "were persuaded" that God would in the future, as He always had done in the past, keep His promises—all of them. He was trustworthy. Thus they willingly and consciously acknowledged the truth of the old spiritual: "This world is not my home; I'm just a passin' through. My treasures are laid up somewhere beyond the blue."

11:14. The next three verses expatiate the theme of the patriarchal pilgrimage. Verse 14 begins with the particle *gar* ("for") which serves as an indication that the verse is designed to explain what was said in the previous verse. The people who admitted they were strangers and temporary residents on the earth revealed (*emphanizousin*) something about themselves. Their confession was an open declaration that they were searching for a fatherland (*patrida*). They felt rootless from an earthly viewpoint because they were not at home. Their roots were in heaven. That was their real home. That is where they would spend eternity.

11:15. The patriarchs of Israel never settled down in Canaan, but it was not because their hearts were in Mesopotamia where Abraham began his wanderings. If that had been the case—that they preferred Mesopotamia to Canaan—they had many opportunities to return. For instance, instead of going down into Egypt, they could easily and more profitably, from a purely human standpoint, have returned to the land of their forefathers and received a more hospitable welcome. To their credit it can be reported they never returned to Ur. They knew they had left in obedience to God's command. To return would be contrary to God's will.

11:16. This verse draws a contrast between what they might have done but did not and the implications of what they actually did do. The "now" (*nun*) is not used in a temporal sense but in a logical sense meaning "since" or "as it is." Instead of settling in Canaan or returning to Mesopotamia, what they actually longed to do (*oregontai*) was to inhabit a city-state (*polin*, verse 10) which had a lifestyle that had come from heaven itself. They wanted something better spiritually than what they had observed in either Ur or Canaan. There was an empty longing in their lives which could only be filled with spiritual reality. Because they possessed this spiritual insight and established their values by it, God was pleased with them. He identified himself with them. He was not afraid to call himself "the God of Abraham, the God of Isaac, and the God of

not having received the promises: . . . although they had not yet received in full, *Norlie* . . . without getting what was promised, *Beck* . . . the blessings promised, *Williams.*

but having seen them afar off: . . . that is, because they really saw them in the far-off future, *Williams* . . . but perceiving them ahead, *Concordant* . . . but they did see them from a distance, *Adams* . . . but having seen and saluted them from a Distance, *Wilson* . . . those things were far in the future, *SEB.*

and were persuaded of [them], and embraced [them]: . . . and hailed them, *Montgomery* . . . and welcomed them, *Williams.*

and confessed that they were strangers and pilgrims on the earth: They openly acknowledged, *TNT* . . . and so professed to be only foreigners and strangers here, *Williams* . . . that they were only strangers and exiles here, *Norlie* . . . who had no permanent home, *Beck.*

14. For they that say such things declare plainly: When people say such things as that, *TNT* . . . people who make such a profession as this show, *Williams.*

that they seek a country: . . . they are looking for, *TNT* . . . they seek a homeland, *Adams* . . . they are seeking a Fatherland, *Montgomery* . . . are in search of a country of their own, *Williams.*

15. And truly, if they had been mindful of: If their hearts had been in, *Beck* . . . been cherishing the memory of, *Williams.*

that [country] from whence they came out: . . . the country they left, *Beck.*

they might have had opportunity to have returned: . . . they might have gone back, *NLT* . . . they might have had a chance to go back, *Klingensmith.*

16. But now they desire a better [country], that is, an heavenly: . . . as it is they are reaching out for, *TNT* . . . The better country that they longed for was nothing less than heaven itself, *Norlie* . . . they were yearning for, *SEB* . . . longing for a better homeland, *Montgomery.*

1498.4 verb 3sing indic pres act	**2016.1** adj gen sing	**1346.1** conj	**3620.2** partic	**1855.2** verb 3sing indic pres mid
ἔστιν]	ἐπουρανίου·	διὸ	οὐκ	ἐπαισχύνεται
estin	*epouraniou*	*dio*	*ouk*	*epaischunetai*
is]	a heavenly;	wherefore	not	is ashamed of

840.8 prs-pron acc pl masc	**3450.5** art nom sing masc	**2296.1** noun nom sing masc	**2296.1** noun nom sing masc	**1926.10** verb inf pres mid
αὐτοὺς	ὁ	θεὸς,	θεὸς	ἐπικαλεῖσθαι
autous	*ho*	*theos*	*theos*	*epikaleisthai*
them		God.	God	to be called

840.1 prs-pron gen pl	**2069.4** verb 3sing indic aor act	**1056.1** conj	**840.2** prs-pron dat pl	**4032.4** noun acc sing fem	**3963.3** noun dat sing fem
αὐτῶν·	ἡτοίμασεν	γὰρ	αὐτοῖς	πόλιν.	**17.** Πίστει
autōn	*hētoimasen*	*gar*	*autois*	*polin*	*Pistei*
their;	he prepared	for	for them	a city.	By faith

4232.18 verb 3sing indic perf act	**11.1** name masc	**3450.6** art acc sing masc	**2439.1** name masc	**3847.12** verb nom sing masc part pres mid
προσενήνοχεν	Ἀβραὰμ	τὸν	Ἰσαὰκ	πειραζόμενος,
prosenēnochen	*Abraam*	*ton*	*Isaak*	*peirazomenos*
has offered up	Abraham		Isaac	being tried,

2504.1 conj	**3450.6** art acc sing masc	**3302.3** adj acc sing masc	**4232.19** verb 3sing indic imperf act	**3450.5** art nom sing masc
καὶ	τὸν	μονογενῆ	προσέφερεν	ὁ
kai	*ton*	*monogenē*	*prosepheren*	*ho*
and	the	only begotten	was offering up	the

3450.15 art acc pl fem	**1845.1** noun fem	**322.1** verb nom sing masc part aor mid	**4242.1** prep	**3614.6** rel-pron acc sing masc
τὰς	ἐπαγγελίας	ἀναδεξάμενος,	**18.** πρὸς	ὃν
tas	*epangelias*	*anadexamenos*	*pros*	*hon*
the	promises	having accepted,	as to	whom

2953.52 verb 3sing indic aor pass	**3617.1** conj	**1706.1** prep	**2439.1** name masc	**2535.52** verb 3sing indic fut pass	**4622.3** prs-pron dat 2sing
ἐλαλήθη,	Ὅτι	ἐν	Ἰσαὰκ	κληθήσεταί	σοι
elalēthē	*Hoti*	*en*	*Isaak*	*klēthēsetai*	*soi*
it was said,		In	Isaac	shall be called	your

4543.1 noun sing neu	**3023.15** verb nom sing masc part aor mid	**3617.1** conj	**2504.1** conj	**1523.2** prep gen
σπέρμα·	**19.** λογισάμενος	ὅτι	καὶ	ἐκ
sperma	*logisamenos*	*hoti*	*kai*	*ek*
seed;	having reckoned	that	even	from among

3361.2 adj gen pl	**1446.4** verb inf pres act	**1409.1** adj nom sing masc	**3450.5** art nom sing masc	**2296.1** noun nom sing masc	**3468.1** adv
νεκρῶν	ἐγείρειν	δυνατὸς	ὁ	θεός,	ὅθεν
nekrōn	*egeirein*	*dunatos*	*ho*	*theos*	*hothen*
dead	to raise	able		God,	whence

840.6 prs-pron acc sing masc	**2504.1** conj	**1706.1** prep	**3712.3** noun dat sing fem	**2837.4** verb 3sing indic aor mid	**3963.3** noun dat sing fem
αὐτὸν	καὶ	ἐν	παραβολῇ	ἐκομίσατο.	**20.** Πίστει
auton	*kai*	*en*	*parabolē*	*ekomisato*	*Pistei*
him	also	in	a sign	he received.	By faith

20.a.**Var:** 01ℵ,06D-org 33,Lach,Treg,Alf,Word We/Ho,Weis,Sod UBS/☆

2504.1 conj	**3875.1** prep	**3165.11** verb gen pl part pres act	**2108.7** verb 3sing indic aor act	**2439.1** name masc
[a☆+ καὶ]	περὶ	μελλόντων	εὐλόγησεν	Ἰσαὰκ
kai	*peri*	*mellontōn*	*eulogēsen*	*Isaak*
[and]	concerning	things coming	blessed	Isaac

Jacob" when He identified himself to Moses (Exodus 3:6). He was pleased because they had been correct in looking for the heavenly city He had "prepared for them."

11:17. In addition to their sojourning life-style there were two other important aspects of their faith: their endurance of trials and their obedience to the Word of God. The two themes are highlighted one against the other. In their pilgrim attitude, which grew out of their faith, they were confronted with hardships and tribulations, but their faith enabled them to keep their eyes on the future which God was preparing for them. With their eyes on that hope, they were able to keep their equilibrium in the midst of the shifting storms of life. God tested Abraham by asking him to sacrifice Isaac who was his *monogenē*, his uniquely born son of the promise, and by faith Abraham proceeded in obedience.

11:18. These words explain the word *monogenē* as it is used of Isaac. In his willingness to sacrifice Isaac, Abraham was letting go of the son of God's promise. Abraham had complained to God because he feared he would die childless and that his servant Eliezer would inherit all of his possessions according to the customs of that day (Genesis 15:2,3ff.). Having an heir was so important to Abraham that he had fathered a son by Sarah's handmaiden Hagar (at Sarah's instigation). Giving up Isaac was no easy thing. God was taking away what He had promised, that which Abraham cherished the most—God's promised son (Genesis 21:12). Abraham had waited and almost given up hope that the promise would be realized. God's demand was costly.

11:19. But Abraham's trust in the Lord was equal to the Lord's demand. The participle *logisamenos* indicates that Abraham thought carefully about his experiences with God and concluded that since He could make a barren Sarah give birth to a child, He also was able to resurrect Isaac after he had been sacrificed. The narrative in Genesis 22 testifies to Abraham's faith in this matter. He assured his servant that both he and Isaac would return, and he was confident that the Lord would furnish a sacrifice on the mountain (Genesis 22:5,8). Abraham believed God could raise Isaac from the dead because Abraham had already received Isaac figuratively from the deadness of Sarah's womb.

11:20. Reliance on God's fulfillment of all which He had promised was also characteristic of Isaac. He had observed the faith of his father Abraham and had seen the faithfulness of the Lord. So, even though he did not experience the complete fulfillment of the promise in his own lifetime, he blessed Jacob and Esau concerning future blessings.

wherefore God is not ashamed to be called their God: This is why, *Williams* . . . Consequently, *Wade* . . . it is no shame to God to be named their God, *BB* . . . was proud to be called their God, *Noli.*

for he hath prepared for them a city: . . . has prepared for them a home in heaven, *Noli* . . . he has made ready a town for them, *BB.*

17. By faith Abraham, when he was tried, offered up Isaac: Through his faith, *Wade* . . . when he was put to the test, *Williams.*

and he that had received the promises: . . . he who had welcomed, *Wade.*

offered up his only begotten [son]: . . . he was ready to offer up, *TNT* . . . was prepared to offer, *Wade* . . . was starting to offer as a sacrifice, *Williams* . . . the only son of his body, *BB.*

18. Of whom it was said: . . . and though he had been told, *TNT.*

That in Isaac shall thy seed be called: Your descendants will come through Isaac, *Adams, SEB* . . . that your posterity will be traced, *Montgomery* . . . Your posterity will arise through, *Noli* . . . shall there be traced a posterity that shall bear thy name, *Wade.*

19. Accounting that God [was] able to raise [him] up, even from the dead: For he considered the fact that God was able to raise people, *Williams* . . . was able even to raise the dead to life, *TNT.*

from whence also he received him in a figure: And in a way he did get him back from the dead, *Beck* . . . Indeed, figuratively, he received him back from death, *Noli* . . . and in a sense he really did receive his son back from death, *TNT* . . . and so from the dead, in a figure, *Williams* . . . in a figurative sense it was from the dead that he recovered him, *Wade.*

20. By faith Isaac blessed Jacob and Esau: Through his faith, *Wade* . . . put his blessings, *Williams.*

concerning things to come: . . . gave news of things to come, *BB* . . . even in connection with things still in the future, *Wade* . . . for the future, *Williams.*

3450.6 art acc sing masc	**2361.1** name masc	**2504.1** conj	**3450.6** art acc sing masc	**2247.1** name masc	**3963.3** noun dat sing fem
τὸν	Ἰακὼβ	καὶ	τὸν	Ἠσαῦ.	**21.** Πίστει
ton	*Iakōb*	*kai*	*ton*	*Esau*	*Pistei*
	Jacob	and		Esau.	By faith

2361.1 name masc	**594.6** verb nom sing masc part pres act	**1524.1** adj sing	**3450.1** art gen pl	**5048.7** noun gen pl masc
Ἰακὼβ	ἀποθνῄσκων	ἕκαστον	τῶν	υἱῶν
Iakōb	*apothnēskōn*	*hekaston*	*tōn*	*huiōn*
Jacob	dying	each	of the	sons

2473.1 name masc	**2108.7** verb 3sing indic aor act	**2504.1** conj	**4210.9** verb 3sing indic aor act	**1894.3** prep	**3450.16** art sing neu
Ἰωσὴφ	εὐλόγησεν	καὶ	προσεκύνησεν	ἐπὶ	τὸ
Iōsēph	*eulogēsen*	*kai*	*prosekunēsen*	*epi*	*to*
of Joseph	blessed	and	worshiped	on	the

204.2 noun sing neu	**3450.10** art gen sing fem	**4321.2** noun gen sing fem	**840.3** prs-pron gen sing	**3963.3** noun dat sing fem	**2473.1** name masc
ἄκρον	τῆς	ῥάβδου	αὐτοῦ.	**22.** Πίστει	Ἰωσὴφ
akron	*tēs*	*rhabdou*	*autou*	*Pistei*	*Iōsēph*
top	of the	staff	his.	By faith	Joseph,

4901.3 verb nom sing masc part pres act	**3875.1** prep	**3450.10** art gen sing fem	**1825.1** noun gen sing fem	**3450.1** art gen pl	**5048.7** noun gen pl masc
τελευτῶν	περὶ	τῆς	ἐξόδου	τῶν	υἱῶν
teleutōn	*peri*	*tēs*	*exodou*	*tōn*	*huiōn*
dying,	concerning	the	exodus	of the	sons

2447.1 name masc	**3285.8** verb 3sing indic aor act	**2504.1** conj	**3875.1** prep	**3450.1** art gen pl	**3609.2** noun gen pl neu
Ἰσραὴλ	ἐμνημόνευσεν,	καὶ	περὶ	τῶν	ὀστέων
Israēl	*emnēmoneusen*	*kai*	*peri*	*tōn*	*osteōn*
of Israel	made mention,	and	concerning	the	bones

840.3 prs-pron gen sing	**1765.3** verb 3sing indic aor mid	**3963.3** noun dat sing fem	**3337.1** name nom masc	**3338.1** name nom masc
αὐτοῦ	ἐνετείλατο.	**23.** Πίστει	ʻ Μωσῆς	[☆ Μωϋσῆς]
autou	*eneteilato*	*Pistei*	*Mōsēs*	*Mōusēs*
his	gave command.	By faith	Moses,	[idem]

1074.17 verb nom sing masc part aor pass	**2900.5** verb 3sing indic aor pass	**4991.1** adj sing neu	**5097.3** prep	**3450.1** art gen pl	**3824.7** noun gen pl masc
γεννηθεὶς	ἐκρύβη	τρίμηνον	ὑπὸ	τῶν	πατέρων
gennētheis	*ekrubē*	*trimēnon*	*hupo*	*tōn*	*paterōn*
having been born,	was hid	three months	by	the	parents

840.3 prs-pron gen sing	**1354.1** conj	**1481.1** verb indic aor act	**785.2** adj sing neu	**3450.16** art sing neu	**3676.1** noun sing masc
αὐτοῦ	διότι	εἶδον	ἀστεῖον	τὸ	παιδίον·
autou	*dioti*	*eidon*	*asteion*	*to*	*paidion*
his	because	they saw	beautiful	the	little child;

2504.1 conj	**3620.2** partic	**5236.13** verb 3pl indic aor pass	**3450.16** art sing neu	**1291.1** noun sing neu	**3450.2** art gen sing
καὶ	οὐκ	ἐφοβήθησαν	τὸ	διάταγμα	τοῦ
kai	*ouk*	*ephobēthēsan*	*to*	*diatagma*	*tou*
and	not	did fear	the	injunction	of the

928.2 noun gen sing masc	**3963.3** noun dat sing fem	**3337.1** name nom masc	**3338.1** name nom masc	**3144.2** adj nom sing masc
βασιλέως.	**24.** Πίστει	ʻ Μωσῆς	[☆ Μωϋσῆς]	μέγας
basileōs	*Pistei*	*Mōsēs*	*Mōusēs*	*megas*
king.	By faith	Moses,	[idem]	great

11:21. Jacob, who had valued the blessing associated with the promise so much that he had schemed and cheated Esau out of his firstborn rights, also died without gaining all of God's promised blessings. Nevertheless, before he died, he passed on the blessing by skipping over his eldest son Reuben and giving the rights of the firstborn to Joseph's younger son Ephraim instead of the elder son, Manasseh (Genesis 48:1,5,16,20). This follows the Septuagint account instead of the Hebrew Masoretic text's account of Genesis 48.

There was a prophetic element in Jacob's blessing upon the sons of Joseph. Even though Manasseh was older than Ephraim, Jacob placed his right hand (signifying the greater blessing) upon the head of Ephraim. It was fulfilled in their later history.

11:22. Likewise, Joseph, when he passed away, exhibited the same faith in God's promises that his fathers had displayed. He was so certain the Lord would give Canaan to his descendants for their possession that he instructed them to carry his bones from Egypt so they could be buried in Canaan. By faith he looked forward to the momentous events of the Exodus by which the Lord would miraculously deliver his progeny from Egypt and mold them into the nation of Israel.

11:23. At this point the account moves into the third and final section of chapter 11 from the patriarchal era to the national era. In doing so the emphasis moves from the faith of those who lived with an unfulfilled promise to the mighty deeds of faith accomplished by the heroes of Israel.

Verse 23 begins with the parents of Moses. Their faith led them to fearlessly disobey Pharaoh's edict to kill all male Hebrew infants. Moses' parents were prompted to risk the penalty for breaking the law because of the striking appearance of the baby. The word *asteion* found here also appears in the Septuagint account (Exodus 2:2) and in Stephen's narrative (Acts 7:20).

11:24. The insight of Moses' parents was vindicated by Moses when he reached adulthood. Moses was raised with all the material and cultural advantages available to a member of the royal family of Egypt. He lived at a time when he himself might have become king (if the Pharaoh's daughter mentioned was Hatshepsut who ruled as Pharaoh and died childless). However, Moses possessed a true understanding of God's promise to his forefathers which enabled him by faith to deny the daughter's claims that he was her son. He had a sense of values which allowed him to reject the temptations of wealth, prestige, influence, and power offered to him by Egypt.

21. By faith Jacob, when he was a dying: . . . when his end was nigh, *Montgomery* . . . when about to die, *Williams.*

blessed both the sons of Joseph: . . . put his blessing on each of Joseph's sons, *Williams.*

and worshipped, [leaning] upon the top of his staff: . . . he bowed in worship, *TNT* . . . leaning on the top of his walking cane, *SEB.*

22. By faith Joseph, when he died: . . . at the end of his life, *Adams* . . . at his decease, *Concordant* . . . as he was dying, *Norlie* . . . when his end was near, *Beck, TNT* . . . at the closing of his life, *Williams.*

made mention of the departing of the children of Israel: . . . referred to, *TNT* . . . remembered the exodus of the sons of Israel, *Wuest* . . . made mention of the future migration of the Israelites, *Williams.*

and gave commandment concerning his bones: . . . gave instructions, *Adams* . . . and gives directions, *Concordant* . . . and said what was to be done with his bones, *TNT* . . . as to the removal of his bones, *Norlie* . . . what to do with his body, *Williams.*

23. By faith Moses, when he was born: . . . at his birth, *Williams* . . . after his birth, *TNT.*

was hid three months of his parents: . . . the parents of Moses hid him for three months, *TNT.*

because they saw [he was] a proper child: . . . was a delightful child, *Adams* . . . he was a handsome child, *Norlie* . . . they saw he was a fine baby, *Beck* . . . he was a beautiful child, *Williams* . . . he was a very lovely child, *TNT.*

and they were not afraid of the king's commandment: . . . they refused to respect the King's order, *TCNT* . . . were not afraid to disobey, *SEB* . . . did not fear the edict of the King, *Wilson* . . . the mandate of, *Concordant* . . . the king's decree, *Montgomery.*

24. By faith Moses, when he was come to years: . . . when he had grown up, *Williams.*

refused to be called the son of Pharaoh's daughter: . . . refused to be known as, *Williams* . . . to decline the title of, *TCNT.*

1090.53 verb nom sing masc part aor mid	714.7 verb 3sing indic aor mid	2978.38 verb inf pres mid	5048.1 noun nom sing masc	2341.2 noun gen sing fem
γενόμενος	ἠρνήσατο	λέγεσθαι	υἱὸς	θυγατρὸς
genomenos	*ērnēsato*	*legesthai*	*huios*	*thugatros*
having become,	refused	to be called	son	of daughter

5166.1 name masc	3095.1 adv comp	141.2 verb nom sing masc part aor mid	4629.1 verb inf pres mid
Φαραώ,	25. μᾶλλον	ἑλόμενος	συγκακουχεῖσθαι
Pharaō	*mallon*	*helomenos*	*sunkakoucheisthai*
Pharaoh's;	rather	having chosen	to suffer affliction with

3450.3 art dat sing	2967.3 noun dat sing masc	3450.2 art gen sing	2296.2 noun gen sing masc	2211.1 conj	4199.3 adj acc sing fem
τῷ	λαῷ	τοῦ	θεοῦ,	ἢ	πρόσκαιρον
tō	*laō*	*tou*	*theou*	*ē*	*proskairon*
the	people		of God,	than	temporary

2174.29 verb inf pres act	264.1 noun fem	613.1 noun acc sing fem	3157.1 adj comp	4009.3 noun acc sing masc
ἔχειν	ἁμαρτίας	ἀπόλαυσιν·	26. μείζονα	πλοῦτον
echein	*hamartias*	*apolausin*	*meizona*	*plouton*
to have	of sin	enjoyment;	greater	riches

26.a.**Txt:** Steph
Var: 01ℵ,06D,018K 020L,025P,byz.Gries Treg,Alf,Word,Tisc We/Ho,Weis,Sod UBS/⋆

2216.15 verb nom sing masc part aor mid	3450.1 art gen pl	1706.1 prep	125.3 name dat fem	125.2 name gen fem
ἡγησάμενος	τῶν	‘ ἐν	Αἰγύπτῳ	[a⋆ Αἰγύπτου]
hēgēsamenos	*tōn*	*en*	*Aiguptō*	*Aiguptou*
having esteemed	than the	in	Egypt	[idem]

2321.6 noun gen pl masc	3450.6 art acc sing masc	3543.1 noun acc sing masc	3450.2 art gen sing	5382.2 name gen masc
θησαυρῶν	τὸν	ὀνειδισμὸν	τοῦ	Χριστοῦ,
thēsaurōn	*ton*	*oneidismon*	*tou*	*Christou*
treasures	the	reproach	of the	Christ;

573.1 verb 3sing indic imperf act	1056.1 conj	1519.1 prep	3450.12 art acc sing fem	3269.1 noun acc sing fem
ἀπέβλεπεν	γὰρ	εἰς	τὴν	μισθαποδοσίαν.
apeblepen	*gar*	*eis*	*tēn*	*misthapodosian*
he was looking away	for	to	the	recompense.

3963.3 noun dat sing fem	2611.3 verb 3sing indic aor act	125.4 name acc fem	3231.1 partic	5236.19 verb nom sing masc part aor pass
27. Πίστει	κατέλιπεν	Αἴγυπτον,	μὴ	φοβηθεὶς
Pistei	*katelipen*	*Aigupton*	*mē*	*phobētheis*
By faith	he left	Egypt,	not	having feared

3450.6 art acc sing masc	2349.3 noun acc sing masc	3450.2 art gen sing	928.2 noun gen sing masc	3450.6 art acc sing masc	1056.1 conj
τὸν	θυμὸν	τοῦ	βασιλέως·	τὸν	γὰρ
ton	*thumon*	*tou*	*basileōs*	*ton*	*gar*
the	indignation	of the	king;	the	for

513.3 adj acc sing masc	5453.1 conj	3571.6 verb nom sing masc part pres act	2565.1 verb 3sing indic aor act	3963.3 noun dat sing fem
ἀόρατον	ὡς	ὁρῶν	ἐκαρτέρησεν.	28. Πίστει
aoraton	*hōs*	*horōn*	*ekarterēsen*	*Pistei*
invisible	as	seeing	he persevered.	By faith

4020.43 verb 3sing indic perf act	3450.16 art sing neu	3818.1 noun sing neu	2504.1 conj	3450.12 art acc sing fem	4236.1 noun acc sing fem
πεποίηκεν	τὸ	πάσχα	καὶ	τὴν	πρόσχυσιν
pepoiēken	*to*	*pascha*	*kai*	*tēn*	*proschusin*
he has kept	the	passover	and	the	pouring

11:25. Moses could have accepted a role in the court of the king of Egypt as the Pharaoh's grandson. He could have disassociated himself completely from his Hebrew kinsmen, but he made a conscious choice not to do so. He observed the affliction and oppression of his own people and decided to identify himself with them. He did this because he knew they were "the people of God." He had heard the promises of God, and he had believed them to be true. It was out of this faith that he reacted when he saw an Egyptian abusing one of his kinsmen (Exodus 2:11,12). It was his faith that God would keep His promise to Abraham and his descendants that led Moses to an understanding of the temporary nature of the things he enjoyed in Egypt. His hope for the fulfillment of all of God's promise enabled him to endure the sufferings he experienced when he identified himself with the Hebrew people.

25. Choosing rather to suffer affliction with the people of God: . . . he preferred to suffer hardships, *Williams* . . . and preferred being mistreated, *Beck* . . . preferring rather to be maltreated, *Concordant* . . . having chosen for himself, *Wuest* . . . to share ill-treatment, *Montgomery* . . . to be mistreated along with God's people, *Adams.*

than to enjoy the pleasures of sin for a season: . . . than to be having sin's enjoyments temporarily, *Wuest* . . . instead of having fun doing sinful things for awhile, *NLT* . . . rather than to have temporary enjoyment of sinful pleasures, *Norlie.*

11:26. Moses was not fooled by the material culture of Egypt. He saw through and beyond it. This was no small accomplishment, as anyone who has seen the King Tut exhibit in the Cairo Museum or visited the Egyptology section of the Louvre can testify. The world is still dazzled by the splendor and wealth accumulated by the royal families of Egypt. Moses was not. He took it all in and concluded that there was greater wealth available in the abuse which he would suffer for the sake of Christ. Moses knew of the promise made to Adam and Eve (Genesis 3:15) and looked for the Christ, i.e., the Anointed One, the promised Deliverer. In the light of the eternal reward promised by the Lord, Moses was able to renounce the promises of Egyptian glory and to endure the reproach and abuse associated with the Hebrews.

26. Esteeming the reproach of Christ: He considered, *Adams* . . . and thought the reproach endured for the Christ, *Williams* . . . he thought that the stigma which attaches to the Christ, *TCNT.*

greater riches than the treasures in Egypt: . . . was of greater value, *TCNT* . . . was greater wealth than all the treasures, *Williams.*

for he had respect unto the recompense of the reward: He examined the pay, *Klingensmith* . . . he was looking ahead to the reward, *Adams, SEB, Beck* . . . for he fixed his eyes on the reward, *Montgomery* . . . for he was looking ahead to the promised reward, *Norlie* . . . kept his eye upon the reward, *Williams.*

11:27. The flight of Moses from Egypt after he killed the Egyptian overseer and was seen by one of his Hebrew kinsmen is not the subject of this verse. It refers rather to the time of the Exodus when he led the Children of Israel out of Egypt in the face of the Pharaoh's protestations. Exodus 2:14 is clear. When Moses left Egypt the first time, he was afraid, but when he led the entire nation at the Exodus, he was bold and unafraid: at that time he was clearly operating by faith. Earlier, he had identified with his people out of faith, but his flight was motivated by self-interest, not faith. His fearless behavior at the time of the Exodus was the result of his newly acquired vision of faith. Having encountered the Lord in the burning bush, he was then able to endure Pharaoh's wrath because he knew the living God who is genuine but unseen.

27. By faith he forsook Egypt: . . . he abandoned Egypt, *Wuest* . . . he left Eygpt, *Williams.*

not fearing the wrath of the king: . . . because he was not afraid of the king's anger, *Williams.*

for he endured, as seeing him who is invisible: . . . for he persevered, *Williams* . . . he "saw" the One Who is unseen, *Adams* . . . as though he could see Him, the unseen King, *Norlie* . . . for he understood the invisible as seen, *Klingensmith.*

11:28. Moses' newly reinforced faith erased his fear of the king. He delivered the Lord's ultimatums and stood up to the king. He rallied the Hebrews, and instead of fearfully sneaking off, he boldly

28. Through faith he kept the passover: . . . he celebrated, *Beck* . . . he instituted the Passover, *Williams.*

and the sprinkling of blood: . . . and put the blood on the doorposts, *Beck* . . . and the pouring of blood upon, *Williams.*

Hebrews 11:29

3450.2 art gen sing	**129.2** noun gen sing neu	**2419.1** conj	**3231.1** partic	**3450.5** art nom sing masc	**3508.1** verb nom sing masc part pres act
τοῦ	αἵματος,	ἵνα	μὴ	ὁ	ʻ ὀλοθρεύων
tou	*haimatos*	*hina*	*mē*	*ho*	*olothreuōn*
of the	blood,	so that	not	the	destroying

28.a.**Txt:** 01ℵ,018K 020L,025P,byz.Tisc We/Ho,Weis,Sod **Var:** 02A,06D,Lach,Alf UBS/⋆

3508.2 verb nom sing masc part pres act	**3450.17** art pl neu	**4274.4** adj pl neu	**2322.2** verb 3sing subj aor act	**840.1** prs-pron gen pl
[a ὀλεθρεύων]	τὰ	πρωτότοκα	θίγῃ	αὐτῶν.
olethreuōn	*ta*	*prōtotoka*	*thigē*	*autōn*
[idem]	the	firstborn	might touch	them.

3963.3 noun dat sing fem	**1218.1** verb 3pl indic aor act	**3450.12** art acc sing fem	**2047.2** name acc fem
29. Πίστει	διέβησαν	τὴν	ἐρυθρὰν θάλασσαν
Pistei	*diebēsan*	*tēn*	*eruthran thalassan*
By faith	they passed through	the	Red Sea

29.a.**Var:** 01ℵ,02A 06D-org,33,bo.Lach Treg,Alf,Word,Tisc We/Ho,Weis,Sod UBS/⋆

5453.1 conj	**1217.2** prep	**3446.3** adj gen sing fem	**1087.2** noun gen sing fem	**3614.10** rel-pron gen sing fem	**3846.1** noun acc sing fem
ὡς	διὰ	ξηρᾶς	[a☆ γῆς,]	ἧς	πεῖραν
hōs	*dia*	*xēras*	*gēs*	*hēs*	*peiran*
as	through	dry;	[land]	of which	trial

2956.27 verb nom pl masc part aor act	**3450.7** art nom pl masc	**124.3** name-adj nom pl masc	**2636.5** verb 3pl indic aor pass	**3963.3** noun dat sing fem
λαβόντες	οἱ	Αἰγύπτιοι	κατεπόθησαν.	**30.** Πίστει
labontes	*hoi*	*Aiguptioi*	*katepothēsan*	*Pistei*
having taken	the	Egyptians	were swallowed up.	By faith

30.a.**Txt:** 06D-corr,018K 020L,byz. **Var:** 01ℵ,02A,06D-org 025P,33,Lach,Treg,Alf Tisc,We/Ho,Weis,Sod UBS/⋆

3450.17 art pl neu	**4886.3** noun pl neu	**2386.1** name fem	**3959.5** verb 3sing indic aor act	**3959.6** verb 3pl indic aor act
τὰ	τείχη	Ἱεριχὼ	ʻ ἔπεσεν,	[a☆ ἔπεσαν]
ta	*teichē*	*Hierichō*	*epesen*	*epesan*
the	walls	of Jericho	fell,	[idem]

2917.4 verb pl neu part aor pass	**1894.3** prep	**2017.1** num card	**2232.1** noun fem	**3963.3** noun dat sing fem
κυκλωθέντα	ἐπὶ	ἑπτὰ	ἡμέρας.	**31.** Πίστει
kuklōthenta	*epi*	*hepta*	*hēmeras*	*Pistei*
having been encircled	for	seven	days.	By faith

4317.1 name fem	**3450.9** art nom sing fem	**4063.1** noun nom sing fem	**3620.3** partic	**4732.1** verb 3sing indic aor mid	**3450.4** art dat pl
Ῥαὰβ	ἡ	πόρνη	οὐ	συναπώλετο	τοῖς
Rhaab	*hē*	*pornē*	*ou*	*sunapōleto*	*tois*
Rahab	the	harlot	not	did perish with	the

540.9 verb dat pl masc part aor act	**1203.15** verb nom sing fem part aor mid	**3450.8** art acc pl masc	**2655.1** noun acc pl masc	**3196.2** prep
ἀπειθήσασιν,	δεξαμένη	τοὺς	κατασκόπους	μετ'
apeithēsasin	*dexamenē*	*tous*	*kataskopous*	*met'*
having disobeyed,	having received	the	spies	with

1503.2 noun gen sing fem	**2504.1** conj	**4949.9** intr-pron sing neu	**2068.1** adv	**2978.1** verb 1sing pres act	**1936.1** verb 3sing indic fut act
εἰρήνης.	**32.** Καὶ	τί	ἔτι	λέγω;	ἐπιλείψει
eirēnēs	*Kai*	*ti*	*eti*	*legō*	*epileipsei*
peace.	And	what	yet	do I say?	Will fail

32.a.**Txt:** p13,p46 06D-corr2,08E,016I 018K,020L,025P,byz. Sod **Var:** 01ℵ,02A,06D-org 33,We/Ho

1056.1 conj	**1466.6** prs-pron acc 1sing	**1466.6** prs-pron acc 1sing	**1056.1** conj	**1328.2** verb acc sing masc part pres mid	**3450.5** art nom sing masc
ʻ γὰρ	με	[a☆ με	γὰρ]	διηγούμενον	ὁ
gar	*me*	*me*	*gar*	*diēgoumenon*	*ho*
for	me	[me	for]	relating	the

led Israel to freedom. By faith, he obeyed God and convinced the people to obey God in the observance of the Passover sacrifice and meal. As a result they were delivered while the Egyptians were thrown into disarray by the slaughter of their firstborn children.

lest he that destroyed the firstborn should touch them: . . . the Angel who was destroying, *Wade* . . . so that the destroyer of the first-born might not touch them, *Williams* . . . to protect the firstborn of Israel from the Angel of destruction, *Noli* . . . would not touch the first-born of Israel, *TNT.*

11:29. Furthermore, it was by the obedience of faith that Moses led the Hebrew people to their triumph over the wily Pharaoh. Seemingly trapped between the army of Pharaoh and the waters of the Red Sea, they were again the ones who benefited from Moses' implicit trust in the Lord. In the face of almost certain disaster, they were delivered by the Lord. The wind blew, the sea parted, and under cover of the divine cloud they passed through the waters on dry ground while the pursuing army drowned. The deliverance of the Hebrew people was accomplished through the unwavering faith of Moses in the face of the powerful Egyptian army and in spite of the cringing fear of the Israelites (Exodus 14:10-12).

29. By faith they passed through the Red sea as by dry [land]: Through their faith...as over dry ground, *Wade* . . . they crossed the Red Sea, *TNT* . . . as though it were, *Williams.*

which the Egyptians assaying to do were drowned: The Egyptians tried it, too, *Beck* . . . who tried to do the same, *Norlie* . . . in attempting it, *Williams* . . . they were swallowed up, *Montgomery* . . . they were engulfed, *Wade.*

11:30. The same kind of deliverance continued to follow the nation of Israel whenever they trusted the Lord. Under the leadership of Joshua, they experienced the remarkable victory over Jericho in their campaign to vanquish the Canaanites and take possession of the land promised to Abraham's descendants. By the apparently foolish tactic of marching around the fortress walls of the city for 7 days in obedience to the Lord's commandment, then shouting in faith, they conquered the well-fortified city.

30. By faith the walls of Jericho fell down: Through faith on the part of Israel, *Wade* . . . collapsed, *Norlie.*

after they were compassed about seven days: . . . after the Israelites had marched round them for seven days, *TNT* . . . they had been encircled, *Adams, Montgomery* . . . being surrounded on, *Concordant* . . . after it had been surrounded, *SEB* . . . after a seige of seven days, *Noli* . . . each of seven days, *Williams* . . . for six days, *Wade.*

11:31. At the same time Israel was trusting God to fight for them at Jericho, within the walls of that same city lived Rahab the prostitute. She had heard of the Lord's exploits on behalf of His people. As a result, she believed that the Lord was the true God. When confronted by Joshua's spies, she cooperated with them and asked for deliverance. She is a prime example of saving faith (James 2:25) and an ancestress of both King David and the Saviour, our Lord Jesus Christ.

31. By faith the harlot Rahab: . . . the prostitute, *Adams.*

perished not with them that believed not: . . . escaped, *Noli* . . . did not die, *Klingensmith* . . . was preserved from perishing along with those who had been defiant, *Wade* . . . didn't perish with her disobedient people, *Beck* . . . was not destroyed with the unbelievers, *TNT* . . . with those who disobeyed God, *Williams.*

when she had received the spies with peace: . . . she had welcomed the scouts as friends, *Williams* . . . she had given the spies a friendly welcome, *TNT* . . . with friendliness, *TCNT* . . . peaceably, *Wade.*

11:32. The inspired writer has already made three points concerning the results of faith, and "time" would not allow more expanded analyses of faith in the lives of individuals, so he said, "And what shall I more say?" But verses 33-40 do say more, without identifying individuals, indicating that, even after entrance into the land of Canaan, faith was necessary during the eras of the judges, kings, and prophets. It is noteworthy that Gideon, Barak, Samson,

32. And what shall I more say?: What further example do I need? *Norlie* . . . why should I continue to mention more? *Williams* . . . What more need I say? *TNT.*

32.b.**Txt:** 06D-corr,018K 020L,025P,byz.
Var: 01א,02A,33,bo. Lach,Treg,Word,Tisc We/Ho,Weis,Sod UBS/☆

32.c.**Txt:** 06D,018K 020L,025P,byz.
Var: 01א,02A,33,bo. Lach,Treg,Tisc,We/Ho Weis,Sod,UBS/☆

5385.1 noun nom sing masc	3875.1 prep	1059.1 name masc	908.1 name masc	4885.1 conj	2504.1 conj	4403.1 name masc
χρόνος	περὶ	Γεδεών,	Βαράκ	⸂b τε	καὶ ⸃	Σαμψών
chronos	*peri*	*Gedeōn*	*Barak*	*te*	*kai*	*Sampsōn*
time	of	Gideon,	Barak	also	and	Samson

2504.1 conj	2398.1 name masc	1132.1 name masc	4885.1 conj	2504.1 conj	4402.1 name masc	2504.1 conj	3450.1 art gen pl
⸂c καὶ ⸃	Ἰεφθάε,	Δαβίδ	τε	καὶ	Σαμουὴλ	καὶ	τῶν
kai	*Iephthae*	*Dabid*	*te*	*kai*	*Samouēl*	*kai*	*tōn*
and	Jephthah,	David	also	and	Samuel	and	of the

4254.5 noun gen pl masc	3614.7 rel-pron nom pl masc	1217.2 prep	3963.2 noun gen sing fem	2581.1 verb 3pl indic aor mid
προφητῶν·	33. οἳ	διὰ	πίστεως	κατηγωνίσαντο
prophētōn	*hoi*	*dia*	*pisteōs*	*katēgōnisanto*
prophets:	who	by	faith	overcame

33.a.**Txt:** 01א-corr,02A 06D-corr,018K,020L 025P,byz.Weis,Sod
Var: 01א-org,06D-org Treg,Tisc,We/Ho UBS/☆

926.1 noun fem	2021.15 verb 3pl indic aor mid	2021.20 verb 3pl indic aor mid	1336.4 noun acc sing fem
βασιλείας,	⸂ εἰργάσαντο	[a ἠργάσαντο]	δικαιοσύνην,
basileias	*eirgasanto*	*ērgasanto*	*dikaiosunēn*
kingdoms,	wrought	[idem]	righteousness,

1997.2 verb 3pl indic aor act	1845.6 noun gen pl fem	5256.1 verb 3pl indic aor act	4601.5 noun pl neu	2997.4 noun gen pl masc
ἐπέτυχον	ἐπαγγελιῶν,	ἔφραξαν	στόματα	λεόντων,
epetuchon	*epangeliōn*	*ephraxan*	*stomata*	*leontōn*
obtained	promises,	stopped	mouths	of lions,

4426.2 verb 3pl indic aor act	1405.4 noun acc sing fem	4300.2 noun gen sing neu	5180.6 verb 3pl indic aor act	4601.5 noun pl neu	3134.2 noun gen sing fem
34. ἔσβεσαν	δύναμιν	πυρός,	ἔφυγον	στόματα	⸂ μαχαίρας,
esbesan	*dunamin*	*puros*	*ephugon*	*stomata*	*machairas*
quenched	power	of fire,	escaped	mouths	of sword,

34.a.**Txt:** 01א-corr 06D-corr,018K,020L 025P,etc.byz.Sod
Var: 01א-org,02A 06D-org,Lach,Treg,Tisc We/Ho,Weis,UBS/☆

3134.7 noun gen sing fem	1727.7 verb 3pl indic aor pass	1406.2 verb 3pl indic aor pass
[☆ μαχαίρης,]	⸂ ἐνεδυναμώθησαν	[a☆ ἐδυναμώθησαν]
machairēs	*enedunamōthēsan*	*edunamōthēsan*
[idem]	acquired strength	[were empowered]

570.3 prep	763.1 noun fem	1090.37 verb 3pl indic aor pass	2451.5 adj nom pl masc	1706.1 prep	4031.2 noun dat sing masc
ἀπὸ	ἀσθενείας,	ἐγενήθησαν	ἰσχυροὶ	ἐν	πολέμῳ,
apo	*astheneias*	*egenēthēsan*	*ischuroi*	*en*	*polemō*
out of	weakness,	became	mighty	in	war,

3787.3 noun acc pl fem	2800.4 verb 3pl indic aor act	243.3 adj gen pl masc	2956.12 verb indic aor act
παρεμβολὰς	ἔκλιναν	ἀλλοτρίων·	35. ἔλαβον
parembolas	*eklinan*	*allotriōn*	*elabon*
armies	made to give way	of strangers.	Received

1129.6 noun nom pl fem	1523.1 prep gen	384.2 noun gen sing fem	3450.8 art acc pl masc	3361.7 adj acc pl masc	840.1 prs-pron gen pl
γυναῖκες	ἐξ	ἀναστάσεως	τοὺς	νεκροὺς	αὐτῶν·
gunaikes	*ex*	*anastaseōs*	*tous*	*nekrous*	*autōn*
women	by	resurrection	the	dead	their;

241.6 adj nom pl masc	1156.2 conj	5019.1 verb 3pl indic aor pass	3620.3 partic	4185.9 verb nom pl masc part aor mid
ἄλλοι	δὲ	ἐτυμπανίσθησαν,	οὐ	προσδεξάμενοι
alloi	*de*	*etumpanisthēsan*	*ou*	*prosdexamenoi*
others	and	were tortured,	not	having accepted

Jephthah, and David all had glaring weaknesses recorded in Scripture. But with all their faults, their faith was eventually displayed in doing what God called them to do. By faith they all accomplished great things for God.

11:33. Verses 33-38 provided a summary of the great deeds of faith accomplished during the time of the judges, kings, and prophets. The descriptions offered are applicable to many Old Testament heroes, not only those named in the previous verse. Most of the judges and many of the kings of Judah and Israel would be among those who "subdued kingdoms." David would of course head the list because he forged a mighty kingdom. He and Solomon ruled over the greatest near-eastern kingdom in their time. Gideon routed the Midianites. Barak (though Deborah was the judge at that time) overthrew the Syrians. Samson harassed the Philistines, and Jephthah smote the Ammonites.

All of these victories came about through faith in the Lord. In setting up the rule of Jehovah in Israel and Judah, those who trusted the Lord performed righteous deeds by setting up equity and justice as standards in governing. Like Abraham, David was singled out by God to be the recipient of special promises: his family, throne, and kingdom were to be established forever (2 Samuel 7:14ff.). Daniel was cast into a den of lions and emerged unharmed because he trusted God to deliver him (Daniel 6). Both David (1 Samuel 17:34f.) and Samson (Judges 14:5,6) were also given power over lions.

11:34. Daniel 3 gives the account of Shadrach, Meshach, and Abednego being cast fully clothed into the flames of Nebuchadnezzar's furnace and emerging unscathed. Countless numbers of believing Jews were delivered from death in battle when they faced overwhelming odds. As a boy David slew the giant Goliath. The blind Samson grew his hair, regained his strength, and pulled the temple of Dagon down on himself and his Philistine tormentors. A timid Gideon and 300 Israelites routed the Midianite armies. By God's power human weakness prevailed over strength. Jonathan single-handedly defeated a Philistine garrison. David surrounded himself with mighty men who fought valiantly for him in the wars which built the kingdom of Judah. The fearful host of Assyria was annihilated in the days of Hezekiah through the faith of the king and angelic intervention (2 Kings 19:35).

11:35. Through the faith of the prophets Elijah and Elisha, the widow's son was raised from the dead (1 Kings 17:17ff.) and the Shunammite's son was resurrected (2 Kings 4:18ff.).

In the period between the Old and New Testaments, during the Jewish revolt against the Seleucid king, Antiochus IV, seven brothers were captured and tortured to death because they refused to be released on condition of violating the Mosaic dietary and sac-

for the time would fail me to tell of Gedeon, and [of] Barak, and [of] Samson, and [of] Jephthae: Time does not allow me, *SEB* . . . There will not be time enough, *Beck* . . . to discourse concerning, *Wilson.*

[of] David also, and Samuel, and [of] the prophets: . . . and of the early preachers, *NLT.*

33. Who through faith subdued kingdoms, wrought righteousness: . . . they won wars, *NLT* . . . conquered kingdoms, brought about justice, *Adams* . . . administered justice, *Williams* . . . established justice, *Norlie* . . . They did what was right, *SEB* . . . did righteous works, *Beck.*

obtained promises, stopped the mouths of lions: . . . received new promises, shut the mouths, *Williams.*

34. Quenched the violence of fire: . . . stopped the force of fire, *Williams* . . . quenched the power of fire, *Montgomery* . . . put out raging fires, *Beck.*

escaped the edge of the sword: . . . from dying by the sword, *Williams.*

out of weakness were made strong: . . . were invigorated from infirmity, *Concordant* . . . found great strength, *Williams.*

waxed valiant in fight: . . . grew mighty, *Williams* . . . became mighty in war, *Adams* . . . they became mighty warriors, *Norlie.*

turned to flight the armies of the aliens: . . . and rounted armies, *Montgomery* . . . They completely defeated foreign armies, *SEB* . . . overturned the Camps of Foreigners, *Wilson.*

35. Women received their dead raised to life again: . . . by a resurrection, *Williams.*

and others were tortured, not accepting deliverance: Others chose to be beaten, *NLT* . . . were broken on the wheel, *Montgomery* . . . they were tortured to death, *SEB* . . . others endured tortures, because they would not accept release, *Williams* . . . were beaten to death, not accepting the deliverance offered, *Wilson* . . . refusing to be delivered, *Adams* . . . not anticipating deliverance, *Concordant* . . . they refused to be freed, *Beck.*

Hebrews 11:36

3450.12 art acc sing fem	623.3 noun acc sing fem	2419.1 conj	2882.1 adj comp gen sing	384.2 noun gen sing fem
τὴν	ἀπολύτρωσιν,	ἵνα	κρείττονος	ἀναστάσεως
tēn	*apolutrōsin*	*hina*	*kreittonos*	*anastaseōs*
the	redemption,	that	a better	resurrection

5018.3 verb 3pl subj aor act	2066.7 adj nom pl masc	1156.2 conj	1685.1 noun gen pl masc	2504.1 conj
τύχωσιν·	**36.** ἕτεροι	δὲ	ἐμπαιγμῶν	καὶ
tuchōsin	*heteroi*	*de*	*empaigmōn*	*kai*
they might obtain;	others	and	of mockings	and

3120.2 noun gen pl fem	3846.1 noun acc sing fem	2956.12 verb indic aor act	2068.1 adv	1156.2 conj	1193.4 noun gen pl
μαστίγων	πεῖραν	ἔλαβον,	ἔτι	δὲ	δεσμῶν
mastigōn	*peiran*	*elabon*	*eti*	*de*	*desmōn*
of scourgings	trial	received,	yet,	moreover,	of bonds

2504.1 conj	5274.2 noun gen sing fem	3008.7 verb 3pl indic aor pass	4108.1 verb 3pl indic aor pass
καὶ	φυλακῆς·	**37.** ἐλιθάσθησαν,	ʻ ἐπρίσθησαν,
kai	*phulakēs*	*elithasthēsan*	*epristhēsan*
and	of imprisonment.	They were stoned,	were sawn asunder,

3847.15 verb 3pl indic aor pass	3847.15 verb 3pl indic aor pass	4108.1 verb 3pl indic aor pass
ἐπειράσθησαν,	[☆ ἐπειράσθησαν,	ἐπρίσθησαν,]
epeirasthēsan	*epeirasthēsan*	*epristhēsan*
were tempted,	[were tempted,	were sawn asunder,]

1706.1 prep	5245.2 noun dat sing masc	3134.2 noun gen sing fem	3134.7 noun gen sing fem	594.9 verb indic aor act
ἐν	φόνῳ	ʻ μαχαίρας	[☆ μαχαίρης]	ἀπέθανον,
en	*phonō*	*machairas*	*machairēs*	*apethanon*
by	slaughter	of sword	[idem]	they died;

3885.1 verb 3pl indic aor act	1706.1 prep	3242.1 noun dat pl fem	1706.1 prep	122.1 adj dat pl neu	1186.1 noun dat pl neu
περιῆλθον	ἐν	μηλωταῖς,	ἐν	αἰγείοις	δέρμασιν,
periēlthon	*en*	*mēlōtais*	*en*	*aigeiois*	*dermasin*
they wandered	in	sheepskins,	in	goats’	skins,

5139.11 verb nom pl masc part pres mid	2323.4 verb nom pl masc part pres mid	2529.1 verb nom pl masc part pres mid	3614.1 rel-pron gen pl
ὑστερούμενοι,	θλιβόμενοι,	κακουχούμενοι,	**38.** ὧν
husteroumenoi	*thlibomenoi*	*kakouchoumenoi*	*hōn*
being destitute,	being oppressed,	being evil treated.	of whom

3620.2 partic	1498.34 verb sing indic imperf act	510.2 adj nom sing masc	3450.5 art nom sing masc	2862.1 noun nom sing masc	1706.1 prep
οὐκ	ἦν	ἄξιος	ὁ	κόσμος,	ʻ ἐν
ouk	*ēn*	*axios*	*ho*	*kosmos*	*en*
not	was	worthy	the	world,	in

38.a.**Txt:** 06D,018K 020L,byz.
Var: 01ℵ,02A,33,Lach Treg,Alf,Tisc,We/Ho Weis,Sod,UBS/☆

1894.3 prep	2030.3 noun dat pl fem	3966.13 verb nom pl masc part pres mid	2504.1 conj	3598.6 noun dat pl neu	2504.1 conj
[a☆ ἐπὶ]	ἐρημίαις	πλανώμενοι	καὶ	ὄρεσιν	καὶ
epi	*erēmiais*	*planōmenoi*	*kai*	*oresin*	*kai*
[on]	deserts	wandering	and	in mountains	and

4546.2 noun dat pl neu	2504.1 conj	3450.14 art dat pl fem	3555.2 noun dat pl fem	3450.10 art gen sing fem	1087.2 noun gen sing fem
σπηλαίοις	καὶ	ταῖς	ὀπαῖς	τῆς	γῆς.
spēlaiois	*kai*	*tais*	*opais*	*tēs*	*gēs*
in caves	and	in the	holes	of the	earth.

rificial laws. By faith they remained true to their God in anticipation of resurrection in the messianic kingdom where they would be allowed to please and obey God rather than man (2 Maccabees 6:18 to 7:11).

Many others suffered at the hands of the Persians, Egyptians, Syrians, Greeks, and Romans during the intertestamental period. Some interpreters feel that the verb "tortured" which is *etumpanisthēsan*, which means "to beat a drum," refers to the martyrdom of Eleazar who was stretched on a drum and beaten to death (2 Maccabees 6:18-30).

11:36. In addition to the martyrs of the Maccabean revolt, others were tested by persecution. The prophet Jeremiah was threatened by priests and prophets because of his prophetic word concerning judgment upon Jerusalem. Later he was imprisoned and beaten by King Zedekiah. Others suffered similar fates when they spoke to Israel concerning the judgment of God. The prophet Urijah, a contemporary of Jeremiah, was executed by King Jehoiakim for preaching the same message as Jeremiah (Jeremiah 26:20-23). All were examples of the endurance made possible by faith in God.

11:37. The description of the hardships suffered by believers continues in this verse. As is seen in the Gospel of John, the Jews were apt to stone people in mob action, and many of God's servants died before an angry crowd. The "sawn asunder" refers to the tradition that the prophet Isaiah died in this gruesome way (*The Ascension of Isaiah the Prophet* 5:1). Execution by sword was common in the ancient world. In 1 Kings 19:10 there is a reference to Elijah's words that Israel had slain many of the Lord's prophets with the sword.

The declaration that God's people "were tempted" (*epeirasthēsan*) is possibly a play on words since the Greek verb referring to sawing in two is *epristhēsan*. Some Greek manuscripts omit *epeirasthēsan*. Those who wandered about lacking food and water, and clothing themselves in animal skins, would include Elijah when he fled from Jezebel and a host of prophets whose messages of judgment were rejected by Israel.

11:38. Before finishing the list of indignities and horrors suffered by the prophets, the inspired writer injected an editorial comment that "the world was not worthy" of these heroes of faith. The people of power, influence, prestige, and wealth who persecuted these saints were in no way equal to them. These persecuted ones understood the invisible and eternal world. They knew that its value was far beyond the wealth of the entire world which surrounded their senses. While they hid from their oppressors in the wilderness and caves, they trusted God and kept their eyes fixed upon the unseen realities of God's kingdom.

that they might obtain a better resurrection: . . . that they might gain, *Wade* . . . that they might rise to a better life, *Williams, TNT* . . . they wanted to inherit a better life after their resurrection, *Noli.*

36. And others had trial of [cruel] mockings and scourgings: . . . had experience of, *Wade* . . . Others knew what it was to be taunted, flogged, *TNT* . . . endured derision, *Noli* . . . stood the test of taunts and tortures, *Williams* . . . had to face taunts and blows, *TCNT.*

yea, moreover of bonds and imprisonment: . . . others were chained and imprisoned, *Adams* . . . and even chains and prisons, *Williams.*

37. They were stoned: . . . stoned to death, *Williams.*

they were sawn asunder: . . . sawn in two, *Williams, TNT.*

were tempted, were slain with the sword: . . . they were tortured to death, *Williams* . . . murdered with, *Beck* . . . slaughtered by the sword, *Norlie* . . . put to death by the sword, *TNT* . . . butchered by the sword, *Wade.*

they wandered about in sheepskins and goatskins: . . . they had to roam about, clad only in, *Wade* . . . With nothing on their bodies but skins of sheep or goats they wandered here and there, *Williams.*

being destitute, afflicted, tormented: They had nothing left, were oppressed, evil treated, *Klingensmith* . . . suffering poverty, oppression and misery, *TNT* . . . suffering from destitution, distress, and ill-usage, *Wade* . . . poor, oppressed, *Norlie* . . . ill-treated, *Adams* . . . persecuted, ill-used, *TCNT* . . . mistreated, *Williams.*

38. (Of whom the world was not worthy:): . . . by the world which was not worthy of them, *Noli.*

they wandered in deserts, and [in] mountains: . . . wandered about in lonely places, *TNT* . . . straying in wildernesses, *Concordant.*

and [in] dens and caves of the earth: . . . and hiding in caverns and underground cavities, *Wade* . . . caves, and holes in the ground, *Williams, TNT.*

2504.1 conj	**3642.7** dem-pron nom pl masc	**3820.7** adj nom pl masc	**3113.38** verb nom pl masc part aor pass
39. Καὶ	οὗτοι	πάντες	μαρτυρηθέντες
Kai	*houtoi*	*pantes*	*marturēthentes*
And	these	all,	having been borne witness to

1217.2 prep	**3450.10** art gen sing fem	**3963.2** noun gen sing fem	**3620.2** partic	**2837.5** verb 3pl indic aor mid	**3450.12** art acc sing fem
διὰ	τῆς	πίστεως,	οὐκ	ἐκομίσαντο	τὴν
dia	*tēs*	*pisteōs*	*ouk*	*ekomisanto*	*tēn*
through	the	faith,	not	did receive	the

1845.4 noun acc sing fem	**3450.2** art gen sing	**2296.2** noun gen sing masc	**3875.1** prep	**2231.2** prs-pron gen 1pl	**2882.5** adj comp sing neu
ἐπαγγελίαν,	**40.** τοῦ	θεοῦ	περὶ	ἡμῶν	κρεῖττόν
epangelian	*tou*	*theou*	*peri*	*hēmōn*	*kreitton*
promise,		God	for	us	better

4948.10 indef-pron sing neu	**4124.1** verb gen sing masc part aor mid	**2419.1** conj	**3231.1** partic	**5400.1** prep	**2231.2** prs-pron gen 1pl
τι	προβλεψαμένου,	ἵνα	μὴ	χωρὶς	ἡμῶν
ti	*problepsamenou*	*hina*	*mē*	*chōris*	*hēmōn*
something	having foreseen,	that	not	apart from	us

4896.11 verb 3pl subj aor pass	**4952.1** partic	**2504.1** conj	**2231.1** prs-pron nom 1pl
τελειωθῶσιν.	**12:1.** Τοιγαροῦν	καὶ	ἡμεῖς
teleiōthōsin	*Toigaroun*	*kai*	*hēmeis*
they should be made perfect.	Therefore	also	we

4965.1 dem-pron acc sing	**2174.19** verb nom pl masc part pres act	**3892.3** verb sing neu part pres mid	**2231.3** prs-pron dat 1pl	**3371.1** noun sing neu
τοσοῦτον	ἔχοντες	περικείμενον	ἡμῖν	νέφος
tosouton	*echontes*	*perikeimenon*	*hēmin*	*nephos*
so great	having	encompassing	us	a cloud

3116.5 noun gen pl masc	**3454.1** noun acc sing masc	**653.4** verb nom pl masc part aor mid	**3820.1** adj	**2504.1** conj	**3450.12** art acc sing fem
μαρτύρων,	ὄγκον	ἀποθέμενοι	πάντα	καὶ	τὴν
marturōn	*onkon*	*apothemenoi*	*panta*	*kai*	*tēn*
of witnesses,	weight	having laid aside	every	and	the

2119.1 adj acc sing fem	**264.4** noun acc sing fem	**1217.1** prep	**5119.2** noun gen sing fem	**4983.5** verb 1pl subj pres act
εὐπερίστατον	ἁμαρτίαν,	δι'	ὑπομονῆς	τρέχωμεν
euperistaton	*hamartian*	*di'*	*hupomonēs*	*trechōmen*
constantly besetting	sin,	with	endurance	we should run

3450.6 art acc sing masc	**4154.3** verb acc sing masc part pres mid	**2231.3** prs-pron dat 1pl	**72.2** noun acc sing masc	**865.1** verb nom pl masc part pres act
τὸν	προκείμενον	ἡμῖν	ἀγῶνα,	**2.** ἀφορῶντες
ton	*prokeimenon*	*hēmin*	*agōna*	*aphorōntes*
the	lying before	us	race,	looking away

1519.1 prep	**3450.6** art acc sing masc	**3450.10** art gen sing fem	**3963.2** noun gen sing fem	**742.1** noun acc sing masc	**2504.1** conj	**4899.1** noun acc sing masc
εἰς	τὸν	τῆς	πίστεως	ἀρχηγὸν	καὶ	τελειωτὴν
eis	*ton*	*tēs*	*pisteōs*	*archēgon*	*kai*	*teleiōtēn*
to	the	of the	faith	leader	and	completer

2400.3 name acc masc	**3614.5** rel-pron nom sing masc	**470.2** prep	**3450.10** art gen sing fem	**4154.4** verb gen sing fem part pres mid	**840.4** prs-pron dat sing
Ἰησοῦν,	ὃς	ἀντὶ	τῆς	προκειμένης	αὐτῷ
Iēsoun	*hos*	*anti*	*tēs*	*prokeimenēs*	*autō*
Jesus:	who	against	the	lying before	him

11:39. Like the patriarchs before them, the judges, kings, and prophets who believed God gained a reputation for righteousness by faith while they lived, but they all died without seeing the Lord fulfill His promise. As was previously argued in 4:8,9, God's promised rest did not arrive when Israel entered Canaan; it is still future for His people.

11:40. This lack of fulfillment of promise was not a failure on God's part. It was part of the divine plan. God actually foresaw (*problepsamenou*) this situation, that is, that there was "something better for us" (NASB). According to God's plan, the age in which He began to fulfill His promise would follow the times of the patriarchs, judges, kings, and prophets. That time began when the eternal Son of God became flesh—"in these last days" (1:2). The Lord spoke His final word through His Son Jesus Christ.

The conclusion is obvious. Since the first coming of Jesus Christ, believers live not in promise but in the age of fulfillment, the new covenant age. It was in God's purpose to make the Old Testament saints wait for the coming of the messianic Son, the establishment of the new covenant, and the exploits of Christian believers, before He establishes His eternal kingdom at the time of the second coming of Jesus Christ. There is a unity between the saints of the two covenants, and it is to be discovered in the person of Jesus, "the author and finisher of our faith" (12:2).

12:1. The first two verses of chapter 12 apply the principles of faith presented in chapter 11. The vast multitude of saints described as heroes of faith were witnesses to the first-century Jewish believers who may have been wondering whether or not they could finish the course which they began when they confessed Jesus as their Messiah. Some of them might have been wondering whether or not their confession was worth all the trouble it was causing them. The testimony of the witnesses marshaled from the Old Testament assures all believers that it is possible to be justified by faith, gain a reputation for righteous living, endure suffering and death without seeing the promise completely fulfilled, and accomplish great things for God. Since they did it, all believers can do it. For the race of life, believers are to trim down, that is, get rid of the sin of unbelief which will impede their progress. Forsaking all other impediments to faith, they are to run the race "with patience," i.e., "endurance" (NASB) (*hupomonēs*). They are to finish what they have begun.

12:2. Like a runner, believers are encouraged not to look back but to fix their gaze upon (*aphorōntes*) Jesus because He is the trailblazing pioneer (*archēgon*), the One who brings faith to com-

39. And these all, having obtained a good report through faith: . . . by their faith won God's approval, *Williams.*

received not the promise: . . . did not obtain the promised blessing, *Wilson* . . . none of them received what He had promised, *Williams.*

40. God having provided some better thing for us: . . . for us God had something still better in mind, *Norlie* . . . With us in mind God had an even better plan, *TNT.*

that they without us should not be made perfect: . . . in order to have them reach their goal with us, *Beck* . . . apart from us might not attain perfection, *Williams* . . . Only with us should they be brought to perfection, *TNT.*

1. Wherefore seeing we also:

are compassed about with so great a cloud of witnesses: . . . figuratively encircled by a great crowd, *Norlie* . . . we are encircled, *Montgomery* . . . by such a large number of witnesses! *SEB* . . . of those who are bearing testimony, *Wuest* . . . so vast a crowd of spectators, *Williams.*

let us lay aside every weight: . . . let us throw off, *Williams* . . . let us get rid of every burden, *Beck* . . . we must put off every, *Adams* . . . putting off every impediment, *Concordant.*

and the sin which doth so easily beset [us]: . . . the sin that clings about us, *Montgomery* . . . the sins that cling to us so closely, *Norlie* . . . Sin can easily tie us up, *SEB* . . . that is so readily found all around us, *Adams* . . . cleverly places itself in an entangling way around us, *Wuest* . . . that easily entangles our feet, *Williams.*

and let us run with patience the race that is set before us: . . . run with endurance, *Williams* . . . the Course marked out for us, *Wilson* . . . that God has planned for us, *NLT.*

2. Looking unto Jesus the author and finisher of [our] faith: . . . keeping our eyes, *Williams* . . . our eyes fixed upon, *TCNT* . . . the pioneer and perfecter, *Montgomery* . . . the Inaugurator and Perfecter of, *Concordant.*

who for the joy that was set before him: . . . instead of the joy which lay before, *Williams.*

2.a.**Var:** p13,p46
06D-org,06D-corr2

5315.2 noun gen sing fem	5116.7 verb 3sing indic aor act	3450.6 art acc sing masc	4567.4 noun acc sing masc	151.2 noun gen sing fem
χαρᾶς	ὑπέμεινεν	[a+ τὸν]	σταυρὸν,	αἰσχύνης
charas	*hupemeinen*	*ton*	*stauron*	*aischunēs*
joy	endured	[the]	cross,	shame

2675.7 verb nom sing masc part aor act	1706.1 prep	1182.5 adj dat sing fem	4885.1 conj	3450.2 art gen sing	2339.2 noun gen sing masc	3450.2 art gen sing
καταφρονήσας,	ἐν	δεξιᾷ	τε	τοῦ	θρόνου	τοῦ
kataphronēsas	*en*	*dexia*	*te*	*tou*	*thronou*	*tou*
having despised,	at	right hand	and	of the	throne	

2.b.**Txt:** Steph
Var: 01ℵ,02A,06D
018K,020L,025P,byz.
Gries,Lach,Treg,Alf
Word,Tisc,We/Ho,Weis
Sod,UBS/☆

2296.2 noun gen sing masc	2495.3 verb 3sing indic aor act	2495.13 verb 3sing indic perf act	355.1 verb 2pl impr aor mid
θεοῦ	⸀ ἐκάθισεν.	[b☆ κεκάθικεν.]	3. ἀναλογίσασθε
theou	*ekathisen*	*kekathiken*	*analogisasthe*
of God	sat down.	[has taken a seat.]	Consider well

3.a.**Txt:** 01ℵ,02A
06D-corr1,044,048,byz.
Var: p13,p46,06D-org

1056.1 conj	3450.6 art acc sing masc	4955.10 dem-pron acc sing fem	5116.10 verb acc sing masc part perf act	5097.3 prep	3450.1 art gen pl
γὰρ	⸂a τὸν ⸃	τοιαύτην	ὑπομεμενηκότα	ὑπὸ	τῶν
gar	*ton*	*toiautēn*	*hupomemenēkota*	*hupo*	*tōn*
for	the	so great	having endured	from	the

3.b.**Txt:** 06D-corr,018K
020L,byz.Sod
Var: 02A,025P,Lach
Treg,Alf,Tisc,Weis
UBS/☆

266.5 adj gen pl masc	1519.1 prep	840.6 prs-pron acc sing masc	1431.6 prs-pron acc sing masc	482.3 noun acc sing fem
ἁμαρτωλῶν	εἰς	⸀ αὐτὸν	[b☆ ἑαυτὸν]	ἀντιλογίαν,
hamartōlōn	*eis*	*auton*	*heauton*	*antilogian*
sinners	against	him	[himself]	opposition,

3.c.**Var:** p13,p46,1739
1881

2419.1 conj	3231.1 partic	2548.2 verb 2pl subj aor act	3450.14 art dat pl fem	5425.7 noun dat pl fem	5050.2 prs-pron gen 2pl
ἵνα	μὴ	κάμητε,	ταῖς	ψυχαῖς	⸂c ὑμῶν ⸃
hina	*mē*	*kamēte*	*tais*	*psuchais*	*humōn*
that	not	you be wearied,	in the	souls	your

3.d.**Var:** p13,p46
06D-org,06D-corr2,1739
1881

1577.2 verb nom pl masc part pres mid	1577.4 verb nom pl masc part perf mid	3632.1 adv	3230.2 prep
⸀☆ ἐκλυόμενοι.	[d ἐκλελυμένοι.]	4. Οὔπω	μέχρις
ekluomenoi	*eklelumenoi*	*Oupō*	*mechris*
fainting.	[having fainted.]	Not yet	unto

129.2 noun gen sing neu	475.1 verb 2pl indic aor act	4242.1 prep	3450.12 art acc sing fem	264.4 noun acc sing fem
αἵματος	ἀντικατέστητε	πρὸς	τὴν	ἁμαρτίαν
haimatos	*antikatestēte*	*pros*	*tēn*	*hamartian*
blood	resisted you	against	the	sin

461.1 verb nom pl masc part pres mid	2504.1 conj	1572.1 verb 2pl indic perf mid	3450.10 art gen sing fem
ἀνταγωνιζόμενοι,	5. καὶ	ἐκλέλησθε	τῆς
antagōnizomenoi	*kai*	*eklelēsthe*	*tēs*
wrestling,	and	you have quite forgotten	the

3735.2 noun gen sing fem	3610.3 rel-pron nom sing fem	5050.3 prs-pron dat 2pl	5453.1 conj	5048.8 noun dat pl masc
παρακλήσεως,	ἥτις	ὑμῖν	ὡς	υἱοῖς
paraklēseōs	*hētis*	*humin*	*hōs*	*huiois*
exhortation,	which	to you,	as	to sons,

1250.1 verb 3sing indic pres mid	5048.5 noun voc sing masc	1466.2 prs-pron gen 1sing	3231.1 partic	3506.1 verb 2sing impr pres act	3672.2 noun gen sing fem
διαλέγεται·	Υἱέ	μου,	μὴ	ὀλιγώρει	παιδείας
dialegetai	*Huie*	*mou*	*mē*	*oligōrei*	*paideias*
he addresses:	Son	my,	not	despise	discipline

pletion (*teleiōtēn*). He set an example for believers under persecution. He endured the agony and suffering of crucifixion and discounted the shamefulness of a criminal execution because He set His gaze on the joys of the Resurrection and His eternal rule at God's side.

12:3. These words reemphasize the exhortation given in the previous verse. The word "for" (*gar*) could well be translated "indeed" in this situation. The word translated "consider" is unusual. In the papyri it was used in reference to the careful comparison of accounts; here it is metaphoric. The Hebrew believers were asked to carefully examine the example set by Jesus in His endurance of the verbal hostility and abuse (*antilogian*) of sinful men. The perfect tense of the verb "endured" stresses the abiding results of His endurance. It is not just a matter of historic interest; it is significant for all believers. Careful consideration of Jesus' endurance of persecution has the power to encourage believers and keep them from gradually fading and dropping out of the race when things get rough.

12:4. The Jewish believers to whom the epistle was written were reminded that even though they had "resisted" (*antikatestēte*, "stood against") the sin of unbelief because of their identification with Jesus, they had not yet been asked to die while struggling (*antagōnizomenoi*, "wrestling against") with the temptation to apostatize. Jesus and the Old Testament saints are reminders to all believers that it is possible to endure such persecution even to the point of dying. The eternal nature of the reward is far superior to anything that can be gained by "giving up in the struggle." To continue living in the present age at the expense of forsaking Christ and His eternal kingdom is to squander the greatest treasure for a mere pittance.

12:5. The fact that some of the Jewish Christians who were recipients of this letter may have been thinking about giving up their confession of Jesus as Messiah indicates they had lost sight of a very important Old Testament teaching. They needed to be reminded of a spiritual truth which they had forgotten. The exhortation given was from Proverbs 3:11,12. The Greek word *paraklēseōs* carries a double-edged impact. It has both the idea of admonition and a sense of comfort and encouragement. Whenever this word is used, it not only confronts believers with their failure to behave in the proper way, but it also reminds them of the provisions which God has made to enable them to do what He desires them to do. And so it is here in Hebrews 12.

endured the cross, despising the shame: . . . and scorned its shame, *Norlie* . . . disregarding the Shame, *Wilson* . . . with no regard for its shame, *Williams* . . . and cared nothing for its shame, *TNT* . . . making light of the ignominy of it, *Wade.*

and is set down at the right hand of the throne of God: . . . and since has taken His seat at, *Williams.*

3. For consider him: Yes...just think of the examples set by Him, *Williams* . . . Think of Jesus, *TNT* . . . consider the steadfastness of Him, *Wade.*

that endured such contradiction of sinners against himself: . . . and the way he bore the bitter enmity of sinful men against himself, *TNT* . . . such opposition from, *Adams* . . . such hostility, *Montgomery* . . . so great opposition aimed at Him by sinful men! *Williams.*

lest ye be wearied and faint in your minds: It will help you not to, *Beck* . . . Then you will not grow tired and lose heart, *TNT* . . . so that you won't get tired and give up, *Adams* . . . to keep from growing weary and fainthearted, *Williams.*

4. Ye have not yet resisted unto blood, striving against sin: So far, in your struggle against sin, you have not had to face death itself, *TNT* . . . as you have struggled on against sin, resisted to the point of pouring out your blood, *Williams* . . . when contending against sin, *Concordant.*

5. And ye have forgotten the exhortation: Have you forgotten that Scripture, *TNT* . . . these words of comfort, *SEB* . . . the encouragement, *Williams* . . . the appeal, *Wade.*

which speaketh unto you as unto children: . . . which reasons with you, *Wade* . . . which is addressed to you as sons, *Williams.*

My son, despise not thou the chastening of the Lord: . . . do not despise the training of the Lord, *Montgomery* . . . think not lightly of the Lord's discipline, *TCNT* . . . don't take it lightly, *SEB* . . . refrain from thinking lightly of the discipline the Lord inflicts, *Williams* . . . of the Lord's training, *Beck.*

Hebrews 12:6

2935.2 noun gen sing masc	3234.1 adv	1577.1 verb 2sing impr pres mid	5097.2 prep	840.3 prs-pron gen sing	1638.9 verb nom sing masc part pres mid
κυρίου,	μηδὲ	ἐκλύου	ὑπ’	αὐτοῦ	ἐλεγχόμενος·
kuriou	mēde	ekluou	hup'	autou	elenchomenos
of Lord,	nor	faint,	by	him	being reproved;

3614.6 rel-pron acc sing masc	1056.1 conj	25.2 verb 3sing pres act	2935.1 noun nom sing masc	3674.2 verb 3sing indic pres act	3118.1 verb 3sing indic pres act
6. ὃν	γὰρ	ἀγαπᾷ	κύριος	παιδεύει·	μαστιγοῖ
hon	gar	agapa	kurios	paideuei	mastigoi
whom	for	loves	Lord	he disciplines,	scourges

1156.2 conj	3820.1 adj	5048.4 noun acc sing masc	3614.6 rel-pron acc sing masc	3720.1 verb 3sing indic pres mid	1479.1 conj
δὲ	πάντα	υἱὸν	ὃν	παραδέχεται.	7. ˊ Εἰ
de	panta	huion	hon	paradechetai	Ei
and	every	son	whom	he receives.	If

7.a.**Txt:** Steph
Var: 01ℵ,02A,06D 018K,020L,025P,Lach Treg,Alf,Tisc,We/Ho Weis,Sod,UBS/☆

1519.1 prep	3672.4 noun acc sing fem	5116.1 verb 2pl pres act	5453.1 conj	5048.8 noun dat pl masc	5050.3 prs-pron dat 2pl
[a☆ εἰς]	παιδείαν	ὑπομένετε,	ὡς	υἱοῖς	ὑμῖν
eis	paideian	hupomenete	hōs	huiois	humin
[For]	discipline	you endure,	as	with sons	with you

7.b.**Txt:** 01ℵ-corr,06D 018K,020L,025P,byz.bo.
Var: 01ℵ-org,02A,025P sa.Lach,Treg,Tisc We/Ho,Weis,UBS/☆

4232.21 verb 3sing indic pres mid	3450.5 art nom sing masc	2296.1 noun nom sing masc	4949.3 intr-pron nom sing	1056.1 conj	1498.4 verb 3sing indic pres act
προσφέρεται	ὁ	θεός·	τίς	γὰρ	ˊb ἐστιν ˋ
prospheretai	ho	theos	tis	gar	estin
is dealing		God;	who	for	is

5048.1 noun nom sing masc	3614.6 rel-pron acc sing masc	3620.3 partic	3674.2 verb 3sing indic pres act	3824.1 noun nom sing masc	1479.1 conj
υἱὸς	ὃν	οὐ	παιδεύει	πατήρ;	8. εἰ
huios	hon	ou	paideuei	patēr	ei
son	whom	not	disciplines	Father?	If

1156.2 conj	5400.1 prep	1498.6 verb 2pl indic pres act	3672.2 noun gen sing fem	3614.10 rel-pron gen sing fem	3223.1 adj nom pl masc
δὲ	χωρίς	ἐστε	παιδείας	ἧς	μέτοχοι
de	chōris	este	paideias	hēs	metochoi
but	without	you are	discipline,	of which	partakers

1090.6 verb 3pl indic perf act	3820.7 adj nom pl masc	679.1 partic	3403.1 adj nom pl masc	1498.6 verb 2pl indic pres act	2504.1 conj	3620.1 partic
γεγόνασιν	πάντες,	ἄρα	νόθοι	ˊ ἐστε	καὶ	οὐχ
gegonasin	pantes	ara	nothoi	este	kai	ouch
have become	all,	then	illegitimate	you are	and	not

5048.6 noun nom pl masc	2504.1 conj	3620.1 partic	5048.6 noun nom pl masc	1498.6 verb 2pl indic pres act	1520.1 adv	3450.8 art acc pl masc
υἱοί.	[☆ καὶ	οὐχ	υἱοί	ἐστε.]	9. εἶτα	τοὺς
huioi	kai	ouch	huioi	este	eita	tous
sons.	[and	not	sons	you are.]	Moreover	the

3173.1 conj	3450.10 art gen sing fem	4418.2 noun gen sing fem	2231.2 prs-pron gen 1pl	3824.9 noun acc pl masc	2174.46 verb 1pl indic imperf act
μὲν	τῆς	σαρκὸς	ἡμῶν	πατέρας	εἴχομεν
men	tēs	sarkos	hēmōn	pateras	eichomen
	the	flesh	of our	fathers	we were having

3673.2 noun acc pl masc	2504.1 conj	1772.6 verb 1pl indic imperf pass	3620.3 partic	4044.3 adj dat sing
παιδευτὰς,	καὶ	ἐνετρεπόμεθα·	οὐ	ˊ πολλῷ
paideutas	kai	enetrepometha	ou	pollō
correctors,	and	we were respecting;	not	much

This Scripture verse is particularly appropriate because it speaks to members of the family of God, to "children" (literally *huiois*, "sons," NASB). It is a gentle reminder that those who are not mature often lose sight of long-range goals in the panic of present difficulties. The Greek word for "despise" is *oligōrei*, and it means "to belittle." So the first part of the admonition is not to belittle the "chastening of the Lord" (*paideias*, the disciplinary instruction given to *paidion*, an infant or child).

12:6. The reason believers are not to belittle God's disciplinary instruction nor fade away in response to His showing them the error of their ways (*elenchomenos*, 12:5) is set forth in the second half of the quotation. The disciplinary instruction of the Lord is a result of His love for His sons. This discipline is described by the verb "scourgeth" (*mastigoi*) which means "to punish by whipping." Without exception, each son whom the Lord "receiveth" (*paradechetai*, "welcomes, accepts") is subject to such discipline. God's love does not overlook the sins of His children; it disciplines them.

12:7. The Greek text does not have an "if" here. It says "you are enduring unto disciplinary instruction." The "ye" is plural and looks at the group as a whole. Since believers are recipients of divine discipline, God is dealing with them as His children. "For what son is he whom the father chasteneth not?" On the basis of the previous statements, the conclusion is obvious. Since "every son" (12:6) is disciplined, those who are not disciplined are not being treated as sons.

12:8. This verse graphically describes those who never experience God's disciplinary instruction: to be without God's discipline is to be a "bastard." When God recognizes someone as His own child, He exercises His discipline in their lives because He loves them. The statement "whereof all are partakers" seems to indicate that the Jews to whom the epistle was sent were for the most part genuine members of the family of God.

12:9. This verse reflects on the comparison inherent in the father/son metaphor which Proverbs 3:11,12 applies to God. There is not only a similarity between God and human fathers, there is also a stark contrast, and it needs to be emphasized. Earthly fathers discipline their children, and they are respected for their efforts. Their training and guidance has the purpose of leading their children into patterns of behavior that are profitable and will keep them out of trouble. Should it not be even more true in regard to the response to the discipline which believers receive from God who is "the Father of spirits"? This title is used for God to heighten the contrast with "fathers of our flesh."

nor faint when thou art rebuked of him: Do not give up, *NLT* . . . nor get weary, *Noli* . . . do not lose heart when he reproves you, *TNT* . . . when you are corrected by Him, *Williams.*

6. For whom the Lord loveth he chasteneth: . . . he disciplines, *Wilson* . . . everyone He loves, *Williams* . . . every child he loves, *Noli.*

and scourgeth every son whom he receiveth: . . . and whips every, *Adams* . . . he acknowledges, *TCNT* . . . chastises...whom He heartily receives, *Williams.*

7. If ye endure chastening: You must submit to discipline, *Williams* . . . endure suffering, *Noli* . . . Your steadfastness serves to discipline you, *Wade* . . . for discipline's sake, *TNT.*

God dealeth with you as with sons: . . . is treating you as, *Noli.*

for what son is he whom the father chasteneth not?: Is there any son whom his father does not discipline? *TNT* . . . who is the son, *Williams* . . . that a father doesn't discipline? *Adams* . . . who does not at times punish his sons? *Norlie* . . . whose father does not train? *Klingensmith* . . . doesn't correct? *Beck.*

8. But if ye be without chastisement: If you do not have the discipline, *TNT* . . . If you lack the discipline, *Noli* . . . without discipline, *Concordant.*

whereof all are partakers: . . . in which all true sons share, *Williams* . . . of which all men have their share, *Wade.*

then are ye bastards, and not sons: . . . your sonship is not legitimate, *Noli* . . . you are Spurious, *Wilson* . . . illegitimate children, *Adams* . . . base-born, *Wade.*

9. Furthermore we have had fathers of our flesh which corrected [us]: We had human fathers, *TNT* . . . Remember that our fathers on earth punished us, *NLT* . . . from our natural fathers, *Wilson* . . . in our earthly fathers we have had disciplinarians, *Wade* . . . our natural fathers used to correct us, *Beck* . . . who disciplined us, *Adams.*

and we gave [them] reverence: . . . we held them in respect, *TNT*

9.a.**Txt:** 06D-corr,018K 020L,byz.
Var: 01ℵ,02A,06D-org 33,Lach,Treg,Alf,Tisc We/Ho,Weis,Sod UBS/☆

9.b.**Txt:** 01ℵ-org,02A 06D-corr2,016I,044,048 byz.Tisc,We/Ho,Sod
Var: p13,p46,01ℵ-corr2 06D-org,1739,1881 UBS/☆

4044.16 adj sing neu	**1156.2** conj	**3095.1** adv comp	**5131.24** verb 1pl indic fut pass	**3450.3** art dat sing
[a☆ πολὺ]	[b☆+ δὲ]	μᾶλλον	ὑποταγησόμεθα	τῷ
polu	*de*	*mallon*	*hupotagēsometha*	*tō*
[idem]	[but]	rather	shall we be in subjection	to the

3824.3 noun dat sing masc	**3450.1** art gen pl	**4011.5** noun gen pl neu	**2504.1** conj	**2180.26** verb 1pl indic fut act	**3450.7** art nom pl masc
πατρὶ	τῶν	πνευμάτων,	καὶ	ζήσομεν;	**10.** οἱ
patri	*tōn*	*pneumatōn*	*kai*	*zēsomen*	*hoi*
Father	of the	spirits,	and	shall live?	The

3173.1 conj	**1056.1** conj	**4242.1** prep	**3504.11** adj acc pl fem	**2232.1** noun fem	**2567.3** prep	**3450.16** art sing neu
μὲν	γὰρ	πρὸς	ὀλίγας	ἡμέρας	κατὰ	τὸ
men	*gar*	*pros*	*oligas*	*hēmeras*	*kata*	*to*
for	indeed	for	a few	days	according to	the

1374.12 verb sing neu part pres act	**840.2** prs-pron dat pl	**3674.6** verb 3pl indic imperf act	**3450.5** art nom sing masc	**1156.2** conj
δοκοῦν	αὐτοῖς	ἐπαίδευον·	ὁ	δὲ
dokoun	*autois*	*epaideuon*	*ho*	*de*
seeming good	to them	were disciplining;	the	but

1894.3 prep	**3450.16** art sing neu	**4702.2** verb sing neu part pres act	**1519.1** prep	**3450.16** art sing neu	**3205.4** verb inf aor act
ἐπὶ	τὸ	συμφέρον,	εἰς	τὸ	μεταλαβεῖν
epi	*to*	*sumpheron*	*eis*	*to*	*metalabein*
for	the	profit,	for	the	to partake

11.a.**Txt:** 01ℵ-corr,02A 06D-corr,018K,020L byz.bo.Weis
Var: 01ℵ-org,025P,33 Tisc,We/Ho,Sod,UBS/☆

3450.10 art gen sing fem	**40.1** noun gen sing fem	**840.3** prs-pron gen sing	**3820.9** adj nom sing fem	**1156.2** conj	**3173.1** conj
τῆς	ἁγιότητος	αὐτοῦ.	**11.** πᾶσα	ʻ δὲ	[a μὲν]
tēs	*hagiotētos*	*autou*	*pasa*	*de*	*men*
of the	holiness	his.	Any	but	

3672.1 noun nom sing fem	**4242.1** prep	**3173.1** conj	**3450.16** art sing neu	**3780.10** verb sing neu part pres act	**3620.3** partic
παιδεία	πρὸς	μὲν	τὸ	παρὸν	οὐ
paideia	*pros*	*men*	*to*	*paron*	*ou*
discipline	for		the	being present	not

1374.5 verb 3sing indic pres act	**5315.2** noun gen sing fem	**1498.32** verb inf pres act	**233.2** conj	**3049.2** noun gen sing fem	**5142.1** adv comp
δοκεῖ	χαρᾶς	εἶναι,	ἀλλὰ	λύπης·	ὕστερον
dokei	*charas*	*einai*	*alla*	*lupēs*	*husteron*
seems	of joy	to be,	but	of grief;	afterwards

1156.2 conj	**2561.3** noun acc sing masc	**1504.1** adj acc sing masc	**3450.4** art dat pl	**1217.1** prep	**840.10** prs-pron gen sing fem
δὲ	καρπὸν	εἰρηνικὸν	τοῖς	δι'	αὐτῆς
de	*karpon*	*eirēnikon*	*tois*	*di'*	*autēs*
but	fruit	peaceable	to the	by	it

1122.2 verb dat pl masc part perf mid	**586.2** verb 3sing indic pres act	**1336.2** noun gen sing fem	**1346.1** conj
γεγυμνασμένοις	ἀποδίδωσιν	δικαιοσύνης.	**12.** Διὸ
gegumnasmenois	*apodidōsin*	*dikaiosunēs*	*Dio*
having been trained	renders	of righteousness.	Wherefore

3450.15 art acc pl fem	**3797.1** verb acc pl fem part perf mid	**5331.8** noun acc pl fem	**2504.1** conj	**3450.17** art pl neu
τὰς	παρειμένας	χεῖρας	καὶ	τὰ
tas	*pareimenas*	*cheiras*	*kai*	*ta*
the	having been wearied	hands	and	the

A contrast is also made between the kinds of response made to an earthly father and the Heavenly Father. The response to the human father is *enetrepometha*, "have regard or respect for"; the response to the Heavenly Father is *hupotagēsometha*, "subjection, subordination." Verse 9 closes by clearly declaring that "subjection" to the Heavenly Father's discipline will produce life in His sons.

. . . we used to treat them with respect, *Williams.*

shall we not much rather: . . . how much more cheerfully should we, *Williams* . . . Should we not be even more willing to, *TNT.*

be in subjection unto the Father of spirits, and live?: . . . submit to, *Williams* . . . our spiritual Father and so gain life? *TNT.*

12:10. Human fathers are fallible. The prevalence of child abuse makes it necessary to emphasize this. Some new believers wrestle with the image of God as their Father because they had earthly fathers who abused them. Verse 10 explicitly says that the discipline of a person's earthly father is limited; it is for "a few days." In addition, their discipline is "after their own pleasure." The Greek here could be translated "according to the standard which seems good to them." The discipline exercised by human fathers varies in its effectiveness. It may be too harsh; it may be too lenient; it may be designed to reach goals which are at odds with what God desires. This is not true of God's disciplinary instruction. Whatever He does by way of discipline is for the believer's benefit.

10. For they verily for a few days chastened [us]: Our human father disciplined us, *TNT* . . . for a short time, *Norlie.*

after their own pleasure; but he for [our] profit: . . . as it seemed right to them; but He for our advantage, *Wilson* . . . but he does it for our good, *Williams.*

that [we] might be partakers of his holiness: . . . so that we may share, *Adams* . . . His holy character, *Williams.*

12:11. Keeping the nature of God's discipline clearly in mind, along with its superiority to the discipline given by human fathers, a basic principle is given. First, there is the acknowledgment that even the discipline of the Heavenly Father has an unpleasant side. Discipline is arduous and sometimes painful. When believers are in the midst of discipline, they are not enjoying themselves. Discipline is not gladness; it is grief. Some children aspire to be Olympic stars, but few are willing to give up their playtime for the rigorous discipline of training, hour upon hour, away from other enjoyable pursuits. There is a sacrifice involved in discipline.

The principle, however, is clearly stated in two significant words: "nevertheless, afterward." After the grief and pain of discipline's sacrifice comes the reward. In the case of God's discipline, the reward is "the peaceable fruit of righteousness." In the end the pursuit of God's righteousness will result in peace and rest from hostility and labor. This result, however, is not the automatic product of divine discipline. The response and attitude of God's children to His discipline is all important. The desired fruit is enjoyed only by "them which are exercised" by God's discipline. The word translated "exercised" is *gegumnasmenois*; it triggers images of athletes training in the gymnasium.

11. Now no chastening for the present seemeth to be joyous: All punishment seems terrible at the time, *SEB* . . . never seems at the time to be pleasant, *TNT* . . . for the time being no discipline seems to be pleasant, *Williams.*

but grievous: nevertheless afterward: . . . it always seems unpleasant and painful, *Beck* . . . it is painful; later on, however, *Williams* . . . yet subsequently, *Concordant.*

it yieldeth the peaceable fruit of righteousness: . . . produces...lives of peace and goodness, *TNT* . . . yields a return, *Wuest* . . . the fruit of peace, *Williams.*

unto them which are exercised thereby: . . . those who have been trained by it, *Adams* . . . trained under it, *Montgomery.*

12:12,13. The athletic image is continued in this verse. In view of the "nevertheless, afterward" principle just stated, believers are to fix their eyes on the goal and to encourage one another when

12. Wherefore lift up the hands which hang down: So tighten the grip of your slipping hands, *Williams* . . . lift your listless hands, *Adams* . . . brace up the wearied hands, *Wilson* . . . your drooping hands, *TNT.*

and the feeble knees: . . . stiffen the stand of your knocking knees, *Williams* . . . the paralyzed knees, *Concordant* . . . and the shaky knees, *Klingensmith* . . . strengthen your weak knees, *TNT.*

Hebrews 12:13

3747.4 verb pl neu part perf mid	1113.3 noun pl neu	458.1 verb 2pl impr aor act	2504.1 conj	5004.1 noun acc pl fem
παραλελυμένα	γόνατα	ἀνορθώσατε	13. καὶ	τροχιὰς
paralelumena	*gonata*	*anorthōsate*	*kai*	*trochias*
having been paralyzed	knees	lift up;	and	paths

13.a.**Txt:** 01ℵ-corr,02A 06D,018K,020L,etc.byz. Sod
Var: p46,01ℵ-org,025P 33,Treg,Tisc,We/Ho Weis,UBS/⋆

3580.2 adj acc pl fem	4020.36 verb 2pl impr aor act	4020.2 verb 2pl pres act	3450.4 art dat pl	4087.6 noun dat pl masc	5050.2 prs-pron gen 2pl
ὀρθὰς	‘ ποιήσατε	[a⋆ ποιεῖτε]	τοῖς	ποσὶν	ὑμῶν,
orthas	*poiēsate*	*poieite*	*tois*	*posin*	*humōn*
straight	make	[idem]	for the	feet	your,

2419.1 conj	3231.1 partic	3450.16 art sing neu	5395.1 adj sing	1610.3 verb 3sing subj aor pass	2367.8 verb 3sing subj aor pass
ἵνα	μὴ	τὸ	χωλὸν	ἐκτραπῇ,	ἰαθῇ
hina	*mē*	*to*	*chōlon*	*ektrapē*	*iathē*
so that	not	the	lame	be turned aside;	it may be healed

1156.2 conj	3095.1 adv comp	1503.4 noun acc sing fem	1371.6 verb 2pl impr pres act	3196.3 prep	3820.4 adj gen pl
δὲ	μᾶλλον.	14. Εἰρήνην	διώκετε	μετὰ	πάντων,
de	*mallon*	*Eirēnēn*	*diōkete*	*meta*	*pantōn*
but	rather.	Peace	pursue	with	all,

2504.1 conj	3450.6 art acc sing masc	38.3 noun acc sing masc	3614.2 rel-pron gen sing	5400.1 prep	3625.2 num card nom masc
καὶ	τὸν	ἁγιασμόν,	οὗ	χωρὶς	οὐδεὶς
kai	*ton*	*hagiasmon*	*hou*	*chōris*	*oudeis*
and	the	sanctification,	which	apart from	no one

3571.31 verb 3sing indic fut mid	3450.6 art acc sing masc	2935.4 noun acc sing masc	1967.1 verb nom pl masc part pres act	3231.1 partic
ὄψεται	τὸν	κύριον·	15. ἐπισκοποῦντες	μή
opsetai	*ton*	*kurion*	*episkopountes*	*mē*
shall see	the	Lord;	looking diligently	not

4948.3 indef-pron nom sing	5139.3 verb nom sing masc part pres act	570.3 prep	3450.10 art gen sing fem	5322.2 noun gen sing fem	3450.2 art gen sing
τις	ὑστερῶν	ἀπὸ	τῆς	χάριτος	τοῦ
tis	*husterōn*	*apo*	*tēs*	*charitos*	*tou*
any	lacking	from	the	grace	

2296.2 noun gen sing masc	3231.1 partic	4948.3 indef-pron nom sing	4347.1 noun nom sing fem	3949.2 noun gen sing fem	504.1 adv
θεοῦ·	μή	τις	ῥίζα	πικρίας	ἄνω
theou	*mē*	*tis*	*rhiza*	*pikrias*	*anō*
of God;	not	any	root	of bitterness	up

15.a.**Txt:** 01ℵ,06D,044 byz.Tisc,Sod
Var: p46,02A,015H 018K,025P,048,6,33,81 104,365,1175,1739 1881,2495

15.b.**Var:** 01ℵ,02A,33 Lach,Treg,Alf,Word Tisc,We/Ho,Weis,Sod UBS/⋆

5289.1 verb nom sing fem part pres act	1760.1 verb 3sing subj pres act	2504.1 conj	1217.2 prep	3642.10 dem-pron gen sing fem
φύουσα	ἐνοχλῇ,	καὶ	‘ διὰ	ταύτης
phuousa	*enochlē*	*kai*	*dia*	*tautēs*
springing	should trouble,	and	by	this

1217.1 prep	840.10 prs-pron gen sing fem	3256.2 verb 3pl subj aor pass	3450.7 art nom pl masc	4044.7 adj nom pl masc
[a⋆ δι’	αὐτῆς]	μιανθῶσιν	[b+ οἱ]	πολλοί·
di’	*autēs*	*mianthōsin*	*hoi*	*polloi*
[by	it]	be defiled	[the]	many;

3231.1 partic	4948.3 indef-pron nom sing	4064.1 noun nom sing masc	2211.1 conj	945.2 adj nom sing masc	5453.1 conj
16. μή	τις	πόρνος	ἢ	βέβηλος,	ὡς
mē	*tis*	*pornos*	*ē*	*bebēlos*	*hōs*
not	any	fornicator	or	profane person,	as

they see discouragement and dispirited living. Verse 13 speaks to the goal of pursuing righteousness on "straight paths." It entails an exhortation to healing through doing what is right. Behaving unrighteously is likened to tripping and twisting or dislocating (*ektrapē*) a joint.

12:14. The figurative language of the previous verse is made explicit here. In line with the heroes of the Faith whom they are to imitate, those who "obtained a good report" (11:2), believers are encouraged to *diōkete,* that is, "pursue, follow hard after" peace. They are also admonished to do the same in regard to holiness because it is absolutely essential for those who will see God. Living by faith in pursuit of a righteous life is not optional; for the Christian it is a necessity.

12:15. The responsibility for self and others is clearly laid on the line by these words. Believers are to oversee one another (*episkopountes*) in order to prevent anyone from falling short (*husterōn,* the same verb found in Romans 3:23) of God's grace. The emphasis here, as it has been throughout the epistle, is on perseverance and endurance. When God's disciplinary instruction comes into believers' lives, some are tempted to become bitter. To complain and rail against His discipline is an improper response. It does not allow for the training and exercise which in the end produces righteousness and peace. Indeed, it is likened to a bitter weed which causes trouble and annoyance; it is a weed which spreads a poisonous contagion. It defiles or stains (*mianthōsin*) many by its presence.

12:16. This verse begins a warning which extends to the end of the chapter (12:29). The seriousness of coming short of God's grace (12:15) evokes the image of Esau. Esau is one of the saddest figures in Bible history. He had so much in his favor, but he failed because he succumbed to fleshly desires—a warning for us against carnality. Believers are to diligently exercise the oversight enjoined in the previous verse in order to keep the immorality and irreligious behavior of Esau from corrupting their congregation.

In one hasty decision, Esau revealed his true character. He was shortsighted. Genesis 25 records how he returned home from the field hungry and for a single meal bartered away his rights as the firstborn son. His exact words were, "Behold, I am at the point to die: and what profit shall this birthright do to me?" (Genesis 25:32). He was not only trading legal privileges and rights of an earthly, material nature, but he was also trampling under foot the covenant of promise which God had made with Abraham. Esau was born as the son of the promise. In trading away his birthright he discounted

13. And make straight paths for your feet: . . . keep your feet in straight paths, *Williams* . . . make level Paths, *Wilson* . . . for your feet to tread in, *Wade.*

lest that which is lame be turned out of the way: Then lameness will not cause your limb, *TNT* . . . so that your lame ankles may not be twisted, *Adams* . . . that the lame limb may not be dislocated through irregularities in the road, *Wade.*

but let it rather be healed: . . . but instead be cured, *Williams.*

14. Follow peace with all [men]: Make it your aim to be at peace with everyone, *TNT* . . . the maintenance of peace, *Wade* . . . Run swiftly after peace, *Montgomery* . . . Try hard to live in peace, *Beck.*

and holiness, without which no man shall see the Lord: Seek holiness, *TNT* . . . and strive for that consecration without which no one, *Williams.*

15. Looking diligently: See to it, *TNT* . . . Continue to look after one another, *Williams* . . . supervising, *Concordant* . . . looking carefully, *Wilson* . . . Keep a watchful eye, *Wade.*

lest any man fail of the grace of God: . . . that no one be wanting of, *Concordant* . . . lest any one fall back from the favor of God, *Wilson* . . . that no one fails to gain God's spiritual blessing, *Williams* . . . that no one falls away from God's grace, *TNT.*

lest any root of bitterness springing up trouble [you]: . . . or some evil like a bitter root, *Williams* . . . no bitterness springs up to cause trouble, *TNT.*

and thereby many be defiled: . . . and be poison to many, *Norlie* . . . and many be stained by it, *Klingensmith* . . . and spoil everybody's life, *TNT* . . . be contaminated by it, *Williams.*

16. Lest there [be] any fornicator, or profane person, as Esau: Let no one be immoral or irreverent, *Norlie* . . . Don't let anyone become a sexual sinner, *SEB* . . . See to it that there is no immoral or worldly person, *TNT* . . . or scorner, *Montgomery* . . . some immoral or godless person like Esau, *Williams.*

Hebrews 12:17

2247.1 name masc	3614.5 rel-pron nom sing masc	470.2 prep	1028.2 noun gen sing fem	1518.6 num card gen fem	586.21 verb 3sing indic aor mid
Ἠσαῦ,	ὃς	ἀντὶ	βρώσεως	μιᾶς	ἀπέδοτο
Esau	*hos*	*anti*	*brōseōs*	*mias*	*apedoto*
Esau,	who	for	meal	one	sold

16.a.**Txt:** 01א-corr 06D-org,018K,020L 025P,byz.Sod **Var:** 01א-org,02A,04C 06D-corr,Lach,Treg,Alf Tisc,We/Ho,Weis UBS/☆

3450.17 art pl neu	4273.1 noun pl neu	840.3 prs-pron gen sing	1431.4 prs-pron gen sing	3471.1 verb 2pl perf act
τὰ	πρωτοτόκια	ˊ αὐτοῦ.	[a ἑαυτοῦ.]	**17.** ἴστε
ta	*prōtotokia*	*autou*	*heautou*	*iste*
the	birthright	his;	[of himself;]	you know

1056.1 conj	3617.1 conj	2504.1 conj	3217.1 adv	2286.12 verb nom sing masc part pres act	2789.8 verb inf aor act
γὰρ	ὅτι	καὶ	μετέπειτα	θέλων	κληρονομῆσαι
gar	*hoti*	*kai*	*metepeita*	*thelōn*	*klēronomēsai*
for	that	also	afterwards,	wishing	to inherit

3450.12 art acc sing fem	2110.4 noun acc sing fem	588.2 verb 3sing indic aor pass	3211.1 noun gen sing fem	1056.1 conj
τὴν	εὐλογίαν	ἀπεδοκιμάσθη·	μετανοίας	γὰρ
tēn	*eulogian*	*apedokimasthē*	*metanoias*	*gar*
the	blessing,	he was rejected,	of repentance	for

4964.4 noun acc sing masc	3620.1 partic	2128.8 verb 3sing indic aor act	2510.1 conj	3196.3 prep	1139.2 noun gen pl neu
τόπον	οὐχ	εὗρεν,	καίπερ	μετὰ	δακρύων
topon	*ouch*	*heuren*	*kaiper*	*meta*	*dakruōn*
place	not	he found,	although	with	tears

1554.5 verb nom sing masc part aor act	840.12 prs-pron acc sing fem	3620.3 partic	1056.1 conj	4193.9 verb 2pl indic perf act
ἐκζητήσας	αὐτήν.	**18.** Οὐ	γὰρ	προσεληλύθατε
ekzētēsas	*autēn*	*Ou*	*gar*	*proselēluthate*
having earnestly sought	it.	Not	for	you have come to

18.a.**Txt:** 06D,018K 020L,byz. **Var:** p46,01א,02A,04C 048,33,it.sa.bo.Lach Treg,Alf,Tisc,We/Ho Weis,Sod,UBS/☆

5419.4 verb dat sing neu part pres mid	3598.3 noun dat sing neu	2504.1 conj	2516.10 verb dat sing neu part perf mid	4300.3 noun dat sing neu
ψηλαφωμένῳ	ˊa ὄρει, ˋ	καὶ	κεκαυμένῳ	πυρὶ,
psēlaphōmenō	*orei*	*kai*	*kekaumenō*	*puri*
being touched	mount	and	having been kindled	with fire,

18.b.**Txt:** 01א-corr 06D-corr,020L,byz. **Var:** 01א-org,02A,04C 06D-org,025P,33,Lach Treg,Alf,Word,Tisc We/Ho,Weis,Sod UBS/☆

2504.1 conj	1099.1 noun dat sing masc	2504.1 conj	4510.2 noun dat sing masc	2200.4 noun dat sing masc	2504.1 conj
καὶ	γνόφῳ,	καὶ	ˊ σκότῳ	[b☆ ζόφῳ]	καὶ
kai	*gnophō*	*kai*	*skotō*	*zophō*	*kai*
and	to obscurity,	and	to darkness,	[to deep gloom]	and

2343.1 noun dat sing fem	2504.1 conj	4393.2 noun gen sing fem	2256.2 noun dat sing neu	2504.1 conj	5292.3 noun dat sing fem
θυέλλῃ,	**19.** καὶ	σάλπιγγος	ἤχῳ,	καὶ	φωνῇ
thuellē	*kai*	*salpingos*	*ēchō*	*kai*	*phōnē*
to tempest,	and	trumpet's	to sound,	and	to voice

4343.5 noun gen pl neu	3614.10 rel-pron gen sing fem	3450.7 art nom pl masc	189.32 verb nom pl masc part aor act	3729.4 verb 3pl indic aor mid
ῥημάτων,	ἧς	οἱ	ἀκούσαντες	παρῃτήσαντο
rhēmatōn	*hēs*	*hoi*	*akousantes*	*parētēsanto*
of words;	which	the	having heard	excused themselves

3231.1 partic	4227.9 verb inf aor pass	840.2 prs-pron dat pl	3030.4 noun acc sing masc	3620.2 partic
μὴ	προστεθῆναι	αὐτοῖς	λόγον·	**20.** οὐκ
mē	*prostethēnai*	*autois*	*logon*	*ouk*
not	to be addressed	to them	word;	not

the spiritual realities inherent in the covenant. In this he was parallel to any of the professing Hebrew believers who were yielding to the pressures around them and abandoning their profession of faith in Jesus as Messiah. In forsaking that profession, they also were abandoning all hope for their eternal future.

who for one morsel of meat sold his birthright: . . . who for a single meal, *Adams* . . . for one feeding, gave up, *Concordant* . . . bartered his birthright, *Wade* . . . he sold his inheritance rights for just one meal! *SEB.*

12:17. The folly of Esau's evaluation and decision is driven home by the reference to his remorse as described in Genesis 27:34,36,38. He did not fully appreciate the uniqueness of the rights which he traded so easily. There was only one birthright. It could not be shared, and Jacob would not give it back because he prized it. Esau's decision was irreversible. Esau gave away a spiritual as well as an earthly inheritance, that is, that the messianic promise might be fulfilled through his line. His loss was irrevocable, he found no place for repentance. Here is a clear warning for us to escape Esau's fate by giving priority to spiritual concerns.

17. For ye know how that afterward: . . . later, *Williams.*

when he would have inherited the blessing, he was rejected: . . . though he wished afterwards, *Wade* . . . he afterward desired to inherit, *Montgomery* . . . wanted to claim, *TNT* . . . he was most anxious to inherit, *Norlie* . . . he wanted to get possession of, *Williams* . . . he was refused, *Wilson* . . . he was turned down, *Klingensmith* . . . his appeal was rejected, *Wade.*

for he found no place of repentance: . . . no opportunity to change his mind, *Adams* . . . he never found an opportunity for repairing his error, *TCNT* . . . He could find no way of undoing what he had done, *TNT* . . . no opportunity of reversing his choice, *Wade.*

though he sought it carefully with tears: . . . though he sought it earnestly, *Montgomery* . . . he tried to get the blessing, *Williams.*

12:18. This verse returns to the same argument used in chapter 2: since believers have received a superior revelation in Jesus Christ, they are subject to a more severe punishment than those who rejected the instructions given when the Lord met with Moses on Mount Sinai. The awesome phenomena and warnings that accompanied the giving of the Law are vividly described. The description depicts the events recorded in Exodus 19:12-25; 20:18. The basic point in Hebrews is in the contrast of verses 18-21 and 22ff. Verse 18 declares, "For ye are not come unto the mount that might be touched." Verses 22-24 stress that believers have come to the heavenly realities associated with Jesus and instituted by Him. The basic thrust then is that disobedience to the heavenly realities will bring a far greater judgment than rejection of the earthly realities that accompanied Moses' institution of the Law. The effect of this contrast is spectacular because of the experience of Israel at Sinai where they were terrified by the fire, smoke, impenetrable darkness, and howling winds.

18. For ye are not come unto the mount that might be touched: . . . tangible in nature, *Wade.*

and that burned with fire: . . . ablaze with fire, *Wade* . . . with its blazing fire that could be felt, *TNT.*

nor unto blackness, and darkness, and tempest: . . . there is now no gloom, or pitch-darkness, or storm, *Norlie* . . . and a whirlwind, *Adams* . . . and to murk, *Wade.*

12:19. In a rising crescendo of trumpets, the thunderous voice of the Lord spoke to Moses, and the people of Israel were filled with dread. In their fear they cried out to Moses, "Speak thou with us, and we will hear: but let not God speak with us, lest we die" (Exodus 20:19).

19. And the sound of a trumpet, and the voice of words: . . . and the blare of a trumpet and an audible voice, *Montgomery* . . . and trumpet-blast, *Williams* . . . and oracular voice, *TNT* . . . a Speaking voice, *Wade.*

which [voice] they that heard entreated: . . . so alarming, *Wade* . . . and a voice whose words made the hearers beg, *Williams.*

that the word should not be spoken to them any more: . . . that not a word more should be added, *Williams* . . . that they should not have to hear any more, *TNT.*

12:20,21. Death by stoning or arrow was the penalty for merely touching Mount Sinai during the time the Lord was speaking to

5179.22 verb 3pl indic imperf act	1056.1 conj	3450.16 art sing neu	1285.1 verb sing neu part pres mid	2550.1 conj
ἔφερον	γὰρ	τὸ	διαστελλόμενον,	Κἂν
epheron	*gar*	*to*	*diastellomenon*	*Kan*
they were bearing	for	the	being commanded:	And

2319.1 noun sing neu	2322.2 verb 3sing subj aor act	3450.2 art gen sing	3598.2 noun gen sing neu	3010.7 verb 3sing indic fut pass
θηρίον	θίγῃ	τοῦ	ὄρους	λιθοβοληθήσεται
thērion	*thigē*	*tou*	*orous*	*lithobolēthēsetai*
if a beast	should touch	the	mountain,	it shall be stoned,

20.a.**Txt:** Steph
Var: 01ℵ,02A,04C,06D 018K,020L,025P,byz. Gries,Lach,Treg,Alf Word,Tisc,We/Ho,Weis Sod,UBS/☆

2211.1 conj	995.1 noun dat sing fem	2669.1 verb 3sing indic fut pass	2504.1 conj	3643.1 adv
(a ἢ	βολίδι	κατατοξευθήσεται·)	**21.** καί,	οὕτως
ē	*bolidi*	*katatoxeuthēsetai*	*kai*	*houtōs*
or	with a dart	shall be shot through;	and,	so

5235.2 adj sing neu	1498.34 verb sing indic imperf act	3450.16 art sing neu	5162.1 verb sing neu part pres mid	3337.1 name nom masc
φοβερὸν	ἦν	τὸ	φανταζόμενον,	‘ Μωσῆς
phoberon	*ēn*	*to*	*phantazomenon*	*Mōsēs*
fearful	was	the thing	appearing	Moses

3338.1 name nom masc	1500.5 verb 3sing indic aor act	1616.1 adj nom sing masc	1498.2 verb 1sing indic pres act	2504.1 conj
[☆ Μωϋσῆς]	εἶπεν,	Ἔκφοβός	εἰμι	καὶ
Mōusēs	*eipen*	*Ekphobos*	*eimi*	*kai*
[idem]	said,	greatly afraid	I am	and

1774.1 adj nom sing masc	233.2 conj	4193.9 verb 2pl indic perf act	4477.1 name fem	3598.3 noun dat sing neu	2504.1 conj
ἔντρομος·	**22.** ἀλλὰ	προσεληλύθατε	Σιὼν	ὄρει,	καὶ
entromos	*alla*	*proselēluthate*	*Siōn*	*orei*	*kai*
trembling:	but	you have come to	Zion	mount;	and

4032.3 noun dat sing fem	2296.2 noun gen sing masc	2180.11 verb gen sing part pres act	2395.2 name fem	2016.5 adj dat sing fem	2504.1 conj
πόλει	θεοῦ	ζῶντος,	Ἰερουσαλὴμ	ἐπουρανίῳ,	καὶ
polei	*theou*	*zōntos*	*Ierousalēm*	*epouraniō*	*kai*
city	of God	living,	Jerusalem	heavenly;	and

3323.3 noun dat pl fem	32.6 noun gen pl masc	3693.1 noun dat sing fem	2504.1 conj	1564.3 noun dat sing fem
μυριάσιν	ἀγγέλων	**23.** πανηγύρει,	καὶ	ἐκκλησίᾳ
muriasin	*angelōn*	*panēgurei*	*kai*	*ekklēsia*
to myriads	of angels,	universal gathering;	and	to assembly

4274.3 adj gen pl masc	1706.1 prep	3636.8 noun dat pl masc	578.3 verb gen pl masc part perf mid
πρωτοτόκων	‘ ἐν	οὐρανοῖς	ἀπογεγραμμένων,
prōtotokōn	*en*	*ouranois*	*apogegrammenōn*
of firstborn	in	heavens	having been registered;

23.a.**Txt:** 0228,byz.Sod
Var: p46,01ℵ,02A,04C 06D,020L,025P,044 048,0121b,33,81,104 365,1175,1739,1881 2495

578.3 verb gen pl masc part perf mid	1706.1 prep	3636.8 noun dat pl masc	2504.1 conj	2896.2 noun dat sing masc
[a☆ ἀπογεγραμμένων	ἐν	οὐρανοῖς,]	καὶ	κριτῇ
apogegrammenōn	*en*	*ouranois*	*kai*	*kritē*
[having been enrolled	in	heavens,]	and	to judge

2296.3 noun dat sing masc	3820.4 adj gen pl	2504.1 conj	4011.7 noun dat pl neu	1337.7 adj gen pl masc
θεῷ	πάντων,	καὶ	πνεύμασιν	δικαίων
theō	*pantōn*	*kai*	*pneumasin*	*dikaiōn*
God	of all;	and	to spirits	of just

Moses. It was applied to both men and beast. The contrast here is the difficulty of approaching God under the old covenant as compared with the easy access through Jesus Christ. The experience was so frightful that even Moses, the peerless leader, feared "exceedingly."

12:22. Verse 22 contrasts God's revelation in the new covenant with the terror and unapproachability of the Lord as He revealed himself in the wilderness. The city which the patriarchal nomads sought had now come. First-century Christians had come to it. They lived at the beginning of the age of fulfillment, not in the age of promise. They entered into the very presence of God in the heavenly sanctuary through Jesus Christ (9:24); they were no longer limited to the annual representation of a dying high priest in an earthly tabernacle or temple. In Christ Jesus they had direct access to the living God at any time. The angels, whom so many of them may have been concerned about because they felt they were a part of the Jewish religious system, were in the presence of the living God by the myriads (tens of thousands). They are still in the service of God for His people (1:14). There is no dread and terror for believers in approaching God. The fire, blackness, smoke, trumpets, and thunderous voice have been replaced by light and splendor. The "do not even touch" has become "come and see."

12:23. The first word of this verse (*panēgurei*) sets the tone of the contrast most specifically; it could be translated "festal assembly." It sets a scene of joy and celebration which easily overshadows the darkness and terror of Sinai. The gathering is styled *ekklēsia prōtotokōn*, "church of the firstborn." This is a picture of the true Church Universal. It is more than an organization, no matter how effective and blessed its ministry may be. It is an organism, composed of all true believers, born into the family of God.

This portrayal has staggering implications. It indicates that all believers are on an equal basis in Jesus Christ. And what a basis it is: they are all firstborn heirs, those to whom a double portion of the inheritance is due. This was no vague hope. Their names were already enrolled in the lists of those who possess citizenship in the heavenly Jerusalem. This was quite a mind-boggling image to Christians in the Early Church who lived in an empire that had many cities composed of 80 percent slaves and only 20 percent citizens. Their God, the living God, is also the One who in the end will judge every man. Christians may be discouraged and downtrodden by the corruption and injustice they are experiencing in this life, but they can be assured of justice in the heavenly city. When they look around Zion, they will meet "the spirits of just men made perfect." They are numbered among the righteous who have been made complete in the Son.

20. (For they could not endure that which was commanded: They could not stand what was ordered, *SEB* . . . they did not try to bear the order, *Williams* . . . could not endure the injunction, *Wilson.*

And if so much as a beast touch the mountain: . . . that even an animal which touched, *TNT* . . . if a wild animal, *Williams.*

it shall be stoned, or thrust through with a dart: . . . it shall be pelted with stones, *Concordant* . . . must be stoned to death, *Williams.*

21. And so terrible was the sight: . . . as he looked at the apalling sight, *Norlie* . . . so terrifying, *Williams* . . . was the scene, *Montgomery.*

[that] Moses said, I exceedingly fear and quake:): I am trembling with fear, *Adams* . . . I am terrified, *Beck* . . . and terror-stricken! *Williams.*

22. But ye are come unto mount Sion: No, you stand before, *TNT.*

and unto the city of the living God, the heavenly Jerusalem:

and to an innumerable company of angels: . . . to myriads of angels, *Adams, Wilson* . . . to countless hosts of angels, *TCNT* . . . and its mighty host of angels, *TNT.*

23. To the general assembly and church of the firstborn: You are in the presence of the joyous assembly, *TNT* . . . to a universal convocation, *Concordant* . . . to the festal gathering and assembly of God's firstborn sons, *Williams* . . . enrolled in heaven, *Klingensmith.*

which are written in heaven: . . . whose names are written, *TNT* . . . enrolled as citizens in heaven, *Williams* . . . registered in heaven, *Montgomery.*

and to God the Judge of all: . . . to a Judge who is the God of all, *Williams* . . . of all men, *TNT.*

and to the spirits of just men made perfect: . . . who have been brought to completeness, *Wuest* . . . of just ones completed, *Klingensmith* . . . of upright men who have attained perfection, *Williams* . . . and the spirits of good men who have been made perfect, *TNT.*

4896.17 verb gen pl masc part perf mid	2504.1 conj	1236.2 noun gen sing fem	3365.3 adj fem	3186.3 noun dat sing masc
τετελειωμένων,	24. καὶ	διαθήκης	νέας	μεσίτῃ
teteleiōmenōn	*kai*	*diathēkēs*	*neas*	*mesitē*
having been perfected;	and	of a covenant	fresh	mediator

24.a.**Txt:** 33,Steph
Var: 01ℵ,02A,04C,06D 018K,020L,025P,byz. Gries,Lach,Treg,Alf Word,Tisc,We/Ho,Weis Sod,UBS/⋆

2400.2 name masc	2504.1 conj	129.3 noun dat sing neu	4330.1 noun gen sing masc	2882.3 adj comp
Ἰησοῦ,	καὶ	αἵματι	ῥαντισμοῦ	' κρεῖττονα
Iēsou	*kai*	*haimati*	*rhantismou*	*kreittona*
to Jesus;	and	to blood	of sprinkling,	better things

25.a.**Txt:** 01ℵ-corr 06D-corr,018K,020L byz.
Var: 01ℵ-org,02A,04C 025P,33,Lach,Treg,Alf Tisc,We/Ho,Weis,Sod UBS/⋆

2882.5 adj comp sing neu	2953.14 verb dat sing masc part pres act	3706.2 prep	3450.6 art acc sing masc	6.2 name masc
[a⋆ κρεῖττον]	λαλοῦντι	παρὰ	τὸν	''Ἄβελ.
kreitton	*lalounti*	*para*	*ton*	*Habel*
[a better thing]	speaking	than		Abel.

25.b.**Txt:** 01ℵ-corr,018K 020L,byz.
Var: 01ℵ-org,02A,04C 025P,33,Lach,Treg,Alf Tisc,We/Ho,Weis,Sod UBS/⋆

984.1 verb 2pl pres act	3231.1 partic	3729.5 verb 2pl subj aor mid	3450.6 art acc sing masc	2953.15 verb acc sing masc part pres act
25. Βλέπετε	μὴ	παραιτήσησθε	τὸν	λαλοῦντα.
Blepete	*mē*	*paraitēsēsthe*	*ton*	*lalounta*
Take heed	not	you refuse	the	speaking.

25.c.**Txt:** Steph
Var: 01ℵ,02A,04C,06D 018K,020L,025P,byz. Gries,Lach,Treg,Alf Word,Tisc,We/Ho,Weis Sod,UBS/⋆

1479.1 conj	1056.1 conj	1552.6 dem-pron nom pl masc	3620.2 partic	5180.6 verb 3pl indic aor act	1614.1 verb indic aor act
εἰ	γὰρ	ἐκεῖνοι	οὐκ	' ἔφυγον,	[a⋆ ἐξέφυγον]
ei	*gar*	*ekeinoi*	*ouk*	*ephugon*	*exephugon*
If	for	those	not	escaped,	[idem]

25.d.**Var:** 01ℵ-org,02A 04C,06D,33,Lach,Treg Alf,Tisc,We/Ho,Weis Sod,UBS/⋆

3450.6 art acc sing masc	1894.3 prep	3450.10 art gen sing fem	1087.2 noun gen sing fem	3729.6 verb nom pl masc part aor mid	3450.6 art acc sing masc
(b τὸν)	ἐπὶ	(c τῆς)	γῆς	παραιτησάμενοι	[d⋆+ τὸν]
ton	*epi*	*tēs*	*gēs*	*paraitēsamenoi*	*ton*
the	on	the	earth	having refused	[the]

25.e.**Txt:** 06D-corr,018K 020L,025P,byz.
Var: 01ℵ,02A,04C 06D-org,33,Lach,Treg Alf,Tisc,We/Ho,Weis Sod,UBS/⋆

5372.1 verb acc sing masc part pres act	4044.3 adj dat sing	4044.16 adj sing neu	3095.1 adv comp	2231.1 prs-pron nom 1pl
χρηματίζοντα,	' πολλῷ	[e⋆ πολὺ]	μᾶλλον	ἡμεῖς
chrēmatizonta	*pollō*	*polu*	*mallon*	*hēmeis*
divinely instructing,	much	[idem]	more	we

3450.7 art nom pl masc	3450.6 art acc sing masc	570.2 prep	3636.7 noun gen pl masc	648.7 verb nom pl masc part pres mid
οἱ	τὸν	ἀπ'	οὐρανῶν	ἀποστρεφόμενοι,
hoi	*ton*	*ap'*	*ouranōn*	*apostrephomenoi*
the	him	from	heavens	turning away from!

3614.2 rel-pron gen sing	3450.9 art nom sing fem	5292.1 noun nom sing fem	3450.12 art acc sing fem	1087.4 noun acc sing fem	4388.2 verb 3sing indic aor act
26. οὗ	ἡ	φωνὴ	τὴν	γῆν	ἐσάλευσεν
hou	*hē*	*phōnē*	*tēn*	*gēn*	*esaleusen*
whose	the	voice	the	earth	shook

4966.1 adv	3431.1 adv	1156.2 conj	1846.7 verb 3sing indic perf mid	2978.15 verb nom sing masc part pres act	2068.1 adv
τότε,	νῦν	δὲ	ἐπήγγελται,	λέγων,	Ἔτι
tote	*nun*	*de*	*epēngeltai*	*legōn*	*Eti*
then;	now	but	he has promised,	saying,	Yet

26.a.**Txt:** 06D,018K 020L,025P,byz.Sod
Var: 01ℵ,02A,04C,33 sa.bo.Lach,Treg,Alf,Tisc We/Ho,Weis,UBS/⋆

526.1 adv	1466.1 prs-pron nom 1sing	4434.1 verb 1sing indic pres act	4434.5 verb 1sing indic fut act	3620.3 partic	3303.1 adv
ἅπαξ	ἐγὼ	' σείω	[a⋆ σείσω]	οὐ	μόνον
hapax	*egō*	*seiō*	*seisō*	*ou*	*monon*
once	I	shake	[will shake]	not	only

12:24. Here, by direct and explicit statement, the inspired writer returned to the previous argument concerning the superiority of Jesus as the Mediator of God's promised new covenant. The words of verse 24 evoke memories of all the blessings secured by the high priesthood of One who has been made an eternal Melchizedekian priest. The blood of Abel, shed by his brother Cain, still cries out in condemnation of Cain; the blood of Jesus, shed by His brethren, still cleanses the consciences of sinners and covers them when they come to God in prayer.

12:25. Since these tremendous benefits belong to those who embrace Jesus the Son, they ought not to reject the message which God is yet delivering through Jesus' "blood of sprinkling" (verse 24). Since the Children of Israel, wandering in the desert with limited access to the Lord, were not able to escape the God of Sinai when they rejected His message, it will be even more impossible for Christians to escape God the Son who came from heaven (John 3:31; 6:38) if they turn aside from Him.

Pondering all this Carter wrote: "A comparison is employed to make vivid and emphatic the distinction between the Mosaic and the Christian eras (cf. Hebrews 2:2, 3). The author reveals that the greater responsibility rests upon the Christian believers because of their higher privileges in Christ. Grace makes the Christian's moral and spiritual responsibility to God greater than was the Jew's under the law. The meaning of the word refuse here appears not to be a stubborn and rebellious rejection of Christ, but rather a sort of begging-off (cf. Luke 14:18; Hebrews 12:1), or excuses and withdrawals (cf. Hebrews 10:38). Such an excusing, evasive, withdrawing, responsibility-shunning attitude is almost certain ultimately to lead the soul to turn away from him that warneth from heaven. When the believer begins to deprecate the blessings and benefits of Christ and the Christian religion, he will end in departing from the living God, unless he experiences a radical change of attitude (cf. Psalm 1:1)" (*The Wesleyan Bible Commentary*, pp.168,169).

12:26. God thundered from Sinai and the earth shook, but the days of dread and doom are not all past. The promise of future judgment of heaven and earth, referred to here, was spoken to the remnant of Jews who were building the temple after they had returned from Babylon (Haggai 2:6). They were few in number and beset on every side by enemies—Arabs, Ammonites, Samaritans, and the governor of the neighboring province. They were discouraged because some of the old-timers remembered the glory of Solomon's Temple and thought the new temple was insignificant in comparison. But through Haggai, the Lord promised the future glory of their temple and His judgment of their enemies. This same promise is yet to be fulfilled and speaks hope to discouraged Christians who think of quitting.

24. And to Jesus the mediator of the new covenant: Now you meet Jesus, *Noli* . . . through whom the new covenant has been made, *TNT* . . . of a fresh covenant, *Concordant.*

and to the blood of sprinkling: . . . you are sprinkled with his blood, *Noli* . . . to his sprinkled Blood, *Montgomery* . . . and whose shed blood, *TNT.*

that speaketh better things than [that of] Abel: . . . has far better things to say to us than Abel's, *TNT* . . . which is more powerful than, *Noli* . . . that speaks in nobler accents, *Wade* . . . whose message cries louder, *Montgomery* . . . which speaks a better message than even, *Williams.*

25. See that ye refuse not him that speaketh: Take care that you do not refuse to hear, *TNT* . . . Be sure you listen to the One Who is speaking, *NLT* . . . lest you should reject Him, *Wilson.*

For if they escaped not: . . . if there was no escape for those, *Wade* . . . have paid the penalty for their disobedience, *Noli.*

who refused him that spake on earth: . . . when they refused to listen to their instructor, *Montgomery* . . . because they refused to listen to him who warned them here on earth, *Williams* . . . uttered His warnings from an earthly Height, *Wade.*

much more [shall not] we [escape]: What chance have we of escaping, *TNT* . . . how much less can we, *Williams* . . . We are going to be punished more severely, *Noli.*

if we turn away from him that [speaketh] from heaven: . . . if we reject, *Williams* . . . if we turn our backs on the one, *TNT* . . . who turn a deaf ear to Him, *Wade* . . . who warns us from heaven, *Beck.*

26. Whose voice then shook the earth: God's voice shook the earth then, *TNT* . . . made the earth to rock, *Wade* . . . at the time, *Noli.*

but now he hath promised, saying: . . . whereas now He has given an assurance in these words, *Wade* . . . Now he has warned us again, *Noli.*

Yet once more I shake: Once more I will make...to tremble, *Williams* . . . again, once for all, I will cause...to quake, *Wade.*

3450.12 art acc sing fem	1087.4 noun acc sing fem	233.2 conj	2504.1 conj	3450.6 art acc sing masc	3636.4 noun acc sing masc
τὴν	γῆν,	ἀλλὰ	καὶ	τὸν	οὐρανόν.
tēn	*gēn*	*alla*	*kai*	*ton*	*ouranon*
the	earth,	but	also	the	heaven.

3450.16 art sing neu	1156.2 conj	2068.1 adv	526.1 adv	1207.1 verb 3sing indic pres act	3450.1 art gen pl
27. Τὸ	δέ	Ἔτι	ἅπαξ,	δηλοῖ	⸂ τῶν
To	*de*	*Eti*	*hapax*	*dēloi*	*tōn*
The	but	Yet	once,	signifies	of the

4388.6 verb gen pl neu part pres mid	3450.12 art acc sing fem	3450.12 art acc sing fem	3450.1 art gen pl	4388.6 verb gen pl neu part pres mid
σαλευομένων	τὴν	[☆ τὴν	τῶν	σαλευομένων]
saleuomenōn	*tēn*	*tēn*	*tōn*	*saleuomenōn*
being shaken	the	[the	of the	being shaken]

3201.3 noun acc sing fem	5453.1 conj	4020.71 verb gen pl part perf mid	2419.1 conj	3176.19 verb 3sing subj aor act	3450.17 art pl neu
μετάθεσιν,	ὡς	πεποιημένων,	ἵνα	μείνῃ	τὰ
metathesin	*hōs*	*pepoiēmenōn*	*hina*	*meinē*	*ta*
removing,	as	having been made,	that	may remain	the

3231.1 partic	4388.5 verb pl neu part pres mid	1346.1 conj	926.4 noun acc sing fem	755.2 adj acc sing fem
μὴ	σαλευόμενα.	**28.** Διὸ	βασιλείαν	ἀσάλευτον
mē	*saleuomena*	*Dio*	*basileian*	*asaleuton*
not	being shaken.	Wherefore	a kingdom	not to be shaken

28.a.**Txt:** p46-corr,02A 04C,06D,0121b,byz. UBS/☆
Var: p46-org,01ℵ,018K 025P,044,6,33,104,326 365,629,1881,2495,Sod

3741.3 verb nom pl masc part pres act	2174.8 verb 1pl subj pres act	2174.5 verb 1pl indic pres act	5322.4 noun acc sing fem	1217.1 prep
παραλαμβάνοντες,	⸀☆ ἔχωμεν	[a ἔχομεν]	χάριν,	δι'
paralambanontes	*echōmen*	*echomen*	*charin*	*di'*
receiving,	may we have	[we have]	grace,	by

28.b.**Txt:** 02A,06D,020L 048,33,326,1739,sa. UBS/☆
Var: 01ℵ,044,0121b,byz.

3614.10 rel-pron gen sing fem	2973.3 verb 1pl subj pres act	2973.13 verb 1pl indic pres act	2081.1 adv
ἧς	⸀☆ λατρεύωμεν	[b λατρεύομεν]	εὐαρέστως
hēs	*latreuōmen*	*latreuomen*	*euarestōs*
which	we may serve	[we serve]	well pleasingly

3450.3 art dat sing	2296.3 noun dat sing masc	3196.3 prep	127.1 noun gen sing fem	2504.1 conj	2105.1 noun gen sing fem
τῷ	θεῷ	μετὰ	⸂ αἰδοῦς	καὶ	εὐλαβείας.
tō	*theō*	*meta*	*aidous*	*kai*	*eulabeias*
	God	with	respect	and	reverence.

28.c.**Txt:** 018K,020L,byz.
Var: 01ℵ-org,02A,04C 06D-org,33,sa.bo.Lach Treg,Alf,Tisc,We/Ho Weis,Sod,UBS/☆

2105.1 noun gen sing fem	2504.1 conj	1183.1 noun gen sing neu	2504.1 conj	1056.1 conj	3450.5 art nom sing masc
[c☆ εὐλαβείας	καὶ	δέους·]	**29.** καὶ	γὰρ	ὁ
eulabeias	*kai*	*deous*	*kai*	*gar*	*ho*
[reverence	and	awe.]	Also	for	

2296.1 noun nom sing masc	2231.2 prs-pron gen 1pl	4300.1 noun sing neu	2624.1 verb sing neu part pres act	3450.9 art nom sing fem
θεὸς	ἡμῶν	πῦρ	καταναλίσκον.	**13:1.** Ἡ
theos	*hēmōn*	*pur*	*katanaliskon*	*Hē*
God	our	a fire	consuming.	The

5197.1 noun nom sing fem	3176.9 verb 3sing impr pres act	3450.10 art gen sing fem	5218.1 noun gen sing fem	3231.1 partic
φιλαδελφία	μενέτω.	**2.** τῆς	φιλοξενίας	μὴ
philadelphia	*menetō*	*tēs*	*philoxenias*	*mē*
brotherly love	let abide;	of the	hospitality	not

12:27. Chapter 12 closes with an explanation of the significance of the quotation from Haggai 2:6 for professing Christians and then draws pointed attention to the value of fear as a deterrent to apostatizing from the Faith. The certainty of God's justice has relevance for the Christian's value system. In the judgment, the Lord will remove everything that is not of lasting value: His enemies, the enemies of believers, pain, death, sickness, drudgery, poverty, famine, disease, sorrow, suffering, and persecution. That which remains will be unshakable. The implication is that if anyone turns aside from his profession of faith in Jesus, he is like Esau—nearsighted. He will be trading short-range fulfillment of desire (escape from his sufferings for Jesus' sake) at the expense of an "eternal weight of glory" (2 Corinthians 4:17), citizenship in God's unshakable kingdom.

12:28. Since Christians are citizens in God's eternal kingdom, they are exhorted to "keep on holding on" (*echōmen*) to God's grace. His grace will see them through their current trials. More importantly, it will enable them to worship and serve God as priests (*latreuōmen*) whose sacrifices, like those offered by Abel, are acceptable to the Lord, because they are offered out of an attitude of reverence (*eulabeias*, recognition of God's greatness, righteousness, and sovereignty).

12:29. The alternative to pious service and endurance by God's grace is apostasy which incurs God's wrath. His wrath is a fire which devours everything in its path. Believers ought to heed the words of Jesus not to fear men but to fear God who is able to destroy them spiritually in hell (Matthew 10:28).

13:1. The first 19 verses of chapter 13 consist of a series of exhortations instructing Christians how to live in obedience to the new covenant by offering their lives as living sacrifices in their priestly service and worship. The first exhortation (verse 1) goes to the heart of the new covenant. Jesus wrapped up the whole Law in commandments by enjoining complete love for God and love for neighbor. In the Upper Room as He prepared His disciples for His imminent death, He declared that the mark which would distinguish believers was a new commandment: loving one another.

Verse 1 is not a random exhortation disconnected from the rest of the epistle; it is a timely reminder of the essential sign of true discipleship. James's epistle says that those who do not live by Jesus' "royal law" (James 2:8) are guilty of living a lie "against the truth" (James 3:14).

13:2. Hospitality (*philoxenias*, "love of strangers"), according to Jesus' Parable of the Good Samaritan, is included in love of neigh-

not the earth only, but also heaven: . . . not only the Earth but also the very Heaven, *Wade* . . . but heaven as well, *TNT.*

27. And this [word], Yet once more: Now that expression, "Once more," *Williams* . . . Yet again, *Wade.*

signifieth the removing of those things that are shaken: . . . implies the final passing away of all that can be shaken, *Wade* . . . the final removal, *Williams.*

as of things that are made: . . . the whole order of created things, *TNT* . . . as being created and material, *Wade.*

that those things which cannot be shaken may remain: . . . in order that the realities which are incapable of being shaken (since they are immaterial) may alone remain, *Wade.*

28. Wherefore we receiving a kingdom which cannot be moved: Accordingly let us who are to receive a Dominion which is proof against any shock, *Wade* . . . accepting an unshakable kingdom, *Concordant* . . . which is unshakable, *Montgomery.*

let us have grace: Let us, therefore, be thankful, *Williams.*

whereby we may serve God acceptably: . . . let us offer him the worship he can accept, *TNT* . . . this will enable us to offer acceptably to God, *Wade.*

with reverence and godly fear: . . . with conscientiousness and awe, *Wade* . . . with holy awe, *Montgomery.*

29. For our God [is] a consuming fire: . . . is a fire that destroys everything, *NLT* . . . is destroying fire, *Klingensmith* . . . is indeed an all-devouring fire, *TNT.*

1. Let brotherly love continue: As brothers in Christ, never cease loving one another, *TNT* . . . Christians, keep on loving one another, *Beck* . . . must be maintained, *Adams* . . . continue to love one another, *Norlie.*

2. Be not forgetful to entertain strangers: Do not neglect to show hospitality, *Montgomery* . . . Don't forget to welcome strangers, *SEB* . . . to open your homes, *TNT* . . . Do not remain neglectful of hospitality to strangers, *Williams.*

1935.1 verb 2pl impr pres mid	**1217.2** prep	**3642.10** dem-pron gen sing fem	**1056.1** conj	**2963.5** verb 3pl indic aor act	**4948.7** indef-pron nom pl masc
ἐπιλανθάνεσθε·	διὰ	ταύτης	γὰρ	ἔλαθόν	τινες
epilanthanesthe	*dia*	*tautēs*	*gar*	*elathon*	*tines*
be forgetful;	by	this	for	unawares	some

3441.3 verb nom pl masc part aor act	**32.8** noun acc pl masc	**3267.2** verb 2pl impr pres mid	**3450.1** art gen pl	**1192.4** noun gen pl masc
ξενίσαντες	ἀγγέλους.	**3.** μιμνῄσκεσθε	τῶν	δεσμίων,
xenisantes	*angelous*	*mimnēskesthe*	*tōn*	*desmiōn*
having entertained	angels.	Be mindful	of the	prisoners,

5453.1 conj	**4737.1** verb nom pl masc part perf mid	**3450.1** art gen pl	**2529.2** verb gen pl masc part pres mid	**5453.1** conj
ὡς	συνδεδεμένοι·	τῶν	κακουχουμένων,	ὡς
hōs	*sundedemenoi*	*tōn*	*kakouchoumenōn*	*hōs*
as	having been bound with;	the	being evil treated,	as

2504.1 conj	**840.7** prs-pron nom pl masc	**1498.23** verb nom pl masc part pres act	**1706.1** prep	**4835.3** noun dat sing neu	**4941.2** adj nom sing masc
καὶ	αὐτοὶ	ὄντες	ἐν	σώματι.	**4.** Τίμιος
kai	*autoi*	*ontes*	*en*	*sōmati*	*Timios*
also	yourselves	being	in	body.	Honorable

3450.5 art nom sing masc	**1055.1** noun nom sing masc	**1706.1** prep	**3820.5** adj dat pl	**2504.1** conj	**3450.9** art nom sing fem	**2818.1** noun nom sing fem
ὁ	γάμος	ἐν	πᾶσιν,	καὶ	ἡ	κοίτη
ho	*gamos*	*en*	*pasin*	*kai*	*hē*	*koitē*
the	marriage	in	every,	and	the	bed

4.a.**Txt:** 04C,06D-corr 018K,020L,byz.
Var: 01ℵ,02A,06D-org 025P,bo.Lach,Treg,Alf Tisc,We/Ho,Weis,Sod UBS/☆

281.1 adj nom sing	**4064.4** noun acc pl masc	**1156.2** conj	**1056.1** conj	**2504.1** conj	**3295.2** noun acc pl masc
ἀμίαντος·	πόρνους	‘ δὲ	[a☆ γὰρ]	καὶ	μοιχοὺς
amiantos	*pornous*	*de*	*gar*	*kai*	*moichous*
undefiled;	fornicators	but	[for]	and	adulterers

2892.25 verb 3sing indic fut act	**3450.5** art nom sing masc	**2296.1** noun nom sing masc	**859.1** adj nom sing masc	**3450.5** art nom sing masc
κρινεῖ	ὁ	θεός.	**5.** Ἀφιλάργυρος	ὁ
krinei	*ho*	*theos*	*Aphilarguros*	*ho*
will judge		God.	Without love of money	the

4999.1 noun nom sing masc	**708.6** verb nom pl masc part pres mid	**3450.4** art dat pl	**3780.11** verb dat pl neu part pres act	**840.5** prs-pron nom sing masc
τρόπος·	ἀρκούμενοι	τοῖς	παροῦσιν·	αὐτὸς
tropos	*arkoumenoi*	*tois*	*parousin*	*autos*
manner of life,	being satisfied	with the	being present;	he

1056.1 conj	**2029.3** verb 3sing indic perf act	**3620.3** partic	**3231.1** partic	**4622.4** prs-pron acc 2sing	**445.2** verb 1sing subj aor act	**3624.2** adv
γὰρ	εἴρηκεν,	Οὐ	μή	σε	ἀνῶ,	οὐδ’
gar	*eirēken*	*Ou*	*mē*	*se*	*anō*	*oud'*
for	has said,	No	not	you	will I leave,	nor

5.a.**Txt:** 06D-org,81,326 365,629,630,945,1175 2495
Var: p46,01ℵ,02A,04C 06D-corr2,044,0121b byz.Tisc

3620.3 partic	**3231.1** partic	**4622.4** prs-pron acc 2sing	**1452.5** verb 1sing subj aor act	**1452.9** verb 1sing indic pres act
οὐ	μή	σε	‘☆ ἐγκαταλίπω.	[a ἐγκαταλείπω.]
ou	*mē*	*se*	*enkatalipō*	*enkataleipō*
not	not	you	will I forsake.	[idem]

5452.1 conj	**2269.4** verb acc pl masc part pres act	**2231.4** prs-pron acc 1pl	**2978.24** verb inf pres act	**2935.1** noun nom sing masc	**1466.5** prs-pron dat 1sing
6. ὥστε	θαρροῦντας	ἡμᾶς	λέγειν,	Κύριος	ἐμοὶ
hōste	*tharrhountas*	*hēmas*	*legein*	*Kurios*	*emoi*
So that	boldly	we	to say,	Lord	to me

bor. Moreover, the patriarchs Abraham and Lot (Genesis 18:2ff.; 19:1ff.) entertained strangers who turned out to be angels sent from the Lord.

13:3. The admonition here was for the Hebrew Christians to continue to identify themselves with those who had been imprisoned because of their faith in Jesus. They were not to abandon these fellow believers out of fear for their own safety. They were one with those who were "in bonds" and must continue to feel their sufferings and needs as their own (6:10; 10:32-34). Since they themselves had not yet entered eternity but remained in their earthly bodies, they could yet face the same sufferings.

13:4. While on the subject of love, the inspired writer spoke of the value of marriage. It is not to be disdained but held in high regard. Perhaps this declaration was necessary because of the influence of the Hellenistic culture which surrounded the early Christians. Many Greek philosophers taught that the body and its sexual functions were either evil or inferior.

This verse places a high value on the marriage relationship. The word *timios,* "honorable," could be translated as "costly." The Christian is to value his relationship with his spouse so highly that he will avoid defiling the *koitē* or marriage "bed" by keeping himself from any kind of sexual relationship outside of the marriage union and from adulterous relationships while married. Premarital sex, sodomy, prostitution, and homosexual acts are all included in the term *pornous,* and, like adultery, they will fall under the judgment of our holy God.

13:5. Since Christians look for a future kingdom which is both unshakable and heavenly, they are not to concentrate their affections and efforts upon the accumulation of worldly wealth. The believer's *tropos,* "life-style," should be "without covetousness," i.e., *aphilarguros,* "without love of silver." A Christian should be satisfied with the things which he already possesses. The primary focus here is not on worldly possessions, but on the spiritual wealth possessed in Jesus Christ, particularly focused in the Lord's promise never to leave His people (Joshua 1:5; also Matthew 28:20).

13:6. The result of the Lord's abiding presence in the midst of His people is courage. Knowing that He is with them, they are filled with confidence and boldness. They echo the words of Psalm

for thereby some have entertained angels unawares: . . . have had angels as their guests, *Norlie* . . . heavenly messengers without knowing it, *Klingensmith* . . . without realizing it, *Adams* . . . unconsciously, *Wilson.*

3. Remember them that are in bonds, as bound with them: . . . remember those who are in prison, as though you were in prison with them, *Williams.*

[and] them which suffer adversity: . . . of those maltreated, *Concordant* . . . and those mistreated, *Klingensmith* . . . ill-treated, *Williams.*

as being yourselves also in the body: . . . since you, too, are liable to similar physical punishment, *Williams.*

4. Marriage [is] honourable in all: The married state should be regarded as, *TCNT* . . . must be honored by everybody, *Adams* . . . should be respected by everyone, *NLT* . . . should think highly of marriage and keep married life pure, *Beck.*

and the bed undefiled: . . . and the marriage bed must be unpolluted, *Adams* . . . and the marriage relations kept sacred, *Williams.*

but whoremongers and adulterers God will judge: Persons who are sexually vicious and immoral God will punish, *Williams.*

5. [Let your] conversation [be] without covetousness: You must not be lovers of money, *Norlie* . . . You must have a turn of mind that is free from avarice, *Williams* . . . May fondness for money not be your manner, *Concordant* . . . Let your life be untainted by love of money, *Montgomery* . . . Don't be greedy, *Beck* . . . Be not of an avaricious disposition, *Wilson.*

[and be] content with such things as ye have: . . . being satisfied with your present circumstances, *Wuest.*

for he hath said:

I will never leave thee, nor forsake thee: . . . nor will I ever abandon you, *TCNT* . . . or desert you, *Beck.*

6. So that we may boldly say: . . . say with complete confidence, *Adams.*

Hebrews 13:7

6.a.**Txt:** 01ℵ-corr,02A 04C-corr,06D,018K 020L,byz.Sod
Var: 01ℵ-org,04C-org 025P,33,bo.Tisc,We/Ho Weis,UBS/☆

991.1 adj nom sing masc	**2504.1** conj	**3620.3** partic	**5236.22** verb 1sing indic fut pass	**4949.9** intr-pron sing neu	**4020.52** verb 3sing indic fut act
βοηθός,	([a] καὶ)	οὐ	φοβηθήσομαι·	τί	ποιήσει
boēthos	*kai*	*ou*	*phobēthēsomai*	*ti*	*poiēsei*
a helper,	and	not	I will be afraid:	what	shall do

1466.4 prs-pron dat 1sing	**442.1** noun nom sing masc	**3285.1** verb 2pl pres act	**3450.1** art gen pl	**2216.8** verb gen pl masc part pres mid
μοι	ἄνθρωπος;	7. Μνημονεύετε	τῶν	ἡγουμένων
moi	*anthrōpos*	*Mnēmoneuete*	*tōn*	*hēgoumenōn*
to me	man?	Remember	the	leaders

5050.2 prs-pron gen 2pl	**3610.2** rel-pron nom pl masc	**2953.30** verb 3pl indic aor act	**5050.3** prs-pron dat 2pl	**3450.6** art acc sing masc	**3030.4** noun acc sing masc
ὑμῶν,	οἵτινες	ἐλάλησαν	ὑμῖν	τὸν	λόγον
humōn	*hoitines*	*elalēsan*	*humin*	*ton*	*logon*
your,	who	spoke	to you	the	word

3450.2 art gen sing	**2296.2** noun gen sing masc	**3614.1** rel-pron gen pl	**331.2** verb nom pl masc part pres act	**3450.12** art acc sing fem
τοῦ	θεοῦ·	ὧν	ἀναθεωροῦντες	τὴν
tou	*theou*	*hōn*	*anatheōrountes*	*tēn*
	of God;	of whom,	considering	the

1532.1 noun acc sing fem	**3450.10** art gen sing fem	**389.1** noun gen sing fem	**3265.2** verb 2pl impr pres mid	**3450.12** art acc sing fem
ἔκβασιν	τῆς	ἀναστροφῆς,	μιμεῖσθε	τὴν
ekbasin	*tēs*	*anastrophēs*	*mimeisthe*	*tēn*
issue	of the	conduct,	imitate	the

8.a.**Txt:** 04C-corr 06D-corr,018K,020L byz.
Var: 01ℵ,02A,04C-org 06D-org,Lach,Treg,Alf Word,Tisc,We/Ho,Weis Sod,UBS/☆

3963.4 noun acc sing fem	**2400.1** name nom masc	**5382.1** name nom masc	**5340.1** adv	**2170.1** adv
πίστιν.	8. Ἰησοῦς	Χριστὸς	(χθὲς	[a☆ ἐχθὲς]
pistin	*Iēsous*	*Christos*	*chthes*	*echthes*
faith.	Jesus	Christ	yesterday	[idem]

2504.1 conj	**4449.1** adv	**3450.5** art nom sing masc	**840.5** prs-pron nom sing masc	**2504.1** conj	**1519.1** prep	**3450.8** art acc pl masc
καὶ	σήμερον	ὁ	αὐτός,	καὶ	εἰς	τοὺς
kai	*sēmeron*	*ho*	*autos*	*kai*	*eis*	*tous*
and	today	the	same,	and	to	the

163.6 noun acc pl masc	**1316.5** noun dat pl fem	**4024.3** adj dat pl fem	**2504.1** conj	**3443.6** adj dat pl fem	**3231.1** partic
αἰῶνας.	9. διδαχαῖς	ποικίλαις	καὶ	ξέναις	μὴ
aiōnas	*didachais*	*poikilais*	*kai*	*xenais*	*mē*
ages.	With teachings	various	and	strange	not

9.a.**Txt:** 018K,020L Steph
Var: 01ℵ,02A,04C,06D 025P,33,Gries,Lach Treg,Alf,Word,Tisc We/Ho,Weis,Sod UBS/☆

3924.3 verb 2pl impr pres act	**3772.3** verb 2pl impr pres mid	**2541.1** adj sing	**1056.1** conj	**5322.3** noun dat sing fem
(περιφέρεσθε·	[a☆ παραφέρεσθε·]	καλὸν	γὰρ	χάριτι
peripheresthe	*parapheresthe*	*kalon*	*gar*	*chariti*
be carried about;	[be carried away;]	good	for	with grace

943.6 verb inf pres mid	**3450.12** art acc sing fem	**2559.4** noun acc sing fem	**3620.3** partic	**1026.6** noun dat pl neu	**1706.1** prep
βεβαιοῦσθαι	τὴν	καρδίαν,	οὐ	βρώμασιν,	ἐν
bebaiousthai	*tēn*	*kardian*	*ou*	*brōmasin*	*en*
to be confirmed	the	heart,	not	foods;	in

3614.4 rel-pron dat pl	**3620.2** partic	**5456.8** verb 3pl indic aor pass	**3450.7** art nom pl masc	**3906.22** verb nom pl masc part aor act
οἷς	οὐκ	ὠφελήθησαν	οἱ	(περιπατήσαντες.
hois	*ouk*	*ōphelēthēsan*	*hoi*	*peripatēsantes*
which	not	were profited	the	having walked.

118:6 which is quoted here. In the middle of distress and suffering, their confidence rests with the Lord. They do not have to be afraid of the pain, injury, or death which men may inflict. This was a strong encouragement and exhortation to any of the Hebrew Christians who may have been disposed to abandon their faith in the face of adversity.

The Lord [is] my helper, and I will not fear: I will dismiss all fear, *Wade.*

what man shall do unto me: What harm can man do, *Wade.*

13:7. In the midst of their temptation to apostatize, the Hebrews were also encouraged to continue remembering their former leaders who guided them and spoke God's words to them. They were to imitate (*mimeisthe,* "follow") the example of their leaders' faith. This may be a reference to the heroes mentioned in chapter 11, or it may refer to the founders of their church who had died. Their lives of victorious faith proved that the Hebrew Christians could also persevere.

7. Remember them which have the rule over you: Remember your pastors, *Norlie* . . . You must not forget your former leaders, *Williams.*

who have spoken unto you the word of God: . . . for it was they who brought you the message of God, *Williams.*

whose faith follow, considering the end of [their] conversation: Consider how they closed their lives, *Williams* . . . take a look at the results of their behavior and imitate their faith, *Adams* . . . Think of the way they lived and died, and imitate their faith, *TNT.*

13:8. Not only do the lives of the heroes and saints witness to the ability of human beings to live by faith in the face of opposition and overwhelming odds, but the example and promises of the Lord Jesus Christ also provide evidence and encouragement to Christians who waver before the enemy. The One who "endured the cross" sits at God's right hand in power and glory (12:2). The One who promised to be with His disciples unto the end of this age (Matthew 28:20) is still the same. Everything else in the life of the believer may change—his job, his family, his self-esteem, his influence, his popularity, his wealth—but Jesus is always the same, and He is always with the believer, encouraging and empowering him to live the life of faith and obedience.

8. Jesus Christ the same yesterday, and to day, and for ever: . . . in the past, in the present, and for all time to come, ever the Same, *Wade.*

13:9. Because Jesus is unchanging, the one fixed point in a world of change, the believer has an anchor in the midst of changing circumstances. Because of the stability the Christian has in Jesus, he can stop being blown around by the novel and alien teachings which constantly arise to oppose the Christian faith. The living, eternal Son continuously channels the grace of God to those who trust Him. Dependence on the Son of God is the source of strength which enables the believer to be courageous when afflicted and persecuted.

The writer is here contrasting the entire gospel economy, under the title "grace," with the Levitical system under the title of "meats." The latter term is appropriate because after certain sacrifices worshipers could have a meal using part of the offering. Instead of being carried away by error and apostatizing, they should become established in the truth of the gospel. Salvation comes only through the grace manifested at Calvary.

9. Be not carried about with divers and strange doctrines: Do not be led astray by them, *Norlie* . . . stop being carried away with varied and strange teachings, *Williams* . . . with different kinds of, *Beck* . . . by high sounding and strange teachings, *Klingensmith.*

For [it is] a good thing: . . . the right course is, *Wade* . . . it is an Excellent thing, *Wilson.*

that the heart be established with grace: . . . to have our resolution braced by a sense of Divine Favour, *Wade* . . . for the heart to be strengthened by God's spiritual strength, *Williams* . . . It is God's grace which strengthens our souls, *TNT.*

not with meats: . . . and not by regulations regarding food, *Montgomery* . . . not by special kinds of food, *Williams* . . . not by restrictions about particular foods, *Wade.*

which have not profited them that have been occupied therein: . . . those who make the observance of such restrictions a rule of conduct have not been benefited thereby, *Wade* . . . from which those adhering to them have gotten no good, *Williams* . . . which never helped anyone who followed them, *TNT.*

9.b.**Txt:** 01ℵ-corr,04C 06D-corr,018K,020L 025P,etc.byz.Sod
Var: 01ℵ-org,02A 06D-org,Lach,Treg,Tisc We/Ho,Weis,UBS/☆

3906.15 verb nom pl masc part pres act	**2174.5** verb 1pl indic pres act	**2356.1** noun sing neu	**1523.1** prep gen
[b☆ περιπατοῦντες.]	**10.** Ἔχομεν	θυσιαστήριον	ἐξ
peripatountes	*Echomen*	*thusiastērion*	*ex*
[walking.]	We have	an altar	of

3614.2 rel-pron gen sing	**2052.25** verb inf aor act	**3620.2** partic	**2174.6** verb 3pl indic pres act	**1833.4** noun acc sing fem	**3450.7** art nom pl masc	**3450.11** art dat sing fem
οὗ	φαγεῖν	οὐκ	ἔχουσιν	ἐξουσίαν	οἱ	τῇ
hou	*phagein*	*ouk*	*echousin*	*exousian*	*hoi*	*tē*
which	to eat	not	they have	authority	the	the

4488.3 noun dat sing fem	**2973.5** verb nom pl masc part pres act	**3614.1** rel-pron gen pl	**1056.1** conj	**1517.6** verb 3sing indic pres mid
σκηνῇ	λατρεύοντες.	**11.** ὧν	γὰρ	εἰσφέρεται
skēnē	*latreuontes*	*hōn*	*gar*	*eispheretai*
tabernacle	serving;	of whose	for	is being brought

2209.4 noun gen pl neu	**3450.16** art sing neu	**129.1** noun sing neu	**3875.1** prep	**264.1** noun fem	**1519.1** prep	**3450.17** art pl neu
ζῴων	τὸ	αἷμα	περὶ	ἁμαρτίας	εἰς	τὰ
zōōn	*to*	*haima*	*peri*	*hamartias*	*eis*	*ta*
animals	the	blood	for	sin	into	the

39.16 adj pl neu	**1217.2** prep	**3450.2** art gen sing	**744.2** noun gen sing masc	**3642.2** dem-pron gen pl	**3450.17** art pl neu	**4835.4** noun pl neu
ἅγια	διὰ	τοῦ	ἀρχιερέως,	τούτων	τὰ	σώματα
hagia	*dia*	*tou*	*archiereōs*	*toutōn*	*ta*	*sōmata*
holies	by	the	high priest,	of these	the	bodies

2588.5 verb 3sing indic pres mid	**1838.1** prep	**3450.10** art gen sing fem	**3787.1** noun gen sing fem	**1346.1** conj
κατακαίεται	ἔξω	τῆς	παρεμβολῆς·	**12.** διὸ
katakaietai	*exō*	*tēs*	*parembolēs*	*dio*
are being burned	outside	the	camp.	Wherefore

2504.1 conj	**2400.1** name nom masc	**2419.1** conj	**37.6** verb 3sing subj aor act	**1217.2** prep	**3450.2** art gen sing	**2375.2** adj gen sing
καὶ	Ἰησοῦς,	ἵνα	ἁγιάσῃ	διὰ	τοῦ	ἰδίου
kai	*Iēsous*	*hina*	*hagiasē*	*dia*	*tou*	*idiou*
also	Jesus,	that	he might sanctify	by	the	his own

129.2 noun gen sing neu	**3450.6** art acc sing masc	**2967.4** noun acc sing masc	**1838.1** prep	**3450.10** art gen sing fem	**4297.2** noun gen sing fem
αἵματος	τὸν	λαόν,	ἔξω	τῆς	πύλης
haimatos	*ton*	*laon*	*exō*	*tēs*	*pulēs*
blood	the	people,	outside	the	gate

3819.11 verb 3sing indic aor act	**4953.1** partic	**1814.30** verb 1pl subj pres mid	**4242.1** prep	**840.6** prs-pron acc sing masc
ἔπαθεν.	**13.** τοίνυν	ἐξερχώμεθα	πρὸς	αὐτὸν
epathen	*toinun*	*exerchōmetha*	*pros*	*auton*
suffered:	therefore	we should go forth	to	him

1838.1 prep	**3450.10** art gen sing fem	**3787.1** noun gen sing fem	**3450.6** art acc sing masc	**3543.1** noun acc sing masc	**840.3** prs-pron gen sing
ἔξω	τῆς	παρεμβολῆς,	τὸν	ὀνειδισμὸν	αὐτοῦ
exō	*tēs*	*parembolēs*	*ton*	*oneidismon*	*autou*
outside	the	camp,	the	reproach	his

5179.8 verb nom pl masc part pres act	**3620.3** partic	**1056.1** conj	**2174.5** verb 1pl indic pres act	**5436.1** adv	**3176.13** verb acc sing fem part pres act
φέροντες·	**14.** οὐ	γὰρ	ἔχομεν	ὧδε	μένουσαν
pherontes	*ou*	*gar*	*echomen*	*hōde*	*menousan*
bearing;	not	for	we have	here	abiding

13:10. The inspired writer now pointed to the mutually exclusive nature of the new covenant sacrifice and the sacrifices offered under the Mosaic Covenant. Christians do not need to identify themselves with the animal sacrifices offered under the Jewish system. Those who continue offering under the old system, which only foreshadowed the reality of Christ's sacrifice, do not possess the *exousian* ("power, right, privilege, authority") to "eat" from the new covenant sacrificial altar.

13:11. In order to accentuate the point about the powerlessness of preoccupation with meats, the writer directed attention to the rites of the Day of Atonement. The bodies of the animals which had been sacrificed were not eaten nor taken into the innermost sanctuary. They were taken outside of the Israelites' camp and burned. It was the blood that was taken "into the sanctuary" and sprinkled on the lid of the ark of the covenant. It was blood, not flesh, that provided ceremonial cleansing under the old covenant.

13:12. The fact that sin offerings and burnt offerings were burned outside the Israelite camp (Exodus 29:14; Leviticus 4:21) leads to another parallel with the sacrifice of Jesus on the cross. Just as those offerings were burned outside the camp, so the death of Christ occurred outside the walls of Jerusalem. It is the shedding of Jesus' blood which cleanses. Emphasis is placed on the idea that His sacrifices took place *exō tēs pulēs* (outside the gate of the city).

13:13. There is a symbolism in the location of the sacrifice of Jesus and that of the animals. Those who go to Calvary, to the altar of Jesus, can no longer serve and worship at the altar of the temple or tabernacle. They must leave Israel, that is, go outside of the camp and away from the Jewish system. Therefore, professing Jewish Christians had to leave the Jewish altar and rites and identify themselves clearly with Jesus. In doing this they accepted the "reproach" (*oneidismon,* see also 11:26) which comes upon those who identify themselves with Christ.

The situation faced by the Hebrew Christians was not new. Moses and all true believers who have come after him suffered because of their allegiance to the Messiah (John 15:19; 16:33; 2 Timothy 3:12). There is a stigma associated with true faith; believers must be prepared to bear it: they cannot be friends with Jesus and partners with the world at the same time.

13:14. Building upon the imagery of the patriarchs which was presented in 11:1,16 and 12:22, the writer explained that believers must be willing to bear the shame of identification with Jesus because they recognize they do not have a permanent city upon earth and look, therefore, for the establishment of God's eternal, heav-

10. We have an altar: As for us, *Noli* . . . Ours is a spiritual altar, *Norlie.*

whereof they have no right to eat which serve the tabernacle: . . . but of the Oblations presented on it they who perform Divine worship in the Tabernacle have no right to eat, *Wade* . . . from which those who officiate in the tent, *TNT* . . . at which the ministers of the Jewish tent of worship, *Williams* . . . the worshipers of the old tabernacle are not allowed, *Noli.*

11. For the bodies of those beasts: That reminds me that, *Noli* . . . those animals, *Williams* . . . For (to draw a parallel from the Mosaic Law) the bodies of the victims, *Wade.*

whose blood is brought into the sanctuary: . . . is taken...into the Holy of Holies, *Wade.*

by the high priest for sin, are burned without the camp: . . . as a sin-offering, *Williams* . . . are not eaten by the worshippers but are burnt, *Wade* . . . outside the precincts of, *Noli* . . . outside the camp, *TNT.*

12. Wherefore Jesus also: That is why, *TNT* . . . Consequently, *Wade* . . . For this reason, *Noli.*

that he might sanctify the people with his own blood: . . . in order that he might make the people holy, *TNT* . . . purify, *TCNT.*

suffered without the gate: . . . and died, *Noli* . . . outside the City-gate, *Wade.*

13. Let us go forth therefore unto him without the camp: . . . let us follow him outside the old camp, *Noli.*

bearing his reproach: . . . enduring the reproach that He endured, *Williams* . . . the same stigma as he, *TCNT* . . . and bear the abuse He suffered, *Beck* . . . and share his disgrace, *TNT* . . . enduring the same obloquy as He endured, *Wade.*

14. For here have we no continuing city: . . . we have no permanent city here below, *Norlie* . . . our permanent home is not here on earth, *Noli* . . . there is no city here on earth that will last forever, *NLT* . . . an abiding city, *Montgomery* . . . no lasting City, *Wade.*

4032.4 noun acc sing fem	233.2 conj	3450.12 art acc sing fem	3165.16 verb acc sing fem part pres act	1919.3 verb 1pl indic pres act
πόλιν,	ἀλλὰ	τὴν	μέλλουσαν	ἐπιζητοῦμεν.
polin	*alla*	*tēn*	*mellousan*	*epizētoumen*
city,	but	the	coming one	we are seeking for.

15.a.**Txt:** 01ℵ-corr2,02A 04C,06D-corr1,0121b byz.
Var: p46,01ℵ-org 06D-org,025P,044

1217.1 prep	840.3 prs-pron gen sing	3631.1 partic	397.2 verb 1pl subj pres act	2355.4 noun acc sing fem
15. Δι'	αὐτοῦ	⸂[a] οὖν ⸃	ἀναφέρωμεν	θυσίαν
Di'	*autou*	*oun*	*anapherōmen*	*thusian*
By	him	therefore	we should offer	sacrifice

133.1 noun gen sing fem	1269.1 adv	1217.2 prep	3820.2 adj gen sing	3450.3 art dat sing	2296.3 noun dat sing masc
αἰνέσεως	⸂ διαπαντὸς	[☆ διὰ	παντὸς]	τῷ	θεῷ,
aineseōs	*diapantos*	*dia*	*pantos*	*tō*	*theō*
of praise	continually	[through	all]		to God,

4969.1 verb	3642.16 dem-pron sing neu	1498.4 verb 3sing indic pres act	2561.3 noun acc sing masc	5327.2 noun gen pl neu
⸂ τουτέστιν,	[☆ τοῦτ'	ἔστιν]	καρπὸν	χειλέων
toutestin	*tout'*	*estin*	*karpon*	*cheileōn*
that is,	[this	is]	fruit	of lips

3533.6 verb gen pl masc part pres act	3450.3 art dat sing	3549.4 noun dat sing neu	840.3 prs-pron gen sing	3450.10 art gen sing fem
ὁμολογούντων	τῷ	ὀνόματι	αὐτοῦ.	**16.** τῆς
homologountōn	*tō*	*onomati*	*autou*	*tēs*
confessing	of the	name	his.	Of the

16.a.**Var:** p46,06D-org 81,2495

1156.2 conj	2120.1 noun gen sing fem	2504.1 conj	3450.10 art gen sing fem	2815.2 noun gen sing fem	3231.1 partic
δὲ	εὐποιΐας	καὶ	[[a]+ τῆς]	κοινωνίας	μὴ
de	*eupoiias*	*kai*	*tēs*	*koinōnias*	*mē*
but	doing good	and	[of the]	of sharing	not

1935.1 verb 2pl impr pres mid	4955.12 dem-pron dat pl fem	1056.1 conj	2355.7 noun dat pl fem	2079.3 verb 3sing indic pres mid
ἐπιλανθάνεσθε·	τοιαύταις	γὰρ	θυσίαις	εὐαρεστεῖται
epilanthanesthe	*toiautais*	*gar*	*thusiais*	*euaresteitai*
be forgetful	with such	for	sacrifices	is well pleased

3450.5 art nom sing masc	2296.1 noun nom sing masc	3844.21 verb 2pl impr pres mid	3450.4 art dat pl	2216.9 verb dat pl masc part pres mid
ὁ	θεός.	**17.** Πείθεσθε	τοῖς	ἡγουμένοις
ho	*theos*	*Peithesthe*	*tois*	*hēgoumenois*
	God.	Obey	the	leading

5050.2 prs-pron gen 2pl	2504.1 conj	5063.1 verb 2pl impr pres act	840.7 prs-pron nom pl masc	1056.1 conj	68.1 verb 3pl indic pres act
ὑμῶν,	καὶ	ὑπείκετε·	αὐτοὶ	γὰρ	ἀγρυπνοῦσιν
humōn	*kai*	*hupeikete*	*autoi*	*gar*	*agrupnousin*
your,	and	be submissive:	they	for	watch

5065.1 prep	3450.1 art gen pl	5425.6 noun gen pl fem	5050.2 prs-pron gen 2pl	5453.1 conj	3030.4 noun acc sing masc
ὑπὲρ	τῶν	ψυχῶν	ὑμῶν	ὡς	λόγον
huper	*tōn*	*psuchōn*	*humōn*	*hōs*	*logon*
for	the	souls	your,	as	account

586.19 verb nom pl masc part fut act	2419.1 conj	3196.3 prep	5315.2 noun gen sing fem	3642.17 dem-pron sing neu	4020.10 verb 3pl subj pres act
ἀποδώσοντες·	ἵνα	μετὰ	χαρᾶς	τοῦτο	ποιῶσιν,
apodōsontes	*hina*	*meta*	*charas*	*touto*	*poiōsin*
being about to render;	that	with	joy	this	they may do,

enly city in the future. Just as the heroes of faith (chapter 11) looked beyond this world in their pilgrimage, so Christians also must break away from the value system of the world and endure persecution because they seek God's approval and reward—not man's.

13:15. Believers have priestly responsibilities under the new covenant. All Christians are priests (1 Peter 2:5). As such they are called upon to offer up sacrifices. But the sacrifices offered under the new covenant are not animal sacrifices; they are spiritual sacrifices. Instead of offering the fruit gathered in the harvest in worship and sacrifice, believer-priests are to worship the Lord by continuously praising Him and giving thanks to Him for their eternal salvation.

13:16. This verse continues to identify some of the spiritual sacrifices Christians are called upon to offer as believer-priests. The first term used here, *eupoiias*, means "doing good." It refers to works of mercy and benevolence which spring from the kindness and generosity of the believer's heart. Those who have received God's grace in forgiveness know what it is to be in need. Their gratitude for God's help in their time of need overflows and leads them to reach out to help others, specifically sharing their material substance with others (*koinōnias*). True Christian religion manifests itself in action. It helps those who cannot help themselves. It opens up both its heart and its wallet (James 1:22-27; 2:15-17; 4:17). God is satisfied and very pleased with sacrifices which possess the qualities presented in these two verses: praise, thanksgiving, helping, giving, and sharing.

13:17. The love for God and for one another which has been under consideration in this section is to be directed also to local church leadership. Because of their position and the relationship of trust which exists, Christians are to "obey" those who are leading (*hēgoumenois*) them. They are to place themselves under ("submit" to) their leaders in a spirit of yieldedness (*hupeikete*). These leaders are alertly watching over the "souls" (*psuchōn*, "lives," "persons") under their care as those who are responsible and who will have to give an account of their guardianship. The reference here is to the general watchful care of local church leaders over the congregation of saints.

The members of the congregation are admonished to follow their leaders in a quiet and gentle manner so the leaders will find the responsibility of oversight an enjoyable task. The alternative is groaning (*stenazontes*)—laborious chafing and struggling under the unpleasant task of shepherding a flock of wayward strays. It is far better for a congregation to follow its leadership peaceably. When there is resistance and rebellion, joy turns into *alusiteles*, something which is confining, inferior, unprofitable, and disadvantageous.

but we seek one to come: . . . we are looking for the city that is yet to come, *TNT* . . . we are searching for that city which is to be ours, *Williams.*

15. By him therefore: So then, through Christ, *Williams.*

let us offer the sacrifice of praise to God continually: . . . let us never cease to offer up, *TNT.*

that is, the fruit of [our] lips giving thanks to his name: . . . the speech of lips, *Williams* . . . praise that springs from lips which acknowledge his name, *TNT* . . . that confess his name, *Montgomery.*

16. But to do good and to communicate forget not: Do not forget to do good and fellowship, *Klingensmith* . . . do not forget to be beneficent and to Distribute, *Wilson* . . . to be kind, *TNT* . . . stop neglecting to do good, *Williams* . . . and to share, *Adams* . . . and to speak the Good Word to others, *Norlie.*

for with such sacrifices God is well pleased: . . . highly pleased, *Williams.*

17. Obey them that have the rule over you, and submit yourselves: Obey your pastors and submit to their will, *Norlie* . . . Continue to obey and to be submissive to your leaders, *Williams* . . . put yourself under their authority, *SEB.*

for they watch for your souls: Day and night they take care of you, *TNT* . . . for they are vigilant for the sake of your souls, *Concordant* . . . they are ever watching in defense of your souls, *Williams.*

as they that must give account: . . . as men who will have to give account of their trust, *Williams* . . . for they are responsible to God for you, *TNT.*

that they may do it with joy, and not with grief: Make this a joy to them and not a burden, *TNT* . . . with lamentation, *Montgomery* . . . and not groaning, *Klingensmith.*

for that [is] unprofitable for you: . . . that wouldn't be to your advantage, *Adams* . . . it is no help to you, *NLT* . . . For that would be worthless to you, *Klingensmith* . . . That would not do you any good, *TNT.*

2504.1 conj	3231.1 partic	4578.3 verb nom pl masc part pres act	253.1 adj sing neu	1056.1 conj	5050.3 prs-pron dat 2pl
καὶ	μὴ	στενάζοντες·	ἀλυσιτελὲς	γὰρ	ὑμῖν
kai	*mē*	*stenazontes*	*alusiteles*	*gar*	*humin*
and	not	groaning,	unprofitable	for	for you

3642.17 dem-pron sing neu		4195.1 verb 2pl pres mid	3875.1 prep	2231.2 prs-pron gen 1pl	3844.11 verb 1pl indic perf act
τοῦτο.	**18.**	Προσεύχεσθε	περὶ	ἡμῶν·	‘ πεποίθαμεν
touto		*Proseuchesthe*	*peri*	*hēmōn*	*pepoithamen*
this.		Pray	for	us:	we are persuaded

18.a.**Txt:** 01ℵ-corr 04C-corr,06D-corr,018K byz.
Var: 02A,04C-org 06D-org,025P,33,Lach Treg,Alf,Word,Tisc We/Ho,Weis,Sod UBS/☆

3844.34 verb 1pl indic pres mid	1056.1 conj	3617.1 conj	2541.8 adj acc sing fem	4743.4 noun acc sing fem	2174.5 verb 1pl indic pres act
[[a]☆ πειθόμεθα]	γὰρ,	ὅτι	καλὴν	συνείδησιν	ἔχομεν,
peithometha	*gar*	*hoti*	*kalēn*	*suneidēsin*	*echomen*
[we are being]	for,	that	a good	conscience	we have,

1706.1 prep	3820.5 adj dat pl	2544.1 adv	2286.16 verb nom pl masc part pres act	388.6 verb inf pres mid
ἐν	πᾶσιν	καλῶς	θέλοντες	ἀναστρέφεσθαι·
en	*pasin*	*kalōs*	*thelontes*	*anastrephesthai*
in	all things	well	wishing	to conduct ourselves.

	3917.2 adv comp	1156.2 conj	3731.1 verb 1sing indic pres act	3642.17 dem-pron sing neu	4020.41 verb inf aor act
19.	περισσοτέρως	δὲ	παρακαλῶ	τοῦτο	ποιῆσαι,
	perissoterōs	*de*	*parakalō*	*touto*	*poiēsai*
	More abundantly	but	I exhort	this	to do,

2419.1 conj	4880.1 adv comp	595.5 verb 1sing subj aor pass	5050.3 prs-pron dat 2pl		3450.5 art nom sing masc	1156.2 conj
ἵνα	τάχιον	ἀποκατασταθῶ	ὑμῖν.	**20.**	Ὁ	δὲ
hina	*tachion*	*apokatastathō*	*humin*		*Ho*	*de*
that	more quickly	I may be restored	to you.		The	and

2296.1 noun nom sing masc	3450.10 art gen sing fem	1503.2 noun gen sing fem	3450.5 art nom sing masc	319.2 verb nom sing masc part aor act
θεὸς	τῆς	εἰρήνης,	ὁ	ἀναγαγὼν
theos	*tēs*	*eirēnēs*	*ho*	*anagagōn*
God	of the	peace	the	having brought again

1523.2 prep gen	3361.2 adj gen pl	3450.6 art acc sing masc	4026.2 noun acc sing masc	3450.1 art gen pl	4122.4 noun gen pl neu
ἐκ	νεκρῶν	τὸν	ποιμένα	τῶν	προβάτων
ek	*nekrōn*	*ton*	*poimena*	*tōn*	*probatōn*
from among	dead	the	Shepherd	of the	sheep

3450.6 art acc sing masc	3144.4 adj acc sing masc	1706.1 prep	129.3 noun dat sing neu	1236.2 noun gen sing fem	164.2 adj gen sing
τὸν	μέγαν	ἐν	αἵματι	διαθήκης	αἰωνίου,
ton	*megan*	*en*	*haimati*	*diathēkēs*	*aiōniou*
the	great	in	blood	of covenant	eternal,

3450.6 art acc sing masc	2935.4 noun acc sing masc	2231.2 prs-pron gen 1pl	2400.3 name acc masc		2645.3 verb 3sing opt aor act
τὸν	κύριον	ἡμῶν	Ἰησοῦν,	**21.**	καταρτίσαι
ton	*kurion*	*hēmōn*	*Iēsoun*		*katartisai*
the	Lord	our	Jesus,		perfect

21.a.**Txt:** 04C,06D-corr 018K,025P,byz.sa.
Var: p46,01ℵ,06D-org,it. bo.Tisc,We/Ho,Weis,Sod UBS/☆

5050.4 prs-pron acc 2pl	1706.1 prep	3820.3 adj dat sing	2024.3 noun dat sing neu	18.4 adj dat sing	1519.1 prep	3450.16 art sing neu
ὑμᾶς	ἐν	παντὶ	(a ἔργῳ)	ἀγαθῷ,	εἰς	τὸ
humas	*en*	*panti*	*ergō*	*agathō*	*eis*	*to*
you	in	every	work	good,	for	the

13:18. As a leader, the inspired writer requested prayer for himself and other leaders. In keeping with the responsibilities of love, all Christians can engage in this positive action on behalf of their leaders. The assembly of believers that prays earnestly and continually for its leadership will be a happily united congregation. Faithful leaders are worthy of the prayers of their congregations because they have a "good (*kalēn,* 'noble, worthy of emulation') conscience, in all things willing to live honestly." In all the areas of their lives they conduct themselves in a way that demonstrates they are open and willing to live exemplary lives before their brethren.

13:19. To the general call to prayer for himself and their leaders, the writer added an urgent appeal. He wished to be present with those to whom the epistle was written, but something was hindering him from doing so. He encouraged them *perissoterōs* ("more earnestly," RSV) to pray for him in order that he might be restored to them at once. The exact cause of this separation was not revealed. But whether it was sickness, imprisonment, bad weather, a change in financial situation, poor traveling conditions, or the pressure of his responsibilities in connection with some other church's problems, it made no difference. He was convinced that prayer could alter his situation and bring him into their midst once again. What a magnificent testimony to the power of prayer in the Church!

13:20. Verses 20 and 21 compose a closing benediction. The blessings of "the God of peace" were invoked upon this group of embattled Hebrew Christians. Nothing could be a more appropriate reminder of God's power to overcome the turmoil in their lives and the surrounding world. His power was demonstrated convincingly in the resurrection of our Lord Jesus Christ. He came back from the dead. He is the Leader whom the sheep follow. Even though the sheep go down into the valley of death, they have nothing to fear because Jesus, the Great Shepherd, will lead them through and out of death. He has been there before them and triumphed. He knows the way and has defeated the foe. Jesus has become the eternal High Priest who always lives to secure the believers' deliverance. The shedding of His blood made possible an eternal covenant. It is a covenant that will never be superseded, because it rests on the final, once-for-all, sin-covering sacrifice of God's unique Son. Christians have nothing to fear.

13:21. The inspired writer prayed that God would, through Jesus Christ, restore and equip (*katartisai*) the Hebrew Christians so they could carry out His will in the performance of the good deeds described in verses 1-19. He also prayed that their performance would gain the approval of God, just as the heroes of faith referred

18. Pray for us: Continue to pray, *Wade*... Keep on praying, *TNT*... for me, *Williams.*

for we trust we have a good conscience: ... since we are becoming more and more persuaded, *Wade* ... We are sure that we have a clear conscience, *TNT*... I am sure that my own conscience is clear, *Noli.*

in all things willing to live honestly: ... since it is our wish to conduct ourselves honourably in every respect, *Wade* ... that I do my best to live a righteous life in every respect, *Noli*... we want to behave well in everything, *Adams* ... in everything I want to live a noble life, *Williams* ... we want to do what is right in all circumstances, *TNT.*

19. But I beseech [you] the rather to do this: And more especially do I beg you to do so, *Williams*... I beg you most earnestly for your prayers, *TNT* ... And I appeal to you all the more earnestly to carry out this request of mine, *Wade.*

that I may be restored to you the sooner: ... so that God may bring me back, *TNT*... so I may be brought back to you the more quickly, *Klingensmith* ... that I may return to you, *Noli.*

20. Now the God of peace: ... who gives us peace, *Williams.*

that brought again from the dead our Lord Jesus: Who brought up from among the dead, *Wade.*

that great shepherd of the sheep: The Great Sheep Herder of the flock, *Klingensmith.*

through the blood of the everlasting covenant: ... with the marks of the Blood shed by Him to make binding an Eternal Covenant, *Wade* ... the blood by which He ratified the everlasting covenant, *Williams* ... in the blood of the ageless agreement, *Klingensmith.*

21. Make you perfect in every good work to do his will: ... may God (I repeat) equip you thoroughly with every good quality, for the accomplishment of His will, *Wade* ... perfectly fit you, *Williams* ... knit you together, *Wilson* ... be adapting you to, *Concordant*... equip you, *Montgomery.*

Hebrews 13:22

4020.41 verb inf aor act	3450.16 art sing neu	2284.1 noun sing neu	840.3 prs-pron gen sing	4020.15 verb nom sing masc part pres act	1706.1 prep
ποιῆσαι	τὸ	θέλημα	αὐτοῦ,	ποιῶν	ἐν
poiēsai	*to*	*thelēma*	*autou*	*poiōn*	*en*
to do	the	will	his,	doing	in

21.b.**Txt:** 04C,025P,it. Sod
Var: p46,01ℵ,02A,06D 018K,33,sa.bo.Tisc We/Ho,Weis,UBS/⋆

5050.3 prs-pron dat 2pl	2231.3 prs-pron dat 1pl	3450.16 art sing neu	2080.4 adj sing	1783.1 prep	840.3 prs-pron gen sing
⸀ ὑμῖν	[b☆ ἡμῖν]	τὸ	εὐάρεστον	ἐνώπιον	αὐτοῦ,
humin	*hēmin*	*to*	*euareston*	*enōpion*	*autou*
you	[us]	the	well pleasing	before	him,

1217.2 prep	2400.2 name masc	5382.2 name gen masc	3614.3 rel-pron dat sing	3450.9 art nom sing fem	1385.1 noun nom sing fem
διὰ	Ἰησοῦ	Χριστοῦ·	ᾧ	ἡ	δόξα
dia	*Iēsou*	*Christou*	*hō*	*hē*	*doxa*
through	Jesus	Christ;	to whom	the	glory

21.c.**Txt:** 01ℵ,02A 0121b,byz.
Var: p46,04C-corr,06D 044,6,104,365,2495

1519.1 prep	3450.8 art acc pl masc	163.6 noun acc pl masc	3450.1 art gen pl	163.4 noun gen pl masc	279.1 intrj
εἰς	τοὺς	αἰῶνας	⸂c τῶν	αἰώνων. ⸃	ἀμήν.
eis	*tous*	*aiōnas*	*tōn*	*aiōnōn*	*amēn*
to	the	ages	of the	ages.	Amen.

3731.1 verb 1sing indic pres act	1156.2 conj	5050.4 prs-pron acc 2pl	79.6 noun nom pl masc	428.1 verb 2pl pres mid	3450.2 art gen sing
22. Παρακαλῶ	δὲ	ὑμᾶς,	ἀδελφοί,	ἀνέχεσθε	τοῦ
Parakalō	*de*	*humas*	*adelphoi*	*anechesthe*	*tou*
I exhort	but	you,	brothers,	bear	the

3030.2 noun gen sing masc	3450.10 art gen sing fem	3735.2 noun gen sing fem	2504.1 conj	1056.1 conj	1217.2 prep
λόγου	τῆς	παρακλήσεως·	καὶ	γὰρ	διὰ
logou	*tēs*	*paraklēseōs*	*kai*	*gar*	*dia*
word	of the	exhortation,	also	for	through

1017.1 adj gen pl masc	1973.1 verb 1sing indic aor act	5050.3 prs-pron dat 2pl	1091.5 verb 2pl indic pres act	3450.6 art acc sing masc
βραχέων	ἐπέστειλα	ὑμῖν.	23. Γινώσκετε	τὸν
bracheōn	*epesteila*	*humin*	*Ginōskete*	*ton*
few words	I wrote	to you.	Know you	the

23.a.**Var:** 01ℵ-org,02A 04C,06D,33,bo.Lach Treg,Alf,Word,Tisc We/Ho,Weis,Sod UBS/⋆

79.4 noun acc sing masc	2231.2 prs-pron gen 1pl	4943.4 name acc masc	624.19 verb acc sing masc part perf mid	3196.1 prep
ἀδελφὸν	[a☆+ ἡμῶν]	Τιμόθεον	ἀπολελυμένον,	μεθ'
adelphon	*hēmōn*	*Timotheon*	*apolelumenon*	*meth'*
brother	[our]	Timothy	having been released;	with

3614.2 rel-pron gen sing	1430.1 partic	4880.1 adv comp	2048.38 verb 3sing subj pres mid	3571.28 verb 1sing indic fut mid	5050.4 prs-pron acc 2pl
οὗ,	ἐὰν	τάχιον	ἔρχηται,	ὄψομαι	ὑμᾶς.
hou	*ean*	*tachion*	*erchētai*	*opsomai*	*humas*
whom,	if	sooner	he should come,	I will see	you.

776.9 verb 2pl impr aor mid	3820.8 adj acc pl masc	3450.8 art acc pl masc	2216.10 verb acc pl masc part pres mid	5050.2 prs-pron gen 2pl
24. Ἀσπάσασθε	πάντας	τοὺς	ἡγουμένους	ὑμῶν,
Aspasasthe	*pantas*	*tous*	*hēgoumenous*	*humōn*
Salute	all	the	leading	your,

2504.1 conj	3820.8 adj acc pl masc	3450.8 art acc pl masc	39.9 adj acc pl masc	776.3 verb 3pl indic pres mid	5050.4 prs-pron acc 2pl
καὶ	πάντας	τοὺς	ἁγίους.	ἀσπάζονται	ὑμᾶς
kai	*pantas*	*tous*	*hagious*	*aspazontai*	*humas*
and	all	the	saints.	Salute	you

to in chapter 11 obtained a good testimony from God concerning their righteousness, faithfulness, and mighty exploits. Such behavior is possible only through the grace mediated by Jesus Christ; therefore, all of the praise and glory will be given to Him as the eternal ages unceasingly roll on.

13:22. After the benediction, the epistle concludes with a few personal remarks and greetings. The Hebrew Christians to whom the epistle was written were asked to bear the exhortations of the epistle with patient endurance (*anechesthe*). The letter was called *tou logou tēs paraklēseōs* (the word of consolation), a strong word of encouragement. The believers were insistently asked to focus their attention on the finality of Jesus' work and encouraged to rest completely in Him.

13:23. Apparently Timothy had been confined in prison and only recently been set free. This seems to throw light on the writer's own circumstances mentioned in 13:19. The matter of the identity of the writer of the Epistle to the Hebrews is debated by Biblical interpreters. On the basis of this verse many would argue that Paul was the inspired writer of this epistle. On the basis of the great differences observed between Hebrews and the letters of the New Testament known to have been written by the apostle Paul, many evangelical scholars are reticent to attribute Hebrews to him. The ideas and themes of the epistle certainly are in agreement with Paul's teachings, but the vocabulary, style, and other linguistic features are quite different from those found in Paul's epistles. Barnabas, Luke, Silas, and many other names have been put forward as suggested writers of Hebrews. Obviously, if Paul did not write this epistle, someone in the Pauline circle did, someone who was associated with Timothy.

Since the writer whom the Spirit used is nowhere identified in the epistle by name, it seems wisest to conclude with the second-century church father, Origen of Alexandria, that "as to who actually wrote the epistle, God knows the truth of the matter." (Cited from the fourth-century church historian, Eusebius, in *Church History*, 6:25:11-14.) But whoever the writer was, he expected Timothy to join him soon, and they planned then to travel and visit the recipients of the epistle.

13:24. The greetings of this verse are as enigmatic as the reference to Timothy in verse 23. There is first the standard epistolary greetings to the leaders of the church to whom the epistle was sent and to the "saints," that is, to the whole assembly of believers. The final sentence is, however, not clear. The words "they of Italy salute you" indicate the greetings were from some natives of Italy. This may mean the epistle was written from Italy and greetings were sent from all the Italian Christians. But it may also mean that he was somewhere other than Italy, and the Italian greetings indicate

working in you that which is wellpleasing in his sight: . . . so that you may do his will, *TNT* . . . accomplishing through you what is pleasing to Him, *Williams.*

through Jesus Christ: May he do in us through Jesus Christ, *TNT.*

to whom [be] glory for ever and ever. Amen: . . . have all the shining greatness forever! Let it be so, *NLT.*

22. And I beseech you, brethren, suffer the word of exhortation: Now I encourage you, *Klingensmith* . . . I beg you, brothers, to listen patiently to this message, *Williams* . . . I urge you, fellow Christians, listen patiently to what I say, *Beck* . . . be patient with my word of, *Norlie* . . . bear patiently with this word of exhortation, *TNT* . . . put up with my word of encouragement, *Adams* . . . bear with the word of entreaty, *Concordant* . . . bear with these words of advice, *TCNT.*

for I have written a letter unto you in few words: . . . for I have written to you briefly, *Montgomery* . . . for I have written you only a short letter, *Williams.*

23. Know ye that [our] brother Timothy is set at liberty: I want you to know, *TNT* . . . You should know that Brother Timothy has been released, *Norlie* . . . Let me inform you that our Brother, *Wade* . . . is out of prison, *NLT* . . . is free again, *Beck.*

with whom, if he come shortly, I will see you: . . . if he comes in time I will bring him with me when I come, *TNT* . . . If he comes soon, he and I will see you together, *Williams* . . . we will visit you together, *TCNT.*

24. Salute all them that have the rule over you, and all the saints: Greet all your leaders, *Adams, Concordant* . . . Give my warm greetings to, *TNT* . . . Remember us to all your leaders and to all the Christians, *Williams* . . . Greet all the officials, *Klingensmith* . . . all the Christian laymembers, *Norlie.*

They of Italy salute you: The Immigrants from Italy send you their kind remembrances, *Wade*

Hebrews 13:25

25.a.**Txt:** 01ℵ-corr,02A 04C,06D,015H,018K 025P,byz.it.bo.Sod
Var: p46,01ℵ-org,33,sa. Tisc,We/Ho,Weis UBS/*

25.b.**Txt:** 018K,byz.
Var: Gries,Lach,Word Tisc,We/Ho,Weis,Sod UBS/*

3450.7 art nom pl masc	**570.3** prep	**3450.10** art gen sing fem	**2455.1** name gen fem	**3450.9** art nom sing fem	**5322.1** noun nom sing fem
οἱ	ἀπὸ	τῆς	Ἰταλίας.	**25.** ἡ	χάρις
hoi	*apo*	*tēs*	*Italias*	*hē*	*charis*
the	from		Italy.	The	grace

3196.3 prep	**3820.4** adj gen pl	**5050.2** prs-pron gen 2pl	**279.1** intrj	**4242.1** prep	**1439.4** name acc pl masc
μετὰ	πάντων	ὑμῶν.	⸂a ἀμήν. ⸃	⸂b Πρὸς	Ἑβραίους
meta	*pantōn*	*humōn*	*amēn*	*Pros*	*Hebraious*
with	all	you.	Amen.	To	Hebrews

1119.21 verb 3sing indic aor pass	**570.3** prep	**3450.10** art gen sing fem	**2455.1** name gen fem	**1217.2** prep	**4943.2** name gen masc
ἐγράφη	ἀπὸ	τῆς	Ἰταλίας,	διὰ	Τιμοθέου. ⸃
egraphē	*apo*	*tēs*	*Italias*	*dia*	*Timotheou*
written	from		Italy,	by	Timothy.

he was writing to people who resided in Italy. There is no easy way to decide the issue. This is one reason Hebrews is called a general epistle. The arguments propounded seem to make the most sense if they are thought of as being directed to professing Jewish Christians.

... Christians from Italy wish to be remembered to you, *Williams* ... Our Italian friends also send you their greetings, *TNT.*

13:25. The magnificent epistle ends with the standard epistolary close used in Christian letters. The full meaning of the word "grace" was artfully presented as the case for the permanent superiority of Christ's saving work as it was argued throughout the epistle. This is a final prayer that the Hebrew Christians would all experience it.

25. Grace [be] with you all. Amen: God's loving favor, *NLT* ... Gracious love, *SEB* ... God's spiritual blessings, *Williams* ... God bless you all, *Laubach* ... May the favor of God, *Macknight* ... God's favor and spiritual blessing, *AmpB.*

THE EPISTLE OF JAMES

Expanded Interlinear
Textual Critical Apparatus
Verse-by-Verse Commentary
Various Versions

2362.2 name gen masc	1976.1 noun nom sing fem
Ἰακώβου	Ἐπιστολή
Iakōbou	*Epistolē*
Of James	Epistle

Textual Apparatus

	2362.1 name nom masc	2296.2 noun gen sing masc	2504.1 conj	2935.2 noun gen sing masc	2400.2 name masc	5382.2 name gen masc
1:1.	Ἰάκωβος	θεοῦ	καὶ	κυρίου	Ἰησοῦ	Χριστοῦ
	Iakōbos	*theou*	*kai*	*kuriou*	*Iēsou*	*Christou*
	James	of God	and	of Lord	Jesus	Christ

1395.1 noun nom sing masc	3450.14 art dat pl fem	1420.1 num card	5279.5 noun dat pl fem	3450.14 art dat pl fem	1706.1 prep	3450.11 art dat sing fem
δοῦλος,	ταῖς	δώδεκα	φυλαῖς	ταῖς	ἐν	τῇ
doulos	*tais*	*dōdeka*	*phulais*	*tais*	*en*	*tē*
slave,	to the	twelve	tribes	the	in	the

1284.2 noun dat sing fem	5299.11 verb inf pres act		3820.12 adj acc sing fem	5315.4 noun acc sing fem	2216.14 verb 2pl impr aor mid
διασπορᾷ	χαίρειν.	2.	Πᾶσαν	χαρὰν	ἡγήσασθε,
diaspora	*chairein*		*Pasan*	*charan*	*hēgēsasthe*
dispersion,	to greet.		All	joy	count,

79.6 noun nom pl masc	1466.2 prs-pron gen 1sing	3615.1 conj	3848.6 noun dat pl masc	3908.2 verb 2pl subj aor act
ἀδελφοί	μου,	ὅταν	πειρασμοῖς	περιπέσητε
adelphoi	*mou*	*hotan*	*peirasmois*	*peripesēte*
brothers	my,	when	temptations	you may fall into

4024.1 adj dat pl masc		1091.12 verb nom pl masc part pres act	3617.1 conj	3450.16 art sing neu	1377.1 noun sing neu	5050.2 prs-pron gen 2pl
ποικίλοις,	3.	γινώσκοντες	ὅτι	τὸ	δοκίμιον	ὑμῶν
poikilois		*ginōskontes*	*hoti*	*to*	*dokimion*	*humōn*
various,		knowing	that	the	proving	of your

3450.10 art gen sing fem	3963.2 noun gen sing fem	2686.2 verb 3sing indic pres mid	5119.4 noun acc sing fem		3450.9 art nom sing fem	1156.2 conj
τῆς	πίστεως	κατεργάζεται	ὑπομονήν·	4.	ἡ	δὲ
tēs	*pisteōs*	*katergazetai*	*hupomonēn*		*hē*	*de*
the	faith	works out	endurance.		The	but

5119.1 noun nom sing fem	2024.1 noun sing neu	4894.1 adj sing	2174.14 verb 3sing impr pres act	2419.1 conj	1498.1 verb 2pl act
ὑπομονὴ	ἔργον	τέλειον	ἐχέτω,	ἵνα	ἦτε
hupomonē	*ergon*	*teleion*	*echetō*	*hina*	*ēte*
endurance	work	perfect	let have,	that	you may be

4894.3 adj nom pl masc	2504.1 conj	3511.1 adj nom pl masc	1706.1 prep	3235.2 num card dat	2981.5 verb nom pl masc part pres mid		1479.1 conj
τέλειοι	καὶ	ὁλόκληροι,	ἐν	μηδενὶ	λειπόμενοι.	5.	Εἰ
teleioi	*kai*	*holoklēroi*	*en*	*mēdeni*	*leipomenoi*		*Ei*
perfect	and	complete,	in	nothing	lacking.		If

1156.2 conj	4948.3 indef-pron nom sing	5050.2 prs-pron gen 2pl	2981.4 verb 3sing indic pres mid	4531.2 noun gen sing fem	153.6 verb 3sing impr pres act
δέ	τις	ὑμῶν	λείπεται	σοφίας,	αἰτείτω
de	*tis*	*humōn*	*leipetai*	*sophias*	*aiteitō*
but	anyone	of you	lack	wisdom,	let him ask

THE EPISTLE OF
JAMES

1:1. From the earliest days of church history it has been believed that the writer of this epistle was James, a brother of Jesus (Matthew 13:55; Galatians 1:19). He was the leader of the infant church (Acts 12:17; 15:13; 21:18; Galatians 2:12).

The writer introduced himself modestly, simply referring to himself as a servant, meaning a bondslave. See Exodus 21:5,6 for the background of this practice. The submission to God and also to the Lord Jesus Christ reminded Jewish believers that Jesus is the Messiah, coequal with God the Father.

The epistle was addressed to Christians (2:1) who were scattered abroad. The dispersion of the 12 tribes of Israel began in Old Testament times through deportations by foreign powers (2 Kings 18:9-12; chapters 24,25). Christians were scattered as a result of persecution following the martyrdom of Stephen (Acts 11:19).

1:2. The Christians to whom James wrote were having problems not of their own making. They fell into them. These various kinds of problems very likely included severe persecution from both Jews and Gentiles (2 Timothy 3:12). The word translated "temptations" can also have the meaning of trials. That which was an external trial of faith could become an internal temptation to sin. Christians were not to react negatively, but to consider it "all joy" (pure joy, free of bitterness) when times of testing came.

1:3. The reason believers were to rejoice when their faith was tested was that the right attitude would result in steadfastness or endurance. Trials are not intended to destroy, but to strengthen.

1:4. Endurance was not an end in itself. Its perfect work was to make believers "perfect and entire." Perfection or maturity was a progressive product of endurance. See Hebrews 6:1. Entirety or completeness indicated symmetrical development of character; no virtue of the fruit of the Spirit (Galatians 5:22,23) was to be lacking.

1:5. "Wanting nothing" (verse 4) is a very high goal. It might still be a future attainment. James followed this statement by saying that if anyone lacked wisdom he could ask God for it. In the process of godly living there will be trials and challenges for which human wisdom is totally inadequate. In addition human wisdom may at

Various Versions

1. James, a servant of God and of the Lord Jesus Christ: . . . bondman, *Darby* . . . slave, *Montgomery* . . . I am a workman owned by God, *NLT.*

to the twelve tribes which are scattered abroad, greeting: . . . that are in exile, *TCNT* . . . scattered over the world, *Laubach* . . . that are in the Dispersion, *Confraternity* . . . Rejoice! *Fenton* . . . Health, *Campbell.*

2. My brethren, count it all joy: . . . esteem it all, *Confraternity* . . . consider it entirely a happy situation, *Adams* . . . Consider it all pleasure, *Fenton.*

when ye fall into divers temptations: . . . when you are encompassed by various trials, *Swann.*

3. Knowing [this], that the trying of your faith: . . . well aware, *Berkeley* . . . these prove, *NLT.*

worketh patience: . . . begets, *Confraternity* . . . develops, *TCNT* . . . is working out endurance, *Norlie* . . . brings out steadfastness, *Berkeley.*

4. But let patience have [her] perfect work: . . . let endurance have, *Montgomery* . . . So let the work of testing go on, *Norlie* . . . have a perfect effect, *Campbell* . . . have full play, *Berkeley.*

that ye may be perfect and entire: . . . until your endurance is perfect in every way, *Norlie* . . . that you may be fully developed and perfectly equipped, *Williams* . . . may be completed and rounded out, *Berkeley* . . . unimpaired, *Concordant.*

wanting nothing: . . . not lacking in anything, *Montgomery* . . . no defects whatever, *Berkeley.*

5. If any of you lack wisdom, let him ask of God: . . . are deficient in, *TCNT.*

3706.2 prep	**3450.2** art gen sing	**1319.6** verb gen sing masc part pres act	**2296.2** noun gen sing masc	**3820.5** adj dat pl	**569.1** adv
παρὰ	τοῦ	διδόντος	θεοῦ	πᾶσιν	ἁπλῶς,
para	*tou*	*didontos*	*theou*	*pasin*	*haplōs*
from	the	giving	God	to all	freely,

2504.1 conj	**3231.1** partic	**3542.1** verb gen sing masc part pres act	**2504.1** conj	**1319.57** verb 3sing indic fut pass	**840.4** prs-pron dat sing
καὶ	μὴ	ὀνειδίζοντος,	καὶ	δοθήσεται	αὐτῷ.
kai	*mē*	*oneidizontos*	*kai*	*dothēsetai*	*autō*
and	not	reproaching,	and	it shall be given	to him:

153.6 verb 3sing impr pres act	**1156.2** conj	**1706.1** prep	**3963.3** noun dat sing fem	**3235.6** num card neu	**1246.8** verb nom sing masc part pres mid
6. αἰτείτω	δὲ	ἐν	πίστει,	μηδὲν	διακρινόμενος·
aiteitō	*de*	*en*	*pistei*	*mēden*	*diakrinomenos*
let him ask	but	in	faith,	nothing	doubting.

3450.5 art nom sing masc	**1056.1** conj	**1246.8** verb nom sing masc part pres mid	**1842.1** verb 3sing indic perf act	**2803.1** noun dat sing masc
ὁ	γὰρ	διακρινόμενος	ἔοικεν	κλύδωνι
ho	*gar*	*diakrinomenos*	*eoiken*	*kludōni*
The	for	doubting	is like	a wave

2258.2 noun gen sing fem	**414.1** verb dat sing masc part pres mid	**2504.1** conj	**4350.1** verb dat sing masc part pres mid	**3231.1** partic
θαλάσσης	ἀνεμιζομένῳ	καὶ	ῥιπιζομένῳ.	**7.** μὴ
thalassēs	*anemizomenō*	*kai*	*rhipizomenō*	*mē*
of sea	being driven by the wind	and	being tossed;	not

1056.1 conj	**3496.1** verb 3sing impr pres mid	**3450.5** art nom sing masc	**442.1** noun nom sing masc	**1552.3** dem-pron nom sing masc	**3617.1** conj
γὰρ	οἰέσθω	ὁ	ἄνθρωπος	ἐκεῖνος,	ὅτι
gar	*oiesthō*	*ho*	*anthrōpos*	*ekeinos*	*hoti*
for	let suppose	the	man	that	that

2956.39 verb 3sing indic fut mid	**2956.45** verb 3sing indic fut mid	**4948.10** indef-pron sing neu	**3706.2** prep	**3450.2** art gen sing
ʻ λήψεταί	[☆ λήμψεταί]	τι	παρὰ	τοῦ
lēpsetai	*lēmpsetai*	*ti*	*para*	*tou*
he shall receive	[idem]	anything	from	the

2935.2 noun gen sing masc	**433.1** noun nom sing masc	**1368.1** adj nom sing masc	**180.1** adj nom sing masc	**1706.1** prep
κυρίου·	**8.** ἀνὴρ	δίψυχος,	ἀκατάστατος	ἐν
kuriou	*anēr*	*dipsuchos*	*akatastatos*	*en*
Lord;	a man	double minded,	unstable	in

3820.15 adj dat pl fem	**3450.14** art dat pl fem	**3461.7** noun dat pl fem	**840.3** prs-pron gen sing	**2714.6** verb 3sing impr pres mid	**1156.2** conj
πάσαις	ταῖς	ὁδοῖς	αὐτοῦ.	**9.** Καυχάσθω	δὲ
pasais	*tais*	*hodois*	*autou*	*Kauchasthō*	*de*
all	the	ways	his.	Let boast	but

9.a.Var: 03B,044

3450.5 art nom sing masc	**79.1** noun nom sing masc	**3450.5** art nom sing masc	**4862.2** adj nom sing masc	**1706.1** prep
ʻa ὁ ˎ	ἀδελφὸς	ὁ	ταπεινὸς	ἐν
ho	*adelphos*	*ho*	*tapeinos*	*en*
the	brother	the	of humble circumstances	in

3450.3 art dat sing	**5149.3** noun dat sing neu	**840.3** prs-pron gen sing	**3450.5** art nom sing masc	**1156.2** conj	**4004.1** adj nom sing masc
τῷ	ὕψει	αὐτοῦ·	**10.** ὁ	δὲ	πλούσιος
tō	*hupsei*	*autou*	*ho*	*de*	*plousios*
the	elevation	his,	the	and	rich

times be evil and contrary to Biblical principles (3:15) and the will of God.

When wisdom is lacking, the believer is to ask God who gives generously. Divine wisdom is a gift of God. But the wisdom which is in view here is what God will give to all believers, not only the spiritual gift which Paul refers to as a "word of wisdom" (1 Corinthians 12:8). They who pray to God will act with more wisdom than they have themselves.

Wisdom can be imparted in various ways. God spoke to Saul of Tarsus in an audible voice (Acts 9:3-6), while He gave Ananias instructions by means of a vision to go and minister to Saul (Acts 9:10). God is sovereign and communicates wisdom in any way He considers appropriate.

The word "ask" as in Matthew 7:7 is in the present tense and means to keep on asking. Lest believers fear that God will become weary with our excessive asking, James indicates He is liberal (gives without reluctance or restraint) and does not upbraid (rebuke or embarrass) the asker for coming often.

1:6. Prayer for wisdom must be in faith which is untainted by doubt. Doubt indicates an unwillingness to rely completely on God. Because of this reluctance the believer is deprived of inner peace. He tosses like a wave between trusting human wisdom and trying to rely on divine wisdom.

1:7,8. In writing about faith, James made a distinction between mental assent and a firm conviction. Demons believe in the existence of God (James 2:19), but the believer who asks of God must not only believe that He exists, but "that he is a rewarder of them that diligently seek him" (Hebrews 11:6).

"That man" indicates a slight contempt for the person who vacillates in trusting God. He is double-minded, trying to look in two directions for help. See Matthew 6:24.

1:9. In the early days of the Church, members were from all classes of people including slaves (Ephesians 6:5) and the destitute (Acts 2:45; 1 Corinthians 11:21). In contrast to those unstable in faith, rather than being filled with resentment, these new believers were encouraged to be delighted because of their exalted position as "fellow citizens with the saints, and of the household of God" (Ephesians 2:19).

1:10. At the Cross all believers whether rich or poor are on an equal footing. The person the world considers disadvantaged is

that giveth to all [men] liberally, and upbraideth not: He is eager to help you, *Laubach* . . . who gives to all men freely and without upbraiding, *Montgomery* . . . who generously gives, *Williams* . . . to all without begrudging anyone, *Norlie* . . . unreservedly, *Adams* . . . who gives freely to all people, *SEB* . . . and reproaches not, *Darby* . . . and does not censure, *Wilson.*

and it shall be given him: Ask, then, and you will receive, *Norlie.*

6. But let him ask in faith, nothing wavering: . . . ask with confidence, *TCNT* . . . for there can be no doubting, *Norlie.*

For he that wavereth is like a wave of the sea: . . . because the doubter, *Fenton* . . . he who hesitates, *Wilson* . . . he who is irresolute, *Campbell* . . . like a surge of the sea, *Montgomery.*

driven with the wind and tossed: . . . tossed to and fro by, *Norlie* . . . driven hither and thither at the mercy of the wind, *TCNT* . . . blown about and broken, *Fenton.*

7. For let not that man think that he shall receive any thing of the Lord: Such a man need not suppose, *Montgomery* . . . cannot expect to get, *Norlie.*

8. A double minded man [is] unstable in all his ways: . . . a hesitating man, *Fenton* . . . vacillating men, irresolute at every turn, *TCNT* . . . turbulent in all his ways, *Concordant* . . . unstable at every turn, *Montgomery* . . . does not himself know what he wants, *Laubach* . . . His heart is divided into two parts, *SEB.*

9. Let the brother of low degree: A Christian brother who has few riches, *NLT* . . . in humble circumstances, *Montgomery* . . . of humble rank, *Fenton* . . . in lowly circumstances, *Adams* . . . who is poor, and tested, *Norlie.*

rejoice in that he is exalted: . . . glory in his exaltation, *Montgomery* . . . be proud of the honor, *Norlie* . . . boast about his high circumstances, *Adams.*

10. But the rich, in that he is made low: . . . the wealthy of his humble place, *Berkeley* . . . but a

1706.1 prep	3450.11 art dat sing fem	4865.2 noun dat sing fem	840.3 prs-pron gen sing	3617.1 conj	5453.1 conj	436.1 noun sing neu
ἐν	τῇ	ταπεινώσει	αὐτοῦ,	ὅτι	ὡς	ἄνθος
en	*tē*	*tapeinōsei*	*autou*	*hoti*	*hōs*	*anthos*
in	the	humiliation	his,	because	as	flower

5363.2 noun gen sing masc	3790.13 verb 3sing indic fut mid	391.3 verb 3sing indic aor act	1056.1 conj	3450.5 art nom sing masc
χόρτου	παρελεύσεται.	**11.** ἀνέτειλεν	γὰρ	ὁ
chortou	*pareleusetai*	*aneteilen*	*gar*	*ho*
grass's	he will pass away.	Rose	for	the

2229.1 noun nom sing masc	4713.1 prep	3450.3 art dat sing	2713.2 noun dat sing masc	2504.1 conj	3445.1 verb 3sing indic aor act	3450.6 art acc sing masc
ἥλιος	σὺν	τῷ	καύσωνι,	καὶ	ἐξήρανεν	τὸν
hēlios	*sun*	*tō*	*kausōni*	*kai*	*exēranen*	*ton*
sun	with	the	burning heat,	and	dried up	the

5363.4 noun acc sing masc	2504.1 conj	3450.16 art sing neu	436.1 noun sing neu	840.3 prs-pron gen sing	1588.3 verb 3sing indic aor act	2504.1 conj
χόρτον,	καὶ	τὸ	ἄνθος	αὐτοῦ	ἐξέπεσεν,	καὶ
chorton	*kai*	*to*	*anthos*	*autou*	*exepesen*	*kai*
grass,	and	the	flower	its	fell,	and

3450.9 art nom sing fem	2123.1 noun nom sing fem	3450.2 art gen sing	4241.2 noun gen sing neu	840.3 prs-pron gen sing	616.22 verb 3sing indic aor mid
ἡ	εὐπρέπεια	τοῦ	προσώπου	αὐτοῦ	ἀπώλετο·
hē	*euprepeia*	*tou*	*prosōpou*	*autou*	*apōleto*
the	beauty	of the	appearance	its	perished:

3643.1 adv	2504.1 conj	3450.5 art nom sing masc	4004.1 adj nom sing masc	1706.1 prep	3450.14 art dat pl fem	4056.2 noun dat pl fem
οὕτως	καὶ	ὁ	πλούσιος	ἐν	ταῖς	πορείαις
houtōs	*kai*	*ho*	*plousios*	*en*	*tais*	*poreiais*
thus	also	the	rich	in	the	goings

840.3 prs-pron gen sing	3105.1 verb 3sing indic fut pass	3079.2 adj nom sing masc	433.1 noun nom sing masc	3614.5 rel-pron nom sing masc
αὐτοῦ	μαρανθήσεται.	**12.** Μακάριος	ἀνὴρ	ὃς
autou	*maranthēsetai*	*Makarios*	*anēr*	*hos*
his	shall wither.	Blessed	man	who

5116.3 verb 3sing indic pres act	3848.4 noun acc sing masc	3617.1 conj	1378.1 adj nom sing masc	1090.53 verb nom sing masc part aor mid
ὑπομένει	πειρασμόν·	ὅτι	δόκιμος	γενόμενος
hupomenei	*peirasmon*	*hoti*	*dokimos*	*genomenos*
endures	temptation;	because	proved	having been

2956.39 verb 3sing indic fut mid	2956.45 verb 3sing indic fut mid	3450.6 art acc sing masc	4586.2 noun acc sing masc	3450.10 art gen sing fem
⸂ λήψεται	[☆ λήμψεται]	τὸν	στέφανον	τῆς
lēpsetai	*lēmpsetai*	*ton*	*stephanon*	*tēs*
he shall receive	[idem]	the	crown	of the

12.a.**Txt:** 04C,018K 020L,025P,byz.Sod **Var:** p23,01ℵ,02A,03B sa.bo.Lach,Treg,Alf,Tisc We/Ho,Weis,UBS/☆

2205.2 noun gen sing fem	3614.6 rel-pron acc sing masc	1846.3 verb 3sing indic aor mid	3450.5 art nom sing masc	2935.1 noun nom sing masc
ζωῆς,	ὃν	ἐπηγγείλατο	⸂a ὁ	κύριος ⸃
zōēs	*hon*	*epēngeilato*	*ho*	*kurios*
life,	which	promised	the	Lord

3450.4 art dat pl	25.4 verb dat pl part pres act	840.6 prs-pron acc sing masc	3235.3 num card nom masc	3847.12 verb nom sing masc part pres mid
τοῖς	ἀγαπῶσιν	αὐτόν.	**13.** Μηδεὶς	πειραζόμενος
tois	*agapōsin*	*auton*	*Mēdeis*	*peirazomenos*
to the	love	him.	No one	being tempted

elevated to a high standing in Christ, and the person the world considers to be in the upper class of society is brought low to the place where his trust is in Christ instead of in riches. People cannot earn a position in the family of God through either poverty or wealth. All are saved by grace through faith apart from works (Ephesians 2:8,9).

Jesus indicated it is hard for a person of wealth to enter into the Kingdom (Matthew 19:16-26). Hard, not because of the wealth, but because of the attitude a desire for wealth can create (1 Timothy 6:9,10). Jesus taught: "Blessed are the poor in spirit: for theirs is the kingdom of heaven" (Matthew 5:3). This is why the rich brother is to rejoice. When he is "made low," that is, becomes so poor in spirit that he makes a complete commitment to Christ, he becomes a fellow member of the household of God (Ephesians 2:19).

The rich brother who is made low has an eternal perspective concerning life and wealth. He has come to see that "the things which are seen are temporal; but the things which are not seen are eternal" (2 Corinthians 4:18). He recognizes that life with all its possessions constitutes a stewardship which brings blessing to the cause of Christ (Acts 4:34-37; 11:27-30).

1:11. The mention of quickly withering grass and flowers to illustrate the transitory nature of life was a figure the readers of James' letter could understand. In that part of the world the brief season of green grass and colorful flowers is often followed by a time of great heat which produces a sudden transformation from beauty to drabness. Jesus also referred to a south wind, the sirocco, which increases the effects of the intense heat (Luke 12:55). Jesus illustrated the suddenness with which life can terminate with the Parable of the Rich Man (Luke 12:16-20). At the time he was concerned with plans for increasing his wealth, his life came to a sudden end.

1:12. The truly blessed or happy believer in this life is not one who is free of trials but the one who endures them and is steadfast during the testings. The structure in the Greek translated "when he is tried" indicates the testing has been concluded and the person has been approved as genuine. After the testing this person receives a crown of life which is promised to those who love God. "Of life" in the expression "crown of life" stands in apposition to "crown." It indicates the believer will receive "the crown, the life." The article "the" before the word "life" refers to the quality of life which follows physical death.

Jesus spoke of the nature of this life when He said to those who are persecuted for righteousness' sake, "Rejoice, and be exceeding glad: for great is your reward in heaven" (Matthew 5:12). Paul referred to this new quality of life when he wrote: "Eye hath not seen, nor ear heard, neither have entered into the heart of man, the things which God hath prepared for them that love him. But God hath revealed them unto us by his Spirit" (1 Corinthians 2:9,10).

rich brother, in his humiliation, *Montgomery* . . . Let also the one who is rich, but humbled, rejoice, *Norlie* . . . in his lowliness, *Clementson* . . . his low condition, *Confraternity.*

because as the flower of the grass he shall pass away: . . . for he too will fade away, *Norlie* . . . like a flower that will die, *NLT* . . . here for only a short while, *SEB.*

11. For the sun is no sooner risen: . . . as the sun comes up, *Montgomery.*

with a burning heat: . . . with its glowing heat, *Berkeley* . . . and brings a scorching wind, *Norlie* . . . with scorching heat, *Wilson.*

but it withereth the grass, and the flower thereof falleth: The grass dries up from it, and the flowers wither one by one, *Norlie* . . . parches the grass, *Confraternity* . . . the herb, *Berkeley.*

and the grace of the fashion of it perisheth: All that lovely sight must go! *Norlie* . . . and all its beauty is gone, *TCNT* . . . It is no longer beautiful, *NLT* . . . The sun's heat destroys their beauty, *SEB* . . . the beauty of its appearance is destroyed, *Adams* . . . the comeliness of its look has perished, *Darby* . . . the beauty of its form disappears, *Fenton* . . . its lovely appearance is ruined, *Berkeley.*

so also shall the rich man fade away in his ways: . . . despite his money, will also come to nothing, *Norlie* . . . he will come to an untimely end, *TCNT* . . . will the rich man wither, *Confraternity* . . . amid his pursuits, *Montgomery* . . . in the middle of his efforts, *Laubach.*

12. Blessed [is] the man that endureth temptation: Happy the man, *Wilson* . . . who holds out in case of trials, *Norlie* . . . who stands firm, *TCNT, Laubach* . . . who sustains trial, *Campbell.*

for when he is tried: . . . when he has stood the test, *Montgomery* . . . having been approved, *Clementson* . . . becoming qualified, *Concordant.*

he shall receive the crown of life: . . . the prize of life, *NLT.*

which the Lord hath promised to them that love him: . . . that is promised, *Berkeley.*

13.a.**Txt:** Steph
Var: 01ℵ,02A,03B,04C 018K,020L,025P,Gries Lach,Treg,Alf,Word Tisc,We/Ho,Weis,Sod UBS/⋆

2978.12 verb 3sing impr pres act	**3617.1** conj	**570.3** prep	**3450.2** art gen sing	**2296.2** noun gen sing masc	**3847.10** verb 1sing indic pres mid
λεγέτω,	Ὅτι	ἀπὸ	(a τοῦ \	θεοῦ	πειράζομαι·
legetō	*Hoti*	*apo*	*tou*	*theou*	*peirazomai*
let say,		From		God	I am being tempted.

3450.5 art nom sing masc	**1056.1** conj	**2296.1** noun nom sing masc	**547.1** adj nom sing masc	**1498.4** verb 3sing indic pres act
ὁ	γὰρ	θεὸς	ἀπείραστός	ἐστιν
ho	*gar*	*theos*	*apeirastos*	*estin*
	For	God	not to be tempted	is

2527.1 adj gen pl	**3847.2** verb 3sing indic pres act	**1156.2** conj	**840.5** prs-pron nom sing masc	**3625.3** num card acc masc	**1524.3** adj nom sing masc
κακῶν,	πειράζει	δὲ	αὐτὸς	οὐδένα.	**14.** ἕκαστος
kakōn	*peirazei*	*de*	*autos*	*oudena*	*hekastos*
by evils,	tempts	and	himself	no one.	Each one

1156.2 conj	**3847.11** verb 3sing indic pres mid	**5097.3** prep	**3450.10** art gen sing fem	**2375.9** adj fem	**1924.1** noun fem
δὲ	πειράζεται,	ὑπὸ	τῆς	ἰδίας	ἐπιθυμίας
de	*peirazetai*	*hupo*	*tēs*	*idias*	*epithumias*
but	is being tempted,	by	the	his own	lust

1811.1 verb nom sing masc part pres mid	**2504.1** conj	**1179.3** verb nom sing masc part pres mid	**1520.1** adv	**3450.9** art nom sing fem
ἐξελκόμενος	καὶ	δελεαζόμενος·	**15.** εἶτα	ἡ
exelkomenos	*kai*	*deleazomenos*	*eita*	*hē*
being drawn away	and	being allured;	then	the

1924.2 noun nom sing fem	**4666.5** verb nom sing fem part aor act	**4936.1** verb 3sing indic pres act	**264.4** noun acc sing fem	**3450.9** art nom sing fem
ἐπιθυμία	συλλαβοῦσα	τίκτει	ἁμαρτίαν·	ἡ
epithumia	*sullabousa*	*tiktei*	*hamartian*	*hē*
lust	having conceived	gives birth to	sin;	the

1156.2 conj	**264.2** noun nom sing fem	**652.1** verb nom sing fem part aor pass	**610.1** verb 3sing indic pres act	**2265.4** noun acc sing masc
δὲ	ἁμαρτία	ἀποτελεσθεῖσα	ἀποκύει	θάνατον.
de	*hamartia*	*apotelestheisa*	*apokuei*	*thanaton*
but	sin	having been completed	brings forth	death.

3231.1 partic	**3966.11** verb 2pl pres mid	**79.6** noun nom pl masc	**1466.2** prs-pron gen 1sing	**27.6** adj pl masc
16. Μὴ	πλανᾶσθε,	ἀδελφοί	μου	ἀγαπητοί·
Mē	*planasthe*	*adelphoi*	*mou*	*agapētoi*
Not	be misled,	brothers	my	beloved.

3820.9 adj nom sing fem	**1388.1** noun nom sing fem	**18.9** adj nom sing fem	**2504.1** conj	**3820.17** adj sing neu	**1427.1** noun sing neu
17. πᾶσα	δόσις	ἀγαθὴ	καὶ	πᾶν	δώρημα
pasa	*dosis*	*agathē*	*kai*	*pan*	*dōrēma*
Every	act of giving	good	and	every	gift

4894.1 adj sing	**505.1** adv	**1498.4** verb 3sing indic pres act	**2568.10** verb sing neu part pres act	**570.3** prep
τέλειον	ἄνωθέν	ἐστιν	καταβαῖνον	ἀπὸ
teleion	*anōthen*	*estin*	*katabainon*	*apo*
perfect	from above	is	coming down	from

3450.2 art gen sing	**3824.2** noun gen sing masc	**3450.1** art gen pl	**5295.4** noun gen pl neu	**3706.1** prep	**3614.3** rel-pron dat sing	**3620.2** partic
τοῦ	πατρὸς	τῶν	φώτων,	παρ'	ᾧ	οὐκ
tou	*patros*	*tōn*	*phōtōn*	*par'*	*hō*	*ouk*
the	Father	of the	lights,	with	whom	not

1:13. Apparently some believers whose faith was being tested allowed the testing to become an occasion of yielding to sinful impulses. Instead of accepting personal responsibility for their failure they were blaming God. This tendency began in Eden when Adam blamed Eve, and God indirectly, and Eve blamed the serpent (Genesis 3:12,13). James was emphatic. Believers were wrong in blaming God.

Because God is absolutely holy, He cannot be tempted with evil. Sometimes He tests believers, but He in no way tempts them to sin. In fact, God will not allow temptation that is greater than the believer can withstand and always provides a way of escape (1 Corinthians 10:13).

1:14. In this verse James took away every excuse anyone might use for not accepting personal responsibility for sin. A person is tempted when he is drawn away by his own lust. Inherent in this statement is recognition of the fact of original sin. Every offspring of Adam and Eve is born with the impulse to sin (Psalm 51:5). It is not external circumstances but the wrong kind of internal desires which lead to sin (Matthew 15:17-20).

Legitimate desires can be drawn out beyond legitimate bounds, and when this happens the person is enticed or trapped. For example, the desire for food is proper, but it is wrong when it becomes gluttony. The same can be said of other God-given desires.

1:15. When desire becomes illegitimate it gives birth to sin, and sin results in death. (See Romans 6:23.) This death can be physical or spiritual. God chastens the sinning believer. While not all sickness is the result of sin, in the case of the Corinthians it was, and God even allowed some to die so their souls might be saved (1 Corinthians 11:28-30). On the other hand, death can be spiritual, that is, resulting in separation from God (Isaiah 59:2; 1 Timothy 5:6).

1:16,17. James commanded believers to cease from the error of blaming God. He made it clear that rather than being the source of temptation to sin, God is the source of nothing but good. "Every good gift" seems to refer to the manner in which God gives. It is liberal, without reluctance or ulterior motives (cf. verse 5). "Every perfect gift" emphasizes the completeness of the gift; nothing is lacking.

To illustrate God's greatness and unchangeableness James used the figure of light. Not only is God the Creator of sun, moon, and stars, but unlike lights of the universe which cast changing shadows or can be obscured by such things as clouds, God never changes

13. Let no man say when he is tempted: . . . he should never say, *Norlie* . . . in the hour of temptation, *TCNT.*

I am tempted of God:

for God cannot be tempted with evil: . . . is incapable of, *Wilson* . . . to do wrong, *Laubach.*

neither tempteth he any man: He Himself tempts no one to do evil, *Norlie.*

14. But every man is tempted, when he is drawn away of his own lust, and enticed: Now each one is undergoing trial when, *Concordant* . . . Rather, each one is tempted by his own evil desires by which he lets himself be enticed and lured, *Norlie* . . . tempted by their own passions—allured and enticed by them, *TCNT* . . . when he is allured by his own evil desire, *Williams* . . . by his own inordinate desire, *Wilson* . . . lusts that allure and entice him, *Montgomery* . . . His selfish desire pulls him away from God, *SEB* . . . by the longing and seducing of his own lust, *Fenton.*

15. Then when lust hath conceived, it bringeth forth sin: . . . evil desire, *Norlie* . . . When he does what his bad thoughts tell him to do, *NLT* . . . and gives birth to sin, *Montgomery* . . . having conceived produces sin, *Wilson.*

and sin, when it is finished: . . . when it is mature, *Montgomery* . . . when it has run its course, *Norlie* . . . is full-grown, *Laubach* . . . fully consummated, *Concordant* . . . the sin grows, *SEB.*

bringeth forth death: . . . and results in death, *SEB* . . . ends in death, *Norlie.*

16. Do not err, my beloved brethren: Do not be deceived, *Montgomery* . . . Make no mistake about it, *SEB* . . . let no one mislead you, *Norlie* . . . do not be fooled about this *NLT.*

17. Every good gift and every perfect gift is from above: Every desire to give, *Norlie* . . . and every perfect boon, *Montgomery* . . . every perfect endowment, *TCNT* . . . Every beneficent gift, *Fenton.*

and cometh down from the Father of lights: . . . the Maker of the Lights in the heavens, *TCNT.*

1746.1 verb 3sing indic pres act	3744.1 noun nom sing fem	2211.1 conj	4998.1 noun gen sing fem	638.1 noun sing neu
ἔνι	παραλλαγὴ,	ἢ	τροπῆς	ἀποσκίασμα.
eni	*parallagē*	*ē*	*tropēs*	*aposkiasma*
there is	variation,	or	of turning	shadow.

1007.15 verb nom sing masc part aor pass	610.2 verb 3sing indic aor act	2231.4 prs-pron acc 1pl	3030.3 noun dat sing masc	223.2 noun gen sing fem
18. βουληθεὶς	ἀπεκύησεν	ἡμᾶς	λόγῳ	ἀληθείας,
boulētheis	*apekuēsen*	*hēmas*	*logō*	*alētheias*
Having willed	he produced	us	by word	of truth,

1519.1 prep	3450.16 art sing neu	1498.32 verb inf pres act	2231.4 prs-pron acc 1pl	532.2 noun acc sing fem	4948.5 indef-pron
εἰς	τὸ	εἶναι	ἡμᾶς	ἀπαρχήν	τινα
eis	*to*	*einai*	*hēmas*	*aparchēn*	*tina*
for	the	to be	us	first fruits	a sort of

18.a.**Txt:** 01ℵ-org,03B byz.
Var: 01ℵ-corr3,02A,04C 025P,044,945,1241 1739

3450.1 art gen pl	840.3 prs-pron gen sing	1431.4 prs-pron gen sing	2910.2 noun gen pl neu	5452.1 conj
τῶν	⸂☆ αὐτοῦ	[a ἑαυτοῦ]	κτισμάτων.	**19.** ⸂ Ὥστε,
tōn	*autou*	*heautou*	*ktismatōn*	*Hōste*
of the	his	[himself]	creatures.	So that,

19.a.**Txt:** 018K,020L 025P,byz.
Var: 01ℵ-corr,02A,03B 04C,it.bo.Lach,Treg,Alf Tisc,We/Ho,Weis,Sod UBS/☆

3471.1 verb 2pl perf act	79.6 noun nom pl masc	1466.2 prs-pron gen 1sing	27.6 adj pl masc	1498.17 verb 3sing impr pres act
[a☆ Ἴστε,]	ἀδελφοί	μου	ἀγαπητοί,	ἔστω
Iste	*adelphoi*	*mou*	*agapētoi*	*estō*
[You know,]	brothers	my	beloved,	let be

19.b.**Var:** 01ℵ,03B,04C 025P-org,it.bo.Lach Treg,Alf,Tisc,We/Ho Weis,UBS/☆

1156.2 conj	3820.6 adj nom sing masc	442.1 noun nom sing masc	4884.1 adj nom sing masc	1519.1 prep	3450.16 art sing neu
[b☆+ δὲ]	πᾶς	ἄνθρωπος	ταχὺς	εἰς	τὸ
de	*pas*	*anthrōpos*	*tachus*	*eis*	*to*
[but]	every	man	swift	to	the

189.36 verb inf aor act	1014.1 adj nom sing masc	1519.1 prep	3450.16 art sing neu	2953.37 verb inf aor act	1014.1 adj nom sing masc	1519.1 prep
ἀκοῦσαι,	βραδὺς	εἰς	τὸ	λαλῆσαι,	βραδὺς	εἰς
akousai	*bradus*	*eis*	*to*	*lalēsai*	*bradus*	*eis*
to hear,	slow	to	the	to speak,	slow	to

3572.4 noun acc sing fem	3572.1 noun nom sing fem	1056.1 conj	433.2 noun gen sing masc	1336.4 noun acc sing fem	2296.2 noun gen sing masc
ὀργήν.	**20.** ὀργὴ	γὰρ	ἀνδρὸς	δικαιοσύνην	θεοῦ
orgēn	*orgē*	*gar*	*andros*	*dikaiosunēn*	*theou*
wrath;	wrath	for	man's	righteousness	God's

20.a.**Txt:** 04C-org,018K 020L,025P,byz.
Var: 01ℵ,02A,03B 04C-corr,Lach,Treg,Alf Tisc,We/Ho,Weis,Sod UBS/☆

3620.3 partic	2686.2 verb 3sing indic pres mid	3620.2 partic	2021.4 verb 3sing indic pres mid	1346.1 conj
⸂ οὐ	κατεργάζεται.	[a☆ οὐκ	ἐργάζεται.]	**21.** Διὸ
ou	*katergazetai*	*ouk*	*ergazetai*	*Dio*
not	works out.	[not	works.]	Wherefore,

653.4 verb nom pl masc part aor mid	3820.12 adj acc sing fem	4364.1 noun acc sing fem	2504.1 conj	3913.2 noun acc sing fem
ἀποθέμενοι	πᾶσαν	ῥυπαρίαν	καὶ	περισσείαν
apothemenoi	*pasan*	*rhuparian*	*kai*	*perisseian*
having laid aside	all	filthiness	and	abounding

2520.2 noun gen sing fem	1706.1 prep	4099.2 noun dat sing fem	1203.12 verb 2pl impr aor mid	3450.6 art acc sing masc
κακίας,	ἐν	πραΰτητι	δέξασθε	τὸν
kakias	*en*	*prautēti*	*dexasthe*	*ton*
of wickedness,	in	gentleness	accept	the

(Malachi 3:6). He is light, and "in him is no darkness at all" (1 John 1:5).

with whom is no variableness: . . . there is not a change of position, *Fenton* . . . not a single change, *Adams* . . . God never changes, *Laubach* . . . is always consistent, *SEB.*

neither shadow of turning: . . . and in His light there are no shadows, *Laubach* . . . nor shadow of eclipse, *Montgomery* . . . neither shadow that is cast by turning, *Clementson* . . . nor shadow of alteration, *Confraternity* . . . or the least Variation, *Wilson.*

1:18. After pointing out in verse 17 that God is the giver of every good gift, James called special attention to the gift of salvation. This was provided of "his own will." God took the initiative. After Adam and Eve sinned God promised a plan of redemption (Genesis 3:15). Jesus made it clear that His followers were the result of divine initiative when He said, "Ye have not chosen me, but I have chosen you" (John 15:16). Paul pointed out that God's plan of salvation was not an afterthought. Man's need of salvation was in God's mind before the foundation of the world (Ephesians 1:4).

"Begat he us" speaks of the new birth, of regeneration. Jesus told Nicodemus, "Except a man be born again, he cannot see the kingdom of God" (John 3:3). Paul pointed out the absolute need of becoming a new creature (Galatians 6:15).

An agency in regeneration is "the word of truth." Peter wrote that believers are born again by the Word of God (1 Peter 1:23). The Holy Spirit is also active in regeneration (John 3:5; Titus 3:5). He works through the Word, reproving man of sin, righteousness, and judgment (John 16:8-11). When man believes the gospel (1 Corinthians 4:15) and accepts Christ as Saviour (John 1:12,13; Galatians 3:26), he becomes a new creature.

"Firstfruits" speaks of the beginning of a harvest which is to follow. James' readers were among the beginning of the great gospel harvest which continues to this day. Paul used the expression in the same way (Romans 16:5).

18. Of his own will begat he us with the word of truth: Because he willed, *Montgomery* . . . He brought us into being, *Norlie.*

that we should be a kind of firstfruits of his creatures: . . . in order that we might be a sample of what He created for Himself, *Fenton* . . . an earnest of still further creations, *TCNT.*

19. Wherefore, my beloved brethren: Mark this well, *Montgomery.*

let every man be swift to hear, slow to speak, slow to wrath: . . . be quick to listen...slow to lose your temper, *Norlie* . . . tardy to speak, *Concordant* . . . in growing angry, *Montgomery.*

20. For the wrath of man worketh not the righteousness of God: Anger is not the way to arrive at the justice God demands, *Norlie* . . . a man's anger does not further the righteous purpose of God, *Montgomery* . . . does not work the justice of, *Confraternity* . . . is not conducive to Divine righteousness, *Fenton.*

1:19,20. Believers are begotten "with the word of truth" (1:18), and because of the importance of the Word believers should be "swift to hear." The Word is not only an agent in regeneration but in sanctification as well (John 17:17; 2 Timothy 3:16,17).

Early congregations of believers were small and often met in homes (Philemon 2). In such informal gatherings there were undoubtedly discussions of Biblical truth. James warned against quick, ill-considered comments which would only lead to confusion.

The word here translated "wrath" seems to imply a continuing resentment. It is tragic but true that ill-considered observations sometimes lead to resentment which does not demonstrate righteousness.

21. Wherefore lay apart all filthiness and superfluity of naughtiness: . . . strip yourselves of everything impure, *Williams* . . . Remove every evil, *SEB* . . . suppress ill-will and all wickedness within you, *Norlie* . . . stripping off all vicious filth, *Fenton* . . . put aside all filthy habits, *TCNT* . . . all that is dirty and wrong, *NLT* . . . superabundance of evil, *Concordant* . . . evil excesses, *Adams.*

and receive with meekness the engrafted word: . . . accept the Word which is planted in you, *Norlie* . . . in a gentle heart, *Berkeley* . . . the implanted Word, *Montgomery.*

1:21. Believers are to lay aside like a garment all moral filth, all that is sordid. "Superfluity of naughtiness" might also be translated "the remains of wickedness." They had already given up some pagan practices and were urged to give up what still remained.

Eager reception of the Word would result in ultimate salvation. Salvation includes deliverance from the penalty of sin (past), from

1705.1 adj acc sing masc	3030.4 noun acc sing masc	3450.6 art acc sing masc	1404.15 verb acc sing masc part pres mid	4834.10 verb inf aor act	3450.15 art acc pl fem
ἔμφυτον	λόγον,	τὸν	δυνάμενον	σῶσαι	τὰς
emphuton	*logon*	*ton*	*dunamenon*	*sōsai*	*tas*
implanted	word,	the	being able	to save	the

5425.8 noun acc pl fem	5050.2 prs-pron gen 2pl	1090.19 verb 2pl impr pres mid	1156.2 conj	4023.2 noun nom pl masc	3030.2 noun gen sing masc
ψυχὰς	ὑμῶν.	22. Γίνεσθε	δὲ	ποιηταὶ	λόγου,
psuchas	*humōn*	*Ginesthe*	*de*	*poiētai*	*logou*
souls	your.	Be you	but	doers	of word,

2504.1 conj	3231.1 partic	3303.1 adv	200.2 noun nom pl masc	200.2 noun nom pl masc	3303.1 adv
καὶ	μὴ	⸂ μόνον	ἀκροαταί,	[☆ ἀκροαταὶ	μόνον]
kai	*mē*	*monon*	*akroatai*	*akroatai*	*monon*
and	not	only	hearers,	[hearers	only]

3745.2 verb nom pl masc part pres mid	1431.8 prs-pron acc pl masc	3617.1 conj	1479.1 conj	4948.3 indef-pron nom sing
παραλογιζόμενοι	ἑαυτούς.	23. ὅτι	εἴ	τις
paralogizomenoi	*heautous*	*hoti*	*ei*	*tis*
deceiving	yourselves.	Because	if	any man

200.1 noun nom sing masc	3030.2 noun gen sing masc	1498.4 verb 3sing indic pres act	2504.1 conj	3620.3 partic	4023.1 noun nom sing masc
ἀκροατὴς	λόγου	ἐστὶν	καὶ	οὐ	ποιητής,
akroatēs	*logou*	*estin*	*kai*	*ou*	*poiētēs*
a hearer	of word	is	and	not	a doer,

3642.4 dem-pron nom sing masc	1842.1 verb 3sing indic perf act	433.3 noun dat sing masc	2627.3 verb dat sing masc part pres act	3450.16 art sing neu
οὗτος	ἔοικεν	ἀνδρὶ	κατανοοῦντι	τὸ
houtos	*eoiken*	*andri*	*katanoounti*	*to*
this	is like	to a man	considering	the

4241.1 noun sing neu	3450.10 art gen sing fem	1071.1 noun gen sing fem	840.3 prs-pron gen sing	1706.1 prep	2054.2 noun dat sing neu
πρόσωπον	τῆς	γενέσεως	αὐτοῦ	ἐν	ἐσόπτρῳ·
prosōpon	*tēs*	*geneseōs*	*autou*	*en*	*esoptrō*
face	the	natural	his	in	a mirror:

2627.4 verb 3sing indic aor act	1056.1 conj	1431.6 prs-pron acc sing masc	2504.1 conj	562.13 verb 3sing indic perf act	2504.1 conj
24. κατενόησεν	γὰρ	ἑαυτὸν	καὶ	ἀπελήλυθεν,	καὶ
katenoēsen	*gar*	*heauton*	*kai*	*apelēluthen*	*kai*
he considered	for	himself	and	has gone away,	and

2091.1 adv	1935.3 verb 3sing indic aor mid	3560.1 intr-pron nom sing masc	1498.34 verb sing indic imperf act	3450.5 art nom sing masc
εὐθέως	ἐπελάθετο	ὁποῖος	ἦν.	25. ὁ
eutheōs	*epelatheto*	*hopoios*	*ēn*	*ho*
immediately	forgot	what like	he was.	The

1156.2 conj	3740.2 verb nom sing masc part aor act	1519.1 prep	3414.4 noun acc sing masc	4894.1 adj sing	3450.6 art acc sing masc
δὲ	παρακύψας	εἰς	νόμον	τέλειον	τὸν
de	*parakupsas*	*eis*	*nomon*	*teleion*	*ton*
but	having looked	into	law	perfect,	the

25.a.**Txt:** 018K,020L 025P,byz.
Var: 01ℵ,02A,03B,04C 33,bo.Lach,Treg,Alf Tisc,We/Ho,Weis,Sod UBS/☆

3450.10 art gen sing fem	1644.2 noun gen sing fem	2504.1 conj	3748.2 verb nom sing masc part aor act	3642.4 dem-pron nom sing masc
τῆς	ἐλευθερίας,	καὶ	παραμείνας,	⸂a οὗτος ⸃
tēs	*eleutherias*	*kai*	*parameinas*	*houtos*
of the	freedom,	and	having continued in,	this

the power of sin (present), and ultimately from the presence of sin (future).

which is able to save your souls: . . . that contains the power to save your souls, *Berkeley.*

1:22. James here began an emphasis on what the believer should do with the "engrafted word" (1:21). It was not enough to be hearers; they were to make sure they became doers of the Word. Hearing is important because faith comes by hearing (Romans 10:17). But unless hearing is followed by obedience, the consequences can be tragic. In the Parable of the Two Builders (Matthew 7:24-27) Jesus emphasized the difference between hearers who acted upon what they heard and those who did nothing about what they heard.

The word translated "deceiving" carries the idea of false reasoning. The "nondoers" rationalized their lack of conformity to the Word. Like the priest and Levite in the Parable of the Good Samaritan who probably justified their disregard of the injured man, "hearers only" were rationalizing their failure to obey what they heard.

22. But be ye doers of the word: Obey the message that you hear, *Norlie* . . . Put that Teaching into practice, *TCNT* . . . Obey the Word of God, *NLT* . . . Do whatever God tells you to do, *Laubach.*

and not hearers only: . . . not merely hearers, *Montgomery* . . . by merely listening, *Berkeley.*

deceiving your own selves: . . . beguiling yourselves, *Concordant* . . . you are only fooling yourselves, *SEB* . . . not deluders of yourselves, *Berkeley.*

1:23,24. James compared the casual hearer of the Word with a man who looks into a mirror and does nothing to improve his appearance. The person who does nothing more than hear the Word disregards changes He needs in character. The word translated "glass" would better be translated "mirror" since it was made of polished metal.

23. For if any be a hearer of the word: Any man who listens to the Word, *Norlie* . . . whoever hears the message, *Berkeley.*

and not a doer: . . . but does not carry out its message, *Norlie* . . . without obeying it, *Williams* . . . without acting upon it, *Berkeley.*

he is like unto a man beholding his natural face in a glass: . . . is similar to the man who observes his own face, *Berkeley* . . . looking at, *Confraternity* . . . contemplating, *Fenton* . . . in a mirror, *Montgomery.*

24. For he beholdeth himself, and goeth his way: . . . he takes a look at himself and goes off, *Berkeley* . . . after he has looked carefully at himself, he goes away, *Montgomery.*

and straightway forgetteth: . . . and presently, *Confraternity* . . . immediately forgets, *Campbell* . . . at once forgets, *Montgomery* . . . then promptly forgets, *Berkeley.*

what manner of man he was: . . . what he is like, *Montgomery* . . . what he looked like, *SEB.*

1:25. The word translated "looketh into" (*parakupsas eis*) is in contrast to the casual beholding of 1:24. It pictures a person stooping over to see something better. It means intent looking and careful examination because the subject under consideration is very important. The same word describes how John and Mary stooped down and looked into the open tomb in which Jesus had been placed (John 20:5,11) because this was a matter of tremendous significance to them.

The person who seriously continues looking "into the perfect law of liberty" is the person who is blessed. The perfect law is described as "the law of liberty."

The Old Testament law was not perfect. It could not give life or righteousness (Galatians 3:21). It was only a shadow of good things to come (Hebrews 10:1). It was only a schoolmaster to lead to Christ so that believers might be justified by faith (Galatians 3:24).

In the Old Testament God promised a new covenant in which He would place His law within the human heart (Jeremiah 31:33). Jesus introduced this new covenant with His atoning death (1 Corinthians 11:25). This perfect law or new covenant was the "engrafted word" (1:21) James' readers had received. This is the law of liberty which sets believers free from the Law as a means of

25. But whoso looketh into: The truly wise man, *Laubach* . . . the man who looks closely, *Montgomery* . . . he who has looked carefully, *Confraternity* . . . looks seriously into, *Berkeley.*

the perfect law of liberty: . . . the Law of Freedom, *TCNT.*

and continueth [therein]: . . . continues looking, *Montgomery* . . . and perseveres, *Campbell* . . . and is faithful to it, *Berkeley.*

3620.2 partic	**200.1** noun nom sing masc	**1938.1** noun gen sing fem	**1090.53** verb nom sing masc part aor mid	**233.2** conj	**4023.1** noun nom sing masc
οὐκ	ἀκροατὴς	ἐπιλησμονῆς	γενόμενος,	ἀλλὰ	ποιητὴς
ouk	*akroatēs*	*epilēsmonēs*	*genomenos*	*alla*	*poiētēs*
not	a hearer	forgetful	having been,	but	a doer

2024.2 noun gen sing neu	**3642.4** dem-pron nom sing masc	**3079.2** adj nom sing masc	**1706.1** prep	**3450.11** art dat sing fem	**4022.1** noun dat sing fem
ἔργου,	οὗτος	μακάριος	ἐν	τῇ	ποιήσει
ergou	*houtos*	*makarios*	*en*	*tē*	*poiēsei*
of work,	this	blessed	in	the	doing

840.3 prs-pron gen sing	**1498.40** verb 3sing indic fut mid	**1479.1** conj	**4948.3** indef-pron nom sing	**1374.5** verb 3sing indic pres act
αὐτοῦ	ἔσται.	**26.** Εἴ	τις	δοκεῖ
autou	*estai*	*Ei*	*tis*	*dokei*
his	shall be.	If	anyone	seems

26.a.**Txt:** 018K,020L,byz. **Var:** 01ℵ,02A,03B,04C 025P,Gries,Lach,Treg Alf,Word,Tisc,We/Ho Weis,Sod,UBS/☆

2334.1 adj nom sing masc	**1498.32** verb inf pres act	**1706.1** prep	**5050.3** prs-pron dat 2pl	**3231.1** partic	**5304.1** verb nom sing masc part pres act
θρησκὸς	εἶναι	⸂a ἐν	ὑμῖν, ⸃	μὴ	χαλιναγωγῶν
thrēskos	*einai*	*en*	*humin*	*mē*	*chalinagōgōn*
religious	to be	among	you,	not	restraining

1094.4 noun acc sing fem	**840.3** prs-pron gen sing	**233.1** conj	**233.2** conj	**534.2** verb nom sing masc part pres act	**2559.4** noun acc sing fem
γλῶσσαν	αὐτοῦ,	⸀ ἀλλ'	[☆ ἀλλὰ]	ἀπατῶν	καρδίαν
glōssan	*autou*	*all'*	*alla*	*apatōn*	*kardian*
tongue	his,	but	[idem]	deceiving	heart

26.b.**Txt:** 01ℵ,02A,04C 018K,020L,etc.byz.Tisc Sod **Var:** 03B,025P,Lach We/Ho,Weis,UBS/☆

840.3 prs-pron gen sing	**1431.4** prs-pron gen sing	**3642.1** dem-pron gen sing	**3124.2** adj nom sing masc	**3450.9** art nom sing fem
⸀ αὐτοῦ,	[b ἑαυτοῦ,]	τούτου	μάταιος	ἡ
autou	*heautou*	*toutou*	*mataios*	*hē*
his,	[of himself,]	of this	futile	the

2333.1 noun nom sing fem	**2333.1** noun nom sing fem	**2485.6** adj	**2504.1** conj	**281.1** adj nom sing	**3706.2** prep
θρησκεία.	**27.** θρησκεία	καθαρὰ	καὶ	ἀμίαντος	παρὰ
thrēskeia	*thrēskeia*	*kathara*	*kai*	*amiantos*	*para*
religion.	Religion	pure	and	undefiled	before

27.a.**Txt:** p74,01ℵ-corr3 02A,03B,04C-corr3 025P,044,33,81,614 630,1739 **Var:** 01ℵ-org,04C-corr2 049,byz.

3450.3 art dat sing	**2296.3** noun dat sing masc	**2504.1** conj	**3824.3** noun dat sing masc	**3642.9** dem-pron nom sing fem	**1498.4** verb 3sing indic pres act
⸂a τῷ ⸃	θεῷ	καὶ	πατρὶ	αὕτη	ἐστίν,
tō	*theō*	*kai*	*patri*	*hautē*	*estin*
	God	and	Father	this	is:

1964.2 verb inf pres mid	**3600.1** adj acc pl masc	**2504.1** conj	**5339.6** noun acc pl fem	**1706.1** prep	**3450.11** art dat sing fem
ἐπισκέπτεσθαι	ὀρφανοὺς	καὶ	χήρας	ἐν	τῇ
episkeptesthai	*orphanous*	*kai*	*chēras*	*en*	*tē*
to visit	orphans	and	widows	in	the

2324.3 noun dat sing fem	**840.1** prs-pron gen pl	**778.1** adj acc sing	**1431.6** prs-pron acc sing masc	**4931.11** verb inf pres act	**570.3** prep
θλίψει	αὐτῶν,	ἄσπιλον	ἑαυτὸν	τηρεῖν	ἀπὸ
thlipsei	*autōn*	*aspilon*	*heauton*	*tērein*	*apo*
tribulation	their,	unspotted	oneself	to keep	from

3450.2 art gen sing	**2862.2** noun gen sing masc	**79.6** noun nom pl masc	**1466.2** prs-pron gen 1sing	**3231.1** partic	**1706.1** prep
τοῦ	κόσμου.	**2:1.** Ἀδελφοί	μου,	μὴ	ἐν
tou	*kosmou*	*Adelphoi*	*mou*	*mē*	*en*
the	world.	Brothers	my,	not	with

righteousness (Romans 10:4) and also from sin (Romans 8:1-4). The law of liberty is not a freedom to sin (Romans 6:1,2; Galatians 5:13) but a freedom to serve God (Romans 6:22). The person who continues in the perfect law and acts accordingly will be the happy person.

he being not a forgetful hearer: . . . who is not a forgetful listener, *Berkeley* . . . a heedless listener who forgets the message, *Norlie* . . . don't merely listen and forget, *Beck.*

but a doer of the work: . . . but an active worker, *Berkeley* . . . a doer who does, *Montgomery.*

this man shall be blessed in his deed: . . . you'll be happy as you do it, *Beck* . . . blessed as a doer, *Norlie* . . . in his practice, *Berkeley.*

1:26. "Seem to be religious" may be translated "thinks of himself as being religious." Self-deception has often been a problem with people who associate with true believers. The words translated "religious" and "religion" refer to the external aspects of a relationship with God. Jesus dealt with this matter when He warned against wrong motives in giving, praying, and fasting (Matthew 6:1-18).

An unbridled tongue is one indication that a person's inner life does not match his outward profession. Just as a horse needs a bridle to control and direct it, the tongue of the believer needs proper control and direction.

The bridled tongue presupposes bridled thinking. The way to bridle the mind and the tongue is to continue to meditate on the Word of God (1:25). Philippians 4:8 gives guidelines for proper thinking: thinking about that which is true, honest, just, pure, lovely, of good report, virtuous, and praiseworthy.

Critical people are often motivated by resentment, jealousy, or bitterness. They fail to speak "the truth in love" (Ephesians 4:15). Their religion is vain. It does not honor God.

26. If any man among you seem to be religious: Whoever supposes he is religious, *Berkeley* . . . thinks that he is, *Norlie.*

and bridleth not his tongue: . . . who does not restrain, *Wilson* . . . but does not control what he says, *SEB.*

but deceiveth his own heart: . . . but deludes his own Heart, *Wilson.*

this man's religion [is] vain: . . . his religious worship, *Williams* . . . a man's religious observances are valueless, *TCNT* . . . is empty, *Montgomery* . . . is worthless, *Norlie* . . . is useless, *Berkeley* . . . does him no good, *Laubach.*

1:27. The words "pure" and "undefiled" present the qualities which should characterize the believer. See Mark 7:3,5,15-23. "Before God and the Father" may be translated "before our God and Father" or "before God who is our Father." Believers are to be more concerned about God's approval than man's.

One example of pure religion is to "visit the fatherless and widows in their affliction." God had expressed a special concern for orphans and widows in His earliest instructions to Israel (Exodus 22:22). In the early days of the Church, deacons were chosen to care for the widows (Acts 6:1-3).

The word "visit" implies more than just making a contribution of material assistance. The church was to support and sustain the orphans in their problems. The less fortunate were to be included in the social life of the church.

Believers should also jealously watch that they do not become spotted or stained by the world. They are in a world of people who are enemies of God. Jesus did not pray that they should be removed from the world but kept from the evil (John 17:15). But believers also have a responsibility. They must guard against conformity to the world. Through meditation on the Word they are to be transformed (Romans 12:2; also see James 1:25).

27. Pure religion and undefiled before God and the Father: What God the Father accepts as pure unpolluted service, *SEB* . . . Your way of worshiping is pure and stainless before God the Father if, *Beck* . . . and without blemish, *Norlie* . . . in agreement with, *Berkeley.*

is this, To visit the fatherless and widows: . . . are things like this, *SEB* . . . to give aid to, *Confraternity* . . . to care for children who have no fathers, *Laubach* . . . to look after orphans, *Montgomery* . . . help orphans, *Norlie.*

in their affliction: . . . in their need, *Norlie* . . . in their hour of trouble, *TCNT* . . . in their distress, *Fenton* . . . in their tribulation, *Confraternity.*

[and] to keep himself unspotted from the world: . . . to keep one's own self unstained, *Williams* . . . to keep personally free from the smut of, *Berkeley* . . . from the contamination of the world, *TCNT* . . . unstained, *Norlie* . . . keep yourself clean from the world's evil ways, *Laubach.*

4240.2 noun dat pl fem	4240.4 noun dat pl fem	2174.2 verb 2pl pres act	3450.12 art acc sing fem
ʽ προσωποληψίαις	[☆ προσωπολημψίαις]	ἔχετε	τὴν
prosōpolēpsiais	*prosōpolēmpsiais*	*echete*	*tēn*
partiality	[idem]	have	the

3963.4 noun acc sing fem	3450.2 art gen sing	2935.2 noun gen sing masc	2231.2 prs-pron gen 1pl	2400.2 name masc	5382.2 name gen masc	3450.10 art gen sing fem
πίστιν	τοῦ	κυρίου	ἡμῶν	Ἰησοῦ	Χριστοῦ	τῆς
pistin	*tou*	*kuriou*	*hēmōn*	*Iēsou*	*Christou*	*tēs*
faith	of the	Lord	our	Jesus	Christ,	of the

2.a.**Txt:** 01ℵ-corr,02A 018K,020L,025P,byz. **Var:** 01ℵ-org,03B,04C Lach,Treg,Alf,Tisc We/Ho,Weis,Sod UBS/☆

1385.2 noun gen sing fem	1430.1 partic	1056.1 conj	1511.7 verb 3sing subj aor act	1519.1 prep	3450.12 art acc sing fem
δόξης·	2. ἐὰν	γὰρ	εἰσέλθῃ	εἰς	ʽa τὴν ˋ
doxēs	*ean*	*gar*	*eiselthē*	*eis*	*tēn*
glory;	if	for	should have come	into	the

4715.4 noun acc sing fem	5050.2 prs-pron gen 2pl	433.1 noun nom sing masc	5389.1 adj nom sing masc	1706.1 prep
συναγωγὴν	ὑμῶν	ἀνὴρ	χρυσοδακτύλιος	ἐν
sunagōgēn	*humōn*	*anēr*	*chrusodaktulios*	*en*
synagogue	your	a man	with gold rings	in

2051.1 noun dat sing fem	2959.3 adj dat sing fem	1511.7 verb 3sing subj aor act	1156.2 conj	2504.1 conj	4292.1 adj nom sing masc
ἐσθῆτι	λαμπρᾷ,	εἰσέλθῃ	δὲ	καὶ	πτωχὸς
esthēti	*lampra*	*eiselthē*	*de*	*kai*	*ptōchos*
apparel	splendid,	may have come in	and	also	a poor

1706.1 prep	4365.1 adj dat sing fem	2051.1 noun dat sing fem	2504.1 conj	1899.2 verb 2pl subj aor act
ἐν	ῥυπαρᾷ	ἐσθῆτι,	3. ʽ καὶ	ἐπιβλέψητε
en	*rhupara*	*esthēti*	*kai*	*epiblepsēte*
in	vile	apparel,	and	you may have looked

3.a.**Txt:** 01ℵ,02A,018K 020L,33,byz.sa.Tisc **Var:** 03B,04C,025P,Alf We/Ho,Weis,Sod UBS/☆

1899.2 verb 2pl subj aor act	1156.2 conj	1894.3 prep	3450.6 art acc sing masc	5246.3 verb acc sing masc part pres act
[a☆ ἐπιβλέψητε	δὲ]	ἐπὶ	τὸν	φοροῦντα
epiblepsēte	*de*	*epi*	*ton*	*phorounta*
[you may have looked	and]	upon	the	wearing

3450.12 art acc sing fem	2051.2 noun acc sing fem	3450.12 art acc sing fem	2959.4 adj acc sing fem	2504.1 conj	1500.10 verb 2pl subj aor act
τὴν	ἐσθῆτα	τὴν	λαμπρὰν,	καὶ	εἴπητε
tēn	*esthēta*	*tēn*	*lampran*	*kai*	*eipēte*
the	apparel	the	splendid,	and	may have said

3.b.**Txt:** 018K,020L 025P,byz. **Var:** 01ℵ,02A,03B,04C 33,Gries,Lach,Treg,Alf Tisc,We/Ho,Weis,Sod UBS/☆

840.4 prs-pron dat sing	4622.1 prs-pron nom 2sing	2493.4 verb 2sing impr pres mid	5436.1 adv	2544.1 adv	2504.1 conj
ʽb αὐτῷ, ˋ	Σὺ	κάθου	ὧδε	καλῶς,	καὶ
autō	*Su*	*kathou*	*hōde*	*kalōs*	*kai*
to him,	You	sit	here	well,	and

3450.3 art dat sing	4292.2 adj dat sing masc	1500.10 verb 2pl subj aor act	4622.1 prs-pron nom 2sing	2449.9 verb 2sing impr aor act	1550.1 adv
τῷ	πτωχῷ	εἴπητε,	Σὺ	στῆθι	ἐκεῖ,
tō	*ptōchō*	*eipēte*	*Su*	*stēthi*	*ekei*
to the	poor	may have said,	You	stand	there,

3.c.**Txt:** 01ℵ,04C-corr 018K,020L,025P,byz.bo. **Var:** 02A,03B,04C-org 33,it.Lach,Treg,Alf,Tisc We/Ho,Weis,Sod UBS/☆

2211.1 conj	2493.4 verb 2sing impr pres mid	5436.1 adv	5097.3 prep	3450.16 art sing neu	5124.1 noun sing neu
ἢ	κάθου	ʽc ὧδε ˋ	ὑπὸ	τὸ	ὑποπόδιόν
ē	*kathou*	*hōde*	*hupo*	*to*	*hupopodion*
or	sit	here	under	the	footstool

2:1. James here continued his emphasis on "pure religion" (1:27) by stating that partiality or favoritism of persons should not be tolerated among believers. The world has always been guilty of partiality, and this form of worldliness can also be carried over into the lives of God's people. This evil was forbidden in Israel's earliest days (Leviticus 19:15; Deuteronomy 1:17). Jesus' critics recognized that He did not show favoritism (Luke 20:21). This was a lesson even Peter had difficulty learning (Acts 10:34; Galatians 2:11-14).

There are various opinions as to the significance of the words "the Lord of glory." Some hold it might mean that Christ now reigns in glory (Luke 24:25), while others see it as an adjective and interpret it "our glorious Lord Jesus Christ."

1. My brethren, have not the faith of our Lord Jesus Christ: . . . since you believe in, *Norlie* . . . do not join faith in, *Confraternity* . . . do not hold the faith, *Montgomery* . . . do not combine faith, *Berkeley* . . . stop trying to maintain your faith, *Williams.*

[the Lord] of glory, with respect of persons: . . . do not show anyone partiality, *Norlie* . . . don't treat people differently, *SEB* . . . don't prefer one person to another, *Beck* . . . in a spirit of caste, *Montgomery* . . . with the worship of rank, *TCNT* . . . while showing favoritism, *Adams.*

2:2. James here gave an illustration of what might have happened in an assembly setting. Then as now there were extremes of wealth and poverty. It was even possible that both a slave holder and his slave(s) would be present. This is why Paul dealt with the responsibilities and relationships of both masters and slaves (Ephesians 6:5-9).

The contrast between rich and poor would have been obvious. "Gold ring" is more literally "gold-fingered." Wealthy Greek and Roman men wore many rings on the fingers of the left hand. Wearing them on the right hand was considered less than masculine. The poor man on the other hand not only lacked fine clothes but was described as wearing vile clothing. In classical Greek the word translated "vile" indicated dry dirt. Apparently some were so poor they had to wear soiled work clothes as they gathered with believers.

The word translated "assembly" would better be translated "synagogue." The Greek is from two words meaning "to bring together." It was a word used to describe any kind of gathering. The Bible refers to synagogues of the Jews (Acts 14:1), of the Libertines (Acts 6:9), and even of Satan (Revelation 2:9; 3:9). It seems that before the word translated "church" came into common usage, a gathering of believing Jews could have been referred to as a synagogue of Christians.

2. For if there come unto your assembly a man with a gold ring: For should there enter into your meeting a gold-ringed man, *Berkeley* . . . Thus, two men may come into your congregation, *Norlie* . . . into your synagogue, *Montgomery, Wilson.*

in goodly apparel: . . . and dazzling clothes, *Montgomery* . . . is well-dressed, *Norlie* . . . in showy clothing, *Swann* . . . in splendid apparel, *Darby* . . . fine apparel, *Confraternity.*

and there come in also a poor man in vile raiment: . . . shabbily clad, *Berkeley* . . . shabby clothes, *Norlie* . . . wearing ragged old clothes, *SEB* . . . in Dirty Clothing, *Wilson* . . . with sordid apparel, *Campbell* . . . mean attire, *Confraternity.*

2:3. James here shifted attention from the hypothetical rich and poor visitors to the reaction of the believers. "Ye have respect" means literally to "look upon" and in this case to give special respectful consideration to the rich man.

In reproving scribes and Pharisees, Jesus indicated they loved the "chief seats in the synagogues" (Matthew 23:1-6). Apparently even in Christian gatherings there were seats of privilege. The rich visitor was courteously invited to occupy such a choice place.

In contrast, the poor person was treated carelessly, if not rudely. He was told either to stand in a given place or sit on the floor at some believer's footstool. The believer did not even offer him a seat. Both men should have received a similar welcome into the gathering where both might have accepted Christ as Saviour.

3. And ye have respect to him that weareth the gay clothing: . . . you are deferential to the man, *TCNT* . . . you pay special attention, *Norlie* . . . you look up to him, *Montgomery* . . . him who is clothed in fine apparel, *Confraternity* . . . to the one well-dressed, *Berkeley.*

and say unto him, Sit thou here in a good place: Here is a fine chair, please be seated, *Norlie* . . . in this fine place! *Montgomery* . . . this place of honor, *Wuest* . . . this good seat, *Adams.*

and say to the poor, Stand thou there: You stand back there, *Laubach.*

or sit here under my footstool: Sit on the floor at my feet! *Montgomery* . . . sit lower than my footstool, *Swann* . . . or crouch under my footstool, *Fenton.*

James 2:4

4.a.**Txt:** 018K,020L 025P,byz.
Var: 01ℵ,02A,03B,04C Lach,Treg,Alf,Tisc We/Ho,Weis,Sod UBS/⋆

1466.2 prs-pron gen 1sing	**2504.1** conj	**3620.3** partic	**1246.12** verb 2pl indic aor pass	**1706.1** prep
μου,	4. ⸂[a] καὶ ⸃	οὐ	διεκρίθητε	ἐν
mou	*kai*	*ou*	*diekrithēte*	*en*
my:	also	not	did you make a difference	among

1431.7 prs-pron dat pl masc	**2504.1** conj	**1090.36** verb 2pl indic aor mid	**2896.4** noun nom pl masc	**1255.5** noun gen pl masc
ἑαυτοῖς,	καὶ	ἐγένεσθε	κριταὶ	διαλογισμῶν
heautois	*kai*	*egenesthe*	*kritai*	*dialogismōn*
yourselves,	and	became	judges	reasonings

4050.4 adj gen pl	**189.29** verb 2pl impr aor act	**79.6** noun nom pl masc	**1466.2** prs-pron gen 1sing	**27.6** adj pl masc
πονηρῶν;	5. Ἀκούσατε,	ἀδελφοί	μου	ἀγαπητοί,
ponērōn	*Akousate*	*adelphoi*	*mou*	*agapētoi*
evil?	Hear,	brothers	my	beloved:

5.a.**Txt:** 02A-corr 04C-corr,018K,020L 025P,byz.
Var: 01ℵ,02A-org,03B 04C-org,Lach,Treg,Alf Word,Tisc,We/Ho,Weis Sod,UBS/⋆

3620.1 partic	**3450.5** art nom sing masc	**2296.1** noun nom sing masc	**1573.3** verb 3sing indic aor mid	**3450.8** art acc pl masc	**4292.7** adj acc pl masc
οὐχ	ὁ	θεὸς	ἐξελέξατο	τοὺς	πτωχοὺς
ouch	*ho*	*theos*	*exelexato*	*tous*	*ptōchous*
not		God	did choose	the	poor

5.b.**Txt:** Steph
Var: 01ℵ,02A,03B,04C 018K,020L,025P,bo. Gries,Lach,Treg,Alf Word,Tisc,We/Ho,Weis Sod,UBS/⋆

3450.2 art gen sing	**2862.2** noun gen sing masc	**3450.3** art dat sing	**2862.3** noun dat sing masc	**3642.1** dem-pron gen sing
⸂ τοῦ	κόσμου	[a⋆ τῷ	κόσμῳ]	⸂b τούτου, ⸃
tou	*kosmou*	*tō*	*kosmō*	*toutou*
of the	world	[in the	world]	this,

4004.6 adj acc pl masc	**1706.1** prep	**3963.3** noun dat sing fem	**2504.1** conj	**2791.5** noun acc pl masc	**3450.10** art gen sing fem
πλουσίους	ἐν	πίστει,	καὶ	κληρονόμους	τῆς
plousious	*en*	*pistei*	*kai*	*klēronomous*	*tēs*
rich	in	faith,	and	heirs	of the

926.1 noun fem	**3614.10** rel-pron gen sing fem	**1846.3** verb 3sing indic aor mid	**3450.4** art dat pl	**25.4** verb dat pl part pres act
βασιλείας	ἧς	ἐπηγγείλατο	τοῖς	ἀγαπῶσιν
basileias	*hēs*	*epēngeilato*	*tois*	*agapōsin*
kingdom	which	he promised	to the	loving

840.6 prs-pron acc sing masc	**5050.1** prs-pron nom 2pl	**1156.2** conj	**812.3** verb 2pl indic aor act	**3450.6** art acc sing masc	**4292.3** adj acc sing masc
αὐτόν;	6. ὑμεῖς	δὲ	ἠτιμάσατε	τὸν	πτωχόν.
auton	*humeis*	*de*	*ētimasate*	*ton*	*ptōchon*
him?	You	but	dishonored	the	poor.

3620.1 partic	**3450.7** art nom pl masc	**4004.4** adj nom pl masc	**2586.1** verb 3pl indic pres act	**5050.2** prs-pron gen 2pl
οὐχ	οἱ	πλούσιοι	καταδυναστεύουσιν	ὑμῶν,
ouch	*hoi*	*plousioi*	*katadunasteuousin*	*humōn*
Not	the	rich	do oppress	you,

2504.1 conj	**840.7** prs-pron nom pl masc	**1657.1** verb 3pl indic pres act	**5050.4** prs-pron acc 2pl	**1519.1** prep	**2895.2** noun pl neu
καὶ	αὐτοὶ	ἕλκουσιν	ὑμᾶς	εἰς	κριτήρια;
kai	*autoi*	*helkousin*	*humas*	*eis*	*kritēria*
and	they	do drag	you	into	courts?

7.a.**Var:** p74,02A,044,33 81,614,630,1505,2495

3620.2 partic	**2504.1** conj	**840.7** prs-pron nom pl masc	**980.3** verb 3pl indic pres act	**3450.16** art sing neu
7. ⸂⋆ οὐκ	[a καὶ]	αὐτοὶ	βλασφημοῦσιν	τὸ
ouk	*kai*	*autoi*	*blasphēmousin*	*to*
not	[also]	they	do blaspheme	the

2:4. "Are ye not then partial in yourselves" could be translated, "Do you then not doubt or waver within your thinking?" The same Greek verb here translated "partial" is used in 1:6 where the idea is doubting or wavering, double-mindedness. When these believers made prejudicial distinctions between classes of people they wavered between the thinking of the world which made class distinctions and the faith they claimed to possess which forbade showing partiality.

In making the distinction between the rich and poor, the believers were setting themselves up as judges. "Judges of evil thoughts" may better be translated "judges with evil thoughts." They had wrong motives and false standards. These standards were not God's, but the world's. They were looking at outward appearances, while God looks on the heart. In anointing a successor to Saul as king of Israel, Samuel was made aware of God's method of evaluating people (1 Samuel 16:7).

2:5. The plea to "hearken" or "listen" indicated the intensity of James' appeal. The problem of partiality was not unimportant.

James then pointed out that God had chosen the poor whom the believers were insulting. Jesus said, "Him that cometh to me I will in no wise cast out" (John 6:37). While God welcomes all who come to Him, these believers were making the poor feel less than welcome (2:6).

The poor were not chosen because they were poor but because they accepted Jesus as Saviour (John 3:16,18). They were chosen before the foundation of the world (Ephesians 1:4), not arbitrarily, but on the basis of what God knew as to how they would respond to Jesus (1 Peter 1:21).

God chose those whom the world classified as poor in order that He might make them rich—not as the world considers riches, but rich in faith. See Luke 12:21; 16:11; 2 Corinthians 8:9. The richness included future blessing as "heirs of the kingdom." There are present (Romans 14:17) and future (Matthew 26:29) blessings of the Kingdom.

2:6. The people the world considered rich were next brought into focus. They were not evil or lost because of their wealth but because they had not accepted Jesus as Saviour (John 3:18). The readers of this letter were not only wrong in flattering the rich because it was incompatible with the Christian faith but because these were the people who oppressed and persecuted them (5:1-6). See Acts 13:50; 16:19; 19:23-41.

2:7. The believers' partiality was further ill-advised because the people they honored were the very ones who dishonored the Christ

4. Are ye not then partial in yourselves: . . . do you not make improper distinctions, *Williams* . . . Are you not contradicting yourselves? *SEB* . . . haven't you discriminated among yourselves, *Adams* . . . Do you not see that you are making class-distinctions among yourselves, *TNT* . . . It is all wrong to make such differences between, *Laubach* . . . do you not make a split among yourselves, *Klingensmith* . . . within your own group? *Norlie.*

and are become judges of evil thoughts?: . . . become men who are wrong in their judgment? *Beck* . . . your standards of judgement are all wrong? *TNT* . . . is there not some evil motive back of such discrimination? *Norlie* . . . from evil Reasonings? *Wilson* . . . with evil deliberations? *Berkeley* . . . of bad ideas? *Klingensmith.*

5. Hearken, my beloved brethren: Listen, *Montgomery* . . . Dear Christian brothers, *NLT* . . . dear fellow Christians, *Beck.*

Hath not God chosen: . . . didn't God choose, *Beck.*

the poor of this world rich in faith: . . . the outcast of the world, *Klingensmith* . . . those whom the world regards as poor, *TNT* . . . to be wealthy in the sphere of faith, *Wuest.*

and heirs of the kingdom: . . . inheritors of the Kingdom, *Klingensmith* . . . to take possession, *TNT* . . . should come to possess, *TCNT.*

which he hath promised to them that love him?:

6. But ye have despised the poor: . . . you insult, *TCNT* . . . you have humiliated, *TNT* . . . you have dishonored the poor man, *Montgomery* . . . you have beaten down the outcast, *Klingensmith.*

Do not rich men oppress you: . . . use their power to oppress you, *Confraternity* . . . who make things hard for you? *Laubach* . . . exploit, oppress, and dominate you, *Wuest* . . . gang up on you, *Klingensmith.*

and draw you before the judgment seats?: . . . and drag you to court? *Montgomery.*

7. Do not they blaspheme that worthy name: . . . good, *Confraternity* . . . glorious, *Montgomery*

2541.1 adj sing	3549.2 noun sing neu	3450.16 art sing neu	1926.17 verb sing neu part aor pass	1894.1 prep	5050.4 prs-pron acc 2pl
καλὸν	ὄνομα	τὸ	ἐπικληθὲν	ἐφ'	ὑμᾶς;
kalon	*onoma*	*to*	*epiklēthen*	*eph'*	*humas*
good	name	the	having been called	upon	you?

1479.1 conj	3175.1 partic	3414.4 noun acc sing masc	4903.2 verb 2pl indic pres act	930.2 adj acc sing masc	2567.3 prep
8. Εἰ	μέντοι	νόμον	τελεῖτε	βασιλικὸν,	κατὰ
Ei	*mentoi*	*nomon*	*teleite*	*basilikon*	*kata*
If	indeed	law	you keep	royal	according to

3450.12 art acc sing fem	1118.4 noun acc sing fem	25.24 verb 2sing indic fut act	3450.6 art acc sing masc	3999.1 adv
τὴν	γραφήν,	Ἀγαπήσεις	τὸν	πλησίον
tēn	*graphēn*	*Agapēseis*	*ton*	*plēsion*
the	scripture,	You shall love	the	neighbor

4622.2 prs-pron gen 2sing	5453.1 conj	4427.4 prs-pron acc sing masc	2544.1 adv	4020.2 verb 2pl pres act	1479.1 conj	1156.2 conj
σου	ὡς	σεαυτόν,	καλῶς	ποιεῖτε·	**9.** εἰ	δὲ
sou	*hōs*	*seauton*	*kalōs*	*poieite*	*ei*	*de*
your	as	yourself,	well	you do.	If	but

4238.1 verb 2pl indic pres act	4238.2 verb 2pl indic pres act	264.4 noun acc sing fem
ʼ προσωποληπτεῖτε,	[☆ προσωπολημπτεῖτε,]	ἁμαρτίαν
prosōpolēpteite	*prosōpolēmpteite*	*hamartian*
you show partiality,	[idem]	sin

2021.1 verb 2pl pres mid	1638.10 verb nom pl masc part pres mid	5097.3 prep	3450.2 art gen sing	3414.2 noun gen sing masc	5453.1 conj
ἐργάζεσθε,	ἐλεγχόμενοι	ὑπὸ	τοῦ	νόμου	ὡς
ergazesthe	*elenchomenoi*	*hupo*	*tou*	*nomou*	*hōs*
you work,	having been convicted	by	the	law	as

3710.3 noun nom pl masc	3610.1 rel-pron nom sing masc	1056.1 conj	3513.1 adj sing	3450.6 art acc sing masc	3414.4 noun acc sing masc
παραβάται.	**10.** ὅστις	γὰρ	ὅλον	τὸν	νόμον
parabatai	*hostis*	*gar*	*holon*	*ton*	*nomon*
transgressors.	Whosoever	for	whole	the	law

10.a.**Txt:** 018K,020L 025P,byz.Sod
Var: 01ℵ,03B,04C,Lach Treg,Alf,Word,Tisc We/Ho,Weis,UBS/☆

4931.27 verb 3sing indic fut act	4275.5 verb 3sing indic fut act	4931.16 verb 3sing subj aor act	4275.6 verb 3sing subj aor act	1156.2 conj
ʼ τηρήσει,	πταίσει	[a☆ τηρήσῃ,	πταίσῃ]	δὲ
tērēsei	*ptaisei*	*tērēsē*	*ptaisē*	*de*
shall keep,	shall stumble	[keeps,	stumbles]	but

1706.1 prep	1518.2 num card dat	1090.3 verb 3sing indic perf act	3820.4 adj gen pl	1761.1 adj nom sing masc	3450.5 art nom sing masc
ἐν	ἑνί,	γέγονεν	πάντων	ἔνοχος.	**11.** ὁ
en	*heni*	*gegonen*	*pantōn*	*enochos*	*ho*
in	one,	he has become	of all	guilty.	The

1056.1 conj	1500.15 verb nom sing masc part aor act	3231.1 partic	3294.6 verb 2sing subj aor act	1500.5 verb 3sing indic aor act
γὰρ	εἰπών,	Μὴ	μοιχεύσῃς,	εἶπεν
gar	*eipōn*	*Mē*	*moicheusēs*	*eipen*
for	having said,	Not	you may commit adultery,	said

2504.1 conj	3231.1 partic	5244.3 verb 2sing subj aor act	1479.1 conj	1156.2 conj	3620.3 partic
καί,	Μὴ	φονεύσῃς·	εἰ	δὲ	οὐ
kai	*Mē*	*phoneusēs*	*ei*	*de*	*ou*
also,	Not	you may commit murder.	If	now	not

after whom Christians were named (Acts 11:26). Paul himself at one time had been one of the world's elite who persecuted the Church (Acts 26:9-11).

. . . excellent, *Darby* . . . noble, *Berkeley* . . . Are not they the ones who scoff at the beautiful name, *Williams* . . . slander the fine Christian name, *Norlie.*

by the which ye are called?: . . . you bear, *Norlie* . . . by which you are distinguished? *Fenton* . . . by which you were called the Lord's own, *Beck.*

2:8. "If ye fulfill" is stronger in the Greek and can be translated "if you really fulfill." Some think believers were claiming to fulfill the "royal law" by honoring the rich, but in reality, they were disobeying the Law by not showing equal honor to the poor.

"The royal law according to the Scripture" is identified as loving a neighbor as oneself. See Leviticus 19:18. Paul showed that this law was a summary of God's moral law (Romans 13:8-10; Galatians 5:14). It is probably called "the royal law" because it presupposes loving God without reservation (see Matthew 22:40 with 1 John 4:20) and because it encompasses all aspects of the moral law.

8. If ye fulfil the royal law according to the scripture: If you are keeping, *Montgomery* . . . If you really observe, *Berkeley* . . . If you really do everything the royal law demands, as it is written, *Beck* . . . The royal command is found in, *SEB.*

Thou shalt love thy neighbour as thyself, ye do well: . . . you do right, *Norlie* . . . you are doing what is right, *TCNT* . . . you are doing splendidly, *Wuest* . . . you behave beautifully, *Berkeley.*

2:9. James made some strong statements concerning the practice of favoritism. He made it clear as in 2:4 that prejudice is not a trifling matter, and here he labeled it sin. The etymology of the Greek word translated "sin" means to miss the mark or target. Those wishing to practice the "royal law" missed the mark completely when showing prejudice or favoritism.

"Convinced of the law" may better be translated "convicted by the law." Discrimination against the poor was condemned in Scripture on several occasions (Leviticus 19:15; Deuteronomy 1:17; 16:19). When believers violated this law they were without excuse; they were convicted by the Law as being guilty of transgression.

The Greek word translated "transgress" means to go beyond. It is a strong word which indicates not inadvertent slipping, but deliberately crossing the clearly marked line of Scripture, in this case, regarding partiality.

9. But if ye have respect to persons, ye commit sin: If you have the spirit of caste, *Montgomery* . . . show partiality to persons, *Norlie* . . . go in for external show, *Swann* . . . show favoritism, *Adams* . . . treat anyone differently, *SEB* . . . prefer one to another, *Beck* . . . you are practicing sin, *Berkeley.*

and are convinced of the law as transgressors: . . . the Law convicts you, *Beck* . . . you stand convicted, *Berkeley* . . . and you are judged as evil-doers by the law, *Norlie* . . . being offenders against it, *TCNT* . . . as culprits, *Fenton.*

2:10. The Pharisees of Jesus' time were rebuked for picking which laws they wished to consider important while neglecting others (Matthew 23:23). It is possible some worldly believers were guilty of the same attitude. James made it clear that no believer had the right to exempt himself from any part of God's law. To deliberately disregard one of God's commandments was to disregard the whole, even though all commandments were not transgressed.

10. For whosoever shall keep the whole law, and yet offend in one [point]: This is the way the law works...but breaks one commandment, *Norlie* . . . yet stumbles, *Montgomery* . . . slips, *Berkeley* . . . shall fail in one point, *Wilson.*

he is guilty of all: . . . may become entangled with all, *Fenton* . . . becomes guilty in every respect, *Berkeley* . . . you're guilty of breaking all of it, *Beck.*

2:11. James here used an extreme illustration of adultery and murder to show how wrong it was to choose which commandments one would keep. The application must have been obvious. Believers

11. For he that said, Do not commit adultery, said also, Do not kill: Do not sin with another man's wife, *Laubach* . . . You must not commit murder, *Williams* . . . Thou shalt not murder, *TCNT.*

James 2:12

11.a.**Txt:** 018K,byz.
Var: 01ℵ,02A,03B,04C Lach,Treg,Alf,Tisc We/Ho,Weis,Sod UBS/☆

3294.7 verb 2sing indic fut act	5244.6 verb 2sing indic fut act	3294.1 verb 2sing indic pres act
⸂ μοιχεύσεις,	φονεύσεις	[a☆ μοιχεύεις,
moicheuseis	*phoneuseis*	*moicheueis*
you shall commit adultery,	shall commit murder	[you commit adultery,

5244.7 verb 2sing indic pres act	1156.2 conj	1090.2 verb 2sing indic perf act	3710.1 noun nom sing masc	3414.2 noun gen sing masc
φονεύεις]	δέ,	γέγονας	παραβάτης	νόμου.
phoneueis	*de*	*gegonas*	*parabatēs*	*nomou*
you murder]	but,	you have become	a transgressor	of law.

3643.1 adv	2953.10 verb 2pl impr pres act	2504.1 conj	3643.1 adv	4020.2 verb 2pl pres act	5453.1 conj	1217.2 prep
12. Οὕτως	λαλεῖτε	καὶ	οὕτως	ποιεῖτε,	ὡς	διὰ
Houtōs	*laleite*	*kai*	*houtōs*	*poieite*	*hōs*	*dia*
So	speak you	and	so	do,	as	by

3414.2 noun gen sing masc	1644.2 noun gen sing fem	3165.13 verb nom pl masc part pres act	2892.32 verb inf pres mid	3450.9 art nom sing fem
νόμου	ἐλευθερίας	μέλλοντες	κρίνεσθαι·	**13.** ἡ
nomou	*eleutherias*	*mellontes*	*krinesthai*	*hē*
law	of freedom	being about	to be judged;	the

13.a.**Txt:** 020L,byz.
Var: 01ℵ,02A,03B,04C 018K,Lach,Treg,Alf Word,Tisc,We/Ho,Weis Sod,UBS/☆

1056.1 conj	2893.1 noun nom sing fem	446.1 adv	413.1 adj nom sing fem	3450.3 art dat sing	3231.1 partic
γὰρ	κρίσις	⸂ ἀνίλεως	[a☆ ἀνέλεος]	τῷ	μὴ
gar	*krisis*	*anileōs*	*aneleos*	*tō*	*mē*
for	judgment	without mercy	[unmerciful]	to the	not

13.b.**Txt:** Steph
Var: 01ℵ-org,03B,04C 018K,020L,byz.Gries Lach,Treg,Alf,Word Tisc,We/Ho,Weis,Sod UBS/☆

4020.38 verb dat sing masc part aor act	1643.2 noun sing neu	2504.1 conj	2590.2 verb 3sing indic pres mid	1643.2 noun sing neu
ποιήσαντι	ἔλεος·	⸂b καὶ ⸃	κατακαυχᾶται	ἔλεος
poiēsanti	*eleos*	*kai*	*katakauchatai*	*eleos*
having wrought	mercy.	And	boasts over	mercy

2893.2 noun gen sing fem	4949.9 intr-pron sing neu	3450.16 art sing neu	3650.1 noun sing neu	79.6 noun nom pl masc	1466.2 prs-pron gen 1sing
κρίσεως.	**14.** Τί	τὸ	ὄφελος,	ἀδελφοί	μου,
kriseōs	*Ti*	*to*	*ophelos*	*adelphoi*	*mou*
judgment.	What	the	profit,	brothers	my,

1430.1 partic	3963.4 noun acc sing fem	2978.7 verb 3sing subj pres act	4948.3 indef-pron nom sing	2174.29 verb inf pres act	2024.4 noun pl neu
ἐὰν	πίστιν	λέγῃ	τις	ἔχειν,	ἔργα
ean	*pistin*	*legē*	*tis*	*echein*	*erga*
if	faith	say	anyone	to have,	works

1156.2 conj	3231.1 partic	2174.7 verb 3sing subj pres act	3231.1 partic	1404.4 verb 3sing indic pres mid	3450.9 art nom sing fem	3963.1 noun nom sing fem
δὲ	μὴ	ἔχῃ;	μὴ	δύναται	ἡ	πίστις
de	*mē*	*echē*	*mē*	*dunatai*	*hē*	*pistis*
but	not	has?	not	is able	the	faith

15.a.**Txt:** 02A,018K 020L,byz.
Var: 01ℵ,03B,33,bo. Treg,Tisc,We/Ho,Weis Sod,UBS/☆

4834.10 verb inf aor act	840.6 prs-pron acc sing masc	1430.1 partic	1156.2 conj	79.1 noun nom sing masc	2211.1 conj
σῶσαι	αὐτόν;	**15.** ἐὰν	⸂a δὲ ⸃	ἀδελφὸς	ἢ
sōsai	*auton*	*ean*	*de*	*adelphos*	*ē*
to save	him?	If	now	a brother	or

15.b.**Txt:** 02A,020L 025P,byz.
Var: 01ℵ,03B,04C 018K,sa.bo.Treg,Alf Tisc,We/Ho,Weis,Sod UBS/☆

78.1 noun nom sing fem	1125.3 adj nom pl masc	5062.3 verb 3pl subj pres act	2504.1 conj	2981.5 verb nom pl masc part pres mid	1498.12 verb 3pl subj pres act
ἀδελφὴ	γυμνοὶ	ὑπάρχωσιν,	καὶ	λειπόμενοι	⸂b ὦσιν ⸃
adelphē	*gumnoi*	*huparchōsin*	*kai*	*leipomenoi*	*ōsin*
a sister	naked	be,	and	lacking	may be

who obeyed most of God's commandments, but deliberately disobeyed by showing partiality, were still transgressors.

2:12. "So speak ye, and so do." In the hypothetical case of the rich man and the poor man (2:2), believers manifested improper speech and action. The believers had become judges with evil motives (2:4). Now James reminded them that they themselves faced coming judgment. See 1 Corinthians 3:11-15; 2 Corinthians 5:10. They should speak and act accordingly.

The New Testament speaks of liberty the believer enjoys (Luke 4:18; John 8:32,36; Romans 8:21; 2 Corinthians 3:17). But this liberty is not freedom to indulge in improper conduct (Romans 6:1- 4). It is freedom to allow the Holy Spirit to manifest Himself in daily life (Romans 8:2-4; Galatians 5:22,23). Believers will be judged on the basis of what they did with this enabling.

2:13. The "royal law" includes showing mercy, which has its own reward (Matthew 5:7). Some early Christians seemed to adopt the attitude of the Pharisees who were meticulous in observing laws and traditions they liked, but disregarded others. They showed no mercy in wanting to impose judgment even when true repentance was demonstrated (John 8:3-11 with Micah 6:8). Failure to show mercy will be a factor in the Day of Judgment (Matthew 7:1,2).

To show mercy is not to condone evil. Paul instructed the church at Corinth to turn an immoral man over to Satan for the destruction of his flesh (1 Corinthians 5:5). The motivation for administering this discipline was to be redemption—"that the spirit may be saved." Then when repentance became evident, Paul in his second letter urged the church to forgive (2 Corinthians 2:5-8).

"Mercy rejoiceth against judgment" is better translated "glorieth" or "triumphs" over judgment. The believer who has received God's mercy and in daily life fulfills the "royal law," which includes mercy, can face coming judgment with confidence.

2:14. James pointed out the uselessness of claiming to have faith if it is not supported by works. Jesus taught that the person who has genuine faith will do the will of God (Matthew 7:21; see also Matthew 25:41-46; Luke 6:46). Lack of love and mercy indicates a lack of true faith. "Can faith save him?" may be translated "Can that faith save him?" There is a difference between claiming to possess faith and true possession.

2:15. The expression "brother or sister" has two implications. Christianity elevated the status of womanhood above that of the existing cultures. The needs of suffering women were recognized along with that of suffering men. It also emphasized the care be-

Now if thou commit no adultery, yet if thou kill: So, in case you commit no adultery, but you kill, *Berkeley* . . . wilt commit murder, *Confraternity.*

thou art become a transgressor of the law: . . . you are guilty of breaking the Law, *NLT* . . . you have become a breaker of, *Berkeley* . . . you are a wrongdoer, *SEB.*

12. So speak ye, and so do: So speak and act, *Montgomery* . . . In your speech and in your actions, *Norlie* . . . Let both your talk and your action be such, *Swann* . . . in such a way, *Berkeley.*

as they that shall be judged by the law of liberty: . . . as are on the verge of being judged by, *Swann* . . . as befits people who are to be, *Berkeley* . . . as men about to be judged by, *Confraternity* . . . by the Law that makes men free, *NLT* . . . the Gospel law, *Norlie.*

13. For he shall have judgment without mercy, that hath showed no mercy: For merciless judgment will be the portion of the merciless man, *Williams* . . . merciless judgment is meted out to the merciless offender, *Norlie* . . . for judgment is merciless for him who has not practised Mercy, *Wilson.*

and mercy rejoiceth against judgment: . . . mercy glories in the face of judgment, *Montgomery* . . . mercy triumphs over judgment, *Adams* . . . Mercy asserts her superiority to Justice, *TCNT.*

14. What [doth it] profit, my brethren, though a man say he hath faith, and have not works?: What is the use, *Berkeley* . . . what good is it if any one says that he has faith, if he has no deeds? *Montgomery* . . . if a person claims he has faith, *SEB* . . . if he has no good deeds to prove it? *Williams* . . . but fails to bring it into practice? *Fenton.*

can faith save him?: This sort of faith can't save him, can it? *Adams.*

15. If a brother or sister be naked: They lack both the needed clothing, *Norlie* . . . is poorly clad, *Berkeley.*

and destitute of daily food: . . . in need of, *Montgomery* . . . in want of daily food, *Confraternity*

3450.10 art gen sing fem τῆς *tēs* of the	**2166.1** adj gen sing fem ἐφημέρου *ephēmerou* daily	**5001.2** noun gen sing fem τροφῆς, *trophēs* food,	**1500.8** verb 3sing subj aor act **16.** εἴπῃ *eipē* say	**1156.2** conj δέ *de* and	**4948.3** indef- pron nom sing τις *tis* anyone
840.2 prs- pron dat pl αὐτοῖς *autois* to them	**1523.1** prep gen ἐξ *ex* from among	**5050.2** prs- pron gen 2pl ὑμῶν, *humōn* you,	**5055.7** verb 2pl impr pres act Ὑπάγετε *Hupagete* Go	**1706.1** prep ἐν *en* in	**1503.3** noun dat sing fem εἰρήνῃ, *eirēnē* peace;
2305.1 verb 2pl impr pres mid θερμαίνεσθε *thermainesthe* be warmed	**2504.1** conj καὶ *kai* and	**5361.2** verb 2pl impr pres pass χορτάζεσθε, *chortazesthe* be filled;	**3231.1** partic μὴ *mē* not	**1319.22** verb 2pl subj aor act δῶτε *dōte* give	**1156.2** conj δὲ *de* but
840.2 prs- pron dat pl αὐτοῖς *autois* to them	**3450.17** art pl neu τὰ *ta* the	**1990.1** adj pl neu ἐπιτήδεια *epitēdeia* necessary things	**3450.2** art gen sing τοῦ *tou* for the	**4835.2** noun gen sing neu σώματος, *sōmatos* body,	**4949.9** intr- pron sing neu τί *ti* what
3450.16 art sing neu τὸ *to* the	**3650.1** noun sing neu ὄφελος; *ophelos* profit?	**3643.1** adv **17.** οὕτως *houtōs* So	**2504.1** conj καὶ *kai* also	**3450.9** art nom sing fem ἡ *hē* the	**3963.1** noun nom sing fem πίστις, *pistis* faith,
1430.1 partic ἐὰν *ean* if	**3231.1** partic μὴ *mē* not	**2024.4** noun pl neu ʻ ἔργα *erga* works	**2174.7** verb 3sing subj pres act ἔχῃ *echē* it has,	**2174.7** verb 3sing subj pres act [☆ ἔχῃ *echē* [it has	**2024.4** noun pl neu ἔργα,] *erga* works,]
3361.8 adj nom sing fem νεκρά *nekra* dead	**1498.4** verb 3sing indic pres act ἐστιν *estin* is	**2567.2** prep καθ' *kath'* by	**1431.11** prs- pron acc sing fem ἑαυτήν. *heautēn* itself.	**233.1** conj **18.** Ἀλλ' *All'* But	**2029.11** verb 3sing indic fut act ἐρεῖ *erei* will say
4948.3 indef- pron nom sing τις *tis* some one,	**4622.1** prs- pron nom 2sing Σὺ *Su* You	**3963.4** noun acc sing fem πίστιν *pistin* faith	**2174.3** verb 2sing indic pres act ἔχεις, *echeis* have,	**2476.3** prs- pron nom κἀγὼ *kagō* and I	**2024.4** noun pl neu ἔργα *erga* works
2174.1 verb 1sing pres act ἔχω· *echō* have.	**1161.9** verb 2sing impr aor act δεῖξόν *deixon* Show	**1466.4** prs- pron dat 1sing μοι *moi* me	**3450.12** art acc sing fem τὴν *tēn* the	**3963.4** noun acc sing fem πίστιν *pistin* faith	**4622.2** prs- pron gen 2sing σου *sou* your
1523.2 prep gen ʻ ἐκ *ek* from	**5400.1** prep [a☆ χωρὶς] *chōris* [without]	**3450.1** art gen pl τῶν *tōn* the	**2024.5** noun gen pl neu ἔργων *ergōn* works	**4622.2** prs- pron gen 2sing ʻb σου, ʼ *sou* your,	**2476.3** prs- pron nom κἀγώ *kagō* and I
1161.6 verb 1sing act ʻ δείξω *deixō* will show	**4622.3** prs- pron dat 2sing σοι *soi* you	**4622.3** prs- pron dat 2sing [☆ σοι *soi* [you	**1161.6** verb 1sing act δείξω] *deixō* will show]	**1523.2** prep gen ἐκ *ek* from	**3450.1** art gen pl τῶν *tōn* the

18.a.**Txt:** 018K,020L,byz. **Var:** 01ℵ,02A,03B,04C 025P,33,Gries,Lach Treg,Alf,Word,Tisc We/Ho,Weis,Sod UBS/☆

18.b.**Txt:** 04C,018K 020L,byz. **Var:** 01ℵ,02A,03B,025P 33,sa.bo.Lach,Treg,Alf Word,Tisc,We/Ho,Weis Sod,UBS/☆

lievers should have for hurting members of the Christian community (Galatians 6:10).

2:16. The ill-clad and hungry brother or sister in James' illustration (2:15) seemed to make people uncomfortable if they had only a profession of faith. One of the group became the spokesman who tried to ease the embarrassment by urging the needy to leave the gathering rather than helping them. It was the common problem of not wanting to get involved.

"Depart in peace" was a customary Jewish parting expression. It had deep meaning when used sincerely, expressing a wish for total well-being. See Mark 5:34; Luke 7:50. When used as a formula for asking someone to leave it was hypocritical and in this case utterly heartless.

"Be ye warmed and filled" indicated an intentional decision not to do anything to provide help. It was expecting that someone else would respond to the need, making the destitute person responsible for finding such a generous person.

The change from the singular "one of you" to the plural "ye" indicates that the entire congregation was guilty of the action even though just one person was the spokesman.

"What doth it profit" indicates the uselessness of an empty profession of faith. When a selfish condition exists, the needy are not cared for, and the able but unwilling persons lose an opportunity to be a blessing and in turn to be blessed. See Psalm 112:9 with 2 Corinthians 9:6-11; Proverbs 19:17; 28:27.

2:17. James here applied the truth of his illustration in 2:15,16. Faith which does not result in works is dead. It is like a lifeless corpse. It does not respond to human need.

While James emphasized the uselessness of faith without works, he was not in conflict with Paul's emphasis on salvation by faith. Paul expressed the importance of works following faith in such passages as Ephesians 2:8-10. Believers are God's workmanship "created in Christ Jesus unto (for) good works." Faith that is genuine will result in good works.

2:18. It seems that in objection to James' emphasis on the inseparability of faith and works, some were taking the position that faith and works were separate entities. In essence the objectors were saying, "Some have the gift of faith and others have the gift of works." It is possible they based their view on teaching such as "there are diversities of gifts" (1 Corinthians 12:4).

James forcefully rejected this attempt to separate faith and works and challenged objectors to give one example of true faith which did not result in good works. This, of course, was impossible. James was not teaching that saving faith is earned by good works, but that true faith results in godly action. A faith which does not result in a change in a believer's life is not truly faith (2:14).

. . . and lacks the day's nourishment, *Berkeley* . . . has nothing to eat, *Klingensmith* . . . has not enough food for one day, *TNT.*

16. And one of you say unto them, Depart in peace, be [ye] warmed and filled: Oh, I am so sorry for you! *Fenton* . . . Go your way, and good luck to you! May you keep warm and get a good, square meal! *Norlie* . . . Goodby, keep yourself warm and eat well, *NLT* . . . find enough to eat, *Laubach* . . . find warmth and food for yourselves, *Montgomery* . . . have a good dinner, *TNT* . . . eat heartily, *Beck.*

notwithstanding ye give them not those things which are needful to the body: Then suppose, too, that you do not give them these very things they need, *Norlie* . . . but at the same time you do not give the necessaries of the body, *Montgomery* . . . without supplying them with their bodily needs, *Berkeley* . . . does nothing at all to make it possible, *TNT* . . . gives nothing the body needs, *Klingensmith.*

what [doth it] profit?: . . . what is the good of that? *TNT* . . . what good would that do them? *Montgomery* . . . What does such talk amount to? *Norlie* . . . what is the use? *Berkeley* . . . what is it worth, *Klingensmith.*

17. Even so faith, if it hath not works: Faith is like that. If there is nothing to show for it, *TNT* . . . the faith that issues in no works, *Berkeley* . . . without deeds to show for it, *Norlie.*

is dead, being alone: . . . is by itself a lifeless thing, *Montgomery* . . . it is just a word, *TNT.*

18. Yea, a man may say, Thou hast faith, and I have works: Some one indeed may say, *Montgomery* . . . and I am a man of action, *TCNT* . . . I have good deeds, *Williams.*

show me thy faith without thy works: I answer, *Montgomery* . . . Prove to me you have faith without any works, *Beck* . . . can you show me your faith apart from, *Norlie* . . . without its practices, *Berkeley.*

and I will show thee my faith by my works: . . . and I will prove to you, *Wuest* . . . by my actions, *TCNT* . . . by the loving deeds that

18.c.**Txt:** 02A,018K 020L,025P,byz.sa.bo. **Var:** 01ℵ,03B,04C,33 Treg,Alf,Word,Tisc We/Ho,Weis,Sod UBS/☆

2024.5 noun gen pl neu	1466.2 prs-pron gen 1sing	3450.12 art acc sing fem	3963.4 noun acc sing fem	1466.2 prs-pron gen 1sing	4622.1 prs-pron nom 2sing
ἔργων	μου	τὴν	πίστιν	⸂c μου.⸃	**19.** σὺ
ergōn	*mou*	*tēn*	*pistin*	*mou*	*su*
works	my	the	faith	my.	You

3961.5 verb 2sing indic pres act	3617.1 conj	3450.5 art nom sing masc	2296.1 noun nom sing masc	1518.3 num card nom masc	1498.4 verb 3sing indic pres act
πιστεύεις	ὅτι	⸀ ὁ	θεός	εἷς	ἐστιν.
pisteueis	*hoti*	*ho*	*theos*	*heis*	*estin*
believe	that		God	one	is.

1518.3 num card nom masc	1498.4 verb 3sing indic pres act	3450.5 art nom sing masc	2296.1 noun nom sing masc	2544.1 adv	4020.4 verb 2sing indic pres act
[εἷς	ἐστὶν	ὁ	θεός;]	καλῶς	ποιεῖς·
heis	*estin*	*ho*	*theos*	*kalōs*	*poieis*
[one	is		God?]	Well	you do;

2504.1 conj	3450.17 art pl neu	1134.3 noun pl neu	3961.3 verb 3pl indic pres act	2504.1 conj	5261.1 verb 3pl indic pres act
καὶ	τὰ	δαιμόνια	πιστεύουσιν,	καὶ	φρίσσουσιν.
kai	*ta*	*daimonia*	*pisteuousin*	*kai*	*phrissousin*
even	the	demons	believe,	and	shudder.

2286.2 verb 2sing indic pres act	1156.2 conj	1091.29 verb inf aor act	5434.1 intrj	442.5 noun voc sing masc	2727.3 adj voc sing masc
20. θέλεις	δὲ	γνῶναι,	ὦ	ἄνθρωπε	κενέ,
theleis	*de*	*gnōnai*	*ō*	*anthrōpe*	*kene*
Will you	but	to know,	O	man	empty,

3617.1 conj	3450.9 art nom sing fem	3963.1 noun nom sing fem	5400.1 prep	3450.1 art gen pl	2024.5 noun gen pl neu	3361.8 adj nom sing fem
ὅτι	ἡ	πίστις	χωρὶς	τῶν	ἔργων	⸀ νεκρά
hoti	*hē*	*pistis*	*chōris*	*tōn*	*ergōn*	*nekra*
that	the	faith	apart from	the	works	dead

20.a.**Txt:** 01ℵ,02A 04C-corr,018K,020L 025P,33,byz.bo.Sod **Var:** 03B,04C-org,it.sa. Lach,Treg,Alf,Tisc We/Ho,Weis,UBS/☆

686.5 adj nom sing fem	1498.4 verb 3sing indic pres act	11.1 name masc	3450.5 art nom sing masc	3824.1 noun nom sing masc
[a☆ ἀργή]	ἐστιν;	**21.** Ἀβραὰμ	ὁ	πατὴρ
argē	*estin*	*Abraam*	*ho*	*patēr*
[barren]	is?	Abraham	the	father

2231.2 prs-pron gen 1pl	3620.2 partic	1523.1 prep gen	2024.5 noun gen pl neu	1338.13 verb 3sing indic aor pass	397.5 verb nom sing masc part aor act
ἡμῶν	οὐκ	ἐξ	ἔργων	ἐδικαιώθη,	ἀνενέγκας
hēmōn	*ouk*	*ex*	*ergōn*	*edikaiōthē*	*anenenkas*
our	not	by	works	was justified,	having offered

2439.1 name masc	3450.6 art acc sing masc	5048.4 noun acc sing masc	840.3 prs-pron gen sing	1894.3 prep	3450.16 art sing neu
Ἰσαὰκ	τὸν	υἱὸν	αὐτοῦ	ἐπὶ	τὸ
Isaak	*ton*	*huion*	*autou*	*epi*	*to*
Isaac	the	son	his	upon	the

2356.1 noun sing neu	984.3 verb 2sing indic pres act	3617.1 conj	3450.9 art nom sing fem	3963.1 noun nom sing fem
θυσιαστήριον;	**22.** βλέπεις	ὅτι	ἡ	πίστις
thusiastērion	*blepeis*	*hoti*	*hē*	*pistis*
altar?	You see	that	the	faith

4753.5 verb 3sing indic imperf act	3450.4 art dat pl	2024.6 noun dat pl neu	840.3 prs-pron gen sing	2504.1 conj	1523.2 prep gen
συνήργει	τοῖς	ἔργοις	αὐτοῦ,	καὶ	ἐκ
sunērgei	*tois*	*ergois*	*autou*	*kai*	*ek*
was working with	the	works	his,	and	by

Verse 18 is another way of stating what Jesus taught when He said, "By their fruits ye shall know them" (Matthew 7:16-20).

2:19. Here James dealt further with the kind of faith he criticized in 2:17,18. These people were orthodox in doctrine. They believed there is one God as opposed to the polytheism of pagans. Orthodox Jewish readers of this epistle had very likely reaffirmed Deuteronomy 6:4 every morning and evening. Gentiles among the readers could have been influenced by their Jewish friends.

James did not criticize the belief in monotheism; he commended the readers for it ("Thou doest well"). What James criticized was the mere intellectual assent without a commensurate change of lifestyle. In answering the scribes concerning the first of all the commandments, Jesus quoted Deuteronomy 6:4 and taught that this belief should affect the believers' relationship with God and man (Mark 12:28-31). Faith must be followed by action.

The writer stated that "the devils also believe, and tremble." This illustrates the tragic result of a correct belief without a proper alignment of life with that belief. The demons have a correct belief about God but do not change their conduct. They recognized Jesus as "the Holy One of God" but trembled or shuddered at the prospect of their ultimate destiny (Mark 1:24). See Matthew 8:29; Mark 5:7; Luke 4:41.

2:20. "But wilt thou know . . . " has the meaning of "Do you desire to know?" The writer here shifts the emphasis to supporting Scripture with which Jewish readers were very familiar. Abraham was claimed as father of the Jews (John 8:39). His faith was prominent in their theological discussions.

The adjective translated "vain" has the thought of being empty, ignorant, lacking in good sense. The word was also used at times to indicate a person trying to make an impression. The King James translators seem to follow this implication by using the word "vain."

2:21. There is no contradiction here between Paul and James. Paul in Romans 3:28; 4:3,19-22, and elsewhere refers to the method of justification. When Abraham was 100 and Sara 90 years old (Genesis 17:17), Abraham believed God would fulfill His promise (Genesis 15:1-6). James (2:21) taught that Abraham's obedience in offering Isaac many years later was the proof of genuine faith (Genesis 22). The context makes it clear that James taught a person is justified by the kind of faith which is genuine and results in obedience.

2:22. "Faith wrought with his works" is literally "worked with his works." His actions were an indication that his faith was at work in all he did. As Phillips points out in his paraphrase, his faith and actions were partners.

I do, *Laubach* . . . through the practices, *Berkeley* . . . I'll prove to you I have faith, *Beck*.

19. Thou believest that there is one God: Do you believe, *Berkeley*. . . that there is only one God? *TNT*.

thou doest well: the devils also believe, and tremble: So far, so good, *Norlie* . . . That's fine! *Beck* . . . That is good, but it is not enough, *Laubach* . . . the demons believe, and they shudder, *Montgomery* . . . and tremble at the thought, *TCNT* . . . and because they do, they shake, *NLT* . . . shake with fear, *SEB*.

20. But wilt thou know, O vain man: . . . do you really need proof, *Norlie* . . . do you really want to understand, *TCNT* . . . do you want to be convinced, O foolish man, *Montgomery* . . . O senseless man! *Wuest* . . . you worthless person, *Adams* . . . O unproductive man, *Berkeley* . . . you foolish fellow, *Beck* . . . You silly man! *TNT* . . . empty person, *Klingensmith*.

that faith without works is dead?: . . . faith apart from deeds is barren? *Montgomery* . . . is empty talk, *Laubach* . . . is worth nothing? *SEB* . . . is unproductive? *Wuest* . . . is useless? *Confraternity* . . . is delinquent? *Berkeley*.

21. Was not Abraham our father justified by works: Think of, *TNT* . . . our ancestor, *Montgomery* . . . made just, *Klingensmith* . . . get to be righteous on the basis of works, *Beck* . . . vindicated by works, *Wuest* . . . made righteous due to his works, *Berkeley*.

when he had offered Isaac his son upon the altar?:

22. Seest thou how faith wrought with his works: His deed, you see, proved that his faith was active and real, *Laubach* . . . see how faith was cooperating with deeds, *Montgomery* . . . You see his faith was active with works, *Beck* . . . how in his case faith and actions went together, *TCNT* . . . faith was spurring him on to do good works, *Norlie* . . . faith worked along with his works, *Confraternity*.

3450.1 art gen pl	**2024.5** noun gen pl neu	**3450.9** art nom sing fem	**3963.1** noun nom sing fem	**4896.9** verb 3sing indic aor pass	**2504.1** conj
τῶν	ἔργων	ἡ	πίστις	ἐτελειώθη,	**23.** καὶ
tōn	*ergōn*	*hē*	*pistis*	*eteleiōthē*	*kai*
the	works	the	faith	was perfected.	And

3997.20 verb 3sing indic aor pass	**3450.9** art nom sing fem	**1118.1** noun nom sing fem	**3450.9** art nom sing fem	**2978.19** verb nom sing fem part pres act
ἐπληρώθη	ἡ	γραφὴ	ἡ	λέγουσα,
eplērōthē	*hē*	*graphē*	*hē*	*legousa*
was fulfilled	the	scripture	the	saying,

23.a.**Txt:** 01ℵ,02A,03B 04C,025P,049,byz.
Var: p20,020L,044,614 623,630,1241,1505 2495

3961.20 verb 3sing indic aor act	**1156.2** conj	**11.1** name masc	**3450.3** art dat sing	**2296.3** noun dat sing masc	**2504.1** conj
Ἐπίστευσεν	⸂a δὲ⸃	Ἀβραὰμ	τῷ	θεῷ,	καὶ
Episteusen	*de*	*Abraam*	*tō*	*theō*	*kai*
Believed	now	Abraham		God,	and

3023.11 verb 3sing indic aor pass	**840.4** prs-pron dat sing	**1519.1** prep	**1336.4** noun acc sing fem	**2504.1** conj	**5224.1** adj nom sing masc
ἐλογίσθη	αὐτῷ	εἰς	δικαιοσύνην,	καὶ	φίλος
elogisthē	*autō*	*eis*	*dikaiosunēn*	*kai*	*philos*
it was reckoned	to him	for	righteousness,	and	friend

24.a.**Txt:** 018K,020L,byz.
Var: 01ℵ,02A,03B,04C 025P,bo.Gries,Lach Treg,Alf,Word,Tisc We/Ho,Weis,Sod UBS/⋆

2296.2 noun gen sing masc	**2535.37** verb 3sing indic aor pass	**3571.1** verb 2pl pres act	**4953.1** partic	**3617.1** conj	**1523.1** prep gen
θεοῦ	ἐκλήθη.	**24.** Ὁρᾶτε	⸂a τοίνυν⸃	ὅτι	ἐξ
theou	*eklēthē*	*Horate*	*toinun*	*hoti*	*ex*
of God	he was called.	You see	then	that	by

2024.5 noun gen pl neu	**1338.9** verb 3sing indic pres mid	**442.1** noun nom sing masc	**2504.1** conj	**3620.2** partic	**1523.2** prep gen
ἔργων	δικαιοῦται	ἄνθρωπος,	καὶ	οὐκ	ἐκ
ergōn	*dikaioutai*	*anthrōpos*	*kai*	*ouk*	*ek*
works	is being justified	a man,	and	not	by

3963.2 noun gen sing fem	**3303.1** adv	**3532.1** adv	**1156.2** conj	**2504.1** conj	**4317.1** name fem	**3450.9** art nom sing fem
πίστεως	μόνον.	**25.** ὁμοίως	δὲ	καὶ	Ῥαὰβ	ἡ
pisteōs	*monon*	*homoiōs*	*de*	*kai*	*Rhaab*	*hē*
faith	only.	In like manner	but	also	Rahab	the

4063.1 noun nom sing fem	**3620.2** partic	**1523.1** prep gen	**2024.5** noun gen pl neu	**1338.13** verb 3sing indic aor pass	**5103.2** verb nom sing fem part aor mid
πόρνη	οὐκ	ἐξ	ἔργων	ἐδικαιώθη,	ὑποδεξαμένη
pornē	*ouk*	*ex*	*ergōn*	*edikaiōthē*	*hupodexamenē*
harlot	not	by	works	was justified,	having received

3450.8 art acc pl masc	**32.8** noun acc pl masc	**2504.1** conj	**2066.11** adj dat sing fem	**3461.3** noun dat sing fem	**1531.21** verb nom sing fem part aor act
τοὺς	ἀγγέλους,	καὶ	ἑτέρᾳ	ὁδῷ	ἐκβαλοῦσα;
tous	*angelous*	*kai*	*hetera*	*hodō*	*ekbalousa*
the	messengers,	and	by another	way	having put forth?

5450.1 conj	**1056.1** conj	**3450.16** art sing neu	**4835.1** noun sing neu	**5400.1** prep	**4011.2** noun gen sing neu
26. ὥσπερ	γὰρ	τὸ	σῶμα	χωρὶς	πνεύματος
hōsper	*gar*	*to*	*sōma*	*chōris*	*pneumatos*
As	for	the	body	apart from	spirit

3361.1 adj sing	**1498.4** verb 3sing indic pres act	**3643.1** adv	**2504.1** conj	**3450.9** art nom sing fem	**3963.1** noun nom sing fem	**5400.1** prep
νεκρόν	ἐστιν,	οὕτως	καὶ	ἡ	πίστις	χωρὶς
nekron	*estin*	*houtōs*	*kai*	*hē*	*pistis*	*chōris*
dead	is,	so	also	the	faith	apart from

"By works was faith made perfect." The goal of true faith is a life in conformity to that faith. The genuineness of Abraham's faith was proven when it reached the goal of obedience to God.

2:23. At the time when Abraham was still childless he believed God's promise that his seed should be as innumerable as the stars of heaven (Genesis 15:5). There must have been many occasions when this faith in God's promise was tested. Willingness to offer Isaac (Genesis 22) was undoubtedly the greatest evidence of this faith. It was not only an act of obedience, but of faith that God could raise his son from the dead if the sacrifice should be required (Hebrews 11:19). When Abraham was willing to offer up the only means by which the promise could be realized, the Scripture was fulfilled that he believed God. In this act it was shown that his faith and works were one. This was faith in full development.

Abraham was called the "Friend of God" (2 Chronicles 20:7; Isaiah 41:8). Jesus indicated the significance of friendship with God when He said: "Ye are my friends, if ye do whatsoever I command you. Hencefore I call you not servants; for the servant knoweth not what his lord doeth; but I have called you friends; for all things that I have heard of my Father I have made known unto you" (John 15:14,15). In Genesis 18:17 there is an example of God revealing to His friend Abraham His intentions concerning Sodom.

2:24. In 2:14 James asked if faith without works can save. Here he gives the answer. No one is saved by the kind of intellectual belief which does not result in appropriate actions. Saving faith is more than mental assent to orthodox doctrine.

2:25. Some readers might have questioned the use of Abraham as an illustration of faith and works because he was such an outstanding person. James next used Rahab the harlot as an illustration. She was as bad as Abraham was good, but she too was justified by a faith (Hebrews 11:31) which resulted in good works. See Joshua 2:8-14. She believed in the God of whom she had heard, and because of this faith she hid the spies and then assisted them in escaping. What was said of Abraham who was at one end of the spectrum was also said of Rahab who was at the other end. They were both justified by an active faith. Their works were evidence of their faith. One indication of the standing Rahab received as a result of her faith is that she was one of only four women listed in the genealogy of Joseph, the husband of Mary of whom Jesus was born (Matthew 1:4,5).

2:26. In chapter 2 James exphasized that mental assent alone is worthless. Now in conclusion he compares faith without works to a body without the spirit. It is like a corpse—dead. To be meaningful, faith and works must go together like spirit and body.

and by works was faith made perfect?: . . . the works, in turn, carried his faith on to perfection, *Norlie* . . . and how faith reached its supreme expression through his works, *Berkeley* . . . by works reached its goal, *Beck* . . . was completed by works, *Adams.*

23. And the scripture was fulfilled which saith, Abraham believed God: And what is written, *Beck* . . . the Scripture came true, *Berkeley* . . . put his trust in, *NLT.*

and it was imputed unto him for righteousness: . . . it was accounted to him, *Berkeley* . . . it was credited to him, *Norlie, Williams* . . . and so God declared him, *SEB* . . . it was reckoned to him as justice, *Confraternity.*

and he was called the Friend of God: God's friend, *Montgomery* . . . God's beloved, *SEB.*

24. Ye see then how that by works a man is justified: This shows, as you must understand...by a faith that works, *Norlie* . . . a person is pronounced righteous due to his works, *Berkeley* . . . a man gets to be righteous on the basis of his works, *Beck* . . . on the principle of works, *Darby.*

and not by faith only: . . . not merely by his faith, *Williams* . . . not on account of faith alone, *Berkeley.*

25. Likewise also was not Rahab the harlot justified by works, when she had received the messengers: Similarly, too, was not Rahab...due to her works, *Berkeley* . . . with the prostitute, *TCNT* . . . In the same way, too, was not Rahab the inkeeper...after having entertained the spies, *Norlie.*

and had sent [them] out another way?: . . . sent them back safely, *Norlie* . . . sending them off by a different road? *Williams.*

26. For as the body without the spirit is dead: . . . which does not have the breath of life, *Laubach* . . . apart from, *Clementson* . . . when separated from its spirit, *Norlie* . . . without breath is lifeless, *Fenton.*

so faith without works is dead also: . . . faith is dead without deeds, *Montgomery* . . . Faith is dead when nothing is done, *NLT* . . . apart from works, *Norlie.*

James 3:1

26.a.**Txt:** 02A,04C,018K 020L,025P,byz. **Var:** 01ℵ,03B,Tisc We/Ho,Weis,Sod UBS/⋆

3450.1 art gen pl	**2024.5** noun gen pl neu	**3361.8** adj nom sing fem	**1498.4** verb 3sing indic pres act		**3231.1** partic	**4044.7** adj nom pl masc
⸂a τῶν ⸃	ἔργων	νεκρά	ἐστιν.	**3:1.**	Μὴ	πολλοὶ
tōn	*ergōn*	*nekra*	*estin*		*Mē*	*polloi*
the	works	dead	is.		Not	many

1314.4 noun nom pl masc	**1090.19** verb 2pl impr pres mid	**79.6** noun nom pl masc	**1466.2** prs-pron gen 1sing	**3471.20** verb nom pl masc part perf act
διδάσκαλοι	γίνεσθε,	ἀδελφοί	μου,	εἰδότες
didaskaloi	*ginesthe*	*adelphoi*	*mou*	*eidotes*
teachers	be,	brothers	my,	knowing

3617.1 conj	**3157.7** adj comp sing neu	**2890.1** noun sing neu	**2956.40** verb 1pl indic fut mid	**2956.46** verb 1pl indic fut mid
ὅτι	μεῖζον	κρίμα	⸀ λημψόμεθα.	[⋆ λημψόμεθα.]
hoti	*meizon*	*krima*	*lēpsometha*	*lēmpsometha*
that	greater	judgment	we shall receive.	[idem]

4044.17 adj pl neu	**1056.1** conj	**4275.2** verb 1pl indic pres act	**533.4** adj nom pl masc	**1479.1** conj	**4948.3** indef-pron nom sing	**1706.1** prep
2. πολλὰ	γὰρ	πταίομεν	ἅπαντες.	εἴ	τις	ἐν
polla	*gar*	*ptaiomen*	*hapantes*	*ei*	*tis*	*en*
Much	for	we stumble	all.	If	anyone	in

3030.3 noun dat sing masc	**3620.3** partic	**4275.1** verb 3sing indic pres act	**3642.4** dem-pron nom sing masc	**4894.2** adj nom sing masc	**433.1** noun nom sing masc
λόγῳ	οὐ	πταίει,	οὗτος	τέλειος	ἀνήρ,
logō	*ou*	*ptaiei*	*houtos*	*teleios*	*anēr*
word	not	stumble,	this	a perfect	man,

1409.1 adj nom sing masc	**5304.2** verb inf aor act	**2504.1** conj	**3513.1** adj sing	**3450.16** art sing neu	**4835.1** noun sing neu
δυνατὸς	χαλιναγωγῆσαι	καὶ	ὅλον	τὸ	σῶμα.
dunatos	*chalinagōgēsai*	*kai*	*holon*	*to*	*sōma*
able	to bridle	also	whole	the	body.

3.a.**Txt:** Steph **Var:** 01ℵ,02A,03B,04C 018K,020L,Lach,Treg Alf,Word,Tisc,We/Ho Weis,Sod,UBS/⋆

1481.20 verb 2sing impr aor mid	**1479.1** conj	**1156.2** conj	**3450.1** art gen pl	**2437.3** noun gen pl masc	**3450.8** art acc pl masc
3. ⸀ Ἰδοὺ	[a⋆ εἰ	δὲ]	τῶν	ἵππων	τοὺς
Idou	*ei*	*de*	*tōn*	*hippōn*	*tous*
Consider,	[if	and]	of the	horses	the

5305.2 noun acc pl masc	**1519.1** prep	**3450.17** art pl neu	**4601.5** noun pl neu	**900.3** verb 1pl indic pres act	**4242.1** prep
χαλινοὺς	εἰς	τὰ	στόματα	βάλλομεν	⸀ πρὸς
chalinous	*eis*	*ta*	*stomata*	*ballomen*	*pros*
bits	in	the	mouths	we put,	for

3.b.**Txt:** 02A,018K,020L 025P,byz.Sod **Var:** 01ℵ,03B,04C,Lach Treg,Alf,Tisc,We/Ho Weis,UBS/⋆

1519.1 prep	**3450.16** art sing neu	**3844.24** verb inf pres mid	**840.8** prs-pron acc pl masc	**2231.3** prs-pron dat 1pl	**2504.1** conj
[b⋆ εἰς]	τὸ	πείθεσθαι	αὐτοὺς	ἡμῖν,	καὶ
eis	*to*	*peithesthai*	*autous*	*hēmin*	*kai*
[to]	the	to obey	them	us,	and

3513.1 adj sing	**3450.16** art sing neu	**4835.1** noun sing neu	**840.1** prs-pron gen pl	**3199.1** verb 1pl indic pres act	**1481.20** verb 2sing impr aor mid
ὅλον	τὸ	σῶμα	αὐτῶν	μετάγομεν.	**4.** Ἰδοὺ
holon	*to*	*sōma*	*autōn*	*metagomen*	*Idou*
whole	the	body	their	we turn about.	Consider,

2504.1 conj	**3450.17** art pl neu	**4003.4** noun pl neu	**4930.4** dem-pron nom pl neu	**1498.18** verb part pres act	**2504.1** conj	**5097.3** prep
καὶ	τὰ	πλοῖα,	τηλικαῦτα	ὄντα,	καὶ	ὑπὸ
kai	*ta*	*ploia*	*tēlikauta*	*onta*	*kai*	*hupo*
also	the	ships,	so great	being,	and	by

3:1. The word "masters" means literally "teachers." Problems existed in the early days of the Church because of false teaching. The conflict concerning faith and works (chapter 2) is a case in point. It seems it was popular to be a teacher, and unqualified, self-righteous people were appointing themselves to this role. They failed to recognize that those endowed by the Spirit with a teaching ministry (1 Corinthians 12:28) are the gifts of Christ to the Church (Ephesians 4:11), as in the case of Acts 13:1. Teachers themselves should have a teachable attitude (Romans 2:1,2) rather than being autocratic and schismatic.

Scripture recognizes that false teaching can come both from without and within the Church (Acts 20:29; 1 Peter 2:1). In this case James spoke to unqualified teachers as "my brethren."

The writer here identified himself as a teacher, and indicated that teachers will have to give an account of their ministry in the future (see Hebrews 13:17). All believers will appear before the judgment seat of Christ (2 Corinthians 5:10; see also 1 Corinthians 3:13-15), and there will be degrees of judgment. More will be required of those who have received much (Luke 12:48). Teachers will be evaluated on a stricter basis because they have had greater opportunity to receive and understand truth.

3:2. James here shifted attention from teachers only and included all believers. James pointed out that without any exception everyone offends or stumbles (same word as in 2:10). This is a strong statement indicating that believers often offend. James 2:10,11 indicates these offenses are blameworthy.

In the previous sentence James had referred to offenses in general. Now he brought offenses of speech into focus. Those who deny that good works accompany true faith are prone to sin in talking. This offending includes attitudes of speech such as sarcasm and impatience (1:19) as well as content.

A person who does not cause stumbling by the wrong use of the tongue "is a perfect man." This does not mean absolute perfection; rather, it means he is a believer of spiritual and moral maturity (see 1:4). The writer goes on to state that such a person is able to "bridle the whole body." He is using the illustration of the way a rider is able to control a horse.

3:3. A bit is a small object, but it controls the entire animal. Likewise, a person who can control his tongue can control his entire being. What is in the heart determines speech content and attitude (Matthew 12:34). If there is genuine faith in the heart, the accompanying works will be both appropriate speech and conduct.

3:4. James further illustrated the relationship of the activity of the tongue to the activity of the entire body with the rudder of a ship. A slight pressure on the rudder of the ship controls its course.

1. My brethren, be not many masters: . . . my fellow Christians, *Beck* . . . not many of you should become, *Norlie* . . . many teachers, *Montgomery.*

knowing that we shall receive the greater condemnation: . . . we are assuming the more accountability, *Berkeley* . . . are criticized all the more severely, *Norlie* . . . we teachers shall be judged by a severer standard than others, *Montgomery* . . . will receive stricter judgment, *Adams* . . . a severer sentence, *Campbell* . . . a greater judgment, *Confraternity* . . . those of us who teach will be judged very carefully, *SEB.*

2. For in many things we offend all: For we all are likely to stumble, *Norlie* . . . in many respects we often stumble, *Montgomery* . . . We all make many mistakes, *NLT, SEB* . . . All of us sin much, *Beck* . . . we all often offend, *Darby* . . . we all make many a slip, *Berkeley.*

If any man offend not in word: One who does not make any slip of the tongue, *Norlie* . . . if any man never stumbles in speech, *Montgomery* . . . If a man controls his tongue, *Laubach* . . . If anyone never slips in speech, *Williams* . . . doesn't sin in what he says, *Beck.*

the same [is] a perfect man: . . . is perfect indeed, *TNT.*

[and] able also to bridle the whole body: A man like that can keep his whole self, *TNT* . . . able as well to control his entire body, *Berkeley* . . . and has control over his whole body as well, *Norlie* . . . able also to lead round by a bridle the whole body, *Confraternity* . . . able to rule, also, *Campbell.*

3. Behold, we put bits in the horses' mouths, that they may obey us: When we control their mouths, *SEB* . . . so that we can make them, *SEB.*

and we turn about their whole body: . . . we guide, *Norlie* . . . we control their whole body also, *Montgomery* . . . so that they are yielding to us, *Concordant.*

4. Behold also the ships, which though [they be] so great, and [are] driven of fierce winds: Notice the ships...driven by violent winds, *Berkeley* . . . Look at the

4497.1 adj gen pl	415.6 noun gen pl masc	415.6 noun gen pl masc	4497.1 adj gen pl	1630.4 verb pl neu part pres mid
ʽ σκληρῶν	ἀνέμων	[☆ ἀνέμων	σκληρῶν]	ἐλαυνόμενα,
sklērōn	*anemōn*	*anemōn*	*sklērōn*	*elaunomena*
violent	winds	[winds	violent]	being driven,

3199.2 verb 3sing indic pres mid	5097.3 prep	1633.4 adj sup gen sing neu	3940.1 noun gen sing neu	3562.1 adv
μετάγεται	ὑπὸ	ἐλαχίστου	πηδαλίου,	ὅπου
metagetai	*hupo*	*elachistou*	*pēdaliou*	*hopou*
are being turned about	by	a very small	rudder,	wherever

4.a.**Txt:** 02A,04C,018K 020L,025P,byz.Sod **Var:** 01ℵ,03B,sa.Treg Tisc,We/Ho,Weis UBS/☆

300.1 partic	3450.9 art nom sing fem	3593.1 noun nom sing fem	3450.2 art gen sing	2096.1 verb gen sing masc part pres act	1007.6 verb 3sing subj pres mid
ʽa ἂν ˎ	ἡ	ὁρμὴ	τοῦ	εὐθύνοντος	ʽ βούληται·
an	*hē*	*hormē*	*tou*	*euthunontos*	*boulētai*
	the	impulse	of the	steering	may will.

4.b.**Txt:** 02A,04C,018K 025P,byz.Sod **Var:** 01ℵ,03B,020L Treg,Tisc,We/Ho,Weis UBS/☆

1007.3 verb 3sing indic pres mid	3643.1 adv	2504.1 conj	3450.9 art nom sing fem	1094.1 noun nom sing fem	3262.1 adj sing
[b☆ βούλεται·]	5. οὕτως	καὶ	ἡ	γλῶσσα	μικρὸν
bouletai	*houtōs*	*kai*	*hē*	*glōssa*	*mikron*
[wills]	Thus	also	the	tongue	a little

5.a.**Txt:** 01ℵ,04C-corr 018K,020L,byz.Sod **Var:** 02A,03B,04C-org 025P,Lach,Treg,Alf Tisc,We/Ho,Weis UBS/☆

3166.1 noun sing neu	1498.4 verb 3sing indic pres act	2504.1 conj	3137.1 verb 3sing indic pres act	3144.17 adj pl neu
μέλος	ἐστὶν,	καὶ	ʽ μεγαλαυχεῖ.	[a☆ μεγάλα
melos	*estin*	*kai*	*megalauchei*	*megala*
member	is,	and	boasts great things.	[great things

5.b.**Txt:** 02A-org 04C-corr,018K,020L,byz. sa.bo. **Var:** 01ℵ,02A-corr,03B 04C-org,025P,Lach Treg,Alf,Word,Tisc We/Ho,Weis,Sod UBS/☆

842.1 verb 3sing indic pres act	1481.20 verb 2sing impr aor mid	3504.1 adj sing	2228.1 intr-pron acc sing masc	4300.1 noun sing neu
αὐχεῖ.]	Ἰδοὺ,	ʽ ὀλίγον	[b☆ ἡλίκον]	πῦρ
auchei	*Idou*	*oligon*	*hēlikon*	*pur*
boasts.]	Behold,	a little	[how great]	fire

2228.2 intr-pron acc sing fem	5049.1 noun acc sing fem	379.1 verb 3sing indic pres act	2504.1 conj	3450.9 art nom sing fem	1094.1 noun nom sing fem
ἡλίκην	ὕλην	ἀνάπτει·	6. καὶ	ἡ	γλῶσσα
hēlikēn	*hulēn*	*anaptei*	*kai*	*hē*	*glōssa*
how large	a wood	it kindles;	and	the	tongue

4300.1 noun sing neu	3450.5 art nom sing masc	2862.1 noun nom sing masc	3450.10 art gen sing fem	92.2 noun gen sing fem
πῦρ,	ὁ	κόσμος	τῆς	ἀδικίας.
pur	*ho*	*kosmos*	*tēs*	*adikias*
fire,	the	world	of the	unrighteousness.

6.a.**Txt:** 020L,025P,byz. **Var:** 01ℵ,02A,03B,04C 018K,sa.bo.Lach,Treg Alf,Word,Tisc,We/Ho Weis,Sod,UBS/☆

3643.1 adv	3450.9 art nom sing fem	1094.1 noun nom sing fem	2497.9 verb 3sing indic pres mid	1706.1 prep	3450.4 art dat pl
ʽa οὕτως ˎ	ἡ	γλῶσσα	καθίσταται	ἐν	τοῖς
houtōs	*hē*	*glōssa*	*kathistatai*	*en*	*tois*
Thus	the	tongue	is being set	in	the

3166.4 noun dat pl neu	2231.2 prs-pron gen 1pl	3450.9 art nom sing fem	4549.1 verb nom sing fem part pres act	3513.1 adj sing	3450.16 art sing neu
μέλεσιν	ἡμῶν,	ἡ	σπιλοῦσα	ὅλον	τὸ
melesin	*hēmōn*	*hē*	*spilousa*	*holon*	*to*
members	our,	the	defiling	whole	the

4835.1 noun sing neu	2504.1 conj	5231.1 verb nom sing fem part pres act	3450.6 art acc sing masc	5005.1 noun acc sing masc	3450.10 art gen sing fem
σῶμα,	καὶ	φλογίζουσα	τὸν	τροχὸν	τῆς
sōma	*kai*	*phlogizousa*	*ton*	*trochon*	*tēs*
body,	and	setting on fire	the	course	of the

The illustration of the ship and rudder added another dimension— fierce winds. James pointed out that no matter how adverse the circumstances, if the rudder can be controlled by the pilot, the entire ship can be controlled. The point of the illustration is that if a believer can maintain control of his tongue in adverse circumstances, he can maintain control over his entire being.

3:5. Here the inspired writer emphasizes how important the tongue is though it is a small member of one's body. Just like the bit which is small in relationship to the size of a horse and the rudder which is small in relationship to a ship, the little tongue can do great things. Some interpret "boasteth" to mean that the tongue is haughty, while others interpret it as reference to accomplishment of great achievements. Peter's proper use of the tongue resulted in the conversion of about 3,000 souls being added to the Church (Acts 2:41).

James has been pointing out that small things can have a beneficial effect. A small bit can be used to guide a horse. A rudder can affect the course of a large ship. Now he goes on to show that small things can also be destructive in their effect.

The word "matter" can refer either to a forest or stacks of lumber. Fire can either have a good or disastrous effect. The point here is that if the tongue is not controlled, careless or evil words, no matter how few, can produce a catastrophe.

3:6. These are strong words used to describe the tongue's activities if it is not curbed. The Holy Spirit is striving to stress how much damage an unbridled tongue can cause. The NIV translates it this way: "The tongue also is a fire, a world of evil among the parts of the body."

The tongue is "a world of iniquity." The entire unrighteous world system can find expression through the tongue. See Psalms 10:7; 12:3,4. The use of the tongue affects the whole body. When the tongue becomes an instrument of evil, the entire personality is stained and polluted. Jesus used a different word (signifying to make ceremonially unholy) to teach the same truth when He said, "That which cometh out of the mouth, this defileth a man" (Matthew 15:11).

"The course of nature" (literally, "the wheel of birth") probably is referring to the entire sphere of human existence. Phillips in his paraphrase suggests an uncontrolled tongue makes "a blazing hell" of life.

The word translated "hell" in the phrase "is set on fire of hell" is *gehenna*. It referred to a constantly burning dump south of Jerusalem. Jesus used this as a figure of hell (Matthew 5:22-29; 10:28). Unrighteous speech has its origin from the kingdom of Satan (cf. Mark 8:33).

ships, too! No matter how big they are or how strong the wind that drives, *Norlie* . . . though they are so large, *Montgomery* . . . being of such proportions, *Concordant* . . . Sailing ships are driven, *NLT* . . . great as they are, and driven by boisterous, *Confraternity.*

yet are they turned about with a very small helm: . . . how they are steered, *Berkeley* . . . tiny rudder, *Williams.*

whithersoever the governor listeth: . . . wherever the impulse of the helmsman wills, *Montgomery* . . . turned about in whatever direction the will of the pilot directs, *Norlie* . . . wherever the touch of the steersman pleases, *Confraternity* . . . to whatever point the impulse of the pilot chooses, *Swann* . . . wherever the helmsman's whim determines, *Berkeley.*

5. Even so the tongue is a little member, and boasteth great things: It is the same with our tongue...it brags about, *SEB* . . . True, the tongue is only a very small member of the body, *Norlie* . . . is a small organ and can talk big, *Berkeley* . . . can boast of great achievements, *Williams* . . . but it boasts mightily, *Confraternity.*

Behold, how great a matter a little fire kindleth!: See how a tiny flame can set a mighty forest afire! *Norlie* . . . Behold, how small a fire—how great a forest it kindles! *Confraternity.*

6. And the tongue [is] a fire, a world of iniquity: . . . is like a spark, *TCNT* . . . a universe, *Fenton* . . . of wickedness, *Norlie* . . . of injustice, *Concordant.*

so is the tongue among our members, that it defileth the whole body: . . . it contaminates, *TCNT* . . . it pollutes, *SEB* . . . it taints, *Berkeley* . . . It can poison the whole body, *Norlie.*

and setteth on fire the course of nature: . . . enflames, *Beck* . . . fires up the whole order of beginnings, *Klingensmith* . . . every power in man's makeup, *Norlie* . . . the whole machinery of existence, *Berkeley* . . . the wheel of nature, *Montgomery* . . . the course of our life, *Confraternity* . . . it sets the whole round of our existence ablaze, *TNT* . . . the entire cycle of our life, *Noli.*

1071.1 noun gen sing fem	**2504.1** conj	**5231.2** verb nom sing fem part pres mid	**5097.3** prep	**3450.10** art gen sing fem	**1060.1** noun gen sing fem
γενέσεως,	καὶ	φλογιζομένη	ὑπὸ	τῆς	γεέννης˙
geneseōs	*kai*	*phlogizomenē*	*hupo*	*tēs*	*geennēs*
nature,	and	being set on fire	by		gehenna.

3820.9 adj nom sing fem	**1056.1** conj	**5285.1** noun nom sing fem	**2319.5** noun gen pl neu	**4885.1** conj	**2504.1** conj	**3932.2** adj gen pl neu
7. πᾶσα	γὰρ	φύσις	θηρίων	τε	καὶ	πετεινῶν,
pasa	*gar*	*phusis*	*thēriōn*	*te*	*kai*	*peteinōn*
Every	for	species	of beasts	both	and	of birds,

2046.2 noun gen pl neu	**4885.1** conj	**2504.1** conj	**1708.1** adj gen pl neu	**1145.2** verb 3sing indic pres mid
ἑρπετῶν	τε	καὶ	ἐναλίων,	δαμάζεται
herpetōn	*te*	*kai*	*enaliōn*	*damazetai*
of creeping things	both	and	things of the sea,	is being subdued

2504.1 conj	**1145.3** verb 3sing indic perf mid	**3450.11** art dat sing fem	**5285.3** noun dat sing fem	**3450.11** art dat sing fem	**440.3** adj dat sing fem
καὶ	δεδάμασται	τῇ	φύσει	τῇ	ἀνθρωπίνῃ˙
kai	*dedamastai*	*tē*	*phusei*	*tē*	*anthrōpinē*
and	has been subdued	by the	species	the	human;

3450.12 art acc sing fem	**1156.2** conj	**1094.4** noun acc sing fem	**3625.2** num card nom masc	**1404.4** verb 3sing indic pres mid	**442.7** noun gen pl masc
8. τὴν	δὲ	γλῶσσαν	οὐδεὶς	ʽ δύναται	ἀνθρώπων
tēn	*de*	*glōssan*	*oudeis*	*dunatai*	*anthrōpōn*
the	but	tongue	no one	is able	of men

1145.1 verb inf aor act	**1145.1** verb inf aor act	**1404.4** verb 3sing indic pres mid	**442.7** noun gen pl masc
δαμάσαι˙	[☆ δαμάσαι	δύναται	ἀνθρώπων˙]
damasai	*damasai*	*dunatai*	*anthrōpōn*
to subdue;	[to subdue	is able	of men;]

8.a.**Txt:** 04C,018K,020L byz.Sod
Var: 01ℵ,02A,03B,025P Lach,Treg,Alf,Word Tisc,We/Ho,Weis UBS/☆

181.1 adj sing neu	**180.2** adj sing neu	**2527.7** adj sing neu	**3194.4** adj nom sing fem
ʽ ἀκατάσχετον	[a☆ ἀκατάστατον]	κακόν,	μεστὴ
akatascheton	*akatastaton*	*kakon*	*mestē*
an unrestrainable	[an unruly]	evil,	full

2423.2 noun gen sing masc	**2264.1** adj gen sing masc	**1706.1** prep	**840.11** prs-pron dat sing fem	**2108.1** verb 1pl indic pres act
ἰοῦ	θανατηφόρου.	**9.** ἐν	αὐτῇ	εὐλογοῦμεν
iou	*thanatēphorou*	*en*	*autē*	*eulogoumen*
of poison	death bringing.	By	this	we bless

9.a.**Txt:** 018K,020L,byz. sa.bo.
Var: 01ℵ,02A,03B,04C 025P,33,Lach,Treg,Alf Tisc,We/Ho,Weis,Sod UBS/☆

3450.6 art acc sing masc	**2296.4** noun acc sing masc	**3450.6** art acc sing masc	**2935.4** noun acc sing masc	**2504.1** conj	**3824.4** noun acc sing masc
ʽ τὸν	Θεὸν	[a☆ τὸν	κύριον]	καὶ	πατέρα,
ton	*Theon*	*ton*	*kurion*	*kai*	*patera*
	God	[the	Lord]	and	Father,

2504.1 conj	**1706.1** prep	**840.11** prs-pron dat sing fem	**2642.1** verb 1pl indic pres mid	**3450.8** art acc pl masc	**442.9** noun acc pl masc
καὶ	ἐν	αὐτῇ	καταρώμεθα	τοὺς	ἀνθρώπους
kai	*en*	*autē*	*katarōmetha*	*tous*	*anthrōpous*
and	by	this	we curse	the	men

3450.8 art acc pl masc	**2567.2** prep	**3531.1** noun acc sing fem	**2296.2** noun gen sing masc	**1090.9** verb acc pl masc part perf act
τοὺς	καθ'	ὁμοίωσιν	θεοῦ	γεγονότας˙
tous	*kath'*	*homoiōsin*	*theou*	*gegonotas*
the	according to	likeness	of God	having been made.

3:7. If there were those who might claim it is impossible to control the tongue, James refers them back to the creation record where God indicated the four categories of creatures over which man was to have dominion (Genesis 1:26,28).

The word here translated "tamed" might more accurately be translated "subdued" (same word as in Mark 5:4). The word can include the idea of domestication. Many animals ranging in size from those smaller than dogs to those as large as elephants have been domesticated and trained to serve mankind. But the word goes beyond domestication and includes the idea of domination over creatures which cannot be domesticated.

3:8. However, the tongue presents a greater problem than the animals. Man who has the power to control the wild nature of animals, apart from God, cannot control his own tongue. "No man" is a strong expression and might be translated "no one of men."

The tongue is an "unruly evil," literally, an evil which cannot be held back. It is like a wild animal restlessly wanting to make an attack. It is like an enemy that cannot be contained by military force. Phillips translates it, "It is an evil always liable to break out."

The tongue is "full of deadly poison." In describing the activities of his enemies, David wrote, "Adders' poison is under their lips" (Psalm 140:3). The untamed tongue prefers speaking evil rather than good (Psalm 52:2-4). It prefers destroying rather than helping (Psalm 64:2-5). It seeks to destroy reputation and morale through slanderous gossip.

3:9. In the previous verse James dealt with the nature of an evil tongue. The tongue, however, is capable of speaking both evil and good. (See Proverbs 10:11,19,31,32; 18:21; Matthew 12:34-37.) In this verse the writer dealt with the inconsistency of the tongue, first blessing God and then cursing man.

To bless means to praise, to extol. Blessing God is the highest function of the tongue, described in Scripture as good and comely (Psalms 33:1; 147:1). But it is absolutely inconsistent for the Christian to bless God and then curse man made in the likeness of God. Believers should not only refrain from cursing but also bless those who curse and persecute them (Luke 6:28; Romans 12:14).

The reason cursing man is evil is that he was made "after the similitude of God," that is, in His likeness. (See Genesis 1:26,27.) The likeness of God in man was not physical or material. Jesus said, "God is a Spirit" (John 4:24), and "a spirit hath not flesh and bones" (Luke 24:39).

The likeness was natural, consisting of intelligence, emotions, and will; and moral, a tendency toward God, though accompanied with the power to make wrong choices. The tendency of fallen man is now away from God, to go his own way. When man sinned in Eden, the likeness to God was severely marred but not lost. Because man retains likeness to God, human life is sacred. To curse man is to curse the likeness of God in man.

and it is set on fire of hell: Its own fire comes from hell itself, *TNT* . . . It turns our existence into an infernal torture, *Noli* . . . as it gets its fire from hell, *Beck* . . . while it is kindled by, *Berkeley* . . . set afire by the junk pile, *Klingensmith* . . . is set on fire by Gehenna, *Wilson* . . . by the flames of the Pit, *TCNT*.

7. For every kind of beasts, and of birds, and of serpents, and of things in the sea, is tamed, and hath been tamed of mankind: For Every Species both of Wild beasts and of Birds, *Wilson* . . . of reptiles and sea animals, *Williams* . . . creatures in the sea, *Beck* . . . can be tamed by the human genius, *Fenton*.

8. But the tongue can no man tame; [it is] an unruly evil: . . . no man has as yet been able to tame the human tongue, this unrestrainable evil, *Norlie* . . . an evil thing, uncontrollable, *TNT* . . . restless evil that it is, *Montgomery* . . . It is a restless plague! *TCNT* . . . a reckless evil, *Adams* . . . an undisciplined evil, *Fenton* . . . this undisciplined mischief, *Berkeley* . . . a turbulent evil, *Concordant* . . . this unruly fiend, *Noli*.

full of deadly poison: It is a store-house of, *TCNT* . . . distended with death-carrying venom, *Concordant*.

9. Therewith bless we God, even the Father: . . . with our tongue, *Beck* . . . With it we bless, *Confraternity* . . . We use it to praise, *TNT* . . . We praise, *Norlie* . . . the Lord and Father, *Berkeley*.

and therewith curse we men: . . . we are accustomed to, *Montgomery* . . . and yet curse human beings, *SEB* . . . with it, we bawl out people, *Klingensmith* . . . other people, *Beck* . . . our fellow men, *Noli*.

which are made after the similitude of God: . . . born in the likeness of, *Klingensmith* . . . who are made in the image of God, *Norlie* . . . who once were made like God, *Beck* . . . made in God's likeness, *TCNT*.

1523.2 prep gen	3450.2 art gen sing	840.3 prs-pron gen sing	4601.2 noun gen sing neu	1814.28 verb 3sing indic pres mid	2110.1 noun nom sing fem
10. ἐκ	τοῦ	αὐτοῦ	στόματος	ἐξέρχεται	εὐλογία
ek	*tou*	*autou*	*stomatos*	*exerchetai*	*eulogia*
Out of	the	same	mouth	goes forth	blessing

2504.1 conj	2641.1 noun nom sing fem	3620.3 partic	5369.1 verb 3sing indic pres act	79.6 noun nom pl masc	1466.2 prs-pron gen 1sing
καὶ	κατάρα.	οὐ	χρή,	ἀδελφοί	μου,
kai	*katara*	*ou*	*chrē*	*adelphoi*	*mou*
and	cursing.	Not	ought,	brothers	my,

3642.18 dem-pron pl neu	3643.1 adv	1090.28 verb inf pres mid	3252.1 partic	3450.9 art nom sing fem	3938.1 noun nom sing fem
ταῦτα	οὕτως	γίνεσθαι.	11. μήτι	ἡ	πηγὴ
tauta	*houtōs*	*ginesthai*	*mēti*	*hē*	*pēgē*
these things	thus	to be.	Not	the	fountain

1523.2 prep gen	3450.10 art gen sing fem	840.10 prs-pron gen sing fem	3555.1 noun gen sing fem	1025.1 verb 3sing indic pres act	3450.16 art sing neu
ἐκ	τῆς	αὐτῆς	ὀπῆς	βρύει	τὸ
ek	*tēs*	*autēs*	*opēs*	*bruei*	*to*
out	of the	same	opening	pours forth	the

1093.1 adj sing neu	2504.1 conj	3450.16 art sing neu	3950.1 adj sing	3231.1 partic	1404.4 verb 3sing indic pres mid
γλυκὺ	καὶ	τὸ	πικρόν;	12. μὴ	δύναται,
gluku	*kai*	*to*	*pikron*	*mē*	*dunatai*
sweet	and	the	bitter?	Not	is able,

79.6 noun nom pl masc	1466.2 prs-pron gen 1sing	4659.1 noun nom sing fem	1623.1 noun fem	4020.41 verb inf aor act	2211.1 conj
ἀδελφοί	μου,	συκῆ	ἐλαίας	ποιῆσαι,	ἢ
adelphoi	*mou*	*sukē*	*elaias*	*poiēsai*	*ē*
brothers	my,	a fig tree	olives	to produce,	or

12.a.**Txt:** 01ℵ,04C-corr 018K,020L,025P,byz. Sod
Var: 02A,03B,04C-org Lach,Treg,Alf,Word Tisc,We/Ho,Weis UBS/⋆

12.b.**Txt:** 018K,020L 025P,byz.
Var: 01ℵ,02A,03B,04C 33,Gries,Lach,Treg,Alf Word,Tisc,We/Ho,Weis UBS/⋆

286.1 noun nom sing fem	4661.2 noun pl neu	3643.1 adv	3625.4 num card nom fem	3938.1 noun nom sing fem	250.1 adj sing neu
ἄμπελος	σῦκα;	(a οὕτως)	(οὐδεμία	πηγὴ	ἁλυκὸν
ampelos	*suka*	*houtōs*	*oudemia*	*pēgē*	*halukon*
a vine	figs?	Thus	no	fountain	salt

2504.1 conj	3641.1 conj	250.1 adj sing neu	1093.1 adj sing neu	4020.41 verb inf aor act	5045.1 noun sing neu
καὶ	[b⋆ οὔτε	ἁλυκὸν]	γλυκὺ	ποιῆσαι	ὕδωρ.
kai	*oute*	*halukon*	*gluku*	*poiēsai*	*hudōr*
and	[neither	salt]	sweet	to produce	water.

4949.3 intr-pron nom sing	4533.1 adj nom sing masc	2504.1 conj	1974.1 adj nom sing masc	1706.1 prep	5050.3 prs-pron dat 2pl
13. Τίς	σοφὸς	καὶ	ἐπιστήμων	ἐν	ὑμῖν;
Tis	*sophos*	*kai*	*epistēmōn*	*en*	*humin*
Who	wise	and	understanding	among	you;

1161.10 verb 3sing impr aor act	1523.2 prep gen	3450.10 art gen sing fem	2541.6 adj gen sing fem	389.1 noun gen sing fem
δειξάτω	ἐκ	τῆς	καλῆς	ἀναστροφῆς
deixatō	*ek*	*tēs*	*kalēs*	*anastrophēs*
let him demonstrate	out of	the	good	conduct

3450.17 art pl neu	2024.4 noun pl neu	840.3 prs-pron gen sing	1706.1 prep	4099.2 noun dat sing fem	4531.2 noun gen sing fem
τὰ	ἔργα	αὐτοῦ	ἐν	πραΰτητι	σοφίας.
ta	*erga*	*autou*	*en*	*prautēti*	*sophias*
the	works	his	in	gentleness	of wisdom;

3:10. Others have pointed out that the tongue is capable of both good and evil expression (Proverbs 18:21). Here, however, the writer points out that it is unnatural for both good and evil to come from believers. James is emphatic, "These things ought not so to be."

James was not writing to unsaved people but to "brethren." A mixture of good and evil speaking can be expected from the natural man, but it is totally out of place for the believer. It should not happen.

10. Out of the same mouth proceedeth blessing and cursing: . . . praise and cursing come from, *Beck* . . . pour forth, *Montgomery.*

My brethren, these things ought not so to be: It is not right, *Norlie* . . . We mustn't do that, my fellow Christians, *Beck.*

3:11. People in Palestine were familiar with the reference to fountains and springs. They were dependent on them for their water supply. Towns were built around springs which provided adequate water in an arid country. The woman of Samaria indicated that her town of Sychar was near the well first used by Jacob (John 4:12).

The people to whom James wrote understood that a spring does not alternate between yielding sweet and bitter water. It was either one or the other, but not both. The reason towns were not built around the Dead Sea is because springs in that region were known to yield only brackish water.

In man, though redeemed and regenerated, the tongue is capable of both good and evil, because he retains his fallen nature along with the new nature. In Galatians 5:17 Paul describes the conflict between the old and new natures. While man cannot tame his own tongue, he can turn the control of it over to the Holy Spirit. When he does this, the Holy Spirit becomes a well of living water in his life (John 7:37,38). When the believer quenches the Spirit, the bitterness of his fallen nature expresses itself.

11. Doth a fountain send forth at the same place: Does a spring pour forth from the same opening, *Montgomery* . . . The spring does not well up...from the same cleft, *Berkeley* . . . discharge, *Norlie* . . . from the same spring mouth? *Klingensmith.*

sweet [water] and bitter?: . . . fresh, *Beck* . . . and salt, *Klingensmith.*

3:12. Just as it is not the nature of the fig tree to bear olives, nor of the vine to bear figs, it is not the nature of the regenerate spirit to speak evil. Whichever nature man allows to dominate his life—the old or the new—determines what his speech will be. This is why it is important to be filled with the Spirit continually (Ephesians 5:18).

12. Can the fig tree, my brethren, bear olive berries?: Nor is it possible, is it, my brothers, *Berkeley* . . . Friends, *Norlie* . . . Do you pick olives from a fig tree? *Klingensmith.*

either a vine, figs?: . . . a grapevine, *Montgomery.*

so [can] no fountain both yield salt water and fresh: Of course not, *TNT* . . . it is impossible to have, *SEB* . . . a salt spring, *Beck* . . . Neither can salt produce, *Berkeley* . . . No more can salt water yield fresh water, *Montgomery* . . . pour out fresh water, *Klingensmith.*

3:13. Now James returned to the responsibility of teachers mentioned in verse 1. Those equipped to be teachers were not only to be knowledgeable but to demonstrate their wisdom with a good conversation, a "good life" (RV).

The teacher is not to use his good conduct to draw attention to himself. This was the sin of hypocrites (Matthew 6:1-5). Jesus demonstrated the true spirit of the teacher when He said, "I am meek and lowly in heart" (Matthew 11:29). The godly teacher will not be selfishly ambitious and arrogant, but mild and gentle.

13. Who [is] a wise man and endued with knowledge among you?: . . . who is truly wise? *SEB* . . . intelligent, *Montgomery* . . . instructed, *Confraternity* . . . discreet among you, *Wilson* . . . understanding, *Berkeley* . . . and knows what is going on, *Klingensmith* . . . in your company? *TNT.*

let him show out of a good conversation: Let him show his deeds by his good life, *Montgomery* . . . he who lives a good life, *Norlie* . . . by good behavior, *Campbell* . . . Let him exhibit it by the nobility of his conduct, *Fenton* . . . Let his life...be an example, *TNT.*

his works with meekness of wisdom: . . . does his deeds in humility? That is wisdom, *Norlie* . . . his actions are carried on with unobtrusive wisdom, *Berkeley* . . . In a gentle spirit of wisdom, *Beck.*

14.a.**Var:** 02A,025P,044 33,81,945,1241,1739 2298

1479.1 conj	**1156.2** conj	**679.1** partic	**2188.4** noun sing	**3950.1** adj sing	**2174.2** verb 2pl pres act
14. εἰ	δὲ	[a+ ἄρα]	ζῆλον	πικρὸν	ἔχετε
ei	*de*	*ara*	*zēlon*	*pikron*	*echete*
if	but	[therefore]	emulation	bitter	you have

2504.1 conj	**2036.3** noun acc sing fem	**1706.1** prep	**3450.11** art dat sing fem	**2559.3** noun dat sing fem	**5050.2** prs-pron gen 2pl	**3231.1** partic
καὶ	ἐριθείαν	ἐν	τῇ	καρδίᾳ	ὑμῶν,	μὴ
kai	*eritheian*	*en*	*tē*	*kardia*	*humōn*	*mē*
and	contention	in	the	heart	your,	not

2590.4 verb 2pl impr pres mid	**2504.1** conj	**5409.4** verb 2pl impr pres mid	**2567.3** prep	**3450.10** art gen sing fem	**223.2** noun gen sing fem
κατακαυχᾶσθε	καὶ	ψεύδεσθε	κατὰ	τῆς	ἀληθείας.
katakauchasthe	*kai*	*pseudesthe*	*kata*	*tēs*	*alētheias*
do boast against	and	lie	against	the	truth.

3620.2 partic	**1498.4** verb 3sing indic pres act	**3642.9** dem-pron nom sing fem	**3450.9** art nom sing fem	**4531.1** noun nom sing fem
15. Οὐκ	ἔστιν	αὕτη	ἡ	σοφία
Ouk	*estin*	*hautē*	*hē*	*sophia*
Not	is	this	the	wisdom

505.1 adv	**2687.8** verb nom sing fem part pres mid	**233.1** conj	**233.2** conj	**1904.2** adj nom sing fem
ἄνωθεν	κατερχομένη,	ʻ ἀλλ’	[☆ ἀλλὰ]	ἐπίγειος,
anōthen	*katerchomenē*	*all’*	*alla*	*epigeios*
from above	coming down,	but	[idem]	earthly,

5426.3 adj nom sing fem	**1135.1** adj nom sing fem	**3562.1** adv	**1056.1** conj	**2188.1** noun sing	**2504.1** conj
ψυχική,	δαιμονιώδης·	**16.** ὅπου	γὰρ	ζῆλος	καὶ
psuchikē	*daimoniōdēs*	*hopou*	*gar*	*zēlos*	*kai*
natural,	demonic.	Where	for	jealousy	and

2036.1 noun nom sing fem	**1550.1** adv	**179.2** noun nom sing fem	**2504.1** conj	**3820.17** adj sing neu	**5175.1** adj sing neu
ἐριθεία,	ἐκεῖ	ἀκαταστασία	καὶ	πᾶν	φαῦλον
eritheia	*ekei*	*akatastasia*	*kai*	*pan*	*phaulon*
contention,	there	commotion	and	every	evil

4088.1 noun sing neu	**3450.9** art nom sing fem	**1156.2** conj	**505.1** adv	**4531.1** noun nom sing fem	**4270.1** adv
πρᾶγμα.	**17.** ἡ	δὲ	ἄνωθεν	σοφία	πρῶτον
pragma	*hē*	*de*	*anōthen*	*sophia*	*prōton*
thing.	The	but	from above	wisdom	first

3173.1 conj	**52.4** adj nom sing fem	**1498.4** verb 3sing indic pres act	**1884.1** adv	**1504.2** adj nom sing fem	**1918.4** adj nom sing fem
μὲν	ἁγνή	ἐστιν,	ἔπειτα	εἰρηνική,	ἐπιεικής,
men	*hagnē*	*estin*	*epeita*	*eirēnikē*	*epieikēs*
	pure	is,	then	peaceful,	gentle,

2118.1 adj nom sing fem	**3194.4** adj nom sing fem	**1643.3** noun gen sing neu	**2504.1** conj	**2561.4** noun gen pl masc	**18.1** adj gen pl
εὐπειθής,	μεστὴ	ἐλέους	καὶ	καρπῶν	ἀγαθῶν,
eupeithēs	*mestē*	*eleous*	*kai*	*karpōn*	*agathōn*
yielding,	full	of mercy	and	of fruits	good,

17.a.**Txt:** 018K,020L,byz. **Var:** 01ℵ,02A,03B,04C 025P,33,Lach,Treg,Alf Tisc,We/Ho,Weis,Sod UBS/☆

86.1 adj nom sing fem	**2504.1** conj	**502.1** adj nom sing fem	**2561.1** noun nom sing masc	**1156.2** conj
ἀδιάκριτος	ʻa καὶ ʼ	ἀνυπόκριτος·	**18.** καρπὸς	δὲ
adiakritos	*kai*	*anupokritos*	*karpos*	*de*
impartial	and	unfeigned.	Fruit	but

3:14. "Envying" is here used to translate *zēlon* which does not have a bad connotation in itself. It is used in a good sense in 2 Corinthians 11:2. Paul calls it "godly jealousy." The adjective "bitter" indicates James was referring to evil jealousy which carnal teachers can harbor. This same Greek word appears in Galatians 5:20 where it is translated "emulations."

"Strife" is translated as "selfish ambition" in the Revised Standard Version. This evil is also listed as a work of the flesh in Galatians 5:20.

If a teacher is dominated by jealousy and selfish ambition, he is instructed to stop being boastful and to stop lying against the truth. He repudiates the truth of the gospel by ungodly attitudes regardless of how wise he claims to be.

3:15. This wisdom is "earthbound" (*NEB*); it "comes from the world" (Phillips). Earthly wisdom originates with man and has only an earthly perspective. "Sensual" means literally "natural, belonging to the soul." It originates in the mind of natural man and stands in contrast to the wisdom of God's Word (2 Timothy 3:16) which is spiritually discerned (1 Corinthians 2:13,14).

Demonic power is the source of some kinds of wisdom. Paul warned that some people would give "heed to seducing spirits, and doctrines of devils" (1 Timothy 4:1; cf. 1 John 4:1).

3:16. James has referred to the evils of envy and strife in verse 14. Now he shows the harm they can produce if allowed to remain —"confusion" (*akatastasia*). It is related to the word translated "unstable" (*akatastatos*) in 1:8. Earthly wisdom results in confusion and instability, while godly wisdom results in harmony and stability.

3:17. It must be understood that God's wisdom is pure from all that is earthly, sensual, and devilish. The wisdom which is from below, from the world, is the complete opposite.

Divine wisdom is "peaceable" in contrast to earthly wisdom which creates confusion. It is peace-loving and produces "peacemakers" (Matthew 5:9). It is "gentle"; that is, it is fair, forbearing and considerate, in contrast to the arrogant spirit produced by earthly wisdom. It is "easy to be entreated," that is, reasonable as opposed to harsh or stubborn. It is "full of mercy and good fruits." God's wisdom results in compassion for the suffering, and produces good works as opposed to the evil work (3:16) resulting from human wisdom. The wisdom from above is "without partiality" (literally "undivided"). There is no indecision about commitment to God. It is "without hypocrisy." There is no attempt to pretend or to make a good impression.

14. But if ye have bitter envying and strife in your hearts: . . . if you cherish, *Williams* . . . jealousy and faction, *Montgomery* . . . bitter jealousy and selfish aims, *Norlie* . . . and rivalry, *Adams.*

glory not, and lie not against the truth: . . . don't brag about it, *SEB* . . . do not pride yourselves in it and play false to the truth, *Berkeley* . . . and be liars against the truth, *Confraternity.*

15. This wisdom descendeth not from above, but [is] earthly, sensual, devilish: Such wisdom does not come down from above; instead it is earthly, animalistic, *Berkeley* . . . terrestrial, soulish, *Concordant* . . . natural, *Darby* . . . the wisdom of demons, *SEB* . . . demoniacal, *Wilson.*

16. For where envying and strife [is]: . . . wherever jealousy and faction exist, *Montgomery* . . . and selfishness, *Norlie* . . . and rivalry, *TCNT* . . . and partyism are, *Swann* . . . and self-seeking exist, *Adams.*

there [is] confusion and every evil work: . . . disorder, *TCNT* . . . instability, *Confraternity* . . . all sorts of evil practices, *Williams* . . . everything base, *Berkeley.*

17. But the wisdom that is from above is first pure, then peaceable, gentle: . . . comes from God, *SEB* . . . comes from on high, *Montgomery* . . . is first of all chaste...moderate, docile, *Confraternity* . . . lenient, *Concordant* . . . courteous, *Berkeley.*

[and] easy to be entreated: . . . compliant, *Adams* . . . listens to reason, *Laubach* . . . open to conviction, *TCNT* . . . conciliatory, *Montgomery* . . . willing to yield, *Williams* . . . easy to be persuaded, *Swann* . . . congenial, *Berkeley.*

full of mercy and good fruits: . . . overflowing with, *Montgomery* . . . bulging with, *Concordant* . . . rich in compassion, *TCNT* . . . good deeds, *Norlie.*

without partiality, and without hypocrisy: . . . free from doubt, *Williams* . . . free from favoritism, *Adams* . . . impartial and sincere, *Norlie* . . . without judging,...dissimulation, *Confraternity* . . . unpretentious, *Berkeley.*

James 4:1

18.a.**Txt:** 018K,byz. **Var:** 01א,02A,03B,04C 020L,025P,Gries,Lach Treg,Alf,Word,Tisc We/Ho,Weis,Sod UBS/☆

3450.10 art gen sing fem	**1336.2** noun gen sing fem	**1706.1** prep	**1503.3** noun dat sing fem	**4540.15** verb 3sing indic pres mid	**3450.4** art dat pl
⸂a τῆς ⸃	δικαιοσύνης	ἐν	εἰρήνῃ	σπείρεται	τοῖς
tēs	*dikaiosunēs*	*en*	*eirēnē*	*speiretai*	*tois*
of the	righteousness	in	peace	is being sown	for the

4020.3 verb dat pl masc part pres act	**1503.4** noun acc sing fem	**4019.1** adv	**4031.4** noun nom pl masc	**2504.1** conj
ποιοῦσιν	εἰρήνην.	**4:1.** Πόθεν	πόλεμοι	καὶ
poiousin	*eirēnēn*	*Pothen*	*polemoi*	*kai*
making	peace.	From where	wars	and

1.a.**Var:** 01א,02A,03B 04C,025P,33,bo.Lach Treg,Alf,Word,Tisc We/Ho,Weis,Sod UBS/☆

4019.1 adv	**3135.1** noun nom pl fem	**1706.1** prep	**5050.3** prs-pron dat 2pl	**3620.2** partic	**1766.1** adv
[a☆+ πόθεν]	μάχαι	ἐν	ὑμῖν;	οὐκ	ἐντεῦθεν,
pothen	*machai*	*en*	*humin*	*ouk*	*enteuthen*
[from where]	fightings	among	you?	Not	from here,

1523.2 prep gen	**3450.1** art gen pl	**2220.2** noun gen pl fem	**5050.2** prs-pron gen 2pl	**3450.1** art gen pl	**4605.7** verb gen pl fem part pres mid
ἐκ	τῶν	ἡδονῶν	ὑμῶν	τῶν	στρατευομένων
ek	*tōn*	*hēdonōn*	*humōn*	*tōn*	*strateuomenōn*
from	the	pleasure	your,	the	warring

1706.1 prep	**3450.4** art dat pl	**3166.4** noun dat pl neu	**5050.2** prs-pron gen 2pl	**1922.3** verb 2pl indic pres act	**2504.1** conj	**3620.2** partic
ἐν	τοῖς	μέλεσιν	ὑμῶν;	**2.** ἐπιθυμεῖτε,	καὶ	οὐκ
en	*tois*	*melesin*	*humōn*	*epithumeite*	*kai*	*ouk*
in	the	members	your?	You desire,	and	not

2174.2 verb 2pl pres act	**5244.1** verb 2pl indic pres act	**2504.1** conj	**2189.1** verb 2pl pres act	**2504.1** conj	**3620.3** partic	**1404.6** verb 2pl indic pres mid
ἔχετε·	φονεύετε	καὶ	ζηλοῦτε,	καὶ	οὐ	δύνασθε
echete	*phoneuete*	*kai*	*zēloute*	*kai*	*ou*	*dunasthe*
have;	you kill	and	covet,	and	not	are able

2.a.**Txt:** 02A,03B,sa.byz. **Var:** 01א,025P,044,322 323,614,623,1243,1505 1852,bo.

1997.3 verb inf aor act	**3136.1** verb 2pl indic pres mid	**2504.1** conj	**4030.2** verb 2pl indic pres act	**2504.1** conj	**3620.2** partic
ἐπιτυχεῖν.	μάχεσθε	καὶ	πολεμεῖτε,	[a+ καὶ]	οὐκ
epituchein	*machesthe*	*kai*	*polemeite*	*kai*	*ouk*
to obtain;	you fight	and	war,	[and]	not

2.b.**Txt:** Steph **Var:** 01א,02A,03B 018K,020L,025P,Gries Lach,Treg,Alf,Tisc We/Ho,Weis,Sod UBS/☆

2174.2 verb 2pl pres act	**1156.2** conj	**1217.2** prep	**3450.16** art sing neu	**3231.1** partic	**153.27** verb inf pres mid
ἔχετε	⸂b δέ, ⸃	διὰ	τὸ	μὴ	αἰτεῖσθαι
echete	*de*	*dia*	*to*	*mē*	*aiteisthai*
you have	but	because	the	not	to ask

5050.4 prs-pron acc 2pl	**153.2** verb 2pl pres act	**2504.1** conj	**3620.3** partic	**2956.1** verb 2pl pres act	**1354.1** conj
ὑμᾶς·	**3.** αἰτεῖτε,	καὶ	οὐ	λαμβάνετε,	διότι
humas	*aiteite*	*kai*	*ou*	*lambanete*	*dioti*
you.	You ask,	and	not	receive,	because

2532.1 adv	**153.24** verb 2pl indic pres mid	**2419.1** conj	**1706.1** prep	**3450.14** art dat pl fem	**2220.3** noun dat pl fem	**5050.2** prs-pron gen 2pl
κακῶς	αἰτεῖσθε,	ἵνα	ἐν	ταῖς	ἡδοναῖς	ὑμῶν
kakōs	*aiteisthe*	*hina*	*en*	*tais*	*hēdonais*	*humōn*
wickedly	you ask,	that	in	the	pleasure	your

4.a.**Txt:** 01א-corr,018K 020L,025P,byz. **Var:** 01א-org,02A,03B 33,it.sa.bo.Lach,Treg Alf,Word,Tisc,We/Ho Weis,Sod,UBS/☆

1154.1 verb 2pl subj aor act	**3295.1** noun nom pl masc	**2504.1** conj	**3291.5** adj nom pl fem	**3620.2** partic
δαπανήσητε.	**4.** ⸂a Μοιχοὶ	καὶ ⸃	μοιχαλίδες,	οὐκ
dapanēsēte	*Moichoi*	*kai*	*moichalides*	*ouk*
you may spend.	Adulterers	and	adulteresses,	not

3:18. In verse 16 James showed that the product of earthly wisdom is confusion and every evil work. In verse 18 he showed that the product of divine wisdom is righteousness. Those endued with divine wisdom are peaceable (3:17). Righteousness is the crop which is then reaped.

4:1. James here dealt with the source of the hostility which existed among some Christians. "Wars and fightings" are plural and indicate that conflict was a continuing condition.

People often blame environment and circumstances for conflicts. But it is not only external conditions but internal inordinate desires which ignite conflicts.

The word "lusts" is used to translate the Greek word *hēdonōn* from which we get the word *hedonism.* James identified personal pleasure and bodily desires at the cost of neighbors' interests as the cause of conflict. Jesus taught that the seeking of the pleasures (same Greek word) of life choked the seed of God's Word (Luke 8:14), and when God's will is ignored, human conflicts result.

People who live only to please themselves cause their own problems. Their desires war against the soul (1 Peter 2:11). Carnal desires strive for supremacy in the believer's life at the cost of displacing Christ's lordship.

4:2. In the original Greek manuscripts there was no punctuation or even separation of words. For this reason commentators have differed as to the correct punctuation in this verse. The NASB translates it as follows: "You lust and do not have; so you commit murder. And you are envious and cannot obtain; so you fight and quarrel."

The reason some people find no satisfaction in life is that they lust after and fight for the things they want instead of asking God for His good and perfect gifts (1:17).

4:3. There is another reason some people do not receive an answer to their prayers. They ask of God, but their motives are wrong. They are not praying according to God's will (1 John 5:14) but according to their own selfish lusts.

4:4. The metaphor of adultery is used in Scripture to describe unfaithfulness to God (Deuteronomy 31:16; Jeremiah 3:20). Hosea's marriage to an adulterous wife was an illustration of Israel's unfaithfulness to God. Jesus spoke of an "evil and adulterous generation" (Matthew 12:39). It is strong language, but a believer who turns away from God is committing spiritual adultery.

18. And the fruit of righteousness is sown in peace: And the harvest, which righteousness yields...comes from a sowing in peace, *Berkeley* . . . of justice, *Confraternity* . . . grows peacefully within, *SEB.*

of them that make peace: . . . by those who are working peace, *Montgomery* . . . those who practise Peace, *Wilson* . . . the peacemakers, *Berkeley.*

1. From whence [come] wars and fightings among you?: What causes wars and feuds, *Norlie* . . . the conflicts and quarrels, *Montgomery.*

[come they] not hence, [even] of your lusts that war in your members?: Do they not come from your passions which are always making war among your bodily members? *Montgomery* . . . from your inordinate passions, *Wuest* . . . from your own selfish desires, *SEB* . . . your own sensual desires, *Norlie* . . . from your vices fighting in your organs? *Fenton.*

2. Ye lust, and have not: ye kill, and desire to have: You continually crave, *Montgomery* . . . You covet...and envy, *Confraternity* . . . You desire, but do not possess, *Swann* . . . There is something that you want but you do not have it, so you get it by killing, *Norlie.*

and cannot obtain:

ye fight and war, yet ye have not, because ye ask not: You engage in conflicts and quarrel, *Wuest* . . . You quarrel and wrangle, *Confraternity* . . . You do not possess, because you do not pray, *Fenton.*

3. Ye ask, and receive not, because ye ask amiss: You continue to ask and do not receive, because you are asking with a wrong purpose, *Montgomery* . . . ye ask evilly, *Clementson.*

that ye may consume [it] upon your lusts: . . . to waste it on, *Adams* . . . you want the things for your own lustful pleasures, *Norlie* . . . that you may expend upon your vices, *Fenton* . . . your passions, *Confraternity* . . . dissolute pleasures, *Berkeley.*

4. Ye adulterers and adulteresses, know ye not: Do you not

James 4:5

3471.6 verb 2pl indic perf act	3617.1 conj	3450.9 art nom sing fem	5210.1 noun nom sing fem	3450.2 art gen sing	2862.2 noun gen sing masc
οἴδατε	ὅτι	ἡ	φιλία	τοῦ	κόσμου,
oidate	*hoti*	*hē*	*philia*	*tou*	*kosmou*
know you	that	the	friendship	of the	world

2171.1 noun nom sing fem	3450.2 art gen sing	2296.2 noun gen sing masc	1498.4 verb 3sing indic pres act	3614.5 rel-pron nom sing masc	300.1 partic
ἔχθρα	τοῦ	θεοῦ	ἐστιν;	ὃς	ʼ ἂν
echthra	*tou*	*theou*	*estin*	*hos*	*an*
enmity		God	is?	Whosoever	

4.b.**Txt:** 01ℵ-corr,02A 018K,020L,byz.
Var: 01ℵ-org,03B,025P Lach,Tisc,We/Ho,Weis Sod,UBS/☆

1430.1 partic	3631.1 partic	1007.14 verb 3sing subj aor pass	5224.1 adj nom sing masc	1498.32 verb inf pres act	3450.2 art gen sing
[b☆ ἐὰν]	οὖν	βουληθῇ	φίλος	εἶναι	τοῦ
ean	*oun*	*boulēthē*	*philos*	*einai*	*tou*
	therefore	be minded	a friend	to be	of the

2862.2 noun gen sing masc	2172.1 adj nom sing masc	3450.2 art gen sing	2296.2 noun gen sing masc	2497.9 verb 3sing indic pres mid	2211.1 conj
κόσμου,	ἐχθρὸς	τοῦ	θεοῦ	καθίσταται.	5. ἢ
kosmou	*echthros*	*tou*	*theou*	*kathistatai*	*ē*
world,	an enemy		of God	is being constituted.	Or

1374.1 verb 2pl pres act	3617.1 conj	2732.1 adv	3450.9 art nom sing fem	1118.1 noun nom sing fem	2978.5 verb 3sing indic pres act
δοκεῖτε	ὅτι	κενῶς	ἡ	γραφὴ	λέγει˙
dokeite	*hoti*	*kenōs*	*hē*	*graphē*	*legei*
think you	that	in emptiness	the	scripture	speaks?

4242.1 prep	5192.4 noun acc sing masc	1955.2 verb 3sing indic pres act	3450.16 art sing neu	4011.1 noun sing neu	3614.16 rel-pron sing neu
Πρὸς	φθόνον	ἐπιποθεῖ	τὸ	πνεῦμα	ὃ
Pros	*phthonon*	*epipothei*	*to*	*pneuma*	*ho*
with	envy	does long	the	Spirit	which

5.a.**Txt:** 018K,020L 025P,byz.it.sa.bo.
Var: p74,01ℵ,02A,03B Lach,Treg,Alf,Tisc We/Ho,Weis,Sod UBS/☆

2700.11 verb 3sing indic aor act	2703.1 verb 3sing indic aor act	1706.1 prep	2231.3 prs-pron dat 1pl	3157.1 adj comp
ʼ κατῴκησεν	[a☆ κατῴκισεν]	ἐν	ἡμῖν;	6. μείζονα
katōkēsen	*katōkisen*	*en*	*hēmin*	*meizona*
dwells	[idem]	in	us?	Greater

1156.2 conj	1319.2 verb 3sing indic pres act	5322.4 noun acc sing fem	1346.1 conj	2978.5 verb 3sing indic pres act	3450.5 art nom sing masc
δὲ	δίδωσιν	χάριν˙	διὸ	λέγει,	ʽΟ
de	*didōsin*	*charin*	*dio*	*legei*	*Ho*
but	he gives	grace.	Wherefore	he says,	

2296.1 noun nom sing masc	5082.2 adj dat pl masc	495.1 verb 3sing indic pres mid	4862.1 adj dat pl	1156.2 conj
θεὸς	ὑπερηφάνοις	ἀντιτάσσεται,	ταπεινοῖς	δὲ
theos	*huperēphanois*	*antitassetai*	*tapeinois*	*de*
God	proud	sets himself against,	to lowly	but

1319.2 verb 3sing indic pres act	5322.4 noun acc sing fem	5131.19 verb 2pl impr aor pass	3631.1 partic	3450.3 art dat sing
δίδωσιν	χάριν.	7. ʽΥποτάγητε	οὖν	τῷ
didōsin	*charin*	*Hupotagēte*	*oun*	*tō*
he gives	grace.	Subject yourselves	therefore	

7.a.**Var:** 01ℵ,02A,03B 33,bo.Lach,Treg,Alf Tisc,We/Ho,Weis,Sod UBS/☆

2296.3 noun dat sing masc	434.3 verb 2pl impr aor act	1156.2 conj	3450.3 art dat sing	1222.3 adj dat sing masc	2504.1 conj
θεῷ.	ἀντίστητε	[a☆+ δὲ]	τῷ	διαβόλῳ,	καὶ
theō	*antistēte*	*de*	*tō*	*diabolō*	*kai*
to God.	Resist	[and]	the	devil,	and

The "friendship of the world" is a desire for a relationship with those who reject God and His Word. When it comes to allegiance there can be no gray area in a believer's life. Either he takes God's point of view (John 15:14) or that of the world. For the believer friendship with the world is more than incompatible; it is enmity, that is, hostility toward God. One of the worst crimes a person can commit is to be a traitor to his country. It is even worse for a believer to give his allegiance to the forces which oppose God.

"Whosoever" in the Greek is emphatic. It indicates a deliberate choice to give allegiance to the world rather than to God. Demas is an illustration of one who chose to desert the cause of Christ because of love for the world (2 Timothy 4:10). Those who choose the world constitute themselves enemies of God.

4:5. James was not quoting any single passage when he said, "Do ye think that the Scripture saith (speaks) in vain . . . ?" It seems he was referring to the general import of various passages dealing with this subject. Either allegiance to the world and God at the same time is impossible, or Scripture is vain, that is, without value.

The word "lusteth" here means to have a strong yearning for what others are or have. There are various translations of this difficult passage. Some hold it is the natural spirit which lusts to envy (see 4:1,2). Others hold it is God who yearns jealously for undivided affection.

4:6. But God "giveth more grace." If the position in verse 5 is taken that it is the natural spirit of man which envies, it follows that regardless of how inordinately man does so, God will give abundant grace to control the desires. If the position is taken that God yearns for the believer's undivided loyalty, it follows that God's grace is sufficient to help the believer be completely loyal. Either way, the believer has no excuse for compromising his loyalty to God. He has a great promise: "Where sin abounded, grace did much more abound" (Romans 5:20).

Believers have a choice to make. The believer's attitude determines whether he will be the object of God's opposition or grace. (See also 1 Peter 5:5.) Those who in arrogant pride reject God's claim of undivided allegiance will find that God opposes them. Pharaoh's experiences illustrate this well. He refused to recognize or give allegiance to God in spite of many evidences of His sovereignty. As a result he found God opposed him over and over again (Exodus 5–14). Those who come to God in humility, however, will receive His abundant grace.

4:7. This verse reveals the two actions which will bring victory: submitting to God and resisting the temptations of Satan. To submit is to place or arrange oneself under, as a good soldier places himself

realize, you apostates, *Berkeley* . . . renegades, *Swann* . . . faithless wives! *Williams.*

that the friendship of the world is enmity with God?: . . . loving this world is hating God? *SEB* . . . is [thereby] constituted an enemy, *Wuest* . . . is hostility to God? *Fenton.*

whosoever therefore will be a friend of the world: . . . whoever determines to be, *Berkeley* . . . wishes to be, *Confraternity.*

is the enemy of God: . . . becomes, *Confraternity* . . . takes his stand as, *Berkeley* . . . is [thereby] constituted, *Wuest* . . . you are against God, *NLT.*

5. Do ye think that the scripture saith in vain: . . . do you think it is mere empty talk when the Scripture says, *Norlie* . . . speaks falsely? *Wilson* . . . unmeaningly, *Fenton* . . . to no purpose? *Berkeley.*

The spirit that dwelleth in us lusteth to envy?: When God put His Spirit in us He is a jealous lover, *Laubach* . . . which has its home in us yearns over us unto jealousy? *Montgomery* . . . that took His abode in us longs for us with holy jealousy, *Norlie* . . . covets unto jealousy, *Confraternity.*

6. But he giveth more grace: But He affords the more, *Berkeley* . . . He keeps on showing us mercy, more and more, *Norlie* . . . gives us more loving favor, *NLT* . . . bestows Superior Favor, *Wilson* . . . gives a more valuable gift, *Fenton* . . . greater grace, *Wuest* . . . greater favor, *Campbell.*

Wherefore he saith: For this reason it says, *Confraternity* . . . as Scripture says, *Norlie.*

God resisteth the proud, but giveth grace unto the humble: . . . against, *SEB* . . . opposes, *Norlie* . . . sets himself in opposition to the Haughty, *Wilson* . . . in battle array against the arrogant, *Wuest.*

7. Submit yourselves therefore to God: . . . ever be subject to God, *Montgomery* . . . put yourselves under God's authority, *SEB.*

Resist the devil, and he will flee from you: Stand up to, *TNT* . . . Stand opposed to the enemy, *Wilson* . . . repel, *Fenton* . . . and he will run away, *NLT.*

5180.9 verb 3sing indic fut mid	570.1 prep	5050.2 prs-pron gen 2pl	1443.11 verb 2pl impr aor act	3450.3 art dat sing	2296.3 noun dat sing masc
φεύξεται	ἀφ’	ὑμῶν·	8. ἐγγίσατε	τῷ	θεῷ,
pheuxetai	*aph'*	*humōn*	*engisate*	*tō*	*theō*
he will flee	from	you.	Draw near		to God,

8.a.**Txt:** 01ℵ,03B,018K 020L,025P,byz.Tisc,Sod **Var:** 02A,We/Ho,Weis UBS/☆

2504.1 conj	1443.16 verb 3sing indic fut act	1443.19 verb 3sing indic fut act	5050.3 prs-pron dat 2pl	2483.8 verb 2pl impr aor act
καὶ	‘ ἐγγιεῖ	[a ἐγγίσει]	ὑμῖν.	καθαρίσατε
kai	*engiei*	*engisei*	*humin*	*katharisate*
and	he will draw near	[idem]	to you.	Cleanse

5331.8 noun acc pl fem	266.4 adj pl masc	2504.1 conj	47.3 verb 2pl impr aor act	2559.1 noun fem
χεῖρας,	ἁμαρτωλοί,	καὶ	ἁγνίσατε	καρδίας,
cheiras	*hamartōloi*	*kai*	*hagnisate*	*kardias*
hands,	sinners,	and	purify	hearts,

1368.2 adj nom pl masc	4854.1 verb 2pl impr aor act	2504.1 conj	3858.6 verb 2pl impr aor act
δίψυχοι.	9. ταλαιπωρήσατε	καὶ	πενθήσατε
dipsuchoi	*talaipōrēsate*	*kai*	*penthēsate*
you double minded.	Be wretched,	and	mourn,

2504.1 conj	2772.16 verb 2pl impr aor act	3450.5 art nom sing masc	1064.1 noun nom sing masc	5050.2 prs-pron gen 2pl	1519.1 prep
καὶ	κλαύσατε.	ὁ	γέλως	ὑμῶν	εἰς
kai	*klausate*	*ho*	*gelōs*	*humōn*	*eis*
and	weep.	The	laughter	your	to

9.a.**Txt:** 01ℵ,02A,044 byz. **Var:** 03B,025P,614,630 945,1241,1739,2495

3859.1 noun sing neu	3214.2 verb 3sing impr aor pass	3216.1 verb 3sing impr aor pass	2504.1 conj
πένθος	‘ μεταστραφήτω,	[a☆ μετατραπήτω,]	καὶ
penthos	*metastraphētō*	*metatrapētō*	*kai*
mourning	let be turned,	[idem]	and

3450.9 art nom sing fem	5315.1 noun nom sing fem	1519.1 prep	2696.1 noun acc sing fem	4864.6 verb 2pl impr aor pass
ἡ	χαρὰ	εἰς	κατήφειαν.	10. ταπεινώθητε
hē	*chara*	*eis*	*katēpheian*	*tapeinōthēte*
the	joy	to	heaviness.	Humble yourselves

10.a.**Txt:** 020L,byz. **Var:** 01ℵ,02A,03B 018K,025P,33,Lach Treg,Alf,Tisc,We/Ho Weis,Sod,UBS/☆

1783.1 prep	3450.2 art gen sing	2935.2 noun gen sing masc	2504.1 conj	5150.5 verb 3sing indic fut act	5050.4 prs-pron acc 2pl
ἐνώπιον	‘a τοῦ `	κυρίου,	καὶ	ὑψώσει	ὑμᾶς.
enōpion	*tou*	*kuriou*	*kai*	*hupsōsei*	*humas*
before	the	Lord,	and	he will exalt	you.

3231.1 partic	2605.4 verb 2pl impr pres act	238.1 prs-pron gen pl	79.6 noun nom pl masc	3450.5 art nom sing masc
11. Μὴ	καταλαλεῖτε	ἀλλήλων,	ἀδελφοί·	ὁ
Mē	*katalaleite*	*allēlōn*	*adelphoi*	*ho*
Not	speak against	one another,	brothers.	The

11.a.**Txt:** 018K,020L,byz. **Var:** 01ℵ,02A,03B,025P sa.bo.Lach,Treg,Alf,Tisc We/Ho,Weis,Sod UBS/☆

2605.5 verb nom sing masc part pres act	79.2 noun gen sing masc	2504.1 conj	2211.1 conj	2892.8 verb nom sing masc part pres act
καταλαλῶν	ἀδελφοῦ,	‘ καὶ	[a☆ ἢ]	κρίνων
katalalōn	*adelphou*	*kai*	*ē*	*krinōn*
speaking against	brother,	and	[or]	judging

3450.6 art acc sing masc	79.4 noun acc sing masc	840.3 prs-pron gen sing	2605.1 verb 3sing indic pres act	3414.2 noun gen sing masc	2504.1 conj
τὸν	ἀδελφὸν	αὐτοῦ,	καταλαλεῖ	νόμου,	καὶ
ton	*adelphon*	*autou*	*katalalei*	*nomou*	*kai*
the	brother	his,	speaks against	law,	and

under an officer of higher rank. It is a voluntary act of humility to submit to God.

It is the humble who will receive God's help, not those who proudly try to resist Satan in their own strength. Satan often causes believers to fail by appealing to their pride. He did so in the Garden of Eden when he told Eve, "Ye shall be as gods" (Genesis 3:5), and Eve did not resist him. When Jesus was tempted by Satan in the wilderness, He provided an example of how believers can triumph. He resisted Satan with Scripture (Luke 4:4,8,12).

4:8. In Old Testament times priests were to approach the symbols of God's presence only at prescribed times. Now, believers are invited to come boldly to the Throne of Grace (Hebrews 4:14-16). They can do this through meditation in the Word and prayer.

Washing was an important ritual of Old Testament priests (Exodus 30:20,21). Today all believers are priests (1 Peter 2:9), and while they abhor sin, they cannot say they never sin (1 John 1:8). They need the cleansing of the blood and "the washing of water by the word" (Ephesians 5:26). Purity of life is important for the believer (Psalm 24:3,4).

A double-minded person is two-faced, trying to look to God and also to the world (cf. 1:8). This person is guilty of spiritual adultery. There is personal responsibility to remove worldly inclinations (1 John 3:3). Notice that it is a matter of the heart. Our love for God determines our relationship with Him.

4:9. Those who boasted of human wisdom (3:14-16) were guilty of wretched behavior (4:1-4) and pride (4:6). James urged them to give evidence of repentance (2 Corinthians 7:9-11). This was not a time for laughter and lighthearted behavior.

4:10. Some readers of this epistle believed exaltation comes through envy, strife, and self-seeking. It is people who humble themselves that will be exalted (Matthew 23:12; Luke 18:14; cf. Matthew 5:5). The opposite is also true. Those who try to promote themselves usually fail.

4:11. James urged the believers, "Speak not evil one of another." They needed to be reminded of Psalm 133:1: "Behold, how good and how pleasant it is for brethren to dwell together in unity!" It reflects badly upon the Christian faith when believers do not live in peace with one another. A slanderer puts himself above the Law

8. Draw nigh to God, and he will draw nigh to you: . . . draw near, *Montgomery* . . . come close, *Norlie* . . . Get close to, *SEB* . . . come near, *TNT.*

Cleanse [your] hands, [ye] sinners: Wash your hands, *Norlie.*

and purify [your] hearts, [ye] double minded: . . . cleanse your hearts, *TNT* . . . you vacillating men! *TCNT* . . . you who have divided hearts, *SEB* . . . you of divided interests, *Berkeley* . . . you doubters, *Beck.*

9. Be afflicted, and mourn, and weep: Become miserable, *Swann* . . . Lament, *Montgomery* . . . Feel your misery, *Berkeley* . . . Now is the time for sorrow, mourning and lamentation, *TNT* . . . Be sorry on account of your sins; grieve over them, *Norlie* . . . and cry for your sins, *Laubach.*

let your laughter be turned to mourning: . . . your worldly laughter give way to, *Norlie* . . . to sorrow, *Berkeley.*

and [your] joy to heaviness: . . . your enjoyment, *Berkeley* . . . your gayety be turned to sadness, *Norlie* . . . your gladness to dejection, *Adams* . . . into gloom! *Montgomery.*

10. Humble yourselves in the sight of the Lord: Take a low position, *Berkeley* . . . before the Lord, *Montgomery* . . . in the presence of the Lord, *Wilson.*

and he shall lift you up: . . . and He will honor you, *Beck* . . . will raise you up, *Montgomery* . . . exalt you, *Confraternity* . . . set you high, *Berkeley.*

11. Speak not evil one of another, brethren: Do not be talking against each other, *Montgomery* . . . do not slander, *Norlie* . . . Do not malign, *Berkeley* . . . Stop defaming, *Wuest* . . . Do not disparage one another, *TCNT* . . . my fellow Christians, *Beck.*

He that speaketh evil of [his] brother, and judgeth his brother: He who gossips about his brother, *Klingensmith* . . . Anyone who talks against his fellow Christian, *Beck* . . . if you disparage, *Noli* . . . says evil against his brother or makes himself his brother's judge, *BB* . . . condemning his brothers, *Montgomery* . . . or criticizing his brother, *Williams* . . . or who passes judgement on him, *TNT.*

James 4:12

2892.5 verb 3sing indic pres act	3414.4 noun acc sing masc	1479.1 conj	1156.2 conj	3414.4 noun acc sing masc	2892.4 verb 2sing indic pres act	3620.2 partic
κρίνει	νόμον·	εἰ	δὲ	νόμον	κρίνεις,	οὐκ
krinei	*nomon*	*ei*	*de*	*nomon*	*krineis*	*ouk*
judges	law.	If	but	law	you judge,	not

1498.3 verb 2sing indic pres act	4023.1 noun nom sing masc	3414.2 noun gen sing masc	233.2 conj	2896.1 noun nom sing masc	1518.3 num card nom masc
εἶ	ποιητὴς	νόμου,	ἀλλὰ	κριτής.	**12.** εἷς
ei	*poiētēs*	*nomou*	*alla*	*kritēs*	*heis*
you are	a doer	of law,	but	a judge.	One

12.a.**Var:** 01ℵ,02A,03B 025P,sa.bo.Gries,Lach Treg,Alf,Tisc,We/Ho Weis,Sod,UBS/☆

1498.4 verb 3sing indic pres act	3450.5 art nom sing masc	3413.1 noun nom sing masc	2504.1 conj	2896.1 noun nom sing masc
ἔστιν	ὁ	νομοθέτης	[a☆+ καὶ	κριτής,]
estin	*ho*	*nomothetēs*	*kai*	*kritēs*
is	the	lawgiver,	[and	judge]

12.b.**Var:** 01ℵ,02A,03B 018K,020L,025P,bo. Gries,Lach,Treg,Alf Tisc,We/Ho,Weis,Sod UBS/☆

3450.5 art nom sing masc	1404.13 verb nom sing masc part pres mid	4834.10 verb inf aor act	2504.1 conj	616.8 verb inf aor act	4622.1 prs-pron nom 2sing
ὁ	δυνάμενος	σῶσαι	καὶ	ἀπολέσαι·	σὺ
ho	*dunamenos*	*sōsai*	*kai*	*apolesai*	*su*
the	being able	to save	and	to destroy:	you

12.c.**Txt:** 018K,020L,byz. Sod **Var:** 01ℵ,02A,03B,025P 33,sa.bo.Lach,Treg,Alf Tisc,We/Ho,Weis UBS/☆

1156.2 conj	4949.3 intr-pron nom sing	1498.3 verb 2sing indic pres act	3614.5 rel-pron nom sing masc	2892.4 verb 2sing indic pres act
[b☆+ δὲ]	τίς	εἶ,	ʻ ὃς	κρίνεις
de	*tis*	*ei*	*hos*	*krineis*
[and]	who	are	that	judges

12.d.**Txt:** 018K,020L,byz. **Var:** 01ℵ,02A,03B,025P sa.bo.Lach,Treg,Alf,Tisc We/Ho,Weis,Sod UBS/☆

3450.5 art nom sing masc	2892.8 verb nom sing masc part pres act	3450.6 art acc sing masc	2066.1 adj sing	3999.1 adv
[c☆ ὁ	κρίνων]	τὸν	ʻ ἕτερον;	[d☆ πλησίον;]
ho	*krinōn*	*ton*	*heteron*	*plēsion*
[the	judging]	the	other?	[neighbor?]

13.a.**Txt:** 02A,018K 020L,025P,byz. **Var:** 01ℵ,03B,33,Elzev Lach,Treg,Tisc,We/Ho Weis,Sod,UBS/☆

70.5 verb 2sing impr pres act	3431.1 adv	3450.7 art nom pl masc	2978.16 verb nom pl masc part pres act	4449.1 adv	2504.1 conj
13. Ἄγε	νῦν	οἱ	λέγοντες,	Σήμερον	ʻ καὶ
Age	*nun*	*hoi*	*legontes*	*Sēmeron*	*kai*
Go to	now,	the	saying,	Today	and

13.b.**Txt:** 018K,020L Steph **Var:** 01ℵ,02A,025P Elzev,Lach,Alf,Word Tisc,We/Ho,Weis UBS/☆

2211.1 conj	833.1 adv	4057.20 verb 1pl subj aor mid	4057.41 verb 1pl indic fut mid
[a☆ ἢ]	αὔριον	ʻ πορευσώμεθα	[b☆ πορευσόμεθα]
ē	*aurion*	*poreusōmetha*	*poreusometha*
[or]	tomorrow	let us go	[we will go]

13.c.**Txt:** 018K,020L Steph **Var:** 01ℵ,02A,025P Elzev,Lach,Alf,Word Tisc,We/Ho,Weis UBS/☆

1519.1 prep	3455.3 dem-pron acc sing fem	3450.12 art acc sing fem	4032.4 noun acc sing fem	2504.1 conj
εἰς	τήνδε	τὴν	πόλιν,	καὶ
eis	*tēnde*	*tēn*	*polin*	*kai*
into	such	the	city	and

13.d.**Txt:** 018K,020L,byz. Weis,Sod **Var:** 01ℵ,03B,025P,sa. bo.Lach,Treg,Tisc We/Ho,UBS/☆

4020.30 verb 1pl subj aor act	4020.53 verb 1pl indic fut act	1550.1 adv	1747.2 noun acc sing masc	1518.4 num card acc masc
ʻ ποιήσωμεν	[c☆ ποιήσομεν]	ἐκεῖ	ἐνιαυτὸν	ʻd ἕνα ˋ
poiēsōmen	*poiēsomen*	*ekei*	*eniauton*	*hena*
let us spend	[we will do]	there	year	one

13.e.**Txt:** 018K,020L Steph **Var:** 01ℵ,02A,025P Elzev,Lach,Alf,Word Tisc,We/Ho,Weis UBS/☆

2504.1 conj	1694.1 verb 1pl subj aor mid	1694.3 verb 1pl indic fut mid	2504.1 conj
καὶ	ʻ ἐμπορευσώμεθα,	[e☆ ἐμπορευσόμεθα]	καὶ
kai	*emporeusōmetha*	*emporeusometha*	*kai*
and	let us do business,	[we will do business]	and

(2:8,10). He acts as though He knows better than the edicts of God's law and in so doing constitutes himself a judge of the Law rather than a doer (1:22-24).

4:12. Readers of this epistle who were slandering their brethren were motivated by pride. They were assuming the prerogative of God in passing judgment on others. By doing this they were rejecting the royal law, "Thou shalt love thy neighbor as thyself" (2:8). They then replaced this with their own law by which they felt justified to judge others. It was necessary for James to remind his readers that God alone is the Judge.

God gave the moral law to Israel at Sinai. Exodus 20:1-17 records the Ten Commandments. Other aspects of the moral law are recorded in subsequent writings of Moses, in Exodus, Leviticus, and Deuteronomy. It is possible James referred to this law, but more likely he referred to what is known as the royal law (see above). Jesus summed up the essence of the Jewish law in two commandments: loving God with all the heart, soul, mind, and strength and loving one's neighbor as himself (Mark 12:28-33).

References to God's power to judge righteously and in turn to save or destroy are found in the Old Testament (Deuteronomy 32:39; 1 Samuel 2:6-10; 2 Kings 5:7). God's power to save or destroy was also demonstrated in New Testament times. Christ brought Lazarus back from the dead (John 11), and Herod was destroyed as a judgment from God (Acts 12:20-23). It would seem, however, that the primary application of this statement is future. When Jesus spoke of persecution to His disciples He said: "Fear not them which kill the body, but are not able to kill the soul: but rather fear him which is able to destroy both soul and body in hell" (Matthew 10:28).

In the Greek the word "you" is in a place of emphasis. It is as though James asked, on the basis of what had just been stated, "And you, who do you think you are to place yourself above this God?"

4:13. In the previous verses James dealt with those who placed themselves above the Law by judging others. In verse 13 he dealt with those who disregarded God in the process of making plans. The folly of these people was not that they planned but that they planned without God. They had no right to say "tomorrow," for they had no assurance of surviving till then. To plan for a year was even worse presumption. It is all right to plan if we include God. Paul made plans, but he did so with full recognition of God's prerogative to change the plans (Acts 16:6-10).

Some of the believers to whom this epistle was written apparently believed that they and they alone would make their life plans. They would determine when they would go ("Today or tomorrow"), where they would go ("into such a city"), and why they would go (to "sell, and get gain"). Instead of looking to God for guidance in the process of planning, they acted as though God did not exist.

speaketh evil of the law, and judgeth the law: . . . talks against...and condemns, *Beck* . . . maligns the Law, *Berkeley* . . . in fact, he is speaking against the law and judges the law, *Norlie* . . . the Law of God, *Noli.*

but if thou judge the law, thou art not a doer of the law, but a judge: If you sit in judgement on the Law, *TNT* . . . by criticising the law, *Norlie* . . . If you condemn the Law, you're not doing what it says but you're being its judge, *Beck* . . . you are not a follower of the law, *SEB* . . . you are not an observer, *Noli* . . . you are not its practicer, *Berkeley* . . . you are not a doer of the law, but a critic, *Klingensmith.*

12. There is one lawgiver, who is able to save and to destroy: You well know that God is the only law-giver...to save and condemn, *Noli* . . . and Critic, *Klingensmith* . . . only one Lawgiver and Judge, *Beck* . . . He who has the power, *Berkeley* . . . who has the power of salvation and of destruction, *BB* . . . and to punish with death, *Norlie.*

who art thou that judgest another?: . . . who are you, to be condemning your neighbor? *Montgomery* . . . that you should pass judgment on your fellow man? *Norlie* . . . that you presume to judge, *Williams.*

13. Go to now, ye that say: Stop a moment, you who say, *Norlie* . . . Behold now, *Confraternity* . . . Come on now, *Fenton* . . . Look out, now, you who are saying, *Klingensmith* . . . Some of you are in the habit of saying, *TNT* . . . How foolish it is to say, *BB.*

To day or to morrow we will go into such a city: . . . we shall proceed to this city, *Wuest* . . . into some city, *Klingensmith* . . . to this or that town, *TNT.*

and continue there a year, and buy and sell, and get gain: . . . spend a year there, and trade and make money, *Montgomery* . . . and do business, *Laubach* . . . and traffic in merchandise, *Campbell* . . . and make a good profit, *Norlie* . . . and become rich, *Fenton.*

13.f.**Txt:** 018K,020L Steph
Var: 01ℵ,02A,025P Elzev,Lach,Alf,Word Tisc,We/Ho,Weis UBS/☆

14.a.**Txt:** 01ℵ,018K 020L,byz.it.Tisc,Sod
Var: 03B,We/Ho,Word Elzev,UBS/☆

14.b.**Txt:** 01ℵ-corr,02A 018K,020L,025P,byz.it. bo.Tisc,Sod
Var: 01ℵ-org,03B We/Ho,Weis,UBS/☆

14.c.**Txt:** 020L,byz.Steph
Var: 02A,03B,018K 025P,Lach,Treg,Alf Word,Tisc,We/Ho,Weis Sod,UBS/☆

14.d.**Txt:** byz.sa.
Var: 01ℵ,02A,03B 018K,Lach,Treg,Alf Tisc,We/Ho,Weis,Sod UBS/☆

15.a.**Txt:** 018K,020L,byz.
Var: 01ℵ,02A,03B,025P Lach,Treg,Alf,Word Tisc,We/Ho,Weis,Sod UBS/☆

15.b.**Txt:** 018K,020L,byz.
Var: 01ℵ,02A,03B,025P Lach,Treg,Alf,Word Tisc,We/Ho,Weis,Sod UBS/☆

2741.6 verb 1pl subj aor act	**2741.11** verb 1pl indic fut act	**3610.2** rel-pron nom pl masc	**3620.2** partic
⸂κερδήσωμεν˙	[f κερδήσομεν˙]	**14.** οἵτινες	οὐκ
kerdēsōmen	*kerdēsomen*	*hoitines*	*ouk*
let us make money,	[we will make money,]	who	not

1971.3 verb 2pl indic pres mid	**3450.16** art sing neu	**3450.10** art gen sing fem	**833.1** adv	**4029.5** intr-pron nom sing fem	**1056.1** conj
ἐπίστασθε	⸂a τὸ ⸃	τῆς	αὔριον˙	ποία	⸂b γὰρ ⸃
epistasthe	*to*	*tēs*	*aurion*	*poia*	*gar*
you know	the	on the	morrow,	what	for

3450.9 art nom sing fem	**2205.1** noun nom sing fem	**5050.2** prs-pron gen 2pl	**816.1** noun nom sing fem	**1056.1** conj	**1498.4** verb 3sing indic pres act
ἡ	ζωὴ	ὑμῶν;	ἀτμὶς	γάρ	⸂ἐστιν
hē	*zōē*	*humōn*	*atmis*	*gar*	*estin*
the	life	your?	A vapor	for	it is,

1498.6 verb 2pl indic pres act	**3450.9** art nom sing fem	**4242.1** prep	**3504.1** adj sing	**5154.11** verb nom sing fem part pres mid	**1884.1** adv
[c☆ ἔστε]	ἡ	πρὸς	ὀλίγον	φαινομένη,	ἔπειτα
este	*hē*	*pros*	*oligon*	*phainomenē*	*epeita*
[you are]	the	for	a little	appearing,	then

1156.2 conj	**2504.1** conj	**846.3** verb nom sing fem part pres mid	**470.2** prep	**3450.2** art gen sing
⸂δὲ	[d☆ καὶ]	ἀφανιζομένη˙	**15.** ἀντὶ	τοῦ
de	*kai*	*aphanizomenē*	*anti*	*tou*
and	[idem]	disappearing,	instead of	the

2978.24 verb inf pres act	**5050.4** prs-pron acc 2pl	**1430.1** partic	**3450.5** art nom sing masc	**2935.1** noun nom sing masc	**2286.27** verb 3sing subj aor act
λέγειν	ὑμᾶς,	Ἐὰν	ὁ	κύριος	θελήσῃ,
legein	*humas*	*Ean*	*ho*	*kurios*	*thelēsē*
to say	your,	If	the	Lord	should will

2504.1 conj	**2180.24** verb 1pl subj aor act	**2180.26** verb 1pl indic fut act	**2504.1** conj	**4020.30** verb 1pl subj aor act
καὶ	⸂ζήσωμεν,	[a☆ ζήσομεν]	καὶ	⸂ποιήσωμεν
kai	*zēsōmen*	*zēsomen*	*kai*	*poiēsōmen*
and	let us live,	[we will live]	also	let us do

4020.53 verb 1pl indic fut act	**3642.17** dem-pron sing neu	**2211.1** conj	**1552.16** dem-pron sing neu	**3431.1** adv	**1156.2** conj
[b☆ ποιήσομεν]	τοῦτο	ἢ	ἐκεῖνο.	**16.** νῦν	δὲ
poiēsomen	*touto*	*ē*	*ekeino*	*nun*	*de*
[we will do]	this	or	that.	Now	but

2714.4 verb 2pl indic pres mid	**1706.1** prep	**3450.14** art dat pl fem	**210.2** noun dat pl fem	**5050.2** prs-pron gen 2pl	**3820.9** adj nom sing fem
καυχᾶσθε	ἐν	ταῖς	ἀλαζονείαις	ὑμῶν˙	πᾶσα
kauchasthe	*en*	*tais*	*alazoneiais*	*humōn*	*pasa*
you boast	in	the	arrogant airs	your:	all

2716.1 noun nom sing fem	**4955.9** dem-pron nom sing fem	**4050.10** adj	**1498.4** verb 3sing indic pres act	**3471.19** verb dat sing masc part perf act
καύχησις	τοιαύτη	πονηρά	ἐστιν.	**17.** εἰδότι
kauchēsis	*toiautē*	*ponēra*	*estin*	*eidoti*
boasting	such	evil	is.	To knowing

3631.1 partic	**2541.1** adj sing	**4020.20** verb inf pres act	**2504.1** conj	**3231.1** partic	**4020.14** verb dat sing part pres act	**264.2** noun nom sing fem
οὖν	καλὸν	ποιεῖν,	καὶ	μὴ	ποιοῦντι,	ἁμαρτία
oun	*kalon*	*poiein*	*kai*	*mē*	*poiounti*	*hamartia*
therefore	good	to do,	and	not	doing,	sin

4:14. The problem with these itinerant merchants was that they acted as though they had ultimate control over their future. They ignored the warning of Scripture, "Boast not thyself of tomorrow; for thou knowest not what a day may bring forth" (Proverbs 27:1). They acted like the man Jesus described in the Parable of the Rich Fool (Luke 12:16-21). He boasted that he had enough wealth to last many years and planned on a hedonistic life-style. That night he died. He had become wealthy in this life but was not rich toward God. He had the wrong kind of riches.

James challenged these readers to consider the transitoriness of life. He said it is like steam which can be seen for a few moments, then vanishes. It is certain life will end, but when this will happen is uncertain.

Throughout the Scriptures figures of speech are used indicating the brevity of life. It is like a "handbreadth" (Psalm 39:5), a "dream" (Psalm 73:20), "a shadow that declineth" (Psalm 102:11), "a flower" (Job 14:2), and like "grass" (1 Peter 1:24). James compared life to a "vapor," something that is visible for just a brief period.

14. Whereas ye know not what [shall be] on the morrow: . . . you who do not know, *Confraternity* . . . what will become of your Life on the morrow, *Wilson* . . . when all the time you do not know what will happen, *Montgomery* . . . What do you know about tomorrow? Nothing, *Norlie.*

For what [is] your life? It is even a vapour: . . . of what character is your life, *Wuest* . . . but a mist, *Montgomery* . . . It is like fog, *NLT* . . . a smoke, *Campbell.*

that appeareth for a little time, and then vanisheth away: . . . visible for awhile, *Fenton* . . . that can be seen for a little while, and then it is gone, *Norlie* . . . appearing for a brief time, *Montgomery* . . . and then disappearing, *TCNT.*

4:15. The writer emphasized the need for considering the will of God in making plans. At one time when Christians wrote of future plans in correspondence they used the letters *D.V.* They stand for the Latin words *Deo volente,* that is, "God willing." Paul recognized that any future plans he might have were subject to God's will. To the Ephesian believers he said, "I will return again unto you, if God will" (Acts 18:21). To the Corinthians he wrote, "I trust to tarry a while with you, if the Lord permit" (1 Corinthians 16:7). Some readers of James' epistle in their pride did not acknowledge any dependence on God.

15. For that ye [ought] to say, If the Lord will, we shall live, and do this, or that: You ought rather to say, *Confraternity* . . . and we are alive, *Norlie.*

4:16. Instead of recognizing dependence on God, these merchants gloried in their arrogant self-confidence. Like the hypocritical Pharisees they were concerned with impressing others with their human ability, rather than humbly pleasing God. This bragging was evil. Boasting is bad at all times, but it is even worse when people do it arrogantly.

16. But now ye rejoice in your boastings: . . . as matters stand, you are proud and you boast, *Norlie* . . . But instead you are proud, *NLT* . . . you are glorying in these insolent boastings, *Montgomery* . . . you pride yourselves on your presumption, *TCNT* . . . you glory in empty presumptions, *Swann* . . . you boast in your proud speeches, *Wilson* . . . in your arrogance, *Confraternity.*

all such rejoicing is evil: All such pride, *NLT* . . . All such bragging, *SEB* . . . boasting, *Confraternity* . . . is sin, *Norlie.*

4:17. Definite acts of sin are deplorable, but they are not the only kind. Here James emphasized the sinfulness of "sins of omission." The merchants (James 4:13-16) failed to walk humbly with God (Micah 6:8). This was as much sin as any positive acts of sin they might have committed. Jesus denounced the Pharisees for the things they had left undone (Matthew 23:23). The priest and Levite who disregarded the needs of the injured traveler were guilty not of a sin of commission, but of omission (Luke 10:30-37). The rich man sinned against Lazarus, not by mistreating him in some aggressive manner, but by neglecting him (Luke 16:19-31).

17. Therefore to him that knoweth to do good: The principle is this, that whoever knows what is right to do, *Norlie* . . . to do right, *Montgomery.*

and doeth [it] not, to him it is sin: . . . and does not perform it, *Wilson* . . . but does not do it, is guilty of sin, *Norlie* . . . commits a sin, *Confraternity.*

James 5:1

840.4 prs-pron dat sing	**1498.4** verb 3sing indic pres act	**70.5** verb 2sing impr pres act	**3431.1** adv	**3450.7** art nom pl masc	**4004.4** adj nom pl masc
αὐτῷ	ἐστιν.	**5:1.** Ἄγε	νῦν	οἱ	πλούσιοι,
autō	*estin*	*Age*	*nun*	*hoi*	*plousioi*
to him	it is.	Go to	now,	the	rich,

2772.16 verb 2pl impr aor act	**3512.1** verb nom pl masc part pres act	**1894.3** prep	**3450.14** art dat pl fem	**4855.2** noun dat pl fem
κλαύσατε	ὀλολύζοντες	ἐπὶ	ταῖς	ταλαιπωρίαις
klausate	*ololuzontes*	*epi*	*tais*	*talaipōriais*
weep,	howling	over	the	miseries

5050.2 prs-pron gen 2pl	**3450.14** art dat pl fem	**1889.6** verb dat pl fem part pres mid	**3450.5** art nom sing masc	**4009.1** noun sing masc	**5050.2** prs-pron gen 2pl
ὑμῶν	ταῖς	ἐπερχομέναις.	**2.** ὁ	πλοῦτος	ὑμῶν
humōn	*tais*	*eperchomenais*	*ho*	*ploutos*	*humōn*
you	the	coming upon.	The	riches	your

4450.1 verb 3sing indic perf act	**2504.1** conj	**3450.17** art pl neu	**2416.4** noun pl neu	**5050.2** prs-pron gen 2pl	**4453.1** adj pl neu
σέσηπεν,	καὶ	τὰ	ἱμάτια	ὑμῶν	σητόβρωτα
sesēpen	*kai*	*ta*	*himatia*	*humōn*	*sētobrōta*
have rotted,	and	the	garments	your	moth eaten

1090.3 verb 3sing indic perf act	**3450.5** art nom sing masc	**5392.1** noun nom sing masc	**5050.2** prs-pron gen 2pl	**2504.1** conj	**3450.5** art nom sing masc
γέγονεν·	**3.** ὁ	χρυσὸς	ὑμῶν	καὶ	ὁ
gegonen	*ho*	*chrusos*	*humōn*	*kai*	*ho*
have become.	The	gold	your	and	the

690.1 noun nom sing masc	**2698.1** verb 3sing indic perf mid	**2504.1** conj	**3450.5** art nom sing masc	**2423.1** noun nom sing masc	**840.1** prs-pron gen pl
ἄργυρος	κατίωται,	καὶ	ὁ	ἰὸς	αὐτῶν
arguros	*katiōtai*	*kai*	*ho*	*ios*	*autōn*
silver	has been eaten away,	and	the	canker	their

1519.1 prep	**3115.1** noun sing neu	**5050.3** prs-pron dat 2pl	**1498.40** verb 3sing indic fut mid	**2504.1** conj	**2052.32** verb 3sing indic fut mid
εἰς	μαρτύριον	ὑμῖν	ἔσται,	καὶ	φάγεται
eis	*marturion*	*humin*	*estai*	*kai*	*phagetai*
for	a testimony	against you	shall be,	and	shall eat

3450.15 art acc pl fem	**4418.6** noun acc pl fem	**5050.2** prs-pron gen 2pl	**5453.1** conj	**4300.1** noun sing neu	**2320.5** verb 2pl indic aor act
τὰς	σάρκας	ὑμῶν	ὡς	πῦρ·	ἐθησαυρίσατε
tas	*sarkas*	*humōn*	*hōs*	*pur*	*ethēsaurisate*
the	flesh	your	as	fire.	You treasured up

1706.1 prep	**2057.10** adj dat pl fem	**2232.7** noun dat pl fem	**1481.20** verb 2sing impr aor mid	**3450.5** art nom sing masc	**3272.1** noun nom sing masc
ἐν	ἐσχάταις	ἡμέραις.	**4.** ἰδοὺ,	ὁ	μισθὸς
en	*eschatais*	*hēmerais*	*idou*	*ho*	*misthos*
in	last	days.	Behold,	the	wage

3450.1 art gen pl	**2023.4** noun gen pl masc	**3450.1** art gen pl	**268.1** verb gen pl masc part aor act	**3450.15** art acc pl fem	**5396.1** noun fem
τῶν	ἐργατῶν	τῶν	ἀμησάντων	τὰς	χώρας
tōn	*ergatōn*	*tōn*	*amēsantōn*	*tas*	*chōras*
of the	workmen	the	having harvested	the	fields

4.a.**Txt:** 02A,03B-corr byz.Sod
Var: 01ℵ,03B-org,Treg Tisc,We/Ho,Weis UBS/☆

5050.2 prs-pron gen 2pl	**3450.5** art nom sing masc	**644.4** verb nom sing masc part perf pass	**872.1** verb nom sing masc part perf mid
ὑμῶν,	ὁ	ʼ ἀπεστερημένος,	[a☆ ἀφυστερημένος]
humōn	*ho*	*apesterēmenos*	*aphusterēmenos*
your,	the	having been kept back	[idem]

5:1. The inspired writer now proceeds to present stern warnings to those who are rich, because of calamities which they will experience. We must remember, however, that in Scripture people are not denounced because of wealth but because of its misuse and abuse. Abraham, a man of great wealth, was a friend of God (2:23). God called Job a perfect and upright man (Job 1:8).

The rich mentioned here, like those in 2:2-6, were apparently not members of the congregations. They were not called to repentance, but rather to "weep and howl" for their coming judgment. It is assumed they will remain unrepentant. The warning came to believers who might be tempted to make wealth their chief object.

5:2. In Bible times objects of wealth included foodstuffs, costly clothing, and precious metals. The corrupted riches here probably refer to grain which had rotted while in storage. The rich fool stored up vast quantities of crops (Luke 12:16-21). While people starved, heartless men allowed food to spoil.

Their beautiful apparel would become spoiled. Elegant, embroidered clothes were prized possessions of the wealthy. The fact that Paul said he "coveted no man's . . . apparel" (Acts 20:33) is an indication that luxurious clothes were objects of envy.

5:3. Their silver and gold would lose their value. They would become as worthless as thoroughly rusted iron. In the Day of Judgment, whatever the nature of the wealth possessed, it would have absolutely no positive value. In fact, the wealth they had dishonestly acquired and selfishly hoarded, and which they valued so highly, would become a witness against them in the Day of Judgment. It would insure their condemnation and intensify the fires of judgment (see Romans 2:5). Only treasures of righteousness will stand the test.

"Ye have heaped treasure together *for* the last days" reads "*in* the last days" in the NIV. At a time when people should be laying up treasures in heaven (Matthew 6:19-21), they were spending time and effort to accumulate inappropriate wealth to live in selfish extravagance.

5:4. In those days there were no labor laws, and the rich often treated workers very unfairly. It appears they had cheated these people out of their just wages. Now, like the blood of Abel (Genesis 4:10), which cried out for vengeance, the defrauded wages in a sense cried out for condemnation of the rich. A just God would not ignore the cry that came from the defrauded workers and defrauded wages. This is why those who had obtained their riches in a way that was illegitimate should weep, because they can anticipate certain judgment (5:1-3).

1. Go to now, [ye] rich men, weep and howl: Look out now, *Klingensmith* . . . Come on you wealthy, weep with loud wailings, *Berkeley* . . . Come now, you rich people, *Beck* . . . you men of wealth, take heed! *Norlie* . . . mark my words, *TNT* . . . Cry out and be very sad, *SEB.*

for your miseries that shall come upon [you]: . . . for the troubles coming upon you, *Klingensmith* . . . that are sure to overtake you, *Williams.*

2. Your riches are corrupted: Your hoarded wealth is rotten, *Fenton* . . . riches lie rotting, *Montgomery* . . . have wasted away, *TCNT* . . . are worth nothing, *NLT* . . . is ruined, *Berkeley* . . . corrode, *Concordant.*

and your garments are motheaten: . . . your clothing has become, *Montgomery* . . . eaten by insects, *Laubach.*

3. Your gold and silver is cankered: . . . covered with rust, *Berkeley* . . . eaten away, *Darby* . . . tarnished, *Beck.*

and the rust of them shall be a witness against you: . . . and their canker, *Darby* . . . tarnish, *Beck* . . . will be for a testimony, *Montgomery* . . . evidence against you, *Berkeley* . . . is witness against you, *Klingensmith.*

and shall eat your flesh as it were fire: . . . consume, *Berkeley* . . . eat your bodies, *Klingensmith* . . . devour...as fire does, *Confraternity.*

Ye have heaped treasure together for the last days: . . . hoarded riches, *Adams* . . . been storing up fire, *Montgomery* . . . You have piled up treasures in these last days, *Beck* . . . You have heaped up as for a fire at the end of your days, *Fenton* . . . that you have stored up against the last days, *Berkeley* . . . You piled up security in last days, *Klingensmith* . . . while the world is coming to an end, *TNT.*

4. Behold, the hire of the labourers: . . . the pay of, *Berkeley* . . . wages of, *Montgomery* . . . the workmen, *Norlie.*

who have reaped down your fields: . . . who mowed, *Montgomery* . . . harvested, *Norlie* . . . gathered your harvests for you, *TNT.*

James 5:5

570.1 prep	5050.2 prs-pron gen 2pl	2869.1 verb 3sing indic pres act	2504.1 conj	3450.13 art nom pl fem	988.1 noun nom pl fem	3450.1 art gen pl
ἀφ'	ὑμῶν	κράζει,	καὶ	αἱ	βοαὶ	τῶν
aph'	*humōn*	*krazei*	*kai*	*hai*	*boai*	*tōn*
by	you,	cries out,	and	the	cries	of the

2302.7 verb gen pl masc part aor act	1519.1 prep	3450.17 art pl neu	3640.2 noun pl neu	2935.2 noun gen sing masc	4376.1 noun masc
θερισάντων	εἰς	τὰ	ὦτα	κυρίου	Σαβαὼθ
therisantōn	*eis*	*ta*	*ōta*	*kuriou*	*Sabaōth*
having reaped,	into	the	ears	of Lord	of Hosts

4.b.**Txt:** 01ℵ,018K,020L byz.Sod
Var: 03B,025P,Lach Treg,Alf,Word,Tisc We/Ho,Weis,UBS/⋆

1511.25 verb 3pl indic perf act	1511.44 verb 3pl indic perf act	5012.1 verb 2pl indic aor act
‘ εἰσεληλύθασιν.	[b☆ εἰσελήλυθαν.]	5. ἐτρυφήσατε
eiselēluthasin	*eiselēluthan*	*etruphēsate*
have entered.	[idem]	You lived in indulgence

1894.3 prep	3450.10 art gen sing fem	1087.2 noun gen sing fem	2504.1 conj	4537.2 verb 2pl indic aor act
ἐπὶ	τῆς	γῆς,	καὶ	ἐσπαταλήσατε.
epi	*tēs*	*gēs*	*kai*	*espatalēsate*
upon	the	earth,	and	lived in self gratification;

5.a.**Txt:** 01ℵ-corr,018K 020L,byz.Sod
Var: 01ℵ-org,02A,03B 025P,33,Lach,Treg,Alf Word,Tisc,We/Ho,Weis UBS/⋆

4982.4 verb 2pl indic aor act	3450.15 art acc pl fem	2559.1 noun fem	5050.2 prs-pron gen 2pl	5453.1 conj	1706.1 prep
ἐθρέψατε	τὰς	καρδίας	ὑμῶν	‘a ὡς ’	ἐν
ethrepsate	*tas*	*kardias*	*humōn*	*hōs*	*en*
you nourished	the	hearts	your	as	in

2232.3 noun dat sing fem	4819.1 noun gen sing fem	2584.2 verb 2pl indic aor act	5244.2 verb 2pl indic aor act
ἡμέρᾳ	σφαγῆς.	6. κατεδικάσατε,	ἐφονεύσατε
hēmera	*sphagēs*	*katedikasate*	*ephoneusate*
a day	of slaughter;	you condemned,	you killed,

3450.6 art acc sing masc	1337.1 adj sing	3620.2 partic	495.1 verb 3sing indic pres mid	5050.3 prs-pron dat 2pl
τὸν	δίκαιον·	οὐκ	ἀντιτάσσεται	ὑμῖν.
ton	*dikaion*	*ouk*	*antitassetai*	*humin*
the	just;	not	he does resist	you.

3086.5 verb 2pl impr aor act	3631.1 partic	79.6 noun nom pl masc	2175.1 conj	3450.10 art gen sing fem
7. Μακροθυμήσατε	οὖν,	ἀδελφοί,	ἕως	τῆς
Makrothumēsate	*oun*	*adelphoi*	*heōs*	*tēs*
Be patient	therefore,	brothers,	till	the

3814.2 noun gen sing fem	3450.2 art gen sing	2935.2 noun gen sing masc	1481.20 verb 2sing impr aor mid	3450.5 art nom sing masc	1086.1 noun nom sing masc
παρουσίας	τοῦ	κυρίου.	ἰδοὺ,	ὁ	γεωργὸς
parousias	*tou*	*kuriou*	*idou*	*ho*	*geōrgos*
coming	of the	Lord.	Behold,	the	farmer

1538.2 verb 3sing indic pres mid	3450.6 art acc sing masc	4941.4 adj acc sing masc	2561.3 noun acc sing masc	3450.10 art gen sing fem	1087.2 noun gen sing fem
ἐκδέχεται	τὸν	τίμιον	καρπὸν	τῆς	γῆς,
ekdechetai	*ton*	*timion*	*karpon*	*tēs*	*gēs*
awaits	the	precious	fruit	of the	earth,

7.a.**Txt:** 01ℵ,025P,33 byz.
Var: 02A,03B,018K 020L,Treg,Alf,Tisc We/Ho,Weis,Sod UBS/⋆

3086.3 verb nom sing masc part pres act	1894.2 prep	840.4 prs-pron dat sing	2175.1 conj	300.1 partic	2956.18 verb 3sing subj aor act
μακροθυμῶν	ἐπ'	αὐτῷ	ἕως	‘a ἂν ’	λάβῃ
makrothumōn	*ep'*	*autō*	*heōs*	*an*	*labē*
being patient	for	it	until		it receive

"Saba-oth" is a transliteration from the Hebrew and means "hosts." It is a powerful expression of God's omnipotence. In the Old Testament He was seen not only as the God of Israel's army, but of heavenly bodies and angelic forces (Judges 5:20; 2 Kings 6:17).

5:5. James says, "Ye have lived in pleasure on the earth and been wanton." Weymouth translates this sentence, "Here on earth you have lived self-indulgent and profligate lives." The living here on earth is in sharp contrast with what these people will face at the judgment.

Without concern about life after death, these rich people lived in selfish luxury. "Wanton" suggests waste. Like the Prodigal Son, they squandered their substance (Luke 15:13) rather than administering it judiciously as a stewardship.

Some understand "ye have nourished your hearts, as in a day of slaughter" to mean unrestrained feasting after a victorious battle. Others, like the RV, omit the word "as" and understand the "day of slaughter" as the Day of Judgment and in contrast to "on the earth." The rich, by presumptuous, unrestrained living, were preparing themselves for the Day of Judgment like animals gorging themselves for the day of slaughter.

5:6. The rich were not satisfied with cheating workers out of their wages. They went so far as to use their influence to condemn and kill righteous people in violation of God's command not to pervert justice (Exodus 23:6; Deuteronomy 24:17). Some who were wrongfully drawn "before the judgment seats" (2:6) were through harsh treatment put to death.

The situation of the poor was so hopeless that they could not or would not resist those who mistreated them. It is possible that they reacted according to the guidance of Paul in Romans 12:19: "Avenge not yourselves." God would avenge them.

5:7. The Greek word translated "be patient" (*makrothumēsate*) basically means "be long-suffering." Just as God suffers long with difficult people (Psalm 86:15; Jonah 4:2; 2 Peter 3:9), believers are to do likewise (1 Thessalonians 5:14). Long-suffering is a fruit of the Spirit (Galatians 5:22).

Believers were assured that oppression would not continue indefinitely. The coming of the Lord would bring about a change. The second coming of Christ is a "blessed hope" for believers (Titus 2:13) and a source of comfort (1 Thessalonians 4:18).

The writer used the work of a farmer to emphasize the need for patience. He would prepare the soil, plant the seed, and wait for the crops to mature. Most of all, he would wait for the rain.

God had promised two rainy seasons in Palestine (Deuteronomy 11:14). The "early rain" came in late October or early November

which is of you kept back by fraud, crieth: You have stolen, *Laubach* . . . you cheated them out of the pay that they deserved, *SEB* . . . you never paid the men, *Beck* . . . which you have withheld from them, *Berkeley* . . . which have been kept back by you unjustly, cry out, *Confraternity* . . . shout out at you, *Adams.*

and the cries of them which have reaped are entered into the ears of the Lord of sabaoth: . . . and the complaints of, *Adams* . . . the outcries of the harvesters, *Norlie* . . . of the reapers, *Berkeley* . . . the groans of those who cut grain have come to the ears, *Beck* . . . of the Lord of Hosts! *TCNT* . . . of the Lord of Armies, *Wilson.*

5. Ye have lived in pleasure on the earth, and been wanton: . . . have lived luxuriously, *Montgomery* . . . have feasted upon earth, *Confraternity* . . . indulged yourselves, *Darby* . . . in luxury and self-gratification, *Norlie* . . . an easy life in the land, *Berkeley* . . . a life of extravagance, *TCNT* . . . and been licentious, *Wilson* . . . and been profligate, *Clementson* . . . and squander, *Concordant.*

ye have nourished your hearts, as in a day of slaughter: . . . fattened your hearts, *Montgomery* . . . on dissipation in the day of slaughter, *Confraternity* . . . as in a day of festivity, *Campbell.*

6. Ye have condemned [and] killed the just: . . . you have murdered, *TCNT* . . . and put to death, *Confraternity* . . . killed the One right with God, *NLT* . . . the upright, *Berkeley* . . . the righteous man, *Montgomery* . . . an innocent man, *SEB.*

[and] he doth not resist you: . . . unresisting, *Montgomery* . . . who did not even oppose you! *Norlie.*

7. Be patient therefore, brethren, unto the coming of the Lord: So, endure patiently, *Berkeley* . . . fellow Christians, *Beck.*

Behold, the husbandman waiteth for the precious fruit of the earth, and hath long patience for it: Note how the farmer awaits the precious produce of the soil, keeping patient about it, *Berkeley* . . . crop on the ground, *Beck.*

James 5:8

7.b.**Txt:** 02A,018K,020L 025P,byz.Sod
Var: p74,03B,sa.Lach Treg,Alf,Tisc,We/Ho Weis,UBS/☆

5046.2 noun acc sing masc	4264.1 adj acc sing masc	4149.1 adj acc sing masc	2504.1 conj	3661.1 adj acc sing masc
⸂b ὑετὸν ⸃	⸀ πρώϊμον	[c☆ πρόϊμον]	καὶ	ὄψιμον·
hueton	*prōimon*	*proimon*	*kai*	*opsimon*
rain	early	[idem]	and	latter.

7.c.**Txt:** 03B-corr,018K 020L,byz.Weis
Var: 01ℵ,02A,03B-org 025P,Treg,Tisc,We/Ho Sod,UBS/☆

3086.5 verb 2pl impr aor act	3631.1 partic	2504.1 conj	5050.1 prs-pron nom 2pl	4592.3 verb 2pl impr aor act
8. μακροθυμήσατε	[a+ οὖν]	καὶ	ὑμεῖς,	στηρίξατε
makrothumēsate	*oun*	*kai*	*humeis*	*stērixate*
Be patient	[therefore]	also	you:	establish

8.a.**Var:** p74,01ℵ,020L

3450.15 art acc pl fem	2559.1 noun fem	5050.2 prs-pron gen 2pl	3617.1 conj	3450.9 art nom sing fem	3814.1 noun nom sing fem
τὰς	καρδίας	ὑμῶν,	ὅτι	ἡ	παρουσία
tas	*kardias*	*humōn*	*hoti*	*hē*	*parousia*
the	hearts	your,	because	the	coming

3450.2 art gen sing	2935.2 noun gen sing masc	1443.15 verb 3sing indic perf act	3231.1 partic	4578.2 verb 2pl impr pres act	2567.1 prep
τοῦ	κυρίου	ἤγγικεν.	**9.** Μὴ	στενάζετε	⸀ κατ'
tou	*kuriou*	*ēngiken*	*Mē*	*stenazete*	*kat'*
of the	Lord	has drawn near.	Not	groan	against

238.1 prs-pron gen pl	79.6 noun nom pl masc	79.6 noun nom pl masc	2567.1 prep	238.1 prs-pron gen pl
ἀλλήλων,	ἀδελφοί,	[☆ ἀδελφοί,	κατ'	ἀλλήλων,]
allēlōn	*adelphoi*	*adelphoi*	*kat'*	*allēlōn*
one another,	brothers,	[brothers,	against	one another,]

9.a.**Txt:** Steph
Var: 01ℵ,02A,03B 018K,020L,025P,Gries Lach,Treg,Alf,Word Tisc,We/Ho,Weis,Sod UBS/☆

2419.1 conj	3231.1 partic	2602.10 verb 2pl subj aor pass	2892.35 verb 2pl subj aor pass	1481.20 verb 2sing impr aor mid
ἵνα	μὴ	⸀ κατακριθῆτε·	[a☆ κριθῆτε·]	ἰδοὺ,
hina	*mē*	*katakrithēte*	*krithēte*	*idou*
that	not	you be condemned.	[you be judged.]	Behold,

9.b.**Var:** 01ℵ,02A,03B 018K,020L,025P,Gries Lach,Treg,Alf,Word Tisc,We/Ho,Weis,Sod UBS/☆

3450.5 art nom sing masc	2896.1 noun nom sing masc	4112.1 prep	3450.1 art gen pl	2351.6 noun gen pl fem	2449.18 verb 3sing indic perf act
[b☆+ ὁ]	κριτὴς	πρὸ	τῶν	θυρῶν	ἕστηκεν.
ho	*kritēs*	*pro*	*tōn*	*thurōn*	*hestēken*
[the]	judge	before	the	door	stands.

5100.2 noun sing neu	2956.24 verb 2pl impr aor act	3450.10 art gen sing fem	2523.1 noun gen sing fem	79.6 noun nom pl masc
10. ⸀Ὑπόδειγμα	λάβετε	⸀ τῆς	κακοπαθείας,	ἀδελφοί,
Hupodeigma	*labete*	*tēs*	*kakopatheias*	*adelphoi*
An example	take	of the	affliction,	brothers

10.a.**Txt:** Steph
Var: 02A,03B,025P We/Ho,UBS/☆

79.6 noun nom pl masc	3450.10 art gen sing fem	2523.1 noun gen sing fem	1466.2 prs-pron gen 1sing	2504.1 conj
[a☆ ἀδελφοί,	τῆς	κακοπαθείας]	μου,	καὶ
adelphoi	*tēs*	*kakopatheias*	*mou*	*kai*
[brothers,	of the	affliction]	my,	and

3450.10 art gen sing fem	3087.2 noun gen sing fem	3450.8 art acc pl masc	4254.7 noun acc pl masc	3614.7 rel-pron nom pl masc
τῆς	μακροθυμίας,	τοὺς	προφήτας	οἳ
tēs	*makrothumias*	*tous*	*prophētas*	*hoi*
of the	patience,	the	prophets	who

10.b.**Var:** 01ℵ,03B,025P Lach,Treg,Tisc,We/Ho Weis,UBS/☆

2953.30 verb 3pl indic aor act	1706.1 prep	3450.3 art dat sing	3549.4 noun dat sing neu	2935.2 noun gen sing masc	1481.20 verb 2sing impr aor mid
ἐλάλησαν	[b☆+ ἐν]	τῷ	ὀνόματι	κυρίου.	**11.** ἰδοὺ,
elalēsan	*en*	*tō*	*onomati*	*kuriou*	*idou*
spoke	[in]	in the	name	of Lord.	Behold,

and provided moisture needed for sowing the seed. The "latter rain" usually came in the early months of the year and was essential for maturing the harvest.

until he receive the early and latter rain: . . . till it has had the spring and summer rains, *TCNT* . . . until the early and late rains come, *TNT, Klingensmith* . . . to get the fall and the spring rains, *Beck* . . . the early and latter harvest, *Wilson* . . . getting the early and late fruit, *Concordant.*

5:8. Here James applied the previous illustration to suffering believers and said, "Be ye also patient." Just as the farmers showed patience because they had learned to trust in God's providential provision, believers were to be patient in their difficult circumstances.

To "stablish your hearts" means to strengthen, make fast, to set firmly so the heart will be unshakable. God through His divine intervention works in believers' lives that "he may stablish your hearts unblamable in holiness before God, even our Father, at the coming of our Lord Jesus Christ with all his saints" (1 Thessalonians 3:13). But believers have a personal responsibility to establish their own hearts. The means by which this is done is the truth of God's Word (1 Peter 2:2).

Believers were not only assured that God heard their cries (5:4), but the Lord was coming to do something about world conditions. When problems exist, time seems to drag by. But time seems shortened for those who have the heavenly perspective.

8. Be ye also patient; stablish your hearts: So you keep waiting patiently, *Berkeley* . . . have great patience, *Klingensmith* . . . You, too, be patient, and keep your courage, *Beck* . . . Fortify your hearts, *Norlie* . . . Firm up your hearts, *Adams* . . . Make your hearts strong, *SEB* . . . strengthen your hearts, *Confraternity.*

for the coming of the Lord draweth nigh: . . . because the Lord will soon be here, *Beck* . . . because the Lord's coming will soon take place, *TNT* . . . the presence of the Lord has come, *Klingensmith* . . . is at hand! *Montgomery.*

5:9. The word translated "grudge" literally means "groan." When people have severe problems, the "groaning" can become murmuring or grumbling, criticizing others for real or imagined grievances. This judging of others is the opposite of the patience James wrote about in the previous verse.

In the Sermon on the Mount Jesus taught, "Judge not, that ye be not judged. For with what judgment ye judge, ye shall be judged: and with what measure ye mete, it shall be measured to you again (Matthew 7:1,2). Sometimes the judgment of those who are critical of others comes in this life. Paul warned the Corinthians, "Neither murmur ye, as some of them also murmured, and were destroyed of the destroyer" (1 Corinthians 10:10). Murmuring deserves no place in a believer's life.

The phrase "the judge standeth before the door" has serious implications. The Judge now stands knocking at the door of hearts seeking redemptive admission (Revelation 3:20); then He will open the door in judgment.

9. Grudge not one against another, brethren: Do not make complaints against each other, *Montgomery* . . . Don't blame your troubles on one another, fellow Christians, *Beck.*

lest ye be condemned: . . . or you will be, *Beck* . . . that you may not be judged, *Confraternity* . . . so you may not come under judgment, *Berkeley.*

behold, the judge standeth before the door: You know, *Beck* . . . Look, *Klingensmith* . . . is here, standing at the door, *TNT* . . . is standing just outside, *SEB* . . . has already stationed Himself at the gates! *Fenton.*

5:10. The experiences of those who have gone before us, and their examples of godly perseverance can be like a beacon to guide us. As these suffering Christians were told to consider the prophets as examples of endurance, they might have thought of people such as Moses (Deuteronomy 18:18), Elijah (1 Kings 17:1), Elisha (1 Kings 19:16), and Jeremiah (Jeremiah 1:1,2). The fact that they had "spoken in the name of the Lord" did not mean they were free from suffering.

10. Take, my brethren, the prophets, who have spoken in the name of the Lord: . . . brothers, think of the prophets, *TNT* . . . fellow Christians, take the prophets who spoke in the Lord's name, *Beck.*

for an example of suffering affliction, and of patience: . . . as an example of labor and patience, *Confraternity* . . . for your example of ill-treatment that was patiently endured, *Berkeley* . . . of patiently suffering wrong, *Beck* . . . the patience of the prophets, *Montgomery* . . . of great suffering and great patience, *Klingensmith.*

11.a.**Txt:** 018K,020L,byz. sa.bo.
Var: 01ℵ,02A,03B,025P Lach,Treg,Alf,Tisc We/Ho,Weis,Sod UBS/☆

3078.1 verb 1pl indic pres act	**3450.8** art acc pl masc	**5116.6** verb acc pl masc part pres act	**5116.14** verb acc pl masc part aor act
μακαρίζομεν	τοὺς	ʻ ὑπομένοντας.	[a☆ ὑπομείναντας·]
makarizomen	*tous*	*hupomenontas*	*hupomeinantas*
we call blessed	the	enduring.	[having enduring.]

3450.12 art acc sing fem	**5119.4** noun acc sing fem	**2465.1** name masc	**189.23** verb 2pl indic aor act	**2504.1** conj
τὴν	ὑπομονὴν	Ἰὼβ	ἠκούσατε,	καὶ
tēn	*hupomonēn*	*Iōb*	*ēkousate*	*kai*
The	endurance	of Job	you have heard of,	and

11.b.**Txt:** 01ℵ,03B-org 018K,614,1505
Var: 02A,03B-corr2 020L,025P,044,049,33 69,81,323,630,945 1241,1739,2495

3450.16 art sing neu	**4904.1** noun sing neu	**2935.2** noun gen sing masc	**1481.6** verb 2pl indic aor act	**1481.15** verb 2pl impr aor act
τὸ	τέλος	κυρίου	ʻ☆ εἴδετε,	[b ἴδετε,]
to	*telos*	*kuriou*	*eidete*	*idete*
the	end	of Lord	you saw;	[you observed]

11.c.**Txt:** 01ℵ,02A,025P 044,81,614,630,945 1739,2495
Var: byz.

3617.1 conj	**4043.1** adj nom sing masc	**1498.4** verb 3sing indic pres act	**3450.5** art nom sing masc	**2935.1** noun nom sing masc
ὅτι	πολύσπλαγχνός	ἐστιν	ʻc☆ ὁ	κύριος ʼ
hoti	*polusplanchnos*	*estin*	*ho*	*kurios*
that	full of tender pity	is	the	Lord

2504.1 conj	**3491.1** adj nom sing masc	**4112.1** prep	**3820.4** adj gen pl	**1156.2** conj	**79.6** noun nom pl masc
καὶ	οἰκτίρμων.	**12.** Πρὸ	πάντων	δέ,	ἀδελφοί
kai	*oiktirmōn*	*Pro*	*pantōn*	*de*	*adelphoi*
and	compassionate.	Before	all things	but	brothers

1466.2 prs-pron gen 1sing	**3231.1** partic	**3523.3** verb 2pl impr pres act	**3250.1** conj	**3450.6** art acc sing masc	**3636.4** noun acc sing masc
μου,	μὴ	ὀμνύετε,	μήτε	τὸν	οὐρανὸν,
mou	*mē*	*omnuete*	*mēte*	*ton*	*ouranon*
my,	not	swear,	neither	the	heaven,

3250.1 conj	**3450.12** art acc sing fem	**1087.4** noun acc sing fem	**3250.1** conj	**241.5** adj acc sing masc	**4948.5** indef-pron	**3590.4** noun acc sing masc
μήτε	τὴν	γῆν,	μήτε	ἄλλον	τινὰ	ὅρκον·
mēte	*tēn*	*gēn*	*mēte*	*allon*	*tina*	*horkon*
nor	the	earth;	nor	other	any	oath;

1498.16 verb 3sing impr pres act	**1156.2** conj	**5050.2** prs-pron gen 2pl	**3450.16** art sing neu	**3346.1** intrj	**3346.1** intrj	**2504.1** conj
ἤτω	δὲ	ὑμῶν	τὸ	Ναὶ,	ναὶ	καὶ
ētō	*de*	*humōn*	*to*	*Nai*	*nai*	*kai*
let be	but	your	the	yes,	yes,	and

12.a.**Txt:** 018K,020L 025P,byz.
Var: 01ℵ,02A,03B,33 sa.bo.Elzev,Gries,Lach Treg,Alf,Word,Tisc We/Ho,Weis,Sod UBS/☆

3450.16 art sing neu	**3620.3** partic	**3620.3** partic	**2419.1** conj	**3231.1** partic	**1519.1** prep	**5110.4** noun acc sing fem	**5097.3** prep
τὸ	Οὔ,	οὔ·	ἵνα	μὴ	ʻ εἰς	ὑπόκρισιν	[a☆ ὑπὸ
to	*Ou*	*ou*	*hina*	*mē*	*eis*	*hupokrisin*	*hupo*
the	no,	no,	that	not	into	hypocrisy	[under

2893.4 noun acc sing fem	**3959.8** verb 2pl subj aor act	**2524.2** verb 3sing indic pres act	**4948.3** indef-pron nom sing	**1706.1** prep
κρίσιν]	πέσητε.	**13.** Κακοπαθεῖ	τις	ἐν
krisin	*pesēte*	*Kakopathei*	*tis*	*en*
judgment]	you may fall.	Does suffer hardships	anyone	among

5050.3 prs-pron dat 2pl	**4195.9** verb 3sing impr pres mid	**2093.1** verb 3sing indic pres act	**4948.3** indef-pron nom sing	**5402.1** verb 3sing impr pres act
ὑμῖν;	προσευχέσθω·	εὐθυμεῖ	τις;	ψαλλέτω.
humin	*proseuchesthō*	*euthumei*	*tis*	*psalletō*
you?	let him pray:	is cheerful	anyone?	let him praise;

5:11. "Behold, we count them happy which endure" is better translated "which *endured.*" This is another element in the encouragement of those presently suffering affliction. Those who have already endured are considered happy or blessed.

The experiences of the patriarch Job and how he came through successfully are a great encouragement to believers. The word here translated "patience" is different from the word so translated in 5:7. There the meaning is long-suffering. Here the meaning is endurance. Job was not always long-suffering with his friends, but he endured. His affirmation, "Though he slay me, yet will I trust in him" (Job 13:15) testified to his steadfastness.

The readers who had heard of Job's endurance were also aware of his vindication. They saw the end which the Lord brought about. Readers could learn from Job's experience that even though believers have much affliction, the final outcome is happy. If the outcome is not always happy in this life, as in the case of Stephen, the heavenly welcome and reward will be of indescribable blessedness (Acts 7:55,56).

The way God dealt with Job reveals His character. It only *seemed* that God had forsaken him; all was well at the last. "Pitiful," very compassionate, refers to God's feeling for man. "Tender mercy" speaks of how He acts toward man.

11. Behold, we count them happy which endure: Remember, we call those happy, *Beck* . . . we count those that were stedfast, *Montgomery* . . . we admire those who have patience, *SEB* . . . we call them blessed who have endured, *Confraternity* . . . who remains faithful to the end, *Laubach* . . . for their way of enduring, *Berkeley.*

Ye have heard of the patience of Job, and have seen the end of the Lord: . . . stedfastness, *Montgomery* . . . how Job endured, and you saw how the Lord finally treated him, *Beck* . . . seen the purpose of, *Confraternity* . . . noticed what conclusion the Lord effected, *Berkeley.*

that the Lord is very pitiful, and of tender mercy: . . . because the Lord is very tenderhearted, *Beck* . . . compassionate and merciful, *Swann* . . . full of tenderness, *Montgomery* . . . tender compassion, *Darby* . . . deeply sympathetic, *Berkeley.*

5:12. Here James comes back to the matter of the believer's speech (see 1:26; 3:2,8; 4:11). As in the words of Jesus to which James referred, the emphasis is on total honesty. It seems dishonesty had become so prevalent that in interpersonal conversation people would affirm statements with an oath. Matthew 23:16-22 indicates how oaths were dishonestly manipulated by the Pharisees so commitments would not be binding.

Some understand that not swearing by an oath applies to all situations including official oaths. Others understand it as calling for total honesty in communication and not applying to legal matters. Alfred Plummer in holding that this verse does not extend to legal matters points out that the Mosaic law "not only allowed, but enjoined the taking of an oath in certain circumstances: and Christ would hardly have abrogated the law, and St. James would hardly have contradicted it without giving some explanation" (*The Expositor's Bible*, 24:305). (See Deuteronomy 6:13; 10:20; Isaiah 65:16; Jeremiah 12:15,16.) Jesus dealt with this matter also (Matthew 5:34-37).

12. But above all things, my brethren, swear not: More than anything else, *SEB* . . . my fellow Christians, *Beck* . . . do not take oaths, *Laubach.*

neither by heaven, neither by the earth, neither by any other oath: . . . any other kind of oath, *Fenton.*

but let your yea be yea; and [your] nay, nay: If you mean yes, say yes, *NLT* . . . let your "yes" mean yes, *Norlie* . . . be just yes, *Beck.*

lest ye fall into condemnation: . . . so you will not fall under, *Montgomery* . . . will escape being judged, *Norlie* . . . may incur no judgment, *Berkeley* . . . or you will be condemned for it, *Beck.*

5:13. As he comes to the close of the epistle, James deals with a series of very personal matters. If believers are afflicted, he says, the answer is to pray instead of complain. If, on the other hand, they are in a happy mood, they should sing unto the Lord. As in the case of Paul and Silas, praying and singing can be combined (Acts 16:25). See also Ephesians 5:19,20.

13. Is any among you afflicted?: When any one of you is, *TCNT* . . . in trouble? *Montgomery* . . . in distress? *Fenton* . . . suffering, *Swann* . . . sad, *Confraternity* . . . suffer evil? *Darby* . . . ill-treatment, *Williams.*

let him pray:

Is any merry?: . . . when any one feels cheerful, *TCNT* . . . in good spirits? *Montgomery* . . . in a happy mood? *Williams.*

let him sing psalms: . . . sing hymns, *TCNT* . . . praises, *Wilson* . . . play music, *Concordant* . . . unto his harp, *Montgomery.*

764.2 verb 3sing indic pres act	**4948.3** indef-pron nom sing	**1706.1** prep	**5050.3** prs-pron dat 2pl	**4200.3** verb 3sing impr aor mid
14. ἀσθενεῖ	τις	ἐν	ὑμῖν;	προσκαλεσάσθω
asthenei	*tis*	*en*	*humin*	*proskalesasthō*
is sick	anyone	among	you?	let him call to

3450.8 art acc pl masc	**4104.2** adj comp acc pl masc	**3450.10** art gen sing fem	**1564.1** noun fem	**2504.1** conj
τοὺς	πρεσβυτέρους	τῆς	ἐκκλησίας,	καὶ
tous	*presbuterous*	*tēs*	*ekklēsias*	*kai*
the	elders	of the	assembly,	and

14.a.**Txt:** 01ℵ,02A,018K 020L,byz.Sod
Var: 03B,025P,Tisc We/Ho,Weis,UBS/☆

4195.23 verb 3pl impr aor mid	**1894.2** prep	**840.6** prs-pron acc sing masc	**216.4** verb nom pl masc part aor act	**840.6** prs-pron acc sing masc
προσευξάσθωσαν	ἐπ'	αὐτὸν,	ἀλείψαντες	⸂a αὐτὸν ⸃
proseuxasthōsan	*ep'*	*auton*	*aleipsantes*	*auton*
let them pray	over	him,	having anointed	him

1624.2 noun dat sing neu	**1706.1** prep	**3450.3** art dat sing	**3549.4** noun dat sing neu	**3450.2** art gen sing	**2935.2** noun gen sing masc	**2504.1** conj
ἐλαίῳ	ἐν	τῷ	ὀνόματι	τοῦ	κυρίου·	**15.** καὶ
elaiō	*en*	*tō*	*onomati*	*tou*	*kuriou*	*kai*
with oil	in	the	name	of the	Lord;	and

3450.9 art nom sing fem	**2152.1** noun nom sing fem	**3450.10** art gen sing fem	**3963.2** noun gen sing fem	**4834.13** verb 3sing indic fut act	**3450.6** art acc sing masc
ἡ	εὐχὴ	τῆς	πίστεως	σώσει	τὸν
hē	*euchē*	*tēs*	*pisteōs*	*sōsei*	*ton*
the	prayer	of the	faith	shall save	the

2548.1 verb acc sing masc part pres act	**2504.1** conj	**1446.13** verb 3sing indic fut act	**840.6** prs-pron acc sing masc	**3450.5** art nom sing masc
κάμνοντα,	καὶ	ἐγερεῖ	αὐτὸν	ὁ
kamnonta	*kai*	*egerei*	*auton*	*ho*
sick one,	and	will raise up	him	the

2935.1 noun nom sing masc	**2550.1** conj	**264.1** noun fem	**1498.10** verb 3sing subj pres act	**4020.47** verb nom sing masc part perf act
κύριος·	κἂν	ἁμαρτίας	ᾖ	πεποιηκώς,
kurios	*kan*	*hamartias*	*ē*	*pepoiēkōs*
Lord;	and if	sins	he may be	having committed,

16.a.**Var:** 01ℵ,02A,03B 018K,025P,sa.bo.Lach Treg,Alf,Tisc,We/Ho Weis,Sod,UBS/☆

856.30 verb 3sing indic fut pass	**840.4** prs-pron dat sing	**1827.3** verb 2pl impr pres mid	**3631.1** partic
ἀφεθήσεται	αὐτῷ.	**16.** ἐξομολογεῖσθε	[a☆+ οὖν]
aphethēsetai	*autō*	*exomologeisthe*	*oun*
it shall be forgiven	him.	Confess	[therefore]

16.b.**Txt:** 018K,020L,byz.
Var: 01ℵ,02A,03B,025P 33,Lach,Treg,Tisc We/Ho,Weis,Sod UBS/☆

238.2 prs-pron dat pl	**3450.17** art pl neu	**3761.6** noun pl neu	**3450.15** art acc pl fem	**264.1** noun fem
ἀλλήλοις	⸂ τὰ	παραπτωματα,	[b☆ τὰς	ἁμαρτίας,]
allēlois	*ta*	*paraptōmata*	*tas*	*hamartias*
to one another	the	faults,	[the	sins,]

16.c.**Txt:** 01ℵ,018K 020L,025P,byz.Tisc,Sod
Var: 02A,03B,Lach We/Ho,Weis,UBS/☆

2504.1 conj	**2153.3** verb 2pl impr pres mid	**4195.1** verb 2pl pres mid	**5065.1** prep	**238.1** prs-pron gen pl
καὶ	⸂ εὔχεσθε	[c προσεύχεσθε]	ὑπὲρ	ἀλλήλων,
kai	*euchesthe*	*proseuchesthe*	*huper*	*allēlōn*
and	pray	[idem]	for	one another,

3567.1 conj	**2367.10** verb 2pl subj aor pass	**4044.16** adj sing neu	**2453.2** verb 3sing indic pres act	**1157.1** noun nom sing fem
ὅπως	ἰαθῆτε.	πολὺ	ἰσχύει	δέησις
hopōs	*iathēte*	*polu*	*ischuei*	*deēsis*
that	you may be healed.	Much	accomplishes	petition

5:14. Here believers have instructions as to what to do in the case of sickness. The word translated "sick" has the idea of being weak. It is the opposite of the word used for strength. The reference seems to be to a feebleness which results in inability to work.

When this sickness develops, the suffering believer is to call for the elders of the church. One title of church leaders in Bible times was *elder.* Apparently they were also known as bishops. See Acts 20:17 with 20:28 where the Greek word for *bishop* is translated "overseer." Because of the debilitating nature of the illness, the elders were to be called to the home rather than have the suffering person come to the congregation. Jesus himself went to the homes of those who were sick (Matthew 8:14; Luke 8:41,42,51).

The elders were not only to pray but to anoint with oil. Anointing the sick with oil was instituted by the Lord. The oil in Scripture is often a type of the Holy Spirit. It is by His power that miracles occur. It was to be done in Jesus' name, that is, by His authority. The Twelve "anointed with oil many that were sick" (Mark 6:13).

5:15. The writer assures his readers that there will be results, that healing will occur. It is not always known who it is that prays the prayer of faith. It might be the sick person as in the case of two blind men who followed Jesus into a house (Matthew 9:27-29); or the faith of sympathetic friends as in the case of the servant of the Roman centurion (Matthew 8:5-13); or the faith of an "elder" as in the case of Dorcas (Acts 9:36-43; 1 Peter 5:1). While there are different ways in which healing comes, it is not man, but the Lord, who raises them up.

In some cases there will be spiritual results also. There are times when sickness is the result of sin. Because of abuses in connection with the Lord's Supper at Corinth, Paul wrote: "For this cause many are weak and sickly among you, and many sleep (die)" (1 Corinthians 11:30). On the other hand, there are times when illness is unrelated to sin. Jesus made it clear there was no sin involved in the case of the man born blind (John 9:1-3). If sin is involved, there is forgiveness (1 John 1:9).

5:16. We are to confess our faults (sins) and pray for one another that we may be healed. Here the matter of sin, sickness, and healing moves beyond the case where elders are called. The confession of sin is to one another. This might be a reference to Jesus' teaching concerning the importance of reconciliation between believers (Matthew 5:23,24). Sickness can be caused by harboring resentment, and it is difficult to pray with ill will in the heart. Removing resentment is a factor in spiritual healing.

Here are stated principles to follow if we desire to have an effective prayer ministry. The prayers of a man who is right with God can accomplish much. The righteous person is the one who practices right living (1 John 3:7). Believers who tolerate sin in their hearts cannot pray effectively (Psalm 66:18).

14. Is any sick among you?: . . . any one of you ill? *Montgomery.*

let him call for the elders of the church: Let him summon, *Fenton* . . . send for, *Montgomery* . . . bring in the presbyters, *Confraternity* . . . of the congregation, *SEB.*

and let them pray over him:

anointing him with oil in the name of the Lord: . . . pouring on oil, *Beck* . . . rubbing him with olive oil, *Concordant.*

15. And the prayer of faith shall save the sick: . . . if you believe, your prayer will make the sick person well, *Beck* . . . that is offered in faith, *Williams* . . . will restore the sick, *Montgomery* . . . heal the sick man, *NLT* . . . save the distressed one, *Clementson.*

and the Lord shall raise him up: . . . restore him to health, *TCNT* . . . make him well, *Laubach* . . . make him healthy, *Beck.*

and if he have committed sins, they shall be forgiven him: . . . if he feels guilty of sins, *Beck* . . . it shall be removed from him, *Fenton.*

16. Confess [your] faults one to another: Admit, *SEB* . . . your sins, *Montgomery.*

and pray one for another, that ye may be healed: . . . pray for one another to be healed, *Beck* . . . may be saved, *Confraternity* . . . be cured, *Berkeley.*

The effectual fervent prayer of a righteous man availeth much: The energetic supplications, *Swann* . . . The Earnest Supplication, *Wilson* . . . by praying vigorously, *Beck* . . . fervent supplication, *Darby* . . . The operative petition of the just, *Concordant* . . . the unceasing prayer of a just man, *Confraternity* . . . The earnest prayer of a good man can do much, *TCNT* . . . from the heart of a man right with God has much power, *NLT* . . . The inwrought prayer of a righteous man exceedingly prevails, *Clementson* . . . Very powerfully productive is the prayer of, *Fenton* . . . the power of his sincere prayer is tremendous...When a person is right with God, *SEB* . . . is mighty in its working, *Montgomery* . . . has great effect, *Berkeley* . . . very powerful effects, *Adams.*

1337.2 adj gen sing	1738.9 verb nom sing fem part pres mid	2226.1 name nom masc	442.1 noun nom sing masc
δικαίου	ἐνεργουμένη.	17. Ἡλίας	ἄνθρωπος
dikaiou	*energoumenē*	*Hēlias*	*anthrōpos*
of a righteous	being made effective.	Elijah	a man

1498.34 verb sing indic imperf act	3526.1 adj nom sing masc	2231.3 prs-pron dat 1pl	2504.1 conj	4194.3 noun dat sing fem
ἦν	ὁμοιοπαθὴς	ἡμῖν,	καὶ	προσευχῇ
ēn	*homoiopathēs*	*hēmin*	*kai*	*proseuchē*
was	of like feelings	to us,	and	with prayer

4195.16 verb 3sing indic aor mid	3450.2 art gen sing	3231.1 partic	1019.5 verb inf aor act	2504.1 conj	3620.2 partic	1019.4 verb 3sing indic aor act
προσηύξατο	τοῦ	μὴ	βρέξαι·	καὶ	οὐκ	ἔβρεξεν
prosēuxato	*tou*	*mē*	*brexai*	*kai*	*ouk*	*ebrexen*
he prayed	the	not	to rain;	and	not	it did rain

1894.3 prep	3450.10 art gen sing fem	1087.2 noun gen sing fem	1747.3 noun acc pl masc	4980.1 num card nom	2504.1 conj	3243.4 noun acc pl masc
ἐπὶ	τῆς	γῆς	ἐνιαυτοὺς	τρεῖς	καὶ	μῆνας
epi	*tēs*	*gēs*	*eniautous*	*treis*	*kai*	*mēnas*
upon	the	earth	years	three	and	months

1787.1 num card	2504.1 conj	3687.1 adv	4195.16 verb 3sing indic aor mid	2504.1 conj	3450.5 art nom sing masc
ἕξ.	18. καὶ	πάλιν	προσηύξατο,	καὶ	ὁ
hex	*kai*	*palin*	*prosēuxato*	*kai*	*ho*
six;	and	again	he prayed,	and	the

3636.1 noun nom sing masc	5046.2 noun acc sing masc	1319.14 verb 3sing indic aor act	2504.1 conj	3450.9 art nom sing fem	1087.1 noun nom sing fem
οὐρανὸς	ὑετὸν	ἔδωκεν,	καὶ	ἡ	γῆ
ouranos	*hueton*	*edōken*	*kai*	*hē*	*gē*
heaven	rain	gave,	and	the	earth

978.2 verb 3sing indic aor act	3450.6 art acc sing masc	2561.3 noun acc sing masc	840.10 prs-pron gen sing fem	79.6 noun nom pl masc
ἐβλάστησεν	τὸν	καρπὸν	αὐτῆς.	19. Ἀδελφοί,
eblastēsen	*ton*	*karpon*	*autēs*	*Adelphoi*
caused to sprout	the	fruit	its.	Brothers,

19.a.**Var:** 01א,02A,03B 018K,025P,sa.bo.Lach Treg,Alf,Tisc,We/Ho Weis,Sod,UBS/☆

1466.2 prs-pron gen 1sing	1430.1 partic	4948.3 indef-pron nom sing	1706.1 prep	5050.3 prs-pron dat 2pl	3966.19 verb 3sing subj aor pass
[a☆+ μου,]	ἐάν	τις	ἐν	ὑμῖν	πλανηθῇ
mou	*ean*	*tis*	*en*	*humin*	*planēthē*
[my,]	if	anyone	among	you	go astray

570.3 prep	3450.10 art gen sing fem	223.2 noun gen sing fem	2504.1 conj	1978.7 verb 3sing subj aor act	4948.3 indef-pron nom sing
ἀπὸ	τῆς	ἀληθείας,	καὶ	ἐπιστρέψῃ	τις
apo	*tēs*	*alētheias*	*kai*	*epistrepsē*	*tis*
from	the	truth,	and	bring back	anyone

20.a.**Txt:** 01א,02A,018K 020L,025P,byz.it.bo.Tisc Sod
Var: 03B,Alf,We/Ho Weis,UBS/☆

840.6 prs-pron acc sing masc	1091.10 verb 3sing impr pres act	1091.5 verb 2pl indic pres act	3617.1 conj	3450.5 art nom sing masc
αὐτόν,	20. ʼ γινωσκέτω	[a☆ γινώσκετε]	ὅτι	ὁ
auton	*ginōsketō*	*ginōskete*	*hoti*	*ho*
him,	let him know	[know you]	that	the

1978.11 verb nom sing masc part aor act	266.3 adj acc sing masc	1523.2 prep gen	3967.2 noun gen sing fem	3461.2 noun gen sing fem
ἐπιστρέψας	ἁμαρτωλὸν	ἐκ	πλάνης	ὁδοῦ
epistrepsas	*hamartōlon*	*ek*	*planēs*	*hodou*
having brought back	a sinner	from	error	of way

5:17. Here is a statement which should boost the spiritual morale of every believer. It was anticipated that some would feel it was natural for a man of heroic achievement to be able to pray effectively, but effective prayer could not be expected of ordinary persons. James made it clear that Elijah was a man with a nature exactly like theirs. The same person who seemed to be so in control on Mount Carmel (1 Kings 18:25-46) was the one who would desire to have God take his life after he heard of Jezebel's threats (1 Kings 19:4). The readers of this epistle could not excuse themselves from praying effectively by elevating Elijah to an exalted status.

The word "earnestly" interprets a Hebrew idiom which means "he prayed with prayer." This Hebraism indicated intensity. While the words he spoke are not recorded, there was an indication of his intensity in his physical posture. "He cast himself down upon the earth, and put his face between his knees" (1 Kings 18:42).

This reference mentions his prayer *for* rain, but he undoubtedly prayed just as earnestly it would *not* rain. There is no discrepancy between the statement "the space of three years and six months" and 1 Kings 18:1 which states "the word of the Lord came to Elijah in the third year." The two rainy seasons in Palestine were about 6 months apart. For the first 6 months Ahab undoubtedly ridiculed Elijah's announcement that there would be no rain. This prophecy would not be verified until the 6-month period between rains had passed and it failed to rain. Jesus also had stated that it did not rain for 3 years and 6 months (Luke 4:25).

5:18. The lesson for readers was that if the earnest prayer of a right-living person could become the instrument by which God controls the weather, this kind of prayer can also be the means by which He grants healing.

5:19. There are some who hold that the erring person in verses 19 and 20 refers to those who were never true converts. First John 2:19 is cited in support of this position. James, however, indicates the possibility of one of the "brethren" erring and needing conversion. While there are Scriptures which indicate God's keeping power, there are also Scriptures which indicate the possibility of people being lost who were once genuinely saved. Revelation 22:19 indicates a condition can develop where a person's name is taken out of the Book of Life. Also see Revelation 3:5. Before a name can be removed from a book, it must first of all be included. The best way to avoid erring from the truth is to have lives anchored in the Word of God.

5:20. Believers are not here commanded to try to rescue the sinner. It is assumed the effort will be made. The reward for the

17. Elias was a man subject to like passions as we are: . . . with feelings just like ours, *Williams* . . . like ourselves, subject to the same infirmities, *Confraternity* . . . of like nature with us, *Clementson* . . . of similar weakness with us, *Berkeley.*

and he prayed earnestly that it might not rain: . . . but when he prayed fervently, *TCNT* . . . he kept on praying, *Klingensmith.*

and it rained not on the earth by the space of three years and six months: . . . there fell no rain on the ground, *Berkeley.*

18. And he prayed again, and the heaven gave rain: Again he prayed earnestly, *Berkeley* . . . heaven sent rain, *Beck* . . . the sky gave, *Montgomery* . . . gives a shower, *Concordant* . . . rain fell from heaven, *Noli.*

and the earth brought forth her fruit: . . . the ground, *Beck* . . . the soil yielded its produce, *Berkeley* . . . germinates her fruit, *Concordant* . . . the soil again produced, *TNT* . . . produced its crops, *Williams.*

19. Brethren, if any of you do err from the truth: My fellow Christians, *Beck* . . . if anybody among you, *Klingensmith* . . . one of you strays, *Montgomery* . . . wanders from, *Laubach* . . . fallen away from the true religion, *Noli.*

and one convert him: . . . if anyone turns him around, *Klingensmith* . . . some one brings him back, *Montgomery* . . . one can turn him back, *Fenton* . . . try to bring him back, *Laubach.*

20. Let him know, that he which converteth the sinner: Remember this, *SEB* . . . be sure of this, *TNT* . . . let him be assured, *Berkeley* . . . know that he who turns the one missing it, *Klingensmith* . . . he ought to know that he who causes a sinner to be brought back, *Confraternity* . . . brings a sinner back, *Montgomery* . . . who turns back a Sinner, *Wilson.*

from the error of his way: . . . from the wandering of his way, *Berkeley* . . . his Path of Error, *Wilson* . . . his misguided way, *Confraternity* . . . his wrong way, *Beck* . . . from his wandering road, *Klingensmith.*

James 5:20

20.b.**Var:** 01ℵ,02A,025P 33,it.bo.Lach,Tisc We/Ho,Sod,UBS/⋆

20.c.**Txt:** 02A,Steph **Var:** Elzev,Gries,Lach Word,Tisc,We/Ho,Weis Sod,UBS/⋆

840.3 prs-pron gen sing αὐτοῦ, *autou* his,
4834.13 verb 3sing indic fut act σώσει *sōsei* shall save
5425.4 noun acc sing fem ψυχὴν *psuchēn* a soul
[b⋆+ **840.3** prs-pron gen sing αὐτοῦ] *autou* [his]
1523.2 prep gen ἐκ *ek* from
2265.2 noun gen sing masc θανάτου, *thanatou* death,

2504.1 conj καὶ *kai* and
2543.3 verb 3sing indic fut act καλύψει *kalupsei* shall cover
3988.1 noun sing neu πλῆθος *plēthos* a multitude
264.6 noun gen pl fem ἁμαρτιῶν. *hamartiōn* of sins.
⌜c **2362.2** name gen masc Ἰακώβου *Iakōbou* Of James

1976.1 noun nom sing fem ἐπιστολή. ⌝ *epistolē* epistle.

effort is knowing a soul is saved from death. If we saw a person was in danger of drowning, we would do all we could to rescue him. How much more should we strive to rescue a person from eternal damnation?

James 5:20

shall save a soul from death: . . . keeps a soul, *BB* . . . will save his soul, *Confraternity* . . . will save that man's soul, *TNT* . . . he has reserved a soul, *Phillips.*

and shall hide a multitude of sins: . . . and veil from God's sight, *Wade* . . . and is the cause of forgiveness for sins without number, *BB* . . . and prevent a multitude of sins, *Fenton* . . . covers up a great number of sins, *Berkeley* . . . and many sins will be forgiven, *NLT* . . . and will cause many sins to be forgiven, *TNT* . . . cover many sins, *Beck* . . . will be covered, *SEB* . . . will "cover a multitude," *Phillips* . . . and will draw a veil over a host of, *Barclay* . . . and bring about the forgiveness of many sins, *TEV* . . . and cover an uncounted number of, *Williams C.K.*

THE FIRST EPISTLE OF PETER

Expanded Interlinear
Textual Critical Apparatus
Verse-by-Verse Commentary
Various Versions

3935.2 name gen masc	1976.1 noun nom sing fem	4272.9 num ord nom sing fem
Πέτρου	Ἐπιστολὴ	Πρώτη
Petrou	*Epistolē*	*Prōtē*
Of Peter	Epistle	First

Textual Apparatus

3935.1 name nom masc	646.1 noun nom sing masc	2400.2 name masc	5382.2 name gen masc	1575.5 adj dat pl masc
1:1. Πέτρος	ἀπόστολος	Ἰησοῦ	Χριστοῦ,	ἐκλεκτοῖς
Petros	*apostolos*	*Iēsou*	*Christou*	*eklektois*
Peter,	apostle	of Jesus	Christ,	to elect

3789.2 adj dat pl masc	1284.1 noun gen sing fem	4054.1 name gen masc	1046.1 name gen fem
παρεπιδήμοις	διασπορᾶς	Πόντου,	Γαλατίας,
parepidēmois	*diasporas*	*Pontou*	*Galatias*
sojourners	of dispersion	of Pontus,	of Galatia,

2558.1 name gen fem	767.2 name gen fem	2504.1 conj	971.1 name gen fem	2567.3 prep
Καππαδοκίας,	Ἀσίας,	καὶ	Βιθυνίας,	**2.** κατὰ
Kappadokias	*Asias*	*kai*	*Bithunias*	*kata*
of Cappadocia,	of Asia,	and	Bithynia,	according to

4127.2 noun acc sing fem	2296.2 noun gen sing masc	3824.2 noun gen sing masc	1706.1 prep	38.2 noun dat sing masc
πρόγνωσιν	θεοῦ	πατρός,	ἐν	ἁγιασμῷ
prognōsin	*theou*	*patros*	*en*	*hagiasmō*
foreknowledge	of God	Father,	by	sanctification

4011.2 noun gen sing neu	1519.1 prep	5056.4 noun acc sing fem	2504.1 conj	4330.2 noun acc sing masc	129.2 noun gen sing neu
πνεύματος,	εἰς	ὑπακοὴν	καὶ	ῥαντισμὸν	αἵματος
pneumatos	*eis*	*hupakoēn*	*kai*	*rhantismon*	*haimatos*
of Spirit,	unto	obedience	and	sprinkling	of blood

2400.2 name masc	5382.2 name gen masc	5322.1 noun nom sing fem	5050.3 prs-pron dat 2pl	2504.1 conj	1503.1 noun nom sing fem
Ἰησοῦ	Χριστοῦ·	χάρις	ὑμῖν	καὶ	εἰρήνη
Iēsou	*Christou*	*charis*	*humin*	*kai*	*eirēnē*
of Jesus	Christ:	Grace	to you	and	peace

3989.6 verb 3sing opt aor pass	2109.1 adj nom sing masc	3450.5 art nom sing masc	2296.1 noun nom sing masc	2504.1 conj
πληθυνθείη.	**3.** Εὐλογητὸς	ὁ	θεὸς	καὶ
plēthuntheiē	*Eulogētos*	*ho*	*theos*	*kai*
may be multiplied.	Blessed	the	God	and

3824.1 noun nom sing masc	3450.2 art gen sing	2935.2 noun gen sing masc	2231.2 prs-pron gen 1pl	2400.2 name masc	5382.2 name gen masc
πατὴρ	τοῦ	κυρίου	ἡμῶν	Ἰησοῦ	Χριστοῦ,
patēr	*tou*	*kuriou*	*hēmōn*	*Iēsou*	*Christou*
Father	of the	Lord	our	Jesus	Christ,

3450.5 art nom sing masc	2567.3 prep	3450.16 art sing neu	4044.16 adj sing neu	840.3 prs-pron gen sing	1643.2 noun sing neu
ὁ	κατὰ	τὸ	πολὺ	αὐτοῦ	ἔλεος
ho	*kata*	*to*	*polu*	*autou*	*eleos*
the	according to	the	great	his	mercy

THE FIRST EPISTLE OF
PETER

1:1. Peter was one of the Twelve whom Jesus called and ordained (1) to be with Him, and (2) to go forth to preach, heal, and cast out devils (Mark 3:14-16). He was a dynamic leader, a spokesman for the Twelve. Three times the New Testament lists the Twelve (Matthew 10:1-4; Mark 3:16-19; Luke 6:12-16), and in each case Peter is mentioned first. However, he never claimed supremacy over the others.

The epistle is addressed to the believers, chiefly Jewish Christians, scattered throughout five Roman provinces of Asia Minor. Peter called them "strangers" (*parepidēmois*, sojourners) because earth is but their temporary home; their permanent abode is heaven. The term "scattered" suggests they were clustered in little church groups here and there.

1:2. The believers are "elect" (*eklektois*, chosen) according to the foreknowledge of God the Father, through sanctification of the Holy Spirit. Only once does *prognōsin* appear elsewhere in the New Testament, and that is in Peter's sermon (Acts 2:23) where he said the arrest of Christ was foreknown by God. The words "sanctification of the Spirit" also appear in 2 Thessalonians 2:13.

The result of the believers' election should be "obedience" (*hupakoēn*, see verse 22) and "sprinkling of the blood of Jesus Christ." *Rantismos* also appears in Hebrews 12:24 in reference to the "blood of sprinkling, that speaketh better things than that of Abel." The "sprinkling" recalls an event recorded in Exodus 24:7,8. On that occasion the people told Moses, "All that the Lord hath said will we do, and be obedient." After they had made this declaration, Moses "took the blood, and sprinkled it on the people." Their pledge of obedience preceded the sprinkling of the blood; similarly Peter's mention of "obedience" comes before "sprinkling of the blood of Jesus Christ," signifying that atonement through His blood is for the obedient.

Peter's wish was that the believers might enjoy "grace" (*charis*, favor) and "peace" (*eirēnē*, tranquility) in abundance.

1:3. Peter honored God the Father as the source of salvation. Out of His abundant "mercy" (*eleos*, compassion) the believers have been begotten again so they have a lively "hope" (*elpida*, expec-

Various Versions

1. Peter, an apostle of Jesus Christ: From Peter, *SEB* . . . a missionary of, *NLT* . . . an ambassador, *Wuest*.

to the strangers scattered throughout Pontus, Galatia, Cappadocia, Asia, and Bithynia: To the exiles, *Noli* . . . to the foreign-born Jews, *Williams* . . . to the elect sojourners, *Clementson* . . . to those who dwell as strangers, *Swann* . . . To God's chosen, homeless people, *SEB* . . . to the chosen expatriates, *Concordant* . . . to the chosen strangers of the Dispersion, *Fenton*.

2. Elect according to the foreknowledge of God the Father: . . . chosen-out ones...having been determined by the foreordination, *Wuest* . . . chosen in accordance with, *Williams* . . . according to the predetermination, *Fenton*.

through sanctification of the Spirit: . . . the setting-apart work of, *Wuest* . . . in their spiritual consecration, *Swann* . . . in holiness of spirit, *Concordant*.

unto obedience and sprinkling of the blood of Jesus Christ: . . . resulting in obedience of faith, *Wuest* . . . in order to obedience, *Campbell* . . . has washed you clean with His blood, *Laubach*.

Grace unto you, and peace, be multiplied: May God bless you more and more, and give you still greater peace, *TCNT* . . . May blessing and peace be abundant to you! *Fenton* . . . May you have complete peace and gracious love, *SEB* . . . Sanctifying grace...and tranquilizing peace, *Wuest* . . . peace to you be increased! *Adams* . . . be to you in increasing measure! *Norlie*.

3. Blessed [be] the God and Father of our Lord Jesus Christ: . . . be eulogized, *Wuest*.

1 Peter 1:4

311.1 verb nom sing masc part aor act	2231.4 prs-pron acc 1pl	1519.1 prep	1667.4 noun acc sing fem	2180.17 verb acc sing fem part pres act
ἀναγεννήσας	ἡμᾶς	εἰς	ἐλπίδα	ζῶσαν
anagennēsas	*hēmas*	*eis*	*elpida*	*zōsan*
having given birth again	us	to	a hope	living

1217.1 prep	384.2 noun gen sing fem	2400.2 name masc	5382.2 name gen masc	1523.2 prep gen
δι'	ἀναστάσεως	Ἰησοῦ	Χριστοῦ	ἐκ
di'	*anastaseōs*	*Iēsou*	*Christou*	*ek*
through	resurrection	of Jesus	Christ	from among

3361.2 adj gen pl	1519.1 prep	2790.3 noun acc sing fem	855.2 adj acc sing	2504.1 conj	281.2 adj acc sing fem
νεκρῶν,	4. εἰς	κληρονομίαν	ἄφθαρτον	καὶ	ἀμίαντον
nekrōn	*eis*	*klēronomian*	*aphtharton*	*kai*	*amianton*
dead,	to	an inheritance	incorruptible	and	undefiled

2504.1 conj	261.1 adj acc sing fem	4931.37 verb acc sing fem part perf mid	1706.1 prep	3636.8 noun dat pl masc	1519.1 prep
καὶ	ἀμάραντον,	τετηρημένην	ἐν	οὐρανοῖς	εἰς
kai	*amaranton*	*tetērēmenēn*	*en*	*ouranois*	*eis*
and	unfading,	having been kept	in	heavens	for

4.a.**Txt:** bo.Steph
Var: 01ℵ,02A,03B,04C 018K,020L,025P,byz. Gries,Lach,Treg,Alf Word,Tisc,We/Ho,Weis Sod,UBS/☆

2231.4 prs-pron acc 1pl	5050.4 prs-pron acc 2pl	3450.8 art acc pl masc	1706.1 prep	1405.3 noun dat sing fem	2296.2 noun gen sing masc
ʿ ἡμᾶς	[a☆ ὑμᾶς]	5. τοὺς	ἐν	δυνάμει	θεοῦ
hēmas	*humas*	*tous*	*en*	*dunamei*	*theou*
us,	[you]	the	by	power	of God

5268.3 verb acc pl masc part pres mid	1217.2 prep	3963.2 noun gen sing fem	1519.1 prep	4843.3 noun acc sing fem	2071.4 adj acc sing fem
φρουρουμένους	διὰ	πίστεως,	εἰς	σωτηρίαν	ἑτοίμην
phrouroumenous	*dia*	*pisteōs*	*eis*	*sōtērian*	*hetoimēn*
being guarded	through	faith,	for	salvation	ready

596.10 verb inf aor pass	1706.1 prep	2511.3 noun dat sing masc	2057.5 adj dat sing masc	1706.1 prep	3614.3 rel-pron dat sing
ἀποκαλυφθῆναι	ἐν	καιρῷ	ἐσχάτῳ·	6. ἐν	ᾧ
apokaluphthēnai	*en*	*kairō*	*eschatō*	*en*	*hō*
to be revealed	in	time	last.	In	which

21.2 verb 2pl pres mid	3504.1 adj sing	732.1 adv	1479.1 conj	1158.3 verb sing neu part pres act
ἀγαλλιᾶσθε,	ὀλίγον	ἄρτι,	εἰ	δέον
agalliasthe	*oligon*	*arti*	*ei*	*deon*
you exult,	for a little while	at present,	if	being necessary

6.a.**Txt:** 01ℵ-corr,02A 04C,018K,020L,025P byz.Sod
Var: 01ℵ-org,03B,Treg Tisc,We/Ho,Weis UBS/☆

1498.4 verb 3sing indic pres act	3048.15 verb nom pl masc part aor pass	1706.1 prep	4024.1 adj dat pl masc
ʿa ἐστὶν, ʾ	λυπηθέντες	ἐν	ποικίλοις
estin	*lupēthentes*	*en*	*poikilois*
it is,	having been put to grief	in	various

3848.6 noun dat pl masc	2419.1 conj	3450.16 art sing neu	1377.1 noun sing neu	5050.2 prs-pron gen 2pl	3450.10 art gen sing fem
πειρασμοῖς,	7. ἵνα	τὸ	δοκίμιον	ὑμῶν	τῆς
peirasmois	*hina*	*to*	*dokimion*	*humōn*	*tēs*
trials,	that	the	proving	your	of the

7.a.**Txt:** 018K,020L,byz.
Var: 01ℵ,02A,03B,04C 025P,Gries,Lach,Treg Alf,Tisc,We/Ho,Weis Sod,UBS/☆

3963.2 noun gen sing fem	4044.16 adj sing neu	4941.7 adj comp sing neu	4046.3 adj comp sing
πίστεως	ʿ πολὺ	τιμιώτερον	[a☆ πολυτιμότερον]
pisteōs	*polu*	*timiōteron*	*polutimoteron*
faith,	much	more precious	[much more precious]

tation) because God raised Jesus Christ from the dead. Peter used the thought of "living" quite often (see 1:23; 2:4,5,24; 4:5,6). No doubt he remembered when his hope was dashed by the Crucifixion; but hope is no longer dead. Due to the Resurrection, believers now have a living hope through the living Christ.

1:4. The believer's inheritance is incorruptible and undefiled unlike some earthly inheritances that disappear before they can be obtained, or that prove to be flawed or defective in their titles. This inheritance is failproof; it "fadeth not away" (*amaranton*, is perpetual). James 1:11 says the rich man shall "fade away" (*maranthēsetai*, pass away, be extinguished), and this word appears in the inscriptions on some ancient tombs. Even these inscriptions will fade away, they are not perpetual; but this inheritance in Christ is "a crown of glory that fadeth not away" (5:4).

1:5. The inheritance is reserved for those who are "kept" (*phrouroumenous*, protected) by the power of God "through faith." God's power protects the believers as they exercise faith. Both the heirs and the inheritance are being guarded; the protective work continues as the believers keep on believing. The outcome is "salvation" (*sōtērian*, deliverance) which is ready to be revealed in the "last time" (*kairō eschatō*, end time). The believers were under great pressure; the persecution instigated by Nero at Rome was spreading in their direction. But Peter assured them that deliverance lay ahead and an eternal inheritance was in their future.

1:6. "Wherein" probably relates to the ultimate deliverance to which Peter referred in verse 5. "Ye greatly rejoice" is not imperative but merely a statement of fact. The believers could "greatly rejoice" (from *agalliaō*, exult) even though "if need be" they had to endure persecution, because their "heaviness" was only "for a season." Though they should encounter "manifold temptations" (*poikilois peirasmois*, various adversities) they could "think it not strange" (4:12), for it was leading to "praise and honor and glory" (1:7).

1:7. Peter said the believers' faith is much "more precious" (*timiōteron*, most valuable, "of great price" as in Matthew 13:46) than gold, for gold "perisheth" (*apollumenou*, is destroyed). Although gold perishes (wears away), it is tested by fire until it proves to be unalloyed. Similarly the believers' faith must undergo testing to remove all the baser elements (impurities) so it may bring praise, honor, and glory to God and to them at the "appearing" (*apokalupsei*, revelation) of Jesus Christ.

which according to his abundant mercy hath begotten us again unto a lively hope by the resurrection of Jesus Christ from the dead: . . . impelled by... caused us to be born again so that we have a hope which is alive, *Wuest* . . . His boundless pity, *Fenton* . . . given us a new Life of undying hope, *TCNT* . . . born anew into a living hope, *Montgomery* . . . regenerated us through the Resurrection, *Wade.*

4. To an inheritance incorruptible, and undefiled: . . . for the enjoyment of an allotment, *Concordant* . . . so that we may share in that imperishable, stainless, *TCNT* . . . will never decay, spoil, *SEB.*

and that fadeth not away: They will never fade or spoil, but will last for ever, *Laubach.*

reserved in heaven for you: They are being kept safe in heaven for us, *NLT* . . . guarded in safe deposit in heaven, *Wuest.*

5. Who are kept by the power of God through faith: . . . are garrisoned, *Concordant* . . . constantly being kept guarded by, *Wuest.*

unto salvation ready to be revealed in the last time: . . . at the end of time, *Fenton* . . . at the final Hour of reckoning, *Wade* . . . in the last era, *Concordant* . . . in a last season which is epochal and strategic in its significance, *Wuest.*

6. Wherein ye greatly rejoice: Exult in this, *Montgomery* . . . you are to be constantly rejoicing with a joy that expresses itself in a triumphant exuberance, *Wuest* . . . be exceedingly glad, *Fenton.*

though now for a season, if need be, ye are in heaviness through manifold temptations: . . . if conditions require it, *Swann* . . . briefly at present, if it must be, being sorrowed by various trials, *Concordant* . . . you are distressed, *Wilson* . . . grieved by numerous trials, *Fenton.*

7. That the trial of your faith, being much more precious than of gold that perisheth: . . . the testing of, *Concordant* . . . the proof of, *Wilson* . . . the genuineness of your faith, *TCNT* . . . for gold can be destroyed, *Laubach.*

5388.2 noun gen sing neu	3450.2 art gen sing	616.21 verb gen sing neu part pres mid	1217.2 prep	4300.2 noun gen sing neu	1156.2 conj
χρυσίου	τοῦ	ἀπολλυμένου,	διὰ	πυρὸς	δὲ
chrusiou	*tou*	*apollumenou*	*dia*	*puros*	*de*
than gold	the	perishing,	by	fire	though

1375.15 verb gen sing neu part pres mid	2128.36 verb 3sing subj aor pass	1519.1 prep	1853.2 noun acc sing masc	2504.1 conj
δοκιμαζομένου,	εὑρεθῇ	εἰς	ἔπαινον	καὶ
dokimazomenou	*heurethē*	*eis*	*epainon*	*kai*
being proved,	be found	to	praise	and

4940.4 noun acc sing fem	2504.1 conj	1385.4 noun acc sing fem	1385.4 noun acc sing fem	2504.1 conj	4940.4 noun acc sing fem	1706.1 prep
⸂ τιμὴν	καὶ	δόξαν,	[☆ δόξαν	καὶ	τιμὴν]	ἐν
timēn	*kai*	*doxan*	*doxan*	*kai*	*timēn*	*en*
honor	and	glory,	[glory	and	honor]	in

597.3 noun dat sing fem	2400.2 name masc	5382.2 name gen masc	3614.6 rel-pron acc sing masc	3620.2 partic	3471.20 verb nom pl masc part perf act
ἀποκαλύψει	Ἰησοῦ	Χριστοῦ·	8. ὃν	οὐκ	⸂ εἰδότες
apokalupsei	*Iēsou*	*Christou*	*hon*	*ouk*	*eidotes*
revelation	of Jesus	Christ,	whom	not	having seen

8.a.**Txt:** 02A,018K,020L 025P,byz.bo.Sod
Var: p72,01ℵ,03B,04C it.sa.Lach,Treg,Alf Word,Tisc,We/Ho,Weis UBS/☆

1481.17 verb nom pl masc part aor act	25.1 verb 2pl pres act	1519.1 prep	3614.6 rel-pron acc sing masc	732.1 adv	3231.1 partic
[a☆ ἰδόντες]	ἀγαπᾶτε,	εἰς	ὃν	ἄρτι	μὴ
idontes	*agapate*	*eis*	*hon*	*arti*	*mē*
[idem]	you love;	on	whom	now	not

3571.7 verb nom pl masc part pres act	3961.13 verb nom pl masc part pres act	1156.2 conj	21.2 verb 2pl pres mid	5315.3 noun dat sing fem
ὁρῶντες,	πιστεύοντες	δὲ,	ἀγαλλιᾶσθε	χαρᾷ
horōntes	*pisteuontes*	*de*	*agalliasthe*	*chara*
looking,	believing,	but	you rejoice	with joy

410.1 adj dat sing fem	2504.1 conj	1386.27 verb dat sing fem part perf mid	2837.2 verb nom pl masc part pres mid
ἀνεκλαλήτῳ	καὶ	δεδοξασμένῃ,	9. κομιζόμενοι
aneklalētō	*kai*	*dedoxasmenē*	*komizomenoi*
inexpressible	and	having been glorified,	receiving

9.a.**Txt:** 01ℵ,02A,04C 018K,020L,025P,byz.bo. Tisc,Sod
Var: 03B,We/Ho,Weis UBS/☆

3450.16 art sing neu	4904.1 noun sing neu	3450.10 art gen sing fem	3963.2 noun gen sing fem	5050.2 prs-pron gen 2pl	4843.3 noun acc sing fem
τὸ	τέλος	τῆς	πίστεως	⸂a ὑμῶν, ⸃	σωτηρίαν
to	*telos*	*tēs*	*pisteōs*	*humōn*	*sōtērian*
the	end	of the	faith	your,	salvation

5425.6 noun gen pl fem	3875.1 prep	3614.10 rel-pron gen sing fem	4843.2 noun gen sing fem	1554.3 verb 3pl indic aor act
ψυχῶν·	10. Περὶ	ἧς	σωτηρίας	ἐξεζήτησαν
psuchōn	*Peri*	*hēs*	*sōtērias*	*exezētēsan*
of souls;	concerning	which	salvation	sought out

2504.1 conj	1813.1 verb 3pl indic aor act	4254.4 noun nom pl masc	3450.7 art nom pl masc	3875.1 prep	3450.10 art gen sing fem	1519.1 prep
καὶ	ἐξηρεύνησαν	προφῆται	οἱ	περὶ	τῆς	εἰς
kai	*exēreunēsan*	*prophētai*	*hoi*	*peri*	*tēs*	*eis*
and	searched out	prophets,	the	of	the	toward

5050.4 prs-pron acc 2pl	5322.2 noun gen sing fem	4253.12 verb nom pl masc part aor act	2028.4 verb nom pl masc part pres act	1519.1 prep
ὑμᾶς	χάριτος	προφητεύσαντες,	11. ἐρευνῶντες	εἰς
humas	*charitos*	*prophēteusantes*	*ereunōntes*	*eis*
you	grace	having prophesied;	searching	to

Peter himself knew something about persecution, both religious and political. He had suffered at the hands both of the Sanhedrin and of Herod Agrippa I, and he had failed the test on one occasion (Luke 22:54-62). But he had recovered, and he was able to strengthen his brethren through this epistle, encouraging them and exhorting them that their "faith fail not" (Luke 22:32).

1:8. The believers had not seen Jesus, but their faith was in Him and they loved Him, so they shared the blessing Jesus promised when He said to Thomas, "Blessed are they that have not seen, and yet have believed" (John 20:29). Since Peter was present when those words were spoken, it is not surprising that he should mention their love for Him whom they have never seen and their belief in Him whom they could not see now.

Peter spoke approvingly of their rejoicing in Jesus Christ. They were jubilant with joy unspeakable and full of "glory" (*dedoxasmenē*, brightness, radiance, splendor, majesty). This word is used of the "glory" of Moses' countenance which shone so brightly the people could not gaze upon it (2 Corinthians 3:7). The joy of salvation is unutterable, indescribable; the Greek word *aneklalētō* does not appear elsewhere in the New Testament although the Authorized Version translates two other words as "unspeakable" in 2 Corinthians 9:15 and 12:4.

1:9. The "salvation" (*sōtērian*, deliverance, preservation, wholeness) Peter wrote of is not conversion but the ultimate fullness of redemption. His readers were already receiving a foretaste of this final salvation of their "souls" (*psuchōn*, whole beings), which is the "end" (*telos*, goal, culmination) of their faith. It is "the grace that is to be brought unto you at the revelation of Jesus Christ" (1:13). This full salvation, which their faith would lead to in the end, actually was theirs all the way to that end, while they appropriated it by faith.

1:10. Peter said the prophets wrote of this salvation. This would reassure the believers, especially the converted Jews who had a profound trust in the Old Testament. The prophets spoke of "the grace that should come unto you" (the grace meant for you), but they did not know what this meant. They were puzzled to understand this gospel of grace which seemed to make their religion of good works and sin offerings outdated, though they "inquired" (*exezētēsan*, sought out, investigated) and "searched diligently" (*exēreunēsan*, explored carefully). John Wesley says of their inquiry, "like miners searching after precious ore, (they searched) after the meaning of the prophecies which they delivered."

though it be tried with fire: . . . be approved by fire-testing, *Wuest* . . . yet, being tested by, *Concordant.*

might be found unto praise and honour and glory at the appearing of Jesus Christ: . . . may redound, *Montgomery* . . . may be discovered after scrutiny to result in, *Wuest* . . . may be found in approval, rectification, and honour and distinction, *Fenton* . . . may be found for applause and glory, *Concordant* . . . when Jesus Christ is revealed, *Berkeley.*

8. Whom having not seen, ye love: You never met him, *Noli* . . . although you have never seen Him, *Williams* . . . not perceiving, *Concordant* . . . because of His preciousness, *Wuest.*

in whom, though now ye see [him] not, yet believing: . . . not seeing at present, *Concordant* . . . have faith in him, *Laubach.*

ye rejoice with joy unspeakable and full of glory: . . . you feel a joy and a glory beyond words to tell, *Laubach* . . . and exult with a triumphant happiness too great for words, *TCNT* . . . inexpressible and glorious, *Wilson* . . . anticipating delight, *Fenton* . . . exalted, *Norlie* . . . glorified, *Wuest.*

9. Receiving the end of your faith: . . . upon the occasion of you receiving, *Wuest* . . . being requited, *Concordant* . . . obtaining the issue of, *Wilson* . . . which is the purpose of, *Adams* . . . the goal of believing, *SEB* . . . the promised consummation, *Wuest* . . . of your faith, *Concordant.*

[even] the salvation of [your] souls: . . . which is the final salvation of, *Wuest.*

10. Of which salvation the prophets have inquired and searched diligently: Concerning which salvation the prophets seek out, *Concordant* . . . prophets conducted an exhaustive inquiry and search, *Wuest* . . . sought out and investigated, *Wilson.*

who prophesied of the grace [that should come] unto you: . . . who predicted in advance, *Wade* . . . concerning the grace which is for you, *Concordant* . . . the particular grace destined for you, *Wuest* . . . of the blessing intended for you, *Berkeley.*

1 Peter 1:12

4949.1	2211.1	4029.1	2511.4	1207.6	3450.16
intr-pron	conj	intr-pron sing	noun acc sing masc	verb 3sing indic imperf act	art sing neu
τίνα	ἢ	ποῖον	καιρὸν	ἐδήλου	τὸ
tina	*ē*	*poion*	*kairon*	*edēlou*	*to*
what	or	what manner of	time	was signifying	the

1706.1	840.2	4011.1	5382.2	4162.1
prep	prs-pron dat pl	noun sing neu	name gen masc	verb sing neu part pres mid
ἐν	αὐτοῖς	πνεῦμα	Χριστοῦ,	προμαρτυρόμενον
en	*autois*	*pneuma*	*Christou*	*promarturomenon*
in	them	Spirit	of Christ,	testifying beforehand of

3450.17	1519.1	5382.4	3667.2	2504.1	3450.15	3196.3
art pl neu	prep	name acc masc	noun pl neu	conj	art acc pl fem	prep
τὰ	εἰς	Χριστὸν	παθήματα,	καὶ	τὰς	μετὰ
ta	*eis*	*Christon*	*pathēmata*	*kai*	*tas*	*meta*
the	to	Christ	sufferings,	and	the	after

3642.18	1385.5	3614.4	596.7	3617.1	3620.1
dem-pron pl neu	noun acc pl fem	rel-pron dat pl	verb 3sing indic aor pass	conj	partic
ταῦτα	δόξας	12. οἷς	ἀπεκαλύφθη	ὅτι	οὐχ
tauta	*doxas*	*hois*	*apekaluphthē*	*hoti*	*ouch*
these	glories;	to whom	it was revealed,	that	not

12.a.**Txt:** 018K,byz.bo.
Var: 01ℵ,02A,03B,04C 020L,025P,Gries,Lach Treg,Alf,Word,Tisc We/Ho,Weis,Sod UBS/☆

1431.7	2231.3	5050.3	1156.2	1241.16
prs-pron dat pl masc	prs-pron dat 1pl	prs-pron dat 2pl	conj	verb 3pl indic imperf act
ἑαυτοῖς,	ʻ ἡμῖν	[a☆ ὑμῖν]	δὲ	διηκόνουν
heautois	*hēmin*	*humin*	*de*	*diēkonoun*
to themselves,	to us	[to you]	but	were serving

840.16	3614.17	3431.1	310.10	5050.3	1217.2
prs-pron pl neu	rel-pron pl neu	adv	verb 3sing indic aor pass	prs-pron dat 2pl	prep
αὐτά,	ἃ	νῦν	ἀνηγγέλη	ὑμῖν	διὰ
auta	*ha*	*nun*	*anēngelē*	*humin*	*dia*
them,	which	now	were announced	to you	by

12.b.**Txt:** 01ℵ,04C,025P byz.
Var: p72,02A,03B,044 33,623-org,1852,2464 We/Ho

3450.1	2076.23	5050.4	1706.1
art gen pl	verb gen pl masc part aor mid	prs-pron acc 2pl	prep
τῶν	εὐαγγελισαμένων	ὑμᾶς	/b ἐν \
tōn	*euangelisamenōn*	*humas*	*en*
the	having announced the good news to	you	by

4011.3	39.3	643.27	570.2	3636.2	1519.1
noun dat sing neu	adj dat sing	verb dat sing neu part aor pass	prep	noun gen sing masc	prep
πνεύματι	ἁγίῳ	ἀποσταλέντι	ἀπ'	οὐρανοῦ,	εἰς
pneumati	*hagiō*	*apostalenti*	*ap'*	*ouranou*	*eis*
Spirit	Holy	having been sent	from	heaven,	into

3614.17	1922.4	32.5	3740.3	1346.1
rel-pron pl neu	verb 3pl indic pres act	noun nom pl masc	verb inf aor act	conj
ἃ	ἐπιθυμοῦσιν	ἄγγελοι	παρακύψαι.	13. Διὸ
ha	*epithumousin*	*angeloi*	*parakupsai*	*Dio*
which	desire	angels	to look.	Wherefore

326.1	3450.15	3613.5	3450.10	1265.1	5050.2
verb nom pl masc part aor mid	art acc pl fem	noun acc pl fem	art gen sing fem	noun gen sing fem	prs-pron gen 2pl
ἀναζωσάμενοι	τὰς	ὀσφύας	τῆς	διανοίας	ὑμῶν,
anazōsamenoi	*tas*	*osphuas*	*tēs*	*dianoias*	*humōn*
having girded up	the	loins	of the	mind	your,

3387.3	4898.1	1666.8	1894.3	3450.12	5179.26
verb nom pl masc part pres act	adv	verb 2pl impr aor act	prep	art acc sing fem	verb acc sing fem part pres mid
νήφοντες,	τελείως	ἐλπίσατε	ἐπὶ	τὴν	φερομένην
nēphontes	*teleiōs*	*elpisate*	*epi*	*tēn*	*pheromenēn*
being sober,	perfectly	hope	in	the	being brought

1:11. The Spirit of Christ in the Old Testament prophets was the Holy Ghost, as made clear in 2 Peter 1:21 (they spoke "as they were moved by the Holy Ghost"). The Third Person of the Trinity has many names, including Spirit of God, Spirit of the Lord, Spirit of His Son, Spirit of Truth, Holy Spirit of God, Comforter, and Promise of the Father. The Spirit within the prophets foretold the sufferings of Christ and the glories (plural) that should follow His sufferings. The prophets sought to know "what (time), or what manner of time" (*eis tina ē poion kairon*) the Spirit "did signify" (*edēlou*, did disclose, point toward). They knew what they were prophesying but not at what time these messianic prophecies would be fulfilled. God only reveals to His servants what they need to know in order that they might be able to trust Him for what they do not know. His faithfulness in the past gives assurance that He will provide all they need in the present and in the future. Like the prophets of old, we do not know all the details of the future, but in His own time God will reveal it unto us, when we no longer "see through a glass, darkly, but then face to face" (1 Corinthians 13:12).

1:12. The prophets could not discover what they sought by searching, but it was revealed to them that their prophecies "did minister" (*diēkonoun*, served), not to themselves but to future believers—to Peter and his peers. Peter reassured believers that the message they had received from preachers like Paul and John was the same gospel the prophets foretold. They prophesied of the things which are now reported to believers by those who have preached the gospel with the same Spirit (whether called Holy Spirit or, as in verse 11, Spirit of Christ) who inspired the prophecies. The Spirit was "sent down from heaven" at Pentecost (see Acts 2:2).

This good news is so wonderful the angels "desire" (*epithumousin*, eagerly long for) to "look into" (*parakupsai*, stoop down and peer into) it. Angels intently watch the plan of redemption unfold, but they cannot participate in it because "Christ died for the ungodly" (Romans 5:6), not for angels.

1:13. In view of their spiritual privileges, Peter called believers to holy living. In those days people wore long, loose robes, and in order to run or do manual work, they had to lift their robes and tuck them in their belts. So Peter directed believers to gird up the "loins" (*osphuas*, hips) of their "mind" (*dianoias*, understanding, comprehension). Since "loins" often denotes procreative powers (as in Acts 2:30; Hebrews 7:5,10), the reference to "loins of your mind" suggests the mind is the procreator of human actions. The thought is father to the deed. Therefore believers should fortify their minds—"having your loins girt about with truth" (Ephesians 6:14). They should "be sober" (*nēphontes*, be alert, self-controlled) and

11. Searching what, or what manner of time the Spirit of Christ which was in them did signify: . . . made inquiry and research to find out, *Berkeley* . . . searching as to what season or character of season the Spirit...was making plain, *Wuest* . . . searching into what or what manner of era the spirit of Christ in them made evident, *Concordant.*

when it testified beforehand the sufferings of Christ: . . . when it predicted the sufferings that were destined for, *Berkeley* . . . surrounding the Messiah, *Fenton.*

and the glory that should follow: . . . which would come after these sufferings, *Wuest* . . . along with them, *Berkeley.*

12. Unto whom it was revealed, that not unto themselves, but unto us they did minister the things: . . . that it was not for their own advantage, *Wade* . . . to you they dispensed them, *Concordant.*

which are now reported unto you by them that have preached the gospel unto you with the Holy Ghost sent down from heaven: . . . were now informed through, *Concordant* . . . who was sent down on a commission from heaven, *Wuest.*

which things the angels desire to look into: . . . into which messengers are yearning to peer, *Concordant* . . . have long wanted to know, *Laubach* . . . have a passionate desire to stoop way down and look into [like the cherubim above the mercy seat who gazed at the sprinkled blood and wondered at its meaning], *Wuest.*

13. Wherefore gird up the loins of your mind: . . . having put out of the way once for all everything that would impede the free action of your mind, *Wuest* . . . of your comprehension, *Concordant* . . . as a means of spiritual preparation, *Williams* . . . get your minds set for action, *Norlie* . . . brace up your minds, and exercise the strictest self-control, *TCNT* . . . keeping level-headed, *Adams* . . . loins of your understanding, *Fenton.*

be sober, and hope to the end for the grace that is to be brought unto you: . . . being vigilant, *Wilson* . . . calm and collected, *Swann* . . . in spirit, *Wuest* . . . expect

5050.3 prs-pron dat 2pl	5322.4 noun acc sing fem	1706.1 prep	597.3 noun dat sing fem	2400.2 name masc	5382.2 name gen masc
ὑμῖν	χάριν	ἐν	ἀποκαλύψει	Ἰησοῦ	Χριστοῦ.
humin	*charin*	*en*	*apokalupsei*	*Iēsou*	*Christou*
to you	grace	at	revelation	of Jesus	Christ;

5453.1 conj	4891.4 noun pl neu	5056.2 noun gen sing fem	3231.1 partic	4816.2 verb nom pl masc part pres mid
14. ὡς	τέκνα	ὑπακοῆς,	μὴ	συσχηματιζόμενοι
hōs	*tekna*	*hupakoēs*	*mē*	*suschēmatizomenoi*
as	children	of obedience,	not	fashioning yourselves

3450.14 art dat pl fem	4245.2 adj comp sing neu	1706.1 prep	3450.11 art dat sing fem	51.2 noun dat sing fem	5050.2 prs-pron gen 2pl	1924.7 noun dat pl fem
ταῖς	πρότερον	ἐν	τῇ	ἀγνοίᾳ	ὑμῶν	ἐπιθυμίαις,
tais	*proteron*	*en*	*tē*	*agnoia*	*humōn*	*epithumiais*
to the	former	in	the	ignorance	your	desires;

233.2 conj	2567.3 prep	3450.6 art acc sing masc	2535.16 verb acc sing masc part aor act	5050.4 prs-pron acc 2pl
15. ἀλλὰ	κατὰ	τὸν	καλέσαντα	ὑμᾶς
alla	*kata*	*ton*	*kalesanta*	*humas*
but	according as	the	having called	you

39.1 adj sing	2504.1 conj	840.7 prs-pron nom pl masc	39.7 adj nom pl masc	1706.1 prep	3820.11 adj dat sing fem	389.2 noun dat sing fem
ἅγιον	καὶ	αὐτοὶ	ἅγιοι	ἐν	πάσῃ	ἀναστροφῇ
hagion	*kai*	*autoi*	*hagioi*	*en*	*pasē*	*anastrophē*
holy,	also	yourselves	holy	in	all	conduct

16.a.**Var:** 03B,We/Ho Weis,Sod,UBS/☆

1090.47 verb 2pl impr aor pass	1354.1 conj	1119.22 verb 3sing indic perf mid	3617.1 conj	39.7 adj nom pl masc
γενήθητε·	**16.** διότι	γέγραπται,	[a☆+ ὅτι]	ʺἍγιοι
genēthēte	*dioti*	*gegraptai*	*hoti*	*Hagioi*
be you;	because	it has been written,		Holy

16.b.**Txt:** 018K,025P,byz. 01ℵ,02A,03B,04C,33 Lach,Treg,Alf,Word Tisc,We/Ho,Weis UBS/☆

1090.48 verb 2pl impr aor mid	1498.42 verb 2pl indic fut mid	3617.1 conj	1466.1 prs-pron nom 1sing	39.5 adj nom sing masc
ʹ γένεσθε,	[b☆ ἔσεσθε,]	ὅτι	ἐγὼ	ἅγιος
genesthe	*esesthe*	*hoti*	*egō*	*hagios*
be you,	[you will be]	because	I	holy

16.c.**Txt:** 02A-corr,04C 018K,020L,025P,byz. Sod **Var:** 01ℵ,02A-org,03B Lach,Treg,Alf,Word Tisc,We/Ho,Weis UBS/☆

1498.2 verb 1sing indic pres act	2504.1 conj	1479.1 conj	3824.4 noun acc sing masc	1926.3 verb 2pl indic pres mid	3450.6 art acc sing masc
ʹc εἰμι. ͵	**17.** Καὶ	εἰ	πατέρα	ἐπικαλεῖσθε	τὸν
eimi	*Kai*	*ei*	*patera*	*epikaleisthe*	*ton*
am.	And	if	Father	you call on	the

672.1 adv	671.1 adv	2892.10 verb acc sing masc part pres act
ʹ ἀπροσωπολήπτως	[☆ ἀπροσωπολήμπτως]	κρίνοντα
aprosōpolēptōs	*aprosōpolēmptōs*	*krinonta*
impartially	[idem]	judging

2567.3 prep	3450.16 art sing neu	1524.2 adj gen sing	2024.1 noun sing neu	1706.1 prep	5238.3 noun dat sing masc
κατὰ	τὸ	ἑκάστου	ἔργον,	ἐν	φόβῳ
kata	*to*	*hekastou*	*ergon*	*en*	*phobō*
according to	the	of each	work,	in	fear

3450.6 art acc sing masc	3450.10 art gen sing fem	3802.1 noun gen sing fem	5050.2 prs-pron gen 2pl	5385.4 noun acc sing masc	388.8 verb 2pl impr aor pass
τὸν	τῆς	παροικίας	ὑμῶν	χρόνον	ἀναστράφητε·
ton	*tēs*	*paroikias*	*humōn*	*chronon*	*anastraphēte*
the	of the	stay	your	time	pass you,

they should "hope" (*elpisate*, expect) "to the end" (*teleiōs*, fully, completely) for the grace that is to be brought to them at the revelation of Jesus Christ.

1:14. As "obedient children" of their Heavenly Father (*hōs tekna hupakoēs*, children of obedience, in contrast to "the children of disobedience" in Ephesians 2:2), believers are to be holy, no longer "fashioning" themselves (from *suschēmatizō*, to conform, as in Romans 12:2) according to the former "lusts" (*epithumiais*, strong desires). Formerly in their "ignorance" (*agnoia*, lack of knowledge) they indulged their natural cravings, but now they are enlightened.

1:15. "Be ye holy" is an imperative, a solemn command. Peter told believers that God who called them is "holy" (*hagion*, pure, blameless), and He is to be their standard or pattern in all "manner of conversation" (*anastrophē*, manner of life, behavior).

1:16. Peter called upon believers' reverence for the Old Testament by referring to Leviticus 19:2, "Ye shall be holy: for I the Lord your God am holy." He says, "It is written" (*gegraptai*, it stands written). The written Word has special force, particularly the Scriptures. This was Christ's defense when tempted by the devil: "It is written" (Luke 4:4).

1:17. The Father, "without respect of persons" (*aprosōpolēptōs*, without partiality), judges "according to every man's work" (*kata to hekastou ergon*, according to the deed of each one). Therefore, if believers wish to call on God the Father, they should monitor their conduct and spend the time of their "sojourning" (from *paroikeō*, dwell as strangers as in Acts 13:17, reside as foreigners) here "in fear" (*phobō*, reverence). As a son fears his father and obeys him, knowing he will be disciplined if he fails to do so, believers should fear the Lord and keep His commandments; but they do not obey Him simply because they are afraid to do otherwise. They keep His commandments because they love Him (John 14:15), and they love Him because He first loved them (1 John 4:19).

Peter emphasized that believers are only "sojourning" on this earth as "strangers and pilgrims" (2:11). They are mere visitors on this planet, passing through as pilgrims en route like Abraham to their permanent home in that "city which hath foundations, whose builder and maker is God" (Hebrews 11:10). Since they are bound for a holy place they should be holy people. They should not fix their hearts on worldly things or copy the people of this world, for it is not their native country.

perfectly, *Concordant* . . . set your hope, *Clementson* . . . with perfect stedfastness, *Darby* . . . which will be offered, *Noli.*

at the revelation of Jesus Christ: . . . upon the occasion of the revelation, *Wuest* . . . at the unveiling of Jesus Christ, *Williams, Concordant.*

14. As obedient children, not fashioning yourselves: Do not obey those low passions, *Laubach* . . . let your lives be shaped, *TCNT* . . . not configuring, *Concordant* . . . stop molding your character, *Williams* . . . assuming an outward expression, *Wuest.*

according to the former lusts in your ignorance: . . . you formerly had in the ignorance of your passionate desires, *Wuest* . . . desires you used to cherish, *Williams* . . . cravings, *Swann* . . . passions which once swayed you, *TCNT* . . . ruled you when you did not know what was right, *Laubach.*

15. But as he which hath called you is holy: . . . but, according as, *Concordant* . . . after the pattern of the One who called you, *Wuest.*

so be ye holy in all manner of conversation: . . . become holy persons in every kind of behavior, *Wuest.*

16. Because it is written: This is exactly what Scripture teaches, *Norlie* . . . and is on record, *Wuest.*

Be ye holy; for I am holy: Become holy, *Fenton* . . . You must be holy, *SEB* . . . You be holy individuals, because, as for myself, *Wuest.*

17. And if ye call on the Father: . . . be careful to approach Him reverently, *Norlie* . . . invoking, *Concordant.*

who without respect of persons: . . . impartially judges, *Wilson* . . . fair to each, *SEB.*

judgeth according to every man's work: . . . impartially by their actions, *Noli.*

pass the time of your sojourning [here] in fear: . . . you may behave, for the time, *Concordant* . . . during your residence as aliens, *Adams* . . . your homelessness, *Swann* . . . your service in reverence, *Fenton* . . . your fleeting stay, *Williams.*

3471.20 verb nom pl masc part perf act	3617.1 conj	3620.3 partic	5186.4 adj dat pl neu	688.3 noun dat sing neu
18. εἰδότες	ὅτι	οὐ	φθαρτοῖς,	ἀργυρίῳ
eidotes	*hoti*	*ou*	*phthartois*	*arguriō*
knowing	that	not	by corruptible things,	by silver

2211.1 conj	5388.3 noun dat sing neu	3056.2 verb 2pl indic aor pass	1523.2 prep gen	3450.10 art gen sing fem	3124.4 adj gen sing fem
ἢ	χρυσίῳ,	ἐλυτρώθητε	ἐκ	τῆς	ματαίας
ē	*chrusiō*	*elutrōthēte*	*ek*	*tēs*	*mataias*
or	by gold,	you were redeemed	from	the	vain

5050.2 prs-pron gen 2pl	389.1 noun gen sing fem	3832.1 adj gen sing fem	233.2 conj
ὑμῶν	ἀναστροφῆς	πατροπαραδότου,	19. ἀλλὰ
humōn	*anastrophēs*	*patroparadotou*	*alla*
your	manner of life	handed down from fathers,	but

4941.1 adj dat sing	129.3 noun dat sing neu	5453.1 conj	284.2 noun gen sing masc	297.1 adj gen sing masc	2504.1 conj
τιμίῳ	αἵματι	ὡς	ἀμνοῦ	ἀμώμου	καὶ
timiō	*haimati*	*hōs*	*amnou*	*amōmou*	*kai*
by precious	blood	as	of a lamb	without blemish	and

778.2 adj gen sing masc	5382.2 name gen masc	4126.3 verb gen sing masc part perf mid	3173.1 conj	4112.1 prep
ἀσπίλου	Χριστοῦ˙	20. προεγνωσμένου	μὲν	πρὸ
aspilou	*Christou*	*proegnōsmenou*	*men*	*pro*
without spot	of Christ:	having been foreknown	indeed	before

2573.1 noun gen sing fem	2862.2 noun gen sing masc	5157.14 verb gen sing masc part aor pass	1156.2 conj	1894.2 prep	2057.1 adj gen pl
καταβολῆς	κόσμου,	φανερωθέντος	δὲ	ἐπ'	ʻ ἐσχάτων
katabolēs	*kosmou*	*phanerōthentos*	*de*	*ep'*	*eschatōn*
foundation	of world,	being manifested	but	at	last

2057.2 adj gen sing	3450.1 art gen pl	5385.5 noun gen pl masc	1217.1 prep	5050.4 prs-pron acc 2pl
[a☆ ἐσχάτου]	τῶν	χρόνων	δι'	ὑμᾶς,
eschatou	*tōn*	*chronōn*	*di'*	*humas*
[idem]	the	times	for the sake of	you,

20.a.**Txt:** 018K,020L 025P,byz.sa.
Var: 01ℵ,02A,03B,04C 33,bo.Lach,Treg,Alf Word,Tisc,We/Ho,Weis Sod,UBS/☆

3450.8 art acc pl masc	1217.1 prep	840.3 prs-pron gen sing	3961.15 verb acc pl masc part pres act	3964.9 adj acc pl masc
21. τοὺς	δι'	αὐτοῦ	ʻ πιστεύοντας	[a☆ πιστοὺς]
tous	*di'*	*autou*	*pisteuontas*	*pistous*
the	by	him	believing	[idem]

21.a.**Txt:** 01ℵ,04C,018K 020L,025P,byz.Sod
Var: 02A,03B,Lach Treg,Alf,Tisc,We/Ho Weis,UBS/☆

1519.1 prep	2296.4 noun acc sing masc	3450.6 art acc sing masc	1446.9 verb acc sing masc part aor act	840.6 prs-pron acc sing masc	1523.2 prep gen
εἰς	θεὸν,	τὸν	ἐγείραντα	αὐτὸν	ἐκ
eis	*theon*	*ton*	*egeiranta*	*auton*	*ek*
in	God,	the	being raised up	him	from among

3361.2 adj gen pl	2504.1 conj	1385.4 noun acc sing fem	840.4 prs-pron dat sing	1319.30 verb acc sing masc part aor act	5452.1 conj
νεκρῶν,	καὶ	δόξαν	αὐτῷ	δόντα,	ὥστε
nekrōn	*kai*	*doxan*	*autō*	*donta*	*hōste*
dead,	and	glory	to him	having given,	so as for

3450.12 art acc sing fem	3963.4 noun acc sing fem	5050.2 prs-pron gen 2pl	2504.1 conj	1667.4 noun acc sing fem	1498.32 verb inf pres act	1519.1 prep
τὴν	πίστιν	ὑμῶν	καὶ	ἐλπίδα	εἶναι	εἰς
tēn	*pistin*	*humōn*	*kai*	*elpida*	*einai*	*eis*
the	faith	your	and	hope	to be	in

1:18. Peter pointed to a further incentive to holy living beyond the holiness and justice of God by stressing the high cost of redemption. He reminded believers they were not redeemed with "corruptible" things (*phthartois,* decayed, perishable) such as silver and gold. If silver and gold were the ransom price, Peter would not have been set free, for he said, "Silver and gold have I none" (Acts 3:6). Slaves were set free by silver and gold, but a greater price was required to redeem believers from the "vain" (*mataias,* empty, profitless) "conversation" (*anastrophēs,* life-style, behavior) they had received by tradition from their fathers. Christ and His apostles taught a life-style superior to that followed by any non-Christians, whether they were Jews or Gentiles.

1:19. The ransom price was the "precious" (*timiō,* most valuable) blood of Christ. As a lamb brought to the slaughter (Isaiah 53:7), He was "without blemish" (*amōmou,* faultless, without blame) and "without spot" (*aspilou,* unstained), fitting the requirements of the Paschal Lamb (see Exodus 12:5). The "Lamb of God" (John 1:29,36) must be perfect. Any lesser sacrifice would be unacceptable (see Leviticus 22:20).

1:20. The messiahship of Jesus was foreordained (or foreseen by God) before the "foundation" (*katabolēs,* founding) of the "world" (*kosmou,* world order). Christ's advent was no afterthought (see Revelation 13:8). It was known from the beginning by both the Father and the preincarnate Son, but they waited for "the fulness of the time" (Galatians 4:4) to put the great plan of redemption into action. Peter said Christ was "manifest" (*phanerōthentos,* made apparent, incarnated) in these "last times" (*eschatōn tōn chronōn,* at the end of time) for the sake of believers ("you"). Jesus was chosen for this mission before the world began, and the believers to whom Peter wrote were "a chosen generation" (1 Peter 2:9).

1:21. Through Christ they have been made believers in God, the One who "raised" (*egeiranta,* awakened, lifted up) Jesus from the dead and who gave Him "glory" (*doxan,* honor, acclaim). Peter emphasized repeatedly how God raised His Son and restored to Him the glory and full expression of His deity He enjoyed before the world was and for which He prayed in the Garden (John 17:5). In his address in Solomon's Porch Peter told how God had glorified His Son Jesus (Acts 3:13). He elaborated on this in his Pentecost sermon (Acts 2:33-36) and mentioned it again when brought before the Council (Acts 5:31). Because Christ was raised and glorified, their "faith" (*pistin,* reliance, assurance) and "hope" (*elpida,* confident expectation) is in God.

18. Forasmuch as ye know that ye were not redeemed with corruptible things, [as] silver and gold: . . . knowing as you do, that not by means of perishable things, little coins, *Wuest* . . . it was not by perishable valuables, *Wade* . . . you were not bought and made free, *NLT.*

from your vain conversation [received] by tradition from your fathers: . . . from the useless behavior patterns, *Adams* . . . your useless ways such as traditionally came down from your forefathers, *Berkeley* . . . from the slavery of your ancestral follies, *Fenton* . . . from your foolish behavior, *Campbell* . . . vain behavior, handed down, *Concordant* . . . transmitted to you from, *Wade* . . . your futile manner of life handed down from generation to generation, *Wuest* . . . your ancestors, *Montgomery.*

19. But with the precious blood of Christ: . . . with Christ's valuable blood, *Adams* . . . the costly blood, *Wuest.*

as of a lamb without blemish and without spot: . . . like that of a perfect lamb, *SEB* . . . without stain, *Norlie* . . . unblemished and immaculate, *Noli* . . . a flawless and unspotted lamb, *Concordant.*

20. Who verily was foreordained before the foundation of the world: . . . provided, *Berkeley* . . . designated in advance, *Wade* . . . foreknown, indeed, before the disruption of the world, *Concordant* . . . before the foundation of the universe was laid, *Wuest.*

but was manifest in these last times for you: . . . disclosed at the end of times, *Berkeley* . . . visibly manifested at the closing years of the times for your sake, *Wuest* . . . for your sakes He has been revealed, *Norlie* . . . at the extremity of the ages, *Fenton.*

21. Who by him do believe in God, that raised him up from the dead, and gave him glory: . . . who rouses Him...and is giving Him glory, *Concordant.*

that your faith and hope might be in God: . . . and expectation is to be, *Concordant* . . . rest in God, *Berkeley.*

1 Peter 1:22

2296.4 noun acc sing masc	3450.15 art acc pl fem	5425.8 noun acc pl fem	5050.2 prs-pron gen 2pl	47.4 verb nom pl masc part perf act
θεόν.	22. Τὰς	ψυχὰς	ὑμῶν	ἡγνικότες
theon	*Tas*	*psuchas*	*humōn*	*hēgnikotes*
God.	The	souls	your	having purified

22.a.**Txt:** 018K,020L 025P,byz.
Var: p72,01ℵ,02A,03B 04C,33,sa.bo.Lach,Treg Alf,Word,Tisc,We/Ho Weis,Sod,UBS/☆

1706.1 prep	3450.11 art dat sing fem	5056.3 noun dat sing fem	3450.10 art gen sing fem	223.2 noun gen sing fem	1217.2 prep
ἐν	τῇ	ὑπακοῇ	τῆς	ἀληθείας	(a διὰ
en	*tē*	*hupakoē*	*tēs*	*alētheias*	*dia*
by	the	obedience	to the	truth	through

4011.2 noun gen sing neu	1519.1 prep	5197.4 noun acc sing fem	502.4 adj acc sing fem	1523.2 prep gen
πνεύματος)	εἰς	φιλαδελφίαν	ἀνυπόκριτον,	ἐκ
pneumatos	*eis*	*philadelphian*	*anupokriton*	*ek*
Spirit	to	brotherly love	unfeigned,	out of

22.b.**Txt:** p72,01ℵ-org 04C,018K,020L,025P 33,byz.sa.bo.Sod
Var: 02A,03B,it.Lach Treg,Alf,Tisc,We/Ho Weis,UBS/☆

2485.7 adj gen sing fem	2559.1 noun fem	238.3 prs-pron acc pl masc	25.18 verb 2pl impr aor act	1605.1 adv
(b καθαρᾶς)	καρδίας	ἀλλήλους	ἀγαπήσατε	ἐκτενῶς·
katharas	*kardias*	*allēlous*	*agapēsate*	*ektenōs*
pure	a heart	one another	love you	fervently.

311.2 verb nom pl masc part perf mid	3620.2 partic	1523.2 prep gen	4554.1 noun gen sing fem	5186.3 adj gen sing fem
23. ἀναγεγεννημένοι	οὐκ	ἐκ	σπορᾶς	φθαρτῆς,
anagegennēmenoi	*ouk*	*ek*	*sporas*	*phthartēs*
Having been begotten again,	not	of	seed	corruptible,

233.2 conj	855.1 adj gen sing	1217.2 prep	3030.2 noun gen sing masc	2180.11 verb gen sing part pres act	2296.2 noun gen sing masc
ἀλλὰ	ἀφθάρτου,	διὰ	λόγου	ζῶντος	θεοῦ
alla	*aphthartou*	*dia*	*logou*	*zōntos*	*theou*
but	of incorruptible,	by	word	living	of God

23.a.**Txt:** 018K,020L 025P,byz.
Var: p72,01ℵ,02A,03B 04C,33,sa.bo.Gries,Lach Treg,Alf,Word,Tisc We/Ho,Weis,Sod UBS/☆

2504.1 conj	3176.11 verb gen sing masc part pres act	1519.1 prep	3450.6 art acc sing masc	163.3 noun acc sing masc	1354.1 conj
καὶ	μένοντος	(a εἰς	τὸν	αἰῶνα.)	24. διότι
kai	*menontos*	*eis*	*ton*	*aiōna*	*dioti*
and	abiding	to	the	age.	Because

24.a.**Txt:** p72,01ℵ-org 03B,04C,025P,049,byz.
Var: 01ℵ-corr2,02A,044 33,323,614,945,1241 1505,1739,2495

3820.9 adj nom sing fem	4418.1 noun nom sing fem	5453.1 conj	5363.1 noun nom sing masc	2504.1 conj	3820.9 adj nom sing fem
πᾶσα	σὰρξ	(a ὡς)	χόρτος,	καὶ	πᾶσα
pasa	*sarx*	*hōs*	*chortos*	*kai*	*pasa*
all	flesh	as	grass,	and	all

24.b.**Txt:** 018K,020L 025P,byz.
Var: p72,01ℵ-corr,02A 03B,04C,Gries,Lach Treg,Alf,Word,Tisc We/Ho,Weis,Sod UBS/☆

1385.1 noun nom sing fem	442.2 noun gen sing masc	840.10 prs-pron gen sing fem	5453.1 conj	436.1 noun sing neu	5363.2 noun gen sing masc
δόξα	(ἀνθρώπου	[b☆ αὐτῆς]	ὡς	ἄνθος	χόρτου.
doxa	*anthrōpou*	*autēs*	*hōs*	*anthos*	*chortou*
glory	of man	[its]	as	flower	of grass.

3445.3 verb 3sing indic aor pass	3450.5 art nom sing masc	5363.1 noun nom sing masc	2504.1 conj	3450.16 art sing neu	436.1 noun sing neu
ἐξηράνθη	ὁ	χόρτος,	καὶ	τὸ	ἄνθος
exēranthē	*ho*	*chortos*	*kai*	*to*	*anthos*
Withered	the	grass,	and	the	flower

24.c.**Txt:** 04C,018K 020L,025P,byz.
Var: 01ℵ,02A,03B,33 Lach,Treg,Word,Tisc We/Ho,Weis,Sod UBS/☆

840.3 prs-pron gen sing	1588.3 verb 3sing indic aor act	3450.16 art sing neu	1156.2 conj	4343.1 noun sing neu	2935.2 noun gen sing masc
(c αὐτοῦ)	ἐξέπεσεν·	25. τὸ	δὲ	ῥῆμα	κυρίου
autou	*exepesen*	*to*	*de*	*rhēma*	*kuriou*
of it	fell away;	the	but	word	of Lord

1:22. Believers have "purified" (*hēgnikotes,* sanctified, made clean) their souls in obeying the truth through the Spirit (see 1:2), as evidenced by their "unfeigned love of the brethren" (*philadelphian,* fraternal affection, brotherly kindness). There is cleansing power in God's truth as it is believed and obeyed. "Brotherly kindness" (*philadelphian*) is mentioned again in 2 Peter 1:7. Peter also mentioned a greater kind of love. He urged them to "love" (*agapēsate*) one another "fervently" (*ektenōs,* intently, earnestly, as also in 4:8). Whereas *philadelphia* is a love based on sentiment, *agapē* is a love based on principle and duty.

Believers love Christ (1:8), and they also love their brethren. In doing this they fulfill God's original purpose for His people: "Thou shalt love the Lord thy God with all thy heart . . . and thy neighbor as thyself" (Luke 10:27).

1:23. Peter's statement that the Word of God "liveth and abideth for ever" is repeated in 1:25. Believers are born of that incorruptible Word (as stated also in James 1:18). They have been "born again" (*anagegennēmenoi,* begotten again, as in 1 Peter 1:3), not by "corruptible seed" (*sporas phthartēs,* parental seed that is perishable), but by the everlasting Word (*logou,* utterance, communication, particularly the Divine Expression as in John 1:1,14; 1 John 1:1; 5:7; Revelation 19:13). They can obey the truth and love one another (1:22) because they have had this new spiritual birth. They no longer have empty, worthless lives like their natural fathers (1:18), for they have been born again into a new family and now they are the children of God.

The holy Scriptures are also the Word of God. When a sinner comes seeking salvation, his faith must be based on what they promise. "Faith cometh by hearing, and hearing by the word of God" (Romans 10:17).

1:24. Peter contrasted the frailty of human nature with the enduring character of God's Word by referring to Isaiah 40:8: "The grass withereth, the flower fadeth: but the word of our God shall stand for ever." All "flesh" (*sarx,* physical being, human nature) is as grass, and all the "glory" (*doxa,* dignity, honor) of man as the "flower" (*anthos,* blossom) of grass. The grass "withereth" (*exērranthē,* shrivels, dries up) and its blossom "falleth away" (*exepesen,* drops off).

1:25. The life of grass is very brief and the life of its blossom is even shorter. That is what man is like, even if he be rich (see James 1:11). But the "word" (*rhēma,* utterances, sayings) of the Lord "endureth" (*menei,* abides, remains) forever. This imperishable

22. Seeing ye have purified your souls in obeying the truth: With your souls purified by obeying the truth, *Berkeley* . . . by means of, *Wuest* . . . the obedience of truth, *Concordant.*

through the Spirit unto unfeigned love of the brethren: . . . resulting in not an assumed but a genuine affection and fondness, *Wuest* . . . that issues into unpretended love of the brotherhood, *Berkeley* . . . unfeigned fondness, *Concordant* . . . a genuine brotherly affection, *TCNT* . . . without hypocrisy, *Montgomery* . . . with sincere brotherly affection, *Fenton* . . . Love one another intensely, *SEB.*

[see that ye] love one another with a pure heart fervently: . . . out of a true heart earnestly, *Concordant* . . . intensely, *Wilson* . . . you should most cordially and consistently love one another, *Berkeley* . . . from the heart love each other with an intense reciprocal love that springs from your hearts because of your estimation of the preciousness of the brethren, and which is divinely self-sacrificial in its essence, *Wuest.*

23. Being born again, not of corruptible seed, but of incorruptible: . . . having been regenerated, *Concordant* . . . not from a germ that perishes, *Williams* . . . not of perishable seed but of imperishable, *Wuest* . . . an imperishable sperm, *Berkeley.*

by the word of God, which liveth and abideth for ever: . . . living and permanent, *Concordant* . . . through God's Living and Lasting Message, *Wade.*

24. For all flesh [is] as grass: The life of all men, *TCNT* . . . All human life is just like, *Williams.*

and all the glory of man as the flower of grass: . . . and all its glory as a grass flower, *Berkeley.*

The grass withereth, and the flower thereof falleth away: . . . was caused to wither away, *Wuest* . . . the bloom, *Berkeley* . . . The flowers drop off, *Williams.*

25. But the word of the Lord endureth for ever: . . . the Lord's message remains forever, *SEB*

1 Peter 2:1

3176.1 verb 3sing indic pres act	1519.1 prep	3450.6 art acc sing masc	163.3 noun acc sing masc	3642.17 dem-pron sing neu	1156.2 conj
μένει	εἰς	τὸν	αἰῶνα.	Τοῦτο	δέ
menei	*eis*	*ton*	*aiōna*	*Touto*	*de*
abides	to	the	age.	This	but

1498.4 verb 3sing indic pres act	3450.16 art sing neu	4343.1 noun sing neu	3450.16 art sing neu	2076.24 verb sing neu part aor pass
ἐστιν	τὸ	ῥῆμα	τὸ	εὐαγγελισθὲν
estin	*to*	*rhēma*	*to*	*euangelisthen*
is	the	word	the	having been announced

1519.1 prep	5050.4 prs-pron acc 2pl	653.4 verb nom pl masc part aor mid	3631.1 partic	3820.12 adj acc sing fem	2520.4 noun acc sing fem
εἰς	ὑμᾶς.	2:1. Ἀποθέμενοι	οὖν	πᾶσαν	κακίαν
eis	*humas*	*Apothemenoi*	*oun*	*pasan*	*kakian*
to	you.	Having laid aside	therefore	all	malice

2504.1 conj	3820.1 adj	1382.4 noun acc sing masc	2504.1 conj	5110.5 noun acc pl fem	2504.1 conj	5192.6 noun acc pl masc
καὶ	πάντα	δόλον	καὶ	ὑποκρίσεις	καὶ	φθόνους
kai	*panta*	*dolon*	*kai*	*hupokriseis*	*kai*	*phthonous*
and	all	deceit	and	hypocrisies	and	envyings

2504.1 conj	3820.16 adj acc pl fem	2606.2 noun acc pl fem	5453.1 conj	733.1 adj pl neu	1018.3 noun pl neu
καὶ	πάσας	καταλαλιάς,	2. ὡς	ἀρτιγέννητα	βρέφη,
kai	*pasas*	*katalalias*	*hōs*	*artigennēta*	*brephē*
and	all	evil speakings,	as	newborn	babes,

3450.16 art sing neu	3024.2 adj sing neu	96.1 adj sing neu	1044.2 noun sing neu	1955.6 verb 2pl impr aor act
τὸ	λογικὸν	ἄδολον	γάλα	ἐπιποθήσατε,
to	*logikon*	*adolon*	*gala*	*epipothēsate*
the	spiritual	unadulterated	milk	long you after,

2.a.**Var:** 01ℵ,02A,03B 04C,018K,025P,bo. Gries,Lach,Treg,Alf Word,Tisc,We/Ho,Weis Sod,UBS/☆

2419.1 conj	1706.1 prep	840.4 prs-pron dat sing	831.14 verb 2pl subj aor pass	1519.1 prep	4843.3 noun acc sing fem
ἵνα	ἐν	αὐτῷ	αὐξηθῆτε,	[a☆+ εἰς	σωτηρίαν,]
hina	*en*	*autō*	*auxēthēte*	*eis*	*sōtērian*
that	by	it	you may grow,	[unto	salvation,]

3.a.**Txt:** 01ℵ-corr,04C 018K,020L,025P,etc.byz. Sod
Var: 01ℵ-org,02A,03B Lach,Treg,Tisc,We/Ho Weis,UBS/☆

1499.1 conj	1479.1 conj	1083.2 verb 2pl indic aor mid	3617.1 conj	5378.1 adj nom sing masc	3450.5 art nom sing masc
3. ‘ εἴπερ	[a☆ εἰ]	ἐγεύσασθε	ὅτι	χρηστὸς	ὁ
eiper	*ei*	*egeusasthe*	*hoti*	*chrēstos*	*ho*
if indeed	[if]	you did taste	that	good	the

2935.1 noun nom sing masc	4242.1 prep	3614.6 rel-pron acc sing masc	4193.15 verb nom pl masc part pres mid	3012.4 noun acc sing masc
κύριος.	4. πρὸς	ὃν	προσερχόμενοι,	λίθον
kurios	*pros*	*hon*	*proserchomenoi*	*lithon*
Lord.	To	whom	coming,	a stone

2180.9 verb part pres act	5097.3 prep	442.7 noun gen pl masc	3173.1 conj	588.4 verb acc sing masc part perf mid
ζῶντα,	ὑπὸ	ἀνθρώπων	μὲν	ἀποδεδοκιμασμένον,
zōnta	*hupo*	*anthrōpōn*	*men*	*apodedokimasmenon*
living,	by	men	indeed	having been rejected,

3706.2 prep	1156.2 conj	2296.3 noun dat sing masc	1575.1 adj sing	1768.2 adj acc sing masc	2504.1 conj	840.7 prs-pron nom pl masc
παρὰ	δὲ	θεῷ	ἐκλεκτόν,	ἔντιμον,	5. καὶ	αὐτοὶ
para	*de*	*theō*	*eklekton*	*entimon*	*kai*	*autoi*
with	but	God	chosen,	precious,	also	yourselves,

Word finds its expression in the "gospel that has been preached" (*euangelisthen*, good news that has been announced, declared) to them.

2:1. In view of the transitory quality of human life and the permanence of the divine Word, Peter exhorted believers to change their life-style. Instead of giving expression to the elements which characterize carnal nature they should hunger for the Word. They should put away all "malice" (*kakian*, badness, trouble-making) and all "guile" (*dolon*, deceit, subtlety) and "hypocrisies" (*hupokriseis*, pretense) and "envies" (*phthonous*, jealousies, grudges) and all "evil speakings" (*katalalias*, backbitings, defamation).

2:2. Peter called believers to be like newborn babes in their desire or craving for milk. He did not say they should *act* like babes, for the Scriptures repeatedly censor believers who act like children rather than grown men (see 1 Corinthians 3:2; 14:20; 16:13; Ephesians 4:14; 6:10). However, believers should never stop growing toward spiritual maturity. They need the "sincere" (*adolon*, without deceit or subtlety) milk "of the word" (*logikon*, of the utterances, sayings).

Some ancient manuscripts add "unto salvation" at the end of 2:2. This seems to indicate that craving for the milk, the unadulterated Word of God, will produce continuous growth until believers receive the inheritance that will be theirs when Jesus returns.

Peter was not contrasting milk with meat or solid food. Instead he was contrasting the pure milk of the Word with food that is mixed (adulterated) with harmful things. Every false cult needs some other book, tradition, dream, or revelation to establish its doctrines. Believers should continually crave the Word in its simplicity and purity, instead of going off into the speculations of false teachers (Horton, pp.23,24).

2:3. Peter said believers have "tasted" (*eguesasthe*, experienced) that the Lord is "gracious" (*chrēstos*, good, kind). Therefore they should lay aside their old life-style and feed their souls on His Word (2:1,2). They should not be content with a taste but should crave it constantly and keep on growing. Fullness of Christian maturity is a goal for the future.

2:4,5. The metaphor now changes from a growing child to a growing building of which Christ is the foundation stone. Peter spoke of Christ as a living stone. The Jews considered Him as being

. . . the declaration...is remaining for the eon, *Concordant* . . . abides for eternity, *Darby* . . . lives on forever, *Williams.*

And this is the word which by the gospel is preached unto you: . . . which in the declaration of the good news was preached, *Wuest.*

1. Wherefore laying aside all malice, and all guile: Putting off, then, *Concordant* . . . cast off all wickedness, *Noli* . . . Free yourselves, then, from, *TCNT* . . . So once for all get rid of all, *Williams* . . . having stripped from you, *Swann* . . . abandoning all vice, and deceit, *Fenton* . . . Put out of your life hate and lying, *NLT* . . . and every craftiness, *Wuest.*

and hypocrisies, and envies, and all evil speakings: . . . vilifications, *Concordant* . . . slanderings, *Wuest.*

2. As newborn babes, desire the sincere milk of the word: . . . as newborn infants do, intensely yearn for, *Wuest* . . . recently born...the unadulterated milk, *Concordant* . . . long for, *Montgomery* . . . crave for pure spiritual milk, *TCNT.*

that ye may grow thereby: . . . by it you may be nourished and make progress in [your] salvation, *Wuest.*

3. If so be ye have tasted that the Lord [is] gracious: . . . in view of the fact that you tasted that the Lord is...loving and benevolent, *Wuest* . . . kind, *Concordant.*

4. To whom coming, [as unto] a living stone: . . . toward whom we are constantly drawing near, himself in character, *Wuest* . . . approaching, *Concordant.*

disallowed indeed of men: . . . rejected indeed, *Montgomery, Concordant* . . . cast away...as worthless by men, *Darby* . . . repudiated after they had tested Him, *Wuest.*

but chosen of God, [and] precious: . . . but in the sight of God a chosen-out One and highly honored and precious, *Wuest* . . . distinguished in the presence of, *Fenton* . . . choice and valuable, *TNT* . . . held in honor, *Concordant.*

1 Peter 2:6

5453.1 conj	3012.5 noun nom pl masc	2180.13 verb nom pl masc part pres act	3481.14 verb 2pl pres mid	3486.1 noun nom sing masc
ὡς	λίθοι	ζῶντες	οἰκοδομεῖσθε,	οἶκος
hōs	*lithoi*	*zōntes*	*oikodomeisthe*	*oikos*
as	stones	living,	are being built up,	a house

5.a.**Var:** p72,01ℵ,02A 03B,04C,bo.Lach,Treg Alf,Tisc,We/Ho,Weis Sod,UBS/☆

4012.2 adj nom sing masc	1519.1 prep	2382.1 noun sing neu	39.1 adj sing	397.7 verb inf aor act
πνευματικὸς	[a☆+ εἰς]	ἱεράτευμα	ἅγιον,	ἀνενέγκαι
pneumatikos	*eis*	*hierateuma*	*hagion*	*anenenkai*
spiritual,	[into]	a priesthood	holy	to offer

5.b.**Txt:** 01ℵ-corr,018K 020L,025P,byz.Sod **Var:** 01ℵ-org,02A,03B 04C,Lach,Treg,Alf,Tisc We/Ho,Weis,UBS/☆

4012.7 adj acc pl fem	2355.1 noun fem	2124.2 adj acc pl fem	3450.3 art dat sing	2296.3 noun dat sing masc
πνευματικὰς	θυσίας	εὐπροσδέκτους	(b τῷ)	θεῷ
pneumatikas	*thusias*	*euprosdektous*	*tō*	*theō*
spiritual	sacrifices	acceptable		to God

6.a.**Txt:** Steph **Var:** 01ℵ,02A,03B,04C 018K,020L,Gries,Lach Treg,Alf,Word,Tisc We/Ho,Weis,Sod UBS/☆

1217.2 prep	2400.2 name masc	5382.2 name gen masc	1346.1 conj	2504.1 conj	1354.1 conj
διὰ	Ἰησοῦ	Χριστοῦ.	6. (Διὸ	καὶ	[a☆ διότι]
dia	*Iēsou*	*Christou*	*Dio*	*kai*	*dioti*
by	Jesus	Christ.	Wherefore	also	[Because]

6.b.**Txt:** 018K,020L 025P,byz. **Var:** 01ℵ,02A,03B,33 Treg,Alf,Tisc,We/Ho Weis,Sod,UBS/☆

3886.1 verb 3sing indic pres act	1706.1 prep	3450.11 art dat sing fem	1118.3 noun dat sing fem	1481.20 verb 2sing impr aor mid
περιέχει	ἐν	(b τῇ)	γραφῇ,	Ἰδοὺ
periechei	*en*	*tē*	*graphē*	*Idou*
it is contained	in	the	scripture:	Behold,

4935.1 verb 1sing indic pres act	1706.1 prep	4477.1 name fem	3012.4 noun acc sing masc	202.2 noun acc sing masc
τίθημι	ἐν	Σιὼν	λίθον	(ἀκρογωνιαῖον,
tithēmi	*en*	*Siōn*	*lithon*	*akrogōniaion*
I place	in	Zion	a stone	corner,

1575.1 adj sing	1575.1 adj sing	202.2 noun acc sing masc	1768.2 adj acc sing masc	2504.1 conj
ἐκλεκτόν,	[☆ ἐκλεκτὸν	ἀκρογωνιαῖον]	ἔντιμον·	καὶ
eklekton	*eklekton*	*akrogōniaion*	*entimon*	*kai*
chosen,	[chosen	corner]	precious:	and

3450.5 art nom sing masc	3961.10 verb nom sing masc part pres act	1894.2 prep	840.4 prs-pron dat sing	3620.3 partic	3231.1 partic
ὁ	πιστεύων	ἐπ'	αὐτῷ	οὐ	μὴ
ho	*pisteuōn*	*ep'*	*autō*	*ou*	*mē*
the	believing	on	him	no	not

2587.5 verb 3sing subj aor pass	5050.3 prs-pron dat 2pl	3631.1 partic	3450.9 art nom sing fem	4940.1 noun nom sing fem
καταισχυνθῇ.	7. Ὑμῖν	οὖν	ἡ	τιμὴ
kataischunthē	*Humin*	*oun*	*hē*	*timē*
should be put to shame.	To you	therefore	the	preciousness

7.a.**Txt:** 02A,018K,020L 025P,byz. **Var:** 01ℵ,03B,04C,Treg Tisc,We/Ho,Weis,Sod UBS/☆

3450.4 art dat pl	3961.3 verb dat pl masc part pres act	540.1 verb dat pl masc part pres act	564.3 verb dat pl masc part pres act	1156.2 conj
τοῖς	πιστεύουσιν·	(ἀπειθοῦσιν	[a☆ ἀπιστοῦσιν]	δὲ
tois	*pisteuousin*	*apeithousin*	*apistousin*	*de*
the	believing;	disobeying	[unbelieving]	but,

7.b.**Txt:** 01ℵ-org 04C-corr,018K,020L 025P,byz.Tisc,Sod **Var:** 01ℵ-corr,02A,03B 04C-org,Lach,Treg,Alf We/Ho,Weis,UBS/☆

3012.4 noun acc sing masc	3012.1 noun nom sing masc	3614.6 rel-pron acc sing masc	588.1 verb 3pl indic aor act	3450.7 art nom pl masc
(λίθον	[b☆ λίθος]	ὃν	ἀπεδοκίμασαν	οἱ
lithon	*lithos*	*hon*	*apedokimasan*	*hoi*
stone	[idem]	which	rejected	the

dead by crucifixion; and as builders might reject an imperfect stone, so they "disallowed" (*apodedokimasmenon*, disapproved, repudiated, rejected) Christ in constructing their religious system. But believers have come to Him knowing He is alive and knowing He is "chosen" (*eklekton*, elect, favorite) of God. He is "precious" (*entimon*, prized, highly esteemed) to God and to them.

God uses what man rejects and often rejects what man approves. Peter brought out this idea in his Pentecost sermon, saying, "God hath made that same Jesus, whom ye have crucified, both Lord and Christ" (Acts 2:36). Jesus himself mentioned the fact when He quoted Psalm 118:22, saying, "The stone which the builders rejected, the same is become the head of the corner" (Matthew 21:42).

God is building a spiritual "house" (*oikos*, dwelling, household, as in 4:17, "house of God") and believers, as living stones, are the material with which He is constructing it. They compose God's house and they also compose the "holy priesthood" (*hierateuma hagion*, sacred body of priests) that ministers in His house. Peter understood that all believers are priests and can approach God directly, as in Hebrews 4:16. All can offer spiritual sacrifices (see also Romans 12:1; Ephesians 5:2; Philippians 2:17; 4:18; Hebrews 13:15,16) which God accepts through His Son.

Paul used the same metaphor of a growing spiritual building in Ephesians 2:21,22. Peter indicated this "spiritual house" includes believers in the five Roman provinces (1 Peter 1:1), recognizing that the church Christ is building (Matthew 16:18) is not merely a localized group but a universal Body.

2:6. Peter referred to Isaiah 28:16: "Behold, I lay in Zion for a foundation a stone, a tried stone, a precious corner stone, a sure foundation." He mentioned only "corner stone." Actually the cornerstone is also a foundation stone and might also mean the keystone at the center of an arch. Christ is the "chief corner stone," and he who builds on Him will never be "confounded" (*kataischunthē*, put to shame, dishonored).

2:7. In his speech at the Beautiful Gate, Peter told the rulers of the Jews, "This is the stone which was set at nought of you builders, which is become the head of the corner" (Acts 4:11). Here he made a similar statement, quoting Psalm 118:22.

He divided mankind into two great classes. To the believers Christ is "precious" (*timē*, most valuable, of high price; like the merchant in Matthew 13:46 who recognized the value of the "pearl of great price" and traded all his possessions for this one great treasure). But to the "disobedient" (*apeithousin*, disbelieving, unpersuadable) Christ is like the stone which expert builders disallowed; they deemed it imperfect and fit only for the rubbish heap. God raised Him from the dead and made Him the head of the "corner" (*gōnias*,

5. Ye also, as lively stones, are built up a spiritual house: . . . into a spiritual Edifice, *Wade.*

an holy priesthood: . . . in which you, like holy priests, *Phillips* . . . for a consecrated Priesthood, *TCNT* . . . a dedicated priesthood, *Berkeley.*

to offer up spiritual sacrifices: . . . bringing up to God's altars, *Wuest.*

acceptable to God by Jesus Christ: . . . through the mediatorship of, *Wuest* . . . are well-pleasing to, *Berkeley.*

6. Wherefore also it is contained in the scripture: For there is a passage of Scripture that runs, *TCNT* . . . There is a passage to this effect, *Phillips* . . . it is included in the scripture, *Concordant.*

Behold, I lay in Sion: I place in Zion, *Berkeley.*

a chief corner stone, elect, precious: . . . a key-stone of great value, *Wade* . . . one that is choice, *Norlie* . . . a choice stone, *TNT* . . . one chosen out...highly honored and precious, *Wuest* . . . a chosen, honored cornerstone, *Berkeley* . . . a corner capstone, chosen, held in honor, *Concordant.*

and he that believeth on him shall not be confounded: . . . whosoever trusts in it, *Campbell* . . . the one who rests his faith on Him, *Wuest* . . . shall never be put to shame, *Montgomery* . . . will never meet with disappointment, *Wade* . . . will never be made ashamed, *SEB* . . . may by no means be disgraced, *Concordant.*

7. Unto you therefore which believe [he is] precious: To you, then, who trust, *Campbell* . . . He is the Distinguished, *Fenton* . . . is of great value, *TNT* . . . is the honor and the preciousness, *Wuest.*

but unto them which be disobedient: . . . to the unbelieving, *Concordant* . . . disbelievers, *Wuest* . . . to those who refuse to believe, *Norlie.*

the stone which the builders disallowed: . . . which the workmen put aside, *NLT* . . . rejected by the builders, *Concordant* . . . did not think was important, *SEB* . . . threw away, *Williams* . . . repudiated, *Wuest.*

3481.6 verb nom pl masc part pres act	3642.4 dem-pron nom sing masc	1090.32 verb 3sing indic aor pass	1519.1 prep	2747.4 noun acc sing fem
οἰκοδομοῦντες,	οὗτος	ἐγενήθη	εἰς	κεφαλὴν
oikodomountes	*houtos*	*egenēthē*	*eis*	*kephalēn*
building,	this	became	to	head

1131.1 noun fem	2504.1 conj	3012.1 noun nom sing masc	4206.2 noun gen sing neu	2504.1 conj	3934.2 noun nom sing fem
γωνίας,	8. καὶ	λίθος	προσκόμματος	καὶ	πέτρα
gōnias	*kai*	*lithos*	*proskommatos*	*kai*	*petra*
of corner,	and	a stone	of stumbling	and	a rock

4480.2 noun gen sing neu	3614.7 rel-pron nom pl masc	4208.2 verb 3pl indic pres act	3450.3 art dat sing	3030.3 noun dat sing masc
σκανδάλου·	οἳ	προσκόπτουσιν	τῷ	λόγῳ
skandalou	*hoi*	*proskoptousin*	*tō*	*logō*
of offense;	who	stumble at	the	word,

540.4 verb nom pl masc part pres act	1519.1 prep	3614.16 rel-pron sing neu	2504.1 conj	4935.32 verb 3pl indic aor pass
ἀπειθοῦντες,	εἰς	ὃ	καὶ	ἐτέθησαν·
apeithountes	*eis*	*ho*	*kai*	*etethēsan*
being disobedient,	to	which	also	they were appointed.

5050.1 prs-pron nom 2pl	1156.2 conj	1079.1 noun sing neu	1575.1 adj sing	927.1 adj sing neu	2382.1 noun sing neu
9. Ὑμεῖς	δὲ	γένος	ἐκλεκτόν,	βασίλειον	ἱεράτευμα,
Humeis	*de*	*genos*	*eklekton*	*basileion*	*hierateuma*
You	but	a race	chosen,	a kingly	priesthood,

1477.1 noun sing neu	39.1 adj sing	2967.1 noun nom sing masc	1519.1 prep	3910.2 noun acc sing fem	3567.1 conj
ἔθνος	ἅγιον,	λαὸς	εἰς	περιποίησιν,	ὅπως
ethnos	*hagion*	*laos*	*eis*	*peripoiēsin*	*hopōs*
a nation	holy,	a people	for	a possession,	that

3450.15 art acc pl fem	697.5 noun acc pl fem	1788.1 verb 2pl subj aor act	3450.2 art gen sing	1523.2 prep gen	4510.3 noun gen sing neu
τὰς	ἀρετὰς	ἐξαγγείλητε	τοῦ	ἐκ	σκότους
tas	*aretas*	*exangeilēte*	*tou*	*ek*	*skotous*
the	virtues	you might set forth	of the	out of	darkness

5050.4 prs-pron acc 2pl	2535.15 verb gen sing masc part aor act	1519.1 prep	3450.16 art sing neu	2275.2 adj sing neu	840.3 prs-pron gen sing
ὑμᾶς	καλέσαντος	εἰς	τὸ	θαυμαστὸν	αὐτοῦ
humas	*kalesantos*	*eis*	*to*	*thaumaston*	*autou*
you	having called	to	the	wonderful	his

5295.1 noun sing neu	3614.7 rel-pron nom pl masc	4077.1 adv	3620.3 partic	2967.1 noun nom sing masc	3431.1 adv	1156.2 conj
φῶς·	10. οἵ	ποτε	οὐ	λαὸς,	νῦν	δὲ
phōs	*hoi*	*pote*	*ou*	*laos*	*nun*	*de*
light;	who	once	not	a people,	now	but

2967.1 noun nom sing masc	2296.2 noun gen sing masc	3450.7 art nom pl masc	3620.2 partic	1640.18 verb nom pl masc part perf mid	3431.1 adv
λαὸς	θεοῦ·	οἱ	οὐκ	ἠλεημένοι,	νῦν
laos	*theou*	*hoi*	*ouk*	*ēleēmenoi*	*nun*
people	God's;	the	not	having received mercy,	now

1156.2 conj	1640.16 verb nom pl masc part aor pass	27.6 adj pl masc	3731.1 verb 1sing indic pres act
δὲ	ἐλεηθέντες.	11. Ἀγαπητοί,	παρακαλῶ
de	*eleēthentes*	*Agapētoi*	*parakalō*
but	having received mercy.	Beloved,	I exhort

angle). Christ is the cornerstone on which the spiritual building rests and which holds the building together.

the same is made the head of the corner: . . . this came to be for, *Concordant.*

2:8. Quoting Isaiah 8:14, Peter said Christ is a "stone of stumbling" (*lithos proskommatos*) to unbelievers. They "stumble" (*proskoptousin*, cut against, as also in Matthew 4:6) at the Word, being unwilling to obey it. He said Christ to them is a "rock of offense" (*petra skandalou*, a rock set to trip someone, as also in Romans 9:33). Whereas *lithos* means a loose stone in the path, *petra* means a ledge rising out of the ground.

Peter said the Jews were "appointed" (*etethēsan*, ordained, as in 1 Timothy 2:7; consigned) to stumble. He could not mean they were predestined to disobey, for God has not appointed anyone to suffer His wrath (1 Thessalonians 5:9); but He has appointed the disobedient to stumble. No one has to be in the category of the disobedient, but those who are cannot avoid the results.

8. And a stone of stumbling, and a rock of offence: . . . a rock of entrapment, *Swann* . . . that will make them fall, *SEB* . . . a Rock that trips the foot, *Wade* . . . a snare rock, *Concordant* . . . an obstacle stone against which one cuts, *Wuest.*

[even to them] which stumble at the word, being disobedient: . . . even to those who because they are non-persuasible, *Wuest* . . . are stumbling also at the word, being stubborn, *Concordant* . . . because they reject the Gospel, *Noli* . . . refusing obedience to it, *Wade.*

whereunto also they were appointed: . . . and this is their appointed doom, *Williams* . . . as they had been predestined to do, *Noli.*

2:9. Those who stumble are not Israel as a nation but those, both Jews and Gentiles, who do not believe. As Israel was God's special treasure (Exodus 19:5,6), so now all who believe share in these privileged positions. In contrast to the fate of the "disobedient" (2:8), Peter said believers are a "chosen generation" (*genos eklekton*, an elect nation) and a "royal priesthood" (*basileion hierateuma*, kingly fraternity of priests). They are a "holy nation" (*ethnos hagion*, sacred race) and a "peculiar people" (*laos eis peripoiēsin*, a people purchased for God's own special possession). "Peculiar" in Old English had this idea of possession.

The purpose of believers' calling is that they might "show forth" (*exangeilēte*, tell out, publish) the "praises" (*aretas*, excellencies) of the Lord who has called them out of "darkness" (*skotous*, shadiness, obscurity) into His "marvelous light" (*thaumaston phōs*, wonderful illumination).

In the Scriptures darkness is often used to symbolize the state in which unbelievers find themselves, under the control of Satan, while light represents God and His kingdom. It is therefore a fitting description of conversion to refer to it as leaving darkness behind and coming into the light of the gospel.

9. But ye [are] a chosen generation, a royal priesthood: . . . select race, *Fenton* . . . elect, *Montgomery* . . . a race chosen out, king-priests, *Wuest.*

an holy nation, a peculiar people: . . . a set-apart nation, a people formed for [God's own] possession, *Wuest* . . . a consecrated class of people, *Noli* . . . purchased people, *Montgomery* . . . an acquired people, *Swann* . . . a procured people, *Concordant* . . . a People for a purpose, *Wilson* . . . for action, *Fenton.*

that ye should show forth the praises: . . . in order that you might proclaim abroad the excellencies, *Wuest* . . . so that you should be recounting the virtues, *Concordant* . . . commissioned to tell forth, *Wade* . . . declare the perfections of him, *Campbell.*

of him who hath called you out of darkness into his marvellous light: . . . called you into participation, *Wuest.*

2:10. Once believers were "not a people," but now they are the "people of God" (see Hosea 2:23). Hosea's words originally dealt with the Jews and their restoration, but Peter applied them to all believers (as Paul did in Romans 9:24-26). Once believers (when disobedient, like the Jews) "had not obtained mercy," but "now have obtained mercy" (*nun de eleēthentes*, now have received compassion).

10. Which in time past [were] not a people, but [are] now the people of God: . . . who formerly, *Campbell* . . . you were disinherited, *Noli.*

which had not obtained mercy, but now have obtained mercy: Once you were outside his mercy, *TNT* . . . have now secured compassion, *Fenton* . . . enjoyed mercy, *Concordant.*

1 Peter 2:12

5453.1 conj	3803.3 adj acc pl masc	2504.1 conj	3789.3 adj acc pl masc	563.9 verb inf pres mid
ὡς	παροίκους	καὶ	ʻ☆ παρεπιδήμους,	ἀπέχεσθαι
hōs	*paroikous*	*kai*	*parepidēmous*	*apechesthai*
as	aliens	and	strangers,	to abstain

11.a.**Txt:** 01ℵ,03B,044 049,sa.byz. **Var:** p72,02A,04C,020L 025P,33,81,623,1241 1243,1852,1881

3789.3 adj acc pl masc	563.8 verb 2pl impr pres mid	3450.1 art gen pl	4416.6 adj gen pl fem
[a παρεπιδήμους,	ἀπέχεσθε]	τῶν	σαρκικῶν
parepidēmous	*apechesthe*	*tōn*	*sarkikōn*
[strangers:	abstain]	from the	fleshly

1924.6 noun gen pl fem	3610.4 rel-pron nom pl fem	4605.3 verb 3pl indic pres mid	2567.3 prep	3450.10 art gen sing fem
ἐπιθυμιῶν,	αἵτινες	στρατεύονται	κατὰ	τῆς
epithumiōn	*haitines*	*strateuontai*	*kata*	*tēs*
desires,	which	war	against	the

5425.2 noun gen sing fem	3450.12 art acc sing fem	389.3 noun acc sing fem	5050.2 prs-pron gen 2pl	1706.1 prep	3450.4 art dat pl
ψυχῆς·	**12.** τὴν	ἀναστροφὴν	ὑμῶν	ἐν	τοῖς
psuchēs	*tēn*	*anastrophēn*	*humōn*	*en*	*tois*
soul;	the	manner of life	your	among	the

1477.6 noun dat pl neu	2174.19 verb nom pl masc part pres act	2541.8 adj acc sing fem	2419.1 conj	1706.1 prep	3614.3 rel-pron dat sing
ἔθνεσιν	ἔχοντες	καλήν,	ἵνα,	ἐν	ᾧ
ethnesin	*echontes*	*kalēn*	*hina*	*en*	*hō*
nations	having	right	that	in	which

2605.2 verb 3pl indic pres act	5050.2 prs-pron gen 2pl	5453.1 conj	2526.2 adj gen pl masc	1523.2 prep gen	3450.1 art gen pl
καταλαλοῦσιν	ὑμῶν	ὡς	κακοποιῶν,	ἐκ	τῶν
katalalousin	*humōn*	*hōs*	*kakopoiōn*	*ek*	*tōn*
they speak against	you	as	evildoers,	through	the

12.a.**Txt:** 02A,018K 020L,025P,byz. **Var:** 01ℵ,03B,04C,Treg Alf,Word,Tisc,We/Ho Weis,Sod,UBS/☆

2541.12 adj gen pl neu	2024.5 noun gen pl neu	2013.1 verb nom pl masc part aor act	2013.2 verb nom pl masc part pres act
καλῶν	ἔργων	ʻ ἐποπτεύσαντες	[a☆ ἐποπτεύοντες]
kalōn	*ergōn*	*epopteusantes*	*epopteuontes*
good	works	having witnessed	[witnessing]

1386.12 verb 3pl subj aor act	3450.6 art acc sing masc	2296.4 noun acc sing masc	1706.1 prep	2232.3 noun dat sing fem	1968.1 noun gen sing fem
δοξάσωσιν	τὸν	θεὸν	ἐν	ἡμέρᾳ	ἐπισκοπῆς.
doxasōsin	*ton*	*theon*	*en*	*hēmera*	*episkopēs*
they may glorify		God	in	day	of visitation.

13.a.**Txt:** 018K,020L 025P,byz. **Var:** 01ℵ,02A,03B,04C 33,Lach,Treg,Alf,Tisc We/Ho,Weis,Sod UBS/☆

5131.19 verb 2pl impr aor pass	3631.1 partic	3820.11 adj dat sing fem	440.3 adj dat sing fem	2909.3 noun dat sing fem
13. Ὑποτάγητε	ʻa οὖν ˎ	πάσῃ	ἀνθρωπίνῃ	κτίσει,
Hupotagēte	*oun*	*pasē*	*anthrōpinē*	*ktisei*
Be in subjection	therefore	to every	human	institution

1217.2 prep	3450.6 art acc sing masc	2935.4 noun acc sing masc	1521.1 conj	928.3 noun dat sing masc	5453.1 conj
διὰ	τὸν	κύριον·	εἴτε	βασιλεῖ,	ὡς
dia	*ton*	*kurion*	*eite*	*basilei*	*hōs*
for the sake of	the	Lord;	whether	to king	as

5080.1 verb dat sing masc part pres act	1521.1 conj	2215.6 noun dat pl masc	5453.1 conj	1217.1 prep	840.3 prs-pron gen sing
ὑπερέχοντι·	**14.** εἴτε	ἡγεμόσιν,	ὡς	δι'	αὐτοῦ
huperechonti	*eite*	*hēgemosin*	*hōs*	*di'*	*autou*
being supreme,	or	to governors	as	by	him

2:11. Peter used the term "dearly beloved" (*agapētoi,* well-loved) often (see 2 Peter 1:17; 3:1,8,14,15,17). He wrote to implore believers as "strangers" (*paroikous,* sojourners, alien residents, noncitizens, as in Ephesians 2:19) and "pilgrims" (*parepidēmous,* temporary residents, as in 1 Peter 1:1) to "abstain" (*apechesthai,* refrain, as in 1 Thessalonians 4:3; 5:22) from "fleshly lusts" (*sarkikōn epithumiōn,* carnal desires, longings for gross sins of the flesh). He said these "war" (*strateuontai,* mobilize to fight, carry on a campaign, as in James 4:1) against the "soul" (*psuchēs,* the whole being).

His readers are followers of Christ, but Peter indicated the war was and is not over. Carnal desires keep arising so they must keep resisting. This struggle between the flesh and the Spirit is pictured vividly by Paul, who wrote, "Walk in the Spirit, and ye shall not fulfil the lust of the flesh" (Galatians 5:16).

2:12. Peter said they should guard their "conversation" (*anastrophēn,* behavior, life-style) to keep it "honest" (*kalēn,* honorable, virtuous) among the "Gentiles" (*ethnesin,* nations, unconverted people, as also in 2:9; 4:3).

False charges were being leveled against them. Neighbors called them enemies of their society. Romans considered them hostile to emperor worship. Many "speak against" them (*katalalousin,* slander, speak evil, as also in 3:16) and call them "evildoers" (*kakopoiōn,* criminals, malefactors). However, by observing believers' "good works" (*kalōn ergōn,* honest and virtuous deeds) they will change their opinion and will glorify God in the "day" (*hēmera,* time) of "visitation" (*episkopēs,* checkup, inspection, confrontation, as in Luke 19:44).

2:13. Although believers are citizens of heaven, they should obey civil laws while on earth. They should "submit" themselves (*hupotagēte,* subordinate, be in subjection, as in 3:22) to every "ordinance" (*ktisei,* institution) of man for the Lord's sake, and should honor the king as being "supreme" (*huperechonti,* prime authority, having superiority) in his earthly realm. Christians should obey their earthly king, Peter said, as long as it did not require disobeying their heavenly King. Sometimes Christians have to choose between the two loyalties (see Acts 4:19,20), but Peter made it clear that Christians should be on the side of law and order.

2:14. "Governors" (*hēgemosin,* chief rulers) are dispatched by the king not only for the "punishment" (*ekdikēsin,* vengeance, retribution) of "evildoers" (*kakopoiōn,* malefactors, criminals) but also for the "praise" (*epainon,* commendation) of those who "do well" (*agathopoiōn,* are virtuous). Therefore, believers should be

11. Dearly beloved, I beseech [you] as strangers and pilgrims: Divinely loved ones...I beg of you, *Wuest* . . . I am entreating you, *Concordant* . . . I implore you...as lodgers and travellers, *Fenton* . . . as only temporary dwellers *Wade* . . . and Sojourners, *Wilson* . . . as resident aliens and refugees, *Adams.*

abstain from fleshly lusts, which war against the soul: . . . be constantly holding yourselves back from the passionate cravings which are fleshly by nature, *Wuest.*

12. Having your conversation honest among the Gentiles: . . . holding your manner of life among the unsaved steadily beautiful in its goodness, *Wuest* . . . your behavior among the nations ideal, *Concordant.*

that, whereas they speak against you as evildoers: . . . in order that in the things in which they defame you as those who do evil, *Wuest.*

they may by [your] good works, which they shall behold, glorify God: . . . by being spectators of ideal acts they should be glorifying God, *Concordant* . . . attracted by your brilliant conduct, praise God whilst witnessing it, *Fenton* . . . because of your works beautiful in their goodness which they are constantly, carefully, and attentively watching, they may glorify God, *Wuest.*

in the day of visitation: . . . when He returns to take care of us, *SEB* . . . when he is revealed to them, *Noli* . . . on the judgment day, *Williams* . . . in the day of His overseeing care, *Wuest.*

13. Submit yourselves to every ordinance of man for the Lord's sake: Put yourselves in the attitude of submission...giving yourselves to the implicit obedience, *Wuest* . . . to every human creation because of the Lord, *Concordant.*

whether it be to the king, as supreme: . . . to the Emperor as supreme ruler, *Montgomery* . . . as one who is supereminent, *Wuest.*

14. Or unto governors, as unto them that are sent by him for the punishment of evildoers: . . . as commissioned by him to bring

14.a.**Txt:** 04C,025P,byz. **Var:** 01ℵ,02A,03B 018K,020L,Gries,Lach Treg,Alf,Word,Tisc We/Ho,Weis,Sod UBS/☆

3854.20 verb dat pl masc part pres mid	**1519.1** prep	**1544.3** noun acc sing fem	**3173.1** conj	**2526.2** adj gen pl masc
πεμπομένοις	εἰς	ἐκδίκησιν	⸂a μὲν ⸃	κακοποιῶν,
pempomenois	*eis*	*ekdikēsin*	*men*	*kakopoiōn*
being sent,	for	vengeance		evildoers,

1853.2 noun acc sing masc	**1156.2** conj	**17.1** adj gen pl masc	**3617.1** conj	**3643.1** adv
ἔπαινον	δὲ	ἀγαθοποιῶν·	**15.** ὅτι	οὕτως
epainon	*de*	*agathopoiōn*	*hoti*	*houtōs*
praise	and	well-doers;	because	so

1498.4 verb 3sing indic pres act	**3450.16** art sing neu	**2284.1** noun sing neu	**3450.2** art gen sing	**2296.2** noun gen sing masc
ἐστὶν	τὸ	θέλημα	τοῦ	θεοῦ,
estin	*to*	*thelēma*	*tou*	*theou*
is	the	will		of God,

15.5 verb acc pl masc part pres act	**5229.1** verb inf pres act	**3450.12** art acc sing fem	**3450.1** art gen pl	**871.5** adj gen pl masc
ἀγαθοποιοῦντας	φιμοῦν	τὴν	τῶν	ἀφρόνων
agathopoiountas	*phimoun*	*tēn*	*tōn*	*aphronōn*
well-doing	to put to silence	the	of the	senseless

442.7 noun gen pl masc	**54.1** noun acc sing fem	**5453.1** conj	**1645.2** adj nom pl masc	**2504.1** conj	**3231.1** partic
ἀνθρώπων	ἀγνωσίαν·	**16.** ὡς	ἐλεύθεροι,	καὶ	μὴ
anthrōpōn	*agnōsian*	*hōs*	*eleutheroi*	*kai*	*mē*
men	ignorance;	as	free,	and	not

5453.1 conj	**1927.1** noun sing neu	**2174.19** verb nom pl masc part pres act	**3450.10** art gen sing fem	**2520.2** noun gen sing fem	**3450.12** art acc sing fem
ὡς	ἐπικάλυμμα	ἔχοντες	τῆς	κακίας	τὴν
hōs	*epikalumma*	*echontes*	*tēs*	*kakias*	*tēn*
as	a cloak	having	of the	malice	the

1644.4 noun acc sing fem	**233.1** conj	**5453.1** conj	**1395.6** noun nom pl masc	**2296.2** noun gen sing masc	**2296.2** noun gen sing masc	**1395.6** noun nom pl masc
ἐλευθερίαν,	ἀλλ'	ὡς	⸂ δοῦλοι	θεοῦ.	[☆ θεοῦ	δοῦλοι.]
eleutherian	*all'*	*hōs*	*douloi*	*theou*	*theou*	*douloi*
freedom,	but	as	slaves	of God.	[of God	slaves.]

3820.8 adj acc pl masc	**4939.9** verb 2pl impr aor act	**3450.12** art acc sing fem	**80.2** noun acc sing fem	**25.1** verb 2pl pres act
17. πάντας	τιμήσατε,	τὴν	ἀδελφότητα	⸂☆ ἀγαπᾶτε,
pantas	*timēsate*	*tēn*	*adelphotēta*	*agapate*
All	honor,	the	brotherhood	love,

17.a.**Var:** 018K,020L 049-org,69,2464,byz.

25.18 verb 2pl impr aor act	**3450.6** art acc sing masc	**2296.4** noun acc sing masc	**5236.6** verb 2pl impr pres mid	**3450.6** art acc sing masc
[a ἀγαπήσατε,]	τὸν	θεὸν	φοβεῖσθε,	τὸν
agapēsate	*ton*	*theon*	*phobeisthe*	*ton*
[idem]		God	fear,	the

928.4 noun acc sing masc	**4939.5** verb 2pl impr pres act	**3450.7** art nom pl masc	**3473.5** noun nom pl masc	**5131.12** verb nom pl masc part pres mid
βασιλέα	τιμᾶτε.	**18.** Οἱ	οἰκέται,	ὑποτασσόμενοι
basilea	*timate*	*Hoi*	*oiketai*	*hupotassomenoi*
king	honor.	The	servants,	being subject

1706.1 prep	**3820.3** adj dat sing	**5238.3** noun dat sing masc	**3450.4** art dat pl	**1197.5** noun dat pl masc	**3620.3** partic	**3303.1** adv
ἐν	παντὶ	φόβῳ	τοῖς	δεσπόταις,	οὐ	μόνον
en	*panti*	*phobō*	*tois*	*despotais*	*ou*	*monon*
with	all	fear	to the	masters,	not	only

in subjection as a good testimony for their Lord, so the rulers will commend them (see also Romans 13:3,4).

criminals to justice, *Berkeley* . . . sent by him to inflict punishment upon those who do evil, *Wuest* . . . for vengeance, *Concordant.*

and for the praise of them that do well: . . . the commendation, *Wade* . . . the applause of doers of good, *Concordant* . . . encourage the well-behaved, *Berkeley.*

2:15. It is God's "will" (*thelēma,* purpose, desire, pleasure, as in Revelation 4:11) that believers should "put to silence" (*phimoun,* muzzle, make speechless, as in Matthew 22:12) their slanderers by "well-doing" (*agathopoiountas,* being virtuous, of good reputation; see also 1 Peter 2:20; 3:16,17). Peter called the slanderers "foolish" men (*aphronōn,* stupid, egotistic, unwise, as in 2 Corinthians 11:16). A believer's only protection against slander is a transparently godly life. This may not save them from trouble but it is its own witness to the truth.

15. For so is the will of God, that with well doing ye may put to silence the ignorance of foolish men: . . . intention of...the senselessness of ignorant men, *Fenton* . . . by doing good you might be reducing to silence...men who are unreflecting and unintelligent, *Wuest* . . . by behaving well you should silence the foolishness of thoughtless people, *Berkeley* . . . muzzle the ignorant talk, *Adams* . . . imprudent men, *Concordant.*

2:16. Peter told believers to submit to civil authority willingly (not of compulsion) as men who are "free" (from *elutheria,* freedom from bondage) and not using that freedom as a "cloak" (*epikalumma,* veil, covering) of "maliciousness" (*kakias,* evil, spite, wickedness, as in 2:1). Instead of using their liberty as a pretext to do evil, they should use it as "servants of God" (*douloi theou,* bondservants of God). Peter and other apostles liked to call themselves slaves of God (see 2 Peter 1:1; Romans 1:1; James 1:1). Everyone is either a servant of God or a slave to sin (see 2 Peter 2:19). No one has absolute personal freedom. To be free indeed the believer must subject himself to the Word of Christ (John 8:31,32).

16. As free, and not using [your] liberty for a cloak of maliciousness: Live like free men, *Williams* . . . doing all this as those who have their liberty, and not as those who are holding their liberty as a cloak of wickedness, *Wuest* . . . veil for evil, *Swann* . . . cover-up, *SEB* . . . some wickedness, *Norlie* . . . as a pretext for vice, *Noli* . . . misconduct, *Montgomery.*

but as the servants of God: . . . as God's slaves, *Concordant* . . . but as those who are God's bondmen, *Wuest.*

2:17. Peter gave four directives which are brief in expression but broad in implementation. He told believers to (1) "honor" (*timēsate,* esteem, respect) all men, whether they deserve it or not; (2) "love" (*agapate,* love much) the "brotherhood" (*adelphotēta,* the Christian fraternity); (3) "fear" (*phobeisthe,* be in awe, revere) God; (4) "honor" (*timate,* esteem, respect) the "king" (*basilea,* sovereign). Though he directed believers to honor all men, Peter specifically mentioned the king; the language used in his first directive indicates that some men deserve more honor than others. In each of the three latter directives the Greek verb denotes continuous action: believers should keep on loving the brotherhood; they should keep on fearing God; they should keep on honoring the king.

17. Honour all [men]: Pay honor, *Wuest*. . . Show respect to everyone, *Norlie* . . . Treat all men, *Campbell* . . . honorably, *Berkeley.*

Love the brotherhood: . . . be loving, *Wuest.*

Fear God: Respect God, *SEB* . . . revere God, *Berkeley.*

Honour the king: Respect the head leader of the country, *NLT* . . . deferential to the king, *TCNT.*

2:18. Many of the believers to whom Peter was writing were slaves, so verses 18-25 are directed to them. He called them "servants" (*oiketai,* a menial domestic, household bondservant, as distinguished from *doulos,* the general term for slaves).

18. Servants, [be] subject to [your] masters with all fear: Domestics may do it by being subject to your owners, *Concordant* . . . Household slaves, put yourselves in constant subjection with every fear in implicit obedience to your absolute lords and masters, *Wuest* . . . showing all respect, *SEB.*

3450.4 art dat pl	18.5 adj dat pl	2504.1 conj	1918.2 adj dat pl masc	233.2 conj	2504.1 conj	3450.4 art dat pl
τοῖς	ἀγαθοῖς	καὶ	ἐπιεικέσιν,	ἀλλὰ	καὶ	τοῖς
tois	*agathois*	*kai*	*epieikesin*	*alla*	*kai*	*tois*
to the	good	and	gentle,	but	also	to the

4501.1 adj dat pl masc	3642.17 dem-pron sing neu	1056.1 conj	5322.1 noun nom sing fem	1479.1 conj	1217.2 prep
σκολιοῖς.	**19.** τοῦτο	γὰρ	χάρις,	εἰ	διὰ
skoliois	*touto*	*gar*	*charis*	*ei*	*dia*
crooked.	This	for	acceptable	if	for sake of

4743.4 noun acc sing fem	2296.2 noun gen sing masc	5135.1 verb 3sing indic pres act	4948.3 indef-pron nom sing	3049.5 noun acc pl fem
συνείδησιν	θεοῦ	ὑποφέρει	τις	λύπας,
suneidēsin	*theou*	*hupopherei*	*tis*	*lupas*
conscience	toward God	endures	anyone	griefs,

3819.7 verb nom sing masc part pres act	94.1 adv	4029.1 intr-pron sing	1056.1 conj	2784.1 noun sing neu	1479.1 conj
πάσχων	ἀδίκως.	**20.** ποῖον	γὰρ	κλέος,	εἰ
paschōn	*adikōs*	*poion*	*gar*	*kleos*	*ei*
suffering	unjustly.	What	for	glory,	if

20.a.**Txt:** 01ℵ-org,02A 03B,04C,byz.
Var: p72,01ℵ-corr2 025P,044,322,323,630 945,1241,1739,2138 2298

262.6 verb nom pl masc part pres act	2504.1 conj	2826.5 verb nom pl masc part pres mid	2822.3 verb nom pl masc part pres mid
ἁμαρτάνοντες	καὶ	ʻ☆ κολαφιζόμενοι	[a κολαζόμενοι]
hamartanontes	*kai*	*kolaphizomenoi*	*kolazomenoi*
sinning	and	being buffeted	[being punished]

5116.11 verb 2pl indic fut act	233.1 conj	1479.1 conj	15.4 verb nom pl masc part pres act	2504.1 conj
ὑπομενεῖτε;	ἀλλ'	εἰ	ἀγαθοποιοῦντες	καὶ
hupomeneite	*all'*	*ei*	*agathopoiountes*	*kai*
you will endure it?	but	if	doing good	and

3819.8 verb nom pl masc part pres act	5116.11 verb 2pl indic fut act	3642.17 dem-pron sing neu	5322.1 noun nom sing fem	3706.2 prep
πάσχοντες	ὑπομενεῖτε,	τοῦτο	χάρις	παρὰ
paschontes	*hupomeneite*	*touto*	*charis*	*para*
suffering	you will endure,	this	acceptable	with

2296.3 noun dat sing masc	1519.1 prep	3642.17 dem-pron sing neu	1056.1 conj	2535.38 verb 2pl indic aor pass	3617.1 conj
θεῷ.	**21.** εἰς	τοῦτο	γὰρ	ἐκλήθητε,	ὅτι
theō	*eis*	*touto*	*gar*	*eklēthēte*	*hoti*
God.	To	this	for	you were called;	because

21.a.**Txt:** p72,02A,03B 04C,025P,byz.
Var: p81,01ℵ,044,623 2464

2504.1 conj	5382.1 name nom masc	3819.11 verb 3sing indic aor act	594.10 verb 3sing indic aor act	5065.1 prep	2231.2 prs-pron gen 1pl
καὶ	Χριστὸς	ʻ☆ ἔπαθεν	[a ἀπέθανεν]	ὑπὲρ	ʻ ἡμῶν,
kai	*Christos*	*epathen*	*apethanen*	*huper*	*hēmōn*
also	Christ	suffered	[died]	for	us.

21.b.**Txt:** bo.Steph
Var: p72,01ℵ,02A,03B 04C,it.sa.Elzev,Gries Lach,Treg,Alf,Tisc We/Ho,Weis,Sod UBS/☆

2231.3 prs-pron dat 1pl	5050.2 prs-pron gen 2pl	5050.3 prs-pron dat 2pl	5115.1 verb nom sing masc part pres act	5099.1 noun acc sing masc
ἡμῖν	[b☆ ὑμῶν,	ὑμῖν]	ὑπολιμπάνων	ὑπογραμμὸν,
hēmin	*humōn*	*humin*	*hupolimpanōn*	*hupogrammon*
us	[you,	you]	leaving	a model,

2419.1 conj	1857.4 verb 2pl subj aor act	3450.4 art dat pl	2460.1 noun dat pl neu	840.3 prs-pron gen sing
ἵνα	ἐπακολουθήσητε	τοῖς	ἴχνεσιν	αὐτοῦ·
hina	*epakolouthēsēte*	*tois*	*ichnesin*	*autou*
that	you should follow after	in the	steps	his;

Peter's statements are imperatives. He directed them to be "subject" (*hupotassomenoi*, obey, be submissive) to their masters with all "fear" (*phobō*, alarm, awe), not only to the "good" (*agathois*, benevolent) and "gentle" (*epieikesin*, moderate, patient, as in James 3:17), but also to the "froward" (*skoliois*, unfair, crooked, as in Philippians 2:15). Some slave owners were kind, others were not. The test of obedience is to believers whose masters are oppressive (see Matthew 5:44-46). Similar directions to bondservants are given in Ephesians 6:5-7; Colossians 3:22-25; 1 Timothy 6:1,2; Titus 2:9.

It was not easy to be a slave in the First Century, even under the best of circumstances. It must have been a great test of a Christian slave to be submissive to a cruel master.

not only to the good and gentle, but also to the froward: ... the benevolent and considerate, *Fenton* ... who are good at heart and sweetly reasonable, satisfied with less than their due, *Wuest* ... lenient, but to the crooked also, *Concordant* ... those who are unfair, *TCNT* ... of cruel disposition, *Norlie* ... unreasonable, *Montgomery* ... perverse, *Clementson* ... arrogant, *Noli.*

2:19. Peter said "this" (obedience to oppressive masters) is "thankworthy" (*charis*, gratifying, cause for thanks, as in Romans 6:17 and 2 Corinthians 2:14). God is pleased if a man or woman will "endure" (*hupopherei*, stay under, bear up, as in 1 Corinthians 10:13 and 2 Timothy 3:11) "grief" (*lupas*, heaviness, sorrows; the word is plural). This must be with a "conscience" (*suneidēsin*, moral consciousness, sense of duty; also in 3:16,21) toward God, "suffering" (*paschōn*, to experience sensation, feel pain) "wrongfully" (*adikōs*, unjustly). If the suffering arises from the servant's faith in the gospel, his patient endurance is all the more "thankworthy."

19. For this [is] thankworthy: ... this is grace, *Concordant* ... is something which is beyond the ordinary course of what might be expected and is therefore commendable, *Wuest.*

if a man for conscience toward God endure grief, suffering wrongfully: ... if, because of conscience...anyone is undergoing sorrows, *Concordant* ... when a person because of the conscious sense of his relation to God bears up under pain, *Wuest* ... unjust ill-treatment, *Noli.*

2:20. What kind of "glory" (*kleos*, renown, praise) is there if, when a person is "buffeted" (*kolaphizomenoi*, beaten physically, as in Matthew 26:67) for his own "faults" (*hamartanontes*, repeated shortcomings, trespasses, sins, offenses), he shall "take it patiently" (*hupomeneite*, stay under, bear up, endure, as in Matthew 10:22 and James 1:12)? Christians may suffer because of misconduct, but only those who suffer for righteousness' sake are martyrs (Matthew 5:11,12). But if a person shall "do well" (*agathopoiountes*, be virtuous, as in 2:15; 3:16,17) and suffer, and if he takes it patiently, this is "acceptable with God" (*charis para theō*, thankworthy, cause for thanks as God looks at it, as in 2:19).

20. For what glory [is it], if, when ye be buffeted for your faults, ye shall take it patiently?: What credit can you claim, *TCNT* ... what sort of fame is it when you fall short of the mark and are pummeled with the fist, *Wuest* ... you are beaten, *NLT* ... sinning and being buffeted, *Concordant* ... you endure, *Wilson* ... endure a beating, *SEB.*

but if, when ye do well, and suffer [for it], ye take it patiently: ... when you are in the habit of doing good and then suffer constantly for it, *Wuest* ... if, doing good and suffering, you will be enduring, *Concordant.*

this [is] acceptable with God: ... this is an unusual and not-to-be-expected action, and therefore commendable, *Wuest* ... beautiful in God's eyes, *TCNT* ... brings honour, *Fenton.*

2:21. "For even hereunto" (to suffer patiently) were they "called" (*eklēthēte*, summoned, as in 1 Peter 1:15; 2:9; 3:9; 5:10; 2 Peter 1:3) because Christ also suffered for them, "leaving" (*hupolimpanōn*, to bequeath) them an "example" (*hupogrammon*, something to copy, a writing-copy for others to imitate) that they should follow his "steps" (*ichnesin*, tracks, footprints, as in Romans 4:12 and 2 Corinthians 12:18). One of the great guidelines a believer may adopt as a standard for behavior in any situation is to ask himself, "What would Jesus do?"

21. For even hereunto were ye called: For this, *Concordant* ... to this very thing, *Wuest.*

because Christ also suffered for us: ... seeing that, *Concordant* ... suffered on your behalf, *TCNT.*

leaving us an example, that ye should follow his steps: ... leaving you a copy, that you should be following up in the footprints of Him, *Concordant.*

3614.5 rel-pron nom sing masc	264.4 noun acc sing fem	3620.2 partic	4020.24 verb 3sing indic aor act	3624.1 conj	2128.32 verb 3sing indic aor pass
22. ὃς	ἁμαρτίαν	οὐκ	ἐποίησεν,	οὐδὲ	εὑρέθη
hos	*hamartian*	*ouk*	*epoiēsen*	*oude*	*heurethē*
who	sin	no	did,	neither	was found

1382.1 noun nom sing masc	1706.1 prep	3450.3 art dat sing	4601.3 noun dat sing neu	840.3 prs-pron gen sing	3614.5 rel-pron nom sing masc
δόλος	ἐν	τῷ	στόματι	αὐτοῦ·	**23.** ὃς
dolos	*en*	*tō*	*stomati*	*autou*	*hos*
deceit	in	the	mouth	his;	who,

3032.3 verb nom sing masc part pres mid	3620.2 partic	483.1 verb 3sing indic imperf act	3819.7 verb nom sing masc part pres act	3620.2 partic
λοιδορούμενος	οὐκ	ἀντελοιδόρει,	πάσχων	οὐκ
loidoroumenos	*ouk*	*anteloidorei*	*paschōn*	*ouk*
being insulted,	not	was not insulting;	suffering	not

542.1 verb 3sing indic imperf act	3722.26 verb 3sing indic imperf act	1156.2 conj	3450.3 art dat sing	2892.9 verb dat sing masc part pres act
ἠπείλει,	παρεδίδου	δὲ	τῷ	κρίνοντι
ēpeilei	*paredidou*	*de*	*tō*	*krinonti*
was threatening;	was giving over	but	to the	judging

1341.1 adv	3614.5 rel-pron nom sing masc	3450.15 art acc pl fem	264.1 noun fem	2231.2 prs-pron gen 1pl
δικαίως·	**24.** ὃς	τὰς	ἁμαρτίας	ἡμῶν
dikaiōs	*hos*	*tas*	*hamartias*	*hēmōn*
righteously;	who	the	sins	our

840.5 prs-pron nom sing masc	397.4 verb 3sing indic aor act	1706.1 prep	3450.3 art dat sing	4835.3 noun dat sing neu	840.3 prs-pron gen sing
αὐτὸς	ἀνήνεγκεν	ἐν	τῷ	σώματι	αὐτοῦ
autos	*anēnenken*	*en*	*tō*	*sōmati*	*autou*
himself	bore	in	the	body	his

1894.3 prep	3450.16 art sing neu	3448.1 noun sing neu	2419.1 conj	3450.14 art dat pl fem	264.7 noun dat pl fem
ἐπὶ	τὸ	ξύλον,	ἵνα	ταῖς	ἁμαρτίαις
epi	*to*	*xulon*	*hina*	*tais*	*hamartiais*
on	the	tree,	that,	to the	sins

576.1 verb nom pl masc part aor mid	3450.11 art dat sing fem	1336.3 noun dat sing fem	2180.24 verb 1pl subj aor act	3614.2 rel-pron gen sing
ἀπογενόμενοι,	τῇ	δικαιοσύνῃ	ζήσωμεν·	οὗ
apogenomenoi	*tē*	*dikaiosunē*	*zēsōmen*	*hou*
having died,	to the	righteousness	we may live;	which

3450.3 art dat sing	3330.1 noun dat sing masc	840.3 prs-pron gen sing	2367.6 verb 2pl indic aor pass	1498.1 verb 2pl act
τῷ	μώλωπι	⸂[a] αὐτοῦ ⸃	ἰάθητε.	**25.** ἦτε
tō	*mōlōpi*	*autou*	*iathēte*	*ēte*
by the	bruise	his	you were healed.	You were

1056.1 conj	5453.1 conj	4122.3 noun pl neu	3966.16 verb pl neu part pres mid	3966.13 verb nom pl masc part pres mid
γὰρ	ὡς	πρόβατα	⸀ πλανώμενα·	[a☆ πλανώμενοι,]
gar	*hōs*	*probata*	*planōmena*	*planōmenoi*
for	as	sheep	going astray,	[idem]

233.1 conj	233.2 conj	1978.17 verb 2pl indic aor pass	3431.1 adv	1894.3 prep	3450.6 art acc sing masc
⸀ ἀλλ'	[☆ ἀλλὰ]	ἐπεστράφητε	νῦν	ἐπὶ	τὸν
all'	*alla*	*epestraphēte*	*nun*	*epi*	*ton*
but	[idem]	were returned	now	to	the

24.a.**Txt:** 01ℵ-org,020L 025P,byz.Tisc
Var: 01ℵ-corr,02A,03B 04C,018K,33,Lach,Treg We/Ho,Weis,Sod UBS/☆

25.a.**Txt:** 04C,018K 020L,025P,byz.
Var: 01ℵ,02A,03B,Lach Treg,Alf,Tisc,We/Ho Weis,Sod,UBS/☆

2:22. As prophesied in Isaiah 53:9, Christ "did no sin." Peter had already pointed to His sinlessness in 1:19. Neither was "guile" (*dolos*, deceit, subtlety, trickery, as also in 1 Peter 2:1; 3:10) "found" (*heurethē*, perceived, discovered after close scrutiny) in His "mouth" (*stomati*, implies speaking, as in 2 Corinthians 13:1).

2:23. The natural reaction to abuse is to retort in anger, trade insult for insult, and threaten to get even. Christ's example is the opposite. When "reviled" (*loidoroumenos*, slander, insult; the language denotes repeated incidents) He reviled not. (See 1 Corinthians 4:12.) When He "suffered" (*paschōn*, experience pain) He did not threaten or menace anyone in return. To follow such an example will require an attitude of forgiveness toward our opponents and of trust toward God. Christ's suffering was undeserved, but He simply "committed himself" (*paredidou*, as an accused man is handed over to a judge) to Him who judges (decides) "righteously" (*dikaiōs*, justly, equitably).

2:24. Christ himself "bare" (*anēnenken*, carry, offer up, a verb commonly used of bringing sacrifices to an altar, as in 1 Peter 2:5) their sins in His own "body" (*sōmati*, as Isaiah 53:12 states, "He bare the sin of many") on the "tree" (*xulon*, timber, not a live tree). The cross became the altar, and Jesus became the perfect sin offering (Hebrews 9:28).

Peter here explained the purpose of Christ's death and resurrection, as Paul did also in Romans 6:1-23. It is that believers, being "dead" to sins (*apogenomenoi*, departed, absent, having renounced all sins) should "live" (*zēsōmen*, vital existence) unto "righteousness" (*dikaiosunē*, equity, doing right, as in Hebrews 1:9; also in 1 Peter 3:14; 2 Peter 1:1; 2:5,21; 3:13).

Referring again to the Crucifixion, Peter said that by Christ's "stripes" (*mōlōpi*, black bruise, bloody wound) they were "healed" (from *iaomai*, heal, make whole). Numerous believers to whom Peter was writing were slaves who may have received such stripes. Usually *iaomai* denotes physical healing, but sometimes, as in Hebrews 12:13, it means spiritual healing. Peter's meaning here is restoration as the context indicates. Christ healed their waywardness and sin so they could be restored to the sheepfold, live righteously, and not be as sheep going astray (2:25).

2:25. Before being healed they were as sheep "going astray" (*planōmena*, seduced, roaming into danger, as in 2 Peter 2:15). Peter was recalling Isaiah 53:6. Now, however, they have "returned" (from *epistrephō*, turn about, convert, come back; used negatively in 2 Peter 2:21,22) unto the "Shepherd" (from *poimēn*,

22. Who did no sin, neither was guile found in his mouth: Nothing false was ever found, *SEB* . . . He was guilty of no sin or the slightest prevarication, *Phillips* . . . neither was Deceit found, *Wilson* . . . He never did anything wrong, nor was anything deceitful ever heard from his lips, *TCNT* . . . who never in a single instance committed a sin...after careful scrutiny, there was found not even craftiness, *Wuest* . . . did not commit sin and never uttered a lie, *TNT*.

23. Who, when he was reviled, reviled not again: When they insulted Christ, *SEB* . . . who when His heart was being wounded with an accursed sting, and when He was being made the object of harsh rebuke and biting, never retaliated, *Wuest* . . . did not revile in return, *Campbell* . . . did not return the insult, *Berkeley*.

when he suffered, he threatened not; but committed [himself] to him that judgeth righteously: . . . did not threaten when abused, *Berkeley* . . . made no threats of revenge...committed his cause to the one who judges fairly, *Phillips* . . . yet gave it over to Him Who is judging justly, *Concordant* . . . kept on delivering all into the keeping of the One, *Wuest*.

24. Who his own self bare our sins in his own body on the tree: . . . who personally in His own body, *Berkeley* . . . carries up our sins in His body on to the pole, *Concordant* . . . on the cross, *Williams*.

that we, being dead to sins, should live unto righteousness: . . . having died with respect to our sins, *Wuest* . . . coming away from sins, *Concordant* . . . so that we might abandon our sins, *Berkeley*.

by whose stripes ye were healed: . . . by whose scars, *Wilson* . . . by Whose welt, *Concordant* . . . By his bleeding wounds, *Swann* . . . by his trickling bruises, *Berkeley* . . . bleeding stripe, *Wuest* . . . His bruising was your healing, *TCNT*.

25. For ye were as sheep going astray: You had wandered away like so many sheep, *Phillips* . . . then you strayed like sheep, *Berkeley*.

4026.2 noun acc sing masc	2504.1 conj	1969.1 noun acc sing masc	3450.1 art gen pl	5425.6 noun gen pl fem	5050.2 prs-pron gen 2pl
ποιμένα	καὶ	ἐπίσκοπον	τῶν	ψυχῶν	ὑμῶν.
poimena	*kai*	*episkopon*	*tōn*	*psuchōn*	*humōn*
shepherd	and	overseer	of the	souls	your.

1.a.**Txt:** 01ℵ-corr,04C 018K,020L,025P,etc.byz. Sod
Var: 01ℵ-org,02A,03B Lach,Treg,Tisc,We/Ho Weis,UBS/☆

3532.1 adv	3450.13 art nom pl fem	1129.6 noun nom pl fem	5131.13 verb nom pl fem part pres mid
3:1. Ὁμοίως,	⸂[a] αἱ ⸃	γυναῖκες,	ὑποτασσόμεναι
Homoiōs	*hai*	*gunaikes*	*hupotassomenai*
Likewise,	the	wives,	being subject

3450.4 art dat pl	2375.5 adj dat pl	433.8 noun dat pl masc	2419.1 conj	2504.1 conj	1479.1 conj
τοῖς	ἰδίοις	ἀνδράσιν,	ἵνα	καὶ	εἴ
tois	*idiois*	*andrasin*	*hina*	*kai*	*ei*
to the	your own	husbands,	that,	even	if

4948.7 indef-pron nom pl masc	540.1 verb 3pl indic pres act	3450.3 art dat sing	3030.3 noun dat sing masc	1217.2 prep	3450.10 art gen sing fem
τινες	ἀπειθοῦσιν	τῷ	λόγῳ,	διὰ	τῆς
tines	*apeithousin*	*tō*	*logō*	*dia*	*tēs*
any	are disobedient	to the	word,	by	the

3450.1 art gen pl	1129.7 noun gen pl fem	389.1 noun gen sing fem	425.1 prep	3030.2 noun gen sing masc
τῶν	γυναικῶν	ἀναστροφῆς	ἄνευ	λόγου
tōn	*gunaikōn*	*anastrophēs*	*aneu*	*logou*
of the	wives	conduct	without	word

1.b.**Txt:** byz.
Var: 01ℵ,02A,03B,04C 018K,020L,025P,Lach Treg,Alf,Tisc,We/Ho Weis,Sod,UBS/☆

2741.9 verb 3pl subj fut pass	2741.12 verb 3pl indic fut pass	2013.1 verb nom pl masc part aor act
⸀ κερδηθήσωνται	[[b]☆ κερδηθήσονται]	**2.** ἐποπτεύσαντες
kerdēthēsōntai	*kerdēthēsontai*	*epopteusantes*
they may be gained,	[they will be gained]	having witnessed

3450.12 art acc sing fem	1706.1 prep	5238.3 noun dat sing masc	52.5 adj acc sing fem	389.3 noun acc sing fem	5050.2 prs-pron gen 2pl
τὴν	ἐν	φόβῳ	ἁγνὴν	ἀναστροφὴν	ὑμῶν·
tēn	*en*	*phobō*	*hagnēn*	*anastrophēn*	*humōn*
the	in	fear	chaste	conduct	your;

3614.1 rel-pron gen pl	1498.17 verb 3sing impr pres act	3620.1 partic	3450.5 art nom sing masc	1839.1 prep	1692.1 noun gen sing fem
3. ὧν	ἔστω	οὐχ	ὁ	ἔξωθεν	ἐμπλοκῆς
hōn	*estō*	*ouch*	*ho*	*exōthen*	*emplokēs*
whose	let it be	not	the	outward	of braiding

3.a.**Txt:** 01ℵ,02A,03B 025P,byz.
Var: p72,04C,044,1852 sa.

2336.4 noun gen pl fem	2504.1 conj	3888.1 noun gen sing fem	5388.4 noun gen pl neu	2211.1 conj	1729.1 noun gen sing fem
⸂[a] τριχῶν, ⸃	καὶ	περιθέσεως	χρυσίων	ἢ	ἐνδύσεως
trichōn	*kai*	*peritheseōs*	*chrusiōn*	*ē*	*enduseōs*
of hair,	and	putting around	of gold,	or	putting on

2416.5 noun gen pl neu	2862.1 noun nom sing masc	233.1 conj	3450.5 art nom sing masc	2899.1 adj nom sing masc	3450.10 art gen sing fem
ἱματίων	κόσμος·	**4.** ἀλλ'	ὁ	κρυπτὸς	τῆς
himatiōn	*kosmos*	*all'*	*ho*	*kruptos*	*tēs*
of garments	adorning;	but	the	hidden	of the

2559.1 noun fem	442.1 noun nom sing masc	1706.1 prep	3450.3 art dat sing	855.3 adj dat sing masc	3450.2 art gen sing
καρδίας	ἄνθρωπος,	ἐν	τῷ	ἀφθάρτῳ	τοῦ
kardias	*anthrōpos*	*en*	*tō*	*aphthartō*	*tou*
heart	man,	in	the	incorruptible	of the

keeper of sheep; translated "pastors" in Ephesians 4:11) and "Bishop" (*episkopon*, overseer, supervisor) of their souls. Here alone is Christ called the believers' Bishop who faithfully watches over His people. This verse recalls Jesus' words in Luke 15:4-7, the Parable of the Lost Sheep. Jesus called himself the Good Shepherd (John 10:11).

but are now returned unto the Shepherd and Bishop of your souls: . . . you turned back to...the Supervisor of, *Concordant* . . . and Guardian, *Montgomery* . . . and [spiritual] Overseer, *Wuest* . . . of your lives, *Wilson.*

3:1. After writing about a servant's duty to be subject to an ungodly master, Peter wrote of a wife's duty toward an unbelieving husband. He directed "wives" (*gunaikes*, a woman, particularly a wife) to be in "subjection" (*hupotassomenai*, submission, under obedience) to their own husbands. *Hupotagēte* is used of submission to God (James 4:7) in contrast to yielding to Satan and again of submission to God's will as a son submits to the authority of his father (Hebrews 12:9). The word implies a voluntary adjustment to authority that is recognized as proper.

The object is that if any husbands are unbelievers—that is, if they "obey not" (*apeithousin*, refuse to believe) the "word" (*logō*, utterance, communication, message; likely means preaching)—they also without a word may be won to God by the "conversation" (*anastrophēs*, behavior) of their wives.

1. Likewise, ye wives, [be] in subjection to your own husbands: . . . you married women, *TCNT, Williams* . . . be subordinate to your respective husbands, *Wade* . . . with implicit obedience, *Wuest.*

that, if any obey not the word: . . . if any are stubborn also, as to the word, *Concordant* . . . even though certain ones obstinately refuse to be persuaded by, *Wuest.*

they also may without the word be won by the conversation of the wives: . . . they will be gained without a word, *Concordant* . . . the behavior, *Montgomery.*

3:2. Though unbelieving husbands may not listen to gospel preaching, Peter said the pure and respectful conduct of their wives is a silent message they cannot easily ignore. They will be won over as they "behold" (*epopteusantes*, inspect, watch, as in 1 Peter 2:12) the wives' "chaste" (*hagnēn*, modest, pure, as in 1 Timothy 5:22) behavior combined with "fear" (*phobō*, awe, reverence; see Ephesians 5:33).

2. While they behold your chaste conversation [coupled] with fear: . . . being spectators of your pure behavior in fear, *Concordant* . . . having viewed attentively your pure manner of life which is accompanied by a reverential fear, *Wuest* . . . and deferential bearing, *Wade.*

3:3. Wives who wish to win their husbands for Christ should not depend on outward adornment such as braiding their hair, wearing gold trinkets, or putting on fine clothes, as worldly women do. *Kosmos* ("adorning") here has its old meaning of ornament, not the common meaning of the world (Robertson, *Word Pictures in the New Testament*, 6:108). Their adorning should not be that outward adorning of "plaiting" (*emplokēs*, elaborate braiding, interweaving; translated "entangled" in 2 Timothy 2:4 and 2 Peter 2:20) the hair. Nor should it be the "wearing" (*peritheseōs*, put around, wrap) of gold (ornaments of gold worn around the hair as nets, as well as on fingers, arms, and ankles) or of putting on of apparel. Peter was not forbidding the use of jewelry any more than the wearing of clothes but was contrasting outward display with inward beauty.

3. Whose adorning let it not be that outward [adorning]: . . . let it not be that external one, *Wilson* . . . which is from without and merely, *Wuest.*

of plaiting the hair: . . . of braiding aught into, *Concordant* . . . an elaborate gathering of the hair into knots, *Wuest* . . . the outer beauty of fancy hairdos, *SEB.*

and of wearing of gold: . . . a lavish display, *Wuest* . . . of decking with gold, *Concordant* . . . golden trinkets, *Fenton.*

or of putting on of apparel: . . . the donning of, *Wuest* . . . the wearing of beautiful dresses, *Montgomery* . . . garments, *Concordant.*

3:4. Their adorning should be the "hidden" man (*kruptos*, secret, concealed, private) of the "heart" (*kardias*, innermost part of the being) in that which is "not corruptible" (*aphthartō*, imperishable,

4. But [let it be] the hidden man of the heart, in that which is not corruptible: . . . the unseen woman, *Fenton* . . . hidden human of the heart, *Concordant* . . . let that adornment be the hidden personality in the heart, imperishable in quality, *Wuest* . . . unfading loveliness, *Noli.*

4098.6 adj gen sing fem	2504.1 conj	2250.2 adj gen sing neu	4011.2 noun gen sing neu	3614.16 rel-pron sing neu	1498.4 verb 3sing indic pres act
πρᾳέος	καὶ	ἡσυχίου	πνεύματος,	ὅ	ἐστιν
praeos	*kai*	*hēsuchiou*	*pneumatos*	*ho*	*estin*
gentle	and	quiet	spirit,	which	is

1783.1 prep	3450.2 art gen sing	2296.2 noun gen sing masc	4045.3 adj sing neu	3643.1 adv	1056.1 conj
ἐνώπιον	τοῦ	θεοῦ	πολυτελές.	5. οὕτως	γάρ
enōpion	*tou*	*theou*	*poluteles*	*houtōs*	*gar*
before		God	of great price.	Thus	for

4077.1 adv	2504.1 conj	3450.13 art nom pl fem	39.14 adj nom pl fem	1129.6 noun nom pl fem	3450.13 art nom pl fem
ποτε	καὶ	αἱ	ἅγιαι	γυναῖκες	αἱ
pote	*kai*	*hai*	*hagiai*	*gunaikes*	*hai*
formerly	also	the	holy	women	the

5.a.**Txt:** 01ℵ,018K,020L byz.
Var: 02A,03B,04C,Lach Treg,Alf,Word,Tisc We/Ho,Weis,Sod UBS/☆

1666.6 verb nom pl fem part pres act	1894.3 prep	3450.6 art acc sing masc	1519.1 prep	2296.4 noun acc sing masc	2858.5 verb 3pl indic imperf act
ἐλπίζουσαι	ʼ ἐπὶ	τὸν	[a☆ εἰς]	θεὸν	ἐκόσμουν
elpizousai	*epi*	*ton*	*eis*	*theon*	*ekosmoun*
hoping	in		[unto]	God	were adorning

1431.13 prs-pron acc pl fem	5131.13 verb nom pl fem part pres mid	3450.4 art dat pl	2375.5 adj dat pl	433.8 noun dat pl masc
ἑαυτάς,	ὑποτασσόμεναι	τοῖς	ἰδίοις	ἀνδράσιν·
heautas	*hupotassomenai*	*tois*	*idiois*	*andrasin*
themselves,	being subject	to the	their own	husbands;

5453.1 conj	4421.1 name nom fem	5057.5 verb 3sing indic aor act	3450.3 art dat sing	11.1 name masc	2935.4 noun acc sing masc
6. ὡς	Σάῤῥα	ὑπήκουσεν	τῷ	Ἀβραάμ,	κύριον
hōs	*Sarrha*	*hupēkousen*	*tō*	*Abraam*	*kurion*
as	Sarah	obeyed		Abraham,	lord

840.6 prs-pron acc sing masc	2535.6 verb nom sing fem part pres act	3614.10 rel-pron gen sing fem	1090.35 verb 2pl indic aor pass	4891.4 noun pl neu
αὐτὸν	καλοῦσα,	ἧς	ἐγενήθητε	τέκνα
auton	*kalousa*	*hēs*	*egenēthēte*	*tekna*
him	calling;	of whom	you became	children,

15.6 verb nom pl fem part pres act	2504.1 conj	3231.1 partic	5236.10 verb nom pl fem part pres mid	3235.5 num card acc fem
ἀγαθοποιοῦσαι	καὶ	μὴ	φοβούμεναι	μηδεμίαν
agathopoiousai	*kai*	*mē*	*phoboumenai*	*mēdemian*
doing good	and	not	fearing	the

4281.1 noun acc sing fem	3450.7 art nom pl masc	433.6 noun nom pl masc	3532.1 adv	4775.1 verb nom pl masc part pres act
πτόησιν.	7. Οἱ	ἄνδρες	ὁμοίως,	συνοικοῦντες
ptoēsin	*Hoi*	*andres*	*homoiōs*	*sunoikountes*
intimidation.	The	husbands	likewise,	dwelling with

2567.3 prep	1102.4 noun acc sing fem	5453.1 conj	766.8 adj comp dat sing neu	4487.2 noun dat sing neu
κατὰ	γνῶσιν,	ὡς	ἀσθενεστέρῳ	σκεύει
kata	*gnōsin*	*hōs*	*asthenesterō*	*skeuei*
according to	knowledge,	as	with a weaker	vessel

3450.3 art dat sing	1128.1 adj dat sing neu	626.1 verb nom pl masc part pres act	4940.4 noun acc sing fem	5453.1 conj	2504.1 conj
τῷ	γυναικείῳ	ἀπονέμοντες	τιμήν,	ὡς	καὶ
tō	*gunaikeiō*	*aponemontes*	*timēn*	*hōs*	*kai*
with the	female,	rendering	honor,	as	also

immortal, as also in 1:4,23). This should include the ornament of a "meek" (*praeos*, humble, mild, gentle) and "quiet" (*hēsuchiou*, peaceable, undisturbed) "spirit" (*pneumatos*, here meaning disposition, temper, as in 1 Corinthians 4:21) which is "of great price" (*poluteles*, very precious, as in Mark 14:3 and 1 Timothy 2:9) "in the sight" of God (*enōpion*, before, in the face of, as in James 4:10). God sees "in secret" (Matthew 6:4,6). He looks not on the outward appearance but on the heart (1 Samuel 16:7). Outward adornments are perishable, but a meek and quiet spirit is a very precious ornament in God's estimation.

3:5. This is how the holy women of ancient times used to adorn themselves. They "trusted" (*elpizousai*, hoped, fixed their expectation, placed their confidence) in God and were "in subjection" (*hupotassomenai*, submissive, under obedience) to their own husbands.

3:6. As a prime example Peter pointed to Sarah who "obeyed" (*hupēkousen*, heed, pay attention to, do as commanded) Abraham, calling him "lord" (*kurion*, master, see Genesis 18:12; this was a general term of respect as in Genesis 23:6,11,15; 31:35; 32:4). Peter said they were true descendants of Sarah if they "do well" (*agathopoiousai*, be virtuous, have a good reputation, as in 1 Peter 2:15) and "are not afraid" (*phoboumenai*, be put in fear) with any "amazement" (*ptoēsin*, terror); that is, are "not afraid of sudden fear" (Proverbs 3:25). Hart suggests that "perhaps Peter regarded Sarah's falsehood as the yielding to a sudden terror for which God rebuked her" (5:64).

3:7. Having described the duties of wives, Peter next turned to husbands. They should "dwell" (*sunoikountes*, reside together) with their wives "according to *knowledge*" (*gnōsin*). Peter did not use the word *ginōskō* which appears in Matthew 1:25 in reference to carnal knowledge but used *gnosin* which indicates a mental understanding. Husbands should understand their wives and show respectful consideration toward them, realizing (1) that wives are "weaker" (*asthenesterō*, more feeble) than their husbands, and (2) that husbands and wives are joint heirs of the "grace" (*charitos*, benefit, favor) of life. Both husband and wife are essential in the marriage partnership; each needs the other, as indicated by Paul: "Neither is the man without the woman, neither the woman without the man" (1 Corinthians 11:11).

Prayers may be "hindered" (*ekkoptesthai*, cut off, hewn down) by wrongdoing or shortcomings in the life of any believer. As examples, Jesus mentioned such problems as a grievance between

[even the ornament] of a meek and quiet spirit, which is in the sight of God of great price: . . . a meek and quiet disposition, *Wuest* . . . in the incorruptibility...is costly, *Concordant* . . . something of surpassing value in God's sight, *Berkeley.*

5. For after this manner: . . . thus formerly, *Wuest* . . . in this way, *Berkeley.*
in the old time:
the holy women also, who trusted in God, adorned themselves: . . . whose expectation was in God, *Concordant* . . . who fixed their hope on God, *Berkeley* . . . sought to make themselves attractive, *Norlie.*
being in subjection unto their own husbands: . . . submissive as they were, *Berkeley* . . . and obeyed their husbands, *Noli.*

6. Even as Sara obeyed Abraham, calling him lord: Sarah, for instance, *Berkeley* . . . was in the habit of rendering obedience to, *Wuest.*
whose daughters ye are, as long as ye do well: . . . whose children you became, doing good, *Concordant* . . . Her genuine daughters you become insofar as you do right, *Berkeley* . . . if the whole course of your life is in the doing of good, *Wuest.*
and are not afraid with any amazement: . . . and let nothing upset you, *Norlie* . . . fearing no intimidation, *Adams* . . . not fearing dismay in anything, *Concordant* . . . not being caused to fear by even one particle of terror, *Wuest* . . . not being frightened by any passionate emotion, *Fenton* . . . yield to no agitating fears, *Wade* . . . are not terrorized by any fear, *Berkeley.*

7. Likewise, ye husbands, dwell with [them] according to knowledge: You married men, *Williams* . . . live in the proper relation, *TCNT* . . . let your home life with them be governed by the dictates of knowledge, *Wuest.*
giving honour unto the wife, as unto the weaker vessel: . . . awarding honor, *Concordant* . . . assigning honour to their feminine nature, *Fenton* . . . as you would for a fragile vase, *Adams.*

7.a.**Txt:** 02A,04C,018K 020L,025P,byz. **Var:** p72,01ℵ-corr,03B 33,it.Treg,Alf,Sod UBS/☆

4640.1 adj nom pl masc	**4640.4** adj dat pl masc	**5322.2** noun gen sing fem	**2205.2** noun gen sing fem
⸀ συγκληρονόμοι	[a☆ συγκληρονόμοις]	χάριτος	ζωῆς,
sunklēronomoi	*sunklēronomois*	*charitos*	*zōēs*
joint heirs	[idem]	of grace	of life,

7.b.**Txt:** 04C-corr,018K 020L,byz. **Var:** 02A,03B,025P Gries,Lach,Treg,Alf Word,We/Ho,Sod UBS/☆

1519.1 prep	**3450.16** art sing neu	**3231.1** partic	**1568.5** verb inf pres mid	**1458.4** verb inf pres mid
εἰς	τὸ	μὴ	⸀ ἐκκόπτεσθαι	[b☆ ἐγκόπτεσθαι]
eis	*to*	*mē*	*ekkoptesthai*	*enkoptesthai*
so as	the	not	to be cut off	[idem]

3450.15 art acc pl fem	**4194.8** noun acc pl fem	**5050.2** prs-pron gen 2pl	**3450.16** art sing neu	**1156.2** conj	**4904.1** noun sing neu	**3820.7** adj nom pl masc
τὰς	προσευχὰς	ὑμῶν.	**8.** Τὸ	δὲ	τέλος,	πάντες
tas	*proseuchas*	*humōn*	*To*	*de*	*telos*	*pantes*
the	prayers	your.	The	and	end,	all

3538.1 adj nom pl masc	**4686.1** adj nom pl masc	**5198.1** adj nom pl masc	**2136.1** adj nom pl masc
ὁμόφρονες,	συμπαθεῖς,	φιλάδελφοι,	εὔσπλαγχνοι,
homophrones	*sumpatheis*	*philadelphoi*	*eusplanchnoi*
of one mind,	sympathizing,	loving the brothers,	tenderhearted,

8.a.**Txt:** 018K,025P,byz. **Var:** 01ℵ,02A,03B,04C bo.Gries,Lach,Treg,Alf Word,Tisc,We/Ho,Weis Sod,UBS/☆

5228.1 adj nom pl masc	**4863.1** adj nom pl	**3231.1** partic	**586.4** verb nom pl masc part pres act
⸀ φιλόφρονες·	[a☆ ταπεινόφρονες,]	**9.** μὴ	ἀποδιδόντες
philophrones	*tapeinophrones*	*mē*	*apodidontes*
friendly,	[humble minded,]	not	rendering

2527.7 adj sing neu	**470.2** prep	**2527.8** adj gen sing neu	**2211.1** conj	**3033.2** noun acc sing fem	**470.2** prep	**3033.1** noun gen sing fem
κακὸν	ἀντὶ	κακοῦ,	ἢ	λοιδορίαν	ἀντὶ	λοιδορίας·
kakon	*anti*	*kakou*	*ē*	*loidorian*	*anti*	*loidorias*
evil	for	evil,	or	insulting	for	insulting;

9.a.**Txt:** 020L,025P,byz. **Var:** 01ℵ,02A,03B,04C 018K,33,Lach,Treg,Alf Tisc,We/Ho,Weis,Sod UBS/☆

4967.1 noun sing neu	**1156.2** conj	**2108.5** verb nom pl masc part pres act	**3471.20** verb nom pl masc part perf act	**3617.1** conj	**1519.1** prep
τοὐναντίον	δὲ	εὐλογοῦντες,	⸂a εἰδότες ⸃	ὅτι	εἰς
tounantion	*de*	*eulogountes*	*eidotes*	*hoti*	*eis*
on the contrary,	but	blessing,	knowing	that	to

3642.17 dem-pron sing neu	**2535.38** verb 2pl indic aor pass	**2419.1** conj	**2110.4** noun acc sing fem	**2789.6** verb 2pl subj aor act
τοῦτο	ἐκλήθητε,	ἵνα	εὐλογίαν	κληρονομήσητε.
touto	*eklēthēte*	*hina*	*eulogian*	*klēronomēsēte*
this	you were called,	that	blessing	you should inherit.

3450.5 art nom sing masc	**1056.1** conj	**2286.12** verb nom sing masc part pres act	**2205.4** noun acc sing fem	**25.11** verb inf pres act	**2504.1** conj
10. ὁ	γὰρ	θέλων	ζωὴν	ἀγαπᾶν,	καὶ
ho	*gar*	*thelōn*	*zōēn*	*agapan*	*kai*
The	for	willing	life	to love,	and

10.a.**Txt:** 01ℵ,018K 020L,025P,byz.bo. **Var:** 02A,03B,04C,33 Lach,Treg,Alf,Tisc We/Ho,Weis,Sod UBS/☆

1481.19 verb inf aor act	**2232.1** noun fem	**18.13** adj acc pl fem	**3835.1** verb 3sing impr aor act	**3450.12** art acc sing fem
ἰδεῖν	ἡμέρας	ἀγαθὰς,	παυσάτω	τὴν
idein	*hēmeras*	*agathas*	*pausatō*	*tēn*
to see	days	good,	let him cause to cease	the

10.b.**Txt:** 020L,025P,byz. bo. **Var:** 01ℵ,02A,03B,04C 018K,33,Lach,Treg,Alf Tisc,We/Ho,Weis,Sod UBS/☆

1094.4 noun acc sing fem	**840.3** prs-pron gen sing	**570.3** prep	**2527.8** adj gen sing neu	**2504.1** conj	**5327.4** noun pl neu	**840.3** prs-pron gen sing
γλῶσσαν	⸂a αὐτοῦ ⸃	ἀπὸ	κακοῦ,	καὶ	χείλη	⸂b αὐτοῦ ⸃
glōssan	*autou*	*apo*	*kakou*	*kai*	*cheilē*	*autou*
tongue	his	from	evil,	and	lips	his

friends (Matthew 5:23) and an unforgiving spirit (Matthew 6:15). Peter indicated a husband's failure to respect his wife as an equal partner may block his prayers and make them ineffective. This warning may apply not only to private prayers but also to a household's united prayers. Family members cannot pray together effectively if there are strained relationships between them. This is particularly true if the misunderstanding or hostility is between husband and wife.

3:8. Peter then addressed all, whether masters or servants, husbands or wives, and exhorts the entire body of believers to be "of one mind" (*homophrones,* like-minded, harmonious). Their attitude toward each other should be one of "compassion" (*sumpatheis,* sympathy, a fellow-feeling), and they should always show brotherly love, be "pitiful" (*eusplanchnoi,* tender-hearted), and "courteous" (*philophrones,* kind and friendly). Whether the believers were failing on these points or not, the instruction probably was not new—for these things were taught very generally by Christ and His apostles—but Peter wished to stir up their pure minds by way of remembrance (2 Peter 3:1). His exhortation would reinforce the teaching and encourage them to obey it.

3:9. Peter said the believers are called to receive a blessing, and in order to receive it they should invoke blessing on others, even those who injure them and revile them. They should not return "evil for evil" (*kakon,* wicked and injurious talk) nor "railing for railing" (*loidorian,* slander, reproach). Instead they should render "blessing" (*eulogountes,* commendation, benediction). As a reward, they will inherit a blessing which is explained in verse 10. This earthly blessing is in addition to their eternal inheritance which is "reserved in heaven" (1:4). Peter is echoing Christ's teaching: "Love your enemies, bless them that curse you, . . . that ye may be the children of your Father which is in heaven: for he maketh his sun to rise on the evil and on the good, and sendeth rain on the just and on the unjust" (Matthew 5:44,45).

3:10. In verses 10-12, Peter explained the "blessing" of verse 9 by quoting David's words in Psalm 34:12-16. He spoke of loving "life" (*zōēn,* life, either literal or figurative; probably he means a prolonged natural life, though he could mean spiritual life) and of seeing good "days" (*hēmeras,* either a 24-hour day or, figuratively, an extended period). To enjoy this full and satisfying life, Peter said the believer should "refrain" (*pausatō,* restrain, quit, cease; as in 4:1, "He that hath suffered in the flesh hath ceased from sin") from speaking "evil" (*kakou,* wicked, harmful talk) and let no words of "guile" (*dolon,* craftiness, subtilty, deceit) escape his lips.

and as being heirs together of the grace of life: . . . fellow-inheritors with you, *Wuest* . . . who are also joint enjoyers of the allotment of the varied grace of life, *Concordant.*

that your prayers be not hindered: . . . and this, in order that no [Satanic] inroads be made into your prayers, *Wuest* . . . may not be denied, *Norlie.*

8. Finally, [be ye] all of one mind, having compassion one of another: Last of all, *NLT* . . . Now, to come to a conclusion, *Wuest* . . . Now the finish: Be all of a like disposition, *Concordant* . . . you should all be united, sympathetic, *TCNT* . . . have unity of spirit, *Noli* . . . be harmonious, *Montgomery* . . . have sympathy, *Norlie* . . . sympathising, *Darby* . . . you must be together in your thinking, *SEB.*

love as brethren, [be] pitiful, [be] courteous: . . . full of brotherly love, *Darby* . . . fond of the brethren, tenderly compassionate, of a humble disposition, *Concordant* . . . tender-hearted ...humble-minded, *Wuest.*

9. Not rendering evil for evil, or railing for railing: . . . not paying back, *Montgomery* . . . not returning wrong for wrong, *Fenton* . . . not giving back evil in exchange for evil, or verbal abuse in exchange for verbal abuse, *Wuest* . . . or abuse for abuse, *TCNT* . . . nor insult for insult, *Noli* . . . reviling for reviling, *Concordant.*

but contrariwise blessing; knowing that ye are thereunto called, that ye should inherit a blessing: . . . be constantly blessing, *Wuest* . . . speaking pleasantly, *Fenton* . . . you should be enjoying the allotment of blessing, *Concordant.*

10. For he that will love life, and see good days: Whoever wants to enjoy life, *Williams* . . . be acquainted with good days, *Concordant* . . . experience happy days, *TCNT.*

let him refrain his tongue from evil, and his lips that they speak no guile: . . . the natural tendency of his tongue, *Wuest* . . . cease from evil, *Concordant* . . . speaking deceit, *Wilson* . . . annoyance, *Fenton.*

1 Peter 3:11

11.a.**Var:** 02A,03B 04C-org,Lach,Treg,Alf We/Ho,Weis,Sod UBS/⋆

3450.2 art gen sing	**3231.1** partic	**2953.37** verb inf aor act	**1382.4** noun acc sing masc	**1565.2** verb 3sing impr aor act	**1156.2** conj
τοῦ	μὴ	λαλῆσαι	δόλον.	**11.** ἐκκλινάτω	[a⋆+ δὲ]
tou	*mē*	*lalēsai*	*dolon*	*ekklinatō*	*de*
the	not	to speak	deceit.	Let him turn aside	[and]

570.3 prep	**2527.8** adj gen sing neu	**2504.1** conj	**4020.35** verb 3sing impr aor act	**18.3** adj sing	**2195.19** verb 3sing impr aor act
ἀπὸ	κακοῦ,	καὶ	ποιησάτω	ἀγαθόν·	ζητησάτω
apo	*kakou*	*kai*	*poiēsatō*	*agathon*	*zētēsatō*
from	evil,	and	let him do	good.	Let him seek

12.a.**Txt:** 04C-corr,Steph **Var:** 01ℵ,02A,03B 04C-org,018K,020L 025P,Lach,Treg,Alf Tisc,We/Ho,Weis,Sod UBS/⋆

1503.4 noun acc sing fem	**2504.1** conj	**1371.17** verb 3sing impr aor act	**840.12** prs-pron acc sing fem	**3617.1** conj	**3450.7** art nom pl masc
εἰρήνην,	καὶ	διωξάτω	αὐτήν.	**12.** ὅτι	⸂a οἱ ⸃
eirēnēn	*kai*	*diōxatō*	*autēn*	*hoti*	*hoi*
peace,	and	let him pursue	it:	because	the

3652.5 noun nom pl masc	**2935.2** noun gen sing masc	**1894.3** prep	**1337.9** adj acc pl masc	**2504.1** conj	**3640.2** noun pl neu
ὀφθαλμοὶ	κυρίου	ἐπὶ	δικαίους,	καὶ	ὦτα
ophthalmoi	*kuriou*	*epi*	*dikaious*	*kai*	*ōta*
eyes	of Lord	on	righteous,	and	ears

840.3 prs-pron gen sing	**1519.1** prep	**1157.4** noun acc sing fem	**840.1** prs-pron gen pl	**4241.1** noun sing neu	**1156.2** conj
αὐτοῦ	εἰς	δέησιν	αὐτῶν·	πρόσωπον	δὲ
autou	*eis*	*deēsin*	*autōn*	*prosōpon*	*de*
his	toward	supplication	their.	Face	but

2935.2 noun gen sing masc	**1894.3** prep	**4020.18** verb acc pl masc part pres act	**2527.9** adj pl neu	**2504.1** conj	**4949.3** intr-pron nom sing
κυρίου	ἐπὶ	ποιοῦντας	κακά.	**13.** Καὶ	τίς
kuriou	*epi*	*poiountas*	*kaka*	*Kai*	*tis*
of Lord	against	doing	evil.	And	who

3450.5 art nom sing masc	**2530.5** verb nom sing masc part fut act	**5050.4** prs-pron acc 2pl	**1430.1** partic	**3450.2** art gen sing	**18.2** adj gen sing
ὁ	κακώσων	ὑμᾶς,	ἐὰν	τοῦ	ἀγαθοῦ
ho	*kakōsōn*	*humas*	*ean*	*tou*	*agathou*
the	shall be injuring	you,	if	of the	good

13.a.**Txt:** 018K,020L 025P,byz. **Var:** 01ℵ,02A,03B,04C 33,Lach,Treg,Alf,Word Tisc,We/Ho,Weis,Sod UBS/⋆

3266.1 noun nom pl masc	**2190.3** noun nom pl masc	**1090.42** verb 2pl subj aor mid	**233.1** conj	**1479.1** conj
⸀ μιμηταὶ	[a⋆ ζηλωταὶ]	γένησθε;	**14.** ἀλλ᾽	εἰ
mimētai	*zēlōtai*	*genēsthe*	*all'*	*ei*
imitators	[zealots]	you should be?	But	if

2504.1 conj	**3819.5** verb 2pl opt pres act	**1217.2** prep	**1336.4** noun acc sing fem	**3079.4** adj nom pl masc
καὶ	πάσχοιτε	διὰ	δικαιοσύνην,	μακάριοι.
kai	*paschoite*	*dia*	*dikaiosunēn*	*makarioi*
also	you should suffer	on account of	righteousness,	blessed;

3450.6 art acc sing masc	**1156.2** conj	**5238.4** noun acc sing masc	**840.1** prs-pron gen pl	**3231.1** partic	**5236.17** verb 2pl subj aor pass
τὸν	δὲ	φόβον	αὐτῶν	μὴ	φοβηθῆτε
ton	*de*	*phobon*	*autōn*	*mē*	*phobēthēte*
the	but	fear	their	not	you should be afraid of,

14.a.**Txt:** 01ℵ,02A,04C 025P,044,byz. **Var:** p72,03B,020L

3234.1 adv	**4866.10** verb 2pl subj aor pass	**2935.4** noun acc sing masc	**1156.2** conj	**3450.6** art acc sing masc
⸂a⋆ μηδὲ	ταραχθῆτε· ⸃	**15.** κύριον	δὲ	τὸν
mēde	*tarachthēte*	*kurion*	*de*	*ton*
neither	should you be troubled;	Lord	but	the

3:11. The believer should not entertain evil thoughts nor expose himself to temptation. On the contrary, he should "eschew" evil (*ekklinatō,* avoid, go out of the way), that is, get out of its way when he sees temptation coming. "Eschew" is from a Norman word (*eschever*) meaning to shun or avoid. The believer should "lean away from" evil; he should bend over backward to avoid it.

More than that, he should take positive steps to do "good" (*agathon,* good, beneficial deeds; as in Galatians 6:10, doing "good" unto all men). Good deeds and good words should mark the believer, and he should be known for good relationships also. He should "seek" peace (*zētēsatō,* desire, seek after; as in Matthew 2:13 where Herod sought the young child to destroy Him). Peter's words echo Hebrews 12:14, "Follow peace with all men." Earnest effort is indicated; the believer should "ensue" peace (*diōxatō,* pursue, follow hard after, as in Philippians 3:14, "I press toward the mark"). The word "ensue" is obsolete; a proper translation is "pursue."

3:12. Peter said the Lord's eyes are *upon* the righteous (not "over" as in the Authorized Version). God looks upon them with favor, and His ears are always open to their prayers. He will faithfully fulfill His promises to grant their petitions; but He will be equally faithful to fulfill His warnings of judgment against evildoers also, for His "face" (*prosōpon,* face, visage, countenance) is against them that do evil. God cannot countenance wrongdoing (Habakkuk 1:13, Berkeley), nor will He listen to the prayers of those who cherish iniquity in their hearts (Psalm 66:18, RSV).

3:13. The word "and" shows cause and effect, basing verse 13 on the preceding verse. Peter indicated that since the believers are righteous and God is watching out for them, no one can "harm" them (*kakōsōn,* injure, damage, hurt; as in Acts 18:10, "No man shall set on thee to hurt thee") as long as they continue to be "followers" (*mimētai,* imitators; as in 1 Corinthians 11:1, "Be ye followers of me, even as I also am of Christ") of that which is good. Peter did not want the believers to feel overwhelmed by persecutions. Though such may come, God will never allow the testing to be more than His servants are able to bear (1 Corinthians 10:13).

3:14. Peter said that if the believers, for righteousness' sake, should "chance to suffer" (as Alford translates it), they are "happy" (*makarioi,* supremely blessed, fortunate; same word as in Matthew 5:10). So they should not fear their enemies' threats; they should not be made "afraid" (*phobēthēte,* alarmed, frightened) by their "terror" (*phobon,* alarm, fear). They need not be "troubled" (*tarachthēte,* disturbed, agitated) nor live in fear of what might possibly happen. The Greek construction ("but and if") suggests that suffering pain for righteousness' sake will be a rare thing; it may happen, but probably not. Believers should be prepared whatever happens.

11. Let him eschew evil, and do good: He must turn away from, *SEB* . . . avoid evil, *Concordant* . . . let him turn aside from vice, *Fenton* . . . do right, *Berkeley.*

let him seek peace, and ensue it: . . . make it his aim, *Wade* . . . and follow after it, *TCNT* . . . pursue it, *Concordant* . . . search for peace and keep after it, *Berkeley.*

12. For the eyes of the Lord [are] over the righteous: . . . are directed in a favorable attitude towards, *Wuest* . . . are on upright men, *Williams* . . . on the just, *Concordant.*

and his ears [are open] unto their prayers: . . . are inclined, *Wuest* . . . and he is listening to their prayers, *SEB* . . . listen to their pleading cries, *Williams* . . . attentive to their prayer, *Fenton* . . . towards their supplications, *Darby* . . . for their petition, *Concordant.*

but the face of the Lord [is] against them that do evil: . . . the Lord frowns upon those who do wrong, *TCNT* . . . those who practice, *Wuest.*

13. And who [is] he that will harm you: . . . will injure you, *Wilson* . . . will be illtreating you, *Concordant* . . . do you evil, *Wuest.*

if ye be followers of that which is good?: . . . if you should become zealous of good? *Concordant* . . . if you become eager for the right? *Berkeley.*

14. But and if ye suffer for righteousness' sake, happy [are ye]: . . . if even you should perchance suffer...you are spiritually prosperous ones, *Wuest* . . . on account of righteousness, you are blessed, *Berkeley.*

and be not afraid of their terror, neither be troubled: Do not let man frighten you; and do not allow yourselves to be distressed, *TCNT* . . . Do not be dismayed, *Noli* . . . do not be affected with fear of them by the fear which they strive to inspire in you, neither become agitated, *Wuest* . . . you may not be afraid with their fear, nor yet be disturbed, *Concordant* . . . nor be alarmed, *Wilson* . . . or be disturbed at it, *Wade* . . . by their threat, *Berkeley.*

15.a.**Txt:** 018K,020L 025P,byz.
Var: p72,01ℵ,02A,03B 04C,33,it.sa.bo.Lach Treg,Alf,Word,Tisc We/Ho,Weis,Sod UBS/☆

2296.4 noun acc sing masc	**5382.4** name acc masc	**37.9** verb 2pl impr aor act	**1706.1** prep	**3450.14** art dat pl fem	**2559.7** noun dat pl fem
ʻ Θεὸν	[a☆ Χριστὸν]	ἁγιάσατε	ἐν	ταῖς	καρδίαις
Theon	*Christon*	*hagiasate*	*en*	*tais*	*kardiais*
God	[Christ]	sanctify	in	the	hearts

15.b.**Txt:** 02A,018K 020L,025P,byz.
Var: 01ℵ,03B,04C,33 bo.Lach,Treg,Tisc We/Ho,Weis,Sod UBS/☆

5050.2 prs-pron gen 2pl	**2071.1** adj nom pl	**1156.2** conj	**103.1** adv	**4242.1** prep	**621.4** noun acc sing fem	**3820.3** adj dat sing
ὑμῶν·	ἕτοιμοι	ʻb δὲ ˋ	ἀεὶ	πρὸς	ἀπολογίαν	παντὶ
humōn	*hetoimoi*	*de*	*aei*	*pros*	*apologian*	*panti*
your,	ready	and	always	for	a defense	to everyone

3450.3 art dat sing	**153.8** verb dat sing masc part pres act	**5050.4** prs-pron acc 2pl	**3030.4** noun acc sing masc	**3875.1** prep	**3450.10** art gen sing fem
τῷ	αἰτοῦντι	ὑμᾶς	λόγον	περὶ	τῆς
tō	*aitounti*	*humas*	*logon*	*peri*	*tēs*
the	asking	you	on account	concerning	the

15.c.**Var:** 01ℵ,02A,03B 04C,33,bo.Lach,Treg Alf,Word,Tisc,We/Ho Weis,Sod,UBS/☆

1706.1 prep	**5050.3** prs-pron dat 2pl	**1667.2** noun gen sing fem	**233.2** conj	**3196.3** prep	**4099.1** noun gen sing fem
ἐν	ὑμῖν	ἐλπίδος,	[c☆+ ἀλλὰ]	μετὰ	πραΰτητος
en	*humin*	*elpidos*	*alla*	*meta*	*prautētos*
in	you	hope,	[but]	with	gentleness

2504.1 conj	**5238.2** noun gen sing masc	**4743.4** noun acc sing fem	**2174.19** verb nom pl masc part pres act	**18.12** adj acc sing fem	**2419.1** conj
καὶ	φόβου·	**16.** συνείδησιν	ἔχοντες	ἀγαθήν,	ἵνα
kai	*phobou*	*suneidēsin*	*echontes*	*agathēn*	*hina*
and	fear;	a conscience	having	good,	that

16.a.**Txt:** 020L,byz.bo.
Var: p72,03B,044,sa.Alf Tisc,We/Ho,Weis,Sod UBS/☆

1706.1 prep	**3614.3** rel-pron dat sing	**2605.3** verb 3pl subj pres act	**2605.6** verb 2pl indic pres mid
ἐν	ᾧ	ʻ καταλαλῶσιν	[a☆ καταλαλεῖσθε]
en	*hō*	*katalalōsin*	*katalaleisthe*
in	which	they may speak against	[you are spoken against]

16.b.**Txt:** 01ℵ,02A,04C 018K,020L,025P,byz.bo.
Var: p72,03B,044,sa.Alf Tisc,We/Ho,Weis,Sod UBS/☆

5050.2 prs-pron gen 2pl	**5453.1** conj	**2526.2** adj gen pl masc	**2587.7** verb 3pl subj aor pass	**3450.7** art nom pl masc
ʻb ὑμῶν ˋ	ὡς	κακοποιῶν,	καταισχυνθῶσιν	οἱ
humōn	*hōs*	*kakopoiōn*	*kataischunthōsin*	*hoi*
you	as	evildoers,	they may be ashamed	the

1893.1 verb nom pl masc part pres act	**5050.2** prs-pron gen 2pl	**3450.12** art acc sing fem	**18.12** adj acc sing fem	**1706.1** prep	**5382.3** name dat masc
ἐπηρεάζοντες	ὑμῶν	τὴν	ἀγαθὴν	ἐν	Χριστῷ
epēreazontes	*humōn*	*tēn*	*agathēn*	*en*	*Christō*
speaking ill of	your	the	good	in	Christ

389.3 noun acc sing fem	**2882.5** adj comp sing neu	**1056.1** conj	**15.5** verb acc pl masc part pres act	**1479.1** conj
ἀναστροφήν.	**17.** κρεῖττον	γὰρ	ἀγαθοποιοῦντας,	εἰ
anastrophēn	*kreitton*	*gar*	*agathopoiountas*	*ei*
manner of life.	Better	for,	doing good,	if

17.a.**Txt:** Steph
Var: 01ℵ,02A,03B,04C 018K,020L,025P,Gries Lach,Treg,Alf,Word Tisc,We/Ho,Weis,Sod UBS/☆

2286.3 verb 3sing indic pres act	**2286.11** verb 3sing opt pres act	**3450.16** art sing neu	**2284.1** noun sing neu	**3450.2** art gen sing	**2296.2** noun gen sing masc
ʻ θέλει	[a☆ θέλοι]	τὸ	θέλημα	τοῦ	θεοῦ,
thelei	*theloi*	*to*	*thelēma*	*tou*	*theou*
wills	[may will]	the	will		of God,

3819.9 verb inf pres act	**2211.1** conj	**2525.2** verb acc pl masc part pres act	**3617.1** conj	**2504.1** conj	**5382.1** name nom masc
πάσχειν,	ἢ	κακοποιοῦντας.	**18.** ὅτι	καὶ	Χριστὸς
paschein	*ē*	*kakopoiountas*	*hoti*	*kai*	*Christos*
to suffer,	than	doing evil;	because	indeed	Christ

3:15. Peter told the believers how to deal with opposition. "Sanctify" (*hagiasate,* hallow, make holy) is a word the pagan Greeks used to describe the setting apart of a temple to be used only for sacred purposes. "The Lord God" (*kurion . . . ton Theon,* God as Lord) might be changed to "Christ as Lord" (*kurion . . . ton Christon,* on the basis of very reliable Greek texts). Peter directed the believers to set Christ apart as Lord in their hearts—as their only Master—and be ready always to give verbal defense of their inner hope. "Be ready" (*hetoimoi,* prepared, adjusted) at all times with an "answer" (*apologian,* a clearing of oneself, defense; as in Acts 22:1, "Hear ye my defense"). They should be able to give the "reason" (*logon,* word, utterance, verbalization) of their inner "hope" (*elpidos,* happy anticipation, expectation).

The Greeks liked to debate issues of all kinds. Peter indicated the believers should be ready to discuss their faith openly. This calls for a clear understanding of their beliefs and for skill in presenting it. It does not negate the need for guidance and inspiration by the Holy Spirit which Jesus promised (Matthew 10:19). On the contrary, Peter said they should give their witness not in a high-handed, cocksure manner but with "meekness" (*prautētos,* humility, mildness) and "fear" (*phobou,* terror, fear, not of man but of God; that is, with reverence and dependence on divine guidance and inspiration).

Believers should not be surprised if they suffer in spite of the fact they are living godly lives. They should be prepared to give the right kind of answer in the face of rejection or persecution. They should not retaliate in self-defense or seek revenge. The best "answer" they can make is to live in such a way no one will believe the accusations.

3:16. In order to give an effective witness, Peter said they need a "good conscience" (*suneidēsin . . . agathēn,* guiltless moral consciousness). This sense of innocence will result from their good "conversation" (*anastrophēn,* manner of life) in Christ. There will be nothing in their lives to make them ashamed; but those who "speak" (*katalalōsin,* speak against, as in 2:12) evil of them will be "ashamed" (*kataischunthōsin,* dishonored, confounded) in the very matter wherein they falsely accuse the believers. "Whereas" may be translated "wherein." Their accusers will be "put to silence" (2:15). "Falsely accuse" is the same strong word (*epēreazō*) used in Luke 6:28; it means revile, insult, slander, spitefully abuse. The answer to false accusations is a godly life.

3:17. If perchance the believers have to suffer, it is "better" (*kreitton,* nobler) to suffer for well-doing than for wrongdoing. This will not happen, however, unless it is within God's "will" (*thelēma,* desire, choice, determination).

15. But sanctify the Lord God in your hearts: But consecrate Christ in your hearts, as Lord, *Montgomery* . . . hallow the Lord Christ, *Concordant* . . . Make a special holy place in your hearts for Christ, *SEB* . . . but set apart Christ, *Wuest.*

and [be] ready always to [give] an answer to every man that asketh you a reason of the hope that is in you: . . . always being those who are ready to present a verbal defense to everyone who asks you for a logical explanation concerning, *Wuest* . . . ever ready with a defense for everyone who is demanding from you an account concerning the expectation, *Concordant.*

with meekness and fear: . . . but give it calmly and respectfully, *TCNT* . . . in a humble and reverent manner, *Norlie* . . . Be gentle as you speak and show respect, *NLT* . . . and a wholesome serious caution, *Wuest.*

16. Having a good conscience: . . . keep your conscience clear, *Williams, Wade* . . . having a conscience unimpaired, *Wuest.*

that, whereas they speak evil of you, as of evildoers: . . . in the very thing in which they defame you, *Wuest* . . . in what they are speaking against you as of evildoers, *Concordant* . . . who slander Your good Conduct in Christ, *Wilson.*

they may be ashamed that falsely accuse: . . . will be ashamed of their slanders, *Noli* . . . they may be put to shame, those who spitefully abuse, insult, *Wuest* . . . they may be mortified, who traduce, *Concordant.*

your good conversation in Christ: . . . when they see the good way you have lived as a Christian, *NLT* . . . your good manner of life, *Clementson* . . . due to your union with Christ, *Wade* . . . your good behavior in Christ, *Concordant.*

17. For [it is] better, if the will of God be so: God may be willing, *Concordant* . . . if perchance it be the will of God, *Wuest.*

that ye suffer for well doing, than for evil doing: . . . it is better when doing good...rather than when doing evil, *Wuest* . . . for doing right, than for doing wrong, *TCNT.*

18.a.**Txt:** 03B,018K 020L,025P,byz.Weis
Var: p72,01ℵ,02A,04C 33,Lach,Treg,Tisc We/Ho,Sod,UBS/⋆

526.1 adv	**3875.1** prep	**264.6** noun gen pl fem	**3819.11** verb 3sing indic aor act	**594.10** verb 3sing indic aor act
ἅπαξ	περὶ	ἁμαρτιῶν	‹ ἔπαθεν,	[a⋆ ἀπέθανεν,]
hapax	*peri*	*hamartiōn*	*epathen*	*apethanen*
once	for	sins	suffered,	[died]

18.b.**Txt:** 01ℵ-corr,02A 04C,018K,020L,sa.bo. Tisc,Sod
Var: p72,03B,025P,044 We/Ho,Weis,UBS/⋆

1337.3 adj nom sing masc	**5065.1** prep	**93.4** adj gen pl masc	**2419.1** conj	**2231.4** prs-pron acc 1pl	**5050.4** prs-pron acc 2pl
δίκαιος	ὑπὲρ	ἀδίκων,	ἵνα	‹ ἡμᾶς	[b ὑμᾶς]
dikaios	*huper*	*adikōn*	*hina*	*hēmas*	*humas*
just	for	unjust,	that	us	[you]

4175.2 verb 3sing subj aor act	**3450.3** art dat sing	**2296.3** noun dat sing masc	**2266.8** verb nom sing masc part aor pass	**3173.1** conj
προσαγάγῃ	τῷ	θεῷ,	θανατωθεὶς	μὲν
prosagagē	*tō*	*theō*	*thanatōtheis*	*men*
he might bring		to God;	having been put to death	

18.c.**Txt:** Steph
Var: 01ℵ,02A,03B,04C 018K,020L,025P,byz. Gries,Lach,Treg,Alf Word,Tisc,We/Ho,Weis Sod,UBS/⋆

4418.3 noun dat sing fem	**2210.7** verb nom sing masc part aor pass	**1156.2** conj	**3450.3** art dat sing	**4011.3** noun dat sing neu
σαρκὶ,	ζῳοποιηθεὶς	δὲ	‹c τῷ ›	πνεύματι,
sarki	*zōopoiētheis*	*de*	*tō*	*pneumati*
in flesh,	having been made alive	but	by the	Spirit,

1706.1 prep	**3614.3** rel-pron dat sing	**2504.1** conj	**3450.4** art dat pl	**1706.1** prep	**5274.3** noun dat sing fem	**4011.7** noun dat pl neu
19. ἐν	ᾧ	καὶ	τοῖς	ἐν	φυλακῇ	πνεύμασιν
en	*hō*	*kai*	*tois*	*en*	*phulakē*	*pneumasin*
in	which	also	to the	in	prison	spirits

4057.24 verb nom sing masc part aor pass	**2756.11** verb 3sing indic aor act	**540.9** verb dat pl masc part aor act	**4077.1** adv
πορευθεὶς	ἐκήρυξεν,	**20.** ἀπειθήσασίν	ποτε,
poreutheis	*ekēruxen*	*apeithēsasin*	*pote*
having gone	he preached,	having disobeyed	sometime,

20.a.**Txt:** Steph
Var: 01ℵ,02A,03B,04C 020L,025P,Gries,Lach Treg,Alf,Word,Tisc We/Ho,Weis,Sod UBS/⋆

3616.1 conj	**526.1** adv	**1538.7** verb 3sing indic imperf mid	**549.6** verb 3sing indic imperf mid	**3450.9** art nom sing fem
ὅτε	‹ ἅπαξ	ἐξεδέχετο	[a⋆ ἀπεξεδέχετο]	ἡ
hote	*hapax*	*exedecheto*	*apexedecheto*	*hē*
when	once	was waiting	[idem]	the

3450.2 art gen sing	**2296.2** noun gen sing masc	**3087.1** noun nom sing fem	**1706.1** prep	**2232.7** noun dat pl fem	**3437.1** name masc
τοῦ	θεοῦ	μακροθυμία	ἐν	ἡμέραις	Νῶε,
tou	*theou*	*makrothumia*	*en*	*hēmerais*	*Nōe*
	of God	patience	in	days	of Noah,

2650.5 verb gen sing fem part pres mid	**2759.2** noun gen sing fem	**1519.1** prep	**3614.12** rel-pron acc sing fem	**3504.10** adj nom pl fem
κατασκευαζομένης	κιβωτοῦ,	εἰς	ἣν	‹ ὀλίγαι,
kataskeuazomenēs	*kibōtou*	*eis*	*hēn*	*oligai*
being prepared	ark,	into	which	few,

20.b.**Txt:** 04C,018K 020L,025P,byz.Sod
Var: 01ℵ,02A,03B,Lach Treg,Alf,Word,Tisc We/Ho,Weis,UBS/⋆

3504.5 adj nom pl masc	**4969.1** verb	**3642.16** dem-pron sing neu	**1498.4** verb 3sing indic pres act	**3501.1** num card
[b⋆ ὀλίγοι,]	‹ τουτεστιν	[⋆ τοῦτ'	ἔστιν]	ὀκτὼ
oligoi	*toutestin*	*tout'*	*estin*	*oktō*
[idem]	that is	[this	is]	eight

5425.5 noun nom pl fem	**1289.4** verb 3pl indic aor pass	**1217.1** prep	**5045.2** noun gen sing neu	**3614.16** rel-pron sing neu	**2504.1** conj
ψυχαί	διεσώθησαν	δι'	ὕδατος,	**21.** ὃ	καὶ
psuchai	*diesōthēsan*	*di'*	*hudatos*	*ho*	*kai*
souls,	were saved	through	water,	which	also

3:18. Peter pointed to Christ to illustrate the nobility of suffering according to "the will of God" (verse 17) which was rewarded with resurrection. Though He was "just" (*dikaios,* innocent, righteous) He suffered "once" (*hapax,* a single time) for the sins of the "unjust" (*adikōn,* wicked, unrighteous). "Bring us to God" (*prosagagē,* approach, conduct) pictures Christ leading sinners to the Father's throne and presenting them there on the basis of His atoning death which has opened the way (Hebrews 10:19,20). Though put to death in the "flesh" (*sarki,* physical body), Christ was "quickened" (*zōopoiētheis,* vitalize, make alive) by the "Spirit" (*pneumati,* ghost, spirit). There is no capitalization in the Greek and some believe Peter was referring to Christ's human spirit, in contrast to His "flesh"; but in view of what follows it seems likely the reference is to the Holy Spirit.

3:19. By the Spirit (or, as some prefer, in spirit) Christ went to the "spirits in prison" and "preached" (*ekēruxen,* publish, proclaim like a town crier) unto them. Presumably this was between His death and His resurrection. Some believe the "spirits in prison" were the fallen angels mentioned in 2 Peter 2:4 and Jude 6. Others speculate that Christ preached to the wicked dead and gave them a second chance to be saved. However, "preached" may mean simply that He reported to the "saints in prison," whoever they be, His vicarious suffering and impending resurrection, the thought being not of appeal but of announcement. The Scriptures offer no "second chance" for those who have died without Christ.

3:20. Nearly all the people of Noah's day were "disobedient" (*apeithēsasin,* refuse to believe) and perished in spite of God's "long-suffering" (*makrothumia,* patience, forbearance). The relationship between verses 19 and 20 is not clear. In fact, the entire passage (verses 19-22) is difficult to interpret. "Men through the ages have struggled with this passage, and still it seems shrouded in mystery. Perhaps it is better to leave it that way. Our own salvation does not depend on our interpretation of this passage, and however we take it we can rejoice in the fact that it reflects the triumph of Christ" (Horton, p.52).

This verse reminds us of God's extreme patience and Noah's remarkable faithfulness. God waited 120 years before sending judgment, giving men a full opportunity to repent—how merciful He is! And Noah, despite ridicule and opposition, preached to his generation. At least he had this satisfaction—his family was saved.

Although Peter raised these questions, they are not answered here. However, the entire passage teaches an important truth. It is that God always gives a full opportunity to men to accept His mercy. He does not send people to hell; they go in spite of all the provisions He has made for their redemption.

18. For Christ also hath once suffered for sins: . . . once died concerning sins, *Concordant* . . . died once for all in relation to sins, *Wuest* . . . once died for sinners, *Berkeley.*

the just for the unjust: . . . the Innocent for the guilty, *Williams* . . . on behalf of, *Wuest* . . . for the sake of the unjust, *Concordant.*

that he might bring us to God: . . . in order that, *Wade* . . . that He may be leading us to God, *Concordant* . . . that He might provide you with an entree into the presence, *Wuest.*

being put to death in the flesh: . . . in His body, *Norlie* . . . put to death as He was physically, *Berkeley.*

but quickened by the Spirit: . . . yet vivified, *Concordant* . . . but raised to life, *Williams C.K.* . . . but made alive in Spirit, *Montgomery* . . . spiritually, *Berkeley.*

19. By which also he went and preached unto the spirits in prison: . . . having proceeded, He made a proclamation to the imprisoned spirits, *Wuest* . . . being gone to the spirits in jail also, He heralds, *Concordant* . . . and made proclamation, *Williams C.K.*

20. Which sometime were disobedient: . . . who were formerly apathetic, *Fenton* . . . They did not obey in the past, *SEB* . . . those once stubborn, *Concordant* . . . who had refused to believe, *Noli* . . . who were at one time rebels, *Wuest.*

when once the longsuffering of God waited: . . . when the patience of God awaited, *Concordant* . . . God's patience was delaying, *Berkeley* . . . was very patient with them, *Norlie.*

in the days of Noah, while the ark was a preparing: This was when the ship was being built, *SEB* . . . was being made, *Wuest* . . . was being got ready, *Wade* . . . being constructed, *Concordant.*

wherein few, that is, eight souls were saved by water: . . . were brought...through the time of deluge, *Wuest* . . . were carried safely through the Water, *Wilson* . . . from the flood, *Norlie.*

21.a.**Txt:** 04C,018K 020L,byz. **Var:** 01ℵ,02A,03B,025P Lach,Treg,Alf,Tisc We/Ho,Weis,Sod UBS/☆

2231.4 prs-pron acc 1pl	**5050.4** prs-pron acc 2pl	**496.1** adj sing neu	**3431.1** adv	**4834.1** verb 3sing indic pres act
ʽ ἡμᾶς	[a☆ ὑμᾶς]	ἀντίτυπον	νῦν	σῴζει
hēmas	*humas*	*antitupon*	*nun*	*sōzei*
us	[you]	counterpart	now	saves

902.1 noun sing neu	**3620.3** partic	**4418.2** noun gen sing fem	**590.1** noun nom sing fem	**4366.1** noun gen sing masc	**233.2** conj
βάπτισμα,	οὐ	σαρκὸς	ἀπόθεσις	ῥύπου,	ἀλλὰ
baptisma	*ou*	*sarkos*	*apothesis*	*rhupou*	*alla*
baptism,	not	of flesh	a putting away	of filth,	but

4743.2 noun gen sing fem	**18.10** adj gen sing fem	**1891.1** noun sing neu	**1519.1** prep	**2296.4** noun acc sing masc	**1217.1** prep
συνειδήσεως	ἀγαθῆς	ἐπερώτημα	εἰς	θεόν,	δι’
suneidēseōs	*agathēs*	*eperōtēma*	*eis*	*theon*	*di’*
of a conscience	good	demand	toward	God,	by

384.2 noun gen sing fem	**2400.2** name masc	**5382.2** name gen masc	**3614.5** rel-pron nom sing masc	**1498.4** verb 3sing indic pres act
ἀναστάσεως	Ἰησοῦ	Χριστοῦ,	22. ὅς	ἐστιν
anastaseōs	*Iēsou*	*Christou*	*hos*	*estin*
resurrection	of Jesus	Christ,	who	is

22.a.**Txt:** 01ℵ-corr,02A 04C,018K,020L,025P etc.byz.Sod **Var:** 01ℵ-org,03B,Treg Tisc,We/Ho,Weis UBS/☆

1706.1 prep	**1182.5** adj dat sing fem	**3450.2** art gen sing	**2296.2** noun gen sing masc	**4057.24** verb nom sing masc part aor pass	**1519.1** prep
ἐν	δεξιᾷ	ʽa τοῦ ˋ	θεοῦ,	πορευθεὶς	εἰς
en	*dexia*	*tou*	*theou*	*poreutheis*	*eis*
at	right hand		of God,	having gone	into

3636.4 noun acc sing masc	**5131.20** verb gen pl masc part aor pass	**840.4** prs-pron dat sing	**32.6** noun gen pl masc	**2504.1** conj
οὐρανόν,	ὑποταγέντων	αὐτῷ	ἀγγέλων	καὶ
ouranon	*hupotagentōn*	*autō*	*angelōn*	*kai*
heaven,	having been subjected	to him	angels	and

1833.6 noun gen pl fem	**2504.1** conj	**1405.6** noun gen pl fem	**5382.2** name gen masc	**3631.1** partic
ἐξουσιῶν	καὶ	δυνάμεων.	4:1. Χριστοῦ	οὖν
exousiōn	*kai*	*dunameōn*	*Christou*	*oun*
authorities	and	powers.	Christ	then

1.a.**Txt:** 01ℵ-corr,02A 018K,020L,025P,byz.bo. Sod **Var:** p72,03B,04C,it.sa. Lach,Treg,Alf,Tisc We/Ho,Weis,UBS/☆

3819.15 verb gen sing masc part aor act	**5065.1** prep	**2231.2** prs-pron gen 1pl	**4418.3** noun dat sing fem	**2504.1** conj	**5050.1** prs-pron nom 2pl
παθόντος	ʽa ὑπὲρ	ἡμῶν ˋ	σαρκί,	καὶ	ὑμεῖς
pathontos	*huper*	*hēmōn*	*sarki*	*kai*	*humeis*
having suffered	for	us	in flesh,	also	you

3450.12 art acc sing fem	**840.12** prs-pron acc sing fem	**1755.1** noun acc sing fem	**3558.1** verb 2pl impr aor mid	**3617.1** conj	**3450.5** art nom sing masc
τὴν	αὐτὴν	ἔννοιαν	ὁπλίσασθε·	ὅτι	ὁ
tēn	*autēn*	*ennoian*	*hoplisasthe*	*hoti*	*ho*
the	same	mind	arm yourselves with;	for	the

1.b.**Txt:** 018K,025P,byz. **Var:** 01ℵ,02A,03B,04C 020L,Lach,Treg,Alf Tisc,We/Ho,Weis,Sod UBS/☆

3819.14 verb nom sing masc part aor act	**1706.1** prep	**4418.3** noun dat sing fem	**3835.9** verb 3sing indic perf mid	**264.1** noun fem
παθὼν	ʽb ἐν ˋ	σαρκί,	πέπαυται	ἁμαρτίας·
pathōn	*en*	*sarki*	*pepautai*	*hamartias*
having suffered	in	flesh	has done with	sin;

1519.1 prep	**3450.16** art sing neu	**3239.1** adv	**442.7** noun gen pl masc	**1924.7** noun dat pl fem	**233.2** conj
2. εἰς	τὸ	μηκέτι	ἀνθρώπων	ἐπιθυμίαις,	ἀλλὰ
eis	*to*	*mēketi*	*anthrōpōn*	*epithumiais*	*alla*
for	the	no longer	men’s	to lusts,	but

3:21. From the final words of verse 20 Peter launched into a discussion of water baptism and made it clear that baptism, like the Flood, is only a "figure" (*antitupon*, counterpart, representation; as in Hebrews 9:24, "Which are the figures of the true"). It takes more than washing in water ("the putting away of the filth of the flesh") to cleanse from sin. There are various views about the meaning of the phrase "saved by water," but all agree that it is not the water itself which saves, but Christ, who is symbolized by the ark. Cleansing comes by the shed blood of the Son of God. "Answer" (*eperōtēma*, inquiry) is a word the Romans used of the senate's approval after inquiry into a matter. God looks beyond the act of baptism and searches to see whether the believer has truly repented and dedicated his life to divine service.

3:22. The disciples saw Christ "go into heaven" (Acts 1:11), and now He is on the "right hand" (*dexias*, right as opposed to left, the right being the hand that usually takes) of God's throne (see Hebrews 8:1). "Angels" (*angelōn*, messenger, either holy or wicked) and "authorities" (*exousiōn*, mastery, jurisdiction) and "powers" (*dunameōn*, might, miracle power) are "made subject" (*hupotagentōn*, under obedience, subordinated) unto Christ.

That Christ is now in heaven in a position of power at God's right hand has been a source of encouragement to believers in every century since the Ascension. Having overcome, He now has supreme authority and is able to supply believers with all that is necessary for them to overcome also.

4:1. Peter next identified himself with the believers. In the light of how Christ has suffered "for us," he told them to "arm yourselves" (*hoplisasthe*, equip yourselves with armor) with the same "mind" (*ennoian*, intent, thinking) as Christ. He "endured the cross, despising the shame" for "the joy that was set before him" (Hebrews 12:2). This same attitude of sacrificing self, enduring patiently, and rejoicing in tribulation will equip the believers to face false accusations and to resist sinful temptation. Peter indicated the reason they suffered persecution was that they had "ceased" (*pepautai*, stop, come to an end) from sin. If they had approved the loose living of their heathen neighbors, they would not have "suffered in the flesh."

4:2. Peter showed that the change salvation brings into a person's life is very real, a complete about-face. No longer will the believer "live" (*biōsai*, spend an existence) the remainder of his "time" (*chronon*, while, season of time) in the "flesh" (*sarki*, physical body) catering to the "lusts" (*epithumiais*, strong desire, craving) of men.

21. The like figure whereunto [even] baptism doth also now save us: . . . the antitype, immersion, *Campbell* . . . a perfect illustration this is of the way you have been admitted to the safety of the Christian ark, *Phillips* . . . as a counterpart now saves, *Wuest* . . . saves you nowadays, *Berkeley.*

(not the putting away of the filth of the flesh . . . not as removal of filth from the physical body, *Norlie* . . . does not mean we wash our bodies clean, *NLT* . . . not being intended for the removal of bodily uncleanness, *Wade* . . . far more than the mere washing of a dirty body, *Phillips.*

but the answer of a good conscience toward God,): . . . the inquiry of, *Concordant* . . . the witness of, *Wuest* . . . by the earnest seeking of a conscience that is clear in God's presence, *Berkeley.*

by the resurrection of Jesus Christ: . . . the virtue of Christ's rising, *Phillips.*

22. Who is gone into heaven, and is on the right hand of God: For he ascended into heaven, *Noli.*

angels and authorities and powers being made subject unto him: . . . there having been made subject to Him, *Wuest* . . . where angelic Beings of every rank yield submission to him, *TCNT* . . . are obeying Him, *NLT.*

1. Forasmuch then as Christ hath suffered for us in the flesh: . . . having suffered for our sakes in flesh, *Concordant* . . . in his human body, *SEB* . . . physically, *Berkeley.*

arm yourselves likewise with the same mind: . . . put on as armor the same mind, *Wuest* . . . with the same attitude, *Norlie* . . . with the same resolve as he did, *TCNT* . . . with a similar intention, *Fenton* . . . with the same determination, *Williams* . . . with the same thought, *Concordant* . . . you should take this same attitude as your weapon, *SEB.*

for he that hath suffered in the flesh hath ceased from sin: . . . has done with sin, *Wuest* . . . has gained relief from sin, *Berkeley.*

2. That he no longer should live the rest of [his] time in the flesh to the lusts of men, but to the will of God: . . . in future, *Montgom-*

3.a.**Txt:** 04C,018K,020L 025P,byz.
Var: p72,01א-corr,02A 03B,it.Lach,Treg,Alf Tisc,We/Ho,Weis,Sod UBS/☆

3.b.**Txt:** 018K,020L 025P,byz.
Var: 01א,02A,03B,04C 33,bo.Lach,Treg,Alf Word,Tisc,We/Ho,Weis Sod,UBS/☆

3.c.**Txt:** 018K,020L 025P,byz.
Var: 01א,02A,03B,04C 33,Lach,Treg,Alf,Word Tisc,We/Ho,Weis,Sod UBS/☆

3.d.**Txt:** 018K,020L 025P,byz.
Var: 01א,02A,03B,04C Lach,Treg,Alf,Word Tisc,We/Ho,Weis,Sod UBS/☆

2284.3 noun dat sing neu	**2296.2** noun gen sing masc	**3450.6** art acc sing masc	**1939.1** adj acc sing masc	**1706.1** prep	**4418.3** noun dat sing fem
θελήματι	θεοῦ	τὸν	ἐπίλοιπον	ἐν	σαρκὶ
thelēmati	*theou*	*ton*	*epiloipon*	*en*	*sarki*
to will	God's	the	remaining	in	flesh

973.1 verb inf aor act	**5385.4** noun acc sing masc	**707.1** adj nom sing masc	**1056.1** conj	**2231.3** prs-pron dat 1pl	**3450.5** art nom sing masc
βιῶσαι	χρόνον.	3. ἀρκετὸς	γὰρ	(a ἡμῖν)	ὁ
biōsai	*chronon*	*arketos*	*gar*	*hēmin*	*ho*
to live	time.	Sufficient	for	for us	the

3790.9 verb nom sing masc part perf act	**5385.1** noun nom sing masc	**3450.2** art gen sing	**972.1** noun gen sing masc	**3450.16** art sing neu
παρεληλυθὼς	χρόνος	(b τοῦ	βίου,)	τὸ
parelēluthōs	*chronos*	*tou*	*biou*	*to*
having past	time	of the	life	the

2284.1 noun sing neu	**1006.3** noun sing neu	**3450.1** art gen pl	**1477.5** noun gen pl neu	**2686.13** verb inf aor mid
(Θέλημα	[c☆ βούλημα]	τῶν	ἐθνῶν	(κατεργάσασθαι,
Thelēma	*boulēma*	*tōn*	*ethnōn*	*katergasasthai*
will	[purpose]	of the	nations	to have worked out,

2686.14 verb inf perf mid	**4057.30** verb acc pl masc part perf mid	**1706.1** prep	**760.4** noun dat pl fem
[d☆ κατειργάσθαι,]	πεπορευμένους	ἐν	ἀσελγείαις,
kateirgasthai	*peporeumenous*	*en*	*aselgeiais*
[idem]	having walked	in	licentiousness,

1924.7 noun dat pl fem	**3495.1** noun dat pl fem	**2943.2** noun dat pl masc	**4083.1** noun dat pl masc	**2504.1** conj
ἐπιθυμίαις,	οἰνοφλυγίαις,	κώμοις,	πότοις,	καὶ
epithumiais	*oinophlugiais*	*kōmois*	*potois*	*kai*
lusts,	wine drinking,	revels,	drinkings,	and

111.1 adj dat pl fem	**1485.3** noun dat pl fem	**1485.6** noun dat pl fem	**1706.1** prep
ἀθεμίτοις	(εἰδωλολατρείαις·	[☆ εἰδωλολατρίαις.]	4. ἐν
athemitois	*eidōlolatreiais*	*eidōlolatriais*	*en*
unhallowed	idolatries.	[idem]	In

3614.3 rel-pron dat sing	**3441.5** verb 3pl indic pres mid	**3231.1** partic	**4788.1** verb gen pl masc part pres act	**5050.2** prs-pron gen 2pl
ᾧ	ξενίζονται,	μὴ	συντρεχόντων	ὑμῶν
hō	*xenizontai*	*mē*	*suntrechontōn*	*humōn*
which	they think it strange	not	running with	your

1519.1 prep	**3450.12** art acc sing fem	**840.12** prs-pron acc sing fem	**3450.10** art gen sing fem	**804.2** noun gen sing fem	**399.1** noun acc sing fem
εἰς	τὴν	αὐτὴν	τῆς	ἀσωτίας	ἀνάχυσιν,
eis	*tēn*	*autēn*	*tēs*	*asōtias*	*anachusin*
to	the	same	of the	dissipation	flood,

980.4 verb nom pl masc part pres act	**3614.7** rel-pron nom pl masc	**586.18** verb 3pl indic fut act	**3030.4** noun acc sing masc
βλασφημοῦντες·	5. οἳ	ἀποδώσουσιν	λόγον
blasphēmountes	*hoi*	*apodōsousin*	*logon*
speaking evil;	who	shall render	account

3450.3 art dat sing	**2072.1** adv	**2174.18** verb dat sing masc part pres act	**2892.20** verb inf aor act	**2180.15** verb acc pl masc part pres act
τῷ	ἑτοίμως	ἔχοντι	κρῖναι	ζῶντας
tō	*hetoimōs*	*echonti*	*krinai*	*zōntas*
to him	ready	having	to judge	living

Instead he will yield himself to the "will" (*thelēmati*, desire, pleasure) of God. Man is self-centered by nature and is under great pressure to be concerned with his own comfort, pleasure, and security; but the believer who copies Christ is concerned with pleasing God, not himself.

4:3. The time before the believers became Christians, Peter said, was long enough and should "suffice" (*arketos*, be sufficient) for them to have "wrought" (*katergasasthai*, work, perform) the pleasures of the "Gentiles" (*ethnōn*, nations, heathen, non-Jewish people). Prior to conversion they "walked" (*peporeumenous*, go, journey) in "lasciviousness" (*aselgeiais*, shocking indecency, unbridled lustful indulgence, as in 2 Peter 2:7), "lusts" (*epithumiais*, strong desire, craving), "excess of wine" (*oinophlugiais*, winebibbing, drunkenness), "revelings" (*kōmois*, rioting, wild parties), "banquetings" (*potois*, carousal, drinking bout), "abominable idolatries" (*athemitois eidōlolatreiais*, lawless, wanton acts that were part of the lewd orgies connected with pagan image-worship). There is no allowance here for Christians to "exercise personal liberty" to drink and carouse. Peter described the lewd idolatries as *athemitois* (abominable, unlawful), the same word he used in Acts 10:28 to describe a Jew's association with a non-Jew. In that case he was referring to Mosaic law, but here he may have been referring to Roman law also, for this lewd behavior was so abhorrent it was forbidden by Roman law as well as God's law.

4:4. When believers refuse to take part in the world's pleasures, their unsaved neighbors think it "strange" (*xenizontai*, unfamiliar, foreign). They are astonished because the believers do not "run" with them (*suntrechontōn*, go along with the crowd) to the same "excess" (*anachusin*, effusion, overflowing) of "riot" (*asōtias*, profligacy, abandonment; as in Luke 15:13 where the prodigal's dissolute life is called "riotous living"). "Speaking evil" (*blasphēmountes*, defame, slander) is a strong word; it is used in Luke 22:65 of the treatment Christ endured. Believers are misunderstood and slandered.

4:5. But Peter said unbelievers will have to give account one day to God who is "ready" (*hetoimōs*, holding himself in readiness) to "judge" (*krinai*, call in question, decide, sentence) every human being whether presently "quick" (*zōntas*, living) or "dead" (*nekrous*, deceased, as in 2 Timothy 4:1, "Who shall judge the quick and the dead"). Peter at Cornelius' house said Christ was ordained "to be the Judge of quick and dead" (Acts 10:42), although in 1 Peter 1:17 he seems to say God the Father will be Judge. The apparent contradiction may be explained by the close association between the Father and the Son, as Christ points out in John 5:19-23.

ery . . . by no means still to spend the rest of his lifetime in the flesh in human desires, *Concordant* . . . live the remaining Time, *Wilson* . . . satisfying human appetites, *Norlie* . . . under the influence of human cravings, *Wade* . . . but for a Divine purpose, *Fenton.*

3. For the time past of [our] life may suffice us: . . . the time which has passed by, *Concordant.*

to have wrought the will of the Gentiles: . . . effected the intention of the nations, *Concordant.*

when we walked in lasciviousness, lusts: . . . gave your life to sex sins and to sinful desires, *NLT* . . . having gone on in wantonness, *Concordant* . . . you lived in shameless lewdness, evil passions, *Williams C.K.* . . . leading lives that are steeped in sensuality, *Williams* . . . living in sexual excess, having evil desires, *SEB* . . . sensuality, *Norlie.*

excess of wine, revellings: . . . hard drinking, *Montgomery* . . . drunkenness, wild partying, *Adams* . . . wild sex parties, *SEB* . . . debauches, revelries, *Concordant* . . . disorderly dancing, *Williams C.K.*

banquetings, and abominable idolatries: . . . dissipation, *Williams* . . . drinking contests, *SEB* . . . drinking bouts, and illicit idolatries, *Concordant* . . . and forbidden idolatries, *Adams.*

4. Wherein they think it strange that ye run not with [them]: . . . people are astonished at your not running, *TCNT* . . . they deem it extraordinary, *Wade* . . . thinking it strange of you not to race together, *Concordant.*

to the same excess of riot: . . . indulge in the same wild orgies, *Norlie* . . . same sink of corruption, *Darby* . . . same loose living and excess, *Williams C.K.* . . . the same puddle of profligacy, *Concordant.*

speaking evil of [you]: . . . say terrible things, *SEB* . . . abuse you, *Williams, Williams C.K.* . . . calumniating, *Concordant.*

5. Who shall give account to him that is ready to judge the quick and the dead: . . . rendering an account to Him Who is holding himself in readiness to judge the living, *Concordant.*

1 Peter 4:6

2504.1 conj	**3361.7** adj acc pl masc	**1519.1** prep	**3642.17** dem-pron sing neu	**1056.1** conj	**2504.1** conj	**3361.6** adj dat pl masc
καὶ	νεκρούς.	**6.** εἰς	τοῦτο	γὰρ	καὶ	νεκροῖς
kai	*nekrous*	*eis*	*touto*	*gar*	*kai*	*nekrois*
and	dead.	To	this	for	also	to dead

2076.16 verb 3sing indic aor pass	**2419.1** conj	**2892.36** verb 3pl subj aor pass	**3173.1** conj
εὐηγγελίσθη,	ἵνα	κριθῶσιν	μὲν
euēngelisthē	*hina*	*krithōsin*	*men*
was the good news announced,	that	they might be judged	indeed

2567.3 prep	**442.9** noun acc pl masc	**4418.3** noun dat sing fem	**2180.4** verb 3pl pres act	**1156.2** conj	**2567.3** prep
κατὰ	ἀνθρώπους	σαρκὶ,	ζῶσιν	δὲ	κατὰ
kata	*anthrōpous*	*sarki*	*zōsin*	*de*	*kata*
as regards	men	in flesh;	might live	but	as regards

2296.4 noun acc sing masc	**4011.3** noun dat sing neu	**3820.4** adj gen pl	**1156.2** conj	**3450.16** art sing neu	**4904.1** noun sing neu
θεὸν	πνεύματι.	**7.** Πάντων	δὲ	τὸ	τέλος
theon	*pneumati*	*Pantōn*	*de*	*to*	*telos*
God	in Spirit.	Of all things	but	the	end

7.a.**Txt:** 018K,020L 025P,byz.
Var: 01ℵ,02A,03B,Lach Treg,Alf,Word,Tisc We/Ho,Weis,Sod UBS/☆

1443.15 verb 3sing indic perf act	**4845.4** verb 2pl impr aor act	**3631.1** partic	**2504.1** conj	**3387.4** verb 2pl impr aor act
ἤγγικεν·	σωφρονήσατε	οὖν	καὶ	νήψατε
ēngiken	*sōphronēsate*	*oun*	*kai*	*nēpsate*
has drawn near:	be sound-minded	therefore,	and	be watchful

8.a.**Txt:** 018K,020L 025P,byz.sa.bo.
Var: 01ℵ,02A,03B,33 Treg,Alf,Tisc,We/Ho Weis,Sod,UBS/☆

1519.1 prep	**3450.15** art acc pl fem	**4194.8** noun acc pl fem	**4112.1** prep	**3820.4** adj gen pl	**1156.2** conj
εἰς	⸂a τὰς ⸃	προσευχάς·	**8.** πρὸ	πάντων	⸂a δὲ ⸃
eis	*tas*	*proseuchas*	*pro*	*pantōn*	*de*
unto	the	prayers;	before	all things	but

3450.12 art acc sing fem	**1519.1** prep	**1431.8** prs-pron acc pl masc	**26.4** noun acc sing fem	**1604.2** adj acc sing fem	**2174.19** verb nom pl masc part pres act
τὴν	εἰς	ἑαυτοὺς	ἀγάπην	ἐκτενῆ	ἔχοντες,
tēn	*eis*	*heautous*	*agapēn*	*ektenē*	*echontes*
the	among	yourselves	love	fervent	having,

8.b.**Txt:** 01ℵ,020L,025P byz.
Var: 02A,03B,018K,bo. Lach,Treg,Alf,Word Tisc,We/Ho,Weis,Sod UBS/☆

3617.1 conj	**26.1** noun nom sing fem	**2543.3** verb 3sing indic fut act	**2543.1** verb 3sing indic pres act	**3988.1** noun sing neu
ὅτι	ἀγάπη	⸀ καλύψει	[b☆ καλύπτει]	πλῆθος
hoti	*agapē*	*kalupsei*	*kaluptei*	*plēthos*
because	love	will cover	[covers]	a multitude

264.6 noun gen pl fem	**5219.2** adj nom pl masc	**1519.1** prep	**238.3** prs-pron acc pl masc	**425.1** prep
ἁμαρτιῶν.	**9.** φιλόξενοι	εἰς	ἀλλήλους	ἄνευ
hamartiōn	*philoxenoi*	*eis*	*allēlous*	*aneu*
of sins;	hospitable	to	one another,	without

9.a.**Txt:** 018K,020L 025P,byz.
Var: 01ℵ,02A,03B,sa. Lach,Treg,Alf,Word Tisc,We/Ho,Weis,Sod UBS/☆

1106.2 noun gen pl masc	**1106.3** noun gen sing masc	**1524.3** adj nom sing masc	**2503.1** conj
⸀ γογγυσμῶν·	[a☆ γογγυσμοῦ·]	**10.** ἕκαστος	καθὼς
gongusmōn	*gongusmou*	*hekastos*	*kathōs*
murmurings;	[murmuring;]	each	according as

2956.14 verb 3sing indic aor act	**5321.1** noun sing neu	**1519.1** prep	**1431.8** prs-pron acc pl masc	**840.15** prs-pron sing neu
ἔλαβεν	χάρισμα,	εἰς	ἑαυτοὺς	αὐτὸ
elaben	*charisma*	*eis*	*heautous*	*auto*
he received	a gift,	to	each other	it

4:6. The inevitability of judgment is not only an incentive to holy living but also an important reason for preaching the gospel. Peter said the gospel was preached to persons now "dead" (*nekrois,* deceased) so that, although ungodly men may have condemned them for their godly way of life, they have received spiritual life from God. All through the epistle Peter was contrasting two classes and telling how the godly should react when persecuted by the ungodly. In 4:14 he contrasted the two classes, believers and unbelievers. In 4:17,18 he contrasted the fate of the one class with that of the other. Here in 4:6 he contrasted being judged by men and being judged by God.

Various interpretations of this verse have been offered. Scholars from Augustine to Luther have said "dead" should be taken spiritually (as in Ephesians 2:1, "dead in trespasses and sins"); but Peter had just used the term literally in the previous sentence. Other scholars suggest some of those to whom Peter was writing may have been concerned over the fate of believers who had died (see 1 Thessalonians 4:15-17) since he said the dead will be judged. Peter reassured them that the deceased will be judged on the same basis as "men in the flesh" (those still living) because the gospel was preached to them while they lived.

4:7. Peter said the "end" (*telos,* culmination) of all things "is at hand" (*ēngiken,* approaching, drawing near). The same word is used in Matthew 3:2 by John and in James 5:8. How near the "end" Peter did not say, but he urged readiness. Believers need to be "sober" (*sōphronēsate,* sane, sound of mind) and "watch" (*nēpsate,* be watchful, discreet) unto "prayers" (*proseuchas,* earnest petitions; the word is plural).

4:8. Readiness for the end calls for constant communion with God through prayers, but also for loving relationships with fellow believers. Above all else, the believers should have "charity" (*agapē,* self-giving love) one toward another, and this Christlike love should be "fervent" (*ektenē,* intense, stretched out). They should extend their love especially toward believers who offend. This forgiving love will cause believers to "cover" (*kalupsei,* conceal, hide) other people's sins rather than expose them.

4:9. Peter said believers should extend this same love to travelers and other believers who need food and shelter. They should show "hospitality" (*philoxenoi,* kindness to visitors) and do it without "grudging" (*gongusmōn,* grumbling, murmuring).

4:10. "Every man" (*hekastos,* every one, male or female) has received a "gift" (*charisma,* favor, spiritual endowment). Paul wrote

6. For for this cause was the gospel preached also to them that are dead: . . . for this purpose, *Wuest* . . . this an evangel is brought to the dead, *Concordant.*

that they might be judged according to men in the flesh: . . . while judged with men physically, *Berkeley* . . . with respect to their physical existence, *Wuest.*

but live according to God in the spirit: . . . they might live with God spiritually, *Berkeley* . . . with respect to their spirit existence, *Wuest.*

7. But the end of all things is at hand: Now the consummation of all, *Concordant* . . . the completion of all, *Fenton* . . . has approached, *Wilson* . . . has drawn near, *Wade.*

be ye therefore sober, and watch unto prayer: Therefore exercise self-restraint, *TCNT* . . . Be self-controlled, *Williams C.K.* . . . Be sane, then, and sober for prayers, *Concordant* . . . Be of sound mind therefore, and be calm and collected in spirit, *Wuest* . . . be wise-minded, and wide awake about prayers, *Swann.*

8. And above all things have fervent charity among yourselves: . . . before all things in order of importance, *Wuest* . . . love each other extensively, *Adams* . . . having earnest love among yourselves, *Concordant* . . . cherish intense love for one another, *Berkeley.*

for charity shall cover the multitude of sins: . . . for love veils, *Montgomery* . . . throws a veil over, *Wade* . . . love makes up for a great many faults, *Norlie* . . . hides an uncounted number of sins, *Williams C.K.* . . . a mass of sins, *Berkeley.*

9. Use hospitality one to another without grudging: Be hospitable, *Concordant* . . . welcome one another to your homes without grumbling, *Williams C.K.* . . . without complaint, *Norlie* . . . complaining about it, *SEB* . . . without murmuring, *Wuest.*

10. As every man hath received the gift: . . . according as he obtained a gracious gift, *Concordant* . . . In whatever quality or quantity each one has received a gift, *Wuest.*

1 Peter 4:11

1241.5 verb nom pl masc part pres act	**5453.1** conj	**2541.4** adj nom pl masc	**3485.3** noun nom pl masc	**4024.2** adj gen sing fem
διακονοῦντες,	ὡς	καλοὶ	οἰκονόμοι	ποικίλης
diakonountes	*hōs*	*kaloi*	*oikonomoi*	*poikilēs*
serving,	as	good	stewards	of various

5322.2 noun gen sing fem	**2296.2** noun gen sing masc	**1479.1** conj	**4948.3** indef-pron nom sing	**2953.2** verb 3sing indic pres act	**5453.1** conj
χάριτος	θεοῦ·	**11.** εἴ	τις	λαλεῖ,	ὡς
charitos	*theou*	*ei*	*tis*	*lalei*	*hōs*
grace	of God.	If	anyone	speaks	as

3025.2 noun pl neu	**2296.2** noun gen sing masc	**1479.1** conj	**4948.3** indef-pron nom sing	**1241.1** verb 3sing indic pres act	**5453.1** conj
λόγια	θεοῦ·	εἴ	τις	διακονεῖ,	ὡς
logia	*theou*	*ei*	*tis*	*diakonei*	*hōs*
oracles	of God;	if	anyone	serves	as

11.a.**Txt:** p72,01ℵ,02A 03B,33,323,945,1241 1739
Var: 025P,byz.

1523.1 prep gen	**2452.2** noun gen sing fem	**3614.10** rel-pron gen sing fem	**5453.1** conj	**5359.1** verb 3sing indic pres act	**3450.5** art nom sing masc
ἐξ	ἰσχύος	☆ ἧς	[a ὡς]	χορηγεῖ	ὁ
ex	*ischuos*	*hēs*	*hōs*	*chorēgei*	*ho*
of	strength	which	[as]	supplies	

2296.1 noun nom sing masc	**2419.1** conj	**1706.1** prep	**3820.5** adj dat pl	**1386.20** verb 3sing subj pres mid	**3450.5** art nom sing masc
θεός·	ἵνα	ἐν	πᾶσιν	δοξάζηται	ὁ
theos	*hina*	*en*	*pasin*	*doxazētai*	*ho*
God;	that	in	all things	may be glorified	

2296.1 noun nom sing masc	**1217.2** prep	**2400.2** name masc	**5382.2** name gen masc	**3614.3** rel-pron dat sing	**1498.4** verb 3sing indic pres act
θεὸς	διὰ	Ἰησοῦ	Χριστοῦ,	ᾧ	ἐστιν
theos	*dia*	*Iēsou*	*Christou*	*hō*	*estin*
God	through	Jesus	Christ,	to whom	is

3450.9 art nom sing fem	**1385.1** noun nom sing fem	**2504.1** conj	**3450.16** art sing neu	**2877.1** noun sing neu	**1519.1** prep	**3450.8** art acc pl masc
ἡ	δόξα	καὶ	τὸ	κράτος	εἰς	τοὺς
hē	*doxa*	*kai*	*to*	*kratos*	*eis*	*tous*
the	glory	and	the	might	to	the

163.6 noun acc pl masc	**3450.1** art gen pl	**163.4** noun gen pl masc	**279.1** intrj	**27.6** adj pl masc	**3231.1** partic
αἰῶνας	τῶν	αἰώνων·	ἀμήν.	**12.** Ἀγαπητοί,	μὴ
aiōnas	*tōn*	*aiōnōn*	*amēn*	*Agapētoi*	*mē*
ages	of the	ages.	Amen.	Beloved,	not

3441.6 verb 2pl impr pres mid	**3450.11** art dat sing fem	**1706.1** prep	**5050.3** prs-pron dat 2pl	**4309.2** noun dat sing fem	**4242.1** prep
ξενίζεσθε	τῇ	ἐν	ὑμῖν	πυρώσει	πρὸς
xenizesthe	*tē*	*en*	*humin*	*purōsei*	*pros*
take as strange	the	among	you	fire	for

3848.4 noun acc sing masc	**5050.3** prs-pron dat 2pl	**1090.23** verb dat sing fem part pres mid	**5453.1** conj	**3443.7** adj gen sing neu	**5050.3** prs-pron dat 2pl
πειρασμὸν	ὑμῖν	γινομένῃ,	ὡς	ξένου	ὑμῖν
peirasmon	*humin*	*ginomenē*	*hōs*	*xenou*	*humin*
trial	to you	taking place,	as if	a strange thing	to you

4670.1 verb gen sing neu part pres act	**233.2** conj	**2498.1** conj	**2814.2** verb 2pl indic pres act	**3450.4** art dat pl
συμβαίνοντος·	**13.** ἀλλὰ	καθὸ	κοινωνεῖτε	τοῖς
sumbainontos	*alla*	*katho*	*koinōneite*	*tois*
happening;	but	according as	you have share	in the

in Romans 12:8 of gifts of giving, of ruling, and of showing mercy which should be exercised cheerfully (without grudging, as Peter said in verse 9). Showing hospitality may be construed as the gift of doing deeds of mercy and kindness. But all believers have not the same gift. As Paul stated in 1 Corinthians 7:7, "Every man hath his proper gift of God, one after this manner, and another after that." Whatever gift one has, he should "minister" it (*diakonountes*, serve) to fellow believers, not neglecting it through carelessness or selfishness, but sharing it for the benefit of others. As good "stewards" (*oikonomoi*, overseer, manager) believers should faithfully dispense God's "grace" (*charitos*, favor, liberality) which is "manifold" (*poikilēs*, diverse) and therefore fits all situations. Whatever we have received we are responsible to use for God's glory.

4:11. The two kinds of gifts mentioned by Peter correspond to the twofold division of service in Acts 6:2-4. One is the speaking kind, the other a less public kind. If a person's gift is to "speak" (*lalei*, talk, preach, give utterance), he should speak as the "oracles" (*logia*, divine utterance, revelation) of God. That is, if he has a speaking gift such as tongues, interpretation, prophecy, the word of wisdom, the word of knowledge, teaching, exhorting, or preaching, he should speak in harmony with God's Word and depend on the Holy Spirit to inspire and guide. If a person's gift is to "minister" (*diakonei*, serve, as in Acts 6:2, "serve tables"), he should do it according to the "ability" (*ischuos*, strength, power) which God gives him. The purpose in all things is that God may be "glorified" (*doxazētai*, honor, magnify, render glorious). "Praise" (*doxa*, honor, worship) and "dominion" (*kratos*, vigor, power, strength) are ascribed to Christ (as in 2 Peter 3:18) for ever and ever. "Amen" (verily, so be it).

4:12. Returning to the subject of suffering for righteousness' sake, Peter said believers should not be surprised or think it "strange" (*xenizesthe*, alien, foreign) that they are undergoing a "fiery trial" (*purōsei*, ordeal; literally, a burning, but the word is used here to refer to a smelting furnace by which gold and silver are purified). He said the purpose of the "fiery trial" (persecution) is to "try" them (*peirasmon*, prove, tempt; as in 2 Peter 2:9, "The Lord knoweth how to deliver the godly out of temptation"). What is happening to them is nothing "strange" (*xenou*, alien, foreign). Christ did not promise His servants a life of ease or immunity from suffering. If the world persecuted Him, it will persecute His followers (John 15:20). But there may be comfort in the salutation "Beloved." It is *agapētoi*, the Greek word which speaks of God's self-giving and infinite love. It may be translated "divinely loved ones," a title that would remind the persecuted believers that they are dear to the heart of God.

[even so] minister the same one to another: Let each one serve the group, *Berkeley* . . . dispensing faithfully, *TCNT* . . . among yourselves, *Concordant.*

as good stewards of the manifold grace of God: . . . like a good manager, *SEB* . . . ideal administrators of the varied grace, *Concordant* . . . God's many mercies, *Norlie* . . . many-sided grace, *Williams C.K.*

11. If any man speak, [let him speak] as the oracles of God: If a man preaches, *NLT*. . . . If speaking, let it be as God's suggestions, *Berkeley* . . . let it be with the power which God has bestowed, *Fenton* . . . one who utters God's truth, *Montgomery.*

if any man minister, [let him do it] as of the ability which God giveth: If a man helps others, *NLT* . . . If serving, let it be with the strength, *Berkeley* . . . dispensing, as out of the strength which God is furnishing, *Concordant* . . . let him do so in reliance on the power which God supplies, *TCNT.*

that God in all things may be glorified through Jesus Christ:

to whom be praise and dominion for ever and ever. Amen: . . . belong Glory and Sovereignth, *Wade* . . . glory and the might for the eons of the eons, *Concordant.*

12. Beloved, think it not strange: Dear friends, *TCNT* . . . Divinely loved ones...stop thinking, *Wuest* . . . Do not be surprised, *NLT* . . . astonished, *Fenton* . . . wonder not, *Campbell.*

concerning the fiery trial which is to try you: . . . because of the fierce struggle you're in, *SEB* . . . conflagration...which is becoming a trial, *Concordant* . . . test by fire is coming upon you, *Williams* . . . smelting process ...which has come to you for the purpose of testing, *Wuest* . . . being applied to you, *Berkeley.*

as though some strange thing happened unto you: . . . an unexpected affair had surprised you, *Fenton* . . . as if you were experiencing something odd, *Berkeley* . . . unexpected misfortune were befalling you, *Noli* . . . a thing alien to you, *Wuest.*

1 Peter 4:14

3450.2 art gen sing	5382.2 name gen masc	3667.4 noun dat pl neu	5299.7 verb 2pl impr pres act	2419.1 conj	2504.1 conj
τοῦ	Χριστοῦ	παθήμασιν,	χαίρετε,	ἵνα	καὶ
tou	*Christou*	*pathēmasin*	*chairete*	*hina*	*kai*
of the	Christ	sufferings,	rejoice,	that	also

1706.1 prep	3450.11 art dat sing fem	597.3 noun dat sing fem	3450.10 art gen sing fem	1385.2 noun gen sing fem	840.3 prs-pron gen sing
ἐν	τῇ	ἀποκαλύψει	τῆς	δόξης	αὐτοῦ
en	*tē*	*apokalupsei*	*tēs*	*doxēs*	*autou*
in	the	revelation	of the	glory	his

5299.20 verb 2pl aor pass	21.5 verb nom pl masc part pres mid	1479.1 conj	3542.8 verb 2pl indic pres mid
χαρῆτε	ἀγαλλιώμενοι.	**14.** εἰ	ὀνειδίζεσθε
charēte	*agalliōmenoi*	*ei*	*oneidizesthe*
you may rejoice	being jubilant.	If	you are being reproached

1706.1 prep	3549.4 noun dat sing neu	5382.2 name gen masc	3079.4 adj nom pl masc	3617.1 conj	3450.16 art sing neu
ἐν	ὀνόματι	Χριστοῦ,	μακάριοι·	ὅτι	τὸ
en	*onomati*	*Christou*	*makarioi*	*hoti*	*to*
in	name	of Christ,	blessed;	because	the

14.a.**Txt:** p72,03B,018K 020L,044,049 **Var:** 01א,02A,029T,33 81,323,945,1241,1739 Sod

3450.10 art gen sing fem	1385.2 noun gen sing fem	2504.1 conj	1405.2 noun gen sing fem	2504.1 conj	3450.16 art sing neu
τῆς	δόξης	[a+ καὶ	δυνάμεως]	καὶ	τὸ
tēs	*doxēs*	*kai*	*dunameōs*	*kai*	*to*
of the	glory	[and	power]	and	the

3450.2 art gen sing	2296.2 noun gen sing masc	4011.1 noun sing neu	1894.1 prep	5050.4 prs-pron acc 2pl	372.4 verb 3sing indic pres mid
τοῦ	θεοῦ	πνεῦμα	ἐφ'	ὑμᾶς	ἀναπαύεται
tou	*theou*	*pneuma*	*eph'*	*humas*	*anapauetai*
	of God	Spirit	upon	you	rests;

14.b.**Txt:** 018K,020L 025P,byz.sa. **Var:** p72,01א,02A,03B 33,bo.Lach,Treg,Alf Tisc,We/Ho,Weis,Sod UBS/☆

2567.3 prep	3173.1 conj	840.8 prs-pron acc pl masc	980.17 verb 3sing indic pres mid	2567.3 prep
⸂b κατὰ	μὲν	αὐτοὺς	βλασφημεῖται,	κατὰ
kata	*men*	*autous*	*blasphēmeitai*	*kata*
according to		them	he is being blasphemed,	according to

1156.2 conj	5050.4 prs-pron acc 2pl	1386.19 verb 3sing indic pres mid	3231.1 partic	1056.1 conj	4948.3 indef-pron nom sing
δὲ	ὑμᾶς	δοξάζεται. ⸃	**15.** μὴ	γάρ	τις
de	*humas*	*doxazetai*	*mē*	*gar*	*tis*
but	you	he is being glorified.	Not	for	anyone

15.a.**Txt:** 01א,02A,03B 018K,020L,025P,044 33,81,323,614,630 1241,1739,2495 **Var:** bo.byz.

5050.2 prs-pron gen 2pl	3819.6 verb 3sing impr pres act	5453.1 conj	5243.1 noun nom sing masc	2211.1 conj	5453.1 conj
ὑμῶν	πασχέτω	ὡς	φονεὺς,	⸂☆ ἢ	[a ὡς]
humōn	*paschetō*	*hōs*	*phoneus*	*ē*	*hōs*
of you	let suffer	as	a murderer,	or	[as]

15.b.**Txt:** 01א,02A,03B 018K,020L,025P,044 33,81,323,614,630 1241,1739,2495 **Var:** p72,bo.byz.

2785.1 noun nom sing masc	2211.1 conj	5453.1 conj	2526.1 adj nom sing masc	2211.1 conj	5453.1 conj
κλέπτης,	⸂☆ ἢ	[b ὡς]	κακοποιὸς,	ἢ	ὡς
kleptēs	*ē*	*hōs*	*kakopoios*	*ē*	*hōs*
thief,	or	[as]	evildoer,	or	as

242.2 noun nom sing masc	242.1 noun nom sing masc
⸂ ἀλλοτριοεπίσκοπος·	[☆ ἀλλοτριεπίσκοπος·]
allotrioepiskopos	*allotriepiskopos*
overlooker of other people's matters;	[a prier into other's affairs;]

4:13. Instead of thinking it a thing alien to them, the believers should expect persecution and should even "rejoice" (*chairete*, be glad, shout for joy; as in Luke 6:23, "Rejoice ye in that day, and leap for joy"). Insofar as the persecution is for the gospel's sake, they can find joy because they are "partakers" (*koinōneite*, share as partners) in Christ's sufferings. No matter how great their sufferings may be, they can look forward to the time of Christ's coming when His glory shall be revealed. At that time they will be glad "with exceeding joy," for since they are suffering with Him in this life, they will reign with Him in the life to come (2 Timothy 2:12). Peter wanted the believers to realize it is an honor to be fellow sufferers with Christ. He had not forgotten the day when he and the other apostles "departed from the presence of the council, rejoicing that they were counted worthy to suffer shame for his (Christ's) name" (Acts 5:41). Living with eternity in view will help us endure hardship.

13. But rejoice, inasmuch as ye are partakers of Christ's sufferings: You should be glad, because it means that you are called to share, *Phillips* . . . insofar as you share in common with, *Wuest* . . . be cheerful for sharing to some degree, *Berkeley* . . . you are participating, *Concordant.*

that, when his glory shall be revealed: . . . the unveiling of His glory, *Concordant* . . . when he shows himself in full splendor to men, *Phillips.*

ye may be glad also with exceeding joy: . . . you may rejoice exultingly, *Wilson* . . . rejoice triumphantly, *Williams* . . . rejoice, that you may be rejoicing, *Concordant* . . . you may be thrilled with, *Wade* . . . the most tremendous joy, *Phillips* . . . with triumphant gladness, *Montgomery* . . . triumphantly cheerful, *Berkeley.*

4:14. "If" does not indicate a hypothetical case. The believers were indeed being "reproached" (*oneidizesthe*, defame, taunt, revile) for the name of Christ; therefore Peter said they were "happy" (*makarioi*, supremely blessed) "for the Spirit of glory and of God" (the Holy Spirit) "resteth" upon them (*anapauetai*, take ease, refresh). A special anointing or refreshing seems to rest upon those who are bearing reproach or suffering for Christ. This has been evident in the deaths of Stephen (Acts 7:55-60) and other martyrs. The Spirit rested on Christ in a special way (see Isaiah 11:2 which Peter quoted here). Peter added, "On their part he is evil spoken of, but on your part he is glorified." There will always be foes of the Christian faith, but we have a special opportunity. Jesus died for our salvation, now we can live in such a way as to bring glory to Him.

14. If ye be reproached for the name of Christ: If men speak bad of you, *NLT* . . . If someone insults you, *SEB* . . . you are defamed, *Berkeley* . . . you have cast in your teeth, as it were, *Wuest* . . . for being Christ's followers, *Phillips.*

happy [are ye]: . . . you are blessed, *Montgomery* . . . spiritually prosperous, *Wuest* . . . that is a great privilege, *Phillips.*

for the spirit of glory and of God resteth upon you: . . . and power...has come to rest, *Concordant* . . . is resting with refreshing power upon you, *Wuest.*

on their part he is evil spoken of, but on your part he is glorified:

4:15. Whatever reproach a believer may suffer, it should result from serving Christ and not from doing wrong. Peter mentioned two specific crimes, murder and thievery, and adds the general classification "evildoer" (*kakopoios*, criminal, malefactor; the same word as in 2:12,14). After the lofty descriptions he had given of the believers' spiritual situation, it may seem incongruous to warn them against such wickedness, but Peter realized they were still human and capable of lapsing back into the flesh, especially since they lived in an extremely immoral society. He also admonished against being "a busybody in other men's matters" (*allotrioepiskopos*, a word not used elsewhere, meaning meddler, one who spies out the affairs of other men). In view of the pressures of persecution, this may be a prohibition against spying or informing on others, something Jesus said some people would do (Matthew 10:21).

15. But let none of you suffer as a murderer, or [as] a thief: . . . none of your number, *Phillips* . . . should have to be punished, *Norlie.*

or [as] an evildoer, or as a busybody in other men's matters: . . . or a poisoner, *Wade* . . . as a profligate, or as a libeller, *Fenton* . . . or a criminal or a meddler, *Berkeley* . . . or a troublemaker, *Norlie* . . . as a spy upon other people's business, *Montgomery* . . . or as a Meddling person, *Wilson* . . . as a self-appointed overseer in other men's matters, *Wuest* . . . an interferer in other's affairs, *Concordant.*

1 Peter 4:16

1479.1 conj	1156.2 conj	5453.1 conj	5381.1 name nom sing masc	3231.1 partic	152.2 verb 3sing impr pres mid
16. εἰ	δὲ	ὡς	Χριστιανός,	μὴ	αἰσχυνέσθω,
ei	*de*	*hōs*	*Christianos*	*mē*	*aischunesthō*
if	but	as	a Christian,	not	let him be ashamed,

16.a.**Txt:** 018K,020L 025P,byz.
Var: 01א,02A,03B,33 bo.Lach,Treg,Alf,Word Tisc,We/Ho,Weis,Sod UBS/⋆

1386.3 verb 3sing impr pres act	1156.2 conj	3450.6 art acc sing masc	2296.4 noun acc sing masc	1706.1 prep	3450.3 art dat sing	3183.3 noun dat sing neu
δοξαζέτω	δὲ	τὸν	θεὸν	ἐν	τῷ	⸂ μέρει
doxazetō	*de*	*ton*	*theon*	*en*	*tō*	*merei*
let him glorify	but		God	in	the	respect

17.a.**Txt:** p72,03B,018K 020L,025P,We/Ho,byz.
Var: 01א,02A,33,81 1852

3549.4 noun dat sing neu	3642.5 dem-pron dat sing masc	3617.1 conj	3450.5 art nom sing masc	2511.1 noun nom sing masc
[a⋆ ὀνόματι]	τούτῳ.	17. ὅτι	⸂a ὁ ⸃	καιρὸς
onomati	*toutō*	*hoti*	*ho*	*kairos*
[name]	this.	Because	the	time

3450.2 art gen sing	751.14 verb inf aor mid	3450.16 art sing neu	2890.1 noun sing neu	570.3 prep	3450.2 art gen sing	3486.2 noun gen sing masc
τοῦ	ἄρξασθαι	τὸ	κρίμα	ἀπὸ	τοῦ	οἴκου
tou	*arxasthai*	*to*	*krima*	*apo*	*tou*	*oikou*
of the	to have begun	the	judgment	from	the	house

3450.2 art gen sing	2296.2 noun gen sing masc	1479.1 conj	1156.2 conj	4270.1 adv	570.1 prep	2231.2 prs-pron gen 1pl	4949.9 intr-pron sing neu
τοῦ	θεοῦ˙	εἰ	δὲ	πρῶτον	ἀφ'	ἡμῶν,	τί
tou	*theou*	*ei*	*de*	*prōton*	*aph'*	*hēmōn*	*ti*
	of God;	if	but	first	from	us,	what

3450.16 art sing neu	4904.1 noun sing neu	3450.1 art gen pl	540.5 verb gen pl masc part pres act	3450.3 art dat sing	3450.2 art gen sing
τὸ	τέλος	τῶν	ἀπειθούντων	τῷ	τοῦ
to	*telos*	*tōn*	*apeithountōn*	*tō*	*tou*
the	end	of the	disobeying	the	

2296.2 noun gen sing masc	2077.3 noun dat sing neu	2504.1 conj	1479.1 conj	3450.5 art nom sing masc	1337.3 adj nom sing masc
θεοῦ	εὐαγγελίῳ;	18. καὶ	εἰ	ὁ	δίκαιος
theou	*euangeliō*	*kai*	*ei*	*ho*	*dikaios*
of God	good news?	And	if	the	righteous

18.a.**Var:** 03B-org We/Ho,Weis,UBS/⋆

3296.1 adv	4834.15 verb 3sing indic pres mid	3450.5 art nom sing masc	1156.2 conj	759.1 adj nom sing masc
μόλις	σῴζεται,	ὁ	[a+ δὲ]	ἀσεβὴς
molis	*sōzetai*	*ho*	*de*	*asebēs*
with difficulty	is being saved,	the	[but]	ungodly

2504.1 conj	266.1 adj nom sing	4085.1 adv	5154.19 verb 3sing indic fut mid	5452.1 conj	2504.1 conj
καὶ	ἁμαρτωλὸς	ποῦ	φανεῖται;	19. ὥστε	καὶ
kai	*hamartōlos*	*pou*	*phaneitai*	*hōste*	*kai*
and	sinner	where	shall appear?	Wherefore	also

3450.7 art nom pl masc	3819.8 verb nom pl masc part pres act	2567.3 prep	3450.16 art sing neu	2284.1 noun sing neu	3450.2 art gen sing
οἱ	πάσχοντες	κατὰ	τὸ	θέλημα	τοῦ
hoi	*paschontes*	*kata*	*to*	*thelēma*	*tou*
the	suffering	according to	the	will	

19.a.**Txt:** 018K,020L 025P,byz.
Var: 01א,02A,03B,33 bo.Lach,Treg,Alf,Tisc We/Ho,Weis,Sod UBS/⋆

2296.2 noun gen sing masc	5453.1 conj	3964.4 adj dat sing masc	2911.1 noun dat sing masc	3769.8 verb 3pl impr pres mid
θεοῦ,	⸂a ὡς ⸃	πιστῷ	κτίστῃ	παρατιθέσθωσαν
theou	*hōs*	*pistō*	*ktistē*	*paratithesthōsan*
of God	as	to a faithful	Creator	let them commit

4:16. The term "Christian" is used in only two other New Testament verses (Acts 11:26; 26:28). It was originally a term given by Gentiles at Antioch; the Jews, who would not acknowledge Jesus to be the Christ (Messiah), would certainly not want to give recognition to that title. By the time this epistle was written, the name *Christian* had become one of reproach and generally used to describe Jesus' followers. The name exposed believers to shame, though systematic persecution had not yet developed. If a man suffers reproach as a Christian, he should not be "ashamed" (*aischunesthō*, feel disgraced) but should thank God for the privilege. Peter had once been ashamed and had denied his Lord (Mark 14:68), but now he had been converted into a man who could strengthen these believers (Luke 22:32).

16. Yet if [any man suffer] as a Christian, let him not be ashamed:
but let him glorify God on this behalf: ... let him give honor, *Norlie* ... for bearing this name, *Williams.*

4:17. Peter evidently was referring to Ezekiel 9:6 where the Lord, in calling for judgment against the evildoers in Jerusalem, said, "And begin at my sanctuary." He said the time had come that "judgment" (*krima*, condemnation, sentencing) should begin at the "house of God," meaning no doubt God's "spiritual house" described in 2:5. Since he realized the coming judgment would be by fire (2 Peter 3:7), he may have been thinking of the believers' "fiery trial" as the beginning of the judgment; and if it "begin" at God's house, what shall be the "end" (*telos*, termination, final destination) of those who reject the gospel!

17. For the time [is come] that judgment must begin at the house of God: ... for punishment to begin, *TCNT* ... for judging starts with God's family, *SEB.*
and if [it] first [begin] at us, what shall the end [be] of them that obey not the gospel of God?: ... and if it starts with us, *Wade* ... who refuse to accept, *Noli* ... who will not accept God's Good News? *Norlie* ... who disobey God's good news? *Adams* ... who are disobedient to the glad tidings of God? *Wilson* ... who are rejecting God's good news? *Williams.*

4:18. Verse 18 is quoted from the Greek (Septuagint) version of Proverbs 11:31. Peter said it is only "scarcely" (*molis*, with difficulty) that the "righteous" (*dikaios*, just, holy, innocent) are "saved" (*sōzetai*, rescue, preserve) in the time of judgment. Since this is so, the fate of the "ungodly" (*asebēs*, irreverent, wicked) and the "sinner" (*hamartōlos*, transgressor) will be dire indeed. The Lord chastens those He loves in order to correct them (Proverbs 3:11,12). If the saved need correction, how much more will the unsaved merit the wrath of God whom they spurned!

18. And if the righteous scarcely be saved: ... with difficulty escape, *Campbell.*
where shall the ungodly and the sinner appear?: ... where will the irreverent, *Swann.*

4:19. Those who are experiencing the "fiery trial" are urged to "commit" (*paratithesthōsan*, put forth, consign) the keeping of their "souls" (*psuchas*, life, heart, mind) to God. The verb form denotes a continuous committing. The Greeks used this word in banking; it means to make a deposit. Peter urged the believers to place their lives in God's safe-deposit box. Their suffering is "according to the will of God" who has allowed it in order to purify their lives. Therefore they can commit themselves to Him with confidence, knowing He who created them will be faithful to fulfill His plan for their lives through all their ordeals.

19. Wherefore let them that suffer according to the will of God:
commit the keeping of their souls [to him] in well doing, as unto a faithful Creator: ... confide their souls to a Reliable Builder, *Fenton.*

1 Peter 5:1

19.b.**Txt:** Steph
Var: 01ℵ,02A,018K 020L,025P,Lach,Treg Alf,Word,Tisc,Weis,Sod UBS/☆

1.a.**Var:** 01ℵ,02A,03B Lach,Treg,Alf,Tisc We/Ho,Weis,Sod UBS/☆

1.b.**Txt:** 01ℵ,018K,020L 025P,byz.bo.Tisc,Sod
Var: 02A,03B,Lach Treg,Alf,We/Ho,Weis UBS/☆

2.a.**Txt:** p72,01ℵ-corr 02A,018K,020L,025P 33,byz.it.bo.Sod
Var: 01ℵ-org,03B,sa. Tisc,We/Ho,Weis UBS/☆

2.b.**Var:** p72,01ℵ,02A 025P,33,it.sa.bo.Lach Treg,Tisc,Weis,Sod UBS/☆

3450.15 art acc pl fem	**5425.8** noun acc pl fem	**1431.2** prs-pron gen pl	**840.1** prs-pron gen pl	**1706.1** prep
τὰς	ψυχὰς	⸂ ἑαυτῶν	[b☆ αὐτῶν]	ἐν
tas	*psuchas*	*heautōn*	*autōn*	*en*
the	souls	of themselves	[their]	in

16.1 noun dat sing fem		**4104.2** adj comp acc pl masc	**3631.1** partic	**3450.8** art acc pl masc
ἀγαθοποιιᾳ.	5:1.	Πρεσβυτέρους	[a☆+ οὖν]	⸂b τοὺς ⸃
agathopoiia		*Presbuterous*	*oun*	*tous*
well-doing.		Elders	[therefore]	the

1706.1 prep	**5050.3** prs-pron dat 2pl	**3731.1** verb 1sing indic pres act	**3450.5** art nom sing masc	**4701.1** noun nom sing masc	**2504.1** conj
ἐν	ὑμῖν	παρακαλῶ	ὁ	συμπρεσβύτερος	καὶ
en	*humin*	*parakalō*	*ho*	*sumpresbuteros*	*kai*
among	you	I exhort	the	a fellow elder	and

3116.1 noun nom sing masc	**3450.1** art gen pl	**3450.2** art gen sing	**5382.2** name gen masc	**3667.3** noun gen pl neu	**3450.5** art nom sing masc
μάρτυς	τῶν	τοῦ	Χριστοῦ	παθημάτων,	ὁ
martus	*tōn*	*tou*	*Christou*	*pathēmatōn*	*ho*
witness	of the	of the	Christ	sufferings,	the

2504.1 conj	**3450.10** art gen sing fem	**3165.15** verb gen sing fem part pres act	**596.6** verb inf pres mid	**1385.2** noun gen sing fem
καὶ	τῆς	μελλούσης	ἀποκαλύπτεσθαι	δόξης
kai	*tēs*	*mellousēs*	*apokaluptesthai*	*doxēs*
also	of the	being about	to be revealed	glory

2817.1 noun nom sing masc		**4025.6** verb 2pl impr aor act	**3450.16** art sing neu	**1706.1** prep	**5050.3** prs-pron dat 2pl	**4028.3** noun sing neu
κοινωνός,	2.	ποιμάνατε	τὸ	ἐν	ὑμῖν	ποίμνιον
koinōnos		*poimanate*	*to*	*en*	*humin*	*poimnion*
partaker:		shepherd	the	among	you	flock

3450.2 art gen sing	**2296.2** noun gen sing masc	**1967.1** verb nom pl masc part pres act	**3231.1** partic	**315.1** adv
τοῦ	θεοῦ,	⸂a ἐπισκοποῦντες ⸃	μὴ	ἀναγκαστῶς,
tou	*theou*	*episkopountes*	*mē*	*anankastōs*
	of God,	exercising oversight	not	by constraint,

233.1 conj	**233.2** conj	**1583.1** adv	**2567.3** prep	**2296.4** noun acc sing masc
⸂ ἀλλ'	[☆ ἀλλὰ]	ἑκουσίως	[b☆+ κατὰ	θεόν,]
all'	*alla*	*hekousiōs*	*kata*	*theon*
but	[idem]	willingly;	[according to	God,]

3234.1 adv	**147.1** adv	**233.2** conj	**4149.1** adv		**3234.2** adv	**5453.1** conj
μηδὲ	αἰσχροκερδῶς,	ἀλλὰ	προθύμως·	3.	μηδ'	ὡς
mēde	*aischrokerdōs*	*alla*	*prothumōs*		*mēd'*	*hōs*
not	for base gain,	but	readily;		not	as

2604.2 verb nom pl masc part pres act	**3450.1** art gen pl	**2792.4** noun gen pl masc	**233.2** conj	**5020.3** noun nom pl masc
κατακυριεύοντες	τῶν	κλήρων,	ἀλλὰ	τύποι
katakurieuontes	*tōn*	*klērōn*	*alla*	*tupoi*
exercising lordship over	of the	possessions,	but	patterns

1090.21 verb nom pl masc part pres mid	**3450.2** art gen sing	**4028.1** noun gen sing neu		**2504.1** conj	**5157.14** verb gen sing masc part aor pass
γινόμενοι	τοῦ	ποιμνίου.	4.	καὶ	φανερωθέντος
ginomenoi	*tou*	*poimniou*		*kai*	*phanerōthentos*
being	of the	flock.		And	having been manifested

5:1. Peter concluded his epistle with solemn exhortations, first to church leaders, then to the general membership. He addressed the "elders" (*presbuterous,* presbyter, senior officer) saying he too was an "elder" (*sumpresbuteros,* copresbyter). He did not call himself pope, nor did he dictate. He identified himself with the local leaders and simply exhorted them (*parakalō,* entreat, beseech). An elder was a pastor or chief administrator in a local assembly. Some evidently were teachers, and others simply saw that teaching was done (1 Timothy 5:17). The terms *elder, presbyter,* and *bishop* were used interchangeably in the Early Church.

Peter was a "witness" (*martus,* martyr, one called to bear witness) for Christ. The word refers not to the act of seeing but the act of testifying to what has been seen, as in Acts 1:8. (In 2 Peter 1:16, where he called himself an eyewitness, the apostle used a different Greek word.) Furthermore, he said he was a "partaker" (*koinōnos,* sharer, partner) of Christ's glory, referring probably to the Transfiguration (Matthew 17:1-9); but he indicated the "glory" (*doxēs,* radiant splendor, honor) was yet to be "revealed" (*apokaluptesthai,* uncover, disclose) so all believers would have the privilege of partaking as he did.

1. The elders which are among you I exhort: . . . to those among you who are pastors, *Norlie.*

who am also an elder, and a witness of the sufferings of Christ: . . . one who actually saw, *TNT* . . . of the Passion of Christ, *Noli.*

and also a partaker of the glory that shall be revealed: . . . that is to be uncovered, *Williams.*

5:2. Peter exhorted the elders to shepherd the believers. Probably he remembered when Christ said to him, "Feed my sheep" (John 21:17). "Feed" (*poimanate,* supervise, tend as a shepherd) includes the duties of guiding and guarding, as well as feeding. The "flock" (*poimnion,* group of sheep) is God's, not theirs. "Taking the oversight thereof" (*episkopountes,* care for, oversee, watch diligently; as in Hebrews 12:15, "Looking diligently lest any man fail"), they are to do it "willingly" (*hekousiōs,* voluntarily, with good will) and not for the sake of "filthy lucre" (*aischrokerdōs,* greedy or dishonest gain). "Lucre" itself is a good word meaning gain, profit, reward. It is not "filthy" unless the gain is ill-gotten. The motive of ministry should be a loving concern for people.

2. Feed the flock of God which is among you: Be shepherds to, *Montgomery* . . . tend the flock, *Wilson* . . . that is committed to your charge, *Wade.*

taking the oversight [thereof], not by constraint, but willingly: . . . not through compulsion, *Montgomery* . . . not out of obligation, *Adams* . . . but voluntarily, *Wilson* . . . by their own free will, *Noli.*

not for filthy lucre, but of a ready mind: . . . not out of eagerness to make a personal profit, but out of eagerness to serve, *Adams* . . . but of your own free will, *TCNT, Williams C.K.* . . . but for the love of the cause, *Norlie* . . . but enthusiastically, *Swann* . . . but in a spirit of enthusiasm, *Wade* . . . but because your heart is in it, *TNT.*

5:3. Elders should not be autocrats, ruling in high-handed fashion. The "heritage" (*klērōn,* allotment, portion, inheritance) they have been called to serve is God's. He has an inheritance (*klēronomias*) in His saints (Ephesians 1:18), and He expects the elders to care for them as faithful overseers. Peter said they should continually be "ensamples" (*tupoi,* type, pattern, model, example; as in 1 Timothy 4:12, "Be thou an example of the believers"). As undershepherds the elders should be living models or patterns of Jesus, the Chief Shepherd (5:4).

3. Neither as being lords over [God's] heritage: Do not domineer, *TNT* . . . not as domineering over the charge entrusted to you, *Fenton* . . . not as masters of those in your keeping, *Williams C.K.*

but being ensamples to the flock: . . . but being Patterns, *Wilson* . . . proving yourselves models for the flock to imitate, *Williams.*

5:4. Peter spoke of Christ, the "chief Shepherd," in a way that recognized the elders as undershepherds. When He shall "appear"

4. And when the chief Shepherd shall appear: . . . is manifested, *Concordant.*

1 Peter 5:5

3450.2 art gen sing	745.1 noun gen sing masc	2837.9 verb 2pl indic fut mid	3450.6 art acc sing masc
τοῦ	ἀρχιποίμενος,	κομιεῖσθε	τὸν
tou	*archipoimenos*	*komieisthe*	*ton*
the	chief shepherd,	you shall receive	the

260.1 adj acc sing masc	3450.10 art gen sing fem	1385.2 noun gen sing fem	4586.2 noun acc sing masc	3532.1 adv
ἀμαράντινον	τῆς	δόξης	στέφανον.	**5.** ῾Ομοίως,
amarantinon	*tēs*	*doxēs*	*stephanon*	*Homoiōs*
unfading	of the	glory	crown.	Likewise,

3365.5 adj comp nom pl masc	5131.19 verb 2pl impr aor pass	4104.7 adj comp dat pl masc	3820.7 adj nom pl masc	1156.2 conj
νεώτεροι,	ὑποτάγητε	πρεσβυτέροις·	πάντες	δὲ
neōteroi	*hupotagēte*	*presbuterois*	*pantes*	*de*
younger,	be subject	to elder,	all	and

5.a.**Txt:** 018K,020L 025P,byz.
Var: 01ℵ,02A,03B,33 bo.Lach,Treg,Alf,Word Tisc,We/Ho,Weis,Sod UBS/☆

5.b.**Txt:** 01ℵ,02A,025P 044,byz.
Var: p72,03B,33

238.2 prs-pron dat pl	5131.12 verb nom pl masc part pres mid	3450.12 art acc sing fem	4863.3 noun acc sing fem
ἀλλήλοις	⸂a ὑποτασσόμενοι ⸃	τὴν	ταπεινοφροσύνην
allēlois	*hupotassomenoi*	*tēn*	*tapeinophrosunēn*
one to another	being subject	the	humility

1456.1 verb 2pl impr aor mid	3617.1 conj	3450.5 art nom sing masc	2296.1 noun nom sing masc	5082.2 adj dat pl masc
ἐγκομβώσασθε·	ὅτι	⸂b ὁ ⸃	θεὸς	ὑπερηφάνοις
enkombōsasthe	*hoti*	*ho*	*theos*	*huperēphanois*
bind on;	because		God	proud

495.1 verb 3sing indic pres mid	4862.1 adj dat pl	1156.2 conj	1319.2 verb 3sing indic pres act	5322.4 noun acc sing fem
ἀντιτάσσεται,	ταπεινοῖς	δὲ	δίδωσιν	χάριν.
antitassetai	*tapeinois*	*de*	*didōsin*	*charin*
sets himself against,	to humble	but	gives	grace.

4864.6 verb 2pl impr aor pass	3631.1 partic	5097.3 prep	3450.12 art acc sing fem	2873.1 adj acc sing fem	5331.4 noun acc sing fem
6. Ταπεινώθητε	οὖν	ὑπὸ	τὴν	κραταιὰν	χεῖρα
Tapeinōthēte	*oun*	*hupo*	*tēn*	*krataian*	*cheira*
Be humbled	therefore	under	the	mighty	hand

3450.2 art gen sing	2296.2 noun gen sing masc	2419.1 conj	5050.4 prs-pron acc 2pl	5150.3 verb 3sing subj aor act	1706.1 prep	2511.3 noun dat sing masc
τοῦ	θεοῦ,	ἵνα	ὑμᾶς	ὑψώσῃ	ἐν	καιρῷ
tou	*theou*	*hina*	*humas*	*hupsōsē*	*en*	*kairō*
	of God,	that	you	he may exalt	in	time;

3820.12 adj acc sing fem	3450.12 art acc sing fem	3178.2 noun acc sing fem	5050.2 prs-pron gen 2pl	1961.1 verb nom pl masc part aor act
7. πᾶσαν	τὴν	μέριμναν	ὑμῶν	⸀ ἐπιῤῥίψαντες
pasan	*tēn*	*merimnan*	*humōn*	*epirrhipsantes*
all	the	care	your	having cast

1961.2 verb nom pl masc part aor act	1894.2 prep	840.6 prs-pron acc sing masc	3617.1 conj	840.4 prs-pron dat sing
[☆ ἐπιρίψαντες]	ἐπ'	αὐτόν,	ὅτι	αὐτῷ
epiripsantes	*ep'*	*auton*	*hoti*	*autō*
[idem]	upon	him,	because	with him

3169.1 verb 3sing indic pres act	3875.1 prep	5050.2 prs-pron gen 2pl	3387.4 verb 2pl impr aor act	1121.9 verb 2pl impr aor act
μέλει	περὶ	ὑμῶν.	**8.** Νήψατε,	γρηγορήσατε,
melei	*peri*	*humōn*	*Nēpsate*	*grēgorēsate*
there is care	about	you.	Be sober,	watch,

(*phanerōthentos*, be made manifest) at His second coming, the Chief Shepherd will reward His faithful undershepherds with a crown, like the Greeks who bestowed crowns on victorious athletes or military heroes. However, the Greeks had crowns made of oak or ivy leaves which would fade, whereas the elders will receive a crown of "glory" (*doxēs*, honor, radiant splendor) that "fadeth not away" (*amarantinon*, fadeless like the *amaranth*, a flower that would not wither quickly like other flowers). The amaranth would revive if moistened with water, so it became a symbol of immortality.

5:5. Proverbs 3:34 states God "giveth grace unto the lowly." Peter said He shows His favor to the "humble" (*tapeinois*, of low degree, lowly in heart; as in Matthew 11:29, "I am meek and lowly in heart"). On the other hand, God "scorneth the scorners" (Proverbs 3:34). He scorns the "proud" (*huperēphanois*, self-exalting) and "resisteth" them (*antitassetai*, oppose). This is a military term used of an army drawn up for battle. It means God's armies are set in opposition to persons who are proud; so it is in the interest of young and old alike that all believers should be "clothed with" humility (*enkombōsasthe*, gird oneself). The apron worn by servants was called *enkombōma*. Peter may have been thinking of the time Jesus girded himself with a towel to teach the disciples a lesson in humility (John 13:4). If the younger believers are humble they will "submit" (*hupotagēte*, be subject, be under obedience) to the older believers. In fact, all should be subject one to another, all esteeming others better than themselves, and all looking for ways they can serve others rather than for ways others can serve them.

5:6. The Greek for "humble yourselves" (*tapeinōthēte*) is passive ("be ye humbled") and indicates they should permit God to humble them. The process He is using to humble them is persecution, and Peter exhorted them to accept it willingly without resentment or rebellion. They are safe in putting themselves under the mighty hand of God, for He is abundantly able to "exalt" (*hupsōsē*, lift up, elevate) them in "due time" (*kairō*, due season, as in Matthew 24:45, "to give them meat in due season"). Humility is not a loss but a gain, for it puts the believer in God's favor and saves him from pride that would destroy him and rob him of future glory.

5:7. Pride makes one self-sufficient, whereas humility is a recognition of one's dependence on God. The believers can show their humility by "casting" (*epirrhipsantes*, throw upon, commit) all their "care" (*merimnan*, concern, anxiety) upon the Lord. Persecution and cares would tempt them to worry, but they have a Good Shepherd who "careth" (*melei*, is concerned) for them.

ye shall receive a crown of glory that fadeth not away: ... you will win no fading wreath, *TCNT* ... you shall be requited with an unfading wreath of glory, *Concordant* ... crown of victory, *TNT.*

5. Likewise, ye younger, submit yourselves unto the elder: In the same way, *NLT* ... you younger communicants, must obey the presbyters, *Noli* ... may be subject, *Concordant* ... be in subjection to the elders, *Wuest* ... accept the authority, *TNT.*

Yea, all [of you] be subject one to another, and be clothed with humility: ... all wear the servile apron of humility with one another, *Concordant.*

for God resisteth the proud: ... is against those, *SEB* ... opposes the proud, *Norlie* ... is opposed to the Haughty, *Wilson* ... resists the arrogant, *Wade* ... opposes himself to those who set themselves above others, *Wuest.*

and giveth grace to the humble: ... to those who are lowly, *Wuest.*

6. Humble yourselves therefore under the mighty hand of God: Be humbled, *Concordant* ... Permit yourselves therefore to be humbled, *Wuest* ... the powerful hand, *Fenton.*

that he may exalt you in due time: He should be exalting you in season, *Concordant* ... when His time comes, *Norlie* ... in an appropriate season, *Wuest.*

7. Casting all your care upon him: ... tossing your entire worry, *Concordant* ... having cast all, *Wilson* ... having deposited with Him, *Wuest* ... Throw all your anxieties upon him, *TCNT* ... Throw all your worries onto, *SEB* ... Cast every worry you have, *Williams* ... all your anxious care on him, *Campbell.*

for he careth for you: ... for he makes you his care, *TCNT* ... He is caring concerning you, *Concordant* ... to Him it is a matter of concern respecting you, *Wuest.*

8. Be sober, be vigilant: Be temperate, *Montgomery* ... Be level-headed, *Adams* ... of a sober mind, be watchful, *Wuest.*

1 Peter 5:9

8.a.**Txt:** 01ℵ-corr,020L 33,byz.
Var: 01ℵ-org,02A,03B 018K,025P,Gries,Lach Treg,Alf,Word,Tisc We/Ho,Weis,Sod UBS/*

3617.1 conj	**3450.5** art nom sing masc	**473.1** noun nom sing masc	**5050.2** prs-pron gen 2pl	**1222.1** adj nom sing masc	**5453.1** conj
(ᵃ ὅτι)	ὁ	ἀντίδικος	ὑμῶν	διάβολος,	ὡς
hoti	*ho*	*antidikos*	*humōn*	*diabolos*	*hōs*
because	the	adversary	your	devil,	as

2997.1 noun nom sing masc	**5445.1** verb nom sing masc part pres mid	**3906.4** verb 3sing indic pres act	**2195.8** verb nom sing masc part pres act	**4949.1** intr-pron
λέων	ὠρυόμενος,	περιπατεῖ,	ζητῶν	τίνα
leōn	*ōruomenos*	*peripatei*	*zētōn*	*tina*
a lion	roaring,	goes about,	seeking	whom

8.b.**Txt:** p72,02A,byz.it.
Var: 01ℵ,018K,020L 025P,Lach,Alf,Tisc We/Ho,Weis,Sod UBS/*

2636.3 verb 3sing subj aor act	**2636.7** verb inf aor act	**3614.3** rel-pron dat sing	**434.3** verb 2pl impr aor act
(καταπίῃ·	[ᵇ* καταπιεῖν·]	9. ᾧ	ἀντίστητε
katapiē	*katapiein*	*hō*	*antistēte*
he may swallow up.	[to devour.]	Whom	resist,

4582.2 adj nom pl masc	**3450.11** art dat sing fem	**3963.3** noun dat sing fem	**3471.20** verb nom pl masc part perf act	**3450.17** art pl neu	**840.16** prs-pron pl neu
στερεοὶ	τῇ	πίστει,	εἰδότες	τὰ	αὐτὰ
stereoi	*tē*	*pistei*	*eidotes*	*ta*	*auta*
firm	in the	faith,	knowing	the	same

9.a.**Var:** 01ℵ,03B,Treg Tisc,We/Ho,Weis UBS/*

3450.1 art gen pl	**3667.3** noun gen pl neu	**3450.11** art dat sing fem	**1706.1** prep	**3450.3** art dat sing	**2862.3** noun dat sing masc
τῶν	παθημάτων	τῇ	ἐν	[ᵃ*+ τῷ]	κόσμῳ
tōn	*pathēmatōn*	*tē*	*en*	*tō*	*kosmō*
the	sufferings,	the	in	[the]	world

9.b.**Txt:** 03B-corr2,025P 044,byz.
Var: 01ℵ,02A,03B-org 018K,0206,33,614,630 1505,2495

5050.2 prs-pron gen 2pl	**80.1** noun dat sing fem	**1989.10** verb inf pres mid	**1989.9** verb 2pl indic pres mid
ὑμῶν	ἀδελφότητι	(* ἐπιτελεῖσθαι.	[ᵇ ἐπιτελεῖσθε.]
humōn	*adelphotēti*	*epiteleisthai*	*epiteleisthe*
your	brotherhood	to be accomplished.	[you are enduring.]

3450.5 art nom sing masc	**1156.2** conj	**2296.1** noun nom sing masc	**3820.10** adj gen sing fem	**5322.2** noun gen sing fem	**3450.5** art nom sing masc
10. Ὁ	δὲ	θεὸς	πάσης	χάριτος,	ὁ
Ho	*de*	*theos*	*pasēs*	*charitos*	*ho*
The	but	God	of all	grace,	the

10.a.**Txt:** 018K,byz.
Var: 01ℵ,02A,03B,020L 025P,bo.Lach,Treg,Alf Word,Tisc,We/Ho,Weis Sod,UBS/*

2535.14 verb nom sing masc part aor act	**2231.4** prs-pron acc 1pl	**5050.4** prs-pron acc 2pl	**1519.1** prep	**3450.12** art acc sing fem
καλέσας	(ἡμᾶς	[ᵃ* ὑμᾶς]	εἰς	τὴν
kalesas	*hēmas*	*humas*	*eis*	*tēn*
having called	us	[you]	to	the

10.b.**Txt:** p72,02A,018K 020L,025P,byz.it.sa.bo. Sod
Var: 01ℵ,03B,Tisc We/Ho,Weis,UBS/*

164.1 adj sing	**840.3** prs-pron gen sing	**1385.4** noun acc sing fem	**1706.1** prep	**5382.3** name dat masc	**2400.2** name masc
αἰώνιον	αὐτοῦ	δόξαν	ἐν	Χριστῷ	(ᵇ Ἰησοῦ,)
aiōnion	*autou*	*doxan*	*en*	*Christō*	*Iēsou*
eternal	his	glory	in	Christ	Jesus,

3504.1 adj sing	**3819.16** verb acc pl masc part aor act	**840.5** prs-pron nom sing masc	**2645.3** verb 3sing opt aor act
ὀλίγον	παθόντας,	αὐτὸς	(καταρτίσαι
oligon	*pathontas*	*autos*	*katartisai*
a little while	having suffered,	himself	may perfect

10.c.**Txt:** 018K,020L 025P,byz.
Var: 01ℵ,02A,03B,Lach Treg,Alf,Word,Tisc We/Ho,Weis,Sod UBS/*

5050.4 prs-pron acc 2pl	**2645.10** verb 3sing indic fut act	**4592.2** verb 3sing opt aor act	**4454.1** verb 3sing opt aor act
ὑμᾶς,	[ᶜ* καταρτίσει,]	(στηρίξαι,	σθενώσαι,
humas	*katartisei*	*stērixai*	*sthenōsai*
you,	[will perfect,]	may he establish,	may he strengthen,

5:8. The believer who is too proud to feel his utter dependence on God is in grave peril, so Peter admonished everyone to be "sober" (*nēpsate,* watchful, mentally calm) and "vigilant" (*grēgorēsate,* alert, awake). An enemy is seeking after them to "devour" them (*katapiē,* swallow), and one of his most effective weapons is pride. Jesus warned Peter against this enemy when He said, "Satan hath desired to have you" (Luke 22:31). Another name for this enemy is the "devil" (*diabolos,* false accuser, slanderer). Peter called him an "adversary" (*antidikos,* opponent in a lawsuit, as in Matthew 5:25). Satan is the great enemy of all the righteous and holy. He is a deceiver and varies his approach, coming sometimes as an "angel of light" (2 Corinthians 11:14) and sometimes as a "roaring lion" (the Greek describes the howl of a wild beast in fierce hunger). When a lion "walketh about" it is time for caution at the sheepfold. The lion's roar creates fear, and a frightened sheep may bolt from the flock to become easy prey. Therefore the shepherd and the sheep need to be on guard. Each sheep needs to stay with the flock and keep close to the shepherd for safety. A sheep is no match for a lion, and we are no match for the devil. But just as David protected his sheep, Jesus will come to the rescue of His people.

because your adversary the devil, as a roaring lion, walketh about: . . . your plaintiff, *Concordant* . . . is working against you, *NLT* . . . always prowling, *Williams.*

seeking whom he may devour: . . . looking for someone to swallow up, *Williams C.K.* . . . as his prey, *Norlie* . . . to devour you, *Wade.*

5:9. A cowardly shepherd may flee when the lion roars, but a courageous one will "resist" (*antistēte,* withstand, as in James 4:7, "Resist the devil, and he will flee from you"). The believer can ward off Satan's attacks if he remains "steadfast" in his faith in God. The Greek *stereoi,* translated "steadfast," means firm, strong, sure, as in 2 Timothy 2:19, "The foundation of God standeth sure." The word was used of a Greek army unit or phalanx presenting a solid front; the soldiers stood in ranks and files that were close and deep, forming a strong defense against the weapons of their day. Peter reminded the believers their fellow Christians in other parts of the world were undergoing as much suffering as they. This would not make their pain any less, but it should keep them from dissipating their strength through self-pity.

9. Whom resist stedfast in the faith: Stand firm against, *TCNT* . . . stand up to him, *TNT* . . . withstand, solid in the faith, *Concordant.*

knowing that the same afflictions are accomplished in your brethren that are in the world: . . . having perceived the same sufferings being completed in your brotherhood, *Concordant* . . . experiencing the same sort of sufferings, *Williams.*

5:10. Believers can find comfort in knowing the "God of all grace" is with them. His grace is "manifold" (4:10) or variegated. God has called them to salvation, and this is "unto" (with a view to) His eternal glory. First they must suffer "a while" (*oligon,* brief period, "a season," as in 1:6), but this will develop their spiritual lives. Peter foretold that through their present suffering God would make them "perfect" (*katartisai,* adjust, putting parts into right relationship and connection, fit together; as in 1 Corinthians 1:10, "That there be no divisions among you; but that ye be perfectly joined together"). He said God would establish them in unity, He would confirm them in spiritual power, and He would put them on a firm foundation.

10. But the God of all grace: . . . from whom all help comes, *TCNT.*

who hath called us unto his eternal glory by Christ Jesus: His eonian glory, *Concordant.*

after that ye have suffered a while, make you perfect: . . . by briefly suffering, He will be adjusting, *Concordant* . . . restore you, *TNT.*

stablish, strengthen, settle [you]: . . . make you firm, *TNT* . . . founding you, *Concordant.*

1 Peter 5:11

10.d.**Txt:** Steph
Var: 01ℵ,02A,03B
018K,020L,025P,Gries
Lach,Treg,Alf,Word
Tisc,We/Ho,Weis,Sod
UBS/☆

10.e.**Txt:** Steph
Var: 01ℵ,018K,020L
025P,byz.Gries,Alf
Word,Tisc,Weis,Sod
UBS/☆

11.a.**Txt:** 01ℵ,020L
025P,byz.sa.Sod
Var: p72,02A,03B,044
Lach,Treg,Alf,Tisc
We/Ho,Weis,UBS/☆

11.b.**Txt:** 01ℵ,02A,025P
044,sa.byz.Tisc,Sod
Var: p72,03B,bo.UBS/☆

4592.5 verb 3sing indic fut act	**4454.2** verb 3sing indic fut act	**2288.2** verb 3sing opt aor act
[d☆ στηρίξει,	σθενώσει,]	ʻ θεμελιώσαι.
stērixei	*sthenōsei*	*themeliōsai*
[he will establish,	he will strengthen,]	may he found:

2288.5 verb 3sing indic fut act	**840.4** prs-pron dat sing	**3450.9** art nom sing fem	**1385.1** noun nom sing fem	**2504.1** conj
[e☆ θεμελιώσει.]	**11.** αὐτῷ	ʻa ἡ	δόξα	καὶ ˎ
themeliōsei	*autō*	*hē*	*doxa*	*kai*
[he will find:]	to him	the	glory	and

3450.16 art sing neu	**2877.1** noun sing neu	**1519.1** prep	**3450.8** art acc pl masc	**163.6** noun acc pl masc	**3450.1** art gen pl
τὸ	κράτος	εἰς	τοὺς	αἰῶνας	ʻb τῶν
to	*kratos*	*eis*	*tous*	*aiōnas*	*tōn*
the	might,	to	the	ages	of the

163.4 noun gen pl masc	**279.1** intrj	**1217.2** prep	**4465.2** name gen masc	**5050.3** prs-pron dat 2pl	**3450.2** art gen sing
αἰώνων. ˎ	ἀμήν.	**12.** Διὰ	Σιλουανοῦ	ὑμῖν	τοῦ
aiōnōn	*amēn*	*Dia*	*Silouanou*	*humin*	*tou*
ages.	Amen.	By	Silvanus,	to you	the

3964.3 adj gen sing masc	**79.2** noun gen sing masc	**5453.1** conj	**3023.2** verb 1sing indic pres mid	**1217.1** prep	**3504.6** adj gen pl masc
πιστοῦ	ἀδελφοῦ,	ὡς	λογίζομαι,	δι'	ὀλίγων
pistou	*adelphou*	*hōs*	*logizomai*	*di'*	*oligōn*
faithful	brother,	as	I reckon,	through	a few

1119.7 verb 1sing indic aor act	**3731.7** verb nom sing masc part pres act	**2504.1** conj	**1942.1** verb nom sing masc part pres act	**3642.12** dem-pron acc sing fem
ἔγραψα,	παρακαλῶν	καὶ	ἐπιμαρτυρῶν	ταύτην
egrapsa	*parakalōn*	*kai*	*epimarturōn*	*tautēn*
I wrote,	exhorting	and	testifying	this

1498.32 verb inf pres act	**225.4** adj	**5322.4** noun acc sing fem	**3450.2** art gen sing	**2296.2** noun gen sing masc	**1519.1** prep
εἶναι	ἀληθῆ	χάριν	τοῦ	θεοῦ,	εἰς
einai	*alēthē*	*charin*	*tou*	*theou*	*eis*
to be	true	grace		of God,	in

12.a.**Txt:** 018K,020L
025P,byz.Weis
Var: 01ℵ,02A,03B,33
Lach,Treg,Alf,Tisc
We/Ho,Sod,UBS/☆

3614.12 rel-pron acc sing fem	**2449.20** verb 2pl indic perf act	**2449.6** verb 2pl aor act	**776.2** verb 3sing indic pres mid
ἣν	ʻ ἑστήκατε.	[a☆ στῆτε.]	**13.** Ἀσπάζεται
hēn	*hestēkate*	*stēte*	*Aspazetai*
which	you stand.	[you stood.]	Greets

5050.4 prs-pron acc 2pl	**3450.9** art nom sing fem	**1706.1** prep	**891.3** name dat fem	**4749.1** adj nom sing fem	**2504.1** conj
ὑμᾶς	ἡ	ἐν	Βαβυλῶνι	συνεκλεκτὴ,	καὶ
humas	*hē*	*en*	*Babulōni*	*suneklektē*	*kai*
you	the	in	Babylon	elected with,	and

3111.1 name nom masc	**3450.5** art nom sing masc	**5048.1** noun nom sing masc	**1466.2** prs-pron gen 1sing	**776.9** verb 2pl impr aor mid
Μάρκος	ὁ	υἱός	μου.	**14.** ἀσπάσασθε
Markos	*ho*	*huios*	*mou*	*aspasasthe*
Mark	the	son	my.	Greet

238.3 prs-pron acc pl masc	**1706.1** prep	**5207.1** noun dat sing neu	**26.2** noun gen sing fem	**1503.1** noun nom sing fem	**5050.3** prs-pron dat 2pl
ἀλλήλους	ἐν	φιλήματι	ἀγάπης.	εἰρήνη	ὑμῖν
allēlous	*en*	*philēmati*	*agapēs*	*eirēnē*	*humin*
one another	with	a kiss	of love.	Peace	with you

5:11. Peter burst into an exclamation of praise as he contemplated the perfection of God's plan for His people. This doxology is similar to that given to the Son in 4:11.

11. To him [be] glory and dominion for ever and ever. Amen: Power belongs to Him, *SEB* . . . might for the eons of the eons, *Concordant* . . . through endless ages! *Norlie.*

5:12. Since we read of only one Silvanus in the Early Church, we may conclude this is the same man who assisted Paul in his missionary travels. In Acts he is called Silas. Due to his prominence among the church leaders in Jerusalem, he was chosen for the important mission to Antioch (Acts 15:22). Silvanus was well acquainted with the churches in Asia Minor to whom Peter was writing, for he helped to establish them; and he was a "faithful brother" to them, "as I suppose," Peter said. This is not conjecture on Peter's part; it is a positive appraisal, for the Greek (*logizomai*) means impute, reckon—not imagine or guess.

Peter had written "briefly"—that is, the epistle is comparatively short, and he was sending it by Silvanus. Possibly it was through Silvanus he had learned about the difficulties these churches were then experiencing, causing him to see the need of "exhorting" them (*parakalōn*, beseech, intreat) and "testifying" (*epimarturōn*, corroborate, attest further) that what they had been taught is "the true grace of God." He admonished them to "stand" in this grace (*histemi*, continue, abide, take a stand; as in Ephesians 6:11, "Stand against the wiles of the devil").

12. By Silvanus, a faithful brother unto you, as I suppose: . . . with the help of, *TNT* . . . I respect very much, *SEB* . . . I reckon him, *TCNT* . . . as I regard him, *Williams.*

I have written briefly, exhorting, and testifying: . . . entreating and deposing, *Concordant.*

that this is the true grace of God wherein ye stand: Hold on to it, *Norlie* . . . unmerited favor, *Williams.*

5:13. What is the city called Babylon here? Some believe Peter was speaking symbolically of Rome. There are many testimonies from the early centuries of the Christian Era to the effect Peter visited Rome and was crucified there. St. Peter's basilica stands above the apostle's supposed burial spot. Our Roman Catholic friends especially hold to this view.

Other scholars, however, believe Peter was writing from Babylon on the Euphrates. Though reduced from its former greatness, the city still had a large population in Peter's day, including many Jews.

Since Peter was the apostle to the Jews, it is understandable that he should have journeyed to that city to preach Christ to them. He said this church at Babylon was "elected together with" them (*suneklektē*, chosen in company with, coelect in Christ) and "saluteth" them (*aspazetai*, greet). And so did "Mark my son," meaning John Mark, his son in the gospel. Early Christian writers state that after leaving his uncle Barnabas, Mark became helper to Peter under whose influence Mark wrote his Gospel.

13. The [church that is] at Babylon, elected together with [you], saluteth you: . . . sends you greetings, *SEB.*

and [so doth] Marcus my son:

5:14. Peter's admonition here is almost identical with Paul's comments in 1 Corinthians 16:20; 2 Corinthians 13:12; Romans 16:16. It was customary in the Early Church, after prayers, for the believers to welcome one another with a holy kiss. However, the custom gave rise to problems; as indicated by Clement of Alex-

14. Greet ye one another with a kiss of charity: Embrace one another, *Fenton* . . . with an affectionate kiss, *Adams* . . . a loving kiss, *SEB* . . . kiss of love, *Concordant.*

Peace [be] with you all that are in Christ Jesus. Amen: Peace be to all true Christians, *Phillips* . . . Every blessing be on you all who belong to Christ, *Barclay* . . . Grace be to you all, *Confraternity* . . . to all of you, *Everyday* . . . are in union with, *TCNT, Wade, Goodspeed* . . . Peace to all those in Christ, *Klingensmith*

1 Peter 5:14

14.a.**Txt:** 01ℵ,018K 020L,025P,byz.bo.Sod **Var:** 02A,03B,044,sa. Lach,Treg,Alf,Tisc We/Ho,Weis,UBS/*

•

14.b.**Txt:** 01ℵ,018K 020L,025P,byz. **Var:** 02A,03B,044,sa.bo. Gries,Lach,Treg,Alf Tisc,We/Ho,Weis,Sod UBS/*

3820.5 adj dat pl	**3450.4** art dat pl	**1706.1** prep	**5382.3** name dat masc	**2400.2** name masc	**279.1** intrj
πᾶσιν	τοῖς	ἐν	Χριστῷ	⸂a Ἰησοῦ. ⸃	⸂b ἀμήν. ⸃
pasin	*tois*	*en*	*Christō*	*Iēsou*	*amēn*
all	the	in	Christ	Jesus.	Amen.

3935.2 name gen masc	**1976.1** noun nom sing fem	**2498.1** adj nom sing masc	**4272.9** num ord nom sing fem
⸂ Πέτρου	ἐπιστολὴ	καθολικὴ.	πρώτη. ⸃
Petrou	*epistolē*	*katholikē*	*prōtē*
Of Peter	Epistle	General	First.

andria, who said, "Love is judged not in a kiss but in good will. Some do nothing but fill the church with noise of kissing. There is another—an impure—kiss full of venom pretending to holiness." So the practice became regulated: men kissed only men, and women kissed only women, and the custom gradually dwindled, though it is still found in some Eastern and European churches. The benediction is peace to all who are committed to Christ Jesus and trusting in Him. "Amen" (verily, so be it).

1 Peter 5:14

. . . Happiness be to all among you who are steadfast in the belief and profession of the gospel, *Macknight* . . . who are in the Messiah, *Murdock* . . . may there be peace—every kind of peace (blessing), especially peace with God, and freedom from fears, agitating passions and moral conflicts. Amen—so be it, *AmpB*.

THE SECOND EPISTLE OF
PETER

Expanded Interlinear
Textual Critical Apparatus
Verse-by-Verse Commentary
Various Versions

1976.1 noun	3935.2 name	1202.4 num ord
nom sing fem	gen masc	nom sing fem
Ἐπιστολὴ	Πέτρου	Δευτέρα
Epistolē	*Petrou*	*Deutera*
Epistle	of Peter	Second

Textual Apparatus

1.a.**Var:** p72,03B,044,69 81,614,623,630,1241 1243,2464,We/Ho

	4677.1	4468.1 name	3935.1 name	1395.1 noun	2504.1
	name masc	nom masc	nom masc	nom sing masc	conj
1:1.	ʿ☆ Συμεὼν	[a Σίμων]	Πέτρος	δοῦλος	καὶ
	Sumeōn	*Simōn*	*Petros*	*doulos*	*kai*
	Simeon	[idem]	Peter,	slave	and

646.1 noun	2400.2	5382.2 name	3450.4	2445.1 adj	2231.3 prs-
nom sing masc	name masc	gen masc	art dat pl	acc sing fem	pron dat 1pl
ἀπόστολος	Ἰησοῦ	Χριστοῦ,	τοῖς	ἰσότιμον	ἡμῖν
apostolos	*Iēsou*	*Christou*	*tois*	*isotimon*	*hēmin*
apostle	of Jesus	Christ,	to the	like precious	with us

2948.3 verb dat pl	3963.4 noun	1706.1	1336.3 noun	3450.2 art	2296.2 noun
masc part aor act	acc sing fem	prep	dat sing fem	gen sing	gen sing masc
λαχοῦσιν	πίστιν	ἐν	δικαιοσύνῃ	τοῦ	θεοῦ
lachousin	*pistin*	*en*	*dikaiosunē*	*tou*	*theou*
having obtained	faith	through	righteousness		of God

2231.2 prs-	2504.1	4842.2 noun	2400.2	5382.2 name	5322.1 noun
pron gen 1pl	conj	gen sing masc	name masc	gen masc	nom sing fem
ἡμῶν	καὶ	σωτῆρος	Ἰησοῦ	Χριστοῦ·	**2.** χάρις
hēmōn	*kai*	*sōtēros*	*Iēsou*	*Christou*	*charis*
our	and	Saviour	Jesus	Christ:	Grace

5050.3 prs-	2504.1	1503.1 noun	3989.6 verb 3sing	1706.1	1907.3 noun	3450.2 art
pron dat 2pl	conj	nom sing fem	opt aor pass	prep	dat sing fem	gen sing
ὑμῖν	καὶ	εἰρήνη	πληθυνθείη	ἐν	ἐπιγνώσει	τοῦ
humin	*kai*	*eirēnē*	*plēthuntheiē*	*en*	*epignōsei*	*tou*
to you	and	peace	be multiplied	in	knowledge	

2.a.**Txt:** p72,03B,04C byz.
Var: 01ℵ,02A,020L 0209,323,945,1739,bo.

2296.2 noun	2504.1	2400.2	5382.2 name	3450.2 art	2935.2 noun
gen sing masc	conj	name masc	gen masc	gen sing	gen sing masc
θεοῦ,	καὶ	ʿ☆ Ἰησοῦ	[a Χριστοῦ]	τοῦ	κυρίου
theou	*kai*	*Iēsou*	*Christou*	*tou*	*kuriou*
of God,	and	of Jesus	[Christ]	the	Lord

3.a.**Var:** 01ℵ,02A,33 Tisc,Weis,UBS/☆

2231.2 prs-	5453.1	3450.17	3820.1	2231.3 prs-	3450.10 art
pron gen 1pl	conj	art pl neu	adj	pron dat 1pl	gen sing fem
ἡμῶν.	**3.** ʿΩς	[a+ τὰ]	πάντα	ἡμῖν	τῆς
hēmōn	*Hōs*	*ta*	*panta*	*hēmin*	*tēs*
our.	As	[the]	all things	to us	the

2281.1 adj	1405.2 noun	840.3 prs-	3450.17	4242.1	2205.4 noun	2504.1
gen sing fem	gen sing fem	pron gen sing	art pl neu	prep	acc sing fem	conj
θείας	δυνάμεως	αὐτοῦ	τὰ	πρὸς	ζωὴν	καὶ
theias	*dunameōs*	*autou*	*ta*	*pros*	*zōēn*	*kai*
divine	power	his	the	to	life	and

2131.4 noun	1426.3 verb gen sing	1217.2	3450.10 art	1907.2 noun
acc sing fem	fem part perf mid	prep	gen sing fem	gen sing fem
εὐσέβειαν	δεδωρημένης,	διὰ	τῆς	ἐπιγνώσεως
eusebeian	*dedōrēmenēs*	*dia*	*tēs*	*epignōseōs*
godliness	having given,	through	the	knowledge

THE SECOND EPISTLE OF
PETER

1:1. The authorship of 2 Peter is questioned by some scholars who believe an unknown follower of Peter wrote it some years after his death. However, we can be confident that the epistle is the work of an apostle. It is full of orthodox and edifying teaching, and there is abundant reason to accept Peter as the author. Evidently this second epistle is an addition to the first and is addressed to the same churches in Asia Minor. It is a kind of farewell message. Peter perceived his death was near and he offered encouraging admonitions. He warned believers against false teachers who deny Christ's redeeming work.

The apostle's name is Simon (Acts 15:14 has Simeon, the Jewish form of the word). Jesus gave him a new name, Peter (*Petros,* "a rock"), which is the Greek form of *Cephas* (from the Hebrew *Kēph*).

Peter called himself a "servant" (*doulos,* bondslave) and an "apostle" (*apostolos,* delegate, ambassador, messenger, one who is sent) of Christ. The "faith" (*pistin,* belief, persuasion, assurance) believers have received and shared in is "like precious" (*isotimon,* similarly precious, of equal value or privilege) with that of Peter and the apostles. They have received this blessed assurance through the "righteousness" (*dikaiosunē,* equitable justification, innocence imputed to all without partiality) of "God and our Saviour Jesus Christ."

1:2. Peter's wish was that they enjoy "grace" (*charis,* gift, favor of God) and "peace" (*eirēnē,* quietness, harmony, well-being) in "multiplied" measure. This will happen through their "knowledge" (*epignōsei*) of the Lord; that is, intimate acquaintance, full discernment, recognition, acknowledgment. This is not merely an intellectual knowledge of Biblical facts, but an experiential knowledge, a personal acquaintance with Jesus Christ as our Saviour and Lord.

1:3. It is possible for believers to have a multiplied measure of grace and peace, seeing that God's divine power has "given" (*dedōrēmenēs,* grant generously, bestow freely) them all the things necessary for "life and godliness." Peter wanted believers to enter into all these potential blessings. They have the capability to "live

Various Versions

1. Simon Peter, a servant and an apostle of Jesus Christ: . . . a slave, *Concordant* . . . a bondslave and an ambassador, *Wuest* . . . and messenger, *Phillips.*

to them that have obtained like precious faith with us: . . . sends this letter to those who have been given a faith as valuable as ours, *Phillips* . . . to those who have been divinely allotted, *Wuest* . . . to them who have reached a faith equally as honorable as ours, *Swann* . . . obtained our common sacred faith, *Noli.*

through the righteousness of God and our Saviour Jesus Christ: . . . by the equitable treatment of, *Wuest.*

2. Grace and peace be multiplied unto you: . . . spiritual blessing and peace be to you in increasing abundance, *Williams* . . . be yours in plenty, *Williams C.K.*

through the knowledge of God, and of Jesus our Lord: . . . as your knowledge...grows deeper, *Phillips* . . . through intimate acquaintance, *Berkeley* . . . in the sphere of and by the experiential knowledge, *Wuest* . . . in an ever-increasing knowledge, *TCNT* . . . in the recognition of, *Concordant.*

3. According as his divine power hath given unto us: He has by his own action, *Phillips* . . . has bestowed on us, *Berkeley* . . . gives it through His great power, *NLT.*

all things that [pertain] unto life and godliness: . . . every requisite, *Berkeley* . . . everything that is necessary for living the truly good life, *Phillips* . . . everything we need for our physical and spiritual life, *Norlie* . . . for leading a good Christian life, *Laubach* . . . tends to life and devoutness, *Concordant* . . . for true religion, *TCNT.*

3450.2 art gen sing	2535.15 verb gen sing masc part aor act	2231.4 prs-pron acc 1pl	1217.2 prep	1385.2 noun gen sing fem	2504.1 conj	697.2 noun gen sing fem
τοῦ	καλέσαντος	ἡμᾶς	ʻ διὰ	δόξης	καὶ	ἀρετῆς,
tou	*kalesantos*	*hēmas*	*dia*	*doxēs*	*kai*	*aretēs*
of the	having called	us	by	glory	and	virtue,

3.b.**Txt:** p72,03B,018K 020L,byz.We/Ho
Var: 01א,02A,04C,025P 044,33,it.sa.bo.Lach Treg,Alf,Word,Tisc Weis,Sod,UBS/☆

2375.10 adj dat sing fem	1385.3 noun dat sing fem	2504.1 conj	697.3 noun dat sing fem	1217.1 prep	3614.1 rel-pron gen pl
[[b]☆ ἰδίᾳ	δόξῃ	καὶ	ἀρετῇ,]	4. δι’	ὧν
idia	*doxē*	*kai*	*aretē*	*di’*	*hōn*
[to his own	glory	and	virtue,]	through	which

3450.17 art pl neu	3147.1 adj sup pl neu	2231.3 prs-pron dat 1pl	2504.1 conj	4941.8 adj pl neu	4941.8 adj pl neu	2504.1 conj
τὰ	ʻ μέγιστα	ἡμῖν	καὶ	τίμια	[☆ τίμια	καὶ
ta	*megista*	*hēmin*	*kai*	*timia*	*timia*	*kai*
the	greatest	to us	and	precious	[precious	and

3147.1 adj sup pl neu	2231.3 prs-pron dat 1pl	1847.2 noun pl neu	1426.2 verb 3sing indic perf mid	2419.1 conj	1217.2 prep
μέγιστα	ἡμῖν]	ἐπαγγέλματα	δεδώρηται,	ἵνα	διὰ
megista	*hēmin*	*epangelmata*	*dedōrētai*	*hina*	*dia*
greatest	to us]	promises	he has given,	that	through

3642.2 dem-pron gen pl	1090.42 verb 2pl subj aor mid	2281.1 adj gen sing fem	2817.3 noun nom pl masc	5285.2 noun gen sing fem
τούτων	γένησθε	θείας	κοινωνοὶ	φύσεως,
toutōn	*genēsthe*	*theias*	*koinōnoi*	*phuseōs*
these	you may become	of divine	sharers	nature,

4.a.**Var:** 01א,02A,03B 020L,Lach,Treg,Tisc We/Ho,Weis,Sod UBS/☆

662.1 verb nom pl masc part aor act	3450.10 art gen sing fem	1706.1 prep	3450.3 art dat sing	2862.3 noun dat sing masc	1706.1 prep
ἀποφυγόντες	τῆς	ἐν	[[a]☆+ τῷ]	κόσμῳ	ἐν
apophugontes	*tēs*	*en*	*tō*	*kosmō*	*en*
having escaped	the	in	[the]	world	through

1924.3 noun dat sing fem	5193.2 noun gen sing fem	2504.1 conj	840.15 prs-pron sing neu	3642.17 dem-pron sing neu	1156.2 conj
ἐπιθυμίᾳ	φθορᾶς.	5. καὶ	αὐτὸ	ʻ☆ τοῦτο	δὲ,
epithumia	*phthoras*	*kai*	*auto*	*touto*	*de*
lust	corruption,	also	same	this	but,

5.a.**Txt:** p72,03B 04C-org,025P,byz.
Var: 01א,04C-corr2,044 33,81,323,614,630,945 1241,1505,1739,2495 Sod

1156.2 conj	3642.17 dem-pron sing neu	4561.3 noun acc sing fem	3820.12 adj acc sing fem	3785.1 verb nom pl masc part aor act
[[a] δὲ	τοῦτο,]	σπουδὴν	πᾶσαν	παρεισενέγκαντες
de	*touto*	*spoudēn*	*pasan*	*pareisenenkantes*
[but	this,]	diligence,	all	having brought in besides,

2007.2 verb 2pl impr aor act	1706.1 prep	3450.11 art dat sing fem	3963.3 noun dat sing fem	5050.2 prs-pron gen 2pl	3450.12 art acc sing fem
ἐπιχορηγήσατε	ἐν	τῇ	πίστει	ὑμῶν	τὴν
epichorēgēsate	*en*	*tē*	*pistei*	*humōn*	*tēn*
supply you	in	the	faith	your	the

697.4 noun acc sing fem	1706.1 prep	1156.2 conj	3450.11 art dat sing fem	697.3 noun dat sing fem	3450.12 art acc sing fem	1102.4 noun acc sing fem
ἀρετήν,	ἐν	δὲ	τῇ	ἀρετῇ	τὴν	γνῶσιν,
aretēn	*en*	*de*	*tē*	*aretē*	*tēn*	*gnōsin*
virtue,	in	and	the	virtue	the	knowledge,

1706.1 prep	1156.2 conj	3450.11 art dat sing fem	1102.3 noun dat sing fem	3450.12 art acc sing fem	1459.4 noun acc sing fem
6. ἐν	δὲ	τῇ	γνώσει	τὴν	ἐγκράτειαν,
en	*de*	*tē*	*gnōsei*	*tēn*	*enkrateian*
in	and	the	knowledge	the	self-control,

godly in Christ Jesus," as 2 Timothy 3:12 describes it. The Lord has "called" (*kalesantos,* bid, summon personally, call by name) believers to His own "glory" (*doxēs,* honor, radiant splendor) and "virtue" (*aretēs,* manliness, holy excellence), thereby to manifest the divine character of Christ in their daily lives.

through the knowledge of him that hath called us to glory and virtue: . . . through the recognition, *Concordant* . . . through the experiential knowledge, *Wuest* . . . in allowing us to know the one who has called us to him, through his own glorious goodness, *Phillips.*

1:4. In giving believers "all things" (verse 3), the Lord has granted them "promises" (*epangelmata,* pledge, self-committal, assurance) that are very valuable and exceedingly great. If believers will claim these precious promises they may, even now, be "partakers" (*koinōnoi,* sharer, partner) in Christ's "nature" (*phuseōs,* genus, lineal descent, native disposition, constitution). Peter was speaking here of regeneration, as in 1 Peter 1:3. This divine nature implanted within the believer by the new birth becomes the source of his new life-style. The new life-style does not come automatically; the believer must make an effort. He must flee away from "lust" (*epithumia,* passionate desire, strong craving—usually for what is forbidden) or he will experience "corruption" (*phthoras,* decay, ruin). "Having escaped" (*apophugontes*) means "escape by flight." God helps those who flee the old life to develop the new life if they cooperate with Him.

4. Whereby are given unto us exceeding great and precious promises: On account of which, *Campbell* . . . through which have been presented to us, *Concordant* . . . the greatest promises of all, *Adams* . . . most honourable promises, *Fenton* . . . and glorious promises, *Williams* . . . promised blessings, *Berkeley.*

that by these ye might be partakers of the divine nature: . . . become participants, *Concordant* . . . to share God's essential nature, *Phillips.*

having escaped the corruption that is in the world through lust: . . . having fled away from, *Wilson* . . . fleeing from the corruption which is in the world by lust, *Concordant* . . . making it possible for you to escape the inevitable disintegration that lust produces in the world, *Phillips* . . . having escaped by flight the corruption which is in the world in the sphere of passionate cravings, *Wuest* . . . that arises from passion, *Berkeley* . . . from the corrupting influences, *TCNT* . . . owing to depraved desire, *Fenton* . . . because of evil desires, *Williams.*

1:5. Spiritual life either grows or dies. Believers should not be content to hold their "faith" (*pistei,* belief, assurance, persuasion, as in verse 1) but should "add" (*epichorēgēsate,* amply furnish, contribute nourishment) to it with wholehearted "diligence" (*spoudēn,* carefulness, intense effort). Peter listed seven supplements needed to round out the believer's faith. Two affect the believer's relationship to God (knowledge, godliness) and five affect his relationship to other people (virtue, temperance, patience, brotherly kindness, love). "Virtue" here is not *dunamis,* the miracle-working power that went out of Jesus (Mark 5:30; Luke 6:19; 8:46). It is *aretēn,* meaning valor, holy excellence, moral power; as in Philippians 4:8, "If there be any virtue . . . think on these things." The word translated "knowledge" is *gnōsin,* meaning awareness, intelligent insight; as in John 15:15, "All things that I have heard of my Father I have made known unto you." As the believer opens his being to the Spirit and the Word, he begins to see truth in its proper perspective.

5. And beside this, giving all diligence: . . . employing all diligence, *Concordant* . . . concentrate all your endeavors upon, *Wade* . . . having added on your part every intense effort, *Wuest* . . . do your utmost, *Berkeley.*

add to your faith virtue: . . . provide lavishly in your faith the aforementioned virtue, *Wuest* . . . supplement your faith with moral character, *Williams* . . . fortitude, *Wilson.*

and to virtue knowledge: . . . intelligence, *Fenton* . . . spiritual knowledge, *Wade* . . . experiential knowledge, *Wuest.*

1:6. "Temperance" (*enkrateian;* cf. Galatians 5:23) relates to the believer's entire life-style, not just drinking. It means self-control, mastery over one's temper, and over all physical appetites. It is the exact opposite of the self-expression and self-indulgence so prevalent in the world. "Patience" (*hupomonēn*) is not a quiet resig-

6. And to knowledge temperance: . . . besides knowledge you must have self-control, *Laubach* . . . self-restraint, *Fenton.*

1706.1 prep	1156.2 conj	3450.11 art dat sing fem	1459.3 noun dat sing fem	3450.12 art acc sing fem	5119.4 noun acc sing fem	1706.1 prep
ἐν	δὲ	τῇ	ἐγκρατείᾳ	τὴν	ὑπομονήν,	ἐν
en	*de*	*tē*	*enkrateia*	*tēn*	*hupomonēn*	*en*
in	and	the	self-control	the	endurance,	in

1156.2 conj	3450.11 art dat sing fem	5119.3 noun dat sing fem	3450.12 art acc sing fem	2131.4 noun acc sing fem	1706.1 prep
δὲ	τῇ	ὑπομονῇ	τὴν	εὐσέβειαν,	7. ἐν
de	*tē*	*hupomonē*	*tēn*	*eusebeian*	*en*
and	the	endurance	the	godliness,	in

1156.2 conj	3450.11 art dat sing fem	2131.3 noun dat sing fem	3450.12 art acc sing fem	5197.4 noun acc sing fem	1706.1 prep
δὲ	τῇ	εὐσεβείᾳ	τὴν	φιλαδελφίαν,	ἐν
de	*tē*	*eusebeia*	*tēn*	*philadelphian*	*en*
and	the	godliness	the	brotherly love,	in

1156.2 conj	3450.11 art dat sing fem	5197.3 noun dat sing fem	3450.12 art acc sing fem	26.4 noun acc sing fem	3642.18 dem-pron pl neu
δὲ	τῇ	φιλαδελφίᾳ	τὴν	ἀγάπην.	8. ταῦτα
de	*tē*	*philadelphia*	*tēn*	*agapēn*	*tauta*
and	the	brotherly love	the	love:	these things

1056.1 conj	5050.3 prs-pron dat 2pl	5062.4 verb part pres act	2504.1 conj	3981.2 verb part pres act	3620.2 partic
γὰρ	ὑμῖν	ὑπάρχοντα	καὶ	πλεονάζοντα,	οὐκ
gar	*humin*	*huparchonta*	*kai*	*pleonazonta*	*ouk*
for	in you	being	and	abounding	neither

686.2 adj acc pl masc	3624.1 conj	173.3 adj acc pl masc	2497.1 verb 3sing indic pres act	1519.1 prep	3450.12 art acc sing fem
ἀργοὺς	οὐδὲ	ἀκάρπους	καθίστησιν	εἰς	τὴν
argous	*oude*	*akarpous*	*kathistēsin*	*eis*	*tēn*
idle	nor	unfruitful	makes	as to	the

3450.2 art gen sing	2935.2 noun gen sing masc	2231.2 prs-pron gen 1pl	2400.2 name masc	5382.2 name gen masc	1907.4 noun acc sing fem
τοῦ	κυρίου	ἡμῶν	Ἰησοῦ	Χριστοῦ	ἐπίγνωσιν·
tou	*kuriou*	*hēmōn*	*Iēsou*	*Christou*	*epignōsin*
of the	Lord	our	Jesus	Christ	knowledge;

3614.3 rel-pron dat sing	1056.1 conj	3231.1 partic	3780.2 verb 3sing indic pres act	3642.18 dem-pron pl neu	5026.1 adj nom sing masc
9. ᾧ	γὰρ	μὴ	πάρεστιν	ταῦτα	τυφλός
hō	*gar*	*mē*	*parestin*	*tauta*	*tuphlos*
with whom	for	not	are present	these things	blind

1498.4 verb 3sing indic pres act	3329.1 verb nom sing masc part pres act	2998.1 noun acc sing fem	2956.25 verb nom sing masc part aor act
ἐστιν,	μυωπάζων,	λήθην	λαβὼν
estin	*muōpazōn*	*lēthēn*	*labōn*
he is,	being shortsighted,	forgetfulness	having taken

3450.2 art gen sing	2484.1 noun gen sing masc	3450.1 art gen pl	3682.1 adv	840.3 prs-pron gen sing	264.6 noun gen pl fem
τοῦ	καθαρισμοῦ	τῶν	πάλαι	αὐτοῦ	‹☆ ἁμαρτιῶν.
tou	*katharismou*	*tōn*	*palai*	*autou*	*hamartiōn*
the	purification	of the	old	of his	sins.

263.3 noun gen pl neu	1346.1 conj	3095.1 adv comp	79.6 noun nom pl masc
[a ἁμαρτημάτων.]	10. Διὸ	μᾶλλον,	ἀδελφοί,
hamartēmatōn	*Dio*	*mallon*	*adelphoi*
[idem]	Wherefore	rather,	brothers,

9.a.**Txt:** p72,03B,04C 020L,025P,byz.
Var: 01ℵ,02A,018K 1175,Tisc

nation to one's fate; it is a heroic perseverance in serving Christ in spite of opposition, as in James 1:3, "The trying of your faith worketh patience." "Godliness" (*eusebeian*; cf. 1 Timothy 6:11) speaks of piety, devoutness, holiness.

Peter had informed the believers that by the new birth they had become partakers of the divine nature; next he showed them how to develop divine character. It means adding those traits which reflect the presence of Christ in our lives.

and to temperance patience: ... endurance, *Concordant.*

and to patience godliness: ... piety, *Wilson* ... devoutness, *Concordant.*

7. And to godliness brotherly kindness: ... brotherly fondness, *Concordant* ... an affection for the brethren, *Wuest.*

and to brotherly kindness charity: ... unselfish concern to, *SEB* ... with universal love, *Williams* ... comprehensive, *Wade* ... divine, *Wuest.*

1:7. "Brotherly kindness" (*philadelphian*) is fraternal affection, fondness for a brother or sister in Christ; "charity" (*agapēn*) is a wider and deeper love. The latter is the kind that enables the believer to love his enemies (Matthew 5:44). The believer is to love others not because he likes them but because they need his love. It is volitional rather than emotional, a love that operates by deliberate choice. It is Calvary love (John 3:16), the love pictured in 1 Corinthians 13:4-7. Believers are to extend to others the kind of love God has shown to them.

8. For if these things be in you, and abound: ... if you possess and progress in these, *Fenton* ... If you possess such virtues, *Norlie* ... who possess these virtues abundantly, *Noli* ... if these things are your natural and rightful possession, and are in superabundance, *Wuest* ... and have them in increasing measure, *Williams C.K.* ... and continually increasing, *Wade.*

they make [you that ye shall] neither [be] barren nor unfruitful: ... to be neither slothful, *Campbell* ... is constituting you not idle nor yet unfruitful, *Concordant* ... they will make you active and productive, *SEB* ... they prevent your being indifferent, *TCNT* ... they will not permit you to be inactive, *Wilson* ... neither be dilatory nor ineffective, *Fenton.*

in the knowledge of our Lord Jesus Christ: ... in the recognition of, *Concordant* ... the experiential knowledge of, *Wuest.*

1:8. Peter indicated the characteristics he enumerated in verses 5-7 should be in them and "abound" (*pleonazonta*, increase exceedingly, overflow). This speaks of the Spirit-filled life which is an overflowing kind, spilling over so others are blessed. It also speaks of Christian character which is formed by developing all these qualities until they are ingrained in one's life. The believer's Christian character is either strong or weak depending on the extent to which he cooperates with the Holy Spirit in developing these qualities in his life.

The goal is to be neither "barren" (*argous*, useless, ineffective) nor "unfruitful" (*akarpous*, unproductive). Believers' "knowledge" (*epignōsin*, intimate acquaintance, full discernment) of Christ should make them active in serving Him, and if they possess these qualities their service will be effective and fruitful.

9. But he that lacketh these things is blind, and cannot see afar off: Whoever does not practice these things, *Laubach* ... he in whom these are not present is blind, closing his eyes, *Concordant* ... lacks these qualities, *Williams* ... he sees only what is under his nose, *Williams C.K.* ... shutting his eyes, *Campbell* ... shortsighted, *Norlie.*

and hath forgotten that he was purged from his old sins: ... getting oblivious of the cleansing from the penalties of his sins of old, *Concordant* ... having taken forgetfulness of the cleansing of, *Wuest* ... choosing to forget the pruning he has received from his old errors, *Fenton* ... his former sinful ways, *Norlie.*

1:9. If a believer does not develop these characteristics he is "blind" (*tuphlos*, sightless, or partly so) and "cannot see afar off" (*muōpazōn*, blink when a light is too bright). In ancient Greek literature *muōpazōn* was used for a nearsighted man. The nearsighted person who lacks these things "hath forgotten" (*lēthēn*, willfully forgotten) that he was "purged" (*katharismou*, cleansed, purified) of the sins he committed prior to his conversion. If he would look back to the life of sin from which he was delivered, and look ahead to the eternal blessings God has promised, he would see the great advantage of developing his Christian character to the fullest extent possible.

4557.6 verb 2pl impr aor act	942.3 adj acc sing fem	5050.2 prs-pron gen 2pl	3450.12 art acc sing fem	2794.4 noun acc sing fem	2504.1 conj
σπουδάσατε	βεβαίαν	ὑμῶν	τὴν	κλῆσιν	καὶ
spoudasate	*bebaian*	*humōn*	*tēn*	*klēsin*	*kai*
be diligent	sure	your	the	calling	and

10.a.**Txt:** p72,03B,04C 025P,byz.
Var: 01ℵ,02A,044,81 614,630,1505,1852 2495

1576.3 noun acc sing fem	4020.66 verb inf pres mid	4020.63 verb 2pl impr pres mid	3642.18 dem-pron pl neu	1056.1 conj
ἐκλογὴν	ʿ☆ ποιεῖσθαι˙	[ª ποιεῖσθε˙]	ταῦτα	γὰρ
eklogēn	*poieisthai*	*poieisthe*	*tauta*	*gar*
election	to make,	[make,]	these things	for

4020.17 verb nom pl masc part pres act	3620.3 partic	3231.1 partic	4275.4 verb 2pl subj aor act	4077.1 adv	3643.1 adv
ποιοῦντες	οὐ	μὴ	πταίσητέ	ποτε.	**11.** οὕτως
poiountes	*ou*	*mē*	*ptaisēte*	*pote*	*houtōs*
doing	no	not	shall you stumble	ever.	Thus

1056.1 conj	4005.1 adv	2007.4 verb 3sing indic fut pass	5050.3 prs-pron dat 2pl	3450.9 art nom sing fem
γὰρ	πλουσίως	ἐπιχορηγηθήσεται	ὑμῖν	ἡ
gar	*plousiōs*	*epichorēgēthēsetai*	*humin*	*hē*
for	richly	shall be supplied	to you	the

1513.1 noun nom sing fem	1519.1 prep	3450.12 art acc sing fem	164.1 adj sing	926.4 noun acc sing fem	3450.2 art gen sing
εἴσοδος	εἰς	τὴν	αἰώνιον	βασιλείαν	τοῦ
eisodos	*eis*	*tēn*	*aiōnion*	*basileian*	*tou*
entrance	into	the	eternal	kingdom	of the

2935.2 noun gen sing masc	2231.2 prs-pron gen 1pl	2504.1 conj	4842.2 noun gen sing masc	2400.2 name masc	5382.2 name gen masc
κυρίου	ἡμῶν	καὶ	σωτῆρος	Ἰησοῦ	Χριστοῦ.
kuriou	*hēmōn*	*kai*	*sōtēros*	*Iēsou*	*Christou*
Lord	our	and	Saviour	Jesus	Christ.

12.a.**Txt:** 018K,020L,byz.
Var: 01ℵ,02A,03B,04C 025P,sa.bo.Lach,Treg Alf,Word,Tisc,We/Ho Weis,Sod,UBS/☆

1346.1 conj	3620.2 partic	270.4 verb 1sing indic fut act	3165.23 verb 1sing indic fut act	5050.4 prs-pron acc 2pl
12. Διὸ	ʿ οὐκ	ἀμελήσω	[ª☆ μελλήσω]	ʿ ὑμᾶς
Dio	*ouk*	*amelēsō*	*mellēsō*	*humas*
Wherefore	not	I will neglect	[I will take care]	you

103.1 adv	103.1 adv	5050.4 prs-pron acc 2pl	5117.2 verb inf pres act	3875.1 prep
ἀεὶ	[☆ ἀεὶ	ὑμᾶς]	ὑπομιμνήσκειν	περὶ
aei	*aei*	*humas*	*hupomimnēskein*	*peri*
always	[always	you]	to put in remembrance	concerning

3642.2 dem-pron gen pl	2510.1 conj	3471.22 verb acc pl masc part perf act	2504.1 conj	4592.8 verb acc pl masc part perf mid
τούτων,	καίπερ	εἰδότας,	καὶ	ἐστηριγμένους
toutōn	*kaiper*	*eidotas*	*kai*	*estērigmenous*
these things,	although	knowing	and	having been established

1706.1 prep	3450.11 art dat sing fem	3780.8 verb dat sing fem part pres act	223.3 noun dat sing fem	1337.1 adj sing	1156.2 conj
ἐν	τῇ	παρούσῃ	ἀληθείᾳ.	**13.** δίκαιον	δὲ
en	*tē*	*parousē*	*alētheia*	*dikaion*	*de*
in	the	being present	truth.	Right	but

2216.1 verb 1sing indic pres mid	1894.1 prep	3607.1 rel-pron sing	1498.2 verb 1sing indic pres act	1706.1 prep	3642.5 dem-pron dat sing masc
ἡγοῦμαι,	ἐφ'	ὅσον	εἰμὶ	ἐν	τούτῳ
hēgoumai	*eph'*	*hoson*	*eimi*	*en*	*toutō*
I count it,	on	which	I am	in	this

1:10. Because of what Peter said in verses 5-9, believers should show all the more diligence in developing these characteristics to assure themselves not only of their "calling" (*klēsin,* invitation, summons) but also of their "election" (*eklogēn,* selection, being chosen).

All are called to be saved, but not all respond by trusting in Christ and living for Him. As Jesus said, "Many are called, but few are chosen" (Matthew 22:14). Jesus made this statement after telling of a guest at the wedding who was ejected; he had accepted the invitation but was not wearing the wedding garment that was required.

Peter said that if believers "do" these things (and keep on doing them, as the Greek indicates), they shall never "fall" (*ptaisēte,* stumble and fall, be tripped up), and their election will be "sure" (*bebaian,* enduring, guaranteed). The word was used by the Greeks in a legal sense to indicate a warranty that protected a buyer.

10. Wherefore the rather, brethren, give diligence: Consequently devote your attention, *Wade* . . . exert yourselves the more, and bend every effort, *Wuest* . . . endeavor through ideal acts, *Concordant* . . . spare no effort, *TCNT.*

to make your calling and election sure: . . . to confirm your calling and choice, *Concordant* . . . to make for yourselves your divine call [into salvation] and your divine selection, *Wuest.*

for if ye do these things, ye shall never fall: . . . if you practice these things, *Berkeley* . . . you will never stumble, *Wuest* . . . you should under no circumstances be tripping at any time, *Concordant.*

1:11. In this way believers will have an entrance into the everlasting kingdom of our Lord (the inheritance of 1 Peter 1:4), and it will be "ministered" (*epichorēgēthēsetai,* amply furnish, contribute) to them "abundantly" (*plousiōs,* copiously, richly). "Ministered" is the same Greek word translated "add" in verse 5. If believers will add the Christian characteristics to their faith, God will add the abundant reward. Only an unmindful and nearsighted person could fail to appreciate such a future.

11. For so an entrance shall be ministered unto you abundantly: . . . you will be triumphantly admitted, *Noli* . . . the entrance shall be richly provided for you, *Wuest* . . . you will find a glorious door opening for you, *Laubach* . . . will be richly supplied to you, *Montgomery.*

into the everlasting kingdom of our Lord and Saviour Jesus Christ: . . . into the eonian kingdom, *Concordant* . . . eternal, *Wuest.*

1:12. The sense of responsibility Peter felt throughout his ministry was intensified as he saw death approaching. He was determined not to be negligent. He knew a minister cannot safely assume his hearers will remember what he has taught them and that it is necessary to repeat familiar truths again and again. He did not condemn them or question their experience; on the contrary, he said they knew ("know," *eidotas,* be aware, perceive) the things he had been telling them, and they were "established" (*estērigmenous,* set fast, make stable) in the truth they now possessed. However, he intended to "put (them) in remembrance" of these things (*hupomimnēskein,* remind quietly), and he would do this "always" (*aei,* ever). He said he would keep on reminding them, for he wanted them to remain firmly fixed in the "truth" (*alētheia,* verity, as in 2:2).

12. Wherefore I will not be negligent: I shall ever be about, *Concordant* . . . take care always, *Berkeley.*

to put you always in remembrance of these things: I think it is right for me to refresh your memory, *SEB* . . . be reminding you concerning these things, *Concordant.*

though ye know [them], and be established in the present truth: . . . even though you are aware of, *Concordant* . . . and have become firmly established...which is present with you, *Wuest* . . . and stand firm in the revealed truth, *Fenton* . . . and are steady-minded in the truth now available, *Berkeley.*

1:13. Peter thought it "meet" (*dikaion,* right) to do this. In other words, it was his duty; he was under obligation "to stir (them) up" (*diegeirein,* awaken, arouse) by reminding them of the truth they had been taught, and he felt he must keep doing this as long as

13. Yea, I think it meet, as long as I am in this tabernacle: Yet I consider it right, *Fenton* . . . I think it my duty, *TCNT* . . . this is the right thing to do, *Norlie* . . . Now I am deeming it just, *Concordant* . . . Indeed, I consider it due you as long as I am in this tent, *Wuest.*

13.a.**Txt:** p72,03B,04C 025P,049,0209,bo.byz. **Var:** 01ℵ,02A,044,623 sa.

3450.3 art dat sing	**4493.2** noun dat sing neu	**1320.3** verb inf pres act	**5050.4** prs-pron acc 2pl	**1706.1** prep	**3450.11** art dat sing fem
τῷ	σκηνώματι,	διεγείρειν	ὑμᾶς	ἐν	[a+ τῇ]
tō	*skēnōmati*	*diegeirein*	*humas*	*en*	*tē*
the	tabernacle,	to stir up	you	by	[the]

5118.1 noun dat sing fem	**3471.18** verb nom sing masc part perf act	**3617.1** conj	**4879.1** adj nom sing fem
ὑπομνήσει·	**14.** εἰδὼς	ὅτι	ταχινή
hupomnēsei	*eidōs*	*hoti*	*tachinē*
putting in remembrance,	knowing	that	imminent

1498.4 verb 3sing indic pres act	**3450.9** art nom sing fem	**590.1** noun nom sing fem	**3450.2** art gen sing	**4493.1** noun gen sing neu
ἐστιν	ἡ	ἀπόθεσις	τοῦ	σκηνώματός
estin	*hē*	*apothesis*	*tou*	*skēnōmatos*
is	the	putting off	of the	tabernacle

1466.2 prs-pron gen 1sing	**2503.1** conj	**2504.1** conj	**3450.5** art nom sing masc	**2935.1** noun nom sing masc	**2231.2** prs-pron gen 1pl	**2400.1** name nom masc
μου,	καθὼς	καὶ	ὁ	κύριος	ἡμῶν	Ἰησοῦς
mou	*kathōs*	*kai*	*ho*	*kurios*	*hēmōn*	*Iēsous*
my,	as	also	the	Lord	our	Jesus

5382.1 name nom masc	**1207.3** verb 3sing indic aor act	**1466.4** prs-pron dat 1sing	**4557.7** verb 1sing indic fut act	**1156.2** conj
Χριστὸς	ἐδήλωσέν	μοι.	**15.** σπουδάσω	δὲ
Christos	*edēlōsen*	*moi*	*spoudasō*	*de*
Christ	signified	to me;	I will be diligent	but

2504.1 conj	**1525.1** adv	**2174.29** verb inf pres act	**5050.4** prs-pron acc 2pl	**3196.3** prep	**3450.12** art acc sing fem	**1684.9** adj acc sing fem
καὶ	ἑκάστοτε	ἔχειν	ὑμᾶς	μετὰ	τὴν	ἐμὴν
kai	*hekastote*	*echein*	*humas*	*meta*	*tēn*	*emēn*
also	at every time	to have	for you	after	the	my

1825.2 noun acc sing fem	**3450.12** art acc sing fem	**3642.2** dem-pron gen pl	**3284.1** noun acc sing fem	**4020.66** verb inf pres mid	**3620.3** partic
ἔξοδον	τὴν	τούτων	μνήμην	ποιεῖσθαι.	**16.** Οὐ
exodon	*tēn*	*toutōn*	*mnēmēn*	*poieisthai*	*Ou*
departure	the	these things	memory	to cause.	Not

1056.1 conj	**4532.2** verb dat pl masc part perf mid	**3316.1** noun dat pl masc	**1795.1** verb nom pl masc part aor act
γὰρ	σεσοφισμένοις	μύθοις	ἐξακολουθήσαντες
gar	*sesophismenois*	*muthois*	*exakolouthēsantes*
for	having been cleverly imagined	myths	having followed out

1101.6 verb 1pl indic aor act	**5050.3** prs-pron dat 2pl	**3450.12** art acc sing fem	**3450.2** art gen sing	**2935.2** noun gen sing masc	**2231.2** prs-pron gen 1pl
ἐγνωρίσαμεν	ὑμῖν	τὴν	τοῦ	κυρίου	ἡμῶν
egnōrisamen	*humin*	*tēn*	*tou*	*kuriou*	*hēmōn*
we made known	to you	the	of the	Lord	our

2400.2 name masc	**5382.2** name gen masc	**1405.4** noun acc sing fem	**2504.1** conj	**3814.4** noun acc sing fem	**233.1** conj
Ἰησοῦ	Χριστοῦ	δύναμιν	καὶ	παρουσίαν,	ἀλλ'
Iēsou	*Christou*	*dunamin*	*kai*	*parousian*	*all'*
Jesus	Christ	power	and	coming,	but

2014.1 noun nom pl masc	**1090.54** verb nom pl masc part aor pass	**3450.10** art gen sing fem	**1552.2** dem-pron gen sing	**3139.1** noun gen sing fem
ἐπόπται	γενηθέντες	τῆς	ἐκείνου	μεγαλειότητος.
epoptai	*genēthentes*	*tēs*	*ekeinou*	*megaleiotētos*
eyewitnesses	having been	of the	that	majesty.

he was in this "tabernacle" (*skēnōmati*, dwelling, tent, tabernacle). Peter described his body as a temporary dwelling.

1:14. Peter was aware that "shortly" (*tachinē*, impending, coming swiftly) he must "put off" (*apothesis*, lay aside, put away) his body. The language corresponds to Christ's statement in John 10:18, "No man taketh it from me, but I lay it down of myself." Peter indicated he would not die under protest; he was willing to lay down his life for the sake of his Lord. He said Christ had made this plain to him. No doubt he was recalling the prophecy (John 21:18,19) that he would die as a prisoner and not as a free man.

1:15. Peter wanted believers to have a written account of his teaching to help them after his death. He was an eyewitness of the life and teachings of Christ. He could testify firsthand to His death, burial, resurrection, and ascension. He could describe the Transfiguration for he was present. Once his generation passed, there would be no eyewitness testimony unless it was preserved in written form. So he said he would "endeavor" (*spoudasō*, be diligent, make every effort) to see that believers have a permanent reminder ("always in remembrance") of these things. His epistles will help meet this need. So will the Gospel of Mark written with his help. In describing his impending death, Peter used two words from the conversation on the Mount of Transfiguration (Luke 9:28-33); namely, *skēnōmatos* (tabernacle, verse 14) and *exodon* (decease, departure, as used in Hebrews 11:22 to describe the Exodus).

1:16. Peter's authority as a teacher depended on his authority as a witness, so he stated his qualifications again. Evidently there were false teachers who were saying the miracles attributed to Christ were only allegories, not facts. Peter emphatically denied this. He said he and the other apostles were not simply following through with "fables" (*muthois*, a fictitious tale, myth) which had been "cunningly devised" (*sesophismenois*, make wise in a good sense, or frame artfully in a bad sense). They were being truthful about Christ's "power" (*dunamin*, might, miracle-working power) and "coming" (*parousian*, advent). This word also appears in 3:4 which states: "Where is the promise of his coming?"

Some may be thinking such a spectacular event as the Second Coming is inconceivable, but Peter entertained no doubts, for he had already glimpsed Christ's glory. He was an "eyewitness" (*epoptai*, spectator, observer) of Christ's "majesty" (*megaleiotētos*, grandeur, mighty power); as Luke 9:43 says: "They were all amazed at the mighty power of God." He had seen the divine aura, and his testimony could not be shaken. The Greek *parousian* is the word used repeatedly by Christ and the apostles to refer to the Second Coming. The same word appears in ancient literature of the coming of any royal visitor.

to stir you up by putting [you] in remembrance: . . . to excite you, *Wilson* . . . to be rousing you by a reminder, *Concordant* . . . to keep you wide-awake by reminding you, *Berkeley.*

14. Knowing that shortly I must put off [this] my tabernacle: . . . being aware, *Concordant* . . . knowing that very soon there is the putting off of my tent, *Wuest* . . . the time for me to strike tent comes swiftly on, *Montgomery.*

even as our Lord Jesus Christ hath showed me: . . . declared to me, *Wilson* . . . made clear to me, *Berkeley* . . . disclosed to me, *Fenton* . . . makes evident to me, *Concordant* . . . gave me to understand, *Wuest.*

15. Moreover I will endeavour that ye may be able after my decease to have these things always in remembrance: Indeed, I will do my best also that on each occasion when you have need after my departure you will be able to call these things to remembrance, *Wuest* . . . I will make every effort to enable each one of you to keep these things in mind after I am gone, *Berkeley* . . . at any time after my departure, *TCNT* . . . to make mention of these things, ever and anon, also, *Concordant.*

16. For we have not followed cunningly devised fables: . . . we did not follow out to their termination, *Wuest* . . . We had nothing to do with man-made stories, *NLT* . . . we did not depend on invented stories, *Williams C.K.* . . . This is no clever invention, *Laubach* . . . cleverly devised stories, *TCNT* . . . wisely made myths, *Concordant* . . . cleverly invented myths, *Norlie, Adams* . . . skilfully invented fables, *Wade* . . . fictitious stories, *Swann.*

when we made known unto you the power and coming of our Lord Jesus Christ: . . . when we acquainted you with the power and coming, *Berkeley* . . . and presence, *Concordant* . . . and personal coming of, *Wuest.*

but were eyewitnesses of his majesty: . . . were Beholders of that Greatness, *Wilson* . . . we saw his greatness! *SEB* . . . by becoming spectators of His magnificence, *Concordant* . . . of His grandeur, *Fenton.*

2956.25 verb nom sing masc part aor act	1056.1 conj	3706.2 prep	2296.2 noun gen sing masc	3824.2 noun gen sing masc	4940.4 noun acc sing fem	2504.1 conj
17. λαβὼν	γὰρ	παρὰ	θεοῦ	πατρὸς	τιμὴν	καὶ
labōn	gar	para	theou	patros	timēn	kai
Having received	for	from	God	Father	honor	and

1385.4 noun acc sing fem	5292.2 noun gen sing fem	5179.29 verb gen sing fem part aor pass	840.4 prs-pron dat sing	4954.1 dem-pron gen sing fem	5097.3 prep
δόξαν,	φωνῆς	ἐνεχθείσης	αὐτῷ	τοιᾶσδε	ὑπὸ
doxan	phōnēs	enechtheisēs	autō	toiasde	hupo
glory,	a voice	having been brought	to him	such	by

3450.10 art gen sing fem	3140.1 adj gen sing fem	1385.2 noun gen sing fem	3642.4 dem-pron nom sing masc	1498.4 verb 3sing indic pres act
τῆς	μεγαλοπρεποῦς	δόξης,	‘ Οὗτός	ἐστιν,
tēs	megaloprepous	doxēs	Houtos	estin
the	very excellent	glory:	This	is

17.a.**Txt:** 01ℵ,02A,04C 018K,020L,etc.byz.it. Tisc,Sod
Var: p72,03B,Alf,We/Ho Weis,UBS/☆

3450.5 art nom sing masc	5048.1 noun nom sing masc	1466.2 prs-pron gen 1sing	3450.5 art nom sing masc	27.3 adj nom sing masc	3450.5 art nom sing masc
ὁ	υἱός	μου	ὁ	ἀγαπητός	[a☆ ὁ
ho	huios	mou	ho	agapētos	ho
the	Son	my	the	beloved,	[The

5048.1 noun nom sing masc	1466.2 prs-pron gen 1sing	3450.5 art nom sing masc	27.3 adj nom sing masc	1466.2 prs-pron gen 1sing	3642.4 dem-pron nom sing masc
υἱός	μου	ὁ	ἀγαπητός	μου	οὗτός
huios	mou	ho	agapētos	mou	houtos
Son	my	the	beloved	my	this

1498.4 verb 3sing indic pres act	1519.1 prep	3614.6 rel-pron acc sing masc	1466.1 prs-pron nom 1sing	2085.5 verb 1sing indic aor act	2504.1 conj
ἐστιν,]	εἰς	ὃν	ἐγὼ	εὐδόκησα.	18. καὶ
estin	eis	hon	egō	eudokēsa	kai
is,]	in	whom	I	have found delight.	And

3642.12 dem-pron acc sing fem	3450.12 art acc sing fem	5292.4 noun acc sing fem	2231.1 prs-pron nom 1pl	189.22 verb 1pl indic aor act	1523.1 prep gen
ταύτην	τὴν	φωνὴν	ἡμεῖς	ἠκούσαμεν	ἐξ
tautēn	tēn	phōnēn	hēmeis	ēkousamen	ex
this	the	voice	we	heard	from

3636.2 noun gen sing masc	5179.30 verb acc sing fem part aor pass	4713.1 prep	840.4 prs-pron dat sing	1498.23 verb nom pl masc part pres act
οὐρανοῦ	ἐνεχθεῖσαν,	σὺν	αὐτῷ	ὄντες
ouranou	enechtheisan	sun	autō	ontes
heaven	having been brought,	with	him	being

18.a.**Txt:** 01ℵ,02A 04C-corr,018K,020L 025P,byz.Tisc,Sod
Var: 03B,04C-org,33 Treg,Alf,We/Ho,Weis UBS/☆

1706.1 prep	3450.3 art dat sing	3598.3 noun dat sing neu	3450.3 art dat sing	39.3 adj dat sing	39.3 adj dat sing	3598.3 noun dat sing neu
ἐν	τῷ	‘ ὄρει	τῷ	ἁγίῳ.	[a☆ ἁγίῳ	ὄρει.]
en	tō	orei	tō	hagiō	hagiō	orei
on	the	mount	the	holy,	[holy	mount.]

2504.1 conj	2174.5 verb 1pl indic pres act	942.4 adj comp acc sing masc	3450.6 art acc sing masc	4255.1 adj acc sing masc
19. καὶ	ἔχομεν	βεβαιότερον	τὸν	προφητικὸν
kai	echomen	bebaioteron	ton	prophētikon
and	we have	more sure	the	prophetic

3030.4 noun acc sing masc	3614.3 rel-pron dat sing	2544.1 adv	4020.2 verb 2pl pres act	4196.3 verb nom pl masc part pres act	5453.1 conj
λόγον,	ᾧ	καλῶς	ποιεῖτε	προσέχοντες,	ὡς
logon	hō	kalōs	poieite	prosechontes	hōs
word,	to which	well	you do	paying attention,	as

1:17. The voice described by Peter is also recorded in Matthew 17:5; Mark 9:7; Luke 9:35. According to Matthew, the voice also said, "Hear ye him," but the other Gospels omit these words. This is not the first time such a message had come from heaven. It was heard at the baptism of Jesus: "This is my Son, whom I love; with him I am well-pleased" (Matthew 3:17, NIV). To Peter (also Paul) the voice from heaven had done more to authenticate Christ's deity than His miracles. No other apostle had seen more miracles than Peter, and he had seen some the other apostles had not seen and yet he offered the voice from heaven rather than the miracles as proof of Christ's authenticity. In the case of Paul (Saul of Tarsus) it was the voice from heaven, not miracles, that convinced him of Jesus' deity (Acts 9:4). When Christ was "transfigured" (Matthew 17:2) He was enveloped in a bright cloud (shekinah) which Peter called "the excellent glory," similar no doubt to the glory cloud which accompanied Israel through the wilderness journey (Exodus 40:34); when the glory cloud filled the temple to such a degree the priests could not minister (1 Kings 8:10); Ezekiel speaks of the cloud that filled the temple so that "the court was full of the radiance of the glory of the Lord" (Ezekiel 10:4, NIV). At the Transfiguration Peter spoke of the voice that came out of the bright cloud which marked God's presence.

1:18. The voice was heard by Peter, James, and John who were with Christ in "the holy mount." The latter words suggest a contrast between the old and new covenants. Sinai was a holy mount where God first revealed himself in His glory. Now there was another "holy mount," the Mount of Transfiguration, made holy by God's manifest presence. Peter remembered the occasion when he, James, and John heard that voice from heaven. They had seen not only Jesus but Moses (the representative of the Law) and Elijah (representing the prophets). Overwhelmed at the magnificent sight, Peter had suggested building three booths for Jesus and the others. But God had said about Jesus, "Hear ye him." A new order had come, the old was passing away. At Sinai God authenticated the law of Moses by fire and smoke, thunder and lightning. On the Transfiguration mount He authenticated the gospel of Christ by the radiant cloud of glory. The contrast is expressed in John 1:17, "For the law was given by Moses, but grace and truth came by Jesus Christ."

1:19. Vivid and valuable though Peter's personal experience with Jesus had been, he said there was something more "sure" (*bebaioteron*, firm, steadfast) and that is the word of "prophecy" (*prophētikon*, foretelling). Old Testament prophecies are a more reliable foundation for faith than signs and wonders. Peter said believers should "take heed" (*prosechontes*, keep in mind, pay attention to)

17. For he received from God the Father honour and glory: . . . from the God of Glorious Majesty, *Laubach* . . . The honor of his glorification was conferred upon him, *Greber* . . . and splendour, *Fenton*.

when there came such a voice to him from the excellent glory: . . . there was borne along by the sublime glory such a voice, *Wuest* . . . the Greatest Glory, *Everyday* . . . being carried to Him in such a way, *Concordant* . . . such a voice was borne to Him from the supreme glory, *Berkeley* . . . brought to him by the magnificent Glory, *Wilson* . . . from the Supreme Majesty, declaring, *Fenton* . . . from the Majestical Glory, *Wade* . . . out of the sublime glory of Heaven, *Phillips*.

This is my beloved Son, in whom I am well pleased: This is My much-loved Son, *NLT* . . . My Son, the beloved One, *Wuest* . . . in whom I delight, *TCNT, Montgomery* . . . am delighted, *Berkeley* . . . toward Whom I am well disposed, *Adams* . . . and I love him. I am very pleased with him, *Everyday*.

18. And this voice which came from heaven we heard: We actually heard that voice speaking, *Phillips* . . . we heard borne along, out from heaven, *Wuest* . . . we hear being carried out of heaven, *Concordant* . . . sounded in our ears, *Greber*.

when we were with him in the holy mount: . . . being together with Him, *Concordant* . . . upon the holy hill, *Fenton* . . . on that sacred mountain, *Williams*.

19. We have also a more sure word of prophecy: The word of prophecy was fulfilled in our hearing! *Phillips* . . . This makes us more sure about the message the prophets gave, *Everyday* . . . we have the message of the prophets more certainly guaranteed, *Williams* . . . we have the prophetic word as a surer foundation, *Wuest* . . . Spoken as they were by the Spirit of God, we consider them absolutely trustworthy, *Greber* . . . we have the prophetic message reaffirmed, *Berkeley* . . . more confirmed, *Concordant* . . . more firmly established, *Swann* . . . which is a still surer guide, *Norlie*.

2 Peter 1:20

3060.3 noun dat sing masc	5154.6 verb dat sing masc part pres act	1706.1 prep	843.1 adj dat sing masc	4964.3 noun dat sing masc	2175.1 conj
λύχνῳ	φαίνοντι	ἐν	αὐχμηρῷ	τόπῳ,	ἕως
luchnō	*phainonti*	*en*	*auchmērō*	*topō*	*heōs*
to a lamp	shining	in	an obscure	place,	until

3614.2 rel-pron gen sing	2232.2 noun nom sing fem	1300.1 verb 3sing subj aor act	2504.1 conj	5294.1 adj nom sing masc	391.4 verb 3sing subj aor act
οὗ	ἡμέρα	διαυγάσῃ,	καὶ	φωσφόρος	ἀνατείλῃ
hou	*hēmera*	*diaugasē*	*kai*	*phōsphoros*	*anateilē*
which	day	should dawn,	and	morning star	should arise

1706.1 prep	3450.14 art dat pl fem	2559.7 noun dat pl fem	5050.2 prs-pron gen 2pl	3642.17 dem-pron sing neu	4270.1 adv
ἐν	ταῖς	καρδίαις	ὑμῶν·	**20.** τοῦτο	πρῶτον
en	*tais*	*kardiais*	*humōn*	*touto*	*prōton*
in	the	hearts	your;	this	first

1091.12 verb nom pl masc part pres act	3617.1 conj	3820.9 adj nom sing fem	4252.2 noun nom sing fem	1118.2 noun gen sing fem
γινώσκοντες,	ὅτι	πᾶσα	προφητεία	γραφῆς
ginōskontes	*hoti*	*pasa*	*prophēteia*	*graphēs*
knowing,	that	all	prophecy	of scripture

2375.9 adj fem	1940.1 noun gen sing fem	3620.3 partic	1090.14 verb 3sing indic pres mid	3620.3 partic	1056.1 conj
ἰδίας	ἐπιλύσεως	οὐ	γίνεται.	**21.** οὐ	γὰρ
idias	*epiluseōs*	*ou*	*ginetai*	*ou*	*gar*
of its own	interpretation	not	is,	not	for

2284.3 noun dat sing neu	442.2 noun gen sing masc	5179.28 verb 3sing indic aor pass	4077.1 adv	4252.2 noun nom sing fem
θελήματι	ἀνθρώπου	ἠνέχθη	ʻ ποτέ	προφητεία,
thelēmati	*anthrōpou*	*ēnechthē*	*pote*	*prophēteia*
by will	of man	was brought	at any time	prophecy,

4252.2 noun nom sing fem	4077.1 adv	233.1 conj	233.2 conj	5097.3 prep
[☆ προφητεία	ποτέ,]	ʻ ἀλλ’	[☆ ἀλλὰ]	ὑπὸ
prophēteia	*pote*	*all’*	*alla*	*hupo*
[prophecy	ever]	but,	[idem]	by

4011.2 noun gen sing neu	39.2 adj gen sing	5179.24 verb nom pl masc part pres mid	2953.30 verb 3pl indic aor act	3450.7 art nom pl masc
πνεύματος	ἁγίου	φερόμενοι	ἐλάλησαν	ʻa οἱ ʼ
pneumatos	*hagiou*	*pheromenoi*	*elalēsan*	*hoi*
Spirit	Holy	being borne,	spoke	the

39.7 adj nom pl masc	570.3 prep	2296.2 noun gen sing masc	442.6 noun nom pl masc	1090.38 verb 3pl indic aor mid
ʻ ἅγιοι	[b☆ ἀπὸ]	θεοῦ	ἄνθρωποι.	**2:1.** Ἐγένοντο
hagioi	*apo*	*theou*	*anthrōpoi*	*Egenonto*
holy	[from]	of God	men.	There were

1156.2 conj	2504.1 conj	5413.4 noun nom pl masc	1706.1 prep	3450.3 art dat sing	2967.3 noun dat sing masc
δὲ	καὶ	ψευδοπροφῆται	ἐν	τῷ	λαῷ,
de	*kai*	*pseudoprophētai*	*en*	*tō*	*laō*
but	also	false prophets	among	the	people,

5453.1 conj	2504.1 conj	1706.1 prep	5050.3 prs-pron dat 2pl	1498.43 verb 3pl indic fut mid	5407.1 noun nom pl masc
ὡς	καὶ	ἐν	ὑμῖν	ἔσονται	ψευδοδιδάσκαλοι,
hōs	*kai*	*en*	*humin*	*esontai*	*pseudodidaskaloi*
as	also	among	you	will be	false teachers,

21.a.**Txt:** Steph
Var: 01ℵ,02A,03B,04C 018K,020L,025P,Gries Lach,Treg,Alf,Word Tisc,We/Ho,Weis,Sod UBS/☆

21.b.**Txt:** 01ℵ,018K 020L,33,byz.it.
Var: p72,03B,025P,bo. Alf,Tisc,We/Ho,Weis UBS/☆

to them for they are like a lamp that lights up a squalid, forbidding place during the long hours before dawn. "Day-star" (*phōsphoros*) means morning star, a reference to Jesus (Revelation 22:16). The morning star is a harbinger of daybreak, welcoming the sun; that is, the "Sun of righteousness" (Malachi 4:2). So they had better pay attention to the lamp of prophecy, without which they will be in the dark.

whereunto ye do well that ye take heed, as unto a light that shineth in a dark place: Pay attention to their words, *Laubach* . . . you, doing ideally...as to a lamp appearing in a dingy place, *Concordant* . . . a lamp which is shining in a squalid place, *Wuest* . . . in a gloomy place, *TCNT* . . . in a dismal place, *Williams.*

until the day dawn, and the day star arise in your hearts: . . . till the day should be breaking and the morning star should be rising, *Concordant* . . . and the Light-bringer may arise, *Wilson.*

1:20. They should heed it, knowing this first, that no prophecy is someone's personal, private idea. "Private" (*idias*) means one's own. "Interpretation" (*epiluseōs*) means solution, explanation. It comes from the verb *epiluō*, to untie, release. In other words, prophecy is of divine, not human, origin. "The interpretation here is not that of the student of scripture, but of the inspired prophet or writer of the scriptures himself, since verse 20 speaks of the method by which these prophecies came with relation to these writers" (Wuest, *Word Studies in the Greek New Testament*, 2:35). As 1 Peter 1:11 states, the prophets did not fully understand what the Spirit within them signified when He "testified beforehand the sufferings of Christ, and the glory that should follow." Now the first part has been fulfilled, and it is like a lamp in the night. When dawn comes, His glory will be seen and the prophecy will be fully understood.

20. Knowing this first, that no prophecy of the scripture:

is of any private interpretation: . . . does not originate from any private explanation, *Wuest* . . . is becoming its own explanation, *Concordant* . . . may be explained by any man's private meaning, *Williams C.K.* . . . ever came about by a prophet's own ideas, *SEB* . . . ever originated as a private solution to someone's problem, *Adams* . . . can be interpreted by man's unaided reason, *TCNT* . . . was ever made up by any man, *NLT* . . . is not of its own Solution, *Wilson* . . . is of a single meaning, *Fenton* . . . is of private impulse, *Campbell.*

1:21. Here is one of the most definitive descriptions of Biblical inspiration. These writers were not inspired like a poet or an artist. They did not decide what or how to write. The Holy Spirit was the divine Author. They were not puppets, with no will of their own. Using their background, personality, and vocabulary, the Third Person of the Trinity moved with them and upon them to bring into being the sacred Scriptures which reveal God and His purposes and plans to man.

The Old Testament prophecies came not by human "will" (*thelēmati*, choice, determination, desire); but dedicated men of God "spake" (*elalēsan*, utter words, talk at length, preach) as they were "moved" (*pheromenoi*, carried, borne along) by the Holy Spirit. Since the Spirit inspired the prophecies, they require His illumination to be understood.

21. For the prophecy came not in old time by the will of man: . . . no prophecy originated from man's own thinking, *Norlie* . . . has ever yet originated in man's will, *Williams* . . . never spoke by their own free will, *Laubach* . . . was never a result of human design, *Fenton* . . . not by the desire of man did prophecy come aforetime, *Wuest.*

but holy men of God spake [as they were] moved by the Holy Ghost: . . . and so spoke at the prompting of God, *TCNT* . . . men spoke words from God who is the ultimate source, *Wuest* . . . while they were being influenced by, *SEB* . . . were inspired by, *Noli.*

2:1. After speaking of the true prophets of the Old Testament (1:21), Peter next warned against false ones. There were false prophets in Jeremiah's day, for example. They shouted, "Thus saith the Lord," but encouraged self-righteousness, denied the truth, and were proved wrong by the events that followed (Jeremiah 14:13-16). Peter warned there would be false teachers who would

1. But there were false prophets also among the people: . . . there arose also, *Wuest.*

even as there shall be false teachers among you: . . . as there will be pretended teachers, *TCNT* . . . will rise up in your midst, *Norlie.*

3610.2 rel-pron nom pl masc	3781.1 verb 3pl indic fut act	138.4 noun pl fem	677.2 noun gen sing fem	2504.1 conj
οἵτινες	παρεισάξουσιν	αἱρέσεις	ἀπωλείας,	καὶ
hoitines	*pareisaxousin*	*haireseis*	*apōleias*	*kai*
who	will bring in stealthily	divisions	destructive,	and

3450.6 art acc sing masc	58.14 verb acc sing masc part aor act	840.8 prs-pron acc pl masc	1197.3 noun acc sing masc	714.5 verb nom pl masc part pres mid
τὸν	ἀγοράσαντα	αὐτοὺς	δεσπότην	ἀρνούμενοι,
ton	*agorasanta*	*autous*	*despotēn*	*arnoumenoi*
the	having bought	them	Master	denying,

1848.1 verb nom pl masc part pres act	1431.7 prs-pron dat pl masc	4879.2 adj acc sing fem	677.3 noun acc sing fem	2504.1 conj
ἐπάγοντες	ἑαυτοῖς	ταχινὴν	ἀπώλειαν·	2. καὶ
epagontes	*heautois*	*tachinēn*	*apōleian*	*kai*
bringing upon	themselves	swift	destruction;	and

4044.7 adj nom pl masc	1795.2 verb 3pl indic fut act	840.1 prs-pron gen pl	3450.14 art dat pl fem	677.4 noun dat pl fem
πολλοὶ	ἐξακολουθήσουσιν	αὐτῶν	ταῖς	‛ ἀπωλείαις,
polloi	*exakolouthēsousin*	*autōn*	*tais*	*apōleiais*
many	will follow out	their	the	destructive ways,

2.a.**Txt:** Steph
Var: 01ℵ,02A,03B,04C
018K,020L,025P,byz.
Gries,Lach,Treg,Alf
Word,Tisc,We/Ho,Weis
Sod,UBS/☆

760.4 noun dat pl fem	1217.1 prep	3614.8 rel-pron acc pl masc	3450.9 art nom sing fem	3461.1 noun nom sing fem
[a☆ ἀσελγείαις,]	δι'	οὓς	ἡ	ὁδὸς
aselgeiais	*di'*	*hous*	*hē*	*hodos*
[licentiousnesses,]	through	whom	the	way

3450.10 art gen sing fem	223.2 noun gen sing fem	980.22 verb 3sing indic fut pass	2504.1 conj	1706.1 prep
τῆς	ἀληθείας	βλασφημηθήσεται·	3. καὶ	ἐν
tēs	*alētheias*	*blasphēmēthēsetai*	*kai*	*en*
of the	truth	will be blasphemed.	And	through

3984.3 noun dat sing fem	3973.1 adj dat pl masc	3030.7 noun dat pl masc	5050.4 prs-pron acc 2pl	1694.2 verb 3pl indic fut mid
πλεονεξίᾳ	πλαστοῖς	λόγοις	ὑμᾶς	ἐμπορεύσονται·
pleonexia	*plastois*	*logois*	*humas*	*emporeusontai*
covetousness	with well-turned	words	you	they will do business:

3614.4 rel-pron dat pl	3450.16 art sing neu	2890.1 noun sing neu	1584.1 adv	3620.2 partic	685.1 verb 3sing indic pres act	2504.1 conj
οἷς	τὸ	κρίμα	ἔκπαλαι	οὐκ	ἀργεῖ,	καὶ
hois	*to*	*krima*	*ekpalai*	*ouk*	*argei*	*kai*
of whom	the	judgment	of old	not	is idle,	and

3.a.**Txt:** p72,01ℵ,02A
03B,04C,025P,323
1241
Var: 044,bo.byz.

3450.9 art nom sing fem	677.1 noun nom sing fem	840.1 prs-pron gen pl	3620.3 partic	3435.1 verb 3sing indic pres act	3435.3 verb 3sing indic fut act
ἡ	ἀπώλεια	αὐτῶν	οὐ	‛☆ νυστάζει.	[a νυστάξει.]
hē	*apōleia*	*autōn*	*ou*	*nustazei*	*nustaxei*
the	destruction	their	not	slumbers.	[will slumber.]

1479.1 conj	1056.1 conj	3450.5 art nom sing masc	2296.1 noun nom sing masc	32.6 noun gen pl masc	262.18 verb gen pl masc part aor act
4. Εἰ	γὰρ	ὁ	θεὸς	ἀγγέλων	ἁμαρτησάντων
Ei	*gar*	*ho*	*theos*	*angelōn*	*hamartēsantōn*
If	for		God	angels	having sinned

4.a.**Txt:** p72,018K,020L
025P,byz.bo.Sod
Var1: 01ℵ,Tisc
Var2: 02A,03B,04C,81
917,We/Ho,UBS/☆

3620.2 partic	5177.4 verb 3sing indic aor mid	233.2 conj	4432.1 noun dat pl fem	4472.1 noun dat pl masc	4472.2 noun dat pl masc
οὐκ	ἐφείσατο,	ἀλλὰ	‛ σειραῖς	[1a σιροῖς	2☆ σειροῖς]
ouk	*epheisato*	*alla*	*seirais*	*sirois*	*seirois*
not	spared,	but	to chains	[in pits	idem]

bring in "heresies" (*haireseis,* sect, division). Heresy means choosing a position contrary to generally accepted belief and thereby causing disunity. Such heresies would be brought in "privily" (*pareisaxousin,* stealthily, smuggled in disguise, perhaps as a mixture of truth and error). They are "damnable" (*apōleias,* ruinous, destructive, deadly), and the false teachers may even deny the Lord who redeemed them; but by so doing they would bring swift "destruction" (*apōleian,* ruin, destruction, damnation) upon themselves.

2:2. Peter compared the false teachers to false prophets of the past. The Lord said His people were "taken away for nought" so His name was "blasphemed" (Isaiah 52:5). Peter foretold that a large number would follow or imitate the "pernicious ways" (*apōleiais,* destructive) of the false teachers and, as a result, the "way of truth" (Christ and His gospel) would be "evil spoken of" (*blasphēmēthēsetai,* slander, revile). "Way" is *hodos* (road, route). "The way of truth" is Jesus, who said, "I am the way (*hodos*), the truth, and the life" (John 14:6).

2:3. The root of the problem is "covetousness" (*pleonexia,* greed, avarice) which would motivate the false teachers to defraud believers. The words of their teaching would be "feigned" (*plastois,* fabricated, formed as from clay or wax; this is where we get our word *plastic*). They would mold words at will to suit their greedy purposes. With fictitious talk they would "make merchandise" of believers. The word *emporeusontai* is the root for *emporium,* our word for a store with a large variety of goods for sale. Jesus used this word concerning the merchants in the temple who were doing business for selfish gain: "Make not my Father's house a house of merchandise (*emporiou*)" (John 2:16). Peter was warning against teachers who are not true servants of God but mere professionals. They make a business of their false teaching to gain something for themselves from the believers. He said "judgment" (*krima,* punishment) is in store for these people. For a long while the judgment "lingereth" not (*argei,* delay, slow down). In other words, they had been ripe for punishment for a long time, and Peter said their damnation (see verse 1) "slumbereth" not (*nustazei,* nod, fall asleep). Their sentence would not be postponed indefinitely.

2:4. The downfall of false teachers is inevitable. Since God did not spare the angels that sinned, He will not spare human beings who are of a lower order of creation. Probably the reference is to the angels who fell when Satan fell (Jude 6). God cast these angels down to "hell" (*tartarōsas,* the deepest abyss of hades). Tartarus for the pagan Greeks was a place of punishment for evil, corresponding to the Gehenna of the Jews. It was the dark and doleful abode of the wicked dead. Peter said the sinning angels were given over into chains of "darkness" (*zophou,* blackness, gloom, mist). The sinning angels are being held in the black pit of "hell" (*tar-*

who privily shall bring in damnable heresies: . . . will stealthily introduce, *Wade* . . . secretly bring in destructive sects, *Montgomery* . . . try to introduce abominable heresies, *Noli* . . . destructive opinions, *SEB* . . . bring in teaching that will destroy you, *Williams C.K.* . . . smuggling in destructive sects, *Concordant* . . . shuffle in destructive errors, *Fenton* . . . insidiously introduce destructive heresies, *Williams.*

even denying the Lord that bought them: . . . denying the sovereign Lord, *Wilson* . . . disowning the Owner who buys them, *Concordant.*

and bring upon themselves swift destruction: . . . sure destruction, *Norlie* . . . swift ruin, *Montgomery.*

2. And many shall follow their pernicious ways: . . . licentious courses, *TCNT* . . . disgusting ways, *Swann* . . . immoral ways, *Williams* . . . follow them into sexual excess, *SEB* . . . following out their wantonness, *Concordant.*

by reason of whom the way of truth: . . . because of whom the glory of the truth, *Concordant.*

shall be evil spoken of: . . . maligned, *Adams* . . . calumniated, *Concordant.*

3. And through covetousness shall they with feigned words make merchandise of you: In their avarice they will exploit you with invented tales, *Williams C.K.* . . . in their libertinism they will exploit you by means of, *Wade* . . . suave words, *Concordant* . . . fabricated stories, *Adams* . . . false arguments, *Noli* . . . make money off you, *SEB.*

whose judgment now of a long time lingereth not: Their conviction, long recorded, will not be deferred, *Fenton* . . . whose judgment of old is not idling, *Concordant.*

and their damnation slumbereth not: . . . nor their Ruin slumbering, *TCNT* . . . on their trail destruction is awake, *Moffatt.*

4. For if God spared not the angels that sinned: . . . when they sinned, *Noli.*

2200.2 noun gen sing masc	4871.1 verb nom sing masc part aor act	3722.10 verb 3sing indic aor act	1519.1 prep
ζόφου	ταρταρώσας	παρέδωκεν	εἰς
zophou	*tartarōsas*	*paredōken*	*eis*
of darkness	having cast to the deepest abyss	delivered	for

4.b.**Txt:** Steph
Var: 03B,04C-org,018K 020L,025P,Gries,Treg Alf,Word,Tisc,We/Ho Weis,Sod,UBS/☆

2893.4 noun acc sing fem	4931.36 verb acc pl masc part perf mid	4931.41 verb acc pl masc part pres mid	2504.1 conj
κρίσιν	ʻ τετηρημένους·	[b☆ τηρουμένους,]	5. καὶ
krisin	*tetērēmenous*	*tēroumenous*	*kai*
judgment	having been kept;	[being kept,]	and

739.3 adj gen sing masc	2862.2 noun gen sing masc	3620.2 partic	5177.4 verb 3sing indic aor mid	233.1 conj	233.2 conj
ἀρχαίου	κόσμου	οὐκ	ἐφείσατο,	ʻ ἀλλ'	[☆ ἀλλὰ]
archaiou	*kosmou*	*ouk*	*epheisato*	*all'*	*alla*
ancient	world	not	spared,	but	[idem]

3453.2 num ord acc sing masc	3437.1 name masc	1336.2 noun gen sing fem	2755.2 noun acc sing masc	5278.8 verb 3sing indic aor act
ὄγδοον	Νῶε	δικαιοσύνης	κήρυκα	ἐφύλαξεν,
ogdoon	*Nōe*	*dikaiosunēs*	*kēruka*	*ephulaxen*
eighth	Noah	of righteousness,	a herald	preserved,

2597.3 noun acc sing masc	2862.3 noun dat sing masc	759.4 adj gen pl masc	1848.2 verb nom sing masc part aor act	2504.1 conj
κατακλυσμὸν	κόσμῳ	ἀσεβῶν	ἐπάξας·	6. καὶ
kataklusmon	*kosmō*	*asebōn*	*epaxas*	*kai*
a flood	to a world	of ungodly	having brought in;	and

4032.5 noun pl fem	4525.2 name gen pl neu	2504.1 conj	1110.2 name gen fem	4925.1 verb nom sing masc part aor act
πόλεις	Σοδόμων	καὶ	Γομόῤῥας	τεφρώσας
poleis	*Sodomōn*	*kai*	*Gomorrhas*	*tephrōsas*
cities	of Sodom	and	Gomorrah	having reduced to ashes

2662.1 noun dat sing fem	2602.4 verb 3sing indic aor act	5100.2 noun sing neu	3165.11 verb gen pl part pres act
καταστροφῇ	κατέκρινεν,	ὑπόδειγμα	μελλόντων
katastrophē	*katekrinen*	*hupodeigma*	*mellontōn*
with an overthrow	condemned,	an example	being about

6.a.**Txt:** 01ℵ,02A,044 byz.Tisc,Sod
Var: p72,03B,025P,614 630,1505,2495

758.1 verb inf pres act	759.5 adj dat pl masc	4935.20 verb nom sing masc part perf act	2504.1 conj	1337.1 adj sing
ʻ ἀσεβεῖν	[a☆ ἀσεβέσιν]	τεθεικώς,	7. καὶ	δίκαιον
asebein	*asebesin*	*tetheikōs*	*kai*	*dikaion*
to live ungodly	[ungodly]	having set;	and	righteous

3063.1 name masc	2639.2 verb acc sing masc part pres mid	5097.3 prep	3450.10 art gen sing fem	3450.1 art gen pl	113.1 adj gen pl masc
Λώτ,	καταπονούμενον	ὑπὸ	τῆς	τῶν	ἀθέσμων
Lōt	*kataponoumenon*	*hupo*	*tēs*	*tōn*	*athesmōn*
Lot,	being oppressed	by	the	of the	lawless

1706.1 prep	760.2 noun dat sing fem	389.1 noun gen sing fem	4363.6 verb 3sing indic aor mid	983.1 noun dat sing neu
ἐν	ἀσελγείᾳ	ἀναστροφῆς,	ἐῤῥύσατο·	8. βλέμματι
en	*aselgeia*	*anastrophēs*	*errhusato*	*blemmati*
in	licentiousness	conduct	he delivered,	through seeing

1056.1 conj	2504.1 conj	187.3 noun dat sing fem	3450.5 art nom sing masc	1337.3 adj nom sing masc	1453.1 verb nom sing masc part pres act
γὰρ	καὶ	ἀκοῇ	ὁ	δίκαιος,	ἐγκατοικῶν
gar	*kai*	*akoē*	*ho*	*dikaios*	*enkatoikōn*
for	and	hearing,	the	righteous,	dwelling

tarōsas) to face "judgment" (*krisin*, tribunal) at the Great White Throne, at which point they will be consigned to the lake of fire (Revelation 20:10) which is prepared for the devil and his angels (Matthew 25:41).

2:5. As a second example of divine judgment, Peter cited the "flood" (*kataklusmon*, deluge, inundation; source of our word *cataclysm*) recorded in Genesis 6 and 7. God destroyed all the people of the ancient world except eight persons (see 1 Peter 3:20). Judgment fell upon the "ungodly" (*asebōn*, irreverent, impious), but Noah, a proclaimer of righteousness, was "saved" (from *phulassō*, preserve, keep safe under guard). Noah warned of the Flood coming upon the people by his example and by his preaching. His obedience in building the ark "condemned the world" (Hebrews 11:7). He warned them of judgment, but they went on with life as usual (Matthew 24:37). He told them God required righteousness, but they despised his preaching. The people perished, but Noah was spared.

2:6. A third example is the fate of Sodom and Gomorrah (Genesis 19:24,25). According to Jude 7 there were other nearby cities which also were destroyed by fire. The cities of the plain were "turned into ashes" (from *tephroō*, incinerate, consume). Strachan prefers to translate it "covered up with ashes," the wording found in a description of the eruption of Vesuvius (*Expositor's Greek Testament*, 5:135). God condemned the wicked cities with an "overthrow" (*katastrophē*, demolition, turning upside down, the word we spell *catastrophe*) thus making them a tragic "ensample" (*hupodeigma*, example, exhibit, specimen) to all who would follow. It shows what is in store for those who live in an "ungodly" manner (*asebein*, act impiously, irreverently, wickedly; as in Jude 15, "To execute judgment upon all, and to convince all that are ungodly among them of all their ungodly deeds").

2:7. But Lot was delivered from Sodom because he was "just" (*dikaion*, righteous, innocent, holy), and he abhorred the "conversation" (*anastrophēs*, behavior, conduct) of the "wicked" (*athesmōn*, outlaw, rebel against God's law). Their conduct was so "filthy" (*aselgeia*, shameless, lascivious, unrestrainedly lustful) that it "vexed" him (*kataponoumenon*, sore distressed, exhaust with toil). It wore him down until he was weary. His soul rebelled against it until he was exhausted.

2:8. Lot was not just a visitor in Sodom; he was "dwelling" there (from *enkatoikeō*, settle down, reside). It was a wicked city when

but cast [them] down to hell: He plunged them down into hell, *Norlie* . . . but flung them into Tartarus, *Wade* . . . thrusting them into the gloomy caverns of Tartarus, *Concordant.*

and delivered [them] into chains of darkness: . . . and locked them in dark prisons, *Laubach* . . . Thick darkness, *Wilson.*

to be reserved unto judgment: . . . to be kept for chastening judging, *Concordant* . . . delivered them over into custody for Judgment, *Wilson.*

5. And spared not the old world: . . . the ancient world, *Norlie.*

but saved Noah the eighth [person], a preacher of righteousness: . . . but preserved Noah, a herald of, *Montgomery.*

bringing in the flood upon the world of the ungodly: . . . bringing a Deluge on a World of Impious men, *Wilson* . . . the irreverent, *Concordant* . . . to destroy a godless world, *Norlie.*

6. And turning the cities of Sodom and Gomorrha into ashes condemned [them] with an overthrow: God also completely destroyed, *Laubach* . . . He burned them up, *SEB* . . . condemns the cities...reducing them to cinders by an overthrow, *Concordant.*

making [them] an ensample unto those that after should live ungodly: . . . having placed them as an example for those about to be irreverent, *Concordant.*

7. And delivered just Lot: . . . he rescued righteous, *TCNT* . . . rescued the good man, *Williams C.K.*

vexed with the filthy conversation of the wicked: . . . who was worn out by the lascivious life, *Montgomery* . . . harried by the behavior of the dissolute in their wantonness, *Concordant* . . . sick and tired of the immoral behavior, *Adams* . . . was very upset about the wild sex life, *SEB* . . . being grievously harassed with the lewd conduct, *Wilson* . . . distressed with the abandoned conversation of the godless, *Darby.*

8. (For that righteous man dwelling among them, in seeing and hearing: . . . observing, *Concordant.*

2 Peter 2:9

1706.1 prep ἐν *en* among | 840.2 prs-pron dat pl αὐτοῖς, *autois* them, | 2232.4 noun acc sing fem ἡμέραν *hēmeran* day | 1523.1 prep gen ἐξ *ex* by | 2232.1 noun fem ἡμέρας *hēmeras* day | 5425.4 noun acc sing fem ψυχὴν *psuchēn* soul | 1337.12 adj acc sing fem δικαίαν *dikaian* righteous

456.1 adj dat pl ἀνόμοις *anomois* with lawless | 2024.6 noun dat pl neu ἔργοις *ergois* works | 922.4 verb 3sing indic imperf act ἐβασάνιζεν· *ebasanizen* was tormenting, | **9.** 3471.4 verb 3sing indic perf act οἶδεν *oiden* knows | 2935.1 noun nom sing masc κύριος *kurios* Lord

2133.3 adj acc pl masc εὐσεβεῖς *eusebeis* godly | 1523.2 prep gen ἐκ *ek* out of | 3848.2 noun gen sing masc πειρασμοῦ *peirasmou* temptation | 4363.4 verb inf pres mid ῥύεσθαι. *rhuesthai* to deliver, | 93.5 adj acc pl masc ἀδίκους *adikous* unrighteous

1156.2 conj δὲ *de* and | 1519.1 prep εἰς *eis* to | 2232.4 noun acc sing fem ἡμέραν *hēmeran* a day | 2893.2 noun gen sing fem κρίσεως *kriseōs* of judgment | 2822.1 verb acc pl masc part pres mid κολαζομένους *kolazomenous* being punished | 4931.11 verb inf pres act τηρεῖν· *tērein* to keep;

10. 3094.1 adv sup μάλιστα *malista* especially | 1156.2 conj δὲ *de* and | 3450.8 art acc pl masc τοὺς *tous* the | 3557.1 adv ὀπίσω *opisō* after | 4418.2 noun gen sing fem σαρκὸς *sarkos* flesh | 1706.1 prep ἐν *en* in

1924.3 noun dat sing fem ἐπιθυμίᾳ *epithumia* lust | 3258.1 noun gen sing masc μιασμοῦ *miasmou* of pollution | 4057.13 verb acc pl masc part pres mid πορευομένους, *poreuomenous* walking, | 2504.1 conj καὶ *kai* and | 2936.1 noun gen sing fem κυριότητος *kuriotētos* lordship

2675.5 verb acc pl masc part pres act καταφρονοῦντας. *kataphronountas* despising. | 4960.1 noun nom pl masc Τολμηταί, *Tolmētai* Daring, | 823.2 adj nom pl masc αὐθάδεις, *authadeis* self-willed; | 1385.5 noun acc pl fem δόξας *doxas* glories | 3620.3 partic οὐ *ou* not

4981.1 verb 3pl indic pres act τρέμουσιν *tremousin* they tremble | 980.4 verb nom pl masc part pres act βλασφημοῦντες· *blasphēmountes* blaspheming; | **11.** 3562.1 adv ὅπου *hopou* where | 32.5 noun nom pl masc ἄγγελοι *angeloi* angels

2452.3 noun dat sing fem ἰσχύϊ *ischui* in strength | 2504.1 conj καὶ *kai* and | 1405.3 noun dat sing fem δυνάμει *dunamei* power | 3157.4 adj comp nom pl masc μείζονες *meizones* greater | 1498.23 verb nom pl masc part pres act ὄντες, *ontes* being, | 3620.3 partic οὐ *ou* not

11.a.**Txt:** 01ℵ,03B,04C 025P,byz.Tisc,We/Ho Sod
Var: p72,1241

5179.3 verb 3pl indic pres act φέρουσιν *pherousin* do bring | 2567.1 prep κατ' *kat'* against | 840.1 prs-pron gen pl αὐτῶν *autōn* them, | 3706.2 prep παρὰ *para* before | 2935.3 noun dat sing masc ‘ κυρίῳ *kuriō* Lord, | 2935.2 noun gen sing masc [a☆ κυρίου] *kuriou* [idem]

982.1 adj acc sing βλάσφημον *blasphēmon* an accusing | 2893.4 noun acc sing fem κρίσιν. *krisin* charge, | **12.** 3642.7 dem-pron nom pl masc οὗτοι *houtoi* These | 1156.2 conj δέ, *de* but, | 5453.1 conj ὡς *hōs* as | 247.2 adj pl neu ἄλογα *aloga* irrational

he chose it (Genesis 13:11-13). As he watched the shameless abandonment of the people and as he listened to their filthy talk, he "vexed his righteous soul." "Vexed" here is *ebasanizen* (torture, torment). Whether he was tortured with a sense of guilt for failing to correct such evil or to protest against it, we are not told, but he must have chastised himself severely for ever choosing to live in such a wicked city.

vexed [his] righteous soul from day to day with [their] unlawful deeds;): . . . he felt tortured in his righteous soul, *SEB* . . . was tortured by their wicked doings, *TCNT* . . . tormented his just soul by their lawless acts, *Concordant.*

2:9. Here Peter made an application from the observations made in verses 4-8. The Lord will always find a way to deliver godly people (like Noah and Lot) out of "temptation" (*peirasmou*, enticement, adversity, trial; as in 1 Peter 4:12, "fiery trial"). Meanwhile He is holding the unjust (like the fallen angels, Noah's wicked neighbors, and the Sodomites) under guard awaiting the day of "judgment" (*kriseōs*, damnation, decision, tribunal) when they will be "punished." The Greek is *kolazomenous* (from *kolazō*), as in Matthew 25:46, "These shall go away into everlasting punishment." The verb form indicates the punishment is continuous. As surely as God delivered Noah and Lot, He will deliver tested believers. Noah's test was to keep believing in the midst of unbelief. It lasted many years but the Lord brought him through. Lot's test was to continue to trust God while enduring great trials. God brought him through successfully.

9. The Lord knoweth how to deliver the godly out of temptations: . . . is acquainted with the rescue of the devout out of trial, *Concordant* . . . a pious man from, *Norlie.*

and to reserve the unjust unto the day of judgment to be punished: . . . keeping the unjust for chastening, *Concordant* . . . to be cut off, *Wilson.*

10. But chiefly them that walk after the flesh in the lust of uncleanness, and despise government: . . . especially those who satisfy their lower nature...who despise authority, *Williams* . . . seek after sensuality, *Fenton* . . . through polluting lust, *Wade* . . . are slaves of low sex habits, *Laubach* . . . indulge in the lust of defiling sensuality, *Noli* . . . the lust of defilement, and in despising all authority, *Montgomery* . . . indulging their polluting passions and despising all control, *TCNT* . . . more especially...who despise Dominion, *Wilson* . . . oppose authority, *Norlie.*

Presumptuous [are they], self-willed: Audacious, *Fenton* . . . given to self-gratification, *Concordant* . . . Daring, headstrong men! *Williams.*

they are not afraid to speak evil of dignities: . . . not afraid to curse the very angels in heaven, *Laubach* . . . do not tremble when they abuse persons of majesty, *Williams* . . . defame Glorious Beings, *Wade* . . . say bad things about the powers in heaven, *NLT* . . . scoff at the glories of the unseen world, *Noli.*

2:10. Peter used strong adjectives to describe false teachers. They are "presumptuous" (*tolmētai*, audacious, brazen, bold) and "self-willed" (*authadeis*, arrogant, self-pleasing). Their independent spirit often strikes out at organization. They "despise" (*kataphronountas*, look down on, scorn) any "government" (*kuriotētos*, dominion, authority). They especially resent the lordship of Christ which is the central theme of all apostolic teaching and practice. To "speak evil of dignities" indicates a rank skepticism regarding the supernatural. "Dignities" is *doxas* (glory, honor, radiant splendor) and probably refers to the angels.

2:11. Angels are greater in strength and ability than the false teachers, yet they do not bring any scurrilous accusation into God's presence against "dignities," not even against Satan or his fallen angels. Jude 9 explains in clearer detail: "Michael the archangel, when contending with the devil he disputed about the body of Moses, durst not bring against him a railing accusation, but said, The Lord rebuke thee" (as in Zechariah 3:2). Even the archangel Michael, who is greater in power and might than other angels, held Satan in such awe he refrained from rebuking him personally.

11. Whereas angels, which are greater in power and might: . . . messengers, being greater in strength and power, *Concordant.*

bring not railing accusation against them before the Lord: . . . bring no abusive charge against them, *Williams C.K.*

2 Peter 2:13

12.a.**Txt:** 018K,020L,byz.
Var: 02A-org,03B,04C
025P,Lach,Treg,Alf
Word,We/Ho,Weis,Sod
UBS/☆

2209.3 noun pl neu	**5282.2** adj pl neu	**1090.67** verb pl neu part perf mid	**1074.28** verb pl neu part perf mid
ζῷα	ʻ φυσικὰ	γεγενημένα	[ᵃ☆ γεγεννημένα
zōa	*phusika*	*gegenēmena*	*gegennēmena*
creatures	natural	having been born	[having been born

5282.2 adj pl neu	**1519.1** prep	**257.1** noun acc sing fem	**2504.1** conj	**5193.4** noun acc sing fem	**1706.1** prep
φυσικὰ]	εἰς	ἅλωσιν	καὶ	φθοράν,	ἐν
phusika	*eis*	*halōsin*	*kai*	*phthoran*	*en*
natural]	for	capture	and	corruption,	in

3614.4 rel-pron dat pl	**49.4** verb 3pl indic pres act	**980.4** verb nom pl masc part pres act	**1706.1** prep	**3450.11** art dat sing fem
οἷς	ἀγνοοῦσιν	βλασφημοῦντες,	ἐν	τῇ
hois	*agnoousin*	*blasphēmountes*	*en*	*tē*
what	they are ignorant of	blaspheming,	in	the

12.b.**Txt:** 01ℵ-corr
04C-corr,018K,020L,byz.
Var: 01ℵ-org,02A,03B
04C-org,025P,Lach
Treg,Alf,Word,Tisc
We/Ho,Weis,UBS/☆

5193.3 noun dat sing fem	**840.1** prs-pron gen pl	**2673.2** verb 3pl indic fut pass	**2504.1** conj
φθορᾷ	αὐτῶν	ʻ καταφθαρήσονται,	[ᵇ☆ καὶ
phthora	*autōn*	*kataphtharēsontai*	*kai*
corruption	their	shall utterly perish,	[indeed

13.a.**Txt:** 01ℵ-corr,02A
04C,018K,020L,33,byz.
it.sa.bo.Tisc,Sod
Var: p72,01ℵ-org,03B
025P,We/Ho,Weis
UBS/☆

5188.9 verb 3pl indic fut pass	**2837.10** verb nom pl masc part fut mid	**90.23** verb nom pl masc part pres mid
φθαρήσονται,]	**13.** ʻ κομιούμενοι	[ᵃ☆ ἀδικούμενοι]
phtharēsontai	*komioumenoi*	*adikoumenoi*
they will perish,]	being about to receive	[suffering wrong]

3272.3 noun acc sing masc	**92.2** noun gen sing fem	**2220.1** noun acc sing fem	**2216.7** verb nom pl masc part pres mid	**3450.12** art acc sing fem
μισθὸν	ἀδικίας,	ἡδονὴν	ἡγούμενοι	τὴν
misthon	*adikias*	*hēdonēn*	*hēgoumenoi*	*tēn*
wage	of unrighteousness;	pleasure	considering	the

1706.1 prep	**2232.3** noun dat sing fem	**5013.2** noun acc sing fem	**4548.2** noun nom pl masc	**2504.1** conj	**3332.1** noun nom pl masc
ἐν	ἡμέρᾳ	τρυφήν,	σπίλοι	καὶ	μῶμοι,
en	*hēmera*	*truphēn*	*spiloi*	*kai*	*mōmoi*
in	daytime	indulgence;	spots	and	blemishes,

13.b.**Txt:** p72,01ℵ
02A-org,04C,018K
020L,025P,bo.byz.
Var: 02A-corr,03B,044
623,1611,sa.

1776.1 verb nom pl masc part pres act	**1706.1** prep	**3450.14** art dat pl fem	**535.4** noun dat pl fem	**26.5** noun dat pl fem	**840.1** prs-pron gen pl
ἐντρυφῶντες	ἐν	ταῖς	ʻ☆ ἀπάταις	[ᵇ ἀγάπαις]	αὐτῶν,
entruphōntes	*en*	*tais*	*apatais*	*agapais*	*autōn*
reveling	in	the	deceits	[love feasts]	their,

4760.1 verb nom pl masc part pres mid	**5050.3** prs-pron dat 2pl	**3652.8** noun acc pl masc	**2174.19** verb nom pl masc part pres act
συνευωχούμενοι	ὑμῖν,	**14.** ὀφθαλμοὺς	ἔχοντες
suneuōchoumenoi	*humin*	*ophthalmous*	*echontes*
feasting with	you;	eyes	having

3194.3 adj acc pl masc	**3291.2** adj gen sing fem	**2504.1** conj	**178.1** adj acc pl masc	**264.1** noun fem
μεστοὺς	μοιχαλίδος	καὶ	ἀκαταπαύστους	ἁμαρτίας,
mestous	*moichalidos*	*kai*	*akatapaustous*	*hamartias*
full	of an adulteress,	and	that cease not	from sin,

1179.2 verb nom pl masc part pres act	**5425.8** noun acc pl fem	**787.2** adj acc pl fem	**2559.4** noun acc sing fem	**1122.3** verb acc sing fem part perf mid
δελεάζοντες	ψυχὰς	ἀστηρίκτους,	καρδίαν	γεγυμνασμένην
deleazontes	*psuchas*	*astēriktous*	*kardian*	*gegumnasmenēn*
alluring	souls	unestablished;	a heart	having been trained

2:12. Indulgence in pride, self-will, contempt for authority—which might be called sins of the spirit—often lead to indulgence in sins of the flesh. Peter said these false teachers act as mere animals born for capture and destruction. Their real desire is to satisfy their physical passions and get material gain. This verse is almost identical with Jude 10 which speaks of ungodly men who creep in secretly to turn liberty into license and deny Christ Jesus the Lord. Jude says they "speak evil of those things which they know not: but what they know naturally, as brute beasts, in those things they corrupt themselves." In their destroying, they themselves shall surely be destroyed. This is often the fate of evil men. Those who choose such a life eventually discover that in the end even that in which they found such pleasure fails to satisfy.

2:13. There is a tragic "reward" (*misthon,* wage) for "unrighteousness" (*adikias,* wrongdoing), and the false teachers will "receive" it (*komioumenoi,* obtain). One charge against them is that they "riot in the daytime." Daylight hours are for productive activity, not revelry; as 1 Thessalonians 5:7 suggests, "They that be drunken are drunken in the night." The false teachers use the day to "riot" (*truphēn,* revel, live in luxury). This is their "pleasure" (*hēdonēn,* hedonism, sensual delight, lust). Peter called them "spots" (from *spilos,* spoil, stain, disfigure) and "blemishes" (*mōmoi,* blot, fault, flaw) that bring disgrace on the Church. "Sporting themselves" is *entruphōntes* (revel, live in luxury). "Deceivings" is *apatais,* but the context suggests it should be *agapais,* meaning love feasts, which would agree with Jude 12.

The Christians customarily ate a meal together before celebrating the Lord's Supper. The purpose was to promote fellowship and express love one for another, so it was called a love feast (feast of charity). The wealthier believers provided the food, but rich and poor ate together. Evidently the false teachers gorged themselves and turned the love feast into a travesty of what God intends this sacred service to be.

The Book of Jude (verses 12,13), almost a parallel passage, says, "These men are blemishes at your love feasts, eating with you without the slightest qualm—shepherds who feed only themselves. They are clouds without rain, blown along by the wind; autumn trees, without fruit and uprooted—twice dead. They are wild waves of the sea, foaming up their shame; wandering stars, for whom blackest darkness has been reserved forever" (NIV).

2:14. Another charge against them is their insatiable lust. They have "eyes full of adultery" (illicit sexual intercourse) and they "cannot cease" from it. Peter painted a vivid picture of a man "who cannot see a woman without lascivious thoughts arising in his heart" (Mayor, p.135). This reminds us of Christ's words about the adul-

12. But these, as natural brute beasts, made to be taken and destroyed: . . . are irrational animals, *Norlie* . . . guided only by instinct, *SEB* . . . to be caught and killed, *Berkeley* . . . born naturally for capture and corruption, *Concordant.*

speak evil of the things that they understand not: . . . uttering blasphemies in the sphere of those things concerning which they are ignorant, *Wuest* . . . while maligning what they do not know, *Berkeley* . . . that in which they are ignorant, *Concordant.*

and shall utterly perish in their own corruption: They will die in their own sinful ways, *NLT* . . . shall in their...destroying surely be destroyed, *Wuest.*

13. And shall receive the reward of unrighteousness: . . . being requited with the wages of injustice, *Concordant* . . . as the hire, *Wuest* . . . rewarded by their own wickedness, *Berkeley.*

[as] they that count it pleasure to riot in the day time: They esteem luxurious festivity, *Wilson* . . . Deeming gratification by day a luxury, *Concordant* . . . deeming luxurious living in the daytime a pleasure, *Wuest* . . . enjoying their deceitful ways, *Adams.*

Spots [they are] and blemishes, sporting themselves with their own deceivings while they feast with you: They are a blot and a disgrace, *Noli* . . . moral blemishes and disgraceful blots, reveling in their deceitful cravings, *Wuest* . . . and flaws, *Concordant* . . . and running sores in our society, *Laubach* . . . they stuff themselves, *SEB.*

14. Having eyes full of adultery, and that cannot cease from sin: . . . having the distended eyes of an adulteress, *Concordant* . . . are full of lust, *Norlie* . . . full of harlots, *Montgomery* . . . and are insatiable for sin, *Swann* . . . and unrestrained sin, *Fenton* . . . They never stop sinning, *SEB* . . . that never have enough of sinning, *Williams C.K.* . . . incessantly sinning, *Campbell.*

beguiling unstable souls: . . . catching unstable souls with bait, *Wuest* . . . entice persons of weak character, *TCNT* . . . unsteady souls, *Montgomery* . . . alluring unestablished, *Darby.*

2 Peter 2:15

14.a.**Txt:** Steph
Var: 01ℵ,02A,03B,04C 018K,020L,025P,Gries Lach,Treg,Alf,Word Tisc,We/Ho,Weis,Sod UBS/☆

15.a.**Txt:** 03B-corr,04C 018K,020L,025P,byz.
Var: 01ℵ,02A,03B-org 33,Tisc,We/Ho,Weis Sod,UBS/☆

15.b.**Txt:** Steph
Var: 01ℵ,02A,03B,04C 018K,020L,025P,byz. Gries,Lach,Treg,Alf Word,Tisc,We/Ho,Weis Sod,UBS/☆

15.c.**Txt:** p72,01ℵ-corr 02A,04C,018K,020L 025P,byz.it.bo.Tisc,Sod
Var: 03B,sa.We/Ho,Weis UBS/☆

3984.6 noun dat pl fem	**3984.2** noun gen sing fem	**2174.19** verb nom pl masc part pres act	**2641.2** noun gen sing fem
ˊ πλεονεξίαις	[a☆ πλεονεξίας]	ἔχοντες,	κατάρας
pleonexiais	*pleonexias*	*echontes*	*kataras*
in covetousnesses	[in covetousness]	having,	of curse

4891.4 noun pl neu	**2611.6** verb nom pl masc part aor act	**2611.13** verb nom pl masc part pres act	**3450.12** art acc sing fem
τέκνα,	15. ˊ καταλιπόντες	[a☆ καταλείποντες]	ˊb τὴν ˋ
tekna	*katalipontes*	*kataleipontes*	*tēn*
children;	having left	[forsaking]	the

2097.2 adj acc sing fem	**3461.4** noun acc sing fem	**3966.18** verb 3pl indic aor pass	**1795.1** verb nom pl masc part aor act	**3450.11** art dat sing fem
εὐθεῖαν	ὁδὸν,	ἐπλανήθησαν,	ἐξακολουθήσαντες	τῇ
eutheian	*hodon*	*eplanēthēsan*	*exakolouthēsantes*	*tē*
straight	way,	they went astray,	having followed	in the

3461.3 noun dat sing fem	**3450.2** art gen sing	**897.1** name masc	**3450.2** art gen sing	**1000.1** name masc	**954.1** name masc
ὁδῷ	τοῦ	Βαλαὰμ	τοῦ	ˊ Βοσόρ,	[c Βεώρ,]
hodō	*tou*	*Balaam*	*tou*	*Bosor*	*Beōr*
way		of Balaam,		of Bosor,	[Beor,]

3614.5 rel-pron nom sing masc	**3272.3** noun acc sing masc	**92.2** noun gen sing fem	**25.14** verb 3sing indic aor act	**1636.1** noun acc sing fem
ὃς	μισθὸν	ἀδικίας	ἠγάπησεν	16. ἔλεγξιν
hos	*misthon*	*adikias*	*ēgapēsen*	*elenxin*
who	reward	of unrighteousness	loved;	reproof

1156.2 conj	**2174.32** verb 3sing indic aor act	**2375.9** adj fem	**3753.1** noun gen sing fem	**5106.1** noun sing neu
δὲ	ἔσχεν	ἰδίας	παρανομίας·	ὑποζύγιον
de	*eschen*	*idias*	*paranomias*	*hupozugion*
but	had	of his own	wickedness,	beast of burden

873.2 adj sing neu	**1706.1** prep	**442.2** noun gen sing masc	**5292.3** noun dat sing fem	**5187.3** verb sing neu part aor mid	**2940.6** verb 3sing indic aor act
ἄφωνον,	ἐν	ἀνθρώπου	φωνῇ	φθεγξάμενον,	ἐκώλυσεν
aphōnon	*en*	*anthrōpou*	*phōnē*	*phthenxamenon*	*ekōlusen*
dumb,	in	man's	voice	having spoken,	forbade

3450.12 art acc sing fem	**3450.2** art gen sing	**4254.2** noun gen sing masc	**3774.1** noun acc sing fem	**3642.7** dem-pron nom pl masc
τὴν	τοῦ	προφήτου	παραφρονίαν.	17. Οὗτοί
tēn	*tou*	*prophētou*	*paraphronian*	*Houtoi*
the	of the	prophet	madness.	These

1498.7 verb 3pl indic pres act	**3938.4** noun nom pl fem	**501.2** adj nom pl fem	**2504.1** conj	**3369.5** noun nom pl fem
εἰσιν	πηγαὶ	ἄνυδροι,	καὶ	ˊ νεφέλαι
eisin	*pēgai*	*anudroi*	*kai*	*nephelai*
are	fountains	without water,	and	clouds

17.a.**Txt:** 020L,byz.
Var: 01ℵ,02A,03B,04C 33,Gries,Lach,Treg,Alf Word,Tisc,We/Ho,Weis Sod,UBS/☆

17.b.**Txt:** 02A,04C,020L 025P,byz.Sod
Var: 01ℵ,03B,sa.bo. Lach,Treg,Alf,Tisc We/Ho,Weis,UBS/☆

2504.1 conj	**3521.1** noun nom pl fem	**5097.3** prep	**2951.2** noun gen sing fem	**1630.3** verb nom pl fem part pres mid
[a☆ καὶ	ὁμίχλαι]	ὑπὸ	λαίλαπος	ἐλαυνόμεναι,
kai	*homichlai*	*hupo*	*lailapos*	*elaunomenai*
[and	mists]	by	storm	being driven,

3614.4 rel-pron dat pl	**3450.5** art nom sing masc	**2200.1** noun nom sing masc	**3450.2** art gen sing	**4510.3** noun gen sing neu	**1519.1** prep
οἷς	ὁ	ζόφος	τοῦ	σκότους	ˊb εἰς
hois	*ho*	*zophos*	*tou*	*skotous*	*eis*
to whom	the	gloom	of the	darkness	to

tery in a lustful gaze (Matthew 5:28). "Beguiling" is *deleazontes* meaning to entrap, catch by bait, entice. "Exercised" is *gegumnasmenēn* (exercising in a gymnasium, training). The false teachers had trained their heart in the practice of "covetousness" (*pleonexiais,* avarice, fraudulency, greediness) and had become children of cursing. They were under a curse and headed for divine judgment.

2:15. Balaam has become known in history as a man who sought to make personal gain at the expense of his ministry (see Numbers 22–24). He is a perfect example of what Peter was dealing with. Balaam sought to manipulate truth so as not to deny it, but to use it for his own advantage. He was not all bad, and much of his message was true; however, he finally lost out completely. He became numbered with the enemies who, according to his own prophecy, were marked for destruction, and his sad end is told in Numbers 31:8. Peter said the false teachers had abandoned the right road. They had gone astray by following in the footsteps of Balaam, the prophet who commercialized his gift. He sought the reward offered by Balak, "the wages of unrighteousness." He loved earthly things more than heavenly things. "Loved" is from *agapaō,* an intense kind of love, the word used in 2 Timothy 4:10: "Demas hath forsaken me, having loved this present world." The final wages of sin is death, though the present pay may seem desirable.

2:16. Balaam's "iniquity" (*paranomias,* transgression) was exposed when his donkey spoke with a human voice. Actually the ass was "dumb" (*aphōnon,* voiceless), and yet it talked to Balaam and restrained him from doing something that was "madness" (*paraphronian,* foolhardy). Balaam had been hired by Balak, king of Moab, to try to turn God against the Israelites so they would not be able to defeat Moab's army. He knew that as long as God was helping the Israelites, his soldiers could not stand against them. So Balaam set out to curse Israel, which was madness indeed. But later he found a way to earn a reward from Balak. He succeeded in luring men of Israel to commit whoredom with women of Moab (see Numbers 25:1-3; 31:16), and this turned God against Israel and brought judgment upon them.

2:17. Peter said the false teachers made an empty profession of faith. He compared them to "wells" (*pēgai,* fountain, spring) without water and to clouds that, instead of giving rain, are "carried" away (*elaunomenai,* driven) by a "tempest" (*lailapos,* squall, hurricane; as in Mark 4:37, the sudden "storm of wind" on the Sea of Galilee that threatened Christ and His disciples). What a disappointment to a thirsty traveler in the desert when he sees a patch of green ahead, only to find when he reaches it that the spring has dried up! Even worse is the plight of spiritually thirsty people who look for the living water, only to be disillusioned by false teachers.

an heart they have exercised with covetous practices; cursed children: . . . their hearts are trained to exploit, *Williams C.K.* . . . exercised with insatiable desires, *Campbell* . . . practised in greed, *Fenton* . . . accursed generation, *Montgomery* . . . Children of a Curse, *Wilson.*

15. Which have forsaken the right way, and are gone astray: Leaving the straight path, they were led astray, *Concordant* . . . Abandoning the straight road, *Wuest* . . . and have taken the wrong road, *Laubach.*

following the way of Balaam [the son] of Bosor, who loved the wages of unrighteousness: . . . in the steps, *TCNT* . . . followed in the tracks, *Berkeley* . . . liked to take a bribe for wrongdoing, *Norlie* . . . the money he got for his sin, *NLT* . . . profits of, *Williams.*

16. But was rebuked for his iniquity: . . . exposed for his own outlawry, *Concordant* . . . the recipient of an effectual rebuke, *Wuest* . . . convicted by his own misdeed, *Berkeley* . . . for his own transgression, *Wade.*

the dumb ass speaking with man's voice forbad the madness of the prophet: . . . a voiceless yoke-beast, uttering with a human voice, forbids the insanity, *Concordant* . . . speaking with, *Fenton* . . . the inarticulate beast of burden...restrained the insanity of, *Wuest* . . . reprimanded, *Campbell* . . . prevented him from carrying out his mad purposes, *Laubach* . . . put an end to the prophet's madness, *Williams C.K.*

17. These are wells without water: . . . waterless fountains, *Norlie* . . . springs, *Montgomery* . . . dried up water holes, *Laubach.*

clouds that are carried with a tempest: . . . mists driven before a gale, *TCNT* . . . fogs driven by a hurricane, *Adams* . . . blown by a storm, *SEB* . . . driven along by a Whirlwind, *Wilson* . . . tempest-tossed, *Fenton.*

to whom the mist of darkness is reserved for ever: . . . for whom the gloom of darkness has been kept, *Concordant* . . . the blackness, *Wuest.*

163.3 noun acc sing masc	4931.34 verb 3sing indic perf mid	5084.1 adj pl neu	1056.1 conj	3125.1 noun gen sing fem
αἰῶνα ⸃	τετήρηται.	**18.** ὑπέρογκα	γὰρ	ματαιότητος
aiōna	*tetērētai*	*huperonka*	*gar*	*mataiotētos*
age	is kept.	Great swelling	for	of futility

5187.1 verb nom pl masc part pres mid	1179.1 verb 3pl indic pres act	1706.1 prep	1924.7 noun dat pl fem	4418.2 noun gen sing fem
φθεγγόμενοι,	δελεάζουσιν	ἐν	ἐπιθυμίαις	σαρκὸς,
phthengomenoi	*deleazousin*	*en*	*epithumiais*	*sarkos*
speaking,	they allure	with	desires	of flesh,

18.a.**Txt:** 01ℵ-org,04C 018K,020L,025P,1739 byz.
Var: p72,01ℵ-corr,02A 03B,33,it.sa.bo.Gries Lach,Treg,Alf,Word Tisc,We/Ho,Weis,Sod UBS/☆

18.b.**Txt:** 018K,020L 025P,byz.
Var: 01ℵ,02A,03B,04C 33,Lach,Treg,Alf,Word Tisc,We/Ho,Weis,Sod UBS/☆

760.4 noun dat pl fem	3450.8 art acc pl masc	3552.1 adv	3506.1 adv
ἀσελγείαις,	τοὺς	⸂ ὄντως	[a☆ ὀλίγως]
aselgeiais	*tous*	*ontōs*	*oligōs*
by licentiousnesses,	the	indeed	[almost]

662.2 verb acc pl masc part aor act	662.3 verb acc pl masc part pres act	3450.8 art acc pl masc	1706.1 prep
⸂ ἀποφυγόντας	[b☆ ἀποφεύγοντας]	τοὺς	ἐν
apophugontas	*apopheugontas*	*tous*	*en*
having escaped from	[escaping from]	the	in

3967.3 noun dat sing fem	388.5 verb acc pl masc part pres mid	1644.4 noun acc sing fem	840.2 prs-pron dat pl
πλάνῃ	ἀναστρεφομένους,	**19.** ἐλευθερίαν	αὐτοῖς
planē	*anastrephomenous*	*eleutherian*	*autois*
error	living,	freedom	them

1846.1 verb nom pl masc part pres mid	840.7 prs-pron nom pl masc	1395.6 noun nom pl masc	5062.7 verb nom pl masc part pres act	3450.10 art gen sing fem
ἐπαγγελλόμενοι,	αὐτοὶ	δοῦλοι	ὑπάρχοντες	τῆς
epangellomenoi	*autoi*	*douloi*	*huparchontes*	*tēs*
promising,	themselves	slaves	being	of the

5193.2 noun gen sing fem	3614.3 rel-pron dat sing	1056.1 conj	4948.3 indef-pron nom sing	2252.2 verb 3sing indic perf mid	3642.5 dem-pron dat sing masc
φθορᾶς·	ᾧ	γάρ	τις	ἥττηται,	τούτῳ
phthoras	*hō*	*gar*	*tis*	*hēttētai*	*toutō*
curruption;	by whom	for	anyone	has been subdued,	by this

19.a.**Txt:** 01ℵ-corr,02A 04C,018K,020L,025P byz.Sod
Var: 01ℵ-org,03B,sa.bo. Tisc,We/Ho,Weis UBS/☆

2504.1 conj	1396.5 verb 3sing indic perf mid	1479.1 conj	1056.1 conj	662.1 verb nom pl masc part aor act
⸂a καὶ ⸃	δεδούλωται.	**20.** εἰ	γὰρ	ἀποφυγόντες
kai	*dedoulōtai*	*ei*	*gar*	*apophugontes*
also	he is held in bondage.	If	for	having escaped

3450.17 art pl neu	3257.1 noun pl neu	3450.2 art gen sing	2862.2 noun gen sing masc	1706.1 prep	1907.3 noun dat sing fem	3450.2 art gen sing
τὰ	μιάσματα	τοῦ	κόσμου	ἐν	ἐπιγνώσει	τοῦ
ta	*miasmata*	*tou*	*kosmou*	*en*	*epignōsei*	*tou*
the	pollutions	of the	world	through	knowledge	of the

20.a.**Txt:** 03B,byz.We/Ho
Var: p72,01ℵ,02A,04C 025P,044,81,323,614 630,945,1505,1739 2495,UBS/☆

2935.2 noun gen sing masc	2231.2 prs-pron gen 1pl	2504.1 conj	4842.2 noun gen sing masc	2400.2 name masc	5382.2 name gen masc
κυρίου	[a☆+ ἡμῶν]	καὶ	σωτῆρος	Ἰησοῦ	Χριστοῦ,
kuriou	*hēmōn*	*kai*	*sōtēros*	*Iēsou*	*Christou*
Lord	[our]	and	Saviour	Jesus	Christ,

3642.3 dem-pron dat pl	1156.2 conj	3687.1 adv	1691.2 verb nom pl masc part aor pass	2252.3 verb 3pl indic pres mid
τούτοις	δὲ	πάλιν	ἐμπλακέντες	ἡττῶνται,
toutois	*de*	*palin*	*emplakentes*	*hēttōntai*
by these	but	again	having been entangled	they are subdued,

2:18. New converts are special targets of false teachers. They "allure" (*deleazousin*, beguile, entrap, entice) those who are just escaping from the ranks of unbelievers who live in error. The false teachers talk in grandiose terms to do this. They are extravagant in their verbosity, and they sway the people with their "great swelling words," but Peter says their words are "vanity" (*mataiotētos*, empty, profitless, insincere). They appeal through carnal desires and through much "wantonness" (*aselgeiais*, lewdness, unrestrained immorality). By encouraging the new converts to compromise, they draw them back into the very life-style from which they recently fled.

Jude's description of the false teachers is even more devastating than Peter's. He said: "These are murmurers, complainers, walking after their own lusts; and their mouth speaketh great swelling words, having men's persons in admiration because of advantage" (Jude 16). Jude further stated: "Clouds they are without water, carried about of winds; trees whose fruit withereth, without fruit, twice dead, plucked up by the roots" (Jude 12). Jude called them "ungodly men, turning the grace of our God into lasciviousness, and denying the only Lord God, and our Lord Jesus Christ" (Jude 4). He stated: "These filthy dreamers defile the flesh, despise dominion, and speak evil of dignities" (Jude 8).

2:19. The false prophets promised "liberty" (*eleutherian*, freedom), but it is not the freedom Christ offered when He said, "The truth shall make you free" (John 8:32). Christ offers freedom from sin, not freedom to sin; and freedom from the Mosaic law, not freedom from the law of divine love. What the false teachers promised was a presumed liberty that amounts to license—a freedom to please oneself regardless of any restraining law. They would use liberty "for an occasion to the flesh" (Galatians 5:13). They would encourage people to sin saying God's grace will cover whatever sins they commit (see Romans 6:1). But Peter said these false teachers themselves really did not enjoy liberty, for they were "servants" (*douloi*, slave) of "corruption" (*phthoras*, depravity, defilement). They had been "overcome" (*hēttētai*, vanquish) by it and therefore were in bondage to it. All who yield themselves to sin are the servants of sin (Romans 6:16).

2:20. Victims of false teachers will end up in a worse state than they were in before they were saved. Jesus made a similar statement in reference to a man from whom an unclean spirit had been cast out: "The last state of that man is worse than the first" (Matthew 12:45). He said the uncleanness becomes seven times worse when the evil spirits return. Similarly believers who, through acknowledging Jesus Christ as Lord and Saviour, have escaped (run away) from worldly "pollutions" (*miasmata*, defilement, uncleanness), if they should become entangled again in those pollutions and be

18. For when they speak great swelling [words] of vanity: They speak their folly in pompous oratory, *Norlie* . . . they say stupid, boastful things, *SEB* . . . uttering extravagant things, *Wuest* . . . make loud foolish boasts about their wicked pleasures, *Laubach.*

they allure through the lusts of the flesh, [through much] wantonness: . . . by using sensual cravings, *Norlie* . . . by an appeal to fleshly desires, *Adams.*

those that were clean escaped from them who live in error: . . . those who are just about escaping from those who are ordering their behavior in the sphere of error, *Wuest* . . . those who are scarcely fleeing from those who are behaving with deception, *Concordant.*

19. While they promise them liberty: They talk about being free, *Laubach* . . . promising them freedom, *Concordant.*

they themselves are the servants of corruption: . . . they are inherently, *Concordant* . . . are slaves to corrupt habits, *TCNT* . . . are slaves of rottenness! *Montgomery.*

for of whom a man is overcome, of the same is he brought in bondage: A person is a slave to whatever has defeated him, *SEB* . . . anyone is discomfited, to this one he has been enslaved also, *Concordant* . . . whom a person has been overcome with the result that he is in a state of subjugation, to this one has he been enslaved with the result that he is in a state of slavery, *Wuest* . . . is the slave of anything which masters him, *Montgomery.*

20. For if after they have escaped the pollutions of the world through the knowledge of the Lord and Saviour Jesus Christ: . . . having escaped from the defilements, *Fenton* . . . while fleeing from, *Concordant* . . . the corrupting ways, *Williams* . . . by an experiential knowledge, *Wuest.*

they are again entangled therein, and overcome: . . . they are again recaptured, *Fenton* . . . they got involved again and were defeated, *SEB* . . . defeated all over again, *Phillips* . . . with the result that they are in a state of subjugation, *Wuest* . . . and succumb to them, *Wade.*

1090.3 verb 3sing indic perf act	**840.2** prs-pron dat pl	**3450.17** art pl neu	**2057.12** adj pl neu	**5337.4** adj comp pl neu	**3450.1** art gen pl
γέγονεν	αὐτοῖς	τὰ	ἔσχατα	χείρονα	τῶν
gegonen	*autois*	*ta*	*eschata*	*cheirona*	*tōn*
has become	to them	the	last	worse	than the

4272.1 num ord gen pl	**2882.5** adj comp sing neu	**1056.1** conj	**1498.34** verb sing indic imperf act	**840.2** prs-pron dat pl	**3231.1** partic
πρώτων.	21. κρεῖττον	γὰρ	ἦν	αὐτοῖς	μὴ
prōtōn	*kreitton*	*gar*	*ēn*	*autois*	*mē*
first.	Better	for	it was	for them	not

1906.16 verb inf perf act	**3450.12** art acc sing fem	**3461.4** noun acc sing fem	**3450.10** art gen sing fem	**1336.2** noun gen sing fem
ἐπεγνωκέναι	τὴν	ὁδὸν	τῆς	δικαιοσύνης,
epegnōkenai	*tēn*	*hodon*	*tēs*	*dikaiosunēs*
to have known	the	way	of the	righteousness,

21.a.**Txt:** 018K,020L,byz.
Var: p72,03B,04C,025P
Lach,Treg,Alf,Tisc
We/Ho,Weis,UBS/⋆

2211.1 conj	**1906.12** verb dat pl masc part aor act	**1978.13** verb inf aor act	**5128.12** verb inf aor act	**1523.2** prep gen
ἢ	ἐπιγνοῦσιν	ʼ ἐπιστρέψαι	[a⋆ ὑποστρέψαι]	ἐκ
ē	*epignousin*	*epistrepsai*	*hupostrepsai*	*ek*
than	having known	to have turned	[idem]	from

3450.10 art gen sing fem	**3722.36** verb gen sing fem part aor pass	**840.2** prs-pron dat pl	**39.11** adj gen sing fem	**1769.2** noun gen sing fem
τῆς	παραδοθείσης	αὐτοῖς	ἁγίας	ἐντολῆς.
tēs	*paradotheisēs*	*autois*	*hagias*	*entolēs*
the	having been delivered	to them	holy	commandment.

22.a.**Txt:** 01ℵ-corr,04C
018K,020L,025P,byz.
Sod
Var: 01ℵ-org,02A,03B
sa.Lach,Treg,Alf,Tisc
We/Ho,Weis,UBS/⋆

4670.5 verb 3sing indic perf act	**1156.2** conj	**840.2** prs-pron dat pl	**3450.16** art sing neu	**3450.10** art gen sing fem
22. συμβέβηκεν	ʼa δὲ ˎ	αὐτοῖς	τὸ	τῆς
sumbebēken	*de*	*autois*	*to*	*tēs*
Has happened	but	to them	the	of the

225.1 adj gen sing	**3804.1** noun gen sing fem	**2938.1** noun nom sing masc	**1978.11** verb nom sing masc part aor act	**1894.3** prep	**3450.16** art sing neu
ἀληθοῦς	παροιμίας,	Κύων	ἐπιστρέψας	ἐπὶ	τὸ
alēthous	*paroimias*	*Kuōn*	*epistrepsas*	*epi*	*to*
true	proverb:	Dog	having returned	to	the

2375.4 adj sing	**1812.1** noun sing neu	**2504.1** conj	**5144.1** noun nom sing fem	**3040.4** verb nom sing fem part aor pass	**1519.1** prep
ἴδιον	ἐξέραμα·	καί,	Ὗς	λουσαμένη,	εἰς
idion	*exerama*	*kai*	*Hus*	*lousamenē*	*eis*
his own	vomit;	and	Sow	having been washed,	to

22.b.**Txt:** 01ℵ,02A,018K
020L,025P,byz.Sod
Var: 03B,04C-org,Treg
Alf,Tisc,We/Ho,Weis
UBS/⋆

2919.1 noun sing neu	**2919.1** noun acc sing masc	**997.1** noun gen sing masc	**3642.12** dem-pron acc sing fem	**2218.1** adv
ʼ κύλισμα	[b⋆ κυλισμὸν]	βορβόρου.	3:1. Ταύτην	ἤδη,
kulisma	*kulismon*	*borborou*	*Tautēn*	*ēdē*
rolling place	[wallowing]	in mire.	This	now,

27.6 adj pl masc	**1202.7** num ord acc sing fem	**5050.3** prs-pron dat 2pl	**1119.1** verb 1sing indic pres act	**1976.4** noun acc sing fem	**1706.1** prep
ἀγαπητοί,	δευτέραν	ὑμῖν	γράφω	ἐπιστολήν,	ἐν
agapētoi	*deuteran*	*humin*	*graphō*	*epistolēn*	*en*
beloved,	a second	to you	I write	epistle,	in

3614.14 rel-pron dat pl fem	**1320.1** verb 1sing indic pres act	**5050.2** prs-pron gen 2pl	**1706.1** prep	**5118.1** noun dat sing fem
αἷς	διεγείρω	ὑμῶν	ἐν	ὑπομνήσει
hais	*diegeirō*	*humōn*	*en*	*hupomnēsei*
which	I stir up	your	in	putting in remembrance

conquered by them, will plunge into sin more deeply than before they were saved and be more helpless to free themselves from its grip. "Entangled" is *emplakentes*, meaning entwine, involve. It is the word used of braiding or plaiting the hair, a very deliberate process, and indicates their return to their former immoral lives is not a rash act but a willful choice on their part.

2:21. There is another way in which those who turn back are worse off than before. It is because they are abandoning or refusing the truth, the holy commandment, God's Word, apart from which they cannot hope for help. In the beginning the truth was new to them, and they were not hardened against it. Now they have become almost immune to its power. Jesus, using the eye as a metaphor, warned against this: "If therefore the light that is in thee be darkness, how great is that darkness" (Matthew 6:23). No one is so blind as he who shuts his eyes to truth! Another warning, that of apostasy, is given in Hebrews 10:26,27. If one willfully rejects God's provision of salvation after receiving the knowledge of the truth, there is no way left by which he can find forgiveness since he is deliberately rejecting Christ's sacrifice, the only sacrifice for sins. The "way of righteousness" is the message John the Baptist preached (Matthew 21:32). It is the way all must follow (1 Timothy 6:11) if they wish to lay hold on eternal life.

2:22. Peter followed the familiar example of Jesus in using homely and vivid illustrations. He described what happens when a believer forsakes the ways of God by the illustrations of a dog and a pig. In each case the point is obvious: the false teachers had "escaped the pollutions of the world" (verse 20) but had not remained in the way of righteousness. When the opportunity arose, they reverted to their old nature and filthy ways. The first illustration is from Proverbs 26:11. The second does not appear in the Old Testament. In view of the Jews' repugnance for swine, it probably is from a Gentile source. There is a story in ancient literature about a hog that went to the public bath with people of high status. However, when coming out he saw a stinking drain and went and rolled himself in it. Peter could not have expressed contempt for false teachers more strongly than to class them with dogs and swine. By using these shocking comparisons, it is hoped believers will recognize deceivers for what they really are and will reject them.

3:1. This, Peter's final letter to believers, stresses the need to keep the Second Coming in mind. It has been mentioned before (1 Peter 4:7), but now it is dealt with more fully. Peter did not tell them anything new but wished to "stir up" (*diegeirō*, arouse them to be wide awake, as in 1:13) their understanding by reminding

the latter end is worse with them than the beginning: . . . their last state, *Darby, Williams C.K.* . . . their last position is far worse, *Phillips* . . . the last things have become to them, *Wuest* . . . their last condition is worse, *Williams* . . . worse than the first, *Concordant.*

21. For it had been better for them not to have known the way of righteousness: . . . to have recognized, *Concordant* . . . to have known the way of goodness at all, *Phillips.*

than, after they have known [it], to turn from the holy commandment delivered unto them: . . . recognizing it, to go back to what was behind, *Concordant* . . . after knowing it to turn their backs on the sacred commandments given to them, *Phillips* . . . than to know it and later turn away, *Laubach* . . . the sacred injunction, *Berkeley* . . . the sacred command committed to their trust, *Williams* . . . transmitted to them, *Wade.*

22. But it is happened unto them according to the true proverb: Alas, for them the old proverbs have come true, *Phillips* . . . In their case the true proverb becomes realized, *Berkeley* . . . these old sayings, *SEB* . . . true saying, *Wuest* . . . has befallen them, *Concordant.*

The dog [is] turned to his own vomit again: A cur turning to, *Concordant.*

and the sow that was washed to her wallowing in the mire: A bathed sow, *Concordant* . . . having been bathed, *Wuest* . . . scrubbed, *Berkeley* . . . went back to roll, *SEB* . . . in the mud, *TCNT* . . . in the muck, *Phillips.*

1. This second epistle, beloved, I now write unto you: This already, *Concordant* . . . the second letter, *Norlie* . . . I have written to you, dear friends of mine, *Phillips* . . . divinely loved ones, *Wuest.*

in [both] which I stir up your pure minds by way of remembrance: . . . in which I am rousing your sincere comprehension by a reminder, *Concordant* . . . stir you up to remember with clear intelligence, *Fenton* . . . in both of them I have tried to stimulate you,

3450.12 art acc sing fem	1496.2 adj acc sing fem	1265.3 noun acc sing fem	3279.9 verb inf aor pass	3450.1 art gen pl
τὴν	εἰλικρινῆ	διάνοιαν,	2. μνησθῆναι	τῶν
tēn	*eilikrinē*	*dianoian*	*mnēsthēnai*	*tōn*
the	pure	mind,	to be mindful	of the

4136.5 verb gen pl neu part perf mid	4343.5 noun gen pl neu	5097.3 prep	3450.1 art gen pl	39.4 adj gen pl
προειρημένων	ῥημάτων	ὑπὸ	τῶν	ἁγίων
proeirēmenōn	*rhēmatōn*	*hupo*	*tōn*	*hagiōn*
having been spoken before	words	by	the	holy

4254.5 noun gen pl masc	2504.1 conj	3450.10 art gen sing fem	3450.1 art gen pl	646.5 noun gen pl masc	2231.2 prs-pron gen 1pl
προφητῶν,	καὶ	τῆς	τῶν	ἀποστόλων	ˊ ἡμῶν
prophētōn	*kai*	*tēs*	*tōn*	*apostolōn*	*hēmōn*
prophets,	and	of the	the	apostles	by us

2.a.**Txt:** Steph
Var: 01ℵ,02A,03B,04C 018K,020L,025P,Lach Treg,Alf,Word,Tisc We/Ho,Weis,Sod UBS/☆

3.a.**Txt:** 018K,020L 025P,byz.
Var: 01ℵ,02A,03B 04C-corr,sa.bo.Lach Treg,Alf,Word,Tisc We/Ho,Weis,Sod UBS/☆

3.b.**Var:** 01ℵ,02A,03B 04C,025P,sa.bo.Gries Lach,Treg,Alf,Word Tisc,We/Ho,Weis,Sod UBS/☆

5050.2 prs-pron gen 2pl	1769.2 noun gen sing fem	3450.2 art gen sing	2935.2 noun gen sing masc	2504.1 conj	4842.2 noun gen sing masc
[a☆ ὑμῶν]	ἐντολῆς,	τοῦ	κυρίου	καὶ	σωτῆρος·
humōn	*entolēs*	*tou*	*kuriou*	*kai*	*sōtēros*
[by you]	commandment	of the	Lord	and	Saviour;

3642.17 dem-pron sing neu	4270.1 adv	1091.12 verb nom pl masc part pres act	3617.1 conj	2048.57 verb 3pl indic fut mid
3. τοῦτο	πρῶτον	γινώσκοντες,	ὅτι	ἐλεύσονται
touto	*prōton*	*ginōskontes*	*hoti*	*eleusontai*
this	first	knowing,	that	will come

1894.2 prep	2057.2 adj gen sing	2057.1 adj gen pl	3450.1 art gen pl	2232.6 noun gen pl fem	1706.1 prep
ἐπ'	ˊ ἐσχάτου	[a☆ ἐσχάτων]	τῶν	ἡμερῶν	[b☆+ ἐν
ep'	*eschatou*	*eschatōn*	*tōn*	*hēmerōn*	*en*
at	last	[idem]	of the	days	[in

1684.1 noun dat sing fem	1687.1 noun nom pl masc	2567.3 prep	3450.15 art acc pl fem	2375.9 adj fem
ἐμπαιγμονῇ]	ἐμπαῖκται,	κατὰ	τὰς	ἰδίας
empaigmonē	*empaiktai*	*kata*	*tas*	*idias*
mocking]	mockers,	according to	the	own

840.1 prs-pron gen pl	1924.1 noun fem	1924.1 noun fem	840.1 prs-pron gen pl	4057.10 verb nom pl masc part pres mid
ˊ αὐτῶν	ἐπιθυμίας	[☆ ἐπιθυμίας	αὐτῶν]	πορευόμενοι,
autōn	*epithumias*	*epithumias*	*autōn*	*poreuomenoi*
their	lusts	[lusts	their]	walking,

2504.1 conj	2978.16 verb nom pl masc part pres act	4085.1 adv	1498.4 verb 3sing indic pres act	3450.9 art nom sing fem
4. καὶ	λέγοντες,	Ποῦ	ἐστιν	ἡ
kai	*legontes*	*Pou*	*estin*	*hē*
and	saying,	Where	is	the

1845.2 noun nom sing fem	3450.10 art gen sing fem	3814.2 noun gen sing fem	840.3 prs-pron gen sing	570.1 prep	3614.10 rel-pron gen sing fem
ἐπαγγελία	τῆς	παρουσίας	αὐτοῦ;	ἀφ'	ἧς
epangelia	*tēs*	*parousias*	*autou*	*aph'*	*hēs*
promise	of the	coming	his?	from	which

1056.1 conj	3450.7 art nom pl masc	3824.6 noun nom pl masc	2810.6 verb 3pl indic aor pass	3820.1 adj	3643.1 adv
γὰρ	οἱ	πατέρες	ἐκοιμήθησαν,	πάντα	οὕτως
gar	*hoi*	*pateres*	*ekoimēthēsan*	*panta*	*houtōs*
for	the	fathers	fell asleep,	all things	thus

them of what they had been taught. This was his purpose "in both"—that is, in this second "epistle" (*epistolēn,* letter) as well as the first. "Pure" is *eilikrinē,* meaning sincere, as in Philippians 1:10: "That ye may be sincere and without offense till the day of Christ." It means genuine; the word speaks of something being examined in full sunlight.

as men with minds uncontaminated by error, by simply reminding you of what you really know already, *Phillips* . . . revive, *Berkeley* . . . to stir up your unsullied minds, *Williams.*

2. That ye may be mindful of the words which were spoken before by the holy prophets: I want you to remember the words spoken of old, *Phillips* . . . so that you may recall, *Wade* . . . to recollect the words previously spoken, *Wilson* . . . to remind you of the declarations which have been declared, *Concordant* . . . of the sayings, *Berkeley.*

and of the commandment of us the apostles of the Lord and Saviour: . . . as well as the commands, *Phillips* . . . of the precept of, *Concordant* . . . also of the commands of the Lord, *Berkeley.*

3:2. In this chapter Peter emphasized two important issues. One is that the Word of God is true and dependable; it means just what it says. The other is that the purpose of prophecy is not to satisfy human curiosity regarding the future but to provide the incentive for holy living. He wanted believers to remember the Old Testament prophecies as well as the teachings of the apostles. "Commandment" does not mean any single precept but the entire gospel—all the teachings of the apostles. A.T. Robertson says a better translation of the Greek is "the commandment of the Lord and Saviour through your apostles" (*Word Pictures in the New Testament,* 6:172). The apostles were not teaching a message of their own but the message they received from Christ.

3. Knowing this first, that there shall come in the last days scoffers: Recognise this fact first, *TCNT* . . . First of all you should understand that...scoffers will come on the scene with their scoffing, *Berkeley* . . . You should never forget that in the last days mockers will undoubtedly come, *Phillips* . . . will make fun, *SEB* . . . will come and mock you, *TNT* . . . and will make sport of our faith, *Laubach* . . . mockers with mockery, *Wuest.*

walking after their own lusts: . . . behaving in line with, *Berkeley* . . . men who live only for their selfish interests, *TNT* . . . men whose only guide in life is what they want for themselves, *Phillips* . . . ordering their manner of life according to their own personal desires, *Wuest* . . . going according to their own desires, *Concordant* . . . their own evil desires, *Norlie.*

3:3. The reason the believers needed to be stirred up and constantly keep sound teachings in mind was that scoffers would arise in the Church. "Scoffers" is *empaiktai,* translated "mockers" in Jude 18, referring to the false teachers. The Greek phrase for "in the last days" is translated in various forms. John 6:39 has "on the last day." James 5:3 gives "for the last days." The Greek literally means "upon the last of the days." Peter was speaking about a future time beyond his own day and ministry.

4. And saying, Where is the promise of his coming?: . . . and they will say, *Phillips* . . . What about his promised coming, *Berkeley* . . . of His appearing? *Fenton* . . . of His presence? *Concordant.*

for since the fathers fell asleep, all things continue as [they were] from the beginning of the creation: Since our ancestors died, *SEB* . . . Since the first Christians fell asleep, *Phillips* . . . went to their rest, *Noli* . . . were put to re-

3:4. Scoffers would ask about the "promise" (*epangelia,* pledge, assurance) of His coming. The reference is to Christ (verse 2). Peter was speaking of the "coming of our Lord Jesus Christ," as in 1:16. "Coming" is *parousias,* Greek for *presence,* meaning His personal arrival, a glorious event. Peter knew that if time went on, some would grow impatient, and scoffers would take advantage of the opportunity to mock the teaching. But the scoffers would be wrong when they said that ever since the forefathers "fell asleep" (passed away) all things remained just as they were from the date of creation.

To correct this mistake Peter referred to the Flood and the change it made in the earth. God had already intervened once, and He will intervene again. But unregenerate men and women do not want any intervention. They wish to pursue their sinful pleasures without interruption. "Fathers" is *pateres,* meaning parent or ancestor. It may refer to the Old Testament prophets who spoke of the Day of the Lord, or to the apostles like Peter who would have died by that time. Peter preached about the second coming of Christ

1259.2 verb 3sing indic pres act	570.2 prep	741.2 noun gen sing fem	2909.2 noun gen sing fem	2963.1 verb 3sing indic pres act	1056.1 conj
διαμένει	ἀπ'	ἀρχῆς	κτίσεως.	5. λανθάνει	γὰρ
diamenei	*ap'*	*archēs*	*ktiseōs*	*lanthanei*	*gar*
continue	from	beginning	of creation.	Is hidden from	for

840.8 prs-pron acc pl masc	3642.17 dem-pron sing neu	2286.18 verb acc pl masc part pres act	3617.1 conj	3636.6 noun nom pl masc	1498.37 verb 3pl indic imperf act
αὐτοὺς	τοῦτο	θέλοντας,	ὅτι	οὐρανοὶ	ἦσαν
autous	*touto*	*thelontas*	*hoti*	*ouranoi*	*ēsan*
them	this,	willing,	that	heavens	were

1584.1 adv	2504.1 conj	1087.1 noun nom sing fem	1523.1 prep gen	5045.2 noun gen sing neu	2504.1 conj	1217.1 prep
ἔκπαλαι,	καὶ	γῆ	ἐξ	ὕδατος	καὶ	δι'
ekpalai	*kai*	*gē*	*ex*	*hudatos*	*kai*	*di'*
of old,	and	an earth	out	of water	and	in

5045.2 noun gen sing neu	4771.11 verb nom sing fem part perf act	3450.3 art dat sing	3450.2 art gen sing	2296.2 noun gen sing masc	3030.3 noun dat sing masc
ὕδατος	συνεστῶσα,	τῷ	τοῦ	θεοῦ	λόγῳ,
hudatos	*sunestōsa*	*tō*	*tou*	*theou*	*logō*
water	having subsisted,	by the		of God	word,

1217.1 prep	3614.1 rel-pron gen pl	3450.5 art nom sing masc	4966.1 adv	2862.1 noun nom sing masc	5045.3 noun dat sing neu
6. δι'	ὧν	ὁ	τότε	κόσμος	ὕδατι
di'	*hōn*	*ho*	*tote*	*kosmos*	*hudati*
through	which	the	then	world	with water

2596.1 verb nom sing masc part aor pass	616.22 verb 3sing indic aor mid	3450.7 art nom pl masc	1156.2 conj	3431.1 adv
κατακλυσθεὶς	ἀπώλετο·	7. οἱ	δὲ	νῦν
kataklustheis	*apōleto*	*hoi*	*de*	*nun*
having been deluged	perished.	The	but	now

7.a.**Txt:** 01ℵ,04C,018K 020L,Steph
Var: 02A,03B,025P Elzev,Lach,Tisc,We/Ho Sod,UBS/⋆

3636.6 noun nom pl masc	2504.1 conj	3450.9 art nom sing fem	1087.1 noun nom sing fem	840.3 prs-pron gen sing	3450.3 art dat sing
οὐρανοὶ	καὶ	ἡ	γῆ	ʻ αὐτοῦ	[a⋆ τῷ
ouranoi	*kai*	*hē*	*gē*	*autou*	*tō*
heavens	and	the	earth	his	[by the

840.4 prs-pron dat sing	3030.3 noun dat sing masc	2320.6 verb nom pl masc part perf mid	1498.7 verb 3pl indic pres act	4300.3 noun dat sing neu
αὐτῷ]	λόγῳ	τεθησαυρισμένοι	εἰσὶν,	πυρί
autō	*logō*	*tethēsaurismenoi*	*eisin*	*puri*
same]	by word	having been treasured up	are,	for fire

4931.30 verb nom pl masc part pres mid	1519.1 prep	2232.4 noun acc sing fem	2893.2 noun gen sing fem	2504.1 conj	677.2 noun gen sing fem
τηρούμενοι	εἰς	ἡμέραν	κρίσεως	καὶ	ἀπωλείας
tēroumenoi	*eis*	*hēmeran*	*kriseōs*	*kai*	*apōleias*
being kept	to	a day	of judgment	and	destruction

3450.1 art gen pl	759.4 adj gen pl masc	442.7 noun gen pl masc	1518.9 num card neu	1156.2 conj	3642.17 dem-pron sing neu
τῶν	ἀσεβῶν	ἀνθρώπων.	8. Ἓν	δὲ	τοῦτο
tōn	*asebōn*	*anthrōpōn*	*Hen*	*de*	*touto*
of the	ungodly	men.	One	but	this thing

3231.1 partic	2963.2 verb 3sing impr pres act	5050.4 prs-pron acc 2pl	27.6 adj pl masc	3617.1 conj	1518.5 num card nom fem
μὴ	λανθανέτω	ὑμᾶς,	ἀγαπητοί,	ὅτι	μία
mē	*lanthanetō*	*humas*	*agapētoi*	*hoti*	*mia*
not	let be hidden	from you,	beloved,	that	one

(Acts 3:20), as Jesus himself did repeatedly (Matthew 24:34) and as the angels promised at the Ascension (Acts 1:11).

3:5. The scoffers would purposely forget the account of the Flood recorded in Genesis 6–8. "Willingly" is *thelontas,* meaning gladly, choice, preference. They would close their eyes to the Biblical account of how God, by the word of His power, created the "heavens" (*ouranoi,* sky, as in Matthew 16:3, "Ye can discern the face of the sky") and the "earth" (*gē,* land, ground). In the beginning all was water. God created the firmament to divide the water in the clouds from the water in the universal sea. Then He caused the sea to "be gathered together unto one place, and let the dry land appear" (Genesis 1:9). The water served to give consistency and coherence to the land; this is one interpretation of Peter's words, though there are others. By this interpretation, "out of the water" refers not to the position of the land but rather to the effect of the water upon the land. "Standing" is from *sunistēmi,* meaning set together, compacted, consist; as in Colossians 1:17, "By him all things consist" (are held together). Water keeps the earth moist and holds it together. Scholars are agreed only on the fact that the meaning is obscure.

3:6. "Whereby" indicates the Flood occurred by means of God's command. By Him the earth was created, and by Him it was inundated (covered with water) so the earth and its inhabitants "perished" (*apōleto,* ruin, destroy fully).

3:7. Divine judgment upon human sins is inevitable, though the earth will never again be destroyed by a flood (Genesis 9:11). This verse says it will be by fire. "The same word" that created the world and that sent the Flood is now saving up the present heavens and earth, holding these elements in store for the fiery judgment which lies ahead. "Kept in store" is *tethēsaurismenoi,* to amass, to treasure up; as in Romans 2:5, "Treasurest up unto thyself wrath against the day of wrath." "Reserved" is *tēroumenoi* (to withhold, to keep in protective custody). "Perdition" is *apōleias* (ruin, loss, perishing). This same Greek word is translated "damnable" and "destruction" in 2:1, and as "pernicious" in 2:2. It is used in the case of Judas, whom Jesus called the "son of perdition" (John 17:12). In applying the word *perdition* to people, the New Testament always makes it clear that the one who is destroyed is responsible for his situation. There is never a fatalistic doom suggested. Even in Judas' case, the Gospels show that as late as the Last Supper, Jesus tried to help Judas to change his mind and purpose.

3:8. "Beloved" (dearly loved) appears six times in Peter's second epistle. He cautioned believers not to forget "this one thing," that

pose, *Concordant* . . . all things are remaining permanently in that state in which they were since the beginning of the creation, *Wuest* . . . everything has remained exactly, *Williams.*

5. For this they willingly are ignorant of: They willfully ignore the fact, *Norlie* . . . They deliberately ignore, *TNT* . . . they want to be oblivious of this, *Concordant* . . . They are deliberately shutting their eyes to a fact that they know very well, *Phillips* . . . they willfully forget, *Wuest.*

that by the word of God the heavens were of old: . . . that there were heavens of old, *Concordant* . . . by God's command ...in the old days, *Phillips* . . . that heavens existed from ancient times, *Wuest.*

and the earth standing out of the water and in the water: . . . become solidified, emerging out of water, *Wade* . . . cohering out of water and through water, *Concordant* . . . and land [standing] out of water, and by means of water, *Wuest.*

6. Whereby the world that then was, being overflowed with water, perished: . . . through which the ordered world of that time, having been deluged by water, was ruined, *Wuest* . . . was also overwhelmed and destroyed, *TNT.*

7. But the heavens and the earth, which are now: . . . this present heaven, *Williams C.K.*

by the same word are kept in store, reserved unto fire: . . . also by God's command, *Phillips* . . . stored with fire, *Concordant* . . . reserved for annihilation by fire, *Wade.*

against the day of judgment and perdition of ungodly men: . . . maintained for the fire of the day of judgment, *Phillips* . . . and destruction of the godless, *TCNT* . . . of irreverent men, *Concordant.*

8. But, beloved, be not ignorant of this one thing: Do not forget, *Montgomery* . . . we must not ignore this lesson of the ages, *Laubach* . . . don't let this fact escape you, *Swann* . . . you are not to be oblivious, *Concordant.*

2 Peter 3:9

2232.2 noun nom sing fem	3706.2 prep	2935.3 noun dat sing masc	5453.1 conj	5343.3 num card neu	2073.3 noun pl neu	2504.1 conj
ἡμέρα	παρὰ	κυρίῳ	ὡς	χίλια	ἔτη,	καὶ
hēmera	*para*	*kuriō*	*hōs*	*chilia*	*etē*	*kai*
day	with	Lord	as	a thousand	years,	and

5343.3 num card neu	2073.3 noun pl neu	5453.1 conj	2232.2 noun nom sing fem	1518.5 num card nom fem	3620.3 partic
χίλια	ἔτη	ὡς	ἡμέρα	μία.	**9.** οὐ
chilia	*etē*	*hōs*	*hēmera*	*mia*	*ou*
a thousand	years	as	day	one.	Not

9.a.**Txt:** 018K,020L,byz.
Var: 01ℵ,02A,03B,04C 025P,33,Lach,Treg,Alf Word,Tisc,We/Ho,Weis Sod,UBS/☆

1012.1 verb 3sing indic pres act	3450.5 art nom sing masc	2935.1 noun nom sing masc	3450.10 art gen sing fem	1845.1 noun fem	5453.1 conj
βραδύνει	⸂a ὁ ⸃	κύριος	τῆς	ἐπαγγελίας,	ὥς
bradunei	*ho*	*kurios*	*tēs*	*epangelias*	*hōs*
does delay	the	Lord	the	promise,	as

4948.7 indef-pron nom pl masc	1015.1 noun acc sing fem	2216.2 verb 3pl indic pres mid	233.2 conj	3086.1 verb 3sing indic pres act
τινες	βραδύτητα	ἡγοῦνται·	ἀλλὰ	μακροθυμεῖ
tines	*bradutēta*	*hēgountai*	*alla*	*makrothumei*
some	delay	count,	but	is patient

9.b.**Txt:** 018K,020L,byz. bo.
Var: p72,01ℵ,02A,03B 04C,025P,33,it.sa.bo. Lach,Treg,Alf,Tisc We/Ho,Weis,Sod UBS/☆

1519.1 prep	2231.4 prs-pron acc 1pl	5050.4 prs-pron acc 2pl	3231.1 partic	1007.8 verb nom sing masc part pres mid
εἰς	⸀ ἡμᾶς,	[b☆ ὑμᾶς,]	μὴ	βουλόμενός
eis	*hēmas*	*humas*	*mē*	*boulomenos*
toward	us,	[you]	not	willing

4948.9 indef-pron acc pl masc	616.26 verb inf aor mid	233.2 conj	3820.8 adj acc pl masc	1519.1 prep	3211.2 noun acc sing fem
τινας	ἀπολέσθαι,	ἀλλὰ	πάντας	εἰς	μετάνοιαν
tinas	*apolesthai*	*alla*	*pantas*	*eis*	*metanoian*
any	to perish,	but	all	to	repentance

10.a.**Txt:** 01ℵ,02A,018K 020L,025P,byz.Weis Sod
Var: 03B,04C,Lach Treg,Alf,Word,Tisc We/Ho,UBS/☆

5397.7 verb inf aor act	2223.7 verb 3sing indic fut act	1156.2 conj	3450.9 art nom sing fem	2232.2 noun nom sing fem	2935.2 noun gen sing masc
χωρῆσαι.	**10.** Ἥξει	δὲ	⸂a ἡ ⸃	ἡμέρα	κυρίου
chōrēsai	*Hēxei*	*de*	*hē*	*hēmera*	*kuriou*
to come.	Shall come	but	the	day	of Lord

10.b.**Txt:** 04C,018K 020L,byz.
Var: 01ℵ,02A,03B,025P 33,sa.bo.Gries,Lach Treg,Alf,Word,Tisc We/Ho,Weis,Sod UBS/☆

5453.1 conj	2785.1 noun nom sing masc	1706.1 prep	3433.3 noun dat sing fem	1706.1 prep	3614.11 rel-pron dat sing fem	3450.7 art nom pl masc
ὡς	κλέπτης	⸂b ἐν	νυκτί, ⸃	ἐν	ᾗ	οἱ
hōs	*kleptēs*	*en*	*nukti*	*en*	*hē*	*hoi*
as	a thief	in	night,	in	which	the

3636.6 noun nom pl masc	4357.1 adv	3790.14 verb 3pl indic fut mid	4598.1 noun pl neu
οὐρανοὶ	ῥοιζηδὸν	παρελεύσονται,	στοιχεῖα
ouranoi	*rhoizēdon*	*pareleusontai*	*stoicheia*
heavens	with rushing noise	shall pass away,	elements

10.c.**Txt:** 02A,018K 020L,byz.
Var: 01ℵ,03B,04C,025P Lach,Treg,Tisc,We/Ho Weis,Sod,UBS/☆

1156.2 conj	2712.1 verb pl neu part pres mid	3061.27 verb 3pl indic fut pass	3061.26 verb 3sing indic fut pass
δὲ	καυσούμενα	⸀ λυθήσονται,	[c☆ λυθήσεται,]
de	*kausoumena*	*luthēsontai*	*luthēsetai*
and	burning with heat	shall be dissolved,	[idem]

2504.1 conj	1087.1 noun nom sing fem	2504.1 conj	3450.17 art pl neu	1706.1 prep	840.11 prs-pron dat sing fem	2024.4 noun pl neu
καὶ	γῆ	καὶ	τὰ	ἐν	αὐτῇ	ἔργα
kai	*gē*	*kai*	*ta*	*en*	*autē*	*erga*
and	earth	and	the	in	it	works

God is very long-suffering. He quoted from Psalm 90:4 to show a thousand years is not very long to the eternal God. When the Bible says "the end of all things is at hand" (1 Peter 4:7), it may mean tomorrow or it may mean a thousand years from now. So believers should not grow impatient if Christ's coming is not as soon as they expect. God's timetable is not synchronized with any earthly clock. Scoffers are ignorant of this. They view time from the standpoint of their own short lives and not from God's standpoint. However long it might be "since the fathers fell asleep" (verse 4), it is not very long in God's sight. Paul evidently expected Christ to return in his own lifetime. He wrote, "We which are alive and remain . . ." (1 Thessalonians 4:17). When it became apparent that he would die prior to Christ's coming, it did not trouble him. He still rejoiced in the crown of righteousness reserved for him and for all those who "love his (Christ's) appearing" (2 Timothy 4:6-8).

that one day [is] with the Lord as a thousand years, and a thousand years as one day: . . . may be equivalent to, *Wade* . . . as a single day, *Fenton.*

3:9. There is a good reason why Christ has not yet returned. He does not wish for anyone to perish. Some will perish (verse 7), but that is not His desire. He patiently provides time and opportunity through the preaching of the gospel, and this is the only reason for the seeming delay in coming as He promised. He is not "slack" (*bradunei,* slow, remiss, tardy) in doing so, but is "long-suffering" (*makrothumei,* forbearing, enduring patiently) toward mankind. Instead of "us-ward," the Greek should be translated "you-ward." "Willing" is *boulomenos,* meaning choice, preference, being so minded; as in 2 Corinthians 1:15, "I was minded to come unto you."

9. The Lord is not slack concerning his promise: . . . not slow in fulfilling, *Norlie* . . . about keeping, *NLT* . . . does not loiter over his promise, *Montgomery* . . . does not delay, *Fenton* . . . is not tardy, *Concordant* . . . to fulfil his promise, *TNT* . . . to do what he has promised, *Williams C.K.*

as some men count slackness: . . . as some people consider him slow, *TCNT.*

but is longsuffering to us-ward: . . . is very patient, *Laubach* . . . is patient with you, *SEB* . . . because of you, *Concordant.*

not willing that any should perish, but that all should come to repentance: . . . does not want anyone to be lost, *TNT* . . . that everyone should be prevailed on to repent, *Norlie* . . . but all to make room for, *Concordant* . . . have an opportunity to repent, *Williams* . . . should come to Reformation, *Wilson.*

3:10. The Day of the Lord will certainly come (the Greek verb carries a positive emphasis). Believers need to remember this and be ready at all times; unbelievers need to realize it also, or they will suffer at the hands of a "thief in the night." Paul used this same expression in 1 Thessalonians 5:2 concerning the Lord's coming. Jesus warned of it, admonishing His disciples to be ready always, "for in such an hour as ye think not the Son of man cometh" (Matthew 24:44). "The day of the Lord" is not a single event but the period of time including the Second Coming, the tribulation period, and the establishment of Christ's kingdom. Peter skipped over all the intervening events and dealt with the final scene when the heavens shall pass away and the earth be burned up. "Elements" is *stoicheia* (basic parts, components). Some say it refers to stars and planets, others to the four elements of which the universe is composed (fire, air, earth, water). Although the atomic structure of chemical elements was not understood in Peter's day, his language may be interpreted in the light of these elements of which all matter is constituted. The picture is one of total destruction of the heavens and the earth.

10. But the day of the Lord will come as a thief in the night: . . . will approach like, *Fenton* . . . will be arriving, *Concordant* . . . will come suddenly and unexpectedly, *Noli* . . . as a robber comes, *NLT.*

in the which the heavens shall pass away with a great noise: . . . the heavenly bodies will burn up and be destroyed, *Williams C.K.* . . . with a crash, *TCNT* . . . in a roaring crash, *Norlie* . . . a shrieking noise, *Adams* . . . rushing, *Darby* . . . whizzing, *SEB* . . . booming, *Concordant.*

and the elements shall melt with fervent heat: . . . and their constituents will be dissolved, *Fenton* . . . by combustion, *Concordant.*

the earth also and the works that are therein shall be burned up: . . . the works in it shall be found, *Concordant* . . . utterly, *Campbell.*

10.d.**Txt:** 02A,020L,byz.lect.bo.Tisc
Var: 01ℵ,03B,018K,025P,Treg,We/Ho,Weis,Sod,UBS/☆

11.a.**Txt:** 01ℵ,02A,018K,020L,byz.it.bo.Tisc
Var: p72,03B,04C,025P,Alf,We/Ho,Weis,Sod,UBS/☆

11.b.**Txt:** p72-corr2,01ℵ-corr2,02A,04C,018K,020L,025P,sa.byz.We/Ho
Var: p72-org,p74,03B,1175

2588.8 verb 3sing indic fut pass	**2128.48** verb 3sing indic fut pass	**3642.2** dem-pron gen pl	**3631.1** partic
⸀ κατακαήσεται.	[d☆ εὑρεθήσεται.]	**11.** Τούτων	⸀ οὖν
katakaēsetai	*heurethēsetai*	*Toutōn*	*oun*
shall be burnt up.	[will be discovered.]	These things	then

3643.1 adv	**3820.4** adj gen pl	**3061.17** verb gen pl neu part pres mid	**4076.3** intr-pron acc pl masc	**1158.1** verb 3sing indic pres act
[a☆ οὕτως]	πάντων	λυομένων,	ποταποὺς	δεῖ
houtōs	*pantōn*	*luomenōn*	*potapous*	*dei*
[thus]	all	being to be dissolved,	what kind of	ought

5062.11 verb inf pres act	**5050.4** prs-pron acc 2pl	**1706.1** prep	**39.15** adj dat pl fem	**389.4** noun dat pl fem	**2504.1** conj
ὑπάρχειν	⸂b ὑμᾶς ⸃	ἐν	ἁγίαις	ἀναστροφαῖς	καὶ
huparchein	*humas*	*en*	*hagiais*	*anastrophais*	*kai*
to be	you	in	holy	life-style	and

2131.5 noun dat pl fem	**4186.7** verb acc pl masc part pres act	**2504.1** conj	**4545.1** verb acc pl masc part pres act	**3450.12** art acc sing fem
εὐσεβείαις,	**12.** προσδοκῶντας	καὶ	σπεύδοντας	τὴν
eusebeiais	*prosdokōntas*	*kai*	*speudontas*	*tēn*
godliness,	expecting	and	hastening	the

3814.4 noun acc sing fem	**3450.10** art gen sing fem	**3450.2** art gen sing	**2296.2** noun gen sing masc	**2232.1** noun fem	**1217.1** prep
παρουσίαν	τῆς	τοῦ	θεοῦ	ἡμέρας	δι'
parousian	*tēs*	*tou*	*theou*	*hēmeras*	*di'*
coming	of the		of God	day	by reason of

3614.12 rel-pron acc sing fem	**3636.6** noun nom pl masc	**4306.2** verb nom pl masc part pres mid	**3061.27** verb 3pl indic fut pass	**2504.1** conj
ἣν	οὐρανοὶ	πυρούμενοι	λυθήσονται,	καὶ
hēn	*ouranoi*	*puroumenoi*	*luthēsontai*	*kai*
which	heavens,	being on fire,	shall be dissolved,	and

4598.1 noun pl neu	**2712.1** verb pl neu part pres mid	**4928.1** verb 3sing indic pres mid	**2508.2** adj acc pl masc	**1156.2** conj
στοιχεῖα	καυσούμενα	τήκεται;	**13.** καινοὺς	δὲ
stoicheia	*kausoumena*	*tēketai*	*kainous*	*de*
elements	burning with heat	shall melt?	New	but

3636.9 noun acc pl masc	**2504.1** conj	**1087.4** noun acc sing fem	**2508.5** adj acc sing fem	**2567.3** prep	**3450.16** art sing neu
οὐρανοὺς	καὶ	γῆν	καινὴν	κατὰ	τὸ
ouranous	*kai*	*gēn*	*kainēn*	*kata*	*to*
heavens	and	earth	a new	according to	the

1847.1 noun sing neu	**840.3** prs-pron gen sing	**4186.1** verb 1pl pres act	**1706.1** prep	**3614.4** rel-pron dat pl
ἐπάγγελμα	αὐτοῦ	προσδοκῶμεν,	ἐν	οἷς
epangelma	*autou*	*prosdokōmen*	*en*	*hois*
promise	his,	we expect,	in	which

1336.1 noun nom sing fem	**2700.2** verb 3sing indic pres act	**1346.1** conj	**27.6** adj pl masc	**3642.18** dem-pron pl neu
δικαιοσύνη	κατοικεῖ.	**14.** Διό,	ἀγαπητοί,	ταῦτα
dikaiosunē	*katoikei*	*Dio*	*agapētoi*	*tauta*
righteousness	dwells.	Wherefore,	beloved,	these things

4186.5 verb nom pl masc part pres act	**4557.6** verb 2pl impr aor act	**778.3** adj nom pl masc	**2504.1** conj	**296.1** adj nom pl masc
προσδοκῶντες,	σπουδάσατε	ἄσπιλοι	καὶ	ἀμώμητοι
prosdokōntes	*spoudasate*	*aspiloi*	*kai*	*amōmētoi*
expecting	be diligent	without spot	and	unblamable

3:11. Peter was more concerned with believers' spiritual condition than with details of what will happen to the heavens and earth. Since this judgment by fire is coming, he says they need to examine their hearts and lives. "Conversation" is *anastrophais* (manner of life, behavior). "Godliness" is *eusebeiais* (holiness, piety, reverence, devoutness). "Dissolved" is *luomenōn* (loosen, disintegrate, melt). It is the New Testament word that best describes atomic disintegration. It is also translated "melt" in 3:12. Since we have become familiar with nuclear power, we know something of "meltdowns," and we can imagine what will take place when all the atoms are smashed. Our knowledge of atomic explosions gives us some idea of the "great noise" (verse 10) which will result from the breakup of all matter.

3:12. The Flood destroyed the earth but not the heavens. Here it says that when the earth is destroyed by fire, the heavens also will be affected: "The heavens being on fire shall be dissolved." So the scoffers are in for an even bigger surprise: there will be a complete destruction by fire, as compared with the partial judgment of the Flood. "Hasting" is *speudontas*, meaning eagerly awaiting as well as speeding. It also carries a sense of hastening His coming. We can do this by going into all the world and preaching the gospel to every creature (Mark 16:15). The purpose of the long-suffering of the Lord (3:9) is to give opportunity for every person on earth to hear the gospel and be saved. This challenge that faced Peter's generation has faced every generation since.

3:13. Believers should not be preoccupied with the flaming destruction of the present heavens and earth but should be looking for new heavens and a new earth in which "righteousness" (*dikaiosunē*, holiness, innocence, equity) "dwelleth" (*katoikei*, reside, make its home). "New" is from *kainos*, meaning fresh. The new heavens and new earth will have a new quality. Some say the heavens and earth will be renewed, rather than being replaced with something brand new. On this question Stanley M. Horton states: "A good case can be made here (verse 10) for taking this as a renovation of the heavens and earth rather than an annihilation. The Bible does speak of 'everlasting hills' (Genesis 49:26; Habakkuk 3:6); the earth 'established forever' (Psalms 78:69; 104:5; 125:1,2), and 'abiding forever' (Ecclesiastes 1:4)" (p.118). Horton goes on to say: "Since fire is often used in the Bible of cleansing or purifying, it may be taken that the heavens and earth are simply renovated, renewed, and restored to a better state by going through the fire" (ibid.).

3:14. Peter exhorted, "Be diligent" (*spoudasate*, eager, zealous, earnest, prompt). The word speaks of intense effort, as in 2 Tim-

11. [Seeing] then [that] all these things shall be dissolved: In view of the fact that all of these things, *Phillips* . . . Since the world will end like this, *Laubach* . . . If the whole universe is to be dissolved in this way, *TNT* . . . All these things in this manner being in process of dissolution, *Wuest.*

what manner [of persons] ought ye to be in [all] holy conversation and godliness: Surely men of good and holy character, *Phillips* . . . to what manner of men must you belong in holy behavior and devoutness, *Concordant* . . . what exotic persons is it necessary in the nature of the case for you to be in the sphere of holy behaviors and pieties, *Wuest* . . . in conduct, *Norlie.*

12. Looking for and hasting unto the coming of the day of God: . . . who live expecting and earnestly longing for, *Phillips* . . . expecting, and earnestly desiring, *Campbell* . . . hoping for and hurrying the presence of God's day, *Concordant.*

wherein the heavens being on fire shall be dissolved: . . . this day will mean that the heavens will disappear in fire, *Phillips.*

and the elements shall melt with fervent heat?: . . . and the stars to melt in the heat, *TNT* . . . elements burning up are being melted, *Wuest* . . . decompose by combustion! *Concordant* . . . through intense heat, *Wade.*

13. Nevertheless we, according to his promise: . . . but our hopes are not set on these, *Phillips.*

look for new heavens and a new earth, wherein dwelleth righteousness: . . . are hoping for, *Concordant* . . . new in quality, *Wuest* . . . will reign, *Noli* . . . in which nothing but good shall live, *Phillips.*

14. Wherefore, beloved, seeing that ye look for such things: So, dear friends, *TNT* . . . On which account, divinely loved ones, *Wuest* . . . while you are waiting, *Norlie* . . . in expectation of these things, *TCNT* . . . whilst you are awaiting these events, *Wade* . . . hoping for these things, *Concordant* . . . for this transformation, *Noli.*

840.4 prs-pron dat sing	**2128.41** verb inf aor pass	**1706.1** prep	**1503.3** noun dat sing fem	**15.** **2504.1** conj	**3450.12** art acc sing fem	**3450.2** art gen sing
αὐτῷ	εὑρεθῆναι	ἐν	εἰρήνῃ,	καὶ	τὴν	τοῦ
autō	*heurethēnai*	*en*	*eirēnē*	*kai*	*tēn*	*tou*
by him	to be found	in	peace;	and	the	of the

2935.2 noun gen sing masc	**2231.2** prs-pron gen 1pl	**3087.4** noun acc sing fem	**4843.3** noun acc sing fem	**2216.3** verb 2pl impr pres mid
κυρίου	ἡμῶν	μακροθυμίαν,	σωτηρίαν	ἡγεῖσθε·
kuriou	*hēmōn*	*makrothumian*	*sōtērian*	*hēgeisthe*
Lord	our	patient,	salvation	count you;

2503.1 conj	**2504.1** conj	**3450.5** art nom sing masc	**27.3** adj nom sing masc	**2231.2** prs-pron gen 1pl	**79.1** noun nom sing masc
καθὼς	καὶ	ὁ	ἀγαπητὸς	ἡμῶν	ἀδελφὸς
kathōs	*kai*	*ho*	*agapētos*	*hēmōn*	*adelphos*
according as	also	the	beloved	our	brother

3834.1 name nom masc	**2567.3** prep	**3450.12** art acc sing fem	**840.4** prs-pron dat sing	**1319.51** verb acc sing fem part aor pass
Παῦλος	κατὰ	τὴν	⸂ αὐτῷ	δοθεῖσαν
Paulos	*kata*	*tēn*	*autō*	*dotheisan*
Paul	according to	the	to him	having been given

1319.51 verb acc sing fem part aor pass	**840.4** prs-pron dat sing	**4531.4** noun acc sing fem	**1119.8** verb 3sing indic aor act	**5050.3** prs-pron dat 2pl
[☆ δοθεῖσαν	αὐτῷ]	σοφίαν	ἔγραψεν	ὑμῖν,
dotheisan	*autō*	*sophian*	*egrapsen*	*humin*
[having been given	to him]	wisdom	wrote	to you,

16.a.**Txt:** 01ℵ,018K 020L,025P,byz.Tisc,Sod
Var: 02A,03B,04C,33 Lach,Treg,Alf,Word We/Ho,Weis,UBS/☆

16. **5453.1** conj	**2504.1** conj	**1706.1** prep	**3820.15** adj dat pl fem	**3450.14** art dat pl fem	**1976.7** noun dat pl fem
ὡς	καὶ	ἐν	πάσαις	⸂a ταῖς ⸃	ἐπιστολαῖς,
hōs	*kai*	*en*	*pasais*	*tais*	*epistolais*
as	also	in	all	the	epistles,

2953.12 verb nom sing masc part pres act	**1706.1** prep	**840.14** prs-pron dat pl fem	**3875.1** prep	**3642.2** dem-pron gen pl
λαλῶν	ἐν	αὐταῖς	περὶ	τούτων·
lalōn	*en*	*autais*	*peri*	*toutōn*
speaking	in	them	concerning	these things,

16.b.**Txt:** 04C,018K 020L,025P,byz.
Var: 01ℵ,02A,03B,33 Lach,Treg,Alf,Word Tisc,We/Ho,Weis,Sod UBS/☆

1706.1 prep	**3614.4** rel-pron dat pl	**3614.14** rel-pron dat pl fem	**1498.4** verb 3sing indic pres act	**1418.1** adj pl neu
ἐν	⸂ οἷς	[b☆ αἷς]	ἐστιν	δυσνόητά
en	*hois*	*hais*	*estin*	*dusnoēta*
among	which	[idem]	are	hard to be understood

4948.5 indef-pron	**3614.17** rel-pron pl neu	**3450.7** art nom pl masc	**259.1** adj nom pl masc	**2504.1** conj	**787.1** adj nom pl masc
τινα,	ἃ	οἱ	ἀμαθεῖς	καὶ	ἀστήρικτοι
tina	*ha*	*hoi*	*amatheis*	*kai*	*astēriktoi*
some things,	which	the	untaught	and	unestablished

4612.1 verb 3pl indic pres act	**5453.1** conj	**2504.1** conj	**3450.15** art acc pl fem	**3036.6** adj acc pl fem	**1118.8** noun acc pl fem	**4242.1** prep
στρεβλοῦσιν,	ὡς	καὶ	τὰς	λοιπὰς	γραφὰς,	πρὸς
streblousin	*hōs*	*kai*	*tas*	*loipas*	*graphas*	*pros*
distort,	as	also	the	remaining	scriptures,	to

3450.12 art acc sing fem	**2375.11** adj acc sing fem	**840.1** prs-pron gen pl	**677.3** noun acc sing fem	**17.** **5050.1** prs-pron nom 2pl	**3631.1** partic
τὴν	ἰδίαν	αὐτῶν	ἀπώλειαν.	Ὑμεῖς	οὖν,
tēn	*idian*	*autōn*	*apōleian*	*Humeis*	*oun*
the	own	their	destruction.	You	therefore,

othy 2:15, "Study (*spoudason*) to show thyself approved unto God." Since believers are expecting a new heaven and new earth pervaded with righteousness, they should prepare themselves to be occupants of such a home so when Christ comes He will find them living in peace, "without spot" (*aspiloi*, unblemished, unstained, undefiled) and "blameless" (*amōmētoi*, faultless, without flaw or blot, untainted by the world).

The second coming of Christ was the great incentive for holy living among believers in the First Century. Peter referred to it here, and Paul often did in his writings. In 1 Corinthians 1:8 he urged believers to be "blameless in the day of our Lord Jesus Christ." In Philippians 1:10 he spoke of being "sincere and without offense till the day of Christ." He also expressed the need for being blameless at Christ's coming in 1 Thessalonians 3:13 and 5:23.

3:15. Believers should refuse to be upset by scoffers, false teachers, or date setters, counting that the long-suffering of the Lord (His patience in granting more time before His coming) is due to His desire that all might repent and obtain salvation. Peter reminded them that Paul said the same thing in his writings. In Romans 2:4, for example: "Despisest thou the riches of his goodness and forbearance and long-suffering; not knowing that the goodness of God leadeth thee to repentance?"

3:16. Peter did not say he could not understand some things in Paul's epistles. He was thinking of people who are "unlearned" (*amatheis*, ignorant) and "unstable" (*astēriktoi*, unfixed, vacillating), who take Scripture passages that seem unclear and "wrest" them (*streblousin*, twist out of context, strain, stretch). They "pervert the gospel of Christ," as Paul said (Galatians 1:7). They even teach people to "continue in sin, that grace may abound" (Romans 6:1), twisting the doctrine of grace. Peter said such teachers bring destruction upon themselves.

This is an important passage, for it shows that Peter considered Paul's writings, like the other Scriptures, to be inspired of God.

3:17. Peter summed up his appeal three times in his final chapter: in verse 11, "Seeing then that all these things shall be dissolved"; in verse 14, "Seeing that ye look for such things"; and verse 17, "Seeing ye know these things before." He saw the need to keep emphasizing basic truths and to keep fortifying believers. Peter had told them many things and had also reminded them of the things Paul taught them. Since they had been forewarned and forearmed with truth concerning all these matters, they were without excuse if they should "fall" (*ekpesēte*, drop away, fall out of, as in Galatians

be diligent that ye may be found of him in peace: . . . do your best, *Wuest* . . . endeavor to be found by Him in peace, *Concordant.*

without spot, and blameless: . . . irreproachable, *Wuest* . . . spotless, *Berkeley* . . . unspotted and flawless, *Concordant* . . . clean and blameless in his sight, *Phillips.*

15. And account [that] the longsuffering of our Lord [is] salvation: . . . consider it as, *Wuest* . . . the continued patience of our Lord for your salvation, *Berkeley* . . . Meanwhile, consider that God's patience is meant to be man's salvation, *Phillips* . . . be deeming the patience of our Lord salvation, *Concordant.*

even as our beloved brother Paul also according to the wisdom given unto him hath written unto you: Paul pointed out in his letter to you, written out of the wisdom God gave him, *Phillips.*

16. As also in all [his] epistles, speaking in them of these things: . . . in his inspired wisdom wrote to you, *TNT* . . . as also in all his letters, speaking in them concerning these things, *Wuest* . . . indeed in all his letters, he referred to these matters, *Phillips* . . . and as well in all the letters in which he mentions these subjects, *Berkeley.*

in which are some things hard to be understood: . . . there are some obscure passages, *Noli* . . . things difficult of being understood, *Wuest* . . . difficult to comprehend, *Wade* . . . hard to apprehend, *Concordant* . . . are hard to think through, *Berkeley.*

which they that are unlearned and unstable wrest: . . . which, unhappily, ill-informed and unbalanced people distort, *Phillips* . . . which the Uninstructed and Unstable pervert, *Wilson* . . . those who are unlearned and lacking stability distort, *Wuest* . . . The untaught and unsteady twist those writings, *Berkeley* . . . of weak character twist, *TCNT* . . . the fickle distort, *Fenton* . . . pervert their meaning, *TNT.*

as [they do] also the other scriptures, unto their own destruction: . . . to their own ruin, *Berkeley.*

27.6 adj pl masc	4126.1 verb nom pl masc part pres act	5278.16 verb 2pl impr pres mid	2419.1 conj	3231.1 partic
ἀγαπητοί,	προγινώσκοντες	φυλάσσεσθε,	ἵνα	μὴ
agapētoi	proginōskontes	phulassesthe	hina	mē
beloved,	knowing beforehand,	beware,	so that	not

3450.11 art dat sing fem	3450.1 art gen pl	113.1 adj gen pl masc	3967.3 noun dat sing fem	4730.3 verb nom pl masc part aor pass
τῇ	τῶν	ἀθέσμων	πλάνῃ	συναπαχθέντες,
tē	tōn	athesmōn	planē	sunapachthentes
with the	of the	lawless	error	having been led away,

1588.6 verb 2pl subj aor act	3450.2 art gen sing	2375.2 adj gen sing	4591.1 noun gen sing masc		831.3 verb 2pl impr pres act
ἐκπέσητε	τοῦ	ἰδίου	στηριγμοῦ·	18.	αὐξάνετε
ekpesēte	tou	idiou	stērigmou		auxanete
you should fall from	the	your own	steadfastness:		grow

1156.2 conj	1706.1 prep	5322.3 noun dat sing fem	2504.1 conj	1102.3 noun dat sing fem	3450.2 art gen sing	2935.2 noun gen sing masc
δὲ	ἐν	χάριτι	καὶ	γνώσει	τοῦ	κυρίου
de	en	chariti	kai	gnōsei	tou	kuriou
but	in	grace,	and	in knowledge	of the	Lord

2231.2 prs-pron gen 1pl	2504.1 conj	4842.2 noun gen sing masc	2400.2 name masc	5382.2 name gen masc	840.4 prs-pron dat sing
ἡμῶν	καὶ	σωτῆρος	Ἰησοῦ	Χριστοῦ.	αὐτῷ
hēmōn	kai	sōtēros	Iēsou	Christou	autō
our	and	Saviour	Jesus	Christ.	To him

3450.9 art nom sing fem	1385.1 noun nom sing fem	2504.1 conj	3431.1 adv	2504.1 conj	1519.1 prep	2232.4 noun acc sing fem	163.1 noun gen sing masc
ἡ	δόξα	καὶ	νῦν	καὶ	εἰς	ἡμέραν	αἰῶνος.
hē	doxa	kai	nun	kai	eis	hēmeran	aiōnos
the	glory	both	now	and	to	day	of age.

279.1 intrj
(a ἀμήν.)
amēn
Amen.

18.a.**Txt:** p72,01ℵ,02A 04C,018K,020L,025P byz.it.sa.bo.Sod
Var: 03B,1241,Tisc We/Ho,Weis,UBS/*

5:4, "Ye are fallen from grace") from their "steadfastness" (*stērigmou*, stability, firmness); so they needed to "beware" (*phulassesthe*, be on guard, a military term). Believers never outlive their need of watchfulness. Paul reminded the Corinthians how Israel failed time after time, and added, "Wherefore let him that thinketh he standeth take heed lest he fall" (1 Corinthians 10:12). Peter indicated the danger is that believers may be "led away" (*sunapachthentes*, seduced, carried off) by the "error" (*planē*, straying, wandering) of the "wicked" (*athesmōn*, lawless). Those who "live in error" (2:18) are those who indulge the lusts of the flesh. Peter suggested that people who are weak along this line can be trapped again and again. He warned against these carnal people in the Church and indicated the believers would be carried away with them unless they remained firm in their faith and commitment to Christ.

It is not easy to breast the tide of compromise when others lower their standards and follow the ways of the world; but "God is faithful, who will not suffer you to be tempted above that ye are able; but will with the temptation also make a way to escape, that ye may be able to bear it" (1 Corinthians 10:13).

3:18. Rather than that they should fall from their steadfastness, Peter admonished them to keep on growing in grace and in the personal, experiential knowledge of Christ. They could know Him not only as "Jesus" (*Iēsou*, Jehovah-saved, the One who saves His people from their sins) and as "Christ" (*Christou*, the Messiah, the One anointed of God to lead His people), but also as "Lord" (*kuriou*, Master, Controller, the One supreme in authority) and as "Saviour" (*sōtēros*, Deliverer, Protector, Preserver, Healer, the One who makes a person whole in body, mind, and spirit). They needed to keep growing in this knowledge, for the best defense against falling is to keep growing stronger. To Christ be "glory" (*doxa*, praise, honor, radiant splendor) both now and for "ever" (*aiōnos*, perpetually, "unto the day of eternity"). If believers follow Peter's instructions and keep growing in virtue, knowledge, temperance, patience, godliness, brotherly kindness, and charity (1:5-7), they will indeed bring glory to Christ. "Amen" (verily, so be it).

17. Ye therefore, beloved, seeing ye know [these things] before: . . . my friends whom I love, are forewarned, *Phillips* . . . dear friends, forewarned as you are, *Berkeley* . . . my loved ones, having knowledge of these things before they take place, *BB* . . . since you have been warned, *Greber* . . . you already know about this, *Everyday* . . . now that you are forewarned, *Norlie* . . . before they happen, *Laubach* . . . knowing in advance, *Swann.*

beware lest ye also, being led away with the error of the wicked: . . . be on guard, *Swann* . . . be careful not to be carried away, *Williams C.K.* . . . be constantly...lest having been carried away by the error of unprincipled men, *Wuest* . . . Do not let those evil people lead you away by the wrong they do, *Everyday* . . . Do not be led astray by idle fancies arising from the errors of godless people, *Greber* . . . take care that you are not turned away by the error of the uncontrolled, *BB* . . . so that you may not be carried away by the stray wanderings of, *Berkeley* . . . by the deceit of the lawless, *Campbell* . . . with the deception of the dissolute, *Concordant* . . . by the errors of lawless men, *Williams* . . . wicked men, *Phillips.*

fall from your own stedfastness: . . . and so lapsing from your present stedfastness, *TCNT* . . . so that you may not lose your firm stand, *Greber* . . . so that you will not fall from your strong faith, *Everyday* . . . Never let them shake your solid faith, *Laubach* . . . and so lose your proper foothold, *Phillips* . . . slip from your own moorings, *Berkeley* . . . from your true faith, *BB.*

18. But grow in grace, and [in] the knowledge of our Lord and Saviour Jesus Christ: But progress in goodness, *Fenton* . . . be constantly growing in the sphere of grace and an experiential knowledge, *Wuest.*

To him [be] glory both now and for ever. Amen: Glory be to him, *Everyday* . . . and unto the Day of Eternity, *Montgomery* . . . as well as for the day of the eon, *Concordant* . . . and until the dawning of the day of eternity! *Phillips* . . . from now until an appointed day in a future era, *Greber.*

THE FIRST EPISTLE OF JOHN

Expanded Interlinear
Textual Critical Apparatus
Verse-by-Verse Commentary
Various Versions

1976.1 noun nom sing fem	2464.2 name gen masc	4272.9 num ord nom sing fem
Ἐπιστολὴ	Ἰωάννου	Πρώτη
Epistolē	*Iōannou*	*Prōtē*
Epistle	of John	First

Textual Apparatus

3614.16 rel-pron sing neu	1498.34 verb sing indic imperf act	570.2 prep	741.2 noun gen sing fem	3614.16 rel-pron sing neu
1:1. Ὃ	ἦν	ἀπ'	ἀρχῆς,	ὃ
Ho	*ēn*	*ap'*	*archēs*	*ho*
What	was	from	beginning,	what

189.38 verb 1pl indic perf act	3614.16 rel-pron sing neu	3571.12 verb 1pl indic perf act	3450.4 art dat pl	3652.7 noun dat pl masc
ἀκηκόαμεν,	ὃ	ἑωράκαμεν	τοῖς	ὀφθαλμοῖς
akēkoamen	*ho*	*heōrakamen*	*tois*	*ophthalmois*
we have heard,	what	we have seen	with the	eyes

2231.2 prs-pron gen 1pl	3614.16 rel-pron sing neu	2277.3 verb 1pl indic aor mid	2504.1 conj	3450.13 art nom pl fem	5331.5 noun nom pl fem	2231.2 prs-pron gen 1pl
ἡμῶν,	ὃ	ἐθεασάμεθα	καὶ	αἱ	χεῖρες	ἡμῶν
hēmōn	*ho*	*etheasametha*	*kai*	*hai*	*cheires*	*hēmōn*
our,	what	we gazed upon	and	the	hands	our

5419.1 verb 3pl indic aor act	3875.1 prep	3450.2 art gen sing	3030.2 noun gen sing masc	3450.10 art gen sing fem	2205.2 noun gen sing fem
ἐψηλάφησαν	περὶ	τοῦ	λόγου	τῆς	ζωῆς·
epsēlaphēsan	*peri*	*tou*	*logou*	*tēs*	*zōēs*
handled	concerning	the	Word	of the	life;

2504.1 conj	3450.9 art nom sing fem	2205.1 noun nom sing fem	5157.10 verb 3sing indic aor pass	2504.1 conj	3571.12 verb 1pl indic perf act
2. καὶ	ἡ	ζωὴ	ἐφανερώθη,	καὶ	ἑωράκαμεν,
kai	*hē*	*zōē*	*ephanerōthē*	*kai*	*heōrakamen*
and	the	life	was manifested,	and	we have seen,

2504.1 conj	3113.4 verb 1pl indic pres act	2504.1 conj	514.1 verb 1pl indic pres act	5050.3 prs-pron dat 2pl	3450.12 art acc sing fem
καὶ	μαρτυροῦμεν,	καὶ	ἀπαγγέλλομεν	ὑμῖν	τὴν
kai	*marturoumen*	*kai*	*apangellomen*	*humin*	*tēn*
and	bear witness,	and	report	to you	the

2205.4 noun acc sing fem	3450.12 art acc sing fem	164.1 adj sing	3610.3 rel-pron nom sing fem	1498.34 verb sing indic imperf act	4242.1 prep
ζωὴν	τὴν	αἰώνιον,	ἥτις	ἦν	πρὸς
zōēn	*tēn*	*aiōnion*	*hētis*	*ēn*	*pros*
life	the	eternal,	which	was	with

3450.6 art acc sing masc	3824.4 noun acc sing masc	2504.1 conj	5157.10 verb 3sing indic aor pass	2231.3 prs-pron dat 1pl	3614.16 rel-pron sing neu
τὸν	πατέρα,	καὶ	ἐφανερώθη	ἡμῖν·	3. ὃ
ton	*patera*	*kai*	*ephanerōthē*	*hēmin*	*ho*
the	Father,	and	was manifested	to us:	what

3.a.**Var:** 01ℵ,02A,03B 04C,025P,33,sa.Lach Treg,Alf,Word,Tisc We/Ho,Weis,Sod UBS/☆

3571.12 verb 1pl indic perf act	2504.1 conj	189.38 verb 1pl indic perf act	514.1 verb 1pl indic pres act	2504.1 conj
ἑωράκαμεν	καὶ	ἀκηκόαμεν,	ἀπαγγέλλομεν	[a☆+ καὶ]
heōrakamen	*kai*	*akēkoamen*	*apangellomen*	*kai*
we have seen	and	have heard	we report	[also]

THE FIRST EPISTLE OF JOHN

1:1. First John is a gateway to the New Testament, presenting the deepest truths in the simplest terms.

The book omits the usual greeting, perhaps because it was intended for a general audience, traditionally the churches in the area of Ephesus. Instead, John opened with a prologue (as in the Gospel of John) which presents his credentials as an eyewitness of Christ and explains his purpose for writing.

John began with a sentence that is not completed until verse 3. His first topic is the Word of life. As in John 1, "the Word" is a title for Jesus Christ, the One who reveals the mind of God to men.

The Word existed from "the beginning," all the way back into eternity (cf. John 1:1). John and the other apostles had both heard and seen the Word, an experience that had given them knowledge which still remained with them (as shown by the Greek perfect tense of the verbs). They could even look back on specific incidents when they inspected the Word carefully; "looked upon" describes an intense scrutiny, and "handled" describes the type of physical contact recorded in John 20:27.

1:2. The second verse is a parenthesis, describing the "life" more fully. John asserted that his ministry of witness was based on the historical event of Christ's appearance as a man. God became man, and the apostles simply testified to what they had experienced. They declared the truth, making an official announcement of what God had done.

The verse gives a more detailed description of "the life." Jesus displayed the kind of endless, glorious life which God himself possesses. After all, He exists "with the Father," a term with a root meaning of "face-to-face with." This intimate relationship was then made known to mankind through witnesses such as John.

1:3. After John finished his parenthesis, he repeated part of the first verse to help his readers pick up the threads of thought which began there. In the phrase "declare we unto you" John finished the main statement of the first verse. The purpose of the epistle was to make known the truth so the readers, as well as the apostles, could benefit from it.

Various Versions

1. That which was from the beginning, which we have heard: We are writing to you about something which has always existed, *Phillips* . . . Christ existed before time began, *Laubach*.

which we have seen with our eyes, which we have looked upon: . . . discerningly seen...gazed upon as a spectacle, *Wuest* . . . something which we had opportunity to observe closely, *Phillips* . . . we have watched it, *Williams C.K.* . . . we contemplated, *Darby*.

and our hands have handled, of the Word of life: . . . even to hold in our hands, *Berkeley* . . . touched with our own hands, *Montgomery* . . . the very message of life, *Williams* . . . Who is the Disclosure of the True Life, *Wade*.

2. (For the life was manifested, and we have seen [it]: That Life was actually made visible, *TCNT* . . . it was life which appeared before us, *Phillips* . . . has been revealed, *Berkeley* . . . seen it with discernment and have it in our mind's eye, *Wuest*.

and bear witness, and show unto you that eternal life: We can prove it, *SEB* . . . are testifying and reporting to you the life eonian, *Concordant* . . . are eyewitnesses of it, *Phillips* . . . are witnessing and are announcing to you, *Berkeley* . . . and bringing back to you a message concerning the life, *Wuest*.

which was with the Father, and was manifested unto us;): . . . which was face to face with, *Montgomery* . . . who existed with the Father, *Berkeley* . . . which is of such a nature as to have been in fellowship with the Father and was made visible to us, *Wuest*.

3. That which we have seen and heard declare we unto you: That which we have seen with discern-

5050.3 prs-pron dat 2pl	**2419.1** conj	**2504.1** conj	**5050.1** prs-pron nom 2pl	**2815.4** noun acc sing fem	**2174.9** verb 2pl subj pres act
ὑμῖν,	ἵνα	καὶ	ὑμεῖς	κοινωνίαν	ἔχητε
humin	*hina*	*kai*	*humeis*	*koinōnian*	*echēte*
to you,	that	also	you	fellowship	may have

3196.1 prep	**2231.2** prs-pron gen 1pl	**2504.1** conj	**3450.9** art nom sing fem	**2815.1** noun nom sing fem	**1156.2** conj	**3450.9** art nom sing fem
μεθ'	ἡμῶν·	καὶ	ἡ	κοινωνία	δὲ	ἡ
meth'	*hēmōn*	*kai*	*hē*	*koinōnia*	*de*	*hē*
with	us;	and	the	fellowship	indeed	the

2233.4 adj nom 1sing fem	**3196.3** prep	**3450.2** art gen sing	**3824.2** noun gen sing masc	**2504.1** conj	**3196.3** prep	**3450.2** art gen sing
ἡμετέρα	μετὰ	τοῦ	πατρὸς	καὶ	μετὰ	τοῦ
hēmetera	*meta*	*tou*	*patros*	*kai*	*meta*	*tou*
our	with	the	Father,	and	with	the

5048.2 noun gen sing masc	**840.3** prs-pron gen sing	**2400.2** name masc	**5382.2** name gen masc	**2504.1** conj	**3642.18** dem-pron pl neu
υἱοῦ	αὐτοῦ	Ἰησοῦ	Χριστοῦ·	4. καὶ	ταῦτα
huiou	*autou*	*Iēsou*	*Christou*	*kai*	*tauta*
Son	his	Jesus	Christ.	And	these things

4.a.**Txt:** 02A-corr,04C 018K,020L,byz.it.bo.
Var: 01ℵ,02A-org,03B 025P,33,Treg,Alf,Tisc We/Ho,Weis,Sod UBS/☆

1119.3 verb 1pl indic pres act	**5050.3** prs-pron dat 2pl	**2231.1** prs-pron nom 1pl	**2419.1** conj	**3450.9** art nom sing fem	**5315.1** noun nom sing fem
γράφομεν	ʼ ὑμῖν	[a☆ ἡμεῖς]	ἵνα	ἡ	χαρὰ
graphomen	*humin*	*hēmeis*	*hina*	*hē*	*chara*
we write	to you	[we]	that	the	joy

2231.2 prs-pron gen 1pl	**1498.10** verb 3sing subj pres act	**3997.32** verb nom sing fem part perf mid	**2504.1** conj	**3642.9** dem-pron nom sing fem
ἡμῶν	ᾖ	πεπληρωμένη.	5. Καὶ	ʼ αὕτη
hēmōn	*ē*	*peplērōmenē*	*Kai*	*hautē*
our	may be	having been fulfilled.	And	this

1498.4 verb 3sing indic pres act	**1498.4** verb 3sing indic pres act	**3642.9** dem-pron nom sing fem	**3450.9** art nom sing fem	**1845.2** noun nom sing fem
ἔστιν	[☆ ἔστιν	αὕτη]	ἡ	ʼ ἐπαγγελία
estin	*estin*	*hautē*	*hē*	*epangelia*
is	[is	the]	the	promise

5.a.**Txt:** 04C,025P,33 byz.sa.bo.
Var: 01ℵ-corr,02A,03B 018K,020L,Gries,Lach Treg,Alf,Word,Tisc We/Ho,Weis,Sod UBS/☆

31.1 noun nom sing fem	**3614.12** rel-pron acc sing fem	**189.38** verb 1pl indic perf act	**570.2** prep	**840.3** prs-pron gen sing	**2504.1** conj
[a☆ ἀγγελία]	ἣν	ἀκηκόαμεν	ἀπ'	αὐτοῦ,	καὶ
angelia	*hēn*	*akēkoamen*	*ap'*	*autou*	*kai*
[message]	which	we have heard	from	him,	and

310.1 verb 1pl indic pres act	**5050.3** prs-pron dat 2pl	**3617.1** conj	**3450.5** art nom sing masc	**2296.1** noun nom sing masc	**5295.1** noun sing neu
ἀναγγέλλομεν	ὑμῖν,	ὅτι	ὁ	θεὸς	φῶς
anangellomen	*humin*	*hoti*	*ho*	*theos*	*phōs*
announce	to you,	that		God	light

1498.4 verb 3sing indic pres act	**2504.1** conj	**4508.1** noun nom sing fem	**1706.1** prep	**840.4** prs-pron dat sing	**3620.2** partic	**1498.4** verb 3sing indic pres act
ἐστιν,	καὶ	σκοτία	ἐν	αὐτῷ	οὐκ	ἔστιν
estin	*kai*	*skotia*	*en*	*autō*	*ouk*	*estin*
is,	and	darkness	in	him	not	is

3625.4 num card nom fem	**1430.1** partic	**1500.9** verb 1pl subj aor act	**3617.1** conj	**2815.4** noun acc sing fem	**2174.5** verb 1pl indic pres act
οὐδεμία.	6. Ἐὰν	εἴπωμεν	ὅτι	κοινωνίαν	ἔχομεν
oudemia	*Ean*	*eipōmen*	*hoti*	*koinōnian*	*echomen*
none.	If	we should say	that	fellowship	we have

Such a proclamation has a purpose: to enable the readers to have fellowship with one another. The present tense of "have" (*echēte*) implies continual fellowship, the relationship based on things shared or held in common like the property of a married couple. For more detail see "koinōnia" in the *Greek-English Dictionary*. This concept of fellowship with other Christians is one of the two major themes of 1 John. The other is introduced in the latter part of the verse: true fellowship among Christians involves fellowship with God as well, both the Father and the Son.

Of all the believers John probably was the one who could understand and appreciate what this kind of fellowship could mean. He was one of the "inner circle," along with Peter and James, who had enjoyed special privileges; for example, witnessing the transfiguration of Jesus. He was very close to Jesus, possibly more than the other apostles (note in 1:1 how he refers to that relationship). He is referred to as "one of his disciples, whom Jesus loved" (John 13:23) and sat next to the Lord at the Last Supper. But he had enjoyed that fellowship for only a little more than 3 years; now he could enjoy it continually through the Spirit.

ment and at present is in our mind's eye, and that which we have heard and at present is ringing in our ears, we are reporting, *Wuest* . . . We repeat, we really saw and heard what we are now writing to you about, *Phillips* . . . We saw Him and we heard Him and are telling you, *Berkeley* . . . we are announcing to you, *Montgomery*.

that ye also may have fellowship with us: We want you to be with us in this, *Phillips* . . . that you may share the dear friendship with Him, *Laubach* . . . you may be participating jointly in common with us, *Wuest*.

and truly our fellowship [is] with the Father, and with his Son Jesus Christ: . . . this fellowship of ours is with, *Berkeley* . . . and our partnership is, *Montgomery* . . . The fellowship we share together is, *Everyday*.

1:4. The prologue climaxes with one of the goals of the epistle (see also 2:1; 5:13)—overflowing joy. While the first three verses deal with John's lifelong work of witness, verse 4 refers specifically to the purpose of this epistle.

John was writing to cause joy (as in John 16:24). He wanted joy for the readers, as some versions suggest. And he wanted to share that joy himself, rejoicing as he saw his spiritual children walking in fellowship with God (3 John 4).

The joy will be "full," a Greek idiom for joy that is filled to the brim and continues to stay full to the point of overflowing.

4. And these things write we unto you, that your joy may be full: We must write and tell you about it, because the more that fellowship extends, the greater the joy it brings to us who are already in it, *Phillips* . . . to make your joy complete, *Norlie* . . . our joy, having been filled completely full in times past may persist in that state of fullness through present time, *Wuest*.

1:5. John moved smoothly from the prologue into the first major strain of thought (1:5 to 2:11)—the truth that God is light, and those who want to have fellowship with Him must live in light. Jesus himself had taught this truth in general terms (cf. John 1:4-9; 3:19-21; 8:12; 9:5; 12:46). Because God is light, the believer must live a life of holiness and of transparency and openness toward God.

The verse concludes with a contrast. Darkness is the opposite of light and thus symbolizes moral evil. Since God is light, John used a double negative to state emphatically that there is no darkness in Him.

5. This then is the message which we have heard of him: Here, then, is the message we heard him give, *Phillips* . . . at present is ringing in our ears, *Wuest*.

and declare unto you: . . . and are proclaiming to you, *Swann* . . . We are passing it on to you, *NLT* . . . and announce to you, *Adams, Wilson* . . . are informing you, *Concordant* . . . bringing back tidings to you, *Wuest*.

that God is light, and in him is no darkness at all: God as to His nature is light, and darkness in Him does not exist, not even one particle, *Wuest* . . . in any measure, *Swann* . . . no darkness whatever, *Berkeley* . . . not the faintest shadow of darkness, *Phillips*.

1:6. The inspired writer developed his basic premise with a series of "if" statements that alternate between right and wrong ways of responding to God's light.

6. If we say that we have fellowship with him, and walk in darkness: Consequently, *Phillips* . . . If we assert that, *Wade* . . . If

3196.2 prep	**840.3** prs-pron gen sing	**2504.1** conj	**1706.1** prep	**3450.3** art dat sing	**4510.4** noun dat sing neu	**3906.7** verb 1pl subj pres act
μετ’	αὐτοῦ,	καὶ	ἐν	τῷ	σκότει	περιπατῶμεν,
met’	*autou*	*kai*	*en*	*tō*	*skotei*	*peripatōmen*
with	him,	and	in	the	darkness	should walk,

5409.2 verb 1pl indic pres mid	**2504.1** conj	**3620.3** partic	**4020.6** verb 1pl indic pres act	**3450.12** art acc sing fem	**223.4** noun acc sing fem
ψευδόμεθα,	καὶ	οὐ	ποιοῦμεν	τὴν	ἀλήθειαν·
pseudometha	*kai*	*ou*	*poioumen*	*tēn*	*alētheian*
we lie,	and	not	do practice	the	truth.

1430.1 partic	**1156.2** conj	**1706.1** prep	**3450.3** art dat sing	**5295.3** noun dat sing neu	**3906.7** verb 1pl subj pres act	**5453.1** conj
7. ἐὰν	δὲ	ἐν	τῷ	φωτὶ	περιπατῶμεν,	ὡς
ean	*de*	*en*	*tō*	*phōti*	*peripatōmen*	*hōs*
If	but	in	the	light	we should walk,	as

840.5 prs-pron nom sing masc	**1498.4** verb 3sing indic pres act	**1706.1** prep	**3450.3** art dat sing	**5295.3** noun dat sing neu	**2815.4** noun acc sing fem
αὐτός	ἐστιν	ἐν	τῷ	φωτί,	κοινωνίαν
autos	*estin*	*en*	*tō*	*phōti*	*koinōnian*
he	is	in	the	light,	fellowship

2174.5 verb 1pl indic pres act	**3196.2** prep	**238.1** prs-pron gen pl	**2504.1** conj	**3450.16** art sing neu	**129.1** noun sing neu	**2400.2** name masc
ἔχομεν	μετ’	ἀλλήλων,	καὶ	τὸ	αἷμα	Ἰησοῦ
echomen	*met’*	*allēlōn*	*kai*	*to*	*haima*	*Iēsou*
we have	with	one another,	and	the	blood	of Jesus

7.a.**Txt:** 02A,018K,020L byz.bo.
Var: 01ℵ,03B,04C,025P sa.Lach,Treg,Alf,Tisc We/Ho,Weis,Sod UBS/⋆

5382.2 name gen masc	**3450.2** art gen sing	**5048.2** noun gen sing masc	**840.3** prs-pron gen sing	**2483.2** verb 3sing indic pres act
⸂a Χριστοῦ⸃	τοῦ	υἱοῦ	αὐτοῦ	καθαρίζει
Christou	*tou*	*huiou*	*autou*	*katharizei*
Christ	the	Son	his	cleanses

2231.4 prs-pron acc 1pl	**570.3** prep	**3820.10** adj gen sing fem	**264.1** noun fem	**1430.1** partic	**1500.9** verb 1pl subj aor act
ἡμᾶς	ἀπὸ	πάσης	ἁμαρτίας.	8. ἐὰν	εἴπωμεν
hēmas	*apo*	*pasēs*	*hamartias*	*ean*	*eipōmen*
us	from	every	sin.	If	we should say

3617.1 conj	**264.4** noun acc sing fem	**3620.2** partic	**2174.5** verb 1pl indic pres act	**1431.8** prs-pron acc pl masc	**3966.2** verb 1pl indic pres act
ὅτι	ἁμαρτίαν	οὐκ	ἔχομεν,	ἑαυτοὺς	πλανῶμεν
hoti	*hamartian*	*ouk*	*echomen*	*heautous*	*planōmen*
that	sin	not	we have,	ourselves	we deceive,

2504.1 conj	**3450.9** art nom sing fem	**223.1** noun nom sing fem	**3620.2** partic	**1498.4** verb 3sing indic pres act	**1706.1** prep	**2231.3** prs-pron dat 1pl
καὶ	ἡ	ἀλήθεια	οὐκ	ἔστιν	ἐν	ἡμῖν.
kai	*hē*	*alētheia*	*ouk*	*estin*	*en*	*hēmin*
and	the	truth	not	is	in	us.

1430.1 partic	**3533.4** verb 1pl subj pres act	**3450.15** art acc pl fem	**264.1** noun fem	**2231.2** prs-pron gen 1pl
9. ἐὰν	ὁμολογῶμεν	τὰς	ἁμαρτίας	ἡμῶν,
ean	*homologōmen*	*tas*	*hamartias*	*hēmōn*
If	we should confess	the	sins	our,

3964.2 adj nom sing masc	**1498.4** verb 3sing indic pres act	**2504.1** conj	**1337.3** adj nom sing masc	**2419.1** conj	**856.14** verb 3sing subj aor act
πιστός	ἐστιν	καὶ	δίκαιος,	ἵνα	ἀφῇ
pistos	*estin*	*kai*	*dikaios*	*hina*	*aphē*
faithful	he is	and	righteous,	that	he may forgive

Verse 6 presents the first such approach: a man who claims fellowship with God yet habitually walks in darkness, hidden from the light of God. Both the claim to have fellowship with God and the walk that avoids His light are in the present tense, showing habitual action. Such a claim is absurd because the two claims are incompatible.

Such a contradictory combination of words and deeds reveals a deep-seated problem of falsehood. The person is a liar in word as well, for his actions are in stark contrast to the claim he has made.

1:7. In contrast to one who merely claims to have fellowship with God, John put forward the case of one who demonstrates the reality of his fellowship with God by a righteous manner of life. This person continually (present tense) walks in the light. God expects each believer to stay on a path of life that is in the sphere of His light, in line with His holy character.

The result of such a holy life is twofold. First, we have fellowship—not only with God, as one might expect, but with each other. Both kinds of fellowship are tied together, as 1:3 declares, and genuine intimacy with God is the only possible basis for deep fellowship with other Christians.

Second, openness to the light cleanses sins, not only through admission to heaven, but as a continual cleansing process in the present life—one needed for any sin.

1:8. A second group of people claims to have no sin, declaring the sin is not a continuing part of their life or their human nature. They may fall into an occasional misstep, but nothing serious enough to deserve the epithet "sinner."

Anyone who believes such a statement is more than a liar; he is deluding himself. "Ourselves" holds an emphatic position, because such people are not innocent victims; they take the lead in deceiving themselves. The New Testament uses "deceive" (Greek, *planōmen*) for serious error, not incidental mistakes. Such a claim demonstrates that the truth of the gospel has not become part of the person's life.

1:9. Rather than denying sin, believers are asked to acknowledge it freely. When we admit our sin, we find, paradoxically, that God removes it. "Confess" (Greek, *homologōmen*) implies we must acknowledge that our sin is sin and admit that we committed it. The plural "sins" shows that confession includes specific acts of sin.

Once we confess sin, the character of God guarantees forgiveness. He is a faithful God who can be trusted to keep His promises (cf. Jeremiah 31:34). He is a righteous God who will forgive our

we claim communion with God, *Noli* . . . if we say we are friends with God, *SEB* . . . we are His dear friends, *Laubach* . . . we enjoy fellowship...while we are walking about in the dark, *Berkeley* . . . things in common we are having with Him, and thus fellowship, and in the sphere of the aforementioned darkness are habitually ordering our behavior, *Wuest.*

we lie, and do not the truth: . . . we speak falsely, *Wilson* . . . we are falsifying and we are not practicing the truth, *Berkeley* . . . we should be both telling and living a lie, *Phillips* . . . and not living in the truth, *Williams C.K.*

7. But if we walk in the light, as he is in the light: . . . if we really are living in the same light in which he eternally exists, *Phillips* . . . if within the sphere of the light we are habitually ordering our behavior, *Wuest* . . . If, however, we walk about, *Berkeley.*

we have fellowship one with another: . . . we have unbroken fellowship, *Williams* . . . we enjoy mutual fellowship, *Berkeley* . . . things in common and thus fellowship we...are having with one another, *Wuest.*

and the blood of Jesus Christ his Son cleanseth us from all sin: . . . and the sacrifice of, *TCNT* . . . keeps continually cleansing us from, *Wuest* . . . continues to cleanse us from all sin, *SEB* . . . will make us clean, *Laubach* . . . will cleanse us from every sin, *Norlie* . . . purifies us from every form of sin, *Wade* . . . every kind of sin, *Williams C.K.*

8. If we say that we have no sin: . . . indwelling, *Wuest.*

we deceive ourselves, and the truth is not in us: . . . we are only fooling ourselves, *SEB* . . . we are deluding ourselves, *Berkeley* . . . ourselves we are leading astray, *Wuest* . . . has no place in us, *TCNT* . . . the truth is not in our hearts, *Williams.*

9. If we confess our sins: . . . if we freely admit that we have sinned, *Phillips* . . . continue to confess, *Wuest* . . . avowing our sins, *Concordant.*

he is faithful and just to forgive us [our] sins: He is to be depended on, *Williams* . . . we find

1 John 1:10

9.a.Var: 01א,04C,044 81,614,623,630,1505 1852,2464,2495

2231.3 prs-pron dat 1pl	3450.15 art acc pl fem	264.1 noun fem	2231.2 prs-pron gen 1pl	2504.1 conj	2483.5 verb 3sing subj aor act
ἡμῖν	τὰς	ἁμαρτίας,	[a+ ἡμῶν,]	καὶ	καθαρίσῃ
hēmin	tas	hamartias	hēmōn	kai	katharisē
us	the	sins,	[our,]	and	may cleanse

2231.4 prs-pron acc 1pl	570.3 prep	3820.10 adj gen sing fem	92.2 noun gen sing fem	1430.1 partic	1500.9 verb 1pl subj aor act
ἡμᾶς	ἀπὸ	πάσης	ἀδικίας.	10. ἐὰν	εἴπωμεν
hēmas	apo	pasēs	adikias	ean	eipōmen
us	from	all	unrighteousness.	If	we should say

3617.1 conj	3620.1 partic	262.21 verb 1pl indic perf act	5418.2 noun acc sing masc	4020.6 verb 1pl indic pres act	840.6 prs-pron acc sing masc
ὅτι	οὐχ	ἡμαρτήκαμεν,	ψεύστην	ποιοῦμεν	αὐτὸν,
hoti	ouch	hēmartēkamen	pseustēn	poioumen	auton
that	not	we have sinned,	a liar	we make	him,

2504.1 conj	3450.5 art nom sing masc	3030.1 noun nom sing masc	840.3 prs-pron gen sing	3620.2 partic	1498.4 verb 3sing indic pres act	1706.1 prep
καὶ	ὁ	λόγος	αὐτοῦ	οὐκ	ἔστιν	ἐν
kai	ho	logos	autou	ouk	estin	en
and	the	word	his	not	is	in

2231.3 prs-pron dat 1pl	4888.1 noun pl neu	1466.2 prs-pron gen 1sing	3642.18 dem-pron pl neu	1119.1 verb 1sing indic pres act
ἡμῖν.	2:1. Τεκνία	μου,	ταῦτα	γράφω
hēmin	Teknia	mou	tauta	graphō
us.	Little children	my,	these things	I write

5050.3 prs-pron dat 2pl	2419.1 conj	3231.1 partic	262.16 verb 2pl subj aor act	2504.1 conj	1430.1 partic	4948.3 indef-pron nom sing
ὑμῖν,	ἵνα	μὴ	ἁμάρτητε·	καὶ	ἐάν	τις
humin	hina	mē	hamartēte	kai	ean	tis
to you,	that	not	you may sin;	and	if	anyone

262.14 verb 3sing subj aor act	3736.2 noun acc sing masc	2174.5 verb 1pl indic pres act	4242.1 prep	3450.6 art acc sing masc
ἁμάρτῃ,	παράκλητον	ἔχομεν	πρὸς	τὸν
hamartē	paraklēton	echomen	pros	ton
should sin,	an Advocate	we have	with	the

3824.4 noun acc sing masc	2400.3 name acc masc	5382.4 name acc masc	1337.1 adj sing	2504.1 conj	840.5 prs-pron nom sing masc
πατέρα,	Ἰησοῦν	Χριστὸν	δίκαιον·	2. καὶ	αὐτὸς
patera	Iēsoun	Christon	dikaion	kai	autos
Father,	Jesus	Christ	righteous;	and	he

2410.1 noun nom sing masc	1498.4 verb 3sing indic pres act	3875.1 prep	3450.1 art gen pl	264.6 noun gen pl fem	2231.2 prs-pron gen 1pl
ἱλασμός	ἐστιν	περὶ	τῶν	ἁμαρτιῶν	ἡμῶν·
hilasmos	estin	peri	tōn	hamartiōn	hēmōn
propitiation	is	for	the	sins	our;

3620.3 partic	3875.1 prep	3450.1 art gen pl	2233.7 adj gen 1pl fem	1156.2 conj	3303.1 adv	233.2 conj	2504.1 conj
οὐ	περὶ	τῶν	ἡμετέρων	δὲ	μόνον,	ἀλλὰ	καὶ
ou	peri	tōn	hēmeterōn	de	monon	alla	kai
not	for	the	ours	but	only,	but	also

3875.1 prep	3513.2 adj gen sing	3450.2 art gen sing	2862.2 noun gen sing masc	2504.1 conj	1706.1 prep	3642.5 dem-pron dat sing masc
περὶ	ὅλου	τοῦ	κόσμου.	3. Καὶ	ἐν	τούτῳ
peri	holou	tou	kosmou	Kai	en	toutō
for	whole	the	world.	And	by	this

sins because the death of Christ has already paid the penalty for them.

God's character leads to forgiveness and cleansing. He forgives sin, as one might release a debtor from his obligation to pay. And He cleanses from all unrighteousness, not only by imputing righteousness to the sinner's account but by gradually producing holy character in daily life.

1:10. While verse 8 describes those who deny that sin is part of their nature, verse 10 tells of another group who deny that they have ever committed a single act of sin. The perfect tense of "have not sinned" makes the sweeping claim that they have maintained complete freedom from sin up to now.

Such a statement defames the character of God and presents Him to the world as a liar, because the whole gospel message rests on the fact that mankind is sinful and needs a Saviour. The claim of sinlessness shows an absence of the Word of God in the speaker's life.

2:1. John changed his format from hypothetical cases involving nonbelievers, and moved to the actual situation of his beloved "little children," a tender greeting to family members. He began by explaining that he did not intend to imply that sin is inevitable. No, he was writing to help them avoid committing even a single act of sin (see aorist tense).

Sin does occur, however, and God has provided a way for believers to respond to it. If anyone sins, Jesus is present to serve as his "advocate," a term often used for one who would testify in a person's favor in court. Christ is face-to-face with the Father making intercession for the Christian on the basis of His own righteousness granted to the believer. What an advantage, to have the Judge's Son as our Advocate!

2:2. This verse expands on the work that Christ did to provide a basis for the intercession mentioned in verse 1. He himself (emphasized in Greek) stands as a propitiation for the believer's sins. "Propitiation" (Greek, *hilasmos*) was used in secular writing for a sacrifice that appeased the wrath of an angered god. Some suggest that the New Testament uses it simply to describe a payment for sin; but the usage seems to include the idea that God is justifiably angry at sin. Christ is the divine sacrifice, provided by God himself, which makes it possible for the Lord to meet man without wrath.

This sacrifice is available to all believers as the basis for dealing with sin, but not just to John and his circle of believers. The verse declares strongly that the benefits of Christ's death are available to the entire world.

God utterly reliable and straightforward—he forgives our sins, *Phillips* . . . be pardoning us our sins, *Concordant.*

and to cleanse us from all unrighteousness: . . . and makes us thoroughly clean from all that is evil, *Phillips* . . . from all wrongdoing, *Montgomery* . . . all injustice, *Concordant.*

10. If we say that we have not sinned: . . . if we take up the attitude, *Phillips* . . . are now in a state where we do not sin, *Wuest.*

we make him a liar, and his word is not in us: . . . we make Him out to be, *Berkeley* . . . we challenge his truthfulness, *Noli* . . . we flatly deny God's diagnosis of our condition and cut ourselves off from what he has to say to us, *Phillips* . . . and his Message has no place in us, *TCNT* . . . Then God's Word does not rule our lives, *Laubach* . . . has made no impression upon us, *Wade.*

1. My little children, these things write I unto you: . . . bairns, *Wuest* . . . the reason I write this to you, *Norlie.*

that ye sin not: . . . to keep you from sinning, *TCNT* . . . that you may not continue to sin, *Montgomery* . . . in order that you may not commit an act of sin, *Wuest.*

And if any man sin, we have an advocate with the Father, Jesus Christ the righteous: . . . if anyone commits an act of sin, One who pleads our cause we constantly have facing the Father, *Wuest* . . . we have a patron, *Darby* . . . we have a Pleader for us, *Wade* . . . a Counsel for defense in the Father's presence, *Berkeley* . . . Who stands face to face with, *Adams* . . . to help defend us before God, *SEB* . . . will ask the Father to forgive you, *Laubach* . . . an Entreater with ...Christ, the Just, *Concordant.*

2. And he is the propitiation for our sins: . . . the means of washing away, *Williams C.K.* . . . is the satisfying-sacrifice, *Swann* . . . is the atonement for, *Norlie* . . . the propitiatory shelter concerned with, *Concordant* . . . an expiatory satisfaction, *Wuest.*

and not for ours only, but also for [the sins of] the whole world: . . . of all mankind, *Noli.*

1091.4 verb 1pl indic pres act	3617.1 conj	1091.33 verb 1pl indic perf act	840.6 prs-pron acc sing masc	1430.1 partic	3450.15 art acc pl fem
γινώσκομεν	ὅτι	ἐγνώκαμεν	αὐτόν,	ἐὰν	τὰς
ginōskomen	hoti	egnōkamen	auton	ean	tas
we know	that	we have known	him,	if	the

1769.7 noun acc pl fem	840.3 prs-pron gen sing	4931.5 verb 1pl subj pres act	3450.5 art nom sing masc	2978.15 verb nom sing masc part pres act
ἐντολὰς	αὐτοῦ	τηρῶμεν.	4. ὁ	λέγων,
entolas	autou	tērōmen	ho	legōn
commandments	his	we keep.	The	saying,

4.a.**Var:** 01ℵ,02A,03B Lach,Treg,Alf,Tisc We/Ho,Weis,Sod UBS/⋆

3617.1 conj	1091.30 verb 1sing indic perf act	840.6 prs-pron acc sing masc	2504.1 conj	3450.15 art acc pl fem	1769.7 noun acc pl fem
[a⋆+ ὅτι]	Ἔγνωκα	αὐτόν,	καὶ	τὰς	ἐντολὰς
hoti	Egnōka	auton	kai	tas	entolas
	I have known	him,	and	the	commandments

840.3 prs-pron gen sing	3231.1 partic	4931.8 verb nom sing masc part pres act	5418.1 noun nom sing masc	1498.4 verb 3sing indic pres act	2504.1 conj	1706.1 prep
αὐτοῦ	μὴ	τηρῶν,	ψεύστης	ἐστίν,	καὶ	ἐν
autou	mē	tērōn	pseustēs	estin	kai	en
his	not	keeping,	a liar	is,	and	in

3642.5 dem-pron dat sing masc	3450.9 art nom sing fem	223.1 noun nom sing fem	3620.2 partic	1498.4 verb 3sing indic pres act	3614.5 rel-pron nom sing masc
τούτῳ	ἡ	ἀλήθεια	οὐκ	ἔστιν·	5. ὃς
toutō	hē	alētheia	ouk	estin	hos
him	the	truth	not	is;	whoever

1156.1 conj	300.1 partic	4931.4 verb 3sing subj pres act	840.3 prs-pron gen sing	3450.6 art acc sing masc	3030.4 noun acc sing masc	228.1 adv
δ'	ἂν	τηρῇ	αὐτοῦ	τὸν	λόγον,	ἀληθῶς
d'	an	tērē	autou	ton	logon	alēthōs
but		may keep	his	the	word,	truly

1706.1 prep	3642.5 dem-pron dat sing masc	3450.9 art nom sing fem	26.1 noun nom sing fem	3450.2 art gen sing	2296.2 noun gen sing masc
ἐν	τούτῳ	ἡ	ἀγάπη	τοῦ	θεοῦ
en	toutō	hē	agapē	tou	theou
in	him	the	love		of God

4896.14 verb 3sing indic perf mid	1706.1 prep	3642.5 dem-pron dat sing masc	1091.4 verb 1pl indic pres act	3617.1 conj	1706.1 prep
τετελείωται.	ἐν	τούτῳ	γινώσκομεν	ὅτι	ἐν
teteleiōtai	en	toutō	ginōskomen	hoti	en
has been perfected.	By	this	we know	that	in

840.4 prs-pron dat sing	1498.5 verb 1pl indic pres act	3450.5 art nom sing masc	2978.15 verb nom sing masc part pres act	1706.1 prep	840.4 prs-pron dat sing
αὐτῷ	ἐσμεν.	6. ὁ	λέγων	ἐν	αὐτῷ
autō	esmen	ho	legōn	en	autō
him	we are.	The	saying	in	him

3176.15 verb inf pres act	3648.3 verb 3sing indic pres act	2503.1 conj	1552.3 dem-pron nom sing masc	3906.18 verb 3sing indic aor act
μένειν,	ὀφείλει,	καθὼς	ἐκεῖνος	περιεπάτησεν,
menein	opheilei	kathōs	ekeinos	periepatēsen
to remain,	ought,	even as	that	walked,

6.a.**Txt:** 01ℵ,04C,025P 044,byz.
Var: 02A,03B,33,623 2464-org

2504.1 conj	840.5 prs-pron nom sing masc	3643.1 adv	3906.17 verb inf pres act	79.6 noun nom pl masc
καὶ	αὐτὸς	⸂a οὕτως ⸃	περιπατεῖν.	7. ⸀ ἀδελφοί,
kai	autos	houtōs	peripatein	adelphoi
also	himself	so	to walk.	Brothers,

2:3. John stated the theme of his next segment in verse 3—there is a test by which one can demonstrate the reality of his relationship to God. The person who truly knows God will keep His commands.

Classical Greek used two words for "know": *oida* was knowledge gained by abstract learning; *ginōskō* was knowledge attained through personal experience. John used *ginōskō* twice in this verse in its classical sense to describe our knowledge of God as a Person, not a set of facts.

"We know him" is perfect tense, which John often used to describe the believer who has come to know God and still retains a personal relationship with God because of the initial encounter with Him. Such a relationship can be tested by looking for consistent obedience to God's commands.

2:4. The apostle took aim at one of the imposters who were plaguing the Early Church, a person who claimed to have the knowledge of God just described. But the promising words were linked with a life of disobedience to God's commands. The verdict is obvious. This person had failed the test of 2:3 and was a liar. His problem went beyond mere confusion; he was actively deceiving others and had no trace of the truth.

2:5. Any Christian may qualify for the contrasting picture in this verse. Whoever habitually keeps the word of God is truly in fellowship with Him, despite the claims of some to be spiritually elite. "Love" appears here for the first of many times in the epistle. It could refer to the love which God has for us, but the context suggests that it means the love we should show toward God. Human love for God is imperfect in this life, but the verse uses a word (Greek, *teteleiōtai*) which means completeness rather than absolute perfection. This is love which becomes complete when it results in loving action (cf. 3:16-18). The final phrase repeats the test of any claim to fellowship with God: obedience to His commands.

2:6. Intimacy with Christ inevitably produces a daily walk that mirrors the pattern of Christ's life. John used the word "abideth," a strong term, to describe a permanent relationship with Jesus, a concept probably drawn from the picture of vine and branches in John 15. Any person who claims to abide in Christ is under obligation to behave in the same way as his Lord. "Ought" and "walk" are both present tense, emphasizing the need to behave in this way continually.

John simply referred to "that one" (*ekeinos*; "he," KJV) without explaining that it referred to Jesus. Christ held such a central place

3. And hereby we do know that we know him, if we keep his commandments: By this token we recognize that we know Him, if we observe His commands, *Berkeley* . . . this we know experientially that we have come to know Him, *Wuest* . . . when we obey God's laws, *Phillips* . . . His precepts, *Concordant.*

4. He that saith, I know him, and keepeth not his commandments: . . . but does not obey, *Norlie* . . . his laws, *Phillips.*

is a liar, and the truth is not in him: . . . truth of God, *Concordant* . . . in this one the truth does not exist, *Wuest* . . . but he lives in self-delusion, *Phillips.*

5. But whoso keepeth his word, in him verily is the love of God perfected: In practice, the more a man learns to obey God's laws, the more truly and fully does he express his love for him, *Phillips* . . . whoever observes His message, in him the love of God has truly reached maturity, *Berkeley* . . . whoever habitually with a solicitous care is keeping His word, truly, in this one the love of God has been brought to its completion, *Wuest* . . . God's love has accomplished its purpose, *Adams* . . . truly in this one, *Concordant.*

hereby know we that we are in him: In this way we recognize that we are in Him, *Berkeley* . . . This is how we know that we are following God, *Everyday* . . . we have an experiential knowledge, *Wuest.*

6. He that saith he abideth in him: Whoever claims, *Williams* . . . He who says, "I live in Christ," *Laubach* . . . saying that he is remaining in Him, *Concordant* . . . The life of a man who professes to be living in God, *Phillips* . . . saying that he as a habit of life is living in close fellowship with and dependence upon Him, *Wuest* . . . God lives in him, *Everyday.*

ought himself also so to walk, even as he walked: . . . is morally obligated just as that One conducted himself, *Wuest* . . . ought personally to live the way He lived, *Berkeley* . . . must bear the stamp of Christ, *Phillips* . . . ought to live as Christ lived, *Laubach.*

1 John 2:8

7.a.**Txt:** 018K,020L,byz.
Var: 01ℵ,02A,03B,04C
025P,sa.bo.Gries,Lach
Treg,Alf,Word,Tisc
We/Ho,Weis,Sod
UBS/☆

27.6 adj pl masc	**3620.2** partic	**1769.3** noun acc sing fem	**2508.5** adj acc sing fem	**1119.1** verb 1sing indic pres act
[a☆ 'Αγαπητοί,]	οὐκ	ἐντολὴν	καινὴν	γράφω
Agapētoi	*ouk*	*entolēn*	*kainēn*	*graphō*
[Beloved]	not	a commandment	new	I write

5050.3 prs-pron dat 2pl	**233.1** conj	**1769.3** noun acc sing fem	**3683.7** adj acc sing fem	**3614.12** rel-pron acc sing fem	**2174.47** verb 2pl indic imperf act
ὑμῖν,	ἀλλ'	ἐντολὴν	παλαιὰν,	ἣν	εἴχετε
humin	*all'*	*entolēn*	*palaian*	*hēn*	*eichete*
to you,	but	commandment	an old,	which	you had

570.2 prep	**741.2** noun gen sing fem	**3450.9** art nom sing fem	**1769.1** noun nom sing fem	**3450.9** art nom sing fem	**3683.4** adj
ἀπ'	ἀρχῆς·	ἡ	ἐντολὴ	ἡ	παλαιά
ap'	*archēs*	*hē*	*entolē*	*hē*	*palaia*
from	beginning:	the	commandment	the	old

7.b.**Txt:** 018K,020L,byz.
Var: 01ℵ,02A,03B,04C
025P,33,sa.bo.Lach
Treg,Alf,Tisc,We/Ho
Weis,Sod,UBS/☆

1498.4 verb 3sing indic pres act	**3450.5** art nom sing masc	**3030.1** noun nom sing masc	**3614.6** rel-pron acc sing masc	**189.23** verb 2pl indic aor act	**570.2** prep
ἐστιν	ὁ	λόγος	ὃν	ἠκούσατε	⸀b ἀπ'
estin	*ho*	*logos*	*hon*	*ēkousate*	*ap'*
is	the	word	which	you heard	from

741.2 noun gen sing fem	**3687.1** adv	**1769.3** noun acc sing fem	**2508.5** adj acc sing fem	**1119.1** verb 1sing indic pres act
ἀρχῆς. ⸃	**8.** πάλιν	ἐντολὴν	καινὴν	γράφω
archēs	*palin*	*entolēn*	*kainēn*	*graphō*
beginning.	Again	a commandment	new	I write

5050.3 prs-pron dat 2pl	**3614.16** rel-pron sing neu	**1498.4** verb 3sing indic pres act	**225.5** adj sing neu	**1706.1** prep	**840.4** prs-pron dat sing	**2504.1** conj
ὑμῖν,	ὅ	ἐστιν	ἀληθὲς	ἐν	αὐτῷ	καὶ
humin	*ho*	*estin*	*alēthes*	*en*	*autō*	*kai*
to you,	which	is	true	in	him	and

1706.1 prep	**5050.3** prs-pron dat 2pl	**3617.1** conj	**3450.9** art nom sing fem	**4508.1** noun nom sing fem	**3717.6** verb 3sing indic pres mid
ἐν	ὑμῖν,	ὅτι	ἡ	σκοτία	παράγεται,
en	*humin*	*hoti*	*hē*	*skotia*	*paragetai*
in	you,	because	the	darkness	is passing away,

2504.1 conj	**3450.16** art sing neu	**5295.1** noun sing neu	**3450.16** art sing neu	**226.1** adj sing	**2218.1** adv
καὶ	τὸ	φῶς	τὸ	ἀληθινὸν	ἤδη
kai	*to*	*phōs*	*to*	*alēthinon*	*ēdē*
and	the	light	the	true	already

5154.2 verb 3sing indic pres act	**3450.5** art nom sing masc	**2978.15** verb nom sing masc part pres act	**1706.1** prep	**3450.3** art dat sing	**5295.3** noun dat sing neu
φαίνει.	**9.** ὁ	λέγων	ἐν	τῷ	φωτὶ
phainei	*ho*	*legōn*	*en*	*tō*	*phōti*
shines.	The	saying	in	the	light

1498.32 verb inf pres act	**2504.1** conj	**3450.6** art acc sing masc	**79.4** noun acc sing masc	**840.3** prs-pron gen sing	**3268.5** verb nom sing masc part pres act
εἶναι,	καὶ	τὸν	ἀδελφὸν	αὐτοῦ	μισῶν,
einai	*kai*	*ton*	*adelphon*	*autou*	*misōn*
to be,	and	the	brother	his	hates,

1706.1 prep	**3450.11** art dat sing fem	**4508.3** noun dat sing fem	**1498.4** verb 3sing indic pres act	**2175.1** conj	**732.1** adv	**3450.5** art nom sing masc
ἐν	τῇ	σκοτίᾳ	ἐστὶν	ἕως	ἄρτι.	**10.** ὁ
en	*tē*	*skotia*	*estin*	*heōs*	*arti*	*ho*
in	the	darkness	is	until	now.	The

in his thought that no further description was necessary (cf. 3:3,5,7,16; 4:17).

2:7. Some may have protested that John was adding his own commands to the Christian faith. But he replied that all he said came directly from the words of Christ himself.

Since verses 9-11 move directly to a discussion of love, it is clear that John was speaking of Christ's command to love other Christians (John 13:34,35). John could speak with conviction, for he had been present when Jesus himself told His disciples He was giving them the commandment. "New" (Greek, *kainēn*) means "new in kind, novel." So the apostle was certainly not inventing new demands; on the contrary, he was repeating standards which the believers had known ever since they began their relationship with Christianity.

2:8. A second look, however, shows that there is a sense in which the commandment is new, in relation to Christ because His death gave new meaning to the word "love." And it has become new to Christians as they experience it in their own lives.

This amazing revolution of love had even begun changing the face of the world. The darkness of sin and hate which was mentioned in 1:5 was passing off the scene, like a column of men disappearing in the distance. The verb should probably be taken in the middle voice, suggesting that the darkness was dissipating of its own accord. In the same way, the genuine light of the gospel was already in the process of shining to dispel the darkness, like a rising sun chasing the shadows.

2:9. John then moved to another test by which we can discover whether our fellowship with God is genuine. As he did in earlier tests, he shifted back and forth between positive and negative statements (cf. 1:6-10; 2:3-6). This verse introduces a person who claims to exist in the sphere of God's light, yet hates his brother. John's verdict is blunt: the man is in the dark, not the light. In fact, he has existed in the darkness all the way to the present moment. There is no room for intermediate attitudes between love and hate in the discussion; a person can either choose to show love by serving others, or refuse to meet their needs. The test applies specifically to fellow Christians, as shown by the mention of "brother."

2:10. Love for fellow Christians is an evidence of a person's position in fellowship with God. And it is significant that the state-

7. Brethren, I write no new commandment unto you, but an old commandment which ye had from the beginning: Divinely loved ones, no commandment new in quality, *Wuest* . . . Dear friends, I am writing...only the old command which you have had, *Berkeley* . . . My loved ones, I do not give you a new law...which you had from the first, *BB* . . . this is no new doctrine...one which you accepted, *Greber.*

The old commandment is the word which ye have heard from the beginning: It is just the old, original command, *Phillips* . . . is identical with the Message, *TCNT* . . . is the word which came to your ears, *BB* . . . is the truth that you have just heard, *Greber.*

8. Again, a new commandment I write unto you, which thing is true in him and in you: On the other hand...one that is real in Him and in you, *Beck* . . . In turn I write...realized in Him, *Berkeley* . . . But in one sense I am sending you a new doctrine. It runs thus, *Greber* . . . I know that it is always new and always true, *Phillips* . . . which fact is true, *Wuest* . . . you can see its truth in Jesus and in yourselves, *Everyday.*

because the darkness is past, and the true light now shineth: I know this because the darkness is passing away and the real light, *Beck* . . . is being caused to pass away, and...the genuine light, *Wuest* . . . for the night is near its end and the true light is even now shining out, *BB* . . . the darkness must yield, and the ray of the true light must shine, *Greber* . . . is beginning to lift, *Phillips* . . . is passing by, and...already is appearing, *Concordant* . . . is already shining, *Norlie.*

9. He that saith he is in the light: A person may claim, *SEB* . . . He who professes, *Wade* . . . Whoever claims to be, *Swann.*

and hateth his brother: . . . and nevertheless harbors hatred of his fellow-man in his heart, *Greber* . . . is habitually hating, *Wuest.*

is in darkness even until now: . . . is still in the darkness, *Norlie* . . . in complete darkness, *Phillips* . . . to this very hour, *TCNT* . . . hitherto, *Concordant* . . . all the while, *Berkeley.*

25.8 verb nom sing masc part pres act	**3450.6** art acc sing masc	**79.4** noun acc sing masc	**840.3** prs-pron gen sing	**1706.1** prep	**3450.3** art dat sing
ἀγαπῶν	τὸν	ἀδελφὸν	αὐτοῦ,	ἐν	τῷ
agapōn	*ton*	*adelphon*	*autou*	*en*	*tō*
loving	the	brother	his,	in	the

5295.3 noun dat sing neu	**3176.1** verb 3sing indic pres act	**2504.1** conj	**4480.1** noun sing neu	**1706.1** prep	**840.4** prs-pron dat sing
φωτὶ	μένει,	καὶ	σκάνδαλον	ἐν	αὐτῷ
phōti	*menei*	*kai*	*skandalon*	*en*	*autō*
light	remains,	and	cause of offense	in	him

3620.2 partic	**1498.4** verb 3sing indic pres act	**3450.5** art nom sing masc	**1156.2** conj	**3268.5** verb nom sing masc part pres act	**3450.6** art acc sing masc
οὐκ	ἔστιν.	**11.** ὁ	δὲ	μισῶν	τὸν
ouk	*estin*	*ho*	*de*	*misōn*	*ton*
not	there is.	The	but	hating	the

79.4 noun acc sing masc	**840.3** prs-pron gen sing	**1706.1** prep	**3450.11** art dat sing fem	**4508.3** noun dat sing fem	**1498.4** verb 3sing indic pres act
ἀδελφὸν	αὐτοῦ,	ἐν	τῇ	σκοτίᾳ	ἐστὶν,
adelphon	*autou*	*en*	*tē*	*skotia*	*estin*
brother	his,	in	the	darkness	is,

2504.1 conj	**1706.1** prep	**3450.11** art dat sing fem	**4508.3** noun dat sing fem	**3906.4** verb 3sing indic pres act	**2504.1** conj	**3620.2** partic
καὶ	ἐν	τῇ	σκοτίᾳ	περιπατεῖ,	καὶ	οὐκ
kai	*en*	*tē*	*skotia*	*peripatei*	*kai*	*ouk*
and	in	the	darkness	walks,	and	not

3471.4 verb 3sing indic perf act	**4085.1** adv	**5055.3** verb 3sing indic pres act	**3617.1** conj	**3450.9** art nom sing fem	**4508.1** noun nom sing fem
οἶδεν	ποῦ	ὑπάγει,	ὅτι	ἡ	σκοτία
oiden	*pou*	*hupagei*	*hoti*	*hē*	*skotia*
knows	where	he goes,	because	the	darkness

5027.1 verb 3sing indic aor act	**3450.8** art acc pl masc	**3652.8** noun acc pl masc	**840.3** prs-pron gen sing	**1119.1** verb 1sing indic pres act
ἐτύφλωσεν	τοὺς	ὀφθαλμοὺς	αὐτοῦ.	**12.** Γράφω
etuphlōsen	*tous*	*ophthalmous*	*autou*	*Graphō*
blinded	the	eyes	his.	I write

5050.3 prs-pron dat 2pl	**4888.1** noun pl neu	**3617.1** conj	**856.29** verb 3pl indic perf mid	**5050.3** prs-pron dat 2pl
ὑμῖν,	τεκνία,	ὅτι	ἀφέωνται	ὑμῖν
humin	*teknia*	*hoti*	*apheōntai*	*humin*
to you,	little children,	because	have been forgiven	you

3450.13 art nom pl fem	**264.5** noun nom pl fem	**1217.2** prep	**3450.16** art sing neu	**3549.2** noun sing neu	**840.3** prs-pron gen sing
αἱ	ἁμαρτίαι	διὰ	τὸ	ὄνομα	αὐτοῦ.
hai	*hamartiai*	*dia*	*to*	*onoma*	*autou*
the	sins	for the sake of	the	name	his.

1119.1 verb 1sing indic pres act	**5050.3** prs-pron dat 2pl	**3824.6** noun nom pl masc	**3617.1** conj	**1091.34** verb 2pl indic perf act
13. Γράφω	ὑμῖν,	πατέρες,	ὅτι	ἐγνώκατε
Graphō	*humin*	*pateres*	*hoti*	*egnōkate*
I write	to you,	fathers	because	you have known

3450.6 art acc sing masc	**570.2** prep	**741.2** noun gen sing fem	**1119.1** verb 1sing indic pres act	**5050.3** prs-pron dat 2pl	**3358.4** noun nom pl masc
τὸν	ἀπ'	ἀρχῆς.	Γράφω	ὑμῖν,	νεανίσκοι,
ton	*ap'*	*archēs*	*Graphō*	*humin*	*neaniskoi*
the	from	beginning.	I write	to you,	young men,

ment begins "He that loveth" rather than "He that saith," since it is describing a person who loves in action, not merely with words. "Abideth" (Greek, *menei*) refers to permanent residence in a location, rather than the temporary stay of a transient. And the present tense of the verb strengthens the emphasis on a permanent relationship.

Such a person is in the light, and there is no "occasion of stumbling" (Greek, *skandalon*) in him. *Skandalon* referred to an animal snare, then to an object that would cause one to trip himself up. The person who loves has nothing in his character that will cause him to stumble into sin.

John Wesley made an interesting comment: "He that hates his brother is an occasion of stumbling to himself. He stumbles against himself, and against all things within and without; while he that loves his brother has a free disencumbered journey" (John Wesley, et al., 1 John 2:10).

2:11. On the other hand, one who hates his brother demonstrates that he is in darkness. First, he exists in darkness (2:9). Second, he walks around in darkness, open to the risk of stumbling over unseen obstacles. Third, he is going away in darkness, not knowing his direction (cf. John 12:35). The obscurity is complete because darkness has blinded his eyes. The aorist tense of "blinded" pictures the decisive moment when the darkness finally overtakes the sinner.

2:12. John opened a new section of the epistle by assuring his readers of their identity in Christ. Because they were genuine members of God's family, they could successfully cope with the spiritual dangers around them. Because of their conversion they had been born into the family of God, having become partakers of His nature. An earthly father considers it his duty to guide and protect his family. God assumes the same responsibility.

Verses 12-14 are a highly structured segment, with the symmetry and repetition of poetry. John presented his point in a pair of triplets, switching from the present tense to aorist at the midpoint, for reasons which are not completely clear.

He wrote first to "little children" (Greek, *teknia*), a term he often used as an affectionate description of all believers. He said he wrote to them because their sins had been forgiven, a fact already accomplished (perfect tense) through the name of Christ.

2:13. Next John addressed the fathers, the more mature believers, and wrote that they had received his message because they had come to know Christ (as in 2:3). He described the Lord as the One who is "from the beginning," the eternally existing One.

The triplet closes with a word to the younger men, a term gen-

10. He that loveth his brother abideth in the light: . . . is remaining, *Concordant* . . . is continually in the light, *Berkeley* . . . lives and moves in the light, *Phillips.*

and there is none occasion of stumbling in him: . . . he will not fall down, *Laubach* . . . has no reason to stumble, *Phillips* . . . there is no stumblingblock in him, *Swann* . . . he is no hindrance to others, *Williams* . . . there is nothing within him to occasion stumbling, *Berkeley* . . . there is no cause for falling, *Williams C.K.* . . . there is no snare in him, *Concordant.*

11. But he that hateth his brother is in darkness, and walketh in darkness: . . . the brother-hater is in the dark and moves in the dark, *Berkeley* . . . as a habit of life hates, *Wuest* . . . and are living in, *TCNT* . . . is shut off from the light and gropes his way in the dark, *Phillips* . . . and is spending his life in the darkness, *Montgomery.*

and knoweth not whither he goeth, because that darkness hath blinded his eyes: . . . he has to grope about, *Norlie* . . . he cannot see in the dark, *Laubach* . . . without seeing where he is going. To move in the dark is to move blindfold, *Phillips.*

12. I write unto you, little children, because your sins are forgiven you for his name's sake: . . . as my dear children, *Phillips* . . . have been put away from you permanently, *Wuest* . . . because of the authority of Jesus, *SEB* . . . on account of his name, *Campbell* . . . through His name, *Concordant.*

13. I write unto you, fathers, because ye have known him [that is] from the beginning: I write to you who are now fathers, because you have known him who has always existed, *Phillips* . . . come to know experientially, *Wuest* . . . the Christ who lived before the world began, *Laubach.*

I write unto you, young men, because ye have overcome the wicked one: Young children, *Campbell* . . . youths, *Concordant* . . . to you vigorous young

13.a.**Txt:** 018K,byz.
Var: 01ℵ,02A,03B,04C 025P,sa.bo.Lach,Treg Alf,Word,Tisc,We/Ho Weis,Sod,UBS/☆

14.a.**Txt:** 01ℵ,02A,03B 04C,020L,025P,044,33 323,614,630,945,1241 1505,1739,2495
Var: byz.

3617.1 conj	**3390.14** verb 2pl indic perf act	**3450.6** art acc sing masc	**4050.1** adj sing	**1119.1** verb 1sing indic pres act
ὅτι	νενικήκατε	τὸν	πονηρόν.	ʻ Γράφω
hoti	*nenikēkate*	*ton*	*ponēron*	*Graphō*
because	you have overcome	the	wicked.	I write

1119.7 verb 1sing indic aor act	**5050.3** prs-pron dat 2pl	**3676.3** noun pl masc	**3617.1** conj	**1091.34** verb 2pl indic perf act
[a ἔγραψα]	ὑμῖν,	παιδία,	ὅτι	ἐγνώκατε
egrapsa	*humin*	*paidia*	*hoti*	*egnōkate*
[I wrote]	to you,	little children,	because	you have known

3450.6 art acc sing masc	**3824.4** noun acc sing masc	**1119.7** verb 1sing indic aor act	**1119.1** verb 1sing indic pres act	**5050.3** prs-pron dat 2pl
τὸν	πατέρα.	14. ʻ☆ Ἔγραψα	[a Γράφω]	ὑμῖν,
ton	*patera*	*Egrapsa*	*Graphō*	*humin*
the	Father.	I wrote	[I write]	to you,

3824.6 noun nom pl masc	**3617.1** conj	**1091.34** verb 2pl indic perf act	**3450.6** art acc sing masc	**570.2** prep	**741.2** noun gen sing fem
πατέρες,	ὅτι	ἐγνώκατε	τὸν	ἀπ᾽	ἀρχῆς.
pateres	*hoti*	*egnōkate*	*ton*	*ap'*	*archēs*
fathers,	because	you have known	the	from	beginning.

1119.7 verb 1sing indic aor act	**5050.3** prs-pron dat 2pl	**3358.4** noun nom pl masc	**3617.1** conj	**2451.5** adj nom pl masc	**1498.6** verb 2pl indic pres act
Ἔγραψα	ὑμῖν,	νεανίσκοι,	ὅτι	ἰσχυροί	ἐστε
Egrapsa	*humin*	*neaniskoi*	*hoti*	*ischuroi*	*este*
I wrote	to you,	young men,	because	strong	you are

2504.1 conj	**3450.5** art nom sing masc	**3030.1** noun nom sing masc	**3450.2** art gen sing	**2296.2** noun gen sing masc	**1706.1** prep	**5050.3** prs-pron dat 2pl
καὶ	ὁ	λόγος	τοῦ	θεοῦ	ἐν	ὑμῖν
kai	*ho*	*logos*	*tou*	*theou*	*en*	*humin*
and	the	word		of God	in	you

3176.1 verb 3sing indic pres act	**2504.1** conj	**3390.14** verb 2pl indic perf act	**3450.6** art acc sing masc	**4050.1** adj sing
μένει,	καὶ	νενικήκατε	τὸν	πονηρόν.
menei	*kai*	*nenikēkate*	*ton*	*ponēron*
abides,	and	you have overcome	the	wicked.

3231.1 partic	**25.1** verb 2pl pres act	**3450.6** art acc sing masc	**2862.4** noun acc sing masc	**3234.1** adv	**3450.17** art pl neu
15. Μὴ	ἀγαπᾶτε	τὸν	κόσμον,	μηδὲ	τὰ
Mē	*agapate*	*ton*	*kosmon*	*mēde*	*ta*
Not	love	the	world,	nor	the things

1706.1 prep	**3450.3** art dat sing	**2862.3** noun dat sing masc	**1430.1** partic	**4948.3** indef-pron nom sing	**25.2** verb 3sing pres act	**3450.6** art acc sing masc
ἐν	τῷ	κόσμῳ,	ἐάν	τις	ἀγαπᾷ	τὸν
en	*tō*	*kosmō*	*ean*	*tis*	*agapa*	*ton*
in	the	world.	If	anyone	should love	the

2862.4 noun acc sing masc	**3620.2** partic	**1498.4** verb 3sing indic pres act	**3450.9** art nom sing fem	**26.1** noun nom sing fem	**3450.2** art gen sing	**3824.2** noun gen sing masc
κόσμον,	οὐκ	ἔστιν	ἡ	ἀγάπη	τοῦ	πατρὸς
kosmon	*ouk*	*estin*	*hē*	*agapē*	*tou*	*patros*
world,	not	is	the	love	of the	Father

1706.1 prep	**840.4** prs-pron dat sing	**3617.1** conj	**3820.17** adj sing neu	**3450.16** art sing neu	**1706.1** prep	**3450.3** art dat sing
ἐν	αὐτῷ·	16. ὅτι	πᾶν	τὸ	ἐν	τῷ
en	*autō*	*hoti*	*pan*	*to*	*en*	*tō*
in	him;	because	all	the	in	the

erally used for those in the 25–40 age group. He wrote to these because they had already encountered Satan, the "wicked one," and had overcome his onslaughts.

Some versions begin verse 14 at this point. But John moves into his second triplet with another statement to "children" (Greek, *paidia*). The new word for children still refers to all believers but emphasizes their immaturity and need of guidance. John acknowledged that these too had come to know the Father.

2:14. The apostle continued his message to the believers, speaking to the "fathers," the more mature members. He repeated the same message he gave them in verse 13.

Then he turned to the younger converts, the "young men," again giving almost the same message as in the prior verse. This time, however, he developed the thought more fully. Strength (Greek, *ischuroi*) is a trait naturally associated with the prime of young manhood, and the word used implies physical strength and ability. Not only did these young men possess great strength, but they also had the Word of God dwelling permanently in them. They had overcome Satan because they were strong. The source of their strength was the Word of God abiding in them. A believer's relationship to the Scriptures invariably determines the quality of his Christian experience. The Bible is called "the sword of the Spirit." Those who have hid God's Word in their hearts have the resources necessary to live an overcoming life and to defeat Satan. When He was tempted, Jesus himself used the Scriptures to defeat the devil.

2:15. An abrupt warning now follows. Christians enjoying such privileges must not center their affections on the world; only God is worthy of their highest devotion.

The command not to love is in the present tense, implying, it appears, that the people have already been developing an affection for the world and need to quench that interest.

The "world" (Greek, *kosmon*) is a word with the general meaning of an orderly arrangement, even used for a woman's adornment in 1 Peter 3:3. It also denotes the universe or the inhabited world. Here, however, it carries an evil connotation, describing the world system which Satan has arranged in his attempt to establish a kingdom without God. Believers are to love neither the world nor the things in it, a concept explained in the following verse. Such love is wrong because God demands we deliberately choose to focus our love on Him.

2:16. John next explained why it is impossible to love both God and the world. The key issue is the fact that a person's attitudes will come from one source or another, either God or the world. Even seemingly neutral items become worldly if they spring from an attitude rooted in the world system, rather than one dependent on God.

men I am writing because you have been strong in defeating the evil one, *Phillips* . . . you have mastered, *TCNT* . . . conquered, *Norlie* . . . gained the victory over the Pernicious One and as a present result are victorious over him, *Wuest.*

I write unto you, little children, because ye have known the Father: Yes, I have written these lines to you all, dear children, *Phillips* . . . children under instruction, *Wuest* . . . you have come to know, *Berkeley.*

14. I have written unto you, fathers, because ye have known him [that is] from the beginning: . . . older men, *Wade* . . . to you fathers because of your experience of the one who has always existed, *Phillips* . . . have learned to know, *Berkeley.*

I have written unto you, young men, because ye are strong: . . . strong with endowed strength, *Wuest* . . . you have all the vigor of youth, *Phillips.*

and the word of God abideth in you: God's Message is always in your thoughts, *TCNT* . . . you have a hold on God's truth, *Phillips* . . . stays in your hearts, *Berkeley* . . . you have kept the divine Gospel, *Noli* . . . treasured in your hearts, *Norlie* . . . lives in you, *Laubach* . . . is always in, *Williams* . . . remains in your thoughts, *Wade.*

and ye have overcome the wicked one: . . . you have gained the victory, *Wuest* . . . You have power over the devil, *NLT* . . . you have conquered the evil one, *Berkeley* . . . you have defeated, *Phillips.*

15. Love not the world, neither the things [that are] in the world: Do not love the ways of the world, *Laubach* . . . Stop considering the world precious with the result that you love it, *Wuest* . . . or what the world has to offer, *TCNT.*

If any man love the world, the love of the Father is not in him: . . . as a habit of life is considering the world precious, *Wuest* . . . Whoever loves the world has not the Father's love in his heart, *Berkeley.*

16. For all that [is] in the world: . . . because everything in the world, *Berkeley.*

2862.3 noun dat sing masc	3450.9 art nom sing fem	1924.2 noun nom sing fem	3450.10 art gen sing fem	4418.2 noun gen sing fem	2504.1 conj	3450.9 art nom sing fem
κόσμῳ,	ἡ	ἐπιθυμία	τῆς	σαρκός,	καὶ	ἡ
kosmō	*hē*	*epithumia*	*tēs*	*sarkos*	*kai*	*hē*
world,	the	desire	of the	flesh,	and	the

1924.2 noun nom sing fem	3450.1 art gen pl	3652.6 noun gen pl masc	2504.1 conj	3450.9 art nom sing fem	210.1 noun nom sing fem
ἐπιθυμία	τῶν	ὀφθαλμῶν,	καὶ	ἡ	ἀλαζονεία
epithumia	*tōn*	*ophthalmōn*	*kai*	*hē*	*alazoneia*
desire	of the	eyes,	and	the	vaunting

3450.2 art gen sing	972.1 noun gen sing masc	3620.2 partic	1498.4 verb 3sing indic pres act	1523.2 prep gen	3450.2 art gen sing	3824.2 noun gen sing masc
τοῦ	βίου,	οὐκ	ἔστιν	ἐκ	τοῦ	πατρός,
tou	*biou*	*ouk*	*estin*	*ek*	*tou*	*patros*
of the	life,	not	is	of	the	Father,

233.1 conj	233.2 conj	1523.2 prep gen	3450.2 art gen sing	2862.2 noun gen sing masc	1498.4 verb 3sing indic pres act
⸂ ἀλλ'	[☆ ἀλλὰ]	ἐκ	τοῦ	κόσμου	ἐστίν.
all'	*alla*	*ek*	*tou*	*kosmou*	*estin*
but	[idem]	of	the	world	is;

2504.1 conj	3450.5 art nom sing masc	2862.1 noun nom sing masc	3717.6 verb 3sing indic pres mid	2504.1 conj	3450.9 art nom sing fem
17. καὶ	ὁ	κόσμος	παράγεται,	καὶ	ἡ
kai	*ho*	*kosmos*	*paragetai*	*kai*	*hē*
and	the	world	is passing away,	and	the

1924.2 noun nom sing fem	840.3 prs-pron gen sing	3450.5 art nom sing masc	1156.2 conj	4020.15 verb nom sing masc part pres act	3450.16 art sing neu
ἐπιθυμία	αὐτοῦ·	ὁ	δὲ	ποιῶν	τὸ
epithumia	*autou*	*ho*	*de*	*poiōn*	*to*
lust	of it,	the	but	doing	the

2284.1 noun sing neu	3450.2 art gen sing	2296.2 noun gen sing masc	3176.1 verb 3sing indic pres act	1519.1 prep	3450.6 art acc sing masc
θέλημα	τοῦ	θεοῦ	μένει	εἰς	τὸν
thelēma	*tou*	*theou*	*menei*	*eis*	*ton*
will		of God	remains	to	the

163.3 noun acc sing masc	3676.3 noun pl masc	2057.8 adj nom sing fem	5443.2 noun nom sing fem	1498.4 verb 3sing indic pres act
αἰῶνα.	18. Παιδία,	ἐσχάτη	ὥρα	ἐστίν·
aiōna	*Paidia*	*eschatē*	*hōra*	*estin*
age.	Little children,	last	hour	it is,

18.a.**Txt:** 01א-corr,02A 018K,020L,byz.Sod
Var: 01א-org,03B,04C Lach,Treg,Alf,Word Tisc,We/Ho,Weis UBS/☆

2504.1 conj	2503.1 conj	189.23 verb 2pl indic aor act	3617.1 conj	3450.5 art nom sing masc	497.1 noun nom sing masc
καὶ	καθὼς	ἠκούσατε	ὅτι	⸀a ὁ ⸃	ἀντίχριστος
kai	*kathōs*	*ēkousate*	*hoti*	*ho*	*antichristos*
and	according as	you heard	that	the	antichrist

2048.34 verb 3sing indic pres mid	2504.1 conj	3431.1 adv	497.3 noun nom pl masc	4044.7 adj nom pl masc	1090.6 verb 3pl indic perf act
ἔρχεται,	καὶ	νῦν	ἀντίχριστοι	πολλοὶ	γεγόνασιν·
erchetai	*kai*	*nun*	*antichristoi*	*polloi*	*gegonasin*
is coming,	even	now	antichrists	many	have arisen,

3468.1 adv	1091.4 verb 1pl indic pres act	3617.1 conj	2057.8 adj nom sing fem	5443.2 noun nom sing fem	1498.4 verb 3sing indic pres act
ὅθεν	γινώσκομεν	ὅτι	ἐσχάτη	ὥρα	ἐστίν
hothen	*ginōskomen*	*hoti*	*eschatē*	*hōra*	*estin*
whence	we know	that	last	hour	it is.

John gave three examples of attitudes that come out of the sphere of the world. First comes the "lust of the flesh," the impulsive desire that originates in the sinful human nature and results in sensuality and other illicit cravings. The second attitude is the "lust of the eyes," the greedy craving that wants whatever it sees. Finally, the "pride of life." John's term for pride is a strong one, carrying the idea of boastful pretensions and bragging beyond the limits of reality. "Life" (Greek, *biou*) refers to mere physical or animal life rather than spiritual or eternal life. It is also used (as in 3:17) to describe the physical possessions that sustain life. The third sin mentioned, then, is that of overconfident pride because of one's possessions. Materialism is always a detriment to spiritual progress.

2:17. A further reason why one should not love the world is that it is temporary. In fact, the present tense of "passing away" shows that the world system had already begun the process of decay that would eventually lead to its disappearance. The middle voice of the verb suggests that the world carries within it the seeds of its own destruction (*paragetai* can be translated as passive or middle voice).

Not only is the world passing away, but so is the "lust" or urgent desire connected with it. The world system only promotes items and values which are part of itself, and since the world is temporary, the things which worldly people want are also temporary.

In contrast, the person who follows the will of God is aligned with something eternal. Both the meaning of "abideth" and the mention of "for ever" underscore the permanence of the godly person. The Greek idiom for "for ever" (literally "into the ages") is a reminder that God's will extends beyond the current age into all the ages yet to come, into the expanse of eternity.

2:18. A new section of the epistle begins here, explaining the fact that God is truth. The rest of the chapter unfolds the need for those who claim fellowship with God to pursue truth, not false teaching.

John addressed his readers as "little children" (Greek, *paidia*), a term emphasizing their immaturity and need to pay attention to the apostle's instructions.

"It is the last time" begins the section, a phrase that only occurs here in the New Testament. Similar terms are used often to describe the age just before Christ's return. The absence of "the" in Greek may suggest that John was not declaring that Christ's coming would certainly be soon; he did observe that his situation was similar to that foretold for the days just prior to the return of Christ.

Several passages in the New Testament describe a specific individual called the Antichrist, who has not yet appeared. Just before the return of Christ to set up His kingdom on earth an individual will arise, called the Antichrist. He will combine in one man to an ultimate degree all the hatred for God and opposition to Him. In John's day a number of people displaying traits like the future

the lust of the flesh, and the lust of the eyes, and the pride of life: . . . the passionate desire of the flesh...the insolent and empty assurance which trusts in the things that serve the creature life, *Wuest* . . . the passions of the flesh, the desires of the eyes and the proud display of life, *Berkeley* . . . the desire seated in the flesh, *Wade* . . . the things that our lower nature and eyes are longing for, *Williams* . . . wanting sinful things to please our bodies, *SEB* . . . the desire of the flesh, and the desire of the eyes, and the ostentation of living, *Concordant* . . . the glory and glamor of life, *Norlie* . . . and a pretentious life, *TCNT* . . . the proud glory of life, *Montgomery* . . . the pride of possessions, *Adams* . . . the vainglory of life, *Clementson* . . . the vain ambitions of life, *Noli.*

is not of the Father, but is of the world: . . . have their origin not from, *Berkeley* . . . from the world as a source, *Wuest.*

17. And the world passeth away, and the lust thereof: . . . and its desire, *Concordant* . . . with its passions is passing away, *Laubach* . . . and its passionate desire, *Wuest.*

but he that doeth the will of God abideth for ever: . . . whoever perseveres in doing God's will, *Williams* . . . will live, *Laubach* . . . will endure, *Noli* . . . is remaining, *Concordant.*

18. Little children, it is the last time: . . . children under instruction, it is a last hour in character, *Wuest* . . . it is the final age of the world, *Norlie* . . . the last hour, *Montgomery* . . . the final Period in the world's history, *Wade.*

and as ye have heard that antichrist shall come: . . . the false-christ is coming, *NLT* . . . have arisen, *Wuest.*

even now are there many antichrists: . . . now also there have come to be many antichrists, *Concordant* . . . many antichrists have already appeared, *Williams* . . . and are here, *Wuest.*

whereby we know that it is the last time: . . . from which we gather certainly that this is, *Berkeley* . . . which confirms my belief that we are near the end, *Phillips* . . . a last hour in character, *Wuest.*

1 John 2:19

19.a.**Txt:** 01ℵ,018K 020L,025P,etc.byz.Weis Sod
Var: 02A,03B,04C,Lach Treg,Alf,Word,Tisc We/Ho,UBS/☆

1523.1 prep gen	2231.2 prs-pron gen 1pl	1814.1 verb indic aor act	1814.41 verb 3pl indic aor act	233.1 conj
19. ἐξ	ἡμῶν	ʻ ἐξῆλθον,	[a☆ ἐξῆλθαν,]	ἀλλ'
ex	*hēmōn*	*exēlthon*	*exēlthan*	*all'*
From among	us	they went out,	[idem]	but

3620.2 partic	1498.37 verb 3pl indic imperf act	1523.1 prep gen	2231.2 prs-pron gen 1pl	1479.1 conj	1056.1 conj	1498.37 verb 3pl indic imperf act	1523.1 prep gen
οὐκ	ἦσαν	ἐξ	ἡμῶν·	εἰ	γὰρ	ʻ ἦσαν	ἐξ
ouk	*ēsan*	*ex*	*hēmōn*	*ei*	*gar*	*ēsan*	*ex*
not	they were	of	us;	if	for	they were	of

2231.2 prs-pron gen 1pl	1523.1 prep gen	2231.2 prs-pron gen 1pl	1498.37 verb 3pl indic imperf act	3176.26 verb 3pl indic plperf act
ἡμῶν,	[☆ ἐξ	ἡμῶν	ἦσαν,]	μεμενήκεισαν
hēmōn	*ex*	*hēmōn*	*ēsan*	*memenēkeisan*
us,	[of	us	they were,]	they would have remained

300.1 partic	3196.1 prep	2231.2 prs-pron gen 1pl	233.1 conj	2419.1 conj	5157.13 verb 3pl subj aor pass
ἂν	μεθ'	ἡμῶν·	ἀλλ'	ἵνα	φανερωθῶσιν
an	*meth'*	*hēmōn*	*all'*	*hina*	*phanerōthōsin*
	with	us,	but	that	they might be made manifest

3617.1 conj	3620.2 partic	1498.7 verb 3pl indic pres act	3820.7 adj nom pl masc	1523.1 prep gen	2231.2 prs-pron gen 1pl	2504.1 conj
ὅτι	οὐκ	εἰσὶν	πάντες	ἐξ	ἡμῶν.	20. καὶ
hoti	*ouk*	*eisin*	*pantes*	*ex*	*hēmōn*	*kai*
that	not	are	all	of	us.	And

5050.1 prs-pron nom 2pl	5380.1 noun sing neu	2174.2 verb 2pl pres act	570.3 prep	3450.2 art gen sing	39.2 adj gen sing	2504.1 conj
ὑμεῖς	χρῖσμα	ἔχετε	ἀπὸ	τοῦ	ἁγίου,	καὶ
humeis	*chrisma*	*echete*	*apo*	*tou*	*hagiou*	*kai*
you	anointing	have	from	the	holy,	and

20.a.**Txt:** 02A,04C,018K 020L,33,byz.it.bo.
Var: 01ℵ,03B,025P,044 sa.Tisc,We/Ho,Weis,Sod UBS/☆

3471.6 verb 2pl indic perf act	3820.1 adj	3820.7 adj nom pl masc	3620.2 partic	1119.7 verb 1sing indic aor act
οἴδατε	ʻ πάντα.	[a☆ πάντες.]	21. οὐκ	ἔγραψα
oidate	*panta*	*pantes*	*ouk*	*egrapsa*
you know	all things.	[idem]	Not	I wrote

5050.3 prs-pron dat 2pl	3617.1 conj	3620.2 partic	3471.6 verb 2pl indic perf act	3450.12 art acc sing fem	223.4 noun acc sing fem	233.1 conj
ὑμῖν	ὅτι	οὐκ	οἴδατε	τὴν	ἀλήθειαν,	ἀλλ'
humin	*hoti*	*ouk*	*oidate*	*tēn*	*alētheian*	*all'*
to you	because	not	you know	the	truth,	but

3617.1 conj	3471.6 verb 2pl indic perf act	840.12 prs-pron acc sing fem	2504.1 conj	3617.1 conj	3820.17 adj sing neu	5414.1 noun sing neu
ὅτι	οἴδατε	αὐτήν,	καὶ	ὅτι	πᾶν	ψεῦδος
hoti	*oidate*	*autēn*	*kai*	*hoti*	*pan*	*pseudos*
because	you know	it,	and	that	any	lie

1523.2 prep gen	3450.10 art gen sing fem	223.2 noun gen sing fem	3620.2 partic	1498.4 verb 3sing indic pres act	4949.3 intr-pron nom sing
ἐκ	τῆς	ἀληθείας	οὐκ	ἔστιν.	22. Τίς
ek	*tēs*	*alētheias*	*ouk*	*estin*	*Tis*
of	the	truth	not	is.	Who

1498.4 verb 3sing indic pres act	3450.5 art nom sing masc	5418.1 noun nom sing masc	1479.1 conj	3231.1 partic	3450.5 art nom sing masc
ἐστιν	ὁ	ψεύστης	εἰ	μὴ	ὁ
estin	*ho*	*pseustēs*	*ei*	*mē*	*ho*
is	the	liar	if	not	the

Antichrist had already appeared, and the "spirit of antichrist" was already present in the world. Only John used the word "antichrist" (in 1 John 2:22; 4:3; 2 John 7), and the prefix *anti* can mean either one who stands openly against the Lord or one who tries to present himself as a substitute for Him, a more subtle form of opposition.

The spirit of Antichrist includes all false teachers and enemies of the truth. This opposition to God may be expected to increase and intensify as time goes on, culminating in the person and activities of one who will gather together under his banner all the anti-God forces in a final attempt to dethrone God. The Book of Revelation depicts his activities and defeat.

2:19. The antichrists of whom John spoke came from the ranks of the believers. John used a play on words when he pointed out that they went out "from us" (Greek, *ex hēmōn*) but were not really "of us" (same Greek phrase). The first use refers to their physical location—they had been in the local churches but had left. The second use refers to the source from which they came—their separation showed that they had never really shared in the same spiritual fellowship as the others. John laid down the rule—those who desert show openly that none of them were truly one with the church.

2:20. Unlike the false brethren, the true believers to whom John wrote had an "unction" or anointing which provided them with the ability to hold to the truth. "Unction" (Greek, *chrisma*) is a play on words—the false "christs" of verse 19 are contrasted with the "chrisma" (empowered saints) of verse 20. In the Old Testament, kings, priests, and prophets were anointed with oil to symbolize the Holy Spirit was empowering them for their task (cf. 1 Samuel 16:13; Isaiah 61:1). This verse speaks of how the Holy Spirit anoints the believer so he will have knowledge which comes from God, the Holy One. Gnostic false teachers claimed to be the sole source of truth, but the Holy Spirit makes it possible for all believers to know the truth.

2:21. John did not write to convey hidden truths which had been concealed from his hearers; his letter was sent to people who simply needed to be reminded of things they already knew. They already knew the gospel, and when they recalled that no lie springs from that source of truth, they would recognize that truth and falsehood cannot coexist.

2:22. The believer's anointing is based on the teachings of the gospel which Christ and His apostles preached. Thus John asked

19. They went out from us, but they were not of us: Out of us they come, *Concordant* . . . went out from our company, it is true, *Phillips* . . . they departed...but they did not belong to us as a source, *Wuest* . . . but they left us, *SEB* . . . never really belonged to us, *Laubach.*

for if they had been of us, they would [no doubt] have continued with us: . . . had they been ours, *Berkeley* . . . If they had really belonged to us they would have stayed, *Phillips* . . . they would have remained with us, *Wilson.*

but [they went out], that they might be made manifest: Because they left, *NLT* . . . but their departure was designed to make it clear, *Wade* . . . it had to become clear, *Berkeley* . . . In fact, their going proves beyond doubt that men like that, *Phillips* . . . they departed in order that they might be plainly recognized, *Wuest.*

that they were not all of us: . . . were revealed as not being of us, *Swann* . . . that all do not belong to us as a source, *Wuest* . . . that it might be shown that none of them belongs to us, *Williams C.K.* . . . they did not belong to our group, *Norlie* . . . were not "our men" at all, *Phillips.*

20. But ye have an unction from the Holy One: Besides, you hold your anointing from, *Berkeley* . . . were anointed by, *Norlie* . . . have been consecrated by, *TCNT* . . . you have received an appointment from, *Williams C.K.*

and ye know all things: . . . all of you have the capacity to know [spiritual truth], *Wuest* . . . you all know the truth, *Laubach* . . . you all are aware, *Concordant.*

21. I have not written unto you because ye know not the truth: The reason I wrote you was not that you do not know the truth, *Berkeley* . . . you are not acquainted with, *Concordant.*

but because ye know it, and that no lie is of the truth: . . . but that you know it and that from truth nothing false originates, *Berkeley* . . . is not out of the truth as a source, *Wuest.*

22. Who is a liar but he that denieth that Jesus is the Christ?: Who is the pre-eminent liar, *Wade*

714.4 verb nom sing masc part pres mid	3617.1 conj	2400.1 name nom masc	3620.2 partic	1498.4 verb 3sing indic pres act	3450.5 art nom sing masc
ἀρνούμενος	ὅτι	Ἰησοῦς	οὐκ	ἔστιν	ὁ
arnoumenos	*hoti*	*Iēsous*	*ouk*	*estin*	*ho*
denying	that	Jesus	not	is	the

5382.1 name nom masc	3642.4 dem-pron nom sing masc	1498.4 verb 3sing indic pres act	3450.5 art nom sing masc	497.1 noun nom sing masc
Χριστός;	οὗτός	ἐστιν	ὁ	ἀντίχριστος
Christos	*houtos*	*estin*	*ho*	*antichristos*
Christ?	This	is	the	antichrist

3450.5 art nom sing masc	714.4 verb nom sing masc part pres mid	3450.6 art acc sing masc	3824.4 noun acc sing masc	2504.1 conj	3450.6 art acc sing masc
ὁ	ἀρνούμενος	τὸν	πατέρα	καὶ	τὸν
ho	*arnoumenos*	*ton*	*patera*	*kai*	*ton*
the	denying	the	Father	and	the

5048.4 noun acc sing masc	3820.6 adj nom sing masc	3450.5 art nom sing masc	714.4 verb nom sing masc part pres mid	3450.6 art acc sing masc
υἱόν.	23. πᾶς	ὁ	ἀρνούμενος	τὸν
huion	*pas*	*ho*	*arnoumenos*	*ton*
Son.	Everyone	the	denying	the

23.a.Var: 01ℵ,02A,03B 04C,025P,sa.bo.Gries Lach,Treg,Alf,Word Tisc,We/Ho,Weis,Sod UBS/☆

5048.4 noun acc sing masc	3624.1 conj	3450.6 art acc sing masc	3824.4 noun acc sing masc	2174.4 verb 3sing indic pres act	3450.5 art nom sing masc
υἱὸν	οὐδὲ	τὸν	πατέρα	ἔχει.	[a☆+ ὁ
huion	*oude*	*ton*	*patera*	*echei*	*ho*
Son,	neither	the	Father	has he.	[the

3533.16 verb nom sing masc part pres act	3450.6 art acc sing masc	5048.4 noun acc sing masc	2504.1 conj	3450.6 art acc sing masc	3824.4 noun acc sing masc
ὁμολογῶν	τὸν	υἱὸν	καὶ	τὸν	πατέρα
homologōn	*ton*	*huion*	*kai*	*ton*	*patera*
confessing	the	Son	also	the	Father

24.a.Txt: 018K,020L,byz. Var: 01ℵ,02A,03B,04C 025P,33,Lach,Treg,Alf Tisc,We/Ho,Weis,Sod UBS/☆

2174.4 verb 3sing indic pres act	5050.1 prs-pron nom 2pl	3631.1 partic	3614.16 rel-pron sing neu	189.23 verb 2pl indic aor act
ἔχει.]	24. ⸀Ὑμεῖς	(a οὖν)	ὃ	ἠκούσατε
echei	*Humeis*	*oun*	*ho*	*ēkousate*
has.]	You	therefore	what	you heard

570.2 prep	741.2 noun gen sing fem	1706.1 prep	5050.3 prs-pron dat 2pl	3176.9 verb 3sing impr pres act	1430.1 partic	1706.1 prep
ἀπ'	ἀρχῆς,	ἐν	ὑμῖν	μενέτω.	ἐὰν	ἐν
ap'	*archēs*	*en*	*humin*	*menetō*	*ean*	*en*
from	beginning,	in	you	let it continue:	if	in

5050.3 prs-pron dat 2pl	3176.19 verb 3sing subj aor act	3614.16 rel-pron sing neu	570.2 prep	741.2 noun gen sing fem	189.23 verb 2pl indic aor act
ὑμῖν	μείνῃ	ὃ	ἀπ'	ἀρχῆς	ἠκούσατε,
humin	*meinē*	*ho*	*ap'*	*archēs*	*ēkousate*
you	should continue	what	from	beginning	you heard,

2504.1 conj	5050.1 prs-pron nom 2pl	1706.1 prep	3450.3 art dat sing	5048.3 noun dat sing masc	2504.1 conj	1706.1 prep	3450.3 art dat sing
καὶ	ὑμεῖς	ἐν	τῷ	υἱῷ	καὶ	ἐν	τῷ
kai	*humeis*	*en*	*tō*	*huiō*	*kai*	*en*	*tō*
also	you	in	the	Son	and	in	the

3824.3 noun dat sing masc	3176.28 verb 2pl indic fut act	2504.1 conj	3642.9 dem-pron nom sing fem	1498.4 verb 3sing indic pres act
πατρὶ	μενεῖτε.	25. καὶ	αὕτη	ἐστὶν
patri	*meneite*	*kai*	*hautē*	*estin*
Father	shall remain.	And	this	is

them to use the truth they already knew to evaluate the message of new teachers. John attacked the heretics who taught that Jesus was a mere man who was indwelt temporarily by the Christ, a divine spirit who left Him just before the Cross. He who denies that Jesus is the Christ is denying the incarnation of Christ, undercutting the truth that God became man. No wonder John declared that such a person is *the* liar (emphatic in Greek)—this teaching would nullify the entire message of the New Testament!

The doctrine of the Incarnation may be considered the foundation stone for all other New Testament truth. "The Word was made flesh, and dwelt among us" (John 1:14) is the great statement which proclaimed God's plan for nullifying the effects of the Fall. If Jesus was not born of a virgin, He was not the Son of God. And He could not be the promised Messiah—Christ. He was not just divine, like God; He was deity himself, the very essence of God in human flesh. To deny this is heresy of the grossest sort.

Those who preached such doctrines evidently claimed to believe the same truths as other teachers concerning the Father, but John warned that anyone who denied the work of Christ was denying the Father as well.

2:23. No one who denies the Son can claim to have a family relationship with the Father; both persons of the Godhead are together inseparably, and both must be accepted together. On the other hand, anyone who acknowledges Jesus as God's Son who became man shows that his Father is God.

This was a very important point to emphasize, especially for the apostle John. In the Gospel he wrote under the inspiration of the Holy Spirit, he had referred to the close relationship between the Father and the Son. When he pointed out that Jesus was the only One who could reveal God to mankind, he wrote, "The only begotten Son, which is in the bosom of the Father, he hath declared him" (John 1:18). To deny this would destroy the truth of the gospel.

2:24. How should a Christian respond to the false teachings of these antichrists? By continuing to believe the truths already learned. The Greek begins with "you," an emphatic contrast with the apostates. Rather than accepting novel ideas, the readers were to hold permanently to the doctrines which they learned in the beginning, when they first heard the gospel.

By obeying, they could remain in a living relationship with God. Abiding permanently with the Son allows us to have fellowship with the Father.

2:25. God promises eternal life to all who remain in the Son. "This" refers to eternal life, as shown by the feminine forms of

. . . And what, I ask you, is the crowning lie? Surely the denial that Jesus is God's anointed one, *Phillips* . . . Who is the liar whom I have in mind? *Greber* . . . if it is not the denier that Jesus is the Christ? *Berkeley* . . . the man who rejects, *TCNT*.

He is antichrist, that denieth the Father and the Son: I say, therefore, that any man who refuses to acknowledge the Father and the Son is an antichrist, *Phillips* . . . is the enemy of Christ, *Everyday* . . . even he who disowns, *Montgomery* . . . because he repudiates both, *Noli* . . . This person is the enemy of Christ, *SEB*.

23. Whosoever denieth the Son, the same hath not the Father: If anyone does not believe in the Son, *Everyday* . . . The man who will not recognize the Son cannot possibly know the Father, *Phillips* . . . who is disowning...neither has, *Concordant*.

[but] he that acknowledgeth the Son hath the Father also: . . . he who confesses, *Montgomery, Laubach* . . . whoever accepts the Son has the Father, too, *Everyday* . . . who is avowing, *Concordant* . . . yet the man who believes in the Son will find that, *Phillips* . . . has the Father as well, *Berkeley* . . . is also in communion with the Father, *Greber*.

24. Let that therefore abide in you, which ye have heard from the beginning: For yourselves I beg you to stick to the original teaching, *Phillips* . . . Be sure that you continue to follow the teaching that you heard from the beginning, *Everyday* . . . live in your heart, *Laubach* . . . be remaining in you, *Concordant* . . . let that stay with you, *Berkeley*.

If that which ye have heard from the beginning shall remain in you: If you do, *Phillips* . . . If you continue in that teaching, *Everyday* . . . let that remain in you, *Williams C.K.* . . . stays with you, *Berkeley*.

ye also shall continue in the Son, and in the Father: . . . you will abide, *Wuest* . . . you will stay, *Everyday* . . . will be remaining in, *Concordant* . . . remain in union with, *Berkeley* . . . you will be living in fellowship with, *Phillips*.

3450.9 art nom sing fem	**1845.2** noun nom sing fem	**3614.12** rel-pron acc sing fem	**840.5** prs-pron nom sing masc	**1846.3** verb 3sing indic aor mid
ἡ	ἐπαγγελία,	ἣν	αὐτὸς	ἐπηγγείλατο
hē	*epangelia*	*hēn*	*autos*	*epēngeilato*
the	promise	which	he	promised

2231.3 prs-pron dat 1pl	**3450.12** art acc sing fem	**2205.4** noun acc sing fem	**3450.12** art acc sing fem	**164.1** adj sing	**3642.18** dem-pron pl neu
ἡμῖν,	τὴν	ζωὴν	τὴν	αἰώνιον.	**26.** Ταῦτα
hēmin	*tēn*	*zōēn*	*tēn*	*aiōnion*	*Tauta*
us,	the	life	the	eternal.	These things

1119.7 verb 1sing indic aor act	**5050.3** prs-pron dat 2pl	**3875.1** prep	**3450.1** art gen pl	**3966.6** verb gen pl masc part pres act	**5050.4** prs-pron acc 2pl
ἔγραψα	ὑμῖν	περὶ	τῶν	πλανώντων	ὑμᾶς.
egrapsa	*humin*	*peri*	*tōn*	*planōntōn*	*humas*
I wrote	to you	concerning	the	leading astray	you:

2504.1 conj	**5050.1** prs-pron nom 2pl	**3450.16** art sing neu	**5380.1** noun sing neu	**3614.16** rel-pron sing neu	**2956.16** verb 2pl indic aor act
27. καὶ	ὑμεῖς	τὸ	χρῖσμα	ὃ	ἐλάβετε
kai	*humeis*	*to*	*chrisma*	*ho*	*elabete*
and	you	the	anointing	which	you received

570.2 prep	**840.3** prs-pron gen sing	**1706.1** prep	**5050.3** prs-pron dat 2pl	**3176.1** verb 3sing indic pres act	**3176.1** verb 3sing indic pres act	**1706.1** prep
ἀπ'	αὐτοῦ,	ʼ ἐν	ὑμῖν	μένει,	[☆ μένει	ἐν
ap'	*autou*	*en*	*humin*	*menei*	*menei*	*en*
from	him,	in	you	remains,	[remains	in

5050.3 prs-pron dat 2pl	**2504.1** conj	**3620.3** partic	**5367.3** noun acc sing fem	**2174.2** verb 2pl pres act	**2419.1** conj	**4948.3** indef-pron nom sing
ὑμῖν,]	καὶ	οὐ	χρείαν	ἔχετε	ἵνα	τις
humin	*kai*	*ou*	*chreian*	*echete*	*hina*	*tis*
you,]	and	not	need	you have	that	anyone

27.a.**Txt:** 02A,018K 020L,byz.bo.
Var: 01ℵ,03B,04C,025P sa.Treg,Alf,Tisc,We/Ho Weis,Sod,UBS/☆

1315.4 verb 3sing subj pres act	**5050.4** prs-pron acc 2pl	**233.1** conj	**5453.1** conj	**3450.16** art sing neu	**840.15** prs-pron sing neu	**840.3** prs-pron gen sing
διδάσκῃ	ὑμᾶς·	ἀλλ'	ὡς	τὸ	ʼ αὐτὸ	[a☆ αὐτοῦ]
didaskē	*humas*	*all'*	*hōs*	*to*	*auto*	*autou*
should teach	you;	but	as	the	same	[idem]

5380.1 noun sing neu	**1315.3** verb 3sing indic pres act	**5050.4** prs-pron acc 2pl	**3875.1** prep	**3820.4** adj gen pl	**2504.1** conj
χρῖσμα	διδάσκει	ὑμᾶς	περὶ	πάντων,	καὶ
chrisma	*didaskei*	*humas*	*peri*	*pantōn*	*kai*
anointing	teaches	you	concerning	all things,	and

225.5 adj sing neu	**1498.4** verb 3sing indic pres act	**2504.1** conj	**3620.2** partic	**1498.4** verb 3sing indic pres act	**5414.1** noun sing neu	**2504.1** conj
ἀληθές	ἐστιν,	καὶ	οὐκ	ἔστιν	ψεῦδος·	καὶ
alēthes	*estin*	*kai*	*ouk*	*estin*	*pseudos*	*kai*
true	is,	and	not	is	a lie;	and

27.b.**Txt:** 018K,020L,byz.
Var: 01ℵ,02A,03B,04C 025P,sa.bo.Lach,Treg Alf,Word,Tisc,We/Ho Weis,Sod,UBS/☆

2503.1 conj	**1315.13** verb 3sing indic aor act	**5050.4** prs-pron acc 2pl	**3176.28** verb 2pl indic fut act	**3176.2** verb 2pl pres act
καθὼς	ἐδίδαξεν	ὑμᾶς,	ʼ μενεῖτε	[b☆ μένετε]
kathōs	*edidaxen*	*humas*	*meneite*	*menete*
even as	it taught	you,	you shall remain	[remain]

1706.1 prep	**840.4** prs-pron dat sing	**2504.1** conj	**3431.1** adv	**4888.1** noun pl neu	**3176.2** verb 2pl pres act	**1706.1** prep
ἐν	αὐτῷ.	**28.** Καὶ	νῦν,	τεκνία,	μένετε	ἐν
en	*autō*	*Kai*	*nun*	*teknia*	*menete*	*en*
in	him.	And	now,	little children,	remain	in

both words. And eternal life is more than infinitely continued existence; it is a quality of life which can be experienced now. Christ himself (note the emphatic "he," Greek *autos*) promised eternal life in such passages as John 3:15,16; 6:40; 17:3.

This is no idle promise. Jesus often showed the relationship between eternal life and the resurrection. At the tomb of Lazarus He told Martha, "I am the resurrection, and the life" (John 11:25). Later in this epistle John states, "He that hath the Son hath life" (5:12). Therefore believers never really die. They are awaiting the resurrection.

25. And this is the promise that he hath promised us, [even] eternal life: And that means sharing his own life for ever, as he has promised, *Phillips* . . . This is the message that he himself brought us, the message of the life hereafter, *Greber* . . . And this is what the Son promised to us—life forever, *Everyday* . . . the life eonian, *Concordant.*

2:26. In the next two verses the apostle repeated some of his major points. First he described the character of the false teachers who were attempting to disturb the churches. He had written "these things" before, primarily in verses 18-25, describing the troublemakers as opponents of Christ and promoters of lies. Now he added the fact that they were deceivers. "Seduce" (Greek, *planontōn*) means to cause someone to go astray. Since the rest of the letter envisions a situation where believers are being approached, but have not succumbed, this present participle may be describing action which is attempted but not completed. The heretics were trying to pull church members off the path but had not yet succeeded in large numbers.

26. These [things] have I written unto you concerning them that seduce you: It is true that I felt I had to write the above about men who would dearly love to, *Phillips* . . . about those people who are trying to lead you the wrong way, *Everyday* . . . those who want to mislead you, *Norlie* . . . those who are deceiving you, *Concordant* . . . who are leading you astray, *Wuest.*

2:27. Next John reviewed the anointing which enables the Christian to recognize truth. He began with an emphatic "you," as in verse 24, showing how different the true believers are from the false teachers. Earlier John asked us to let the anointing remain (2:24); here he asserted that it actually does remain in the believer.

This anointing implies the presence of the Holy Spirit, who makes it possible for us to escape dependence on human teachers. Of course John did not want to abolish teachers; he was functioning as a teacher when he wrote his book! But a Spirit-led Christian can detect truth and error without aid from any new breed of teacher.

The rest of the verse develops the command to abide in Christ. The Holy Spirit teaches the things a Christian needs to know, and His instruction is always true, not a lie. Then John repeated the fact that this anointing teaches the Christian, this time using the aorist tense to refer to the teaching ministry of Christ. The final phrase gives a command, "Abide in him." This is a reference to Christ, as shown by verse 28.

27. But the anointing which ye have received of him abideth in you: Yet I know that the touch of his Spirit never leaves you, *Phillips* . . . Christ gave you a special gift. You still have this gift in you, *Everyday* . . . which Christ poured upon you, *Laubach* . . . is remaining in you, *Concordant.*

and ye need not that any man teach you: . . . having that anyone be constantly teaching you, *Wuest* . . . you stand in no need of teaching from anyone, *Berkeley* . . . and you don't really need a human teacher, *Phillips.*

but as the same anointing teacheth you of all things: The Holy Spirit is able to teach you, *NLT* . . . The gift he gave you teaches you about everything, *Everyday* . . . instructs you about everything, *Berkeley.*

and is truth, and is no lie: The Holy Spirit teaches only the truth, *Laubach* . . . This gift is true, *Everyday* . . . and is no falsehood, *Berkeley.*

and even as it hath taught you, ye shall abide in him: . . . be constantly abiding, *Wuest* . . . remain in Him, *Concordant* . . . continue to live in Christ, as his gift taught you, *Everyday* . . . hold faithfully to that which it has taught you, *Greber.*

2:28. As John began another new section, he added a new concept to the command to abide: the second coming of the Lord. Christians should maintain an abiding relationship with Jesus so

28. And now, little children, abide in him: . . . his teaching urges you to live in Christ, *Phillips* . . . remain in union, *Wade.*

28.a.**Txt:** 018K,020L,byz.
Var: 01ℵ,02A,03B,04C 025P,33,sa.bo.Lach Treg,Alf,Tisc,We/Ho Weis,Sod,UBS/☆

840.4 prs-pron dat sing	**2419.1** conj	**3615.1** conj	**1430.1** partic	**5157.12** verb 3sing subj aor pass	**2174.8** verb 1pl subj pres act
αὐτῷ·	ἵνα	‘ ὅταν	[a☆ ἐὰν]	φανερωθῇ,	‘ ἔχωμεν
autō	*hina*	*hotan*	*ean*	*phanerōthē*	*echōmen*
him,	that	when	[if]	he be manifested	we may have

28.b.**Txt:** 01ℵ-org,018K 020L,byz.
Var: 01ℵ-corr,02A,03B 04C,025P,Lach,Treg Alf,Tisc,We/Ho,Weis Sod,UBS/☆

2174.53 verb 1pl subj aor act	**3816.4** noun acc sing fem	**2504.1** conj	**3231.1** partic	**152.3** verb 1pl subj aor pass	**570.2** prep
[b☆ σχῶμεν]	παῤῥησίαν,	καὶ	μὴ	αἰσχυνθῶμεν	ἀπ'
schōmen	*parrhēsian*	*kai*	*mē*	*aischunthōmen*	*ap'*
[idem]	boldness,	and	not	be put to shame	from

840.3 prs-pron gen sing	**1706.1** prep	**3450.11** art dat sing fem	**3814.3** noun dat sing fem	**840.3** prs-pron gen sing	**1430.1** partic	**3471.17** verb 2pl subj perf act
αὐτοῦ,	ἐν	τῇ	παρουσίᾳ	αὐτοῦ.	**29.** Ἐὰν	εἰδῆτε
autou	*en*	*tē*	*parousia*	*autou*	*Ean*	*eidēte*
him	at	the	coming	his.	If	you know

29.a.**Var:** 01ℵ,02A,04C 025P,33,sa.Treg,Alf Tisc,Weis,Sod,UBS/☆

3617.1 conj	**1337.3** adj nom sing masc	**1498.4** verb 3sing indic pres act	**1091.5** verb 2pl indic pres act	**3617.1** conj	**2504.1** conj
ὅτι	δίκαιός	ἐστιν,	γινώσκετε	ὅτι	[a☆+ καὶ]
hoti	*dikaios*	*estin*	*ginōskete*	*hoti*	*kai*
that	righteous	he is,	you know	that	[also]

3820.6 adj nom sing masc	**3450.5** art nom sing masc	**4020.15** verb nom sing masc part pres act	**3450.12** art acc sing fem	**1336.4** noun acc sing fem
πᾶς	ὁ	ποιῶν	τὴν	δικαιοσύνην,
pas	*ho*	*poiōn*	*tēn*	*dikaiosunēn*
everyone	the	practicing	the	righteousness

1523.1 prep gen	**840.3** prs-pron gen sing	**1074.23** verb 3sing indic perf mid	**1481.15** verb 2pl impr aor act	**4076.5** intr-pron acc sing fem
ἐξ	αὐτοῦ,	γεγέννηται.	**3:1.** Ἴδετε	ποταπὴν
ex	*autou*	*gegennētai*	*Idete*	*potapēn*
of	him	has been born.	See	what manner

26.4 noun acc sing fem	**1319.33** verb 3sing indic perf act	**2231.3** prs-pron dat 1pl	**3450.5** art nom sing masc	**3824.1** noun nom sing masc	**2419.1** conj
ἀγάπην	δέδωκεν	ἡμῖν	ὁ	πατὴρ,	ἵνα
agapēn	*dedōken*	*hēmin*	*ho*	*patēr*	*hina*
love	has given	to us	the	Father,	that

1.a.**Var:** 01ℵ,02A,03B 04C,025P,33,it.sa.bo. Lach,Treg,Alf,Tisc We/Ho,Weis,Sod UBS/☆

4891.4 noun pl neu	**2296.2** noun gen sing masc	**2535.40** verb 1pl subj aor pass	**2504.1** conj	**1498.5** verb 1pl indic pres act
τέκνα	θεοῦ	κληθῶμεν·	[a☆+ καὶ	ἐσμέν.]
tekna	*theou*	*klēthōmen*	*kai*	*esmen*
children	of God	we should be called.	[and	we are.]

1217.2 prep	**3642.17** dem-pron sing neu	**3450.5** art nom sing masc	**2862.1** noun nom sing masc	**3620.3** partic	**1091.3** verb 3sing indic pres act
διὰ	τοῦτο	ὁ	κόσμος	οὐ	γινώσκει
dia	*touto*	*ho*	*kosmos*	*ou*	*ginōskei*
On account of	this	the	world	not	knows

1.b.**Txt:** p74,01ℵ-corr2 02A,03B,044,33,323 614,630,945,1505,1739 2495
Var: 01ℵ-org,04C,025P byz.

2231.4 prs-pron acc 1pl	**5050.4** prs-pron acc 2pl	**3617.1** conj	**3620.2** partic	**1091.17** verb 3sing indic aor act	**840.6** prs-pron acc sing masc
‘☆ ἡμᾶς,	[b ὑμᾶς,]	ὅτι	οὐκ	ἔγνω	αὐτόν.
hēmas	*humas*	*hoti*	*ouk*	*egnō*	*auton*
us,	[you,]	because	not	it knew	him.

27.6 adj pl masc	**3431.1** adv	**4891.4** noun pl neu	**2296.2** noun gen sing masc	**1498.5** verb 1pl indic pres act	**2504.1** conj	**3632.1** adv
2. Ἀγαπητοί,	νῦν	τέκνα	θεοῦ	ἐσμεν,	καὶ	οὔπω
Agapētoi	*nun*	*tekna*	*theou*	*esmen*	*kai*	*oupō*
Beloved,	now	children	of God	are we,	and	not yet

they can stand before Him unashamed when He returns. "Confidence" (Greek, *parrhēsian*) was used to describe the free citizens of Athens who were permitted to speak their minds boldly in the assembly. In contrast, a person with no abiding tie to God will shrink away in shame when the Monarch of the universe arrives.

2:29. John began a new cycle of teaching here, which took the same themes he had already handled, and developed the thoughts a little further. For instance, he deepened the thought of fellowship to the concept of sonship (3:9; 4:7; 5:1,4,18). After establishing our identity as family members, he moved on to show that the tests of true sonship are holiness, love, and truth.

The first topic is holiness (2:29 to 3:10). If we know the doctrinal fact that the character of God is righteous, we will be able to learn by experience the practical truth that those in His family must also have righteousness.

In context, it appears that the "he" of the first part of the verse refers to Jesus who has a righteous character. In the second part, "him" refers to the Father as the source of the new birth. Anyone who continually practices the righteousness which Christ displayed is demonstrating that he has received birth from God, stamping him with the divine likeness.

3:1. When John considered our place as children of God, he burst out in excitement. "Behold!" is a sharp command to pay attention to the marvelous kind of love which God has permanently bestowed. "What manner of" originally meant "from what country," and later became an exclamation of surprise and wonder (cf. Mark 13:1). This love (Greek, *agapē*) is God's way of showing mercy to man, not merely an emotional reaction. It is a special kind of love. The Greek language contains other words which may be translated "love," but they are less in meaning than agape love. They can mean just physical love, on an animal level. Another is best translated "affection," which can be strong. But God's kind of love is given without measure, does not ask for reciprocation. As a result of His love, we enjoy the status of God's children. And not in word only; many manuscripts add "we are," to show that the title is real.

Belonging to God's family implies suffering the world's misunderstanding. Opposition often arises, because men and women in the world system find God a mystery. They feel ill at ease and develop hostility toward God and His people.

3:2. Here John compared the present and future of God's people. Our present reality is the privilege of a position as children of God (not "sons," as in KJV). The future is still obscure, but we can know

that, when he shall appear, we may have confidence: So that if he were suddenly to reveal himself we should still know exactly where we stand, *Phillips* . . . if he is manifested, we may have boldness, *Swann* . . . in order that whenever He is made visible, we may have instant freedom of speech, *Wuest* . . . we can face him proudly, *Noli.*

and not be ashamed before him at his coming: . . . without shrinking from him in shame, *Noli* . . . and not hide from him in shame, *Williams C.K.* . . . and not be put to shame by Him, *Concordant* . . . not be made to shrink away from Him in shame at His coming and personal presence, *Wuest.*

29. If ye know that he is righteous: If you know in an absolute manner that, *Wuest* . . . you should be perceiving that He is just, *Concordant* . . . God is really good, *Phillips.*

ye know that every one that doeth righteousness is born of him: . . . who practices, *Berkeley* . . . is begotten of Him, *Concordant* . . . a true child of God, *Phillips* . . . from Him has been born, with the present result that that one is a born-one, *Wuest.*

1. Behold, what manner of love the Father hath bestowed upon us: Perceive, *Concordant* . . . Consider the incredible love that, *Phillips* . . . See what amazing love, *Adams* . . . what transcendent love, *Wade* . . . what a wealth of love the Father has lavished on us, *Berkeley* . . . what exotic [foreign to the human heart] love the Father has permanently, *Wuest.*

that we should be called the sons of God: . . . in allowing us to be called, *Phillips* . . . to the end that we may be named children, *Wuest* . . . children, *Concordant.*

therefore the world knoweth us not, because it knew him not: . . . does not recognize us, *TNT* . . . because it has not come into an experiential knowledge of Him, *Wuest* . . . it did not know Him, *Berkeley.*

2. Beloved, now are we the sons of God: Divinely loved ones, now born-ones of, *Wuest* . . . we are God's children now, *Berkeley.*

1 John 3:3

2.a.**Txt:** 018K,020L,byz.
Var: 01א,02A,03B,04C 025P,sa.Lach,Treg,Alf Word,Tisc,We/Ho,Weis Sod,UBS/⋆

5157.10 verb 3sing indic aor pass	**4949.9** intr-pron sing neu	**1498.41** verb 1pl indic fut mid	**3471.5** verb 1pl indic perf act	**1156.2** conj	**3617.1** conj
ἐφανερώθη	τί	ἐσόμεθα	οἴδαμεν	⸂a δὲ ⸃	ὅτι
ephanerōthē	*ti*	*esometha*	*oidamen*	*de*	*hoti*
was it manifested	what	we shall be;	we know	but	that

1430.1 partic	**5157.12** verb 3sing subj aor pass	**3527.3** adj nom pl masc	**840.4** prs-pron dat sing	**1498.41** verb 1pl indic fut mid	**3617.1** conj
ἐὰν	φανερωθῇ,	ὅμοιοι	αὐτῷ	ἐσόμεθα,	ὅτι
ean	*phanerōthē*	*homoioi*	*autō*	*esometha*	*hoti*
if	he be manifested,	like	him	we shall be,	for

3571.32 verb 1pl indic fut mid	**840.6** prs-pron acc sing masc	**2503.1** conj	**1498.4** verb 3sing indic pres act	**2504.1** conj	**3820.6** adj nom sing masc
ὀψόμεθα	αὐτὸν	καθώς	ἐστιν.	3. καὶ	πᾶς
opsometha	*auton*	*kathōs*	*estin*	*kai*	*pas*
we shall see	him	as	he is.	And	everyone

3450.5 art nom sing masc	**2174.17** verb nom sing masc part pres act	**3450.12** art acc sing fem	**1667.4** noun acc sing fem	**3642.12** dem-pron acc sing fem	**1894.2** prep
ὁ	ἔχων	τὴν	ἐλπίδα	ταύτην	ἐπ'
ho	*echōn*	*tēn*	*elpida*	*tautēn*	*ep'*
the	having	the	hope	this	in

840.4 prs-pron dat sing	**47.1** verb 3sing indic pres act	**1431.6** prs-pron acc sing masc	**2503.1** conj	**1552.3** dem-pron nom sing masc	**52.1** adj nom sing masc
αὐτῷ,	ἁγνίζει	ἑαυτὸν,	καθὼς	ἐκεῖνος	ἁγνός
autō	*hagnizei*	*heauton*	*kathōs*	*ekeinos*	*hagnos*
him,	purifies	himself,	even as	that one	pure

1498.4 verb 3sing indic pres act	**3820.6** adj nom sing masc	**3450.5** art nom sing masc	**4020.15** verb nom sing masc part pres act	**3450.12** art acc sing fem
ἐστιν.	4. Πᾶς	ὁ	ποιῶν	τὴν
estin	*Pas*	*ho*	*poiōn*	*tēn*
is.	Everyone	the	practicing	the

264.4 noun acc sing fem	**2504.1** conj	**3450.12** art acc sing fem	**455.4** noun acc sing fem	**4020.5** verb 3sing indic pres act	**2504.1** conj
ἁμαρτίαν,	καὶ	τὴν	ἀνομίαν	ποιεῖ,	καὶ
hamartian	*kai*	*tēn*	*anomian*	*poiei*	*kai*
sin,	also	the	lawlessness	practices;	and

3450.9 art nom sing fem	**264.2** noun nom sing fem	**1498.4** verb 3sing indic pres act	**3450.9** art nom sing fem	**455.1** noun nom sing fem	**2504.1** conj
ἡ	ἁμαρτία	ἐστὶν	ἡ	ἀνομία.	5. καὶ
hē	*hamartia*	*estin*	*hē*	*anomia*	*kai*
the	sin	is	the	lawlessness.	And

3471.6 verb 2pl indic perf act	**3617.1** conj	**1552.3** dem-pron nom sing masc	**5157.10** verb 3sing indic aor pass	**2419.1** conj	**3450.15** art acc pl fem
οἴδατε	ὅτι	ἐκεῖνος	ἐφανερώθη,	ἵνα	τὰς
oidate	*hoti*	*ekeinos*	*ephanerōthē*	*hina*	*tas*
you know	that	that	was manifested,	that	the

5.a.**Txt:** 01א,04C,018K 020L,byz.sa.Sod
Var: 02A,03B,025P,33 it.bo.Lach,Treg,Alf,Tisc We/Ho,Weis,UBS/⋆

264.1 noun fem	**2231.2** prs-pron gen 1pl	**142.12** verb 3sing subj aor act	**2504.1** conj	**264.2** noun nom sing fem
ἁμαρτίας	⸂a ἡμῶν ⸃	ἄρῃ·	καὶ	ἁμαρτία
hamartias	*hēmōn*	*arē*	*kai*	*hamartia*
sins	our	he might take away;	and	sin

1706.1 prep	**840.4** prs-pron dat sing	**3620.2** partic	**1498.4** verb 3sing indic pres act	**3820.6** adj nom sing masc	**3450.5** art nom sing masc
ἐν	αὐτῷ	οὐκ	ἔστιν.	6. πᾶς	ὁ
en	*autō*	*ouk*	*estin*	*pas*	*ho*
in	him	not	is.	Anyone	the

something about it. One great fact stands out—we will be like Christ. The great transformation will take place when He returns, and the Christian will be able to look upon the Lord just as He is in reality. The view of Christ is the secret to Christlikeness. Of course no one achieves perfect likeness, but "like" denotes a marked similarity of attributes.

Because believers have been made "partakers of the divine nature" (2 Peter 1:4), they possess a potential for manifesting the attributes of the Christ who dwells within them by His Spirit. In a sense the Son of God can live himself out of their lives by helping them act as He himself would in given situations. They are His representatives.

and it doth not yet appear what we shall be: . . . not yet has it been made visible what we shall be, *Wuest* . . . We don't know what we shall become in the future, *Phillips* . . . has not yet been shown, *Berkeley.*

but we know that, when he shall appear, we shall be like him: We are aware that, if He should be manifested, *Concordant* . . . We only know that, if reality were to break through, we should reflect his likeness, *Phillips* . . . whenever it is made visible, like ones to Him we shall be, *Wuest* . . . when He has been revealed we shall resemble Him, *Berkeley.*

for we shall see him as he is: . . . according as, *Concordant.*

3:3. This future hope produces holy behavior. Without exception, a Christian who maintains his hope of being made righteous like Jesus will discipline himself to seek purity. When John began a verse with "every man" (Greek, *pas ho*), he was often refuting some group like the early Gnostics who set themselves up as a special class above the need for holiness. But the apostle showed that holiness brooks no exceptions.

3. And every man that hath this hope in him purifieth himself, even as he is pure: . . . who has this expectation, *Concordant* . . . resting on Him, *Berkeley* . . . continually set on Him is constantly purifying himself, *Wuest* . . . lives a pure life, *Laubach* . . . Everyone who has at heart a hope like that keeps himself pure, for he knows how pure Christ is, *Phillips.*

3:4. A person who is born from God habitually lives a righteous life; logically, a person living in sin is demonstrating that he has *not* been born into the family of God. A literal rendering of the first clause would be, "Everyone who commits sin also commits lawlessness." John went on to conclude the verse by pointing out that sin *is* lawlessness. The two words are virtually interchangeable.

Why belabor these definitions? "Sin" (Greek, *hamartian*) has a root idea of "missing the mark," while "lawlessness" (Greek, *anomian*) implies a more serious offense of purposely disregarding the law of God. The false teachers John mentioned may have been playing down the seriousness of "minor" offenses. But the apostle insisted that any form of sin is rebellion against God.

4. Whosoever committeth sin transgresseth also the law: . . . who habitually commits sin, also habitually commits lawlessness, *Wuest* . . . practices lawbreaking, *Berkeley* . . . is guilty of lawlessness, *Norlie* . . . is doing sin is doing lawlessness, *Concordant* . . . is also acting in defiance of Law, *TCNT* . . . breaks the law, *Williams C.K.*

for sin is the transgression of the law: That is what sin is—breaking the law, *Laubach* . . . by definition—a breaking of God's law, *Phillips* . . . for sin is lawlessness, *Norlie* . . . is the violation of divine Law, *Noli.*

3:5. How can a Christian tolerate sin when the very purpose of Christ's coming was to do away with sin? John's readers were well aware that the Lord became a man for the purpose of doing away with sins. The plural "sins" indicates that John was thinking not only of Christ's atonement for sin, but also of His power to remove acts of sin from the lives of His people.

Beyond that, Christ's very nature is sinless. John denied that sin had any place in the life of Jesus. The verb "is" portrays Christ as sinless in past, present, and future. Thus His people must abstain from sin.

5. And ye know that he was manifested to take away our sins: . . . you are aware, *Concordant* . . . you know absolutely, *Wuest* . . . He appeared, *Williams* . . . that He came in visible form, *Berkeley* . . . Christ became man for the purpose of removing sin, *Phillips.*

and in him is no sin: . . . sin in Him does not exist, *Wuest* . . . and that he himself was quite free from sin, *Phillips.*

1706.1 prep	**840.4** prs-pron dat sing	**3176.10** verb nom sing masc part pres act	**3620.1** partic	**262.2** verb 3sing indic pres act	**3820.6** adj nom sing masc
ἐν	αὐτῷ	μένων	οὐχ	ἁμαρτάνει·	πᾶς
en	*autō*	*menōn*	*ouch*	*hamartanei*	*pas*
in	him	abiding	not	is sinning:	anyone

3450.5 art nom sing masc	**262.4** verb nom sing masc part pres act	**3620.1** partic	**3571.11** verb 3sing indic perf act	**840.6** prs-pron acc sing masc	**3624.1** conj
ὁ	ἁμαρτάνων	οὐχ	ἑώρακεν	αὐτὸν,	οὐδὲ
ho	*hamartanōn*	*ouch*	*heōraken*	*auton*	*oude*
the	sinning	not	has seen	him,	nor

1091.32 verb 3sing indic perf act	**840.6** prs-pron acc sing masc	**4888.1** noun pl neu	**3235.3** num card nom masc	**3966.3** verb 3sing impr pres act
ἔγνωκεν	αὐτόν.	7. Τεκνία,	μηδεὶς	πλανάτω
egnōken	*auton*	*Teknia*	*mēdeis*	*planatō*
has known	him.	Little children,	no one	let lead astray

5050.4 prs-pron acc 2pl	**3450.5** art nom sing masc	**4020.15** verb nom sing masc part pres act	**3450.12** art acc sing fem	**1336.4** noun acc sing fem
ὑμᾶς·	ὁ	ποιῶν	τὴν	δικαιοσύνην,
humas	*ho*	*poiōn*	*tēn*	*dikaiosunēn*
you;	the	practicing	the	righteousness,

1337.3 adj nom sing masc	**1498.4** verb 3sing indic pres act	**2503.1** conj	**1552.3** dem-pron nom sing masc	**1337.3** adj nom sing masc	**1498.4** verb 3sing indic pres act
δίκαιός	ἐστιν,	καθὼς	ἐκεῖνος	δίκαιός	ἐστιν.
dikaios	*estin*	*kathōs*	*ekeinos*	*dikaios*	*estin*
righteous	is,	even as	that one	righteous	is.

3450.5 art nom sing masc	**4020.15** verb nom sing masc part pres act	**3450.12** art acc sing fem	**264.4** noun acc sing fem	**1523.2** prep gen	**3450.2** art gen sing
8. ὁ	ποιῶν	τὴν	ἁμαρτίαν,	ἐκ	τοῦ
ho	*poiōn*	*tēn*	*hamartian*	*ek*	*tou*
The	practicing	the	sin,	of	the

1222.2 adj gen sing masc	**1498.4** verb 3sing indic pres act	**3617.1** conj	**570.2** prep	**741.2** noun gen sing fem	**3450.5** art nom sing masc
διαβόλου	ἐστίν·	ὅτι	ἀπ'	ἀρχῆς	ὁ
diabolou	*estin*	*hoti*	*ap'*	*archēs*	*ho*
devil	is;	because	from	beginning	the

1222.1 adj nom sing masc	**262.2** verb 3sing indic pres act	**1519.1** prep	**3642.17** dem-pron sing neu	**5157.10** verb 3sing indic aor pass
διάβολος	ἁμαρτάνει.	εἰς	τοῦτο	ἐφανερώθη
diabolos	*hamartanei*	*eis*	*touto*	*ephanerōthē*
devil	sins.	For	this	was manifested

3450.5 art nom sing masc	**5048.1** noun nom sing masc	**3450.2** art gen sing	**2296.2** noun gen sing masc	**2419.1** conj	**3061.9** verb 3sing subj aor act
ὁ	υἱὸς	τοῦ	θεοῦ,	ἵνα	λύσῃ
ho	*huios*	*tou*	*theou*	*hina*	*lusē*
the	Son		of God,	that	he might destroy

3450.17 art pl neu	**2024.4** noun pl neu	**3450.2** art gen sing	**1222.2** adj gen sing masc	**3820.6** adj nom sing masc	**3450.5** art nom sing masc
τὰ	ἔργα	τοῦ	διαβόλου.	9. Πᾶς	ὁ
ta	*erga*	*tou*	*diabolou*	*Pas*	*ho*
the	works	of the	devil.	Everyone	the

1074.26 verb nom sing masc part perf mid	**1523.2** prep gen	**3450.2** art gen sing	**2296.2** noun gen sing masc	**264.4** noun acc sing fem	**3620.3** partic
γεγεννημένος	ἐκ	τοῦ	θεοῦ	ἁμαρτίαν	οὐ
gegennēmenos	*ek*	*tou*	*theou*	*hamartian*	*ou*
having been born	of		God,	sin	not

3:6. Next the writer makes a bold statement—everyone who abides in Christ does not sin. John generally used the word *abide* as a synonym for regeneration; he who abides is a child of God. Now he claimed that no child of God is going to sin. "Sinneth" is in the present tense, which normally emphasizes the continuing nature of an action. As 1:8 to 2:1 teaches, believers may commit an act of sin, but one genuinely born from God will not make it a continued practice.

The opposite also holds true. No one who continually sins has come to know God in a permanent relationship. The secret for overcoming is abiding in Christ.

3:7. Some were trying to twist the concept of holiness and lead believers astray, so John gave a direct warning against such predators. Regardless of any contrary teaching, it remains true that only the person who actually lives a righteous life deserves the title "righteous." Words are insufficient; we must live according to Christ's pattern.

3:8. Sin is serious because of its source. Much as he earlier spoke about Christians who were born "from God," John now declared that the source of life for the habitual sinner is "of (from) the devil." From the dawn of earth's history, the adversary has continued his career of revolt against God. And God is so opposed to Satan's activity that one of the chief reasons for Christ's incarnation was to break up the devil's works. Jesus Christ came to do away with sins (3:5).

3:9. The writer here makes his strongest statement about the standard of holiness expected in children of God. The verse follows his common pattern of stating truth both in a negative and positive form. The first half of the verse makes a blanket declaration: no one who has been born of God commits sin. The perfect tense of "born" is used once again as a synonym for regeneration, and "of God" refers to Him as the source of spiritual life, just as in earlier verses.

The problem arises when this verse is placed alongside other verses which declare that no one is free from sin (1:8,10; 2:1). In addition, even the saintliest believers have testified that they could not live completely free from sin. How can these facts be reconciled?

Some have suggested that John referred to a special class of believers or a particular kind of sin. Others think that he spoke only of the ideal of the Christian life, or was actually giving a veiled command. But such interpretations require one to read meanings into the text beyond what it actually says. The explanation which

6. Whosoever abideth in him sinneth not: No one who keeps in union with Him, *Norlie* . . . constantly abiding, *Wuest* . . . who remains in Him does not sin, *Berkeley* . . . does not habitually sin, *Montgomery.*

whosoever sinneth hath not seen him, neither known him: . . . whoever lives in sin, *Montgomery* . . . The regular sinner has never seen or, *Phillips* . . . practices sinning has neither looked on Him nor, *Berkeley* . . . has not with discernment seen Him, *Wuest.*

7. Little children, let no man deceive you: Little born-ones, stop allowing anyone to be leading you astray, *Wuest* . . . You, my children, are younger than I am, and I don't want you to be taken in by any clever talk just here, *Phillips* . . . lead you astray, *Norlie, TNT* . . . into the wrong way, *NLT.*

he that doeth righteousness is righteous, even as he is righteous: . . . practices righteousness, *Berkeley* . . . who lives a consistently good life is a good man, as surely as God is good, *Phillips* . . . who habitually does righteousness, *Wuest.*

8. He that committeth sin is of the devil: The person who keeps on sinning belongs to, *NLT* . . . the man whose life is habitually sinful is spiritually a son of, *Phillips* . . . under the control of, *Laubach* . . . is of the enemy, *Wilson* . . . is doing sin is of the Adversary, *Concordant* . . . is out of the devil as a source, *Wuest.*

for the devil sinneth from the beginning: . . . devil is behind all sin, as he always has been, *Phillips.*

For this purpose the Son of God was manifested: On this account, *Norlie* . . . came to earth, *Phillips* . . . appeared, *Berkeley.*

that he might destroy the works of the devil: . . . should be annulling the acts, *Concordant* . . . with the express purpose of liquidating the devil's activities, *Phillips* . . . to break up, *Berkeley* . . . bring to naught, *Wuest* . . . undo the devil's deeds, *Adams.*

9. Whosoever is born of God doth not commit sin: . . . who is begotten of God is not doing sin,

1 John 3:10

4020.5 verb 3sing indic pres act	3617.1 conj	4543.1 noun sing neu	840.3 prs-pron gen sing	1706.1 prep	840.4 prs-pron dat sing
ποιεῖ,	ὅτι	σπέρμα	αὐτοῦ	ἐν	αὐτῷ
poiei	*hoti*	*sperma*	*autou*	*en*	*autō*
practicing,	because	seed	his	in	him

3176.1 verb 3sing indic pres act	2504.1 conj	3620.3 partic	1404.4 verb 3sing indic pres mid	262.10 verb inf pres act	3617.1 conj
μένει·	καὶ	οὐ	δύναται	ἁμαρτάνειν,	ὅτι
menei	*kai*	*ou*	*dunatai*	*hamartanein*	*hoti*
abides,	and	not	he is able	to sin,	because

1523.2 prep gen	3450.2 art gen sing	2296.2 noun gen sing masc	1074.23 verb 3sing indic perf mid	1706.1 prep	3642.5 dem-pron dat sing masc
ἐκ	τοῦ	θεοῦ	γεγέννηται.	**10.** ἐν	τούτῳ
ek	*tou*	*theou*	*gegennētai*	*en*	*toutō*
of		God	has been born.	In	this

5156.4 adj	1498.4 verb 3sing indic pres act	3450.17 art pl neu	4891.4 noun pl neu	3450.2 art gen sing	2296.2 noun gen sing masc	2504.1 conj
φανερά	ἐστιν	τὰ	τέκνα	τοῦ	θεοῦ	καὶ
phanera	*estin*	*ta*	*tekna*	*tou*	*theou*	*kai*
manifest	are	the	children		of God	and

3450.17 art pl neu	4891.4 noun pl neu	3450.2 art gen sing	1222.2 adj gen sing masc	3820.6 adj nom sing masc	3450.5 art nom sing masc	3231.1 partic
τὰ	τέκνα	τοῦ	διαβόλου.	πᾶς	ὁ	μὴ
ta	*tekna*	*tou*	*diabolou*	*pas*	*ho*	*mē*
the	children	of the	devil.	Everyone	the	not

10.a.**Txt:** 01ℵ,03B,byz.
Var: 02A,04C,018K
025P,69,81,323,945
1241,1739

4020.15 verb nom sing masc part pres act	3450.12 art acc sing fem	1336.4 noun acc sing fem	3620.2 partic	1498.4 verb 3sing indic pres act
ποιῶν	[a+ τὴν]	δικαιοσύνην	οὐκ	ἔστιν
poiōn	*tēn*	*dikaiosunēn*	*ouk*	*estin*
practicing	[the]	righteousness	not	is

1523.2 prep gen	3450.2 art gen sing	2296.2 noun gen sing masc	2504.1 conj	3450.5 art nom sing masc	3231.1 partic	25.8 verb nom sing masc part pres act
ἐκ	τοῦ	θεοῦ,	καὶ	ὁ	μὴ	ἀγαπῶν
ek	*tou*	*theou*	*kai*	*ho*	*mē*	*agapōn*
of		God,	and	the	not	loving

3450.6 art acc sing masc	79.4 noun acc sing masc	840.3 prs-pron gen sing	3617.1 conj	3642.9 dem-pron nom sing fem	1498.4 verb 3sing indic pres act
τὸν	ἀδελφὸν	αὐτοῦ.	**11.** Ὅτι	αὕτη	ἐστὶν
ton	*adelphon*	*autou*	*Hoti*	*hautē*	*estin*
the	brother	his.	Because	this	is

11.a.**Txt:** 02A,03B,049
byz.
Var: 01ℵ,04C,025P,044
323,614,630,945,1241
1505,1739,2495

3450.9 art nom sing fem	31.1 noun nom sing fem	1845.2 noun nom sing fem	3614.12 rel-pron acc sing fem	189.23 verb 2pl indic aor act
ἡ	☆ ἀγγελία	[a ἐπαγγελία]	ἣν	ἠκούσατε
hē	*angelia*	*epangelia*	*hēn*	*ēkousate*
the	message	[promise]	which	you heard

570.2 prep	741.2 noun gen sing fem	2419.1 conj	25.3 verb 1pl pres act	238.3 prs-pron acc pl masc	3620.3 partic
ἀπ'	ἀρχῆς,	ἵνα	ἀγαπῶμεν	ἀλλήλους·	**12.** οὐ
ap'	*archēs*	*hina*	*agapōmen*	*allēlous*	*ou*
from	beginning;	that	we should love	one another:	not

2503.1 conj	2506.1 name masc	1523.2 prep gen	3450.2 art gen sing	4050.2 adj gen sing	1498.34 verb sing indic imperf act	2504.1 conj
καθὼς	Κάϊν	ἐκ	τοῦ	πονηροῦ	ἦν,	καὶ
kathōs	*Kain*	*ek*	*tou*	*ponērou*	*ēn*	*kai*
as	Cain	of	the	wicked	was,	and

adheres closest to the text is the one that points to the present tense used in the verbs. This and all the other passages dealing with the topic use the present tense, which normally describes habitual or continued action. In contrast, 2:1 uses the aorist tense, describing an isolated act of sin. God has provided a means of dealing with an occasional act of sin, but anyone who belongs to God's family will be unable to maintain a continual practice of sin.

A believer cannot remain in sin because "his seed remaineth in him." Some think that "seed" means God's offspring, and that His children remain in Him. But the context makes better sense when the verse is understood as God's seed remaining in the believer. As a parent's sperm passes on the family resemblance, the Father passes His nature on to His children.

Scientists who specialize in the field of genetics report that genes, passed on from generation to generation, greatly determine the nature and characteristics of offspring. If this is true in the natural, how much more so is it true in the spiritual realm. It might be said that when believers are born into the family of God, they receive, with the new nature, divine characteristics. It is the believer's responsibility, then, to develop these traits until he reaches spiritual maturity.

3:10. This verse sums up the preceding section on holiness (2:29 to 3:9) and makes a transition to the next section on love (3:11-24). By means of "this," namely, the test of holiness, it is possible to distinguish the children of God from the children of the devil. The hidden nature of a person's heart reveals itself in two symptoms: if a person fails to continually do what is righteous or if he fails to habitually love his brother, he is not connected to God as the source of life.

3:11. The closing phrase of verse 10 leads into a discussion of love as a trait of God's children. The command to love is nothing new; it dates back to the beginning of their Christian experience (cf. John 13:34,35). Believers are to love all, but 1 John focuses specifically on love for other Christians. In the First Century, believers were an "endangered species." Since the Roman emperors were considered gods, Christians were considered "atheists" and were to be exterminated. Only by demonstrating love could believers survive.

3:12. John argued for the need to love one another by citing the bad example of Cain (Genesis 4). Cain's character was based on a relation to Satan, much as Christians are "of (from) God." His character expressed itself when he violently slaughtered his brother. Jesus linked hatred with murder (Matthew 5:21-28), naming Satan

Concordant . . . When God makes someone his child, that person does not go on sinning, *Everyday* . . . does not practice sin, *Phillips.*

for his seed remaineth in him: God's nature is in Him, *Laubach* . . . The new life God gave that person stays in him, *Everyday* . . . for a sperm divine remains within him, *Berkeley* . . . because the God-given life-principle continues to live in him, *Williams* . . . is in him, for good, *Phillips.*

and he cannot sin, because he is born of God: . . . is not able, *Wuest* . . . can't go on sinning, *Adams* . . . and such a heredity is incapable of sin, *Phillips* . . . he cannot practice sinning, *Berkeley* . . . Because he has been begotten by God, *Wilson* . . . he has become a child of God, *SEB.*

10. In this the children of God are manifest: This is the way to distinguish God's children from the devil's, *Williams* . . . Here we have a clear indication as to who are, *Phillips* . . . we can see who God's children are, *Everyday* . . . are plainly distinguished by this, *Wade* . . . distinguished from, *TCNT* . . . are known apart, *Norlie* . . . are distinguished in this way, *TNT* . . . are apparent, *Concordant* . . . are discovered, *Campbell.*

and the children of the devil: . . . and who the devil's children are, *Everyday.*

whosoever doeth not righteousness is not of God: Anyone who does not practice righteousness, *Berkeley* . . . The man who does not lead a good life, *Phillips* . . . Those who do not do what is right are not children of God, *Everyday.*

neither he that loveth not his brother: . . . who fails to love, *Phillips* . . . with a divine and self-sacrificial love, *Wuest.*

11. For this is the message that ye heard from the beginning, that we should love one another: . . . this is the basic commandment, *Noli* . . . This is the teaching, *Everyday.*

12. Not as Cain, [who] was of that wicked one, and slew his brother: Do not be like Cain who belonged to, *Everyday* . . . We are none of us to have the spirit...who was a son of the devil, *Phillips*

4821.1 verb 3sing indic aor act	3450.6 art acc sing masc	79.4 noun acc sing masc	840.3 prs-pron gen sing	2504.1 conj	5320.1 prep
ἔσφαξεν	τὸν	ἀδελφὸν	αὐτοῦ·	καὶ	χάριν
esphaxen	*ton*	*adelphon*	*autou*	*kai*	*charin*
murdered	the	brother	his;	and	on account of

4949.4 intr-pron gen sing	4821.1 verb 3sing indic aor act	840.6 prs-pron acc sing masc	3617.1 conj	3450.17 art pl neu	2024.4 noun pl neu
τίνος	ἔσφαξεν	αὐτόν;	ὅτι	τὰ	ἔργα
tinos	*esphaxen*	*auton*	*hoti*	*ta*	*erga*
what	murdered he	him?	because	the	works

840.3 prs-pron gen sing	4050.10 adj	1498.34 verb sing indic imperf act	3450.17 art pl neu	1156.2 conj	3450.2 art gen sing	79.2 noun gen sing masc
αὐτοῦ	πονηρὰ	ἦν,	τὰ	δὲ	τοῦ	ἀδελφοῦ
autou	*ponēra*	*ēn*	*ta*	*de*	*tou*	*adelphou*
his	wicked	were,	the	and	of the	brother

13.a.**Txt:** 02A,03B,byz. We/Ho
Var: 01ℵ,04C-vid,025P 044,323,945,1241,1739

840.3 prs-pron gen sing	1337.14 adj pl neu	2504.1 conj	3231.1 partic	2273.1 verb 2pl pres act
αὐτοῦ	δίκαια.	13. [a☆+ Καὶ]	Μὴ	θαυμάζετε,
autou	*dikaia*	*Kai*	*Mē*	*thaumazete*
his	righteous.	[And]	Not	wonder,

13.b.**Txt:** 018K,020L,byz. sa.bo.
Var: 01ℵ,02A,03B,04C 025P,Lach,Treg,Alf Word,Tisc,We/Ho,Weis Sod,UBS/☆

79.6 noun nom pl masc	1466.2 prs-pron gen 1sing	1479.1 conj	3268.3 verb 3sing indic pres act	5050.4 prs-pron acc 2pl	3450.5 art nom sing masc
ἀδελφοί	⸂b μου, ⸃	εἰ	μισεῖ	ὑμᾶς	ὁ
adelphoi	*mou*	*ei*	*misei*	*humas*	*ho*
brothers	my,	if	hates	you	the

2862.1 noun nom sing masc	2231.1 prs-pron nom 1pl	3471.5 verb 1pl indic perf act	3617.1 conj	3197.7 verb 1pl indic perf act
κόσμος.	14. ἡμεῖς	οἴδαμεν	ὅτι	μεταβεβήκαμεν
kosmos	*hēmeis*	*oidamen*	*hoti*	*metabebēkamen*
world.	We	know	that	we have passed

1523.2 prep gen	3450.2 art gen sing	2265.2 noun gen sing masc	1519.1 prep	3450.12 art acc sing fem	2205.4 noun acc sing fem	3617.1 conj
ἐκ	τοῦ	θανάτου	εἰς	τὴν	ζωήν,	ὅτι
ek	*tou*	*thanatou*	*eis*	*tēn*	*zōēn*	*hoti*
from	the	death	to	the	life,	because

25.3 verb 1pl pres act	3450.8 art acc pl masc	79.9 noun acc pl masc	3450.5 art nom sing masc	3231.1 partic	25.8 verb nom sing masc part pres act
ἀγαπῶμεν	τοὺς	ἀδελφούς·	ὁ	μὴ	ἀγαπῶν
agapōmen	*tous*	*adelphous*	*ho*	*mē*	*agapōn*
we love	the	brothers.	The	not	loving

14.a.**Txt:** 04C,018K 020L,025P,byz.bo.Sod
Var: 01ℵ,02A,03B,33,it. Lach,Treg,Alf,Word Tisc,We/Ho,Weis UBS/☆

3450.6 art acc sing masc	79.4 noun acc sing masc	3176.1 verb 3sing indic pres act	1706.1 prep	3450.3 art dat sing	2265.3 noun dat sing masc
⸂a τὸν	ἀδελφόν, ⸃	μένει	ἐν	τῷ	θανάτῳ.
ton	*adelphon*	*menei*	*en*	*tō*	*thanatō*
the	brother,	resides	in	the	death.

3820.6 adj nom sing masc	3450.5 art nom sing masc	3268.5 verb nom sing masc part pres act	3450.6 art acc sing masc	79.4 noun acc sing masc	840.3 prs-pron gen sing
15. πᾶς	ὁ	μισῶν	τὸν	ἀδελφὸν	αὐτοῦ,
pas	*ho*	*misōn*	*ton*	*adelphon*	*autou*
Everyone	the	hating	the	brother	his

441.1 noun nom sing masc	1498.4 verb 3sing indic pres act	2504.1 conj	3471.6 verb 2pl indic perf act	3617.1 conj	3820.6 adj nom sing masc
ἀνθρωποκτόνος	ἐστίν,	καὶ	οἴδατε	ὅτι	πᾶς
anthrōpoktonos	*estin*	*kai*	*oidate*	*hoti*	*pas*
a murderer	is,	and	you know	that	every

as a murderer (John 8:44). To hate someone is sinful and murderous, for the one who hates requires only opportunity before he actually commits the crime.

Next, John described Cain's motive (and at the same time hinted at the motivation for the persecution of believers in his own age). Cain's works were evil, while his brother's were righteous—so Cain killed Abel. Similarly, a Christian's good example is a standing rebuke to the one who cannot claim a life-style of righteousness. It reminds him of what he is like in comparison with what he ought to be. His attitude is irrational, like the king in ancient times who killed a messenger who brought him bad news.

. . . whose motivation was from the evil one and he murdered his brother, *Berkeley* . . . was out of the Pernicious One, and killed his brother by severing his jugular vein, *Wuest* . . . and butchered his brother, *Williams.*

And wherefore slew he him?: And for what reason did he murder him? *Berkeley* . . . Have you realized his motive? *Phillips* . . . on what account, *Wuest* . . . on behalf of what, *Concordant* . . . And why did he kill him? *Norlie.*

Because his own works were evil, and his brother's righteous: It was just because he realized the goodness of his brother's life and the rottenness of his own, *Phillips* . . . his own deeds were wicked, *Laubach* . . . his acts were wicked, yet those of his brother, just, *Concordant* . . . those of his brother were virtuous, *Berkeley.*

3:13. Cain showed the attitude characteristic of most members of the world system, and John immediately applied the principle to his audience.

The present tense of the command to stop being amazed suggests that the readers were surprised by the opposition they met, and John explained that hatred is the standard reaction of the world toward Christianity. Even the form of "if" implies that such a hatred is a fact.

13. Marvel not, my brethren, if the world hate you: You must not be surprised, *Williams* . . . do not be, *Norlie, NLT* . . . Do not feel, *Berkeley* . . . Stop marveling, *Wuest* . . . when the people of this world, *Everyday.*

3:14. The next two verses return to the test of faith which he set forth in 2:9-11—love for the brethren. "We" (Greek, *hēmeis*) is emphatic, marking the contrast with the world. The believer loves other Christians, while the world hates them.

John introduced a new description of salvation, picturing Christians as people who have "passed from death unto life." The verb *metabebēkamen* means a move from one location to another and is an apt description of the way salvation transfers a person from the sphere of darkness to the realm of light. The perfect tense once again describes the past conversion which introduces a person to a continuing relationship with Christ.

Continued love for other believers demonstrates that this transfer is genuine. Anyone who does not display that love is giving evidence that he has never come out of the sphere of death into which he was born.

14. We know that we have passed from death unto life: . . . we have crossed the frontier, *Phillips* . . . we have proceeded, *Concordant* . . . we have made the transfer out of, *Berkeley* . . . we have passed over permanently out of the death, *Wuest.*

because we love the brethren: . . . the brothers, *Berkeley.*

He that loveth not [his] brother abideth in death: The man that does not love, *Williams C.K.* . . . The man without love for his brother is living in death already, *Phillips* . . . loving in this manner is abiding in the sphere of the death, *Wuest* . . . remains in death, *Norlie.*

3:15. This verse shows why hatred is a valid test of whether a person is unregenerate, though it may seem like a harsh standard. A person who continues to hate someone else (note the present tense) is actually a murderer. *Anthrōpoktonos* occurs only here and in John 8:44 where Jesus said that the devil is also a murderer. Elsewhere the Lord equated hatred with murder (Matthew 5:21,22), since the one who hates another actually has the same desire as a murderer but lacks the opportunity to carry out his wish. For John

15. Whosoever hateth his brother is a murderer: . . . who actively hates his brother, *Phillips* . . . commits murder in his heart, *Laubach* . . . is a potential murderer, *Noli* . . . is a man-killer, *Concordant* . . . manslayer, *Campbell.*

441.1 noun nom sing masc	3620.2 partic	2174.4 verb 3sing indic pres act	2205.4 noun acc sing fem	164.1 adj sing	1706.1 prep
ἀνθρωποκτόνος	οὐκ	ἔχει	ζωὴν	αἰώνιον	ἐν
anthrōpoktonos	*ouk*	*echei*	*zōēn*	*aiōnion*	*en*
murderer	not	has	life	eternal	in

15.a.**Txt:** 03B,018K,33 323,614,1241 **Var:** 01ℵ,02A,04C,025P 044,byz.Tisc,Sod

840.4 prs-pron dat sing	1431.5 prs-pron dat sing masc	3176.13 verb acc sing fem part pres act	1706.1 prep	3642.5 dem-pron dat sing masc
ʿ☆ αὐτῷ	[a ἑαυτῷ,]	μένουσαν.	**16.** Ἐν	τούτῳ
autō	*heautō*	*menousan*	*En*	*toutō*
him	[himself,]	abiding.	By	this

1091.33 verb 1pl indic perf act	3450.12 art acc sing fem	26.4 noun acc sing fem	3617.1 conj	1552.3 dem-pron nom sing masc	5065.1 prep
ἐγνώκαμεν	τὴν	ἀγάπην,	ὅτι	ἐκεῖνος	ὑπὲρ
egnōkamen	*tēn*	*agapēn*	*hoti*	*ekeinos*	*huper*
we have known	the	love,	because	that	for

2231.2 prs-pron gen 1pl	3450.12 art acc sing fem	5425.4 noun acc sing fem	840.3 prs-pron gen sing	4935.10 verb 3sing indic aor act	2504.1 conj
ἡμῶν	τὴν	ψυχὴν	αὐτοῦ	ἔθηκεν·	καὶ
hēmōn	*tēn*	*psuchēn*	*autou*	*ethēken*	*kai*
us	the	life	his	laid down;	and

2231.1 prs-pron nom 1pl	3648.4 verb 1pl indic pres act	5065.1 prep	3450.1 art gen pl	79.7 noun gen pl masc	3450.15 art acc pl fem
ἡμεῖς	ὀφείλομεν	ὑπὲρ	τῶν	ἀδελφῶν	τὰς
hēmeis	*opheilomen*	*huper*	*tōn*	*adelphōn*	*tas*
we	ought	for	the	brothers	the

16.a.**Txt:** 018K,020L,byz. **Var:** 01ℵ,02A,03B,04C 025P,Lach,Treg,Alf Word,Tisc,We/Ho,Weis Sod,UBS/☆

5425.8 noun acc pl fem	4935.7 verb inf pres act	4935.17 verb inf aor act	3614.5 rel-pron nom sing masc	1156.1 conj	300.1 partic
ψυχὰς	ʿ τιθέναι.	[a☆ θεῖναι.]	**17.** ὃς	δ'	ἂν
psuchas	*tithenai*	*theinai*	*hos*	*d'*	*an*
lives	to lay down.	[idem]	Whoever	but	

2174.7 verb 3sing subj pres act	3450.6 art acc sing masc	972.2 noun acc sing masc	3450.2 art gen sing	2862.2 noun gen sing masc	2504.1 conj
ἔχῃ	τὸν	βίον	τοῦ	κόσμου,	καὶ
echē	*ton*	*bion*	*tou*	*kosmou*	*kai*
may have	the	means of life	the	world's,	and

2311.6 verb 3sing subj pres act	3450.6 art acc sing masc	79.4 noun acc sing masc	840.3 prs-pron gen sing	5367.3 noun acc sing fem	2174.15 verb part pres act
θεωρῇ	τὸν	ἀδελφὸν	αὐτοῦ	χρείαν	ἔχοντα,
theōrē	*ton*	*adelphon*	*autou*	*chreian*	*echonta*
may see	the	brother	his	need	having,

2504.1 conj	2781.4 verb 3sing subj aor act	3450.17 art pl neu	4551.1 noun pl neu	840.3 prs-pron gen sing	570.2 prep	840.3 prs-pron gen sing
καὶ	κλείσῃ	τὰ	σπλάγχνα	αὐτοῦ	ἀπ'	αὐτοῦ,
kai	*kleisē*	*ta*	*splanchna*	*autou*	*ap'*	*autou*
and	may shut up	the	bowels	his	from	him,

4316.1 adv	3450.9 art nom sing fem	26.1 noun nom sing fem	3450.2 art gen sing	2296.2 noun gen sing masc	3176.1 verb 3sing indic pres act	1706.1 prep
πῶς	ἡ	ἀγάπη	τοῦ	θεοῦ	μένει	ἐν
pōs	*hē*	*agapē*	*tou*	*theou*	*menei*	*en*
how	the	love		of God	resides	in

18.a.**Txt:** 018K,020L,byz. sa.bo. **Var:** 01ℵ,02A,03B,04C 025P,Lach,Treg,Alf Word,Tisc,We/Ho,Weis Sod,UBS/☆

840.4 prs-pron dat sing	4888.1 noun pl neu	1466.2 prs-pron gen 1sing	3231.1 partic	25.3 verb 1pl pres act
αὐτῷ;	**18.** Τεκνία	ʿa μου, ʾ	μὴ	ἀγαπῶμεν
autō	*Teknia*	*mou*	*mē*	*agapōmen*
him?	Little children	my,	not	we should love

there was no middle ground. Anyone who carries such an attitude around is demonstrating that eternal life does not reside in him.

and ye know that no murderer hath eternal life abiding in him: . . . no man-killer at all has life eonian remaining, *Concordant* . . . has everlasting life remaining in him, *Williams C.K.* . . . continuing within him, *Berkeley.*

3:16. Since love is a test of true Christianity, it is important to describe the characteristics of the love that passes the test.

The question is not difficult to answer, for every Christian has already come to know by experience the sort of love which God requires. The perfect tense of "perceive" points both to the cross, where Christ performed the supreme act of love, and to the experience of His love in our lives.

When John spoke of the One who "laid down his life for us," he made it obvious that he meant the death of Christ. This idiom describes a voluntary act of self-sacrifice. The death of Jesus was no accident, as He himself had said in John 10:17,18 and 15:13.

Just as the Lord laid down His life for mankind, believers have a moral obligation to lay down their lives for other Christians, following His example (John 15:12). This, of course, does not mean that a Christian dies to atone for the sins of others; rather, it shows the extent of the sacrifices that love may demand.

16. Hereby perceive we the love [of God], because he laid down his life for us: We understand the meaning of love from this, that He laid down his own life on our behalf, *Berkeley* . . . In Christ we saw what real love is, *Laubach* . . . we know what love is and can do, *Norlie* . . . He, for our sakes, lays down His soul, *Concordant.*

and we ought to lay down [our] lives for the brethren: . . . as for us, we have a moral obligation on behalf of our brethren, *Wuest* . . . our souls for the sake of, *Concordant.*

3:17. The perfect example of Jesus is contrasted with the example of one who falsely claims to follow the Lord. The writer condemns the one who claims to be ready to die for a brother in an emergency, yet refuses to show practical love in the routines of life.

Such a person "hath this world's good(s)." "Whoso" is a broad expression, including anyone who fits the criteria. The word "good" comes from the Greek *bios* which describes the sort of physical life which an animal possesses, and it was later used, as here, to describe the physical possessions necessary to sustain life. The person has ample material resources. Second, the person "seeth his brother have need." The verb for seeing (Greek, *theōrē*) describes the careful gaze that makes one fully aware of the brother's difficulty. The present tense verbs show a continuing knowledge of a continuing need. Third, the person closes his heart against the needy brother. There is a change to the aorist tense when speaking of the man who "shutteth" his heart and chooses not to help. The "bowels" are mentioned because ancient writers thought of the internal organs such as the heart, lungs, and liver as the seat of the emotions, much as modern man uses the word *heart.*

Anyone who fits all three of these descriptions has failed the test of love. John asked his readers to be the judge: how can a person claim to have God's love as part of his person and react in such a calloused manner?

17. But whoso hath this world's good, and seeth his brother have need: . . . whoever has as a constant possession the necessities of life, *Wuest* . . . is rich enough to have all the things he needs, *SEB* . . . whoso may have the world's substance, *Darby* . . . possesses the world's resources, and notices that his brother suffers need, *Berkeley* . . . whoever may be having a livelihood in this world, and may be beholding his brother, *Concordant* . . . the life-sustaining things, *Swann.*

and shutteth up his bowels [of compassion] from him: . . . and snaps shut his heart from, *Wuest* . . . shuts up his pity against him, *Williams C.K.* . . . steels his heart against him, *TCNT* . . . yet he closes his heart against him, *Norlie* . . . stifles his emotions toward him, *Adams* . . . and then locks his deep sympathies away from, *Berkeley* . . . locking his compassions from, *Concordant.*

how dwelleth the love of God in him?: . . . can have no divine love in his heart, *Noli* . . . is abiding in him? *Wuest* . . . lodging in him? *Berkeley.*

3:18. John urged his beloved children in the Lord to avoid such hypocrisy. They must avoid the kind of love that is only talk. In-

18. My little children, let us not love in word, neither in tongue: Dear children, *Berkeley* . . . we should not be loving, *Concordant* . . . our love must not be, *TNT* . . . we must not manifest our love only in fine words on the

18.b.**Var:** 02A,03B,04C 018K,020L,Gries,Lach Treg,Alf,Word,Tisc We/Ho,Weis,Sod UBS/⋆

3030.3 noun dat sing masc	**3234.1** adv	**3450.11** art dat sing fem	**1094.3** noun dat sing fem	**233.1** conj	**233.2** conj
λόγῳ	μηδὲ	[b⋆+ τῇ]	γλώσσῃ,	ʼ ἀλλ᾽	[⋆ ἀλλὰ]
logō	*mēde*	*tē*	*glōssē*	*all'*	*alla*
in word,	nor	[with the]	with tongue,	but	[idem]

18.c.**Var:** 01ℵ,02A,03B 04C,020L,025P,byz. Gries,Lach,Treg,Alf Word,Tisc,We/Ho,Weis Sod,UBS/⋆

1706.1 prep	**2024.3** noun dat sing neu	**2504.1** conj	**223.3** noun dat sing fem		**2504.1** conj	**1706.1** prep
[c⋆+ ἐν]	ἔργῳ	καὶ	ἀληθείᾳ.	**19.**	ʼa Καὶ ˎ	ἐν
en	*ergō*	*kai*	*alētheia*		*Kai*	*en*
[in]	in work	and	in truth.		And	by

19.a.**Txt:** 01ℵ,04C,018K 020L,025P,byz.sa.Tisc Sod
Var: 02A,03B,it.bo.Lach We/Ho,Weis,UBS/⋆

3642.5 dem-pron dat sing masc	**1091.4** verb 1pl indic pres act	**1091.58** verb 1pl indic fut mid	**3617.1** conj	**1523.2** prep gen
τούτῳ	ʼ γινώσκομεν	[b⋆ γνωσόμεθα]	ὅτι	ἐκ
toutō	*ginōskomen*	*gnōsometha*	*hoti*	*ek*
this	we know	[we will know]	that	of

19.b.**Txt:** 018K,020L,byz.
Var: 01ℵ,02A,03B,04C 025P,Lach,Treg,Alf Word,Tisc,We/Ho,Weis Sod,UBS/⋆

3450.10 art gen sing fem	**223.2** noun gen sing fem	**1498.5** verb 1pl indic pres act	**2504.1** conj	**1699.1** prep	**840.3** prs-pron gen sing
τῆς	ἀληθείας	ἐσμέν,	καὶ	ἔμπροσθεν	αὐτοῦ
tēs	*alētheias*	*esmen*	*kai*	*emprosthen*	*autou*
the	truth	we are,	and	before	him

19.c.**Txt:** 01ℵ,02A-corr 04C,018K,020L,025P byz.bo.Tisc,Sod
Var: 02A-org,03B,sa. We/Ho,Weis,UBS/⋆

3844.17 verb 1pl indic fut act	**3450.15** art acc pl fem	**2559.1** noun fem	**3450.12** art acc sing fem	**2559.4** noun acc sing fem
πείσομεν	ʼ τὰς	καρδίας	[c⋆ τὴν	καρδίαν]
peisomen	*tas*	*kardias*	*tēn*	*kardian*
shall persuade	the	hearts	[the	hearts]

2231.2 prs-pron gen 1pl		**3617.1** conj	**1430.1** partic	**2578.1** verb 3sing subj pres act	**2231.2** prs-pron gen 1pl	**3450.9** art nom sing fem
ἡμῶν˙	**20.**	ὅτι	ἐὰν	καταγινώσκῃ	ἡμῶν	ἡ
hēmōn		*hoti*	*ean*	*kataginōskē*	*hēmōn*	*hē*
our,		that	if	should condemn	our	the

2559.2 noun nom sing fem	**3617.1** conj	**3157.2** adj comp nom sing	**1498.4** verb 3sing indic pres act	**3450.5** art nom sing masc	**2296.1** noun nom sing masc
καρδία,	ὅτι	μείζων	ἐστὶν	ὁ	θεὸς
kardia	*hoti*	*meizōn*	*estin*	*ho*	*theos*
heart,	that	greater	is		God

3450.10 art gen sing fem	**2559.1** noun fem	**2231.2** prs-pron gen 1pl	**2504.1** conj	**1091.3** verb 3sing indic pres act	**3820.1** adj
τῆς	καρδίας	ἡμῶν	καὶ	γινώσκει	πάντα.
tēs	*kardias*	*hēmōn*	*kai*	*ginōskei*	*panta*
of the	heart	our	and	knows	all things.

21.a.**Txt:** 01ℵ,04C,018K 020L,byz.it.Tisc
Var: 02A,03B,044,33 Lach,Treg,We/Ho,Weis Sod,UBS/⋆

	27.6 adj pl masc	**1430.1** partic	**3450.9** art nom sing fem	**2559.2** noun nom sing fem	**2231.2** prs-pron gen 1pl	**3231.1** partic
21.	᾿Αγαπητοί,	ἐὰν	ἡ	καρδία	ʼa ἡμῶν ˎ	μὴ
	Agapētoi	*ean*	*hē*	*kardia*	*hēmōn*	*mē*
	Beloved,	if	the	heart	our	not

21.b.**Txt:** 01ℵ,02A,018K 020L,byz.it.sa.bo.Tisc
Var: 03B,04C,We/Ho Weis,Sod,UBS/⋆

2578.1 verb 3sing subj pres act	**2231.2** prs-pron gen 1pl	**3816.4** noun acc sing fem	**2174.5** verb 1pl indic pres act	**4242.1** prep
καταγινώσκῃ	ʼb ἡμῶν, ˎ	παῤῥησίαν	ἔχομεν	πρὸς
kataginōskē	*hēmōn*	*parrhēsian*	*echomen*	*pros*
should condemn	us,	confidence	we have	toward

3450.6 art acc sing masc	**2296.4** noun acc sing masc		**2504.1** conj	**3614.16** rel-pron sing neu	**1430.1** partic	**153.5** verb 1pl subj pres act
τὸν	θεόν,	**22.**	καὶ	ὃ	ἐὰν	αἰτῶμεν,
ton	*theon*		*kai*	*ho*	*ean*	*aitōmen*
	God,		and	whatever		we may ask,

stead, their love should show itself in actions. And since even good deeds can be done with a hypocritical attitude or false motives, he added that the works of love should be done in truth. Sometimes "works" have received a bad name, but there is nothing wrong with them if done with the right motive.

3:19. This verse begins by looking back at the message just given—that love for other Christians is a test of genuine membership in God's family. It goes on to assert that this love enables the believer to know with certainty that he is indeed "of the truth," one whose life originates in the truth of the gospel. In addition, the presence of love for other Christians allows us to pacify our troubled conscience and stand in the presence of God with confidence. Verse 22 connects this boldness to prayer.

3:20. The grammar of this verse is difficult because of the two uses of the Greek term *hoti,* translated "for" and then left untranslated in the KJV. The opening phrase could be rendered "whatever our heart condemns" or "because, if our heart condemns, *we know* that God is . . . ." In either case, the thought is that an oversensitive conscience can plague a Christian with unjustified guilt feelings, even though he passes such tests as the demand to love. In such a case, we can still come to God with confidence, even though our conscience condemns us. God is greater in knowledge than our conscience, and He is the final authority (cf. 1 Corinthians 4:3-5).

3:21. On the other hand, a person who does not suffer from an accusing conscience can have boldness toward God. "Confidence" (Greek, *parrhēsian*) means freedom and openness in speech, and though it referred to the return of Christ in 2:28, here it leads naturally into the topic of prayer in verse 22. "Toward God" (Greek, *pros ton theon*) often implies face-to-face intimacy, as one would enjoy in prayer to the Father.

3:22. When a Christian is confident of his place in God's family, regardless of any emotions of guilt or unworthiness, he can communicate with his Father in prayer with the assurance that he is being heard. The truth that God will answer that believer's prayer, whatever may be requested, is a strong promise.

The rest of the verse, however, adds restrictions to the promise. The reason one can ask and receive is because he has fulfilled the

tongue, *Greber* . . . in the sphere of word, *Wuest* . . . do not let our love be mere words, *TCNT* . . . or talk, *SEB* . . . or speech only, *Norlie* . . . in theory, *Noli.*

but in deed and in truth: . . . in act, *Concordant* . . . and in reality, *Noli* . . . let us love in sincerity and in practice! *Phillips* . . . we should show that love by what we do, *Everyday* . . . as divine truth teaches us, *Greber.*

19. And hereby we know that we are of the truth, and shall assure our hearts before him: If we live like this, we shall know that we are children of the truth and can reassure ourselves in the sight of God, *Phillips* . . . In this way we shall become fully aware that to the truth we owe our lives, and in His presence our hearts shall be at peace, *Berkeley* . . . we belong to the way of truth, *Everyday* . . . persuading our hearts in front of Him, *Concordant* . . . in His presence shall tranquilize our hearts in whatever our hearts condemn us, *Wuest.*

20. For if our heart condemn us, God is greater than our heart, and knoweth all things: . . . our heart should be censuring us, *Concordant* . . . even if our own hearts make us feel guilty...God is infinitely greater, *Phillips* . . . is wiser than, *Laubach* . . . our conscience, *Norlie* . . . He knows everything, *Berkeley.*

21. Beloved, if our heart condemn us not, [then] have we confidence toward God: Divinely loved ones...a fearless confidence we constantly have facing God the Father, *Wuest* . . . if we do not feel that we are doing wrong, we can be without fear when we come to God, *Everyday* . . . when we realize this our hearts no longer accuse us, we may have the utmost confidence in God's presence, *Phillips* . . . in case our hearts do not condemn us, then we draw near to God with confidence, *Berkeley* . . . we can face God fearlessly, *Noli* . . . we have boldness, *Concordant.*

22. And whatsoever we ask, we receive of him: . . . whatsoever we may be requesting, we are obtaining, *Concordant* . . . And God gives us the things we ask for,

1 John 3:23

22.a.**Txt:** 018K,020L,byz.
Var: 01א,02A,03B,04C
33,Lach,Treg,Alf,Tisc
We/Ho,Weis,Sod
UBS/☆

2956.5 verb 1pl indic pres act	**3706.1** prep	**570.2** prep	**840.3** prs-pron gen sing	**3617.1** conj	**3450.15** art acc pl fem
λαμβάνομεν	⸂ παρ'	[a☆ ἀπ']	αὐτοῦ,	ὅτι	τὰς
lambanomen	*par'*	*ap'*	*autou*	*hoti*	*tas*
we receive	from	[idem]	him,	because	the

1769.7 noun acc pl fem	**840.3** prs-pron gen sing	**4931.3** verb 1pl indic pres act	**2504.1** conj	**3450.17** art pl neu
ἐντολὰς	αὐτοῦ	τηροῦμεν,	καὶ	τὰ
entolas	*autou*	*tēroumen*	*kai*	*ta*
commandments	his	we are keeping,	and	the things

695.2 adj pl neu	**1783.1** prep	**840.3** prs-pron gen sing	**4020.6** verb 1pl indic pres act	**2504.1** conj
ἀρεστὰ	ἐνώπιον	αὐτοῦ	ποιοῦμεν.	23. καὶ
aresta	*enōpion*	*autou*	*poioumen*	*kai*
pleasing	before	him	we are practicing.	And

3642.9 dem-pron nom sing fem	**1498.4** verb 3sing indic pres act	**3450.9** art nom sing fem	**1769.1** noun nom sing fem	**840.3** prs-pron gen sing	**2419.1** conj
αὕτη	ἐστὶν	ἡ	ἐντολὴ	αὐτοῦ,	ἵνα
hautē	*estin*	*hē*	*entolē*	*autou*	*hina*
this	is	the	commandment	his,	that

23.a.**Txt:** 03B,018K
020L,byz.We/Ho,Weis
UBS/☆
Var: 01א,02A,04C,Lach
Treg,Tisc,Sod

3961.26 verb 1pl subj aor act	**3961.63** verb 1pl subj pres act	**3450.3** art dat sing	**3549.4** noun dat sing neu	**3450.2** art gen sing
⸂ πιστεύσωμεν	[a πιστεύωμεν]	τῷ	ὀνόματι	τοῦ
pisteusōmen	*pisteuōmen*	*tō*	*onomati*	*tou*
we should believe	[idem]	on the	name	of the

5048.2 noun gen sing masc	**840.3** prs-pron gen sing	**2400.2** name masc	**5382.2** name gen masc	**2504.1** conj	**25.3** verb 1pl pres act
υἱοῦ	αὐτοῦ	Ἰησοῦ	Χριστοῦ,	καὶ	ἀγαπῶμεν
huiou	*autou*	*Iēsou*	*Christou*	*kai*	*agapōmen*
Son	his	Jesus	Christ,	and	should love

23.b.**Txt:** 01א,02A,03B
04C,044,0245,33,81
323,614,630,1241,1739
2495
Var: 049,byz.

238.3 prs-pron acc pl masc	**2503.1** conj	**1319.14** verb 3sing indic aor act	**1769.3** noun acc sing fem	**2231.3** prs-pron dat 1pl
ἀλλήλους,	καθὼς	ἔδωκεν	ἐντολὴν	⸂b ἡμῖν. ⸃
allēlous	*kathōs*	*edōken*	*entolēn*	*hēmin*
one another,	even as	he gave	commandment	to us.

2504.1 conj	**3450.5** art nom sing masc	**4931.8** verb nom sing masc part pres act	**3450.15** art acc pl fem	**1769.7** noun acc pl fem
24. καὶ	ὁ	τηρῶν	τὰς	ἐντολὰς
kai	*ho*	*tērōn*	*tas*	*entolas*
And	the	keeping	the	commandments

840.3 prs-pron gen sing	**1706.1** prep	**840.4** prs-pron dat sing	**3176.1** verb 3sing indic pres act	**2504.1** conj	**840.5** prs-pron nom sing masc	**1706.1** prep
αὐτοῦ,	ἐν	αὐτῷ	μένει,	καὶ	αὐτὸς	ἐν
autou	*en*	*autō*	*menei*	*kai*	*autos*	*en*
his,	in	him	remains,	and	he	in

840.4 prs-pron dat sing	**2504.1** conj	**1706.1** prep	**3642.5** dem-pron dat sing masc	**1091.4** verb 1pl indic pres act	**3617.1** conj	**3176.1** verb 3sing indic pres act
αὐτῷ˙	καὶ	ἐν	τούτῳ	γινώσκομεν	ὅτι	μένει
autō	*kai*	*en*	*toutō*	*ginōskomen*	*hoti*	*menei*
him:	and	by	this	we know	that	he resides

1706.1 prep	**2231.3** prs-pron dat 1pl	**1523.2** prep gen	**3450.2** art gen sing	**4011.2** noun gen sing neu	**3614.2** rel-pron gen sing	**2231.3** prs-pron dat 1pl
ἐν	ἡμῖν,	ἐκ	τοῦ	πνεύματος	οὗ	ἡμῖν
en	*hēmin*	*ek*	*tou*	*pneumatos*	*hou*	*hēmin*
in	us,	by	the	Spirit	which	to us

conditions given: keeping God's commandments and doing the things which please Him. The "commandments" refer to the explicit demands made by God, while "things that are pleasing" covers a broader range of acts that may not be directly mentioned in the Bible. Both "keep" and "do" are present tense verbs and imply a habitual obedience to God's will as a prerequisite for answered prayer. (See also 5:14,15.)

A life lived in yieldedness to the will of God is the secret to a successful Christian experience. The reason believers can expect answers to prayer is that as far as they know they are asking in accordance with the will of God (they certainly would not ask for anything contrary to His will). The result is that God gives them what they ask for, and if not, something better. There are many occasions in this life when we do not receive the answer we have expected. But our heavenly Father knows best, and when on the other side we know as we are known, we will learn that every time God answered in a way which was best for us. When our faith seems weak, we can always trust God to do what is right.

3:23. If answered prayer depends on keeping God's commands, then what are those commands? They can be summed up in the twin pillars of the epistle: faith and love. God wants man to believe in the name (and thus the Person) of His Son, and the aorist tense points to initial conversion. This is to be accompanied by a continual (present tense) practice of loving one another, just as Christ himself instructed in John 13:34; 15:12. Since, as John states in the next chapter, the very nature of God is love, and by the new birth believers receive of that nature, love should characterize them.

3:24. This verse returns to a discussion of the significance of keeping those commandments. The person who habitually observes the requirements which God has laid down is the one who genuinely abides in God. "Him" in verse 24 refers to God the Father, as it did in verses 22 and 23.

The relationship goes in two directions—the believer abides in God and God abides in the believer—to underscore that intimacy with God can exist. Keeping God's commands is not the prerequisite for a relationship, but it does provide evidence of such a relationship.

A person who rests his assurance of salvation on an imperfect obedience to God's commands is likely to suffer from frequent doubts. So a second witness confirms the believer's standing with God. We can know in experience that God abides in us because of the presence of the Holy Spirit which comes only as a gift from Him (Romans 8:14-16). John did not explain how the Spirit's presence becomes obvious. His indwelling can be detected by spiritual people.

Everyday . . . And he gives us all our requests, *BB* . . . and get from Him anything we ask, *Beck.*

because we keep his commandments: . . . we are keeping His precepts, *Concordant* . . . we observe His injunctions, *Berkeley* . . . we are obeying his orders, *Phillips* . . . because we obey God's commands, *Everyday* . . . because we keep all his laws, *BB* . . . with solicitous care, *Wuest.*

and do those things that are pleasing in his sight: . . . and practice what pleases him, *Noli* . . . which are pleasing in His penetrating gaze, *Wuest* . . . in his eyes, *BB.*

23. And this is his commandment, That we should believe on the name of his Son Jesus Christ: His orders are that we should put our trust in, *Phillips* . . . And this is his law, that we have faith in the name of his Son, *BB* . . . And this is His injunction, that we put our faith in, *Berkeley* . . . Put your trust in, *NLT.*

and love one another, as he gave us commandment: . . . as he himself instructed us, *Noli* . . . as He enjoined us, *Berkeley* . . . as we used to hear him say in person, *Phillips* . . . as he taught us, *Greber* . . . even as he said to us, *BB* . . . as He has ordered us to do, *Beck.*

24. And he that keepeth his commandments dwelleth in him, and he in him: . . . the one who as a habit of life exercises, *Wuest* . . . He who obeys His commands remains in Him, *Berkeley* . . . who does what He orders, *Beck* . . . will remain in communion with God, and God in communion with him, *Greber* . . . lives in God, *Everyday.*

And hereby we know that he abideth in us: We know that He really lives in us, *Laubach* . . . How do we know that God lives in us? *Everyday* . . . that God is in communion with us we know, *Greber* . . . By this we know that He remains in us, *Berkeley* . . . the guarantee of his presence within us, *Phillips* . . . our witness that he is in us, *BB.*

by the Spirit which he hath given us: . . . from the Spirit as a source whom He gave to us, *Wuest* . . . by the spirit-world that He has granted to us, *Greber.*

1 John 4:1

1319.14 verb 3sing indic aor act		27.6 adj pl masc	3231.1 partic	3820.3 adj dat sing	4011.3 noun dat sing neu
ἔδωκεν.	4:1.	Ἀγαπητοί,	μὴ	παντὶ	πνεύματι
edōken		Agapētoi	mē	panti	pneumati
he gave.		Beloved,	not	every	spirit

3961.2 verb 2pl pres act	233.2 conj	1375.1 verb 2pl pres act	3450.17 art pl neu	4011.4 noun pl neu	1479.1 conj
πιστεύετε,	ἀλλὰ	δοκιμάζετε	τὰ	πνεύματα,	εἰ
pisteuete	alla	dokimazete	ta	pneumata	ei
believe,	but	prove	the	spirits,	if

1523.2 prep gen	3450.2 art gen sing	2296.2 noun gen sing masc	1498.4 verb 3sing indic pres act	3617.1 conj	4044.7 adj nom pl masc
ἐκ	τοῦ	θεοῦ	ἐστιν˙	ὅτι	πολλοὶ
ek	tou	theou	estin	hoti	polloi
of		God	they are;	because	many

5413.4 noun nom pl masc	1814.24 verb 3pl indic perf act	1519.1 prep	3450.6 art acc sing masc	2862.4 noun acc sing masc
ψευδοπροφῆται	ἐξεληλύθασιν	εἰς	τὸν	κόσμον.
pseudoprophētai	exelēluthasin	eis	ton	kosmon
false prophets	have gone out	into	the	world.

2.a.**Txt:** 01ℵ-corr2,02A 03B,04C,020L 044-corr3,33,614,945 1739,1852,1881 **Var:** 044-org,byz.

1706.1 prep	3642.5 dem-pron dat sing masc	1091.5 verb 2pl indic pres act	1091.41 verb 3sing indic pres mid	3450.16 art sing neu
2. ἐν	τούτῳ	☆ γινώσκετε	[a γινώσκεται]	τὸ
en	toutō	ginōskete	ginōsketai	to
By	this	you know	[he is being known]	the

4011.1 noun sing neu	3450.2 art gen sing	2296.2 noun gen sing masc	3820.17 adj sing neu	4011.1 noun sing neu	3614.16 rel-pron sing neu
πνεῦμα	τοῦ	θεοῦ˙	πᾶν	πνεῦμα	ὃ
pneuma	tou	theou	pan	pneuma	ho
Spirit		of God:	every	spirit	which

3533.2 verb 3sing indic pres act	2400.3 name acc masc	5382.4 name acc masc	1706.1 prep	4418.3 noun dat sing fem	2048.29 verb acc sing masc part perf act
ὁμολογεῖ	Ἰησοῦν	Χριστὸν	ἐν	σαρκὶ	ἐληλυθότα
homologei	Iēsoun	Christon	en	sarki	elēluthota
confesses	Jesus	Christ	in	flesh	having come,

1523.2 prep gen	3450.2 art gen sing	2296.2 noun gen sing masc	1498.4 verb 3sing indic pres act	2504.1 conj	3820.17 adj sing neu	4011.1 noun sing neu
ἐκ	τοῦ	θεοῦ	ἐστιν.	3. καὶ	πᾶν	πνεῦμα
ek	tou	theou	estin	kai	pan	pneuma
of		God	is;	and	every	spirit

3.a.**Txt:** 01ℵ,018K,020L byz. **Var:** 02A,03B,1241,bo. Gries,Lach,Treg,Alf We/Ho,Weis,UBS/☆

3614.16 rel-pron sing neu	3231.1 partic	3533.2 verb 3sing indic pres act	3450.6 art acc sing masc	2400.3 name acc masc	5382.4 name acc masc
ὃ	μὴ	ὁμολογεῖ	τὸν	Ἰησοῦν	a Χριστὸν
ho	mē	homologei	ton	Iēsoun	Christon
which	not	confesses		Jesus	Christ

1706.1 prep	4418.3 noun dat sing fem	2048.29 verb acc sing masc part perf act	1523.2 prep gen	3450.2 art gen sing	2296.2 noun gen sing masc	3620.2 partic
ἐν	σαρκὶ	ἐληλυθότα,	ἐκ	τοῦ	θεοῦ	οὐκ
en	sarki	elēluthota	ek	tou	theou	ouk
in	flesh	come,	of		God	not

1498.4 verb 3sing indic pres act	2504.1 conj	3642.17 dem-pron sing neu	1498.4 verb 3sing indic pres act	3450.16 art sing neu	3450.2 art gen sing
ἐστιν˙	καὶ	τοῦτό	ἐστιν	τὸ	τοῦ
estin	kai	touto	estin	to	tou
is:	and	this	is	the	of the

4:1. At this point the epistle begins a new strain of thought, arguing that sonship can be demonstrated by adherence to truth, particularly the truth about the person of Christ. Evidently false teachers who were harassing the churches with doctrines characteristic of the Gnostic heresy.

The opening command asks believers to stop putting faith in "every spirit," referring to people claiming to get their message from a supernatural source. Christians need to realize that not every spirit represents God. Instead of being gullible, they need to "try" (*dokimazete*, test) any prophet who claims to speak as a mouthpiece for the Spirit of God (cf. Deuteronomy 18:20-22). It was foolish to assume that all claimants truly have their origin in God, because a large number of false prophets were already in circulation, promoting their teachings throughout the world.

No one would deny that believers can receive guidance from the Holy Spirit. Jesus said of Him, "He will guide you into all truth" (John 16:13). But the human spirit may be involved, or even an evil spirit. This is the reason we have the right and the obligation to "try (test) the spirits," to see if their guidance conforms to the Word of God.

1. Beloved, believe not every spirit: . . . dear friends of mine, *Phillips* . . . do not put trust in every Inspired Utterance, *Wade* . . . do not trust every inspiration, *TCNT* . . . do not put faith in, *Berkeley* . . . every so-called spiritual utterance, *Williams.*

but try the spirits whether they are of God: . . . test the spirits, *Concordant* . . . put the spirits to the test, *Berkeley* . . . to see whether they are of Divine origin, *Wade* . . . to discover whether they come from, *Phillips* . . . for the purpose of approving them if they are, and finding that they meet the specifications laid down, *Wuest.*

because many false prophets are gone out into the world: . . . the world is full of false prophets, *Phillips* . . . many false preachers, *NLT* . . . have been traveling over the world, *Laubach* . . . have been let out into the world, *Berkeley.*

4:2. The question is, How does one test such people? The inspired writer gave a practical way to determine the truth—by examining the content of the prophet's message. If a spirit-inspired utterance is truly from God, it will be an open acknowledgment of Jesus, the Christ or Anointed One who became human. Gnostic teachers asserted that the divine Christ was separate from the man Jesus and merely indwelt Him temporarily. John opposed their view by demanding that genuine Christians accept Jesus and Christ as the same person. He also specified that Christ came "in flesh," omitting any article to emphasize the kind of nature He assumed. And the perfect participle "is come" shows that Christ's action in becoming man was more than a temporary arrangement.

2. Hereby know ye the Spirit of God: In this you know, *Concordant* . . . By this we recognize, *Berkeley* . . . Here is the way in which to recognize, *TCNT* . . . You can test them in this simple way, *Phillips.*

Every spirit that confesseth that Jesus Christ is come in the flesh is of God: . . . which is avowing, *Concordant* . . . says, "I believe that Jesus is the Christ who came to earth and became a man," *Everyday* . . . who agrees...that Jesus Christ has come in the sphere of the flesh...and still remains incarnate, *Wuest* . . . as having come incarnate, *Berkeley* . . . actually became man, *Phillips* . . . that man speaks for God, *Laubach.*

4:3. The test of truth is continued here in negative form. If a person claims to reveal truth, yet refuses to acknowledge the apostolic doctrine of Christ, he is a deceiver. The present tense of "confesseth" (Greek, *homologei*) speaks of a habitual practice, and the meaning of the word implies a personal conviction openly expressed. The definite article before Jesus refers back to the fuller openly expressed. The definite article before Jesus refers back to the fuller statement of faith previously given in verse 2; the false spirits are those which deny that Jesus is the divine Christ who became man.

If such speakers were not inspired by the Holy Spirit, their message must come from a different spirit. This spirit is identified as the "spirit of antichrist" (cf. 2:18). The italicized word *spirit* (mean-

3. And every spirit that confesseth not that Jesus Christ is come in the flesh is not of God: Another spirit refuses to say this, *SEB* . . . who denies that, *Noli* . . . refuses to say this about Jesus, *Everyday* . . . that does not acknowledge Jesus, *Berkeley* . . . this aforementioned Jesus, *Wuest* . . . has come in a human body, *NLT* . . . does not come from God, *Phillips.*

and this is that [spirit] of antichrist: . . . it is the utterance of Antichrist, *Williams.*

497.2 noun gen sing masc	3614.16 rel-pron sing neu	189.39 verb 2pl indic perf act	3617.1 conj	2048.34 verb 3sing indic pres mid
ἀντιχρίστου,	ὃ	ἀκηκόατε	ὅτι	ἔρχεται,
antichristou	*ho*	*akēkoate*	*hoti*	*erchetai*
antichrist,	which	you have heard	that	it comes,

2504.1 conj	3431.1 adv	1706.1 prep	3450.3 art dat sing	2862.3 noun dat sing masc	1498.4 verb 3sing indic pres act	2218.1 adv
καὶ	νῦν	ἐν	τῷ	κόσμῳ	ἐστὶν	ἤδη.
kai	*nun*	*en*	*tō*	*kosmō*	*estin*	*ēdē*
and	now	in	the	world	is it	already.

5050.1 prs-pron nom 2pl	1523.2 prep gen	3450.2 art gen sing	2296.2 noun gen sing masc	1498.6 verb 2pl indic pres act	4888.1 noun pl neu
4. Ὑμεῖς	ἐκ	τοῦ	θεοῦ	ἐστε,	τεκνία,
Humeis	*ek*	*tou*	*theou*	*este*	*teknia*
You	of		God	are,	little children,

2504.1 conj	3390.14 verb 2pl indic perf act	840.8 prs-pron acc pl masc	3617.1 conj	3157.2 adj comp nom sing	1498.4 verb 3sing indic pres act
καὶ	νενικήκατε	αὐτούς·	ὅτι	μείζων	ἐστὶν
kai	*nenikēkate*	*autous*	*hoti*	*meizōn*	*estin*
and	have overcome	them,	because	greater	is

3450.5 art nom sing masc	1706.1 prep	5050.3 prs-pron dat 2pl	2211.1 conj	3450.5 art nom sing masc	1706.1 prep	3450.3 art dat sing
ὁ	ἐν	ὑμῖν	ἢ	ὁ	ἐν	τῷ
ho	*en*	*humin*	*ē*	*ho*	*en*	*tō*
the	in	you	than	the	in	the

2862.3 noun dat sing masc	840.7 prs-pron nom pl masc	1523.2 prep gen	3450.2 art gen sing	2862.2 noun gen sing masc	1498.7 verb 3pl indic pres act
κόσμῳ.	5. αὐτοὶ	ἐκ	τοῦ	κόσμου	εἰσίν,
kosmō	*autoi*	*ek*	*tou*	*kosmou*	*eisin*
world.	They	of	the	world	are;

1217.2 prep	3642.17 dem-pron sing neu	1523.2 prep gen	3450.2 art gen sing	2862.2 noun gen sing masc	2953.5 verb 3pl indic pres act	2504.1 conj
διὰ	τοῦτο	ἐκ	τοῦ	κόσμου	λαλοῦσιν,	καὶ
dia	*touto*	*ek*	*tou*	*kosmou*	*lalousin*	*kai*
because of	this	of	the	world	they talk,	and

3450.5 art nom sing masc	2862.1 noun nom sing masc	840.1 prs-pron gen pl	189.5 verb 3sing indic pres act	2231.1 prs-pron nom 1pl	1523.2 prep gen
ὁ	κόσμος	αὐτῶν	ἀκούει.	6. ἡμεῖς	ἐκ
ho	*kosmos*	*autōn*	*akouei*	*hēmeis*	*ek*
the	world	them	hears.	We	of

3450.2 art gen sing	2296.2 noun gen sing masc	1498.5 verb 1pl indic pres act	3450.5 art nom sing masc	1091.11 verb nom sing masc part pres act	3450.6 art acc sing masc
τοῦ	θεοῦ	ἐσμεν·	ὁ	γινώσκων	τὸν
tou	*theou*	*esmen*	*ho*	*ginōskōn*	*ton*
	God	are;	the	knowing	

2296.4 noun acc sing masc	189.5 verb 3sing indic pres act	2231.2 prs-pron gen 1pl	3614.5 rel-pron nom sing masc	3620.2 partic	1498.4 verb 3sing indic pres act
θεὸν,	ἀκούει	ἡμῶν·	ὃς	οὐκ	ἔστιν
theon	*akouei*	*hēmōn*	*hos*	*ouk*	*estin*
God,	hears	us;	who	not	is

1523.2 prep gen	3450.2 art gen sing	2296.2 noun gen sing masc	3620.2 partic	189.5 verb 3sing indic pres act	2231.2 prs-pron gen 1pl	1523.2 prep gen
ἐκ	τοῦ	θεοῦ,	οὐκ	ἀκούει	ἡμῶν.	ἐκ
ek	*tou*	*theou*	*ouk*	*akouei*	*hēmōn*	*ek*
of		God,	not	hears	us.	By

ing it was supplied by the KJV translators) is the most logical way to translate the Greek construction. The very spirit which will empower the future "man of sin" was already at work in these false teachers.

Such subtle deception should have been no surprise to these believers, for the problem had already begun in John's day.

whereof ye have heard that it should come; and even now already is it in the world: . . . which you were warned would come, *Phillips* . . . of whose coming you have heard. Right now he is in the world, *Berkeley* . . . Now he and his agents are, *Noli* . . . and it is now active in the world, *Wade.*

4:4. The genuine believers who received the letter stood in strong contrast to those deluded by the spirit of Antichrist. They had God as the source of their spiritual life. These "little children" had been born into God's family. In addition they had overcome "them," namely, the false prophets of verse 1. The perfect tense of "overcome" shows that they had withstood the lure of false doctrine in the past and were still standing firm at the time of the epistle's writing. But they still needed to be on guard to maintain their purity in the future.

The reason they could overcome the power of evil was because the One who indwelt them was greater than the one indwelling the world. This phrase continues the contrast between the Holy Spirit and the "spirit of antichrist."

It is a great encouragement to be reminded of the power available to believers. Satan is an active force in the world, he has great power and many ways of attacking the people of God. It is good, then, to remind ourselves that though the devil is mighty, God is almighty. Satan may be powerful, but God is all-powerful.

4. Ye are of God, little children, and have overcome them: As for you, out of God you are, little born-ones, and you have gained a complete victory over them and are still victors, *Wuest* . . . you belong to God, *SEB* . . . and you have successfully resisted such men as these, *TCNT* . . . you have refuted these false teachers, *Norlie* . . . You have won a victory over the false spirits, *Laubach* . . . you have conquered them, *Concordant* . . . and have defeated them, *Berkeley.*

because greater is he that is in you, than he that is in the world: He who is in our hearts is greater, *Williams* . . . is mightier than, *Norlie* . . . is far stronger than the antichrist, *Phillips.*

4:5. The false teachers who had harassed the churches based their work on a different source. They were creatures of the satanic world system, thoroughly at home in this view of life. Since their thoughts were in tune with the world, they found a ready audience when they spoke to other world-dwellers. They spoke the world's language and found easy acceptance.

5. They are of the world: therefore speak they of the world: The agents of the antichrist are children of the world; they speak the world's language, *Phillips* . . . so they talk from a worldly point of view, *Berkeley* . . . out of the world as a source they are constantly speaking, *Wuest.*

and the world heareth them: . . . and the world listens to them, *Wuest, Berkeley* . . . of course, pays attention to what they say, *Phillips.*

4:6. John spotlighted the readers in verse 4 and the heretics in verse 5. Here the focus is on the teachers of the truth. Like you, he claimed, "we are of God." And those who were in tune with God would listen to men like the apostles who had received their message from Him. Those who thought in the world's thought patterns would, of course, not care to hear the truth.

In conclusion one may see that there is another test of truth—the type of people who welcome a message give a clue to its nature. People who love truth will respond to a spirit characterized by truth; those who are already deluded will respond to a spirit of delusion.

6. We are of God: he that knoweth God heareth us: We are God's children and only the man who knows God hears our message, *Phillips* . . . Whoever has acquaintance with God, *Berkeley* . . . will listen to us, *Norlie.*

he that is not of God heareth not us: . . . what we say means nothing to the man who is not himself a child of God, *Phillips* . . . will turn a deaf ear to us, *Norlie* . . . doesn't listen to us, *Adams.*

3642.1 dem-pron gen sing	1091.4 verb 1pl indic pres act	3450.16 art sing neu	4011.1 noun sing neu	3450.10 art gen sing fem	223.2 noun gen sing fem
τούτου	γινώσκομεν	τὸ	πνεῦμα	τῆς	ἀληθείας
toutou	*ginōskomen*	*to*	*pneuma*	*tēs*	*alētheias*
this	we know	the	spirit	of the	truth

2504.1 conj	3450.16 art sing neu	4011.1 noun sing neu	3450.10 art gen sing fem	3967.2 noun gen sing fem	27.6 adj pl masc
καὶ	τὸ	πνεῦμα	τῆς	πλάνης.	7. Ἀγαπητοί,
kai	*to*	*pneuma*	*tēs*	*planēs*	*Agapētoi*
and	the	spirit	of the	error.	Beloved,

25.3 verb 1pl pres act	238.3 prs-pron acc pl masc	3617.1 conj	3450.9 art nom sing fem	26.1 noun nom sing fem	1523.2 prep gen
ἀγαπῶμεν	ἀλλήλους·	ὅτι	ἡ	ἀγάπη	ἐκ
agapōmen	*allēlous*	*hoti*	*hē*	*agapē*	*ek*
let us love	one another;	because	the	love	of

3450.2 art gen sing	2296.2 noun gen sing masc	1498.4 verb 3sing indic pres act	2504.1 conj	3820.6 adj nom sing masc	3450.5 art nom sing masc
τοῦ	θεοῦ	ἐστιν,	καὶ	πᾶς	ὁ
tou	*theou*	*estin*	*kai*	*pas*	*ho*
	God	is,	and	everyone	the

25.8 verb nom sing masc part pres act	1523.2 prep gen	3450.2 art gen sing	2296.2 noun gen sing masc	1074.23 verb 3sing indic perf mid	2504.1 conj
ἀγαπῶν,	ἐκ	τοῦ	θεοῦ	γεγέννηται,	καὶ
agapōn	*ek*	*tou*	*theou*	*gegennētai*	*kai*
loving,	of		God	has been born,	and

1091.3 verb 3sing indic pres act	3450.6 art acc sing masc	2296.4 noun acc sing masc	3450.5 art nom sing masc	3231.1 partic	25.8 verb nom sing masc part pres act
γινώσκει	τὸν	θεόν.	8. ὁ	μὴ	ἀγαπῶν,
ginōskei	*ton*	*theon*	*ho*	*mē*	*agapōn*
knows		God.	The	not	loving,

3620.2 partic	1091.17 verb 3sing indic aor act	3450.6 art acc sing masc	2296.4 noun acc sing masc	3617.1 conj	3450.5 art nom sing masc
οὐκ	ἔγνω	τὸν	θεόν·	ὅτι	ὁ
ouk	*egnō*	*ton*	*theon*	*hoti*	*ho*
not	knew		God;	because	

2296.1 noun nom sing masc	26.1 noun nom sing fem	1498.4 verb 3sing indic pres act	1706.1 prep	3642.5 dem-pron dat sing masc	5157.10 verb 3sing indic aor pass
θεὸς	ἀγάπη	ἐστίν.	9. ἐν	τούτῳ	ἐφανερώθη
theos	*agapē*	*estin*	*en*	*toutō*	*ephanerōthē*
God	love	is.	In	this	was manifested

3450.9 art nom sing fem	26.1 noun nom sing fem	3450.2 art gen sing	2296.2 noun gen sing masc	1706.1 prep	2231.3 prs-pron dat 1pl	3617.1 conj
ἡ	ἀγάπη	τοῦ	θεοῦ	ἐν	ἡμῖν,	ὅτι
hē	*agapē*	*tou*	*theou*	*en*	*hēmin*	*hoti*
the	love		of God	to	us,	that

3450.6 art acc sing masc	5048.4 noun acc sing masc	840.3 prs-pron gen sing	3450.6 art acc sing masc	3302.3 adj acc sing masc	643.17 verb 3sing indic perf act
τὸν	υἱὸν	αὐτοῦ	τὸν	μονογενῆ	ἀπέσταλκεν
ton	*huion*	*autou*	*ton*	*monogenē*	*apestalken*
the	Son	his	the	only begotten	has sent

3450.5 art nom sing masc	2296.1 noun nom sing masc	1519.1 prep	3450.6 art acc sing masc	2862.4 noun acc sing masc	2419.1 conj	2180.24 verb 1pl subj aor act
ὁ	θεὸς	εἰς	τὸν	κόσμον,	ἵνα	ζήσωμεν
ho	*theos*	*eis*	*ton*	*kosmon*	*hina*	*zēsōmen*
	God	into	the	world,	that	we might live

4:7. An abrupt change in theme marks the beginning of a new section here, one which focuses on the requirement that a genuine Christian must display love. The apostle had listed love before as a test of faith (2:7-11; 3:10-24); now the logic behind the test is explained.

John began by calling his readers "beloved," people who have experienced love. The opening phrase may be translated as a statement ("we love") or an exhortation ("let us love"). The later seems to fit better, for it was used in that way in 3:18. The present tense of the verb demands a continual practice of love toward one another.

The second part of the verse explains why Christians should exhibit such love. The love which was being discussed comes only from God; anyone who is habitually marked by this distinctive kind of love gives evidence of a relationship with God. He has been given a place in the Father's family which he still holds; in addition, he has a knowledge of God which is fed by personal experience of His presence.

4:8. The opposite case also holds true: if a person has a pattern of life which does not include *agapē*-type love, he shows that he never made the initial acquaintance of God. The aorist tense of "knoweth" is evidently an ingressive aorist which describes the beginning of a relationship.

The reason for such a sweeping statement is then explained. God is love; love is part of His essential nature. The lack of a definite article before "love" shows that the inspired writer was emphasizing the quality of love rather than attempting to define God's nature. Since love is an integral part of the divine nature, a person devoid of love shows that he has not been affected by contact with God. He is separate from God.

4:9. A statement reminiscent of John 3:16 describes the way in which God has expressed His love in action. "In this" refers to the sending of the Son which is described in the balance of the verse. Love had always been part of the divine attributes, but it was not until the incarnation of Christ that God's love was fully revealed. The definite article before "love" identifies it as the particular love which characterizes the Lord. The phrase "toward us" (Greek, *en hēmin*) may be rendered "in us," or more appropriately, "among us." Jesus' coming displayed God's love among the members of the human race.

The second phrase of the verse begins with "his only begotten Son" in the Greek word order, stressing the marvelous nature of this gift. Jesus is the divine Son, the unique One (Greek, *monogenē*) unlike any other. He was sent (Greek, *apestalken*) with a mission to perform, one which has continuing results, as shown by the

Hereby know we the spirit of truth, and the spirit of error: By this we may distinguish, *Montgomery* . . . This gives us a ready means of distinguishing the true from the false, *Phillips* . . . This is the way to distinguish a true spiritual utterance from one that is false, *Williams* . . . the inspiration that is Real and the inspiration that is delusive, *Wade* . . . has the true spirit or the false, *Laubach* . . . spirit of deception, *Concordant.*

7. Beloved, let us love one another: for love is of God: Dear friends, *Everyday* . . . To you whom I love I say, let us go on loving, *Phillips* . . . we should be loving, *Concordant* . . . because love springs from, *Berkeley* . . . with a divine and self-sacrificial love, because this aforementioned love is out of God as a source, *Wuest* . . . because love originates with God, *Williams* . . . our love is of divine origin, *Greber.*

and every one that loveth is born of God, and knoweth God: . . . has been born with the present result that he is regenerated and knows God in an experiential way, *Wuest* . . . is God's son and has some knowledge of him, *Phillips* . . . has become God's child, *Everyday* . . . and possesses the true conception of God, *Greber.*

8. He that loveth not knoweth not God; for God is love: He who is not loving, *Berkeley* . . . He who is lacking in love has no understanding of God's nature, *Greber* . . . cannot know him at all, *Phillips* . . . has not come to know God, because God as to His nature is love, *Wuest.*

9. In this was manifested the love of God toward us: As for us, the love of God was revealed by the fact that, *Berkeley* . . . the greatest demonstration of God's love for us has been, *Phillips* . . . was clearly shown the love of God in our case, *Wuest* . . . among us, *Concordant.*

because that God sent his only begotten Son into the world: . . . that God has dispatched, *Concordant* . . . the uniquely begotten One, God sent off into the world on a mission in order, *Wuest.*

1 John 4:10

1217.1 prep	840.3 prs-pron gen sing	1706.1 prep	3642.5 dem-pron dat sing masc	1498.4 verb 3sing indic pres act	3450.9 art nom sing fem
δι'	αὐτοῦ.	10. ἐν	τούτῳ	ἐστὶν	ἡ
di'	*autou*	*en*	*toutō*	*estin*	*hē*
through	him.	In	this	is	the

26.1 noun nom sing fem	3620.1 partic	3617.1 conj	2231.1 prs-pron nom 1pl	25.15 verb 1pl indic aor act	3450.6 art acc sing masc
ἀγάπη,	οὐχ	ὅτι	ἡμεῖς	ἠγαπήσαμεν	τὸν
agapē	*ouch*	*hoti*	*hēmeis*	*ēgapēsamen*	*ton*
love,	not	that	we	loved	

2296.4 noun acc sing masc	233.1 conj	3617.1 conj	840.5 prs-pron nom sing masc	25.14 verb 3sing indic aor act	2231.4 prs-pron acc 1pl	2504.1 conj
θεόν,	ἀλλ'	ὅτι	αὐτὸς	ἠγάπησεν	ἡμᾶς,	καὶ
theon	*all'*	*hoti*	*autos*	*ēgapēsen*	*hēmas*	*kai*
God,	but	that	he	loved	us,	and

643.8 verb 3sing indic aor act	3450.6 art acc sing masc	5048.4 noun acc sing masc	840.3 prs-pron gen sing	2410.2 noun acc sing masc	3875.1 prep
ἀπέστειλεν	τὸν	υἱὸν	αὐτοῦ	ἱλασμὸν	περὶ
apesteilen	*ton*	*huion*	*autou*	*hilasmon*	*peri*
sent	the	Son	his	a propitiation	for

3450.1 art gen pl	264.6 noun gen pl fem	2231.2 prs-pron gen 1pl	27.6 adj pl masc	1479.1 conj	3643.1 adv
τῶν	ἁμαρτιῶν	ἡμῶν.	11. Ἀγαπητοί,	εἰ	οὕτως
tōn	*hamartiōn*	*hēmōn*	*Agapētoi*	*ei*	*houtōs*
the	sins	our.	Beloved,	if	so

3450.5 art nom sing masc	2296.1 noun nom sing masc	25.14 verb 3sing indic aor act	2231.4 prs-pron acc 1pl	2504.1 conj	2231.1 prs-pron nom 1pl
ὁ	θεὸς	ἠγάπησεν	ἡμᾶς,	καὶ	ἡμεῖς
ho	*theos*	*ēgapēsen*	*hēmas*	*kai*	*hēmeis*
	God	loved	us,	also	we

3648.4 verb 1pl indic pres act	238.3 prs-pron acc pl masc	25.11 verb inf pres act	2296.4 noun acc sing masc	3625.2 num card nom masc
ὀφείλομεν	ἀλλήλους	ἀγαπᾶν.	12. θεὸν	οὐδεὶς
opheilomen	*allēlous*	*agapan*	*theon*	*oudeis*
ought	one another	to love.	God	no one

4312.1 adv	2277.13 verb 3sing indic perf mid	1430.1 partic	25.3 verb 1pl pres act	238.3 prs-pron acc pl masc
πώποτε	τεθέαται·	ἐὰν	ἀγαπῶμεν	ἀλλήλους,
pōpote	*tetheatai*	*ean*	*agapōmen*	*allēlous*
ever	has seen;	if	we should love	one another,

3450.5 art nom sing masc	2296.1 noun nom sing masc	1706.1 prep	2231.3 prs-pron dat 1pl	3176.1 verb 3sing indic pres act	2504.1 conj	3450.9 art nom sing fem
ὁ	θεὸς	ἐν	ἡμῖν	μένει,	καὶ	ἡ
ho	*theos*	*en*	*hēmin*	*menei*	*kai*	*hē*
	God	in	us	resides,	and	the

26.1 noun nom sing fem	840.3 prs-pron gen sing	4896.18 verb nom sing fem part perf mid	1498.4 verb 3sing indic pres act	1706.1 prep
ἀγάπη	αὐτοῦ	τετελειωμένη	‘ ἐστιν	ἐν
agapē	*autou*	*teteleiōmenē*	*estin*	*en*
love	his	having been perfected	is	in

2231.3 prs-pron dat 1pl	1706.1 prep	2231.3 prs-pron dat 1pl	1498.4 verb 3sing indic pres act	1706.1 prep	3642.5 dem-pron dat sing masc
ἡμῖν.	[☆ ἐν	ἡμῖν	ἐστιν.]	13. Ἐν	τούτῳ
hēmin	*en*	*hēmin*	*estin*	*En*	*toutō*
us.	[in	us	is.]	By	this

perfect tense of the verb. God's purpose was to make eternal life possible for His people.

that we might live through him: . . . to give us life through him, *Phillips, Everyday* . . . so that through him we might obtain spiritual life, *Greber.*

4:10. The discussion of love moves forward by explaining what love really is. It is found "herein" or "in this," the facts described in the remainder of the verse. The specific kind of love described thus far may be seen in its pure form, not in human affection, but in the love displayed by God himself.

The "we" in "we loved God" is emphasized in the Greek and placed in contrast with "he," the great Lover. The love which believers must have is not love which man originates. It is more than any affection which we have felt toward God. On the contrary, love originates with God. He is the initiator, the One who not only loved mankind, but translated love into deed by sending His Son on a mission to provide propitiation (see 2:2) as a way of making reconciliation with God possible.

10. Herein is love, not that we loved God, but that he loved us: We see real love, *Phillips* . . . His love for us was not occasioned by our having loved God first, *Greber* . . . which love exists in this, *Berkeley* . . . True love is God's love for us, not our love for God, *Everyday.*

and sent his Son [to be] the propitiation for our sins: . . . dispatches...a propitiatory shelter concerned with our sins, *Concordant* . . . sent off His Son, an expiatory satisfaction concerning our sins, *Wuest* . . . to make personal atonement for, *Phillips* . . . to be the atoning sacrifice for our sins, *Norlie* . . . to be the way to take away our sins, *Everyday.*

4:11. God's love stands as an example for His children. He demonstrated His love through the Incarnation and by His provision of salvation (4:9,10), and "so" points back to this fact. "So" is a small word, but note how much it includes here. Think of the suffering of the Father in letting Jesus suffer. Think of the honor He bestows in making us part of His family. Amazing love! The form of "if" used in this verse assumes the truth of the statement; God has indeed loved us.

God's love places a moral obligation on all believers to maintain a pattern of love for one another.

11. Beloved, if God so loved us, we ought also to love one another: Loved ones, *Berkeley* . . . dear friends! *Everyday* . . . If God loved us as much as that, surely we, in our turn, should love one another! *Phillips* . . . since in that manner and to that extent did God love us, also, as for us, we are under moral obligation to be constantly loving one another, *Wuest.*

4:12. At this point John inserted the well-known fact that God is invisible; in fact, no one has ever seen His essence. The word "God" appears first in the Greek word order for emphasis, and it appears without a definite article to refer to the nature of God's being. The statement appears to be an abrupt shift in thought but actually sets the stage for a discussion of the way in which God may actually be known. Some might have been claiming to have visions in which they received special knowledge of the Lord, but the apostle denied their claims. Rather than revealing himself to a select few, God makes himself available to all who trust Him and show their faith by loving one another.

When a person habitually shows love to other Christians, it gives evidence that God has taken up a lasting relationship with that person. In addition, it demonstrates that the love which God gives has accomplished its intended purpose by producing a person who gives love to others. The combination of verbs emphasizes the existing result of God's past work in the person's life.

12. No man hath seen God at any time: No one has ever seen God, *Williams C.K.* . . . It is true that no human being has ever had a direct vision of God, *Phillips* . . . God in His [invisible] essence no one has ever yet beheld, *Wuest* . . . has ever gazed upon God, *Concordant.*

If we love one another, God dwelleth in us: In case we love one another, God remains in us, *Berkeley* . . . Yet if we love one another God does actually live in us, *Phillips* . . . makes His abode in us, *Norlie* . . . has full sway in us, *Swann.*

and his love is perfected in us: . . . and only then does our love for Him become complete in our hearts, *Greber* . . . and His love runs its full course in us, *Berkeley* . . . and his love grows in us toward perfection, *Phillips* . . . has reached its goal. It is made perfect in us, *Everyday.*

1091.4 verb 1pl indic pres act	**3617.1** conj	**1706.1** prep	**840.4** prs-pron dat sing	**3176.5** verb 1pl indic pres act	**2504.1** conj	**840.5** prs-pron nom sing masc
γινώσκομεν	ὅτι	ἐν	αὐτῷ	μένομεν,	καὶ	αὐτὸς
ginōskomen	*hoti*	*en*	*autō*	*menomen*	*kai*	*autos*
we know	that	in	him	we reside,	and	he

1706.1 prep	**2231.3** prs-pron dat 1pl	**3617.1** conj	**1523.2** prep gen	**3450.2** art gen sing	**4011.2** noun gen sing neu	**840.3** prs-pron gen sing
ἐν	ἡμῖν,	ὅτι	ἐκ	τοῦ	πνεύματος	αὐτοῦ
en	*hēmin*	*hoti*	*ek*	*tou*	*pneumatos*	*autou*
in	us,	because	of	the	Spirit	his

1319.33 verb 3sing indic perf act	**2231.3** prs-pron dat 1pl	**2504.1** conj	**2231.1** prs-pron nom 1pl	**2277.14** verb 1pl indic perf mid	**2504.1** conj
δέδωκεν	ἡμῖν.	**14.** καὶ	ἡμεῖς	τεθεάμεθα	καὶ
dedōken	*hēmin*	*kai*	*hēmeis*	*tetheametha*	*kai*
he has given	to us.	And	we	have seen	and

3113.4 verb 1pl indic pres act	**3617.1** conj	**3450.5** art nom sing masc	**3824.1** noun nom sing masc	**643.17** verb 3sing indic perf act
μαρτυροῦμεν	ὅτι	ὁ	πατὴρ	ἀπέσταλκεν
marturoumen	*hoti*	*ho*	*patēr*	*apestalken*
bear witness	that	the	Father	has sent

3450.6 art acc sing masc	**5048.4** noun acc sing masc	**4842.4** noun acc sing masc	**3450.2** art gen sing	**2862.2** noun gen sing masc	**3614.5** rel-pron nom sing masc
τὸν	υἱὸν	σωτῆρα	τοῦ	κόσμου.	**15.** Ὃς
ton	*huion*	*sōtēra*	*tou*	*kosmou*	*Hos*
the	Son	Saviour	of the	world.	Whoever

300.1 partic	**3533.10** verb 3sing subj aor act	**3617.1** conj	**2400.1** name nom masc	**1498.4** verb 3sing indic pres act	**3450.5** art nom sing masc
ἂν	ὁμολογήσῃ	ὅτι	Ἰησοῦς	ἐστιν	ὁ
an	*homologēsē*	*hoti*	*Iēsous*	*estin*	*ho*
	may confess	that	Jesus	is	the

5048.1 noun nom sing masc	**3450.2** art gen sing	**2296.2** noun gen sing masc	**3450.5** art nom sing masc	**2296.1** noun nom sing masc	**1706.1** prep
υἱὸς	τοῦ	θεοῦ,	ὁ	θεὸς	ἐν
huios	*tou*	*theou*	*ho*	*theos*	*en*
Son		of God,		God	in

840.4 prs-pron dat sing	**3176.1** verb 3sing indic pres act	**2504.1** conj	**840.5** prs-pron nom sing masc	**1706.1** prep	**3450.3** art dat sing	**2296.3** noun dat sing masc
αὐτῷ	μένει,	καὶ	αὐτὸς	ἐν	τῷ	θεῷ.
autō	*menei*	*kai*	*autos*	*en*	*tō*	*theō*
him	abides,	and	he	in		God.

2504.1 conj	**2231.1** prs-pron nom 1pl	**1091.33** verb 1pl indic perf act	**2504.1** conj	**3961.40** verb 1pl indic perf act	**3450.12** art acc sing fem
16. καὶ	ἡμεῖς	ἐγνώκαμεν	καὶ	πεπιστεύκαμεν	τὴν
kai	*hēmeis*	*egnōkamen*	*kai*	*pepisteukamen*	*tēn*
And	we	have known	and	have believed	the

26.4 noun acc sing fem	**3614.12** rel-pron acc sing fem	**2174.4** verb 3sing indic pres act	**3450.5** art nom sing masc	**2296.1** noun nom sing masc	**1706.1** prep
ἀγάπην	ἣν	ἔχει	ὁ	θεὸς	ἐν
agapēn	*hēn*	*echei*	*ho*	*theos*	*en*
love	which	has		God	to

2231.3 prs-pron dat 1pl	**3450.5** art nom sing masc	**2296.1** noun nom sing masc	**26.1** noun nom sing fem	**1498.4** verb 3sing indic pres act	**2504.1** conj
ἡμῖν.	Ὁ	θεὸς	ἀγάπη	ἐστίν,	καὶ
hēmin	*Ho*	*theos*	*agapē*	*estin*	*kai*
us.		God	love	is,	and

4:13. Another thought is added to this discussion of love: the believer can be confident of his relationship with God because of the presence of the Holy Spirit in his life. As usual, "hereby" looks toward the following phrase and shows the test by which one can know by experience that he is in a reciprocal relationship of fellowship with God.

The evidence is that God has given some measure of the work of the Holy Spirit, perhaps in the form of spiritual gifts, or simply His indwelling presence (contrast John 3:34).

4:14. The epistle has just been discussing the truth that man can live in intimate relationship with God—and not merely a privileged few, but anyone who comes to Him in faith. Such an opportunity is almost too good to be true, and John paused briefly to declare that his words are indeed reliable. He opened with an emphatic "we" to underscore his personal knowledge of Christ's work. In words that recall 1:1, he declared that he and his fellow eyewitnesses had seen the great work of God which they testified about. The incarnation of Christ stands as an objective proof that we do indeed have the privilege of "abiding" in God.

Though no one has seen God directly (verse 12), John had seen (Greek, *tetheametha*) His work; the perfect tense shows that the sights were still registered in his mind. He could confidently claim accuracy as he now gave testimony.

The core of his message was the fact that the Father had sent His Son to become the "Saviour" of the world. *Saviour* (Greek, *sōtēra*) was used in various ways in secular Greek but occurs in Scripture primarily as a title for judges who rescued Israel from oppressors, and as the description for Jesus who came to deliver mankind from eternal death.

4:15. Although verse 14 makes it clear that Christ provided salvation which is available to the world as a whole, it is not automatically applied to the whole population. So verse 15 follows with a statement that throws the doors wide open to any who will approach on God's terms—acknowledging that Jesus Christ is the Son of God.

The word for "confess" (Greek, *homologēsē*) implies a personal acceptance, not merely verbal assent. And the aorist tense describes a simple act of confession, perhaps the initial decision of accepting Jesus as the Son of God. The formula given (as in 4:2,3) would effectively eliminate from the body of believers the Gnostic heretics who denied that the human Jesus was either the Christ or truly the Son of God.

4:16. Although this verse sounds similar to verse 14, the words used ("known" and "believed") are different. So the "we" in verse 16 undoubtedly refers to John and his readers, rather than to the apostles. They had learned the facts of God's love shown in the

13. Hereby know we that we dwell in him, and he in us, because he hath given us of his Spirit: From this we know, *Berkeley* . . . This is how we know...He has given us some of His Spirit, *Beck* . . . we are remaining in Him, *Concordant* . . . the guarantee of our living in him and his living in us is the share of his own Spirit which he gives us, *Phillips* . . . we recognize from the fact that He has sent us spirits from His kingdom, *Greber* . . . a portion of, *Adams* . . . has given us a share in his Spirit, *Williams C.K.*

14. And we have seen and do testify: Besides, we ourselves have seen and we are bearing witness, *Berkeley* . . . are eyewitnesses able and willing to, *Phillips* . . . we have gazed upon Him, *Concordant* . . . and can tell the truth, *Beck* . . . we testify to that fact, *Norlie* . . . as for us, we have deliberately and steadfastly contemplated, *Wuest* . . . That is what we teach, *Everyday.*

that the Father sent the Son [to be] the Saviour of the world: . . . as the world's Savior, *Berkeley* . . . to save the world, *Phillips* . . . the universe, *Greber.*

15. Whosoever shall confess that Jesus is the Son of God: Whoever acknowledges, *TCNT* . . . Everyone who says openly, *BB* . . . If someone says, *Everyday* . . . If anyone will acknowledge, *Norlie* . . . whoever agrees with the statement that, *Wuest* . . . should be avowing, *Concordant.*

God dwelleth in him, and he in God: . . . finds that God lives in him, *Phillips* . . . has God in him, *BB* . . . with him God remains in union, *Berkeley.*

16. And we have known and believed the love that God hath to us: . . . and have trusted, *Adams* . . . we have seen and had faith in the love, *BB* . . . We have perceived the love that God cherishes for us and placed all our trust in it, *Greber* . . . So we have come to know and trust the love God has for us, *Phillips* . . . And so we know the love that God has for us, and we trust that love, *Everyday* . . . put faith in the love which God cherishes in us, *Berkeley* . . . we have believed and at present maintain that attitude, *Wuest.*

3450.5 art nom sing masc	3176.10 verb nom sing masc part pres act	1706.1 prep	3450.11 art dat sing fem	26.3 noun dat sing fem	1706.1 prep	3450.3 art dat sing
ὁ	μένων	ἐν	τῇ	ἀγάπῃ,	ἐν	τῷ
ho	*menōn*	*en*	*tē*	*agapē*	*en*	*tō*
the	abiding	in	the	love,	in	

2296.3 noun dat sing masc	3176.1 verb 3sing indic pres act	2504.1 conj	3450.5 art nom sing masc	2296.1 noun nom sing masc	1706.1 prep	840.4 prs-pron dat sing
θεῷ	μένει,	καὶ	ὁ	θεὸς	ἐν	αὐτῷ.
theō	*menei*	*kai*	*ho*	*theos*	*en*	*autō*
God	abides,	and		God	in	him.

16.a.**Var:** 01ℵ,03B 018K,020L,sa.bo.Lach Alf,Tisc,We/Ho,Weis Sod,UBS/☆

3176.1 verb 3sing indic pres act	1706.1 prep	3642.5 dem-pron dat sing masc	4896.14 verb 3sing indic perf mid	3450.9 art nom sing fem
[a☆+ μένει.]	**17.** ἐν	τούτῳ	τετελείωται	ἡ
menei	*en*	*toutō*	*teteleiōtai*	*hē*
[abides.]	In	this	has been perfected	the

26.1 noun nom sing fem	3196.1 prep	2231.2 prs-pron gen 1pl	2419.1 conj	3816.4 noun acc sing fem	2174.8 verb 1pl subj pres act
ἀγάπη	μεθ'	ἡμῶν,	ἵνα	παῤῥησίαν	ἔχωμεν
agapē	*meth'*	*hēmōn*	*hina*	*parrhēsian*	*echōmen*
love	with	us,	that	confidence	we may have

1706.1 prep	3450.11 art dat sing fem	2232.3 noun dat sing fem	3450.10 art gen sing fem	2893.2 noun gen sing fem	3617.1 conj	2503.1 conj
ἐν	τῇ	ἡμέρᾳ	τῆς	κρίσεως,	ὅτι	καθὼς
en	*tē*	*hēmera*	*tēs*	*kriseōs*	*hoti*	*kathōs*
in	the	day	of the	judgment,	that	even as

1552.3 dem-pron nom sing masc	1498.4 verb 3sing indic pres act	2504.1 conj	2231.1 prs-pron nom 1pl	1498.5 verb 1pl indic pres act	1706.1 prep	3450.3 art dat sing
ἐκεῖνός	ἐστιν,	καὶ	ἡμεῖς	ἐσμεν	ἐν	τῷ
ekeinos	*estin*	*kai*	*hēmeis*	*esmen*	*en*	*tō*
that	is,	also	we	are	in	

2862.3 noun dat sing masc	3642.5 dem-pron dat sing masc	5238.1 noun nom sing masc	3620.2 partic	1498.4 verb 3sing indic pres act	1706.1 prep
κόσμῳ	τούτῳ.	**18.** φόβος	οὐκ	ἔστιν	ἐν
kosmō	*toutō*	*phobos*	*ouk*	*estin*	*en*
world	this.	Fear	not	there is	in

3450.11 art dat sing fem	26.3 noun dat sing fem	233.1 conj	3450.9 art nom sing fem	4894.6 adj nom sing fem	26.1 noun nom sing fem	1838.1 prep
τῇ	ἀγάπῃ,	ἀλλ'	ἡ	τελεία	ἀγάπη	ἔξω
tē	*agapē*	*all'*	*hē*	*teleia*	*agapē*	*exō*
the	love,	but	the	perfect	love	out

900.2 verb 3sing indic pres act	3450.6 art acc sing masc	5238.4 noun acc sing masc	3617.1 conj	3450.5 art nom sing masc	5238.1 noun nom sing masc
βάλλει	τὸν	φόβον,	ὅτι	ὁ	φόβος
ballei	*ton*	*phobon*	*hoti*	*ho*	*phobos*
casts	the	fear;	because	the	fear

2824.1 noun acc sing fem	2174.4 verb 3sing indic pres act	3450.5 art nom sing masc	1156.2 conj	5236.7 verb nom sing masc part pres mid	3620.3 partic
κόλασιν	ἔχει·	ὁ	δὲ	φοβούμενος	οὐ
kolasin	*echei*	*ho*	*de*	*phoboumenos*	*ou*
torment	has,	the	and	fearing	not

4896.14 verb 3sing indic perf mid	1706.1 prep	3450.11 art dat sing fem	26.3 noun dat sing fem	2231.1 prs-pron nom 1pl
τετελείωται	ἐν	τῇ	ἀγάπῃ.	**19.** ἡμεῖς
teteleiōtai	*en*	*tē*	*agapē*	*hēmeis*
has been made perfect	in	the	love.	We

gospel and had then trusted the message for themselves. This gospel announces the love which God has "to us" (Greek, *en hēmin*); the phrase goes beyond a mere description of the Father's love toward man and could be rendered "love which God has in us," a love which the believer can experience in his own life.

John repeated his statement (4:8) that God is love and used it to summarize this segment explaining the source of love. Since love is bound up with the essential nature of God, a person who dwells in that kind of love must also be dwelling in God, since He alone is the source of that love.

Note that the inspired writer did not say "love is God," for there is much which goes under that description which is not true love or the highest kind of love. Rather, since God is the very essence of love, all that He does issues from that nature. And since in the new birth believers are caused to share the divine nature, love will be their chief trademark.

4:17. One of the results of experiencing God's love is confidence in our relation to Him, a theme which the next verses explore. The mutual indwelling of God and the believer described in verse 16 is the means for God's love to reach a state of completion. "Made perfect" (Greek, *teteleiōtai*) does not mean absolute perfection; it generally describes that which is complete or fully developed, reaching its intended goal. As the child of God lives in intimacy with the Father, God's love eventually reaches the place where it has its intended effect (cf. 4:12).

Divine love will enable a believer to stand before God with confidence at the Day of Judgment. At the future day when we are evaluated by the Lord, we can know that there is no danger of condemnation. We can have this assurance because of the certain similarity between Christ and His people. In this context, the point of likeness is probably the fact that a Christian loves, just as Christ loves.

4:18. Turning to the opposite side of the subject, the inspired writer stated that there is no kind of fear (no definite article) in the type of love he had been describing. The two attitudes counteract each other.

Instead of coexisting with fear, love expels it. The apostle was careful to specify that he is talking about the love which has become complete by learning to give love (cf. 4:12). When a person finds God's love being expressed through his deeds, he has no reason to fear God, as verse 17 mentions. After all, fear comes from the knowledge that punishment is coming. "Torment" (Greek, *kolasin*) consistently refers to punishment of various kinds, and John's description seems to include fear itself as part of the punishment. One who lives in fear of facing God shows that God's love has not taken its proper place in his heart.

God is love; and he that dwelleth in love dwelleth in God, and God in him: . . . who is remaining in love is remaining in God, *Concordant* . . . he who continues in love, *Berkeley* . . . the man whose life is lived in love does, in fact live in God, *Phillips.*

17. Herein is our love made perfect: So our love for him grows more and more, *Phillips* . . . this has been brought to completion the aforementioned love which is in us...which love exists in its completed state, *Wuest* . . . perfected with us, *Concordant.*

that we may have boldness in the day of judgment: . . . filling us with complete confidence for the day, *Phillips* . . . we can wait without any fear, *Laubach* . . . that we face the judgment day confidently, *Berkeley* . . . resulting in our having unreservedness of speech at the day, *Wuest.*

because as he is, so are we in this world: . . . because we are living His way in this world, *Berkeley* . . . for we realize that our life in this world is actually his life lived in us, *Phillips.*

18. There is no fear in love; but perfect love casteth out fear: On the contrary, *TCNT* . . . Love contains no fear—indeed fully developed love expels every particle of fear, *Phillips* . . . instead, perfect love expels fear, *Berkeley* . . . love which exists in its completed state throws fear outside, *Wuest* . . . Love knows no fear. Perfect love drives out fear, *Norlie* . . . pushes out fear, *SEB* . . . banishes fear, *Wade.*

because fear hath torment: . . . for fear implies punishment, *TCNT* . . . involves torture, *Berkeley* . . . Restraint, *Wilson* . . . suggests painful punishment, *Norlie* . . . carries a penalty, *Swann* . . . has chastening, *Concordant* . . . always contains some of the torture of feeling guilty, *Phillips.*

He that feareth is not made perfect in love: So long as a man is afraid that God will punish him, he shows that his love is not yet perfect, *Laubach* . . . has not reached love's perfection, *Berkeley* . . . has not been brought to completion in the sphere of this love, and is not in that state at present, *Wuest.*

19.a.**Txt:** 018K,020L,byz.
Var: 02A,03B,1241
1739,Lach,Treg,Alf
Word,Tisc,We/Ho,Weis
Sod,UBS/*

25.3 verb 1pl pres act	**840.6** prs-pron acc sing masc	**3617.1** conj	**840.5** prs-pron nom sing masc	**4272.5** num ord nom sing masc
ἀγαπῶμεν	⸂[a] αὐτὸν ⸃	ὅτι	αὐτὸς	πρῶτος
agapōmen	*auton*	*hoti*	*autos*	*prōtos*
love	him	because	he	first

25.14 verb 3sing indic aor act	**2231.4** prs-pron acc 1pl	**1430.1** partic	**4948.3** indef-pron nom sing	**1500.8** verb 3sing subj aor act	**3617.1** conj
ἠγάπησεν	ἡμᾶς.	**20.** Ἐάν	τις	εἴπῃ,	Ὅτι
ēgapēsen	*hēmas*	*Ean*	*tis*	*eipē*	*Hoti*
loved	us.	If	anyone	should say,	

25.5 verb 1sing indic pres act	**3450.6** art acc sing masc	**2296.4** noun acc sing masc	**2504.1** conj	**3450.6** art acc sing masc	**79.4** noun acc sing masc
Ἀγαπῶ	τὸν	θεόν,	καὶ	τὸν	ἀδελφὸν
Agapō	*ton*	*theon*	*kai*	*ton*	*adelphon*
I love		God,	and	the	brother

840.3 prs-pron gen sing	**3268.4** verb 3sing subj pres act	**5418.1** noun nom sing masc	**1498.4** verb 3sing indic pres act	**3450.5** art nom sing masc	**1056.1** conj
αὐτοῦ	μισῇ,	ψεύστης	ἐστίν·	ὁ	γὰρ
autou	*misē*	*pseustēs*	*estin*	*ho*	*gar*
his	should hate,	a liar	he is.	The	for

3231.1 partic	**25.8** verb nom sing masc part pres act	**3450.6** art acc sing masc	**79.4** noun acc sing masc	**840.3** prs-pron gen sing	**3614.6** rel-pron acc sing masc
μὴ	ἀγαπῶν	τὸν	ἀδελφὸν	αὐτοῦ	ὃν
mē	*agapōn*	*ton*	*adelphon*	*autou*	*hon*
not	loving	the	brother	his	whom

3571.11 verb 3sing indic perf act	**3450.6** art acc sing masc	**2296.4** noun acc sing masc	**3614.6** rel-pron acc sing masc	**3620.1** partic	**3571.11** verb 3sing indic perf act
ἑώρακεν,	τὸν	θεὸν	ὃν	οὐχ	ἑώρακεν,
heōraken	*ton*	*theon*	*hon*	*ouch*	*heōraken*
he has seen,		God	whom	not	he has seen,

20.a.**Txt:** 02A,018K
020L,33,byz.it.bo.
Var: 01ℵ,03B,044,sa.
Lach,Treg,Alf,Tisc
We/Ho,Weis,Sod
UBS/*

4316.1 adv	**3620.3** partic	**1404.4** verb 3sing indic pres mid	**25.11** verb inf pres act	**2504.1** conj	**3642.12** dem-pron acc sing fem
⸂ πῶς	[[a]* οὐ]	δύναται	ἀγαπᾶν;	**21.** καὶ	ταύτην
pōs	*ou*	*dunatai*	*agapan*	*kai*	*tautēn*
how	[not]	is he able	to love?	And	this

3450.12 art acc sing fem	**1769.3** noun acc sing fem	**2174.5** verb 1pl indic pres act	**570.2** prep	**840.3** prs-pron gen sing	**2419.1** conj	**3450.5** art nom sing masc
τὴν	ἐντολὴν	ἔχομεν	ἀπ'	αὐτοῦ,	ἵνα	ὁ
tēn	*entolēn*	*echomen*	*ap'*	*autou*	*hina*	*ho*
the	commandment	we have	from	him,	that	the

25.8 verb nom sing masc part pres act	**3450.6** art acc sing masc	**2296.4** noun acc sing masc	**25.2** verb 3sing pres act	**2504.1** conj	**3450.6** art acc sing masc
ἀγαπῶν	τὸν	θεὸν	ἀγαπᾷ	καὶ	τὸν
agapōn	*ton*	*theon*	*agapa*	*kai*	*ton*
loving		God	loves	also	the

79.4 noun acc sing masc	**840.3** prs-pron gen sing	**3820.6** adj nom sing masc	**3450.5** art nom sing masc	**3961.10** verb nom sing masc part pres act
ἀδελφὸν	αὐτοῦ.	**5:1.** Πᾶς	ὁ	πιστεύων
adelphon	*autou*	*Pas*	*ho*	*pisteuōn*
brother	his.	Everyone	the	believing

3617.1 conj	**2400.1** name nom masc	**1498.4** verb 3sing indic pres act	**3450.5** art nom sing masc	**5382.1** name nom masc	**1523.2** prep gen
ὅτι	Ἰησοῦς	ἐστιν	ὁ	Χριστὸς	ἐκ
hoti	*Iēsous*	*estin*	*ho*	*Christos*	*ek*
that	Jesus	is	the	Christ,	of

4:19. In contrast, genuine believers habitually show love, not because of their innate ability to show affection, but because God himself loved them, giving them the potential of displaying love in their own lives. The aorist tense of "loved" points back to the great demonstration of God's love: the incarnation and sacrifice of Christ.

This is a concept almost too great for the human mind to fathom. There is, in God, so much to love, and in us so little. The normal order would be to love Him. But, like a human parent, yet to a greater degree, God looks beyond our imperfections and loves us, not merely as a sentiment but demonstrating it by His actions.

19. We love him, because he first loved us: As for us, let us be constantly loving, *Wuest* . . . We have the power of loving, because he first had love for us, *BB.*

20. If a man say, I love God, and hateth his brother: If someone says, *Berkeley* . . . I am constantly loving God, *Wuest*. . . and yet habitually hates his brother, *Williams* . . . and yet hates his fellow-man, *Greber.*

he is a liar: . . . his words are false, *BB.*

for he that loveth not his brother whom he hath seen: . . . for how can any one who does not love his neighbor whom he sees with his physical eyes, *Greber* . . . whom he has seen with discernment and at present has within the range of his vision, *Wuest*. . . He can see his brother, but he hates him, *Everyday* . . . who has no love for his brother whom he has seen, *BB* . . . before his eyes, *Phillips.*

how can he love God whom he hath not seen?: . . . is not able to, *Berkeley* . . . cannot possibly love God, *Wade*. . . at present does not have within the range of his vision he is not able to be loving, *Wuest* . . . the one beyond his sight? *Phillips.*

4:20. The idea already introduced in 3:16-18 is further developed. A person who genuinely possesses God's love will express it toward others. John presented the hypothetical case of a person who claims to love God, yet acts in a way that contradicts his words. He habitually hates one who should have been considered his brother. There is no need to waste time analyzing the problem; this fellow is a liar, one who intentionally deceives others. The logic is simple: no one can love an invisible God when he cannot do the easier task of loving a brother whom he is able to see.

4:21. As he had done previously in this epistle (2:7,8; 3:23), the apostle John declared that the command to love is nothing new, nothing that he had dreamed up himself. It is the very command which the Church already has received from God himself.

"This commandment" refers to the demand given in the latter part of the verse—to love one's brother as well as God. The "him" from whom we receive the command could be Jesus, as in some earlier parts of the epistle. However, God the Father appears in the immediate context, so it is likely that the commandment is one that comes from the Father. It may be a reference to the two great commands related by Jesus in Matthew 22:37-40.

While verse 20 asked how a person could love God and hate His children, verse 21 shows that one who loves God should love others simply because the God he claims to love has commanded love for brothers and sisters.

21. And this commandment have we from him, That he who loveth God love his brother also: . . . we have this conclusion from, *Swann* . . . this is the word...he who has love for God is to have the same love for his brother, *BB* . . . And this is the order He gave us: If you love God, love your brother, *Beck* . . . it is his explicit command that the one, *Phillips* . . . It is from God that we have received the command that he who would love God must love his fellow-man also, *Greber* . . . that the lover of God, *Berkeley* . . . should constantly be loving also, *Wuest.*

5:1. The new chapter continues the same line of thought, demonstrating that genuine love for God inevitably produces love for other Christians. First, all who maintain a belief in Jesus as the divine Christ are born of God. The same doctrinal test had been used earlier (2:22; 4:2,3,15) to distinguish true believers from false Gnostic teachers. The man Jesus is the divine Anointed One who had been promised in the Old Testament, and those who believe this truth show they have been born from God. The perfect tense

1. Whosoever believeth that Jesus is the Christ is born of God: Everyone who has faith that, *Berkeley*. . . that Jesus is the Messiah is one of God's children, *Greber* . . . is the promised Savior, *Beck* . . . is a child of God, *Williams C.K.* . . . is God's child, *Everyday* . . . is the Christ begotten of God, *Concordant* . . . out

3450.2 art gen sing	2296.2 noun gen sing masc	1074.23 verb 3sing indic perf mid	2504.1 conj	3820.6 adj nom sing masc	3450.5 art nom sing masc
τοῦ	θεοῦ	γεγέννηται·	καὶ	πᾶς	ὁ
tou	*theou*	*gegennētai*	*kai*	*pas*	*ho*
	God	has been born;	and	everyone	the

1.a.**Txt:** 01ℵ,02A,018K 020L,025P,byz.bo.Tisc Sod
Var: 03B,044,33,it.sa. We/Ho,Weis,UBS/★

25.8 verb nom sing masc part pres act	3450.6 art acc sing masc	1074.7 verb acc sing masc part aor act	25.2 verb 3sing pres act	2504.1 conj
ἀγαπῶν	τὸν	γεννήσαντα	ἀγαπᾷ	(ᵃ καὶ)
agapōn	*ton*	*gennēsanta*	*agapa*	*kai*
loving	the	having begotten,	loves	also

3450.6 art acc sing masc	1074.25 verb sing part perf mid	1523.1 prep gen	840.3 prs-pron gen sing	1706.1 prep	3642.5 dem-pron dat sing masc
τὸν	γεγεννημένον	ἐξ	αὐτοῦ.	2. ἐν	τούτῳ
ton	*gegennēmenon*	*ex*	*autou*	*en*	*toutō*
the	having been born	of	him.	By	this

1091.4 verb 1pl indic pres act	3617.1 conj	25.3 verb 1pl pres act	3450.17 art pl neu	4891.4 noun pl neu	3450.2 art gen sing
γινώσκομεν	ὅτι	ἀγαπῶμεν	τὰ	τέκνα	τοῦ
ginōskomen	*hoti*	*agapōmen*	*ta*	*tekna*	*tou*
we know	that	we love	the	children	

2296.2 noun gen sing masc	3615.1 conj	3450.6 art acc sing masc	2296.4 noun acc sing masc	25.3 verb 1pl pres act	2504.1 conj
θεοῦ,	ὅταν	τὸν	θεὸν	ἀγαπῶμεν	καὶ
theou	*hotan*	*ton*	*theon*	*agapōmen*	*kai*
of God,	when		God	we love	and

2.a.**Txt:** 01ℵ,018K,020L 025P,byz.
Var: 03B,044,1739,sa.bo. Lach,Treg,Alf,Word Tisc,We/Ho,Weis,Sod UBS/★

3450.15 art acc pl fem	1769.7 noun acc pl fem	840.3 prs-pron gen sing	4931.5 verb 1pl subj pres act	4020.73 verb 1pl subj pres act
τὰς	ἐντολὰς	αὐτοῦ	(τηρῶμεν.	[ᵃ★ ποιῶμεν.]
tas	*entolas*	*autou*	*tērōmen*	*poiōmen*
the	commandments	his	keep.	[do.]

3642.9 dem-pron nom sing fem	1056.1 conj	1498.4 verb 3sing indic pres act	3450.9 art nom sing fem	26.1 noun nom sing fem	3450.2 art gen sing	2296.2 noun gen sing masc
3. αὕτη	γάρ	ἐστιν	ἡ	ἀγάπη	τοῦ	θεοῦ,
hautē	*gar*	*estin*	*hē*	*agapē*	*tou*	*theou*
This	for	is	the	love		of God,

2419.1 conj	3450.15 art acc pl fem	1769.7 noun acc pl fem	840.3 prs-pron gen sing	4931.5 verb 1pl subj pres act	2504.1 conj
ἵνα	τὰς	ἐντολὰς	αὐτοῦ	τηρῶμεν·	καὶ
hina	*tas*	*entolas*	*autou*	*tērōmen*	*kai*
that	the	commandments	his	we should keep;	and

3450.13 art nom pl fem	1769.4 noun nom pl fem	840.3 prs-pron gen sing	920.2 adj nom pl fem	3620.2 partic	1498.7 verb 3pl indic pres act
αἱ	ἐντολαὶ	αὐτοῦ	βαρεῖαι	οὐκ	εἰσίν.
hai	*entolai*	*autou*	*bareiai*	*ouk*	*eisin*
the	commandments	his	burdensome	not	are.

3617.1 conj	3820.17 adj sing neu	3450.16 art sing neu	1074.25 verb sing part perf mid	1523.2 prep gen	3450.2 art gen sing
4. ὅτι	πᾶν	τὸ	γεγεννημένον	ἐκ	τοῦ
hoti	*pan*	*to*	*gegennēmenon*	*ek*	*tou*
Because	all	the	having been born	of	

2296.2 noun gen sing masc	3390.1 verb 3sing indic pres act	3450.6 art acc sing masc	2862.4 noun acc sing masc	2504.1 conj	3642.9 dem-pron nom sing fem
θεοῦ	νικᾷ	τὸν	κόσμον·	καὶ	αὕτη
theou	*nika*	*ton*	*kosmon*	*kai*	*hautē*
God	overcomes	the	world;	and	this

of "born" shows that this believer has entered God's family at a point in the past and still enjoys that family relationship. When a person is born again, he becomes a member of God's family, with God the Father and His Son the Elder Brother. Other believers are part of that family, and often that relationship becomes closer than natural family ties, because of a common bond.

If everyone who believes in Christ has a relationship with God by birth, then it is impossible to separate the child from the parent. And that is precisely the point in the second half of the verse. Anyone who loves God, the parent, must have a special place of affection for God's child. The aorist tense of "begat" is used to describe the act of God in producing a new child, then a switch is made back to the perfect tense of the same verb (Greek, *gegennēmenon*). This describes the believer's experience of the new birth with its abiding results.

5:2. This verse summarizes the discussion of the link between love for God and love for fellow Christians. There is a tightly-woven connection between three ideas that were featured in the previous verses: love for the children of God, love for God, and obedience to the commands of God.

The inseparable joining of these ideas may be learned from "this"—the teaching of 4:21 to 5:1 about God's command and the believer's place in God's family. When we know these truths, we also know that people who love God's children are the very ones who love God himself and do what He commands.

5:3. In verse 2 obedience is linked with love; now we learn that one leads to the other. The definite article identifies "love" here as the distinctive love (Greek, *agapē*) which has been discussed all through the epistle, and "of God" specifies the love which a believer has toward the Father (as in 5:2). When we love God in the way this epistle requires, we will habitually obey His commands.

These commands are not "grievous" (*bareiai*, heavy, difficult to carry). Jesus contrasted the heavy loads that Pharisees put on people (Matthew 23:4) with the light burden He would give (Matthew 11:30).

5:4. Note that God's commands are simple. They are easy to bear because of the new birth. The neuter "whatsoever" (*pan*) is used to stress that victory comes from the fact of regeneration, not the strength of the reborn person. The perfect tense of "born" is used to describe the new life that a believer now has as a result of being born of God.

This power to overcome the world comes from "our faith." The

from God has been born, *Wuest* . . . proves himself one of God's family, *Phillips.*

and every one that loveth him that begat: . . . every one who loves the Father, *Montgomery* . . . whoever loves the Parent, *Adams.*

loveth him also that is begotten of him: . . . loves the child born of Him, *Adams* . . . loves the Father's children, *Everyday* . . . has love for his child, *BB.*

2. By this we know that we love the children of God: The test of the genuineness of our love for God's family lies in this question, *Phillips* . . . In this way, we are certain that we have love for, *BB* . . . How do we know that we love God's children? *Everyday* . . . we are habitually loving the born-ones, *Wuest.*

when we love God, and keep his commandments: . . . do we love God himself and do we obey his commands? *Phillips* . . . and keep his laws, *BB* . . . and practise, *Wilson.*

3. For this is the love of God, that we keep his commandments: For true love of God means this, *Berkeley* . . . loving God means obeying his commands, *Phillips, Everyday* . . . and with solicitous care guarding and observing, *Wuest* . . . means to obey His Word, *NLT.*

and his commandments are not grievous: . . . they are not hard to keep, *Laubach* . . . are not burdensome, *Norlie, Wilson* . . . are not irksome, *Montgomery* . . . aren't annoying, *Adams* . . . not too hard for us, *SEB* . . . are not heavy, *Williams C.K.*

4. For whatsoever is born of God overcometh the world: This is the power that has mastered the world, *TCNT* . . . Everyone who is a child of God has the power to win against the world, *Everyday* . . . Anything which comes from God is able to overcome the world, *BB* . . . for God's "heredity" within us will always conquer the world outside us, *Phillips* . . . continues to conquer, *Williams* . . . defeats the world, *Adams* . . . is constantly coming off victorious over the world, *Wuest* . . . overcome the power of the world with ease, *Greber.*

1 John 5:5

1498.4 verb 3sing indic pres act	3450.9 art nom sing fem	3391.1 noun nom sing fem	3450.9 art nom sing fem	3390.11 verb nom sing fem part aor act	3450.6 art acc sing masc
ἐστὶν	ἡ	νίκη	ἡ	νικήσασα	τὸν
estin	*hē*	*nikē*	*hē*	*nikēsasa*	*ton*
is	the	victory	the	having overcame	the

2862.4 noun acc sing masc	3450.9 art nom sing fem	3963.1 noun nom sing fem	2231.2 prs-pron gen 1pl	4949.3 intr-pron nom sing	1498.4 verb 3sing indic pres act
κόσμον,	ἡ	πίστις	ἡμῶν·	5. τίς	ἐστιν
kosmon	*hē*	*pistis*	*hēmōn*	*tis*	*estin*
world,	the	faith	our.	Who	is

5.a.**Var:** 03B,We/Ho Weis,UBS/☆

1156.2 conj	3450.5 art nom sing masc	3390.3 verb nom sing masc part pres act	3450.6 art acc sing masc	2862.4 noun acc sing masc	1479.1 conj
[[a]☆+ δέ]	ὁ	νικῶν	τὸν	κόσμον,	εἰ
de	*ho*	*nikōn*	*ton*	*kosmon*	*ei*
[and]	the	overcoming	the	world,	if

3231.1 partic	3450.5 art nom sing masc	3961.10 verb nom sing masc part pres act	3617.1 conj	2400.1 name nom masc	1498.4 verb 3sing indic pres act
μὴ	ὁ	πιστεύων	ὅτι	Ἰησοῦς	ἐστιν
mē	*ho*	*pisteuōn*	*hoti*	*Iēsous*	*estin*
not	the	believing	that	Jesus	is

3450.5 art nom sing masc	5048.1 noun nom sing masc	3450.2 art gen sing	2296.2 noun gen sing masc	3642.4 dem-pron nom sing masc	1498.4 verb 3sing indic pres act
ὁ	υἱὸς	τοῦ	θεοῦ;	6. Οὗτός	ἐστιν
ho	*huios*	*tou*	*theou*	*Houtos*	*estin*
the	Son		of God?	This	is

3450.5 art nom sing masc	2048.13 verb nom sing masc part aor act	1217.1 prep	5045.2 noun gen sing neu	2504.1 conj	129.2 noun gen sing neu	2400.1 name nom masc
ὁ	ἐλθὼν	δι'	ὕδατος	καὶ	αἵματος,	Ἰησοῦς
ho	*elthōn*	*di'*	*hudatos*	*kai*	*haimatos*	*Iēsous*
the	having come	by	water	and	blood,	Jesus

6.a.**Txt:** Steph
Var: 01ℵ,02A,03B 018K,020L,025P,byz. Treg,Alf,Word,Tisc We/Ho,Weis,Sod UBS/☆

3450.5 art nom sing masc	5382.1 name nom masc	3620.2 partic	1706.1 prep	3450.3 art dat sing	5045.3 noun dat sing neu	3303.1 adv
⌜a ὁ ⌝	Χριστός·	οὐκ	ἐν	τῷ	ὕδατι	μόνον,
ho	*Christos*	*ouk*	*en*	*tō*	*hudati*	*monon*
the	Christ;	not	by	the	water	only,

6.b.**Var:** 02A,03B,020L 025P,33,Lach,Treg,Alf Word,Tisc,We/Ho,Weis Sod,UBS/☆

233.1 conj	1706.1 prep	3450.3 art dat sing	5045.3 noun dat sing neu	2504.1 conj	1706.1 prep	3450.3 art dat sing	129.3 noun dat sing neu
ἀλλ'	ἐν	τῷ	ὕδατι	καὶ	[[b]☆+ ἐν]	τῷ	αἵματι·
all'	*en*	*tō*	*hudati*	*kai*	*en*	*tō*	*haimati*
but	by		water	and	[in]	the	blood.

2504.1 conj	3450.16 art sing neu	4011.1 noun sing neu	1498.4 verb 3sing indic pres act	3450.16 art sing neu	3113.14 verb sing neu part pres act
καὶ	τὸ	πνεῦμά	ἐστιν	τὸ	μαρτυροῦν
kai	*to*	*pneuma*	*estin*	*to*	*marturoun*
And	the	Spirit	it is	the	bearing witness,

3617.1 conj	3450.16 art sing neu	4011.1 noun sing neu	1498.4 verb 3sing indic pres act	3450.9 art nom sing fem	223.1 noun nom sing fem
ὅτι	τὸ	πνεῦμά	ἐστιν	ἡ	ἀλήθεια.
hoti	*to*	*pneuma*	*estin*	*hē*	*alētheia*
because	the	Spirit	is	the	truth.

7.a.**Txt:** Steph
Var: 01ℵ,02A,03B 018K,020L,025P,044 048,33,byz.lect.sa.bo. Gries,Lach,Treg,Alf Word,Tisc,We/Ho,Weis Sod,UBS/☆

3617.1 conj	4980.1 num card nom	1498.7 verb 3pl indic pres act	3450.7 art nom pl masc	3113.10 verb nom pl masc part pres act	1706.1 prep
7. ὅτι	τρεῖς	εἰσιν	οἱ	μαρτυροῦντες,	⌜a ἐν
hoti	*treis*	*eisin*	*hoi*	*marturountes*	*en*
Because	three	there are	the	bearing witness	in

aorist "overcometh" points to a past victory, either the finished work of Christ on the cross (cf. John 16:33) or the moment when a person places faith in Christ's work in order to become part of the Christian family. There is also a continuing aspect of this victorious life. The faith which enables a person to receive Christ as Saviour will also enable him to maintain his Christian experience.

5:5. The emphasis switches from the general fact to a very specific rhetorical question: Who can overcome the world other than one who believes the truth about Jesus? Obviously, no one. Continued victory over the world and its temptations comes not from vague faith in an unspecified direction, but faith in the Jesus who is the "Son of God." Again, the inspired writer contends for the combination of humanity and deity in Jesus, in opposition to the Gnostic heresy.

5:6. Verses 6-12 focus on the truth concerning the person of Christ. The discussion begins with the somewhat obscure declaration that Jesus Christ came by both water and blood. Some have taught that these two terms refer to baptism and the Lord's Supper, or to the water and blood flowing from Christ's body at the Crucifixion (John 19:34). But John was more likely referring to the baptism and death of Jesus. The apostle may well have been opposing the Gnostic idea that the divine Christ merely came upon the human Jesus at the Baptism, departing before the Crucifixion. On the contrary, it was Jesus the Christ who experienced both the water of baptism and the blood of death—not baptism alone.

Greek New Testaments often divide the verses at this point. The writer went on to show that the Holy Spirit acts as witness to this truth. The Spirit descended on Jesus at His baptism in the form of a dove, and Christ himself said that the Spirit's work was to bear witness of Him (John 15:26). And who could be a more reliable witness than the One who is the Spirit of Truth?

5:7,8. The key thought of 5:6-12, the final section on Christ's person, is that of witness. The writer explains how God has provided testimony to the true identity of Jesus Christ. Verse 6 introduces the Holy Spirit as the first witness, then verses 7 and 8 add two others—water and blood.

The fact that there are three witnesses is the main point of the sentence. Jewish law required two or three witnesses before a person could be convicted of a serious crime (Deuteronomy 17:6; 19:15; Matthew 18:16), so John presents three witnesses who are called upon to attest to the point. The present tense of "bear record" shows that all three testify continually.

and this is the victory that overcometh the world, [even] our faith: It is our faith which conquers, *SEB* . . . In fact, this faith of ours is the only way in which the world has been conquered, *Phillips* . . . What gives us our victory over the powers of the world is our faith, *Greber* . . . And this is the conquest, *Concordant* . . . that has come off victorious, *Wuest* . . . that has triumphed over, *Berkeley* . . . is victorious over the world, *Wade.*

5. Who is he that overcometh the world: The only one who triumphs over the powers of the world is, *Greber* . . . who could ever be said to conquer the world, *Phillips* . . . who is conquering, *Concordant* . . . Who is the world's victor, *Berkeley* . . . who is constantly coming off victorious, *Wuest* . . . the one who wins against the world, *Everyday.*

but he that believeth that Jesus is the Son of God?: . . . except the man who really believes that the Jesus who entered the world is, *Phillips* . . . is the person who believes that Jesus is the Son of God, *Everyday.*

6. This is he that came by water and blood, [even] Jesus Christ: . . . came with the double sign of, *Phillips* . . . through the instrumentality, *Wuest* . . . with the testimony of, *Greber.*

not by water only, but by water and blood: . . . the water of his baptism as man and the blood of the atonement that he made by his death, *Phillips* . . . and in the blood, *Berkeley* . . . both bore witness to him, *Greber.*

And it is the Spirit that beareth witness, because the Spirit is truth: . . . which is testifying, *Concordant* . . . endorses this as true, *Phillips* . . . appeared as an unimpeachable witness on his behalf, *Greber.*

7. For there are three that bear record in heaven: The witness therefore is a triple one, *Phillips* . . . three witnesses, *Berkeley* . . . three there are that are constantly bearing testimony, *Wuest* . . . are in one accord, *Swann* . . . that bears convincing witness, *Wade* . . . that are testifying, *Concordant* . . . that tell us about Jesus, *Everyday.*

1 John 5:8

3450.3 art dat sing τῷ *tō* the	3636.3 noun dat sing masc οὐρανῷ, *ouranō* heaven,	3450.5 art nom sing masc ὁ *ho* the	3824.1 noun nom sing masc πατήρ, *patēr* Father,	3450.5 art nom sing masc ὁ *ho* the	3030.1 noun nom sing masc λόγος, *logos* Word,

2504.1 conj καὶ *kai* and	3450.16 art sing neu τὸ *to* the	39.1 adj sing ἅγιον *hagion* Holy	4011.1 noun sing neu πνεῦμα· *pneuma* Ghost;	2504.1 conj καὶ *kai* and	3642.7 dem-pron nom pl masc οὗτοι *houtoi* these	3450.7 art nom pl masc οἱ *hoi* the

4980.1 num card nom τρεῖς *treis* three	1518.9 num card neu ἕν *hen* one	1498.7 verb 3pl indic pres act εἰσιν. *eisin* are.	2504.1 conj **8.** καὶ *kai* And	4980.1 num card nom τρεῖς *treis* three	1498.7 verb 3pl indic pres act εἰσιν *eisin* there are

3450.7 art nom pl masc οἱ *hoi* the	3113.10 verb nom pl masc part pres act μαρτυροῦντες *marturountes* bearing witness	1706.1 prep ἐν *en* on	3450.11 art dat sing fem τῇ *tē* the	1087.3 noun dat sing fem γῇ, ˋ *gē* earth,	3450.16 art sing neu τὸ *to* the

4011.1 noun sing neu πνεῦμα *pneuma* Spirit,	2504.1 conj καὶ *kai* and	3450.16 art sing neu τὸ *to* the	5045.1 noun sing neu ὕδωρ, *hudōr* water,	2504.1 conj καὶ *kai* and	3450.16 art sing neu τὸ *to* the	129.1 noun sing neu αἷμα, *haima* blood;	2504.1 conj καὶ *kai* and

3450.7 art nom pl masc οἱ *hoi* the	4980.1 num card nom τρεῖς *treis* three	1519.1 prep εἰς *eis* to	3450.16 art sing neu τὸ *to* the	1518.9 num card neu ἕν *hen* one	1498.7 verb 3pl indic pres act εἰσιν. *eisin* are.	1479.1 conj **9.** εἰ *ei* If

3450.12 art acc sing fem τὴν *tēn* the	3114.3 noun acc sing fem μαρτυρίαν *marturian* witness	3450.1 art gen pl τῶν *tōn* of the	442.7 noun gen pl masc ἀνθρώπων *anthrōpōn* men	2956.5 verb 1pl indic pres act λαμβάνομεν, *lambanomen* we receive,

3450.9 art nom sing fem ἡ *hē* the	3114.1 noun nom sing fem μαρτυρία *marturia* witness	3450.2 art gen sing τοῦ *tou*	2296.2 noun gen sing masc θεοῦ *theou* of God	3157.2 adj comp nom sing μείζων *meizōn* greater	1498.4 verb 3sing indic pres act ἐστίν· *estin* is.

3617.1 conj ὅτι *hoti* Because	3642.9 dem-pron nom sing fem αὕτη *hautē* this	1498.4 verb 3sing indic pres act ἐστὶν *estin* is	3450.9 art nom sing fem ἡ *hē* the	3114.1 noun nom sing fem μαρτυρία *marturia* witness	3450.2 art gen sing τοῦ *tou*

9.a.**Txt:** 018K,020L 025P,byz.
Var: 01ℵ,02A,03B,33 sa.bo.Lach,Treg,Alf Word,Tisc,We/Ho,Weis Sod,UBS/☆

2296.2 noun gen sing masc θεοῦ, *theou* of God	3614.12 rel-pron acc sing fem ʽ ἣν *hēn* which	3617.1 conj [a☆ ὅτι] *hoti* [because]	3113.27 verb 3sing indic perf act μεμαρτύρηκεν *memarturēken* he has witnessed	3875.1 prep περὶ *peri* concerning

3450.2 art gen sing τοῦ *tou* the	5048.2 noun gen sing masc υἱοῦ *huiou* Son	840.3 prs-pron gen sing αὐτοῦ. *autou* his.	3450.5 art nom sing masc **10.** ὁ *ho* The	3961.10 verb nom sing masc part pres act πιστεύων *pisteuōn* believing	1519.1 prep εἰς *eis* on

Some writers have understood "water and blood" to refer to the ordinances of baptism and the Lord's Supper, pointing to the present participle as evidence that historical events cannot be meant. But since the same terms in verse 6 seem to mean the baptism and crucifixion of Jesus Christ, it would seem unwise to change the meaning so quickly. The three witnesses are all based on events in the life of Christ which continue to testify to His person whenever they are proclaimed (compare John's use of such testimony in 1:1-3).

The Spirit may refer to the descent in the form of a dove at the baptism of Jesus, since John the Baptist took this as proof of Jesus' deity (John 1:32-34). The water is likely a reference to His baptism again, particularly to the voice from heaven declaring Jesus to be God's beloved Son. And the blood refers to the death of Christ, a clear demonstration of His humanity that simultaneously showed Him to be more than merely a man. John took the pivotal events in the Gnostic version of Jesus' life and used them to bear witness to the divine-human Son of God. He added that all three witnesses agree in their testimony—literally, "the three are unto the one."

The King James Version contains an additional statement in these verses, calling on the Father, Son, and Holy Spirit as witnesses. Modern versions omit this segment because it did not appear in any Greek manuscripts prior to the 14th Century and did not exist in the Latin Vulgate translation until A.D. 800. The truth of these statements, however, are indubitable.

5:9. Evaluating such testimony, the writer called on his readers to move from the lesser to the greater. They accepted testimony from human witnesses (the form of the "if" clause assumes the statement to be true). Two or three witnesses were all that were required for legal proof. Therefore, they should accept the even better testimony of God himself. His word is more trustworthy than any human witness, and the triple testimony of Spirit, water, and blood is God's testimony. And since it is God's witness concerning His own Son, who could be better qualified to give testimony?

The writer has already mentioned, in verse 7, the three who "bear record in heaven" (the "Word," of course, refers to Jesus the Son of God). Jesus' life on earth was a testimony to His deity. Twice the Father testified to His Son, at His baptism and at the Transfiguration. And now the Spirit "beareth witness with our spirit, that we are the children of God" (Romans 8:16).

5:10. In the last few verses the writer presented objective witnesses to the truth of the gospel. Now the text presents the subjective side of the issue: the necessity for each person to place faith in the Jesus who has been presented. All that God the Father has done to provide redemption, and all that God the Son has done

the Father, the Word, and the Holy Ghost: and these three are one: . . . the three support one conclusion, *Wade.*

8. And there are three that bear witness in earth: There is a threefold testimony, *TCNT* . . . Thus we have three witnesses for him, *Greber.*

the Spirit, and the water, and the blood: and these three agree in one: . . . the Spirit in our own hearts, the signs of the water of baptism and the blood of atonement, *Phillips* . . . The aforementioned three concur, *Wuest* . . . These three speak the same thing, *NLT* . . . and the three are in unison, *Berkeley* . . . and these three agree in their testimony, *Greber* . . . and these three have one purpose, *Beck.*

9. If we receive the witness of men, the witness of God is greater: If we accept the testimony of men, *Norlie* . . . We believe people when they say something is true. But what God says, *Everyday* . . . We accept human evidence on these terms, and surely the evidence of God has still greater weight, *Barclay* . . . If we are prepared to accept human testimony, God's own testimony...is surely infinitely more valuable, *Phillips* . . . we accept the evidence of men, *Laubach, Williams C.K.* . . . If we welcome the witness of men the witness of God is greater, *Klingensmith* . . . as authentic, how much more highly must we regard the testimony of God! *Greber* . . . more important, *NLT* . . . of still greater weight, *Wade.*

for this is the witness of God which he hath testified of his Son: And such testimony is available in the words with which God testified to us concerning His Son, *Greber* . . . because God's testimony is the truth He told about His Son, *Beck* . . . This is the evidence that he has given in regard to his Son, *Barclay* . . . that He has borne testimony concerning His Son, *Wuest* . . . And he has told us the truth about his own Son, *Everyday* . . . which God has given about his Son, *BB* . . . that he witnessed about his Son, *Klingensmith* . . . that he has borne witness concerning his Son, *Confraternity.*

3450.6 art acc sing masc	5048.4 noun acc sing masc	3450.2 art gen sing	2296.2 noun gen sing masc	2174.4 verb 3sing indic pres act	3450.12 art acc sing fem
τὸν	υἱὸν	τοῦ	θεοῦ	ἔχει	τὴν
ton	*huion*	*tou*	*theou*	*echei*	*tēn*
the	Son		of God	has	the

10.a.**Txt:** 01ℵ,044,it. Steph
Var: 02A,03B,018K 020L,025P,byz.Treg,Alf Tisc,Weis,Sod,UBS/⋆

3114.3 noun acc sing fem	1706.1 prep	1431.5 prs-pron dat sing masc	840.4 prs-pron dat sing	3450.5 art nom sing masc	3231.1 partic
μαρτυρίαν	ἐν	ʿ ἑαυτῷ˙	[a⋆ αὐτῷ˙]	ὁ	μὴ
marturian	*en*	*heautō*	*autō*	*ho*	*mē*
witness	in	himself;	[him;]	the	not

3961.10 verb nom sing masc part pres act	3450.3 art dat sing	2296.3 noun dat sing masc	5418.2 noun acc sing masc	4020.43 verb 3sing indic perf act	840.6 prs-pron acc sing masc
πιστεύων	τῷ	θεῷ	ψεύστην	πεποίηκεν	αὐτόν,
pisteuōn	*tō*	*theō*	*pseustēn*	*pepoiēken*	*auton*
believing		God	a liar	has made	him,

3617.1 conj	3620.3 partic	3961.39 verb 3sing indic perf act	1519.1 prep	3450.12 art acc sing fem	3114.3 noun acc sing fem
ὅτι	οὐ	πεπίστευκεν	εἰς	τὴν	μαρτυρίαν,
hoti	*ou*	*pepisteuken*	*eis*	*tēn*	*marturian*
because	not	he has believed	in	the	witness

3614.12 rel-pron acc sing fem	3113.27 verb 3sing indic perf act	3450.5 art nom sing masc	2296.1 noun nom sing masc	3875.1 prep
ἣν	μεμαρτύρηκεν	ὁ	θεὸς	περὶ
hēn	*memarturēken*	*ho*	*theos*	*peri*
which	has witnessed		God	concerning

3450.2 art gen sing	5048.2 noun gen sing masc	840.3 prs-pron gen sing	2504.1 conj	3642.9 dem-pron nom sing fem	1498.4 verb 3sing indic pres act
τοῦ	υἱοῦ	αὐτοῦ.	11. καὶ	αὕτη	ἐστὶν
tou	*huiou*	*autou*	*kai*	*hautē*	*estin*
the	Son	his.	And	this	is

3450.9 art nom sing fem	3114.1 noun nom sing fem	3617.1 conj	2205.4 noun acc sing fem	164.1 adj sing	1319.14 verb 3sing indic aor act
ἡ	μαρτυρία	ὅτι	ζωὴν	αἰώνιον	ἔδωκεν
hē	*marturia*	*hoti*	*zōēn*	*aiōnion*	*edōken*
the	witness,	that	life	eternal	gave

2231.3 prs-pron dat 1pl	3450.5 art nom sing masc	2296.1 noun nom sing masc	3450.5 art nom sing masc	2296.1 noun nom sing masc	2231.3 prs-pron dat 1pl
ʿ ἡμῖν	ὁ	θεός˙	[ὁ	θεὸς	ἡμῖν,]
hēmin	*ho*	*theos*	*ho*	*theos*	*hēmin*
to us		God;		[God	to us,]

2504.1 conj	3642.9 dem-pron nom sing fem	3450.9 art nom sing fem	2205.1 noun nom sing fem	1706.1 prep	3450.3 art dat sing	5048.3 noun dat sing masc
καὶ	αὕτη	ἡ	ζωὴ	ἐν	τῷ	υἱῷ
kai	*hautē*	*hē*	*zōē*	*en*	*tō*	*huiō*
and	this	the	life	in	the	Son

840.3 prs-pron gen sing	1498.4 verb 3sing indic pres act	3450.5 art nom sing masc	2174.17 verb nom sing masc part pres act	3450.6 art acc sing masc
αὐτοῦ	ἐστιν.	12. ὁ	ἔχων	τὸν
autou	*estin*	*ho*	*echōn*	*ton*
his	is:	the	having	the

5048.4 noun acc sing masc	2174.4 verb 3sing indic pres act	3450.12 art acc sing fem	2205.4 noun acc sing fem	3450.5 art nom sing masc	3231.1 partic
υἱὸν,	ἔχει	τὴν	ζωήν˙	ὁ	μὴ
huion	*echei*	*tēn*	*zōēn*	*ho*	*mē*
Son,	has	the	life:	the	not

by His death to make salvation possible will be of no value unless the individual acts to receive God's gift.

The person who places trust in Christ receives a confirming inner testimony to support the external proofs. The Holy Spirit chose words carefully here to specify faith that goes beyond a mere whim. In 3:23 the aorist tense of "believe" refers to the initial moment of accepting Christ as Saviour; here the present tense describes a faith that continues to trust in God's Son as a pattern for living. The phrase used for faith is *believe in* (Greek, *pisteuōn eis*), an expression which occurs numerous times in the Gospel of John and appears in the epistle here and in 5:13. While one might *believe* a person simply by accepting one of his statements, *believing in* a person implies a settled confidence in his overall trustworthiness. The phrase describes a faith that commits itself to Jesus, relying on Him to provide salvation and obeying His dictates as Lord.

Anyone who places such faith in Jesus as the Son of God finds that an inward testimony joins the outward evidences already mentioned in verses 8 and 9. These are the three witnesses—Spirit, water, and blood—which look to the historical events of Christ's life that prove His divine-human nature. Faith may begin by looking at factual evidence; it is confirmed by an inner conviction of truth which comes from the Holy Spirit.

The alternative is presented as well. Refusal to believe God is tantamount to calling God a liar (cf. 1:10). "Believeth" in the phrase "he that believeth not God" occurs without an accompanying "in" (Greek, *eis*) and means that the person refuses to accept the truth of the statements which God has made concerning His Son. This person does not even reach the point of personal trust in Christ. One who refuses to believe God has made Him out to be a liar; the perfect tense reminds the readers that such an insult to God's character continues as long as the man's decision to reject Christ remains unchanged. God has not changed His testimony, and the one who persists in rejecting it is impugning the Lord's truthfulness.

10. He that believeth on the Son of God hath the witness in himself: Consequently, whoever believes in the Son of God can defend his faith by appealing to God's testimony, *Greber* . . . He who has faith in, *BB* . . . The believer in the Son of God possesses the witness within himself, *Berkeley* . . . has the proof right in his heart, *Laubach* . . . possesses this testimony in his heart, *Noli* . . . will find God's testimony in his own heart, *Phillips* . . . has the truth that God told us, *Everyday*.

he that believeth not God hath made him a liar: He who disbelieves God, *Berkeley* . . . but whoever does not believe even the testimony of God, brands God as a liar, *Greber* . . . made Him a liar, and as a result considers Him to be such, *Wuest* . . . makes him false, *BB*.

because he believeth not the record that God gave of his Son: Such is the case with him who refuses to believe God's own testimony on behalf of His Son, *Greber* . . . he is deliberately refusing to accept the testimony concerning his own Son that God is prepared to give him, *Phillips* . . . because he has not faith in the witness which God has given about, *BB* . . . he has put no faith in the evidence, *Berkeley* . . . by not accepting the testimony, *Norlie* . . . with the result that he is in a settled state of unbelief, *Wuest* . . . does not believe what God told us about his Son, *Everyday* . . . which God has testified concerning His Son, *Concordant*.

5:11. This verse focuses on the internal witness which the apostle mentioned in verse 10. It is the fact that God gave us eternal life. The aorist tense of "given" joins with the lack of a definite article for "eternal life" to show that a believer enjoys eternal life now. It is not merely a never-ending extension of our current existence; it is a quality of life which belongs properly to the God who inhabits eternity—but He chooses to give it to us at the moment we trust His Son who came as the sole source of this life.

11. And this is the record, that God hath given to us eternal life: And his witness is this, *BB* . . . the evidence: God has granted us, *Berkeley* . . . This testimony also contains the truth that God has restored to us the life hereafter, *Greber*.

and this life is in his Son: . . . this real life is to be found only in, *Phillips* . . . only in communion with His Son, *Greber*.

5:12. The inspired writer summarized his discussion of the witnesses to Christ's person by drawing a simple, inescapable conclusion—since eternal life comes solely from the Son of God, he who has the Son is the one who possesses life.

12. He that hath the Son hath life: It follows naturally that any man who has genuine contact with Christ has this life, *Phillips* . . . Those who find the Son find Life, *TCNT* . . . Accordingly, he who is in close communion with the Son has Spiritual life, *Greber*.

2174.17 verb nom sing masc part pres act	3450.6 art acc sing masc	5048.4 noun acc sing masc	3450.2 art gen sing	2296.2 noun gen sing masc	3450.12 art acc sing fem
ἔχων	τὸν	υἱὸν	τοῦ	θεοῦ,	τὴν
echōn	*ton*	*huion*	*tou*	*theou*	*tēn*
having	the	Son		of God,	the

2205.4 noun acc sing fem	3620.2 partic	2174.4 verb 3sing indic pres act	3642.18 dem-pron pl neu	1119.7 verb 1sing indic aor act	5050.3 prs-pron dat 2pl
ζωὴν	οὐκ	ἔχει.	**13.** Ταῦτα	ἔγραψα	ὑμῖν
zōēn	*ouk*	*echei*	*Tauta*	*egrapsa*	*humin*
life	not	has.	These things	I wrote	to you

13.a.**Txt:** 018K,020L 025P,byz.
Var: 01ℵ,02A,03B Gries,Lach,Treg,Alf Word,Tisc,We/Ho,Weis Sod,UBS/☆

3450.4 art dat pl	3961.3 verb dat pl masc part pres act	1519.1 prep	3450.16 art sing neu	3549.2 noun sing neu	3450.2 art gen sing
⸂a τοῖς	πιστεύουσιν	εἰς	τὸ	ὄνομα	τοῦ
tois	*pisteuousin*	*eis*	*to*	*onoma*	*tou*
the	believing	on	the	name	of the

5048.2 noun gen sing masc	3450.2 art gen sing	2296.2 noun gen sing masc	2419.1 conj	3471.17 verb 2pl subj perf act	3617.1 conj	2205.4 noun acc sing fem
υἱοῦ	τοῦ	Θεοῦ, ⸃	ἵνα	εἰδῆτε	ὅτι	ζωὴν
huiou	*tou*	*Theou*	*hina*	*eidēte*	*hoti*	*zōēn*
Son		of God,	that	you may know	that	life

13.b.**Txt:** 018K,020L 025P,byz.
Var: 01ℵ-org,03B,Treg Alf,Tisc,We/Ho,Weis Sod,UBS/☆

2174.2 verb 2pl pres act	164.1 adj sing	2504.1 conj	2419.1 conj	3961.8 verb 2pl subj pres act	3450.4 art dat pl
ἔχετε	αἰώνιον,	⸂ καὶ	ἵνα	πιστεύητε	[b☆ τοῖς
echete	*aiōnion*	*kai*	*hina*	*pisteuēte*	*tois*
you have	eternal,	and	that	you may believe	[the

3961.3 verb dat pl masc part pres act	1519.1 prep	3450.16 art sing neu	3549.2 noun sing neu	3450.2 art gen sing	5048.2 noun gen sing masc
πιστεύουσιν]	εἰς	τὸ	ὄνομα	τοῦ	υἱοῦ
pisteuousin	*eis*	*to*	*onoma*	*tou*	*huiou*
believing]	on	the	name	of the	Son

3450.2 art gen sing	2296.2 noun gen sing masc	2504.1 conj	3642.9 dem-pron nom sing fem	1498.4 verb 3sing indic pres act	3450.9 art nom sing fem
τοῦ	θεοῦ.	**14.** καὶ	αὕτη	ἐστὶν	ἡ
tou	*theou*	*kai*	*hautē*	*estin*	*hē*
	of God.	And	this	is	the

3816.1 noun nom sing fem	3614.12 rel-pron acc sing fem	2174.5 verb 1pl indic pres act	4242.1 prep	840.6 prs-pron acc sing masc	3617.1 conj
παῤῥησία	ἣν	ἔχομεν	πρὸς	αὐτόν,	ὅτι
parrhēsia	*hēn*	*echomen*	*pros*	*auton*	*hoti*
confidence	which	we have	toward	him,	that

1430.1 partic	4948.10 indef-pron sing neu	153.25 verb 1pl subj pres mid	2567.3 prep	3450.16 art sing neu	2284.1 noun sing neu
ἐάν	τι	αἰτώμεθα	κατὰ	τὸ	θέλημα
ean	*ti*	*aitōmetha*	*kata*	*to*	*thelēma*
if	anything	we may ask	according to	the	will

840.3 prs-pron gen sing	189.5 verb 3sing indic pres act	2231.2 prs-pron gen 1pl	2504.1 conj	1430.1 partic	3471.5 verb 1pl indic perf act	3617.1 conj
αὐτοῦ,	ἀκούει	ἡμῶν·	**15.** καὶ	ἐὰν	οἴδαμεν	ὅτι
autou	*akouei*	*hēmōn*	*kai*	*ean*	*oidamen*	*hoti*
his,	he hears	us.	And	if	we know	that

15.a.**Txt:** 02A,03B,018K byz.Sod
Var: 01ℵ,020L,025P Tisc,We/Ho,Weis UBS/☆

189.5 verb 3sing indic pres act	2231.2 prs-pron gen 1pl	3614.16 rel-pron sing neu	300.1 partic	1430.1 partic	153.25 verb 1pl subj pres mid
ἀκούει	ἡμῶν,	ὃ	⸂ ἂν	[a☆ ἐὰν]	αἰτώμεθα,
akouei	*hēmōn*	*ho*	*an*	*ean*	*aitōmetha*
he hears	us,	whatsoever			we may ask,

"Having the Son" (cf. 1 John 2:23; 2 John 9) is used as a synonym for having a personal relationship with Jesus Christ. The one who has Christ also has life, and the present tense of the verb *echei* indicates once more that this life is a present reality, not merely a future possibility. This is one of the most simple, yet profound, statements of what salvation means. In John 1:12 Christ speaks of receiving Him, and in Revelation 3:20 He speaks of standing at the door and knocking and coming in at a sinner's invitation. When we have Him we have life, His life.

The latter part of the verse presents a strong contrast with the first statement. It is an illusion to believe anyone can have eternal life apart from the Son of God.

[and] he that hath not the Son of God hath not life: . . . and if he has not, then he does not possess this life at all, *Phillips* . . . and he who lacks this communion with the Son of God also lacks spiritual life, *Greber.*

5:13. This verse begins the conclusion to the epistle. As he did in his Gospel (John 20:31), John closed his letter by stating his purpose for writing. While John's Gospel intended to bring people to faith, his epistle aims to help believers besieged by opposing views of Christianity, to enable them to know confidently that they have followed the truth. The word for "know" (Greek, *eidēte*) was often used for knowledge characterized by certainty.

"These things" refers most directly to the immediately preceding verses but also embraces the themes of the whole letter. The tests of faith presented throughout the epistle give the believer a basis for assurance that his relationship with God is a reality. The final phrase of the verse underscores the test most recently put forward: belief in Jesus as the Son of God. (See 5:10 for "believe on.")

13. These things have I written unto you that believe on the name of the Son of God: . . . to have you see that you, who have faith in the name of God's Son, *Berkeley* . . . so as to make you aware, *Greber* . . . who already believe, *Phillips* . . . in the authority of, *SEB* . . . in the Self-revelation, *Wade.*

that ye may know that ye have eternal life: . . . may be perceiving, *Concordant* . . . in order that you may know with an absolute knowledge, *Wuest* . . . so that you may be quite sure that, here and now, you possess eternal life, *Phillips* . . . obtain life in the beyond, *Greber.*

and that ye may believe on the name of the Son of God: . . . if you believe, *Greber.*

5:14. When we know that we are children of God, it is natural to have confidence when we approach Him in prayer. A believer may have the "confidence" (Greek, *parrhēsia*) that allows him to speak openly (the original meaning of the word). The phrase "in him" (Greek, *pros auton*) might be translated more clearly as "toward Him," since *pros* has a root meaning of "face-to-face" and often describes intimate personal relationships, as in John 1:1.

The believer knows that God hears any request with a favorable attitude, as long as it is in accord with His will. This passage is one of several that describe conditions for answered prayer (1 John 3:22; cf. John 14:14; 15:7).

14. And this is the confidence that we have in him: Our hearts are filled with great confidence, *Greber* . . . this is the boldness, *Darby, Concordant* . . . the assurance, *Wuest* . . . we have resting on Him, *Berkeley* . . . We can come to God with no doubts, *Everyday.*

that, if we ask any thing according to his will, he heareth us: . . . we are certain that he hears every request that is made in accord with his own plan, *Phillips* . . . if we make request for anything, *Wade* . . . if we petition anything in agreement with, *Berkeley* . . . for ourselves, *Wuest* . . . This means that when we ask God for things (and those things agree with what God wants for us), then God cares about what we say, *Everyday.*

5:15. When we know that God has heard our request favorably, His power and love assure us that we have the answer we have asked. An unusual construction is used here for "if we know," linking *ean* with an indicative verb (but the combination did occur in some secular writings) which assumes that the condition is true. We know God has heard, thus we know that He will answer. In

15. And if we know that he hear us, whatsoever we ask: He listens to us whatever we may petition, *Berkeley* . . . And since we know that he invariably gives his attention to our prayers, whatever they are about, *Phillips* . . . God listens to us every time we ask him. So we know that he gives us the things that we ask from him, *Everyday* . . . whatever we may be requesting, *Concordant.*

15.b.**Txt:** 02A,018K 020L,025P,byz.Sod
Var: 01ℵ,03B,33,Lach Treg,Tisc,We/Ho,Weis UBS/☆

3471.5 verb 1pl indic perf act	**3617.1** conj	**2174.5** verb 1pl indic pres act	**3450.17** art pl neu	**154.2** noun pl neu	**3614.17** rel-pron pl neu
οἴδαμεν	ὅτι	ἔχομεν	τὰ	αἰτήματα	ἃ
oidamen	*hoti*	*echomen*	*ta*	*aitēmata*	*ha*
we know	that	we have	the	requests	which

153.19 verb 1pl indic perf act	**3706.1** prep	**570.2** prep	**840.3** prs-pron gen sing	**1430.1** partic	**4948.3** indef-pron nom sing
ᾐτήκαμεν	ʼ παρ'	[b☆ ἀπ']	αὐτοῦ.	**16.** Ἐάν	τις
ētēkamen	*par'*	*ap'*	*autou*	*Ean*	*tis*
we have asked	from	[idem]	him.	If	anyone

1481.10 verb 3sing subj aor act	**3450.6** art acc sing masc	**79.4** noun acc sing masc	**840.3** prs-pron gen sing	**262.5** verb acc sing masc part pres act
ἴδῃ	τὸν	ἀδελφὸν	αὐτοῦ	ἁμαρτάνοντα
idē	*ton*	*adelphon*	*autou*	*hamartanonta*
should see	the	brother	his	sinning

264.4 noun acc sing fem	**3231.1** partic	**4242.1** prep	**2265.4** noun acc sing masc	**153.20** verb 3sing indic fut act	**2504.1** conj
ἁμαρτίαν	μὴ	πρὸς	θάνατον,	αἰτήσει,	καὶ
hamartian	*mē*	*pros*	*thanaton*	*aitēsei*	*kai*
a sin	not	to	death,	he shall ask,	and

1319.38 verb 3sing indic fut act	**840.4** prs-pron dat sing	**2205.4** noun acc sing fem	**3450.4** art dat pl	**262.8** verb dat pl masc part pres act	**3231.1** partic
δώσει	αὐτῷ	ζωήν,	τοῖς	ἁμαρτάνουσιν	μὴ
dōsei	*autō*	*zōēn*	*tois*	*hamartanousin*	*mē*
he shall give	him	life	to the	sinning	not

4242.1 prep	**2265.4** noun acc sing masc	**1498.4** verb 3sing indic pres act	**264.2** noun nom sing fem	**4242.1** prep	**2265.4** noun acc sing masc
πρὸς	θάνατον.	ἔστιν	ἁμαρτία	πρὸς	θάνατον·
pros	*thanaton*	*estin*	*hamartia*	*pros*	*thanaton*
to	death.	There is	a sin	to	death;

3620.3 partic	**3875.1** prep	**1552.10** dem-pron gen sing fem	**2978.1** verb 1sing pres act	**2419.1** conj	**2049.11** verb 3sing subj aor act
οὐ	περὶ	ἐκείνης	λέγω	ἵνα	ἐρωτήσῃ·
ou	*peri*	*ekeinēs*	*legō*	*hina*	*erōtēsē*
not	concerning	that	do I say	that	he should ask.

3820.9 adj nom sing fem	**92.1** noun nom sing fem	**264.2** noun nom sing fem	**1498.4** verb 3sing indic pres act	**2504.1** conj
17. πᾶσα	ἀδικία	ἁμαρτία	ἐστίν,	καὶ
pasa	*adikia*	*hamartia*	*estin*	*kai*
Every	unrighteousness	sin	is;	and

1498.4 verb 3sing indic pres act	**264.2** noun nom sing fem	**3620.3** partic	**4242.1** prep	**2265.4** noun acc sing masc	**3471.5** verb 1pl indic perf act
ἔστιν	ἁμαρτία	οὐ	πρὸς	θάνατον.	**18.** Οἴδαμεν
estin	*hamartia*	*ou*	*pros*	*thanaton*	*Oidamen*
there is	a sin	not	to	death.	We know

3617.1 conj	**3820.6** adj nom sing masc	**3450.5** art nom sing masc	**1074.26** verb nom sing masc part perf mid	**1523.2** prep gen	**3450.2** art gen sing	**2296.2** noun gen sing masc
ὅτι	πᾶς	ὁ	γεγεννημένος	ἐκ	τοῦ	θεοῦ
hoti	*pas*	*ho*	*gegennēmenos*	*ek*	*tou*	*theou*
that	anyone	the	having been born	of		God

3620.1 partic	**262.2** verb 3sing indic pres act	**233.1** conj	**3450.5** art nom sing masc	**1074.17** verb nom sing masc part aor pass	**1523.2** prep gen
οὐχ	ἁμαρτάνει·	ἀλλ'	ὁ	γεννηθεὶς	ἐκ
ouch	*hamartanei*	*all'*	*ho*	*gennētheis*	*ek*
not	is sinning,	but	the	having been born	of

fact, the present tense of "have" is used because God's promise is as certain as the actual event would be.

we know that we have the petitions that we desired of him: . . . then the requests we ask of Him are assured us, *Berkeley* . . . we can rest assured that He will give us, *Norlie* . . . we can be quite sure that our prayers will be answered, *Phillips.*

5:16. Although most discussion of verses 16 and 17 focuses on the "sin unto death," it is important to note that the primary emphasis of the passage is on the other side of the question, the "sin not unto death." In view of verses 13-15, these two verses are primarily an example of one area in which Christians can pray confidently according to the will of God.

When a person sees a brother sinning, he can pray for that brother knowing that his prayer is in line with God's will. The term "brother" consistently refers to fellow Christians, so the "sin not unto death" is one which a believer might commit. It is a sin which other Christians can see. And it is a sin which is repeated (note the present tense of "sin"). The epistle has consistently declared that a genuine Christian cannot continue a pattern of sin; God will not allow it to keep on. Thus a person can pray for a sinning brother, and God will answer by giving that brother life, a restored life of fellowship with God.

There is such a thing as a sin which leads to death, and John did not instruct his readers to pray for forgiveness in such a case, because this would not be in accord with God's will. The sin unto death is not described, but it has been much discussed by later commentators. It may refer to the sin of a believer who persists in sin to the point where God judges him or her by physical death (cf. Acts 5:1-11; 1 Corinthians 11:30). Or it may refer to the sin of unbelievers such as the apostate teachers and their faction, who habitually committed sins which John cataloged as the marks of an unbeliever. In this case, the death involved would be spiritual death. Neither option would be a situation where a person would pray for God to forgive apart from repentance on the sinner's part.

16. If any man see his brother sin a sin [which is] not unto death: In case someone sees his brother commit a sin, not fatal, *Berkeley* . . . which has not killed his soul, *Laubach* . . . which does not lead to eternal death, *SEB* . . . that is not deadly sin, *Williams C.K.* . . . which is not in its tendency towards death, *Wuest* . . . I don't mean deliberately turning his back on God and embracing evil, *Phillips.*

he shall ask, and he shall give him life for them that sin not unto death: . . . he should pray to God for him and secure fresh life for the sinner, *Phillips* . . . he will petition and will obtain life for him, *Berkeley.*

There is a sin unto death: I do not say that he shall pray for it: There is a deadly sin, *Montgomery* . . . True, there are mortal sins, *Noli* . . . a sin that means death; I advise no prayer for that, *Berkeley* . . . that leads to spiritual death—that is not the sort of sin I have in mind when I recommend prayer for the sinner, *Phillips* . . . I do not urge you to make intercession for that, *Norlie* . . . make a request about that, *Adams* . . . Not concerning that one [sin] do I say that he should ask, *Wuest.*

5:17. There is no implication that sin is condoned by saying that some sins are less serious than others. Rather, like the statement in 3:4, there is the declaration that all unrighteousness is sin. "Unrighteousness" (Greek, *adikia*) refers to any behavior which does not measure up to God's standard. Thus any deviation from God's will or character is sin. If a believer sins, to avoid physical or spiritual death—or both, he must repent and find forgiveness.

17. All unrighteousness is sin: and there is a sin not unto death: Any wrongdoing is sin, *Williams* . . . Every failure to obey God's laws is sin, of course, but there is sin that does not preclude repentance and forgiveness, *Phillips* . . . there is sin which does not involve death, *Berkeley.*

5:18. The apostle closed his letter with a triple "We know," a threefold statement of bedrock truths.

First, we know that everyone who has been given birth from God does not keep on sinning—a restatement of 3:9. On the contrary, he is guarded from the "wicked one." The aorist tense of "he that

18. We know that whosoever is born of God sinneth not: We know absolutely, *Wuest* . . . that every one, *Swann* . . . who has derived his Life from God, *TCNT* . . . the true child of God, *Phillips* . . . is not habitually committing sin, *Montgomery* . . . does not continue to sin, *SEB* . . . practices no sinning, *Berkeley.*

1 John 5:19

18.a.**Txt:** 01ℵ,02A-corr 018K,020L,025P,33,byz. Weis,Sod
Var: 02A-org,03B,Treg Alf,Tisc,We/Ho,UBS/☆

3450.2 art gen sing τοῦ *tou* God — 2296.2 noun gen sing masc θεοῦ *theou* God — 4931.2 verb 3sing indic pres act τηρεῖ *tērei* keeps — 1431.6 prs-pron acc sing masc ⸀ ἑαυτόν, *heauton* himself, — 840.6 prs-pron acc sing masc [a☆ αὐτόν,] *auton* [him,] — 2504.1 conj καὶ *kai* and

3450.5 art nom sing masc ὁ *ho* the — 4050.6 adj nom sing masc πονηρὸς *ponēros* wicked — 3620.1 partic οὐχ *ouch* not — 674.4 verb 3sing indic pres mid ἅπτεται *haptetai* does touch — 840.3 prs-pron gen sing αὐτοῦ. *autou* him.

19. 3471.5 verb 1pl indic perf act οἴδαμεν *oidamen* We know — 3617.1 conj ὅτι *hoti* that — 1523.2 prep gen ἐκ *ek* of — 3450.2 art gen sing τοῦ *tou* — 2296.2 noun gen sing masc θεοῦ *theou* God — 1498.5 verb 1pl indic pres act ἐσμεν, *esmen* we are, — 2504.1 conj καὶ *kai* and — 3450.5 art nom sing masc ὁ *ho* the

2862.1 noun nom sing masc κόσμος *kosmos* world — 3513.4 adj nom sing masc ὅλος *holos* whole — 1706.1 prep ἐν *en* in — 3450.3 art dat sing τῷ *tō* the — 4050.3 adj dat sing πονηρῷ *ponērō* wicked — 2719.2 verb 3sing indic pres mid κεῖται. *keitai* lies.

20.a.**Txt:** 01ℵ,03B,bo. byz.
Var: 02A,044,33,81,323 614,630,1505,1739 2495,sa.Sod

20. 3471.5 verb 1pl indic perf act ⸀☆ οἴδαμεν *oidamen* We know — 1156.2 conj δὲ *de* and — 2504.1 conj [a καὶ *kai* [And — 3471.5 verb 1pl indic perf act οἴδαμεν] *oidamen* we know] — 3617.1 conj ὅτι *hoti* that — 3450.5 art nom sing masc ὁ *ho* the

5048.1 noun nom sing masc υἱὸς *huios* Son — 3450.2 art gen sing τοῦ *tou* — 2296.2 noun gen sing masc θεοῦ *theou* of God — 2223.2 verb 3sing indic pres act ἥκει, *hēkei* is come, — 2504.1 conj καὶ *kai* and — 1319.33 verb 3sing indic perf act δέδωκεν *dedōken* has given — 2231.3 prs-pron dat 1pl ἡμῖν *hēmin* us

20.b.**Txt:** 03B-corr2,044 byz.
Var: 01ℵ,02A,03B-org 020L,025P,049,33,81 614,Tisc,We/Ho,Sod

1265.3 noun acc sing fem διάνοιαν *dianoian* an understanding — 2419.1 conj ἵνα *hina* that — 1091.7 verb 1pl subj pres act ⸀☆ γινώσκωμεν *ginōskōmen* we might know — 1091.4 verb 1pl indic pres act [b γινώσκομεν] *ginōskomen* [we know]

3450.6 art acc sing masc τὸν *ton* the — 226.1 adj sing ἀληθινόν· *alēthinon* true; — 2504.1 conj καὶ *kai* and — 1498.5 verb 1pl indic pres act ἐσμὲν *esmen* we are — 1706.1 prep ἐν *en* in — 3450.3 art dat sing τῷ *tō* the — 226.3 adj dat sing masc ἀληθινῷ, *alēthinō* true,

1706.1 prep ἐν *en* in — 3450.3 art dat sing τῷ *tō* the — 5048.3 noun dat sing masc υἱῷ *huiō* Son — 840.3 prs-pron gen sing αὐτοῦ *autou* his, — 2400.2 name masc Ἰησοῦ *Iēsou* Jesus — 5382.3 name dat masc Χριστῷ. *Christō* Christ. — 3642.4 dem-pron nom sing masc οὗτός *houtos* This

20.c.**Txt:** Steph
Var: 01ℵ,02A,03B,33 Lach,Treg,Alf,Tisc We/Ho,Weis,Sod UBS/☆

1498.4 verb 3sing indic pres act ἐστιν *estin* is — 3450.5 art nom sing masc ὁ *ho* the — 226.2 adj sing masc ἀληθινὸς *alēthinos* true — 2296.1 noun nom sing masc θεὸς, *theos* God, — 2504.1 conj καὶ *kai* and — 3450.9 art nom sing fem ⸂c ἡ ⸃ *hē* the

2205.1 noun nom sing fem ζωὴ *zōē* life — 164.3 adj nom sing αἰώνιος. *aiōnios* eternal.

21. 4888.1 noun pl neu Τεκνία, *Teknia* Little children, — 5278.12 verb 2pl impr aor act φυλάξατε *phulaxate* keep — 1431.8 prs-pron acc pl masc ⸀ ἑαυτοὺς *heautous* yourselves

is begotten" may well refer to Christ rather than the believer, and the most common rendering of "himself" is "him" (Greek, *auton*). The Son of God guards the believer so Satan cannot take hold of him to drag him into sin.

but he that is begotten of God keepeth himself: . . . guards himself, *Wilson* . . . knows how to protect himself, *Noli* . . . maintains a watchful guardianship, *Wuest* . . . retains hold on him, *Berkeley* . . . he is in the charge of God's own Son, *Phillips* . . . The Son of God keeps him safe, *Everyday.*

and that wicked one toucheth him not: . . . the Pernicious One, *Wuest* . . . and the Evil One cannot hurt him, *Everyday* . . . and the evil one must keep his distance, *Phillips* . . . does not lay hold on him, *Campbell* . . . does not get a grip on him, *Berkeley.*

5:19. The second truth that a Christian may know with absolute certainty is the fact that he is connected to God and in opposition to the devil. Whereas verse 18 spoke of the theological principle that believers could overcome sin, verse 19 shifts to a more personal statement—"we" are from God. John placed himself with his readers as those who have God as the source of their life. Regardless of any doubts that their opponents may have kindled, they can be assured that they belong to the Father.

This is in sharp contrast to a second relationship, the tie between the world and Satan. The world (Greek, *kosmos*) refers to the entire system of society which Satan has built up in opposition to God. The entire civilization lies in "the wicked one," a standard translation of *tō ponērō*, resting passive and helpless in his control.

19. [And] we know that we are of God, and the whole world lieth in wickedness: . . . we ourselves are children of God, and we also know that the world around us, *Phillips* . . . We know that we belong to God. But the Evil One controls the whole world, *Everyday* . . . is under the power of, *Williams* . . . lies in the grip of the evil one, *Adams* . . . lies under the dominance of, *Berkeley.*

5:20. The third foundation truth which we know is that God has provided a way for us to escape from Satan's realm. Jesus Christ, the Son of God, has come and has given us understanding—both statements use verbs which look back to the historical event of Christ's incarnation and couple it to the benefits which His coming still provides. The Son not only became man, He revealed the truth. He gave "understanding" (Greek, *dianoian*), the capacity to receive spiritual truth.

It is good to have a certainty about our relationship with God. A believer does not practice sin. He has confidence that he is a child of God. And he knows he is a part of God, like a vine and its branches.

The goal of His coming was to make it possible to know truth personified, God the Father. The Gnostics could offer no secrets that could compare with this. The word "true" (Greek, *alēthinos*) emphasizes the fact that Jesus introduced the genuine God, in contrast to the pseudodeities of the cults.

Not only does the believer come to know the true God, but he also enjoys such an intimate relationship with Him that John can say "we are in him." And this bond to the Father comes from the fact that we are likewise "in" the Son. Knowing Jesus is the introduction to knowing His Father.

The sum of the whole matter is that the One whom John declared is the genuine God and the fountain of eternal life.

20. And we know that the Son of God is come, and hath given us an understanding, that we may know him that is true: . . . has actually come to this world, and has shown us the way to know the one who is true, *Phillips* . . . with an absolute knowledge...given us a permanent understanding in order that we may be knowing in an experiential way the One who is genuine, *Wuest* . . . has given us a comprehension, *Concordant* . . . has given us discernment to recognize the True God, *TCNT* . . . has given us insight to recognize the true One, *Berkeley* . . . Who is the Real God, *Wade.*

and we are in him that is true, [even] in his Son Jesus Christ: We know that our real life is, *Phillips* . . . our lives are in that true God, *Everyday* . . . in union with the true One, *Berkeley* . . . we are in the Genuine One, *Wuest.*

This is the true God, and eternal life: . . . the genuine God and life eternal, *Wuest* . . . This is the real God and this is real, eternal life, *Phillips.*

5:21. The final statement is a warning. John prefaced it with his term of affection, "Little children," because he was deeply con-

21. Little children, keep yourselves from idols. Amen: Dear children, *Berkeley* . . . My chil-

1 John 5:21

21.a.**Txt:** 01ℵ-corr,02A 018K,025P,byz.
Var: 01ℵ-org,03B,020L Lach,Treg,Tisc,We/Ho Weis,Sod,UBS/☆

21.b.**Txt:** 018K,020L 025P,byz.
Var: 01ℵ,02A,03B,33,it. sa.bo.Gries,Lach,Treg Alf,Word,Tisc,We/Ho Weis,Sod,UBS/☆

21.c.**Txt:** Steph
Var: Elzev,Gries,Lach Word,Tisc,We/Ho,Weis Sod,UBS/☆

1431.17 prs-pron pl neu	**570.3** prep	**3450.1** art gen pl	**1487.4** noun gen pl neu	**279.1** intrj	**2464.2** name gen masc
[a☆ ἑαυτὰ]	ἀπὸ	τῶν	εἰδώλων.	⌈b ἀμήν ⌉	⌈c Ἰωάννου
heauta	*apo*	*tōn*	*eidōlōn*	*amēn*	*Iōannou*
[idem]	from	the	idols	Amen.	Of John

1976.1 noun nom sing fem	**2498.1** adj nom sing masc	**4272.9** num ord nom sing fem
ἐπιστολὴ	καθολικὴ	πρώτη. ⌉
epistolē	*katholikē*	*prōtē*
epistle	general	first.

cerned for them with fatherly love. But the command itself is stern. "Guard yourselves from idols!" The aorist tense makes the tone even sharper. The idols meant could have been the actual idols which filled every Roman city, but were more likely to have been the false gods presented by Gnostic teachers.

Though John's readers faced great pressure from those who claimed to have the truth, he provided them with tests of holiness, love, and truth by which they could be confident that they truly belonged to the family of God.

dren, keep yourselves from, *Noyes* . . . put yourselves beyond the reach of, *Williams* . . . guard yourselves, *Montgomery* . . . But be on your guard...against every false god! *Phillips* . . . away from, *SEB* . . . beware of false gods! *Norlie* . . . guard yourselves from symbols, *Klingensmith* . . . from false divinities, *Noli* . . . from misrepresentations of God, *Wade* . . . from idolatry, *Murdock* . . . from communication with evil spirits, *Greber* . . . false gods, [from anything and everything that would occupy the place in your heart due to God, from any sort of substitute for Him that would take first place in your life], *AmpB* . . . My sons, avoid all idolatrous imitations, *Wand* . . . keep yourselves from worshipping false gods and images, *Macknight.*

THE SECOND EPISTLE OF JOHN

Expanded Interlinear
Textual Critical Apparatus
Verse-by-Verse Commentary
Various Versions

1976.1 noun nom sing fem	2464.2 name gen masc	1202.4 num ord nom sing fem
Ἐπιστολὴ	Ἰωάννου	Δευτέρα
Epistolē	*Iōannou*	*Deutera*
Epistle	of John	Second

Textual Apparatus

3450.5 art nom sing masc	4104.3 adj comp nom sing masc	1575.8 adj dat sing fem	2932.1 noun dat sing fem	2504.1 conj	3450.4 art dat pl
1:1. Ὁ	πρεσβύτερος	ἐκλεκτῇ	κυρίᾳ	καὶ	τοῖς
Ho	*presbuteros*	*eklektē*	*kuria*	*kai*	*tois*
The	elder	to elect	lady	and	the

4891.6 noun dat pl neu	840.10 prs-pron gen sing fem	3614.8 rel-pron acc pl masc	1466.1 prs-pron nom 1sing	25.5 verb 1sing indic pres act	1706.1 prep
τέκνοις	αὐτῆς,	οὓς	ἐγὼ	ἀγαπῶ	ἐν
teknois	*autēs*	*hous*	*egō*	*agapō*	*en*
children	her,	whom	I	love	in

223.3 noun dat sing fem	2504.1 conj	3620.2 partic	1466.1 prs-pron nom 1sing	3304.2 adj nom sing masc	233.2 conj	2504.1 conj
ἀληθείᾳ,	καὶ	οὐκ	ἐγὼ	μόνος,	ἀλλὰ	καὶ
alētheia	*kai*	*ouk*	*egō*	*monos*	*alla*	*kai*
truth,	and	not	I	only,	but	also

3820.7 adj nom pl masc	3450.7 art nom pl masc	1091.37 verb nom pl masc part perf act	3450.12 art acc sing fem	223.4 noun acc sing fem	1217.2 prep
πάντες	οἱ	ἐγνωκότες	τὴν	ἀλήθειαν,	**2.** διὰ
pantes	*hoi*	*egnōkotes*	*tēn*	*alētheian*	*dia*
all	the	having known	the	truth,	for sake of

3450.12 art acc sing fem	223.4 noun acc sing fem	3450.12 art acc sing fem	3176.13 verb acc sing fem part pres act	1706.1 prep	2231.3 prs-pron dat 1pl
τὴν	ἀλήθειαν	τὴν	μένουσαν	ἐν	ἡμῖν,
tēn	*alētheian*	*tēn*	*menousan*	*en*	*hēmin*
the	truth	the	residing	in	us,

2504.1 conj	3196.1 prep	2231.2 prs-pron gen 1pl	1498.40 verb 3sing indic fut mid	1519.1 prep	3450.6 art acc sing masc	163.3 noun acc sing masc
καὶ	μεθ'	ἡμῶν	ἔσται	εἰς	τὸν	αἰῶνα·
kai	*meth'*	*hēmōn*	*estai*	*eis*	*ton*	*aiōna*
and	with	us	shall be	to	the	age.

1498.40 verb 3sing indic fut mid	3196.1 prep	2231.2 prs-pron gen 1pl	5322.1 noun nom sing fem	1643.2 noun sing neu	1503.1 noun nom sing fem	3706.2 prep
3. ἔσται	μεθ'	ἡμῶν	χάρις,	ἔλεος	εἰρήνη	παρὰ
estai	*meth'*	*hēmōn*	*charis*	*eleos*	*eirēnē*	*para*
Shall be	with	us	grace,	mercy,	peace,	from

3.a.**Txt:** 01א,018K,020L 025P,byz.bo.
Var: 02A,03B,048,it.sa. Lach,Treg,Alf,Word Tisc,We/Ho,Weis,Sod UBS/⋆

2296.2 noun gen sing masc	3824.2 noun gen sing masc	2504.1 conj	3706.2 prep	2935.2 noun gen sing masc	2400.2 name masc
θεοῦ	πατρός	καὶ	παρὰ	⸂a κυρίου ⸃	Ἰησοῦ
theou	*patros*	*kai*	*para*	*kuriou*	*Iēsou*
God	Father,	and	from	Lord	Jesus

5382.2 name gen masc	3450.2 art gen sing	5048.2 noun gen sing masc	3450.2 art gen sing	3824.2 noun gen sing masc	1706.1 prep	223.3 noun dat sing fem
Χριστοῦ	τοῦ	υἱοῦ	τοῦ	πατρός,	ἐν	ἀληθείᾳ
Christou	*tou*	*huiou*	*tou*	*patros*	*en*	*alētheia*
Christ,	the	Son	of the	Father,	in	truth

THE SECOND EPISTLE OF JOHN

1. Second John provides an opportunity to observe the way the apostle John applied the principles taught in 1 John to a concrete situation. As usual, he chose to remain unnamed, simply introducing himself as "the elder." At the probable date of this epistle John would be the last surviving apostle and would need no elaborate introduction. His choice of "elder" refers both to his advanced age and to his position in the church.

The epistle is addressed to "the elect lady." Many have concluded that the "lady" was a local church, addressed figuratively as a woman. Her "children" would be the church members and the "elect sister" in verse 13 would be a sister church. Others believe the letter was intended for an individual Christian woman and her family. Either view is possible. The admonitions would be appropriate for either a person or for a congregation of believers.

The apostle declared that he loved this lady and her children in truth. The plural "whom" shows that the entire family was included in his love. He strengthened his statement by adding that she and her children also enjoyed the affection of all believers. Believers are described as "all they that have known the truth." The perfect tense is used to describe those who have gained a knowledge which produces a lasting relationship. *Ginōskō* often refers to the knowledge of God gained by personal experience of salvation.

2. John went on to explain why Christians love this lady. It was not merely because of her unusual personality, but because "the truth" of the gospel had become part of every believer's life. Once the truth comes to reside in a person's life, it produces love for other Christians. It is the driving force of the Christian life, and the woman addressed in 2 John shared in that love. The Greek phrase "to the age" is the usual idiom for "for ever."

3. Second John follows the customary letter format, first listing the writer and the recipient, then giving a greeting. Early Christians often used distinctively meaningful greetings like the one used here. Unlike other writers, who express their greetings as a wish, John stated his greeting in the future tense as a prediction. This woman and her household would enjoy grace, mercy, and peace.

Various Versions

1. The elder unto the elect lady and her children: From the pastor, *Norlie* . . . I, a Ruler in the church, *BB* . . . The Presbyter to a Mother Church, *Wade* . . . The old man to the Chosen Lady, *Fenton* . . . The Lady whom God called, *Laubach* . . . selected out by sovereign grace for salvation, *Wuest* . . . to Electa Cyria, *Campbell* . . . From the Officer of the Church, *TCNT* . . . This letter comes to a certain Christian lady and her children, *Phillips*.

whom I love in the truth; and not I only: . . . as for myself, I love in the sphere of the truth, *Wuest* . . . I love all of you in the truth, *Everyday* . . . of whom I am truly fond, *Greber* . . . held in the highest affection not only by me, *Phillips*.

but also all they that have known the truth: . . . at present possess a knowledge of it, *Wuest* . . . all those who recognize, *Berkeley* . . . all who have attained to knowledge of, *Greber*.

2. For the truth's sake, which dwelleth in us: Because of this true knowledge, *BB* . . . that remains in us, *Berkeley* . . . We love you because of the truth—the truth that lives in us, *Everyday*.

and shall be with us for ever: . . . which even now we know and which will be our companion for ever, *Phillips* . . . which will remain united with us for all time to come, *Greber* . . . will exist with us, *Fenton* . . . to eternity, *Darby*.

3. Grace be with you, mercy, [and] peace, from God the Father: Loving favor and loving-kindness, *NLT*.

and from the Lord Jesus Christ, the Son of the Father, in truth and love: . . . the Father's Son, *Phillips* . . . with whom you are united by truth and peace, *Greber*.

2504.1 conj	**26.3** noun dat sing fem	**5299.15** verb 1sing indic aor pass	**3003.1** adv	**3617.1** conj	**2128.22** verb 1sing indic perf act
καὶ	ἀγάπῃ.	4. Ἐχάρην	λίαν	ὅτι	εὕρηκα
kai	*agapē*	*Echarēn*	*lian*	*hoti*	*heurēka*
and	love.	I rejoiced	exceedingly	that	I have found

1523.2 prep gen	**3450.1** art gen pl	**4891.5** noun gen pl neu	**4622.2** prs-pron gen 2sing	**3906.16** verb acc pl masc part pres act	**1706.1** prep
ἐκ	τῶν	τέκνων	σου	περιπατοῦντας	ἐν
ek	*tōn*	*teknōn*	*sou*	*peripatountas*	*en*
of	the	children	your	walking	in

223.3 noun dat sing fem	**2503.1** conj	**1769.3** noun acc sing fem	**2956.15** verb 1pl indic aor act	**3706.2** prep	**3450.2** art gen sing
ἀληθείᾳ,	καθὼς	ἐντολὴν	ἐλάβομεν	παρὰ	τοῦ
alētheia	*kathōs*	*entolēn*	*elabomen*	*para*	*tou*
truth,	as	commandment	we received	from	the

3824.2 noun gen sing masc	**2504.1** conj	**3431.1** adv	**2049.2** verb 1sing indic pres act	**4622.4** prs-pron acc 2sing	**2932.2** noun nom sing fem	**3620.1** partic
πατρός.	5. καὶ	νῦν	ἐρωτῶ	σε,	κυρία,	οὐχ
patros	*kai*	*nun*	*erōtō*	*se*	*kuria*	*ouch*
Father.	And	now	I beseech	you,	lady,	not

5.a.**Txt:** Steph
Var: 01ℵ,02A,03B 018K,020L,025P,byz. Elzev,Gries,Lach,Treg Alf,Word,Tisc,We/Ho Weis,Sod,UBS/☆

5453.1 conj	**1769.3** noun acc sing fem	**1119.1** verb 1sing indic pres act	**1119.32** verb nom sing masc part pres act	**4622.3** prs-pron dat 2sing
ὡς	ἐντολὴν	‛ γράφω	[a☆ γράφων]	σοι
hōs	*entolēn*	*graphō*	*graphōn*	*soi*
as	a commandment	I write	[writing]	to you

2508.5 adj acc sing fem	**233.2** conj	**3614.12** rel-pron acc sing fem	**2174.46** verb 1pl indic imperf act	**570.2** prep	**741.2** noun gen sing fem
καινὴν,	ἀλλὰ	ἣν	εἴχομεν	ἀπ'	ἀρχῆς,
kainēn	*alla*	*hēn*	*eichomen*	*ap'*	*archēs*
new,	but	which	we were having	from	beginning,

2419.1 conj	**25.3** verb 1pl pres act	**238.3** prs-pron acc pl masc	**2504.1** conj	**3642.9** dem-pron nom sing fem	**1498.4** verb 3sing indic pres act
ἵνα	ἀγαπῶμεν	ἀλλήλους.	6. καὶ	αὕτη	ἐστὶν
hina	*agapōmen*	*allēlous*	*kai*	*hautē*	*estin*
that	we should love	one another.	And	this	is

3450.9 art nom sing fem	**26.1** noun nom sing fem	**2419.1** conj	**3906.7** verb 1pl subj pres act	**2567.3** prep	**3450.15** art acc pl fem
ἡ	ἀγάπη,	ἵνα	περιπατῶμεν	κατὰ	τὰς
hē	*agapē*	*hina*	*peripatōmen*	*kata*	*tas*
the	love,	that	we should walk	according to	the

1769.7 noun acc pl fem	**840.3** prs-pron gen sing	**3642.9** dem-pron nom sing fem	**1498.4** verb 3sing indic pres act	**3450.9** art nom sing fem
ἐντολὰς	αὐτοῦ.	αὕτη	‛ ἐστιν	ἡ
entolas	*autou*	*hautē*	*estin*	*hē*
commandments	his.	This	is	the

1769.1 noun nom sing fem	**3450.9** art nom sing fem	**1769.1** noun nom sing fem	**1498.4** verb 3sing indic pres act	**2503.1** conj
ἐντολή,	[☆ ἡ	ἐντολή	ἐστιν,]	καθὼς
entolē	*hē*	*entolē*	*estin*	*kathōs*
commandment,	[the	commandment	is,]	even as

189.23 verb 2pl indic aor act	**570.2** prep	**741.2** noun gen sing fem	**2419.1** conj	**1706.1** prep	**840.11** prs-pron dat sing fem
ἠκούσατε	ἀπ'	ἀρχῆς,	ἵνα	ἐν	αὐτῇ
ēkousate	*ap'*	*archēs*	*hina*	*en*	*autē*
you heard	from	beginning,	that	in	it

"Grace" refers to undeserved favor from God, "mercy" describes help bestowed on the helpless, and "peace" is both the fact of blessing and the subjective calm that springs from it.

These blessings come from a divine source: both Jesus Christ and God the Father. The apostle may have stressed this connection because of the tendency of some false teachers to separate the Father from the Son. The final phrase shows that the three blessings are administered with a balance between truth and love, which the rest of the letter strives to maintain. Both qualities are necessary. Truth which is not administered in love is too harsh to be fully effective. On the other hand, love which operates without a proper regard for truth can be mere sentimentality.

4. Like many letter writers of his day, John moved to a word of commendation. He declared that he rejoiced to discover good news about some of the lady's children. They were walking in truth. The perfect tense of "found" shows that his information remained true, and the present participle "walking" implies a continued pattern of healthy spiritual life. As a spiritual parent to many believers, John was always concerned about their welfare. The fact that only some are mentioned does not imply that the others were unfaithful, merely that John had not heard reports about them. These younger believers were walking or carrying out their daily actions in the sphere of the truth.

The next phrase forges a link between the lives of these believers and the command of God. Their walk in the truth was the kind of life which God demands. This phrase refers to the overall teaching of Scripture, rather than a specific verse.

5. At this point John turned to the immediate reason for the letter, the need to regain a proper balance between the demands of truth and love. He phrased his message as a formal request, not a command or a plea.

The apostle asked nothing new; he simply reaffirmed the command which Christians have obeyed since the Church began—to love one another. Christ gave the command in John 13:34,35, and John repeated it in 1 John 3:11.

6. Love, however, must be exercised within the guidelines of obedience. The first phrase here defines love more narrowly, as behavior that continually moves according to the standard of God's commands. Love is more than an uncontrollable emotion. It is action for the good of another, functioning within the limits of all God's other commands. The second part of the verse reiterates that this was the original intent of Christ's command to love.

4. I rejoiced greatly that I found: It has made me very happy, *Norlie* . . . I was very happy to find, *Williams C.K.* . . . was greatly delighted, *Fenton* . . . I feel extremely happy to have found, *Berkeley* . . . I am happy to find, *Williams* . . . I was delighted that I found, *Adams* . . . I was filled with joy when I met, *Laubach.*

of thy children walking in truth: . . . among your children those who live in a true way, *Berkeley* . . . conducting themselves, *Wuest* . . . living in the truth, *Williams C.K.*

as we have received a commandment from the Father: . . . instruction, *Berkeley* . . . from the presence of, *Wuest* . . . the Father himself, *Phillips.*

5. And now I beseech thee, lady: . . . now I entreat you, *Wuest* . . . now I beg of you, Princess, *Fenton* . . . I beg you now, dear lady, *Phillips.*

not as though I wrote a new commandment unto thee: . . . not by way of writing you a new injunction, *Berkeley* . . . not as though I were issuing any new order, *Phillips* . . . which is new in quality, *Wuest.*

but that which we had from the beginning: . . . but instead, *Berkeley* . . . simply reminding you of the original one, *Phillips.*

that we love one another: . . . with a divine love sacrificial in its essence, *Wuest.*

6. And this is love, that we walk after his commandments: You must live in love, *Laubach* . . . that we keep on living in accordance, *Williams* . . . consists in our behaving in agreement with His suggestions, *Berkeley* . . . we should be ordering our behavior dominated by his commandments, *Wuest* . . . according to His precepts, *Concordant.*

This is the commandment, That, as ye have heard from the beginning: . . . the very same command...the way you heard from the first, *Berkeley* . . . which you learnt from the first, *Fenton.*

ye should walk in it: . . . to behave exactly, *Berkeley* . . . in its sphere you should be ordering your behavior, *Wuest* . . . live in love, *TNT.*

2 John 7

3906.8 verb 2pl subj pres act	**3617.1** conj	**4044.7** adj nom pl masc	**3969.2** adj nom pl masc	**1511.1** verb indic aor act
περιπατῆτε˙	7. ὅτι	πολλοὶ	πλάνοι	ʻ εἰσῆλθον
peripatēte	*hoti*	*polloi*	*planoi*	*eisēlthon*
you might walk.	Because	many	deceivers	entered

7.a.**Txt:** 018K,020L 025P,byz.
Var: 01ℵ,03B,Weis,Sod UBS/☆

1814.1 verb indic aor act	**1519.1** prep	**3450.6** art acc sing masc	**2862.4** noun acc sing masc	**3450.7** art nom pl masc	**3231.1** partic
[a☆ ἐξῆλθον]	εἰς	τὸν	κόσμον,	οἱ	μὴ
exēlthon	*eis*	*ton*	*kosmon*	*hoi*	*mē*
[went]	into	the	world,	the	not

3533.5 verb nom pl masc part pres act	**2400.3** name acc masc	**5382.4** name acc masc	**2048.42** verb sing part pres mid	**1706.1** prep
ὁμολογοῦντες	Ἰησοῦν	Χριστὸν	ἐρχόμενον	ἐν
homologountes	*Iēsoun*	*Christon*	*erchomenon*	*en*
confessing	Jesus	Christ	coming	in

4418.3 noun dat sing fem	**3642.4** dem-pron nom sing masc	**1498.4** verb 3sing indic pres act	**3450.5** art nom sing masc	**3969.1** adj nom sing masc	**2504.1** conj
σαρκί˙	οὗτός	ἐστιν	ὁ	πλάνος	καὶ
sarki	*houtos*	*estin*	*ho*	*planos*	*kai*
flesh,	this	is	the	deceiver	and

3450.5 art nom sing masc	**497.1** noun nom sing masc	**984.1** verb 2pl pres act	**1431.8** prs-pron acc pl masc	**2419.1** conj	**3231.1** partic
ὁ	ἀντίχριστος.	8. βλέπετε	ἑαυτούς,	ἵνα	μὴ
ho	*antichristos*	*blepete*	*heautous*	*hina*	*mē*
the	antichrist.	See to	yourselves,	that	not

8.a.**Txt:** 018K,020L 025P,byz.
Var: 01ℵ-corr,02A,03B 33,it.sa.bo.Lach,Treg Alf,Word,Tisc,We/Ho Weis,Sod,UBS/☆

616.15 verb 1pl subj aor act	**616.32** verb 2pl subj aor act	**3614.17** rel-pron pl neu	**2021.14** verb 1pl indic aor mid
ʻ ἀπολέσωμεν.	[a☆ ἀπολέσητε]	ἃ	ʻ εἰργασάμεθα,
apolesōmen	*apolesēte*	*ha*	*eirgasametha*
we may lose	[you may lose]	what things	we achieved,

8.b.**Txt:** 03B,025P,sa.byz.
Var: 01ℵ,02A,044,33 81,323,630,1241,1505 1739,2495,Tisc,Sod

2021.23 verb 2pl indic aor mid	**233.2** conj	**3272.3** noun acc sing masc	**3994.3** adj acc sing masc	**612.7** verb 1pl subj aor act
[b εἰργάσασθε,]	ἀλλὰ	μισθὸν	πλήρη	ʻ ἀπολάβωμεν.
eirgasasthe	*alla*	*misthon*	*plērē*	*apolabōmen*
[you achieved]	but	a reward	full	we may receive.

8.c.**Txt:** 018K,020L 025P,byz.
Var: 01ℵ-corr,02A,03B 33,it.sa.bo.Lach,Treg Alf,Word,Tisc,We/Ho Weis,Sod,UBS/☆

612.12 verb 2pl subj aor act	**3820.6** adj nom sing masc	**3450.5** art nom sing masc	**3707.3** verb nom sing masc part pres act
[c☆ ἀπολάβητε.]	9. πᾶς	ὁ	ʻ παραβαινων,
apolabēte	*pas*	*ho*	*parabainōn*
[you may receive.]	All	who	transgressing,

9.a.**Txt:** 018K,020L 025P,byz.Sod
Var: 01ℵ,02A,03B,Lach Treg,Alf,Word,Tisc We/Ho,Weis,UBS/☆

4113.3 verb nom sing masc part pres act	**2504.1** conj	**3231.1** partic	**3176.10** verb nom sing masc part pres act	**1706.1** prep	**3450.11** art dat sing fem
[a☆ προάγων]	καὶ	μὴ	μένων	ἐν	τῇ
proagōn	*kai*	*mē*	*menōn*	*en*	*tē*
[going forward]	and	not	continuing	in	the

9.b.**Txt:** 018K,020L 025P,byz.bo.
Var: 01ℵ,02A,03B,33 sa.Lach,Treg,Alf,Word Tisc,We/Ho,Weis,Sod UBS/☆

1316.3 noun dat sing fem	**3450.2** art gen sing	**5382.2** name gen masc	**2296.4** noun acc sing masc	**3620.2** partic	**2174.4** verb 3sing indic pres act
διδαχῇ	ʻb τοῦ	Χριστοῦ, ʼ	θεὸν	οὐκ	ἔχει˙
didachē	*tou*	*Christou*	*theon*	*ouk*	*echei*
teaching	of the	Christ,	God	not	has.

3450.5 art nom sing masc	**3176.10** verb nom sing masc part pres act	**1706.1** prep	**3450.11** art dat sing fem	**1316.3** noun dat sing fem	**3450.2** art gen sing
ὁ	μένων	ἐν	τῇ	διδαχῇ	τοῦ
ho	*menōn*	*en*	*tē*	*didachē*	*tou*
The	abiding	in	the	teaching	of the

7. There is a reason the explanation of verses 5 and 6 was necessary. Many deceivers had appeared, hoping to take advantage of the hospitality and love shown by unsuspecting Christians. Believers are indeed to love one another, but they must love discriminately.

These false teachers had already spread out into the world and posed a serious threat to the truth. John provided a test by which to detect such deceivers. These men did not acknowledge that Jesus Christ came in the flesh. They represented early gnosticism, a heresy which started from the position that all physical matter is inherently evil. The Gnostics could not accept a genuine Incarnation, in which God became man and took on human flesh. So John selected this key doctrine as the test of the false teacher. Anyone who denied the Incarnation was a representative of the deceiver par excellence, an antichrist who opposed the true Christ with an alternative message.

8. Here in verse 8 we find the first command in the letter: a warning to beware, to be on guard. This serves as the focus of John's message. *Blepete* is present tense and demands continual watchfulness to prevent disaster. Its plural form shows that both the woman and her household needed to watch themselves, to keep from being led astray by false teachers.

The purpose of John's warning was to prevent two harmful results from taking place. First, he wanted to forestall the destruction of his work. *Eirgasametha* carries the idea of work that involves labor and exertion; the people who had brought the gospel invested much time and energy in the task of winning converts such as the family addressed in this letter, and John did not want that work to be destroyed. He used a word that means to ruin or make useless; it is also used to describe the fate of unbelievers who perish eternally. Second, John did not want these believers to lose their rewards. His words do not suggest that they will lose everything, but they may fail to receive their full wages.

9. The next verse lays down general principles which explain the importance of the issues. Even though the men who came asking for hospitality all claimed to be representatives of the gospel, not all of them deserved that status.

He began with a negative statement. Any person who showed certain characteristics was a person who did not have God. Such a person kept running forward, adding his own ideas to the teachings of Christ. The Gnostic teachers loved to boast of the hidden truths of salvation which they alone could reveal. They showed no desire to remain "in the doctrine (teaching) of Christ." Whether this phrase refers to the things which Christ taught or the things which His apostles taught about Him, these deceivers refused to stay within the framework of the original gospel. They insisted on adding their own concepts. John's verdict on all such people: they do not have God.

7. For many deceivers are entered into the world: For the world is becoming full of, *Phillips* . . . there are many impostors, *TCNT* . . . Many false teachers, *Norlie* . . . went forth, *Wuest* . . . have gone out, *Berkeley.*

who confess not: They won't admit, *SEB* . . . do not agree, *Wuest.*

that Jesus Christ is come in the flesh: . . . as having come incarnated, *Berkeley* . . . came as a human being, *TNT* . . . sphere of flesh, *Wuest* . . . really became man, *Phillips.*

This is a deceiver and an antichrist: . . . the misleader and the antagonist of Christ, *Fenton* . . . the very spirit of deceit, *Phillips* . . . what I call the work of the impostors, *Noli.*

8. Look to yourselves: Ever be keeping a watchful eye upon, *Wuest* . . . Look out for, *Berkeley* . . . Take care of, *Phillips.*

that we lose not those things which we have wrought: Don't lose the reward, *SEB* . . . so you may not lose the results of, *Berkeley* . . . that which you have worked for, *Adams* . . . that we are working for, *Laubach* . . . the things we accomplish, *Wuest.*

but that we receive a full reward: . . . instead, make sure of a full reward, *Berkeley* . . . but may receive full wages, *Darby* . . . you may be getting full wages, *Concordant* . . . but persevere till God gives you your reward, *Phillips.*

9. Whosoever transgresseth, and abideth not in the doctrine of Christ: Everybody who goes beyond, *Adams* . . . Whoever wanders away, *Noli* . . . The man who is so "advanced" that he is not content with what Christ taught, *Phillips* . . . Whoever assumes leadership, and does not remain in the doctrine, *Berkeley* . . . beyond the limits [of true doctrine] and does not remain in the aforementioned teaching with reference to the Christ, *Wuest.*

hath not God: . . . does not possess God, *Wuest* . . . has repudiated God, *Noli* . . . has in fact no God, *Phillips.*

He that abideth in the doctrine of Christ: The one who remains, *Wuest* . . . keeps moving in the sphere of, *Berkeley* . . . bases his life on Christ's teaching, *Phillips.*

5382.2 name gen masc	**3642.4** dem-pron nom sing masc	**2504.1** conj	**3450.6** art acc sing masc	**3824.4** noun acc sing masc	**2504.1** conj
Χριστοῦ,	οὗτος	καὶ	τὸν	πατέρα	καὶ
Christou	*houtos*	*kai*	*ton*	*patera*	*kai*
Christ,	this	both	the	Father	and

3450.6 art acc sing masc	**5048.4** noun acc sing masc	**2174.4** verb 3sing indic pres act	**1479.1** conj	**4948.3** indef-pron nom sing	**2048.34** verb 3sing indic pres mid
τὸν	υἱὸν	ἔχει.	**10.** εἴ	τις	ἔρχεται
ton	*huion*	*echei*	*ei*	*tis*	*erchetai*
the	Son	has.	If	anyone	comes

4242.1 prep	**5050.4** prs-pron acc 2pl	**2504.1** conj	**3642.12** dem-pron acc sing fem	**3450.12** art acc sing fem	**1316.4** noun acc sing fem	**3620.3** partic
πρὸς	ὑμᾶς,	καὶ	ταύτην	τὴν	διδαχὴν	οὐ
pros	*humas*	*kai*	*tautēn*	*tēn*	*didachēn*	*ou*
to	you,	and	this	the	teaching	not

5179.2 verb 3sing indic pres act	**3231.1** partic	**2956.1** verb 2pl pres act	**840.6** prs-pron acc sing masc	**1519.1** prep	**3477.4** noun acc sing fem
φέρει,	μὴ	λαμβάνετε	αὐτὸν	εἰς	οἰκίαν,
pherei	*mē*	*lambanete*	*auton*	*eis*	*oikian*
does bring,	not	do receive	him	into	house,

2504.1 conj	**5299.11** verb inf pres act	**840.4** prs-pron dat sing	**3231.1** partic	**2978.2** verb 2pl pres act	**3450.5** art nom sing masc	**1056.1** conj
καὶ	χαίρειν	αὐτῷ	μὴ	λέγετε·	**11.** ὁ	ʻ γὰρ
kai	*chairein*	*autō*	*mē*	*legete*	*ho*	*gar*
and	To rejoice!	to him	not	say;	the	for

2978.15 verb nom sing masc part pres act	**2978.15** verb nom sing masc part pres act	**1056.1** conj	**840.4** prs-pron dat sing	**5299.11** verb inf pres act
λέγων	[☆ λέγων	γὰρ]	αὐτῷ	χαίρειν,
legōn	*legōn*	*gar*	*autō*	*chairein*
saying	[saying	for]	to him	To rejoice!

2814.1 verb 3sing indic pres act	**3450.4** art dat pl	**2024.6** noun dat pl neu	**840.3** prs-pron gen sing	**3450.4** art dat pl	**4050.5** adj dat pl
κοινωνεῖ	τοῖς	ἔργοις	αὐτοῦ	τοῖς	πονηροῖς.
koinōnei	*tois*	*ergois*	*autou*	*tois*	*ponērois*
shares	in the	works	his	the	evil.

4044.17 adj pl neu	**2174.17** verb nom sing masc part pres act	**5050.3** prs-pron dat 2pl	**1119.5** verb inf pres act	**3620.2** partic
12. Πολλὰ	ἔχων	ὑμῖν	γράφειν,	οὐκ
Polla	*echōn*	*humin*	*graphein*	*ouk*
Many things	having	to you	to write,	not

1007.12 verb 1sing indic aor pass	**1007.18** verb 1sing indic aor pass	**1217.2** prep	**5325.1** noun gen sing masc	**2504.1** conj
ʻ ἠβουλήθην	[a☆ ἐβουλήθην]	διὰ	χάρτου	καὶ
ēboulēthēn	*eboulēthēn*	*dia*	*chartou*	*kai*
I would	[idem]	with	paper	and

3158.1 adj gen sing neu	**233.2** conj	**1666.1** verb 1sing indic pres act	**2048.23** verb inf aor act	**1090.63** verb inf aor mid	**4242.1** prep
μέλανος·	ἀλλὰ	ἐλπίζω	ʻ ἐλθεῖν	[b☆ γενέσθαι]	πρὸς
melanos	*alla*	*elpizō*	*elthein*	*genesthai*	*pros*
ink;	but	I hope	to come	[to be]	to

5050.4 prs-pron acc 2pl	**2504.1** conj	**4601.1** noun sing neu	**4242.1** prep	**4601.1** noun sing neu	**2953.37** verb inf aor act	**2419.1** conj
ὑμᾶς,	καὶ	στόμα	πρὸς	στόμα	λαλῆσαι,	ἵνα
humas	*kai*	*stoma*	*pros*	*stoma*	*lalēsai*	*hina*
you,	and	mouth	to	mouth	to speak,	that

12.a.**Txt:** byz.
Var: 01ℵ,02A,03B 018K,020L,025P,Lach Treg,Alf,Word,Tisc We/Ho,Weis,Sod UBS/☆

12.b.**Txt:** 018K,020L 025P,byz.sa.
Var: 01ℵ,02A,03B,33 Lach,Treg,Alf,Word Tisc,We/Ho,Weis,Sod UBS/☆

The verse moves on to state the positive side of the contrast. One who remains within the boundaries of the original teachings of Christ is the one who truly has God. In fact, he has both the Son and the Father (cf. 1 John 2:23,24).

he hath both the Father and the Son: . . . this one possesses both, *Wuest* . . . as his God, *Phillips.*

10. John applied the general command to the particular situation which his friend now faced. The form of "if" used assumes that the sentence is a statement of reality. False teachers actually were coming to this home, men who did not carry with them the genuine teaching of Christ. When this happened, John's command was clear. Do not receive them! The present tense suggests that the lady may have been welcoming such people indiscriminately in the past, so John called on her to stop doing so. She was not to bring them into her home, and she was not to provide them with the hospitality and help that went with a formal greeting in that culture.

10. If there come any unto you: In case anyone approaches you, *Berkeley* . . . If any teacher comes to you, *Phillips.*

and bring not this doctrine: . . . who is disloyal to what Christ taught, *Phillips* . . . is not bearing, *Wuest* . . . this teaching, *SEB.*

receive him not into [your] house: . . . do not receive him in your home, *Berkeley* . . . don't have him inside, *Phillips.*

neither bid him God speed: Do not even say hello to him, *NLT* . . . And stop giving him greeting, *Wuest* . . . or wish him well, *TCNT* . . . nor wish Him success, *Wilson* . . . nor extend him your greeting, *Berkeley.*

11. John concluded by giving the reason it is wrong to provide loving hospitality for such people. More is involved than mere obedience to the command to love. It may seem harmless to speak words of greeting. But when such a greeting becomes participation in the evil deeds of an apostate, it is wrong. *Koinōnei* means "to share, participate" and implies close union and active participation, not just a superficial involvement. John forbade any variety of love that makes a believer a coworker with a false teacher. Opening one's home to such a person simply provided a heretic with a base for operations.

The overall message is clear. Christians are expected to display love for one another, but that love must be tempered by discriminating regard for truth. Harboring apostates is never approved by God.

11. For he that biddeth him God speed: . . . who gives him a friendly greeting, *Norlie* . . . who bids him prosperity, *Swann* . . . he who wishes him success, *Campbell* . . . bids him welcome, *Berkeley.*

is partaker of his evil deeds: . . . unless you want to share in the evil that he is doing, *Phillips* . . . makes himself a sharer of those, *Berkeley* . . . partakes in his wicked works, *Darby* . . . is a partner in his works which are pernicious, *Wuest* . . . himself participates in his wicked doings, *Fenton* . . . shares in his evil works, *Swann* . . . his wicked acts, *Concordant.*

12. The epistle comes to a close in almost the same way as 3 John. John had many items he would have liked to discuss with his friend, topics not specified in the text. But when he composed the letter, he decided not to pursue them in writing.

He mentioned his writing materials, paper and ink. The letter was probably written on a single sheet of papyrus, the most common writing material of the time, manufactured from the stem of the papyrus reed. The ink was made of lampblack or soot mixed with water and gum, then hardened into sticks, to be cut and moistened for use as needed.

Rather than trust all his thoughts to writing, John hoped to make a visit to the household. At that time they would be able to talk face-to-face. The literal Greek idiom "mouth to mouth" is even more intimate than the English rendering. The result of this personal

12. Having many things to write unto you: Although I have, *Berkeley* . . . I have much to communicate to you, *Wade* . . . I have a lot that I could write to you, *Phillips.*

I would not [write] with paper and ink: I would rather not use, *Berkeley* . . . did not, after giving the matter mature consideration, desire to do so with, *Wuest.*

but I trust to come unto you: . . . but I hope to come, *Fenton, TNT* . . . I am expecting to come, *Concordant* . . . am hoping to be present with you, *Wuest* . . . but I hope to have a visit with you, *Berkeley.*

and speak face to face: . . . and talk with you, *Berkeley* . . . and speak by word of mouth, *Fenton.*

3450.9 art nom sing fem	5315.1 noun nom sing fem	2231.2 prs-pron gen 1pl	1498.10 verb 3sing subj pres act	3997.32 verb nom sing fem part perf mid
ἡ	χαρὰ	ἡμῶν	⸀ᾖ	πεπληρωμένη·
hē	chara	hēmōn	ē	peplērōmenē
the	joy	our	may be	having been fulfilled.

3997.32 verb nom sing fem part perf mid	1498.10 verb 3sing subj pres act	776.2 verb 3sing indic pres mid	4622.4 prs-pron acc 2sing
[☆ πεπληρωμένη	ᾖ.]	13. Ἀσπάζεταί	σε
peplērōmenē	ē	Aspazetai	se
[having been fulfilled	may be]	Greets	you

13.a.**Txt:** 018K,020L,byz. **Var:** 01ℵ,02A,03B,025P 33,it.sa.bo.Gries,Lach Treg,Alf,Word,Tisc We/Ho,Weis,Sod UBS/☆

13.b.**Txt:** 020L,Steph **Var:** Elzev,Gries,Lach Word,Tisc,We/Ho,Weis Sod,UBS/☆

3450.17 art pl neu	4891.4 noun pl neu	3450.10 art gen sing fem	78.2 noun gen sing fem	4622.2 prs-pron gen 2sing	3450.10 art gen sing fem
τὰ	τέκνα	τῆς	ἀδελφῆς	σου	τῆς
ta	tekna	tēs	adelphēs	sou	tēs
the	children	of the	sister	your	the

1575.7 adj gen sing fem	279.1 intrj	2464.2 name gen masc	1976.1 noun nom sing fem	1202.4 num ord nom sing fem
ἐκλεκτῆς.	⸂a ἀμήν. ⸃	⸂b Ἰωάννου	ἐπιστολὴ	δευτέρα. ⸃
eklektēs	amēn	Iōannou	epistolē	deutera
elect.	Amen.	Of John	epistle	second.

encounter would be an opportunity for both to experience a thoroughly joyful meeting. The combination of perfect tense and a form of the verb "to be" pictures a joy that is brought to fullness, then continues to be full to the point of overflowing. The same construction appears in 1 John 1:4.

that our joy may be full: . . . our happiness may be complete, *Berkeley* . . . our joy, having been filled completely full, might persist in that state of fullness through present time, *Wuest* . . . and our joy will be all the greater, *Greber* . . . so that you may be very happy, *Beck* . . . for then our joy will be complete, *Barclay* . . . your joy may be complete, *Kliest* . . . so that your joy might run over, *Klingensmith* . . . and how we shall enjoy that! *Phillips* . . . That will make us very happy, *Everyday* . . . that your happiness may be complete, *Goodspeed.*

13. In John's closing statement, he passed on greetings from the woman's nieces and nephews. "The children of thy elect sister greet thee." There is no greeting from the sister herself, who may have been absent or deceased. Some commentators have taken the position that the verse describes members of a sister church, probably the one where John resided. In any case, the "sister" is known as a "chosen" one, called by God to be a member of His family.

This epistle offers a powerful corrective to the tendency to overlook the importance of truth in our zeal to show love.

13. The children of thy elect sister greet thee. Amen: There greet you the born-ones of your sister, the selected-out one, *Wuest* . . . of your beloved sister, *Campbell* . . . your noble sister, who is of God's selection, *BB* . . . Your sister's children send their love, *Phillips* . . . thy sister, Elect, *Confraternity* . . . whom God has chosen, *Beck* . . . of your chosen sister send you their love, *Everyday* . . . chosen by God, send you their good wishes, *Barclay* . . . send their hearty greetings, *Greber* . . . salute thee, *Noyes* . . . sends you regards, *Fenton* . . . send you greetings, *Berkeley* . . . wish to be remembered to you, *Williams, Goodspeed* . . . Grace be with you, *Murdock.*

THE THIRD EPISTLE OF
JOHN

Expanded Interlinear
Textual Critical Apparatus
Verse-by-Verse Commentary
Various Versions

1976.1 noun nom sing fem	2464.2 name gen masc	4995.4 num ord nom sing fem
Ἐπιστολὴ	Ἰωάννου	Τρίτη
Epistolē	*Iōannou*	*Tritē*
Epistle	of John	Third

Textual Apparatus

3450.5 art nom sing masc	4104.3 adj comp nom sing masc	1043.1 name dat masc	3450.3 art dat sing	27.2 adj dat sing
1:1. Ὁ	πρεσβύτερος	Γαΐῳ	τῷ	ἀγαπητῷ,
Ho	*presbuteros*	*Gaiō*	*tō*	*agapētō*
The	elder	to Gaius	the	beloved,

3614.6 rel-pron acc sing masc	1466.1 prs-pron nom 1sing	25.5 verb 1sing indic pres act	1706.1 prep	223.3 noun dat sing fem	27.5 adj voc sing masc
ὃν	ἐγὼ	ἀγαπῶ	ἐν	ἀληθείᾳ.	2. Ἀγαπητέ,
hon	*egō*	*agapō*	*en*	*alētheia*	*Agapēte*
whom	I	love	in	truth.	Beloved,

3875.1 prep	3820.4 adj gen pl	2153.1 verb 1sing indic pres mid	4622.4 prs-pron acc 2sing	2117.3 verb inf pres mid
περὶ	πάντων	εὔχομαί	σε	εὐοδοῦσθαι
peri	*pantōn*	*euchomai*	*se*	*euodousthai*
concerning	all things	I wish	you	to prosper

2504.1 conj	5039.9 verb inf pres act	2503.1 conj	2117.1 verb 3sing indic pres mid	4622.2 prs-pron gen 2sing	3450.9 art nom sing fem
καὶ	ὑγιαίνειν,	καθὼς	εὐοδοῦταί	σου	ἡ
kai	*hugiainein*	*kathōs*	*euodoutai*	*sou*	*hē*
and	to be in health,	even as	prospers	your	the

5425.1 noun nom sing fem	5299.15 verb 1sing indic aor pass	1056.1 conj	3003.1 adv	2048.47 verb gen pl masc part pres mid
ψυχή.	3. ἐχάρην	γὰρ	λίαν	ἐρχομένων
psuchē	*echarēn*	*gar*	*lian*	*erchomenōn*
soul.	I rejoiced	for	exceedingly,	coming

79.7 noun gen pl masc	2504.1 conj	3113.11 verb gen pl masc part pres act	4622.2 prs-pron gen 2sing	3450.11 art dat sing fem
ἀδελφῶν	καὶ	μαρτυρούντων	σου	τῇ
adelphōn	*kai*	*marturountōn*	*sou*	*tē*
brothers	and	bearing witness	of your	the

223.3 noun dat sing fem	2503.1 conj	4622.1 prs-pron nom 2sing	1706.1 prep	223.3 noun dat sing fem	3906.3 verb 2sing indic pres act
ἀληθείᾳ,	καθὼς	σὺ	ἐν	ἀληθείᾳ	περιπατεῖς.
alētheia	*kathōs*	*su*	*en*	*alētheia*	*peripateis*
truth,	even as	you	in	truth	walk.

3156.1 adj comp acc sing fem	3642.2 dem-pron gen pl	3620.2 partic	2174.1 verb 1sing pres act	5315.4 noun acc sing fem	2419.1 conj
4. μειζοτέραν	τούτων	οὐκ	ἔχω	χαράν,	ἵνα
meizoteran	*toutōn*	*ouk*	*echō*	*charan*	*hina*
Greater	than these things	not	I have	joy,	that

4.a.**Var:** 02A,03B 04C-org,Lach,Treg,Alf Word,Tisc,We/Ho,Weis Sod,UBS/☆

189.1 verb 1sing pres act	3450.17 art pl neu	1684.12 adj pl neu	4891.4 noun pl neu	1706.1 prep	3450.11 art dat sing fem	223.3 noun dat sing fem
ἀκούω	τὰ	ἐμὰ	τέκνα	ἐν	[a☆+ τῇ]	ἀληθείᾳ
akouō	*ta*	*ema*	*tekna*	*en*	*tē*	*alētheia*
I hear	the	my	children	in	[the]	truth

THE THIRD EPISTLE OF
JOHN

1. Even though 3 John is a short book, it teaches some crucial concepts of Christian life. As in his other letters, John remained anonymous, introducing himself simply as "the elder," referring both to his age and his status as the last surviving apostle.

The Gaius who received this letter remains unknown apart from the letter itself. The verse emphasizes John's love for Gaius. Even the word "I" is emphatic.

John loved Gaius "in the truth." The repeated use of "truth" here, as in his other writings, shows that truth was a central idea in the apostle's thoughts. He repeated the phrase both with the Greek definite article (verses 3,4,8,12) and without it (verses 1 and 3). Secular writings often used the phrase as a synonym for "truly," but the usage in 2 and 3 John suggests that here it refers to the specific truth that comes from God.

2. John used verses 2-4 to compliment Gaius for Christian virtues; the rest of the letter encouraged him to keep displaying those same virtues.

It opens with the warm greeting "beloved," which begins almost every paragraph (verses 2,5,11). Then John shared his prayer for Gaius—that he would be as prosperous in all areas of life as he had been in his spiritual life. The word "prosper" carries images of a successful journey, while the other verb describes good physical health.

3. John knew of Gaius through the reports of traveling Christians who had passed through Gaius' hometown and brought word to John's location (traditionally Ephesus). These travelers consistently testified that Gaius was living in a way that matched the pattern set forth by God's truth. The verse closes with an added confirmation. The reality of the man's life matched the reports, for he actually walked in the truth.

4. Nothing gave John greater joy than to hear that his spiritual children continued to walk in line with the truth of the gospel. "My children" is emphatic and suggests that Gaius may have come to Christ through the ministry of John. And John wanted all the believers within his family to live godly lives.

Various Versions

1. The elder unto the well-beloved Gaius: The Presbyter, *Noli* . . . The old man to his friend, *Fenton* . . . My dear friend, *Laubach* . . . to the esteemed, *Berkeley.*

whom I love in the truth: . . . whom, as for myself, I love in the sphere of the truth, *Wuest* . . . with sincere love, *Phillips.*

2. Beloved, I wish above all things that thou mayest prosper and be in health: My heartfelt prayer for you, my very dear friend, is that you may be as healthy and prosperous, *Phillips* . . . I pray that you may have good success, *Laubach.*

even as thy soul prospereth: . . . in the same way that your soul is prospering, *Adams.*

3. For I rejoiced greatly: I felt extremely happy, *Berkeley* . . . I was delighted, *Phillips.*

when the brethren came: . . . constantly coming, *Wuest* . . . brothers arrived, *Phillips.*

and testified of the truth that is in thee: . . . and bearing witness of, *Wuest* . . . and testified to your fidelity to the Truth, *TCNT* . . . and spoke so highly of the sincerity of your life, *Phillips.*

even as thou walkest in the truth: . . . obviously you are living in, *Phillips* . . . as for you, in the sphere of the truth you are conducting yourself, *Wuest* . . . as indeed you are living the true life, *Berkeley.*

4. I have no greater joy: Nothing pleases me more than, *Adams* . . . Nothing affords me more enjoyment, *Berkeley* . . . no greater satisfaction, *Wade.*

than to hear that my children walk in truth: . . . are habitually ordering their behavior, *Wuest* . . . conduct themselves, *Fenton* . . . follow the truth, *Laubach.*

3906.11 verb part pres act	27.5 adj voc sing masc	3964.1 adj sing	4020.4 verb 2sing indic pres act	3614.16 rel-pron sing neu
περιπατοῦντα.	5. Ἀγαπητέ,	πιστὸν	ποιεῖς	ὃ
peripatounta	*Agapēte*	*piston*	*poieis*	*ho*
walking.	Beloved,	faithfully	you do	whatever

1430.1 partic	2021.16 verb 2sing subj aor mid	1519.1 prep	3450.8 art acc pl masc	79.9 noun acc pl masc
ἐὰν	ἐργάσῃ	εἰς	τοὺς	ἀδελφοὺς
ean	*ergasē*	*eis*	*tous*	*adelphous*
	you may have accomplished	toward	the	brothers

5.a.**Txt:** 018K,020L 025P,byz.
Var: 01ℵ,02A,03B,04C Lach,Treg,Alf,Word Tisc,We/Ho,Weis,Sod UBS/☆

2504.1 conj	1519.1 prep	3450.8 art acc pl masc	3642.17 dem-pron sing neu	3443.5 adj acc pl masc	3614.7 rel-pron nom pl masc
καὶ	‘ εἰς	τοὺς	[a☆ τοῦτο]	ξένους,	6. οἳ
kai	*eis*	*tous*	*touto*	*xenous*	*hoi*
and	toward	the	[this]	strangers,	who

3113.18 verb 3pl indic aor act	4622.2 prs-pron gen 2sing	3450.11 art dat sing fem	26.3 noun dat sing fem	1783.1 prep
ἐμαρτύρησάν	σου	τῇ	ἀγάπῃ	ἐνώπιον
emarturēsan	*sou*	*tē*	*agapē*	*enōpion*
witnessed	of your	the	love	before

1564.1 noun fem	3614.8 rel-pron acc pl masc	2544.1 adv	4020.51 verb 2sing indic fut act	4170.5 verb nom sing masc part aor act
ἐκκλησίας·	οὓς	καλῶς	ποιήσεις	προπέμψας
ekklēsias	*hous*	*kalōs*	*poiēseis*	*propempsas*
assembly	whom	well	you will do	having set forward

512.1 adv	3450.2 art gen sing	2296.2 noun gen sing masc	5065.1 prep	1056.1 conj	3450.2 art gen sing	3549.3 noun gen sing neu
ἀξίως	τοῦ	θεοῦ·	7. ὑπὲρ	γὰρ	τοῦ	ὀνόματος
axiōs	*tou*	*theou*	*huper*	*gar*	*tou*	*onomatos*
worthily		of God;	on behalf of	for	the	name

7.a.**Txt:** 02A,04C,018K 020L,025P,byz.Weis Sod
Var: 01ℵ,03B,Lach Treg,Tisc,We/Ho UBS/☆

1814.1 verb indic aor act	1814.41 verb 3pl indic aor act	3235.6 num card neu	2956.9 verb nom pl masc part pres act	570.3 prep
‘ ἐξῆλθον	[a ἐξῆλθαν]	μηδὲν	λαμβάνοντες	ἀπὸ
exēlthon	*exēlthan*	*mēden*	*lambanontes*	*apo*
they went forth,	[idem]	nothing	taking	from

7.b.**Txt:** 018K,020L 025P,byz.sa.
Var: 01ℵ,02A,03B,04C bo.Lach,Treg,Alf,Word Tisc,We/Ho,Weis,Sod UBS/☆

3450.1 art gen pl	1477.5 noun gen pl neu	1475.3 adj gen pl masc	2231.1 prs-pron nom 1pl	3631.1 partic
τῶν	‘ ἐθνῶν.	[b☆ ἐθνικῶν.]	8. ἡμεῖς	οὖν
tōn	*ethnōn*	*ethnikōn*	*hēmeis*	*oun*
the	nations.	[Gentiles.]	We	therefore

8.a.**Txt:** 04C-corr,018K 020L,025P,byz.
Var: 01ℵ,02A,03B 04C-org,33,Lach,Treg Alf,Word,Tisc,We/Ho Weis,Sod,UBS/☆

3648.4 verb 1pl indic pres act	612.3 verb inf pres act	5112.5 verb inf pres act	3450.8 art acc pl masc
ὀφείλομεν	‘ ἀπολαμβάνειν	[a☆ ὑπολαμβάνειν]	τοὺς
opheilomen	*apolambanein*	*hupolambanein*	*tous*
ought	to receive	[to welcome]	the

4955.8 dem-pron acc pl masc	2419.1 conj	4754.4 adj nom pl masc	1090.16 verb 1pl subj pres mid	3450.11 art dat sing fem
τοιούτους,	ἵνα	συνεργοὶ	γινώμεθα	τῇ
toioutous	*hina*	*sunergoi*	*ginōmetha*	*tē*
such,	that	fellow workers	we may be	with the

9.a.**Var:** 01ℵ-org,02A 03B,048,sa.bo.Lach Treg,Alf,Word,Tisc We/Ho,Weis,Sod UBS/☆

223.3 noun dat sing fem	1119.7 verb 1sing indic aor act	4948.10 indef-pron sing neu	3450.11 art dat sing fem	1564.3 noun dat sing fem
ἀληθείᾳ.	9. Ἔγραψά	[a☆+ τι]	τῇ	ἐκκλησίᾳ·
alētheia	*Egrapsa*	*ti*	*tē*	*ekklēsia*
truth.	I wrote	[something]	to the	assembly;

5. John next encouraged Gaius to maintain the specific virtue of hospitality. The opening phrase confirms the fact that God approved the ministry Gaius had already carried out.

John used two words to describe the deeds of Gaius. *Poieis* simply states that he actually carried out tasks, and the present tense shows that hospitality was a habit with him. *Ergasē* adds the idea of wearying labor, with an aorist form that sums up Gaius' whole history of service. His home had been open to Christian brothers, even those who were strangers to him.

Hospitality was one of the accepted virtues of the ancient world, as well as a command of Scripture (Titus 1:8; Hebrews 13:2). Christian workers traveled long distances, and public inns were expensive and primitive. So the Early Church developed an informal hospitality network, aided by believers' generosity.

6. More than one itinerant Christian had confirmed not only the truth (verse 3) but the love displayed by Gaius. *Agapē* means more than emotion or words; it is action.

The verb changes to future tense—"thou shalt do well" if you continue to show such love. This common phrase was a polite idiom like the English *please.* Gaius should continue to help those who came to him. *Propempsas* includes receiving a person, entertaining him for the night, and providing the supplies needed for the next stage of the journey. Gaius was to do this in a manner worthy of God, welcoming them in a manner appropriate for one who represents the Lord.

7. John explained the reasons these brothers deserved help. Their purpose was worthy; they went forth for the sake of the Name, either the name of Christ or of God the Father. They were missionaries, proclaiming the glorious person of God.

In addition, they did not take money from their hearers, as the typical religion-peddlers of the day did.

8. This verse states a principle: believers must support such men. The unsaved need not pay for the gospel; instead, Christians are obligated to undertake the task of providing protection and resources. Such a ministry allows believers to become fellow workers with the truth. God's truth moves forward, and Christians have the privilege of sharing in the progress.

9. This verse marks an abrupt shift in mood, descending with a jolt to deal with a difficult situation. John had written a prior letter, now lost, to Gaius' church.

Surprisingly, the letter was rejected. Opposition was led by Diotrephes, whose aristocratic name meant "nurtured by Zeus." John

5. Beloved, thou doest faithfully whatsoever thou doest: Beloved friend, you are acting faithfully when you do anything, *Berkeley* . . . You practise faith, friend, when you bestow benefits, *Fenton* . . . You are acting loyally, my friend, *Williams C.K.* . . . you are doing a work of faith, whatever you are performing, *Wuest.*

to the brethren, and to strangers: . . . for the brothers, and specially for the strangers, *Berkeley.*

6. Which have borne witness of thy charity before the church: . . . bore testimony of your love before the assembly, *Wuest* . . . They have testified before the church about your friendship, *Berkeley.*

whom if thou bring forward on their journey after a godly sort, thou shalt do well: . . . whom you are doing well to provide with the necessities of travel...on their journey in a manner worthy of God, *Wuest* . . . to forward them on their journey in a way befitting God's service, *Berkeley* . . . on their trip in a manner that is worthy of God, *Adams.*

7. Because that for his name's sake they went forth: . . . for the sake of that Name, *Fenton* . . . on behalf of that Name they have gone out, *Berkeley* . . . they have started out, *Montgomery.*

taking nothing of the Gentiles: . . . without accepting anything from, *Berkeley* . . . taking not even one thing from the pagans, *Wuest* . . . from their heathen converts, *TCNT* . . . they refused help from any one except Christians, *Laubach.*

8. We therefore ought to receive such: Hence we ought to support such, *Montgomery* . . . as a moral obligation to underwrite such as these, *Wuest* . . . we owe it to support such as these, *Swann* . . . ought to entertain such, *Wilson, Wade* . . . to show hospitality to such men, *Williams.*

that we might be fellowhelpers to the truth: . . . in order to be...in the truth, *Berkeley* . . . fellow workers, *Wuest.*

9. I wrote unto the church: I have written, *Berkeley* . . . the assembly, *Wuest.*

233.1 conj	3450.5 art nom sing masc	5220.1 verb nom sing masc part pres act	840.1 prs-pron gen pl	1355.1 name nom masc
ἀλλ'	ὁ	φιλοπρωτεύων	αὐτῶν	Διοτρεφὴς
all'	*ho*	*philoprōteuōn*	*autōn*	*Diotrephēs*
but	the	loving to be first	of them	Diotrephes,

3620.2 partic	1911.1 verb 3sing indic pres mid	2231.4 prs-pron acc 1pl	1217.2 prep	3642.17 dem-pron sing neu	1430.1 partic
οὐκ	ἐπιδέχεται	ἡμᾶς.	**10.** διὰ	τοῦτο,	ἐὰν
ouk	*epidechetai*	*hēmas*	*dia*	*touto*	*ean*
not	receives	us.	On account of	this,	if

2048.6 verb 1sing subj aor act	5117.4 verb 1sing indic fut act	840.3 prs-pron gen sing	3450.17 art pl neu	2024.4 noun pl neu
ἔλθω,	ὑπομνήσω	αὐτοῦ	τὰ	ἔργα
elthō	*hupomnēsō*	*autou*	*ta*	*erga*
I come,	I will bring to remembrance	his	the	works

3614.17 rel-pron pl neu	4020.5 verb 3sing indic pres act	3030.7 noun dat pl masc	4050.5 adj dat pl	5233.1 verb nom sing masc part pres act
ἃ	ποιεῖ,	λόγοις	πονηροῖς	φλυαρῶν
ha	*poiei*	*logois*	*ponērois*	*phluarōn*
which	he does,	with words	evil	talking nonsense

2231.4 prs-pron acc 1pl	2504.1 conj	3231.1 partic	708.5 verb nom sing masc part pres mid	1894.3 prep	3642.3 dem-pron dat pl	3641.1 conj
ἡμᾶς·	καὶ	μὴ	ἀρκούμενος	ἐπὶ	τούτοις,	οὔτε
hēmas	*kai*	*mē*	*arkoumenos*	*epi*	*toutois*	*oute*
us;	and	not	being satisfied	with	these,	neither

840.5 prs-pron nom sing masc	1911.1 verb 3sing indic pres mid	3450.8 art acc pl masc	79.9 noun acc pl masc	2504.1 conj	3450.8 art acc pl masc
αὐτὸς	ἐπιδέχεται	τοὺς	ἀδελφούς,	καὶ	τοὺς
autos	*epidechetai*	*tous*	*adelphous*	*kai*	*tous*
himself	receives	the	brothers,	and	the

1007.11 verb acc pl masc part pres mid	2940.1 verb 3sing indic pres act	2504.1 conj	1523.2 prep gen	3450.10 art gen sing fem	1564.1 noun fem
βουλομένους	κωλύει,	καὶ	ἐκ	τῆς	ἐκκλησίας
boulomenous	*kōluei*	*kai*	*ek*	*tēs*	*ekklēsias*
desiring	he forbids,	and	from	the	assembly

1531.3 verb 3sing indic pres act	27.5 adj voc sing masc	3231.1 partic	3265.1 verb 2sing impr pres mid	3450.16 art sing neu	2527.7 adj sing neu
ἐκβάλλει.	**11.** Ἀγαπητέ,	μὴ	μιμοῦ	τὸ	κακὸν,
ekballei	*Agapēte*	*mē*	*mimou*	*to*	*kakon*
casts out.	Beloved,	not	do imitate	the	evil,

233.2 conj	3450.16 art sing neu	18.3 adj sing	3450.5 art nom sing masc	15.3 verb nom sing masc part pres act	1523.2 prep gen
ἀλλὰ	τὸ	ἀγαθόν.	ὁ	ἀγαθοποιῶν,	ἐκ
alla	*to*	*agathon*	*ho*	*agathopoiōn*	*ek*
but	the	good.	The	doing good,	of

3450.2 art gen sing	2296.2 noun gen sing masc	1498.4 verb 3sing indic pres act	3450.5 art nom sing masc	1156.2 conj	2525.1 verb nom sing masc part pres act
τοῦ	θεοῦ	ἐστιν·	ὁ	(a δὲ)	κακοποιῶν
tou	*theou*	*estin*	*ho*	*de*	*kakopoiōn*
	God	is;	the	but	doing evil

11.a.**Txt:** 020L,bo.Steph
Var: 01ℵ,02A,03B,04C 018K,025P,byz.Gries Lach,Treg,Alf,Word Tisc,We/Ho,Weis,Sod UBS/⋆

3620.1 partic	3571.11 verb 3sing indic perf act	3450.6 art acc sing masc	2296.4 noun acc sing masc	1210.2 name dat masc
οὐχ	ἑώρακεν	τὸν	θεόν.	**12.** Δημητρίῳ
ouch	*heōraken*	*ton*	*theon*	*Dēmētriō*
not	has seen		God.	To Demetrius

introduced him as one who loved to have preeminence, to enjoy first place. In contrast, Colossians 1:18 declares that only Christ rightly holds first place.

10. The apostle intended to make a visit and deal with the situation. Though he used the word "if," only the timing is uncertain. When John arrived, he would show Diotrephes' actions in their true light—as rebellion.

The indictment against Diotrephes falls into two categories. First, he spoke against John and his associates. *Phluarōn* pictures empty or foolish speech like a pot that boils over, throwing up a froth of bubbles. But more than mere foolishness was involved. These unjust accusations were aggressive, evil attacks. Second, Diotrephes went beyond words to actions. He refused to accept the Christian workers who came from John. He moved to prevent any other Christians in the assembly from helping the itinerants. And he expelled any who refused to be intimidated.

11. Verses 11 and 12 focus on an important point of the letter. Verse 11 gives the first command contained in the letter. In the face of opposition from Diotrephes, Gaius must have been tempted to stop helping the missionaries. So John encouraged Gaius to imitate the good, not the evil.

Agathon describes that which is morally and spiritually good. *Kakon* is a weaker word, used for something inferior, lacking the qualities it should have.

The reason for John's command is that the only source of genuine good is contact with God (1 John 2:29; 3:9; 4:7; 5:1,18). In contrast, a person with habitually bad behavior shows that he has never come to know God. John often used such terms to distinguish saved and unsaved people. Diotrephes did not show the evidence of being a regenerate man.

12. A new character abruptly appears. At the end of a discussion on the duty of hospitality and a warning to do what is right rather than following the bad example of Diotrephes, John now introduced Demetrius. The immediate purpose of the letter was evidently to introduce Demetrius as the bearer of the letter, a man worthy of Gaius' hospitality.

John provided a threefold recommendation for Demetrius who does not appear elsewhere in the New Testament. The first two testimonies are in the perfect tense, showing that he had a reputation that went back into the past. The first testimony is the general witness of those who know Demetrius. This is seconded by the testimony of the truth itself; his life matched the truth of the gospel

but Diotrephes, who loveth to have the preeminence among them: . . . the one who is fond of being the pre-eminent one among them, *Wuest* . . . who is eager to be a leader, *Norlie* . . . wants to be the head of the church himself, *Laubach* . . . likes to make himself prominent among them, *Fenton.*

receiveth us not: . . . declines to recognize us, *TCNT* . . . refuses to acknowledge my authority, *Norlie* . . . is not accepting us, *Wuest* . . . refuses to listen to me, *Williams* . . . does not accept what we say, *Swann* . . . doesn't recognize our authority, *Adams* . . . rejected us, *SEB.*

10. Wherefore, if I come, I will remember his deeds which he doeth: On this account, if I should come, I shall bring to remembrance, *Wuest* . . . I will denounce his actions, *Noli.*

prating against us with malicious words: . . . all his noisy talk against us, *Williams C.K.* . . . sneering at us with vile expressions, *Fenton* . . . talking wicked nonsense about us, *Wade* . . . in making empty charges against us with evil words, *Swann* . . . pernicious words, *Wuest* . . . in ridiculing us with his wicked tongue, *TCNT* . . . the evil words that he babbles about us! *Adams.*

and not content therewith, neither doth he himself receive the brethren: He does not stop with that, *Laubach* . . . accept the brethren, *Wuest.*

and forbiddeth them that would: . . . and those who after mature consideration desire to do so, he prevents, *Wuest* . . . he interferes with those who wish to welcome them, *Williams.*

and casteth [them] out of the church: . . . excludes them, *Wade* . . . and out of the assembly he throws them, *Wuest* . . . expels them from the assembly, *Norlie.*

11. Beloved, follow not that which is evil, but that which is good: . . . don't copy what is bad, *SEB* . . . do not follow bad examples, *Williams, Noli* . . . do not have the habit of imitating the evil, *Wuest.*

He that doeth good is of God: . . . is out of God, *Wuest.*

but he that doeth evil hath not seen God:

3113.39 verb 3sing indic perf mid	5097.3 prep	3820.4 adj gen pl	2504.1 conj	5097.2 prep	5097.3 prep
μεμαρτύρηται	ὑπὸ	πάντων,	καὶ	⸀ὑπ'	[☆ ὑπὸ]
memarturētai	*hupo*	*pantōn*	*kai*	*hup'*	*hupo*
witness has been borne	by	all,	and	by	[idem]

840.10 prs-pron gen sing fem	3450.10 art gen sing fem	223.2 noun gen sing fem	2504.1 conj	2231.1 prs-pron nom 1pl	1156.2 conj
αὐτῆς	τῆς	ἀληθείας·	καὶ	ἡμεῖς	δὲ
autēs	*tēs*	*alētheias*	*kai*	*hēmeis*	*de*
itself	the	truth;	and	we	also

12.a.**Txt:** 018K,020L 025P,byz.
Var: 01ℵ,02A,03B,04C sa.bo.Lach,Treg,Alf,Tisc We/Ho,Weis,Sod UBS/☆

3113.4 verb 1pl indic pres act	2504.1 conj	3471.6 verb 2pl indic perf act	3471.3 verb 2sing indic perf act	3617.1 conj	3450.9 art nom sing fem
μαρτυροῦμεν,	καὶ	⸀οἴδατε	[a☆ οἶδας]	ὅτι	ἡ
marturoumen	*kai*	*oidate*	*oidas*	*hoti*	*hē*
bear witness,	and	you know	[idem]	that	the

3114.1 noun nom sing fem	2231.2 prs-pron gen 1pl	225.2 adj nom sing	1498.4 verb 3sing indic pres act	4044.17 adj pl neu
μαρτυρία	ἡμῶν	ἀληθής	ἐστιν.	13. Πολλὰ
marturia	*hēmōn*	*alēthēs*	*estin*	*Polla*
witness	our	true	is.	Many things

13.a.**Txt:** 018K,020L 025P,byz.
Var: 01ℵ,02A,03B,04C sa.bo.Lach,Treg,Alf Word,Tisc,We/Ho,Weis Sod,UBS/☆

2174.42 verb indic imperf act	1119.5 verb inf pres act	1119.15 verb inf aor act	4622.3 prs-pron dat 2sing	233.1 conj	3620.3 partic
εἶχον	⸀γράφειν,	[a☆ γράψαι	σοι,]	ἀλλ'	οὐ
eichon	*graphein*	*grapsai*	*soi*	*all'*	*ou*
I had	to write,	[to write	to you,]	but	not

2286.1 verb 1sing pres act	1217.2 prep	3158.1 adj gen sing neu	2504.1 conj	2534.2 noun gen sing masc	4622.3 prs-pron dat 2sing	1119.15 verb inf aor act
θέλω	διὰ	μέλανος	καὶ	καλάμου	σοι	⸀γράψαι·
thelō	*dia*	*melanos*	*kai*	*kalamou*	*soi*	*grapsai*
I will	with	ink	and	pen	to you	to write;

13.b.**Txt:** 018K,020L 025P,byz.
Var: 01ℵ,02A,03B,04C Lach,Treg,Alf,Word Tisc,We/Ho,Weis,Sod UBS/☆

1119.5 verb inf pres act	1666.1 verb 1sing indic pres act	1156.2 conj	2091.1 adv	1481.19 verb inf aor act
[b☆ γράφειν·]	14. ἐλπίζω	δὲ	εὐθέως	⸀ἰδεῖν
graphein	*elpizō*	*de*	*eutheōs*	*idein*
[idem]	I hope	but	immediately	to see

4622.4 prs-pron acc 2sing	4622.4 prs-pron acc 2sing	1481.19 verb inf aor act	2504.1 conj	4601.1 noun sing neu	4242.1 prep	4601.1 noun sing neu
σε,	[☆ σε	ἰδεῖν,]	καὶ	στόμα	πρὸς	στόμα
se	*se*	*idein*	*kai*	*stoma*	*pros*	*stoma*
you,	[you	to see,]	and	mouth	to	mouth

2953.41 verb 1pl indic fut act	1503.1 noun nom sing fem	4622.3 prs-pron dat 2sing	776.3 verb 3pl indic pres mid	4622.4 prs-pron acc 2sing
λαλήσομεν.	Εἰρήνη	σοι.	ἀσπάζονταί	σε
lalēsomen	*Eirēnē*	*soi*	*aspazontai*	*se*
we shall speak.	Peace	to you.	Greet	you

3450.7 art nom pl masc	5224.4 adj nom pl masc	776.4 verb 2sing impr pres mid	3450.8 art acc pl masc	5224.7 adj acc pl masc	2567.1 prep	3549.2 noun sing neu
οἱ	φίλοι.	ἀσπάζου	τοὺς	φίλους	κατ'	ὄνομα.
hoi	*philoi*	*aspazou*	*tous*	*philous*	*kat'*	*onoma*
the	friends.	Greet	the	friends	by	name.

15.a.**Txt:** Steph
Var: Elzev,Gries,Lach Word,Tisc,We/Ho,Weis Sod,UBS/☆

2464.2 name gen masc	1976.1 noun nom sing fem	2498.1 adj nom sing masc	4995.4 num ord nom sing fem
⸂a Ἰωάννου	ἐπιστολὴ	καθολικὴ	τρίτη. ⸃
Iōannou	*epistolē*	*katholikē*	*tritē*
Of John	epistle	general	third.

so well that the resemblance was obvious. John offered his personal testimony as the third witness, giving assurance that Demetrius' exemplary character was still being maintained in the present. Gaius no doubt knew from past experience that John's recommendations were reliable, and Gaius could confidently offer help to Demetrius.

13. John ended the epistle quickly after he had made his request for the hospitality Demetrius needed. The closing verses of the book are remarkably similar to the end of 2 John.

Like so many writers, John had much to say, but neither the time nor inclination to put it on paper. The imperfect tense of *eichon* refers to the time when he was writing the letter and had many matters which could have been included. But when he had completed the epistle, there were several topics which he deliberately chose to omit, reserving them for a later date when he could say them more effectively in person.

John's writing instruments were ink and pen. The ink (literally "black") was made of soot and water thickened with gum, while the pen was actually made from the sharpened stem of a reed. Though writers of the day often used secretaries, the mention of ink and pen may hint that John wrote the letter in his own hand—perhaps a reason for its brevity.

14. John hoped to visit Gaius soon and speak more fully. The use of the word "hope" does not imply wavering; it merely acknowledges the fact that God is the One who controls our plans. The apostle planned to arrive soon to deal with the problems of the church and to speak personally to Gaius. The literal Greek rendering, "mouth to mouth," is the equivalent of the English idiom *face-to-face.*

John closed with "Peace be to thee," a traditional Jewish blessing that had been adopted by the early Christians. As usual, he selected a form suited to the situation. Peace was the blessing needed by the church in Gaius' city.

The last two greetings follow customary patterns. John first passed on greetings from believers in his own area who were friends of Gaius. Then he took the opportunity to ask Gaius to pass on his good wishes to mutual friends in the area. John made a point of asking that they be greeted by name, a phrase used elsewhere in the New Testament, only in John 10:3, to describe the good shepherd calling his sheep by name. John had a shepherd's heart, caring enough to pen this letter to one believer who faced a difficult situation.

Third John provides a case study in Christian living, showing how the broad principles outlined in 1 John may be applied to a specific problem. While 2 John is a warning against an unthinking kind of fellowship which extends hospitality to false teachers, 3 John gives guidance for the opposite problem: the temptation to retreat from the responsibility of offering fellowship when such a ministry leads to opposition.

12. Demetrius hath good report of all [men], and of the truth itself: Everyone has a good word to say for Demetrius, and the very truth speaks well of him, *Phillips* . . . says good things about...And the truth agrees with what they say, *Everyday* . . . there has been borne testimony by all, *Wuest* . . . has won a good reputation, *Wade* . . . enjoys a good reputation from everyone and from truth itself, *Berkeley* . . . is being praised by every one, *Laubach.*

yea, and we [also] bear record; and ye know that our record is true: We add our testimony too, *Berkeley* . . . Also, we say good about him. And you know that what we say is true, *Everyday* . . . He has our warm recommendation also, and you know you can trust what we say about anyone, *Phillips* . . . you know that our evidence is reliable, *Fenton* . . . and this testimony still holds true, *Wuest* . . . is trustworthy, *Wade.*

13. I had many things to write: There is a great deal I want to say to you, *Phillips* . . . I want to tell you, *Everyday.*

but I will not with ink and pen write unto thee: . . . but I can't put it down in black and white, *Phillips* . . . but I am unwilling to communicate to you, *Fenton* . . . but I do not desire to be writing to you, *Wuest.*

14. But I trust I shall shortly see thee: I am hoping shortly, *Wuest* . . . I hope to see you before long, *Phillips* . . . I hope to visit you soon, *Everyday.*

and we shall speak face to face: . . . and we will have a heart-to-heart talk, *Phillips* . . . Then we can be together and talk, *Everyday.*

Peace [be] to thee. [Our] friends salute thee: All our friends here send love, *Phillips* . . . The friends here with me send their love, *Everyday.*

Greet the friends by name: Remember the friends, *Fenton* . . . Remember us to, *Wade* . . . Remember me to our friends individually, *Williams* . . . please give ours personally to all our friends at your end, *Phillips* . . . Please give our love to each one of the friends there, *Everyday* . . . to the friends one by one, *Williams C.K.*

THE EPISTLE OF JUDE

Expanded Interlinear
Textual Critical Apparatus
Verse-by-Verse Commentary
Various Versions

1976.1 noun nom sing fem / 3450.2 art gen sing / 2430.2 name masc

Ἐπιστολή Τοῦ Ἰούδα

Epistolē Tou Iouda

Epistle of Jude

Textual Apparatus

1:1. Ἰούδας (2430.1 name nom masc; *Ioudas*; Jude,) Ἰησοῦ (2400.2 name masc; *Iēsou*; of Jesus) Χριστοῦ (5382.2 name gen masc; *Christou*; Christ) δοῦλος, (1395.1 noun nom sing masc; *doulos*; slave,) ἀδελφὸς (79.1 noun nom sing masc; *adelphos*; brother) δὲ (1156.2 conj; *de*; and)

Ἰακώβου, (2362.2 name gen masc; *Iakōbou*; of James,) τοῖς (3450.4 art dat pl; *tois*; to the) ἐν (1706.1 prep; *en*; in) θεῷ (2296.3 noun dat sing masc; *theō*; God) πατρὶ (3824.3 noun dat sing masc; *patri*; Father) ‘ ἡγιασμένοις (37.18 verb dat pl masc part perf mid; *hēgiasmenois*; having been sanctified)

1.a.**Txt:** 018K,020L 025P,byz. **Var:** p72,01ℵ,02A,03B it.sa.bo.Lach,Treg,Alf Word,Tisc,We/Ho,Weis Sod,UBS/⋆

[a⋆ ἠγαπημένοις] (25.35 verb dat pl masc part perf mid; *ēgapēmenois*; [having been loved]) καὶ (2504.1 conj; *kai*; and) Ἰησοῦ (2400.2 name masc; *Iēsou*; in Jesus) Χριστῷ (5382.3 name dat masc; *Christō*; Christ)

τετηρημένοις (4931.35 verb dat pl masc part perf mid; *tetērēmenois*; having been kept) κλητοῖς· (2795.3 adj dat pl masc; *klētois*; called.)

2. ἔλεος (1643.2 noun sing neu; *eleos*; Mercy) ὑμῖν (5050.3 prs-pron dat 2pl; *humin*; to you) καὶ (2504.1 conj; *kai*; and) εἰρήνη (1503.1 noun nom sing fem; *eirēnē*; peace,)

καὶ (2504.1 conj; *kai*; and) ἀγάπη (26.1 noun nom sing fem; *agapē*; love) πληθυνθείη. (3989.6 verb 3sing opt aor pass; *plēthuntheiē*; may be multiplied.)

3. Ἀγαπητοί, (27.6 adj pl masc; *Agapētoi*; Beloved,) πᾶσαν (3820.12 adj acc sing fem; *pasan*; all)

σπουδὴν (4561.3 noun acc sing fem; *spoudēn*; diligence) ποιούμενος (4020.64 verb nom sing masc part pres mid; *poioumenos*; using) γράφειν (1119.5 verb inf pres act; *graphein*; to write) ὑμῖν (5050.3 prs-pron dat 2pl; *humin*; to you) περὶ (3875.1 prep; *peri*; concerning)

3.a.**Var:** p72,01ℵ,02A 03B,sa.Lach,Treg,Alf Tisc,We/Ho,Weis,Sod UBS/⋆

τῆς (3450.10 art gen sing fem; *tēs*; the) κοινῆς (2812.2 adj gen sing fem; *koinēs*; common) [a⋆+ ἡμῶν] (2231.2 prs-pron gen 1pl; *hēmōn*; [our]) σωτηρίας, (4843.2 noun gen sing fem; *sōtērias*; salvation,) ἀνάγκην (316.4 noun acc sing fem; *anankēn*; necessity)

ἔσχον (2174.30 verb indic aor act; *eschon*; I had) γράψαι (1119.15 verb inf aor act; *grapsai*; to write) ὑμῖν, (5050.3 prs-pron dat 2pl; *humin*; to you,) παρακαλῶν (3731.7 verb nom sing masc part pres act; *parakalōn*; exhorting) ἐπαγωνίζεσθαι (1849.1 verb inf pres mid; *epagōnizesthai*; to contend earnestly)

τῇ (3450.11 art dat sing fem; *tē*; for the) ἅπαξ (526.1 adv; *hapax*; once) παραδοθείσῃ (3722.37 verb dat sing fem part aor pass; *paradotheisē*; having been delivered) τοῖς (3450.4 art dat pl; *tois*; to the) ἁγίοις (39.8 adj dat pl masc; *hagiois*; saints) πίστει. (3963.3 noun dat sing fem; *pistei*; faith.)

THE EPISTLE OF

JUDE

1. The Book of Jude has been called the Acts of the Apostates because it provides such a graphic description of the false teachers who plagued the Christian community in the First Century.

Jude's name was literally *Judas*. He was one of several men by that name in the New Testament. The second phrase, "servant of Jesus Christ," is a fascinating display of humility in light of the final identification, "brother of James." The only James prominent enough to stand without further identification was the writer of the Epistle of James, the brother of Christ himself (James 1:1; Galatians 1:19). Thus Jude was the brother of both James and Jesus himself (Mark 6:3).

The book was addressed to a general audience, defined by spiritual condition rather than a physical location. The recipients were described in three phrases. They were "loved by God the Father (NIV)," positioned within the sphere of God's love. The perfect tense of "loved" (see variant in *Interlinear*) describes a love based on God's past love which continues to the present. They were "preserved in ('kept by,' NIV) Jesus Christ." This phrase is also in the perfect tense, showing that they were safe now because Christ long before had taken up the task of keeping them. *Tetērēmenois* implies close attention and watchful care. Jude addressed his readers as "called." The word may be used for a summons to a feast or a call to judgment, but in this verse it describes the way God calls men and women to come to Him for salvation.

2. Jude's greeting contains three elements. He prayed that believers might experience God's mercy, peace, and love (*eleos, eirēnē*, and *agapē*). Jude wanted believers to be filled to their capacity with all three graces.

3. In verse 3 Jude explained the reason for his writing the epistle. It was vital that he write a letter urging these Christians to struggle to defend the Faith. *Epagōnizesthai* comes from the fierce competition of the athletic field. Believers must fight with all their strength to preserve "the faith" which has been handed down to them. *Hapax* means "once for all," because the message of Christianity was given to the Church at the beginning; it had not come in installments. The content of the apostolic gospel is fixed, not to be revised for each new era.

Various Versions

1. Jude, the servant of Jesus Christ, and brother of James: I am a workman owned by, *NLT.*

to them that are sanctified by God the Father: To those who accepted the heavenly invitation, *Noli* . . . have been loved and are the permanent objects of His love, *Wuest.*

and preserved in Jesus Christ, [and] called: . . . and are safeguarded through union with, *Wade* . . . in a position of being carefully guarded, to those who were divinely summoned, *Wuest.*

2. Mercy unto you, and peace and love, be multiplied: . . . and love—abundantly, *SEB* . . . be yours increasingly, *Wade.*

3. Beloved, when I gave all diligence to write unto you: . . . although I was making all haste, *Montgomery* . . . I was anxious to write to you, *Williams C.K.* . . . I have been striving hard to write to you, *Norlie.*

of the common salvation: . . . about the salvation we share, *SEB* . . . possessed in common by all of us, *Wuest.*

it was needful for me to write unto you: I was impelled, *Fenton* . . . I found it necessary, *Williams* . . . had constraint laid upon me, *Wuest.*

and exhort [you] that ye should earnestly contend for the faith: . . . beseeching you to contend with intensity and determination, *Wuest* . . . to exhort you to fight earnestly, *Norlie* . . . urge you to carry on a vigorous defense of, *Williams* . . . to strive energetically, *Fenton* . . . to be strenuous in defence of, *Wade.*

which was once delivered unto the saints: . . . that was delivered to the saints in a full and final way, *Adams* . . . entrusted into the safe-keeping of the saints, *Wuest* . . . to God's people, *Williams.*

Jude 4

4.a.**Txt:** 01ℵ,02A,04C 018K,020L,025P,etc.byz. Tisc,Sod
Var: 03B,We/Ho,Weis UBS/☆

4.b.**Txt:** 01ℵ,04C,018K 020L,025P,etc.byz.Sod
Var: 02A,03B,Lach Treg,Alf,Word,Tisc We/Ho,Weis,UBS/☆

4.c.**Txt:** 018K,020L 025P,byz.
Var: p72,01ℵ,02A,03B 04C,sa.bo.Gries,Lach Treg,Alf,Word,Tisc We/Ho,Weis,Sod UBS/☆

5.a.**Txt:** 01ℵ,018K,020L byz.Weis
Var: 02A,03B,04C-corr 33,sa.bo.Lach,Treg,Alf Word,Tisc,We/Ho,Sod UBS/☆

5.b.**Txt:** 018K,020L,byz.
Var: 01ℵ,02A,03B,04C 33,bo.Lach,Treg,Alf Word,Tisc,We/Ho,Weis Sod,UBS/☆

5.c.**Txt:** 018K,020L,byz. Sod
Var: 01ℵ,02A,03B 04C-org,Treg,Alf,Tisc We/Ho,Weis,UBS/☆

5.d.**Txt:** 01ℵ,044,byz.
Var: 02A,03B,33,81 2344

3783.1 verb 3pl indic aor act	**3783.2** verb 3pl indic aor act	**1056.1** conj	**4948.7** indef-pron nom pl masc
4. ⸂ παρεισέδυσαν	[a☆ παρεισέδυησαν]	γάρ	τινες
pareisedusan	*pareiseduēsan*	*gar*	*tines*
Came in stealthily	[Crept in]	for	certain

442.6 noun nom pl masc	**3450.7** art nom pl masc	**3682.1** adv	**4129.3** verb nom pl masc part perf mid
ἄνθρωποι,	οἱ	πάλαι	προγεγραμμένοι
anthrōpoi	*hoi*	*palai*	*progegrammenoi*
men,	the	of old	having been before marked out

1519.1 prep	**3642.17** dem-pron sing neu	**3450.16** art sing neu	**2890.1** noun sing neu	**759.3** adj pl masc	**3450.12** art acc sing fem	**3450.2** art gen sing
εἰς	τοῦτο	τὸ	κρίμα,	ἀσεβεῖς	τὴν	τοῦ
eis	*touto*	*to*	*krima*	*asebeis*	*tēn*	*tou*
to	this	the	sentence,	ungodly	the	

2296.2 noun gen sing masc	**2231.2** prs-pron gen 1pl	**5322.4** noun acc sing fem	**5322.6** noun acc sing fem	**3216.1** verb nom pl masc part pres act
θεοῦ	ἡμῶν	⸂ χάριν	[b☆ χάριτα]	μετατιθέντες
theou	*hēmōn*	*charin*	*charita*	*metatithentes*
of God	our	grace	[idem]	changing

1519.1 prep	**760.3** noun acc sing fem	**2504.1** conj	**3450.6** art acc sing masc	**3303.1** adv	**1197.3** noun acc sing masc
εἰς	ἀσέλγειαν	καὶ	τὸν	μόνον	δεσπότην
eis	*aselgeian*	*kai*	*ton*	*monon*	*despotēn*
into	licentiousness	and	the	only	master,

2296.4 noun acc sing masc	**2504.1** conj	**2935.4** noun acc sing masc	**2231.2** prs-pron gen 1pl	**2400.3** name acc masc	**5382.4** name acc masc
⸂c Θεὸν ⸃	καὶ	κύριον	ἡμῶν	Ἰησοῦν	Χριστὸν
Theon	*kai*	*kurion*	*hēmōn*	*Iēsoun*	*Christon*
God	and	Lord	our	Jesus	Christ

714.5 verb nom pl masc part pres mid	**5117.3** verb inf aor act	**1156.2** conj	**5050.4** prs-pron acc 2pl	**1007.1** verb 1sing indic pres mid
ἀρνούμενοι.	**5.** Ὑπομνῆσαι	δὲ	ὑμᾶς	βούλομαι,
arnoumenoi	*Hupomnēsai*	*de*	*humas*	*boulomai*
denying.	To put in remembrance	but	you	I would,

3471.22 verb acc pl masc part perf act	**5050.4** prs-pron acc 2pl	**526.1** adv	**3642.17** dem-pron sing neu	**3820.1** adj
εἰδότας	⸂a ὑμᾶς ⸃	ἅπαξ	⸂ τοῦτο,	[b☆ πάντα,]
eidotas	*humas*	*hapax*	*touto*	*panta*
knowing	you	once	this,	[all things,]

3617.1 conj	**3450.5** art nom sing masc	**2935.1** noun nom sing masc	**2400.1** name nom masc	**2967.4** noun acc sing masc	**1523.2** prep gen
ὅτι	⸂c ὁ ⸃	⸂ κύριος	[d Ἰησοῦς]	λαὸν	ἐκ
hoti	*ho*	*kurios*	*Iēsous*	*laon*	*ek*
that	the	Lord	[Jesus]	a people	out of

1087.2 noun gen sing fem	**125.2** name gen fem	**4834.8** verb nom sing masc part aor act	**3450.16** art sing neu	**1202.8** num ord sing neu
γῆς	Αἰγύπτου	σώσας,	τὸ	δεύτερον
gēs	*Aiguptou*	*sōsas*	*to*	*deuteron*
land	of Egypt	having saved,	in the	second place

3450.8 art acc pl masc	**3231.1** partic	**3961.34** verb acc pl masc part aor act	**616.3** verb 3sing indic aor act	**32.8** noun acc pl masc	**4885.1** conj
τοὺς	μὴ	πιστεύσαντας	ἀπώλεσεν,	**6.** ἀγγέλους	τε
tous	*mē*	*pisteusantas*	*apōlesen*	*angelous*	*te*
the	not	having believed	he destroyed.	Angels	and

4. Here Jude began to go into detail. He had learned of a serious threat to the Church. A new breed of leader had slipped into the congregations. They appeared attractive but posed serious dangers. In 2 Peter 2, a parallel passage, the threat was still future, but by Jude's time the apostasy had begun. *Pareisedusan* was used for one who entered a place without being noticed. Like thieves, heretics were making a stealthy entrance through the side door. Jude wrote to warn his fellow Christians of the true character of these men.

This was not a new problem. Jesus had a Judas among His followers. Paul had found it necessary to warn the church about this danger. When he met with the elders of Ephesus on his way to Jerusalem, he told them, "I know this, that after my departing shall grievous wolves enter in among you, not sparing the flock" (Acts 20:29). The Book of Galatians was written to deal with the heresy of the Judaizers. And the danger is not diminished in our day. Leaders need to be on guard against heresy and teach believers so they will not be led away and "devoured" by false teachers. Satan is so subtle in his approach that believers must be aware of his tactics and be prepared to resist him.

Verse 4 summarizes the major themes expounded in the rest of the book. First, such men were under the judgment of God. Their doom was determined long before Jude wrote his epistle (see Isaiah 8:19-22; Zephaniah 3:1-8). Second, they were degraded in character and conduct. *Asebeis* is a central concept of the epistle, occurring five times. It describes one who fails to treat God with the worship and reverence He deserves. Beyond this ungodliness, false teachers distort Christian teaching. They twist God's grace into a license to sin (ignoring Titus 2:11-13). The final step in their shameful path is to deny Jesus as their Lord and Master. *Kurion* is a title of honor; *despotēn* emphasizes a master's power over his subjects. The apostates about whom Jude wrote denied the lordship of Christ.

4. For there are certain men crept in unawares: . . . entered, *Wuest* . . . have slipped in surreptitiously, *Adams* . . . have sneaked in, *Williams* . . . into the Church, *Noli* . . . by secret means, *Laubach* . . . furtively, *Wade.*

who were before of old ordained to this condemnation: . . . of whom in the long ago this condemnation was set forth in advance, *Berkeley* . . . men predestined in ancient prophecies, *Montgomery* . . . their doom was written down long ago, *Williams* . . . predicted with reference to this judgment, *Wuest.*

ungodly men, turning the grace of our God into lasciviousness: . . . godless persons, *Williams* . . . impious ones, who pervert the grace of our God into unbridled lust, *Berkeley* . . . men destitute of reverential awe...perverting the grace of our God into moral anarchy and lack of self-restraint, *Wuest* . . . they twist the mercy of God to mean that they can practice sex vice, *Laubach* . . . twisting the grace of our God into a reason for debauchery, *Adams* . . . into license for debauchery, *Wade* . . . giving us an excuse to live in uncontrolled immorality, *Norlie* . . . into what is disgusting, *Swann* . . . into profligacy, *Fenton* . . . to orgies, *SEB.*

and denying the only Lord God, and our Lord Jesus Christ: . . . and denying the only absolute Master, *Wuest* . . . disown our only Master, *Williams C.K.*

5. In the next three verses Jude moved into a series of examples from the Old Testament, each demonstrating the fact that God deals with such rebellion. (Compare a similar set of illustrations in 2 Peter 2.)

First, believers were asked to remember Israel's experience during the Exodus. The story was familiar to them. They knew the details. But Jude extracted the main points. The Lord rescued His people from their bondage in Egypt, but when they reached the threshold of Canaan, they refused to believe God could give them possession of the land (Numbers 13). So God turned them back to the desert to wander until they died (Numbers 14:20-35; cf. 1 Corinthians 10:1-11). Despite their privileges, God judged them when they rebelled.

5. I will therefore put you in remembrance: I desire to remind you, *Berkeley* . . . I must remind you that God's patience has a limit, *Laubach* . . . after mature consideration I desire to remind you, *Wuest.*

though ye once knew this: . . . although you have a full and final knowledge about it, *Adams* . . . since once you were quite familiar with all the facts, *Berkeley.*

how that the Lord, having saved the people out of the land of Egypt: . . . after rescuing the people, *Berkeley.*

afterward destroyed them that believed not: . . . destroyed at the next occasion those who practiced on faith, *Berkeley.*

6. Jude's second illustration came from the angels who rebelled. The exact Old Testament source for the verse is debated: some

3450.8 art acc pl masc	3231.1 partic	4931.20 verb acc pl masc part aor act	3450.12 art acc sing fem	1431.2 prs-pron gen pl	741.4 noun acc sing fem
τοὺς	μὴ	τηρήσαντας	τὴν	ἑαυτῶν	ἀρχὴν,
tous	*mē*	*tērēsantas*	*tēn*	*heautōn*	*archēn*
the	not	having kept	the	their own	first state,

233.2 conj	614.2 verb acc pl masc part aor act	3450.16 art sing neu	2375.4 adj sing	3476.1 noun sing neu	1519.1 prep
ἀλλὰ	ἀπολιπόντας	τὸ	ἴδιον	οἰκητήριον,	εἰς
alla	*apolipontas*	*to*	*idion*	*oikētērion*	*eis*
but	having left	the	their own	dwelling,	unto

2893.4 noun acc sing fem	3144.10 adj gen sing fem	2232.1 noun fem	1193.5 noun dat pl	126.1 adj dat pl masc	5097.3 prep
κρίσιν	μεγάλης	ἡμέρας	δεσμοῖς	ἀϊδίοις	ὑπὸ
krisin	*megalēs*	*hēmeras*	*desmois*	*aidiois*	*hupo*
judgment	of great	day	in bonds	eternal	under

2200.3 noun acc sing masc	4931.24 verb 3sing indic perf act	5453.1 conj	4525.1 name pl neu	2504.1 conj	1110.1 name
ζόφον	τετήρηκεν˙	7. ὡς	Σόδομα	καὶ	Γόμοῤῥα,
zophon	*tetērēken*	*hōs*	*Sodoma*	*kai*	*Gomorrha*
darkness	he 'is kept;	as	Sodom	and	Gomorrah,

2504.1 conj	3450.13 art nom pl fem	3875.1 prep	840.13 prs-pron acc pl fem	4032.5 noun pl fem	3450.6 art acc sing masc
καὶ	αἱ	περὶ	αὐτὰς	πόλεις,	τὸν
kai	*hai*	*peri*	*autas*	*poleis*	*ton*
and	the	around	them	cities,	

3527.1 adj sing	3642.3 dem-pron dat pl	4999.3 noun acc sing masc	4999.3 noun acc sing masc	3642.3 dem-pron dat pl
ὅμοιον	‹ τούτοις	τρόπον	[☆ τρόπον	τούτοις]
homoion	*toutois*	*tropon*	*tropon*	*toutois*
in like	with them	manner	[manner	like]

1595.1 verb nom pl fem part aor act	2504.1 conj	562.11 verb nom pl fem part aor act
ἐκπορνεύσασαι,	καὶ	ἀπελθοῦσαι
ekporneusasai	*kai*	*apelthousai*
having given themselves to sexual immorality	and	having gone

3557.1 adv	4418.2 noun gen sing fem	2066.10 adj gen sing fem	4154.2 verb 3pl indic pres mid	1159.1 noun sing neu
ὀπίσω	σαρκὸς	ἑτέρας,	πρόκεινται	δεῖγμα,
opisō	*sarkos*	*heteras*	*prokeintai*	*deigma*
after	flesh	other,	are set forth as	an example,

4300.2 noun gen sing neu	164.2 adj gen sing	1343.2 noun acc sing fem	5092.1 verb nom pl fem part pres act	3532.1 adv
πυρὸς	αἰωνίου	δίκην	ὑπέχουσαι.	8. Ὁμοίως
puros	*aiōniou*	*dikēn*	*hupechousai*	*Homoiōs*
of fire	eternal	penalty	undergoing.	Yet

3175.1 partic	2504.1 conj	3642.7 dem-pron nom pl masc	1781.1 verb nom pl masc part pres mid	4418.4 noun acc sing fem
μέντοι	καὶ	οὗτοι	ἐνυπνιαζόμενοι,	σάρκα
mentoi	*kai*	*houtoi*	*enupniazomenoi*	*sarka*
in like manner	also	these	dreaming	flesh

3173.1 conj	3256.1 verb 3pl indic pres act	2936.2 noun acc sing fem	1156.2 conj	114.4 verb 3pl indic pres act	1385.5 noun acc pl fem
μὲν	μιαίνουσιν,	κυριότητα	δὲ	ἀθετοῦσιν,	δόξας
men	*miainousin*	*kuriotēta*	*de*	*athetousin*	*doxas*
	defile,	lordship	and	set aside,	glories

teach that it refers to the sin of angels ("sons of God," Genesis 6:2) or to the original fall of Satan and the angels, while others say it refers to an event preserved only in tradition. In any case, Jude declared that a group of angels sinned by refusing to keep the original position of authority and power given to them by God. Instead, they deserted their own assigned dwelling place. Despite their high rank, God judged them. They would not keep their place, so He has kept them imprisoned, waiting for the great Day of Judgment at the end of time. The darkness mentioned here is a deep, dense blackness, a fit picture of separation from God.

The fate of these angels teaches us a solemn lesson: They had been created holy by the hand of God and loved as His creation, for He who is holy loves holiness. But the relationship changed when by their own voluntary will they turned away from the God who created and loved them. They have lost their high place of privilege, and now await judgment. There are none so holy they cannot fail and fall.

7. Jude's third example came from the account of Sodom and Gomorrah which included three smaller towns in the vicinity: Admah and Zeboim, as well as Zoar, which was preserved at Lot's request (Genesis 19:1-25; Deuteronomy 29:23).

The text draws a close comparison between Sodom and the angels of verse 6. Both groups shared the same judgment; it is possible that they may have committed similar sins.

Sodom's specific sin was sexual immorality. *Ekporneusasai* is an intensified form of the usual word for sexual sin, and the seriousness of their sin is underlined by the phrase that follows: "going after strange (of a different kind) flesh," a clear reference to the homosexual sin practiced in Sodom.

Like other sinners described in these verses, Sodom and Gomorrah felt God's wrath. They are a perpetual demonstration of God's judgment on sin. They underwent doom by fire, a fire described by Jude as eternal because it corresponds to the fires of hell.

8. This verse begins a section that moves from rebels of the past to a description of the deceivers about whom Jude was troubled. He used several words to emphasize the shift in thought. *Homoiōs* draws a parallel between the Old Testament sinners and the ones about whom Jude was writing. These men shared several unsavory characteristics. First, they "defile the flesh"—their immorality caused a moral stain. Second, they "despise dominion" (reject lordship)—they deliberately rejected any form of established authority that hindered their impulses. Third, they "speak evil of dignities" (blaspheme glories)—they condemned beings who possess high degrees of glory. The connection with verse 9 suggests that angelic beings may be meant here. Beyond these traits, the apostates were dreamers. Their distorted view of reality caused their rebellious attitudes.

6. And the angels which kept not their first estate: . . . who did not stay in their appointed place, *Norlie* . . . who did not keep their first domain, *Montgomery* . . . had not kept their own original state, *Darby* . . . who kept not their own Principality, *Wilson* . . . that did not remain in their own high office, *Williams C.K.* . . . who did not preserve their original rank, *Williams* . . . did not keep their first position, *SEB* . . . did not guard their own dominion, *Fenton.*

but left their own habitation: . . . and left their proper home, *TCNT* . . . but left their proper dwelling place, *Adams* . . . abandoned their proper duty, *Fenton* . . . deserted their heavenly homeland, *Noli.*

he hath reserved in everlasting chains under darkness unto the judgment of the great day: He reserves in custody, *Fenton* . . . kept in perpetual chains, *Norlie, Wilson* . . . of the lower world, *Swann.*

7. Even as Sodom and Gomorrha, and the cities about them:

in like manner, giving themselves over to fornication: . . . glutted themselves in sensuality, *Montgomery* . . . gave themselves over to sexual sin, *SEB* . . . indulged in grossest immorality, *Williams.*

and going after strange flesh: . . . even perversion, *SEB* . . . after foul sensuality, *Fenton* . . . and homosexuality, *Norlie* . . . and unnatural vice, *Montgomery.*

are set forth for an example, suffering the vengeance of eternal fire: . . . enduring the retributive justice of an aionian Fire, *Wilson.*

8. Likewise also these [filthy] dreamers: . . . by their dreamings, *Adams.*

defile the flesh, despise dominion: . . . make their flesh foul with sin, *Laubach* . . . pollute our human nature, reject control, *TCNT* . . . disgrace their bodies, defy their creator, *Noli* . . . discard authority, *Williams.*

and speak evil of dignities: . . . and scoff at, *Montgomery* . . . and speak disparagingly, *TCNT* . . . and insult glorious beings, *Adams* . . . and deride the majesties, *Williams* . . . and revile their angels, *Noli.*

1156.2 conj	980.3 verb 3pl indic pres act		3450.5 art nom sing masc	1156.2 conj	3277.1 name masc	3450.5 art nom sing masc
δὲ	βλασφημοῦσιν.	9.	ὁ	δὲ	Μιχαὴλ	ὁ
de	*blasphēmousin*		*ho*	*de*	*Michaēl*	*ho*
and	blaspheme.			But	Michael	the

738.1 noun nom sing masc	3616.1 conj	3450.3 art dat sing	1222.3 adj dat sing masc	1246.8 verb nom sing masc part pres mid
ἀρχάγγελος,	ὅτε	τῷ	διαβόλῳ	διακρινόμενος
archangelos	*hote*	*tō*	*diabolō*	*diakrinomenos*
archangel,	when	with the	devil	disputing

1250.7 verb 3sing indic imperf mid	3875.1 prep	3450.2 art gen sing	3337.2 name gen masc	4835.2 noun gen sing neu	3620.2 partic
διελέγετο	περὶ	τοῦ	Μωσέως	σώματος,	οὐκ
dielegeto	*peri*	*tou*	*Mōseōs*	*sōmatos*	*ouk*
he was reasoning	about	the	of Moses	body,	not

4958.5 verb 3sing indic aor act	2893.4 noun acc sing fem	2002.3 verb inf aor act	981.1 noun fem	233.1 conj
ἐτόλμησεν	κρίσιν	ἐπενεγκεῖν	βλασφημίας,	ἀλλ'
etolmēsen	*krisin*	*epenenkein*	*blasphēmias*	*all'*
did dare	a charge	to bring against	accusing,	but

1500.5 verb 3sing indic aor act	1992.5 verb 3sing opt aor act	4622.3 prs-pron dat 2sing	2935.1 noun nom sing masc		3642.7 dem-pron nom pl masc
εἶπεν,	Ἐπιτιμήσαι	σοι	κύριος.	10.	οὗτοι
eipen	*Epitimēsai*	*soi*	*kurios*		*houtoi*
said,	Rebuke	you	Lord.		These

1156.2 conj	3607.8 rel-pron pl neu	3173.1 conj	3620.2 partic	3471.8 verb 3pl indic perf act	980.3 verb 3pl indic pres act
δὲ	ὅσα	μὲν	οὐκ	οἴδασιν	βλασφημοῦσιν·
de	*hosa*	*men*	*ouk*	*oidasin*	*blasphēmousin*
but,	whatever things		not	they know	they blaspheme;

3607.8 rel-pron pl neu	1156.2 conj	5283.1 adv	5453.1 conj	3450.17 art pl neu	247.2 adj pl neu
ὅσα	δὲ	φυσικῶς,	ὡς	τὰ	ἄλογα
hosa	*de*	*phusikōs*	*hōs*	*ta*	*aloga*
whatever things	but	naturally,	as	the	irrational

2209.3 noun pl neu	1971.4 verb 3pl indic pres mid	1706.1 prep	3642.3 dem-pron dat pl	5188.6 verb 3pl indic pres mid
ζῷα,	ἐπίστανται,	ἐν	τούτοις	φθείρονται.
zōa	*epistantai*	*en*	*toutois*	*phtheirontai*
creatures	they understand,	in	these things	they corrupt themselves.

	3622.1 intrj	840.2 prs-pron dat pl	3617.1 conj	3450.11 art dat sing fem	3461.3 noun dat sing fem	3450.2 art gen sing	2506.1 name masc
11.	οὐαὶ	αὐτοῖς·	ὅτι	τῇ	ὁδῷ	τοῦ	Κάϊν
	ouai	*autois*	*hoti*	*tē*	*hodō*	*tou*	*Kain*
	Woe	to them!	because	in the	way		of Cain

4057.17 verb 3pl indic aor pass	2504.1 conj	3450.11 art dat sing fem	3967.3 noun dat sing fem	3450.2 art gen sing	897.1 name masc
ἐπορεύθησαν,	καὶ	τῇ	πλάνῃ	τοῦ	Βαλαὰμ
eporeuthēsan	*kai*	*tē*	*planē*	*tou*	*Balaam*
they went,	and	to the	error		of Balaam

3272.2 noun gen sing masc	1619.3 verb 3pl indic aor pass	2504.1 conj	3450.11 art dat sing fem	482.2 noun dat sing fem	3450.2 art gen sing
μισθοῦ	ἐξεχύθησαν,	καὶ	τῇ	ἀντιλογίᾳ	τοῦ
misthou	*exechuthēsan*	*kai*	*tē*	*antilogia*	*tou*
for reward	rushed,	and	in the	rebellion	

9. Jude illustrated the depth of their arrogance by pointing to an encounter between the two highest angels, Michael the archangel and the devil himself. The name of Michael, the chief angel, means "Who is like God?" He has the task of opposing Satan and defending Israel (Daniel 10:13,21;12:1; Revelation 12:7-9). Satan began his career as perhaps the highest of all angels (cf. Isaiah 14:12-20).

The incident Jude described in verse 9 is not mentioned in the Old Testament, and no further details are known about it. Whether Jude knew of it through oral tradition or an apocryphal writing, the Holy Spirit guided his selection of facts, and its historicity need not be doubted.

Michael and Satan were involved in a dispute regarding the body of Moses which had been buried by God himself. Despite his high rank, Michael did not dare lay down a condemnation using blasphemous or slanderous words. Instead, he merely replied that God himself would rebuke Satan.

9. Yet Michael the archangel: when contending with the devil he disputed about the body of Moses: . . . when in his encounter with the devil, *Berkeley* . . . in his controversy with, *Wade* . . . when he was arguing, *TCNT* . . . he reasoned about, *Wilson.*

durst not bring against him a railing accusation: . . . did not dare to bring a reviling judgment, *Swann* . . . did not venture to pronounce sentence on his blasphemies, *Berkeley* . . . bring a sentence of judgment that would impugn his [original] dignity, *Wuest* . . . indulge in an abusive defence, *Fenton* . . . an insulting accusation, *Adams* . . . in defamatory terms, *Wade.*

but said, The Lord rebuke thee: . . . but simply said, *Fenton.*

10. Jude was dealing with blasphemers who coupled arrogance with ignorance. When they slandered beings higher than themselves (note verses 8,9), they did not know the seriousness of their offense.

They understood very little, and the knowledge they did have was the kind that would destroy them. *Epistantai* is the knowledge that comes through instinct or the five senses; it is no better than the capacity of an animal. These men only understood their own physical lusts, and they were headed for ruin as a result of indulging those desires. These men were a clear example of the saying, "A little knowledge is a dangerous thing." The only dependable knowledge is that which comes from God's Word.

10. But these speak evil of those things which they know not: . . . sneer at anything they do not understand, *Berkeley* . . . are cursing anything they cannot understand, *Laubach* . . . on the one hand, revile as many things concerning which they do not have absolute knowledge, *Wuest.*

but what they know naturally, as brute beasts: . . . while whatever they do know sensually as reasonless brutes, *Berkeley* . . . on the other hand, revile as many things by instinct like the unreasoning animals, which they understand, *Wuest.*

in those things they corrupt themselves: . . . by these they are being brought to ruin, *Wuest* . . . by those things they are corrupted, *Berkeley* . . . they can understand only sensual lusts, *Noli* . . . they destroy themselves, *NLT* . . . they ruin themselves, *Adams.*

11. Jude wrote, "Woe unto them!" He then referred to three Old Testament characters to show how such sin leads to destruction.

The false teachers had followed "the way of Cain" who tried to approach God on his own terms and found his offering rejected (Genesis 4). He lacked an attitude of faith (Hebrews 11:4) and may have refused to offer the blood sacrifice God demanded.

Like the rushing waters of a breached reservoir, these false teachers hurried to follow Balaam's deceiving ways. When the prophet found himself unable to curse Israel, he earned his fee by suggesting a plan to destroy the people by luring them into sexual relations with pagan women (Numbers 22–25).

The false teachers were like Korah who led a revolt against Moses and Aaron (Numbers 16), refusing to recognize the authorities God had placed over them, just as the apostates despised any higher power. The result was judgment; Jude's word "perished" goes beyond physical death to describe eternal separation from God.

11. Woe unto them! for they have gone in the way of Cain: Alas for them! *Wilson* . . . Terrible will be their end, *Laubach* . . . they have marched the way of, *Fenton.*

and ran greedily after the error of Balaam for reward: . . . led astray by Balaam's love of gain, *TCNT* . . . they abandoned themselves for a reward, *Wuest* . . . They think of nothing but making money, *Laubach.*

and perished in the gainsaying of Core: . . . have destroyed themselves in Korah's rebellion! *Adams.*

Jude 12

12.a.**Var:** 01ℵ-corr,02A 03B,020L,33,Lach,Treg Alf,Tisc,We/Ho,Weis Sod,UBS/☆

2852.1 name masc	**616.23** verb 3pl indic aor mid	**3642.7** dem-pron nom pl masc	**1498.7** verb 3pl indic pres act	**3450.7** art nom pl masc	**1706.1** prep
Κόρε	ἀπώλοντο.	**12.** οὗτοί	εἰσιν	[a☆+ οἱ]	ἐν
Kore	*apōlonto*	*houtoi*	*eisin*	*hoi*	*en*
of Korah	perished.	These	are	[the]	in

3450.14 art dat pl fem	**26.5** noun dat pl fem	**5050.2** prs-pron gen 2pl	**4547.1** noun nom pl fem	**4760.1** verb nom pl masc part pres mid
ταῖς	ἀγάπαις	ὑμῶν	σπιλάδες,	συνευωχούμενοι
tais	*agapais*	*humōn*	*spilades*	*suneuōchoumenoi*
the	love feasts	your	sunken rocks,	feasting together

863.1 adv	**1431.8** prs-pron acc pl masc	**4025.4** verb nom pl masc part pres act	**3369.5** noun nom pl fem	**501.2** adj nom pl fem
ἀφόβως,	ἑαυτοὺς	ποιμαίνοντες˙	νεφέλαι	ἄνυδροι,
aphobōs	*heautous*	*poimainontes*	*nephelai*	*anudroi*
fearlessly,	themselves	pasturing;	clouds	without water,

12.b.**Txt:** Steph
Var: 01ℵ,02A,03B,04C 018K,020L,Gries,Lach Treg,Alf,Word,Tisc We/Ho,Weis,Sod UBS/☆

5097.3 prep	**415.6** noun gen pl masc	**3924.5** verb nom pl fem part pres mid	**3772.4** verb nom pl fem part pres mid
ὑπὸ	ἀνέμων	‹ περιφερόμεναι˙	[b☆ παραφερόμεναι,]
hupo	*anemōn*	*peripheromenai*	*parapheromenai*
by	winds	being carried about,	[being carried away,]

1180.2 noun pl neu	**5189.1** adj pl neu	**173.4** adj pl neu	**1361.1** adv	**594.19** verb pl neu part aor act
δένδρα	φθινοπωρινὰ	ἄκαρπα	δὶς	ἀποθανόντα
dendra	*phthinopōrina*	*akarpa*	*dis*	*apothanonta*
trees	autumnal,	without fruit,	twice	having died,

1597.3 verb pl neu part aor pass	**2922.1** noun pl neu	**65.2** adj pl neu	**2258.2** noun gen sing fem
ἐκριζωθέντα˙	**13.** κύματα	ἄγρια	θαλάσσης
ekrizōthenta	*kumata*	*agria*	*thalassēs*
having been rooted up;	waves	wild	of sea,

1875.1 verb pl neu part pres act	**3450.15** art acc pl fem	**1431.2** prs-pron gen pl	**151.4** noun acc pl fem	**786.4** noun nom pl masc
ἐπαφρίζοντα	τὰς	ἑαυτῶν	αἰσχύνας˙	ἀστέρες
epaphrizonta	*tas*	*heautōn*	*aischunas*	*asteres*
foaming out	the	their own	shames;	stars

3968.1 adj nom pl masc	**3614.4** rel-pron dat pl	**3450.5** art nom sing masc	**2200.1** noun nom sing masc	**3450.2** art gen sing	**4510.3** noun gen sing neu
πλανῆται,	οἷς	ὁ	ζόφος	τοῦ	σκότους
planētai	*hois*	*ho*	*zophos*	*tou*	*skotous*
wandering,	to whom	the	gloom	of the	darkness

13.a.**Txt:** 018K,byz.
Var: 01ℵ,02A,03B,04C 020L,Gries,Lach,Treg Alf,Word,Tisc,We/Ho Weis,Sod,UBS/☆

1519.1 prep	**3450.6** art acc sing masc	**163.3** noun acc sing masc	**4931.34** verb 3sing indic perf mid	**4253.8** verb 3sing indic aor act
εἰς	‹a τὸν ›	αἰῶνα	τετήρηται.	**14.** ‹ Προεφήτευσεν
eis	*ton*	*aiōna*	*tetērētai*	*Proephēteusen*
to	the	age	has been kept.	Prophesied

14.a.**Txt:** 02A,04C,018K 020L,byz.Sod
Var: 03B,Treg,Tisc We/Ho,Weis,UBS/☆

4253.16 verb 3sing indic aor act	**1156.2** conj	**2504.1** conj	**3642.3** dem-pron dat pl	**1436.2** num ord nom sing masc	**570.3** prep
[a ἐπροφήτευσεν]	δὲ	καὶ	τούτοις	ἕβδομος	ἀπὸ
eprophēteusen	*de*	*kai*	*toutois*	*hebdomos*	*apo*
[idem]	and	also	to these	seventh	from

75.1 name masc	**1786.1** name masc	**2978.15** verb nom sing masc part pres act	**1481.20** verb 2sing impr aor mid	**2048.3** verb 3sing indic aor act
Ἀδὰμ	Ἑνὼχ,	λέγων,	Ἰδοὺ,	ἦλθεν
Adam	*Henōch*	*legōn*	*Idou*	*ēlthen*
Adam,	Enoch,	saying,	Behold,	came

12. The next two verses contain a cluster of vivid descriptions of the apostates, all drawn from nature.

These men were like rocks (see *Interlinear*) submerged just below the surface, ready to tear the hull of a ship. The danger was real, even though hidden. Such men took part in the love feasts, the fellowship meals which accompanied the Lord's Supper in the first-century Church, and eventually abused it to the point that it was discontinued. Some versions translate *spilades* as "spots," but this definition did not develop until after the New Testament period. The deceivers feasted without any fear they would be called to account for their sins.

They were shepherds who took care of their own needs, rather than the needs of the sheep (cf. Ezekiel 34:8). They were like clouds carrying the promise of rain for a parched land, but with not a drop of water in reality. They had no stability, but went wherever the winds blew them. They were like trees "without fruit" in the late autumn when fruit was expected. They were doubly dead, dead all the way to the root; their fate was to be uprooted. Similarly, the false teachers promised great benefits, but produced no legitimate results.

13. The apostates were like the turbulent waves of a polluted lake, casting up seaweed and rubbish on the beach. They spewed out openly the things most people would hide with shame.

The final comparison from nature pictured them as "wandering stars," shooting stars that flash for a moment and are then engulfed in darkness. *Planētai* refers to that which leads astray or causes one to wander from the path.

14. Jude described the troublemakers by using Old Testament examples and by metaphors from nature. Next he quoted an ancient prophet to show their doom was sure. The prophecy cited in verse 14 appears nowhere in the Old Testament. The text is quite close to a passage in the Book of Enoch. But whether Jude was quoting from the Book of Enoch or citing information he had received from some other source, the fact that it is included in the letter demonstrates its historic accuracy.

Enoch was seventh in line in the genealogy of Adam (Genesis 5). The record says Enoch was a man who walked so close to God that he was taken to heaven without passing through death. He also provides the only example of prophecy in the era before the Flood. His prophecy proves that rebels against God will be punished.

Enoch prophesied, "Behold, the Lord cometh." He employed the aorist tense of *come* (*ēlthen*) to describe an event still future, because its accomplishment is certain. From a New Testament perspective, it is clear the prophecy refers to the Second Coming.

The Lord will come accompanied by myriads of holy ones. "Myriads" (see *Interlinear*) was often used to denote 10,000 soldiers but

12. These are spots in your feasts of charity: These are like hidden rocks, *Norlie* . . . the stains, *Berkeley* . . . are blots on your love feasts, *Adams.*

when they feast with you, feeding themselves without fear: . . . in your company they shamelessly gorge themselves, *Berkeley* . . . carousing shamelessly, and feasting gluttonously, *Noli* . . . feast sumptuously without scruple, *Montgomery* . . . banqueting with you without a qualm, *Adams* . . . without reverence, *Fenton* . . . as shepherds leading themselves to pasture, *Wuest.*

clouds [they are] without water, carried about of winds: . . . rainless clouds, *Berkeley* . . . carried past by the tempests, *Swann* . . . but they have no rain, *SEB.*

trees whose fruit withereth, without fruit: . . . trees that are leafless, *TCNT* . . . leafless autumn trees, devoid of fruit, *Wade* . . . dead trees which bear no fruit, *Laubach* . . . fruitless, *Berkeley.*

twice dead, plucked up by the roots: . . . doubly dead! *Adams* . . . having died twice, rooted up, *Wuest* . . . pulled up by, *Williams C.K.* . . . uprooted, *Berkeley.*

13. Raging waves of the sea: Their sins are like the dirty water along the shore, *NLT* . . . are wild waves, *Norlie* . . . wildly raging, *Berkeley* . . . untamed sea waves, *Wuest.*

foaming out their own shame: . . . waves which throw on the shore the foul smelling things beneath the sea, *Laubach* . . . foaming out their shameful debris, *Adams* . . . throwing up to the surface their own shameful desires, *Williams C.K.* . . . their own disgrace, *Berkeley.*

wandering stars: . . . straying, *Berkeley* . . . wandering meteors, *Wuest.*

to whom is reserved the blackness of darkness for ever: . . . for whom the gloom of the abyss has been reserved, *Noli* . . . the gloom of darkness is forever reserved, *Berkeley* . . . doomed to utter darkness, *Williams.*

14. And Enoch also, the seventh from Adam, prophesied of these, saying: . . . seventh generation, *Berkeley* . . . there prophesied also with respect to these, *Wuest.*

2935.1 noun nom sing masc	1706.1 prep	3323.3 noun dat pl fem	39.15 adj dat pl fem	39.15 adj dat pl fem	3323.3 noun dat pl fem
κύριος	ἐν	ʼ μυριάσιν	ἁγίαις	[☆ ἁγίαις	μυριάσιν]
kurios	*en*	*muriasin*	*hagiais*	*hagiais*	*muriasin*
Lord	in	myriads	holy	[holy	myriads]

15.a.**Txt:** Steph
Var: 01ℵ,02A,03B,04C
018K,020L,Lach,Treg
Alf,Tisc,We/Ho,Weis
Sod,UBS/☆

840.3 prs-pron gen sing	4020.41 verb inf aor act	2893.4 noun acc sing fem	2567.3 prep	3820.4 adj gen pl	2504.1 conj
αὐτοῦ,	**15.** ποιῆσαι	κρίσιν	κατὰ	πάντων,	καὶ
autou	*poiēsai*	*krisin*	*kata*	*pantōn*	*kai*
his,	to execute	judgment	against	all,	and

15.b.**Txt:** 02A,03B,04C
044,33,81,323,630
1241,1505,1739,2495
Var: p72,01ℵ,sa.

1810.1 verb inf aor act	1638.13 verb inf aor act	3820.8 adj acc pl masc	3450.8 art acc pl masc	3820.12 adj acc sing fem
ʼ ἐξελέγξαι	[a☆ ἐλέγξαι]	ʼ πάντας	τοὺς	[b☆ πᾶσαν
exelenxai	*elenxai*	*pantas*	*tous*	*pasan*
to convict	[to reprove]	all	the	[every

15.c.**Txt:** 018K,020L,byz.
Tisc
Var: 01ℵ,02A,03B,04C
sa.bo.Lach,Treg,Alf
We/Ho,Weis,Sod
UBS/☆

5425.4 noun acc sing fem	759.3 adj pl masc	840.1 prs-pron gen pl	3875.1 prep	3820.4 adj gen pl	3450.1 art gen pl
ψυχὴν]	ἀσεβεῖς	ʼc αὐτῶν ˎ	περὶ	πάντων	τῶν
psuchēn	*asebeis*	*autōn*	*peri*	*pantōn*	*tōn*
soul]	ungodly	of them	concerning	all	the

2024.5 noun gen pl neu	757.1 noun fem	840.1 prs-pron gen pl	3614.1 rel-pron gen pl	758.2 verb 3pl indic aor act	2504.1 conj
ἔργων	ἀσεβείας	αὐτῶν	ὧν	ἠσέβησαν,	καὶ
ergōn	*asebeias*	*autōn*	*hōn*	*ēsebēsan*	*kai*
works	of ungodliness	their	which	they did ungodlily,	and

3875.1 prep	3820.4 adj gen pl	3450.1 art gen pl	4497.1 adj gen pl	3614.1 rel-pron gen pl	2953.30 verb 3pl indic aor act
περὶ	πάντων	τῶν	σκληρῶν	ὧν	ἐλάλησαν
peri	*pantōn*	*tōn*	*sklērōn*	*hōn*	*elalēsan*
concerning	all	the	hard	which	spoke

2567.1 prep	840.3 prs-pron gen sing	266.4 adj pl masc	759.3 adj pl masc	3642.7 dem-pron nom pl masc	1498.7 verb 3pl indic pres act
κατ'	αὐτοῦ	ἁμαρτωλοὶ	ἀσεβεῖς.	**16.** Οὗτοί	εἰσιν
kat'	*autou*	*hamartōloi*	*asebeis*	*Houtoi*	*eisin*
against	him	sinners	ungodly.	These	are

1107.1 noun nom pl masc	3172.1 adj nom pl masc	2567.3 prep	3450.15 art acc pl fem	1924.1 noun fem
γογγυσταί,	μεμψίμοιροι,	κατὰ	τὰς	ἐπιθυμίας
gongustai	*mempsimoiroi*	*kata*	*tas*	*epithumias*
murmurers,	complainers,	after	the	lusts

16.a.**Txt:** 01ℵ,02A,03B
018K,044,33,81,630
945,1505,Tisc,We/Ho
Sod,UBS/☆
Var: p72-corr3,04C
020L,025P,1,323,1241
1739,2495,UBS/☆

840.1 prs-pron gen pl	1431.2 prs-pron gen pl	4057.10 verb nom pl masc part pres mid	2504.1 conj	3450.16 art sing neu	4601.1 noun sing neu
ʼ αὐτῶν	[a☆ ἑαυτῶν]	πορευόμενοι·	καὶ	τὸ	στόμα
autōn	*heautōn*	*poreuomenoi*	*kai*	*to*	*stoma*
their	[themselves]	walking;	and	the	mouth

840.1 prs-pron gen pl	2953.2 verb 3sing indic pres act	5084.1 adj pl neu	2273.5 verb nom pl masc part pres act	4241.4 noun pl neu
αὐτῶν	λαλεῖ	ὑπέρογκα,	θαυμάζοντες	πρόσωπα
autōn	*lalei*	*huperonka*	*thaumazontes*	*prosōpa*
their	speaks	inflated,	admiring	faces

5455.2 noun gen sing fem	5320.1 prep	5050.1 prs-pron nom 2pl	1156.2 conj	27.6 adj pl masc
ὠφελείας	χάριν.	**17.** Ὑμεῖς	δέ,	ἀγαπητοί,
ōpheleias	*charin*	*Humeis*	*de*	*agapētoi*
profit	for the sake of.	You	but,	beloved,

could also refer to an indefinite large number. The "saints" (holy ones) mentioned in verse 14 may include angels (as in Matthew 25:31) or human believers (as in Colossians 3:4) or both.

Behold, the Lord cometh with ten thousands of his saints: . . . with myriads, *Montgomery* . . . holy myriads, *Wuest* . . . of His people, *Williams* . . . holy angels, *Campbell.*

15. Verse 15 continues the quotation from the prophecy of Enoch. One purpose of the Lord's coming is to mete out judgment against all and end the planet's rebellion. This judgment will be directed against sinful men and may also include the evil angels mentioned elsewhere in Jude. God will not only perform an act of judgment, He will also convict ("convince") all the ungodly of their wickedness.

The rest of the verse catalogs the depth of evil that will be judged. The world at Christ's return will be "ungodly," lacking in reverence for God and living in defiance of His will. Their deeds are ungodly, the manner in which they do the deeds is ungodly, and their harsh words against God are ungodly.

15. To execute judgment upon all: He will judge the world, *Laubach.*

and to convince all that are ungodly among them: . . . and to convict all, *Norlie* . . . effectually convict all those who are destitute of a reverential awe towards God, *Wuest.*

of all their ungodly deeds which they have ungodly committed: . . . concerning all their works of impiety which they impiously performed, *Wuest* . . . of which they have been notoriously guilty, *Fenton.*

and of all their hard [speeches]: . . . all the harsh things, *SEB.*

which ungodly sinners have spoken against him: . . . which impious sinners spoke against Him, *Wuest.*

16. Jude concluded with a final list of phrases describing the seducers who had crept into the churches. The verse expands on the sins of speech that are mentioned at the end of Enoch's prophecy.

These men were grumblers ("murmurers"), much like the Israelites during their sojourn in the wilderness (cf. 1 Corinthians 10:10). By its pronunciation the word *gongustai* suggests a low rumbling of discontent, and it describes smoldering discontent that has not come out into the open. Such an attitude is one of the distinguishing marks of the godless person.

Such individuals are faultfinders, dissatisfied with their lot in life. The man who always cursed his luck was a standard character in classical Greek literature, and these apostates fit that stereotype. Like the angels mentioned in verse 6, they forgot to be grateful to God and wanted a role different from the one allotted to them.

They lived according to their own lusts, just as the people of Sodom and Gomorrah followed their sensual cravings. The present tense shows a continual pattern of life governed by the dictates of physical desires rather than the will of God. They speak puffed-up words. Their speech is pompous, bombastic oratory designed to impress, but empty of value. Hoping to gain an advantage for themselves, they pay excessive attention to influential people. *Thaumazontes* literally means "to be amazed." The false teachers are described here as flatterers, fawning on anyone who can help them reach their coveted places of honor. In setting themselves above the need to worship God, they worshiped men.

The central section of Jude, from verse 8 to verse 17, gives a chilling description of the apostates. In the beginning few of these traits would be obvious, and believers might welcome men of such seeming importance. But the rottenness beneath the surface must be uncovered. That was Jude's task.

16. These are murmurers, complainers: These wicked men are always complaining, *Laubach* . . . complaining against their lot, *Wuest* . . . grumblers, malcontents, *Adams* . . . inveterate fault-finders, *Fenton* . . . blaming others, *SEB.*

walking after their own lusts: . . . pursuing their way at the prompting of their own passions, *Wade* . . . ordering their course of conduct in accordance with their own passionate cravings, *Wuest* . . . proceeding in accordance with their own inordinate desires, *Fenton* . . . They live to satisfy their evil passions, *Williams.*

and their mouth speaketh great swelling [words]: . . . they have arrogant words upon their lips, *TCNT* . . . talk arrogantly, *Noli* . . . speak arrogantly, *Adams* . . . speaks immoderate, extravagant things, *Wuest.*

having men's persons in admiration because of advantage: . . . catering to personalities for the sake of advantage, *Wuest* . . . flattering people to gain favor, *Adams* . . . flatter men for their own advantage, *Williams C.K.* . . . for the sake of profit, *Darby.*

3279.8 verb 2pl impr aor pass	3450.1 art gen pl	4343.5 noun gen pl neu	3450.1 art gen pl	4136.5 verb gen pl neu part perf mid
μνήσθητε	τῶν	ῥημάτων	τῶν	προειρημένων
mnēsthēte	*tōn*	*rhēmatōn*	*tōn*	*proeirēmenōn*
remember	the	words	the	having been spoken before

5097.3 prep	3450.1 art gen pl	646.5 noun gen pl masc	3450.2 art gen sing	2935.2 noun gen sing masc	2231.2 prs-pron gen 1pl
ὑπὸ	τῶν	ἀποστόλων	τοῦ	κυρίου	ἡμῶν
hupo	*tōn*	*apostolōn*	*tou*	*kuriou*	*hēmōn*
by	the	apostles	of the	Lord	our

18.a.**Txt:** 02A,04C,018K 020L-corr,025P,byz.Sod
Var: 01ℵ,03B,020L-org Lach,Tisc,We/Ho,Weis UBS/☆

18.b.**Txt:** 018K,020L 025P,byz.
Var: 01ℵ,02A,03B,04C 33,Lach,Tisc,Weis,Sod UBS/☆

2400.2 name masc	5382.2 name gen masc	3617.1 conj	2978.25 verb indic imperf act	5050.3 prs-pron dat 2pl
Ἰησοῦ	Χριστοῦ·	**18.** ὅτι	ἔλεγον	ὑμῖν,
Iēsou	*Christou*	*hoti*	*elegon*	*humin*
Jesus	Christ,	that	they were saying	to you,

3617.1 conj	1706.1 prep	2057.2 adj gen sing	5385.3 noun dat sing masc	1894.2 prep	2057.2 adj gen sing
ʽa ὅτι ʼ	ʽ ἐν	ἐσχάτου	χρόνῳ	[b☆ Ἐπ'	ἐσχάτου
hoti	*en*	*eschatou*	*chronō*	*Ep'*	*eschatou*
that	in	last	time	[At	last

3450.2 art gen sing	5385.2 noun gen sing masc	1498.43 verb 3pl indic fut mid	1687.1 noun nom pl masc	2567.3 prep	3450.15 art acc pl fem
τοῦ	χρόνου]	ἔσονται	ἐμπαῖκται	κατὰ	τὰς
tou	*chronou*	*esontai*	*empaiktai*	*kata*	*tas*
of the	time]	there will be	mockers,	after	the

1431.2 prs-pron gen pl	1924.1 noun fem	4057.10 verb nom pl masc part pres mid	3450.1 art gen pl	757.3 noun gen pl fem
ἑαυτῶν	ἐπιθυμίας	πορευόμενοι	τῶν	ἀσεβειῶν.
heautōn	*epithumias*	*poreuomenoi*	*tōn*	*asebeiōn*
their own	desires	walking	of the	ungodlinesses.

3642.7 dem-pron nom pl masc	1498.7 verb 3pl indic pres act	3450.7 art nom pl masc	587.1 verb nom pl masc part pres act	5426.2 adj nom pl masc
19. Οὗτοί	εἰσιν	οἱ	ἀποδιορίζοντες,	ψυχικοί,
Houtoi	*eisin*	*hoi*	*apodiorizontes*	*psuchikoi*
These	are	the	setting apart,	natural,

4011.1 noun sing neu	3231.1 partic	2174.19 verb nom pl masc part pres act	5050.1 prs-pron nom 2pl	1156.2 conj	27.6 adj pl masc
πνεῦμα	μὴ	ἔχοντες.	**20.** ὑμεῖς	δέ,	ἀγαπητοί,
pneuma	*mē*	*echontes*	*humeis*	*de*	*agapētoi*
Spirit	not	having.	You	but,	beloved,

3450.11 art dat sing fem	39.17 adj sup dat sing fem	5050.2 prs-pron gen 2pl	3963.3 noun dat sing fem	2010.2 verb nom pl masc part pres act
ʽ τῇ	ἁγιωτάτῃ	ὑμῶν	πίστει	ἐποικοδομοῦντες
tē	*hagiōtatē*	*humōn*	*pistei*	*epoikodomountes*
on the	most holy	your	faith	building up

1431.8 prs-pron acc pl masc	2010.2 verb nom pl masc part pres act	1431.8 prs-pron acc pl masc	3450.11 art dat sing fem	39.17 adj sup dat sing fem
ἑαυτοὺς,	[☆ ἐποικοδομοῦντες	ἑαυτοὺς	τῇ	ἁγιωτάτῃ
heautous	*epoikodomountes*	*heautous*	*tē*	*hagiōtatē*
yourselves,	[building up	yourselves	in the	most holy

5050.2 prs-pron gen 2pl	3963.3 noun dat sing fem	1706.1 prep	4011.3 noun dat sing neu	39.3 adj dat sing	4195.13 verb nom pl masc part pres mid
ὑμῶν	πίστει,]	ἐν	πνεύματι	ἁγίῳ	προσευχόμενοι,
humōn	*pistei*	*en*	*pneumati*	*hagiō*	*proseuchomenoi*
your	faith,]	in	Spirit	Holy	praying,

17. A new section begins here. How should the Church respond to this terrible threat? Jude gave a series of instructions for dealing with the problem.

He began with "But, beloved," a dramatic switch from the renegades to the faithful Christians. Jude instructed believers to remember the warnings they had already heard. "Remember" is the first command given in the letter. The believers' first line of defense was the realization that the original apostles had predicted such an invasion of heretics.

Though Jude did not quote a particular passage from the New Testament, he gave the general sense of the apostolic teaching recorded in Scripture in such passages as Acts 20:29,30; 1 Timothy 4:1; 2 Timothy 3:1-9; 4:3,4; and 1 John 2:18. God is not surprised; believers should not be taken by surprise either.

18. Jude next quoted the specific warning which the apostles had given. The imperfect tense shows that this warning was given repeated emphasis in the early teaching.

The phrase "the last time" refers to the period before the return of Christ. Since that return can occur at any time, Jude applied it to his own era. At that time, "mockers" were predicted, as in 2 Peter 3:3. Mockers are those who ridicule God's Word and laugh at those who refuse to follow their lustful life-style. Despite their claims of freedom, "mockers" walk around enslaved by their desires for ungodly things.

19. These false teachers were the real cause of division, though they probably accused any protester of being unloving.

The apostates considered themselves spiritual and called common Christians *psuchikoi,* limited to the level of life that even plants shared. But Jude turned the tables and declared that *they* were the ones on the lower level.

Such individuals do not have the Spirit. In the light of Romans 8:9 the phrase shows these false teachers were not regenerate.

20. Jude turned next to positive commands. Verses 20 and 21 declare the Christian's responsibility toward himself.

Jude again began with "But ye, beloved" to draw a contrast between genuine Christians and the false teachers. The primary command appears in verse 21, surrounded by three secondary instructions.

First, a believer should build himself up in the "most holy faith" rather than tearing it down as the apostates did. "Most holy faith" pictures the objective truth of the gospel as something utterly separate from any human doctrine.

Second, believers must pray in the Holy Spirit. Christians can claim the aid of the Holy Spirit in prayer (Romans 8:26,27) as they oppose the enemies of God (Ephesians 6:18).

17. But, beloved, remember ye the words: . . . do remember, dear friends, *Phillips* . . . you must recollect, *TCNT* . . . remember the predictions of, *Noli* . . . remember the suggestions, *Berkeley.*

which were spoken before of the apostles of our Lord Jesus Christ: . . . that the messengers of Jesus Christ gave us beforehand, *Phillips* . . . what was foretold, *TCNT* . . . that were given heretofore by, *Berkeley.*

18. How that they told you there should be mockers in the last time: At the end of this period there will be scoffers, *Adams* . . . when they said, *Phillips.*

who should walk after their own ungodly lusts: . . . whose lives are guided by their own impious passions, *Berkeley* . . . who will live to satisfy their own godless passions, *Williams* . . . who live according to their own Godless desires, *Phillips* . . . guided by their own sinful desires, *Norlie.*

19. These be they who separate themselves: They are men who will create factions, *Norlie* . . . These are the agitators, *Berkeley* . . . These are the men who split communities, *Phillips* . . . who are making trouble, *SEB* . . . that set up divisions, *Williams C.K.* . . . who are causing divisions among, *Laubach.*

sensual, having not the Spirit: They are only physical, *SEB* . . . for they are led by human emotions and never by the Spirit of God, *Phillips* . . . living an animal life, *Williams C.K.* . . . they ignore their human spirit which has to do with the spiritual, religious part of a person's life, *Wuest* . . . mere animals, destitute of any spiritual nature, *Williams* . . . the worldly, who lack the Spirit, *Berkeley.*

20. But ye, beloved, building up yourselves on your most holy faith: . . . you, dear friends of mine, build yourselves up on the foundation of your most holy faith, *Phillips* . . . building yourselves up constantly in the sphere of and by means of, *Wuest.*

praying in the Holy Ghost: . . . and as constantly, *Wuest* . . . and are worshiping by, *Berkeley* . . . praying with a holy spirit, *Fenton.*

1431.8 prs-pron acc pl masc	1706.1 prep	26.3 noun dat sing fem	2296.2 noun gen sing masc	4931.19 verb 2pl impr aor act
21. ἑαυτοὺς	ἐν	ἀγάπῃ	θεοῦ	ʻ☆ τηρήσατε,
heautous	*en*	*agapē*	*theou*	*tērēsate*
yourselves	in	love	of God	keep,

21.a.**Txt:** 01ℵ,02A,025P byz.
Var: p72,03B,04C-org 044,1505,1611,1852 2495,bo.

4931.42 verb 1pl subj aor act	4185.5 verb nom pl masc part pres mid	3450.16 art sing neu	1643.2 noun sing neu	3450.2 art gen sing
[a τηρήσωμεν,]	προσδεχόμενοι	τὸ	ἔλεος	τοῦ
tērēsōmen	*prosdechomenoi*	*to*	*eleos*	*tou*
[let us keep,]	awaiting	the	mercy	of the

2935.2 noun gen sing masc	2231.2 prs-pron gen 1pl	2400.2 name masc	5382.2 name gen masc	1519.1 prep	2205.4 noun acc sing fem	164.1 adj sing
κυρίου	ἡμῶν	Ἰησοῦ	Χριστοῦ,	εἰς	ζωὴν	αἰώνιον.
kuriou	*hēmōn*	*Iēsou*	*Christou*	*eis*	*zōēn*	*aiōnion*
Lord	our	Jesus	Christ	unto	life	eternal.

2504.1 conj	3614.8 rel-pron acc pl masc	3173.1 conj	1640.5 verb 2pl impr pres act	1246.10 verb nom pl masc part pres mid
22. καὶ	οὓς	μὲν	ʻ ἐλεεῖτε	διακρινόμενοι·
kai	*hous*	*men*	*eleeite*	*diakrinomenoi*
And	whom		pity,	making a difference

22.a.**Txt:** 018K,020L 025P,byz.lect.
Var: 01ℵ,03B,04C-corr We/Ho,Weis,Sod UBS/☆

1635.1 verb 2pl impr pres act	1246.17 verb acc pl masc part pres mid	3614.8 rel-pron acc pl masc	1156.2 conj	1706.1 prep
[a☆ ἐλεᾶτε	διακρινομένους,]	23. ʻ οὓς	δὲ	ἐν
eleate	*diakrinomenous*	*hous*	*de*	*en*
[pity you	doubting,]	whom	but	with

5238.3 noun dat sing masc	4834.2 verb 2pl impr pres act	1523.2 prep gen	3450.2 art gen sing	4300.2 noun gen sing neu	720.3 verb nom pl masc part pres act
φόβῳ,	σῴζετε,	ἐκ	τοῦ	πυρὸς	ἁρπάζοντες,
phobō	*sōzete*	*ek*	*tou*	*puros*	*harpazontes*
fear	save,	out of	the	fire	snatching;

23.a.**Txt:** 018K,020L 025P,byz.lect.Steph
Var: 01ℵ,02A,03B We/Ho,Weis,Sod UBS/☆

4834.2 verb 2pl impr pres act	1523.2 prep gen	4300.2 noun gen sing neu	720.3 verb nom pl masc part pres act	3614.8 rel-pron acc pl masc	1156.2 conj
[a☆ σῴζετε	ἐκ	πυρὸς	ἁρπάζοντες,	οὓς	δὲ
sōzete	*ek*	*puros*	*harpazontes*	*hous*	*de*
[save	out of	fire	seizing,	whom	but

1635.1 verb 2pl impr pres act	1706.1 prep	5238.3 noun dat sing masc	3268.6 verb nom pl masc part pres act	2504.1 conj	3450.6 art acc sing masc
ἐλεᾶτε	ἐν	φόβῳ,]	μισοῦντες	καὶ	τὸν
eleate	*en*	*phobō*	*misountes*	*kai*	*ton*
pity	with	fear,]	hating	even	the

570.3 prep	3450.10 art gen sing fem	4418.2 noun gen sing fem	4549.2 verb acc sing masc part perf mid	5345.2 noun acc sing masc	3450.3 art dat sing
ἀπὸ	τῆς	σαρκὸς	ἐσπιλωμένον	χιτῶνα.	24. Τῷ
apo	*tēs*	*sarkos*	*espilōmenon*	*chitōna*	*Tō*
by	the	flesh	spotted	garment.	To the

24.a.**Txt:** 018K,025P,byz.
Var: 01ℵ,03B,04C,020L bo.Elzev,Gries,Lach Treg,Word,Tisc,We/Ho Weis,Sod,UBS/☆

1156.2 conj	1404.14 verb dat sing masc part pres mid	5278.13 verb inf aor act	840.8 prs-pron acc pl masc	5050.4 prs-pron acc 2pl
δὲ	δυναμένῳ	φυλάξαι	ʻ αὐτοὺς	[a☆ ὑμᾶς]
de	*dunamenō*	*phulaxai*	*autous*	*humas*
but	being able	to keep	them	[you]

673.1 adj acc pl masc	2504.1 conj	2449.15 verb inf aor act	2684.1 prep	3450.10 art gen sing fem
ἀπταίστους,	καὶ	στῆσαι	κατενώπιον	τῆς
aptaistous	*kai*	*stēsai*	*katenōpion*	*tēs*
without stumbling,	and	to set	before	the

21. The primary command of the sentence appears next: "Keep yourselves in the love of God." Verse 1 describes God's part in keeping the believer, verse 21 the human side. The Christian is to keep himself in the sphere of God's love, the place where His blessings are available.

Finally, the believer must wait eagerly for the mercy of God to be displayed. This is probably a reference to Christ's return.

22. Verses 22 and 23 move to a different area: the Christian's duty toward others in the face of apostasy. In the situation Jude envisioned, some people will be doubters, open to truth, but confused. In dealing with a sincere doubter, the believer must show mercy, leading him gently to truth.

23. There are others who are more deeply committed to a false teaching than those mentioned in verse 22. In dealing with such people, a Christian may need to use a more direct approach. *Harpazontes* has the idea of "snatching" with some violence, just as you would snatch a child away from a flame. Lot's experience at the destruction of Sodom is an illustration. The "fire" in this verse probably refers to eternal fire, as in verse 7.

A third type of person mentioned in this verse calls for very careful treatment. Confirmed sinners must be approached with a combination of pity and fear. Their sin is so deep that believers must be aware of the danger of being defiled themselves. Believers are to hate even the "garment spotted (polluted) by the flesh." The picture comes from the Old Testament laws concerning lepers (Leviticus 13:47-59). The *chitōna* was the inner garment, the one next to the body. A leper's disease could cause his very clothing to be infected, and the garment would be burned to prevent the spread of infection. In the same way, some sinners seem to defile all who even touch them.

24. The epistle concludes with a magnificent benediction and doxology. In the face of distressing problems, it is vital to know the God who is able to keep the Christian from falling. God is able to keep the believer "from falling" in the same way a sentry keeps watch to warn an army against attack. The Lord's watchcare over His children can enable them to walk surefootedly, like a horse picking its way through uneven terrain. With God on guard, no believer need be ambushed by temptations to immorality or by doctrinal deceptions.

Because He guards the believer from stumbling, God will also carry the process to completion. Christians can stand before Him in the presence of His glory in heaven and shout with excited joy, because they come to the Throne blameless. *Amōmous* is used in 1 Peter 1:19 to describe Christ, the spotless Lamb sacrificed to enable the believer to stand blameless before God.

21. Keep yourselves in the love of God: . . . with watchful care, *Wuest* . . . Cling to, *Noli* . . . within the shelter of God's love, *Wade.*

looking for the mercy of our Lord Jesus Christ unto eternal life: Wait patiently for...which will bring you to, *Phillips* . . . all the while awaiting, *Berkeley* . . . Wait for the Lord Jesus Christ with his mercy to give you life forever, *Everyday* . . . expectantly looking for...resulting in life eternal, *Wuest.*

22. And of some have compassion, making a difference: For some of these men you can feel pity and you can treat them differently, *Phillips* . . . on some...be showing mercy, on those who are in doubt, *Wuest* . . . Convince certain ones who separate themselves, *Berkeley.*

23. And others save with fear, pulling [them] out of the fire: Try to save them from hell fire, *Laubach* . . . Others you must try and save by fear, snatching them as it were, *Phillips* . . . show mercy to others with caution, *Adams* . . . by dragging them out of, *Montgomery.*

hating even the garment spotted by the flesh: . . . on still others have pity mingled with great caution, loathing even the clothing that has been, *Berkeley* . . . hating even the undergarment, *Wuest* . . . Pity those who are slaves to animal passions, *Laubach* . . . while hating the very garments their deeds have befouled, *Phillips* . . . even if you hate to touch their sin-soaked garments, *Noli* . . . Hate even their clothes which are dirty from sin, *Everyday* . . . stained with their evil nature, *SEB* . . . befouled by their lusts, *Norlie* . . . polluted with sensuality, *Fenton.*

24. Now unto him that is able to keep you from falling: . . . can help you not to fall, *Everyday* . . . to guard you, *Fenton* . . . without stumbling, *Darby* . . . from stumbling, *Montgomery.*

and to present [you] faultless: . . . and to make you stand, *Williams* . . . without fault, *Phillips* . . . can bring you before his glory without any wrong in you, *Everyday.*

Jude 25

25.a.**Txt:** 018K,020L 025P,byz.
Var: 01ℵ,02A,03B,04C 33,Gries,Lach,Treg,Alf Word,Tisc,We/Ho,Weis Sod,UBS/*

25.b.**Var:** 01ℵ,02A,03B 04C,020L,bo.Gries,Lach Treg,Alf,Word,Tisc We/Ho,Weis,Sod UBS/*

25.c.**Txt:** 018K,020L 025P,byz.
Var: 01ℵ,02A,03B,04C Lach,Treg,Alf,Word Tisc,We/Ho,Weis,Sod UBS/*

25.d.**Var:** 01ℵ,02A,03B 04C,020L,sa.bo.Lach Treg,Alf,Word,Tisc We/Ho,Weis,Sod UBS/*

25.e.**Txt:** 025P,Steph
Var: Elzev,Gries,Lach Word,Tisc,We/Ho,Weis Sod,UBS/*

1385.2 noun gen sing fem	**840.3** prs-pron gen sing	**297.4** adj acc pl masc	**1706.1** prep	**20.3** noun dat sing fem	**3304.4** adj dat sing masc
δόξης	αὐτοῦ	ἀμώμους	ἐν	ἀγαλλιάσει,	**25.** μόνῳ
doxēs	*autou*	*amōmous*	*en*	*agalliasei*	*monō*
glory	his	blameless	with	exultation,	to only

4533.2 adj dat sing masc	**2296.3** noun dat sing masc	**4842.3** noun dat sing masc	**2231.2** prs-pron gen 1pl	**1217.2** prep	**2400.2** name masc
(a σοφῷ)	θεῷ	σωτῆρι	ἡμῶν,	[b*+ διὰ	Ἰησοῦ
sophō	*theō*	*sōteri*	*hēmōn*	*dia*	*Iēsou*
wise	God	Saviour	our,	[through	Jesus

5382.2 name gen masc	**3450.2** art gen sing	**2935.2** noun gen sing masc	**2231.2** prs-pron gen 1pl	**1385.1** noun nom sing fem	**2504.1** conj
Χριστοῦ	τοῦ	κυρίου	ἡμῶν]	δόξα	(c καὶ)
Christou	*tou*	*kuriou*	*hēmōn*	*doxa*	*kai*
Christ	the	Lord	our]	glory	and

3142.1 noun nom sing fem	**2877.1** noun sing neu	**2504.1** conj	**1833.2** noun nom sing fem	**4112.1** prep	**3820.2** adj gen sing
μεγαλωσύνη,	κράτος	καὶ	ἐξουσία,	[d*+ πρὸ	παντὸς
megalōsunē	*kratos*	*kai*	*exousia*	*pro*	*pantos*
greatness,	might	and	authority	[before	all

3450.2 art gen sing	**163.1** noun gen sing masc	**2504.1** conj	**3431.1** adv	**2504.1** conj	**1519.1** prep	**3820.8** adj acc pl masc	**3450.8** art acc pl masc
τοῦ	αἰῶνος]	καὶ	νῦν	καὶ	εἰς	πάντας	τοὺς
tou	*aiōnos*	*kai*	*nun*	*kai*	*eis*	*pantas*	*tous*
the	age]	both	now,	and	to	all	the

163.6 noun acc pl masc	**279.1** intrj	**1976.1** noun nom sing fem	**2430.2** name masc	**2498.1** adj nom sing masc
αἰῶνας.	ἀμήν.	(e Ἐπιστολὴ	Ἰούδα	καθολική.)
aiōnas	*amēn*	*Epistolē*	*Iouda*	*katholikē*
ages.	Amen.	Epistle	of Jude	general.

This does not mean believers have never had a fault, for only Jesus lived a faultless life. Rather, it means that the faults of the past have been repented of and have been brought to the Cross where the blood of God's Son cleanses from all sin. What joy there will be to know that all has been forgiven, and now the faults are not imputed to our account. The faults which filled us with despair, doubts, and apprehension are now forgiven and forgotten. Matthew Henry says, "Where there is no sin there will be no sorrow; where there is the perfection of holiness, there will be the perfection of joy" (p.1117).

25. Such a God deserves all praise. The epistle ends with a doxology. Jude addressed it to God the Father, who is the Saviour of man. Salvation comes through Jesus Christ who serves as the divine channel through whom man comes to the Father, thus bringing praise to the Father.

Jude ascribed four glories to God. "Glory" is the term for the visible display of God's attributes, His excellence. "Majesty" pictures the royal dignity of the King of the universe. "Dominion" describes the infinite control God exerts over the world. "Power" (authority) speaks of God's right to do as He pleases with His creation.

These characteristics belong to the Lord eternally, in eternity past, in the present, and throughout the eternal future.

before the presence of his glory with exceeding joy: . . . exultant before the radiant glory of His eyes, *Greber* . . . before His glory, *Wand* . . . give you a place in his glory, *BB* . . . great joy before His glory, *Beck* . . . to stand you before his glory, *Klingensmith* . . . the manifestation of his glory at the day of judgment, *Macknight* . . . his majesty, *Murdock* . . . his glorious presence, *Williams* . . . the presence of His glory with abounding joy, *Berkeley* . . . in his presence irreproachable and triumphant, *Goodspeed* . . . in gladness, *Confraternity* . . . with glad rejoicing, *Barclay* . . . in triumphant joy, *Norlie* . . . with exquisite delight, *Fenton* . . . with rejoicing, *Williams C.K.* . . . and with unspeakable joy, *Phillips* . . . with unspeakable, ecstatic delight, *AmpB* . . . and give you great joy, *Everyday.*

25. To the only wise God our Saviour: . . . namely, the only God...by means of Jesus the Messiah, *Murdock* . . . to the only omniscient God, *Noli* . . . to God alone, *Wilson* . . . He is the One who saves us, *Everyday* . . . Who is our Deliverer through our Lord Jesus Christ, *Greber.*

[be] glory and majesty, dominion and power: . . . belong, *Confraternity* . . . be praise, *Murdock* . . . be ascribed the glory of infinite perfection, and the majesty of empire absolutely universal; strength to govern that empire, and right to do whatever seemeth to himself good, *Macknight* . . . let us give...honour, *BB* . . . great honor, strength, *Klingensmith* . . . might, and authority, *Montgomery* . . . greatness, *Everyday.*

both now and for ever. Amen: . . . for all time past, *Everyday* . . . before every aeon, *Hanson* . . . before all time, *Wuest, Confraternity* . . . as in time immemorial, *Greber* . . . before time was, now, and in all ages, *Phillips* . . . and now, and to all ages, *Alford* . . . from everlasting, so be it now and forever, *Beck* . . . and now, and forever more, *Berkeley* . . . before time began, is now, and shall be for all time to come, *TCNT* . . . both now and all time to come, *Klingensmith* . . . until time ends, *Barclay.*

Overview–Hebrews

The *Overview* is a significant section of the *Study Bible.* It offers important background information concerning each book. It usually provides a comprehensive outline of the book, then presents in-depth studies on themes which relate to the subject matter. Since it serves as a background, it does not necessarily cover every chapter or section. It provides material for which there would not be enough space in the *Verse-by-Verse Commentary.*

The literary style of the Epistle to the Hebrews is immediately striking. Without any greeting or opening, the author introduces his main theme: Christ is the fulfillment and completion of the revelation of God which began in the Old Testament. The letter does, however, close in keeping with epistolary style and custom, with a series of personal greetings and wishes for the recipients' well-being.

One notes the absence of any biographical opening comments about the author of the letter to the Hebrews. Although almost certainly the author was known and respected by his recipients, his identity has nonetheless been forgotten. Even the Early Church had to be content with speculating as to his identity. Some thought it was Paul (e.g., Clement of Alexandria, died ca. 215), while others contended it was Barnabas or another of Paul's coworkers.

Despite the inclusion of Hebrews in the Pauline corpus as early as the Third Century by the Eastern church, it was not until the Fourth Century that the West included it in the New Testament Scripture collection as the 14th letter of Paul. Even as late as the Reformation, however, questions concerning the canonicity of Hebrews persisted. When Luther resisted placing Hebrews among the "correct certain main books" of Scripture, his decision was linked to a particular doctrinal issue, one that had been debated in the Church since ancient times. Some believe 6:4-6 teaches there is no possibility of being saved after once falling from faith. Such a strong viewpoint greatly affected the general attitude and practice of the Church towards repentance. It further led to a decrease in the letter's reputation. By virtue of its own immanent truth, however, the letter to the Hebrews did manage to survive and has proved to be one of the pillars of New Testament revelation.

The question of authorship is unanswerable. One of the best hypotheses is Luther's theory that it was Apollos. According to Acts 18:24-28, Apollos, who worked in Ephesus, was a Jewish Christian from Alexandria: "an eloquent man . . . mighty in the Scriptures." Both of these qualifications, knowledge of the Scriptures and eloquence of speech (a by-product of his Hellenistic culture) could be applied to the author of Hebrews. But as readers of the Bible we must be content with what the letter itself tells us, and it does not tell us its author's name. Some scholars aver that although the style is different from Paul's other writings he may be the author of this book.

We do learn that he knows Timothy (13:23) and that he was with believers from Italy (13:24). From this some have concluded that the letter was sent to the church in Rome or to a group within it.

Since portions of the letter to the Hebrews appear in 1 Clement, it is clear that it was written before A.D. 95. Perhaps it was penned as early as the midsixties, since we read nothing in it about the destruction of the temple.

The letter indicates that the writer was disturbed by the spiritual condition of some of his readers. At a time when they should have been prepared to teach others, it was still necessary to teach them the fundamental truths of the Faith (5:12). Their problem was that they were "dull of hearing" (5:11). The seriousness of the situation is reflected in the author's repeated warnings of the risk of backsliding (6:4-8; 10:26-31; 12:15-17). There was apparently some tendency towards schism (10:25), as well as a spiritual weakening and faintheartedness (12:3). The main issue was that second generation Christians (2:3) needed to be strengthened in their faith.

As the Greek title (*pros hebraious*, added in the Second Century) indicates, the letter probably was addressed to a church body largely made up of Jewish Christians. Under the pressure of persecution and discouragement because the coming of the Lord had not occurred (10:32-39), they were being enticed to return to Judaism. In light of this, the author admonished them to hold fast to their profession of faith (4:14-16). They must not throw away their confidence, which held a promise of great reward (10:35). The warnings are so general, though, they can apply to Christians of all generations.

The Distinct Trait of the Epistle to the Hebrews

In order to understand properly the Epistle to the Hebrews, one must scrutinize the text and read it in connection with the rest of the New Testament. No New Testament writing stands alone, isolated from the rest. The great contribution of the New Testament Scriptures is their united testimony to Jesus Christ as Lord and Saviour. Their dependence on one another, though, varies considerably.

Of all of the epistolary literature, the Epistle to the Hebrews stands apart as the one most distinctly referring to the earthly life of Jesus. Here we encounter a clear recognition that Jesus is God incarnate, that He was tempted, that He agonized in Gethsemane (5:7), that He suffered and died. We also detect some doctrinal correspondence with the Gospel of John: (1) the preexistent Jesus takes part in creation (cf. John's prologue); (2) Jesus is portrayed as the priestly intercessor (John 17, the high priestly prayer); and (3) like John, the author of Hebrews is concerned about properly worshiping God in spirit and truth (cf. John 4:23).

In the same way the letter shares a close affinity with Paul's theology. Both emphasize the inability of the Law to save or atone for sin (Romans 3:20; Hebrews 10:1f.). Both contrast Sinai and the heavenly Jerusalem (Galatians 4:24f.; Hebrews 12:18f.), and both understand Jesus' death to be a sacrifice. Paul, however, does not portray Jesus as the High Priest. This is an important distinction that characterizes the Epistle to the Hebrews.

More than any other letter in the New Testament, Hebrews is oriented around the cultic, ritualistic system of Judaism. The presentation builds upon images of sacrifice and atonement. Taking the Old Testament's guidelines for ritual sacrifice and priestly service as a starting point, the author portrays Christ to his readers as the One who makes atonement, the ultimate High Priest, whose self-sacrifice secured, once and for all, our eternal redemption (9:12).

The Epistle to the Hebrews shows how the old covenant and its temple cultus had attained its end and fulfillment in Christ. The chain of logic here is reminiscent of Paul's dispute with Judaism over the proper understanding of the Law. Now the ritual of the Old Testament sacrificial system is being exposed as just as inadequate as the Old Testament Law to atone and redeem mankind from its sin. Such redemption requires a far superior sacrifice than that which the high priest offered on the Day of Atonement. Instead of taking away sins, these offerings only succeeded in being a reminder of sin (10:1-4). But, because Christ offered himself as a pure sacrifice to God (9:14), He cleansed us from our sins (1:3). He has given us the ability to approach the Holy of Holies with boldness (10:19) and to serve God (12:28).

Hebrews provides a proper understanding of the two covenants. It is handled in such a way that the old covenant is not consequently viewed as superfluous. God is the source of both covenants. That there should be two covenants is also according to the counsel of God; it is part of His plan of salvation. Hebrews also emphasizes that believers, even of that era, were living in the last days (1:2) when God in a decisive way had graciously intervened in the history of His people, in accordance with His promises. All the promises were fulfilled in Christ, God's Son. Therefore, solely because Christ had come, the inspired writer could challenge the most time-honored institutions of the Jewish religion—the tabernacle, the priesthood, and the sacrificial system.

The Old Testament, however, retains its significance, since it forms the background for the ultimate revelation of God in Christ. So the entire thesis is constructed on the Old Testament, which is viewed from a messianic perspective.

Hebrews must be viewed in light of first-century circumstances, especially in reference to Judaism outside of Palestine, i.e., Hellenistic Judaism, which flourished in the Greek culture. Perhaps the foremost representative of Hellenistic Judaism would be Philo, who lived in Alexandria from around 20 B.C. to A.D. 45. But Hebrews does not follow Philo, as the altogether different use of Scripture makes plain.

Even though Philo considered the Old Testament to be divine Scripture and knew its contents, he used an allegorical method to interpret it. This enabled him to interpret Scripture according to his own philosophical premises rather than according to Biblical teachings. In contrast to Philo, Hebrews does not interpret Old Testament texts philosophically, but messianically. In company with the other witnesses of the New Testament, it proclaims the message of the Bible as a record of God's saving act in Christ. Each quotation from the Old Testament is carefully interpreted in light of its fulfillment in the new covenant.

Typically, this reflects a typological method according to which persons and institutions of the Old Testament are interpreted as "types" or "patterns" that occur in the New Testament. Melchizedek is thus presented as a type of Christ, as the true High Priest (chapter 7); the tabernacle a picture of the heavenly sanctuary (chapter 9). The main point is that the realization or fulfillment of the types began with Christ; the Law was just a shadow of the good things to come, not the things themselves (10:1).

The Outline of the Epistle to the Hebrews

The arrangement of this epistle is precise and clear-cut. The first major section extends to chapter 5 and discusses the superiority of the revelation of the new covenant over the old. Christ surpasses the angels (chapter 1) as well as Moses (chapter 3). The second major section extends from 4:14 to 10:31 and gives a thorough description of the high priestly office of Jesus and His work of atonement. The third and final main section is made up largely of admonitions (10:32 to 13:17). This is not to imply that admonishing is limited to only the final three chapters; on the contrary, the letter's entire structure of sections of instruction interspersed with pastoral advice suggests this is a prime concern. The structure of the letter does not alter its primary goal: to encourage the readers to persevere in and better understand their faith.

OUTLINE

I. THE NEW, FINAL REVELATION OF GOD (1:1–4:13)
   A. God Has Spoken by His Son (1:1-4)
   B. Christ's Superiority to the Angels (1:5-14)
   C. Warning Against Falling From Salvation (2:1-4)
   D. The Temporary Humbling of Christ (2:5-18)
   E. Christ's Superiority to Moses (3:1-6)
   F. Warning Against Stubbornness (3:7-19)
   G. Continuation of the Sabbath Rest (4:1-10)
   H. Praise of the Word of God (4:11-13)

II. CHRIST AS THE TRUE HIGH PRIEST (4:14–10:31)
   A. Christ the Compassionate High Priest (4:14-16)
   B. In the Manner of Melchizedek (5:1-10)
   C. Renewed Rebuke of Readers (5:11–6:8)
   D. God's Covenant Faithfulness (6:9-20)
   E. Jesus Is High Priest Just Like Melchizedek (7:1-28)
   F. Jesus Is High Priest in the Heavenly Sanctuary (8:1-13)
   G. The Perfect Sacrifice of Jesus (9:1–10:18)
   H. The Danger of Apostasy (10:19-31)

III. STANDING FIRM IN THE FAITH (10:32–13:25)
   A. Keeping One's Confidence (10:32-39)
   B. The Power of Faith in the Lives of the Patriarchs (11:1-40)
   C. Christ the Author and Finisher of the Faith (12:1-11)
   D. Warning Against Rejecting the Grace of God (12:12-17)
   E. The Glory of the New Covenant (12:18-29)
   F. Social Responsibilities (13:1-6)
   G. Religious Gatherings (13:7-17)
   H. Personal Applications (13:18-25)

THE NEW, FINAL REVELATION OF GOD (1:1–4:13)

Understanding the significance of the names of Jesus is essential for understanding the Book of Hebrews. The name characterizing the human nature of the Lord, "Jesus," is used no less than nine times:

"But we see Jesus, who was made a little lower than the angels" (2:9). By virtue of His incarnation Jesus was restricted in time and space; He had to comply with the restrictions of His humanity and at last was handed over to certain men and the powers that stood behind them. The fact that He humbled himself and became obedient unto death (Philippians 2:8) is the basis for His being crowned with glory and honor.

"Consider the Apostle and High Priest of our profession, Christ Jesus" (3:1). Jesus brought together in His person the roles of both Moses and Aaron under the old covenant. As the "one sent" (*apostolon*, "apostle") from God, Jesus relates to us the Word of God. As the true High Priest, He has covered our sins and given to us the grace of God.

Jesus entered behind the veil (i.e., into the Holy of Holies) as a forerunner for us (6:20). In His ministry as High Priest He retains His true humanity, thus He is not inferior to the Aaronic high priest who alone was allowed to enter the Most Holy Place.

Jesus represents a better covenant (7:22). He became the guarantee of a new and better covenant as a true man.

Because of the sacrifice of Christ, we are given confidence ("boldness") to enter the Holy of Holies (10:19). By virtue of the sacrifice of the One who shared our nature, we have gained access to God (cf. Romans 5:1ff.).

As we fix our eyes on Jesus, the author and finisher of our faith, we see that looking to Him is the source of our strength (12:2). Through His obedience, He provided the perfect model of faith.

We have come to the mediator of a new covenant, Jesus (12:24, see 7:22).

Christ suffered outside the gate (13:12). Once again we see how the name *Jesus* is related to His suffering and death.

The God of peace brought the Great Shepherd of the flock, even our Lord Jesus, up from the dead (13:20). The Resurrection, which is otherwise not mentioned in Hebrews, is explicitly mentioned here. Its truth is affirmed by the presence of the earthly name, Jesus, in reference to it. We should observe here that the name *Jesus* has a unique relationship to the bodily appearance of the Lord, His humbling of himself, His suffering, and His death. The redemptive act on history is not based on some pagan myth of redemption.

God Has Spoken by His Son

A fundamental event for the Hebrews' argument is the reality of the Incarnation. God became man in Jesus. This view closely corresponds with the one found in the "Christ hymn" of Philippians 2:6-11. As the Son, Jesus learned obedience, and in every way Christ subjected himself to the will of God (5:8). Only after He had suffered everything necessary in the plan of God could He become the source of our eternal salvation (5:9). By suffering Jesus demonstrated that through the cross He was the perfect offering for sin. Obedience marked His service to God and made available forgiveness of sins and salvation.

The Book of Hebrews takes very seriously the need for humanity to be saved. All human beings are subject to death. Death is not regarded as natural, however, but an unnatural consequence of the power of sin. There is no escaping death's power as long as the devil has authority over death and over all those subject to death. If there is to be any salvation, the devil must be conquered on his own terms: on earth by a human being. This is why Christ had to come as a man and share in "flesh and blood" (2:14).

Christ's incarnation and subsequent death has a twofold sense: (1) Through His death as a man He overcame the ruler of death, the devil (2:14). (2) Christ redeemed mankind, which has always been enslaved to the fear of death (2:15). Because Christ submitted willingly to every consequence of being human, including being tempted, He is able to be a true high priest, who is merciful and faithful (2:17,18).

In explicit statements Hebrews provides a rough draft of the life of Christ. Christ calls men His brothers (2:11); He partakes of flesh and blood (2:14). His being "made like his brethren" expresses an identification with humanity, including things common to men—temptation, suffering, and death. It is as the One who was tempted and who suffered that Jesus offers comfort to those who are tempted (2:18).

Also descriptive of the work of Jesus are names like "Christ," "Lord," "Son of God." The title *Son* especially permeates the Book of Hebrews, as does *Son of God*. The opening verses reflect this fact: "God, who at sundry times and in divers manners spake in time past unto the fathers by the prophets, hath in these last days spoken unto us by his Son" (1:1,2).

All of God's former saving work among the

people of Israel pointed toward the final revelation of the Son. Incarnation, thus, was the goal of God's revelation. The new age could begin; the time of fulfillment had arrived, just as the prophets foretold. Once again God was speaking, now through His Son, "whom he hath appointed heir of all things, by whom also he made the worlds; who being the brightness of his glory, and the express image of his person, and upholding all things by the word of his power, when he had by himself purged our sins, sat down on the right hand of the Majesty on high" (1:2,3).

This opening description of the nature and work of the Son shows how exalted this position is in the history of salvation. Christ is not just the Redeemer who "had by himself purged our sins," He is also the One by whom all of creation came into existence. To the same degree as other New Testament writings, Hebrews emphasizes that Christ participated in the creation of the universe (as well as in maintaining its existence; cf. John 1:3; Colossians 1:17).

But first and foremost, Christ is the Redeemer. He has cleansed us from our sins (1:3). Sin prevents men from approaching God; it is only removed when purification is made. Christ provided such cleansing by His perfect sacrifice. By virtue of His saving work, Christ has been exalted to the right hand of God. Moreover, it is noteworthy that as early as this introduction Christ is portrayed in His threefold role of Prophet (God has spoken to us by His Son), Priest (He, by himself, cleansed us from sin), and King (He sat down at the right hand of the Majesty).

Whether Christ is called by His earthly name, Jesus, or His divine title, Son of God, He is one person. The divine will is disclosed in one person, according to Hebrews, the Son (2:10). God speaks to us through His Son, and it is the Son, who having cleansed us from sin, sits at the right hand of God (1:1-4).

Although Hebrews repeatedly refers to the "Son," God is called "Father" on only one occasion (Hebrews 1:5, a quote from 2 Samuel 7:14). God is the exalted Majesty from whom Christ receives all. God installed Christ as heir (1:2). Christ also receives the office of High Priest, since He did not presume such honor for himself (5:5).

The essential relationship between the Son and God comes through in the following statement: "Who being the brightness of his glory, and the express image of his person" (1:3). The divine status of Christ is not based on adoption, but on His nature. Christ reveals the Father. He is a reflection (*apaugasma*) of His glory and a perfect image, representation (*charaktēr*) of the nature of God, i.e., what God is really like (cf. John 5:19,30; 14:9).

In virtually the same breath Hebrews presents the Son's relationship to the world. He participated in creation—"by whom also he made the worlds"—and in the providence of God—"upholding all things by the word of his power." Finally Christ is the heir of all things. The created world did not only come into existence through Christ, it would fall into utter chaos without Him. Because Christ became heir, it is further implied that creation first attains consummation in Him (cf. 1:13; 10:13).

Corresponding to the aforementioned titles, Christ's work is viewed from a twofold perspective: His earthly life and His service in heaven, in the heavenly sanctuary.

Since the "children" have "flesh and blood," He partook of their nature as well (2:14; cf. 7:14). Hebrews stresses that as representative of all mankind, Christ's humanity was total; in every way He had to be like His "brothers and sisters" (cf. 2:17). His tasting of death was to the advantage of all (2:9). Although He is fully human, this in no way detracts from His being fully God. The Incarnation began a brief temporary period during which Christ willingly submitted to the will of the Father. For a little while He was made a little lower than the angels (Hebrews 2:7,9; cf. Philippians 2:7).

Temptation, tears, and suffering are characteristics of any human life. Except for the Gospels, it is the Epistle to the Hebrews which most realistically captures the earthly life of Jesus (4:15; 5:7f.; 7:26). Christ's being subject to earthly trials enables Him in His glorified humanity to have compassion upon the weak (4:15). But Christ is different from humankind in one distinct way: He is without sin (4:15; 7:26). Moreover, the book adds some other virtues: Jesus trusted God (2:13; 5:7ff.); He was faithful (2:17; 3:2); He was merciful and compassionate (2:17; 4:15); and He had great faith (12:2).

At no time, however, is the human nature of Jesus stressed in reference to His sacrificing of himself. He is God and man in one and the same person, Jesus Christ. In a passage resembling the testimony of John the apostle that Christ has the power to lay down His life and to take it up again (John 10:18), the Epistle to the Hebrews stresses that it was by virtue of the eternal Spirit that Christ offered himself up as a spotless offering (9:14; cf. 7:16).

The Epistle to the Hebrews draws a close relationship between the earthly obedience of Christ and His exaltation to the right hand of God in heaven (cf. 2:9; 12:2). The book looks back on the humility and suffering that took place in the past, and at the same time looks forward to the worldwide dominion of Christ which is yet to be revealed.

Unlike the writings of the apostle Paul, Hebrews gives themes like the Resurrection (13:20) and Second Coming (9:28; 10:37) only a moderate role. It attaches much more significance to the Ascension (4:14; 6:20; 7:26; 9:11f.,24) and to Christ's being seated on the throne at the right hand of God in heaven (1:3; 8:1; 10:12; 12:2). This is where Christ exercises His role as eternal High Priest on our behalf (9:24; cf. 7:25). From here He also encourages those who are tempted (2:18). The consummation of the work of atonement makes possible Christ's ascension to the heavenly throne (1:3).

Warnings in the Epistle

One distinguishing feature of the Epistle to the Hebrews is that its teaching is often interrupted by warning sections (3:1-4,16; 5:11 to 6:20; 10:19,39; 12:1-13,17). Based on what he knew was occurring among his readers, the author offered some practical advice and warning. But rather than appearing to be "interruptions," they may reflect key passages for unlocking the meaning of the letter as a whole. One is immediately struck by the elaborate explanations of the priesthood and sacrificial system. This presentation, it should be realized, is addressing a particular, definite problem of believers. The actual situation is best reconstructed by looking at the warning sections.

The heart of the Book of Hebrews is that Christ is sacrificed, once and for all, and through this He has provided cleansing for our sins and access to God's throne (9:19,22). In keeping with this theme, Christ is the forerunner who leads His people into the heavenly land of promise (6:20; 11:13-16). The Christian is responsible to strive by faith and perseverance for this heavenly goal, according to the pattern provided by Christ's own life and death (12:1-3; 13:12,13).

Christ's Superiority to the Angels

Many Scripture references are presented in 1:5-14 to show Christ's superiority to the angels. Chapter 2 opens with an admonition not to be lured away from salvation. The Holy Spirit intends to divert believers from such disaster by reminding them that Christian revelation is proclaimed, not by angels, but by the Lord himself. Moreover, it is confirmed by mighty deeds (2:3,4) and has an explicit relationship with the world to come (2:5).

According to Jewish thinking the law of Moses had been mediated by angels (cf. Galatians 3:10; Acts 7:53). This undoubtedly had influenced some of the believers; they were thus in jeopardy of forfeiting their salvation and denying the revelation of God in Jesus Christ. In the world to come dominion belongs solely to Christ.

Warning Against Backsliding

The believer's life-style should be governed by an awareness of the powers of the coming age (3:1ff.). As those having a share in the heavenly calling, they are obligated to hold fast to their Christian hope with confidence and conviction (3:1,6). And once more, Christ is their pattern for this.

Certainly Moses' faithfulness is an encouraging example, but as the Son of God, Jesus has an authority that exceeds that of Moses by far (3:2-6).

Warning Against Stubbornness

The crisis facing the believers was best compared with the situation Israel experienced in the wilderness. In actuality, the Christian life is itself an "exodus" whose goal is to experience the Scriptures' promise of rest (3:7-11). Psalm 95:7-11 offers a sharp caution. The "today" of the Psalms did not lose its relevance for the readers of Hebrews. It summoned the hearer to seize the eternal moment announced by Jesus, and to complete the journey that began by believing in Him. The risk consists in the fact that like ancient Israel, some will harden themselves and will not attain "rest" because of their unbelief (3:12-19).

Continuation of the Sabbath Rest

The writer offers a more encouraging word in chapter 4. The promise of entering God's rest is still in force. No one should think that it is too late (4:1). Again the author recalls Psalm 95, which is essentially the invitation given to the wilderness generation and which is now given to us. The Israelites forfeited the promise because of unbelief. But the Word of God is not ineffective. Even though they declined the invitation, the invitation is still in effect (4:6-9). Therefore, no one should think that he or she will be abandoned if by faith one seizes God's promise for his or her own.

Nevertheless, the author does not deny that the call for decision is urgent. He warns his readers against the danger of backsliding so they too do not become an example of disobedience (4:11). Note that throughout the letter the threat of falling was viewed as very present (cf. 6:4-6; 10:26-31; 12:15-17).

An interesting "digression" occurs in 5:11 to 6:20. Here the author pauses to shift his teaching to the spiritual level of his listeners. Having frequently referred to Christ as the true High Priest, the writer is ready to give a basic description of Christ's role as High Priest. This is difficult, though, for the readers are "dull of hearing" (5:11). He reproaches them, because instead of making progress in Christian understanding, they have to be instructed in the most basic principles of the Faith (Hebrews 5:12-14; cf. 1 Corinthians 2:6ff.; 3:1ff.; 1 Peter 2:2).

The "basic foundations" ("elementary teachings," NIV) of faith are listed in 6:1,2. There are six aspects, paired in three groups: "repentance and faith," "teaching on baptisms and laying on of hands," and "the resurrection of the dead and eternal judgment." The first two are linked to the basic articles of the Gentile mission (Windisch), and are probably indicative that the author is first thinking of Gentile Christian readers. However, nothing would prevent them from being Jews either. "Repentance and faith" belong together and represent the response to the preaching demanded by Jesus himself (cf. Matthew 5:20; Mark 1:15; John 14:1). "Teachings concerning baptisms and the laying on of hands" also belong together. "Baptisms" here probably refers to "absolutions, washings, or other ritual purifications, such as Jewish proselyte baptism or the baptism of John.

Christian baptism may be meant, although the plural is used (cf. the use with Apollos in Acts 18:24-26). The Book of Acts frequently depicts the Spirit as being given through the laying on of hands at baptism or by an apostle. It was critical that Jewish converts be instructed about the resurrection of the dead and eternal judgment, since Christian revelation gave these events new significance (Manson, pp.62,63).

The writer is reaching a climax in his argument. His readers should have grown in their faith, but instead they are still immature. As a result of their immaturity the threat of backsliding is even greater. But the author is not totally discounting their possibility of salvation (6:9). They once demonstrated their Christian faith and love in their actions (6:10; cf. 10:32). The critical issue now is that they show a similar zeal and enduring faith so the promises of God might be realized (6:11,12). With warning as well as encouragement the Scriptures have awakened the spiritual sensitivity of the believers.

We encounter the same combination of encouragement and admonition in the second large admonishing section (10:19-39). On the one hand, the writer urges his readers to enter boldly into the Holy of Holies and to carry out the priestly duties to which they have been called. On the other hand, he warns them against falling into (i.e., being judged by) the hands of the living God. The shift in the voice of the verb reflects the pastoral concern of the writer. By virtue of Christ's sacrifice access to God is made possible. The potential for worshiping God and loving one's neighbor is made available. Therefore, there is a repeated invitation to enter the Holy of Holies (10:19), to draw near to God (10:22), and to encourage one another toward love and good deeds (10:24). But the readers must also be aware of the terrible judgment that awaits them if they ignore God's promise of grace in Christ (10:26f.).

Finally, chapter 13 contains a series of admonitions that first involve relations with society (13:1-6) and then congregational concerns (13:7-17). Among the social obligations of believers one finds hospitality (Hebrews 13:2; cf. Romans 12:13; 1 Peter 4:9), care of prisoners (Hebrews 13:3), and respect for marriage (Hebrews 13:4; cf. 1 Corinthians 6:9).

In later verses the readers are urged to remember the example left to them by the patriarchs and their forebears. They are not to be "carried away by all kinds of strange teachings" (13:9, NIV). Of the utmost importance is that they—because of their total dependence on Christ—offer the sacrifice of praise which pleases God (13:15,16).

The closing chapters give some important clues as to the background of the letter. It seems that the author is especially concerned about some divisiveness that is threatening the church. He thus warns against neglecting the assembling together for common worship (10:25). He also warns them not to succumb to false teachings (13:9). In conjunction with this he advises them to pay close attention to their leaders (13:17; cf. 13:7).

"Salvation" in the Hebrews Epistle

Salvation is deliverance from the power of death; indeed, it is a rescue from every power or force that opposes God (5:7). But this is the negative side of salvation. Positively, salvation means a realization of the promises of God. This can be experienced in the present (6:9), but it will reach its total fulfillment in the eschatological consummation (1:14; 9:28).

Based upon the overall understanding of the Epistle to the Hebrews, the concept of salvation might best be described as "rest" (4:9,10). Rest is the fulfillment of God's promises. Especially is this so in the eschatological sense of physical and spiritual blessing. The expression *Sabbath rest* is best understood in relation to the Jewish concept that the Sabbath was a prototype of the future age to come.

If it is legitimate to describe salvation in terms of location, salvation is one's "homeland" (11:14,16); it is a "city" (11:10,16; 12:22; 13:14). Christian hope is thus directed toward an eternal heavenly goal. As a background to this, all the earthly institutions, such as the tabernacle, the Law, and the temple, are only shadows of the future heavenly reality. Abraham waited patiently for a "city which hath foundations, whose builder and maker is God" (11:10). This is why Abraham became a model of the Christian pilgrim, "For here have we no continuing city, but we seek one to come" (13:14).

The Old Testament shows that God is faithful. Some of the patriarchs and forebears were allowed to see the promises fulfilled. Abraham and Sarah were two such heroes of the Faith (6:15; cf. 11:11). But, in relation to the sending of the Son in the last days, any notion of fulfillment of the Old Testament promises can only be interpreted as models for the much more glorious fulfillment of the coming consummation (11:40). Against this backdrop the urgency of the author to the Hebrews is better appreciated. Salvation is infinite in scope from God's point of view. To reject it will inevitably lead to judgment (2:3).

Even though the Epistle to the Hebrews does not contain the word *Saviour* (*sōtēr*), Christ is explicitly presented as the "pioneer of salvation" (2:10) and the "author of eternal salvation" (5:9). The life and work of Christ create the possibility of salvation for mankind. Through His obedience He clears a path for His "brothers and sisters" to approach God.

CHRIST AS THE TRUE HIGH PRIEST (4:14–10:31)

What sets the Son apart from all others, and what typifies His role in salvation, is that having offered a cleansing sacrifice for our sins, He placed himself at the right hand of the Majesty on high (1:3). With this saying the Epistle to the Hebrews succeeds in combining in a unique way the priestly and kingly offices of the ministry of Christ. This unique perspective has its most distinct form in the presentation of Christ as our High Priest.

The Ministry of the High Priest

Humanity exists for the purpose of having fellowship with God. God created mankind in His own image (Genesis 1:27) to share a relationship based on love with his Creator and to enter into His rest (Hebrews 4:9). But humanity rebelled against God and rejected the Creator through acts of sin and disobedience.

Fallen humanity works hard trying to reestablish the severed ties with God, to rediscover the fellowship with and access to God that was lost because of Adam's fall. It is the duty of the priest to be the instrument of this "reconnection." Hebrews reflects the longing for perfection (7:11; 9:9) that is the basis for the high priest's service. The priest is the intermediary between God and man. The Jewish high priest represented the people to God and at the same time represented God to the people.

The revelation at Sinai held the promise that Israel would one day become a kingdom of priests and a holy people for God (Exodus 19:6). The people were thus concerned about such a relationship, but the priesthood was only performed by members of the priestly tribe, Aaron, his sons, and the Levites (Numbers 3:6-13).

The priest had several responsibilities. The Bible describes a few of the priestly duties that were linked to the Law, to teaching, and to the authority to judge (Leviticus 10:8-11; Deuteronomy 17:8,9). It also describes those duties centering around the tabernacle service, such as placing the showbread (Leviticus 24:5-9), burning incense (Exodus 30:7,8), sacrificing (especially the sprinkling of the blood, Leviticus 1:5), and blessing (Numbers 6:22-27).

The high priest represented all the people. This role was especially evident on the great Day of Atonement when he entered into the most holy area of the temple to make atonement for himself as well as for the sins of all Israel (Leviticus 16). The chain of reasoning was that through the person of the high priest the people themselves appeared before God in the very place (Holy of Holies) where His divine presence appeared in such a special way.

The Epistle to the Hebrews pays particular attention to the sacrifice offered on the Day of Atonement, because this event serves as a model for the work of Christ. At the same time, it was unmistakable proof of the inadequacy of the old covenant (10:1-4). In contrast to the sacrifice of the high priest, which had to be performed on a yearly basis, the sacrifice of Christ was "once for all" (10:10). The eternal sacrifice bears witness to the end of the old age and the establishment of the new covenant (9:15).

In 5:1-4 the writer explains the nature of the high priestly office, including its duties and place in the covenant arrangement. To be qualified to be a high priest, one must be chosen among men (5:1); he must understand human problems (5:2,3); and he must be called by God (5:4). The verses that follow show that Christ more than fulfills these requirements (5:5-10; cf. 2:17; 3:1; 4:14,15). The requirement that the high priest be a descendant of Aaron is not discussed here but is given special attention in chapter 7.

The Eternal Priesthood of Christ

The fundamental text proving the high priestly status of Christ is Psalm 110:4: "Thou art a priest for ever after the order of Melchizedek." This passage is cited in Hebrews 5:6,10; 7:17,21 and is united with Psalm 2:7, a key text for interpreting the Epistle to the Hebrews.

The citations from the Psalms demonstrate the legitimacy of Christ's claim to the high priesthood, even though the Book of Hebrews is the only New Testament book to make such an assertion. The context for this unique witness of the Book of Hebrews must be sought in Jesus' own intimation that His death was a sacrifice (Mark 10:45; 14:24). Sacrifice is naturally connected with a priest who sacrifices (cf. John 17:19). In the same way, there is a close connection between Jesus' saying that He would build a temple not made by hands (Mark 14:58; 15:29; Matthew 26:61; John 2:19) and the concept in Hebrews of Jesus as the High Priest who enters into the heavenly sanctuary (9:24).

It is crucial to realize that everything implied in the concept of high priest—historically as well as theologically—is fulfilled once and for all in Christ. Christian confession since ancient times stands on this statement: Jesus is the true High Priest who has opened the way for us to the Most Holy Place (6:20; 10:19,20).

This explains why the high priestly office assumed by Christ is modeled not only after the Levitical priesthood, but also from the superior priesthood of the priest-king Melchizedek. Beginning with a Biblical promise: "Thou art a priest for ever after the order of Melchizedek" (Psalm 110:4; cf. Hebrews 5:6,10), the writer of Hebrews repeats in the early verses of chapter 7 what the Bible says concerning Melchizedek. This serves as the background for the perfect priesthood of Christ.

Who was Melchizedek? Point by point the writer lists what the Bible says about him in Genesis 14:17-20. He begins with Melchizedek's name and titles. Melchizedek is a messianic name, literally meaning "king of righteousness" (cf. Zechariah 9:9), as well as "king of peace" (cf. Isaiah 9:6). In connection with this king of Salem (i.e., Jerusalem), it is told that after the battle he met with Abraham with bread and wine and blessed him as a priest of the Most High. Abraham gave Melchizedek his tithe, thus signifying his acceptance of the God of this stranger and his authority as a priest.

When Melchizedek is described as being "without father, without mother, without descent, having neither beginning of days nor end of life, but made like unto the Son of God" (7:3), it appears to refer to the Jewish religion. According to Judaism, only one with a spotless and pure descent could become a priest (Ezra 2:61-63; Nehemiah 7:63-65). Thus Melchizedek did not meet the requirements. He was "unfit" for priestly service! But, it is perfectly clear that Melchizedek is a priest of a heavenly, unexplainable order. The logic of Hebrews does not always rest on Psalm 110:4. Melchizedek is a priest eternally; he thus lives continually and does not have a beginning or end.

One might ask whether the author of Hebrews detracts from Jesus by emphasizing the uniqueness of Melchizedek. But the contrary is true. The more he relates about Melchizedek, the more the glory of the Son of God shines through. Those numerous sayings about this ancient priest all have a messianic fulfillment and all point toward the Son of God. What occurred in ancient time is a prelude to what "in the last days" had become a reality in Christ. It is proper to say that because of Christ, new light is shed on the ancient, mysterious story of Melchizedek in Genesis 14.

That the priesthood of Melchizedek is superior to the Levitical priesthood is brought out by the writer's observation that Abraham offered a tithe to Melchizedek. Obviously the one who receives the tithe is superior to the one who gives it (7:4-8). We also find here a thought of great significance in the Scriptures. When Abraham met Melchizedek and gave him a tenth of his goods, in a unique way, as a descendant of Abraham, Levi was present too. The offspring is affected by his ancestor's actions. Thus Levi indirectly acknowledged the superior priesthood of Melchizedek (7:9,10).

The same kind of reasoning occurs on a higher plane. Adam was the first member of the human family. This made his fall even more catastrophic, because Adam is a corporate expression of all mankind to come. The many are going to be disobedient because of the fall of the one (Romans 5:17). This is why salvation had to be accomplished by one who could represent all humanity. Christ's duty was to restore what Adam had forfeited. Through His obedience He established a totally new race of people justified through His blood (Romans 5:9).

The account of Melchizedek serves as the first indication of the end of the old priesthood and the beginning of the new order. The Levitical priesthood was inadequate. The fact that Scriptures speak of a priest of another kind (other than those before), like Melchizedek, shows this. Undeniably a reorganization of the priesthood has occurred; the office is now the responsibility of the tribe of Judah. Scripture does not speak of priests from that tribe, but Christ did not acquire His status as High Priest through the Law, which required a certain parentage. Rather, He is the One with eternal existence. He alone is worthy of the testimony: "Thou art a priest for ever after the order of Melchizedek" (7:13-17).

Chapter 7 concludes the critical discussion of the superiority of Christ's priesthood to the Aaronic service (7:20ff.). The writer earlier showed that Christ has the qualifications of the ideal high priest. He is faithful, merciful, and compassionate (2:17,18; 4:15; 5:8; 7:26), and He received His position by virtue of a divine calling (5:5).

Moreover, as High Priest, Christ has several advantages over the Aaronic priesthood: (1) He was installed by an oath (7:21). (2) His priesthood cannot perish because He remains forever (Hebrews 7:23,24; cf. Psalm 110:4). (3) He is not affected by evil; He is perfect, unlike the Aaronic priest (7:26-28). (4) His sanctuary is not on earth, but in heaven (8:1; 9:11). (5) His sacrifice was given once and for all (*ephapax*); in contrast, the Jewish high priest had to offer sacrifice every year (9:12; 10:11). (6) The sacrifice of Christ reflects His total consecration (7:27; 10:10).

The writer reaches a brief climax in 8:1 when he states that we "have such a high priest, who is set on the right hand of the throne of the Majesty in the heavens." On a par with what is said in 1:3, this text shows how Christ unites the two offices of priest and king in His person. Having provided one offering for sins and thereby placing himself forever at the right hand of God, Christ now waits for the dominion that He secured to be finally established (10:11-14). These statements unite the priestly and kingly offices.

That Christ is forever at the right hand of God further signifies that His royal priesthood is eternal: "Jesus Christ the same yesterday, and today, and forever" (13:8). As High Priest He stands between humanity and God; as King He represents God to humanity. Both roles are in effect eternally, because in perfectly fulfilling the will of God, Christ has taken His place at the right hand of the throne of God (12:2).

As our eternal and true High Priest, Christ can intercede to God on our behalf (7:25; 9:24; cf. Romans 8:34). We may ever bring God offerings of praise through Him (13:15). Christ provides access to the throne of God. "Let us therefore come boldly unto the throne of grace, that we may obtain mercy, and find grace to help in time of need" (4:16). We have this confidence through the sacrifice of Christ (10:19-22). Thus Christ fulfilled and surpassed the model provided by the Levitical priesthood. Eternal redemption was won by the One who is both sacrifice and priest.

The Earthly and Heavenly Sanctuary

It is natural that in conjunction with the priesthood of Christ the Book of Hebrews discusses the sanctuary. The high priest and sanctuary are closely connected. Christ is said to serve in the sanctuary, the true tabernacle (8:2). With the additional comment that the sanctuary was not constructed by human hands but by the Lord himself, a contrast is obviously being drawn between the heavenly and earthly sanctuaries. Earthly priests serve in the earthly sanctuary, which is only a pattern and a shadow of the heavenly (8:5).

The reference is almost certainly to the portable, Mosaic tabernacle of Israel's wilderness journeys. The tabernacle sanctuary that Moses ordered to be built is the pattern of the coming perfect sanctuary (Exodus 25:9; 25:40; Hebrews 8:5).

The earthly sanctuary is described as a "tabernacle" (*skēnēn*; 8:5; 9:21; 13:10). The two parts of the tabernacle were the first room, called the Holy Place, and the second room, called the Most Holy Place (Holy of Holies; 9:2ff.). The Epistle to the Hebrews closely adheres to the language of the Septuagint at this juncture. Accordingly, *skēnēn* refers to the tabernacle as a whole. Besides *skēnēn*, the Book of Hebrews also utilizes the expression *to hagion* in connection with the earthly sanctuary (9:1). The Septuagint as well as Josephus and Philo also use this expression in this way.

Of decisive importance for the Epistle to the Hebrews is the idea that the heavenly sanctuary was a model for the earthly sanctuary. This idea is expressed as early as Exodus 25:40 (cf. Hebrews 8:5). Christ carries out His priestly duties in the heavenly sanctuary, in the true tabernacle. Hebrews 9:11 and 24 further emphasize that the heavenly sanctuary is not made by hands; in other words, it does not belong to this world. The heavenly temple is the true temple; the earthly tabernacle is just a reflection, a shadow of this. The logical outcome of such reasoning is fully realized in Christ.

Hebrews 9:1-5 gives the floor plan of the earthly tabernacle. The various parts are listed according to the information in Exodus 25 and 26. This provides a realistic background for the later description of the sacrificial service.

In the first room (Holy Place) the lampstand stood, as did the table and the bread of Presence (showbread). Behind this front room, separated by a veil, was the place of God's presence. There too was located the ark of the covenant containing the tables of the Decalogue. Inside the Most Holy Place cherubim watched over the mercy seat, the cover for the ark of the covenant and the place of atonement. Here atonement was made for the sins of the people. "There I will meet with thee, and I will commune with thee from above the mercy seat, from between the two cherubim which are upon the ark of the testimony, of all things which I will give thee in commandment unto the children of Israel" (Exodus 25:22; cf. 30:6). This is why this room was the most holy of all places.

"Sacrifice" in the Hebrews Epistle

As is the case with other themes in the Epistle to the Hebrews, our understanding of sacrifice will be enhanced by recognizing the contrast between the old and new covenants. The Levitical sacrificial offering has its counterpart in the atoning sacrifice of Christ the High Priest. Hebrews reveals something majestic and significant in the Mosaic rituals of divine worship. Christians need not think otherwise; rather, if they acknowledge the beauty and significance of the Law, they will understand the gospel even better (Westcott).

It is important to recognize the time frame associated with the rituals and commands of the old covenant. They were in effect "until the time of the new order" (9:10, NIV). The nature of worship under the first covenant was not counter to the will of God. God had specifically overseen their implementation through Moses. However, because of its inability to secure complete atonement (i.e., including one's conscience; 9:9), the order of worship under the old covenant proved its own inadequacy. Since under the first covenant the priests had only limited access to the sanctuary—and the people had none at all—it had to be admitted that access to the heavenly sanctuary was not truly open (9:6-8). Through the Holy Spirit, we have a better understanding of the nature of the old covenant (Michel).

The Book of Hebrews views the Christ event as initiating and completing the transition from one age to the next. Until Calvary the place of sacrifice was in the earthly tabernacle. The new age involves worship of God in the heavenly sanctuary, where Christ has entered as forerunner. In the same manner, under the leadership of Christ, believers are able to enter the Most Holy Place (10:19; 13:14). The signs of the new age to come are present already; it is up to men and women to prepare themselves (8:13; 9:9; 13:12ff.).

The new covenant coming through Christ is spoken of in 9:11-14. Just as the earthly high priest entered the Holy of Holies on the Day of Atonement (e.g., especially Leviticus 16), Christ as High Priest has entered heaven itself. And just as the high priest brought the sacrificed blood of goats and oxen, Christ has presented a sacrifice too—His own blood.

Similarities between the Aaronic high priest and Christ our High Priest are obvious, but Christ's role as High Priest is distinctive: (1) Christ has not entered an earthly but a heavenly sanctuary (9:11). (2) He has not presented the blood of bulls and goats, but His own blood (9:12). (3) He does not enter the sanctuary every year, but did so "once for all" (10:10; cf. 9:12,26,28). (4) Through His sacrifice, Christ has secured eternal redemption for those who believe in Him. Through the Cross, sin as the force which separates humanity from God has been overcome; access to the throne of God has been made freely possible (9:26).

The sacrificial system of the Old Testament was unable to secure any permanent atonement. That it had to be repeated each year proves this. Rather than removing the transgressions of the people, the Day of Atonement only reminded them of their perpetual sinfulness (10:1-4).

Naturally, the author of Hebrews regards the sacrificial system of the old covenant as typical of the perfect atoning work of Christ. When he associates Christ's offering of His blood with that of the various sacrifices of the old covenant, we should realize that the former sacrifices can only appear as ineffective, imperfect (10:1-14). But we must have a proper understanding of this effect. The old covenant sacrifices pointed to something beyond themselves. They were a model for the perfect atoning sacrifice that Christ would bring. That is why the old sacrificial system is described in such negative terms; it is to highlight the superiority of Christ's sacrifice, which began on the "night in which he was betrayed" (1 Corinthians 11:23). The old rituals of course served their purpose in their day, until the new covenant could be introduced. They thereby helped prepare God's people for their total fulfillment in Christ.

Under the former sacrificial system there was a sharp distinction between the offering of an animal and the presentation of its blood. Usually the sacrifice was butchered by the one on whose behalf the sacrifice was made; or, if it was a public sacrifice, by the representative of the people (i.e., the priest). But the sprinkling of blood on the altar could only be performed by a high priest. Under the new covenant Christ is both the sacrifice as well as the High Priest. Thus when He presents himself as a spotless sacrifice to God, He fulfills both roles by virtue of the Spirit (cf. 9:14). He consequently also fulfilled in His dual nature as God-man the purpose of human existence. He purified our conscience from dead works and enabled us to serve the living God. He is therefore the Mediator of a new covenant, so they which are called might receive the promise of eternal inheritance (9:14,15).

Before leaving the Book of Hebrews' teaching on sacrifice, we will outline in detail the ritual that took place on the Day of Atonement, because, as it was noted, it plays a significant role in preparing for the work of Christ.

The Day of Atonement was celebrated on the 10th day in the 7th month (tishri, equivalent to October). It is described in detail in Leviticus 16 (cf. Leviticus 23:26ff.; Numbers 29:7ff.; Ezekiel 45:17ff.). The rituals on the Day of Atonement reflected an understanding of the many views of sacrifice, which according to divine decree were established to afford mankind entrance to God (Westcott).

The central figure was the high priest. All general priestly duties were performed on this day by the high priest. He prepared himself to fulfill these obligations a full 7 days in advance. On the day itself, after cleansing himself he dressed in sacred garments (Leviticus 16:4). The sacrificial animals were prepared: "And he shall take of the congregation of the children of Israel two kids of the goats for a sin offering, and one ram for a burnt offering. And Aaron shall offer his bullock of the sin offering, which is for himself, and make an atonement for himself, and for his house" (Leviticus 16:5,6).

Then the high priest entered the Most Holy Place and sprinkled some of the blood of the bullock on the lid of the mercy seat. As he did this, smoke from the lighted incense veiled the lid of the mercy seat covering the ark of the testimony. This prevented him from dying as he performed the ritual (Leviticus 16:12-14). The high priest was to do the same thing as he offered the goat as a sin offering for the people. He thus provided atonement for all the sins of the Israelites (Leviticus 16:15,16).

When the high priest had obtained atonement for his house, himself, and the entire congregation of Israel, a general confession of sins followed. When the high priest put his hands on the head of a live goat and confessed the sins and transgressions of the people, by faith the sins were transferred to the goat, which was then led into the desert (Leviticus 16:20-22).

The ritual concluded when the high priest took off his linen clothes, washed himself, and sacrificed a burnt offering for himself and for the people. He thereby obtained atonement for himself and for them (Leviticus 16:23-25). Finally the corpses of the animals that had been sacrificed were burned outside of the camp (Leviticus 16:27). Each year this event was repeated in an effort to reestablish the covenant relationship with God that had been destroyed because of the sins of the people.

The points of similarity between the high priest of the old covenant and that of the new are obvious. It is not necessary to review the several differences again. The differences remind one of the stars, whose light pales when the sun rises. The Epistle to the Hebrews testifies to the perfect nature of Christ's atoning sacrifice.

Conscience and Perfection

The deficiency of the old covenant lay first and foremost in the inability of its offerings to "make him that did the service perfect, as pertaining to the conscience" (9:9). We come face-to-face here with a major concern: conscience and perfection. Both terms occur rather late in the Scriptures.

The expression "conscience" does not occur in the Old Testament. An individual might recognize his wrongdoing (e.g., David, 2 Samuel 12), but the Old Testament does not advance any dogmatic theory that man is intrinsically equipped with a moral awareness or ethical principle. From the Biblical perspective, humanity stands guilty in the presence of the will of God as it is revealed in the Law. As far as the Gospels are concerned, a similar idea is presented. The term "conscience" does not occur, but when Jesus taught He appealed to the personal discernment of His listeners (Luke 12:57; cf. Luke 10:36,37).

Now, outside the Gospels we find the term "conscience" (*suneidēsis*) in Acts, Romans, 1 and 2 Corinthians, the Pastoral Epistles, Hebrews, and 1 Peter. Paul's writings reflect a somewhat classical understanding of "conscience" as the inner voice that guides individuals concerning what is right and wrong. The Gentiles give evidence, suggests Paul in Romans 2:15, that what the Law requires is written on the hearts of the Gentiles, as their conscience bears witness to it. Men are obligated, therefore, to submit to authorities "not only for wrath, but also for conscience' sake" (Romans 13:5). Thus, Paul writes, conscience can be a witness or a judge between himself and others (cf. 2 Corinthians 1:12; 4:2; 5:11).

In the Pastoral Epistles, conscience plays a special role as a characteristic of proper Christian faith. Paul's coworker, Timothy, is admonished to fight the good fight, holding faith and a good conscience (1 Timothy 1:18,19; cf. 4:2; Titus 1:15). It is the apostle's duty to promote "charity out of a pure heart, and of a good conscience, and of faith unfeigned" (1 Timothy 1:5; cf. 3:9; 2 Timothy 1:3).

In the Epistle to the Hebrews conscience also plays a significant role. It is the response of the conscience which lays bare the insufficiency of the old sacrificial system (9:9; cf. 10:2). Conversely, the perfect sacrifice of Christ purifies the conscience and allows the believer to praise and serve God (9:14; 10:22). Now one can know for sure that he or she has a good conscience (13:18).

The expression *perfection* or *completion* (*teleiōsis*) is equally important. Like the term *conscience, perfection* occurs five times in the Epistle to the Hebrews; in addition one finds the related term *finisher* (*teleiotēs*) applied to Christ. From the Biblical point of view, *perfection* involves undivided devotion to God, especially in the covenant relationship. Therefore, the prayer in Psalm 119:80 reads: "Let my heart be sound in thy statutes." This idea of undivided devotion to God is the background for Jesus' words in Matthew 5:48, "Be ye therefore perfect, even as your Father which is in heaven is perfect."

The expression *completion* acquired a new and unique dimension when used in conjunction with the revelation in Christ. The hidden counsel of God, His plan of salvation, was on the brink of fulfillment. With the birth of the Son of God that fulfillment, the "fulness of time," came (Galatians 4:4; cf. Ephesians 1:10). Jesus' work was a carrying out of the will and plan of God (John 4:34). It culminated in His death (John 19:28,30). "It is finished," He cried out.

From such a viewpoint the author of Hebrews testifies to the perfection of Christ and to humanity's "perfection" or "completion" by faith in Christ (cf. Colossians 1:17,18). A fundamental prerequisite to Christ's saving death was His following the path of suffering. "For it became him, for whom are all things, and by whom are all things, in bringing many sons unto glory, to make the captain of their salvation perfect through sufferings" (2:10). That Christ had to suffer and debase himself poses no inconsistency with the fact of His honor and authority as God. There was no other way to salvation than incarnation and suffering (cf. 2:14-18). Through this, Christ became the "pioneer" of salvation and the source of eternal salvation (5:10).

The life and work of Christ determine our salvation. Christ is the author of faith as well as the One who perfects it (12:2). As the One who has been made perfect forever, Christ can lead others to perfection (5:9; cf. 11:40; 12:23).

A New Covenant

On several occasions the author uses the term *covenant.* Christ is the guarantor of a "better covenant" (7:22); specifically, the "better" covenant is based upon "better" promises (8:6). The expression "covenant" (*diathēkēs*) in Hebrews, as in the Septuagint, reflects the Hebrew term *b*[e]*rîth. B*[e]*rîth* and *diathēkē* indicate God's initiative in making an agreement with humanity. According to the common Hellenistic understanding, *diathēkē* denotes a "last will." The decisive factor is that *diathēkē* is used with both meanings in Hebrews.

As a mediator (*mesitēs*), Christ is contrasted with Moses, who was a mediator between God and His people under the old covenant (Hebrews 8:6; cf. Galatians 3:9). The writer emphasizes the reality of the new covenant. The idea that the new covenant is based on better promises is merely the logical outcome of the fact that the Biblical promises are fulfilled in Christ.

The promise of a new covenant goes back to Jeremiah 31. There it is prophesied that the days would come when the Lord would establish a new covenant with the house of Israel and the house of Judah. Then He would write His commands in their minds and hearts and create a totally new relationship with God. God would also blot out all their sins (Jeremiah 31:31f.; Hebrews 8:8-12).

These "better promises" are superior to those promises of God which depended on the obedience of the people. If they failed, the promises were nullified (8:9). But, on one critical point the old and new covenants agree: covenants are sealed with the offering of sacrifices (and offering meals; Hebrews 9:15ff.; cf. Genesis 15:17,18; 31:43-54; Exodus 24:1-11).

The term *covenant* or *testament* presupposes that the one who initiated the agreement must die before the agreement is put into effect (9:16,17). The old covenant was also established with the shedding of blood, since Moses sprinkled blood on the people, the scroll of the commandments, the tabernacle, and all the vessels of the divine worship (9:18-22).

Nonetheless, the sacrifice of Christ is different from and superior to the offerings of the old covenant. Again the Scripture shows the effect of Christ's perfect sacrifice (9:23-28). He offers His own blood in the heavenly sanctuary (9:24,25) and does away with sin, once and for all (9:26).

The idea of covenant does not merely guarantee a link to Israel's history; it also offers a new plan of salvation that builds on the perfect redemptive work of Christ. By virtue of this, men and women can stand before God and serve Him as He desires (10:19f.; 12:28).

STANDING FIRM IN THE FAITH (10:32–13:25)

"Faith" in the Hebrews Epistle

Hebrews 11 is rightfully called the "Faith Chapter." In it one receives a basic introduction to the nature of faith. But there is more. One also sees the power of faith manifested in terms of heroes of faith under the old covenant.

The "Faith Chapter" is designed to support and to encourage the readers to enduring faith. The appeal to persevere in faith occurs immediately prior to this section (10:36ff.). The writer presents a rough draft of the sacred history of the Old Testament from one unique vantage point. He presents the most well-known characters of the Old Testament as models of faith and faithfulness.

But what is faith? Our writer tells us: "Look at the ancestors of the Faith." The forebears include the heroes of Israel's faith. These models can teach us two things: (1) how great and valuable is the gift of faith, and (2) the power that faith exhibits.

Those trusting and believing in God never turned to Him in vain. Because they received God's help and blessing, it is obvious for later generations that the exploits of the heroes of faith were done according to God's will. Why did they receive grace? Because they believed God. In other words, they trusted in God's promises; they clung to the promise in hope, despite the fact they never saw the realization of their faith. The line of reasoning in Hebrews is similar to Paul's testimony of the Christian hope. "We are saved by hope: but hope that is seen is not hope: for what a man seeth, why doth he yet hope for? But if we hope for that we see not, then do we with patience wait for it" (Romans 8:24,25).

Israel's relationship with God was always intended to be by faith. None of the patriarchs could serve God half-heartedly; they could only serve fully trusting Him by faith. Just a glance at the ancestors of faith tells that they always trusted in what was not seen and that God rewarded them. Everything significant and wonderful in Israel's history was received by faith as God's gift to those who believed.

Hebrews 11:1 defines faith: "Faith is the substance of things hoped for, the evidence of things not seen." Once again we notice a close relationship between faith and hope. If there is no human hope, there is little chance for man to be stirred to believe. That is why the word and promise of God lay the foundations for human faith. Faith and hope are directed toward the invisible God, His word, and His promises. In faith, those things in question are precisely those things that are not seen, "for we walk by faith, not by sight" (2 Corinthians 5:7).

"Faith is the substance of things hoped for." Here there is help in distinguishing between faith and illusion. Faith is the full assurance of something and is reflected in everything we do. Thus faith is a power in our lives, a power that leads us to action.

Faith also involves conviction. The power and influence of the visible world is actually much less than the voice of the invisible. The tangible and concrete do not have the ability to support us, carry us, and give us a share in the riches of Christ. It is encouraging to know that the invisible comes to us and convinces us of the truth of God.

With this definition of the nature of faith, not only is the history of heroes of the Faith illuminated, but also the road which believers must travel—by faith not sight—is brought into perspective. In the natural we see only that God has summoned Christ to heaven where He is exalted to the right hand and installed as High Priest. There He helps us. We cannot see this, but we believe it by faith.

Faith in what is not seen and in the future are the main point. "For by it the elders obtained a good report" (11:2). The Word of God often expressly describes an individual as "righteous" or as having "found favor with God." This indicates that he or she trusted God and His promises.

We marvel at God's visible hand throughout Creation; what we see in Creation causes us to praise God. However, what we see as "visible" was created out of the invisible through the power of the Living Word. Hebrews 11:3 attaches a special significance to this understanding of creation. We should not be astonished that God wants us to fix our desires and heart on what is invisible, since what is seen originates in the invisible Word of God. We are to find fulfillment not in the visible, material world, but in the invisible.

A long list of the heroes of faith follows this introduction. The first true example of faith is Abel. We are told that he placed his offering on the altar. If the point is that only the visible is important, Abel acted unreasonably. Why sacrifice his animal? The answer: he longed for the invisible and sought blessings which he could only hope to attain. The sacrifice of Abel (and his entire life) are a testimony to his faith (11:4).

The second example of faith is Enoch (11:5). The Bible only tells us that he "walked with God" (Genesis 5:22-24). But the author of Hebrews sees a new relationship in this comment. Enoch possessed a faith that was pleasing to God. "Without faith it is impossible to please him" (11:6). Literally, he *set himself* to walk with God. His will was involved.

The story of the life of Noah was still well known in the time of Jesus (cf. Matthew 24:37ff.). The ancient account also shows how Noah built his ark in the midst of an unconcerned and faithless generation. What caused him to take such a "strange" action? From a human vantage point there was no immediate danger, but Noah listened to God's warning and did not pay attention to the jeering world. He "condemned the world, and became heir of the righteousness which is by faith" (11:7).

More than anyone else in history, the ancestors testify of the nature and character of faith. All the patriarchs, Abraham, Isaac, and Jacob demonstrated faith. They had received the promise of the land, but they nonetheless never actually possessed it. All the time they patiently looked forward to the heavenly land that they had not yet entered (11:8-16).

Abraham is a particularly noteworthy example. The New Testament clearly shows him as the greatest Old Testament example of faith (Romans 4:3; Galatians 3:6; James 2:23; cf.

Acts 7:5). Abraham demonstrated his faith early in his career, when he left his homeland and people in order to go to the land God had promised to show him (11:9).

Perhaps even more thrilling than this, however, is the account of his offering of Isaac (11:17-19). We recall that Abraham was commanded to offer his only son, the son given as the realization of the promise of God (11:11,12). During this episode it seems as if God had reneged on His promise to Abraham. This brought Abraham into the strongest struggle of faith; indeed, it was his greatest test. He realized, however, that under the circumstances there was no alternative but to trust God, believe on Him fully to fulfill His promise, even though Isaac should die. Consequently, Hebrews pictures Abraham's offering of Isaac as a figurative foreshadowing of the Resurrection. Here, for the first time we have the idea that God can "raise" from the dead (11:19).

The next name on the roll call is Moses. His life story is also a tremendous testimony to his faith (11:23-29). Five examples from his life are given: (1) His being delivered at his birth from the infanticide ordered by the evil pharaoh (11:23); (2) his willingness to share the fate of God's people (11:24-26); (3) his faithfulness toward the invisible God rather than the visible and powerful pharaoh (11:27); (4) his institution of Passover (11:28); and (5) the crossing of the Red Sea together with the Israelites (11:29).

The following verses contain an additional series of examples of faith from Israel's history. By faith the walls of Jericho fell (11:30). According to Joshua 6, the walls fell on the seventh day of the siege, when, following the divine command, Israel walked around the city seven times, the priests blew their trumpets, and the people gave a loud shout. Their faith was exhibited in the conviction that their extraordinary actions would indeed accomplish what God said they would. Rahab, a prostitute, is also mentioned because of her great faith (cf. Matthew 1:5).

Under the heading of the prophets and those who gave their lives for their faith, the list of heroes of the Faith draws to a close. Now the writer gives other examples without elaborating on the nature of their faith. The power of faith and faith expressed in trial are the primary subjects discussed in this section (11:32-38). Victory as well as "defeat" (death, torture) are by-products of the same faith. Triumph and God's intervention are not the only criteria of genuine faith. The courage to suffer, even a willingness to die, are not in any way inferior demonstrations of faith.

The way God related to men and women of old varied greatly. At times He visibly intervened on their behalf; on other occasions it appeared as if He did not help at all. Some saw mighty miracles; others did not. Nonetheless, both groups were faithful. Some glorified God through their lives; others did so through their deaths. We observe that faith enables one to overcome but also to be overcome; to live but also to die. Faith follows wherever God leads.

The concluding verses of chapter 11 underscore even further that faith looks toward the future. This is reflected in the statement: "And these all, having obtained a good report through faith, received not the promise" (11:39). They waited until "now," "that they without us should not be made perfect" (11:40).

The Old Testament is repeatedly seen as a document of promise. Faith was indeed present in Old Testament times, but it was directed toward what occurs in Christ. God's plan concerns all His chosen ones (9:15). Therefore, one group cannot attain perfection without the other.

The Life of the Church

The Book of Hebrews gives the impression that it is speaking to a church in danger of giving up the Faith (cf. 12:12,13). This explains the constant attempt to stir up, encourage, and warn believers.

As in the writings of the apostle Paul, Hebrews depicts the life of the Christian believer as a race (cf. 1 Corinthians 9:24,25; Philippians 3:13,14; 2 Timothy 4:7). The goal lies ahead, hidden in the Word and promises of God. Therefore, it is necessary to lay aside anything that might keep one from running or finishing the race (i.e., sin; 12:1). We must also accept the available help. The Old Testament heroes of faith were mentioned in chapter 11. How much more help is there when we fix our eyes upon Jesus, the author and finisher of our faith (12:2,3)! His invitation is this: "Come unto me, all ye that labor and are heavy laden" (Matthew 11:28). He is able to give the soul new courage.

Having described the life of the Church as a race, the Scripture now turns to the image of a struggle (12:4). With the expression, "You have not yet resisted to the point of shedding your blood" (NIV), the readers are given brief warning that even more perilous times may lie ahead. They have endured great trials and suffered loss of property and honor (10:32-34), but they have not yet given their lives. This possibility must be acknowledged; believers should not be surprised if hardships come to that point (cf. 1 Peter 4:12). Instead of being ashamed of such a fate, believers must come to understand that it is because they are children (cf. Proverbs 3:11,12). An earthly father who loves his children will indeed discipline them (12:4-8).

The analogy between the earthly father and the Heavenly Father (here "Father of spirits"), is elaborated on in 12:9ff. in an effort to show that the goal of divine discipline is to promote holiness (12:10), righteousness (12:11), and peace (12:14).

Believers are particularly portrayed as having free access to God through the sacrifice of Christ. Christ thus opened a new and living entrance to God through the "veil" ("curtain," NIV) which is His body (10:20). The imagery comes from the temple. A veil or curtain separated the outer sanctuary from the Holy of Holies. The veil is allegorically understood to represent the body of Christ. Figuratively, His body was "torn in pieces" at His death when His blood was shed. The giving of His life enables us to enter the presence of God.

That believers now have free access to God is a main theme in the Epistle to the Hebrews. Under the old covenant entrance was not possible. Now, however, because of the sacrifice of Christ, an entrance free of all obstacles has been provided. Now we can truly worship God.

The Meaning of Worship

The Epistle to the Hebrews shows that the Old Testament's rituals and priesthood were fulfilled in Christ. In the Early Church there was no high priest. Christ was the true, eternal High Priest.

But what does the Epistle to the Hebrews say about the Early Church's understanding of worship? In what practical ways does the letter show that "the way to the sanctuary," thanks to the work of Christ, is open?

Believers are people of the new covenant. Their worship is not a return to the former arrangement under the old covenant given at Sinai. On the contrary, they approach heaven itself, the place where God has chosen to establish His name (Deuteronomy 12:5). This is the true Mount Zion, the heavenly Jerusalem. There, in a sense, the earthly people of God join the crowds which stand before the Ancient of Days (Daniel 7:10). They also join with the Church of the Firstborn who are able to stand before the Son of Man (Luke 21:36). There they encounter the eternal God and the mediator Jesus Christ, who bears the blood of the new and eternal covenant. In the presence of God they receive an unshakable kingdom, one more reason why they owe thanks and acceptable service to God (12:28).

Here we catch a glimpse of the meaning of worship as revealed in Hebrews. Worship under the new covenant takes place in heaven (12:22). This is a consequence of Christ's having once and for all entered the Holy of Holies; of His offering His own blood as a sacrifice for our sins; and of His having obtained our eternal redemption (9:12). This is the basis for understanding the priestly access to God the people of the new covenant enjoy: "Having therefore, brethren, boldness to enter into the holiest by the blood of Jesus, by a new and living way, which he hath consecrated for us, through the veil, that is to say, his flesh; and having a high priest over the house of God; let us draw near with a true heart" (10:19-22).

This may be why the reader's attention is constantly directed to the riches that belong to those in Christ Jesus. They need to understand also the value of being able to worship God. They have an altar from which they who serve at the tabernacle had no right to eat. This suggests that their worship, even in its sacrificial meal, was in every way superior to the old covenant. We also do not lack an altar; we have one from which we receive strength and power.

The following verses show that the suffering of the Lord "outside the camp" had a sanctifying effect (13:12). Christians can partake of this holiness if they are willing to go with Him "outside the camp" and bear His reproach (13:13). There is a distinct, vital relationship between the sacrifice of Christ and the "sacrifice" of believers in choosing the way of self-denial and rejection of the world's values. The "sacrifices" the believer has to offer to this relationship are shown: "By him therefore let us offer the sacrifice of praise to God continually, that is, the fruit of our lips, giving thanks to his name. But to do good and to communicate forget not: for with such sacrifices God is well pleased" (13:15,16).

The key to the church's worship is contained in the phrase "by him." It emphasizes the unique privilege of believers. It is "by Christ"—"the Way" that we have access to God. It is only "by Him" that we can offer anything pleasing to God (cf. 1 Peter 2:5; Romans 1:8; 16:27; Colossians 3:17).

When 13:14 emphasizes that we seek a coming city, it also reflects a certain view of worship. While believers wait for the time when they join Christ in heaven, where He has ascended (4:14; 8:1), they are already experiencing the heavenly glory anticipated by the signs Christ has given. Thus, in a certain sense the altar of 13:10 is in heaven, where Christ has offered His own blood, the eternal sacrifice for redemption. But, precisely because the issue is one of sacrifice, Christians approach this altar as they gather around the table of the Lord in the Communion service.

Use of the Old Testament in Hebrews

The Book of Hebrews makes extensive use of the Old Testament. There are many direct quotes and even more allusions. Portions from the Pentateuch are cited 12 times; the Psalms, 11; the Prophets, 4; and there is 1 quotation from Proverbs. Of the 29 quotations, 23 are from either the Pentateuch or Psalms. It is odd that there are not more references to the prophetic writings, especially in those passages where he speaks of the Old Testament sacrificial system. The person and work of Christ is primarily illuminated from passages in the Psalms.

Most of the quotations in Hebrews do not occur elsewhere in the New Testament. This holds true for 21 out of 29 of the quotations. Of the remaining eight, one is cited in the Synoptic Gospels, while the others appear in Acts, Paul's epistles, and Revelation.

Hebrews presents the Old Testament as a divine oracle from start to finish. The Biblical account is the voice of God's word; the Word is thus alive in Scripture (4:12f.). Scripture, therefore, is not merely a "book"; it is a living word from God to people of all time. The words of the Bible and its promises also extend beyond the time of their writing. The consistent use of the present tense in the citations also underscores this truth: "He is not ashamed to call them brethren, saying . . ." (2:11,12); "as the Holy Ghost saith . . ." (3:7); "ye have forgotten the exhortation which speaketh unto you as unto children" (12:5).

There is no parallel in the New Testament to this style of quotation. Usually when the present tense of "says" appears, it is connected to the name of the prophet (e.g., Isaiah "says," Romans 10:16) or to Scripture (Romans 9:17). This feature verifies that the Book of Hebrews views God as speaking personally and precisely in the Old Testament.

Further investigation reveals that the writer regularly relies upon the Septuagint translation. Many citations, however, do follow the Hebrew text. On eight occasions the citation differs from the Hebrew but corresponds with the Greek. Finally, some quotations do not correspond with either the Septuagint or the Hebrew (6:13,14; 9:20; 10:30). Here perhaps a later, traditional form is being used. This reveals a view that Scripture contains a deep spiritual meaning. Scripture is handled very carefully, and the deeper meaning of passages appear.

The final revelation of God—in His Son—is totally perfect, "but the word of the oath, which was since the law, maketh the Son, who is consecrated for evermore" (7:28). It is therefore a serious offense to neglect such a great salvation (2:3) or to refuse Him who speaks (12:25). The saying, "Today if ye will hear his voice," (3:15) is thus applicable to Christians of all time.

The numerous Old Testament quotations also illuminate the theme "fulfillment of promise" (cf. the story of Abraham, Genesis 22:16, 17; Hebrews 6:13,14; 11:8f.). Abraham is a unique example of obedience (Hebrews 11:8), patience (Hebrews 11:9f.), and faith (Hebrews 11:17f.; cf. Romans 4:18). The patriarchs who also received the promise demonstrated the same kind of faith as Abraham (11:9).

The next step in the history of revelation is the account of the giving of the Law at Sinai. The Epistle to the Hebrews records this in 3:7ff. and in 4:1ff., using words from Psalm 95:7ff.: "Today if ye will hear his voice." The word of God is alive and speaks even to this day. Even though the disobedient wilderness generation fell, the promise of God was still in effect. The fulfillment of the promises awaits those who are repentant: "Today if ye will hear his voice, harden not your hearts" (4:7).

The giving of the Law is referred to in Hebrews 12:18ff. (cf. Exodus 19:12,13; Deuteronomy 4:11,12). The concluding of the giving of the covenant is also mentioned in Hebrews 9:19,20 and 10:29 (cf. Exodus 24:8). The occupation of Canaan is mentioned as a sign of the true and lasting rest (4:8; cf. 11:30,31).

The religious institutions of the Old Testament, e.g., the tabernacle and the worship therein, and especially the Day of Atonement, are given special attention (Hebrews 8:5f.; 9:1f.; cf. Exodus 25:40; 26:33; 30:10). All of this was merely a foreshadowing of the heavenly temple and its ritual, which was to be finalized when the new order was introduced.

The fulfillment of the promise of a new covenant is the final step in the ancient revelation (Jeremiah 31:31ff.; cf. Hebrews 8:8f.; 10:15f.). The new fellowship between God and mankind is based on God's forgiveness and presupposes personal acknowledgment of God. What remains to be fulfilled is the promise of Haggai 2:6 (cf. Hebrews 12:26f.).

The declaration that Christ is the Son of God rests first and foremost on Psalm 2:7 and 2 Samuel 7:14 (cf. Hebrews 1:5; 5:5). In the light of this confession, Christ stands as unique from any other of God's messengers.

That Christ is King is demonstrated from Psalm 45:7,8 (cf. Hebrews 1:8,9). The people of God's new covenant build the certainty of inheriting an unshakable kingdom on this fact (Hebrews 12:28; cf. Daniel 7:27). A more elaborate understanding of Christ's work is provided in the model of the priest-king Melchizedek (Hebrews 5:6,10; 6:20; 7:11f.; cf. Psalm 110:4). This unusual king shows that the work of Christ extends to others besides Israel.

Finally, according to Psalm 8:4ff., Christ is the Son of Man (Hebrews 2:6ff.). In Him humanity discovers its true potential. Christ is not ashamed to call men His brothers (Hebrews 2:11,12; cf. Psalm 22:23). His faithfulness exceeds that of Moses (Hebrews 3:1f.; cf. Numbers 12:7). Through His total obedience Christ summons a new humanity. These are those who because of their faith and obedience to Him will inherit salvation (5:9).

The Old Testament was written for our instruction. The reality of this fact is driven home by the Epistle to the Hebrews. It makes a call to leave comfortable, secure positions and participate in the soon coming perfect joy. We see this plan realized best in the history of the people of Israel. There we find solace to endure the tension between the difficulties of the present and the future bliss.

Overview–James

OPENING

The Epistle of James belongs to the so-called General (Catholic) Epistles. The books were given this designation because most of them are not addressed to any specific individual or local church. The author presents himself as James; the epistle is sent "to the twelve tribes which are scattered abroad." This phrase is thought to address a group of Jewish-Christian readers living in the Diaspora (the regions of the dispersion). Since the epistle was written in Greek, it is plain that it spoke to Greek-speaking Jews who believed Jesus to be the Messiah.

On the Day of Pentecost, many Jews from other parts of the Roman Empire visited Jerusalem. These, believing in the proclamation of the apostles, carried the gospel back to their homeland in the Diaspora (cf. Acts 2:9-11; 9:2; 11:19; 13:1).

The author describes himself simply as "James, a servant of God and of the Lord Jesus Christ." This is enough for his readership to recognize him. During the early Christian Era there was only one James who could consider himself that familiar to the Jewish Christian constituency, namely James the brother of Jesus, leader of the church in Jerusalem (cf. Galatians 2:12). The Jews of the Diaspora were used to receiving religious advice and guidance from the church in Jerusalem. This made it easy for them to accept instruction from James. Because of his location in the holiest city of Judaism and the hub of the Christian faith as well, James could contact Jewish Christians throughout the Roman Empire, especially during the pilgrimage feasts when travelers would come to Jerusalem (e.g., Acts 2). Thus, there may have been some personal contact between James and his readers. The authoritative as well as brotherly tone of his letter shows James was a highly esteemed and beloved Christian leader.

There is a strong argument from tradition that James the brother of the Lord authored this epistle. Some contend for two other apostles of the same name. James the son of Alpheus was probably too unrecognized to claim such authority for himself. John's brother, James the son of Zebedee, died as a martyr as early as A.D. 44. However, this need not exclude him from having authored the epistle, since much of the evidence suggests that it was written before the apostolic council in Jerusalem (A.D. 49–50). It could have been written in the midforties.

Nevertheless, in all probability the author is the Jerusalem church leader James, the brother of our Lord. The unique style and manner of the epistle itself support this position, especially when compared with the correspondence from the council recorded in Acts 15. (1) Both have the same form of greeting (cf. James 1:1; Acts 15:23). (2) Both use the same Greek word for "to visit" (cf. James 1:27; Acts 15:14). (3) Both have the same Greek expression for turning back to God (James 5:19,20; Acts 15:19). (4) The idea that "by the name of the Lord believers are 'called' " is the same in James 2:7 and Acts 15:17.

The Epistle of James was known relatively early in the Early Church, but it was included among the "disputed letters" for a time. Origen first attributed the letter to James the brother of the Lord and accepted it as Holy Writ. Athanasius, Jerome, and Augustine also acknowledged the epistle as genuine. At the councils of Hippo (A.D. 393) and Carthage (A.D. 397) the epistle was accepted as canonical. One of the chief reasons for the delay in its inclusion was almost certainly its appeal to Jewish Christians. Gentile Christians, who largely controlled the Church in later years, were perhaps reluctant to include books other than those used by their own missionaries and apostles. An apparent contrast between Paul and James may have also contributed to the delay.

Even as late as the Reformation the question of the canonicity of the epistle was raised again. Since more than 400 years of evangelical Christianity have preceded us, the question may seem superfluous. But to the Reformers, who in effect "rediscovered" the Scriptures, the issue was quite different. Should the canon of the Roman Catholic Church be adopted wholesale? As we learn from history, they did not adopt such a policy; some books of the Roman Catholic canon are not in the Protestant Bible. When the Synod of Trent accepted the apocryphal books into the canon, Protestants did not. But the Epistle of James was retained, in keeping with the process of canonization in the Early Church. With respect to the question of the authenticity of the epistle today there is almost no strong difference of opinion.

It is not easy to outline this epistle; some even consider it impossible. Those structures that have been attempted usually are lists of themes. James has a somewhat loose structure, arranged around one central theme. Its message is crystal clear and forms the background for interpreting the entire letter. Its central theme comes to the fore in 2:14-26, the main section of the letter: Faith and obedience are inseparable.

THE LITERARY STYLE OF THE EPISTLE

Knowing the literary style of the epistle is a vital step towards understanding its message. The epistle reflects a particular type of literature known as paraenesis. During the First Century paraenetic writings were commonplace in the Jewish and Greco-Roman cultures (Dibelius Hermeneia, James, p.3). This kind of writing is characterized by ethical instruction and rules for living. Normally these are somewhat loosely joined together according to major themes. It is important to keep in mind the relationship to these themes.

This type of writing is reminiscent of Jewish wisdom writings; for example the short, pithy style and the frequent use of the imperative mood. Furthermore, useful illustrations and applications are interspersed; vices and virtues are listed. Often dialogue takes place between imagined opponents. This technique, known as diatribe, was also used by the Greeks.

Many places in the New Testament show evidence of this paraenetic style, especially the writings of Paul and James. They both employ paraenetic lists (Galatians 5:19-23; James 3:13-18), and both hold debates with imagined opponents whom they drive into a corner during the course of debate (Romans 3:1-20; James 2:14-26). The admonition sections of Paul's letters often contain paraenesis; James, also, contains paraenetic instruction.

THE RELATIONSHIP WITH OTHER SCRIPTURES

Numerous similarities between the contents of the Epistle of James and contemporary Jewish and Greek writings can be demonstrated. There are also some striking similarities between James and Old Testament sayings, Gospel passages, and other New Testament letters. James, however, was no "compiler" of tradition; rather, he was an independent and original inspired writer, guided by the Holy Spirit in what he wrote.

In his brief letter James makes a number of citations or allusions to the Old Testament, including the Pentateuch, Joshua, 1 Kings, Job, Psalms, Proverbs, Ecclesiastes, Isaiah, Jeremiah, Ezekiel, Daniel, Hosea, Joel, Amos, Jonah, Micah, Zechariah, and Malachi. Thus we see in James a beautiful illustration of the unity of the Bible and of the hermeneutics of the Holy Spirit. The deity of Jesus is emphasized as His words are accorded the same authority as those of God in the Old Testament Scriptures.

The parallels with the Gospels is one of the most distinctive features of the Epistle of James. If one compares one of Paul's letters with James, their differences in style and content will be readily apparent. There would be a different response if one compared James with the Gospels, especially Matthew. Then their similarities would be striking. Ryrie finds no less than 15 references to the Sermon on the Mount alone (p.137). Mussner points out 12 points of contact with the Gospels. He goes on to cite G. Kittel's finding of some 26 similar points of contact with the Gospels (pp.47f.). E. Thidemann has compiled the correspondences: James 1:2 and Matthew 5:11; James 1:4 and Matthew 5:48; James 1:5 and Matthew 7:7; James 1:6 and Matthew 9:29; James 1:17 and Matthew 7:11; James 1:22 and Matthew 7:24; James 1:23 and Matthew 7:26; James 2:5 and Matthew 5:3,5; James 2:6 and Luke 18:3, 20:47, Mark 12:40; James 2:8 and Matthew 22:39; James 2:11 and Matthew 5:21; James 2:13 and Matthew 5:7; James 2:14f. and Matthew 25:21-46; James 2:15 and Matthew 6:25; James 3:1f. and Matthew 5:9; James 4:2 and Matthew 5:21; James 4:3 and Matthew 7:7; James 4:4 and Matthew 12:39; James 4:9 and Luke 6:25; James 4:10 and Matthew 23:12; James 4:11 and Matthew 7:1; James 4:13-15 and Matthew 6:34; James 4:17 and Luke 12:47; James 5:1 and Luke 6:24; James 5:2 and Matthew 6:19; James 5:5 and Luke 16:19; James 5:6 and Luke 6:37; James 5:7 and Mark 4:26-29; James 5:9 and Mark 13:29, Matthew 24:33; James 5:10 and Matthew 5:12; James 5:12 and Matthew 5:34; James 5:17 and Luke 4:25; James 5:19 and Luke 17:3, Matthew 18:15.

These parallels indicate a close relationship with the events described in the Gospels. Not all of these parallels are equally significant, but collectively they cannot be dismissed outrightly. It is virtually impossible that these similarities occurred by chance. The writer was intimately associated with Jesus and had the advantage of personal observation. This also supports the view that the writer was the brother of Jesus.

It is evident that James had extensive knowledge of Jesus' sayings, both from his own memory and from common knowledge among those who had been with Him. The Holy Spirit could recall Jesus' teachings to James, according to His purpose in this epistle. It may have been written prior to any of the Gospels, and perhaps, as some contend, it is the earliest document of the New Testament.

Apart from the four Gospels, no other New Testament writings contain such a clear echo of the Gospel words of Jesus. In reality the whole epistle is knit together with sayings of Jesus. These form the background for the Christology and soteriology (doctrine of salvation) of the Epistle of James.

CHRISTOLOGY

The Epistle of James is very clear in its presentation of those doctrines it is concerned with. It was not intended to cover every doctrine of the Christian faith. However, this is not as unique as some have tried to argue; other New Testament writings are similar. The Bible is not designed so every document repeats what every other one says. The doctrine of the sufficiency of Scripture concerns Scripture as a unit, not each book.

Since the beginning of Christianity the Church followed the teachings of the apostles (Acts 2:42). In this epistle the essential apostolic teaching about divine revelation and redemption are presumed to be known by believers. Thus, we see why Jude, without any explanation, challenges his readers to strive for "the faith which was once delivered unto the saints" (Jude 3). If this holds true for Jude, which deals with Christian doctrine, why is it strange to some that James—a letter concerned about Christian life-style—should do the same?

In commenting on James in this way it should be emphasized that the epistle does have an abundance of Biblical advice that is unique in its Christian content, but which modifies Jewish material. The very concept of God in James is "Christianized." God is "Father" (2:17; 3:9); He has revealed himself in the Son, Jesus Christ. The letter further has a rather sophisticated Christology and soteriology.

James proclaims Jesus Christ is Lord (1:1; 2:1; 5:8). This is called the first Christian symbol (Romans 10:9; Philippians 2:11), and we find it as early as James. When the first Christians called Jesus "Lord," *kurios,* they adopted the Old Testament's language (cf. John 20:28). James interchanges the name Lord with God the Father and the Son; at times it is difficult to determine just which is meant (e.g., 5:7-15). And when in his opening James referred to himself as a "servant of God and of the Lord Jesus Christ," it was an equation of Jesus with God. This was asserting the deity of Jesus Christ. Furthermore, we note that James presented Jesus Christ as the object of faith; He is the One in whom we trust (2:1). Like the rest of the New Testament authors, according to James the faith that saves us is faith in Christ. Of course, this includes faith in God (2:23).

James refers to this Jesus in whom we trust as "Jesus Christ the Lord of glory" (2:1). Particularly for James, as brother to the Lord and as a witness of Jesus' humanity and humbleness during their days in Nazareth, this designation must have been among James' most natural expressions for his faith in Jesus Christ. But from other New Testament passages we see that Christ's death, resurrection, and ascension are the heart of the Christian faith (Acts 4:33). The death of Christ—the Cross—is implicit in the preaching of His resurrection (cf. 1 Corinthians 1:18; 15:3-5). In Ephesians 1:19 and 2:10 the message of the resurrection and ascension of Christ capture the entire message of the gospel. Salvation is there described as being "made alive in Christ" (2:5). Paul adds in Ephesians 4:9 the comment that the exaltation of Christ would have been of no consequence to us had He not first humbled himself in His humanity.

It is precisely because Christ died for our sins that in Romans 10:9 Paul can state that faith in the resurrection of Jesus is saving faith (cf. 1 Thessalonians 1:10). James' understanding of "the faith of our Lord Jesus Christ, the Lord of glory" must have included the dimension of faith in the person and work of Jesus Christ. The phrase thus summarizes the Christian faith. The glorified Lord in whom the Church believes is none other than the Lord who answers prayers (James 5:14,15; cf. Mark 16:17; Acts 3:16; Colossians 3:17).

Connected to the Christology of the epistle is an eschatology that places the return of Christ in the center of the events of the last days: "The coming of the Lord draweth nigh" (5:8). This reflects the vibrant expectation of the Early Church (cf. John 21:23; 1 Thessalonians 1:10; Hebrews 10:37). Believers saw themselves as living in the last days (1 Corinthians 10:11; Hebrews 1:2); Christ's return was imminent. During trials and persecutions the coming of the Lord was the sustaining hope of the Church. They anticipated the coming of Christ the Saviour. The eschatology and soteriology of the epistle are founded on its Christology.

SOTERIOLOGY

Soteriology, or the doctrine of salvation, is proclaimed by the Epistle of James in much the same language and terms as in the rest of the New Testament. It can be described as justification (2:23), with the corresponding concepts of grace (4:5) and forgiveness of sins (5:15). Likewise, the idea of a new birth is discussed (1:18). God is said to be mighty to save (4:12). With reference to the new birth, it is said to take place by faith. The idea of faith in James is especially faith in Jesus Christ (2:1). The believer belongs to the name that called him (James 2:7; cf. Acts 4:12, where the name of Jesus is the only name given whereby men can be saved). These unique elements comprise the background for understanding some difficult passages in the letter.

At issue in the Epistle of James is the concept of justification. James speaks of justification by faith as well as justification by works (2:21-25). If one hopes to comprehend this paradox, the letter's teaching about the way to salvation must be understood. Then the reader will discover that James does not allow humanity the least hope of self-justification. James' view of the fallen nature of humankind forbids any such notion.

The prime difference between the Mosaic law and the gospel of Christ was that the former was based on works and the latter on grace. Under both systems individuals had to choose for themselves whether to serve God or not. Men are born with a corrupt, sinful nature, because of Adam's sin. This imposes on them a tendency toward unrighteousness and sin. Unless they find a means of atonement, only judgment can be their lot.

God has always provided a way for men to obtain forgiveness. Under the Law there was an elaborate system of sacrifice, with the great one on Yom Kippur, the Day of Atonement. On that occasion, once a year, the high priest offered a bullock for the sins of the entire nation, sprinkling the blood on the mercy seat in the Holy of Holies. Then a scapegoat was brought, and laying his hands on its head, the high priest confessed over the goat "all the iniquities of the children of Israel, and all their transgressions in all their sins" (Leviticus 16:21). Then the goat was sent into the wilderness, never to return, symbolizing God's forgiveness.

Note that the atonement was made for all the sins of all the people; however, individuals had to enter by faith into the reality of that atonement by their own decision, by an act of their own will. The other sacrifices provided this opportunity.

In Jesus' day some of the Pharisees had the idea they could be justified by fully keeping the Law. This is why they developed a detailed collection of rules, the "traditions of the elders," to interpret the Law. But Jesus revealed they could not even keep the first commandment, to love God wholly. Paul, a former Pharisee, could testify that he had reached the point of being "blameless" as far as the "righteousness which is in the law" was concerned (Philippians 3:6)—but he had not found salvation!

The same principle holds true concerning salvation under the gospel. Christ died for the sins of the whole world, so atonement has been made for all mankind. "God is not willing that any should perish" (2 Peter 3:9). But each individual must choose for himself. By the Holy Spirit, God is seeking to draw all men, but He does not force men to accept. Neither does he arbitrarily reject any. Man has a free will by which he may choose.

The Scriptures say, "There is none righteous, no, not one" (Romans 3:10). James emphasizes this truth by his discussion of the tongue (3:1-12). "The tongue can no man tame. It is an unruly evil, full of deadly poison" (verse 8). And back of the tongue stands the heart. Whatever the tongue says reflects the voice of the heart . It is impossible to "tame" the tongue, because man cannot control his sinful nature. Only by acquiring a new nature can victory come. And this is what God does for men through the new birth, making them "partakers of the divine nature" (2 Peter 1:4).

Jesus stated that a bad tree cannot bring forth good fruit. This is a central theme in His teaching; it is also one proclaimed by the apostles who followed Him. Peter wrote of an empty way of life received by tradition from their fathers (1 Peter 1:18). John wrote: "If we say that we have no sin, we deceive ourselves" (1 John 1:8). Paul tells us that the "carnal mind is enmity against God: for it is not subject to the law of God, neither indeed can be" (Romans 8:7). Skimming a series of passages in James shows that he totally agreed with this viewpoint which challenged the Jewish understanding of justification. Consequently, we see that there is no basis for thinking that James believed one can be justified by works. Such a notion is just as unthinkable as believing a bad tree could bear good fruit or that a bitter fountain could provide fresh water (3:12).

Such a radical but Biblical view of the sinful nature of humanity forms the backdrop for all that James—in concert with the other New Testament authors and Jesus—understood to take place at salvation. Salvation is the unmerited forgiveness of sin and the justification (i.e., pronouncing as righteous) of the guilty party (2:23; 5:15). Moreover, it involves such a radical transformation of the individual's personality and disposition that it is called "rebirth, regeneration, or re-creation." It is part of Jesus' own message: "Ye must be born again(!)" (John 3:7). Paul put it this way: "If any man be in Christ, he is a new creature: old things are passed away; behold, all things are become new" (2 Corinthians 5:17). Peter said that God "according to his abundant mercy hath begotten us again unto a lively hope by the resurrection of Jesus Christ from the dead" (1 Peter 1:3). John wrote: "Whosoever believeth that Jesus is the Christ is born of God" (1 John 5:1).

James joined in this harmonious proclamation: "Of his own will begat he us with the word of truth that we should be a kind of firstfruits of his creatures" (1:18). The original wording of the Greek is an emphatic expression, which in the New Testament uniquely denotes regeneration. It signifies the new birth from above; "that which is born of the Spirit is spirit" (John 3:6). We were dead spiritually, separated from the life of God, but have been made alive in Christ (Ephesians 2:1,5).

Because James opened his epistle with this understanding of salvation as regeneration, a clear light is shed on his later comments about justification. When the nature of the tree is altered, should it then be able to produce fruit of a different kind? When the fountain is cleansed, should it not be able to give fresh water? When a person becomes a new creature in Christ and has partaken of the very divine nature, should this not lead to a new life-style (cf. Romans 6:4)?

Justification cannot be divorced from regeneration. What kind of faith could possibly justify without regenerating? None. The faith that justifies also brings new birth and the transformation of the individual. That is why any faith not expressed in good works is dead and useless (i.e., not faith at all). Faith that does not cause renewal will neither cause righteousness. James brings his discussion to a climactic close with the formulation: "justified by works." The one justified by faith will also be justified by his works.

AGAINST ANTINOMIANISM

The Epistle of James is also a polemical document directed against antinomianism (lit., "anti-law," a rejection of the law which leads to immorality). It is a grand monument to the moral sensibility and integrity of the Early Church.

Within the Jewish-Christian and Gentile churches of the early Christian Era, many shared common struggles. The Gentile believers were confronted by their own heritage of Greek philosophies and "wisdom," while the Jewish Christians felt pressure from their Jewish heritage. These influences circulated throughout the Diaspora. Jewish Christians as well as Gentile Christians had to make a fundamental break with their past. It is easy to understand, though, that many brought with them the mind-set and habits of their days outside of Christ. Related to this tendency is the curious fact that both Jewish and Gentile elements eventually manifest themselves in the area of practical living.

Even more strangely, they appear in two diametrically opposed forms. On the one hand, there is the false asceticism and on the other, licentious libertinism. Jewish Christians were prone to both excessive legalism and overt rejection of all laws. Legalism was an attempt to attain righteousness through the works of the Law; lawlessness appealed to a salvation solely based on faith and void of any obedience.

The New Testament Scriptures combat both legalists and antinomians, whether they originated in Jewish legalism or Gentile philosophical systems. The Epistle to the Galatians is the strongest attack on a Jewish righteousness-by-works mentality, while the Epistle of James is a confrontation with the problem of antinomianism. It may seem that James contrasts with Galatians and argues for the validity of works, but upon closer scrutiny we see that the New Testament as a whole endorses obedience (i.e., "works"). John the Baptist demanded "fruits meet for repentance" (Matthew 3:8). Jesus himself concluded His Sermon on the Mount by underscoring the necessity of both hearing and acting on His Word (Matthew 7:24ff.). Paul the apostle shaped his preaching to both Jews and Gentiles so "that they should repent and turn to God, and do works meet for repentance" (Acts 26:20.). Peter exhorted his audience to maintain good behavior so the Gentiles could see their good deeds (1 Peter 2:12). John wrote: "Let us not love in word, neither in tongue; but in deed and in truth" (1 John 3:18).

James too calls for works. Christian character becomes manifest in works and vice-versa. Patience must lead to works (1:4). To listen to the Word must promote good deeds (1:22). Faith also leads to works (2:14), as does compassion (2:15,16). Wisdom is to make itself known through works (3:13). Such required good deeds are not exactly the converse of "bad deeds," but of a faith in God that is expressed only in words. "Therefore to him that knoweth to do good, and doeth it not, to him it is sin" (4:17).

JAMES AND PAUL

The contrast that some have maintained exists between James and Paul is usually supported by setting certain texts over against others. For example, what Paul said in Romans 3:28: "We conclude that a man is justified by faith without the deeds of the law," is contrasted with what James said in 2:24: "Ye see then how that by works a man is justified, and not by faith only." It must be admitted, if this were the only comment either of these authors wrote, it would be difficult to reconcile them. But both of these detached texts fall in unique contexts; both are conclusions to a certain chain of logic, and they are intelligible only in light of their immediate context. Paul rejected works of the Law as "dead works" (cf. Hebrews 9:14) as far as justification is concerned. James rejected faith without works, "dead faith," as a means of justification.

It is important to understand what the two authors did *not* mean. James could not possibly have meant that a person becomes righteous in God's eyes through his own efforts to fulfill the Law. He consistently asserted in his letter that all of us fail in many things (3:2). Moreover, he noted explicitly that a single violation of the Law means one is guilty of violating all of the Law (2:10). Thus James dismissed any notion that righteousness is attained through keeping the Law as vigorously as Paul did in Galatians 3:10 and 5:2-4. James knew no way to salvation other than rebirth through the word of truth, i.e., the gospel (1:18), and through justification by faith (2:23).

Paul, for his part, was not saying that the faith which justifies is a faith unrelated to works (obedience). Did he not conclude his comments in Romans 3:21-31 by asking: "Do we then make void the law through faith? God forbid: yea, we establish the law"?

The phrase "God forbid" surfaces throughout the Epistle to the Romans. In many instances it functions precisely to reject the notion that a Christian can "continue in sin" (6:1, 2,15). Paul indignantly opposed any who twisted his message in such a manner (3:8). For Paul, faith that justifies is faith that "worketh by love" (Galatians 5:6), and although one may have all faith, it is nothing without love (1 Corinthians 13:2). Thus, Paul and James fully correspond in their understanding of justification. James does not teach salvation without faith, and Paul does not teach salvation without the works of faith.

A contrast between James and Paul can actually be contrived only if one adopts an interpretation of salvation that places both of them in opposition to what is otherwise taught by the rest of the New Testament. Moreover, such an interpretation would make them inconsistent within their own writings. It is plain that Paul understood "works" in two different senses: there are "works of the law" and "good works." It is equally obvious that James understood works in only one sense—as the fruit of faith.

Of course, it is rather easy to create a false contrast between the two if these distinctions are not maintained. If one compares what Paul said about works of the Law with James' comments about works of faith; and if one also places what Paul said about true faith alongside what James said about dead faith, then it is possible to make it appear as if the two are diametrically opposed to one another.

However, it would be just as easy to make them appear to contradict themselves. The same Paul who said in Romans 3:28 that man is justified by faith without deeds, said in 1 Corinthians 7:19 that keeping the commandments of God is essential to faith. Moreover, James wrote in 2:21 that Abraham was justified by works, but in verse 23 James goes on to say Abraham was justified by faith. Neither Paul nor James, however, seemed to see any contradiction in their words. On the contrary, it appears as if Paul took it for granted that those saved by grace, not works, are saved to do good works (Ephesians 2:9,10). Likewise, James viewed justification by works not in contrast to, but as a confirmation of and in fulfillment of justification by faith (2:21-24).

Some of those who do not agree that the

Epistle of James is a response to Paul, still think that the letter may be a correction to a misunderstood "Paulism" similar to the kind Paul himself combated. This should probably be viewed as anachronistic, since there is much to indicate that James was written prior to Galatians and Romans. The kind of antinomianism James attacked does not necessarily have to be a result of some misunderstanding of Paul.

What James might call justification by works is actually the practical outworking of the doctrine of justification by faith. The Epistle of James uses both the notion of faith and works in the same context; one does not negate the other. In this connection it is important to recognize that James is neither the first nor the last to speak of righteousness by works. Jesus himself did, as did Paul. Jesus said that on the day of judgment a person will be condemned or justified according to his works (Matthew 12:37). Similarly, Paul referred to a judgment according to works (Romans 2:16; 14:10; 1 Corinthians 4:4,5; 2 Corinthians 5:10).

Two possibilities are latent in the expression "judgment according to works," either condemnation or justification. The term *justification* comes from the language of the courts and denotes a decision of "innocent" by a judge. At the last day the sentence will be passed according to works; this does not nullify that we are justified by faith. No. James notes that when Abraham was justified by works it was the fulfillment (practical outworking) of justification by faith (2:22,23).

The same holds true for justification by works on judgment day. James says that faith was made perfect by works. The faith that is demonstrated in deed becomes perfect. When faith is manifest through works the tension between faith and works disappears. Then our being justified by faith and judged by works is consistent.

We are saved apart from anything we might do, but we receive what we deserve at the Judgment. Justification by faith is the basis of salvation; justification by works is the fruit of salvation. Though Abraham was justified by faith (Genesis 15:6), he was justified by works 30 years later when he offered Isaac in sacrifice (Genesis 22:12). At that time Abraham had lived as the friend of God (Genesis 18:17). He lived a holy life (Genesis 17:1). Through his life he confirmed the pronouncement of justification given to him by God because of his faith.

Overview–1 Peter

Peter is often referred to as the apostle of hope, Paul the apostle of faith, and John the apostle of love. In his epistles Peter addressed particular problems, as did Paul and John. Together these apostles dealt with the entire spectrum of the Christian faith.

Peter's epistles contain a wealth of doctrine and encouragement. The flow of 1 Peter is smooth and even; 2 Peter is somewhat more uneven. In many ways the differences in form and style remind one of the differences between Paul's epistles to the Romans and Galatians. First Peter is didactic and gives warning. Second Peter is quite polemic. Nonetheless, in both letters the predominant concern is the care of the believer.

CANONICITY

Christians of the First Century were actively engaged in determining the authenticity and apostolicity of the epistles. Peter's first epistle satisfied the two main criteria for acceptance as Holy Scripture: It was apostolic and it had since the outset been accepted as Holy Scripture by the Early Church.

It is among the best attested documents in the New Testament. The first witness to its authenticity comes from the Bible itself. Peter himself referred to it when he used the words "second epistle" (2 Peter 3:1).

According to the church historian Eusebius of Caesarea the epistle was commonly regarded as genuine. Some believe there is an echo of 1 Peter in 1 Clement (ca. A.D. 96), Ignatius (ca. A.D. 110), the Shepherd of Hermas, and the Epistle of Barnabas. Papias (A.D. 125) also used 1 Peter. From that same time (A.D. 125) there are probable allusions to 1 Peter in Polycarp. Other Second Century writers also appear to refer to the letter and ascribe it to Peter the apostle (e.g., Basil [125], Theodotion [160], and Irenaeus [180]).

It was not until more recent times that the authenticity of the epistle was questioned. Modern Biblical criticism based the objection to the authenticity of 1 Peter on historical and dogmatic questions as well as on the linguistic style.

Historical objections culminate for the most part in the supposed improbability that Peter, the apostle to the Jews, would write a letter to churches in Asia Minor, the supposed "jurisdiction" of Paul. But Paul himself endorsed Peter's authority or perhaps "popularity" among his churches (1 Corinthians 1:12). It is further argued that the letter presupposes a persecution in Asia Minor (ca. during the reign of Domitian, 81–96), which did not actually occur until after Peter's death. However, nothing in the epistle itself suggests that such a state-backed persecution of Christians was under way. The contrary is true (cf. 2:13,14). But still it is clear from the Book of Acts and the Epistles that Christians faced opposition from the very beginning, much like Peter wrote about in his letter.

Arguments against the authenticity of the letter based on linguistic style question the ability of a Galilean fisherman to write such excellent Greek. Peter understood and used Greek, but it is very likely that Silas (Silvanus; cf 1 Peter 5:12), the old friend and coworker of Paul and the coauthor of the letters to the Thessalonians, also coauthored 1 Peter.

Objections raised because the First Epistle of Peter used the Septuagint rather than the Hebrew Bible (Masoretic Text) are of little consequence, since the Qumran texts have shown other texts which could have been the basis here. On the other hand, it is still quite likely that the Septuagint did indeed serve as the basis of the Scripture citations in 1 Peter. Peter simply used the text of his audience.

Dogmatic objections to Petrine authorship concern the distinct similarities between some of Paul's writings, particularly Ephesians and Romans. Without question there are similarities, but this only proves that in the Early Church there was a unified doctrinal foundation as well as fruitful dialogue among leaders. Peter acknowledged the letters of Paul and knew them well (2 Peter 3:15,16). His first epistle also indicates some points of contact with Hebrews and the Epistle of James.

The objections raised against the authenticity of Peter's first epistle are of even less consequence in light of the stronger external and internal witnesses to its authenticity. The external witnesses mentioned above are so reliable that it seems no book of the New Testament has an earlier, stronger, or better attestation. Furthermore, we have the epistle's own testimony and some strong internal reasons for accepting it as genuine.

AUTHORSHIP

Peter, the apostle of Jesus Christ, introduced himself as the author (1:1). He asserted his apostolic authority and claimed equal status with the leaders of the Church by describing himself as "also an elder" (5:1). When he admonished those guarding the "flock" of God, his words implied that such action was his duty—a reminder of the pastoral calling given to Peter by the Lord following His resurrection (John 21:15-17).

One interesting feature is that the words used to describe the sufferings of Christ correspond more closely to Mark's Gospel than to any of the other Synoptics. It is a well-known and ancient tradition that Mark relied on Peter as his principal source.

There is a striking similarity between the sermons and speeches of Peter recorded in the Book of Acts and his words in the epistle. Related to this is the consistent understanding that the Christ-event was the fulfillment of Old Testament prophecies (1 Peter 1:10,12; cf. Acts 3:18-24). Further, both relate that God makes no distinction between people (1 Peter 1:17; cf. Acts 10:34) and that Christ is the stone rejected by the builders (1 Peter 2:7,8; Acts 4:10,11). Finally, there is similar importance attached to the name of the Lord (1 Peter 4:14,16; cf. Acts 3:6,16; 4:10,12; 10:43).

Suffering is a central theme in 1 Peter, especially the suffering of Christ. It is interesting to compare what the letter says with what Peter said as reported in the Gospels and Acts. The Gospels relate that Peter resisted the fact that Jesus had to follow the way of suffering (Matthew 16:21f.). However, in the Book of Acts, a focal point of Peter's preaching is that "Christ should suffer" (3:18; cf. 2:23). In his first epistle Peter equated "suffering" with "the death of Christ." He described himself as a "witness of the sufferings of Christ" (5:1). He wrote that Christ was "put to death in the flesh" (3:18), but his tendency was to emphasize the suffering aspect of that death (cf. 2:21; 3:18; 5:1). He stressed the fact that the prophets "testified beforehand the sufferings of Christ" (1:11).

The epistle indicates that believers are to share in these sufferings; it is the way to glory (4:13). They are to enter this glory "after that ye have suffered a while" (5:10; cf. 1:6,7). Peter was a man traveling in the shadow of the Cross. Like his Master, he knew a cross awaited him at the end of his journey. Peter differed in this respect from his fellow apostles. During most of their apostolic service their personal hope was for the return of Christ. Of John it was said: "that disciple should not die" (John 21:23). Paul could say that he did not wish to be unclothed, but clothed with his heavenly dwelling (2 Corinthians 5:4). He felt it better to remain until the coming of the Lord than to die a natural death. He could say: "We which are alive and remain unto the coming of the Lord" (1 Thessalonians 4:15). But paradoxically, the very one known as the apostle of hope could not entertain a personal hope that he would escape death. Peter knew he would glorify God through his death (John 21:18,19); he also knew it would not be long in coming (2 Peter 1:14). It was the Peter who approached the day when he would be led where he did not want to go who wrote these epistles.

After he met Jesus, Peter's life fell into three sections: (1) the years when he accompanied Jesus; (2) after the Resurrection, until he left Jerusalem—during this time (ca. A.D. 45–48), he was the major leader of the Church (Acts 1-12); (3) very little is known of the third period during which he was one of the pillars of the Church until his death (Galatians 2:9). The legacy of these two letters are the apostle's last will to Christianity.

RECIPIENTS OF THE EPISTLE

The epistle is addressed "To God's elect, strangers in the world, scattered throughout Pontus, Galatia, Cappadocia, Asia and Bithynia" (1:1, NIV). These words indicate the initial readers lived in the Roman provinces in the northwestern section of Asia Minor. The term "strangers" is understood by some to refer to Christian Jews of the Diaspora. Others regard the term as a symbol for the believer's status as a "stranger" in the world. Many references in the epistle indicate that the latter interpretation is preferred. For example, formerly believers lived in ignorance (1:14) and shared in abominable idolatries (4:3). Perhaps the most vivid illustration is that they were formerly "not a people" (2:10). Most likely the churches that received the letter were of mixed, Jewish-Gentile congregations.

Apparently the believers were facing strong harassment from outsiders. Peter used the terms "suffer" or "suffering" no less than 16 times. Although the outsiders had slandered the believers as evildoers, there is no evidence that this was a state-sponsored persecution. The authorities were not seen in a hostile light but rather as a police force to punish the evildoers and praise those who did well. Evidently the Christians were still being protected by the authorities (2:13-17), but the opposition was beginning. Peter wrote to encourage his brothers and sisters (cf. Luke 22:32).

TIME AND PLACE

The closing words of the epistle (5:13) indicate that it originated in "Babylon." If this is to be taken literally, it probably refers to Babylon on the Euphrates. There was a Roman military outpost in Egypt with this name, but it is unlikely that this obscure defense post was the place referred to by Peter. In Mesopotamia there was an ancient, rather large Jewish settlement, and even though the city of Babylon was largely destroyed, some Jews still lived in this region. It would not be out of the question to assume that Peter, the apostle to the Jews, had visited this place. If his letter originated here it would account for the east-to-west listing of regions in the opening greeting.

If Babylon is to be understood figuratively, the meaning is without question "Rome." It is not easy to understand why the apostle would choose such cryptic language, but the two other figurative expressions in the verse favor such an understanding. The text literally reads: "She, that is at Babylon, elected together with you, salute you, and so does Marcus my son" (5:13). The word "she" is understood figuratively as the church. "Marcus" was undoubtedly, like Silas, "Mark," Paul's coworker. He was the "son" of Peter only in a spiritual sense. When the two expressions are taken figuratively, it makes good sense to take Babylon in the same way. If this is the case, as in Revelation 16:19; 17:18; 18:2,10, "Babylon" refers to Rome. An ancient tradition indicates Peter was martyred at Rome during Nero's persecution of Christians in the fall of A.D. 64. The time of the apostle's death is therefore established sometime between 64 and 67; the two letters sometime before this. During this time, Paul was imprisoned in Rome; in Jerusalem, earlier, James had been put to death by the Jews. Peter must have thought his own death was drawing near, and he must have wanted to reach his friends with a word of warning and encouragement.

SURVEY AND STRUCTURE

As we find in Paul's writings, there are distinct teaching portions and encouragement sections in 1 Peter. In the first section (1:1 to 2:11), doctrinal matters are presented. The remainder of the letter is devoted primarily to practical admonition and advice. Nonetheless, there is no truly sharp distinction between teaching and advice. Peter described his writing as an encouragement and a testimony (5:12). Doctrine is the basis for encouragement and admonition. Because God has begotten us again (1:3), we should live holy lives "as obedient children" (1:14-17). Believers are to follow Christ's example, walking in His footsteps (2:21). Because Christ took our sins, we are to be dead to them (2:24). The thought of reward can be motivation to holy service (5:2-4). Thus the Christian is to seek God's acceptance.

The strong emphasis on humility and submissiveness was virtually at odds with the Greek notion of human dignity. The manner in which good works are portrayed in this epistle did not coincide with either Jewish or Greek thought. It is a unique Christian ethic, modeled on Christ's example presented in this epistle.

Because teaching and advice are so interwoven, it is not easy to distinguish a clear-cut structure or outline. Interpreters have used their own points of view and different thematic interests to create a structure. Many are useful and insightful; many are similar. One should not force the epistle into some rigid arrangement. However, the following outline should be helpful in seeing the main content:

I. Salvation in Christ (1:1–2:10)
II. The Conduct of the Christian (2:11–3:12)
III. The Sufferings of the Christian (3:13–4:19)
IV. Final Encouragement (5:1ff.)

THE THEOLOGY OF PETER

Since Peter was one of the closest followers of Jesus during His public ministry, it is reasonable to assume much of what he wrote echoes the teaching of the Lord. At the same time there is a strong undercurrent of Pauline theology. This suggests that during the apostolic period much of the teaching was shared by the body of Christ as a whole (cf. Galatians 2:1ff.). There is a significant amount of theology in 1 Peter. In this Overview only the main points can be mentioned.

(1) The Trinitarian View of the Godhead

The epistle opens with a clearly expressed faith in the Trinity: "Elect according to the foreknowledge of God the Father, through sanctification of the Spirit, unto obedience and sprinkling of the blood of Jesus Christ" (1:2). The great trinitarian doxology of 1:3-12 delineates the role of each of the three Persons of the Godhead in salvation. These verses give one of the clearest trinitarian statements in the New Testament.

(2) God the Father

Peter used the phrase "God the Father" (1:2) in much the same way John's Gospel speaks of God as "Father" in the absolute sense, i.e., as a member of the Godhead. This is markedly underscored in 1:3: "the God and Father of our Lord Jesus Christ." Here faith in God is linked to Christology. The God preached by Peter is the One who beforehand spoke through the prophets and who anticipated the coming of Christ (1:10,11). In these last times God the Father has revealed himself in the Son (1:5). God is the "faithful Creator" (4:19). He is holy and expects holiness from His people (1:15). He judges without respect of persons (1:17). Believers have been brought "to God" and into right relationship with Him through the suffering and death of Christ (3:18). It is through Christ that believers have faith in God, and this faith means hope in God for eternal glory (1:21).

(3) Christology

Peter's theology is fundamentally Christological. It is so comprehensive that it covers virtually every main element of the New Testament's teaching about the person and work of Christ. First Peter includes most of the major soteriological (doctrine of salvation) and eschatological (doctrine of last things) teachings as well. Within this brief letter the apostle Peter emerges as one of the great teachers of the Christian faith. The following can be mentioned:

Preexistence of Christ (1:20)

Before the foundation of the world Christ was. This was an actual preexistence and a real manifestation in time (cf. John 1:1-14). Even in His preexistence Christ was the spotless Lamb who was to redeem mankind with His blood (1 Peter 1:19; cf. Revelation 13:8).

Prophecy of His Coming (1:11)

Old Testament prophets prophesied that Christ would come. They testified to His sufferings as well as to His humiliation and subsequent glorification. Actually, through the Holy Spirit (here the Spirit of Christ), Christ himself testified to His coming. That the Spirit bore witness as the Spirit of Christ centuries, indeed thousands of years, before the coming of Christ is reminiscent of Hebrews 11:26. Long before Christ's coming, Moses considered the dishonor of associating with Christ of more value than the treasures of Egypt.

Christ—Messiah

The most often used title for the Lord in 1 Peter is simply "Christ" (1:11,19; 2:21; 3:15,16,18; 4:1,13,14; 5:1,10,14). The combination "Jesus Christ" is not used as often (1:1,2,3,7,13; 2:5; 3:21; 4:11). Although Peter used the title "Christ" as a proper name, he could not have done so without being fully aware that the name meant "Messiah," the "anointed one." Peter's dramatic confession at Caesarea Philippi, "Thou art the Christ, the Son of the living God" (Matthew 16:16), indicated that awareness. Such a messianic proclamation was also a distinct feature of Peter's sermons in Acts (Acts 2:14-16; 3:12-26, etc.).

The Incarnation

Peter viewed Jesus' birth as well as His return as a "revelation" (1:20; cf. 1:7,13; 4:13; 5:4). At His birth the preexistent Christ entered the human sphere. This corresponds with Paul's use of the phrase "manifest in the flesh" (1 Timothy 3:16). Other New Testament writers took the same position (e.g., Paul, 1 Timothy 3:16; cf. 2 Thessalonians 1:7; the author of Hebrews, 9:26; cf. verse 28; John, 1 John 3:5,8; cf. 2:28; 3:2).

Christ's Sinlessness

The apostle Peter was an eyewitness to the words and ministry of the only sinless Person ever to live on earth. Christ is the only One who could ever issue the challenge: "Which of you convinceth me of sin?" (John 8:46). Peter repeatedly emphasized that Christ was free from sin ("who did no sin," 2:22). Christ was the "lamb without blemish" (without innate sin) and "without spot" (without external sin). He alone could offer sacrifice for others (1:19), the "just for the unjust" (3:18).

Christ's Example

God's holiness was revealed and demonstrated in Jesus Christ as He lived out His perfect life among men. Peter presented Christ's holiness as the model for believers, "Leaving us an example, that ye should follow his steps" (2:21). He argued (1:15,16) that God's own holiness should be incentive for holy lives among His people.

Substitutionary Death

Not for one minute did Peter entertain the idea that merely by example Christ secured salvation for the believer. As soon as he presented Christ as example (2:21-23), he moved on to write of Jesus as the One who atoned for sin, "who his own self bare our sins in his own body on the tree" (2:24). Christ's death was a substitutional death, "the just for (*huper*) the unjust" (3:18). The Greek term *huper*, here means "instead of," "in place of," "for." It functions in much the same way as it does in Philemon 13, "that in thy stead he might have ministered unto me." The issue, then, is full substitution. Christ takes the place of the sinner.

Peter further underscored this in 1:19, where he referred to Christ as the blameless sacrificial Lamb. This recalls the symbolic, substitutional nature of the Levitical sacrifices. However, in contrast to the repeated sacrifices of the priests, Christ "hath once suffered" (3:18), i.e., "once and for all" (cf. Romans 6:9,10; Hebrews 9:28; 10:10-12). Christ offered the perfect sacrifice for our sins. It does not have to be repeated. He offered himself in our place to "bring us to God" (3:18), to grant us access to God (cf. Hebrews 10:19,20). He gave himself that "we, being dead to sins, should live unto righteousness" (2:24).

In the original language the term for "redeemed" is *lutroō*, which implies a redemption based on a ransom. (Cf. Matthew 20:28, where Jesus said the Son of Man would give His life as a ransom for many [*lutron anti*, "ransom instead of" to be precise]; cf. also 1 Timothy 2:6: "Who gave himself a ransom for all" [*antilutron huper*, literally "ransom instead of"].)

Descent to the Realm of the Dead (3:18-20)

Most interpreters unite these verses with those texts referring to Christ's descent to the kingdom of death following His death on the cross. Jesus promised the repentant thief he would join Him in paradise (Luke 23:43), which is understood as the habitation of the righteous after death. Peter mentioned Christ's descent into the kingdom of death, but he emphasized the fact that Christ did not remain there (Acts 2:27,31). Paul also wrote of Christ's visit to the kingdom of the dead during the time between His death and resurrection (Romans 10:7). The context of 3:18-22 concerns Christ's death, resurrection, and ascension. If one takes this to mean that as a part of salvation history Jesus departed and preached to the spirits in prison (cf. 1 Peter 4:6; 2 Peter 2:4-9; Jude 6), it raises a number of questions. These will be addressed later in a separate section.

The Resurrection

Three times in his first epistle Peter mentioned the Resurrection. He wrote that the basis of the believer's hope is that God raised Jesus from the dead and gave Him glory (1:21). He stated (1:3) that God has "begotten us again unto a lively hope by the resurrection of Jesus Christ." Possibly, the expression "quickened by the Spirit" (3:18, i.e., "made alive") refers to the Resurrection.

Ascension

Christ's ascension into heaven is portrayed in Scripture as a visible, tangible event (Acts 1:9). Peter was an eyewitness of the Ascension (Acts 1:22; 3:22). His words in his first epistle echo his sermon in Solomon's Porch in which he declared that Christ will remain in heaven until the time of His return and the restoration of all things (Acts 3:20,21).

Exaltation

Christ did not have to wait until His return to receive glory (1 Peter 1:11,21; 4:13; cf. 1 Timothy 3:16). He has already entered "into his glory" (cf. Luke 24:26). Peter reported that He now "is on the right hand of God, angels and authorities and powers being made subject unto him" (3:22). He is a "living stone, disallowed indeed of men, but chosen of God, and precious" (2:4). God's response to the world's rejection of His Son (2:21ff.; 3:18) is that He exalted Christ and gave Him the name "Lord" (1 Peter 1:3; cf. Philippians 2:9-11). Christ is also to be honored in the Church of God in this way (3:14).

The concept of Christ seated at the right hand of God is central to New Testament teaching. Peter concluded his sermon on the Day of Pentecost with this picture (Acts 2:33-36). Paul united it with the exaltation of Christ above all authorities (Ephesians 1:20ff.). In Hebrews 8:1ff., and 1 John 2:1,2, this concept is joined with the truth that Christ is High Priest and Advocate for His people.

The Return of Christ

Christ's glory is closely associated with His exaltation and will be revealed when He returns (4:13). Peter encouraged believers to set their hope fully on the grace that will become their portion at His revelation (1:13). His return is called the "salvation ready to be revealed in the last time" (1:5). The trial of their faith will result in praise and honor (1:7). Faithful servants of the Lord will receive the unfading crown of glory (5:4). But the Lord's return will also mean judgment, for He will be "ready to judge the quick and the dead" (4:5). Judgment has already begun at the house of God, "and if the righteous scarcely be saved, where shall the ungodly and the sinner appear?" (4:17,18).

These strong words warn of the eschatological judgment Peter wrote about in his second epistle. But in 1 Peter the apostle encouraged believers who were experiencing persecution and opposition. Their trials were only for "a season" (1:6). When the Lord returns, believers will receive joy in exchange for their sufferings (4:13), and delight in the incorruptible inheritance reserved for them in heaven (1:4).

(4) The Holy Spirit (Pneumatology)

In keeping with the trinitarian understanding of God in this letter, the unity of the Godhead is strengthened by Peter's reference to the Spirit as the Spirit of God (4:14), the Spirit of Christ (1:11), and the Holy Spirit (1:12). During the time of the old covenant, the Spirit of Christ through the messianic prophecies (1:11) testified of the sufferings of Christ and the glory that would follow. In the present age the Spirit works through the preaching of the gospel (1 Peter 1:12; cf. 1 Thessalonians 1:5). He performs a sanctifying work in believers (1 Peter 1:2; cf. the fruit of the Spirit, Galatians 5:22). In times of trial, when believers are scorned because of the name of Christ, the Spirit watches over and strengthens them (1 Peter 4:14; cf. Matthew 5:11).

(5) Holy Scripture

There are several pertinent comments relevant to Holy Scripture in 1 Peter. The apostle used the expression "the scripture" (2:6) as synonymous with "the word" (2:8), "the word of God" (1:23), or "the word of the Lord" (1:25). This Word is the divine seed which gives new birth (1:23; cf. 1:3). Those who reject Christ do not believe the Word (1 Peter 2:8; cf. John 5:46,47). Those who refuse to believe the Word will "stumble," "whereunto also they were appointed" (2:8). God will judge those who reject His Word by handing them over to their own unbelief (cf. Luke 16:31; 2 Thessalonians 2:10-12). The Word of God is alive; it can therefore give new life (1:23). The Word of the Lord is the true, spiritual "milk" that allows the new believer to grow in the knowledge of their salvation (2:2). The Word of the Lord endures forever (1 Peter 1:25; cf. Matthew 5:18; Luke 21:33; John 10:35).

First Peter points out that the Old Testament prophecies were not the result of mechanical dictation, but were both a divine and human effort. The prophets inquired and searched diligently concerning what the Spirit revealed to them (1:10-12). The authority of Scripture is emphasized in 4:11 in that those who speak in the church are to do so as if speaking the Word of God.

(6) Personal Salvation

The objective side of salvation is an integral part of the Christology of the letter and was discussed earlier in that section. Here it will only be noted that Peter explicitly pointed out that personal salvation is "by grace." The people of God are those who have obtained mercy (2:10) and who stand in the grace of God (5:12). The humble are given grace (5:5). Unlike those who stumble because of unbelief, the faithful will not be confounded (2:6-8). Believers are chosen by God (1:1) and called (1:15). They have returned to God (2:25). They believe in Christ (1:8; 2:7) and have been born again (1:23). They testify to their salvation by water baptism (3:21). They are to pattern their lives after Christ's example (2:21). The consummation of their salvation will be experienced in the eternal kingdom of God (1:9).

(7) The Church (Ecclesiology)

Peter wrote to "churches" (plural) which were cared for by elders (5:1,2). This presupposes local church structure. "The church that is at Babylon" was very likely a local church (5:13). Elsewhere, the Church universal was in the mind of the apostle. The Church is the flock of God scattered throughout the land (5:2). Believers are compared with living stones that are part of a "spiritual house" (commonly understood as temple imagery, 1 Peter 2:5; cf. 1 Corinthians 3:16,17). Believers are also called a "holy priesthood" (2:5,9). They are the new people of God (2:9,10), a concept peculiar to the New Testament.

The wide range of Peter's theology cannot be limited to what has been discussed above. Only the most significant aspects could be presented. Such a concentration of "theological doctrine" in one place is perhaps paralleled only in Ephesians and 1 John. These three small documents illustrate the depth of apostolic preaching.

THE SPIRITS IN PRISON

First Peter 3:19 is a frequently debated text. It refers to Christ's having "preached unto the spirits in prison." Since ancient times a variety of interpretations have been offered. Three have become especially prominent and deserve our attention. A short survey of each will be of value.

(1) The View of the Early Church

During the first two centuries, the Early Church apparently viewed 3:19 as a reference to Christ's descending to the kingdom of death during the time between His death and resurrection. There, announcing the victory of the Cross, He redeemed the righteous who lived under the old covenant. For example, the Shepherd of Hermas and Irenaeus both refer to an apocryphal saying about Jeremiah: "With Jeremiah he makes his death and his descension to Hades (the kingdom of death) known by saying: 'The Lord, the Holy One of Israel, did remember his dead ones, they who earlier did sleep in the dust of the earth, and descended to them in order to preach glad tidings and to deliver them' " (Irenaeus). "I will penetrate all the lower parts of the earth and I will visit all those who are asleep (i.e., the dead), and I will inform all those who are waiting for the Lord" (Shepherd of Hermas, *Similitude* 9:16:6,24,25).

The primary thrust of this view is that Christ was not idle during His visit to the realm of the dead like His counterpart Jonah the prophet. Instead, Christ subdued the kingdom of death and assaulted and conquered the forces of Satan. He took the "keys of hell and death" (cf. Revelation 1:18), and thereby attained power to release death's prisoners. This viewpoint is expressed in the creedal phrase, "went down to the kingdom of death."

Whether or not one accepts this interpretation as valid, however, it does not explain why Christ preached to the stubborn and rebellious of the generation of the Flood, i.e., Noah's contemporaries. Many attempts have been made to overcome this inadequacy.

(2) The View of Augustine

Augustine's interpretation of 3:19, later followed by theologians of the Middle Ages, was already implicit in the Latin translation (Vulgate) of the verse. According to the Vulgate, Christ's "preaching" is understood to have taken place during the time of Noah, while God waited patiently. This view is accepted by many theologians today.

To support this view many appeal to the fact that the grammatical form of the sentence concerning those who "sometime were disobedient" refers to the period in which the action took place. According to this view, Christ's preaching then did not take place in hell but, by virtue of His preexistence, He preached by the Spirit (Genesis 6:3) through Noah, "the preacher of righteousness" (2 Peter 2:5). This preaching as well as the resistance to it took place "when once the longsuffering of God waited in the days of Noah, while the ark was a preparing" (3:20). Since only eight were saved, it is evident that most refused to heed Noah's message. By referring to this in verse 21, Peter hoped to stimulate the Christians to work fearlessly, even though there might be little result.

The fact that the gospel was preached to the dead (4:6) can then be understood in the same way. Even those who died had the opportunity to hear the "gospel" through God's messengers before they died, as Christ preached through Jonah (see above). Those who died, who were no longer "in the flesh," could not be judged as if they were "in the flesh." Thus the preaching of the gospel had to have taken place in times past. To be "judged according to men in the flesh" probably refers to their death (cf. Hebrews 9:27).

Theologians who reject the Augustinian interpretation find it too "artificial." They believe it is exegetically arbitrary. The Greek term *poreutheis* occurs twice in this passage. First, in 3:19 it is used of Christ's descent into hell. Second, in 3:22 it refers to Christ's ascension. This leads many to disagree that the expression "he went" (*poreutheis*) in verse 19 refers to the preexistence of Christ.

(3) The Hypothesis Concerning Angels

In 1890, F. Spitta introduced a theory which gained many followers. His hypothesis had its origins in Jewish pseudepigrapha and other writings of the pre-Christian period, such as the Book of Enoch, the Apocalypse of Baruch, the Testaments of the Twelve Patriarchs, and Jubilees. Some of these apocryphal writings indicate that, according to Genesis 6:2ff., fallen angels had sexual relations with women of the human race. The Biblical text refers to "sons of God" who had relations with the "daughters of men" (Genesis 6:2; cf. Jude 6,7). Their offspring were the "Nephilim," or "giants" (Genesis 6:4). The hypothesis is that the Flood came as a result of this intercourse between fallen angels and humankind. According to the Book of Enoch, the fallen angels and their offspring were the origin and source of all paganism. They became sort of evil "guardian angels" to kings and powerful world figures. Enoch indicates that such "giants" were imprisoned in the deepest darkness.

Those interpreters who contend for this "angel hypothesis" think Peter's first epistle expresses the view that Jesus, following His death, went and announced His victory to these demonic spirits. Therefore, they state, paganism's power was thereby shattered, causing the princes of the spiritual realm to admit Christ's dominion. More recent interpreters have frequently united such a view with the doctrine of the "restoration of all things" (*apokatastatis*). This teaching maintains that eventually even the evil spirits will be saved. But this view goes too far.

Many of those who accept this theory believe Christ's preaching in hell was a proclamation of judgment, a demonstration of His triumph. They contend that Peter used this to remind and encourage Christians to proclaim the gospel boldly, to men and women presently controlled by these forces. They cite 3:22 as a proof text of their theory.

However, many interpreters reject any theory along these lines. They consider such theories "fables of Jewish Gnostic Haggadah." They maintain that any "angel theory" is inconsistent with Jesus' words that angels neither marry nor are given in marriage (Mark 12:25). Those who insist that Christ preached salvation to evil spirits in hell encounter the direct opposition of Scripture.

Summation

There is little hope of making some definitive choice among these various options; the problem is simply too complex. Nevertheless, it is helpful to be aware that differing views exist. This should encourage careful study of the choices before making a decision. One need not feel compelled to understand completely everything in Scripture.

One conclusion can be drawn: this passage gives no basis for any such universalistic teaching or for salvation after death.

Overview–2 Peter

Simon Peter introduced himself as "a servant and apostle of Jesus Christ." He addressed the letter to "them that have obtained like precious faith with us"—i.e., a faith equally precious. This unique form emphasized that the faith of the recipients, which had come to them through the hearing of the gospel, was no less precious than the faith of those who had been eyewitnesses of Christ and His ministry (cf. John 20:29). Gentiles who were accepting Christ were in no way deficient or inferior to Jewish believers.

The author referred to an earlier letter (3:1). The most obvious and natural understanding of this is that it refers to 1 Peter. If so, it means that the recipients were a group of churches in Asia Minor. The apostle Peter's death was rapidly approaching (1:14). Perhaps he was already in prison. Based on this, it is reasonable to assume the letter was written in the midsixties, shortly before Peter was martyred. Second Peter 3:15,16 suggests the apostle Paul was still alive; this also supports an early dating of the letter.

No mention is made of the geographic origin of the letter. The "Babylon" of 1 Peter 5:13 probably applies to the second letter as well (see *Overview* for 1 Peter). If this is the case, not much time elapsed between the writing of the two letters.

Canonicity

The authenticity of 1 Peter is among the best attested in the New Testament. It was accepted by the Early Church without any doubt. Second Peter, however, belongs to a group of writings which were disputed for a long time before they were included in the holy canon. Initially, it seems as if the letter was not widely known. It is difficult to determine where it first appeared. There are some indications it was known by 1 and 2 Clement (ca. A.D. 95), Aristedes, Valentinus, Hippolytus, Irenaeus, Justin Martyr, Barnabas, Polycarp, and Hermas. While these are uncertain allusions, the letter was cited as Holy Writ by Theophilus of Antioch who died in 183. Origen, around the year 240, first attributed the letter to Peter although he mentioned it was disputed by others. However, long before Origen, it was used in Egypt since it was included in the Sahidic version.

It is also significant that both 1 and 2 Peter appear in the Bodmer papyrus designated p72, dated sometime around A.D. 200. It is among the oldest uncials (a manuscript written in capital letters) in existence. It should also be pointed out that p72 includes only portions of 1 and 2 Peter and Jude. No other New Testament book is part of this manuscript. In light of its inclusion in p72, it is probable that it was read in some churches in certain regions of the world. This agrees with what church historian Eusebius wrote concerning Clement of Alexandria (died ca. 220) including 2 Peter in his Bible. This represents the ancient Egyptian tradition. A few Old Latin manuscripts dating from the 6th to the 11th centuries include parts of 2 Peter.

The external witnesses to the letter are thus not as weak as is sometimes asserted. Some suggest that on the basis of external testimony alone one would be compelled to accept the book as highly valued by early writers.

In the years immediately preceding the canonization of Scripture there was a wide acceptance of the epistle, e.g., Cyril of Jerusalem, Athanasius, Augustine, etc. Jerome included the letter in his Vulgate version. The epistle was also accepted as canon by the church councils at Laodicia (366), Hippo (393), and by the two councils at Carthage (397 and 419). As a result of the decisions of the last councils the Western Church accepted the same canon as had Athanasius in 367.

Not everyone is fully aware of how seriously the Early Church viewed the difficult task of determining the canon of the New Testament. Their intense and persistent debates only indicated their thoughtful concern. Acceptance by an ecclesiastical council did not in any way "make" a book Holy Scripture. The councils' decisions only acknowledged the immanence of the document, its apostolic origin, and its place in the Church. The process of canonization was final and irreversible. No one in a later era of church history would have the knowledge or sources available to the Early Church. The body of sacred writings accepted by the Early Church as canon was passed on to later generations as Holy Scripture.

QUESTIONS CONCERNING AUTHORSHIP

The following is a survey of recent objections to the authenticity of 2 Peter as well as the responses to these arguments. The issues can be divided into five main groups.

(1) The Self-Testimony of the Author

The letter itself claims to be written by Simon

Peter, the apostle of Christ (1:1). The author testified that he had been an eyewitness of Christ's majesty and that he had seen His glory on the "holy mount" (2 Peter 1:16-19; cf. Matthew 17:1f.). He reminded his readers that Jesus had told him ahead of time that he would die within a short time (2 Peter 1:14; cf. John 21:18). He also referred to a previous letter addressed to his readers (2 Peter 3:1; cf. 1 Peter 1:1). All of this seems to confirm the authenticity of the epistle. However, some seem to use such information as an argument against the genuineness of the letter. They accuse the author of being a pseudepigrapher who intentionally introduced these facts into the text in order to give it the appearance of Petrine authorship.

One thing is clear: The only alternative to being genuine is being false. Either the book was written by the apostle of Christ, or it was written by someone claiming to be him. Such a pretense was a literary form that was common in antiquity. In late Judaism numerous works were ascribed to individuals who could not have possibly written them. Likewise, many "gospels," "acts of apostles," "letters," and "apocalypses" which purported to be from apostles circulated in the Early Church.

It is asserted by some that during this time such falsification was harmless "pious fiction." Such an opinion is doubtful. It is one thing to say that literary falsifications occurred and that men were deceived; it is an entirely different matter to assert that such forgeries were accepted as authentic and ethically proper. Not even the Greeks tolerated such falsification. One Greek actor was fined 10 talents for inserting a line in a play. Herodotus reported that one Onamachritus was exiled because he added a verse to a poem by Musaeus. How can one suggest that Christians would be any more tolerant?

There are many examples of the church fathers distancing themselves from such practices. Irenaeus indignantly reproached the heretics for using forged epistles they had manufactured themselves. Tertullian wrote of a presbyter in Asia Minor who had authored the apocryphal "Acts of Paul and Thecla." Because this man had improperly used Paul's name in a document that represented his own fancies and thoughts rather than the words of Paul, he was promptly removed from his post. His excuse that he had done it out of love for Paul fell on deaf ears. Bishop Serapion of Antioch (ca. 180) responded similarly when he learned that one of the churches in his care was interested in the "Gospel of Peter." Immediately he placed a prohibition against using it and said, "For our part, brethren, we do receive Peter and the other apostles like Christ. But the epistles which falsely carry their name, we reject as experienced men because we know that they were not presented us by them."

It is not at all correct to say that the Early Church accepted literary forgeries. Even less correct is the view that such spurious writings were canonized! Writing letters in the name of someone else was not acceptable. The canonization process involved refusing to accept those writings not considered apostolic. How can anyone argue, then, that forgeries were commonly accepted? Of course false apostolic letters circulated in the Ancient Church. The apostle Paul warned against false apostolic letters that were being circulated in the Early Church (2 Thessalonians 2:2). Perhaps one of the reasons Paul signed his letters with his own hand was to prevent such forgeries (2 Thessalonians 3:17,18).

False epistles represented a twofold deceit. First, the author's name was false; second, he published his forgery as an apostolic word from God. Such deceit brought him under God's judgment of false prophets (Deuteronomy 18:20-22; Jeremiah 23:21). If 2 Peter is a forgery of this kind, what right would the author have to rebuke the false teachers (2:1)?

(2) Inconsistencies Between 1 and 2 Peter

One argument used against the authenticity of 2 Peter is that its form and style are different from 1 Peter. First Peter contains some of the most sophisticated Greek of the New Testament. The same cannot be said for 2 Peter. Early theologians realized this. Jerome offered a possible explanation. Silvanus was Peter's scribe for his first letter (1 Peter 5:12). For his second letter he used another scribe or wrote it himself.

However, the gap between the two epistles is not as great as some would make it appear. Not everything is inconsistent. Some points have extraordinary similarities. The wording in 1 and 2 Peter is just as much alike as 1 Timothy and Titus, for example. To use linguistic differences as a basis for rejecting Petrine authorship of 2 Peter is therefore absurd.

(3) The Reference to Paul

Another argument directed against the authenticity of 2 Peter concerns the mention of Paul in 3:15,16. Some find it unthinkable that Peter would refer to his fellow apostle as "our beloved brother Paul." But this should not seem so strange. New Testament epistolary literature regularly named persons. Paul did so in his letters (e.g., Romans 16). So did the apostle John (3 John 9,12). The same can be said of the letter to the Hebrews (Hebrews 13:23). Paul named Peter several times (1 Corinthians 3:22; 9:5; 15:6; Galatians 1:18; 2:7ff.). Why, then, should Peter's mention of Paul be disallowed? This is not a valid argument against the genuineness of the letter.

Some contend there was rivalry between Paul and Peter. Peter had been corrected by Paul in Antioch (Galatians 2:11ff.). But Peter had defended Paul before the apostolic council in Jerusalem (Acts 15:7) and extended to him the right hand of fellowship (Galatians 2:9). Those who assert it is unlikely Peter would speak so kindly of Paul in his second epistle (3:15) underestimate the character of this apostle.

Some think the very mention of Paul's letters suggests 2 Peter belongs to a later time period. These assume that Peter knew of a collection of Paul's letters, but a *Corpus Paulinium* ("body of Pauline writings") was not an issue until late in the First Century. This was long after the death of Peter. But Peter did not say anything about a "collection" of Paul's writings. He spoke only of "all of his (Paul's) epistles" (3:15), noting only that he and Paul shared similar understandings concerning Christ's return. It is true that Peter values Paul's letters as "other Scriptures." The reference to "other scriptures" (3:16) refers to the Old Testament as well as to other New Testament writings used in the church gatherings. The early Christians considered the teaching of the apostles of equal value to the Old Testament. Thus it is no anachronism to equate apostolic Scriptures with the rest of Holy Writ.

(4) The Relationship With the Epistle of Jude

Most of the content of the Epistle of Jude bears a striking similarity with portions of 2 Peter (Jude 5-19; cf. 2 Peter 2:1 to 3:3). There are similar vocabulary, concepts, and illustrations. Although copying is not implied, the correspondences are so evident that it seems there is some kind of relationship between the two epistles. Explanations for these similarities vary. Some contend the author of Peter borrowed material from Jude; others take the opposite view. Some regard the differences as a consequence of a revision. Others assert that one of the authors merely repeated the other from memory. Several interpreters believe the similarities and differences can be explained best by presuming a common source. For example, there might have been a common "catechism" or teaching condemning heretics (e.g., Reicke, *The Anchor Bible*, 37:147; Wheaton, 1251). Great debates have raged over "who used whom?" or "did anybody use anybody?"

The resolution to these interesting problems is a "toss-up." It is difficult to see how any of this affects the authenticity of the Scriptures. Both writers took responsibility for what they had written. Neither made any attempt to conceal his identity. The content may be similar but it is not identical. Jude claimed the apostles stood behind some of what he wrote (Jude 17,18; cf. 2 Peter 3:3). Both books were received by the Early Church as Holy Scripture. In essence they both say the same thing, exemplifying the scriptural principle that by "the mouth of two witnesses, or at the mouth of three witnesses, shall the matter be established" (Deuteronomy 19:15; Matthew 18:16; cf. Genesis 41:32).

(5) The Anti-Gnosticism of the Epistle

One of the more serious objections to the authenticity of 2 Peter is that the letter opposes the kind of heresy belonging to a later period. However, it should be noted that the letter addresses a future problem. It speaks against false teachers who are to come (2:2). Like Paul, Peter wrote of the seductions of the "last days" (cf. 1 Timothy 4:1-3; cf. Acts 20:29-30). Church history confirms how accurate these predictions were and how important were the warnings.

Paul, as well as Peter, understood that seductions belong not only to the future. Both men were aware that the "mystery of lawlessness" was already at work (cf. 2 Thessalonians 2:7). Paul merged his prophetic word for the future with a description of the present (2 Timothy 3:1-9). The same combination of present and future tenses appears in the second chapter of 2 Peter. The apostle John wrote of antichrists already present in the world and the Antichrist who was to come (1 John 2:18). It is no coincidence that prophetic passages break the bonds of time; on the contrary, it is the nature of prophetic speech.

The assertion is unfounded that the kind of heresy opposed by Peter in his second epistle was not present during the early years of the apostle's life. Also, the heresies he described involved aberrations in both life and teaching. It is quite possible that there are Gnostic elements in the opposition's teaching in both 2 Peter and Jude. Peter's emphasis on Christian knowledge may be in response to this. It has been acknowledged for a long time that "protognostic" strains existed in some first-century churches. Colossians especially evidences this. The unique features of second-century gnosticism are not reflected in 2 Peter's attacks against its opponents. The polemic elements of 2 Peter cannot be used to undermine the authenticity of the letter.

The Content of the Epistle

According to the custom of that day, the epistle opens with the author introducing himself and greeting his readers (1:1,2). Next he admonished believers to live a life of godliness according to the divine power given them in salvation. Through the power available in Christ, believers can escape the corruption of the world. They can become partakers of the divine nature and gain admittance into the eternal kingdom of Jesus Christ. Peter reminded his readers (1:12-21) he was an eyewitness of the glory and majesty of Jesus at the "holy mount." He emphasized the truth that it was the Holy Spirit who inspired the prophecies of Scripture.

Over against the Spirit-inspired prophecies stand the false prophecies of the heretics and their followers. The apostle commented on the inevitable destruction towards which they were heading (2:1-3). A warning was sounded in 2:4-22 of how the condemnation of these false prophets was anticipated by Holy Scripture. God did not spare the angels that sinned, but placed them in prison in caverns of darkness until the judgment. Neither did He spare the "ancient world" (pre-Noahic), except for Noah and seven others. Sodom and Gomorrah also faced certain destruction. Only "righteous Lot" was delivered from God's judgment on the immoral people around him. These examples show how the Lord delivers the righteous from trial. They also show how the ungodly, especially those who revile the Lord and slander heavenly beings, are kept for the Day of Judgment. The ungodly will perish as "irrational beasts." As those who "revel in daylight" they are full of adultery and greed, and are "accursed." They are like Balaam who wanted to be paid for unrighteousness. They are arrogant, rude, and have fallen back into the corruption from which they were delivered by Christ. Their final fate is worse than their first.

The apostle denounced those who mock the message of the Lord's return and say He is not coming (3:1-10). Just as the first flood overcame the world's inhabitants, so too will the coming of the Lord—the flood of fire—overcome the ungodly. New heavens and a new earth will come (3:12). That time is postponed only because the Lord is patient towards the ungodly. His desire is that all would repent.

Second Peter falls into three natural divisions which are reflected in the modern chapter breaks. The following outline can be made:

I. "The True Knowledge" (chapter 1)
  (1) Admonition to fear God (1:3-11)
  (2) An eyewitness (1:12-18)
  (3) The prophetic word (1:19-21)

II. The False Teachers (chapter 2)
  (1) False teachers will come (2:1-3)
  (2) Judgment of false teachers (2:4-9)
  (3) The character of false teachers (2:10-22)

III. The Return of Christ (chapter 3)
  (1) The mockers of the last days (3:1-4)
  (2) The Day of the Lord (3:5-10)
  (3) The call for holiness (3:11-18)

Overview–1 John

Although First John is commonly called an "epistle," it does not have some of the features that were typical of Greek letters of that period. It does not indicate the writer or the persons to whom the letter was sent. There is no greeting or closing. However, there is much throughout the epistle that reveals the type of community to whom the letter was sent. In addition, one can discern the personal and intimate bond between the writer and his readers.

Some scholars believe the epistle was a circular letter written to several churches in a particular region. In this respect it could be compared to 1 Peter and perhaps Ephesians. Such a theory might also explain the general tone of the letter as well as the intimate relationship implied between the writer and the recipients. Some describe 1 John as a tract, a homily (sermon), or a treatise of some kind.

THE WRITER

The language, style, theological concepts, and thought world of the writer of 1 John indicates a close relationship to the Gospel of John. Because of this, the question of authorship must be resolved in connection with the discussion of the authorship of the Gospel. Attempts to demonstrate that a different person wrote the three letters and the Gospel have been vigorously challenged. First John is actually anonymous since the writer did not mention his name. However, the first readers of the epistle had no doubts as to the identity of the writer.

Second and Third John only indirectly identify the writer as "the elder" (*ho presbuteros*). This is probably not some official title (the "presbyter" being an elder on a council of elders). The definite article (*ho*) argues against it being an official title. Some interpreters hold that it denotes a person who bears apostolic tradition or a disciple of the apostle. Ancient tradition tells us the apostle John lived for a long time. As the only surviving apostle he might have chosen to call himself "the elder" or, in other words, the "chief elder."

The three most common solutions to the identity of the author are: (1) John the apostle, the son of Zebedee; (2) an otherwise unknown elder named John; (3) a former disciple of John who was the "editor" of the material.

The least viable option is solution number 2. The traditional solution, which clearly does not find much endorsement from contemporary scholarship, is that John the apostle was the author.

PLACE AND TIME OF WRITING

The First Epistle of John gives no indication of its geographic origin. According to Irenaeus, the apostle John spent his last years in Ephesus. It is possible, therefore, that the epistle was written from somewhere in Asia Minor. This was the ancient tradition.

The letter can probably be dated sometime between A.D. 75 and 100. Since it was known in the first quarter of the Second Century, it cannot have been written any later. Some think it was composed prior to A.D. 70. That a Palestinian Jew should be familiar with the thought world of a different culture should not necessarily be surprising. A parallel is found in the Qumran writings (Dead Sea Scrolls).

On the other hand, some expressions are best explained as the author's turning his opponents' language to his own purposes while rejecting their theology. For example, the language shows some affinity with Gnostic thought, but the writer has thoroughly "Christianized" his understanding of those concepts. The author's shaping of Hellenistic Judaism's language and Gnostic concepts in no way implies that he endorsed such systems. He used the language of his hearers and interpreted their concepts, thoughts, and theology in a Christian light. The language thus became a weapon against his opponents.

STRUCTURE

It is difficult to structure 1 John since the writer interwove the two themes of faith and love throughout the letter. The two basic themes were examined from different vantage points. This interrelationship between the various sections of the epistle has been described as "concentric circles." Perhaps a better description would be a "spiral," since there is movement and progression in each section. It is difficult to determine where one section ends and another begins. Moreover, one stylistic trait of the author was to introduce a series of associated ideas as the letter progressed. This might explain the seemingly "illogical"—or at least "surprising"—transitions and shifts of thought.

Without suggesting that the author had such a plan in mind when he wrote, we can still offer a brief outline illuminating the content of the letter.

I. THE PROLOGUE: THE OBJECT OF PREACHING, ITS BASIS AND PURPOSE (1:1-4)

II. FELLOWSHIP WITH GOD AND WALKING IN THE LIGHT (1:5–2:17)
  A. Fellowship With God and Sin (1:5–2:2)
    1. God Is Light
    2. False Doctrine: Improper Attitudes Toward Sin
    3. The Work of Jesus Christ—A Compendium
  B. To Know God Is To Keep the Commandments (2:3-6)
  C. The Old and the New Commandments (2:7-11)
  D. You Own Everything—Therefore Do Not Love the World (2:12-17)

III. THE BATTLE AGAINST ANTI-CHRISTS, FALSE CHRISTOLOGY, AND SIN (2:18–3:24)
  A. Concerning Antichrists (2:18-27)
  B. Righteousness and the Hope of Glory (2:28–3:3)
  C. The Christian Does Not Sin (3:4-10)
  D. Concerning Love of the Brethren (3:11-18)
  E. The Fruit of Love (3:19,20)
  F. When the Heart Does Not Condemn (3:21-24)

IV. FAITH IN CHRIST AND LOVE (4:1–5:12)
  A. Test the Spirits Confessing Christ (4:1-6)
  B. We Love Because He Loved Us First (4:7-21)
  C. The Triumph of Faith (5:1-5)
  D. The Three Witnesses (5:6-12)

V. EPILOGUE (5:13-21)

THE CRISES IN THE CHURCH

First John was addressed to one or more churches in serious crisis. The struggle was not between Judaism and Christianity or between paganism and Christianity, but between true and false believers. The activity that had generated the crisis was that a group of prominent members—including teachers and prophets—of the church or churches were spreading their syncretistic version of Christianity. This mixture of Greek, Jewish, and Christian concepts was the source of the problem.

The comment in 2:19, "They went out from us but did not belong to us," is best interpreted as a schism within the church. Possibly those with whom John was contending had been excommunicated from the community. It is also possible they had willingly left the church. How many the "many" antichrists were cannot be determined (2:18; 4:1). As this quasi-Christian group which had left the church attempted to promote its ideals, another group still within the church community were sympathizing with these "heretics." The crisis was not only in the church, it was in the hearts of some believers.

First John speaks to this crisis. The author's main purpose was pastoral and positive. He reminded his readers of all they possessed in Jesus Christ, the Son of God. He encouraged them to remain in the true faith. The polemic leveled at the heretics was not against them but against their false theology which was nearly fatal to the church. Prior to 2:18 the polemic against the heretics is indirect; after that it takes on a more direct nature.

THE HERETICS

The heretics were falsifiers of the Christian faith. They did not teach the truth, but a lie, since they had been seduced by the spirit of delusion. They were not of God but of the world. They were nothing other than antichrists and false prophets. They considered themselves "true" Christians, "superior" to those in the church who had not "advanced" as they had. It is not clear whether John was combating a unified group or whether there were several factions with a variety of common false theologies.

John began his attack on two fronts: one Christological, the other ethical. The apostle emphasizes that Jesus is the Word of Life (1:1); Christ (2:22; 5:1); the Son of God (4:15; 5:5; cf. also 2:23; 3:23; 5:11-13,20). He stressed that Jesus is the Christ, come in the flesh (1 John 4:2; 2 John 7); He came by water and blood (1 John 5:6). From 2:22 it seems that the heretics' Christology derived from the Jewish denial that Jesus was Messiah.

The main issue, however, was not whether Jesus was Messiah, but the relationship between the humanity of Jesus on the one hand, and the divinity of the Son of God on the other. Possibly, the false teachers did not directly deny the Incarnation, but from John's point of view they rejected it. They may have accepted the Incarnation without incorporating it into a doctrine of atonement. John, however, stressed the truth that the atoning sacrifice of Christ was the climax of God's love.

The heretics may have thought the Messiah, the Son of God, was united with the human

Jesus only for a period. But this view in effect denied the Incarnation. Thus they had said "No" to God's salvation. The Christological understanding of the heretics is perhaps most clearly outlined in 5:6. They could agree that Jesus "came by water," which refers to Jesus' baptism. But John emphasized that Jesus came "not by water only, but by water and blood."

The ultimate heresy from John's perspective was to say the unity between the human and the divine was only temporary in Christ. It was not only the man Jesus who died on the cross but the God-man Jesus Christ, the Son of God. For the false teachers, Jesus' death did not matter at all.

Often the name *Cerinthus* appears in connection with the heretics John opposed. Cerinthus lived in Ephesus at the same time tradition says John lived in that city. Cerinthus denied the Virgin Birth and asserted that the "Christ nature" descended on Jesus at His baptism and departed before He was crucified.

Any actual docetic system in which Jesus was only a shell for the divine nature was *not* Cerinthus' position nor that of John's opponents. This development can be found only in the Second Century. For example, Ignatius of Antioch combated such Docetists who scorned the idea that God became flesh (*sarx*). Even though it is not possible to make a positive identification of the heresy opposed in 1 John, it does seem closely related, although not necessarily identical, to the teaching of Cerinthus. John insisted that to speak falsely of Christ was to be labeled a heretic. Any dissolution of the union between Jesus and Christ—even at His death—nullifies God's gospel of love.

Ethics, the Christian's relationship to his fellow believers, was John's other main concern. That relationship will be governed totally by his Christology. To walk in the light, to keep God's commandments to love one another, to do righteousness, and so on, are all expressions showing that faith in Jesus is inextricably bound to one's ethical life-style. They are not the cause of one's relationship with God, but they do characterize it.

Faith and ethics are inseparable elements of the Christian life. The commandment in 3:23 to exercise faith in Jesus and brotherly love toward others summarizes the entire Christian faith. To know God is to keep His commands (2:3). Faith in Christ and love for fellow believers are inseparable. Those who put aside faith in Jesus as the Christ are also rejecting the love of God. Those who fail to love the community of God are also neglecting to love God.

The manifestation of love is the sign of the genuine Christian. The love John wrote about is divine love, not love on a human level. Divine love is denied when one sets aside loving God's people. The sign of the world—and the heretics—is hate. The world cannot do otherwise (3:13)!

First John teaches that faith must manifest itself in the mundane affairs of day-to-day living, such as when a fellow believer is in need (3:16f.). The New Testament usually applies the term *brother* to Christians, not neighbors in general. The brotherly love of which John wrote involves love for fellow believers especially (3:11,23; 4:7,11,12).

However, love of all people—the world—was strongly underlined by John. In demonstration of this principle, John did not show hatred for those opposing and persecuting the Christian community to whom he wrote. There is insufficient evidence for calling them "amoral" or "libertines." Perhaps at best they should be understood as "elitist pneumatics," whose arrogance led them to moral indifference. For the most part they were well-satisfied with their so-called knowledge (*gnōsis*).

Overview–2 John

AUTHOR AND DATE

This epistle can best be described as a letter to the Church. Its length resembles that of the private letters of that day. The style, language, and thought world of 2 and 3 John prove both were written by the same person. Both also bear a relationship with 1 John. In both there is an abundance of Johannine expressions and concepts. Some of these are terms like "love, truth, to witness, testimony, commandment, a new commandment, and antichrist," as well as concepts like "to abide in, to walk in, to be of God, to see God." Those who have attempted to show two different authors of 1 John, and 2 and 3 John cannot be taken seriously.

Both 2 and 3 John can be dated around the same time (ca. A.D. 80–100). There is virtually no justification for identifying the epistle mentioned in 3 John 9 as 2 John. The church mentioned in 2 John is entirely different from the one to which Gaius (the recipient of 3 John) belonged. It can be surmised that both churches were located in Asia Minor. Comments concerning the "elder" can be found in the overview of 1 John.

Canonicity

It is more noteworthy that these two short apostolic letters were included in the canon than that some placed them among the antilegomena, the disputed epistles.

As late as the beginning of the Fourth Century, Eusebius classified 2 and 3 John as among the "disputed." Sometime around the beginning of the Fifth Century, the Peshitta, the Syrian translation of the Bible, included 1 John but not the other two.

However, these two short letters were known and used in the Church, and they are included among the most ancient manuscripts in existence. Numerous theologians of the Early Church either paraphrased, cited, or interpreted verses or passages from all three epistles of John. Apparently 2 John was more widely used than 3 John. Further, it is difficult to imagine anyone putting himself in the awkward position of trying to honor the apostle by writing something that was directly against that which the letters themselves speak out against!

Even though they were disputed for a long time, those two letters did become part of the canon. Men of the Third and Fourth Century were convinced that 2 and 3 John were of apostolic origin.

The Second Epistle of John can be outlined in the following manner:

OUTLINE

(1) The opening (verses 1-3)
(2) The children of the church—the joy of the elder (verse 4)
(3) The challenge to mutual love (verses 5-6)
(4) The warning against heretics (verses 7-9)
(5) A "no" to heretics (verses 10,11)
(6) Conclusion

THE CENTRAL TEACHING OF THE EPISTLE

The conceptual framework and mode of expression in 2 John is strongly reminiscent of 1 John. Both speak of the relationship between genuine confession of Christ and loving one another. Also, in both texts although the writer spoke with authority, he did so with a warm and fatherly warmth. Nevertheless, there are some differences. Whereas the church mentioned in 1 John was experiencing a crisis because of the threat of false teachers, it appears as though the church addressed by 2 John had not yet undergone attack (verse 10) although the author cautioned that many deceivers had gone out into the world.

Verse 4 commends some of the members of the church whom the author knew. Their Christian walk caused him to rejoice "greatly." Their practical Christian living led him to believe the general situation of the church was good. However, he emphasized that walking in the truth and keeping the commandment cannot be divorced from faith in Christ and confessing His name. The close relationship between ethics and Christology was again stressed as "from the beginning" (cf. verses 5,6). Jesus had given the commandment, the apostles preached it, and those to whom the epistle was sent had heard it "from the beginning," i.e., from the first time they heard the gospel of love. The false teachers were denouncing this relationship. These "transgresseth" (verse 9). Perhaps the writer was using the opponents' own vocabulary in a sarcastic manner. Any so-called "progress" of the heretics was actually "regression." Their "enlightenment" was actually "darkness." They had "advanced" so far they had left God entirely.

These "deceivers" (verse 7) rejected the Incarnation as well as the Atonement. As a result they undermined the Christian commandment—indeed the power of—to love one another. They were probably confessing Jesus as

"Lord," but at the same time were denying His lordship and His true nature as God-man. Therefore, the apostle wrote they were to be rejected immediately if they surfaced in the church and attempted to propagate their "faith." Their denouncement must be seen in the light of the love of God. Because they were actually spurning the love of God revealed in Jesus Christ "come in the flesh," the apostle of love had to correct them. Not to do so would have been unloving.

The apostle gave explicit instructions concerning those who attempted to enter the church but rejected apostolic doctrine (verse 10). They were not to be welcomed. "Into your house" here most certainly refers to the local church gathering, not someone's home. There is no disparity between what John taught in this epistle and what Jesus taught concerning loving one's enemies. Jesus' own definition of love rejected sharply any twisted concepts concerning God. His conflicts with the Pharisees aptly illustrate this (e.g., Matthew 23). The decisive "no" directed at the heretics was equally a "yes" to the love of God. If the heretics had been given free rein under the pretense of love for God it would not have shown love for God or His children.

The heretics had threatened the relationship between God the Father and His children. This explains John's harsh reaction. He closed his epistle with an expression of hope that he would be able to visit them and elaborate more fully on the teaching he had given in the letter.

Overview–3 John

Third John is a personal letter written by "the elder" to an individual named Gaius. However, instead of addressing personal concerns, the letter deals with life in the church. In all of John's writings the term *ekklēsia*, "assembly," often used for the "church," occurs only in this little letter (verses 6,9,10). (Concerning the date and the place the epistle has in the canon, see the discussion in the overview of 2 John.)

In contrast to the First and Second Epistles of John, 3 John makes no mention of heretics, unless the resistance of Diotrephes is a result of his sympathizing with the deceivers. This, however, cannot be verified by the letter.

Even though 3 John does not discuss any deep theological issues, it remains valuable for the Church since it offers lucid insight into some of the difficulties facing a late First Century church (probably in Asia Minor). The epistle also presents a picture of lively missionary activity and a glimpse of how the gospel was supported financially.

Third John can be outlined as follows:

(1) Opening (verse 1)
(2) Gaius—the Joy of the Elder (verses 2-4)
(3) The Challenge to Support Missionaries (verses 5-8)
(4) Diotrephes—the Perpetrator of Strife (verses 9,10)
(5) The Recommendation of Demetrius (verses 11,12)
(6) Closing (verses 13,14)

THE MAIN THEME OF THE EPISTLE

The letter centers around three persons: Gaius, Diotrephes, and Demetrius.

(1) Gaius, to whom the letter was addressed, must have been an influential person in the church. Fellow Christians or itinerant preachers had brought "the elder" the good report concerning Gaius' Christian life-style. The writer praised Gaius for welcoming the traveling brethren, and for his "walk in the truth." He let Gaius know he was depending on him to welcome his own "evangelists." They were to be shown hospitality and supported materially so that those to whom they ministered would not have to pay to hear them. This was the case among many Hellenistic itinerant philosophers and preachers. Because missionaries go forth in the name of Jesus, without asking for financial support from their listeners, those who send them must support them. The author included himself in this responsibility. He and Gaius were coworkers in the truth.

(2) Diotrephes was the ringleader of the opposition. He was the exact opposite of Gaius. He did not acknowledge the authority of the elder, so letters were of little consequence. Almost certainly John had written before but with little effect. Because of Diotrephes, the letter may not even have been read to the church.

Diotrephes' position in the church is not known. However, he certainly had significant influence. He had tried to oust those in the church who supported the traveling preachers (verse 10). No doubt he was a very self-reliant individual. Perhaps he was the leader of a group of elders. A close examination of the text indicates he was not a theological threat but a threat to authority.

Because Diotrephes did not accept the authority of the writer of the epistle, he spoke "malicious words" against him, but John promised that when he arrived he would remind the church of Diotrephes' works. It is not clear whether the strife was resolved. However, the fact that 3 John has survived through the centuries seems to indicate that "the elder" did achieve the desired results.

The situation may be summarized in three points: (a) Diotrephes was slandering "the elder." He disagreed with the missions strategy of "the elder." (b) He would not receive traveling missionaries. His negative attitude was hindering the spread of the gospel. (c) He was excluding some from the church. The present tense of "forbiddeth" and "casteth" may indicate what he was trying to do.

(3) Demetrius, the third main character, was probably one of the leaders of the itinerant missionaries. Perhaps he delivered the epistle. Gaius could address him candidly. Just as Gaius received a positive testimony from the itinerant missionaries, Demetrius also was spoken well of by all. His positive recommendation is a contrast to the false confessors of Christ (2 John 10,11), who were not to be received. Even though the "good report" concerning Demetrius widened the rift between Diotrephes and Gaius, the writer of the epistle indicated no action was to be taken for the wrong reasons.

Closing

The greeting which closed the epistle reflects its private character. The greeting was from friend to friend, not from one church to another. The absence of a greeting to the church was probably because of the position Diotrephes had usurped for himself.

Overview–Jude

The epistle of Jude is the seventh and last of the so-called General Epistles. It concludes the epistolary literature of the presently arranged New Testament. Although no particular addressee is identified, its contents suggest it was directed to a certain church or group of churches facing a particular problem. As is often the case in the New Testament, the letter was intended to oppose false teaching which threatened the Church.

AUTHOR AND DATE OF COMPOSITION

The author called himself "Jude," the "servant (literally, 'slave') of Jesus Christ and brother of James." Doubtless, he was the Jude, who (in Matthew 13:55 and Mark 6:3) with *Jacob* (James) was identified as the brother of Jesus. Even though Jude was the only writer in the New Testament who referred to such a relationship, he did so in humility. He not only avoided directly calling himself Jesus' brother, he also placed himself in the shadow of his more well-known brother, James.

James was so well known by the recipients of the letter that no further explanation was needed. At that time there was only one James who fit this description, James the brother of Jesus and overseer of the church in Jerusalem (Galatians 1:19; 2:12; cf. Acts 12:17; 15:13).

Some have asserted this Jude was Judas Thaddeus or "the brother of James" (Luke 6:16; Acts 1:13). The genitive case, however, is ordinarily taken to mean the "son" of James, not "brother." Besides, it is out of the question that the apostle Jude is meant, for the writer placed himself out of the apostolic group (verse 17).

Jesus' brothers and sisters did not believe in Him during His earthly ministry (John 7:5). Following the Resurrection, Jesus revealed himself to James (1 Corinthians 15:8), and after the Ascension Jesus' brothers were with His mother and the apostles (Acts 1:14). Paul wrote that the brothers of the Lord became heralds of the gospel (1 Corinthians 9:5). Other than this there is little known about Jude.

In Eusebius' Church History, he explained that according to Hegesippus (ca. A.D. 180), two of the grandchildren of Jude had to appear before Emperor Domitian because they were from the royal lineage of David. It was feared they might lead some kind of Jewish rebellion. The emperor released them as harmless. His concerns were eased when he saw their hands marked by hard work and when he learned they lived as poor farmers in the land of the Jews. It is told, though, that they eventually became bishops in the Church.

The Epistle of Jude was strongly attested in the Early Church. Portions of it may appear in 1 Clement, the Shepherd of Hermas, the Epistle of Barnabas, the Didache, and in the writings of Polycarp. All of these are dated around the end of the First or beginning of the Second Century. The Muratorian Canon included Jude. Athenagoras and Tertullian knew it, and Clement of Alexandria referred to it in his book *Hupotuposes* ("Sketches"). Didymus defended its genuineness. A tract by Cyprian cited a verse from Jude as Holy Scripture. Origen appealed numerous times to the letter as a work by the brother of the Lord. He commended it as "certainly short," but dressed in a vigorous language by divine grace.

There seems to be little question that the epistle is authentic, but there was a question as to whether or not it should be included in the canon of the New Testament. Later scholars doubted the authorship and asserted it was written in the post-apostolic period. It is virtually impossible, however, to imagine a pseudepigrapher in the Second Century choosing the obscure name of Jude in an effort to give his writing credibility. Nothing in the content of the letter supports that idea. On the contrary, it can be observed that the writer, rather than appealing to his own authority, appealed to the words of the apostles (verse 17).

The origin of the epistle and its destination cannot be definitively determined. The time of writing is also uncertain. If Jude worked chiefly in Jewish regions it is more likely that he addressed churches in the Jewish regions of Syria. But, since Paul's words in 1 Corinthians 9:5 seem to indicate that the brothers of the Lord were known by the church there, it is possible and even likely, that their territory covered a wider range. Since the epistle is written in Greek it could have had a wide audience.

Even though the date of the writing of this epistle cannot be established with certainty, its contents seem to indicate it belongs to the later writings of the New Testament, probably between A.D. 65 and 80. Jude could still have been alive at this time. He appears among the last in the lists of Jesus' brothers, perhaps indicating he was one of the youngest.

The Epistle of Jude cites a text from the Apocrypha. This would have been acceptable during the First Century, but it caused uncertainty in later centuries. Eventually this led to its being a disputed letter. However, it was accepted into the canon at the Council of Laodicia in A.D. 364 and later at the Council of Carthage in A.D. 397.

Apparently Jude used at least two sayings from the Old Testament Apocrypha. Material from the Book of Enoch occurs in verses 6 and 13, and in verse 15 it is almost verbatim. Verse 9 contains some material from the Assumption (ascension) of Moses. It is also possible that something from the Testament of Naphtali appears in verse 6, and from the Testament of Asher in verse 8. Much of the Jewish apocrypha and pseudepigrapha were highly regarded during this time. Ancient Jewish traditions were embedded in these writings. Moreover, Jude was not the only Biblical writer to use sources outside of Scripture. The Old Testament refers to other historical works. Paul alluded to pagan poets (Acts 17:28; 1 Corinthians 15:32,33; Titus 1:12). He also alluded to a rabbinic midrash on the "rock in the desert" (1 Corinthians 10:4). He identified "Jannes and Jambres" as the Egyptian sorcerers who opposed Moses; that information did not come from the Biblical account. The use of other sources occurs in Acts 7:22; Galatians 3:19; Hebrews 2:2; 11:37; and James 5:17. This is not to say that pagan philosophers or Jewish pseudepigrapha were given canonical authority.

Another striking feature of Jude is its resemblance to 2 Peter, especially chapter 2. Much of the content is the same. There are too many differences to speak of "copying," but at the same time, the two epistles are so obviously related that some kind of dependency is undeniable. There are basically three theories purporting to explain this.

Some assert that 2 Peter used Jude; others take the opposite view. A third option is that both epistles came from a common source. These options have little impact on an understanding of the letter. Many interpreters point out that Peter wrote of "coming" ("shall be") false teachers (2 Peter 2:1), whereas Jude wrote of false teachers who had "crept in unawares" (verse 4). This might suggest that Peter viewed the danger as future, but Jude saw it as already present. Such an argument might have some validity, but it must be remembered that Peter often shifted between present and future tenses. Moreover, in verse 18 Jude spoke of the apostles warning that scoffers would come in the last days. Perhaps he was alluding to Peter's words in 3:3. That would indicate 2 Peter preceded Jude; however, this cannot be determined for certain.

CONTENTS

The Epistle of Jude is both a defense of the gospel and a polemical treatise. The author explained that his purpose was to write about their "common salvation." Compelled by circumstances, however, Jude forfeited that goal and instead he admonished his readers to "earnestly contend for the faith which was once delivered unto the saints." He gave a prophetic word, not from the will of men but the God of Scripture who inspired him to write (cf. 2 Peter 1:21).

The occasion for Jude's writing was that heretics had infiltrated the Church and were spreading their damaging doctrines. Just as it is useless for a farmer to continue sowing if the weeds have not been pulled, so it is fruitless to announce the truth if the lie is not confronted. These two factors go hand in hand.

The Epistle of Jude is the only book in the Bible whose sole objective is to combat the apostasy that will come prior to Christ's return. Its placement in the Bible makes it an introduction to the Book of Revelation. This provides the spiritual rationale for the apocalyptic judgments unveiled in the final book of the Bible. The Biblical teaching about apostasy is epitomized by Jude. With panoramic immensity this tiny epistle of only 25 verses surveys the history of apostasy in heaven and earth. Jude recalled the backsliding of angels and men. He gave examples from before the Flood as well as from Israel's history. He addressed the problem of apostasy in his contemporary Church and spoke of the falling away of the last days. In the latter, he particularly corresponds with the teaching of Jesus and His apostles.

Jesus said the last days would be characterized by seductions: "When the Son of man cometh, shall he find faith on the earth?" (Luke 18:8). Paul referred to the "falling away" (2 Thessalonians 2:3; cf. 1 Timothy 4:1), and he described the last days as a time when "sound teaching" would not be endured (2 Timothy 4:3). The apostle Peter wrote that false teachers would appear who "privily shall bring in damnable heresies" that would lead to destruction (2 Peter 2:1). Jude added his final, urgent appeal to the Church to "contend for the faith which was once delivered unto the saints."

This faith was delivered "once" (verse 3), that

is, "once and for all," totally, completely. Sacred truth and the divine history of salvation are transmitted by Holy Scripture. When the apostolic canon was completed, nothing could be added or subtracted.

Jude is unique in both form and content. Two features of its composition are particularly exceptional. First, it is based on groups of three that are interspersed throughout the letter. Second, its argumentation is based on contrasts between "these" and "you."

The first and most significant main section describes the false teachers: their doctrine, character, and the judgment facing them. Against the continual "these" (i.e., the false teachers, verses 8,10,11,12,14,16,19) stands the antithetical "but beloved" (verses 17,20). The first section is characterized by "these," while the second largely features "you."

The following outline can be made:

I. OPENING (1-3)
- (1) Sender and Addressees (verse 1)
- (2) Blessing Wish (verse 2)
- (3) Motive (verse 3)

II. HERETICS DESCRIBED (4-19)
- (1) Three Distinguishing Features (verse 4)
  - (a) Ungodly
  - (b) Lawless
  - (c) Denying the Lord
- (2) Three Examples of Judgment (5-7)
  - (a) Israel in the Desert (verse 5)
  - (b) Angels That Sinned (verse 6)
  - (c) Sodom and Gomorrah (verse 7)
- (3) Three Main Sins (8-10)
  - (a) "Dreamers" (verse 8)
  - (b) Defilers of the Body (verse 8)
  - (c) Arrogant Mockers (verses 8-10)
- (4) Three Examples of Error (11)
  - (a) The Way of Cain
  - (b) The Error of Balaam
  - (c) The Rebellion of Korah (Core)
- (5) Five Images From Nature (12,13)
  - (a) A Submerged Reef (verse 12)
  - (b) Clouds Without Rain (verse 12)
  - (c) Trees Without Fruit (verse 12)
  - (d) Wild Waves of the Sea (verse 13)
  - (e) Wandering Stars (verse 13)
- (6) The Prophecy of Enoch (14-16)
- (7) The Prophecies of the Apostles (17-19)

III. BELIEVERS EXHORTED (20-23)
- (1) Three Exhortations (20,21)
  - (a) Build Yourselves Up (verse 20)
  - (b) Pray in the Spirit (verse 20
  - (c) Abide in God's Love (verse 21)
- (2) Three Prescriptions for Helping (22,23)
  - (a) With Sympathy (verse 22)
  - (b) With Boldness (verse 23)
  - (c) With Fear (verse 23)

IV. CLOSING DOXOLOGY (24,25)

HERETICS DESCRIBED

The kind of violence the Biblical writers directed against opponents and deceivers may be shocking to some. But Jesus himself used vigorous condemnation of the Pharisees and scribes. He called them "serpents," a "brood of vipers," and those following them "children of hell" (Matthew 23:15,33). The apostles did not exercise restraint in condemning their opponents. Paul pronounced a curse upon those who preached another gospel (Galatians 1:8,9). He called his opponents "dogs" and "workers of evil" (Philippians 3:2). Peter compared the false teachers to "brute beasts" and called them "cursed children" whose judgment was certain (2 Peter 2:1,3,12,14). Jude expressed the same harsh attitude when he attacked the false teachers who had infiltrated the church.

(1) Three Distinguishing Features (verse 4)

First, Jude described the false teachers as "ungodly," that is, without reverence or fear of God. Their godlessness was not passive, it was active, willful, and shameless. Furthermore, the heretics were lawless and mocked God's grace (cf. Romans 6:1f.) instead of allowing His grace to train them in living a holy life (Titus 2:12). Jesus' brothers, James and Jude, both stated explicitly that faith must be demonstrated in works. James showed that good works testify to a saving faith. Jude maintained that evil works are a sign of falling away from the Faith. The third feature of the heretics was that they denied Christ.

(2) Three Examples of Judgment (verses 5-7)

Jude continued by reminding his readers how the Lord had previously executed judgment over sinners. He gave three examples: first, *Israel in the desert* (verse 5; cf. Numbers 14:26-38; 1 Corinthians 10:1-13; Hebrews 3:7; 4:11). Next he referred to God's judgment on the *fallen angels* (verse 6). Once these angels sang the praises of God; now they are chained in utter darkness. Two types of sin caused their fall—pride and lust. The third warning example is *Sodom and Gomorrah* (verse 7). The kind of judgment portrayed here is not for a godless world but for religious deceivers.

(3) Three Main Sins (verses 8-11)

Jude went to the root of the false teachers' error when he called them *dreamers;* they were fanatics without spiritual sobriety. Their visionary experiences led them astray by diverting them into a spiritual realm of delusion; they were under the control of evil forces. They believed these experiences condoned their ungodly life-style. While they took pride in their false spirituality, they *corrupted themselves* with immorality in a way resembling some later Gnostic practices. Jude described them as having an *arrogant attitude.* They did not submit to higher authorities and even derided them.

(4) Three Examples of Error (verse 11)

Verse 11 pronounces a woe upon these false teachers (cf. Matthew 11:21; 23:13ff.). They are compared with three tragic figures of the Old Testament. They were following the *way of Cain,* who rejected true worship of God and tried to approach Him with an unacceptable offering. Cain was of the Evil One and killed his brother. The errorists were also like *Balaam,* who thought fear of God was a means of monetary gain (cf. 1 Timothy 6:5), and who led Israel into sin (cf. Revelation 2:14). The *gainsaying of Core* refers to Korah's rebellion against Moses' and Aaron's God-given authority, and he, and "they and all that appertained to them, went down alive into the pit" (Numbers 16:33). Korah's destruction presents a picture of the judgment awaiting Antichrist, the last ultimate deceiver (Revelation 19:20).

(5) Five Images From Nature (verses 12,13)

Heaven, earth, and sea all give vivid descriptions of these deceivers. They were like *submerged reefs* (*The Amplified Bible*) which, unseen, by sailors, cause their destruction. They were also like *clouds without water* which pass overhead without giving rain. They were like *unfruitful trees,* lacking any life or root (cf. Luke 13:6-9). Like *wild waves of the sea,* the false teachers brought garbage and debris onto the "shore" of the Faith. They were like *wandering stars* which have strayed from their courses and wander aimlessly in the night sky.

(6) The Prophecy of Enoch (verses 14-16)

According to the Scriptures, Enoch did not die but was translated to heaven by the Lord (cf. Hebrews 11:5). He is a pattern for those who will be "caught up" at the coming of the Lord. Jude 14 explains that Enoch prophesied about the coming of the Christ, thereby confirming the ancient tradition written in the Book of Enoch. Enoch's prophecy concerned the judgment of the ungodly. They are to be judged not only because of their ungodly works, but also because of the bitter and rebellious words they have spoken against the Lord.

(7) The Prophecies of the Apostles (verses 17-19)

Believers are not to be discouraged or disappointed because of persecutions; these must come (cf. Matthew 18:7). The apostles foretold that mockers would emerge during the last days (2 Peter 2:1; 3:3). But they also prophesied of the victory of God's kingdom. God's people are to hold fast and cling to the admonition of the Word and to be patient (cf. Revelation 3:10). Jesus offered words of encouragement to believers undergoing trials and the deceptions of the last days: "But he that shall endure unto the end, the same shall be saved" (Matthew 24:13).

BELIEVERS EXHORTED

Most of the epistle addressed the problem of deceivers, but in closing Jude added a short section encouraging believers to continue in the Faith. He concluded with resounding praise to God.

(1) Three Exhortations (verses 20,21)

While the children of God wait for Christ's coming, they must take care of their spiritual well-being. They must *build themselves up* in their holy faith through the truth revealed in Jesus Christ and passed on by the apostles. Furthermore, they are to *pray in the Holy Spirit.* The Word and prayer belong together, and through them the believer can *keep himself in the love of God* (cf. John 15:9). They are *sanctified by the Father* (verse 1), but they must stay within the bounds of God's love.

(2) Three Prescriptions for Helping (verses 22,23)

Believers are not merely to concern themselves with their own spirituality. They are to care for others also. Some who had been enticed by the false teachers were in desperate need of help. Help must be administered according to each situation. Some need compassion and understanding; others must be "snatched" from the "fire" of heresy, just as one might save someone from a burning building. Others had drifted so far from the truth as to give themselves over to sin and impurity. They could be helped only with extreme caution (cf. Galatians 6:1). Love for the sinner must be joined with an uncompromising hatred for the sin, so the impurity of the sin would not infect the believer.

Following these exhortations, Jude closed his epistle with praise to God to whom belongs all "glory, majesty, dominion and power, both now and ever."

Manuscripts

Egyptian Papyri

Note: (a) designates the section of the New Testament on which the manuscript is based; (b) designates the century in which it is believed the manuscript was written (using the Roman numerals); (c) provides information on the present location of the manuscript.

p1 (a) Gospels; (b) III; (c) Philadelphia, University of Pennsylvania Museum, no. E2746.

p2 (a) Gospels; (b) VI; (c) Florence, Museo Archeologico, Inv. no. 7134.

p3 (a) Gospels; (b) VI, VII; (c) Vienna, Österreichische Nationalbibliothek, Sammlung Papyrus Erzherzog Rainer, no. G2323.

p4 (a) Gospels; (b) III; (c) Paris, Bibliothèque Nationale, no. Gr. 1120, suppl. 2°.

p5 (a) Gospels; (b) III; (c) London, British Museum, P. 782 and P. 2484.

p6 (a) Gospels; (b) IV; (c) Strasbourg, Bibliothèque de la Université, 351r, 335v, 379, 381, 383, 384 copt.

p7 (a) Gospels; (b) V; (c) now lost, was in Kiev, library of the Ukrainian Academy of Sciences.

p8 (a) Acts; (b) IV; (c) now lost; was in Berlin, Staatliche Museen, P. 8683.

p9 (a) General Epistles; (b) III; (c) Cambridge, Massachusetts, Harvard University, Semitic Museum, no. 3736.

p10 (a) Paul's Epistles; (b) IV; (c) Cambridge, Massachusetts, Harvard University, Semitic Museum, no. 2218.

p11 (a) Paul's Epistles; (b) VII; (c) Leningrad, State Public Library.

p12 (a) General Epistles; (b) late III; (c) New York, Pierpont Morgan Library, no. G. 3.

p13 (a) General Epistles; (b) III, IV; (c) London, British Museum, P. 1532 (verso), and Florence, Biblioteca Medicea Laurenziana.

p14 (a) Paul's Epistles; (b) V (?); (c) Mount Sinai, St. Catharine's Monastery, no. 14.

p15 (a) Paul's Epistles; (b) III; (c) Cairo, Museum of Antiquities, no. 47423.

p16 (a) Paul's Epistles; (b) III, IV; (c) Cairo, Museum of Antiquities, no. 47424.

p17 (a) General Epistles; (b) IV; (c) Cambridge, England, University Library, gr. theol. f. 13 (P), Add. 5893.

p18 (a) Revelation; (b) III, IV; (c) London, British Museum, P. 2053 (verso).

p19 (a) Gospels; (b) IV, V; (c) Oxford, Bodleian Library, MS. Gr. bibl. d. 6 (P.).

p20 (a) General Epistles; (b) III; (c) Princeton, New Jersey, University Library, Classical Seminary AM 4117 (15).

p21 (a) Gospels; (b) IV, V; (c) Allentown, Pennsylvania, Library of Muhlenberg College, Theol. Pap. 3.

p22 (a) Gospels; (b) III; (c) Glasgow, University Library, MS. 2-x. 1.

p23 (a) General Epistles; (b) early III; (c) Urbana, Illinois, University of Illinois, Classical Archaeological and Art Museum, G. P. 1229.

p24 (a) Revelation; (b) IV; (c) Newton Center, Massachusetts, Library of Andover Newton Theological School.

p25 (a) Gospels; (b) late IV; (c) now lost, was in Berlin, Staatliche Museen, P. 16388.

p26 (a) Paul's Epistles; (b) c. 600; (c) Dallas, Texas, Southern Methodist University, Lane Museum.

p27 (a) Paul's Epistles; (b) III; (c) Cambridge, England, University Library, Add. MS. 7211.

p28 (a) Gospels; (b) III; (c) Berkeley, California, Library of Pacific School of Religion, Pap. 2.

p29 (a) Acts; (b) III; (c) Oxford, Bodleian Library, MS. Gr. bibl. g. 4 (P.).

p30 (a) Paul's Epistles; (b) III; (c) Ghent, University Library, U. Lib. P. 61.

p31 (a) Paul's Epistles; (b) VII; (c) Manchester, England, John Rylands Library, P. Ryl. 4.

p32 (a) Paul's Epistles; (b) c. 200; (c) Manchester England, John Rylands Library, P. Ryl. 5.

p33 (a) Acts; (b) VI; (c) Vienna, Österreichische Nationalbibliothek, no. 190.

p34 (a) Paul's Epistles; (b) VII; (c) Vienna, Österreichische Nationalbibliothek, no. 191.

p35 (a) Gospels; (b) IV (?); (c) Florence, Biblioteca Medicea Laurenziana.

p36 (a) Gospels; (b) VI; (c) Florence, Biblioteca Medicea Laurenziana.

p37 (a) Gospels; (b) III, IV; (c) Ann Arbor, Michigan, University of Michigan Library, Invent. no. 1570.

p38 (a) Acts; (b) c. 300; (c) Ann Arbor, Michigan, University of Michigan Library, Invent. no. 1571.

p39 (a) Gospels; (b) III; (c) Chester, Pennsylvania, Crozer Theological Seminary Library, no. 8864.

p40 (a) Paul's Epistles; (b) III; (c) Heidelberg, Universitätsbibliothek, Inv. Pap. graec. 45.

p41 (a) Acts; (b) VIII; (c) Vienna, Österreichische Nationalbibliothek, Pap. K.7541-8.

p42 (a) Gospels; (b)VII, VIII; (c) Vienna, Österreichische Nationalbibliothek, KG 8706.

p43 (a) Revelation; (b) VI, VII; (c) London, British Museum, Pap. 2241.

p44 (a) Gospels; (b) VI, VII; (c) New York, Metropolitan Museum of Art, Inv. 14-1-527.

p45 (a) Gospels, Acts; (b) III; (c) Dublin, Chester Beatty Museum; and Vienna, Osterreichische Nationalbibliothek, P. Gr. Vind. 31974.

p46 (a) Paul's Epistles; (b) c. 200; (c) Dublin, Chester Beatty Museum, and Ann Arbor, Michigan, University of Michigan Library, Invent. no. 6238.

p47 (a) Revelation; (b) late III; (c) Dublin, Chester Beatty Museum.

p48 (a) Acts; (b) late III; (c) Florence, Museo Medicea Laurenziana.

p49 (a) Paul's Epistles; (b) late III; (c) New Haven, Connecticut, Yale University Library, P. 415.

p50 (a) Acts; (b) IV, V; (c) New Haven, Connecticut, Yale University Library, P. 1543.

p51 (a) Paul's Epistles; (b) c. 400; (c) London British Museum.

p52 (a) Gospels; (b) early II; (c) Manchester, John Rylands Library, P. Ryl. Gr. 457.

p53 (a) Gospels, Acts; (b) III; (c) Ann Arbor, Michigan, University of Michigan Library, Invent. no. 6652.

p54 (a) General Epistles; (b) V, VI; (c) Princeton, New Jersey, Princeton University Library, Garrett Depos. 7742.

p55 (a) Gospels; (b) VI, VII; (c) Vienna, Österreichische Nationalbibliothek, P. Gr. Vind. 26214.

p56 (a) Acts; (b) V, VI; (c) Vienna, Österreichische Nationalbibliothek, P. Gr. Vind. 19918.

p57 (a) Acts; (b) IV, V; (c) Vienna, Österreichische Nationalbibliothek, P. Gr. Vind. 26020.

p58 (a) Acts; (b) VI; (c) Vienna, Österreichische Nationalbibliothek, P. Gr. Vind. 17973, 36133[54], and 35831.

p59 (a) Gospels; (b) VII; (c) New York, New York University, Washington Square College of Arts and Sciences, Department of Classics, P. Colt. 3.

p60 (a) Gospels; (b) VII; (c) New York, New York University, Washington Square College of Arts and Sciences, Department of Classics, P. Colt. 4.

p61 (a) Paul's Epistles; (b) c. 700; (c) New York, New York University, Washington Square College of Arts and Sciences, Department of Classics, P. Colt. 5.

p62 (a) Gospels; (b) IV; (c) Oslo, University Library.

p63 (a) Gospels; (b) c. 500; (c) Berlin, Staatliche Museen.

p64 (a) Gospels; (b) c. 200; (c) Oxford, Magdalen College Library.

p65 (a) Paul's Epistles; (b) III; (c) Florence, Biblioteca Medicea Laurenziana.

p66 (a) Gospels; (b) c. 200; (c) Cologny/Genève, Bibliothèque Bodmer.

p67 (a) Gospels; (b) c. 200; (c) Barcelona, Fundación San Lucas Evangelista, P. Barc. 1.

p68 (a) Paul's Epistles; (b) VII (?); (c) Leningrad, State Public Library, Gr. 258.

p69 (a) Gospels; (b) III; (c) place (?)

p70 (a) Gospels; (b) III; (c) place (?)

p71 (a) Gospels; (b) IV; (c) place (?)

p72 (a) General Epistles; (b) III, IV; (c) Cologny/Genève, Bibliothèque Bodmer.

p73 (a) Gospels; (b)—; (c) Cologny/Genève, Bibliothèque Bodmer.

p74 (a) Acts, General Epistles; (b) VII; (c) Cologny/Genève, Bibliothèque Bodmer.

p75 (a) Gospels; (b) early III; (c) Cologny/Genève, Bibliothèque Bodmer.

p76 (a) Gospels; (b) VI; (c) Vienna, Österreichische Nationalbibliothek, P. Gr. Vind. 36102.

Major Codices

01, aleph:	Sinaiticus
02, A:	Alexandrinus
03, B:	Vaticanus
04, C:	Ephraemi Rescriptus
05, D:	Bezae Cantabrigiensis
06, E:	Claromontanus

Majuscules

No.	Contents	Century
01, *aleph*	Total New Testament	4th
02, A	Total New Testament	5th
03, B	New Testament, Revelation	4th
04, C	Total New Testament	5th
05, D	Gospels, Acts	6th
06, D	Paul's Epistles	6th
07, E	Gospels	8th
08, E	Acts	6th
09, F	Gospels	9th
010, F	Paul's Epistles	9th
011, G	Gospels	9th
012, G	Paul's Epistles	9th
013, H	Gospels	9th
015, H	Paul's Epistles	6th
016, I	Paul's Epistles	5th
017, K	Gospels	9th
018, K	Acts, Paul's Epistles	9th
019, L	Gospels	8th
020, L	Acts, Paul's Epistles	9th
021, M	Gospels	9th
022, N	Gospels	6th
023, O	Gospels	6th
024, P	Gospels	6th
025, P	Acts, Paul's Epistles, Revelation	9th
026, Q	Gospels	5th
028, S	Gospels	10th
029, T	Gospels	9th
030, U	Gospels	9th
031, V	Gospels	9th
032, W	Gospels	5th
033, X	Gospels	10th
034, Y	Gospels	9th
036,	Gospels	10th
037,	Gospels	9th
038,	Gospels	9th
039,	Gospels	9th
040,	Gospels	6th-8th
041,	Gospels	9th
042,	Gospels	6th
043,	Gospels	6th
044,	Gospels, Acts, Paul's Epistles	8th-9th

In addition to these manuscripts identified by a letter (letter uncials), there are 200 other numbered majuscule manuscripts. Even though most of these manuscripts are very valuable, there is not enough room to list them all. Our apparatus gives the official numbers, 046, 047 etc.

Minuscules

There are about 2800 of these. A total classification of these is only possible in specialized literature dealing with textual criticism.

Early Versions

it	Itala, early Latin	II-IV
vul	Vulgate	IV-V
old syr	Old Syrian	II-III
syr pesh	"peshitta"	V
got	Gothic	IV
arm	Armenian	IV-V
geo	Georgian	V
cop	Coptic	VI
nub	Nubian	VI
eth	Ethiopian	VI

Early Church Fathers

Ambrosius, deacon of Alexandria, and intimate friend of Origen, died 250.

Athanasius, was bishop of Alexandria, 326; died in 373.

Athenagoras, a Christian philosopher of Athens, flourished in 178.

Augustine, 354-430.

Basil the Great, bishop of Caesarea, born in Cappadocia, 329; died 379.

Bede, the Venerable, born 673.

Chrysostom, bishop of Constantinople, born 344; died 407.

Clemens Alexandrinus, Clement of Alexandria, the preceptor of Origen, died 212.

Clemens Romanus, Clement of Rome, *supposed* to have been fellow laborer with Peter and Paul, and bishop of Rome, 91.

Cyprian, bishop of Carthage, in 248; was martyred, 258.

Cyrillus Alexandrinus, this Cyril was patriarch of Alexandria 412; died 444.

Cyrillus Hierosolymitanus, Cyril, bishop of Jerusalem, was born 315; died 386.

Ephraim Syrus, Ephraim the Syrian, was deacon of Edessa; and died 373.

Eusebius of Caesarea, c.260-340.

Gregory the Great, bishop of Rome, flourished in 590.

Gregory Thaumaturgus, was a disciple of Origen, and bishop of Neocaesarea in 240.

Hippolytus, a Christian bishop, flourished 230; died 235.

Ignatius, bishop of Antioch, was martyred about 110.

Irenaeus, disciple of Polycarp; born in Greece about 140; martyred 202.

Jerome, also called Hieronymus, one of the most eminent of the Latin fathers; author of the translation of the Scriptures called the Vulgate; born about 342, died in 420.

Justin Martyr, a Christian philosopher, martyred 165.

Origen, one of the most eminent of the Greek fathers, 185-254.

Tertullian, a most eminent Latin father, died about 220.

Books of the New and Old Testament and the Apocrypha

New Testament Books

Matthew
Mark
Luke
John
Acts
Romans
1 Corinthians
2 Corinthians
Galatians
Ephesians
Philippians
Colossians
1 Thessalonians
2 Thessalonians
1 Timothy
2 Timothy
Titus
Philemon
Hebrews
James
1 Peter
2 Peter
1 John
2 John
3 John
Jude
Revelation

Old Testament Books

Genesis
Exodus
Leviticus
Numbers
Deuteronomy
Joshua
Judges
Ruth
1 Samuel
2 Samuel
1 Kings
2 Kings
1 Chronicles
2 Chronicles
Ezra
Nehemiah
Esther
Job
Psalms
Proverbs
Ecclesiates
Song of Solomon
Isaiah
Jeremiah
Lamentations
Ezekiel
Daniel
Hosea
Joel
Amos
Obadiah
Jonah
Micah
Nahum
Habakkuk
Zephaniah
Haggai
Zechariah
Malachi

Books of the Apocrypha

1 & 2 Esdras
Tobit
Judith
Additions to Esther
Wisdom of Solomon
Ecclesiasticus or the Wisdom of Jesus Son of Sirach
Baruch
Prayer of Azariah and the Song of the Three Holy Children
Susanna
Bel and the Dragon
The Prayer of Manasses
1–4 Maccabees

Bibliography

Modern Greek Texts.

Aland, K. et al. in cooperation with the Institute for New Testament Textual Research. *The Greek New Testament.* 2nd ed. London: United Bible Societies. 1968.

Aland, K. et al. in cooperation with the Institute for New Testament Textual Research. *The Greek New Testament.* 3rd ed. New York: United Bible Societies. 1975.

Nestle, E. and K. Aland. *Novum Testamentum Graece.* 25th ed. Stuttgart: Deutsche Bibelstiftung. 1963.

Nestle, E. and K. Aland. et al. *Novum Testamentum Graece.* 26th ed. Stuttgart: Deutsche Bibelstiftung. 1979.

General Reference Sources with Abbreviations.

BAGD
Bauer, W. *A Greek-English Lexicon of the New Testament and Other Early Christian Literature.* 2nd ed. Revised and augmented by F. Wilbur Gingrich and Frederick W. Danker from Walter Bauer's Fifth Edition, Chicago: University of Chicago Press. 1958.

NIDNTT
Brown, Colin. ed. *The New International Dictionary of New Testament Theology.* Grand Rapids: Zondervan. 1975.

TDNT
Kittel, G. and G. Friedrich. *Theological Dictionary of the New Testament.* Trans. G.W. Bromiley. Grand Rapids: Wm. B. Eerdmans. 1964-. Vols. I-IV were edited by G. Kittell (1933-42), and Vols. V-IX by G. Friedrich (1954-72).

LSJ
Lidell, H.G. and R. Scott. *A Greek-English Lexicon.* 9th ed., H. Stuart Jones and R. McKenzie. Oxford: Clarendon. 1940.

M-M
Moulton, J.H. and G. Milligan. *The Vocabulary of the Greek Testament Illustrated from the Papyri and Other Non-Literary Sources.* London: Hodder and Stoughton. 1914-30; Grand Rapids: Eerdmans. 1985.

General Bibliography

Barclay, William. *The Letter to the Hebrews. The Daily Study Bible.* Philadelphia: The Westminster Press. 1957.

Brown, Raymond E. *The Epistles of John.* Vol. 30 of *The Anchor Bible.* Ed. by W. F. Albright and D. N. Freedman. Garden City: Doubleday and Company, Inc. 1982.

Bruce, A. B. *The Epistle to the Hebrews.* 2nd. ed. Edinburgh: T. and T. Clark. 1899.

Bruce, F. F. *The Epistles of John.* Old Tappan, NJ: Revell. 1970.

Buchanan, George Wesley. *To the Hebrews.* Vol. 36 of *The Anchor Bible.* Ed. by W. F. Albright and D. N. Freedman. Garden City: Doubleday and Company, Inc. 1978.

Bullinger, E. W. *Great Cloud of Witnesses.* London: Eyre and Spottiswoode. 1911. Reprint. Grand Rapids: Kregel Publications. 1979.

Calvin, John. *Commentaries of the Epistle of Paul to the Hebrews. Calvin's Commentaries.* Trans. by John Owen. Grand Rapids: William B. Eerdmans Publishing Co. 1948.

Carter, Charles W. *The Epistle to the Hebrews.* In *Hebrews - Revelation.* Vol. 6 of *The Wesleyan Bible Commentary.* Ed. by Ralph Earle. Grand Rapids: William B. Eerdmans Publishing Co. 1972.

Clarke, Adam. *The General Epistle of James.* In *Romans to the Revelation.* Vol. 6, *Clarke's Commentary.* Nashville: Abingdon Press. N.d.

Cross, Frank Moore. *The Ancient Library of Qumran and Modern Biblical Studies.* Garden City: Doubleday and Company, Inc. Reprint. Grand Rapids: Baker Book House. 1980.

Dibelius, Martin. *James.* Trans. by Michael A. Williams. *Hermeneia.* Ed. by Helmut Koester. Philadelphia: Fortress Press. 1976.

Eusebius. *The History of the Church.* Trans. by G. A. Williamson. New York: Penguin Books. 1981.

Green, M. *The Second Epistle General of Peter and the General Epistle of Jude. Tyndale New Testament Commentaries.* Ed. by R. V. G. Tasker. Grand Rapids: William B. Eerdmans Publishing Co. 1968.

Hart, J. H. A. *The First Epistle General of Peter.* In *First Peter - Revelation.* Vol. 5 of *The Expositor's Greek Testament.* Ed. by W. Robertson Nicoll. Grand Rapids: William B. Eerdmans Publishing Co. 1951.

Henry, Matthew. *Acts to Revelation.* Vol. 6, *Matthew Henry's Commentary on the Whole Bible.* New York: Flemming H. Revell Company. N.d.

Horton, Stanley. *Ready Always: A Devotional Commentary on the Epistles of Peter.* Springfield, MO: Gospel Publishing House. 1974.

Hughes, Graham. *Hebrews and Hermeneutics.* Vol. 36 of *Society for New Testament Studies Monograph Series.* Ed. by M. Wilson and M. E. Thrall. New York: Cambridge University Press. 1979.

Kaiser, Walter C. *The Use of the Old Testament in the New.* Chicago: Moody Press. 1985.

Kaseman, Ernst. *The Wandering People of God.* Trans. by R. A. Harrisville and I. L. Sandberg. Minneapolis: Augsburg Publishing House. 1984.

Kelly, J. N. D. *A Commentary on the Epistles of Peter and Jude. Black's New Testament Commentaries.* London: A. and C. Black. 1969.

Luther, Martin. *The Catholic Epistles.* Vol. 30 of *Luther's Works.* Ed. by Jaroslav Pelikan and Walter Hansen. St. Louis: Concordia Publishing House. 1967.

Manson, William. *The Epistle to the Hebrews.* London: Hodder and Stoughton Ltd. 1951.

Martin, Ralph P. *James.* Vol. 48 of *Word Biblical Commentary.* Ed. by Ralph P. Martin. Waco: Word Books. 1988.

Mayor, Joseph B. *The Epistle of St. Jude and Second Epistle of Peter.* MacMillan and Company. 1907. Reprint. Minneapolis: Klock and Klock Christian Publishers. 1978.

Michel, Otto. *Der Brief and die Hebraer. Kritisch - Exegetischer Kommentar uber Das Neue Testament.* Gottingen: Vandenhoeck and Ruprecht. 1975.

Milligan, George. *The Theology of the Epistle to the Hebrews.* London: T. and T. Clark. 1899. Reprint. Minneapolis: James Family Publishing Company. 1978.

Moffatt, James. *Critical and Exegetical Commentary on the Epistle to the Hebrews. The International Critical Commentary.* Ed. by Alfred Plummer. Edinburgh: T. and T. Clark. 1975.

Moffatt, James. *The General Epistles. The Moffatt New Testament Commentary.* Garden City: Doubleday, Doran and Company, Inc. 1928.

Moulton, James Hope, and George Milligan. *The Vocabulary of the Greek New Testament.* Reprint. Grand Rapids: William B. Eerdmans Publishing Co. 1972.

Mussner, Franz. *Der Jakobusbrief. Herders Theologischer Kommentar zum Neuen Testament.* Freiburg: Herder. 1975.

Odeberg, Hugo. *Pharisaism and Christianity.* Trans. by J. M. Moe. St. Louis: Concordia Publishing House. 1964.

Pfeiffer, Charles F. *The Epistle to the Hebrews.* Chicago: Moody Press. 1962.

Plummer, Alfred. *The Epistles of St. John. Cambridge Greek Testament.* Cambridge University Press. 1886.

Plummer, Alfred. *The General Epistles of James and Jude.* In *James, Jude, Peter.* Vol. 24, *The Expositor's Bible.* Ed. by W. Robertson Nicoll. New York: Funk and Wagnalls Company. 1900.

Plumptre, E. H. *The General Epistle of James. The Cambridge Bible.* Ed. by J. J. S. Perowne. Cambridge: The University Press. 1901.

Reicke, Bo. *The Epistles of James, Peter, and Jude.* Vol. 37 of *The Anchor Bible.* Ed. by W. F. Albright and D. N. Freedman. Garden City: Doubleday and Company, Inc. 1973.

Robertson, A. T. *The First Epistle General of Peter.* In *The General Epistles and the Revelation of John.* Vol. 6 of *Word Pictures in the New Testament.* Nashville: Broadman Press. 1933.

Ropes, James Hardy. *The Epistle of St. James. The International Critical Commentary.* Ed. by Alfred Plummer and Francis Brown. Edinburgh: T. and T. Clark. 1968.

Ryrie, Charles Caldwell. *Biblical Theology of the New Testament.* Chicago: Moody Press. 1959.

Sidebottom, E. M. *James, Jude, and 2 Peter.* Vol. 49 of *New Century Bible.* Ed. by H. H. Rowley and Matthew Black. London: Thomas Nelson and Sons, Ltd. 1967.

Stott, John R. W. *The Epistles of John.* Vol. 19 of *Tyndale New Testament Commentaries.* Ed. by R. V. G. Tasker. Grand Rapids: William B. Eerdmans Publishing Co. 1964.

Strachan, R. H. *The Second Epistle General of Peter.* In *First Peter - Revelation.* Vol. 5 of *The Expositor's Greek Testament.* Ed. by W. Robertson Nicoll. Grand Rapids: William B. Eerdmans Publishing Co. 1951.

Taylor, Richard S. *The Epistle to the Hebrews.* In *Hebrews - Revelation.* Vol. 10 of *Beacon Bible Commentary.* Ed. by Ralph Earle. Kansas City: Beacon Hill Press. 1967.

Testaments of the Twelve Patriarchs. In *The Old Testament Pseudepigrapha.* Ed. by James H. Charlesworth. Garden City: Doubleday and Company, Inc. 1983.

The Ascension of Isaiah the Prophet. In *The Old Testament Pseudepigrapha.* Ed. by James H. Charlesworth. Garden City: Doubleday and Company, Inc. 1983.

Vermes, G., trans. *The Dead Sea Scrolls in English.* Baltimore: Penguin Books. 1975.

Wesley, John, et.al. *One Volume New Testament Commentary.* Grand Rapids: Baker Book House. 1957.

Westcott, Brooke Foss. *The Epistle to the Hebrews.* Reprint. Grand Rapids: William B. Eerdmans Publishing Co. 1984.

Wheaton, David H. *2 Peter.* In *The New Bible Commentary.* Ed. by Donald Guthrie. Rev. ed. Grand Rapids: William B. Eerdmans Publishing Co. 1970.

Windisch, H. *Der Hebraerbrief. Handbook zum Neuen Testament.* Tubingen: 1931.

Wuest, Kenneth S. *In the Last Days.* In *Philippians - Hebrews - The Pastoral Epistles - First Peter: In the Last Days.* Vol. 2 of *Wuest's Word Studies from the Greek New Testament.* Grand Rapids: William B. Eerdmans Publishing Co. 1973.

Various Versions Acknowledgments

Scripture quotations found in Various Versions were taken from the following sources with special permssion as indicated. The sources listed may be found in one or all of the volumes of THE COMPLETE BIBLICAL LIBRARY.

AB

Fitzmyer, Joseph A., S.J., trans. *The Gospel According to Luke I- IX; (Anchor Bible).* New York: Doubleday & Company, Inc. 1985. Reprinted with permission. ©1981, 1985.

ADAMS

Adams, Jay E. *The Christian Counselor's New Testament: a New Translation in Everyday English with Notations, Marginal References, and Supplemental Helps.* Grand Rapids, MI: Baker Book House. 1977. Reprinted with permission. ©1977.

ALBA

Condon, Kevin. *The Alba House New Testament.* Staten Island, NY: Alba House, Society of St. Paul copublished with The Mercier Press Ltd. 1972. Reprinted with permission. *The Mercier New Testament.* 4 Bridge Street. Cork, Ireland: The Mercier Press Ltd. ©1970.

ALFORD

Alford, Henry. *The New Testament of Our Lord and Saviour Jesus Christ: After the Authorized Version.* Newly compared with the original Greek, and revised. London: Daldy, Isbister. 1875.

AMPB

The Amplified Bible. Grand Rapids, MI: Zondervan Publishing House. 1958. Reprinted with permission from the *Amplified New Testament.* © The Lockman Foundation. 1954, 1958.

ASV

(American Standard Version) The Holy Bible Containing the Old and New Testaments: Translated out of the original tongues; being the version set forth A.D. 1611, compared with the most ancient authorities and rev. A.D. 1881-1885. New York: Thomas Nelson Inc., Publishers. 1901, 1929.

BARCLAY

Barclay, William. *The New Testament: A New Translation.* Vol. 1, *The Gospels and the Acts of the Apostles.* London: William Collins Sons & Co. Ltd. 1968. Reprinted with permission. ©1968.

BB

The Basic Bible: Containing the Old and New Testaments in Basic English. New York: Dutton. 1950. Reprinted with permission. *The Bible In Basic English.* © Cambridge University Press. 1982.

BECK

Beck, William F. *The New Testament in the Language of Today.* St. Louis, MO: Concordia Publishing House. 1963. Reprinted with permission. © Mrs. William Beck, *An American Translation.* Leader Publishing Company: New Haven, MO.

BERKELEY

The Holy Bible: the Berkeley Version in Modern English Containing the Old and New Testaments. Grand Rapids: Zondervan Publishing House. 1959. Used by permission. ©1945, 1959, 1969.

BEZA

Iesv Christi, D.N. Novum Testamentum. Geneva: Henricus Stephanus. 1565.

BLACKWELL

Blackwell, Boyce W. *Letters from Paul: An Exegetical Translation.* Anderson, IN: Warner Press, 1971.

BRUCE

Bruce, F.F. *The Letters of Paul: An Expanded Paraphrase Printed in Parallel with the RV.* Grand Rapids: William B. Eerdmans Publishing Co. 1965. Reprinted with permission. F.F. Bruce. *An Expanded Paraphrase of the Epistles of Paul.* The Paternoster Press: Exeter, England. ©1965, 1981.

CAMPBELL

Campbell, Alexander. *The Sacred Writings of the Apostles and Evangelists of Jesus Christ commonly styled the New Testament:* Translated from the original Greek by Drs. G. Campbell, J. Macknight & P. Doddridge with prefaces, various emendations and an appendix by A. Campbell. Grand Rapids: Baker Book House. 1951 reprint of the 1826 edition.

CKJB

The Children's 'King James' Bible: New Testament. Translated by Jay Green. Evansville, IN: Modern Bible Translations, Inc. 1960.

CLEMENTSON

Clementson, Edgar Lewis. *The New Testament: a Translation.* Pittsburg, PA: Evangelization Society of Pittsburgh Bible Institute. 1938.

CONCORDANT

Concordant Version: The Sacred Scriptures: Designed to put the Englished reader in possession of all the vital facts of divine revelation without a former knowledge of Greek by means of a restored Greek text. Los Angeles: Concordant Publishing Concern. 1931. Reprinted with permission. *Concordant Literal New Testament.* Concordant Publishing Concern. 15570 Knochaven Road, Canyon Country, CA 91351. ©1931.

CONFRATERNITY

The New Testament of Our Lord and Savior Jesus Christ: Translated from the Latin Vulgate, a revision of the Challoner-Rheims Version edited by Catholic scholars under the patronage of the Episcopal Committee of the Confraternity Christian Doctrine. Paterson, NJ: St. Anthony Guild Press. 1941. Reprinted with permission by the Confraternity of Christian Doctrine, Washington, DC. ©1941.

CONYBEARE

Conybeare, W.J. and Rev. J.S. Howson D.D. *The Life and Epistles of St. Paul.* Rev. ed. 2 vols. London: Longman, Green, Longman, and Roberts. 1862.

COVERDALE

The New Testament: The Coverdale Version. N.p. 1535(?), 1557.

CRANMER

Cranmer or Great Bible. *The Byble in Englyshe, . . .* translated after the veryte of the Hebrue and Greke text, by ye dilygent studye of dyverse excellent learned men, expert in the forsayde tonges. Prynted by Richard Grafton & Edward Whitchurch. Cum privilegio ad Imprimendum solum. 1539.

DARBY

Darby, J.N. *The Holy Scriptures A New Translation from the Original Languages.* Lansing, Sussex, England: Kingston Bible Trust. 1975 reprint of the 1890 edition.

DOUAY

The Holy Bible containing the Old and New Testaments: Translated from the Latin Vulgate . . . and with the other translations diligently compared, with annotations, references and an historical and chronological index. New York: Kennedy & Sons. N.d.

ET

Editor's Translation. Gerard J. Flokstra, Jr., D.Min.

EVERYDAY

The Everyday Bible: New Century Version. Fort Worth: Worthy Publishing. 1987. Reprinted with permission. World Wide Publications. *The Everyday Study Bible: Special New Testament Study Edition.* Minneapolis: World Wide Publications. 1988.

FENTON

Fenton, Farrar. *The Holy Bible in Modern English.* London: A. & C. Black. 1944 reprint of the 1910 edition.

GENEVA

The Geneva Bible: a facsimile of the 1560 edition. Madison, WI: University of Wisconsin Press. 1969.

GENEVA (1557)

The Nevve Testament of Ovr Lord Iesus Christ. Printed by Conrad Badius. 1557.

GOODSPEED

The Bible: An American Translation. Translated by Edgar J. Goodspeed. Chicago: The University of Chicago Press. 1935.

GREBER

The New Testament: A New Translation and Explanation Based on the Oldest Manuscripts. Translated by Johannes Greber. New York: John Felsberg, Inc. 1937.

HANSEN

Hansen, J.W. The New Covenant. 2nd. ed. 2 vols. Boston: Universalist Publishing House. 1888.

HBIE

The Holy Bible containing the Old and New Testaments: an improved edition (based in part on the Bible Union Version). Philadelphia: American Baptist Publication Society 1913.

HISTNT

The Historical New Testament: Being the literature of the New Testament arranged in the order of its literary growth and according to the dates of the documents: a new translation by James Moffatt. Edinburgh: T & T Clark. 1901.

HOERBER

Hoerber, Robert G. *Saint Paul's Shorter Letters.* Fulton, MO: Robert G. Hoerber. 1954.

JB

The Jerusalem Bible. Garden City, NY: Darton, Longman & Todd, Ltd. and Doubleday and Co, Inc. 1966. Reprinted by permission of the publisher. ©1966.

KJII

King James II New Testament. Grand Rapids: Associated Publishers and Authors, Inc. ©Jay P. Green. 1970.

KLEIST

The New Testament Rendered from the Original Greek with Explanatory Notes. Translated by James A. Kleist and Joseph L. Lilly. Milwaukee: The Bruce Publishing Company. 1954.

KLINGENSMITH

Klingensmith, Don J. *Today's English New Testament.* New York: Vantage Press. 1972. Reprinted by permission of author. ©Don J. Klingensmith, 1972.

KNOX

Knox, R.A. *The New Testament of our Lord and Saviour Jesus Christ: A New Translation.* New York: Sheen and Ward. 1946. Reprinted by permission of The Liturgy Commission.

LAMSA

Lamsa, George M. *The Holy Bible From Ancient Eastern Text.* Translated from original Aramaic sources. Philadelphia: Holman. 1957. From *The Holy Bible From Ancient Eastern Text* by George Lamsa. ©1933 by Nina Shabaz; renewed 1961 by Nina Shabaz. ©1939 by Nina Shabaz; renewed 1967 by Nina Shabaz. ©1940 by Nina Shabaz; renewed 1968 by Nina Shabaz. ©1957 by Nina Shabaz. Reprinted by permission of Harper & Row, Publishers, Inc.

LATTIMORE

Lattimore, Richmond. *Four Gospels and The Revelation:* Newly translated from the Greek.

New York: Farrar, Straus, Giroux, Inc. 1979. Reprinted by permission of the publisher. © Richard Lattimore, 1962, 1979.

LAUBACH

Laubach, Frank C. *The Inspired Letters in Clearest English.* Nashville: Thomas Nelson Publishers. 1956.

LIVB

The Living Bible: Paraphrased. Wheaton, IL: Tyndale House Publishers. 1973. Used by permission of the publisher. © Tyndale House Publishers. 1971.

LOCKE

Locke, John. *A Paraphrase and Notes on the Epistles of St. Paul to the Galatians, First and Second Corinthians, Romans, and Ephesians:* To which is prefixed an essay for the understanding of St. Paul's Epistles. Campbridge, England: Brown, Shattuck; Boston: Hilliard, Gray, and Co. 1832.

MACKNIGHT

Macknight, James. *New Literal Translation:* From the original Greek, of all the Apostolical Epistles, with a commentary, and notes, philological, critical, explanatory, and practical. Philadelphia: Wardkem. 1841.

MACKNIGHT

Macknight, James. *Harmony of the Four Gospels:* 2 vols. in which the natural order of each is preserved, with a paraphrase and notes. London: Longman, Hurst, Rees, Orme and Brown. 1819.

MJV

English Messianic Jewish Version. May Your Name Be Inscribed in the Book of Life. Introduction and footnotes by The Messianic Vision. Washington, D.C.: ©1981. Bible text by Thomas Nelson, Inc. Nashville: Thomas Nelson Publishing Company. ©1979.

MOFFATT

The New Testament: A New Translation. New York: Harper and Row Publishers, Inc.; Kent, England: Hodder and Stoughton Ltd. c.1912. Reprinted with permission.

MONTGOMERY

Montgomery, Helen Barrett. *The Centenary Translation of the New Testament:* Published to signalize the completion of the first hundred years of work of the American Baptist Publication Society. Philadelphia: American Baptist Publishing Society. 1924. Used by permission of Judson Press. *The New Testament in Modern English* by Helen Barrett Montgomery. Valley Forge: Judson Press. 1924, 1952.

MURDOCK

Murdock, James. *The New Testament: The Book of the Holy Gospel of our Lord and Our God, Jesus the Messiah:* A literal translation from the Syriac Peshito version. New York: Stanford and Swords. 1851.

NAB

The New American Bible. Translated from the original languages with critical use for all the ancient sources by members of the Catholic Biblical Association of America. Encino, California: Benzinger. 1970.

NASB

The New American Standard Bible. Anaheim, CA: Lockman Foundation. 1960. Reprinted with permission. © The Lockman Foundation 1960, 1962, 1963, 1968, 1971, 1972, 1973, 1975, 1977.

NEB

The New English Bible: New Testament. Cambridge, England: Cambridge University Press. 1970. Reprinted by permission. ©The Delegates of the Oxford University Press and The Syndics of the Cambridge University Press 1961, 1970.

NIV

The Holy Bible: New International Version. Grand Rapids: Zondervan Publishing House. 1978. Used by permission of Zondervan Bible Publishers. ©1973, 1978, International Bible Society.

NKJB

The New King James Bible, New Testament. Nashville, TN: Royal Pub. 1979. Reprinted from *The New King James Bible-New Testament.* ©1979, 1982, Thomas Nelson, Inc., Publishers.

NLT

The New Life Testament. Translated by Gleason H. Ledyard. Canby, Oregon: Christian Literature Foundation. 1969.

NOLI

Noli, S. *The New Testament of Our Lord and Savior Jesus Christ: Translated into English from the Approved Greek Text of the Church of Constantinople and the Church of Greece.* Boston: Albanian Orthodox Church in America. 1961.

NORLIE

Norlie, Olaf M. *Simplified New Testament: In plain English for today's reader: A new translation from the Greek.* Grand Rapids: Zondervan Publishing House. 1961. Used by permission. ©1961.

NORTON

Norton, Andrews. *A Translation of the Gospels with Notes.* Boston: Little, Brown. 1856.

NOYES

Noyes, George R. *The New Testament:* Translated from the Greek text of Tischendorf. Boston: American Unitarian Association. 1873.

NTPE

The New Testament: A New Translation in Plain English. Translated by Charles Kingsley Williams. Grand Rapids: Wm. B. Eerdmans Publishing Company. 1963.

PANIN

Panin, Ivan., ed. *The New Testament from the Greek Text as Established by Bible Numerics.* Toronto, Canada: Clarke, Irwin. 1935.

PHILLIPS

Phillips, J.B., trans. *The New Testament in Modern English.* Rev. ed. New York: Macmillan Publishing Company, Inc. 1958. Reprinted with permission. ©J.B. Phillips 1958, 1960, 1972.

PNT

A Plain Translation of the New Testament by a Student. Melbourne, Australia: McCarron, Bird. 1921.

RHEIMS

The Nevv Testament of Iesus Christ. Translated faithfully into English, out of the authentical Latin, . . . In the English College of Rhemes. Printed at Rhemes by Iohn Fogny. Cum privilegio. 1582.

RIEU

Rieu, E.V. *The Four Gospels.* London: Penguin Books Ltd. 1952. Reprinted with permission. ©E.V. Rieu, 1952.

ROTHERHAM

Rotherham, Joseph B. *The New Testament:* Newly translated (from the Greek text of Tregelles) and critically emphasized, with an introduction and occasional notes. London: Samual Bagster. 1890.

RPNT

Johnson, Ben Cambell. *The Heart of Paul: A Relational Paraphrase of the New Testament.* Vol. 1. Waco: Word Books. 1976.

RSV

Revised Standard Version; The New Covenant commonly called the New Testament of our Lord and Saviour Jesus Christ: Translated from the Greek being the version set forth A.D. 1611, revised A.D. 1881, A.D. 1901. New York: Thomas Nelson Inc. Publishers. 1953. Used by permission. ©1946, 1952, 1971, 1973 by the Division of Christian Education of the National Council of the Churches of Christ in the U.S.A.

RV

The New Testament of our Lord and Savior Jesus Christ: Translated out of the Greek . . . being the new version revised 1881. St. Louis, MO: Scammell. 1881.

SAWYER

Sawyer, Leicester Ambrose. *The New Testament: Translated from the original Greek,* with chronological arrangement of the sacred books, and improved divisions of chapters and verses. Boston: Walker, Wise. 1861.

SCARLETT

Scarlett, Nathaniel. *A translation of the New Testament from the original Greek:* humbly attempted. London: T. Gillett. 1798.

SEBNT

The Simple English™ Bible, New Testament: American edition. New York: International Bible Translators, Inc. 1981. Used by permission from International Bible Translators, Inc.

SWANN

Swann, George. *New Testament of our Lord and Saviour Jesus Christ.* 4th. ed. Robards, KY: George Swann Company. 1947.

TCNT

The Twentieth Century New Testament: a Translation into Modern English Made from the Original Greek: (Westcott & Hort's text). New York: Revell. 1900.

TEV

The Good News Bible, Today's English Version. New York: American Bible Society. 1976. Used by permission. © American Bible Society, 1966, 1971, 1976.

TNT

The Translator's New Testament. London: The British and Foreign Bible Society. 1973.

TORREY

Torrey, Charles Cutler. *The Four Gospels: A New Translation.* New York: Harper and Row Publishers Inc. 1933. Reprinted by permission. ©1933.

TYNDALE

Tyndale, William. *The Newe Testament dylygently corrected and compared with the Greke.* and fynesshed in the yere of oure Lorde God anno M.D. and XXXIIII in the month of Nouember. London: Reeves and Turner. 1888.

TYNDALE (1526)

The First New Testament in the English Language (1525 or 1526). Reprint. Bristol. 1862. Or Clevland: Barton. N.d.

WADE

Wade, G. W. *The Documents of the New Testament: Translated and Historically Arranged with Critical Introductions.* N.p., n.d.

WAY

Way, Arthur S., trans. *Letters of St. Paul: To seven churches and three friends with the letter to the Hebrews.* 8th ed. Chicago: Moody. 1950 reprint of the 1901 edition.

WESLEY

Wesley, John. *Explanatory notes upon the New Testament.* London: Wesleyan-Methodist Book-room. N.d.

WEYMOUTH

Weymouth, Richard Francis. *The New Testament in Modern Speech:* An idiomatic translation into everyday English from the text of the "Resultant Greek Testament." Revised by J. A.

Robertson. London: James Clarke and Co. Ltd. and Harper and Row Publishers Inc. 1908. Reprinted by permission.

WILLIAMS

Williams, Charles B. *The New Testament: A Translation in the Language of the People.* Chicago: Moody Bible Institute of Chicago. 1957. Used by permission of Moody Press. Moody Bible Institute of Chicago. ©1937, 1966 by Mrs. Edith S. Williams.

WILLIAMS C. K.

Williams, Charles Kingsley. *The New Testament: A New Translation in Plain English.* Grand Rapids: William B. Eerdmans Publishing Co. 1963.

WILSON

Wilson, Benjamin. *The Emphatic Diaglott containing the original Greek Text of what is commonly styled the New Testament* (according to the recension of Dr. F.F. Griesback) with interlineary word for word English translation. New York: Fowler & Wells. 1902 reprint edition of the 1864 edition.

WORRELL

Worrell, A.S. *The New Testament: Revised and Translated:* With notes and instructions; designed to aid the earnest reader in obtaining a clear understanding of the doctrines, ordinances, and primitive assemblies as revealed. Louisville, KY: A.S. Worrell. 1904.

WUEST

Wuest, Kenneth S. *The New Testament: An Expanded Translation.* Grand Rapids: Wm. B. Eerdmans Publishing Company. 1961. Used by permission of the publisher. ©1961.

WYCLIF

Wyclif(fe), John. *The Holy Bible containing the Old and New Testaments with the Apocryphal Books:* in the earliest English version made from the Latin Vulgate by John Wycliffe and his followers. London: Reeves and Turner. 1888.

YOUNG

Young, Robert. *Young's Literal Translation of the Holy Bible.* Grand Rapids: Baker Book House.1953 reprint of the 1898 3rd edition.